THE CRB COMMODITY YEARBOOK
2005

 Commodity Research Bureau

WILEY

John Wiley & Sons, Inc.

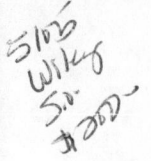
CRB believes that the information and opinions contained herein are reliable, but CRB does not make any warranties whatsoever, expressed or implied, and CRB assumes no liability for reliance on or use of information and opinion contained herein.

Commodity Research Bureau
330 South Wells Street, Suite 612
Chicago, Illinois 60606-7110 USA
800.621.5271 or 312.554.8456
Fax: 312.939.4135
Website: www.crbtrader.com
Email: info@crbtrader.com

TABLE OF CONTENTS

Commodity Research Bureau Product Overview

Commodity Research Bureau is the oldest and most respected information provider in the industry. CRB was founded in 1934 and is widely recognized in the industry for its accurate and professional products.

CRB's products are tailored for individual traders and brokerage firms. All of our products are available to brokerage firms on a bulk and private-label basis.

Product samples and pricing are located on our web site at www.crbtrader.com.

Please contact us for a free consultation about how our products can help your trading or your business.

Call 312.554.8456, or e-mail us at info@crbtrader.com

Commodity Research Bureau

330 South Wells Street, Suite 612
Chicago, IL 60606-7110

Phone: 800.621.5271 or
312.554.8456
Fax: 312.939-4135
E-mail: info@crbtrader.com

Fundamental Futures Research	
Futures Market Service	Weekly 8-page newsletter on futures market fundamentals available in print or PDF formats.
Commodity Yearbook	Annual publication of fundamental data on over 100 commodity markets. Available as a hardcover book with CD.

Trading System Recommendations	
Electronic Futures Trend Analyzer	Computerized daily trading system started in 1963 with specific entry and exit points for the futures markets.

Charts	
Futures Perspective	Weekly 104-page magazine of charts on over 70 futures markets. Available in print or PDF formats.
Historical Wall Charts	Large poster-size charts on 35 futures markets with volume/open interest and Commitment of Traders data. Published annually each fall or on demand with your logo.
Historical Desk Sets	Spiral-bound set of 86 charts on 48 markets with volume/open interest and Commitment of Traders data. Published each spring and fall.
Commodity Index Report	Weekly publication covering the Commodity Research Bureau Futures and Spot Indexes in both tabular and graphical format.

Price Data and Charting Software	
CRB DataCenter	End-of-day daily price files on futures, options, options volatility, equities and mutual funds. Available in various text formats for direct upload to your chart/analysis software.
CRB InfoTech CD	The most comprehensive collection of commodity market information available anywhere, with decades of prices on over 600 cash, futures, foreign exchange, index markets, and option implied volatilities.
Custom Historical Data	Order a one-time package of price information according to your needs.
PowerSignals	Powerful charting and technical analysis software for end-of-day traders.
BarchartX	Real-time charting and technical analysis software with data feed direct from our state-of-the-art live data center.
ddfplus	Enterprise-class equity and futures data feed for client-based enterprise applications.

Booklets	
Understanding Booklets	Booklets customizable with your firm's logo with titles including: Understanding the Futures Markets, Understanding the Options Markets, and Understanding the Securities Markets.

ACKNOWLEDGEMENTS

The editors wish to thank the following for source material:

Agricultural Marketing Service (AMS)

Agricultural Research Service (ARS)

American Bureau of Metal Statistics, Inc. (ABMS)

American Forest & Paper Association (AF & PA)

The American Gas Association (AGA)

American Iron and Steel Institute (AISI)

American Metal Market (AMM)

Bureau of the Census

Bureau of Economic Analysis (BEA)

Bureau of Labor Statistics (BLS)

Chicago Board of Trade (CBT)

Chicago Mercantile Exchange (CME / IMM / IOM)

Coffee, Sugar & Cocoa Exchange (CSCE)

Commodity Credit Corporation (CCC)

Commodity Futures Trading Commision (CFTC)

The Conference Board

Economic Research Service (ERS)

Edison Electric Institute (EEI)

E D & F Man Cocoa Ltd

Farm Service Agency (FSA)

Federal Reserve Bank of St. Louis

Fiber Economics Bureau, Inc.

Florida Department of Citrus

Food and Agriculture Organization of
   the United Nations (FAO)

Foreign Agricultural Service (FAS)

Futures Industry Association (FIA)

International Cotton Advisory Committee (ICAC)

International Rubber Study Group (IRSG)

Johnson Matthey

Kansas City Board of Trade (KCBT)

Leather Industries of America

MidAmerica Commodity Exchange (MidAm)

Minneapolis Grain Exchange (MGE)

National Agricultural Statistics Service (NASS)

National Coffee Association of U.S.A., Inc. (NCA)

New York Cotton Exchange (NYCE / NYFE / FINEX)

New York Mercantile Exchange (NYMEX)
   Commodity Exchange, Inc. (COMEX)

Oil World

The Organisation for Economic Co-Operation
   and Development (OECD)

Random Lengths

The Silver Institute

The Society of the Plastics Industry, Inc. (SPI)

United Nations (UN)

United States Department of Agriculture (USDA)

United States Geological Survey (USGS)

Wall Street Journal (WSJ)

Winnipeg Commodity Exchange (WCE)

THE COMMODITY PRICE TREND

The Reuters-Commodity Research Bureau Futures Index in 2004 closed the year up +11.2% at 283.90. That was the third consecutive yearly gain and followed the +8.9% gain in 2003 and the +23.0% gain in 2002. In the previous recessionary year of 2001, the Reuters-CRB Futures Index fell −16.3%.

Four of the six Reuters-CRB Futures Price Sub-indices posted gains in 2004: Softs (+37.2%), Livestock (+27.7%), Energy (+27.5%), and Precious Metals (+8.9%). Two of the six Sub-indices posted declines: Grains (-21.6%) and the Industrials (-9.6%). The only real weakness in commodity prices in 2004 was tied to a sharp decline in soybean, corn, wheat and cotton prices as ideal summer growing conditions led to bumper crops.

The Reuters-CRB Futures Index was driven higher in 2004 by the weakness in the dollar, strong commodity demand from the US and China, and the sharp rally in oil prices. Crude oil futures prices in 2004 soared by 34% to a close of $43.45 per barrel. Meanwhile, the dollar index fell sharply by −7.2% in 2004, which boosted the price of real goods such as commodities. US GDP growth was strong in 2004 at +4.4%, and Chinese GDP growth remained extremely strong at +9.5%.

Energy

The Reuters-CRB Futures Price Energy Sub-index, which is comprised of Crude Oil, Heating Oil, and Natural Gas, accounts for 18% of the overall Index. The Energy Sub-index in 2004 closed +27.5% yr/yr, adding to the +11.9% gain seen in 2003 and the +56.5% gain seen in 2002. Crude oil and heating oil showed sharp gains during the year, while natural gas closed slightly lower on the year by −0.6% yr/yr. Crude oil rallied sharply during 2004 due to very strong demand, lagging oil production, and Hurricane Ivan in September which reduced US oil production in the Gulf of Mexico by about 25% for several months by damaging under-water pipelines.

Grains

The Reuters-CRB Futures Price Grains and Oilseeds Sub-index, which is comprised of Corn, Soybeans, and Wheat, accounts for 18% of the overall Index. The Grains and Oilseeds Sub-index in 2004 closed −21.6% yr/yr, falling back after the sharp gains of +19.9% in 2003 and +18.4% in 2002. Soybean, corn and wheat prices plunged in the latter half of 2004 as it became obvious that ideal growing conditions in the US in the summer of 2004 would be ideal and would lead to bumper crops. There were record corn and soybean crops, and wheat prices were hurt by a large crop and heavy export competition.

Industrials

The Reuters-CRB Futures Price Industrials Sub-index, which is comprised of Copper and Cotton, accounts for 12% of the overall Index. The Industrials Sub-index showed a −9.6% decline in 2004, which reversed part of the +45.3% gain seen in 2003 and the +24.5% gain in 2002. Copper soared by 43% in 2004, driven higher by very strong demand from the US and particularly China, combined with lagging mining output. That created a supply deficit of about 750,000 metric tons in 2004. Cotton, on the other hand, fell sharply in 2004 due to ideal growing conditions and a record US cotton crop.

Livestock

The Reuters-CRB Futures Price Livestock Sub-index, which is comprised of Live Cattle and Lean Hogs, accounts for 12% of the overall Index. The Livestock Sub-index closed +27.7% in 2004 following the three previous relatively flat years (-5.3% in 2003, +1.4% in 2002, and −2.4% in 2001). Live cattle prices rallied 16% in 2004. Although US exports to Japan and the rest of Asia remained shut down in 2004 due to mad cow disease, the US border also remained closed to imports from Canada (which reduced supply) and US consumers showed strong demand for beef during the year, thus keeping beef prices high. Lean hog prices soared by 43% during 2004, driven higher by strong domestic and overseas demand and by the lack of much herd expansion.

Precious Metals

The Reuters-CRB Futures Price Precious Metals Sub-index, which is comprised of Gold, Platinum, and Silver, accounts for 17% of the overall Index. The Precious Metals Sub-index rallied by +8.9% in 2004, adding to the rallies of +25.9% seen in 2003 and +17.1% seen in 2002. Bullish factors centered on the weak dollar combined with strong jewelry and industrial demand due to the relatively strong world economy.

Softs

The Reuters-CRB Futures Price Softs Sub-index, which is comprised of Cocoa, Coffee, Orange Juice, and Sugar #11, accounts for 23% of the overall Index. The Softs Sub-index in 2004 closed sharply higher by +37.2%, more than reversing the sharp −17.5% decline seen in 2003. Bullish factors centered on the weak dollar and relatively strong world demand. In 2004, cocoa closed +2% yr/yr, coffee closed +60%, sugar closed +59%, and orange juice closed +42%. Cocoa production fell about 6% in 2004 and coffee production fell by about 9%, thus supporting the prices of cocoa and coffee. There was a production deficit of sugar in 2004 of about 1.8 million metric tons, which pushed sugar prices higher. Orange juice soared on the 4 hurricanes that hit the southeastern US in 2004 in late summer and early fall, which caused a 33% reduction in the US orange crop in 2004.

Reuters-CRB Futures Index (weekly close) as of December 31, 2004

Monthly Reuters-CRB Futures Index   High, Low and Close (1967=100)

Year		Jan.	Feb.	Mar.	Apr.	May	June	July	Aug.	Sept.	Oct.	Nov.	Dec.	Range
1995	High	237.96	236.16	236.89	237.70	237.12	238.00	235.90	240.27	245.81	242.67	244.49	246.47	246.47
	Low	232.58	230.97	231.07	233.16	229.55	232.18	229.31	231.71	239.38	238.32	240.85	240.93	229.31
	Close	232.78	234.25	232.94	235.30	232.72	233.38	233.23	239.97	241.73	242.22	241.84	243.18	----
1996	High	247.56	251.21	253.50	263.79	261.24	252.92	251.90	252.04	250.35	249.59	247.08	246.85	263.79
	Low	238.63	245.62	242.72	250.19	251.79	246.64	240.09	242.83	243.10	237.78	235.99	238.12	235.99
	Close	247.53	248.77	251.40	256.09	254.07	248.67	241.99	249.46	245.63	237.83	243.36	239.61	----
1997	High	244.30	243.91	248.01	249.00	254.79	249.98	243.38	245.30	244.50	247.62	243.52	238.39	254.79
	Low	238.93	236.14	241.64	237.64	245.54	238.52	232.01	236.69	240.03	238.34	235.27	228.84	228.84
	Close	238.99	242.41	245.17	248.29	250.96	239.42	242.75	241.98	243.06	240.04	235.92	229.14	----
1998	High	235.36	236.08	231.74	229.09	226.67	216.75	216.75	207.48	205.03	206.57	206.73	197.29	236.08
	Low	221.56	223.97	223.04	223.42	214.03	208.42	205.99	195.18	196.31	201.34	195.18	187.89	187.89
	Close	234.28	227.65	228.88	223.99	215.90	214.63	206.00	195.68	203.30	203.28	195.42	191.22	----
1999	High	198.96	191.45	193.28	192.89	193.99	193.43	192.91	199.59	209.41	209.91	207.54	206.20	209.91
	Low	187.18	182.76	183.38	187.14	185.05	185.07	182.67	190.14	199.03	199.66	202.23	200.74	182.67
	Close	189.74	182.95	191.83	192.39	186.72	191.54	190.36	199.35	205.19	201.52	204.07	205.14	----
2000	High	213.70	215.29	217.88	214.15	226.12	227.29	225.69	228.02	232.20	234.38	231.46	233.37	234.38
	Low	201.43	206.74	209.61	207.61	211.86	222.23	217.42	217.76	224.74	218.38	220.93	225.46	201.43
	Close	210.46	208.78	214.37	211.03	222.27	223.93	218.61	227.41	226.57	219.28	229.79	227.83	----
2001	High	232.58	228.34	225.75	216.39	219.29	212.39	209.27	202.90	202.34	191.09	192.74	193.94	232.58
	Low	223.02	219.68	210.24	208.87	208.43	203.86	201.84	197.02	188.24	182.83	181.83	187.73	181.83
	Close	224.12	221.78	210.26	214.50	209.00	205.56	202.70	199.63	190.49	185.66	192.66	190.61	----
2002	High	195.97	193.53	205.45	208.39	205.33	209.33	215.10	219.24	229.62	231.67	231.83	238.39	238.39
	Low	186.38	187.19	192.26	195.21	197.42	199.56	207.24	208.46	217.60	223.82	223.29	230.17	186.38
	Close	187.29	192.33	204.92	201.16	204.20	209.29	210.97	219.20	226.53	228.91	230.64	234.52	----
2003	High	248.92	251.59	247.23	236.62	242.16	238.25	237.20	243.74	246.07	250.67	257.54	263.60	263.60
	Low	234.58	245.39	228.10	228.77	231.26	231.39	230.36	233.96	236.79	241.68	244.79	249.60	228.10
	Close	248.45	247.25	232.15	232.53	235.55	233.78	234.21	243.70	243.66	247.58	248.44	255.29	----
2004	High	271.08	275.02	285.28	284.42	277.94	282.03	275.38	278.10	285.37	289.29	292.49	291.02	292.49
	Low	257.49	258.94	270.52	268.53	266.80	264.34	265.50	265.20	269.12	280.53	280.20	276.15	257.49
	Close	262.57	274.73	283.77	272.54	277.25	265.94	267.78	276.50	284.98	283.70	290.94	283.90	----

Source: Reuters

CRB INDEXES

Reuters-CRB Futures Index
(monthly close) through December 2004

Index Value

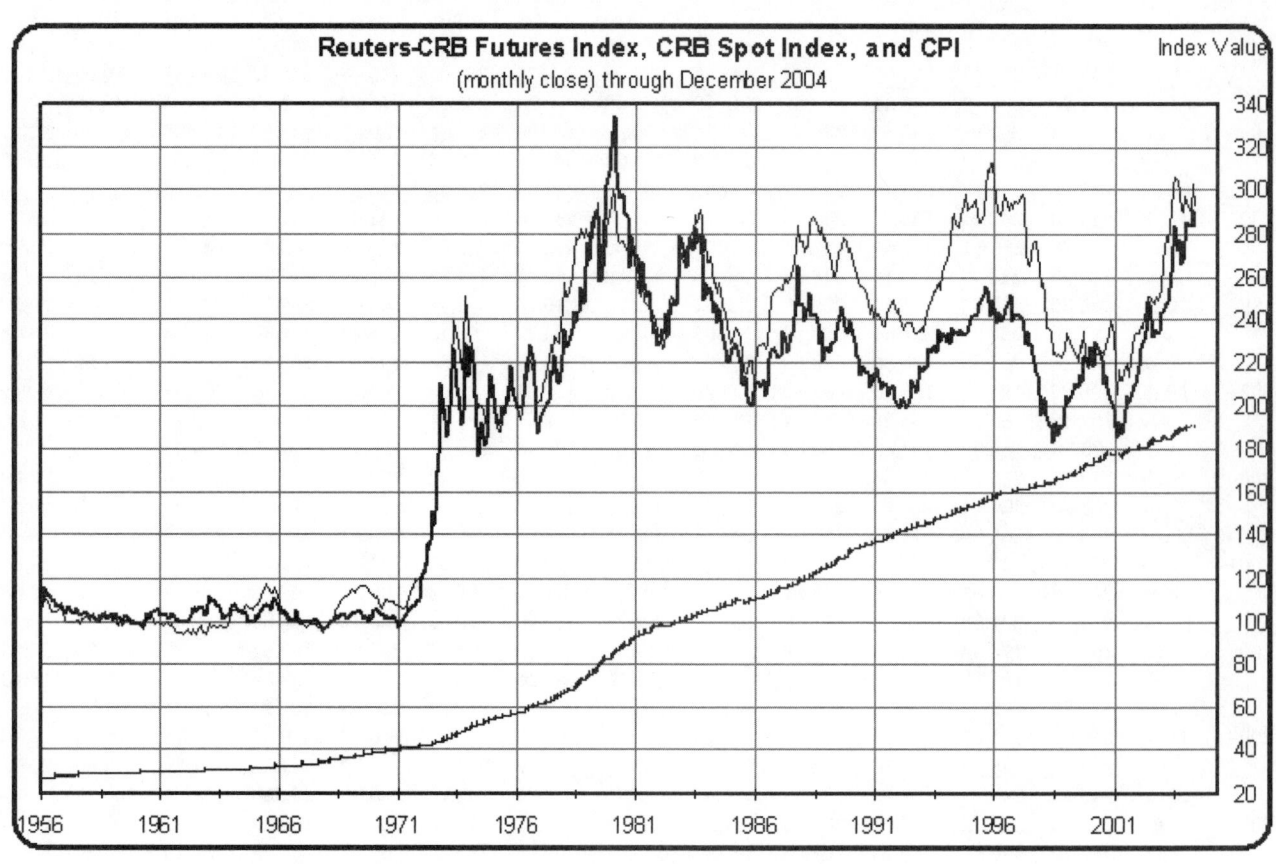

Reuters-CRB Futures Index, CRB Spot Index, and CPI
(monthly close) through December 2004

Index Value

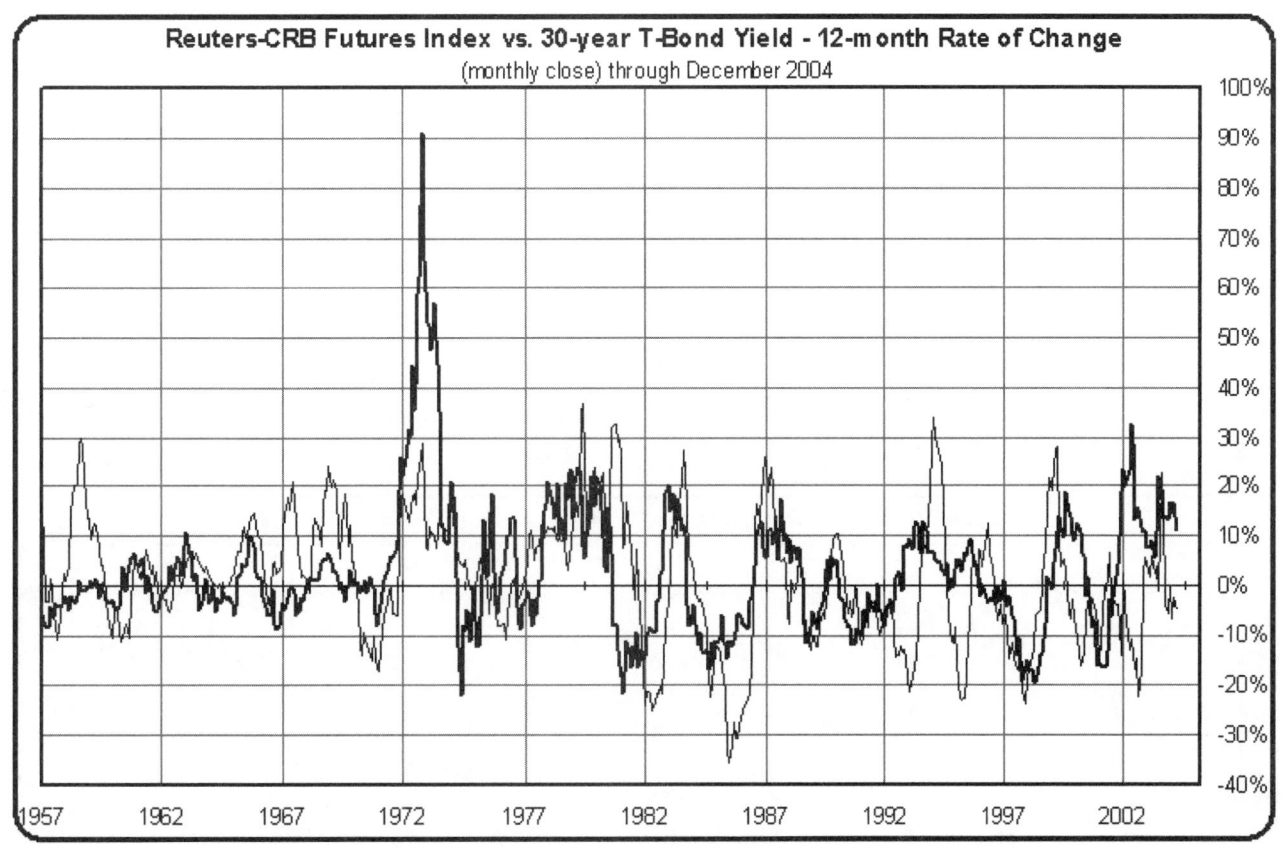

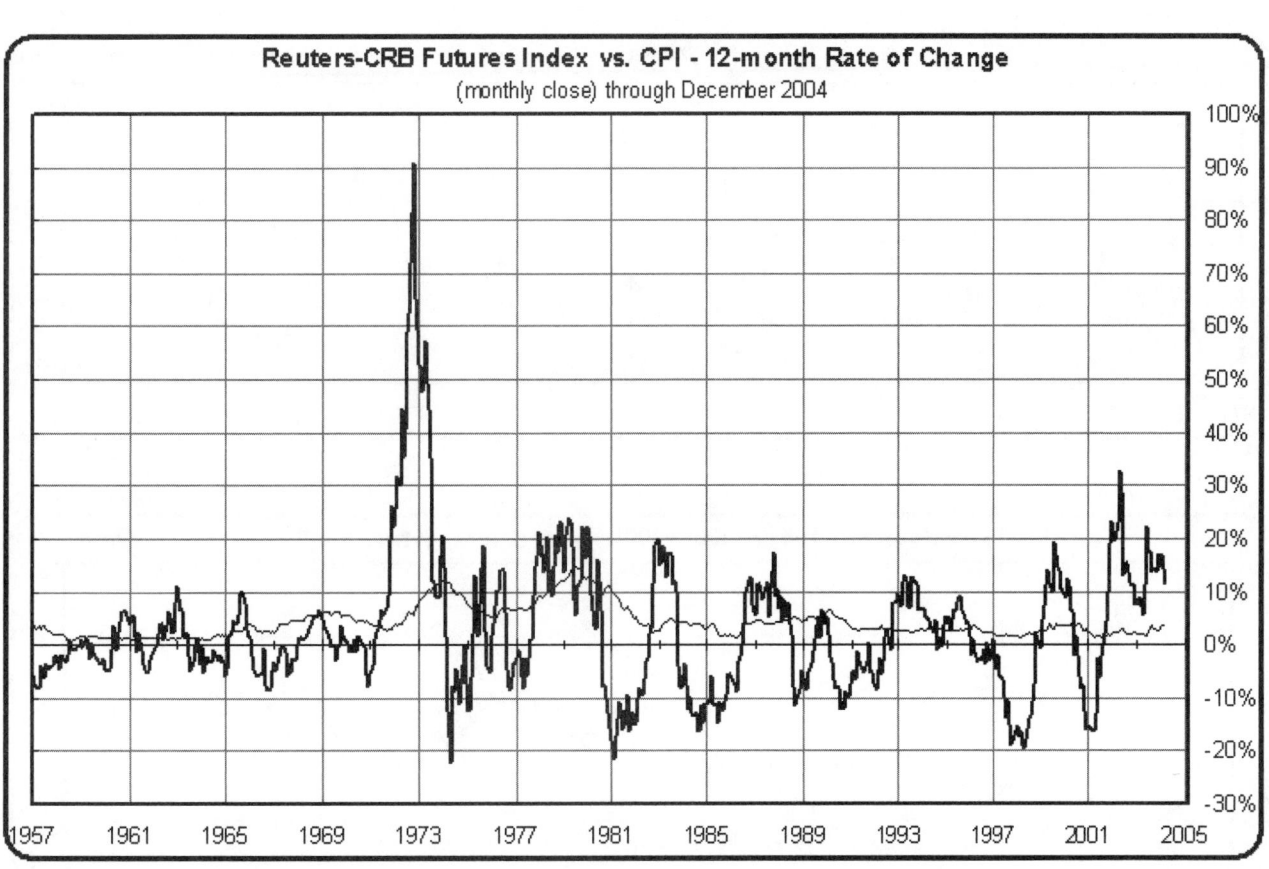

CRB INDEXES

Reuters-CRB Total Return Index (monthly close) through December 2004

Reuters-CRB Total Return Index (weekly close) as of December 31, 2004

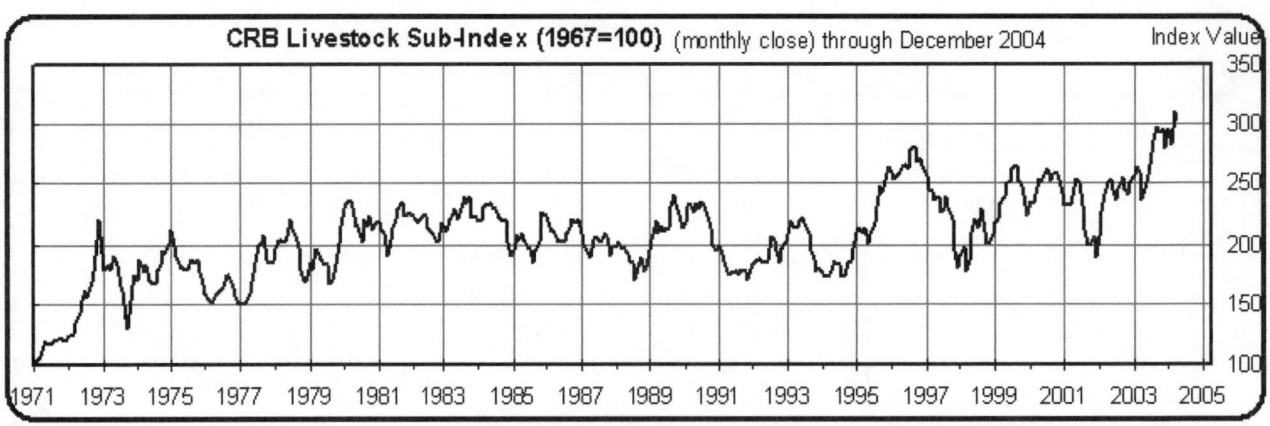

CRB Livestock Sub-Index (1967=100) (monthly close) through December 2004

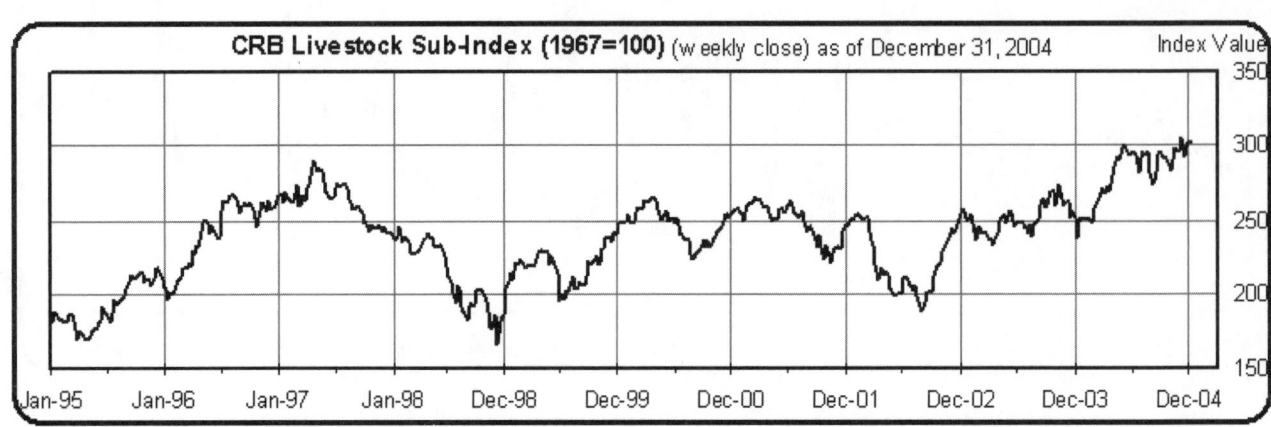

CRB Livestock Sub-Index (1967=100) (weekly close) as of December 31, 2004

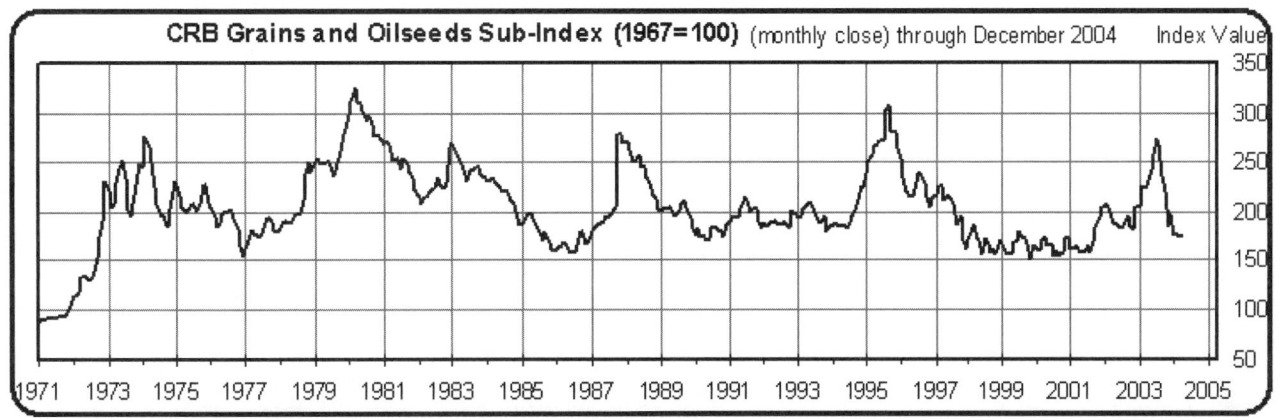

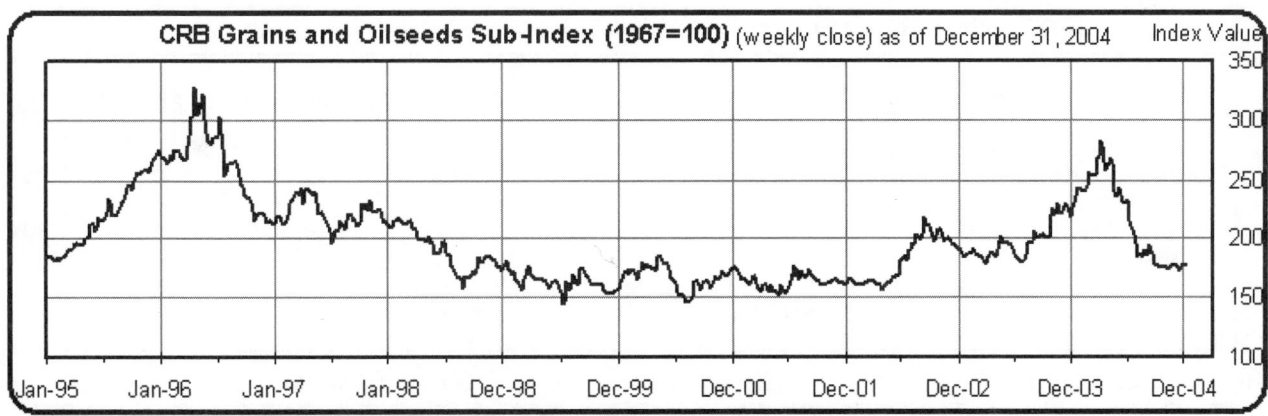

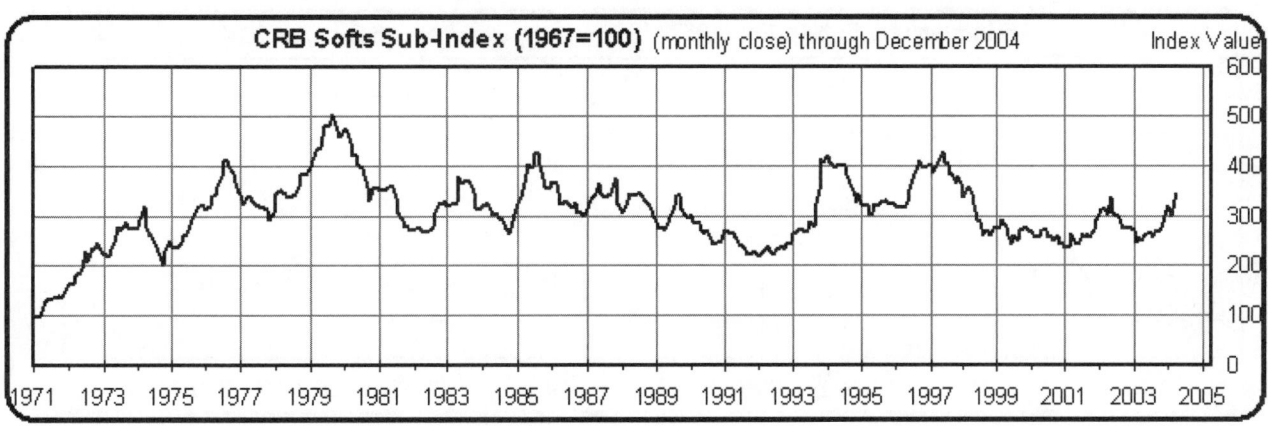

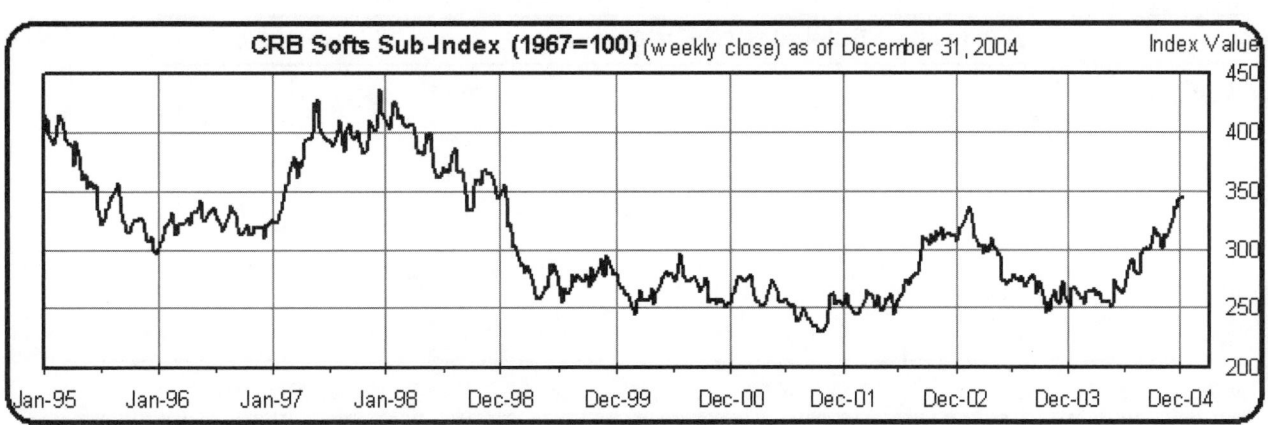

CRB INDEXES

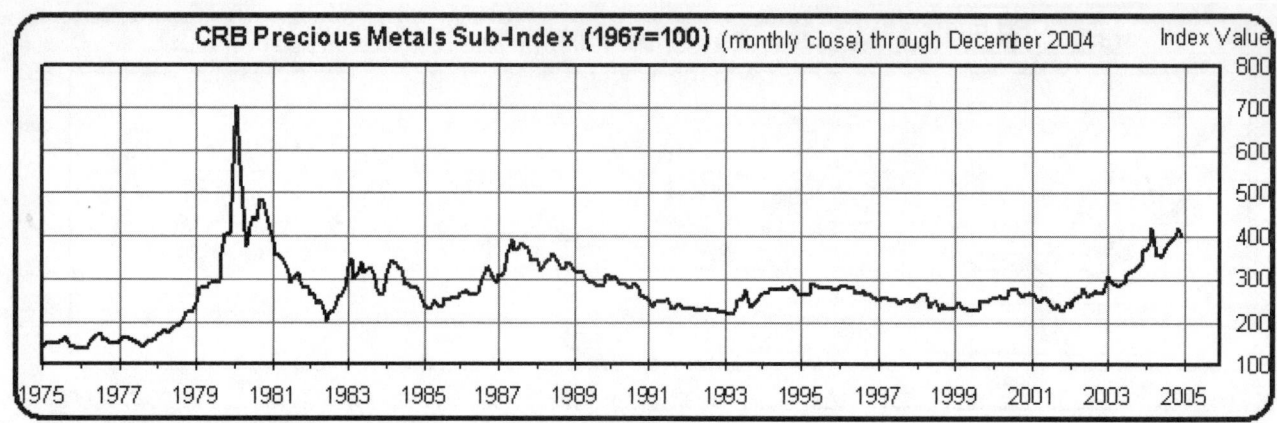

CRB Precious Metals Sub-Index (1967=100) (monthly close) through December 2004   Index Value

CRB Precious Metals Sub-Index (1967=100) (weekly close) as of December 31, 2004   Index Value

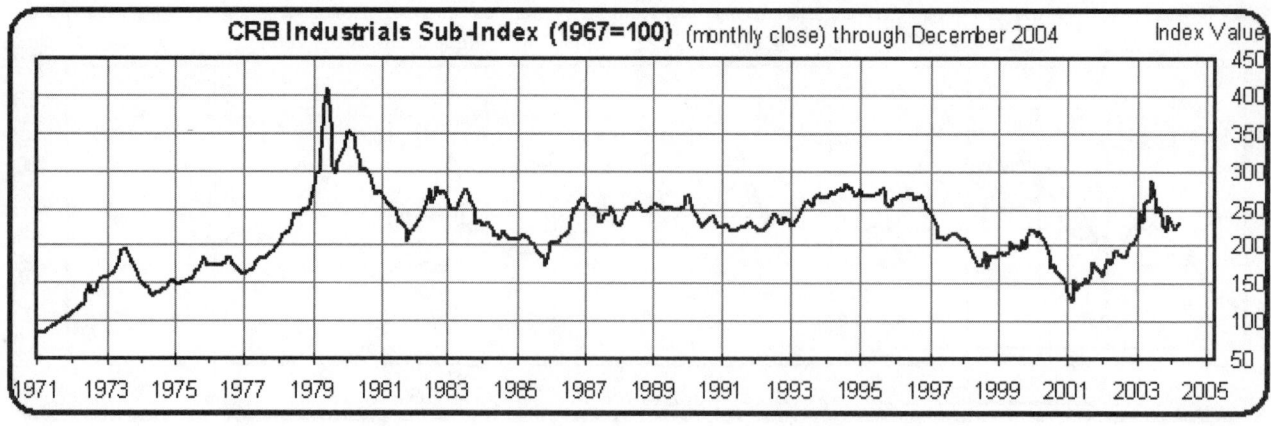

CRB Industrials Sub-Index (1967=100) (monthly close) through December 2004   Index Value

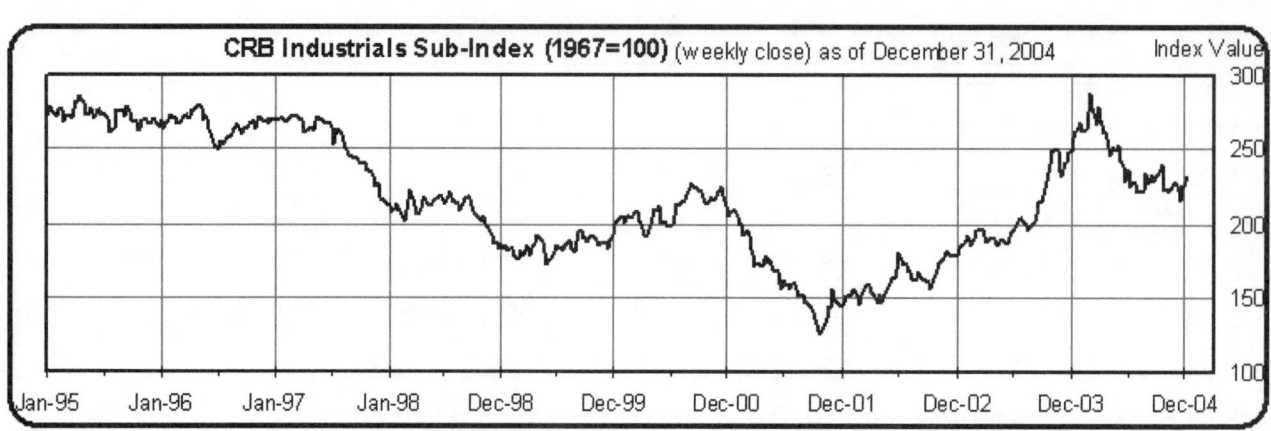

CRB Industrials Sub-Index (1967=100) (weekly close) as of December 31, 2004   Index Value

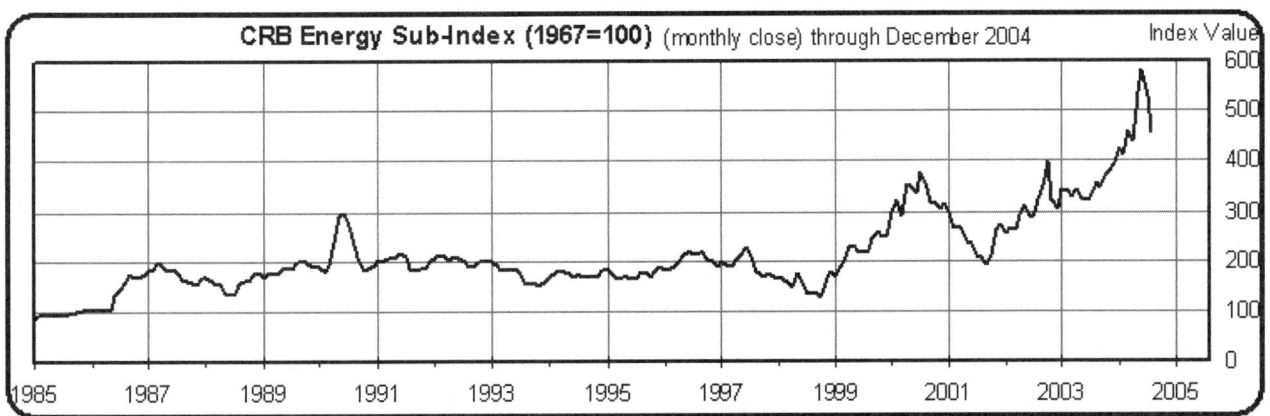

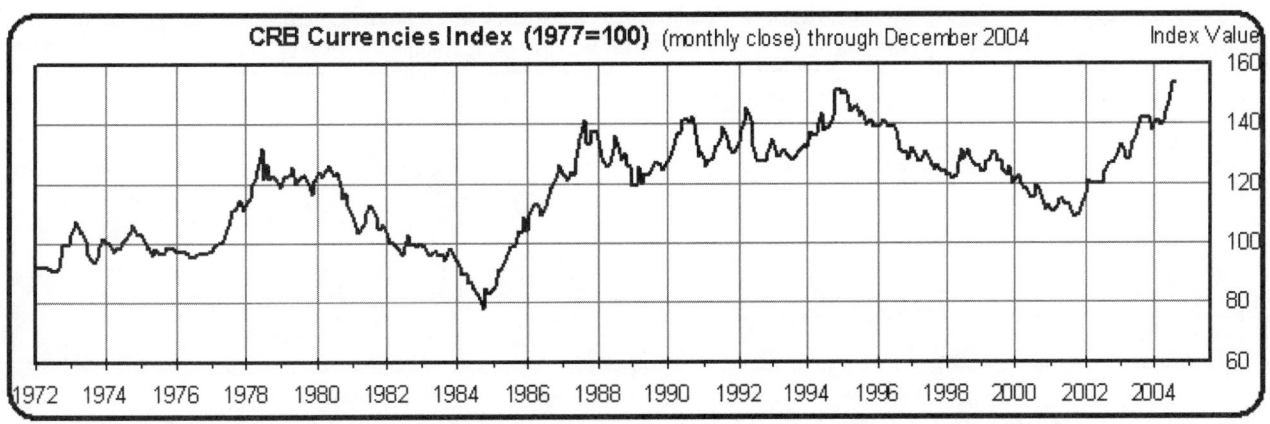

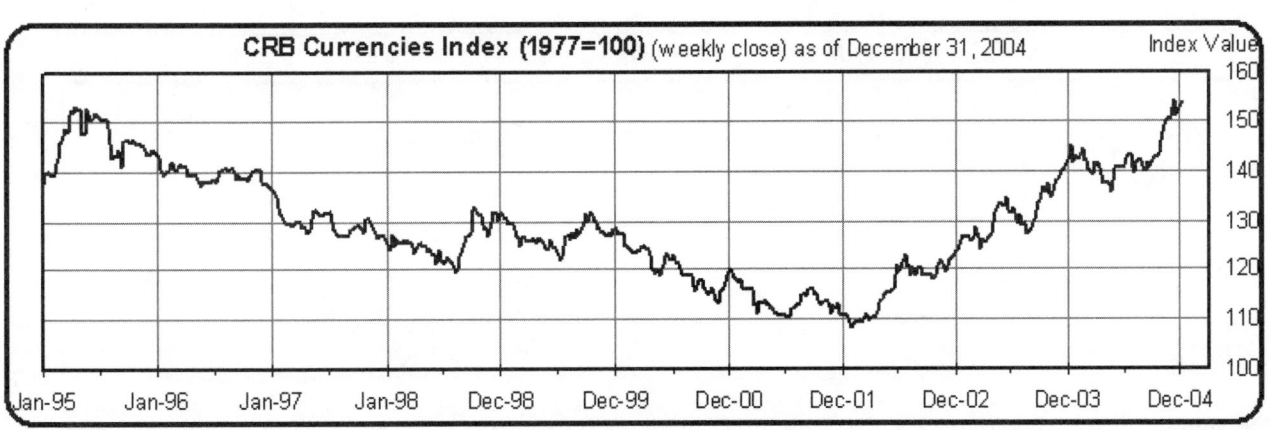

CRB INDEXES

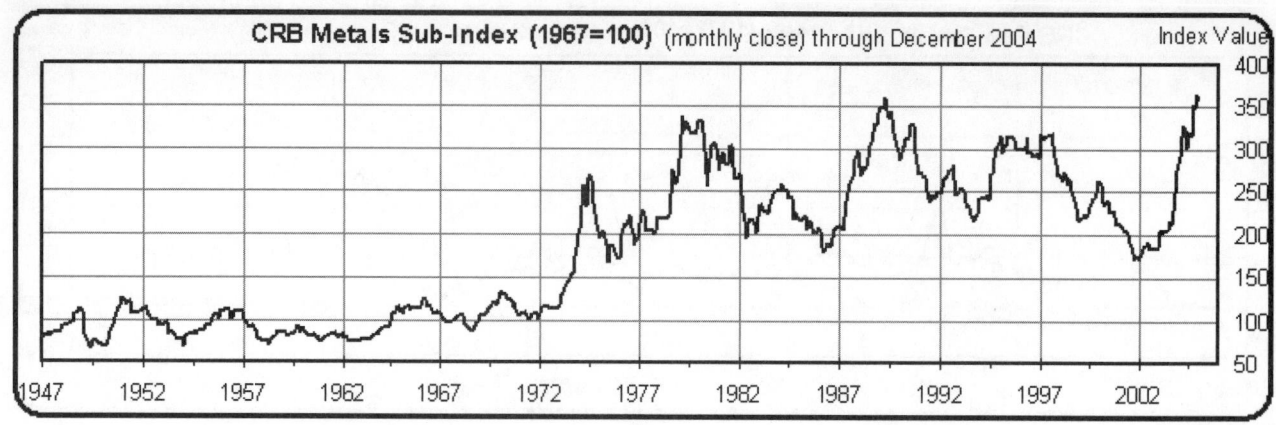

CRB Metals Sub-Index (1967=100) (monthly close) through December 2004

Index Value

CRB Metals Sub-Index (1967=100) (weekly close) as of December 31, 2004

Index Value

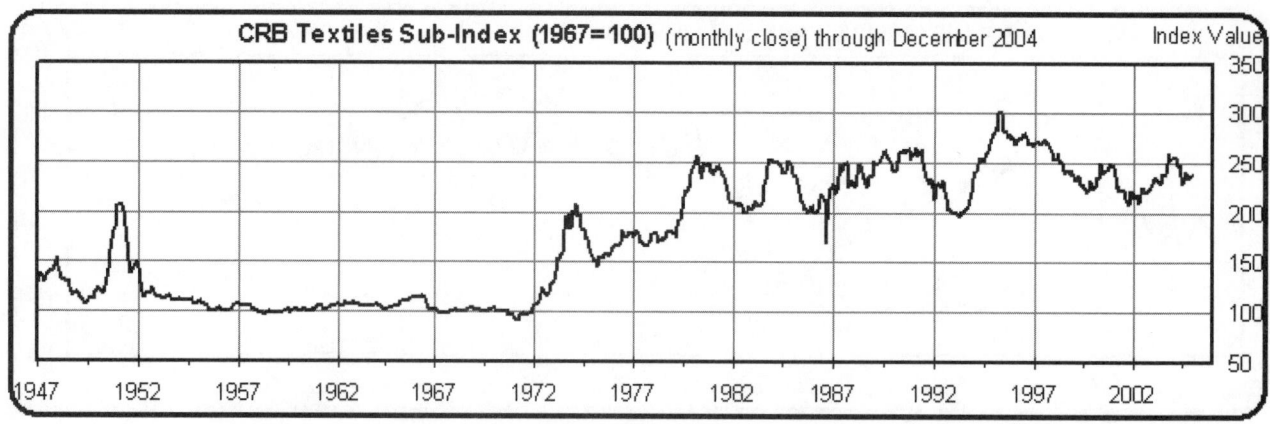

CRB Textiles Sub-Index (1967=100) (monthly close) through December 2004

Index Value

CRB Textiles Sub-Index (1967=100) (weekly close) as of December 31, 2004

Index Value

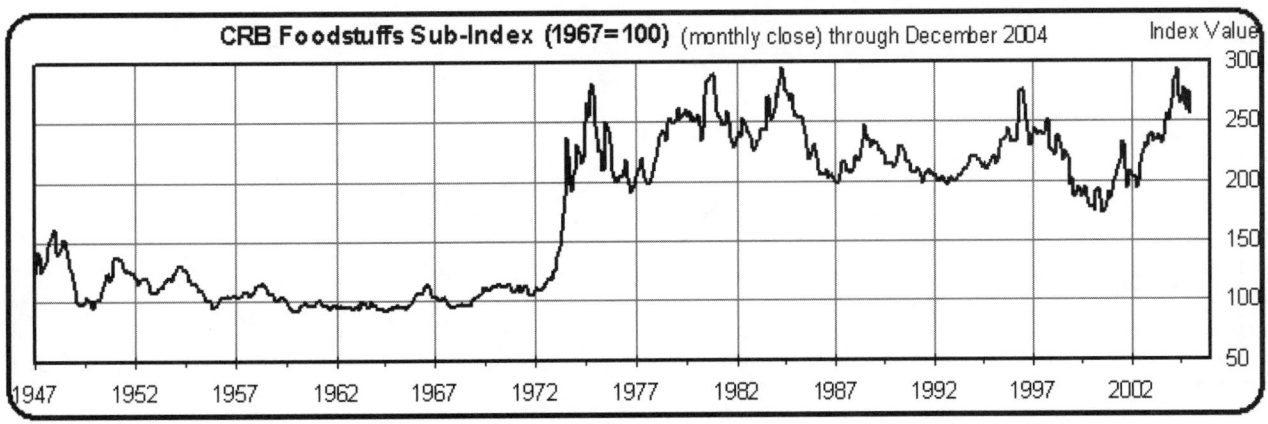

CRB INDEXES

CRB Fats & Oils Sub-Index (1967=100) (monthly close) through December 2004

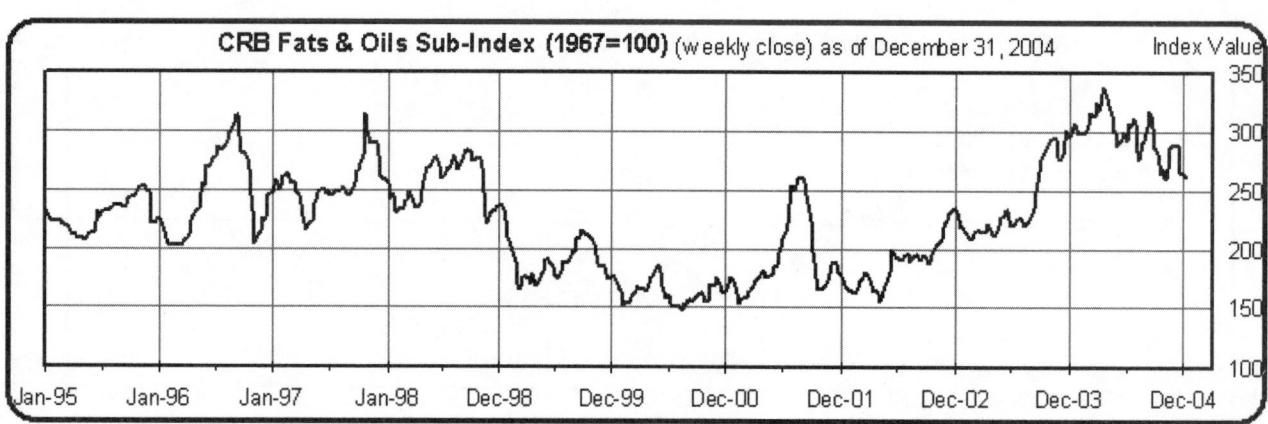

CRB Fats & Oils Sub-Index (1967=100) (weekly close) as of December 31, 2004

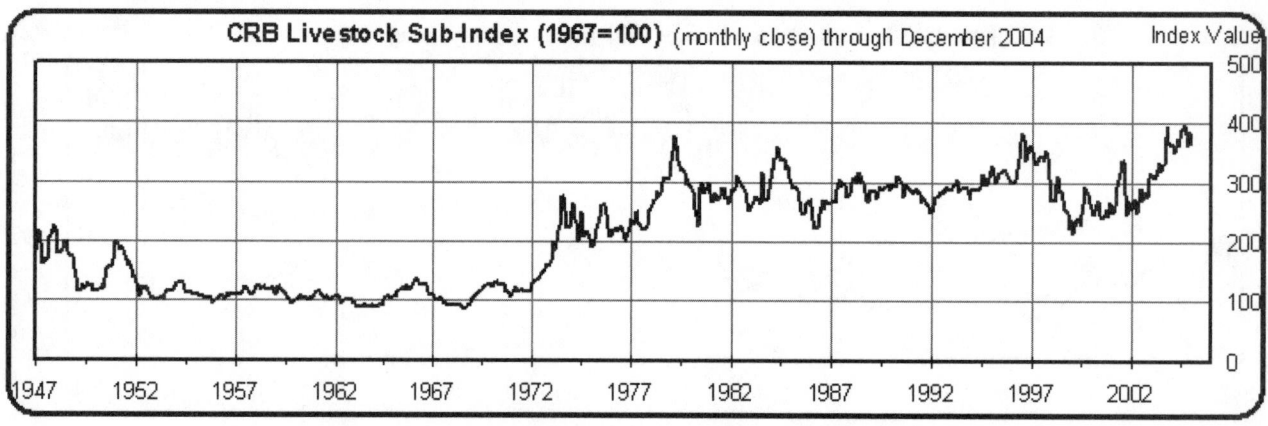

CRB Livestock Sub-Index (1967=100) (monthly close) through December 2004

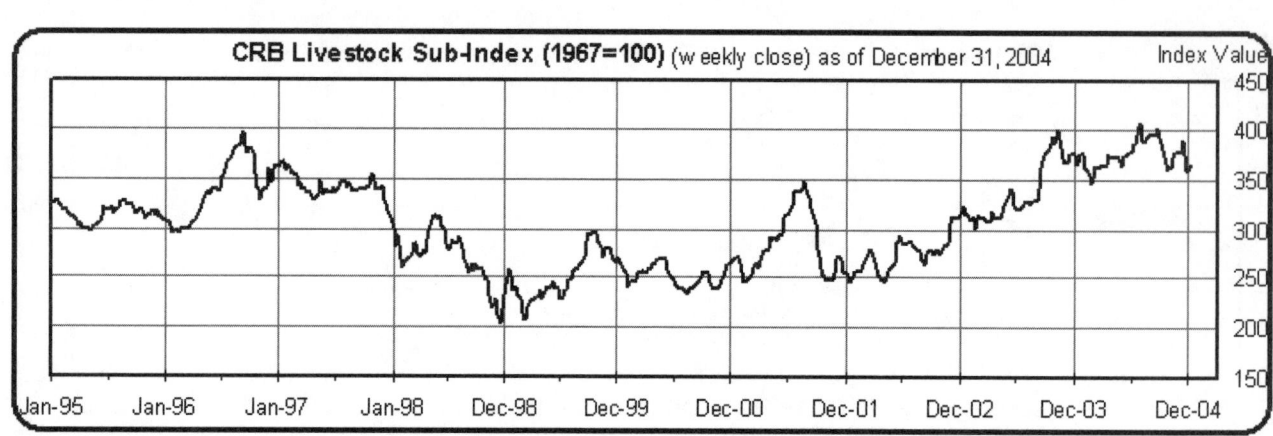

CRB Livestock Sub-Index (1967=100) (weekly close) as of December 31, 2004

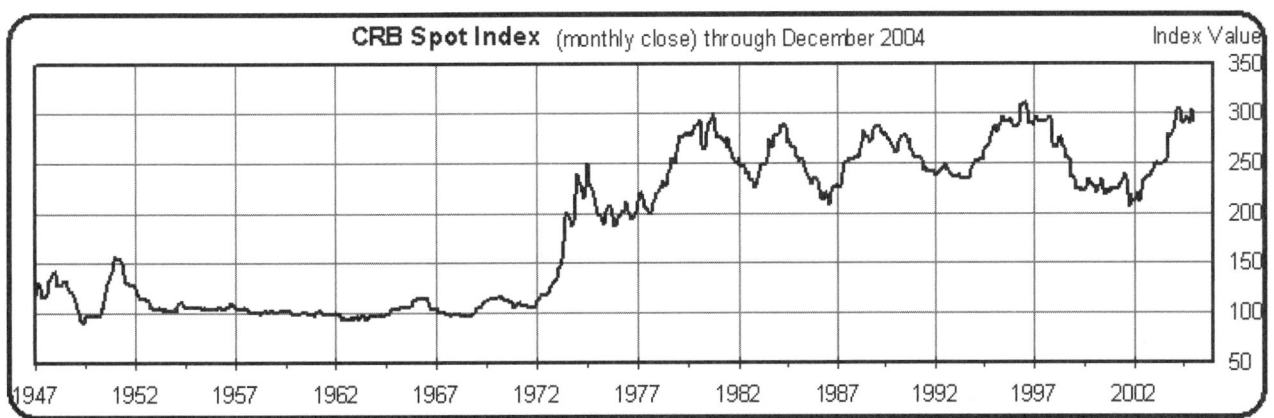

CRB Spot Index (monthly close) through December 2004

CRB Spot Index (weekly close) as of December 31, 2004

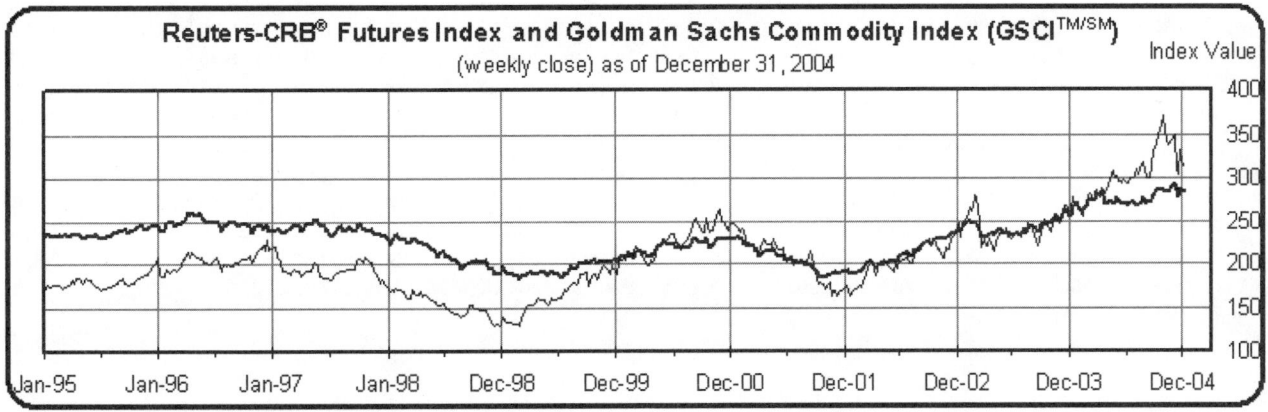

Reuters-CRB® Futures Index and Goldman Sachs Commodity Index (GSCI™/SM)
(weekly close) as of December 31, 2004

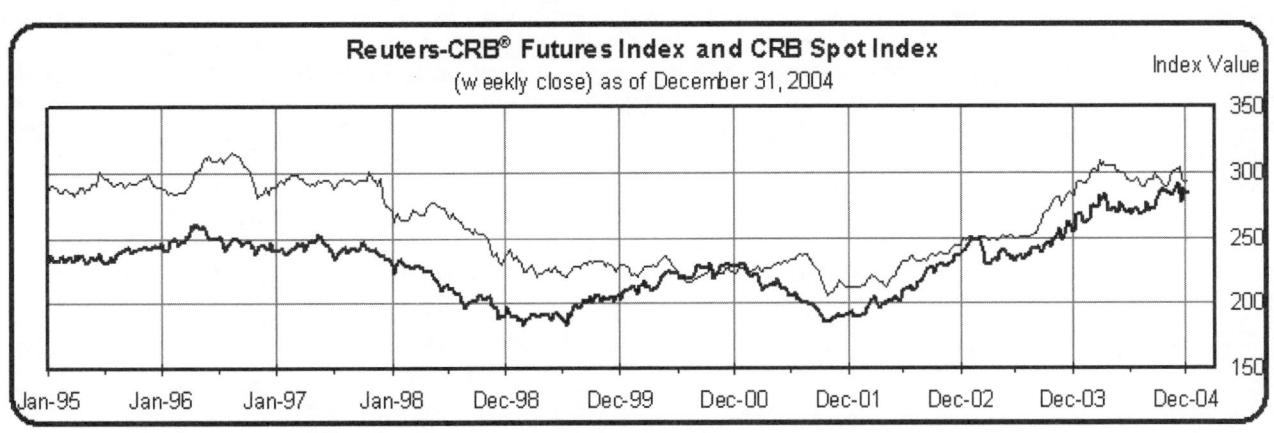

Reuters-CRB® Futures Index and CRB Spot Index
(weekly close) as of December 31, 2004

CRB INDEXES

Reuters-CRB Futures Index   (1967=100)

Year	Jan.	Feb.	Mar.	Apr.	May	June	July	Aug.	Sept.	Oct.	Nov.	Dec.	Average
1995	234.92	233.85	233.97	236.16	233.45	234.87	232.43	236.01	241.64	241.01	242.67	244.30	237.11
1996	243.22	248.65	248.38	257.84	257.85	249.64	245.88	248.27	246.26	244.56	241.95	242.55	247.92
1997	241.57	239.75	245.29	244.60	250.45	243.78	236.30	240.99	242.24	243.67	240.06	234.27	241.91
1998	228.96	230.59	227.27	225.62	221.19	213.19	209.86	202.06	202.19	203.75	201.76	191.76	213.18
1999	192.49	187.21	188.50	189.83	190.04	191.16	187.16	196.72	202.20	203.88	203.90	204.10	194.77
2000	207.65	211.28	213.87	211.29	220.42	224.73	220.51	220.84	228.23	226.36	226.56	228.98	220.06
2001	228.30	223.42	218.06	213.43	214.69	208.37	204.98	200.18	195.34	186.20	188.42	190.42	205.98
2002	191.44	190.91	201.86	200.74	201.69	203.92	211.42	214.01	226.00	227.52	228.54	234.62	211.06
2003	242.04	247.89	237.81	231.73	237.38	235.11	234.05	238.13	241.44	246.15	250.66	258.44	241.74
2004	266.65	264.93	278.19	276.48	272.78	270.78	270.41	271.18	276.47	285.36	286.02	283.28	275.21

Average.   *Source: Reuters*

Reuters-CRB Total Return Index   (01/02/1982 = 100)

Year	Jan.	Feb.	Mar.	Apr.	May	June	July	Aug.	Sept.	Oct.	Nov.	Dec.	Average
1995	169.98	169.52	172.28	176.46	176.31	176.97	174.80	177.88	181.54	182.10	185.24	187.54	177.55
1996	188.83	195.24	198.53	208.97	212.70	208.38	207.94	210.28	210.51	209.04	208.71	210.91	205.84
1997	213.40	214.34	220.88	220.95	227.21	222.93	217.83	224.70	226.54	229.04	227.08	223.55	222.37
1998	218.70	220.31	216.50	216.38	212.56	203.76	198.67	190.58	188.10	188.33	185.97	175.45	201.28
1999	174.03	168.19	167.75	168.26	167.90	167.79	162.71	170.56	174.40	176.55	176.57	176.74	170.95
2000	179.91	184.26	185.75	184.91	192.79	196.58	193.58	194.90	200.34	201.69	201.20	203.34	193.27
2001	203.36	201.01	195.92	192.85	193.22	187.33	184.07	180.47	175.05	166.56	167.80	168.76	184.70
2002	168.68	167.57	176.25	175.30	175.60	176.90	182.67	184.84	193.03	193.63	194.30	199.36	182.34
2003	206.09	212.02	204.98	200.88	205.98	203.97	203.20	206.86	209.00	213.19	217.06	224.06	208.94
2004	232.53	232.63	243.99	243.01	239.65	238.51	237.98	239.34	242.08	249.59	249.77	248.58	241.47

Average.   *Source: Reuters*

Reuters-CRB Livestock Sub-Index   (1967=100)

Year	Jan.	Feb.	Mar.	Apr.	May	June	July	Aug.	Sept.	Oct.	Nov.	Dec.	Average
1995	185.34	182.37	182.24	173.59	173.43	184.03	185.86	195.55	208.75	213.69	209.00	215.05	192.41
1996	201.57	207.41	216.98	230.40	248.31	241.82	258.82	264.31	260.11	253.94	256.55	260.00	241.69
1997	266.08	264.82	262.53	279.54	282.22	268.15	271.58	265.42	257.26	245.92	244.43	242.39	262.53
1998	239.60	234.03	226.72	235.29	235.76	229.99	207.42	197.30	189.93	199.85	186.52	180.88	213.61
1999	206.47	220.47	218.75	222.97	226.14	219.14	198.18	206.89	209.31	221.68	227.97	239.13	218.09
2000	247.36	249.80	257.10	262.53	256.37	251.37	243.94	229.65	228.34	233.64	239.69	251.99	245.98
2001	254.81	254.62	262.97	259.27	252.40	257.32	257.15	248.31	240.83	230.82	227.86	237.26	248.64
2002	249.43	251.46	243.59	216.16	209.26	199.59	206.70	196.98	197.76	217.97	234.73	247.80	222.62
2003	252.70	242.32	240.06	237.27	251.07	248.86	245.33	244.63	261.29	264.33	264.96	255.07	250.66
2004	248.90	250.53	266.53	274.15	291.60	294.91	292.29	285.44	287.72	287.29	296.26	297.60	281.10

Average.   *Source: Reuters*

Reuters-CRB Grains and Oilseeds Sub-Index   (1967=100)

Year	Jan.	Feb.	Mar.	Apr.	May	June	July	Aug.	Sept.	Oct.	Nov.	Dec.	Average
1995	184.82	183.20	189.04	195.61	201.36	210.98	225.25	222.79	237.96	249.06	256.38	266.37	218.57
1996	267.57	271.40	271.53	301.95	307.91	282.07	278.63	263.07	253.05	232.64	219.07	214.39	263.61
1997	215.98	221.87	237.07	238.69	230.18	215.02	205.02	212.19	216.58	224.63	226.06	218.68	221.83
1998	214.52	214.79	213.25	199.56	196.08	190.83	182.58	166.56	169.78	179.47	184.47	177.89	190.82
1999	174.76	165.92	170.54	166.69	163.22	163.11	152.45	166.33	170.88	161.96	158.72	155.35	164.16
2000	167.48	170.65	174.94	174.44	180.96	169.12	152.62	150.32	160.91	162.60	167.06	171.37	166.87
2001	171.45	163.23	164.33	158.41	155.93	156.71	170.42	168.74	167.95	161.37	163.22	162.14	163.66
2002	164.09	160.38	163.97	160.53	162.97	171.11	188.10	199.34	213.65	204.33	200.95	193.39	181.90
2003	187.57	189.29	183.12	185.98	194.62	193.35	181.84	192.82	201.68	209.28	222.27	226.46	197.36
2004	237.68	243.83	261.79	267.95	247.24	234.25	203.40	188.28	186.93	176.69	176.41	175.24	216.64

Average.   *Source: Reuters*

Reuters-CRB Softs Sub-Index   (1967=100)

Year	Jan.	Feb.	Mar.	Apr.	May	June	July	Aug.	Sept.	Oct.	Nov.	Dec.	Average
1995	405.39	399.28	399.95	384.85	364.22	351.55	329.05	345.29	325.52	321.52	322.60	304.13	354.45
1996	307.43	325.93	319.41	327.69	331.92	330.58	322.33	328.79	320.57	316.11	317.36	317.84	322.16
1997	327.64	350.54	372.52	382.78	413.76	401.03	394.65	398.59	399.18	389.98	401.19	419.17	387.59
1998	415.43	413.98	404.35	387.22	393.07	365.64	367.69	372.51	348.36	351.86	365.91	353.12	378.26
1999	337.91	307.51	285.94	267.35	264.74	281.81	263.21	272.47	277.53	276.51	285.29	284.51	283.73
2000	268.52	254.77	259.39	260.26	267.91	280.26	285.20	273.72	270.43	270.05	257.94	255.68	267.01
2001	269.11	274.59	265.27	254.72	268.62	255.68	251.01	244.01	238.45	231.91	254.36	254.63	255.20
2002	256.23	246.71	259.73	256.73	254.63	252.54	270.15	278.25	307.15	311.84	311.53	311.73	276.44
2003	320.55	326.00	302.23	302.05	293.41	272.95	275.12	273.77	271.84	257.57	258.78	263.99	284.86
2004	265.93	259.29	265.98	259.39	256.91	266.95	285.81	289.61	304.70	309.01	318.42	339.23	285.10

Average.   *Source: Reuters*

Reuters-CRB Precious Metals Sub-Index   (1967=100)

Year	Jan.	Feb.	Mar.	Apr.	May	June	July	Aug.	Sept.	Oct.	Nov.	Dec.	Average
1995	265.73	263.63	265.16	289.98	285.47	282.94	277.71	279.13	280.28	275.22	274.70	272.07	276.00
1996	282.94	287.42	282.22	277.93	276.71	269.07	267.44	271.57	264.94	262.25	259.36	253.98	271.32
1997	247.53	253.11	258.96	247.44	250.59	253.42	239.26	246.69	250.85	255.18	245.16	246.46	249.55
1998	248.47	264.43	260.37	268.39	249.46	237.82	245.86	236.52	233.80	231.20	231.77	229.92	244.83
1999	234.41	242.14	236.84	232.19	232.87	225.71	224.55	225.82	232.58	253.20	246.60	246.81	236.14
2000	247.16	266.43	256.51	253.53	255.44	268.03	267.08	266.97	269.50	263.47	261.97	266.96	261.92
2001	265.48	259.23	253.04	252.17	261.28	254.87	243.70	232.22	239.24	232.66	227.06	237.71	246.56
2002	241.90	245.33	254.47	261.61	266.59	276.27	268.03	264.27	269.19	267.88	272.29	281.24	264.09
2003	295.57	298.35	290.78	279.76	295.52	294.54	302.39	310.85	321.35	321.26	333.13	355.31	308.23
2004	377.11	375.30	400.41	390.82	351.29	354.67	366.98	380.85	377.08	394.42	408.67	402.12	381.64

Average.   *Source: Reuters*

Reuters-CRB Industrials Sub-Index   (1967=100)

Year	Jan.	Feb.	Mar.	Apr.	May	June	July	Aug.	Sept.	Oct.	Nov.	Dec.	Average
1995	274.98	274.94	272.16	282.57	276.51	274.19	267.31	269.46	276.06	266.12	267.70	268.28	272.52
1996	267.19	269.93	270.69	274.19	274.91	257.12	253.62	261.06	263.27	266.47	267.86	268.97	266.27
1997	270.41	270.19	270.85	263.10	268.38	267.49	258.50	251.84	243.77	238.57	230.50	215.60	254.10
1998	210.53	207.84	217.25	210.75	212.15	217.89	215.99	211.93	216.96	206.76	200.15	188.18	209.70
1999	182.97	178.44	180.15	184.41	184.94	176.40	182.58	184.71	191.68	190.18	187.34	187.10	184.24
2000	201.37	202.67	204.59	194.18	207.18	200.83	207.37	217.64	224.10	217.16	217.11	219.27	209.46
2001	206.86	199.04	186.19	174.20	173.72	162.54	158.63	153.43	145.27	131.33	140.85	146.56	164.89
2002	150.49	151.21	156.49	152.31	152.59	167.27	172.54	164.08	161.79	162.28	176.79	178.53	162.20
2003	185.33	190.29	193.39	188.69	186.75	190.80	201.85	198.23	212.04	236.48	243.08	244.56	205.96
2004	262.68	269.43	273.02	256.62	249.14	234.34	224.38	226.27	233.50	227.52	223.80	223.54	242.02

Average.   *Source: Reuters*

Reuters-CRB Energy Sub-Index   (1967=100)

Year	Jan.	Feb.	Mar.	Apr.	May	June	July	Aug.	Sept.	Oct.	Nov.	Dec.	Average
1995	171.21	172.70	172.83	181.95	182.70	174.42	167.23	170.54	171.54	165.92	169.85	177.15	173.17
1996	172.90	172.23	180.81	188.88	184.71	182.51	190.10	197.32	211.80	222.07	215.48	220.02	194.90
1997	220.04	202.43	197.71	191.95	200.26	190.52	192.73	205.97	212.80	225.03	211.70	188.21	203.28
1998	172.94	174.02	167.87	175.68	167.64	160.86	159.57	150.85	166.17	163.45	153.67	133.38	162.18
1999	134.58	129.41	146.56	169.80	174.02	180.31	196.88	219.08	228.80	225.66	225.76	223.94	187.90
2000	231.38	245.97	254.09	244.62	278.91	308.81	301.39	328.52	366.18	356.34	366.76	361.93	303.74
2001	345.00	328.00	312.27	319.96	308.23	292.65	267.20	269.05	253.17	232.68	214.70	206.92	279.15
2002	195.20	202.12	243.96	262.72	269.34	258.24	260.08	274.04	301.33	301.49	278.41	311.52	263.20
2003	337.33	375.64	346.99	313.78	328.18	342.51	332.71	343.58	317.98	338.95	331.81	361.52	339.25
2004	371.45	355.20	376.02	384.99	426.01	419.28	438.34	459.75	475.69	574.75	535.62	475.97	441.09

Average.   *Source: Reuters*

CRB INDEXES

Reuters-CRB Currencies Index   (1977=100)

Year	Jan.	Feb.	Mar.	Apr.	May	June	July	Aug.	Sept.	Oct.	Nov.	Dec.	Average
1995	139.31	140.54	147.85	152.52	150.20	150.85	150.58	145.41	143.89	146.33	145.21	143.83	146.38
1996	141.69	141.01	141.12	139.61	138.11	138.37	139.53	140.52	139.51	138.74	139.92	137.47	139.63
1997	134.61	130.30	129.56	128.71	130.83	131.75	130.14	126.84	128.02	129.07	129.58	126.93	129.70
1998	125.06	126.10	125.65	124.96	124.33	122.86	121.89	120.65	126.18	130.98	128.86	130.69	125.68
1999	130.97	128.48	126.37	125.74	125.32	124.63	124.08	126.89	128.89	130.66	128.24	127.71	127.33
2000	127.65	124.37	124.01	123.43	119.42	122.54	121.59	119.04	117.11	115.99	114.89	117.55	120.63
2001	118.42	116.58	114.25	113.01	112.24	110.92	111.29	114.02	115.21	114.04	112.69	112.01	113.72
2002	110.20	109.38	110.40	111.33	114.54	117.39	121.30	119.68	119.54	119.02	120.77	121.97	116.29
2003	125.37	126.36	126.61	126.42	132.07	133.04	130.30	128.77	130.93	135.96	136.23	140.44	131.04
2004	143.44	143.23	140.68	139.36	137.62	140.48	141.81	140.92	141.25	144.04	149.66	152.54	142.92

Average.   *Source: Reuters*

Reuters-CRB Interest Rates Index   (1977=100)

Year	Jan.	Feb.	Mar.	Apr.	May	June	July	Aug.	Sept.	Oct.	Nov.	Dec.	Average
1995	104.56	106.24	107.34	108.11	110.87	113.49	112.66	111.53	113.26	114.58	115.45	116.96	111.25
1996	117.19	116.20	112.99	111.43	110.52	109.76	110.19	111.53	110.24	111.89	113.96	113.43	112.44
1997	111.73	112.69	110.78	109.74	111.02	112.12	113.61	113.14	113.73	114.68	115.77	116.46	112.96
1998	117.89	117.38	116.89	116.99	116.87	118.00	118.13	119.09	121.67	122.67	121.23	122.33	119.10
1999	121.32	119.62	118.11	118.56	116.57	112.78	112.32	110.71	108.79	106.42	107.46	104.56	113.10
2000	100.05	101.51	102.61	103.99	101.80	103.65	104.12	105.21	105.10	105.57	105.94	108.44	104.00
2001	108.79	108.94	109.86	108.61	107.69	107.90	108.24	109.63	110.74	112.26	112.29	108.97	109.49
2002	109.51	110.34	107.65	108.31	109.04	110.08	111.45	114.14	116.24	115.54	115.44	115.27	111.92
2003	115.27	116.68	116.88	116.13	119.22	120.42	116.27	113.02	113.86	NA	NA	NA	116.42
2004	NA	NA	123.94	118.47	115.30	114.52	117.46	119.91	121.02	121.71	121.25	120.64	119.42

Average.   Index not calculated for September 16, 2003 to March 17, 2004 due the non-trading status of the 90-day T-Bill futures .   *Source: Reuters*

Reuters-CRB Energy Index   (1977=100)

Year	Jan.	Feb.	Mar.	Apr.	May	June	July	Aug.	Sept.	Oct.	Nov.	Dec.	Average
1995	164.14	165.53	164.81	173.68	175.03	166.48	158.37	161.43	162.35	156.59	160.74	168.23	164.78
1996	164.97	163.44	171.10	179.54	174.63	171.72	178.55	184.68	196.42	206.02	201.08	206.38	183.21
1997	206.58	190.96	186.85	179.95	186.96	177.03	179.48	183.81	181.21	189.93	184.01	172.65	184.95
1998	161.58	157.72	151.69	154.94	153.95	146.54	140.94	133.79	143.89	140.22	131.31	118.14	144.56
1999	121.00	116.39	136.44	152.20	153.53	157.52	176.40	185.48	196.52	192.71	202.36	207.81	166.53
2000	220.53	237.09	241.29	221.42	247.72	263.67	255.40	268.97	292.15	287.36	286.70	249.86	256.01
2001	251.05	256.70	246.06	258.47	264.15	248.51	231.56	238.47	231.53	201.64	180.55	180.49	232.43
2002	185.01	190.86	224.68	234.25	233.13	226.56	234.70	240.27	256.04	250.75	228.78	258.02	230.25
2003	279.06	307.09	282.73	243.10	243.92	256.78	264.31	275.82	248.55	265.44	271.25	284.02	268.51
2004	300.37	298.35	314.50	322.72	359.33	342.21	367.52	389.41	402.57	460.54	430.64	389.95	364.84

Average.   *Source: Reuters*

CRB Metals Sub-Index   (1967=100)

Year	Jan.	Feb.	Mar.	Apr.	May	June	July	Aug.	Sept.	Oct.	Nov.	Dec.	Average
1995	313.63	299.01	298.04	303.14	303.64	311.24	314.25	318.17	308.45	303.26	305.74	301.53	306.68
1996	299.42	299.46	301.22	301.43	308.34	300.32	291.72	294.20	293.15	289.90	290.94	289.87	296.66
1997	301.63	314.62	313.30	307.82	314.72	316.61	316.07	319.28	310.95	296.58	290.01	271.76	306.11
1998	268.29	264.16	267.94	272.68	270.55	265.39	261.89	255.45	243.16	232.73	224.78	218.73	253.81
1999	213.74	221.29	220.66	222.50	227.01	223.50	234.41	237.06	243.65	242.77	247.19	253.77	232.30
2000	261.71	248.29	240.26	237.57	241.56	239.24	232.04	226.20	228.82	225.15	216.25	215.36	234.37
2001	212.47	212.90	210.59	204.94	205.14	205.60	197.04	188.09	181.32	179.50	172.96	173.80	195.36
2002	174.76	176.41	181.22	186.31	189.12	189.38	192.66	184.51	184.03	185.61	183.21	186.27	184.46
2003	199.71	204.17	206.72	202.78	205.57	207.77	212.24	214.09	220.24	240.20	248.49	266.70	219.06
2004	287.40	306.07	320.96	321.90	314.73	308.28	312.29	318.21	333.97	350.45	359.77	361.92	324.66

Average.   *Source: Commodity Research Bureau*

CRB Textiles Sub-Index (1967=100)

Year	Jan.	Feb.	Mar.	Apr.	May	June	July	Aug.	Sept.	Oct.	Nov.	Dec.	Average
1995	280.48	282.37	291.19	296.05	299.12	302.66	292.36	279.76	277.13	275.23	279.43	275.91	285.97
1996	276.49	272.70	273.40	275.41	276.87	277.40	275.16	279.64	277.22	273.05	269.86	268.40	274.63
1997	269.52	271.25	274.25	271.49	270.16	270.89	271.97	273.21	272.06	270.64	269.23	262.34	270.58
1998	257.45	253.08	259.10	254.41	249.87	250.57	249.00	246.35	244.38	243.39	242.46	240.31	249.20
1999	237.40	233.67	235.09	234.94	234.45	229.24	225.02	226.43	222.21	223.51	227.73	222.63	229.36
2000	226.56	227.69	234.87	234.25	242.70	243.76	241.28	243.73	244.33	244.90	248.17	248.57	240.07
2001	244.74	241.84	233.40	225.97	224.47	222.12	222.44	218.55	214.74	207.79	215.86	218.99	224.24
2002	218.08	216.84	218.40	214.72	211.21	220.16	222.95	221.74	219.02	220.10	225.85	227.76	219.74
2003	231.25	235.31	235.04	234.64	231.66	235.24	240.88	237.50	244.30	256.99	257.59	254.25	241.22
2004	257.58	253.15	252.37	247.97	249.74	242.65	233.48	233.58	237.31	235.03	235.88	236.39	242.93

Average.   *Source: Commodity Research Bureau*

CRB Raw Industrials Sub-Index   (1967=100)

Year	Jan.	Feb.	Mar.	Apr.	May	June	July	Aug.	Sept.	Oct.	Nov.	Dec.	Average
1995	347.95	340.48	344.60	350.13	352.09	354.17	345.59	339.41	334.33	332.30	339.24	333.59	342.82
1996	330.62	327.90	330.35	333.51	340.92	336.13	334.42	343.27	343.73	334.71	330.34	333.02	334.91
1997	339.39	344.54	340.99	333.63	336.84	337.30	334.89	340.47	337.33	334.47	327.64	310.56	334.84
1998	299.61	296.85	302.89	301.25	305.40	299.72	295.56	290.17	280.98	275.73	268.88	265.94	290.25
1999	262.81	259.65	255.03	251.75	250.07	248.91	253.43	255.96	262.56	266.37	270.39	267.30	258.69
2000	267.85	260.91	260.39	258.23	265.37	261.78	255.19	255.69	258.81	257.29	252.58	256.00	259.17
2001	254.54	248.53	246.35	244.03	244.29	245.92	244.22	238.10	228.30	220.52	218.94	221.57	237.94
2002	219.05	222.33	231.03	230.38	231.81	243.72	245.38	240.53	240.77	240.68	243.04	248.21	236.41
2003	255.85	258.59	260.97	258.79	257.65	260.47	263.77	263.99	273.24	291.18	295.88	302.30	270.22
2004	312.24	309.54	316.77	318.52	312.98	308.40	308.84	307.54	315.25	315.13	320.52	322.65	314.03

Average.   *Source: Commodity Research Bureau*

CRB Foodstuffs Sub-Index   (1967=100)

Year	Jan.	Feb.	Mar.	Apr.	May	June	July	Aug.	Sept.	Oct.	Nov.	Dec.	Average
1995	219.46	221.47	218.29	214.13	215.95	226.31	235.27	234.61	237.28	243.42	244.23	238.39	229.07
1996	233.28	232.57	233.26	246.69	265.58	274.54	276.66	276.53	265.72	251.50	229.80	230.02	251.35
1997	235.11	237.80	244.45	240.91	238.45	241.03	237.75	239.92	239.66	247.60	251.08	238.97	241.06
1998	227.01	224.06	227.68	229.62	239.15	238.54	229.77	223.56	221.42	224.02	209.87	193.10	223.98
1999	206.75	196.53	189.81	187.94	191.60	195.96	182.09	191.60	192.12	190.13	183.46	178.24	190.52
2000	180.37	175.68	183.76	189.88	194.32	190.42	176.52	171.63	175.02	183.53	186.75	186.58	182.87
2001	189.68	192.93	200.48	203.57	210.24	213.09	222.61	232.42	224.06	199.51	200.24	203.40	207.69
2002	203.33	202.39	204.04	197.88	195.85	207.11	218.25	222.32	226.98	230.63	230.76	237.99	214.79
2003	238.60	237.01	234.16	234.55	239.15	239.53	232.81	234.30	244.69	251.04	255.36	257.99	241.60
2004	263.90	275.85	287.49	287.41	285.33	278.05	273.83	270.42	272.10	257.76	268.47	261.77	273.53

Average.   *Source: Commodity Research Bureau*

CRB Fats and Oils Sub-Index   (1967=100)

Year	Jan.	Feb.	Mar.	Apr.	May	June	July	Aug.	Sept.	Oct.	Nov.	Dec.	Average
1995	229.67	222.52	217.45	210.30	209.21	220.48	231.42	236.49	236.69	245.02	251.26	229.05	228.30
1996	218.89	204.00	204.69	217.16	241.13	268.92	282.65	296.26	301.95	264.15	216.42	232.10	245.69
1997	251.33	258.86	251.94	227.72	232.31	248.87	248.32	249.72	252.10	283.11	288.95	269.92	255.26
1998	243.27	234.23	243.63	242.61	268.84	271.10	265.68	272.81	280.06	277.37	249.93	231.77	256.78
1999	230.99	194.96	172.59	174.97	176.78	187.84	178.61	191.19	209.68	209.53	194.38	177.98	191.63
2000	171.15	154.77	161.97	165.37	177.74	171.57	152.26	153.11	157.52	160.41	165.44	167.35	163.22
2001	170.49	158.27	165.77	177.63	177.95	196.02	232.89	259.60	237.33	177.05	174.66	184.78	192.70
2002	169.64	165.91	177.34	167.61	164.38	193.38	193.29	192.85	193.20	193.90	211.97	230.05	187.79
2003	222.39	209.89	215.72	216.91	219.56	229.01	225.83	223.36	251.40	285.47	288.08	292.22	239.99
2004	305.30	300.47	318.53	330.54	302.31	295.32	304.60	290.52	302.51	267.12	279.42	271.36	297.33

Average.   *Source: Commodity Research Bureau*

CRB INDEXES

CRB Livestock Sub-Index   (1967=100)

Year	Jan.	Feb.	Mar.	Apr.	May	June	July	Aug.	Sept.	Oct.	Nov.	Dec.	Average
1995	325.84	318.16	310.08	302.19	300.38	311.58	318.07	323.56	322.51	317.12	313.58	312.26	314.61
1996	302.41	296.63	301.21	310.30	334.30	338.42	358.24	379.90	386.88	360.36	338.92	352.93	338.38
1997	361.37	356.89	343.71	333.09	338.67	338.44	343.09	342.90	338.44	344.87	340.87	323.03	342.11
1998	286.77	265.73	279.13	280.03	309.09	301.80	281.81	281.60	258.47	256.56	232.29	217.99	270.94
1999	249.71	231.27	216.59	231.92	236.71	241.07	235.92	254.64	274.60	294.16	279.97	272.14	251.56
2000	261.83	245.67	252.65	258.44	268.41	260.53	241.72	238.62	245.35	252.78	240.45	259.65	252.18
2001	267.57	250.14	261.05	273.14	288.88	306.84	329.73	341.78	313.84	260.77	252.97	264.23	284.25
2002	251.61	260.32	274.95	257.32	256.33	289.40	288.22	279.03	274.13	276.94	288.86	313.14	275.85
2003	316.67	308.65	310.49	311.25	320.03	333.29	324.58	327.63	361.30	386.60	385.63	372.48	338.22
2004	372.16	353.19	362.41	369.65	369.31	374.28	395.48	392.33	395.40	365.68	373.69	370.63	374.52

Average.   *Source: Commodity Research Bureau*

CRB Spot Index   (1967=100)

Year	Jan.	Feb.	Mar.	Apr.	May	June	July	Aug.	Sept.	Oct.	Nov.	Dec.	Average
1995	288.25	285.63	285.97	286.41	288.36	294.95	295.37	291.91	290.66	292.67	296.66	290.84	290.64
1996	286.76	285.00	286.60	294.89	307.90	309.50	309.55	314.30	309.47	297.86	284.84	286.33	297.75
1997	292.16	296.14	297.68	292.11	292.54	294.07	291.18	295.14	293.41	295.82	294.16	279.06	292.79
1998	267.54	264.66	269.59	269.67	276.42	273.07	266.71	260.89	254.96	253.34	242.99	233.36	261.10
1999	238.31	231.76	226.07	223.61	224.55	225.83	221.44	227.35	231.10	232.12	230.78	226.54	228.29
2000	227.91	222.00	225.85	227.78	233.68	229.89	219.54	217.28	220.60	224.15	223.29	224.99	224.75
2001	225.75	224.13	226.51	226.66	229.81	231.98	235.20	235.83	226.62	211.72	211.15	214.01	224.95
2002	212.55	214.02	219.65	216.54	216.43	228.09	233.96	232.98	235.10	236.59	238.01	244.06	227.33
2003	248.72	249.60	249.73	248.66	250.00	251.77	250.71	251.49	261.25	274.11	278.66	283.38	258.17
2004	291.55	295.38	304.54	305.49	301.44	295.70	294.10	291.86	296.90	290.35	298.19	296.26	296.81

Average.   *Source: Commodity Research Bureau*

Goldman Sachs Commodity Index (GSCI)   (12/31/1969=100)

Year	Jan.	Feb.	Mar.	Apr.	May	June	July	Aug.	Sept.	Oct.	Nov.	Dec.	Average
1995	176.83	176.82	176.88	182.64	182.62	178.49	173.90	177.20	182.06	180.71	186.06	197.06	180.94
1996	194.61	195.08	200.85	212.77	209.40	202.05	202.81	199.12	202.64	209.63	210.81	220.70	205.04
1997	214.62	194.88	192.88	191.24	198.60	186.50	185.35	194.25	197.20	205.75	199.35	181.94	195.21
1998	170.94	168.98	164.28	165.89	161.48	154.50	149.22	141.12	148.40	149.57	144.64	131.72	154.23
1999	135.29	132.37	143.86	155.40	156.81	158.22	165.21	177.60	187.64	184.89	191.84	194.62	165.31
2000	200.14	211.15	214.19	200.42	219.11	230.07	222.13	230.88	247.73	243.67	251.82	244.79	226.34
2001	239.18	231.54	220.13	222.86	222.32	213.26	202.89	203.76	197.04	178.07	169.63	167.74	205.70
2002	168.97	172.75	193.58	199.87	200.65	197.07	203.12	208.76	223.69	222.70	212.18	230.03	202.78
2003	241.74	264.19	246.70	221.68	228.18	235.01	233.18	241.35	228.54	242.22	246.24	261.23	240.86
2004	269.18	266.23	280.10	284.06	303.19	292.63	298.97	308.01	315.29	356.70	341.12	314.25	302.48

Average.   *Source: Goldman Sachs*

CRB InfoTech CD

Historical Price Data on CD

Instant Access to Decades of Historical Price Data

CRB InfoTech CD provides the widest variety of financial and commodity data available in one electronic source. Nowhere else can you access data on over 600 cash futures, indices and FOREX markets along with options volatility. It's the only source available for many underlying cash markets offering prices extending back to the 50s, 40s, and even earlier. Compiled from major worldwide exchanges, trade associations and government agencies.

InfoTech helps you Perform Analysis, Back-Testing, Modeling, Presentations

InfoTech includes DataXtract, which enables you to download entire trading histories from your CD-ROM in a variety of formats for your own independent analysis. You can create nearby contracts, continuation contracts and synthetic contracts, along with years of cash prices and volatility studies.

Includes PowerSignals Lite - Advanced Technical Charting

Features include 10 chart styles, 7 Line tools, more than 30 built-in studies and Design Studio. One of the **most powerful features** built into PowerSignals is the Technical Study Design Studio. With it, you can create studies that manipulate your price data in almost any way you want. You can take the results of your studies and display them as lines on an existing chart, on a brand new chart with its own scales, or as tabular displays of the raw data. All of the Technical Studies that are included in the PowerSignals software have been created in the Design Studio, exposing properties such as line colors, numbers of periods in calculations and even the underlying formulas to you. If you would prefer some study to be calculated differently than the built-in formula, you can modify the study as desired and save it for future use. If you want to make a brand new study, you can use the existing studies as models for your study.

Update Your Database with Final Markets

InfoTech can be updated with a subscription to Final Markets, our end-of-day data from the CRB DataCenter. You'll receive futures/cash and option volatility data from over 50 major worldwide exchanges.

For more information, visit www.crbtrader.com, or call 800-621-5271

CRB Futures Perspective

Each 104-page issue of *Futures Perspective* is packed with uncluttered, easy-to-read charts. You'll find all the market information you need for a thorough technical analysis of the markets, including daily and weekly bar charts displaying open, high, low and settlement prices. Our special quarterly Long Range Charts section of monthly price charts is included each January, April, July and October.

With *Futures Perspective's* exclusive format, you won't need to flip back and forth between pages, because an entire market is charted on facing pages. Easy-to-update gridlines, multiple contracts, and studies assist you in your analysis. But there's more to *Futures Perspective* than our popular charts. You'll also find:

- Complete Technical Studies Including:
    - Relative Strength Index (9-day)
    - Stochastic (9-day)
    - Bullish Consensus
    - Commitments of Traders data
    - Historical Open Interest (6-year)
- Market Movers Calendar
- Trading Systems Overview
- Stock Market Momentum Indicator
- CRB's own Electronic Futures Trend Analyzer

Our information is tailored to your trading needs. CRB Futures Perspective is available in three different editions and frequencies - so you receive only the information you want and need. Choose from Full, Financial or Agricultural edition; select weekly, biweekly or monthly frequencies. Whichever edition or frequency you prefer, your issues are printed each Friday after the markets close and mailed to you immediately the same night.

For more information, visit www.crbtrader.com, or call 800-621-5271

CRB Wall Charts and Desk Sets

Designed to help you easily spot market reversals and critical turning points, CRB Historical Wall Charts and Desk Sets will show you in one quick look how seasonal patterns and long-term trends create profitable trading opportunities. Our charts let you plot trendlines according to actual market performance, rather than charting on market averages. Each chart offers plenty of room for updating and adding trendlines.

Historical Wall Charts

Printed each fall, Wall Charts are available for the top 35 markets. More than just a poster measuring 22½"h x 34"w, these ten-year charts use the nearest futures contract and show open/high/low/settle prices with total volume and total open interest and Commitment of Traders data for each week through the last week of September.

> **Agricultural Markets**: Corn, Oats, Soybeans, Soybean Meal, Soybean Oil, Wheat, Kansas City Wheat, Cotton #2, Cocoa, Coffee, Sugar #11, Feeder Cattle, Live Cattle, Lean Hogs and Pork Bellies.
>
> **Financial Markets**: U.S. Dollar Index, British Pound, Canadian Dollar, Euro FX, Japanese Yen, Swiss Franc, Eurodollars, 5-Year T-Notes, 10-Year T-Notes 30-Year T-Bonds, Copper, Gold Silver, Crude Oil, Heating Oil #2, Unleaded Gasoline Natural Gas, S&P 500 Index, NASDAQ 100 Index and Dow Jones Industrials

Historical Desk Sets

Printed each spring and fall, the Desk Set includes 48 markets*. By allowing you to take the longest possible view of these markets, our Desk Set helps you identify potential trends and plan your strategy accordingly. Measuring 12½"h x 17"w, this spiral-bound set includes 10 years of weekly trading ranges with total volume and open interest and Commitment of Traders data and 30 years of monthly price activity with total volume and open interest on adjacent pages.

> ***Additional Markets**: Lumber, Orange Juice, Australian Dollar, Mexican Peso, 2-Year T-Notes, Palladium, Platinum, SPI 200 Index, DAX Index, Hang Seng Index, Nikkei 225 Index, FTSE 100 Index and Reuters-CRB Futures Index.

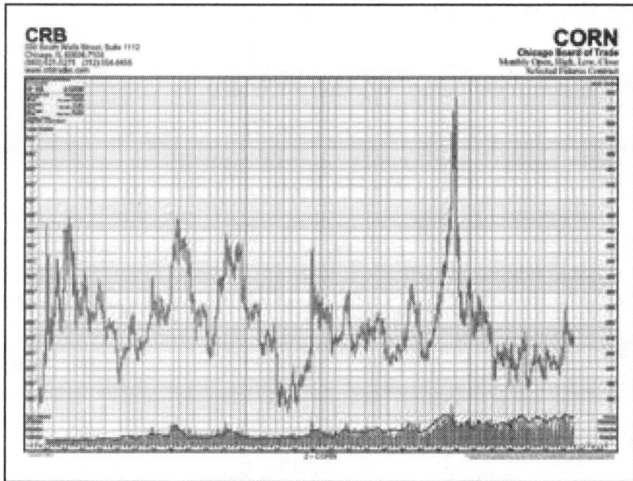 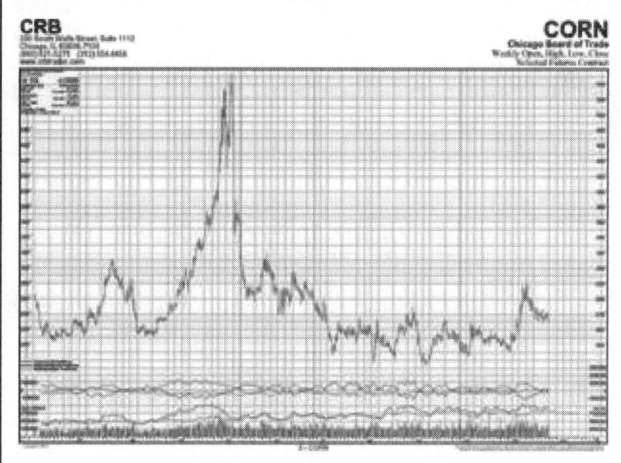

For more information, visit www.crbtrader.com, or call 800-621-5271

Commodity Research Bureau • 330 South Wells Street, Suite 612 • Chicago IL, 60606 USA
Phone: 312.554.8456 or 800.621.5271 • Fax: 312.939.4135 • info@crbtrader.com • www.crbtrader.com

MAJOR COMMODITY BULL MARKET CONTINUES IN 2004

The Reuters-CRB index in 2004 rallied sharply by +11.2% to a new 24-year high and extended the rally seen in the previous two years. In the overall bull market that began in October 2001, the Reuters-CRB index rallied by a total of +60.0% through the end of 2004. That kept the rally in its position as the third largest in post-war history.

The two larger rallies both occurred in the 1970s. The 1971-74 rally was the largest and totaled 146.7%. The 1977-80 rally was the second largest and totaled 82.8%. The current rally has a long way to go before challenging those rallies. However, the duration of the 2001-04 rally is now 39 months and has been longer than the 1971-74 rally and has matched the 1977-80 rally.

The Reuters-CRB index ended 2004 at levels not seen since 1981 when Ronald Reagan was President and Paul Volcker was in his second year as Fed Chairman (Volcker's term was 1979-87). Commodity prices during the 1970s surged mainly because of a serious inflation outbreak driven by an expansive fiscal policy, the surge in oil prices, and an overly easy Fed monetary policy. The CPI finally peaked at +14.8% in March 1980 when Mr. Volcker's monetary crackdown started to succeed in slowing inflation. The Fed's crack-down on inflation caused the double-dip recessions of 1979-80 and 1981-82, and also caused commodity prices to fall sharply in the first half of the 1980s.

In the current commodity bull market, by contrast, the US CPI index has been relatively well-behaved and ended 2004 at only +3.0%. During the entire 2001-04 commodity bull market, the CPI has averaged a modest +2.2%, which is well below the average of +4.9% seen during the 1971-74 rally and the +10.2% average seen during the 1977-80 rally. The nearby chart shows how the Reuters-CRB index has shown much stronger growth than the CRB index since 1992 and particularly during the 2001-04 commodity bull market.

The modest behavior of inflation during the current commodity bull market suggests that other factors are driving commodity prices higher. In fact, the main driver has been the weak dollar. The dollar plunged by 33% over the time-frame of the 2001-04 commodity bull market. Commodities, as real assets, typically rise in price when the currency in which they are quoted depreciates in value.

The strong relationship between the Reuters-CRB index and the US Dollar Index can be seen in the nearby chart. This chart shows how the Reuters-CRB index has risen sharply over the same time frame that the dollar has plunged. In fact, the weekly correlation of the Reuters-CRB index and the dollar index over the course of the 2001-04 commodity bull market has shown a remarkably strong negative correlation of −0.95. That shows how closely tied commodity prices and the dollar are in moving in opposite directions.

Commodity Bull Markets Ranked by Percentage Gain (1960-2004)

	---------- Low ----------		---------- High ----------		Percent Rally	Rally Duration (months)	Avg CPI (yr-yr%)
1971-74	October 1971	96.40	February 1974	237.80	146.7%	28	4.9%
1977-80	August 1977	184.70	November 1980	337.60	82.8%	39	10.2%
2001-04	October 2001	182.83	November 2004	292.49	60.0%	39	2.2%
1986-88	July 1986	196.16	June 1988	272.19	38.8%	23	3.2%
1992-96	August 1992	198.17	April 1996	263.79	33.1%	44	2.8%

Source: Commodity Research Bureau

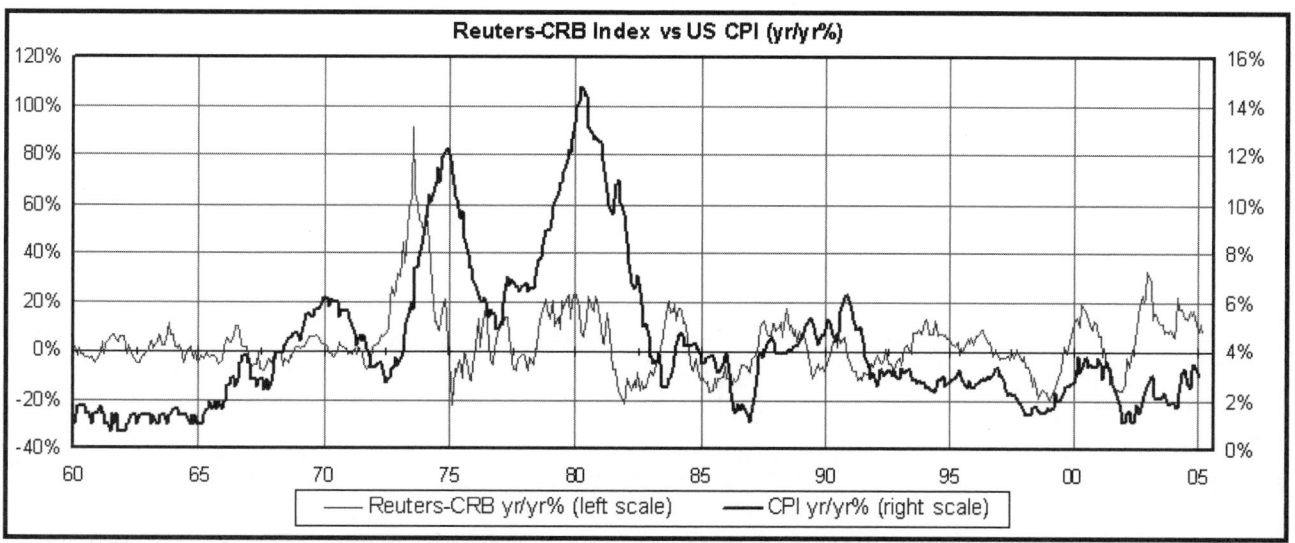

Reuters-CRB Index vs US CPI (yr/yr%)

— Reuters-CRB yr/yr% (left scale)　　— CPI yr/yr% (right scale)

Precious metals prices provide a good illustration of how the dollar has driven commodity prices higher. That is because a key component of precious metals prices is their "store of value." When the currency in which the precious metal is quoted depreciates, there is a quick market effect in raising the price of that precious metal. Over the 2001-04 bull market, gold prices rallied by 79% and showed a very strong negative weekly correlation of −0.96 with the dollar index.

There has, however, been more behind the 3-year commodity bull market than just the dollar. The world economy has shown increasing strength in the past 3 years, and that has led to higher demand across the board for commodities. China in particular has been a major cause of commodity strength in recent years. In 2004, the Chinese economy showed a very strong GDP growth of +9.5%. China has been a key buyer for crude oil and also for industrial metals and construction supplies. Copper provides an excellent example of Chinese demand, and copper prices soared again in 2004 to a new 16-year high.

The crude oil market was the component of the Reuters-CRB index that showed the strongest growth during 2004. The crude oil market rallied on increased Chinese demand, stronger worldwide demand for oil due to the stronger global economy (+5.1% world GDP in 2004), various supply disruptions from non-OPEC producers, and limited OPEC supply as OPEC bumped up against its capacity limits.

The outlook continues to look strong for commodity prices going forward . The world economy is expected to remain strong near +4.3% in 2005, according to the IMF, thus keeping demand alive for commodities. In addition, there is little reason to believe that the dollar's decline will end in the near future given the massive US current

account deficit. As long as the dollar moves lower, commodity prices will move higher. The main threat to higher commodity prices comes from China as Chinese authorities try to slow their economy to a more sustainable long-term growth rate. If they fail and cause a hard-landing, that will cause a sharp drop in commodity prices. However, such a decline would probably be only temporary and worldwide demand for commodities would likely reemerge before long, thus keeping commodity prices underpinned.

Richard W. Asplund, CRB Chief Economist

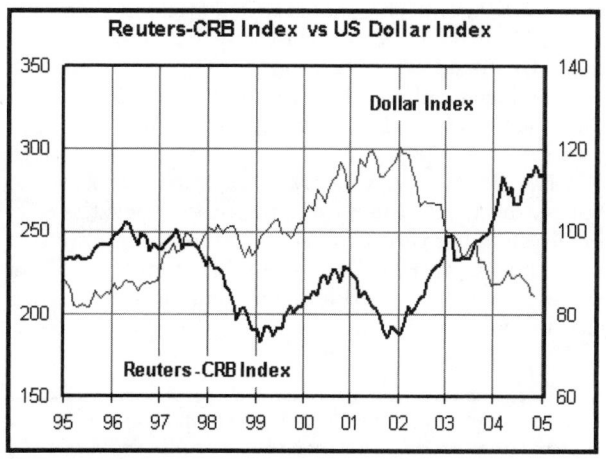

Reuters-CRB Index vs US Dollar Index

Dollar Index

Reuters-CRB Index

CRUDE OIL PRICES HAVE NEARLY TRIPLED IN LAST 3 YEARS

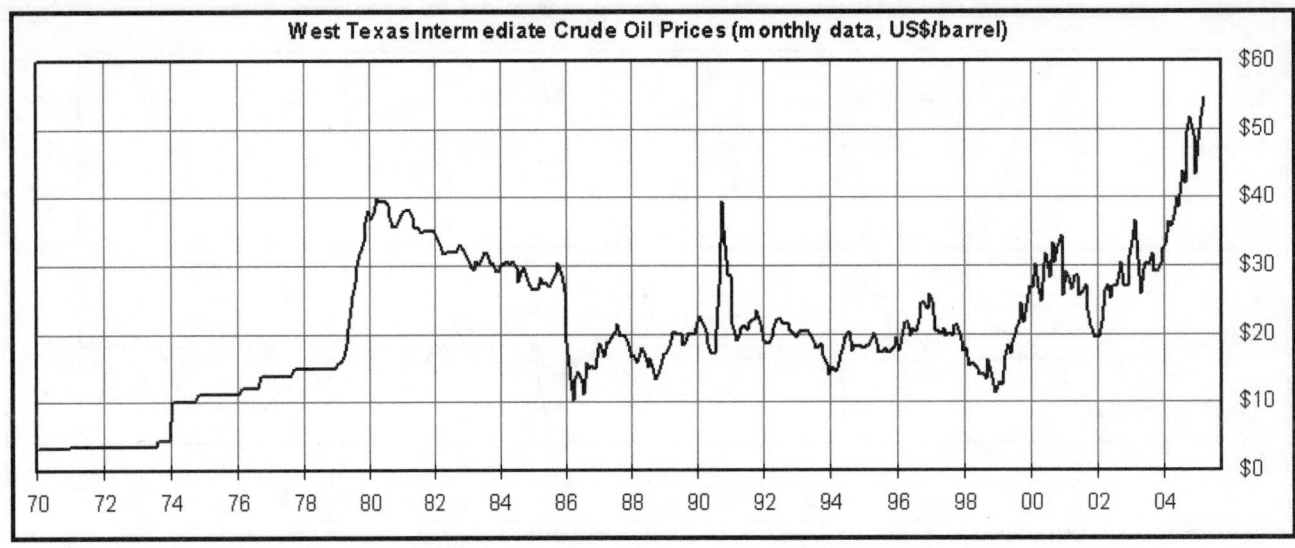

West Texas Intermediate Crude Oil Prices (monthly data, US$/barrel)

Crude oil prices have rallied very sharply in the past three years, recently reaching a new record high of over $55 per barrel. The rally has been instrumental in pushing up the overall Reuters-CRB index. In addition, the rally has important implications for the US and global economies and global stock markets. Higher oil prices are particularly damaging for stock prices because high oil prices have a double-whammy for profits, hurting revenues through a slower economy and also raising input costs.

The marketplace has been remarkably sanguine about the run-up in crude oil prices thus far. Economists have not significantly revised downward their estimates for US GDP growth because of the oil price rally, and the S&P 500 index has been able to rally to a new 3-1/2 year high. One reason for this is that the US economy is only half as dependent on oil as it was when OPEC shocked the world with its oil embargo back in 1973.

The Treasury note market has generally shown a bullish reaction to the rally in oil prices. While the rally in oil prices temporarily pushes up the overall inflation statistics, the more important effect is that the rally in oil prices hurts the US economy and thus cools GDP growth and core inflation.

Monetarist theory states that if the Federal Reserve holds its monetary policy steady, a rise in the price of one commodity like oil will be offset by a decline in the prices of other consumer products, thus leaving the overall price level unchanged. Otherwise stated, a sharp rise in crude oil prices will be deflationary for the prices of other goods, assuming the Federal Reserve leaves monetary policy unchanged. If on the other hand the Federal Reserve panics and tries to offset the rise in crude oil prices with an easier monetary policy, as it did during the 1970s, then a rally in crude oil prices can kick off a generalized rise in inflation. In the current instance, the Federal Reserve is slowly tightening monetary policy and is not accommodating the rise in oil prices. Bond market participants are therefore not concerned that the rise in oil prices will cause a generalized inflation outbreak.

Demand is clearly the reason for the rally in oil prices in the past three years, and particularly new demand from China. The nearby chart shows how Chinese demand for imported oil has doubled since mid-2002. Not coincidently, the rally in oil prices that began in 2002 coincided with the sharp rise in Chinese buying of crude oil imports. In addition, world demand for oil has increased, even aside from Chinese demand, as world economic growth recovered from the 2001 recession. The

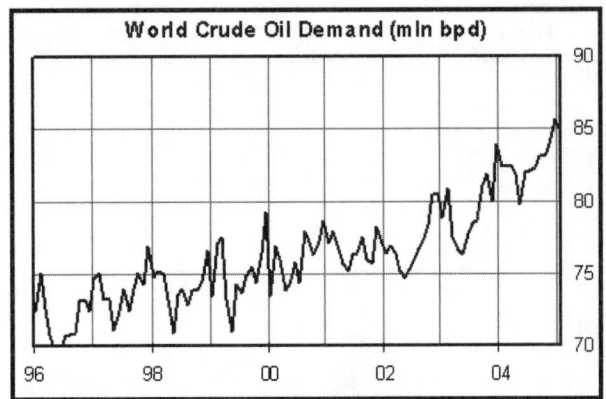

World Crude Oil Demand (mln bpd)

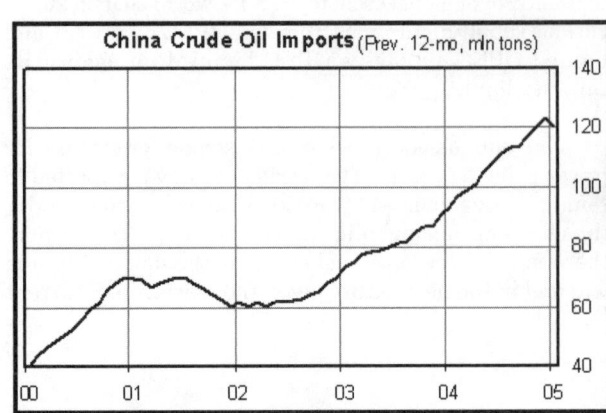

China Crude Oil Imports (Prev. 12-mo, mln tons)

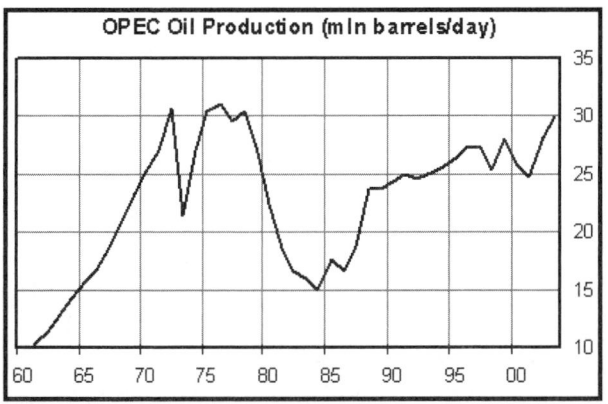

OPEC Oil Production (mln barrels/day)

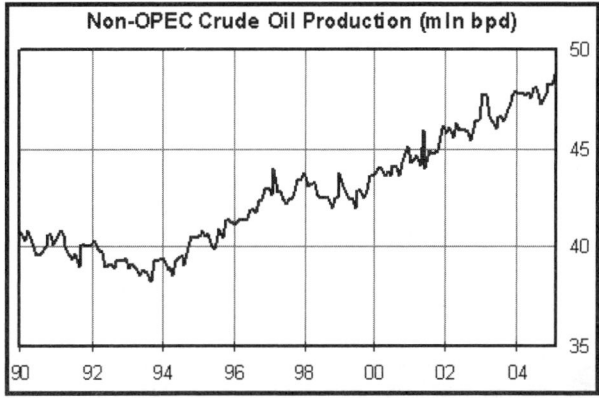

Non-OPEC Crude Oil Production (mln bpd)

nearby chart shows how world oil demand rose from 75 million barrels per day in early 2002 to roughly 85 million barrels per day more recently, an increase of 13%.

Meanwhile, production has had trouble keeping pace with demand. OPEC boosted its production to 30.54 million barrels per day in October 2004, which was the highest production level since the late-1970s. OPEC in autumn 2004 raised production to offset the temporary 25% drop in US Gulf of Mexico oil production that occurred after Hurricane Ivan severely damaged under-water pipelines in the Gulf of Mexico. OPEC scaled back its production to the mid-29 million bpd level in December 2004 through February 2005 as oil prices stabilized and production from the Gulf of Mexico normalized.

However, the events of late 2004 made it clear that OPEC was constrained in raising production any further because of the physical limits of its existing production facilities. OPEC had very little excess spare capacity to use to temporarily control and cap oil prices. Events in late 2004 made clear to market participants the possibility for large upward spikes in oil prices and the danger of being caught short crude oil.

OPEC also learned in 2004 that oil prices near $50 did not create a crisis in the world stock markets or cause a global recession. OPEC in January 2005 therefore dropped its target band of $22-28 per barrel for an OPEC blend of crude oil (which equates to about $23-31 for West Texas Intermediate crude oil) as essentially obsolete. Even Saudi Arabia, the most pro-Western of the OPEC nations now believes that OPEC can safely target oil prices

near or above $40 without causing economic damage.

Crude oil production from non-OPEC countries has steadily risen in the past decade, as the nearby chart shows. However, in late 2004 there was some weakness in non-OPEC production tied to continued insurgent attacks on oil production in Iraq, and also tied to a small decline in Russian oil production as a result of the Russian government's effective expropriation of key production assets from Yukos in 2004 for back taxes.

US crude oil inventories fell sharply from June through September 2004, as world oil production failed to keep up with demand (see nearby chart). However, OPEC geared up production through the end of 2004 and there was a recovery in crude oil inventories in Q4-2004. By March 2005, US oil inventories had risen to a new 8-month high. But despite the higher level of inventories, crude oil futures prices in March 2005 nearly matched the record high of $55.67 posted back in October 2004. In addition, crude oil demand was expected to ease in the second quarter in the awkward time between winter home heating oil demand and summer gasoline demand.

The rally in oil prices in early March 2005, even in the face of rising inventories and expected weaker spring demand, highlighted the extent to which speculative buying has pushed oil prices higher. While the effect of speculative buying is difficult to quantify, that buying has clearly had a bullish impact on crude oil prices in recent years. Some observers believe that there is as much as a $10 speculative premium built into oil prices.

We believe that the long-term outlook for crude oil prices is bullish due to growing demand combined with lagging investment in new production facilities. There is the possibility of sharp, temporary upward spikes in oil prices given that nearly all oil producers are running at full capacity and have very little excess capacity to offset any supply snafus. Nevertheless, within the context of the secular bull market in crude oil prices, there is also the possibility of temporary downdrafts tied to the periodic washout of speculative long positions and the possibility of any stumbles in world or Chinese economic growth.

Richard W. Asplund, CRB Chief Economist

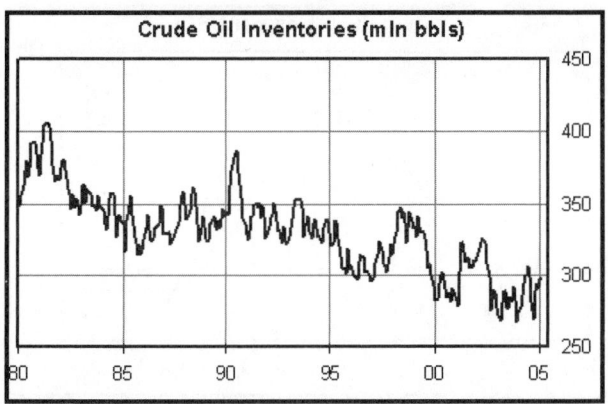

Crude Oil Inventories (mln bbls)

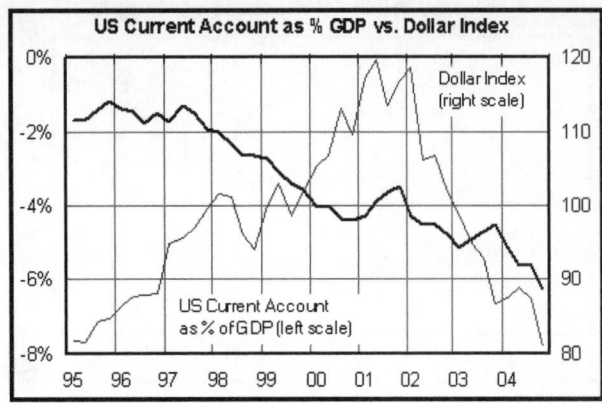

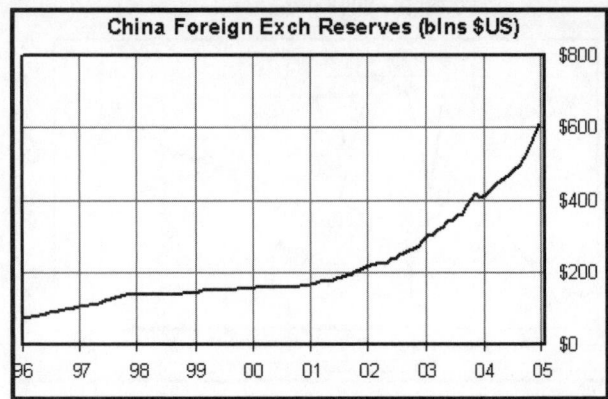

The weak US dollar has been the main factor driving commodity prices higher in the past 3 years, as detailed in the previous article. Over the course of the 2001-04 commodity bull market of +60.0%, the dollar index has depreciated by 33%. The extremely close negative correlation between the dollar index and the Reuters-CRB index seen over that bull market of –0.95 attests to the driving influence of the weak dollar on the rally in commodity prices. The bottom line is that the direction of the dollar is at least as important in forecasting commodity prices as the usual supply/demand factors.

The main bearish factor for the US dollar has been the sharp increase in the US current account deficit seen since 1997. The current account balance is the broadest measure of US trade with the rest of the world and includes goods, services, and transfer payments. The US dollar managed to rally in the late-1990s despite the rising US current account deficit because of the roaring bull market in US stocks and the inflow of foreign investment to take advantage of US investment returns. However, the dollar peaked not long after the US stock market bubble burst in 2000. Since 2001, the dollar has plunged as the US current account deficit has ballooned to record levels. As of late 2004, the US current account deficit approached 6% of US GDP, which is an all-time record.

In any other country, or in previous decades, a country would not have been able to sustain a current account deficit as large as 6% of GDP without a massive currency depreciation. In order for such a current account deficit to exist without a currency crash, foreign investors must

be willing to hold huge amounts of currency of the nation, meaning that nation must have very attractive investment returns and extremely deep capital markets for investing the currency.

Fortunately, the US has so far qualified as such a country. Foreign investors have been willing to hold large amounts of US dollars because US investment returns are strong and are among the least risky in the world. In addition, the US dollar has become the de-facto world currency, which means there is a huge demand for dollar paper currency throughout the world for conducting transactions. However, if foreign recipients of dollars decide they don't want to reinvest those dollars into dollar-denominated investments and instead decide to sell those dollars on the open market, then the dollar will depreciate. A weaker currency should, in theory, lead to a smaller current account deficit as imports become more expensive and fall, and as exports become cheaper and rise.

However, in the current case, the dollar hasn't shown the full force of depreciation that would normally be seen because the Asian central banks are holding dollars, rather than selling them in exchange for their own currencies. They are doing that because they are trying to keep their currencies at artificially low levels in order to make their exports more attractive in the world marketplace.

China has taken the export growth model to a new level following Japan's demonstrated success in using the export growth model to build an economic powerhouse after World War II. China is relying on its huge export

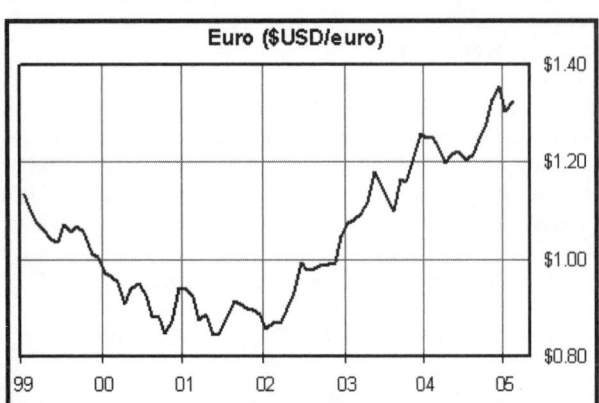

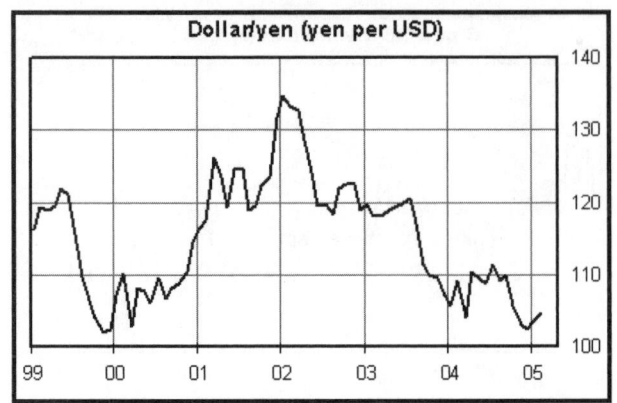

US Export & Import Growth (yoy%)

Export Growth — Import Growth

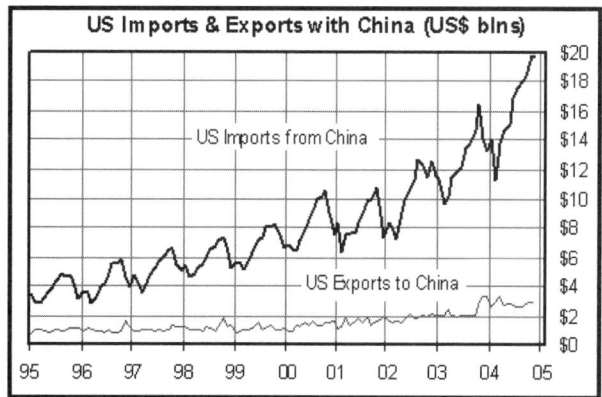

US Imports & Exports with China (US$ blns)

US Imports from China

US Exports to China

sector to provide wages and profits to local companies, which in turn creates domestic household wealth and demand. China has fixed its currency at an artificially low level of 8.3 yuan per dollar in order to keep its exports cheap in the world market and to fuel its booming export sector.

The byproduct of this policy, however, is that China has acquired a huge quantity of dollar reserves, as seen in the nearby chart. China's foreign exchange reserves rose 52% in 2004 and now total $609 billion, and Japan's reserves rose 26% in 2004 to reach $824 billion. More generally, foreign purchases of US securities have totaled over $4 trillion in the past decade. During 2004, foreign central banks purchased a remarkably high 42% of all new US Treasury notes and bonds.

The US dollar hinges on the willingness of the Asian central banks to hold and even acquire more dollar reserves as new dollars come in the door from their trade surplus with the US. There has been talk in Japan and South Korea about diversifying their foreign exchange reserves, and the dollar dropped sharply on that news. The market remains very nervous about any hint that foreign central banks might lighten up their dollar reserves since that would mean more dollars being dumped on the world's forex exchange markets. However, the Asian central banks are not likely to sell their existing dollar reserves since any hint of such selling could lead to a plunge in the dollar and by extension the value of their portfolios. Thus, the central banks are likely to make only a slow and incremental shift away from the dollar going forward.

There isn't likely to be much relief for the US in its trade deficit with countries such as China or India or other low-labor-cost producers. That is because of the dramatic size of their competitive advantage in producing products cheaply. As the nearby chart shows, US imports from China have soared since 2000 and have far outstripped US exports to China. This is due to (1) China's artificially undervalued currency, (2) China's low-wage production advantage, and (3) the lifting of world trade barriers. Chinese apparel imports, for example, have soared in early 2005 as the former global textile export restrictions were removed by agreement at the end of 2004. In January

2005, the US trade deficit with China account for one-fourth of the overall US trade deficit. The comparative advantage of low-wage countries in fact is likely to accelerate in coming years, providing a continued source of upward pressure on the US trade deficit.

While the comparative advantage of low-cost-labor nations is clearly a factor behind the US current account deficit, it is also important to analyze the foreign investment flows that finance the current account deficit. These investment flows, which are the flip-side of the current account deficit, are called the "capital account surplus" and by definition equal the current account deficit of goods and services. Thus, when the capital account surplus rises, the US current account deficit rises as well.

There are some who believe that the US current account deficit is being driven not so much by trade in goods and services as by investment flows. Federal Reserve Governor Ben Bernanke delivered an important speech on March 10, 2005 in which he argued that the US current account deficit is being caused, not so much by the terms of trade in goods and services, but by a huge glut of global savings. Those savings are being directed to the US due to the safety and attractiveness of US investment returns and the depth of the markets. To the extent that foreign investors buy US investments, the US capital account surplus rises, and by definition the current account deficit rises as well.

It is fortunate for the US that this glut of world savings exists and that foreign investors view the US markets as an attractive investment destination because the US desperately needs that capital to cover its shortage of domestic savings. Domestic savings in the US are scarce because of the poor US household savings rate and the huge US federal budget deficit.

If Mr. Bernanke's thesis is correct, then the implication is that the US current account deficit does not represent a crisis and will in fact correct downward by itself once overseas capital finds better uses at home through economic development and higher interest rates.

To summarize, there are multiple reasons for the massive US current account deficit. Reasons include both

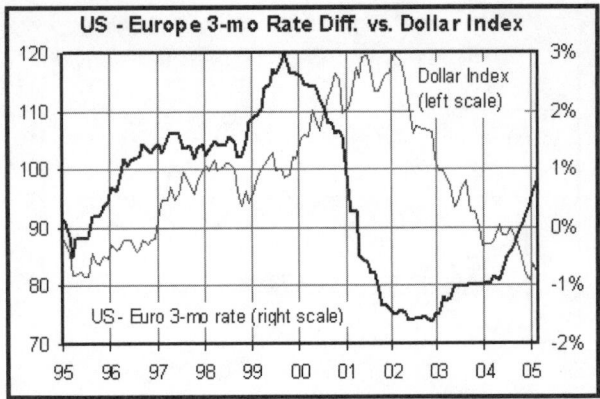

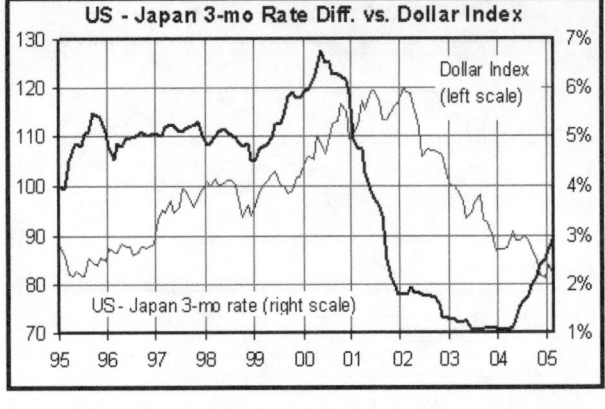

short-term cyclical factors that will reverse in due course, and long-term structural factors that won't correct for years or even decades. Short-term factors include (1) the surge in oil prices seen in the past 3 years which has sharply boosted the dollar value of imported oil, (2) the fact that the US business cycle remains ahead of its key trading partners which means that US demand for imports is relatively strong and foreign demand for US exports is relatively weak, and (3) importers into the US have not raised prices substantially in response to the weak dollar but have instead accepted lower profit margins, meaning import prices haven't risen far enough to slash import demand.

Long-term structural factors behind the US current account deficit include (1) the huge US appetite for foreign imported oil, (2) the improved comparative advantage of nations such as China and India which have cheap labor and the resources to employ that labor into export powerhouses, and (3) the poor US household savings rate and the massive US federal budget deficit, which means the US must import a huge amount of capital to cover its capital needs (boosting the capital account surplus and the US current account deficit as well).

There are few indications that there will be any significant downward adjustment in the US current account deficit any time in the near future. Most of the factors mentioned above are likely to persist in coming quarters and even years. This suggests that the US dollar will remain in a secular bear market.

In fact, it is easy to spin a nightmare scenario for the dollar and for the US economy that could occur if the US current account deficit continues to surge and causes a loss of confidence among foreign investors in the dollar. The dollar could go into a downward spiral in which dollar weakness begets more dollar weakness and panic emerges as foreign investors dump their US stock and bond holdings. That scenario would involve a triple plunge in the dollar, US stocks, and US bonds, combined with a heavy dose of import inflation. If that were to happen, the Federal Reserve would be forced to step in with sharply higher interest rates to stop the dollar's plunge, thus bringing on an economic recession.

The US is skirting near the edge of this scenario. However, there is cause for optimism that the US will be able to muddle through its current account situation without a debacle because the Fed is likely to continue raising US interest rates through the end of 2005. That is a fundamentally bullish factor for the dollar since higher short-term interest rates attract foreign capital into dollar-denominated bank deposits.

The nearby chart shows how dramatically US interest rate differentials are improving relative to European interest rates which have been flat for two years. The US interest rate advantage over Japan is even more dramatic since Japanese short-term interest rates have been near or below 0.5% for the past 10 years. US interest rate differentials are likely to rise further through 2005 as US short-term interest rates go up and Japanese and European rates go sideways.

Another key bullish factor for the dollar is that the US economy and the US stock market continue to look very healthy, and that will continue to attract foreign capital into the US for equity investment purposes. As long as foreign capital looks favorably on US investment returns, the US can stave off disaster from its current account deficit since foreigners will want to hold dollar-denominated investments.

On balance, we look for the secular dollar bear market to continue in 2005 due to the current account deficit situation. However, periodic counter-trend rallies in the dollar cannot be ruled out based on rising US interest rate differentials and the strong US economy. As seen in the late 1990s, the dollar can rally sharply even in the face of a rising current account deficit. Thus, while we are moderately bearish on the dollar, we also believe there will be periodic counter-trend rallies in the dollar in 2005 as the foreign exchange market periodically shifts its focus back and forth from the current account deficit to rising US interest rate differentials.

Richard W. Asplund, CRB Chief Economist

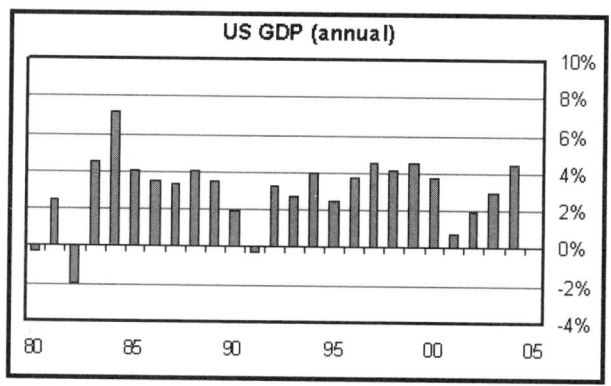

US GDP (annual)

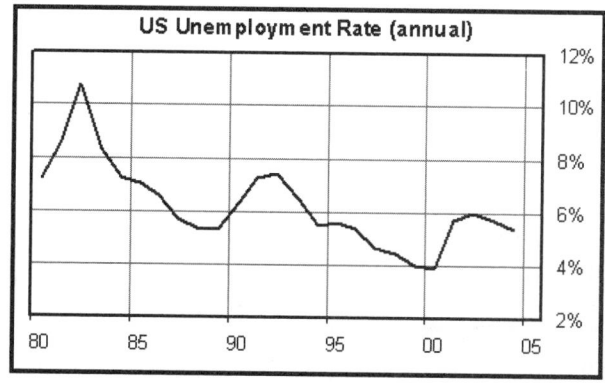

US Unemployment Rate (annual)

The US economy in 2004 showed strong real GDP growth of +4.4%, improving significantly from the weak growth rates seen in 2001-03 (+0.8% in 2001, +1.9% in 2002, +3.0% in 2003). US real GDP growth in 2005 is expected to settle back a bit to +3.7%, but that is still slightly above the +3.6% average US GDP growth rate seen since 1950.

There are several key factors that should support the US economy in 2005 including strong business investment, an improving US labor market, historically low interest rates, continued strength in the housing market even though mortgage rates are likely to rise somewhat, a continued stimulative fiscal policy, and continued strength in the US stock market which should support household wealth and business confidence.

Business investment appears to be off to a good start in 2005 since businesses are generally confident about the economy and consumer demand. Business investment in equipment and software in Q4-2004 was very strong at +18.0% and has averaged about +15% in the past 4 quarters. Orders have started off 2005 at a relatively strong level, providing confidence that business investment will remain strong through 2005.

Consumer spending continues at steady and relatively strong levels. Consumer spending held up the economy during the 2001-02 slow period, and US consumers are continuing to provide a solid underpinning for the overall economy. Personal consumption spending in Q1-2005 is expected to be a firm +3.1% following a strong +4.2% pace in Q4. Retail sales have been strong on a year-on-year basis near +7.0% in January and February 2005.

The improving labor market should continue to support consumer confidence and spending. Payroll growth was weak in the second half of 2004 with an average monthly payroll gain of +162,000. However, February payrolls picked up to +262,000 and consensus expectations call for average monthly payroll growth near +180,000 through 2005. The unemployment rate is likely to drop only slightly in 2005 because formerly discouraged workers are coming back into the labor market to look for a job as economic conditions improve. This will expand the labor pool and make it difficult for the unemployment rate to drop, even though new jobs are being created. The US unemployment rate in January 2005 was at a 3-year low of 5.2%.

The housing sector showed record growth in 2004 and should remain relatively strong in 2005, though down from 2004 levels due to higher mortgage rates. There is continued debate about whether there is a bubble in housing prices, but the housing market should remain stable as long as the US economy remains relatively firm and there is no sharp drop-off in consumer income to pay mortgages.

The inflation outlook continues to point upward, which is why the Federal Reserve is expected to continue ratcheting up interest rates through the end of the year. The Federal Reserve continues to claim in its statements that inflation is "well contained." The Fed's preferred measure of the inflation is the core personal consumption expenditure deflator and that series has in fact remained in the narrow range of +1.4% to +1.6% over the past year. However, the PPI and CPI statistics are clearly pointing upward. The core PPI (year-on-year) has risen sharply in the past two years from a trough of –0.5% in December

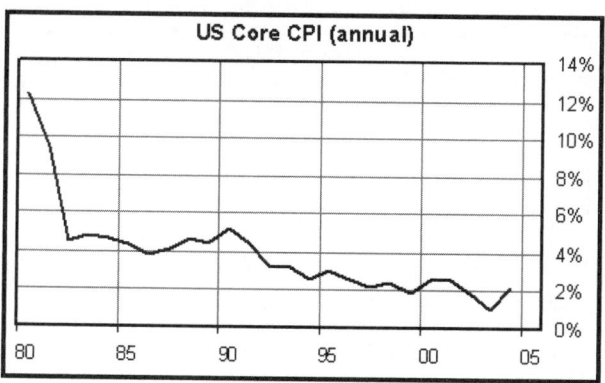

US Core CPI (annual)

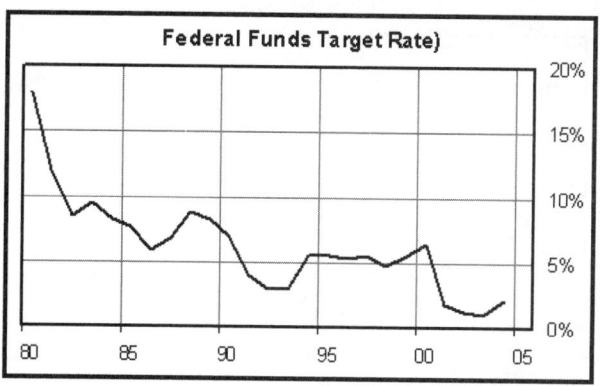

Federal Funds Target Rate)

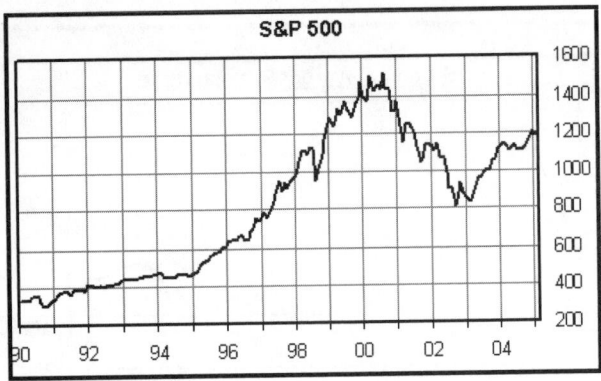

S&P 500

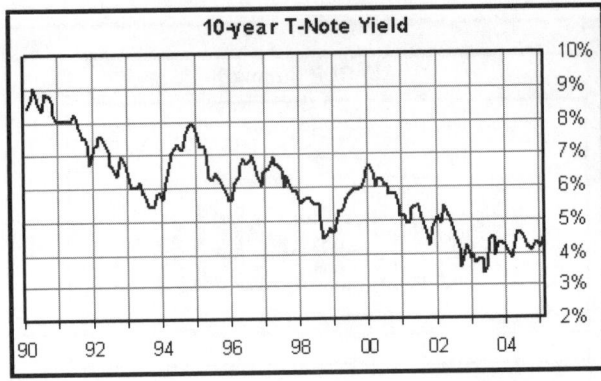

10-year T-Note Yield

2002 to the a 9-year high of +2.7% in February 2005. The core CPI has risen sharply in the past year from its trough of +1.1% in early 2004 to a 2-year high of +2.3% in February 2005.

The Federal Reserve in 2004 raised its federal funds rate target by a total of 125 basis points from 1.00% in June 2004 to 2.25% in December 2004. As of March 2005, the markets were expecting the Fed in 2005 to raise the funds rate target by another 150 basis points to 3.75% by the end of 2005. Even a 3.75% funds rate target by year-end, however, would be a lower funds rate target than has been seen for most of the last 4 decades. That would also be a lower funds rate target than the average of about 5% seen in the latter half of the 1990s when GDP averaged a strong +4.0%.

The US financial markets have provided a favorable backdrop for the US economy. The S&P 500 index has rallied by about 60% in the past 2 years, thus boosting household wealth and supporting business and consumer confidence. Even after that rally, the stock market remains at relatively reasonable valuation levels, suggesting that the market can sustain and perhaps even extend its gains in 2005. Corporate earnings growth in 2005 is expected at +10%, which is above the long-term average of about +7%. Earnings growth in 2005 comes on top of the very strong earnings growth rates of +20% seen in 2004 and +18% in 2003.

Short-term US interest rates are likely to rise significantly in 2005, in line with expectations for the Fed to tighten by a total of 150 basis points in 2005. However, long-term rates have remained remarkable low so far, even after the 50 basis point rise in 10-year yields seen in February and early-March 2005. The current 10-year T-

note yield near 4.50% is still more commensurate with the 1960s than with any subsequent decade. In the second half of the 1990s, when US GDP growth averaged a strong +4.0%, the 10-year T-note yield averaged about 6%, well above current levels. Low US interest rates should continue to provide a sustained boost to the US economy, even though rates are rising from the extremely low levels seen in 2001-03.

The two main threats to the US economy in 2005 are the dollar and the possibility of even higher crude oil prices. The weak dollar will only become an issue in the unlikely event that a downward spiral in the dollar develops which the Fed is forced to halt with a sharp increase in short-term interest rates. Higher oil prices present a more likely threat. High oil prices trimmed US GDP growth in 2004 by as much as three-quarters of a percentage point. However, the US economy is now only half as dependent on oil as it was when past oil shocks caused US recessions. Thus, the likelihood of a US recession being caused by higher oil prices seems remote at this point. The markets in any case remain on guard for unexpected shocks such as another major terrorist attack or a sudden economic stumble in China.

In general, we remain optimistic about the macroeconomic outlook for the US in 2005. The Fed is slowly moving to a neutral federal funds rate target, the US stock market is strong, the inflation outlook is relatively contained, and US interest rates remain historically low. The favorable US macroeconomic picture should provide a strong demand backdrop for commodity prices in 2005.

Richard W. Asplund, CRB Chief Economist

US Dollar Index

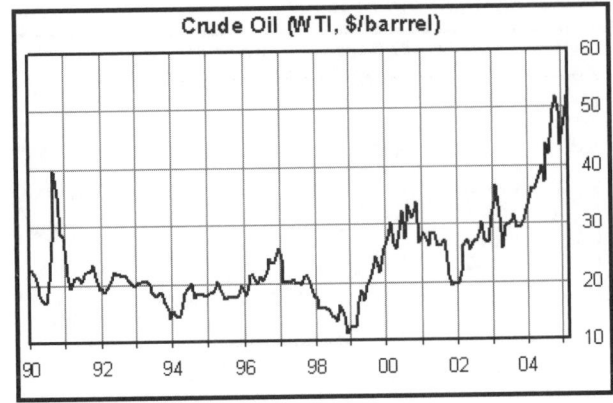

Crude Oil (WTI, $/barrrel)

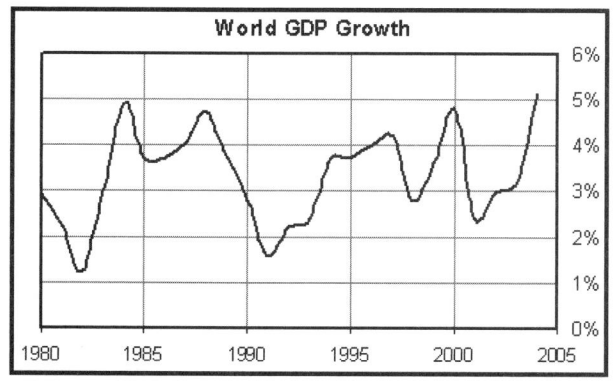

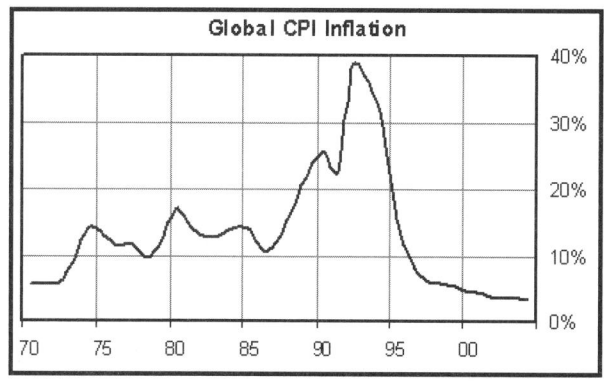

World GDP growth is expected to ease to +4.3% in 2005 from +5.1% in 2004, according to IMF forecasts released in March 2005. Lower economic growth forecasts stem from high oil prices and lagging economic performance in Japan and Europe. World GDP growth in 2004 was very strong as the world economy continued to recover from the slow-growth period seen in 2001-03.

Japan's economy is likely to see growth of only +0.8% in 2005 and Europe's economy is likely to see growth of only +1.6% in 2005, according to IMF forecasts. World economic growth in 2005 will continue to be led by China and the US. Chinese GDP growth in 2005 is likely to remain strong in the +8.5% area, showing a modest slowdown from +9.5% in 2004. The IMF is forecasting US GDP growth in 2005 near +3.7%, down from +4.4% in 2004, but still an above-trend performance.

World inflation in 2005 is likely to remain subdued near the 2004 rate of about +3.2%, held down by slower economic growth. The favorable inflation outlook will allow the world's key central banks to maintain a relatively easy monetary policy. The European Central Bank may end up leaving its monetary policy unchanged all year with its refinancing rate at 2.00%. The Bank of Japan will likely leave its monetary policy unchanged all year with its overnight rate near zero, where it has been since 1999. The markets expect the US Federal Reserve to tighten by a total of 150 basis points in 2005, but that would still leave the federal funds rate target at 3.75% by year-end, still a relatively low rate.

World bond yields should remain subdued in 2005 as economic growth is capped by high crude oil prices and strong non-dollar currencies. The MSCI World Developed 10-year Government Bond yield in January 2005 fell to a new low of 4.59%. Low world interest rates should help the world economy to perform above-trend in 2005.

The world stock markets in 2005 should maintain their balance, although major gains are unlikely. The world stock market has rallied by 63% in the past 2 years on the sharp growth in corporate profits. Corporate profit growth should continue at an above-trend rate in 2005, but stock market gains will be more difficult considering the sharp gains already seen in the past 2 years. World stock markets are still at reasonable valuations, meaning there is little risk of a major sell-off as long as no shocks emerge to hurt corporate earnings performance.

There are risks, however, for global growth in 2005 from the possibilities of a further surge in oil prices, or from a stumble in China's attempt to slow its economic growth to a more balanced rate. But on the whole, we are optimistic about the prospects for world economic growth in 2005. That suggests that world commodity demand should remain relatively strong in 2005, underpinning support for commodity prices.

Richard W. Asplund, CRB Chief Economist

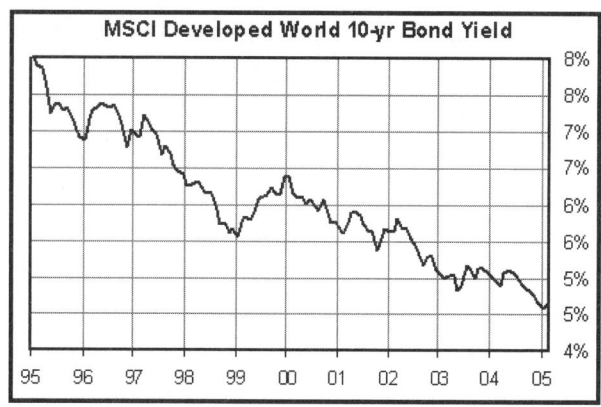

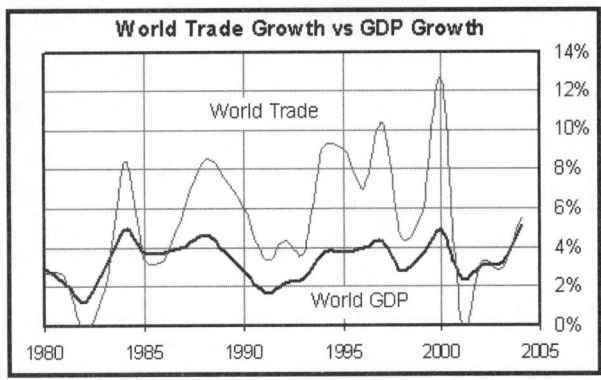

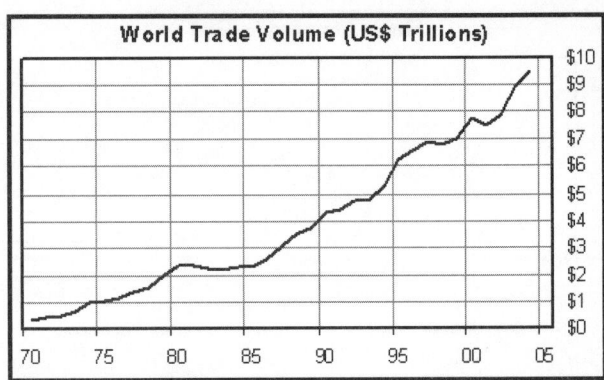

Three-quarters of business leaders in 91 countries believe it is "very important" for their companies and for their domestic economies that the Doha Round of world trade talks gets back on track. That was the outcome of an April 2004 survey sponsored by the International Chamber of Commerce. Free trade provides enormous benefits in efficiency and productivity and results in an overall increase of world economic growth. Free trade also provides good news for consumers who get access to products with lower prices. As Federal Reserve Chairman Greenspan has argued, a further expansion of free trade and globalization is also critical to allow the US to finance its current account deficit.

The nearby chart shows how world trade has nearly quintupled in the past 15 years. Trade has soared because of lower protectionist barriers, greatly improved world information and transportation systems, and the fall of communism and centrally-planned economies, which has brought literally billions of people into the world consumer economy.

Yet the Doha Round of world trade talks which began in 2001 remains stalled. The talks broke down in September 2003 when Brazil and a bloc of developing countries walked out of the talks to protest the huge subsidies and protectionist measures that G7 countries provide to their domestic agricultural producers. Wealthy nations provide some $300 billion in subsidies annually to their farmers.

After walking out of global trade talks, Brazil filed an action against the US on cotton at the World Trade

Organization. Brazil ended up winning the first ruling against a wealthy nation's agricultural subsidies, and that ruling provided an important precedent for other commodities. Brazil successfully argued that the $10 billion in subsidies that the US provides to US cotton producers results in the dumping of subsidized cotton supply onto the world market, thus depressing cotton prices and harming cotton farmers in the rest of the world. The WTO ruling against the US on cotton has forced the wealthy nations to be more flexible on the issue of reducing agricultural subsidies. Europe in 2004 also showed flexibility by curbing its artificial price system for sugar that is designed to support European sugar beet farmers.

The impact of reduced farm subsidies in the US and Europe will be reduced production, higher global prices, and smaller agricultural trade surpluses for the US and Europe. In fact, the USDA has projected that the US agricultural trade surplus in fiscal 2005 will fall to a 3-decade low of $4.5 billion (see nearby chart).

The impact of reducing trade barriers was clearly seen as Chinese clothing exports surged in early 2005 after the elimination of textile quotas starting January 1, 2005. That was a clear example of how the specialization and division of labor, freed from artificial barriers to trade, produces higher productivity and lower prices for consumers.

The Bush administration in its second term should place a very high priority on a successful conclusion of the Doha Round of world trade talks. Former US Trade Representative Robert Zoellick has left to become Deputy Secretary of State, and US trade policy will have to wait for direction from a new US Trade Representative. The new US Trade Representative should place more emphasis on the world trade talks than on being side-tracked by regional trade agreements. Completing the world trade talks would be the single best way for the Bush administration to promote the goals of world economic growth and the spread of democracy and individual economic liberty.

Richard W. Asplund, CRB Chief Economist

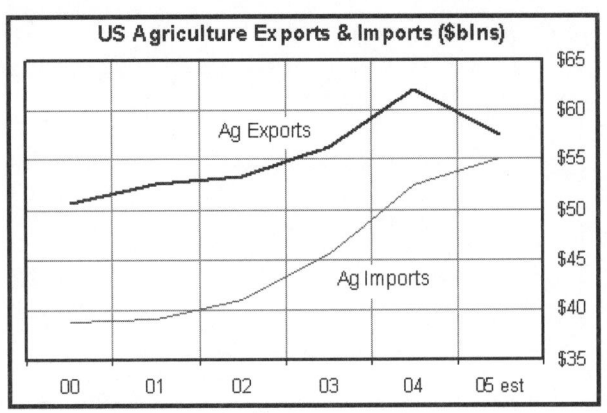

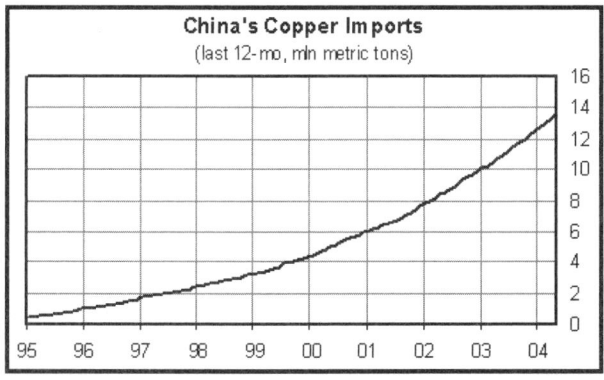

China's Copper Imports
(last 12-mo, mln metric tons)

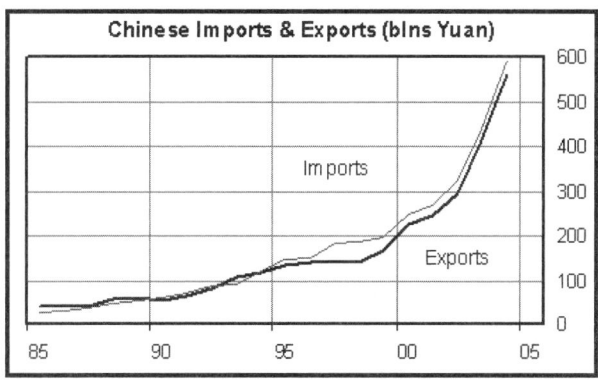

Chinese Imports & Exports (blns Yuan)

Chinese demand is a key factor that has driven a broad list of commodity prices higher in recent years. The nearby chart, for example, shows the dramatic effect of China on the copper market, with Chinese imports in the past decade rising from virtually nothing in 1995 to about 14 million metric tons per year by mid-2004. Copper prices remained subdued until 2001, but then more than doubled to a 16-year high from 2001-04 as Chinese demand converged with a weak dollar to cause copper prices to go through the roof. Similar events have occurred in other industrial metals markets (aluminum, nickel), in energy (Chinese crude oil imports have doubled in the past 2-1/2 years), and in construction materials such as lumber and cement.

China has been growing on a scale that is difficult for Westerners to comprehend. There is a massive migration of people moving from poor, rural areas of China into urban areas. China is building new urban areas equal to the size of more than two New York Cities every year in order to house the rural immigrants. That is the source of the huge demand for construction raw materials such as cement, lumber, and copper. Moreover, China's roaring export sector is also a heavy importer of raw materials for a wide variety of manufactured goods.

Clearly, the course of China's economic growth and demand is a key factor in forecasting the path of commodity prices. China's GDP growth in 2004 was very strong at +9.5%, mildly above the 10-year average of +8.6%. Chinese authorities in 2004 tried to slow the economy to a more sustainable growth rate near 8% by imposing credit curbs on hot sectors such as autos, steel,

and others. However, the credit curbs had little effect and the Chinese central bank finally raised interest rates a notch. China's GDP growth in Q1-2005 was expected to slow a bit to +8.5%.

The key figure to watch in China is inflation. As long as inflation remains below about 5%, the Chinese authorities can claim that they have the economy under control. However, if inflation starts to move upward toward or above 5%, then the Chinese authorities will be forced to clamp down on the monetary brakes. China does not have a particularly good history of engineering soft landings, which means there is an ever-present threat that the Chinese economy could take a sudden tumble.

Chinese authorities are juggling many balls at once in an economy that has many problems including left-over state-run companies and related labor market rigidities, inadequate infrastructure, a poorly-functioning equity market, corruption, serious bad loan problems in the banking system, and a command-type psychology toward trying to control the economy. At the same time, Chinese authorities are trying to maintain their artificially-low yuan peg to the dollar, which is causing a massive buildup in dollar reserves.

China could quickly become the source of significant volatility in the global markets if the Chinese economy suddenly stumbles. However, any stumble is likely to be temporary, and China is likely to remain the key driver of world commodity markets in coming years.

Richard W. Asplund, CRB Chief Economist

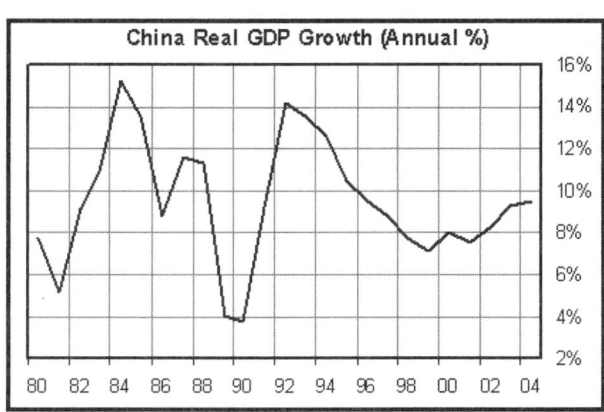

China Real GDP Growth (Annual %)

China CPI Inflation Rate (yr/yr%)

Volume U.S.

U.S. Futures Volume Highlights
2004 in Comparison with 2003

2004 Rank	Top 50 Contracts Traded in 2004	2004 Contracts	%	2003 Contracts	%	2003 Rank
1	Eurodollars (3-month), CME	297,284,038	22.90%	208,771,164	20.42%	1
2	T-Notes (10-year), CBT	196,119,150	15.10%	146,745,281	14.35%	3
3	E-Mini S&P 500 Index, CME	167,202,962	12.88%	161,176,639	15.76%	2
4	T-Notes (5-year), CBT	105,469,410	8.12%	73,746,445	7.21%	4
5	E-Mini NASDAQ 100, CME	77,168,513	5.94%	67,888,938	6.64%	5
6	T-Bonds (30-year), CBT	72,949,053	5.62%	63,521,507	6.21%	6
7	Crude Oil, NYMEX	52,883,200	4.07%	45,436,931	4.44%	7
8	Corn, CBT	24,038,233	1.85%	19,118,715	1.87%	9
9	Mini ($5) Dow Jones Industrial Index, CBT	20,695,848	1.59%	10,859,690	1.06%	16
10	Euro FX, CME	20,456,672	1.58%	11,193,922	1.09%	14
11	Soybeans, CBT	18,846,021	1.45%	17,545,714	1.72%	11
12	Natural Gas, NYMEX	17,441,942	1.34%	19,037,118	1.86%	10
13	E-Mini Russell 2000 Index, CME	17,121,233	1.32%	3,878,935	0.38%	31
14	S&P 500 Index, CME	16,175,584	1.25%	20,175,462	1.97%	8
15	Gold (100 oz.), COMEX Div. of NYMEX	14,959,617	1.15%	12,235,689	1.20%	12
16	Heating Oil #2, NYMEX	12,884,511	0.99%	11,581,670	1.13%	13
17	Unleaded Regular Gas, NYMEX	12,777,442	0.98%	11,172,050	1.09%	15
18	Federal Funds (30-day), CBT	11,940,120	0.92%	8,271,726	0.81%	17
19	Sugar #11, NYBOT	9,766,550	0.75%	7,140,724	0.70%	21
20	T-Notes (2-year), CBT	9,454,774	0.73%	4,415,906	0.43%	28
21	Soybean Meal, CBT	8,569,243	0.66%	8,158,445	0.80%	18
22	Wheat, CBT	7,955,155	0.61%	6,967,416	0.68%	22
23	Soybean Oil, CBT	7,593,314	0.58%	7,417,340	0.73%	20
24	Japanese Yen, CME	7,395,322	0.57%	6,085,209	0.60%	23
25	Long-Short TRAKRS Index II, CME	5,693,223	0.44%			
26	Canadian Dollar, CME	5,611,328	0.43%	4,219,618	0.41%	29
27	Henry Hub Swap, NYMEX	5,353,792	0.41%	2,356,600	0.23%	39
28	Silver (5,000 oz), COMEX Div. of NYMEX	5,006,125	0.39%	4,111,190	0.40%	30
29	TRAKRS Gold, CME	4,868,842	0.37%	6,065,013	0.59%	24
30	British Pound, CME	4,676,512	0.36%	2,595,155	0.25%	37
31	Live Cattle, CME	4,510,128	0.35%	4,436,089	0.43%	25
32	Coffee C, NYBOT	4,193,303	0.32%	3,211,031	0.31%	33
33	TRAKRS Commodity, CME	4,138,262	0.32%	7,424,763	0.73%	19
34	Swiss Franc, CME	4,067,767	0.31%	3,596,658	0.35%	32
35	NASDAQ 100, CME	4,011,983	0.31%	4,421,221	0.43%	26
36	E-mini S&P SmallCap 600 Index	3,282,347	0.25%	1,417,513	0.14%	45
37	Mexican Peso, CME	3,247,222	0.25%	2,123,623	0.21%	42
39	High Grade Copper, COMEX Div. of NYMEX	3,190,625	0.25%	3,089,270	0.30%	34
40	Cotton #2, NYBOT	3,156,018	0.24%	3,035,992	0.30%	35
41	LIBOR (1-month), CME	2,886,987	0.22%	1,138,358	0.11%	47
42	Wheat, KCBT	2,833,370	0.22%	2,632,033	0.26%	36
43	T-Notes (10-year), EUREX	2,818,977	0.22%			
44	Australian Dollar, CME	2,672,733	0.21%	1,609,289	0.16%	44
45	Dow Jones Industrial Index, CBOT	2,577,138	0.20%	4,416,302	0.43%	27
46	Cocoa, NYBOT	2,389,050	0.18%	2,128,206	0.21%	41
47	T-Notes (5-year), EUREX	2,332,942	0.18%			
48	Single Stock Futures, ONECHI	1,890,097	0.15%	1,488,573	0.15%	
49	Wheat, MGE	1,378,694	0.11%	1,066,489	0.10%	48
50	TRAKRS Euro Currency Index, CME	1,248,272	0.10%	1,196,525	0.12%	46
50	TRAKRS Index, CME	994,756	0.16%	2,469,467	0.39%	34
	Top 50 Contracts	1,298,387,830		1,022,486,302*		
	Contracts Below the Top 50	25,639,702	1.94%	20,482,362	1.96%	
	TOTAL	**1,324,027,532**	**100.00%**	**1,042,968,664**	**100.00%**	

* For 2003 Top 50 contracts totaled 1,027,270,647 including 4 contracts that are not among 2004's Top 50.

U.S. Futures Volume Highlights
2004 in Comparison with 2003

2004 RANK	EXCHANGE	2004 CONTRACTS	%	2003 CONTRACTS	%	2003 RANK
1	Chicago Mercantile Exchange (CME)	664,884,607	50.22%	530,989,007	50.91%	1
2	Chicago Board of Trade (CBT)	489,230,144	36.95%	373,669,290	35.83%	2
3	New York Mercantile Exchange (NYMEX)**	133,284,248	10.07%	111,789,658	10.72%	3
4	New York Board of Trade (NYBOT)*	23,955,212	1.81%	18,822,048	1.80%	4
5	EUREX US	6,186,008	0.47%	0	0.00%	
6	Kansas City Board of Trade (KCBT)	2,834,799	0.21%	2,634,424	0.25%	5
7	OneChicago	1,922,726	0.15%	1,619,194	0.16%	6
8	Minneapolis Grain Exchange (MGE)	1,381,456	0.10%	1,087,020	0.10%	8
9	NASDAQ LIFFE Markets (NQLX)	257,000	0.02%	858,900	0.08%	9
10	CBOE Futures Exchange (CFE)	91,332	0.01%	0	0.00%	
11	BrokerTec Futures Exchange	0	0.00%	1,356,825	0.13%	7
12	MidAmerica Commodity Exchange	0	0.00%	142,298	0.01%	10
	TOTAL	**1,324,027,532**	**100.00%**	**1,042,968,664**	**100.00%**	

** Includes Comex Division.

* Includes the New York Futures Exchange, New York Cotton Exchange and Coffee, Sugar and Cocoa Exchange.

Chicago Board of Trade (CBT)

FUTURE	CONTRACT UNIT	2004	2003	2002	2001	2000
Wheat	5,000 bu	7,955,155	6,967,416	6,872,891	6,801,541	6,407,531
Mini Wheat	1,000 bu	31,044	22,288			
Corn	5,000 bu	24,038,233	19,118,715	18,132,447	16,728,748	17,185,442
Mini Corn	1,000 bu	86,771	53,404			
Oats	5,000 bu	416,448	318,898	415,140	440,854	402,190
Soybeans	5,000 bu	18,846,021	17,545,714	14,475,100	12,150,369	12,627,950
Mini Soybeans	1,000 bu	362,829	250,447			
Soybean Oil	60,000 lbs	7,593,314	7,417,340	6,816,483	6,034,325	5,369,903
Soybean Meal	100 tons	8,569,243	8,158,445	7,174,507	6,743,772	6,317,988
Rice	200,000 lbs	168,165	265,234	193,723	121,661	169,133
Mini Silver	1,000 oz	204,255	34,804	7,723	1,087	
Mini Gold	33.2 troy oz	420,604	145,173	9,024	717	
Silver	5,000 oz	12,398		72	161	66
Gold	100 oz	89,539		55	4,867	7,173
T-Bonds (30-year)	100,000 USD	72,949,053	63,521,507	56,082,284	58,579,290	62,750,843
Mini T-Bonds (30-year)	50,000 USD	11,373	15,707	10,009	4,383	
T-Notes (10-year)	100,000 USD	196,119,150	146,745,281	95,786,299	57,585,828	46,700,538
Mini T-Notes (10-year)	50,000 USD	82	49	96	213	
T-Notes (5-year)	100,000 USD	105,469,410	73,746,445	50,512,085	31,122,401	23,331,981
T-Notes (2-year)	200,000 USD	9,454,774	4,415,906	3,203,855	2,389,165	1,477,253
WHEN Issued T-Notes (2-Year)		1				
Mini Eurodollars	500,000 USD	91	543	1,541	483	
Interest Rate Swap (10-year)	100,000 USD	856,968	1,038,777	661,527	58,884	
Interest Rate Swap (5-year)	100,000 USD	243,353	110,275	53,030		
Municipal Note Index (10-year)	100,000 USD	65,026	94,541	8,678		
30-Day Federal Funds	5,000,000 USD	11,940,120	8,271,726	6,285,789	4,686,695	1,443,665
Bund	100,000 EUR	2,303				
Bobl	100,000 EUR	3,219				
Schatz	100,000 EUR	4,306				
Dow Jones Industrial Index	10 USD x Index	2,577,138	4,416,302	6,485,501	4,901,949	3,572,428
Mini ($5) Dow Jones Industrial Index	5 USD x Index	20,695,848	10,859,690	2,224,757		
Dow Jones US Total Market Index	500 USD x Index	3,028				
Dow Jones AIGCI Index	100 x Index	40,882	43,321	14,782	4,292	
Total Futures		**489,230,144**	**373,669,290**	**276,316,119**	**209,988,002**	**189,662,407**

Eurex US

FUTURE	CONTRACT UNIT	2004	2003	2002	2001	2000
T-Notes (2-year)	200,000 USD	53,663				
T-Notes (5-year)	200,000 USD	2,332,942				
T-Notes (10-year)	200,000 USD	2,818,977				
T-Bonds	200,000 USD	980,426				
Total Futures		**6,186,008**				

Chicago Mercantile Exchange (CME)

Future	Contract Unit	2004	2003	2002	2001	2000
Lean Hogs	40,000 lbs	3,204,186	2,164,155	1,931,260	2,018,339	2,111,807
Pork Bellies, Frozen	40,000 lbs	151,949	161,329	152,054	196,359	309,576
Butter	40,000 lbs	6,167	8,544	5,897	1,374	5,366
Nonfat Dry Milk	44,000 lbs	114	230	12	48	
Class III Milk	200,000 lbs	345,973	191,351	103,375		
Class IV Milk	200,000 lbs	690	137	4,714	6,513	4,868
Live Cattle	40,000 lbs	4,510,128	4,436,089	3,851,736	4,279,273	3,681,512
Feeder Cattle	44,000 lbs	741,265	704,852	585,517	616,988	582,279
Random Lumber	80,000 bd ft	242,873	223,891	164,423	206,840	221,168
Diamonium Phosphate	100 tons	62				
Urea Ammonium Nitrate	100 tons	218				
Urea	100 tons	300	585,517	616,988	582,279	650,071
Eurodollar (3-month)	1,000,000 USD	297,284,038	208,771,164	202,080,832	184,015,496	108,114,998
Eurodollar FRA (3-month)	1,000,000 USD	328				
Euroyen	1,000,000,000 JPY	224,821	179,573	231,723	494,519	1,079,074
2-Year SWAP		26,240	6,640	5,671		
5-Year SWAP		56,438	43,616	13,301		
10-Year SWAP		65,281	40,030	7,234		
Consumer Price Index	2,500 USD x CPI	5,264				
Mexican CETES	400,000 MXN	2				
One Month LIBOR	3,000,000 USD	2,886,987	1,138,358	110,934	1,315,593	896,269
Australian Dollar	100,000	2,672,733	1,609,289	1,049,220	832,707	749,555
British Pound	62,500	4,676,512	2,595,155	2,166,469	2,078,834	2,029,542
Brazilian Real	100,000	2,911	277	4	3,937	2,067
Canadian Dollar	100,000	5,611,328	4,219,618	3,134,963	2,961,680	2,460,134
CME $ Index	1,000 USD x Index	306	457			
Czech Koruna		31				
Euro FX	125,000	20,456,672	11,193,922	6,986,600	5,898,429	4,267,408
E-Mini Euro FX	62,500	190,554	16,860	7,252	13,244	29,942
Hungarian Forint	30,000,000	10				
Japanese Yen	12,500,000	7,395,322	6,085,209	4,394,982	4,552,599	3,965,377
E-Mini Japanese Yen	6,250,000	5,466	2,740	2,557	2,023	6,166
Mexican Peso	500,000	3,247,222	2,123,623	1,354,256	1,069,327	1,117,304
New Zealand Dollar	100,000	162,370	120,235	54,148	21,766	32,862
Norwegian Krone	227,000	2,122	388	303		
Polish Zloty	500,000	4,461				
Russian Ruble	2500000	30,620	4,420			
South African Rand	500,000	65,749	73,542	55,275	65,327	40,701
Swedish Krona	193,600	812	4	1		
Swiss Franc	125,000	4,067,767	3,596,658	2,830,738	2,901,939	3,241,207
Australian Dollar / Canadian Dollar	200,000 AUD	676	220	16		
Australian Dollar / Japanese Yen	200,000 AUD	1,066	94	16		
Australian Dollar / New Zealand Dollar	200,000 AUD	639				
British Pound / Japanese Yen	125,000 GBP	651	894	519		
British Pound / Swiss Franc	125,000 GBP	689	103	263		
Canadian Dollar / Japanese Yen	200,000 CAD	344	102			
Swiss Franc / Japanese Yen	250,000 CHF	110	247	54		
Euro / Australian Dollar	125,000 EUR	769	554	306		
Euro / Canadian Dollar	125,000 EUR	901	247	5		
Euro / Norwegian Krone	125,000 EUR	98				
Euro / Polish Zloty	500,000	3,859				
Euro / British Pound	125,000 EUR	43,635	65,696	7,166	127	973
Euro / Japanese Yen	125,000 EUR	118,614	161,600	58,768	98,970	4,289
Euro / Swedish Krona	125,000 EUR	318				
Euro / Swiss Franc	125,000 EUR	7,290	1,794	949	182	2
Nikkei 225 Index (USD)	5 USD x Index	1,239,010	765,463	571,241	476,274	455,298
Nikkei 225 Index (JPY)	5 USD x Index	260,128				
S&P 500 Index	500 USD x Index	16,175,584	20,175,462	23,699,667	22,478,152	22,467,859
E-Mini S&P 500 Index	50 USD x Index	167,202,962	161,176,639	115,741,691	39,434,843	19,211,355
S&P 500 Barra Growth Index	500 USD x Index	2,754	5,119	7,756	12,408	16,733
S&P 500 Barra Value Index	500 USD x Index	8,852	14,131	17,238	24,319	31,121
S&P Financial Sector Index	125 USD x Index	2,527	4,093	5,052		
S&P Technology-Telecomm Sector Index	125 USD x Index	197	60	1,410		
S&P MidCap 400 Index	500 USD x Index	260,764	302,817	387,800	378,526	332,438
S&P SmallCap 600 Index	200 USD x Index	2,354	1,635	191		
E-mini S&P SmallCap 600 Index	100 USD x Index	3,282,347	1,417,513	343,087		
X-Fund 2	1,000 USD x Index	1				
NASDAQ 100 Index	500 USD x Index	4,011,983	4,421,221	4,903,287	5,586,750	5,094,042
E-Mini NASDAQ 100 Index	20 USD x Index	77,168,513	67,888,938	54,491,180	32,550,233	10,817,277
E-Mini NASDAQ Composite Index	20 USD x Index	445	6,444			

Chicago Mercantile Exchange (CME) (Continued)

Future	Contract Unit	2004	2003	2002	2001	2000
Russell 2000 Index	500 USD x Index	614,040	655,778	843,479	714,259	508,726
E-Mini Russell 2000 Index	100 USD x Index	17,121,233	3,878,935	859,885	26,012	
Russell 1000 Index	100 USD x Index	51,437	14,941			
Long-Short TRAKRS Index	1 USD x Index	1,070,408	994,756	2,469,467		
Long-Short TRAKRS Index II	1 USD x Index	5,693,223				
TRAKRS Select 50 Index	1 USD x Index	676,801	2,436,069	4,614,721		
LMC TRAKRS Index	1 USD x Index	460,246	1,803,316	2,697,494		
TRAKRS Commodity	1 USD x Index	4,138,262	7,424,763			
TRAKRS Euro Currency	1 USD x Index	1,248,272	1,196,525			
TRAKRS Gold	1 USD x Index	4,868,842	6,065,013			
HDD Weather	20 USD x Index	16,404	6,058	2,334	131	67
HDD Seasonal Weather	20 USD x Index	2,080	225			
CDD Weather	20 USD x Index	23,656	8,176	1,831		20
CDD Seasonal Weather	20 USD x Index	2,395				
Euro HDD Weather	20 GBP x Index	2,015	375			
Euro CAT Weather	20 GBP x Index	535				
Euro HDD Seasonal Weather	20 GBP x Index	350				
Goldman Sachs Commodity Index	250 USD x Index	450,036	371,473	518,323	479,646	1,002,673
Total Futures		**664,584,607**	**530,989,007**	**443,537,987**	**315,971,885**	**195,106,470**

Kansas City Board of Trade (KCBT)

FUTURE	CONTRACT UNIT	2004	2003	2002	2001	2000
Wheat	5,000 bu	2,833,370	2,632,033	2,738,536	2,357,004	2,427,950
Value Line Index	100 USD x Index	1,429	2,391	17,370	17,773	9,954
Total Futures		**2,834,799**	**2,634,424**	**2,755,949**	**2,375,133**	**2,446,607**

Minneapolis Grain Exchange (MGE)

FUTURE	CONTRACT UNIT	2004	2003	2002	2001	2000
Spring Wheat	5,000 bu	1,378,694	1,066,489	1,199,149	967,666	955,659
Hard Red Spring Wheat Index	5,000 bu	56				
Hard Red Winter Wheat Index	5,000 bu	2,521	16,535			
Soft Red Winter Wheat Index	5,000 bu	69				
National Corn Index	5,000 bu	116	3,996	2,253		
Total Futures		**1,381,456**	**1,087,020**	**1,201,543**	**968,699**	**958,420**

NASDAQ LIFFE Markets (NQLX)

FUTURE	CONTRACT UNIT	2004	2003	2002	2001	2000
Single Stock Futures		234,392	576,765	72,897		
Exchange Traded Funds		22,608	282,135	17,194		
Total Futures		**257,000**	**858,900**	**90,091**		

New York Board of Trade (NYBOT)

FUTURE	CONTRACT UNIT	2004	2003	2002	2001	2000
Coffee 'C'	37,500 lbs	4,193,303	3,211,031	2,718,508	2,199,371	2,134,961
Mini Coffee	12,500 lbs	276	332	784		
Sugar #11	112,000 lbs	9,766,550	7,140,724	6,173,756	5,150,329	5,933,850
Sugar #14	112,000 lbs	114,619	133,811	141,017	116,733	122,976
Cocoa	10 metric tons	2,389,050	2,128,206	2,079,980	2,005,817	2,110,048
Cotton #2	50,000 lbs	3,156,018	3,035,992	2,327,960	2,259,665	2,597,757
Ethanol	7,750 US Gallons	1,371				
Orange Juice, Frozen Concentrate	15,000 lbs	970,437	652,715	577,757	577,496	712,204
Orange Juice, Frozen Concentrate - Diff			10			
US Dollar / Canadian Dollar	200,000 USD	2,949	2,458	2,581	1,854	2,825
US Dollar / Swedish Krona	200,000 USD	11,654	12,377	2,983	2,564	2,423
US Dollar / Norwegian Krone	200,000 USD	17,016	11,350	1,178	746	58
US Dollar / Swiss Franc	200,000 USD	8,513	26,119	11,159	10,737	16,671
US Dollar / Japanese Yen	200,000 USD	46,433	43,351	58,583	16,338	30,353
US Dollar / British Pound	125,000 GBP	49,150	40,467	31,956	17,379	14,202
US Dollar / Czech Koruna	200,000 USD	9,852	527			
US Dollar / Hungarian Forint	200,000 USD	9,283	1,120			
US Dollar / South African Rand	100,000 USD	71,332	31,272	11,081	4,793	9,984
Canadian Dollar / Japanese Yen	200,000 CAD	16,604	16,440	8,593	18,865	5,380
Australian Dollar / US Dollar	100,000 AUD	13,141	6,061	8,043	2,640	44,307
Australian Dollar / Canadian Dollar	200,000 AUD	9,178	15,104	5,181	17,886	2,064
Australian Dolar / New Zealand Dollar	200,000 AUD	34,904	16,357	9,525	12,673	15,333
New Zealand Dollar / US Dollar	100,000 NZD	37,899	26,395	13,289	24,426	23,866
Australian Dollar / Japanese Yen	200,000 AUD	66,006	41,468	21,870	31,250	32,390
Norwegian Krone / Swedish Koruna	500,000 NOK	10,192				

VOLUME U.S.

New York Board of Trade (NYBOT)   (Continued)

FUTURE	CONTRACT UNIT	2004	2003	2002	2001	2000
British Pound / Swiss franc	125,000 GBP	31,151	20,503	13,204	21,379	11,061
British Pound / Japanese Yen	125,000 GBP	68,519	52,145	30,925	42,651	85,530
Swiss Franc / Japanese Yen	200,000 CHF	41,614	22,193	9,038	15,196	13,662
Euro	200,000 EUR	65,808	60,926	81,998	64,431	97,032
Euro / US Dollar, Small	100,000 EUR	12,409	5,365	2,560	2,299	6,508
Euro / Australian Dollar	100,000 EUR	44,000	30,466	14,635	17,006	7,674
Euro / Canadian Dollar	100,000 EUR	52,496	49,890	17,731	11,712	8,396
Euro / Czech Koruna	100,000 EUR	28,093	2,774			
Euro / Hungarian Forint	100,000 EUR	17,640	24			
Euro / Japanese Yen	100,000 EUR	363,069	346,751	337,756	294,733	278,119
Euro / Swedish Krona	100,000 EUR	64,334	49,977	45,757	30,354	54,076
Euro / British Pound	100,000 EUR	226,404	117,989	124,485	112,727	159,862
Euro / Norwegian	100,000 EUR	29,536	29,815	17,670	4,488	2,461
Euro / Swiss Franc	100,000 EUR	143,274	133,218	69,057	44,162	69,538
Small British Pound / US Dollar	62,500 GBP	6,006				
Small US Dollar / Canadian Dollar	100,000 USD	247				
Small US Dollar / Japanese Yen	100,000 USD	5,664				
Small US Dollar / Swiss Franc	100,000 USD	41				
US Dollar Index	1,000 USD x Index	748,204	563,032	411,571	342,948	297,745
Revised NYSE Composite Index	50 USD x Index	14,678	7,143			
Russell 1000 Index	500 USD x Index	961,771	677,626	646,455	313,318	94,736
Russell 1000 Growth Index	500 USD x Index	2,442	836			
Russell 1000 Value Index	500 USD x Index	2,392	415			
Russell 2000 Index	500 USD x Index	424	10			
Russell 2000 Growth Index	500 USD x Index	4				
Russell 2000 Value Index	500 USD x Index	2				
Russell 3000 Index	500 USD x Index	20	96			
Reuters-CRB Futures Index	500 USD x Index	19,230	23,156	14,283	16,878	63,494
Total Futures		**23,955,212**	**18,822,048**	**16,272,144**	**14,034,168**	**15,214,853**

New York Mercantile Exchange (NYMEX)

COMEX Division

FUTURE	CONTRACT UNIT	2004	2003	2002	2001	2000
Gold	100 oz	14,959,617	12,235,689	9,018,183	6,785,340	6,643,464
Silver	5,000 oz	5,006,125	4,111,190	3,135,564	2,569,198	3,117,017
High Grade Copper	25,000 lbs	3,190,625	3,089,270	2,807,286	2,856,641	2,778,124
Aluminum	44,000 lbs	72,169	107,490	74,000	43,089	46,099
Total Futures		**23,228,536**	**19,543,639**	**15,035,033**	**12,258,659**	**12,626,367**

NYMEX Division

FUTURE	CONTRACT UNIT	2004	2003	2002	2001	2000
Palladium	100 oz	267,552	95,613	41,053	25,925	50,766
Platinum	50 oz	295,695	268,305	219,771	205,969	320,924
No. 2 Heating Oil, NY	1,000 bbl	12,884,511	11,581,670	10,695,202	9,264,472	9,631,376
Unleaded Gasoline, NY	1,000 bbl	12,777,442	11,172,050	10,979,736	9,223,510	8,645,182
Crude Oil	1,000 bbl	52,883,200	45,436,931	45,679,468	37,530,568	36,882,692
E-Mini Crude Oil	400 bbl	720,421	277,411	210,228		
Brent Crude Oil	1,000 bbl	135,385	30	1,516	49,565	
Propane	42,000 gal	14,764	14,710	12,826	10,566	26,075
Natural Gas	10,000 MMBTU	17,441,942	19,037,118	24,357,792	16,468,355	17,875,013
E-Mini Natural Gas	4,000 MMBTU	136,123	115,502	67,981		
PJM Monthly		234,207	142,859			
Coal	1,500 tons	7,490	5,235	4,124	2,209	
NYISO A		91,067	88,826	1,268		
NYISO G		26,018	52,996	4,848		
NYISO J		13,214	10,245	758		
PJM Daily		190,591	30,221			
PJM Weekly		18,725	3,963			
Dow Jones Mid-Columbia		3,310				
Dow Jones NP15		3,770				
Dow Jones SP15		6,594				
Dow Jones Palo Verde		1,510				
ISO New England Peak LMP Swap		4,030				
WTI Midland Crude		200				
WTI Crude Oil Calendar Swap		152,680	33,785			
NY Harbor Residual Fuel 1.0% Sulfur Swap		625	375			
US Gulf Coast No 2 Crack Spread Calendar		1,375				
NY Harbor No 2 Crack Spread Calendar Swap		120,780				
Gulf Coast Gas vs Heating Oil Spread Swap		3,650				
Gulf Coast Jet vs NYMEX HO Spread Swap		1,750				

New York Mercantile Exchange (NYMEX) (Continued)
NYMEX Division

FUTURE	CONTRACT UNIT	2004	2003	2002	2001	2000
Gulf Coast No 6 Fuel Oil 3.0% Swap		200				
NY Harbor Conv Gas vs NY Harbor Gas Spread Swap		900				
NY Harbor Heating Oil Calendar Swap		51,347	2,355			
Gasoline vs. Heating Oil Swap		20,795	150			
NYMEX Gasoline Calendar Swap		20,279				
US Gulf Coast Unleaded 87 Crack Spread Calendar		45,775				
NY Harbor Unleaded Crack Spread Calendar		45,336				
Unleaded 87 Up-Down Calendar Swap		6,675				
Henry Hub Basis Swap		98,408				
AECO-C/NIT Basis Swap		488,699				
Chicago Basis Swap		174,498				
ANR - Oklahoma Basis		52,967	8,235	856		
Columbia Gulf Onshore Basis		24,272	3,526			
TETCO ELA Basis		24,755	4,872			
Michigan Basis		94,137	81,074	856		
TETCO STX Basis		19,790	13,132			
Transco Zone 3 Basis Swap		56,993	2,750			
Houston Ship Channel Basis Swap		429,266				
San Juan Basis Swap		62,048				
Sumas Basis		320,144	172,313	5,890		
NGPL Mid-Continent		69,854	32,580	1,666		
WAHA Basis		184,909	134,632			
CIG Rockies		69,555	7,026			
Henry Hub Swap		5,353,792	2,356,600			
Northwest Rockies Basis Swap		652,511				
Natural Gas Penultimate Swap		294,011				
Social Basis Swap		569,540				
Texas Eastern Zone M-3 Basis		278,235	178,591	7,702		
NGPL Louisiana Basis		3,724	2,260			
TRANSCO Zone 6 Basis Swap		480,197				
PG&E Malin Basis		334,230	241,769	11,564		
PG&E Citygate Basis		209,906	110,812	186		
NGPL TEX/OK Basis		60,266	13,418	2,072		
Northern Natural Gas Demarcation Basis		17,651	35,901	4,950		
Northern Natural Gas Ventura Basis		21,771	65,843	5,525		
Dominion Transmission - Appalachian Basis		247,191	95,595	1,898		
Panhandle Basis Swap		224,329				
Permian Basis		128,814	211,397	1,340		
TCO Basis		244,049	103,343	3,610		
Chicago Swing		102				
Henry Hub Swing		40,102				
Panhandle Swing		599				
Houston Ship Channel Swing		1,078				
WAHA Swing		1,310				
El Paso, Permian Index Swap		2,250				
Henry Hub Index Swap		65,860				
Houston Ship Channel Index Swap		12,791				
Panhandle Index Swap		1,798				
WAHA Index Swap		4,549				
Chicago Index Swap		1,581				
No 2 Up-Down Spread Calendar Swap		2,352				
Total Futures		110,054,812	92,246,019	92,324,686	72,781,325	73,461,273
Total Futures**		133,283,348	111,789,658	107,359,719	85,039,984	86,087,640

ONECHICAGO

FUTURE	CONTRACT UNIT	2004	2003	2002	2001	2000
Single Stock Futures		1,890,097	1,488,573	151,878		
Exchange Traded Funds		29,585	127,424	32,203		
Dow Jones MicroSector Index		3,044	3,197			
Total Futures		1,922,726	1,619,194	184,081		

Total US Futures Volume

	2004	2003	2002	2001	2000
TOTAL FUTURES	1,324,027,532	1,042,968,664	851,310,387	629,212,715	491,451,073
PERCENT CHANGE	26.95%	22.51%	35.30%	28.03%	2.83%

* Includes the New York Futures Exchange, New York Cotton Exchange and Coffee, Sugar and Cocoa Exchange.

** Includes Commodity Exchange, Inc.

VOLUME U.S.

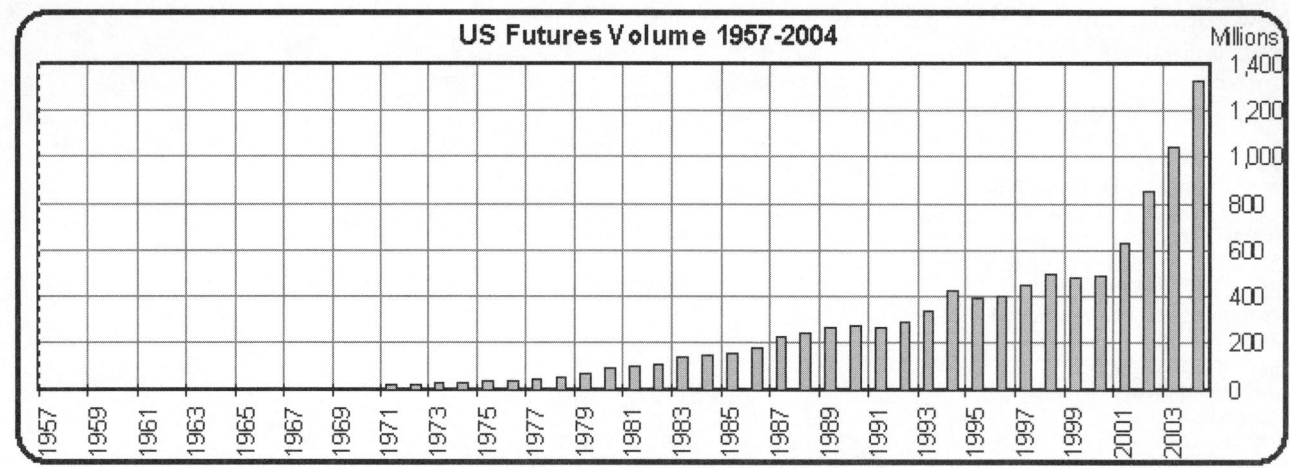

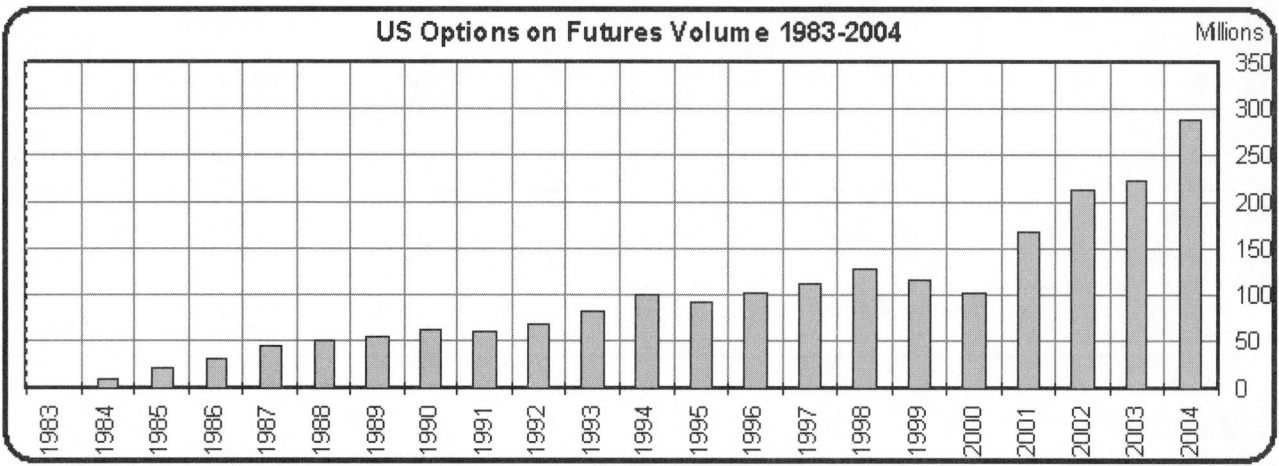

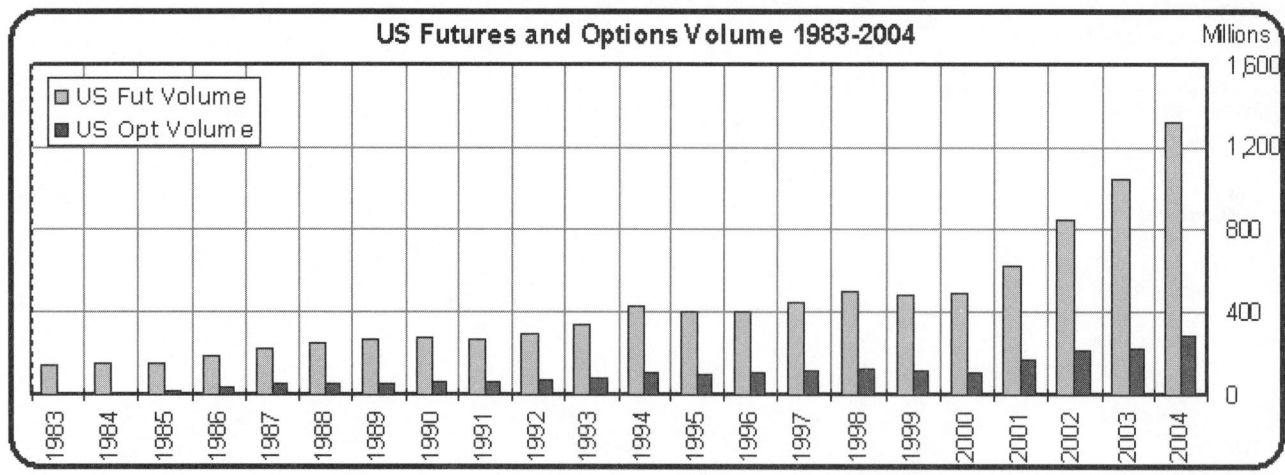

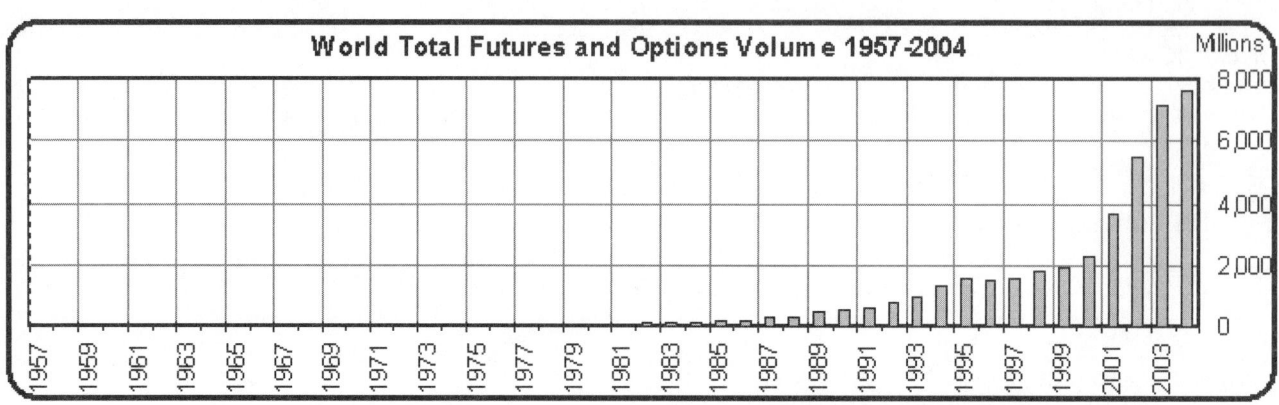

Options Traded on U.S. Securities Exchanges Volume Highlights
2004 in Comparison with 2003

2004 RANK	EXCHANGE	2004 CONTRACTS	%	2003 CONTRACTS	%	2003 RANK
1	Chicago Board of Options Exchange	361,086,774	30.55%	283,946,495	31.28%	1
2	International Securities Exchange	360,852,519	30.53%	244,968,190	26.98%	2
3	American Stock Exchange	202,680,929	17.15%	180,074,778	19.84%	3
4	Philadelphia Stock Exchange	133,401,278	11.29%	112,705,597	12.41%	4
5	Pacific Stock Exchange	103,262,458	8.74%	86,152,637	9.49%	5
6	Boston Options Exchange	20,741,271	1.75%	0	0.00%	
	Total Options	**1,182,025,229**	**100.00%**	**907,847,697**	**100.00%**	

Options Traded on U.S. Futures Exchanges Volume Highlights
2004 in Comparison with 2003

2004 RANK	EXCHANGE	2004 CONTRACTS	%	2003 CONTRACTS	%	2003 RANK
1	Chicago Mercantile Exchange (CME)	140,457,074	48.57%	109,220,627	49.27%	1
2	Chicago Board of Trade (CBT)	110,764,242	38.31%	80,521,459	36.32%	2
3	New York Mercantile Exchange (NYMEX)	29,873,559	10.33%	25,435,781	11.47%	3
4	New York Board of Trade (NYBOT)	7,774,379	2.69%	6,010,110	2.71%	4
5	Kansas City Board of Trade (KCBT)	254,304	0.09%	465,381	0.21%	5
6	Minneapolis Grain Exchange (MGE)	34,826	0.01%	46,711	0.02%	6
7	EUREX US	800	0.00%	0	0.00%	
	Total Options	**289,159,184**	**100.00%**	**221,700,069**	**100.00%**	

** Includes Commodity Exchange, Inc.

* Includes the New York Futures Exchange, New York Cotton Exchange and Coffee, Sugar and Cocoa Exchange.

Options Volume on U.S. Futures Exchange 2000-2004
Chicago Board of Trade (CBT)

Option	Contract Unit	2004	2003	2002	2001	2000
Wheat	5,000 bu	1,465,760	1,788,500	1,773,559	1,714,041	1,563,557
Corn	5,000 bu	7,593,355	4,515,240	5,397,748	4,864,294	5,135,111
Oats	5,000 bu	36,498	36,163	90,780	70,218	52,760
Soybeans	5,000 bu	6,045,952	4,885,399	4,227,445	3,829,236	3,890,510
Soybean Oil	60,000 lbs	947,383	665,532	659,302	672,284	490,666
Soybean Meal	100 tons	971,335	546,267	404,351	606,187	657,709
Rice	200,000 lbs	22,064	34,978	35,272	23,233	32,955
T-Bonds	100,000 USD	13,788,908	15,180,025	15,324,548	13,478,771	17,267,458
T-Notes (10-year)	100,000 USD	56,878,013	41,165,629	31,741,521	19,983,876	10,629,021
T-Notes (5-year)	100,000 USD	17,215,903	9,697,455	7,533,556	4,681,604	3,733,542
T-Notes (2-year)	200,000 USD	10,206	11,874	32,468	44,185	3,824
30-Day Federal Funds	5,000,000 USD	4,707,103	1,614,319			
Flexible US T-Bonds		193,663	57,442	38,456	38,160	18,781
Flexible T-Notes (10-year)		96,192	56,920	60,577	45,700	24,670
Flexible T-Notes (5-year)		29,900	200	4,225	2,200	12,160
Dow Jones Industrial Index	10 USD x Index	190,708	263,629	234,219	288,364	200,379
Mini ($5) Dow Jones Industrial Index	5 USD x Index	571,299				
Total Options		**110,764,242**	**80,521,459**	**67,566,482**	**50,345,068**	**43,866,151**

Chicago Mercantile Exchange (CME)

Option	Contract Unit	2004	2003	2002	2001	2000
Lean Hogs	40,000 lbs	179,093	129,227	156,699	171,472	161,931
Pork Bellies, Frozen	40,000 lbs	4,010	7,991	5,595	6,901	29,712
Butter	50,000 lbs	401	800	259	38	385
Mini BFP Milk	100,000 lbs	1,654	1,269	2,107	2,836	263
Class III Milk	200,000 lbs	122,014	79,901	23,852		
Class IV Milk	200,000 lbs	15	41	543	1,448	656
Live Cattle	40,000 lbs	500,927	664,291	476,467	688,149	622,590
Feeder Cattle	44,000 lbs	142,638	179,347	121,226	186,247	132,086
Random Lumber	80,000 bd ft	20,056	18,139	14,665	25,752	19,413
Euroyen	100,000,000 JPY	437	53	318	2,225	9,756
Eurodollar (3-month)	1,000,000 USD	130,598,377	100,823,779	105,580,961	88,174,799	28,590,428
Eurodollar Bundle (5-year)	1-5 yr ED Bundle	52				

VOLUME U.S.

Chicago Mercantile Exchange (CME) (Continued)

Option	Contract Unit	2004	2003	2002	2001	2000
One Month LIBOR	3,000,000 USD	201	4,191	395	2,106	2,236
British Pound	62,500	166,360	156,569	121,443	147,205	174,928
Canadian Dollar	100,000	190,976	206,862	153,329	109,908	75,934
Japanese Yen	12,500,000	465,261	489,123	849,646	839,069	567,896
Mexican Peso	500,000	3,664	5,050	5,688	5,331	5,741
Swiss Franc	125,000	55,596	53,766	82,285	119,051	125,360
Australian Dollar	100,000	60,593	42,495	18,098	30,050	10,337
Euro FX	125,000 EUR	1,492,887	1,187,819	929,518	655,991	371,737
Nikkei 225	5 USD x Index	8,774	8,564	4,197	3,339	4,270
S&P 500 Index	500 USD x Index	5,834,225	4,986,456	5,235,388	4,381,924	4,352,249
E-Mini S&P	50 USD x S&P Index	477,712	112,864	46,355	21,777	18,814
S&P MidCap 400 Index	500 USD x Index	375	780	2,573	4,007	2,911
NASDAQ 100 Index	100 USD x Index	37,612	50,439	71,991	121,895	699,264
E-Mini NASDAQ 100 Index	20 USD x Index	10,015				
Russell 2000	500 USD x Index	6,205	4,048	4,602	10,941	8,047
CDD Weather	100 x CDD	3,475	230	32		
HDD Weather	100 x HDD	11,527	501	281		
HDD Seasonal Weather	100 x HDDSW	39,650	3,390			
CDD Seasonal Weather	100 x CDDSW	5,650	150			
Euro HDD Weather	20 GBP x Index	850				
Euro CAT Weather	20 GBP x Index	450				
Euro HDD Seasonal Weather	20 GBP x Index	13,950				
Goldman Sachs Commodity Index	250 USD x Index	1,392	1,492	1,318	3,343	3,281
Total Options		**140,457,074**	**109,220,627**	**113,909,833**	**95,740,352**	**36,007,913**

Kansas City Board of Trade (KCBT)

Option	Contract Unit	2004	2003	2002	2001	2000
Wheat	5,000 bu	254,304	465,381	570,823	24,311	218,052
Total Options		**254,304**	**465,381**	**570,887**	**24,356**	**218,062**

New York Board of Trade (NYBOT)**

Option	Contract Unit	2004	2003	2002	2001	2000
Coffee 'C'	37,500 lbs	1,970,068	1,328,081	1,063,090	799,506	909,251
Sugar #11	112,000 lbs	2,854,683	1,690,190	1,380,300	1,305,470	2,027,581
Cocoa	10 metric tons	429,769	497,188	743,237	436,295	495,221
Cotton #2	50,000 lbs	1,725,982	2,157,441	1,171,843	1,025,578	1,027,002
Ethanol	7,750 US Gallons	10				
Orange Juice Frozen Concentrate	15,000 lbs	554,432	195,541	175,794	170,756	237,673
US Dollar Index	500 USD x Index	57,189	29,532	28,694	15,365	14,650
Euro	200,000 EUR	352	578	69	932	676
Australian Dollar / Canadian Dollar	200,000 AUD	2	3	1		
Euro / British Pound	100,000 EUR	67	253	14	936	1,232
Euro / Swiss Franc	100,000 EUR	300				
Euro / Japanese Yen	100,000 EUR	40	776	104	685	1,492
British Pound / Japanese Yen	125,000 GBP	17	209	156	16	0
US Dollar / Canadian Dollar	200,000 USD	45	60	140	1,492	5,200
British Pound / Japanese Yen	125,000 GBP	209	156	16	0	291
New Zealand Dollar / US Dollar	200,000 NZD	13	3			
US Dollar / Canadian Dollar	200,000 USD	60	140			
US Dollar / South African Rand	100,000 USD	170	1	600		
US Dollar / Japanese Yen	12,500,000 JPY	12	112	70	867	0
US Dollar / British Pound	125,000 GBP	25	31			
US Dollar / Swiss Franc	200,000 USD	1				
NYSE Composite Index	500 USD x Index	5,573	25,320	89,791	78,053	93,912
Revised NYSE Composite Index	50 USD x Index	26,952	18,912			
Russell 1000 Growth Index	500 USD x Index	273	358			
Russell 1000 Value Index	500 USD x Index	6	1,578			
Russell 1000 Index	500 USD x Index	103,944	61,264	1,449	9,905	48,245
Russell 2000 Index	500 USD x Index	36,305	734			
Russell 3000 Index	500 USD x Index	4,647				
Reuters-CRB Futures Index	500 USD x Index	3,515	1,913	974	891	3,306
Total Options**		**7,774,379**	**6,010,110**	**4,656,335**	**3,857,721**	**4,922,626**

Minneapolis Grain Exchange (MGEX)

Option	Contract Unit	2004	2003	2002	2001	2000
American Spring Wheat	5,000 bu	34,260	39,764	61,086	29,112	41,441
Hard Red Spring Wheat Index	5,000 bu	30				
Hard Red Winter Wheat Index	5,000 bu	416	5,773			
Soft Red Winter Wheat Index	5,000 bu	120				
Total Options		**34,826**	**46,711**	**61,226**	**29,830**	**42,658**

New York Mercantile Exchange (NYMEX)*

COMEX Division

Option	Contract Unit	2004	2003	2002	2001	2000
Gold	100 oz	4,667,523	4,310,318	1,948,564	1,975,019	2,083,414
Silver	5,000 oz	1,022,348	560,018	530,831	483,386	579,085
High Grade Copper	25,000 lbs	216,350	47,326	37,315	50,826	65,043
Total Options		**5,906,221**	**4,920,341**	**2,516,710**	**2,509,231**	**2,727,542**

NYMEX Division

Option	Contract Unit	2004	2003	2002	2001	2000
Platinum	50 oz	637	633	456	1,813	7,065
Heating Oil	42,000 gal	800,277	668,859	602,170	704,972	1,385,968
Heating Oil 1-month CSO		1,880	2,430	747		
Heating Oil APO		1,134				
Unleaded Gasoline	1,000 bbl	904,466	616,245	721,932	1,040,030	1,012,460
Unleaded Gasoline 1-month CSO		3,175	3,465	1,087		
Unleaded Gasoline APO		300				
Crude Oil	1,000 bbl	11,512,918	10,237,121	11,460,857	7,726,076	7,460,052
Crude Oil 1-month CSO		357,156	164,928	92,603		
Crude Oil 12-month CSO		9,600	825	2,905		
Crude Oil APO		23,622	131			
Natural Gas	10,000 MMBTU	8,071,967	8,742,277	10,966,023	5,974,240	5,335,800
Natural Gas 1-month CSO		47,328	13,557	4,636		
Natural Gas 3-month CSO		500		200		
Natural Gas 6-month CSO		50				
Natural Gas 12-month CSO		100				
Gas-Crude Oil Spread	1,000 bbl	79,664	35,797	6,521	14,992	16,348
Heating Oil-Crude Oil Spread	1,000 bbl	98,503	28,747	6,364	13,014	42,363
PJM Monthly		3,985				
European Style Natural Gas		2,012,703				
European Style Crude Oil		17,080				
European Style Heating Oil		8,023				
European Style Unleaded Gasoline		12,270				
Total Options		**23,967,338**	**20,515,440**	**23,868,006**	**15,475,878**	**15,260,056**
Total Options*		**29,873,559**	**25,435,781**	**26,384,716**	**17,985,109**	**17,987,598**

Total US Options Volume

	2004	2003	2002	2001	2000
TOTAL OPTIONS	289,159,184	221,700,069	213,149,576	168,211,323	103,065,376
PERCENT CHANGE	30.43%	4.01%	26.72%	63.21%	-10.38%

* Includes the New York Futures Exchange, New York Cotton Exchange and Coffee, Sugar and Cocoa Exchange.

** Includes Commodity Exchange, Inc.

Volume Worldwide

Australian Stock Exchange (ASX), Australia

	2004	2003	2002	2001	2000
S&P/ASX Index	66,256	67,769			
All Futures on Individual Equities	460,501	267,630			
Total Futures	**526,757**	**335,399**			
S&P / ASX Index	794,121	578,066			
All Options on Individual Equities	19,164,851	15,988,740			
Total Options	**19,958,972**	**16,566,806**			

Bolsa de Mercadorias & Futuros (BM&F), Brazil

	2004	2003	2002	2001	2000
Arabica Coffee	620,997	478,544	446,115	475,034	390,513
Robusta Conillon Coffee	20	405	475		
Live Cattle	225,200	113,473	152,939	92,365	149,795
Live Cattle (WTr)	6				
Feeder Cattle	1,024	9,475	1,295		
Sugar Crystal	47,347	40,257	48,326	93,904	52,552
Cotton	60	172	75	15	306
Corn	52,600	43,902	16,616	4,588	8,084
Soybean Futures	7,225	2,917	624	83	2,257
Gold Forward	15	483	4,425	484	1,520
Gold	2,742				
Gold Spot	57,609	98,386	65,892	42,971	95,494
Anhydrous Fuel Alcohol	40,453	49,158	62,896	67,527	53,963
Bovespa Stock Index Futures	7,063,923	6,630,407	5,231,780	5,151,572	7,000,335
INrX-50	6,265	85			
Bovespa Mini Index	2,892,016	1,158,155	592,342	110,943	
Interest Rate	1,002,920,263	57,641,625	48,568,401	46,241,111	37,626,151
Interest Rate Swap	1,005,212	888,957	474,713	964,419	6,656,112
Interest Rate x Exchange Rate Swap	1,189,805	3,520,170	3,185,443	3,645,863	2,216,247
Interest Rate x Reference Rate Swap	9,762	5,052	1,628	27,953	33,753
Interest Rate x Price Index Swap (formerly Inflation)	775,591	666,988	183,647	99,900	67,468
Interest Rate x Ibovespa Index Swap	1,175	435	224	1,392	33
Exchange Rate Swap	27,069	9,778	1		
Price Index	14,255	13,200			
ID x US Dollar Spread Futures	536,358	731,544	586,143	1,375,846	5,059,141
FRA on ID x US Dollar Spread	33,326,518	22,823,905	18,571,494	16,524,996	
ID x US Dollar Spread Swap	126,525	234,958	981,454		
ID x US Dollar MIni Swap with reset	189,441	1,057,259			
ID Forward with Reset	5	50	8,986	602,431	370,747
Global 2040	79,645	160			
C-Bond	25,919	35,903	13,696	2,605	983
US Dollar	23,943,757	16,784,939	16,132,798	18,636,578	20,208,454
Mini US Dollar	608,772	625,382	182,673	10,845	0
US Dollar forward points	365,914	227,097	116,199		
Euro	20	300	125	170	
Total Futures	**1,076,163,508**	**113,895,061**	**95,912,579**	**94,175,252**	**80,073,865**
Gold on Actuals	236,058	173,142	213,130	156,447	119,512
Gold Exercise	62,378	82,728	102,904	58,316	34,114
US $ Denominated Arabica Coffee	50,148	37,423	34,689	12,818	8,137
US $ Denominated Arabica Coffee Exercise	3,206	1,143	2,720	1,130	1,041
Live Cattle	550	764		1,204	1,533
Live Cattle Exercise	2	42			
Anhydrous Fuel Alcohol	100				
Anhydrous Fuel Alcohol Exercise	50				
Bovespa Stock	21,730				
Bovespa Stock Exercise	11,350				
Bovespa Stock Volatility	56,885				
Interest Rate	1,253,545	182,183			
Interest Rate (IDI)	2,224,832	1,772,583	2,539,353	1,129,060	661,218
Interest Rate (IDI) Exercise	154,100	155,263	15,910	89,013	58,100
Interest Rate (volatility)	879,575	9,810			
IDI Index (exercise)	131,099				
IDI Index (volatility)	143,180	1,185			
Fexible Bovespa Stock Index	687,412	1,216,418	578,467	273,888	116,976
US Dollar on Actuals	2,708,961	2,148,440	947,759	1,211,601	1,328,215
US Dollar Exercise	147,645	130,187	152,174	139,057	75,685
US Dollar Volatility	255,150	30,030			
Flexible Currency	866,474	949,200	1,098,543	570,739	458,631
Total Options	**9,894,430**	**6,890,541**	**5,703,209**	**3,696,233**	**3,455,810**

BOVESPA, Brazil

	2004	2003	2002	2001	2000
Ibovespa Index	1,586,762	1,600,261	1,144,628		
Mini Ibovespa Index	3,003				
Exchange Traded Funds	36				
All Options on Individual Equities	233,759,713	175,622,679	89,740,269		
Total Options	**235,349,514**	**177,223,140**	**90,884,897**		

Budapest Commodity Exchange (BCE), Hungary

	2004	2003	2002	2001	2000
Corn	9,617	12,513	9,450	15,733	41,956
CE Corn	6				
Feed Wheat	1,351	711	1,316	2,403	726
CE Feed Wheat	1				
Feed Barley	366	354	118	433	1,369
CE Feed Barley	1				
Wheat	4,246	6,883	9,271	14,987	21,345
CE Wheat	1				
Sunflower Seed	1,909	1,031	392	1,101	845
CE Sunflower Seed	1				
Rapeseed	270	24			
Ammonium Nitrate	1	3	2	17	67
US Dollar	401,800	1,153,307	389,001	425,125	486,860
Japanese Yen	57,980	197,763	179,650	226,639	232,844
EUR	615,144	1,602,075	698,888	1,840,127	1,306,688
British Pound	26,134	62,270	4,410	15,426	42,380
Czech Koruna	310	3,370	8,720		
Polish Zloty	1,258	3,565	1,330		
Swiss Franc	44,930	188,786	32,780	63,010	38,901
EURCHF	215	111			
EURUSD	5,255	937			
EURJPY	578	373			
EURPLN	2,441	433			
GBPCHF	551	27			
GBPJPY	1,825				
GBPUSD	2,896	68			
USDCHF	231	86			
USDJPY	620	139			
USDPLN	1,249	719			
3-Month BUBOR	4,320	1,540	3,400	7,585	
Total Futures	**1,185,507**	**3,237,088**	**1,338,846**	**2,612,788**	**2,174,480**
Corn	432	888	305	511	697
Wheat	90	242	150	164	19
EUR	113,970	414,095	260,850	11,000	
EUR/PLN	225				
EUR/USD	44	15			
GBP/JPY	10				
USD/PLN	448				
Total Options	**115,219**	**436,890**	**285,555**	**11,675**	**859**

Budapest Stock Exchange (BSE), Hungary

	2004	2003	2002	2001	2000
Budapest Stock Index (BUX)	376,679	400,003	292,128	1,236,405	839,978
Budapest Stock Mid & SmallCap Index (BUMIX)	51				
3-Month BUBOR	3,445	150			
EUR/HUF	38,069	178,460	74,800	41,722	22,536
JPY/HUF	41,350	67,390	3,761	3,084	
CHF/HUF	71,800	326,090	75,150	7,064	7,064
CZK/HUF	26,410	3,770			
EUR/HUF	512,991	514,451			
GBP/HUF	28,000	1,000	1,600	1,000	1,000
PLN/HUF	42,092	1,800			
USD/HUF	227,235	36,586	125,689	116,176	74,790
GBP/USD	197,560	72,350	3,100		
GBP/CHF	100,630	33,000			
GBP/JPY	311,030	4,800			
GBP/SEK	33,800	23,300			
EUR/CHF	38,700	43,575			
EUR/CZK	2,200				
EUR/GBP	17,500	25,100			
EUR/NOK	18,600	23,900			
EUR/JPY	46,200	8,200			
EUR/PLN	28,300	24,200			
EUR/ROL	5,000				
EUR/SEK	51,200	2,039,000			
EUR/TRL	1,500				
EUR/USD	501,448	249,750	41,800		
USD/CHF	117,700	16,440	249,750	41,800	
USD/JPY	666,030	146,525	1,700		
USD/PLN	5,400				
USD/TRL	3,800				
All Futures on Individual Equities	707,875	694,553	452,638	879,049	456,510
Total Futures	**4,222,595**	**4,939,893**	**1,072,566**	**2,286,300**	**1,402,378**

Dalian Commodity Exchange (DCE), China

	2003	2003	2002	2001	2000
Corn	5,828,045				
No 1 Soybeans	57,340,803	60,000,808	12,689,935		
No 2 Soybeans	114,347				
Soybean Meal	24,750,958	14,953,398	4,404,134		
Total Futures	**88,034,153**	**74,973,493**	**48,407,404**		

VOLUME WORLDWIDE

EUREX, Frankfurt, Germany

(formerly DTB and SOFFEX)	2004	2003	2002	2001	2000
DAX	29,229,847	27,181,218	19,996,503	14,686,359	11,524,330
HEX 25	24,934	32,589	44,524		
NEMAX 50	124,411	750,125	4,704,283	5,409,482	702,873
TecDAX	456,346	181,954			
DJ Global Titans 50	333	2,017	965	871	
DJ Global Italy Titans 50	70,403				
DJ Euro STOXX 50	121,661,944	116,035,326	86,354,731	37,828,500	14,315,518
DJ Euro STOXX Automobiles	99,776	152,714	83,677		
DJ Euro STOXX Banks	243,541	483,451	560,757	113,478	
DJ Euro STOXX Basic Resources	18,018	10,185			
DJ Euro STOXX Chemicals	5,254	54			
DJ Euro STOXX Construction	573	481			
DJ Euro STOXX Cyclical Goods and Services	5,358	40			
DJ Euro STOXX Energy	118,457	105,614	77,762		
DJ Euro STOXX Financial Services	1,050	995	110		
DJ Euro STOXX Food and Beverage	16,382	8,538			
DJ Euro STOXX Healthcare	4,288	3,281	9,037	2,399	
DJ Euro STOXX Industry Goods and Services	844	230			
DJ Euro STOXX Insurance	236,325	323,207	151,250		
DJ Euro STOXX Media	8,863	8,339	698		
DJ Euro STOXX Non-Cyclical Goods and Services	2,035	444			
DJ Euro STOXX Media	1,983	42			
DJ Euro STOXX Technology	160,160	281,967	303,315	82,321	
DJ Euro STOXX Telecom	182,949	192,907	279,535	47,967	
DJ Euro STOXX Utilities	12,705	16,927	1,304		
DJ STOXX 50	798,106	970,107	690,719	452,830	355,801
DJ STOXX 600 Banks	32,222	8,595	25,376	11,259	
DJ STOXX 600 Basic Resources	647				
DJ STOXX 600 Oil & Gas	3,261				
DJ STOXX 600 Financial Services	166				
DJ STOXX 600 Food & Beverage	347				
DJ STOXX 600 Healthcare	70,931	41,394	100,674	11,968	
DJ STOXX 600 Industrial G&S	1,527				
DJ STOXX 600 Insurance	18,803	170			
DJ STOXX 600 Media	305				
DJ STOXX 600 Technology	15,887	8,331	13,306	5,152	
DJ STOXX 600 Telecom	19,596	20,537	20,403	6,900	
DJ STOXX 600 Utilities	29,622	9,651			
Swiss Market Index (SMI)	8,098,575	8,969,235	7,019,626	5,099,537	4,586,219
Exchange Traded Funds	78,393	187,996	56,126		
Swiss Government Bond (CONF)	308,206	284,809	275,392	416,883	479,350
Euro-BUND	239,787,517	244,414,274	191,263,413	178,011,304	151,326,295
Euro-BOBL	159,166,394	150,087,139	114,678,996	99,578,068	62,502,582
3-Month Euribor	585,142	503,951	527,815	663,980	1,224,877
Euro-SCHATZ	122,928,076	117,370,528	108,760,955	92,637,630	42,822,290
Total Futures	**684,630,502**	**668,650,028**	**536,013,920**	**435,141,707**	**289,952,183**
DAX	42,184,611	41,521,920	44,027,830	44,102,502	31,941,562
HEX 25	1,050	7,128	14		
NEMAX 50	210	48,969	634,195	1,726,251	473,297
TecDAX	27,370	13,477			
DJ Global Titans 50	29	48	40	104	
DJ Euro STOXX 50	71,406,377	61,794,673	39,477,430	19,046,893	8,197,999
DJ Euro STOXX Automobile	24,536	50,673	35,303		
DJ Euro STOXX Banks	150,913	413,834	898,989	20,434	
DJ Euro STOXX Chemicals	2	2			
DJ Euro STOXX Energy	46,243	63,427	64,012		
DJ Euro STOXX Financial Services	160	307	146		
DJ Euro STOXX Food and Beverage	300				
DJ Euro STOXX Healthcare	600	19	2,456	96	
DJ Euro STOXX Insurance	91,371	269,736	114,021		
DJ Euro STOXX Media	799				
DJ Euro STOXX Technology	28,102	86,830	382,141	19,031	
DJ Euro STOXX Telecom	39,396	110,664	314,976	9,677	
DJ STOXX 50	14,952	55,417	39,594	44,400	61,530
DJ STOXX 600 Banks	1,865				
DJ STOXX 600 Basic Resources	3,850				
DJ STOXX 600 Healthcare	20,017	11,270	45,040		
DJ STOXX 600 Technology	1,000	4			
DJ STOXX 600 Telecom	3,405	2			
DJ STOXX 600 Utilities	1,000	1,633			
Swiss Market Index (SMI)	3,645,596	3,983,918	4,230,082	3,179,143	3,474,369
Euro-BUND	30,896,920	27,316,536	18,125,981	22,054,064	26,291,123
Euro-SCHATZ	9,782,863	11,723,090	8,954,263	10,075,031	1,954,183
Euro-BOBL	10,829,250	10,498,534	4,529,387	6,188,962	2,436,491
All Options on Individual SMI Component Equities	47,714,268	46,302,221	34,496,338	35,239,133	35,648,521
All Options on Nordic Equities	17,836,215	13,265,471	20,601,113	16,165,675	4,536,186
All Options on Dutch Equities	8,364,977	6,862,703	2,708,256	835,418	
All Options on Exchange Traded Funds	85,478	70,350	6,069		
All Options on French Equities	2,743,950	1,487,428	246,562		
All Options on German Equities	134,857,678	120,211,761	85,111,674	276,825	9,905
All Options on Italian Equities	187,948	80,041	16,675		
All Options on US Equities	15,207	30,198	123,966	38,196	
Total Options	**381,008,508**	**346,282,284**	**265,186,953**	**239,052,063**	**164,119,313**

EURONEXT, Amsterdam

(Formerly EOE, AFM and AEX, Netherlands)	2004	2003	2002	2001	2000
Live Hogs (AVC)	33	1,257	4,959	32,437	32,020
Potatoes (APC)	14,397	40,265	39,285	61,184	63,184
Potatoes (FAP)	11,876				
AEX Stock Index (FTI)	5,651,747	5,215,465	4,231,053	3,317,913	2,674,824
Light AEX Stock Index (FTIL)	5,827	6,639	12,401	8,211	20,700
Euro/US Dollar (FED)	2,026	1,405	568	2,346	989
US Dollar/Euro (FDE)	1,959	1,088	1,077	2,234	3,656
All Futures on Individual Equities	13,257	32,429	37,042	8,387	773
Total Futures	**5,701,122**	**5,298,861**	**4,328,952**	**3,437,501**	**2,801,241**
Potato (OPA)	2,426				
Euro / US Dollar (EDX)	139,758	74,279	21,692	29,760	30,835
US Dollar / Euro	99,322	64,045	40,677	39,790	63,560
EOE Stock Index	17,093,573	14,120,099	9,133,875	6,569,129	4,953,037
Light AEX Stock Index (AEXL)	34,539	131,209	86,403	50,241	37,782
All Options on Individual Equities	60,196,898	59,754,703	64,076,106	56,348,323	50,345,697
Total Options	**77,566,516**	**74,145,895**	**73,368,051**	**63,065,039**	**55,488,681**

EURONEXT, United Kingdom

(LCE merged with LIFFE in 1996)	2004	2003	2002	2001	2000
3-Month Short Sterling	51,324,125	42,323,094	34,307,727	34,945,053	22,606,948
3-Month Euroswiss	7,296,932	5,009,460	4,976,206	4,694,391	4,621,559
3-Month Euroyen Tibor	736				
1-Month Eonia	35,152	58,341			
3-Month Euribor	157,746,684	137,692,190	105,756,584	91,083,198	58,016,852
3-Month Eurodollar	4,666,508				
Long Gilt	14,045,404	10,150,267	7,789,011	6,710,557	5,350,705
2-Year Swapnote EUR	458,492	580,516	977,127	686,450	
5-Year Swapnote EUR	688,952	1,022,358	1,437,955	1,502,104	
10-Year Swapnote EUR	653,046	1,031,016	1,613,672	1,967,221	
2-Year Swapnote USD	1	1,120	8,191		
5-Year Swapnote USD	430	17,660	13,399		
10-Year Swapnote USD	2,968	28,595	50,102		
Japanese Government Bond	80,569	44,613	37,723	72,182	379,541
FTSE 100 Index	20,772,878	20,252,114	17,238,726	12,698,908	10,142,828
FTSE Eurotop 100 Index	88,475	109,846	129,414	130,824	153,792
FTSE Eurotop 300 Index	814,030	344,100			
FTSEurofirst 80 Index	277,661	210,171			
MSCI Euro Index	60,414	107,207	114,576	124,202	77,140
MSCI Pan-Euro Index	474,949	563,944	552,460	373,259	166,135
FTSE Mid 250 Index	32,896	5,422	804	559	8,706
Cocoa #7	2,643,199	2,328,609	1,802,142	1,514,384	1,636,322
Robusta Coffee	3,054,386	2,320,831	1,905,319	1,547,838	1,470,980
Wheat	75,455	91,387	80,784	95,676	87,387
White Sugar	1,251,233	1,062,494	1,044,806	898,261	907,399
All Futures on Individual Equities	12,929,406	6,349,198	3,935,121	2,325,744	
Total Futures	**279,474,981**	**231,708,154**	**184,026,644**	**161,522,775**	**105,712,717**
3-Month Short Sterling	16,139,006	14,162,149	7,364,057	7,692,455	4,167,648
3-Month Sterling Mid-curve	1,461,723	967,384	346,001	427,975	127,080
3-Month Euroswiss	49,251	65,925	81,467	82,145	68,922
3-Month Euribor	52,245,463	57,733,239	33,481,758	21,643,698	7,900,121
3-Month Euribor Mid Curve	6,433,100	4,907,879	1,419,271	963,417	432,445
3-Month Eurodollar	376				
Euro Bund	72				
2-Year Swapnote	1,400	15,904	8,816	450	
5-Year Swapnote	2,516	2,452	5,992	1,730	
10-Year Swapnote	540	7,888	2,730	2,429	
FTSE 100 Index (ESX)	17,866,310	14,619,893	13,263,116	11,848,155	6,285,819
FTSE 100 Index (SEI)	10,766	55,215	110,800	320,461	531,389
FTSEurofirst 80 Index	521	1,841			
FTSEurofirst 100 Index	20	1,166			
FTSE 100 Index FLEX	1,178,067	1,066,997	595,486	229,152	71,898
Cocoa	170,079	188,822	194,682	94,505	7,119
US Dollar Coffee	248,990	143,148	139,394	80,197	119,200
Wheat	2,387	3,262	8,092	12,693	15,610
White Sugar	94,705	66,561	43,900	70,526	121,671
All Options on Individual Equities	11,578,961	10,108,068	12,889,422	10,725,183	5,484,873
Total Options	**107,484,253**	**104,117,793**	**69,954,984**	**54,225,252**	**25,342,092**

VOLUME WORLDWIDE

EURONEXT, Brussels

(Formerly BELFOX)	2004	2003	2002	2001	2000
Bel 20 Index	379,855	328,673	507,229	543,501	780,301
Total Futures	**379,855**	**328,673**	**2,653,399**	**3,438,621**	**30,299,351**
Bel 20 Index	271,717	320,540	747,161	727,853	911,275
All Options on Individual Equities	326,844	319,850	450,734	404,559	589,218
Total Options	**598,561**	**640,390**	**1,197,895**	**1,132,412**	**1,503,453**

EURONEXT, Lisbon

	2004	2003	2002	2001	2000
PSI-20 Index	114,955	214,415	346,134		
All Futures on Individual Equities	520,966	560,224	2,928,883		
Total Futures	**635,921**	**774,639**	**3,275,017**		
All Options on Individual Equities	28,152	74,664	5,228		
Total Options	**28,152**	**74,664**	**6,755**		

EURONEXT, Paris

(Formerly MATIF and MONEP, France)	2004	2003	2002	2001	2000
Wheat #2	160,200	114,758	107,602	57,159	33,038
Corn	71,124	90,973	98,654	57,664	27,677
Rapeseed	191,644	174,538	165,462	135,655	115,840
CAC 40 Stock Index 10 Euro	24,058,528	29,319,624	26,411,321	22,923,597	18,249,903
Total Futures	**24,481,496**	**29,711,816**	**26,991,450**	**42,042,673**	**62,968,563**
Rapeseed	8,075	7,003	9,834	7,554	5,313
Wheat	7,109	7,643	1,679		
CAC 40 Index (Long Term)	63,152,339	73,668,131	84,342,670	107,251,388	84,036,775
All Options on Individual Equities*	230,863,609	174,487,319	246,165,884	178,330,328	89,434,383
Total Options	**294,031,132**	**248,170,096**	**330,520,413**	**285,592,240**	**173,531,463**

Helsinki Exchanges (HEX), Finland

(formerly the Finnish Options Market Exchange)	2003	2002	2001	2000	1999
STOX Stock Future	1,648,009	2,157,347	988,503	853,872	820,574
HEXTech Index	79	282	41		
Total Futures	**1,648,088**	**2,157,629**	**988,544**	**874,862**	**1,101,616**
All Options on Individual Equities (STOX)	320,255	486,581	152,052	324,526	1,263,363
Total Options	**320,255**	**486,729**	**155,092**	**332,154**	**1,533,496**

Copenhagen Stock Exchange / The FUTOP Market, Denmark

	2004	2003	2002	2001	2000
KFX Stock Index	555,052	610,908	434,163	459,007	995,934
Total Futures	**555,052**	**610,908**	**434,163**	**459,007**	**1,029,369**
KFX Stock Index	1,299	8,440	7,722	5,529	10,277
All Options on Individual Equities	147,655	142,702	94,911	26,041	3,838
Total Options	**148,954**	**151,142**	**102,633**	**31,570**	**16,503**

International Petroleum Exchange (IPE), United Kingdom

	2004	2003	2002	2001	2000
Crude Oil	25,458,259	24,012,969	21,493,486	18,396,069	17,297,974
Gasoil	9,355,767	8,429,981	8,156,358	7,230,408	7,115,435
Natural Gas - Seasons	15,090	600	450	1,005	50
Natural Gas - Quarters	24,045	1,590	4,155	3,900	1,465
Natural Gas BOM	90	1,455	90	2,570	2,555
Natural Gas Daily (NBP)	90	74,180	180	1,540	5,440
Natural Gas Monthly (NBP)	609,350	737,610	578,925	462,665	515,305
Electricity Baseload - Monthly	1,070				
Electricity Baseload - Quarters	900				
Electricity Baseload - Seasons	2,280				
Total Futures	**35,466,941**	**33,258,385**	**30,233,664**	**26,098,207**	**24,938,224**
Crude Oil	28,688	49,520	146,809	252,217	452,284
Gasoil	45,154	33,339	61,001	60,240	100,631
Total Options	**73,842**	**82,859**	**207,810**	**312,457**	**552,915**

Italian Derivatives Market of the Italian Stock Exchange, Italy

	2004	2003	2002	2001	2000
MIB 30 Index	3,331,843	4,263,886	4,877,464	4,634,329	4,260,085
Mini FIB 30 Index	1,485,112	2,570,238	2,132,937	1,400,135	358,439
All Futures on Individual Equities	1,734,256	468,083	59,853		
Total Futures	**6,551,211**	**7,302,565**	**7,071,028**	**6,035,207**	**4,620,568**
MIB 30 Index	2,220,807	2,505,351	2,588,402	2,716,271	2,843,986
All Options on Individual Equities	9,500,498	7,924,078	7,587,199	8,329,533	5,875,138
Total Options	**11,721,305**	**10,429,429**	**10,175,601**	**11,045,804**	**8,719,124**

Korea Futures Exchange (KFE), Korea

* Transferred from KSE	2004	2003	2002	2001	2000
Korea Treasury Bonds	7,352,307	10,285,042	12,777,991	9,323,430	1,538,507
5-Year Treasury Bond	61	171,538			
Monetary Stabilization Bond	2,621	207,209	1,688		
*KOPSI 200	55,608,856	62,204,783	42,868,164	31,502,184	19,666,518
KOSDAQ 50 Index	206,221	727,997	380,491	466,479	
Gold	969	56,998		608	62,936
US Dollar	2,090,291	1,506,123	1,434,591	1,676,979	1,355,730
Total Futures	**65,261,326**	**75,159,690**	**57,465,025**	**42,971,090**	**22,626,492**
*KOPSI 200 Index	2,521,557,274	2,837,724,953	1,889,823,786	823,289,608	193,829,070
KOSDAQ 50 Index	1	3	44	85	
*All Options on Individual Equities	1	8,159	57,918		
Total Options	**2,521,557,276**	**2,837,734,344**	**1,889,908,138**	**823,289,693**	**193,845,775**

Korea Stock Exchange (KSE), Korea

	2003	2002	2001	2000	1999
KOPSI 200	62,204,783	42,868,164	31,502,184	19,666,518	17,200,349
Total Futures	**62,204,783**	**42,868,164**	**31,502,184**	**19,666,518**	**17,200,349**
KOPSI 200 Index	2,837,724,953	1,889,823,786	823,289,608	193,829,070	79,936,658
All Options on Individual Equities	8,159	57,918			
Total Options	**2,837,733,112**	**1,889,881,704**	**823,289,608**	**193,829,070**	**79,936,658**

London Metal Exchange (LME), United Kingdom

	2003	2002	2001	2000	1999
High Grade Primary Aluminum	26,953,102	22,330,491	23,767,595	25,443,980	22,211,729
Aluminum Alloy	703,356	895,726	819,206	643,659	740,955
North American Special Aluminum Alloy	833,022	173,127			
Copper - Grade A	19,437,740	16,579,090	17,797,929	17,565,260	16,789,674
Standard Lead	4,504,246	3,411,156	3,096,929	3,222,766	3,310,109
Primary Nickel	4,220,434	3,187,275	3,194,758	5,126,919	5,396,342
Special High Grade Zinc	10,470,171	8,100,114	6,113,484	7,549,121	7,341,620
Tin	1,448,083	1,625,470	1,432,814	1,846,413	1,770,807
Total Futures	**68,570,154**	**56,303,779**	**56,224,495**	**61,413,076**	**57,563,009**
High Grade Primary Aluminum	1,618,895	877,429	1,547,829	2,437,147	1,502,276
Aluminum Alloy	541	379	5,787	3,101	1,037
North American Special Aluminum Alloy	50	22			
Copper - Grade A	1,239,523	888,068	1,053,373	1,172,551	1,156,929
Standard Lead	95,967	50,413	86,098	76,256	114,498
Primary Nickel	144,489	67,781	133,039	415,373	250,823
Special High Grade Zinc	386,652	300,347	188,147	555,127	520,942
Tin	8,070	14,671	27,150	71,845	147,615
Primary Aluminum TAPOS	137,598	74,943	80,244	251,846	299,167
Copper Grade A TAPOS	90,381	32,939	39,472	46,498	41,261
Lead TAPOS	1,551	1,697	1,512	329	
Nickel TAPOS	4,950	6,642	10,937		
NASAA TAPOS	768				
Special High Grade Zinc TAPOS	8,738	14,884	14,807	1,948	
Total Options	**3,738,173**	**2,330,225**	**3,188,755**	**5,032,171**	**4,034,548**

Malaysia Derivatives Exchange, Malaysia

(formerly the KLCE and KLOFFE)	2004	2003	2002	2001	2000
Crude Palm Oil	1,378,334	1,434,713	911,015	479,799	308,622
3-Month KLIBOR	141,969	126,289	61,369	54,914	44,812
3-Year Malaysian Gov't Securities (FMG3)	4,327	781			
5-Year Malaysian Gov't Securities (FMG5)	19,494	116,221	72,959		
KLSE Composite Index (FKLI)	1,088,419	331,445	231,444	287,528	366,942
Total Futures	**2,632,543**	**2,009,460**	**1,276,787**	**822,241**	**720,376**

VOLUME WORLDWIDE

MEFF Renta Fija (RF), Spain

	2004	2003	2002	2001	2000
10-Year Notional Bond	95	1,382	46,771	290,608	1,094,548
Total Futures	**95**	**1,382**	**46,771**	**290,608**	**1,094,922**

MEFF Renta Variable (RV), Spain

	2004	2003	2002	2001	2000
IBEX 35 Plus Index	4,354,868	3,545,942	3,896,643	4,305,035	4,183,028
Mini IBEX 35 Index	1,182,497	1,070,853	724,424	22,423	
All Futures on Individual Equities	12,054,799	12,492,568	12,645,186	8,766,165	
Total Futures	**17,592,164**	**17,109,363**	**17,267,294**	**13,108,293**	**4,183,028**
IBEX 35 Plus Index	2,947,529	2,981,593	2,693,086	557,306	766,078
All Options on Individual Equities	8,200,314	11,378,992	18,701,248	22,628,132	16,580,519
Total Options	**11,147,843**	**14,360,585**	**24,068,192**	**23,628,446**	**17,346,597**

Mercado a Termino de Rosario (ROFEX), Argentina

	2004	2003	2002	2001	2000
Wheat	36	859	1,913	11,632	
Rosafe Soybean Index (ISR)	56,468	11,912	11,811	145,655	
Rosafe Corn Index (IMR)	309	615	555	1,107	
US Dollar (DLR)	7,679,077	2,694,348	385,139		
Total Futures	**7,735,890**	**2,708,313**	**399,432**	**159,935**	
Wheat	24	128	2	7,596	
Rosafe Soybean Index (ISR)	59,449	1,134	4,636	55,304	
US Dollar (DLR)	368,182	132,871	3,957		
Total Options	**427,655**	**134,183**	**9,038**	**63,898**	

Mexican Derivatives Exchange (MEXDER), Mexico

	2004	2003	2002	2001	2000
US Dollar	1,289,386	81,395	52,108		
IPC Stock Index	327,942	220,731	49,243		
CETE 91	2,418,381	11,398,544	3,568,951		
TIIE 28	206,027,203	162,077,312	80,595,463		
M10 Bond	278,644	38,279			
UDI Inflation Index	20				
All Futures on Individual Equities	13,455				
Total Futures	**210,355,031**	**173,820,944**	**84,274,979**		
IPC Stock Index	35,943				
All Options on Individual Equities	4,290				
Total Options	**40,233**				

Montreal Exchange (ME), Canada

	2004	2003	2002	2001	2000
3-Month Bankers Acceptance (BAX)	7,765,060	6,578,451	4,789,319	4,234,236	4,992,957
30-Day Overnight Repo Rate (ONX)	1,480	6,055	6,817		
Canadian Government Bonds (OBA)	605	3,754			
2-Year Canadian Gov't Bond (CGZ)	218,069				
10-Year Canadian Gov't Bond (CGB)	3,005,359	2,397,119	1,803,420	1,835,229	1,501,264
S&P Canada 60 Index (SXF)	1,906,038	1,681,994	1,450,860	1,174,328	1,272,244
Gold Index (SXA)	774	1,454	739		
Banking Index (SXB)	186	110	187		
Information Technology Index (SXH)	726	6,890	7,071		
Energy Index (SXY)	2,524	452	85		
Total Futures	**12,900,821**	**10,676,279**	**8,058,498**	**7,260,999**	**7,766,687**
3-Month Bankers Acceptance (OBX)	265,937	341,245	57,950	89,339	249,976
10-Year Canadian Gov't Bond (OBK,OBV,OBZ)	8	744	3,774	20,369	8,877
S&P Canada 60 Index (SXF)	38,892	38,221	47,749	35,585	88,923
i60 Index (XIU)	120,502	130,508	237,325	127,731	120,556
Barclays iUnits S&P/TSX Capped Gold Index Fund (XGD)	54,561	18,199			
Barclays iUnits S&P/TSX Capped Financials Index Fund (XFN)	73,006	101,914			
Barclays iUnits S&P/TSX Capped IT Index Fund (XIT)	11,800	9,721			
Barclays iUnits S&P/TSX Capped Energy Index Fund (XEG)	37,783	10,917			
All Options on Individual Equities	8,311,818	6,355,251	6,086,675	5,099,894	4,753,495
Total Options	**8,914,307**	**7,006,720**	**6,433,473**	**5,372,930**	**5,221,827**

National Stock Exchange of India

	2004	2003	2002	2001	2000
S&P CNX Nifty Index	23,354,782	10,557,024	1,641,779	750,956	
All Futures on Individual Equities	44,051,780	25,573,756	8,557,332	435,701	
Total Futures	**67,406,562**	**36,141,561**	**10,199,111**	**1,186,657**	
S&P CNX Nifty Index	2,812,109	1,332,417	314,478	7,596	
All Options on Individual Equities	4,874,958	5,607,990	2,773,524	55,304	
Total Options	**7,687,067**	**6,940,407**	**3,088,002**	**62,900**	

New Zealand Futures Exchange (NZFOE), New Zealand

	2004	2003	2002	2001	2000
NZ Broad Wool	104				
10-Year Government Stock	788	735	2,000	32,319	8,024
90-Day Bank Bill	491,706	484,263	607,453	915,225	781,074
FoX15 Gross Share Price Index	68				
Total Futures	**492,666**	**486,120**	**614,831**	**1,010,852**	**794,502**
90-Day Bank Bill	4,515	7,130	8,909	18,320	22,906
Total Options	**4,515**	**7,130**	**12,187**	**34,932**	**88,296**

OM Stockholm (OMS), Sweden

	2004	2003	2002	2001	2000
Interest Rate	6,546,035	6,674,408	5,586,173	7,033,675	5,371,720
OMX Index	16,460,920	14,567,900	13,331,795	14,906,505	11,477,162
All Futures on Individual Equities	4,257,168	1,424,890	1,290,181	1,468,018	2,144,767
Total Futures	**27,264,123**	**24,315,286**	**22,365,778**	**24,396,742**	**19,868,571**
OMX Index	8,946,939	6,371,381	4,916,726	4,587,544	4,167,448
All Options on Individual Equities	58,171,571	43,098,768	35,795,942	34,729,075	30,691,587
Total Options	**67,118,510**	**49,790,404**	**41,199,397**	**39,482,711**	**35,206,729**

Oslo Stock Exchange (OSE), Norway

	2004	2003	2002	2001	2000
Forwards	1,071,127	436,943	191,374	302,497	260,521
OBX	677,615	764,376	689,904	521,314	750,264
Total Futures	**1,748,742**	**1,201,319**	**881,278**	**837,341**	**1,024,266**
OBX	681,783	543,090	700,313	662,394	1,025,027
All Options on Individual Equities	2,921,209	2,079,405	1,594,138	2,346,339	2,062,350
Total Options	**3,602,992**	**2,622,495**	**2,294,451**	**3,008,733**	**3,087,377**

Shanghai Metal Exchange, China

	2004	2003	2002	2001	2000
Copper	21,248,370	11,166,288	5,796,300	4,088,943	2,674,016
Aluminum	6,829,499	2,155,498	2,355,796	1,448,192	455,206
Rubber	9,680,649	26,757,964	4,020,987	73,200	1,000,299
Fuel Oil	2,818,855				
Total Futures	**40,577,373**	**40,079,750**	**12,173,083**	**5,610,335**	**4,129,521**

Singapore Exchange (SGX), Singapore

	2004	2003	2002	2001	2000
Eurodollar	8,241,545	18,802,104	19,504,044	17,684,054	10,083,633
Singapore Dollar Interest Rate	42,486	58,353	128,034	111,210	61,300
Nikkei 225 Index	7,769,675	7,098,920	4,857,565	4,573,348	4,484,978
Straits Times Index	1,830	6,601	7,329	20,023	47,106
S&P CNX Nifty Index	38			1,800	20,403
MSCI Singapore Index	1,658,600	1,046,326	711,687	488,489	479,486
MSCI Taiwan Index	6,998,626	5,455,812	4,628,247	3,902,738	3,390,153
Euroyen TIBOR	2,490,390	2,015,211	1,812,175	2,711,826	7,149,469
Euroyen LIBOR	34,547	110,529	255,256	452,559	326,849
5-Year Singapore Gov't Bond	446	14,598	68,327	79,246	
10-Year Japanese Gov't Bond	86	92	360		
Mini Japanese Gov't Bond	931,110	745,091	630,761	545,189	718,353
Total Futures	28,169,379	35,356,776	32,623,190	30,606,546	26,804,964
All Futures on Individual Equities	549	13,690	6,575		
Total Futures	**35,356,776**	**32,623,190**	**30,606,546**	**26,804,964**	**24,480,004**
Japanese Government Bond	1,990	2,074	247	228	299
MSCI Taiwan Index	41,971	40,274	47,897	42,899	1,107
Nikkei 225 Index	205,417	249,087	201,206	291,052	708,498
Total Options	**249,378**	**291,448**	**264,205**	**383,316**	**766,999**

Taiwan Futures Exchange, Taiwan

	2004	2003	2002	2001	2000
TAIEX	8,861,278	6,514,691	4,132,040	2,844,707	1,339,908
Mini TAIEX	1,943,269	1,316,712	1,044,058	413,343	
Taiwan Stock Exchange Electronic Sector Index	1,568,391	990,752	834,920	635,661	409,706
Taiwan Stock Exchange Bank & Insurance Sector Index	2,255,478	1,126,895	366,790	452,541	177,175
Taiwan 50 Index	6,157	4,068			
10-Year Government Bond	67,705				
30-Day Commercial Paper Interest Rate	209,561				
Total Futures	**14,911,839**	**9,953,118**	**6,377,808**	**4,346,252**	**1,926,789**
TAIEX	43,824,511	21,720,083	15,664,464	5,137	
All Options on Individual Equities	6,237,079	201,733			
Total Options	**50,061,590**	**21,921,816**	**15,664,464**	**5,137**	

JSE Securities Exchange (SAFEX), South Africa

	2004	2003	2002	2001	2000
White Maize (WMAZ)	969,838	1,160,919	918,764	563,510	245,396
Yellow Maize (YMAZ)	228,709	249,691	290,921	77,933	57,666
WEAT	200,663	186,942	86,057	23,992	9,279
SUNS	56,285	61,055	60,271	25,249	5,751
SOYA	3,054	536	464		
All Share Index	9,289,443	8,521,365	6,975,380	8,044,557	5,817,231
Industrial Index	37,117	79,270	480,497	2,304,176	3,303,760
Gold Mining Index (GLDX)	9	1,072	6,505		
Financial Index (FINI)	15,931	41,198	146,945	10,585	25,788
Financial Industrial Index (FINDI)	4,892				
Government Bond Index (GOVI)	3,103	344	668		
FTSE/JSE Capped Top 40 Index (CTOP)	34,938				
FTSE/JSE Shareholder Weighted Top 40 Index (DTOP)	37,596				
JBAR	951	2			
RESI	2,004	12,053	35,249	2,933	460
Kruger Rand (KGRD)	15,798	36,323			
R 153	8,332	5,844	4,065	1,788	1,063
R 157	1,942	1,340	846		
R 194	3,872	1,856			
All Futures on Individual Equities	8,897,187	4,585,919	2,224,684	811,156	29,991
Total Futures	**19,811,664**	**14,947,523**	**11,233,002**	**11,868,242**	**9,505,060**
White Maize (WMAZ)	333,285	535,408	443,624	269,887	116,714
Yellow Maize (YMAZ)	33,385	82,062	120,599	27,785	12,117
WEAT	62,434	22,306	41,192	8,694	3,429
SUNS	5,089	7,224	7,207	5,775	1,904
SOYA	52	80	170		
All Share Index	11,267,046	10,501,861	10,916,338	17,926,295	12,137,585
Financial Industrial Index (FINDI)	1,717				
R 153	3,349	16,785	19,119	9,449	3,099
R 157	2,227	2,430	3,567		
R 194	80	1,980	1,800		
All Options on Individual Equities	6,827,533	6,877,254	8,102,185	5,705,719	1,992,579
Total Options	**18,536,197**	**18,054,220**	**19,733,581**	**24,307,477**	**15,178,641**

Sydney Futures Exchange (SFE), Australia

	2004	2003	2002	2001	2000
SPI 200	4,622,139	4,288,848	3,761,904	3,881,745	3,824,860
Australian Dollar	41,862	25,566	29,076	40,654	
30-Day Interbank Cash Rate	659,926	53,141			
90-Day Bank Bills	14,213,188	11,435,471	8,486,560	9,108,108	7,700,381
3-Year Treasury Bonds	22,805,279	19,246,934	16,459,043	15,718,248	12,359,076
3-Year Interest Rate Swaps	12,000	401	300		
10-Year Treasury Bonds	8,557,437	6,705,904	5,200,290	5,296,233	4,981,880
d-cypha NSW Base Load Electricity	3,700	2,730	160		
d-cypha VIC Base Load Electricity	2,693	2,766	100		
d-cypha QLD Base Load Electricity	1,378	1,335	80		
d-cypha SA Base Load Electricity	1,630	1,420			
d-cypha NSW Peak Period Electricity	1,142	1,927	310		
d-cypha VIC Peak Period Electricity	1,466	1,762	160		
d-cypha QLD Peak Period Electricity	994	660	230		
d-cypha SA Peak Period Electricity	358	235	45		
d-cypha VIC Base $300 CAP	10				
Fine Wool	2,013	2,467	1,755	2,385	3,063
Broad Wool	826	2,003	2,756	944	417
Greasy Wool	9,520	9,095	14,180	8,621	11,126
MLA/SFE Cattle	1,354	1,175	175		
All Futures on Individual Equities	29,986	47,822	29,286	12,545	8,817
Total Futures	**50,968,901**	**41,831,862**	**33,987,967**	**34,075,508**	**28,901,368**
SPI 200	518,511	585,620	414,598	516,432	1,098,919
SPI 200 Intra Day Cash Settled	4,917				
90-Day Bank Bills	175,286	250,876	227,208	267,808	326,638
3-Year Treasury Bond	369,708	220,382	237,509	301,782	319,383
Overnight 3-Year Treasury Bond	1,262,942	1,151,097	1,048,753	618,011	477,192
3-Year Bonds Intra-Day	534,302	583,719	277,905		
10-Year Treasury Bonds	60,619	38,972	24,037	36,341	104,948
10-Year Bonds Intra-Day	1,845	6,307	1,880		
Overnight 10-Year Treasury Bond	71,140	86,313	22,629	29,671	47,373
d-cypha SA Peak Period Electricity	50	10			
d-cypha VIC Peak Period Electricity	65	5			
Greasy Wool	1,159	177	1,038	20	3
Total Options	**3,000,544**	**2,923,478**	**2,255,557**	**1,770,371**	**2,375,579**

Tel-Aviv Stock Exchange (TASE), Israel

	2004	2003	2002	2001	2000
TA-25 Index	8,291	10,210	32,214	53,198	
Shekel-Dollar Rate	44	85	67		
Total Futures	**8,335**	**10,295**	**32,281**	**53,198**	
TA-25 Index	36,921,511	29,352,985	29,425,456	26,871,775	
TA-Banks Index	596	610	3,453	35,940	
Shekel-Dollar Rate	5,847,295	8,343,368	11,542,803	6,049,954	
Shekel-Euro Rate	598,206	391,221	415,712	23,940	
Total Options	**43,367,608**	**38,088,184**	**41,387,424**	**32,981,609**	

Wiener Borse - Derivatives Market of Vienna, Austria

(formerly the AFOE)	2004	2003	2002	2001	2000
ATX Index	50,743	49,441	99,397	271,741	431,048
ATF Index	25,607				
CeCe (5 Eastern European Indices)	40,108	63,439	68,542	164,278	227,829
All Futures on Individual Equities	7,862				
Total Futures	**124,320**	**112,880**	**167,939**	**436,019**	**658,877**
ATX Index	36,738	27,608	68,903	123,757	205,286
ATF Index	4,097				
All Options on Individual Equities	2,077,320	1,252,041	1,090,225	1,239,969	
Total Options	**2,118,155**	**1,279,649**	**1,159,145**	**1,365,633**	**218,099**

Winnipeg Commodity Exchange (WCE), Canada

	2004	2003	2002	2001	2000
Wheat	87,758	59,194	89,136	166,932	164,981
Flaxseed	90	4,438	25,586	72,476	101,216
Canola (Rapeseed)	1,737,972	1,547,283	1,828,122	2,424,973	1,858,773
Western Barley	204,635	200,701	212,019	237,574	266,077
Total Futures	**2,030,455**	**1,811,616**	**2,155,796**	**2,903,826**	**2,391,565**
Western Barley	3,273	2,778	1,819	5,728	6,656
Canola	20,568	28,368	35,470	125,236	63,641
Total Options	**23,841**	**31,160**	**37,487**	**133,507**	**76,944**

Hong Kong Futures Exchange (HKFE), Hong Kong

	2004	2003	2002	2001	2000
Hang Seng Index	8,601,559	6,800,360	4,802,422	4,400,071	4,023,138
Mini Hang Seng Index	1,457,681	1,248,295	1,107,964	769,886	120,165
H-Shares Index	1,743,700	47,941			
Dow Jones Industrial Average	2,673	9,091	6,773		
1-Month HIBOR	733	310	970	14,315	12,075
3-Month HIBOR	58,307	47,799	280,257	629,491	325,155
3-Year Exchange Fund Note	2,225	2,012	3,673	1,175	
All Futures on Individual Equities	17,274	18,654	21,056	7,756	3,322
Total Futures	**11,884,152**	**8,174,652**	**6,228,037**	**5,830,672**	**4,521,926**
Hang Seng Index	2,029,068	2,118,792	1,070,431	716,114	544,047
Mini Hang Seng Index	26,882	32,131	6,176		
H-Shares Index	77,758				
All Options on Individual Equities	5,611,832	4,220,638	3,724,760	4,002,655	4,188,702
Total Options	**7,745,540**	**6,371,561**	**4,801,367**	**4,718,880**	**4,738,644**

Fukuoka Futures Exchange (FFE), Japan

(Formerly KCE)	2004	2003	2002	2001	2000
Red Beans	8,297	40,675	42,650	54,845	37,689
Imported Soybeans	31,310	28,938	30,108	122,429	307,676
Non-GMO Soybeans	308,943	499,526	824,629	1,478,070	1,284,179
Refined Sugar	1,427	1,421	1,432	1,437	1,443
Corn	2,406,808	1,881,771	1,331,933	2,016,968	2,357,240
Broiler	92,022	44,376	754,626	2,693,858	2,443,593
Soybean Meal	187,926	242,676	185,608		
Total Futures	**3,036,733**	**2,739,383**	**3,170,986**	**6,367,607**	**6,431,820**

Tokyo International Financial Futures Exchange (TIFFE), Japan

	2004	2003	2002	2001	2000
3-Month Euroyen TIBOR	7,259,779	4,155,800	4,470,763	7,624,711	17,077,791
3-Month Euroyen LIBOR	3,000	3,000		2,904	8,255
5-Year Yen Swapnote	245,049	205,092			
10-Year Yen Swapnote	147,482	408,025			
US Dollar /Japanese Yen	200			1,294	3,900
Total Futures	**7,655,510**	**4,771,917**	**4,470,763**	**7,628,909**	**17,089,946**

VOLUME WORLDWIDE

Kansai Agricultural Commodities Exchange (KANEX), Japan

(Formerly OGE, OSE and KGE)	2003	2002	2001	2000	1999
Red Beans	12,080	45,786	30,069	47,563	177,039
Imported Soybeans	41,126	161,244	465,057	872,373	1,245,358
Non-GMO Soybeans	622,337	767,206	971,980	856,623	
Refined Sugar	2,842	2,864	2,874	2,886	2,842
Raw Sugar	18,956	42,736	94,961	231,550	462,427
Raw Silk (formerly at Kobe Raw Silk Exchange)	8,009	69,609	269,199	188,091	178,114
Frozen Shrimp	1,144,264	1,937,842			
Corn 75 Index	317,561	499,912	263,520		
Coffee Index	1,274,190	961,715	371,272		
Total Futures	**3,441,365**	**4,488,914**	**2,901,551**	**2,447,652**	**2,442,440**
Raw Sugar	2,931	3,040	6,097	12,388	30,363
Total Options	**2,931**	**3,040**	**6,097**	**12,388**	**30,363**

Central Japan Commodity Exchange (CJCE), Japan

(formerly NGSE, NTE, and TDCE)	2004	2003	2002	2001	2000
Red Beans	1,439	30,100	71,057	29,614	45,297
Non-GMO Soybeans	12,398	418,476	18,419	22,471	65,642
Hen Egg	798,308	399,167	338,291	596,415	590,274
Gasoline	15,869,951	16,705,638	15,212,512	14,392,478	11,048,071
Gas Oil	1,056,257				
Kerosene	15,454,906	13,984,740	14,338,356	12,346,595	8,714,440
Total Futures	**33,193,259**	**31,538,530**	**30,011,863**	**27,846,712**	**21,328,867**

Osaka Securities Exchange(OSE), Japan

	2004	2003	2002	2001	2000
Nikkei 225 Index	14,415,884	13,058,425	10,841,300	9,516,875	7,426,478
Nikkei 300 Index	167,399	172,862	293,438	961,566	1,281,029
Total Futures	**14,583,283**	**13,231,287**	**11,134,754**	**10,478,441**	**8,707,853**
Nikkei 225 Index	16,560,874	14,958,100	9,428,235	6,953,222	5,715,856
Nikkei 300 Index	491	234	568	609	674
All Options on Individual Equities	1,481,415	45,412	21,415	38,077	103,556
Total Options	**18,042,780**	**15,003,746**	**9,450,218**	**6,991,908**	**5,820,086**

Osaka Mercantile Exchange (OME), Japan

(formerly KRE and OTE)	2004	2003	2002	2001	2000
Rubber (RSS3)	756,411	1,550,423	1,300,492	710,872	1,404,451
Rubber (TSR20)	826,045	1,985,225	587,641	66,268	213,758
Rubber Index	814,328	1,423,491	1,885,262	967,915	1,561,707
Aluminum	1,101,198	963,464	1,285,419	1,438,450	1,695,737
Nickel	344,571	220,618	69,133		
Total Futures	**3,842,553**	**6,162,589**	**5,207,652**	**3,387,170**	**5,142,913**

Tokyo Commodity Exchange (TOCOM), Japan

	2004	2003	2002	2001	2000
Gold	17,385,766	26,637,897	20,506,652	9,791,711	7,841,692
Silver	1,473,370	1,160,565	930,886	660,864	558,770
Platinum	13,890,300	14,211,824	14,436,155	16,244,583	13,577,201
Palladium	438,934	275,322	87,883	117,098	1,007,307
Aluminum	321,131	329,565	513,892	735,366	543,015
Gasoline	23,648,587	25,677,079	20,866,237	16,441,056	14,370,266
Kerosene	13,036,277	13,208,350	10,482,433	8,301,559	6,741,173
Crude Oil	2,284,572	1,809,711	2,037,215	911,597	
Gas Oil	235,844	372,977			
Rubber	1,732,645	3,568,929	5,551,837	3,334,411	6,195,440
Total Futures	**74,447,426**	**87,252,219**	**75,413,190**	**56,538,245**	**50,851,882**
Gold	64,308				
Total Options	**64,308**				

Tokyo Stock Exchange (TSE), Japan

	2004	2003	2002	2001	2000
10-Year Government Yen Bond	8,025,268	6,465,073	6,356,612	7,377,641	9,909,127
TOPIX Stock Index	10,305,318	9,359,047	7,131,178	5,071,946	4,148,776
Electric Appliance Index	741	724	466	350	2,610
Bank Index	601	140,331	141,751	13,298	50,545
Total Futures	**18,331,928**	**15,965,175**	**13,630,046**	**12,465,433**	**14,254,348**
TOPIX	17,643	98,137	93,249	7,623	2,630
10-Year Government Yen Bond	1,262,994	972,518	1,036,395	1,062,235	1,271,887
Total Options	**1,280,637**	**1,070,655**	**1,129,644**	**1,069,858**	**1,274,517**

Tokyo Grain Exchange (TGE), Japan

	2004	2003	2002	2001	2000
American Soybeans	2,125,458	1,745,697	1,001,747	1,740,613	2,355,163
Non-GMO Soybeans	9,971,499	6,735,421	3,416,660	3,342,542	2,875,667
Soybean Meal	43,553	52,039	210,829	268,513	
Arabic Coffee	4,293,422	5,019,572	4,844,715	4,465,044	4,231,369
Red Beans	363,328	555,190	593,087	1,093,922	680,751
Corn	8,122,448	5,984,743	7,431,128	10,341,897	8,341,227
Refined Sugar	2,854	2,842	2,864	2,874	2,886
Robusta Coffee	427,466	617,327	460,507	420,873	729,618
Raw Sugar	355,659	371,896	709,394	1,031,530	1,561,657
Total Futures	**25,705,687**	**21,084,727**	**18,670,931**	**22,707,808**	**20,778,338**
American Soybean	17,758	17,548	21,515	19,040	84,819
Corn	16,072	12,214	16,511	52,012	113,888
Raw Sugar	5,405	5,979	19,309	37,544	85,957
Total Options	**39,235**	**35,741**	**57,335**	**108,596**	**284,664**

Yokohama Commodity Exchange (YCE), Japan

(formerly Maebashi Dried Cocoon & Yokohama Raw Silk Ex.)	2004	2003	2002	2001	2000
Raw Silk	239,446	919,049	698,321	602,727	789,795
International Raw Silk	8,470	11,581	40,935	241,004	387,081
Dried Cocoon	91	27,368	29,385	69,789	208,119
Potato	869,589	894,160	738,569	399,351	
Vegetables	47,215				
Total Futures	**1,164,811**	**1,852,158**	**1,507,210**	**1,312,871**	**1,384,995**

	2004	2003	2002	2001	2000
Total Futures	**2,139,293,501**	**1,927,572,093**	**1,473,598,607**	**1,173,022,823**	**952,905,056**
Percent Change	**10.98%**	**30.81%**	**25.62%**	**23.10%**	**21.89%**
Total Options	**3,907,764,474**	**4,012,673,793**	**2,898,783,708**	**1,630,793,276**	**722,899,112**
Percent Change	**-2.61%**	**38.43%**	**77.75%**	**125.59%**	**38.18%**
Total Futures and Options	**6,047,057,975**	**5,940,203,225**	**4,372,382,315**	**2,803,816,099**	**1,675,804,168**
Percent Change	**1.80%**	**35.86%**	**55.94%**	**67.31%**	**28.42%**

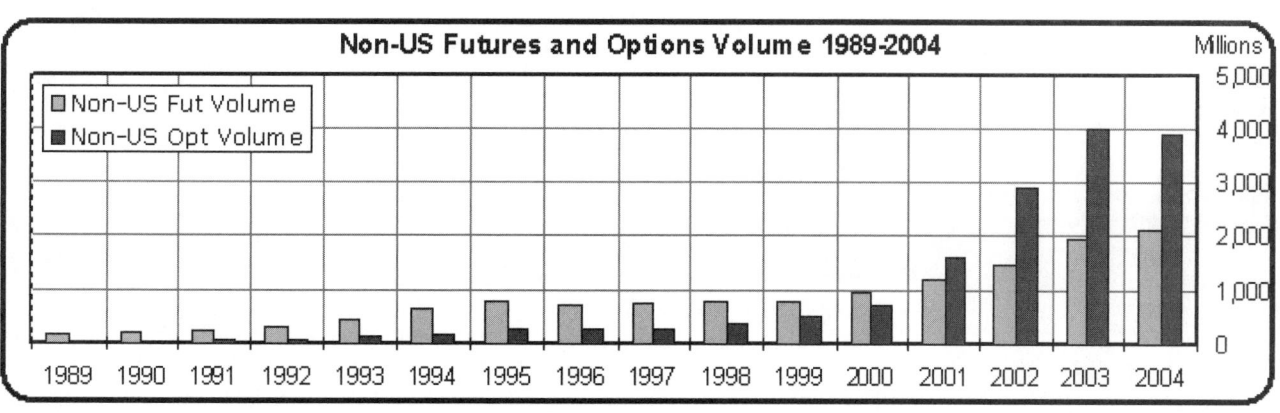

Conversion Factors

Commonly Used Agricultural Weights and Measurements

Bushel Weights:
wheat and soybeans = 60 lbs.
corn, sorghum and rye = 56 lbs.
barley grain = 48 lbs.
barley malt = 34 lbs.
oats = 32 lbs.

Bushels to tonnes:
wheat and soybeans = bushels X 0.027216
barley grain = bushels X 0.021772
corn, sorghum and rye = bushels X 0.0254
oats = bushels X 0.014515

1 tonne (metric ton) equals:
2204.622 lbs.
1,000 kilograms
22.046 hundredweight
10 quintals

1 tonne (metric ton) equals:
36.7437 bushels of wheat or soybeans
39.3679 bushels of corn, sorghum or rye
45.9296 bushels of barley grain
68.8944 bushels of oats
4.5929 cotton bales (the statistical bale used by the USDA and ICAC contains a net weight of 480 pounds of lint)

Area Measurements:
1 acre = 43,560 square feet = 0.040694 hectare
1 hectare = 2.4710 acres = 10,000 square meters
640 acres = 1 square mile = 259 hectares

Yields:
wheat: bushels per acre X 0.6725 = quintals per hectare
rye, corn: bushels per acre X 0.6277 = quintals per hectare
barley grain: bushels per acre X 0.538 = quintals per hectare
oats: bushels per acre X 0.3587 = quintals per hectare

Commonly Used Weights

The troy, avoirdupois and apothecaries' grains are identical in U.S. and British weight systems, equal to 0.0648 gram in the metric system. One avoirdupois ounce equals 437.5 grains. The troy and apothecaries' ounces equal 480 grains, and their pounds contain 12 ounces.

Troy weights and conversions: 100 kilograms = 1 quintal
24 grains = 1 pennyweight
20 pennyweights = 1 ounce
12 ounces = 1 pound
1 troy ounce = 31.103 grams
1 troy ounce = 0.0311033 kilogram
1 troy pound = 0.37224 kilogram
1 kilogram = 32.1507 troy ounces
1 tonne = 32,151 troy ounces

Avoirdupois weights and conversions:
27 11/32 grains = 1 dram
16 drams = 1 ounce
16 ounces = 1 lb.
1 lb. = 7,000 grains
14 lbs. = 1 stone (British)
100 lbs. = 1 hundredweight (U.S.)
112 lbs. = 8 stone = 1 hundredweight (British)
2,000 lbs. = 1 short ton (U.S. ton)
2,240 lbs. = 1 long ton (British ton)
160 stone = 1 long ton
20 hundredweight = 1 ton
1 lb. = 0.4536 kilogram
1 hundredweight (cwt.) = 45.359 kilograms
1 short ton = 907.18 kilograms
1 long ton = 1,016.05 kilograms

Metric weights and conversions:
1,000 grams = 1 kilogram

1 tonne = 1,000 kilograms = 10 quintals
1 kilogram = 2.204622 lbs.
1 quintal = 220.462 lbs.
1 tonne = 2204.6 lbs.
1 tonne = 1.102 short tons
1 tonne = 0.9842 long ton

U.S. dry volumes and conversions:
1 pint = 33.6 cubic inches = 0.5506 liter
2 pints = 1 quart = 1.1012 liters
8 quarts = 1 peck = 8.8098 liters
4 pecks = 1 bushel = 35.2391 liters
1 cubic foot = 28.3169 liters

U.S. liquid volumes and conversions:
1 ounce = 1.8047 cubic inches = 29.6 milliliters
1 cup = 8 ounces = 0.24 liter = 237 milliliters
1 pint = 16 ounces = 0.48 liter = 473 milliliters
1 quart = 2 pints = 0.946 liter = 946 milliliters
1 gallon = 4 quarts = 231 cubic inches = 3.785 liters
1 milliliter = 0.033815 fluid ounce
1 liter = 1.0567 quarts = 1,000 milliliters
1 liter = 33.815 fluid ounces
1 imperial gallon = 277.42 cubic inches = 1.2 U.S. gallons = 4.546 liters

ENERGY CONVERSION FACTORS

U.S. Crude Oil (average gravity)
1 U.S. barrel = 42 U.S. gallons
1 short ton = 6.65 barrels
1 tonne = 7.33 barrels

Barrels per tonne for various origins

Abu Dhabi	7.624
Algeria	7.661
Angola	7.206
Australia	7.775
Bahrain	7.335
Brunei	7.334
Canada	7.428
Dubai	7.295
Ecuador	7.58
Gabon	7.245
Indonesia	7.348
Iran	7.37
Iraq	7.453
Kuwait	7.261
Libya	7.615
Mexico	7.104
Neutral Zone	6.825
Nigeria	7.41
Norway	7.444
Oman	7.39
Qatar	7.573
Romania	7.453
Saudi Arabia	7.338
Trinidad	6.989
Tunisia	7.709
United Arab Emirates	7.522
United Kingdom	7.279
United States	7.418
Former Soviet Union	7.35
Venezuela	7.005
Zaire	7.206

Barrels per tonne of refined products:

aviation gasoline	8.9
motor gasoline	8.5
kerosene	7.75
jet fuel	8
distillate, including diesel	7.46
(continued above)	

residual fuel oil	6.45
lubricating oil	7
grease	6.3
white spirits	8.5
paraffin oil	7.14
paraffin wax	7.87
petrolatum	7.87
asphalt and road oil	6.06
petroleum coke	5.5
bitumen	6.06
LPG	11.6

Approximate heat content of refined products:
(Million Btu per barrel, 1 British thermal unit is the amount
of heat required to raise the temperature of 1 pound of
water 1 degree F.)

Petroleum Product	Heat Content
asphalt	6.636
aviation gasoline	5.048
butane	4.326
distillate fuel oil	5.825
ethane	3.082
isobutane	3.974
jet fuel, kerosene	5.67
jet fuel, naptha	5.355
kerosene	5.67
lubricants	6.065
motor gasoline	5.253
natural gasoline	4.62
pentanes plus	4.62

Petrochemical feedstocks:

naptha less than 401*F	5.248
other oils equal to or greater than 401*F	5.825
still gas	6
petroleum coke	6.024
plant condensate	5.418
propane	3.836
residual fuel oil	6.287
special napthas	5.248
unfinished oils	5.825
unfractionated steam	5.418
waxes	5.537

Source: U.S. Department of Energy

Natural Gas Conversions

Although there are approximately 1,031 Btu in a cubic foot of gas, for most applications, the following conversions are sufficient:

Cubic Feet			MMBtu		
1,000	(one thousand cubic feet)	=	1 Mcf	=	1
1,000,000	(one million cubic feet)	=	1 MMcf	=	1,000
10,000,000	(ten million cubic feet)	=	10 MMcf	=	10,000
1,000,000,000	(one billion cubic feet)	=	1 Bcf	=	1,000,000
1,000,000,000,000	(one trillion cubic feet)	=	1 Tcf	=	1,000,000,000

CRB Futures Market Service

CRB's *"Futures Market Service"* is a weekly publication designed to make you a more powerful trader through an understanding of the fundamental factors moving the commodity and financial futures markets.

The CRB *Futures Market Service* has stood the test of time with its status as the industry's oldest and most respected fundamental newsletter. The first edition was published on February 3, 1934.

Most traders make their trading decisions based on technical analysis and technical trading systems. However, combining both fundamentals and technicals gives you an even more powerful trading approach to the markets. Understanding the fundamentals helps you to gauge market direction, how far the market may move, and when the market may move.

We help you to understand these factors through our fundamental commentary and our weekly commodity and financial calendars. We analyze factors such as Fed policy, inflation, interest rates, stock market earnings and valuation, the dollar, metal and petroleum fundamentals, crop reports and global crop conditions, and livestock and softs fundamentals. We also use the Commitment of Traders to analyze how the big funds are impacting the markets.

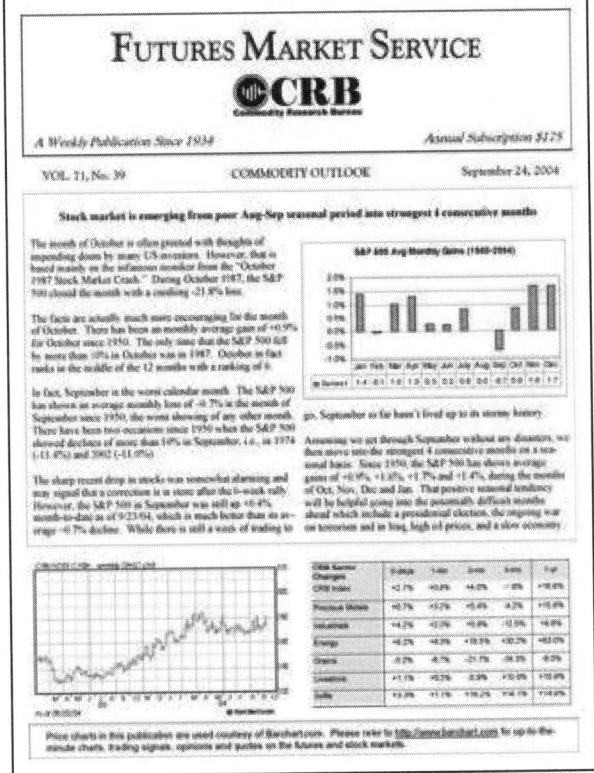

Also included in the service is a weekly version of CRB's *Electronic Futures Trend Analyzer*, which is an automated trading system providing specific trade recommendations with exact market entry and exit points.

For more information, visit www.crbtrader.com, or call

Commodity Research Bureau • 330 South Wells Street, Suite 612 • Chicago IL, 60606 USA
Phone: 312.554.8456 or 800.621.5271 • Fax: 312.939.4135 • info@crbtrader.com • www.crbtrader.com

Aluminum

Aluminum (symbol Al) is a silvery, lightweight metal that is the most abundant metallic element in the earth's crust. Aluminum was first isolated in 1825 by a Danish chemist, Hans Christian Oersted, using a chemical process involving a potassium amalgam. A German chemist, Friedrich Woehler, improved Oersted's process by using metallic potassium in 1827. He was the first to show aluminum's lightness. In France, Henri Sainte-Claire Deville isolated the metal by reducing aluminum chloride with sodium and established a large-scale experimental plant in 1854. He displayed pure aluminum at the Paris Exposition of 1855. In 1886, Charles Martin Hall in the US and Paul L.T. Heroult in France simultaneously discovered the first practical method for producing aluminum through electrolytic reduction, which is still the primary method of aluminum production today.

By volume, aluminum weighs less than a third as much as steel. This high strength-to-weight ratio makes aluminum a good choice for construction of aircraft, railroad cars, and automobiles. Aluminum is used in cooking utensils and the pistons of internal-combustion engines because of its high heat conductivity. Aluminum foil, siding, and storm windows make excellent insulators. Because it absorbs relatively few neutrons, aluminum is used in low-temperature nuclear reactors. Aluminum is also useful in boat hulls and various marine devices due to its resistance to corrosion in salt water.

Aluminum futures and options are traded on the New York Mercantile Exchange (NYMEX) and the London Metal Exchange. Aluminum futures are traded on the Tokyo Commodity Exchange (TOCOM), the Osaka Mercantile Exchange (OME), and the Shanghai Futures Exchange (SHFE).

The NYMEX aluminum futures contract calls for the delivery of 44,000 pounds of aluminum and the contract is priced in terms of cents per pound.

Prices – NYMEX aluminum futures prices showed continued strength in 2004, rallying from 75 cents per pound at the beginning of 2004 to 94 cents at the end of the year, for a rally of about 25%. Aluminum at the end of 2004 was up by more than 50% from the major low of about 60 cents posted at the end of 2001.

Supply – World production of aluminum rose 6.5% yr/yr in 2003, the latest reporting year, to a record high of 27.700 million metric tons. The world's largest producers of aluminum are China with 20% of world production in 2003, Russia (13%), US (10%), Canada (10%), and Australia (7%). US production of primary aluminum in 2004 (through November, annualized) fell –7.0% yr/yr to 2.514 million metric tons, which was only about one-half of the record high of 4.654 million metric tons produced in 1980. US production of aluminum from secondary sources in 2003 fell –3.8% yr/yr to 2.820 million metric tons.

Demand – World consumption of aluminum in 2001, the latest reporting year for the series, fell –4.8% yr/yr to 23.613 million metric tons, which was moderately below the record high of 24.811 million metric tons consumed in 2000. US consumption of aluminum in 2003 fell –3.0% yr/yr to 6.130 million metric tons, which was a new 11-year low.

Trade – US exports in 2003 fell –3.1% yr/yr to 1.540 million metric tons, which was moderately below the record high of 1.760 million metric tons in 2000. US imports of aluminum in 2003 rose +1.7% yr/yr to a record high of 4.130 million metric tons. The US relied on imports for 41% of its consumption in 2003.

World Production of Primary Aluminum   In Thousands of Metric Tons

Year	Australia	Brazil	Canada	China	France	Germany	Norway	Russia	Spain	United Kingdom	United States	Vene-zuela	World Total
1995	1,297	1,188	2,172	1,680	372	575	847	2,724	361	238	3,375	630	19,668
1996	1,372	1,195	2,283	1,770	380	576	863	2,874	362	240	3,577	629	20,800
1997	1,495	1,200	2,327	1,960	399	572	919	2,906	360	248	3,603	634	21,700
1998	1,627	1,208	2,374	2,340	424	612	996	3,005	362	258	3,713	585	22,600
1999	1,718	1,250	2,390	2,530	455	634	1,020	3,146	364	272	3,779	570	23,600
2000	1,769	1,277	2,373	2,800	441	644	1,026	3,245	366	305	3,668	571	24,300
2001	1,797	1,140	2,583	3,250	462	652	1,068	3,300	376	341	2,637	571	24,300
2002[1]	1,836	1,318	2,709	4,300	463	653	1,096	3,347	380	344	2,707	605	26,000
2003[2]	1,857	1,381	2,792	5,450	450	650	1,150	3,478	385	325	2,703	601	27,700

[1] Preliminary.   [2] Estimate.   Source: U.S. Geological Survey (USGS)

Production of Primary Aluminum (Domestic and Foreign Ores) in the U.S.   In Thousands of Metric Tons

Year	Jan.	Feb.	Mar.	Apr.	May	June	July	Aug.	Sept.	Oct.	Nov.	Dec.	Total
1995	281	253	280	272	285	277	288	286	280	289	285	299	3,375
1996	301	283	303	293	303	293	301	302	292	304	295	305	3,577
1997	305	277	307	295	304	296	305	304	294	307	298	310	3,603
1998	309	280	312	305	316	307	319	318	309	315	307	317	3,713
1999	315	287	320	309	319	310	319	324	310	323	316	328	3,779
2000	329	308	327	316	327	299	296	296	291	300	289	291	3,668
2001	256	220	232	225	229	215	214	212	206	214	208	205	2,637
2002	210	197	220	216	228	225	238	237	227	235	232	241	2,707
2003	242	220	238	225	228	221	226	225	217	224	215	221	2,702
2004[1]	216	202	217	209	217	204	209	210	203	211	206		2,513

[1] Preliminary.   Source: U.S. Geological Survey (USGS)

ALUMINUM

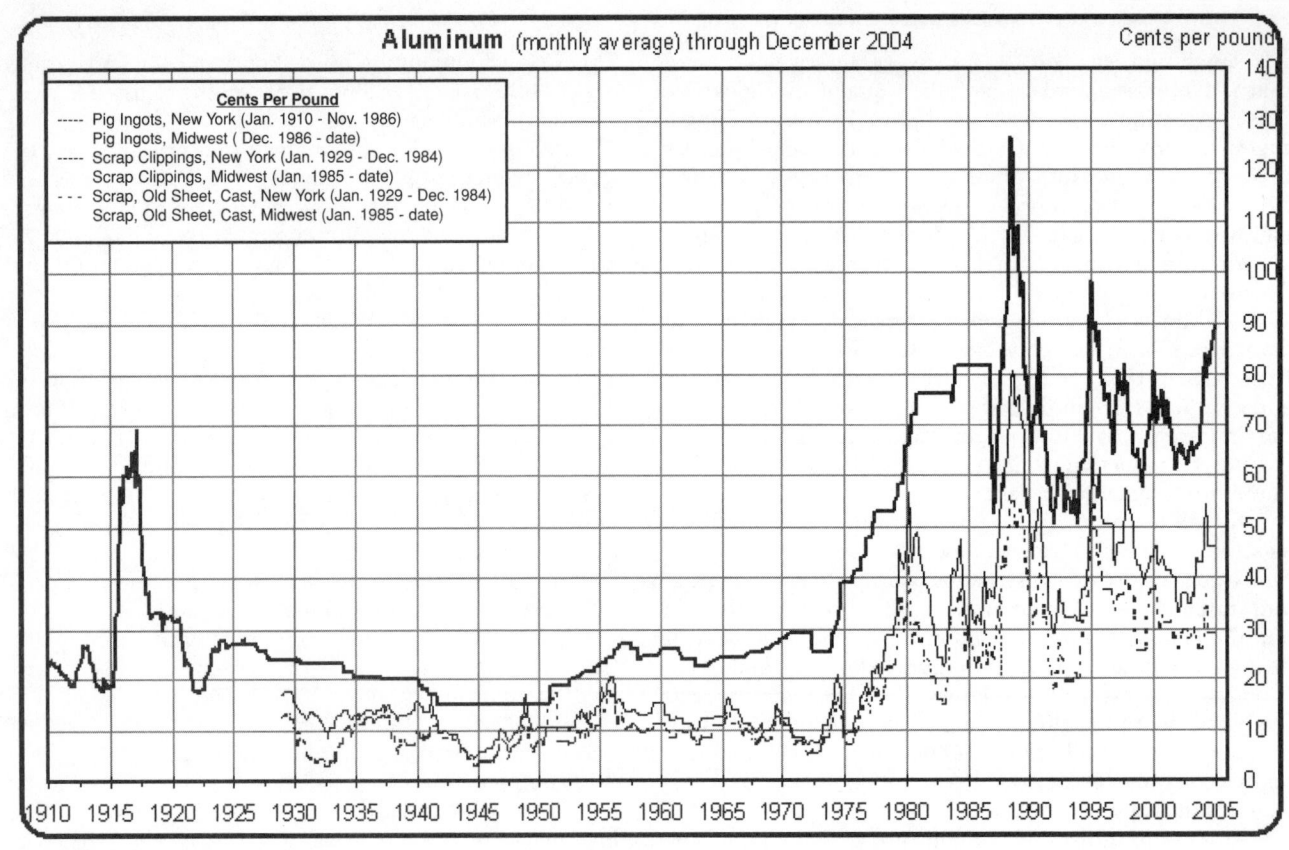

Aluminum (monthly average) through December 2004 — Cents per pound

Cents Per Pound
----- Pig Ingots, New York (Jan. 1910 - Nov. 1986)
Pig Ingots, Midwest (Dec. 1986 - date)
----- Scrap Clippings, New York (Jan. 1929 - Dec. 1984)
Scrap Clippings, Midwest (Jan. 1985 - date)
- - - Scrap, Old Sheet, Cast, New York (Jan. 1929 - Dec. 1984)
Scrap, Old Sheet, Cast, Midwest (Jan. 1985 - date)

Salient Statistics of Aluminum in the United States   In Thousands of Metric Tons

	Net Import Reliance as a % of Apparent	--- Production ---		Primary Ship-	Recovery from ------ Scrap ------		Apparent Con-	Plate, Sheet, Foil	Rolled Structural Shapes[3]	Ex- truded Shapes[4]		Perma- nent Mold	Castings		Total All Net	Total All Net Ship-
Year	Consumption	Primary	Second- ary	ments	OLd	New	sumption				All		Die	Sand	All	ments
1994	30	3,299	3,086	8,169	1,500	1,583	6,879	4,810	296	1,420	6,690	247	551	208	1,050	7,740
1995	23	3,375	3,189	8,258	1,510	1,684	6,295	4,900	526	1,540	7,130	442	627	207	1,440	8,580
1996	22	3,577	3,310	8,330	1,570	1,730	6,610	4,430	350	1,540	6,480	473	612	180	1,390	7,860
1997	23	3,603	3,550	8,880	1,530	2,020	6,720	4,710	315	1,610	6,800	468	670	153	1,410	8,210
1998	25	3,713	3,440	9,260	1,500	1,950	7,090	4,760	551	1,560	7,040	511	584	134	1,350	8,390
1999	30	3,779	3,700	9,840	1,570	2,120	7,770	5,000	549	1,640	7,360	484	1,020	158	1,790	9,150
2000	33	3,668	3,450	9,830	1,370	2,080	7,530	4,840	592	1,640	7,240	549	991	152	1,850	9,080
2001	35	2,637	2,970	9,310	1,210	1,760	6,230	4,370	512	1,550	6,580	484	873	251	1,760	8,340
2002	39	2,707	2,930	9,640	1,170	1,750	6,320	4,450	559	1,550	6,710	536	953	244	1,890	8,600
2003[1]	41	2,703	2,820	9,700	1,070	1,750	6,130	4,390	514	1,530	6,580	NA	NA	NA	NA	NA

------- Net Shipments[5] by Producers ------- (Wrought Products / Castings)

[1] Preliminary.   [2] To domestic industry.   [3] Also rod, bar & wire.   [4] Also rod, bar, tube, blooms & tubing.   [5] Consists of total shipments less shipments to other mills for further fabrication.   NA = Not available.   E = Net exporter.   *Source: U.S. Geological Survey (USGS)*

Supply and Distribution of Aluminum in the United States   In Thousands of Metric Tons

Year	Apparent Consump- tion	---- Production ---- Primary	From Old Scrap	Imports	Exports	Inventories -- December 31 -- Private	Govern- ment[2]	Year	Apparent Consump- tion	---- Production ---- Primary	From Old Scrap	Imports	Exports	Inventories -- December 31 -- Private	Govern- ment[2]
1992	5,715	4,042	1,612	1,725	1,453	2,156	57	1998	7,090	3,713	1,500	3,550	1,590	1,930	----
1993	6,612	3,695	1,632	2,545	1,207	2,209	57	1999	7,770	3,779	1,570	4,000	1,650	1,870	----
1994	6,879	3,299	1,503	3,382	1,365	2,149	57	2000	7,530	3,668	1,370	3,910	1,760	1,550	----
1995	6,295	3,375	1,505	2,975	1,610	2,099	57	2001	6,230	2,637	1,210	3,740	1,590	1,300	----
1996	6,610	3,577	1,570	2,810	1,500	1,860	57	2002[1]	6,320	2,707	1,170	4,060	1,590	1,320	----
1997	6,720	3,603	1,530	3,080	1,570	1,860	[4]	2003[2]	6,130	2,703	1,070	4,130	1,540	1,400	----

[1] Preliminary.   [2] Estimate.   [3] National Defense Stockpile.   [4] Less than 1/2 unit.   Source: U.S. Geological Survey (USGS)

Aluminum Products Distribution of End-Use Shipments in the United States — In Thousands of Metric Tons

Year	Building & Construction	Consumer Durables	Containers & Packaging	Electrical	Exports	Machinery & Equipment	Trans-portaion	Other	Total
1994	1,400	647	2,270	682	1,200	572	2,310	276	9,360
1995	1,220	621	2,310	657	1,310	570	2,610	279	9,570
1996	1,330	655	2,180	671	1,290	569	2,640	291	9,610
1997	1,320	694	2,220	708	1,360	626	2,990	318	10,200
1998	1,390	725	2,270	714	1,260	629	3,250	273	10,500
1999	1,470	760	2,320	739	1,330	661	3,600	293	11,200
2000	1,450	767	2,260	771	1,280	679	3,600	293	11,100
2001	1,500	681	2,250	686	902	641	3,190	367	10,200
2002	1,560	722	2,260	677	1,070	616	3,410	390	10,700
2003[1]	1,560	719	2,240	655	857	621	3,520	385	10,600

[1] Preliminary.   Source: U.S. Geological Survey (USGS)

World Consumption of Primary Aluminum — In Thousands of Metric Tons

Year	Brazil	Canada	China	France	Germany	India	Italy	Japan	Rep. of Korea	Russia	United Kingdom	United States	World Total
1992	377.1	420.4	1,253.8	730.5	1,457.1	414.3	660.0	2,271.6	397.0	1,242.0	550.0	4,616.9	18,529.5
1993	378.9	492.5	1,339.9	667.2	1,150.7	475.3	554.0	2,138.3	524.8	657.0	540.0	4,877.1	18,122.6
1994	414.1	559.0	1,500.1	736.3	1,370.3	475.0	660.0	2,344.8	603.9	470.0	570.0	5,407.1	19,670.8
1995	500.6	611.9	1,941.6	743.8	1,491.3	581.0	665.4	2,335.6	675.4	476.0	620.0	5,054.8	20,480.9
1996	497.0	619.9	2,135.3	671.7	1,355.4	584.8	585.1	2,392.6	674.3	443.8	571.0	5,348.0	20,596.4
1997	478.6	628.2	2,260.3	724.2	1,558.4	553.4	671.0	2,434.3	666.3	469.2	583.0	5,390.0	21,721.8
1998	521.4	720.6	2,425.4	733.8	1,519.0	566.5	675.4	2,082.0	505.7	489.2	579.0	5,813.6	21,797.2
1999	463.1	777.2	2,925.9	774.2	1,438.6	569.5	735.3	2,112.3	814.0	562.8	496.8	6,203.3	23,323.0
2000	513.8	798.7	3,499.1	780.4	1,490.3	602.4	780.3	2,224.9	822.6	748.4	575.5	6,079.5	24,811.4
2001[1]	550.8	759.6	3,545.4	772.9	1,590.9	558.0	770.4	2,014.0	849.6	786.2	433.3	5,117.0	23,612.8

[1] Preliminary.   Source: American Metal Market (AMM)

Salient Statistics of Recycling Aluminum in the United States

Year	Percent Recycled	New Scrap[1]	Old Scrap[2]	Recycled Metal[3]	Apparent Supply	New Scrap[1]	Old Scrap[2]	Recycled Metal[3]	Apparent Supply
		In Thousands of Metric Tons				Value in Millions of Dollars			
1993	37	1,310	1,630	2,940	7,920	1,540	1,920	3,460	9,300
1994	36	1,580	1,500	3,090	8,460	2,480	2,360	4,840	13,300
1995	40	1,680	1,510	3,190	7,980	3,190	2,850	6,040	15,100
1996	40	1,730	1,570	3,310	8,340	2,730	2,480	5,200	13,100
1997	41	2,020	1,530	3,550	8,740	3,430	2,590	6,020	14,800
1998	38	1,950	1,500	3,440	9,040	2,810	2,160	4,970	13,100
1999	37	2,120	1,570	3,700	9,890	3,070	2,280	5,350	14,300
2000	36	2,080	1,370	3,450	9,610	3,420	2,260	5,670	15,800
2001	37	1,760	1,210	2,970	7,990	2,670	1,830	4,500	12,100
2002	36	1,750	1,170	2,930	8,060	2,510	1,680	4,190	11,500

[1] Scrap that results from the manufacturing process.   [2] Scrap that results from consumer products.   [3] Metal recovered from new plus old scrap.
Source: U.S. Geological Survey (USGS)

Producer Prices for Aluminum Used Beverage Can Scrap — In Cents Per Pound

Year	Jan.	Feb.	Mar.	Apr.	May	June	July	Aug.	Sept.	Oct.	Nov.	Dec.	Average
1995	74.85	72.24	65.00	65.00	65.00	65.00	65.00	67.98	64.80	58.45	57.00	58.50	64.91
1996	57.73	56.00	56.24	58.90	59.00	49.70	47.50	49.25	50.20	48.50	49.03	53.50	52.96
1997	56.98	59.00	59.00	58.27	58.05	58.05	58.32	59.60	59.50	59.13	59.00	57.12	58.50
1998	54.53	57.00	57.00	52.95	49.85	47.09	45.50	44.50	46.21	44.50	44.50	46.14	49.15
1999	44.50	44.50	44.20	45.68	47.45	46.50	48.40	49.00	49.00	53.79	55.50	57.64	48.84
2000	58.58	62.90	61.50	56.85	54.50	54.50	56.50	57.00	57.00	56.20	53.50	53.50	56.88
2001	54.26	55.50	55.45	54.50	54.23	50.79	46.93	45.50	45.50	44.63	44.50	44.50	49.71
2002	44.50	44.66	47.21	49.41	48.68	48.50	46.89	45.06	46.36	47.07	49.76	50.29	47.37
2003	50.50	52.30	52.45	49.43	50.17	49.75	49.22	49.83	47.43	50.17	52.00	53.73	50.58
2004	57.44	61.64	61.65	63.00	57.85	60.00	62.23	60.57	59.48	62.07	61.45	63.81	60.93

Source: American Metal Market (AMM)

ALUMINUM

Average Price of Cast Aluminum Scrap (Crank Cases) in Chicago   In Cents Per Pound

Year	Jan.	Feb.	Mar.	Apr.	May	June	July	Aug.	Sept.	Oct.	Nov.	Dec.	Average
1995	53.53	54.08	49.02	48.50	44.41	42.50	43.76	45.80	45.05	39.27	37.50	37.50	45.08
1996	37.50	37.50	37.50	37.50	37.50	37.50	37.50	36.50	35.40	33.80	33.50	33.50	36.27
1997	36.09	36.50	36.50	36.50	36.50	36.50	36.50	39.36	38.60	38.50	38.50	38.07	37.34
1998	37.50	37.50	37.50	35.95	35.50	31.59	25.50	25.50	25.50	25.50	25.50	25.50	30.71
1999	25.50	25.50	25.50	25.50	26.45	29.23	36.83	37.50	37.50	37.50	37.50	37.50	31.87
2000	37.50	37.50	37.50	35.55	31.09	30.32	30.30	32.00	32.00	31.09	31.00	31.00	33.04
2001	31.00	31.00	31.00	31.00	31.00	31.00	28.29	28.00	28.00	28.00	26.40	26.00	29.25
2002	26.00	27.47	28.95	30.00	30.00	30.00	30.00	29.64	28.00	28.00	28.00	28.00	28.67
2003	28.10	30.00	30.00	29.00	29.00	27.90	26.68	26.00	26.00	26.00	26.00	26.00	27.56
2004	30.00	31.26	36.00	36.00	33.00	29.00	29.00	29.00	29.00	29.00	29.00	29.00	30.77

Source: American Metal Market (AMM)

Aluminum Exports of Crude Metal and Alloys from the United States   In Thousands of Metric Tons

Year	Jan.	Feb.	Mar.	Apr.	May	June	July	Aug.	Sept.	Oct.	Nov.	Dec.	Total
1995	26.1	32.7	25.4	31.1	31.4	20.7	26.6	39.2	38.9	33.0	30.4	33.6	369.1
1996	23.1	27.9	31.2	34.3	46.2	54.3	36.3	33.7	30.2	40.3	33.2	26.2	416.9
1997	31.0	25.5	22.5	33.0	24.1	34.9	23.9	33.2	34.4	26.5	33.0	30.0	352.0
1998	21.2	21.4	21.8	17.4	22.6	21.8	20.9	21.5	28.0	23.9	20.4	24.7	265.6
1999	18.6	26.7	23.9	22.7	25.2	27.7	23.7	27.5	26.1	31.4	30.3	34.8	318.6
2000	18.7	27.2	30.2	21.9	24.4	22.4	20.5	24.2	20.5	20.7	20.7	21.6	273.0
2001	19.6	16.1	18.9	14.7	16.8	15.6	12.4	14.5	12.6	18.9	16.7	15.1	191.9
2002	17.1	15.2	15.6	16.4	19.4	18.3	15.0	15.5	17.5	19.8	19.4	16.4	205.6
2003	14.3	14.8	14.5	16.9	17.0	17.8	16.5	20.4	18.7	22.9	20.4	19.7	213.9
2004[1]	18.2	20.8	24.3	25.2	25.1	27.6	23.7	23.0	28.3	26.9			291.7

[1] Preliminary.   *Source: U.S. Geological Survey (USGS)*

Aluminum General Imports of Crude Metal and Alloys into the United States   In Thousands of Metric Tons

Year	Jan.	Feb.	Mar.	Apr.	May	June	July	Aug.	Sept.	Oct.	Nov.	Dec.	Total
1995	214.0	168.0	204.0	195.0	184.0	172.0	136.0	134.0	117.0	137.0	139.0	133.0	1,933.0
1996	158.0	150.0	148.0	188.0	176.0	169.0	139.0	149.0	136.0	170.0	147.0	180.0	1,910.0
1997	145.0	147.0	209.0	196.0	198.0	167.0	157.0	152.0	150.0	175.0	146.0	222.0	2,060.0
1998	220.0	204.0	202.0	200.0	189.0	243.0	170.0	204.0	198.0	198.0	189.0	177.0	2,394.0
1999	191.0	200.0	240.0	311.0	281.0	258.0	213.0	219.0	178.0	202.0	178.0	180.0	2,651.0
2000	246.0	213.0	206.0	211.0	233.0	234.0	250.0	206.0	189.0	186.0	181.0	137.0	2,490.0
2001	193.0	200.0	237.0	197.0	209.0	179.0	201.0	198.0	252.0	220.0	248.0	227.0	2,561.0
2002	272.0	205.0	223.0	221.0	221.0	263.0	228.0	279.0	235.0	196.0	264.0	186.0	2,793.0
2003	215.0	246.0	350.0	202.0	265.0	261.0	233.0	194.0	215.0	210.0	233.0	243.0	2,867.0
2004[1]	211.0	288.0	248.0	254.0	282.0	309.0	297.0	225.0	279.0	286.0			3,214.8

[1] Preliminary.   *Source: U.S. Geological Survey (USGS)*

Average Open Interest of Aluminum Futures in New York   In Contracts

Year	Jan.	Feb.	Mar.	Apr.	May	June	July	Aug.	Sept.	Oct.	Nov.	Dec.
1999	----	----	----	----	1,032	1,461	1,875	1,984	1,767	1,244	625	615
2000	794	580	254	326	965	2,035	3,938	4,803	4,580	4,598	3,587	2,046
2001	2,446	3,173	3,450	3,529	3,269	3,724	3,891	3,459	2,753	3,728	3,644	3,276
2002	3,277	2,744	2,738	2,250	2,397	2,902	3,903	4,618	4,643	5,139	8,057	10,479
2003	9,573	9,163	6,960	7,190	7,686	8,529	8,402	8,445	7,655	7,283	8,434	9,427
2004	8,815	7,384	9,666	10,575	10,363	10,370	9,626	10,287	10,292	10,035	9,706	8,879

Source: New York Mercantile Exchange (NYMEX), COMEX Division

Volume of Trading of Aluminum Futures in New York   In Contracts

Year	Jan.	Feb.	Mar.	Apr.	May	June	July	Aug.	Sept.	Oct.	Nov.	Dec.	Total
1999	----	----	----	----	6,179	5,875	5,275	3,373	3,114	2,801	639	722	27,978
2000	1,224	2,394	1,664	1,901	3,859	3,566	6,295	3,767	5,993	6,365	5,055	4,016	46,099
2001	7,361	1,694	4,410	2,822	2,853	4,634	4,404	3,794	1,428	2,887	4,251	2,551	43,089
2002	2,774	4,635	4,924	2,593	5,388	5,389	8,953	4,194	2,571	7,328	16,185	9,066	74,000
2003	12,565	9,625	8,163	5,440	10,567	8,463	11,797	9,451	5,119	6,222	8,536	11,542	107,490
2004	9,425	9,621	9,548	9,770	5,438	5,453	5,280	2,063	5,533	4,822	2,525	2,691	72,169

Source: New York Mercantile Exchange (NYMEX), COMEX Division

Antimony

Antimony (symbol Sb) is a lustrous, extremely brittle and hard crystalline semi-metal that is silvery white in its most common allotropic form. Antimony is a poor conductor of heat and electricity. In nature, antimony has a strong affinity for sulfur and for such metals as lead, silver, and copper. Antimony is primarily a byproduct of the mining, smelting and refining of lead, silver, and copper ores. There is no longer any mine production of antimony in the US.

The most common use of antimony is in antimony trioxide, a chemical that is used as a flame retardant in textiles, plastics, adhesives and building materials. Antimony trioxide is also used in battery components, ceramics, bearings, chemicals, glass, and ammunition.

Prices – Antimony prices in 2004 rallied sharply by 18% to an average of 131.03 cents per pound from the 2003 average of 110.89 cents. That was an 8-year high. Antimony prices in 2004 were double the 32-year low of 66.05 cents posted as recently as 1999. Bullish factors included stronger US and global economic growth, the weak dollar, and tight supplies.

Supply – World mine production of antimony in 2003 fell sharply by 28% to 81,600 metric tons from 113,000 metric tons in 2002. Production in 2003 was roughly half the record production level seen in 2001 of 157,000 metric tons. China accounted for 86% of world antimony production in 2003, down from 91% in 2002. After China, the only significant producers are South Africa (6.5% of world production) and Bolivia (2.8%). World production fell mainly because Chinese production in 2003 plunged by 30% to 70,000 metric tons. US secondary production of antimony in 2004 rose slightly to 5,600 metric tons from 5,350 metric tons in 2002.

Demand – US industrial consumption of antimony in 2003 fell by 20% to 9,230 metric tons from 11,500 metric tons in 2002. Of consumption in 2003, 51% was used for flame-retardants, 26% was used for metal products, and 23% was used for non-metal products.

Trade – US imports of antimony ore in 2003 plunged by 68% (gross weight fell by 67.6% to 428 metric tons, and antimony content fell by 68.5% to 412 metric tons). Imports of antimony oxide in 2003 showed a comparatively small 7% decline to 26,000 metric tons from 27,900 metric tons in 2002. US exports of antimony oxide fell by 11% to 2,910 metric tons from 3,260 metric tons in 2002.

World Mine Production of Antimony (Content of Ore)   In Metric Tons

Year	Australia	Bolivia	Canada	China[2]	Guat-emala	Kyrgy-zstan	Mexico[3]	Peru[4]	Russia	South Africa	Thai-land	Turkey	World Total
2000	1,511	1,907	364	110,000	-----	150	39	461	4,500	4,104	84	360	125,000
2001	1,380	2,264	234	140,000	-----	150	----	274	4,500	4,927	40	370	157,000
2002[1]	1,200	2,336	143	100,000	-----	150	----	356	NA	5,746	10	370	113,000
2003[2]	1,300	2,300	143	70,000	-----	40	----	356	NA	5,310	40	350	81,600

[1] Preliminary.   [2] Estimate.   [3] Includes antimony content of miscellaneous smelter products.   [4] Recoverable.
Source: U.S. Geological Survey (USGS)

Salient Statistics of Antimony in the United States   In Metric Tons

Year	Avg. Price cents/lb. CIF U.S. Ports	Production[3] Primary[2] Mine	Primary[2] Smelter	Secondary (Alloys)[2]	Ore Gross Weight	Ore Antimony Content	Oxide (Gross Weight)	Exports (Oxide)	Industry Stocks, December 31[3] Metallic	Oxide	Sulfide	Other	Total[4]
2000	65.5	W	13,300	7,700	4,630	3,690	28,500	6,040	2,540	3,970	W	270	6,780
2001	64.7	----	9,080	5,380	2,610	2,290	27,700	5,880	645	4,090	W	256	4,990
2002[1]	88.4	----	W	5,350	1,320	1,310	27,900	3,260	729	4,080	W	254	5,060
2003[2]	107.5	----	W	5,600	428	412	26,000	2,910	587	3,580	W	2,200	6,370

[1] Preliminary.   [2] Estimate.   [3] Antimony content.   [4] Including primary antimony residues & slag.   W = Withheld proprietary data.
Source: U.S. Geological Survey (USGS)

Industrial Consumption of Primary Antimony in the United States   In Metric Tons (Antimony Content)

Year	Metal Products Ammu-nition	Antimonial Lead	Sheet & Pipe	Bearing Metal & Bearings	Solder	Total All Metal Products	Flame Retardents Plastics	Flame Retardents Total	Non-Metal Products Ceramics & Glass	Pigments	Plastics	Total	Grand Total
2000	W	1,040	W	42	135	2,980	8,940	9,910	1,020	620	1,330	3,490	16,400
2001	W	1,060	W	52	78	2,800	6,210	7,570	518	653	1,050	2,760	13,100
2002	W	887	W	42	89	2,760	4,930	6,310	505	565	837	2,460	11,500
2003[1]	W	910	W	43	85	2,410	3,680	4,720	487	597	532	2,100	9,230

[1] Preliminary.   [2] Estimated coverage based on 77% of the industry.   W=Withheld proprietary data.   *Source: U.S. Geological Survey (USGS)*

Average Price of Antimony[1] in the United States   In Cents Per Pound

Year	Jan.	Feb.	Mar.	Apr.	May	June	July	Aug.	Sept.	Oct.	Nov.	Dec.	Average
2001	84.90	75.00	75.00	75.00	75.00	75.00	75.00	75.00	73.26	69.50	69.50	69.50	74.31
2002	69.50	69.50	69.50	69.50	64.22	65.13	73.09	86.97	113.24	149.59	141.91	135.25	92.28
2003	121.53	109.15	118.48	119.49	119.77	119.07	107.86	105.01	105.01	105.01	102.76	97.52	110.89
2004	110.10	122.47	132.83	133.81	133.81	126.23	125.87	133.81	138.35	138.35	138.35	138.35	131.03

[1] Prices are for antimony metal (99.65%) merchants, minimum 18-ton containers, c.i.f. U.S. Ports.   *Source: American Metal Market (AMM)*

Apples

The apple tree is the common name of trees from the rose family, Rosaceae, and the fruit that comes from them. The apple tree is a deciduous plant and grows mainly in the temperate areas of the world. The apple tree is believed to have originated in the Caspian and Black Sea area. Apples were the favorite fruit of the ancient Greeks and Romans. The early settlers brought apple seeds with them and introduced them to America. John Champman, also known as Johnny Appleseed, was responsible for extensive planting of apple trees in the Midwestern United States.

Prices – The average monthly price of apples received by growers in the US rose by +9.2% yr/yr to 28.1 cents per pound in 2004, which was a record high.

Supply – World apple production in the 2004-05 marketing year fell –12.9% yr/yr to 38.981 million metric tons, which was a 9-year low. The world's largest apple producers in 2004-05 were the US (with 11% of world production), Turkey (6%), Italy (5%), France (5%), and Germany (5%). US apple production in 2004-05 rose +9.8% yr/yr to 4.290 million metric tons, recovering further from the 2-decade low of 3.866 million metric tons posted in 2002-03.

Demand – The utilization breakdown of the 2003 apple crop showed that 63% of apples were for fresh consumption, 18% for juice and cider, 14% for canning, 2% for dried apples, and 3% for frozen apples. US per capita apple consumption in 2000 was 17.9 pounds.

World Production of Apples[3], Fresh (Dessert & Cooking)   In Thousands of Metric Tons

Year	Argentina	Canada	France	Germany	Hungary	Italy	Japan	Netherlands	South Africa	Spain	Turkey	United States	World Total
1999-00	847	582	2,166	1,936	420	2,196	928	575	581	887	2,500	4,822	47,575
2000-1	1,331	532	2,300	2,631	700	2,267	800	500	668	699	2,400	4,801	47,935
2001-2	900	467	2,055	1,522	605	2,220	931	500	591	962	2,450	4,274	45,440
2002-3	1,000	402	2,060	1,563	540	2,206	926	370	682	683	2,200	3,866	43,660
2003-4[1]	900	379	2,080	1,518	500	1,878	842	385	701	826	2,600	3,907	44,752
2004-5[2]	NA	382	NA	1,842	680	2,106	881	NA	720	645	2,300	4,290	38,981

[1] Preliminary.   [2] Estimate.   [3] Commercial crop.   *Source: Foreign Agricultural Service, U.S. Department of Agriculture (FAS-USDA)*

Salient Statistics of Apples[2] in the United States

Year	Production Total	Production Utilized	Growers Prices Fresh cents/lb.	Growers Prices Processing $/ton	Fresh	Canned	Dried	Frozen	Juice & Cider	Other[3]	Avg. Farm Price cents /lb.	Farm Value Million $	Exports Fresh	Imports Fresh Dried[5] & Dried[5]	Fresh Per Capita Consumption Lbs.
	— Millions of Pounds —												— Metric Tons —		
1998	11,646	10,763	17.3	95.1	6,413	1,174	330	266	2,485	95	12.2	1,316.2	660.3	15.7 171.8	19.0
1999	10,632	10,447	21.3	128.0	5,996	1,319	263	271	2,473	126	15.0	1,563.6	571.9	21.5 195.3	18.5
2000	10,581	10,320	17.8	101.0	6,266	1,184	248	196	2,334	93	12.8	1,320.8	743.6	33.3 180.6	17.5
2001	9,423	9,209	22.9	108.0	5,468	1,257	221	249	1,945	71	15.8	1,453.1	593.0	21.2 193.9	15.6
2002	8,524	8,374	25.8	130.0	5,366	1,079	208	192	1,479	51	18.9	1,572.2	572.3	26.2 170.4	16.0
2003[1]	8,613	8,523	29.5	130.0	5,342	1,196	162	213	1,515	96	20.9	1,729.9	528.5	186.8	16.5

Utilization of Quantities Sold; Processed[5]; Foreign Trade[4]; Domestic

[1] Preliminary.   [2] Commercial crop.   [3] Mostly crushed for vinegar, jam, etc.   [4] Year beginning July.   [5] Fresh weight basis.
Source: Economic Research Service, U.S. Department of Agriculture (ERS-USDA)

Price of Apples Received by Growers (for Fresh Use) in the United States   In Cents Per Pound

Year	Jan.	Feb.	Mar.	Apr.	May	June	July	Aug.	Sept.	Oct.	Nov.	Dec.	Average
1999	15.8	15.0	15.3	14.1	13.3	12.7	16.3	22.7	21.6	24.3	22.9	23.2	18.1
2000	21.8	20.3	19.8	19.3	17.8	16.1	16.2	19.5	23.3	21.8	18.5	18.1	19.4
2001	15.8	15.2	14.6	15.7	15.2	14.9	15.2	17.3	21.2	24.8	23.5	23.1	18.0
2002	22.1	21.6	22.0	21.8	21.5	22.0	20.6	24.5	30.0	30.1	26.8	26.3	24.1
2003	25.8	24.6	22.6	23.4	21.8	22.4	20.8	34.6	27.1	27.9	29.7	27.9	25.7
2004[1]	30.4	29.4	30.7	29.9	29.4	30.1	29.5	27.3	27.2	27.1	23.9	22.3	28.1

[1] Preliminary.   Source: Economic Research Service, U.S. Department of Agriculture (ERS-USDA)

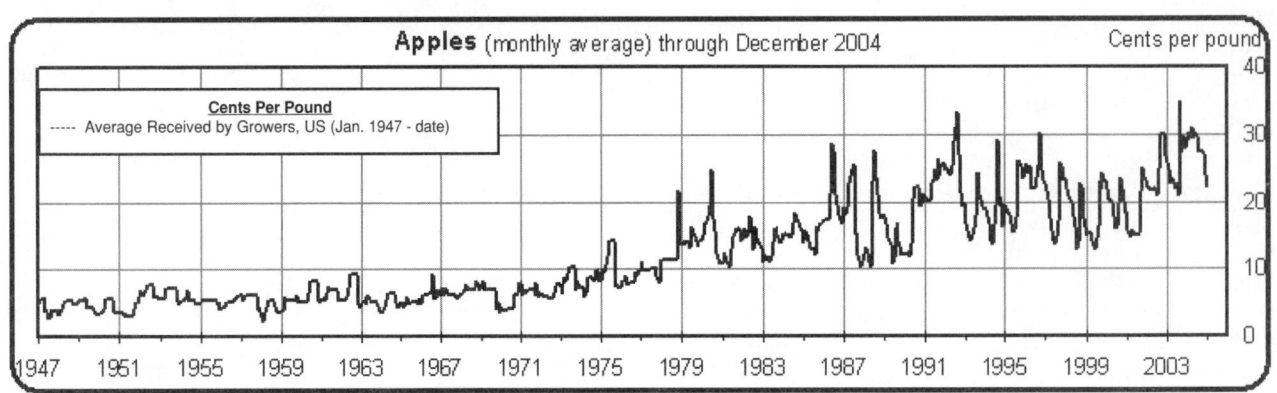

Apples (monthly average) through December 2004 — Cents per pound

Cents Per Pound
----- Average Received by Growers, US (Jan. 1947 - date)

Arsenic

Arsenic (symbol As) is a silver-gray, extremely poisonous, semi-metallic element. Arsenic, which is odorless and flavorless, has been known since ancient times, but it wasn't until the Middle Ages that its poisonous characteristics first became known. Metallic arsenic was first produced in the 17th century by heating arsenic with potash and soap. Arsenic is rarely found in nature in its elemental form and is generally recovered as a by-product of ore processing. Recently, small doses of arsenic have been found to put some forms of cancer into remission. It can also help thin blood. Homoeopathists have successfully used undetectable amounts of arsenic to cure stomach cramps.

The US does not produce any arsenic and instead imports all its consumption needs for arsenic metals and compounds. More than 95 percent of the arsenic consumed in the US is in compound form, mostly as arsenic trioxide, which in turn is converted into arsenic acid. Production of chromated copper arsenate, a wood preservative, accounts for about 90% of the domestic consumption of arsenic trioxide. Three companies in the US manufacture chromate copper arsenate. Another company used arsenic acid to produce an arsenical herbicide. Arsenic metal is used to produce nonferrous alloys, primarily for lead-acid batteries.

One area where there is increased consumption of arsenic is in the semiconductor industry. Very high-purity arsenic is used in the production of gallium arsenide. High speed and high frequency integrated circuits that use gallium arsenide have better signal reception and lower power consumption. An estimated 30 metric tons per year of high-purity arsenic is used in the production of semiconductor materials.

Since roughly 90% of US arsenic production is for wood preservative treatments, the demand for arsenic is closely tied to new home construction, home renovation, and deck construction. However, future demand for arsenic is questionable given its toxicity and the possibility of tighter environmental regulations in the future.

Supply – World production of white arsenic (arsenic trioxide) in 2003 rose slightly by 0.3% to 35,100 metric tons from the 23-year low of 35,000 seen in 2002. The world's largest producer by far is China with 46% of world production, followed by Chile with 23% of world production, Peru with 9%, Mexico with 6%, and Russia with 4%. China's production of arsenic has been constant at 16,000 metric tons in the past five consecutive years. US supply of arsenic in 2003 rose +10% to 21,700 metric tons from the 18-year low of 19,700 metric tons posted in 2002 due to recessionary economic conditions.

Demand – US demand for arsenic in 2003 rose by +10% to 21,600 metric tons from the 18-year low of 19,600 metric tons posted in 2002. Of that demand, 89% was for wood preservatives, 3% was for glass, 3% was for non-ferrous alloys and electric usage, and 5% was for other uses.

Trade – US imports of trioxide arsenic in 2003 rose by +10.5% to 27,300 metric tons from 24,700 metric tons in 2002. US exports of trioxide arsenic were negligible at 173 metric tons, up from 100 metric tons in 2002. Regarding arsenic imports, the import of arsenic in metal form rose +12.6% to 990 metric tons in 2003 and the import of arsenic in compound form rose +10.6% to 20,800 metric tons.

World Production of White Arsenic (Arsenic Trioxide)   In Metric Tons

Year	Belgium	Bolivia	Canada[4]	Chile	China	France	Germany	Mexico	Namibia[3]	Peru	Phillippines	Russia[5]	World Total
1994	2,000	341	250	4,050	18,000	6,000	300	4,400	3,047	286	----	1,500	46,800
1995	2,000	362	250	4,076	21,000	5,000	250	3,620	1,661	285	----	1,500	47,000
1996	2,000	255	250	8,000	15,000	3,000	250	2,942	1,559	111	----	1,500	42,900
1997	2,000	282	250	8,350	15,000	2,500	250	2,999	1,297	637	----	1,500	42,000
1998	1,500	284	250	8,400	15,500	2,000	200	2,573	175	624	----	1,500	40,300
1999	1,500	437	250	8,000	16,000	1,000	200	2,419	----	1,611	----	1,500	41,800
2000	1,500	318	250	8,000	16,000	1,000	200	2,522	----	2,495	----	1,500	38,800
2001	1,000	846	250	8,000	16,000	1,000	100	2,381	----	2,800	----	1,500	35,900
2002[1]	1,000	237	250	8,000	16,000	1,000	100	1,946	----	2,970	----	1,500	35,000
2003[2]	1,000	250	250	8,000	16,000	1,000	100	2,000	----	3,000	----	1,500	35,100

[1] Preliminary.   [2] Estimate.   [3] Output of Tsumeb Corp. Ltd. only.   [4] Includes low-grade dusts that were exported to the U.S. for further refining.   [5] Formerly part of the U.S.S.R.; not reported separately until 1992.   *Source: U.S. Geological Survey (USGS)*

Salient Statistics of Arsenic in the United States   In Metric Tons (Arsenic Content)

Year	Supply — Imports Metal	Supply — Imports Compounds	Industry Stocks Jan. 1	Total	Distribution — Apparent Demand	Industry Stocks Dec. 31	Agricultural Chemicals	Glass	Wood Preservatives	Non-Ferrous Alloys & Electric	Other	Total	Trioxide Mexican (Cents/Pound)	Metal Chinese (Cents/Pound)	Imports Trioxide[3]	Exports
1994	1,330	20,300	----	21,630	21,500	----	1,200	700	18,000	1,300	300	21,500	32	40	26,800	79
1995	557	22,100	----	22,700	22,300	----	1,000	700	19,600	600	400	22,300	33	66	29,000	430
1996	252	21,200	----	21,400	21,400	----	950	700	19,200	250	300	21,400	33	40	28,000	36
1997	909	22,800	----	23,700	23,700	----	1,400	700	20,000	900	300	23,700	31	32	30,000	61
1998	997	29,300	----	30,300	30,100	----	1,500	900	26,500	1,200	300	30,100	30	40	38,600	177
1999	1,300	22,100	----	23,400	22,000	----	1,100	600	19,500	850	200	22,000	----	----	29,100	1,350
2000	830	23,600	----	24,500	24,400	----	----	700	21,800	700	250	24,400	----	----	31,100	41
2001	1,030	23,900	----	25,000	24,900	----	----	750	21,900	1,000	250	24,900	----	----	31,500	57
2002[1]	879	18,800	----	19,700	19,600	----	----	700	17,300	650	200	19,600	----	----	24,700	100
2003[2]	990	20,800	----	21,700	21,600	----	----	660	19,200	660	200	21,600	----	----	27,300	173

[1] Preliminary.   [2] Estimate.   [3] For Consumption.   Source: U.S. Geological Survey (USGS)

Barley

Barley is the common name for the genus of cereal grass and is native to Asia and Ethiopia. Barley is an ancient crop and was grown by the Egyptians, Greek, Romans and Chinese. Barley is now the world's fourth largest grain crop, after wheat, rice, and corn. Barley is planted in the spring in most of Europe, Canada and the United States. The U.S. barley crop year begins June 1. It is planted in the autumn in parts of California, Arizona and along the Mediterranean Sea. Barley is hardy and drought resistant and can be grown on marginal cropland. Salt-resistant strains are being developed for use in coastal regions. Barley grain, along with hay, straw, and several by-products are used for animal feed. Barley is used for malt beverages and in cooking. Barley, like other cereals, contains a large proportion of carbohydrate (67%) and protein (12.8%). Barley futures are traded on the Winnipeg Commodity Exchange (WCE), the London International Financial Futures and Options Exchange (LIFFE) and the Budapest Commodity Exchange.

Prices – The monthly average price for all barley received by US farmers in the 2004-05 marketing year (through December 2005) fell sharply by –10.4% yr/yr to $2.52 per bushel. That was moderately below the 2-decade high of $2.94 per bushel posted in 1995/96.

Supply – World barley production in the 2004-05 marketing year rose by +7.1% to 152.515 million metric tons, recovering further from the 4-year low of 133.792 million metric tons seen in 2002-03. The world's largest barley crop of 179.162 million metric tons occurred in 1990-01. The

world's largest barley producers are Russia with 11.5% of world production in 2004-05, Canada (8.7%), Germany (8.5%), France (7.3%), Spain (7.0%), Turkey (4.7%), Australia (4.6%), and the US (4.0%).

US barley production in the 2004-05 marketing year rose by +0.3% to 279.253 million bushels, which was a 4-year high. That was less than one-half of the record US barley crop of 608.532 million bushels seen in 1986-87. US farmers harvested 4.021 million acres of barley in 2004-05, which was the lowest acreage since the late 1800's (specifically, since 1894-95). However, the barley yield in 2004-05 rose to a record high of 69.4 bushels per acre. Ending stocks for the 2004-05 marketing year rose +2.5% to a 6-year high of 123.0 million bushels.

Demand – U.S. total barley disappearance in 2004-05 rose +19.8% yr/yr to 297.0 million bushels, which was a 4-year high. Regarding the utilization breakdown, 70% of barley is used for food and alcoholic beverages, 27% for animal feed, and 3% for seed, according the latest available figures from 2002-03.

Trade – World exports of barley in 2004-05 rose by +1.1% yr/yr to 15.250 million metric tons, recovering from the 7-year low of 15.079 million metric tons seen in 2003-04. The largest world exporters of barley in 2004-05 were Australia with 22% of world exports, the European Union with 22%, Canada with 11%, and the US with only 3%. The single largest importer of barley is Saudi Arabia with 6.500 million metric tons of imports in 2004-05.

World Barley Supply and Demand   In Thousands of Metric Tons

Year	Australia	Canada	EC-15	Total Non-US	U.S.	Total Exports	Saudi Arabia	Unaccounted	Total Imports	Russia	U.S.	Total Utilization	Canada	U.S.	Total Stocks
1995-6	3,375	2,596	2,480	18,347	1,182	19,529	3,876	214	19,172	17,566	7,635	150,965	1,749	2,168	19,700
1996-7	3,967	3,442	6,183	21,798	1,214	23,012	5,887	737	22,342	16,435	8,459	149,480	2,919	2,383	23,761
1997-8	2,838	1,897	2,990	11,755	1,071	12,826	4,026	483	12,826	16,494	6,879	146,037	2,459	2,596	32,137
1998-9	4,241	1,185	8,894	17,235	550	17,785	5,814	809	17,785	12,900	7,207	138,916	2,737	3,084	28,850
1999-00	2,870	1,806	10,443	17,927	853	18,780	5,900	110	18,780	11,441	6,752	132,559	2,838	2,424	24,026
2000-1	3,924	1,956	6,275	15,842	1,068	16,910	5,100	537	16,910	12,700	6,407	134,173	2,516	2,314	22,755
2001-2	4,590	1,126	3,236	17,072	517	17,589	6,000	489	17,589	14,250	5,661	135,842	2,047	2,006	28,263
2002-3	2,159	304	6,307	16,249	552	16,801	7,502	39	16,801	15,500	5,179	135,448	1,475	1,510	26,607
2003-4[1]	6,105	1,935	1,000	14,722	357	15,079	5,700	305	15,079	18,600	4,991	147,168	2,106	2,619	21,822
2004-5[2]	3,300	1,700	3,300	14,800	450	15,250	6,500	345	15,250	16,400	6,139	145,242	3,026	2,668	29,095

[1] Preliminary.   [2] Estimate.   *Source: Foreign Agricultural Service, U.S. Department of Agriculture (FAS-USDA)*

World Production of Barley   In Thousands of Metric Tons

Year	Australia	Canada	China	Denmark	France	Germany	India	Russia	Spain	Turkey	United Kingdom	United States	World Total
1995-6	5,823	13,035	4,089	3,864	7,739	11,891	1,730	15,800	5,200	6,900	6,833	7,824	142,095
1996-7	6,696	15,562	4,000	3,953	9,540	12,074	1,510	15,900	9,600	7,200	7,780	8,544	143,541
1997-8	6,482	13,527	4,000	3,887	10,181	13,399	1,462	20,800	8,600	7,300	7,828	7,835	154,491
1998-9	5,987	12,709	2,656	3,565	10,591	12,512	1,680	9,800	10,902	7,500	6,630	7,667	135,586
1999-00	5,032	13,196	2,970	3,680	9,540	13,300	1,470	10,600	7,430	6,600	6,580	6,103	127,735
2000-1	6,743	13,172	2,646	3,980	9,950	12,110	1,447	14,100	11,280	7,400	6,490	6,919	132,883
2001-2	8,280	10,846	2,893	3,970	9,810	13,500	1,432	19,500	6,250	6,900	6,660	5,407	141,350
2002-3	3,865	7,489	3,322	4,120	10,990	10,930	1,500	18,700	8,330	7,200	6,130	4,940	133,792
2003-4[1]	10,287	12,328	3,400	3,770	9,960	10,670	1,410	18,000	8,700	6,900	6,370	6,059	142,383
2004-5[2]	7,000	13,200	3,450	3,800	11,200	13,000	1,370	17,500	10,600	7,100	5,900	6,080	152,515

[1] Preliminary.   [2] Estimate.   *Source: Foreign Agricultural Service, U.S. Department of Agriculture (FAS-USDA)*

Barley Acreage and Prices in the United States

Year Begin- ning June 1	Acreage ----- 1,000 Acres ----- Planted	Harvested for Grain	Yield Per Harvested Acre -- Bushels --	------ Seasonal Prices ------ Received by Farmers[3] All	Feed[4]	Malting[4] Dollars per Bushel	Portland No. 2 Western	National Average Loan Rate	Target Price	Put Under Support (mil. Bu.)	% of Pro- duction
1997-8	6,706	6,198	58.1	2.33	1.86	2.69	2.49	1.57	NA	33.3	9.3
1998-9	6,337	5,864	60.0	1.95	1.55	2.33	1.96	1.56	NA	25.9	7.4
1999-00	5,194	4,734	59.2	2.10	1.65	2.50	2.11	1.59	NA	13.6	4.9
2000-1	5,864	5,213	61.1	2.11	1.74	2.36	2.25	1.62	NA	16.0	5.0
2001-2	4,967	4,289	58.2	2.18	1.74	2.58	2.31	1.65	NA	10.6	4.2
2002-3	5,008	4,123	55.0	2.68	2.16	2.96	2.71	1.88	2.21	10.4	4.6
2003-4[1]	5,348	4,727	58.9	2.82	2.27	3.07		1.88	2.21		
2004-5[2]	4,527	4,021	69.4	2.51	1.82	2.82					

[1] Preliminary. [2] Estimate. [3] Excludes support payments. [4] Duluth through May 1998. *Source: Economic Research Service, U.S. Department of Agriculture (ERS-USDA)*

Salient Statistics of Barley in the United States   In Millions of Bushels

Year Begin- ning June 1	Supply Beginning Stocks	Produc- tion	Imports	Total Supply	Disappearance Domestic Use Food & Acohol Beverages	Seed	Feed & Residual	Total	Exports	Total Disap- pearance	Ending Stocks Gov't Owned[3]	Privately Owned[4]	Total Stocks
1997-8	109.5	360.0	40.3	509.6	161.6	10.4	144.0	316.0	74.4	390.3	0	119.2	119.2
1998-9	119.2	359.9	29.8	501.2	161.4	8.6	161.1	331.1	28.5	359.5	0.3	141.4	141.7
1999-00	141.7	352.1	25.0	448.5	162.5	9.5	136.0	308.0	30.0	338.0	0	111.0	111.0
2000-1	111.0	318.7	29.0	459.0	164.0	8.0	122.0	294.0	58.0	353.0	0	106.0	106.0
2001-2	106.0	249.4	24.0	379.0	164.0	8.0	88.0	260.0	26.0	286.0	0	92.0	92.0
2002-3	92.0	226.9	18.0	337.0	164.0	9.0	65.0	238.0	30.0	268.0	0	69.0	69.0
2003-4[1]	69.0	278.3	21.0	368.0	163.0	9.0	65.0	237.0	19.0	248.0	0	120.0	120.0
2004-5[2]	120.0	279.3	20.0	420.0			110.0		15.0	295.0	0	125.0	125.0

[1] Preliminary. [2] Estimate. [3] Uncommitted inventory. [4] Includes quantity under loan & farmer-owned reserve. *Source: Economic Research Service, U.S. Department of Agriculture (ERS-USDA)*

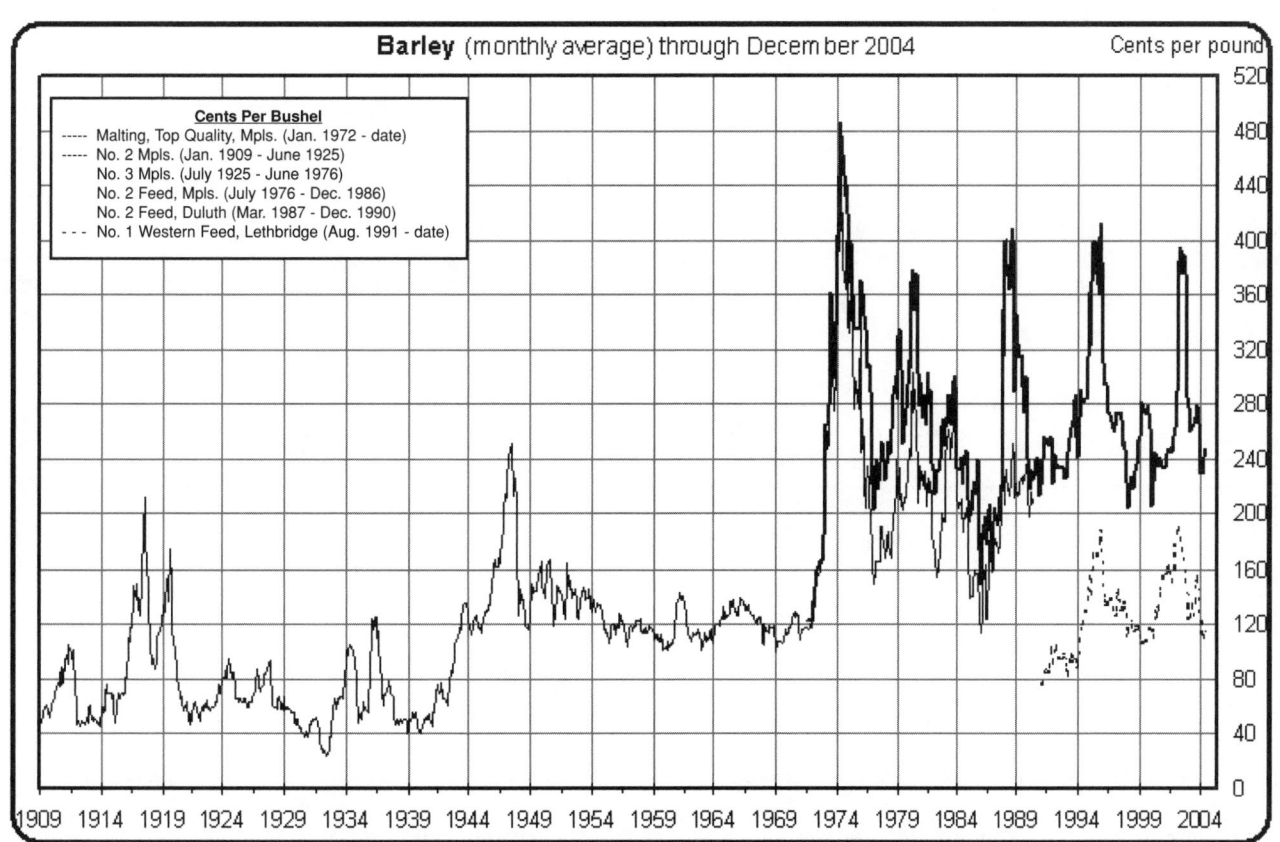

BARLEY

Average Price Received by Farmers for All Barley in the United States   In Dollars Per Bushel

Year	June	July	Aug.	Sept.	Oct.	Nov.	Dec.	Jan.	Feb.	Mar.	Apr.	May	Average
1997-8	2.26	2.27	2.35	2.38	2.44	2.61	2.43	2.42	2.40	2.13	2.16	2.13	2.33
1998-9	1.93	2.01	2.07	2.01	1.91	2.05	2.03	1.89	1.90	2.00	1.78	1.82	1.95
1999-00	1.70	2.04	2.37	2.03	1.96	2.14	2.25	2.04	2.13	2.23	2.09	2.19	2.10
2000-1	2.04	2.70	2.23	1.81	1.97	2.15	2.22	2.00	2.10	2.07	2.05	2.12	2.12
2001-2	1.98	2.00	2.41	2.24	2.29	2.30	2.21	2.09	2.17	2.17	2.09	2.24	2.18
2002-3	2.09	2.14	2.68	2.64	2.64	2.79	2.91	2.85	2.87	2.83	2.85	2.91	2.68
2003-4	2.99	2.74	2.91	2.88	2.74	2.83	2.93	2.69	2.72	2.79	2.78	2.78	2.82
2004-5[1]	2.64	2.54	2.79	2.43	2.29	2.51	2.47	2.37					2.51

[1] Preliminary.   *Source: Economic Research Service, U.S. Department of Agriculture (ERS-USDA)*

Average Price Received by Farmers for Feed Barley in the United States   In Dollars Per Bushel

Year	June	July	Aug.	Sept.	Oct.	Nov.	Dec.	Jan.	Feb.	Mar.	Apr.	May	Average
1997-8	2.31	2.04	2.10	2.29	2.05	1.98	1.66	1.58	1.56	1.51	1.42	NQ	1.86
1998-9	1.82	1.62	1.49	1.40	1.46	1.47	1.55	1.58	1.60	1.49	1.54	1.62	1.55
1999-00	1.55	1.48	1.50	1.64	1.61	1.66	1.64	1.63	1.68	1.78	1.68	1.94	1.65
2000-1	1.73	1.71	1.50	1.54	1.71	1.87	1.90	1.80	1.77	1.76	1.73	1.91	1.74
2001-2	1.77	1.63	1.54	1.71	1.86	1.79	1.77	1.67	1.69	1.75	1.79	1.89	1.74
2002-3	1.83	1.88	2.05	2.23	2.26	2.32	2.14	2.17	2.20	2.30	2.20	2.33	2.16
2003-4	2.33	2.22	2.39	2.27	2.24	2.43	2.26	2.15	2.16	2.20	2.16	2.39	2.27
2004-5[1]	2.20	2.21	1.87	1.64	1.57	1.78	1.64	1.66					1.82

[1] Preliminary.   *Source: National Agricultural Statistical Service, U.S. Department of Agriculture (NASS-USDA)*

Average Open Interest of Western Feed Barley Futures in Winnipeg   In Contracts

Year	Jan.	Feb.	Mar.	Apr.	May	June	July	Aug.	Sept.	Oct.	Nov.	Dec.
1997	22,718	19,290	15,080	14,620	14,385	12,291	10,023	13,641	12,909	13,147	14,473	13,576
1998	15,789	17,337	18,039	14,706	12,666	10,847	9,915	10,384	11,420	11,460	11,338	8,622
1999	8,231	10,635	10,579	9,713	8,333	8,993	10,348	11,959	13,206	15,014	15,662	15,031
2000	16,709	20,500	21,100	22,501	20,299	17,402	15,128	15,095	15,885	14,921	17,192	19,605
2001	19,453	20,515	19,163	19,458	16,020	15,778	16,475	17,202	16,926	13,577	11,407	10,480
2002	9,771	10,653	11,255	11,113	11,141	11,068	11,271	13,046	13,845	12,172	9,000	8,027
2003	8,559	8,203	8,546	9,028	9,631	10,290	10,676	9,580	8,409	7,154	7,524	5,346
2004	6,731	6,881	6,262	9,779	10,497	9,930	9,992	9,743	11,140	11,956	12,786	10,916

Source: Winnipeg Commodity Exchange (WCE)

Volume of Trading of Western Barley Futures in Winnipeg   In Contracts

Year	Jan.	Feb.	Mar.	Apr.	May	June	July	Aug.	Sept.	Oct.	Nov.	Dec.	Total
1997	30,608	30,298	25,910	23,511	17,228	18,912	15,615	21,993	23,291	29,418	31,629	16,201	284,614
1998	23,954	23,472	23,904	23,553	17,395	20,273	21,011	18,101	16,097	21,330	21,589	8,315	238,994
1999	15,463	17,539	13,853	17,179	8,911	16,294	17,936	15,837	29,141	16,662	26,445	16,117	211,377
2000	23,371	22,598	21,563	23,631	19,816	24,298	15,230	11,981	23,105	23,447	42,529	14,508	266,077
2001	26,836	18,732	16,962	24,993	26,361	20,465	20,849	20,137	19,735	21,276	14,926	6,302	237,574
2002	14,268	16,370	15,924	17,663	21,440	18,349	19,860	23,436	22,431	14,471	17,035	10,772	212,019
2003	10,555	18,933	13,069	18,879	13,900	15,153	13,293	29,799	19,438	18,937	17,768	10,977	200,701
2004	11,405	16,265	12,784	23,806	13,179	27,081	15,326	14,933	23,072	15,790	22,516	8,478	204,635

Source: Winnipeg Commodity Exchange (WCE)

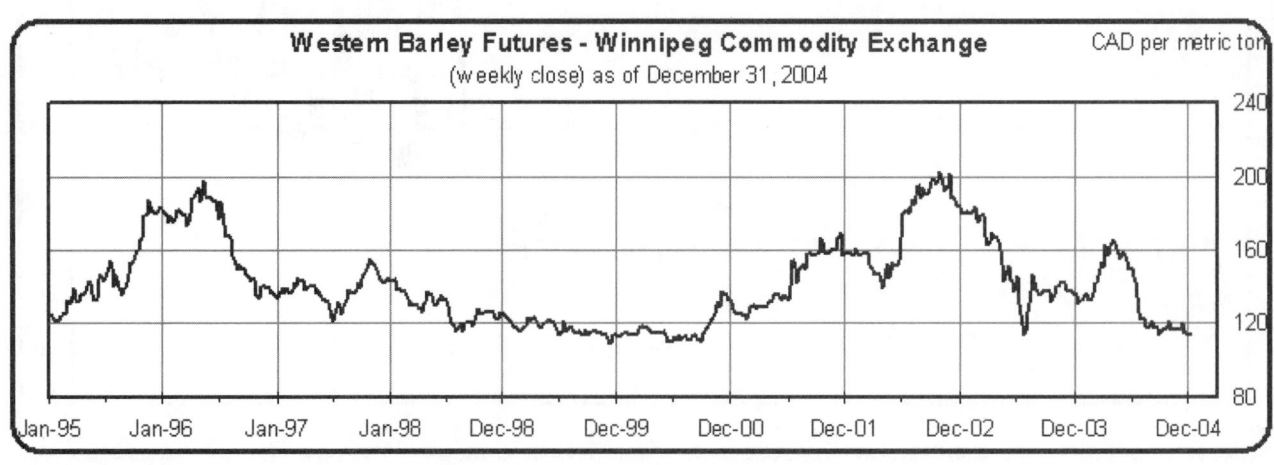

Western Barley Futures - Winnipeg Commodity Exchange   CAD per metric ton
(weekly close) as of December 31, 2004

Bauxite

Bauxite is a naturally occurring, heterogeneous material comprised of one or more aluminum hydroxide minerals plus various mixtures of silica, iron oxide, titanium, alumina-silicates, and other impurities in trace amounts. Bauxite is an important ore of aluminum and forms by the rapid weathering of granite rocks in warm, humid climates. It is easily purified and can be converted directly into either alum or metallic aluminum. It is a soft mineral with hardness varying from 1 to 3, and specific gravity from 2 to 2.55. Bauxite is dull in appearance and may vary in color from white to brown. It usually occurs in aggregates in pea-sized lumps.

Bauxite is the only raw material used in the production of alumina on a commercial scale in the United States. Bauxite is classified according to the intended commercial application, such as abrasive, cement, chemical, metallurgical, and refractory. Of all the bauxite mined, about 95 percent is converted to alumina for the production of aluminum metal with some smaller amounts going to nonmetal uses as various forms of specialty alumina. Small amounts are used in non-metallurgical bauxite applications. Bauxite is also used to produce aluminum chemicals and is used in the steel industry.

Supply – World production of bauxite rose 2.1% yr/yr in 2003 to a new record high 146 million metric tons. The world's largest producer of bauxite is Australia with 38% of world production in 2003, followed by Guinea (11%), Jamaica (9.2%), Brazil (.09%), and China (8.6%). Chinese production of bauxite has quadrupled in the past 10 years. India's bauxite production has also risen rapidly and is more than triple the amount seen 15 years ago.

Demand – US consumption of bauxite in 2003 rose by 12.2% yr/yr to 11.200 million metric tons from 9.770 million metric tons in 2001, which was well below the record high of 15.962 million metric tons seen in 1980. The alumina industry took 95% of bauxite production in 2003, or 10.600 million metric tons. The refractory industry took 1.3% of US bauxite supply in 2003 (150,000 metric tons), the abrasive industry took 0.5% (53,000 metric tons), and the chemical industry took the remainder.

Trade – The US relies on imports for virtually 100% of its consumption needs. Domestic ore, which provides less than 1 percent of the US requirement for bauxite, was mined by one company from surface mines in the states of Alabama and Georgia. US imports of bauxite rose +14.8% yr/yr to 8.697 million metric tons in 2003, which was well below the record of 14.976 million metric tons seen in 1974. US exports of bauxite were negligible at 77,000 metric tons.

World Production of Bauxite   In Thousands of Metric Tons

Year	Australia	Brazil	China	Greece	Guinea	Guyana[2]	Hungary	India	Jamaica[3]	Russia[3]	Sierra Leone	Suriname	World Total
1994	41,733	8,673	3,700	2,196	13,300	1,732	836	4,809	11,564	3,000	735	3,772	106,000
1995	42,655	10,214	5,000	2,200	15,800	2,028	1,015	5,240	10,857	3,100	----	3,530	112,000
1996	43,063	10,998	6,200	2,452	15,600	2,475	1,044	5,757	11,863	3,300	----	3,695	117,000
1997	44,465	11,671	8,000	1,877	16,359	2,467	743	6,019	11,987	3,350	----	3,877	122,000
1998	44,553	11,961	8,200	1,823	15,570	2,267	1,138	6,102	12,646	3,450	----	3,931	123,000
1999	48,416	14,372	8,500	1,883	15,590	2,359	935	6,712	11,688	3,750	----	3,715	129,000
2000	53,802	13,866	9,000	1,991	15,700	2,471	1,047	7,562	11,127	4,200	----	3,610	136,000
2001	53,799	13,790	9,800	2,052	15,100	1,950	1,000	7,864	12,370	4,000	----	4,394	138,000
2002[1]	54,024	13,189	12,000	2,492	15,300	1,690	720	9,647	13,120	3,800	----	4,002	143,000
2003[2]	55,602	13,148	12,500	2,418	15,500	1,500	666	10,002	13,444	4,000	----	4,215	146,000

[1] Preliminary.   [2] Estimate.   [3] Dry Bauxite equivalent of ore processed.   *Source: U.S. Geological Survey (USGS)*

Salient Statistics of Bauxite in the United States   In Thousands of Metric Tons

Year	Net Import Reliance as a % of Apparent Consumption	Average Price FOB Mine $ per Ton	Consumption by Industry Total	Alumina	Abrasive	Chemical	Refractory	Dry Equivalent Imports[3] (for Consumption)	Exports[3]	Consumption	Stocks, December 31 Producers & Consumers	Government	Total
1994	99	15-24	11,200	10,400	197	192	350	11,349	129	11,200	1,560	17,200	18,800
1995	99	15-18	10,900	10,100	133	201	394	10,582	108	10,900	1,730	16,300	18,100
1996	100	15-18	11,000	10,300	117	W	380	10,552	132	11,000	1,930	15,700	17,600
1997	100	15-18	11,500	10,700	98	W	466	11,069	85	11,500	2,260	14,300	16,500
1998	100	25	12,700	12,000	135	W	332	11,393	99	12,700	1,860	11,000	12,800
1999	100	23	11,700	11,100	113	W	251	10,189	149	11,700	1,440	6,800	8,250
2000	100	22	10,800	10,100	111	W	160	8,860	142	10,800	1,300	5,710	7,000
2001	100	23	9,770	9,010	61	W	175	8,542	81	9,770	1,740	2,070	3,810
2002[1]	100	20	9,980	9,290	52	W	115	7,577	42	9,980	1,280	1,770	3,050
2003[2]	100	20	11,200	10,600	53	W	150	8,697	77	11,200	959	66	1,030

[1] Preliminary.   [2] Estimate.   [3] Including concentrates.   W = Withheld to avoid disclosing company proprietary data.
Source: U.S. Geological Survey (USGS)

11

Bismuth

Bismuth (symbol Bi) is a rare metallic element with a pinkish tinge. Bismuth has been known since ancient times, but it was confused with lead, tin, and zinc until the middle of the 18th century. Among the elements in the earth's crust, bismuth is ranked about 73rd in natural abundance. This makes bismuth about as rare as silver. Most industrial bismuth is obtained as a by-product of ore extraction.

Bismuth is useful for castings because of the unusual way that it expands after solidifying. Some of bismuth's alloys have unusually low melting points. Bismuth is one of the most difficult of all substances to magnetize. It tends to turn at right angles to a magnetic field. Because of this property, it is used in instruments for measuring the strength of magnetic fields.

Bismuth finds a wide variety of uses such as pharmaceutical compounds, ceramic glazes, crystal ware, and chemicals and pigments. Bismuth is found in household pharmaceuticals and is used to treat stomach ulcers. Bismuth is opaque to X-rays and can be used in fluoroscopy. Bismuth has also found new use as a nontoxic substitute for lead in various applications such as brass plumbing fixtures, crystal ware, lubricating greases, pigments, and solders. There has been environmental interest in the use of bismuth as a replacement for lead used in shot for waterfowl hunting and in fishing sinkers. Another use has been for galvanizing to improve drainage characteristics of galvanizing alloys. Zinc-bismuth alloys have the same drainage properties as zinc-lead without being as hazardous.

Prices – The dealer price of bismuth in 2003 fell to a 10-year low of $2.87 per pound from $3.14 per pound in 2002. The low price was due to the continued weak global economy in 2003.

Supply – World mine production of bismuth in 2003 rose +3.3% to 3,810 metric tons from the 7-year low of 3,690 metric tons mined in 2003. The world's largest producer in 2003 was Mexico with 32% of world production, followed by China with 26%, Peru with 26%, and Canada with 5%. Regarding production of the refined metal, Mexico had 26% of production (up from 23% in 2002), Belgium had 22%, China had 17%, and Peru had 12% in 2003. The US does not have any significant domestic refinery production of bismuth.

Demand – US consumption of bismuth in 2003 fell 8.6% to a 4-year low of 2,120 metric tons from 2,320 metric tons in 2002. Of that consumption, 39.2% went for metallurgical additives, 30.5% for fusible alloys, 29.1% for chemicals, and 1.3% for other uses.

Trade – US imports of bismuth rose +20.2% to 2,320 metric tons in 2003 from the 7-year low of 1,930 metric tons in 2002. Of US imports, 34% came from Belgium and 23% came from Mexico. US exports of bismuth and alloys were negligible in 2003 at 108 metric tons, down 18% from 131 metric tons in 2002.

World Production of Bismuth   In Metric Tons (Mine Output=Metal Content)

| | Mine Output, Metal Content | | | | | | Refined Metal | | | | | | |
Year	Canada	China	Japan	Mexico	Peru	Total	Belgium	China	Kazak-hastan	Japan	Mexico	Peru	Total
1996	150	610	169	1,070	1,000	3,600	800	750	50	562	957	939	4,180
1997	196	550	30	1,642	1,000	4,360	800	760	50	550	990	774	4,070
1998	186	240	24	1,204	1,000	3,980	700	820	50	479	1,030	832	4,330
1999	311	2,680	24	548	1,000	4,860	700	860	55	481	412	705	3,570
2000	243	1,120	26	1,112	1,000	3,790	700	770	55	520	1,083	744	4,230
2001	258	1,250	28	1,390	1,000	4,420	700	1,230	130	551	1,390	640	5,050
2002[1]	189	950	24	1,126	1,000	3,690	1,000	700	130	474	1,126	568	4,400
2003[2]	200	1,000	27	1,200	1,000	3,810	1,000	800	130	530	1,200	570	4,630

[1] Preliminary.   [2] Estimate.   *Source U.S. Geological Survey (USGS)*

Salient Statistics of Bismuth in the United States   In Metric Tons

| | Bismuth Consumed, By Uses | | | | | | | Imports from | | | | Dealer Price $ Per Pound |
| | Metal-lurgical Additives | Other Alloys & Uses | Fusible Alloys | Chemicals[3] | Total Consumption | Consumer Stocks Dec. 31 | Exports of Metal & Alloys | Metallic Bismuth from | | | | |
Year								Belgium	Mexico	Peru	Total	
1996	231	35	401	855	1,520	122	151	584.0	453.0	19.5	1,490	3.65
1997	252	31	593	655	1,530	213	206	691.0	601.0	163.0	2,170	3.50
1998	335	32	741	884	1,990	175	245	739.0	807.0	68.8	2,720	3.60
1999	340	31	823	855	2,050	130	257	742.0	277.0	6.8	2,110	3.85
2000	346	34	889	861	2,130	118	491	832.0	516.0	20.4	2,410	3.70
2001	369	45	981	805	2,200	95	541	728.0	605.0	----	2,220	3.74
2002[1]	388	50	1,070	813	2,320	111	131	724.0	518.0	19.5	1,930	3.14
2003[2]	831	25	646	616	2,120	278	108	778.0	532.0	0.1	2,320	2.87

[1] Preliminary.   [2] Estimate.   [3] Includes pharmaceuticals.   *Source: U.S. Geological Survey (USGS)*

Average Price of Bismuth (99.99%) in the United States   In Dollars Per Pound

Year	Jan.	Feb.	Mar.	Apr.	May	June	July	Aug.	Sept.	Oct.	Nov.	Dec.	Average
2001	----	----	4.15	----	----	3.73	----	----	3.58	----	----	3.43	3.72
2002	----	3.20	3.20	3.10	3.05	3.05	2.94	2.90	2.90	2.90	2.90	2.90	3.00
2003	2.90	2.90	2.90	2.92	2.98	2.98	2.98	2.98	2.98	2.98	2.98	2.98	2.96
2004	2.98	2.98	2.98	2.98	2.98	2.98	2.98	2.98	2.98	2.98	2.98	2.98	2.98

Source: American Metal Market (AMM)

Broilers

Broiler chickens are raised for meat rather than for eggs. The broiler industry was started in the late 1950's when chickens were selectively bred for meat production. Broiler chickens are housed in massive flocks mainly between 20,000 and 50,000 birds, with some flocks reaching over 100,000 birds. Broiler chicken farmers usually rear five or six batches of chickens per year.

After just six or seven weeks, broiler chickens are slaughtered (a chicken's natural lifespan is around seven years). Chickens marketed as pouissons, or spring chickens, are slaughtered after four weeks. A few are kept longer than seven weeks to be sold as the larger roasting chickens.

Prices – The average monthly price received by farmers for broilers (live weight) rose sharply in 2004 by +27.8% yr/yr to a new record high of 45.2 cents per pound. The average monthly price for wholesale broilers (ready-to-cook) in 2004 (through November) rose sharply by +20.5% to 74.69 cents per pound, which was also a new record high.

Supply – Total production of broilers in 2004 rose by +4.2% yr/yr to 34.135 billion pounds, which was a record high. The number of broilers raised for commercial production in 2004 rose by +2.8% yr/yr to a new record of 8.757 billion birds. The average weight per bird rose by 1.4% to 5.26 pounds, which was a new record high and was nearly 50% heavier than the average bird weight of 3.62 pounds seen in 1970, attesting to the increased efficiency of the industry.

Demand – US per capita consumption of broilers in 2004 rose to a new record high of 85.3 pounds (ready-to-cook) per person per year. US consumption of chicken has nearly doubled in the past two decades, up from 47.0 pounds in 1980, as consumers have increased their consumption of chicken because of the focus on low-carb diets and because chicken is a leaner and healthier meat than either beef or pork.

Broiler Supply and Prices in the United States

Year & Quarters	Number (Millions)	Average Weight (Pounds)	Liveweight Pounds (Mil. Lbs.)	Certified RTC Weight (Mil. Lbs.)	Total Production RTC[3] (Mil. Lbs.)	Per Capita Consumption RTC Basis (Mil. Lbs.)	Farm	Geogia Dock[4]
							Cents per Pound	
1999	8,112	4.99	40,444	29,741	29,741	77.0	36.89	58.75
2000	8,239	5.00	38,417	30,397	30,495	77.4	35.20	58.14
2001	8,387	5.04	42,337	31,257	31,266	76.6	39.58	62.08
2002	8,511	5.12	43,529	32,190	32,240	80.5	30.42	61.65
2003[1]	8,522	5.19	44,247	32,700	32,749	81.6	35.33	64.80
2004[2]	8,762	5.26	46,096	34,063	34,134	85.3	45.17	74.69
I	2,138	5.20	11,128	8,208	8,208	20.8	45.67	70.76
II	2,197	5.23	11,488	8,491	8,491	21.2	50.00	76.10
III	2,267	5.27	11,956	8,834	8,835	21.8	46.00	78.33
IV	2,159	5.34	11,525	8,531	8,600	21.4	39.00	73.58

[1] Preliminary. [2] Estimate. [3] Total production equals federal inspected slaughter plus other slaughter minus cut-up & further processing condemnation. [4] Ready-to-cook basis. *Source: Economic Research Service, U.S. Department of Agriculture (ERS-USDA)*

Salient Statistics of Broilers in the United States

Year	Commercial Production Number (Mil. Lbs.)	Commercial Production Liveweight (Mil. Lbs.)	Average Liveweight Per Bird (Pounds)	Average Price (Cents/Lb.)	Value of Production (Mil. $)	Federally Inspected	Other Chickens	Total	Storage Stocks January 1	Exports	Broiler Feed Ratio (Pounds)	Total (Mil. Lbs.)	Per Capita[4] (Pounds)
						In Millions of Pounds							
1998	7,934	38,554	4.86	39.3	15,147	27,612	525	28,137	614	4,787	7.2	23,254	72.60
1999	8,146	40,830	5.01	37.1	15,129	29,468	554	30,022	717	4,978	6.7	24,965	77.00
2000	8,263	41,516	5.02	33.6	13,989	30,209	531	31,740	804	5,138	7.8	25,606	77.40
2001	8,389	42,446	5.06	39.3	16,696	30,938	515	31,453	807	5,737	5.5	25,819	76.60
2002	8,591	44,059	5.13	30.5	13,437	31,895	547	32,442	720	4,941	5.4	27,467	80.50
2003[1]	8,493	43,958	5.18	34.6	15,215	32,313	502	32,815	768	5,034	5.9	27,966	81.60
2004[2]						33,542	490	34,032	609	5,375	7.4	28,678	84.60

[1] Preliminary. [2] Estimate. [3] Ready-to-cook. [4] Retail weight basis. *Source: Economic Research Service, U.S. Department of Agriculture (ERS-USDA)*

Average Wholesale Broiler[1] Prices RTC (Ready-to-Cook) (In Cents Per Pound)

Year	Jan.	Feb.	Mar.	Apr.	May	June	July	Aug.	Sept.	Oct.	Nov.	Dec.	Average
1998	54.66	56.40	58.10	58.52	60.08	64.26	68.53	72.13	70.53	68.04	64.13	60.45	62.99
1999	59.33	58.23	56.79	55.08	60.02	60.33	59.46	57.65	57.15	54.87	59.52	58.42	58.07
2000	55.43	53.84	54.48	55.39	55.71	56.01	56.61	55.47	58.35	57.22	58.22	57.23	56.16
2001	56.87	57.47	58.95	58.46	59.40	59.88	60.43	60.90	61.93	60.17	58.89	55.98	59.11
2002	56.86	55.91	55.17	53.47	56.42	58.44	57.47	55.72	55.88	52.97	53.42	54.74	55.54
2003	60.46	60.49	60.02	57.78	59.44	61.56	62.80	63.20	64.08	63.59	64.45	65.71	61.97
2004[2]	68.66	74.96	75.94	76.40	79.54	82.00	81.59	75.44	70.07	68.79	68.08	68.01	74.12

[1] 12-city composite wholesale price. [2] Preliminary. *Source: Economic Research Service, U.S. Department of Agriculture (ERS-USDA)*

Butter

Butter is a dairy product produced by churning the fat from milk, usually cow's milk, until it solidifies. In some parts of the world, butter is also made from the milk of goats, sheep, and even horses. Butter has been in use since at least 2,000 BC. Today butter is used principally as a food item, but in ancient times it was used more as an ointment, medicine, or illuminating oil. Butter was first churned in skin pouches thrown back and forth over the backs of trotting horses.

It takes about 10 quarts of milk to produce 1 pound of butter. The manufacture of butter is the third largest use of milk in the US. California is generally the largest producing state, followed closely by Wisconsin, with Washington as a distant third. Commercially finished butter is comprised of milk fat (80% to 85%), water (12% to 16%), and salt (about 2%). Although the price of butter is highly correlated with the price of milk, it also has its own supply and demand dynamics.

The consumption of butter has dropped in recent decades because pure butter has a high level of animal fat and cholesterol that have been linked to obesity and heart disease. The primary substitute for butter is margarine, which is produced from vegetable oil rather than milk fat. US per capita consumption of margarine has risen from 2.6 pounds in 1930 to recent levels near 8.3 pounds, much higher than US butter consumption.

Futures on butter are traded at the Chicago Mercantile Exchange (CME). The CME's butter futures contract calls for the delivery of 40,000 pounds of Grade AA butter and is priced in cents per pound.

Prices – The average monthly price of butter at the Chicago Mercantile Exchange in 2004 (through October) rallied very sharply by 59% to a new record high of 181.67 cents per pound. That was sharply higher than the 8-year low of 110.59 cents posted in 2002.

Supply – World production of butter in 2005 is forecasted to rise +4.3% yr/yr to 6.960 million metric tons, which would be the highest production level since the record high of 7.271 million metric tons was posted in 1986. The world's largest producers of butter are India with 41% of projected world production in 2005, the United States with 8%, New Zealand with 6%, and Russia with 4%. Production of creamery butter by US factories in 2004 (monthly average through November) fell –2.8% to a new 5-year low of 1.208 billion pounds. That was far below the record of 1.365 billion pounds seen in 1992.

Demand – US usage of butter in 2003 fell by –7.8% yr/yr to 1.192 billion pounds. That was only about one-half of the usage levels above 2 billion seen in the 1930s and 1940s, illustrating the downtrend in US butter consumption. Per capita consumption of butter in the US in 2000, the latest reporting year for the series, was 4.6 pounds per person per year, little changed from 1980 but sharply lower than 7.5 pounds in 1960 and 17.3 pounds in 1930.

Trade – US imports of butter in 2003 fell by –8.8% yr/yr to 31.73 million pounds, accounting for only a very small portion of US usage. US butter exports in 2003 rose +267% to a 6-year high of 22 million pounds.

Supply and Distribution of Butter in the United States   In Millions of Pounds

	------------------------ Supply ------------------------				----------------------------------- Distribution -----------------------------------							-------- 93 Score --------	
		Cold Storage				-- Domestic Disappearance --		--- Department of Agriculture ---				AA Wholesale Price	
Year	Pro-duction	Stocks[3] Jan. 1[5]	Imports	Total Supply	Total	Per Capita (Pounds)	Exports	Jan. 1 Stocks[4]	Dec. 31 Stocks[4]	Removed by USDA Programs	Total Use	California ----- $ per Pound -----	Chicago
1995	1,264	80	1.537	1,348	1,186	4.5	100	68	3	77.8	1,329	----	.8188
1996	1,174	19	10.545	1,204	1,148	4.3	83	3	0	0.1	1,190	----	1.0824
1997	1,151	14	24.154	1,177	1,115	4.1	46	0	0	38.4	1,156	----	1.1625
1998	1,082	21	70.369	1,243	1,220	4.4	33	0	0	12.6	1,229	----	1.7685
1999	1,167	26	39.813	1,337	1,307	4.7	20	0	0	3.7	1,314	----	1.2396
2000	1,274	25	32.400	1,331	1,329	4.5	9	0	0	8.8	1,289	----	1.1768
2001	1,237	24	75.000	1,336	1,268	4.4	8	0	0	0	1,275	----	1.6630
2002[1]	1,355	56	34.800	1,446	1,293	4.4	6	0	1	0	1,288	----	1.1059
2003[2]	1,242	158	31.733	1,432	1,192		22	1		37.1		----	1.1450

[1] Preliminary.   [2] Estimates.   [3] Includes butter-equivalent.   [4] Includes butteroil.   [5] *Includes stocks held by USDA.*
Source: Economic Research Service, U.S. Department of Agriculture (ERS-USDA)

Commercial Disappearance of Creamery Butter in the United States   In Millions of Pounds

Year	First Quarter	Second Quarter	Third Quarter	Fourth Quarter	Total	Year	First Quarter	Second Quarter	Third Quarter	Fourth Quarter	Total
1993	224.6	231.5	271.9	312.7	1,040.6	1999	299.3	316.4	318.3	374.8	1,308.8
1994	261.7	254.9	285.0	298.3	1,097.3	2000	300.8	286.9	332.3	380.6	1,300.6
1995	335.7	269.0	261.2	304.9	1,186.0	2001	290.9	278.4	316.1	397.0	1,282.4
1996	325.6	301.8	237.5	310.3	1,180.0	2002	313.5	263.5	317.4	393.4	1,287.8
1997	302.7	250.7	265.8	287.6	1,109.0	2003	304.2	275.4	317.2	411.8	1,308.6
1998	289.0	276.3	255.3	308.6	1,137.0	2004[1]	286.3	295.7	333.6	420.8	1,336.4

[1] Preliminary.   *Source: Economic Research Service, U.S. Department of Agriculture (ERS-USDA)*

World (Total) Butter[3] Production   In Thousands of Metric Tons

Year	Australia	France	Germany	India	Ireland	Netherlands	New Zealand	Poland	Russia	Ukraine	United Kingdom	United States	World Total
1997	147	466	442	1,470	145	134	307	178	280	109	139	522	5,171
1998	154	463	426	1,600	145	149	343	183	270	113	137	530	5,336
1999	176	448	427	1,750	143	140	316	168	260	108	143	579	5,513
2000	180	453	426	1,950	144	126	344	169	265	135	132	570	5,814
2001	160	450	425	2,250	131	128	352	181	270	156	130	559	6,145
2002	164	450	420	2,400	132	120	370	180	280	131	132	615	6,555
2003[1]	163	NA	NA	2,450	NA	NA	392	185	280	148	NA	563	6,608
2004[2]	132	NA	NA	2,600	NA	NA	407	NA	270	170	NA	550	6,676

[1] Preliminary.   [2] Forecast.   [3] Factory (including creameries and dairies) & farm.   *Source: Foreign Agricultural Service, U.S. Department of Agriculture (FAS-USDA)*

Production of Creamery Butter in Factories in the United States   In Millions of Pounds

Year	Jan.	Feb.	Mar.	Apr.	May	June	July	Aug.	Sept.	Oct.	Nov.	Dec.	Total
1997	127.6	108.6	105.4	118.3	102.7	82.0	80.0	68.8	79.3	83.3	89.1	106.0	1,151.3
1998	117.8	105.7	106.7	107.1	92.6	69.9	63.8	64.3	68.2	88.5	91.1	106.3	1,081.9
1999	123.3	111.5	113.7	106.4	104.7	86.0	75.8	66.1	78.8	93.0	90.4	117.2	1,166.8
2000	139.9	128.2	121.0	111.7	108.9	89.1	85.4	83.7	89.9	103.9	100.4	111.6	1,273.6
2001	127.4	111.8	111.4	109.0	111.0	86.8	84.2	75.6	86.7	109.9	100.1	123.0	1,236.8
2002	140.1	124.2	127.7	131.6	125.5	95.8	94.4	88.9	92.8	102.6	103.9	127.6	1,355.1
2003[1]	141.9	128.1	126.4	122.8	114.9	84.2	80.1	70.9	73.3	96.8	88.4	114.6	1,242.4
2004[2]	131.9	105.8	96.7	96.5	106.6	97.0	91.2	88.6	92.1	101.5	97.5	111.9	1,217.4

[1] Preliminary.   [2] Estimate.   *Source: Economic Research Service, U.S. Department of Agriculture (ERS-USDA)*

Cold Storage Holdings of Creamery Butter on First of Month in the United States   In Millions of Pounds

Year	Jan.	Feb.	Mar.	Apr.	May	June	July	Aug.	Sept.	Oct.	Nov.	Dec.
1997	13.7	23.2	36.0	50.3	86.8	104.2	93.7	85.6	69.5	43.9	26.6	15.4
1998	20.8	34.2	44.2	55.9	67.4	72.7	60.6	51.0	41.1	34.1	31.2	28.7
1999	25.9	60.8	95.0	108.4	125.5	136.6	120.6	123.6	90.7	71.5	64.2	30.2
2000	25.1	82.4	107.8	114.0	126.9	138.2	145.8	136.9	101.3	85.0	58.3	27.3
2001	24.1	68.4	86.1	96.2	112.3	138.0	153.5	151.1	118.0	110.9	100.8	57.9
2002	55.9	99.2	130.1	145.2	196.6	226.8	243.0	245.3	229.5	209.1	164.6	135.6
2003	157.8	204.8	239.9	249.0	263.7	298.0	301.4	283.9	253.9	207.2	170.2	122.5
2004[1]	99.6	152.4	158.1	158.1	155.7	178.7	187.2	193.5	161.0	133.0	107.2	57.2

[1] Preliminary.   *Source: Agricultural Statistics Board, U.S. Department of Agriculture (ASB-USDA)*

Average Price of Butter at Chicago Mercantile Exchange[1]   In Cents Per Pound

Year	Jan.	Feb.	Mar.	Apr.	May	June	July	Aug.	Sept.	Oct.	Nov.	Dec.	Average
1997	81.9	98.4	106.3	95.6	86.1	105.5	102.7	102.5	101.6	135.3	148.8	120.1	116.2
1998	109.2	139.8	134.1	136.4	153.2	186.7	203.1	216.6	273.1	242.3	187.9	140.8	177.6
1999	144.4	133.1	130.3	103.9	111.0	147.7	134.7	141.4	135.8	113.8	109.6	94.2	125.0
2000	91.6	92.9	99.7	108.7	122.2	128.6	120.3	120.3	119.1	116.9	151.7	150.0	118.5
2001	122.3	138.1	154.9	174.7	190.4	197.4	192.4	204.5	219.7	151.9	135.2	130.2	167.6
2002	134.5	124.3	124.7	117.1	105.9	104.3	103.0	97.5	96.4	103.2	104.3	112.0	110.6
2003	108.2	104.1	109.2	109.1	109.2	111.4	119.9	117.1	117.3	118.5	120.6	129.7	114.5
2004	143.2	171.3	213.5	222.0	203.6	193.0	174.6	154.1	176.6	164.8	192.4	170.8	181.7

[1] Data from June 1998 through December 2001 are for Wholesale Price of 92 Score Creamery (Grade A) Butter, Central States; prior to June 1998 are for Grade AA in Chicago.   *Source: Economic Research Service, U.S. Department of Agriculture (ERS-USDA)*

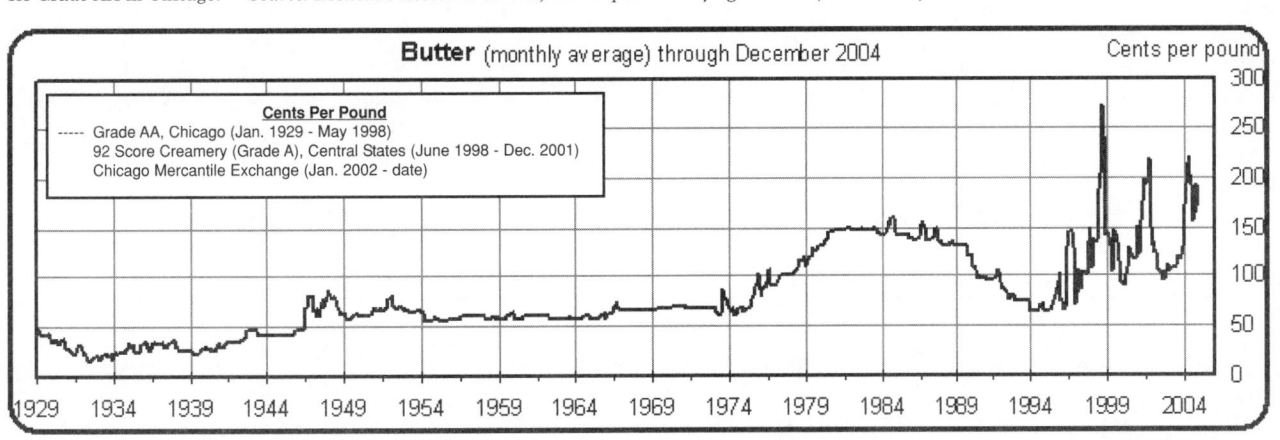

Butter (monthly average) through December 2004   Cents per pound

Cents Per Pound
----- Grade AA, Chicago (Jan. 1929 - May 1998)
92 Score Creamery (Grade A), Central States (June 1998 - Dec. 2001)
Chicago Mercantile Exchange (Jan. 2002 - date)

Cadmium

Cadmium (symbol Cd) is a soft, bluish-white, metallic element that can easily be shaped and cut with a knife. Cadmium melts at 321 degrees Celsius and boils at 765 degrees Celsius. Cadmium burns brightly in air when heated, forming the oxide CdO. In 1871, the German chemist Friedrich Stromeyer discovered cadmium in incrustations in zinc furnaces.

Rare greenockite is the only mineral bearing cadmium. Cadmium occurs most often in small quantities associated with zinc ores, such as sphalerite. Electrolysis or fractional distillation is used to separate the cadmium and zinc. About 80% of world cadmium output is a by-product from zinc refining. The remaining 20% comes from secondary sources and recycling of cadmium products. Cadmium recycling is practical only from nickel-cadmium batteries and from some alloys and dust from electric-arc furnaces.

Cadmium is used primarily for metal plating and coating operations in transportation equipment, machinery, baking enamels, photography, and television phosphors. It is also used in pigments and lasers, and in nickel-cadmium and solar batteries.

Prices – Cadmium prices in the past 7 years have been at severely depressed levels, reflecting the decreased demand for the substance. Cadmium prices in 2003 fell to 50 cents per pound from 52 cents per pound in 2002. That was up sharply from the record low of 14 cents in 1999 but it was still far below the 20-year average price of $1.59 per pound and the record high of $6.91 per pound in 1988.

Supply – World cadmium production in 2003 rose +0.6% yr/yr to 16,900 metric tons, up from the 3-decade low of 16,800 metric tons in 2002. China and Japan were the largest producers of cadmium in 2003, each producing about 2,500 metric tons, representing 15% of world production. US production of cadmium in 2003 fell -4.3% yr/yr to 670 metric tons, which was a new record low. The US production level in 2003 was less than half the level seen as recently as 2000. The US in 2003 accounted for just 4% of world cadmium production.

Demand – Consumption of cadmium has been declining fairly steeply in the last few years due to environmental concerns. US cadmium consumption fell by –5.5% yr/yr in 2003 to a record low of 530 metric tons. Of the total apparent consumption, about 75% is used for batteries, 12% for pigments, 8% for coatings and plating, 4% for nonferrous alloys, and 1% for other uses.

Trade – The US in 2003 relied on imports for virtually none of its cadmium usage, down from 38% as recently as 1998. US imports of cadmium have plunged in recent years and in 2003 fell to a negligible 18 metric tons from 425 metric tons as recently as 2000. US exports of cadmium rose sharply to 558 metric tons in 2003 from 168 metric tons in 2002.

World Refinery Production of Cadmium   In Metric Tons

Year	Australia	Belgium	Canada	China	Finland	Germany	Italy	Japan	Kazak-hstan	Mexico	United Kingdom	United States[3]	World Total
1996	639	1,579	2,537	1,570	648	1,150	296	2,344	800	784	541	1,530	18,900
1997	632	1,420	2,260	1,980	650	1,145	287	2,473	745	1,223	455	2,060	20,300
1998	585	1,318	2,090	2,130	520	1,020	328	2,337	1,622	1,218	440	1,240	20,200
1999	462	1,235	1,911	2,150	700	1,145	360	2,567	1,246	1,275	547	1,190	20,000
2000	552	1,148	1,941	2,370	683	1,130	284	2,472	1,250	1,268	503	1,890	20,800
2001	378	1,236	1,429	2,510	604	540	312	2,460	1,250	1,241	485	680	18,800
2002[1]	350	117	1,400	2,440	----	422	391	2,444	1,300	1,382	450	700	16,800
2003[2]	350	120	1,400	2,500	----	450	100	2,497	1,351	1,400	450	670	16,900

[1] Preliminary.   [2] Estimate.   [3] Primary and secondary metal.   *Source: U.S. Geological Survey (USGS)*

Salient Statistics of Cadmium in the United States   In Metric Tons of Contained Cadmium

Year	Net Import Reliance as a % of Apparent Consumption	Production (Metal)	Producer Shipments	Cadmium Sulfide Production	Production Other Compounds	Imports of Cadmium Metal[3]	Exports[4]	Apparent Consumption	Industry Stocks Dec. 31[5]	New York Dealer Price $ per Pound
1996	32	1,530	1,310	119	720	843	201	2,250	1,140	1.24
1997	19	2,060	1,370	113	607	790	554	2,510	1,090	.51
1998	38	1,240	1,570	125	638	514	180	2,100	729	.28
1999	9	1,190	1,020	64	604	294	20	1,850	893	.14
2000	6	1,890	1,580	42	417	425	314	2,010	1,200	.16
2001	3	680	954	31	----	107	272	659	1,110	.23
2002[1]	0	700	776	33	----	25	168	561	1,780	.52
2003[2]	0	670	320	----	----	18	558	530	1,460	.50

[1] Preliminary.   [2] Estimate.   [3] For consumption.   [4] Cadmium metal, alloys, dross, flue dust.   [5] Metallic, Compounds, Distributors.
[6] Sticks & Balls in 1 to 5 short ton lots.   E = Net exporter.   *Source: U.S. Geological Survey (USGS)*

Average Price of Cadmium (99.95%) in the United States   In Dollars Per Pound

Year	Jan.	Feb.	Mar.	Apr.	May	June	July	Aug.	Sept.	Oct.	Nov.	Dec.	Average
2002	----	30.50	30.07	27.50	27.50	27.50	27.59	29.50	31.15	43.15	56.58	64.52	35.96
2003	58.33	55.00	55.00	55.00	59.29	67.50	67.50	67.50	67.50	63.15	57.50	57.50	60.90
2004	57.50	62.24	62.50	62.50	62.50	62.50	62.50	62.50	62.50	62.50	62.50	62.50	62.06

Source: American Metal Market (AMM)

Canola (Rapeseed)

Canola is a genetic variation of rapeseed that was developed by Canadian plant breeders specifically for its nutritional qualities and its low level of saturated fat. The term *Canola* is a contraction of "Canadian oil." The history of canola oil begins with the rapeseed plant, a member of the mustard family. The rape plant is grown both as feed for livestock and birdfeed. For 4,000 years, the oil from the rapeseed was used in China and India for cooking and as lamp oil. During World War II, rapeseed oil was used as a marine and industrial lubricant. After the war, the market for rapeseed oil plummeted. Rapeseed growers needed other uses for their crop, and that stimulated the research that led to the development of canola. In 1974, Canadian plant breeders from the University of Manitoba produced canola by genetically altering rapeseed. Each canola plant produces yellow flowers, which then produce pods. The tiny round seeds within each pod are crushed to produce canola oil. Each canola seed contains approximately 40% oil. Canola oil is the world's third largest source of vegetable oil accounting for 13% of world vegetable oils, following soybean oil at 32%, and palm oil at 28%. The rest of the seed is processed into canola meal, which is used as high protein livestock feed.

The climate in Canada is especially suitable for canola plant growth. Today, over 13 million acres of Canadian soil are dedicated to canola production. Canola oil is Canada's leading vegetable oil. Due to strong demand from the US for canola oil, approximately 70% of Canada's canola oil is exported to the US. Canola oil is used as a salad oil, cooking oil, and for margarine as well as in the manufacture of inks, biodegradable greases, pharmaceuticals, fuel, soap, and cosmetics.

Canola futures and options are traded at the Winnipeg Exchange. The futures contract calls for the delivery of 20 metric tons of canola and 5 contracts are together called a "1 board lot." The contract is priced in Canadian dollars per metric ton.

Prices – Canola prices on the Winnipeg nearest-futures chart rallied early in 2004 to post a 2-year high of CD$444 per metric ton, but then plunged by 40% during 2004 along with other North American grain prices to a 4-year low of CD$260 by January 2005. The average monthly wholesale price of canola oil in the Midwest in 2003 (through September) rose +0.1% yr/yr to 27.20 cents per pound, which was a 4-year high. The average monthly wholesale price of canola meal (36% delivery Pacific Northwest) rose sharply by 31% to $188.46 per short ton in 2003, but then faded to $138.81 by February 2004.

Supply – World canola production in the 2004-05 marketing year rose by +9.1% yr/yr to a new record high of 43.027 million metric tons. The world's largest canola producers are China with 28% of world production in 2004-05, Canada (18%), India (14%), Germany (12%), and France (9%). US production of canola in 2004-05 fell –10.6% yr/yr to a 7-year low of 613,000 metric tons.

Regarding canola products, world production of canola oil in 2004-05 rose +7.7% to 15.168 million metric tons, which was a new record high. US production of canola oil in 2004-05 rose +2.4% to 255,000 metric tons, which was a record high. World production of canola meal in 2004-05 rose +7.7% to a new record high of 23.589 million metric tons.

Demand – World crush demand for canola in 2004-05 rose +8.0% yr/yr to 39.447 million metric tons, which was a new record high. World consumption of canola oil in 2004-05 rose +7.3% yr/yr to a new record high of 15.092 million metric tons. World consumption of canola meal in 2004-05 rose +7.4% to 23.348 million metric tons, which was a new record high.

Trade – World canola exports in 2004-05 rose +9.2% to 5.910 million metric tons, world canola oil exports rose +5.0% to 1.389 million metric tons, and world canola meal exports fell –15.4% yr/yr to 2.015 million metric tons. World canola imports in 2004-05 rose +8.9% to 5.632 million metric tons, world canola oil imports rose +4.5% to 1.316 million metric tons, and world canola meal imports fell –16.8% to 1.825 million metric tons. Regarding US canola trade, US canola imports in 2004-05 rose +44.0% to 350,000 metric tons and US exports fell –28.0% to 219,000 metric tons.

World Production of Canola (Rapeseed)   In Thousands of Metric Tons

Year	Austrlia	Canada	China	Czecho-slovakia	France	Germany	India	Pakistan	Poland	Sweden	United Kingdom	Former USSR	World Total
1993-4	305	5,480	6,940	377	1,550	2,848	5,390	225	594	313	1,136	211	26,735
1994-5	309	7,233	7,492	452	1,800	2,837	5,884	225	756	214	1,298	244	30,310
1995-6	557	6,436	9,777	662	2,700	3,127	6,000	255	1,377	215	1,330	252	34,435
1996-7	624	5,062	9,200	521	2,870	2,150	6,942	255	449	139	1,410	226	31,531
1997-8	856	6,392	9,578	575	3,496	2,867	4,935	286	595	132	1,527	221	33,108
1998-9	1,690	7,643	8,300	680	3,734	3,388	4,900	292	1,099	129	1,566	339	35,885
1999-00	2,460	8,798	10,132	931	4,392	4,285	5,110	279	1,132	154	1,737	135	42,483
2000-1	1,775	7,205	11,381	844	3,481	3,286	3,725	297	958	112	1,157	148	37,405
2001-2	1,756	5,017	11,331	973	2,874	4,160	4,500	231	1,064	112	1,159	140	36,037
2002-3[1]	871	4,178	10,552	710	3,360	3,830	3,600	221	950	160	1,470	115	32,508
2003-4[2]	1,691	6,771	11,420	390	3,410	3,640	6,800	235	790	130	1,770	192	39,428
2004-5[3]	1,300	7,700	12,000	850	3,900	5,200	5,900	241	1,500	200	1,600	120	43,027

[1] Preliminary.   [2] Estimate.   [3] Forecast.   *Source: Economic Research Service, U.S. Department of Agriculture (ERS-USDA); The Oil World*

CANOLA

Volume of Trading of Canola Futures in Winnipeg   In Contracts

Year	Jan.	Feb.	Mar.	Apr.	May	June	July	Aug.	Sept.	Oct.	Nov.	Dec.	Total
1995	75,068	87,113	86,340	67,937	95,447	85,126	94,576	70,904	94,794	126,210	84,991	107,177	1,075,683
1996	99,542	95,034	76,704	128,169	148,189	103,892	135,652	87,896	108,490	161,894	90,105	110,453	1,346,020
1997	121,433	133,056	131,473	148,647	117,219	116,117	80,867	72,602	93,967	150,065	97,984	124,245	1,387,675
1998	100,926	144,309	110,708	140,789	130,551	121,829	107,816	89,457	121,573	181,002	127,120	181,278	1,557,358
1999	129,758	59,772	132,732	143,282	102,838	134,179	94,256	113,913	130,505	184,973	157,428	179,798	1,563,434
2000	137,528	182,744	163,038	169,807	168,164	152,358	79,071	91,762	146,890	208,639	154,727	204,045	1,858,773
2001	196,137	292,226	286,463	247,744	205,798	188,175	163,901	155,531	143,220	205,016	174,910	165,852	2,424,973
2002	164,945	179,753	166,889	159,981	133,202	139,256	132,524	174,527	131,034	170,873	105,661	169,477	1,828,122
2003	129,903	152,738	108,991	153,528	120,178	152,979	90,909	66,768	109,760	217,310	90,950	153,269	1,547,283
2004	145,339	204,567	178,516	192,429	120,218	128,843	73,417	97,483	113,368	175,776	110,922	196,094	1,736,972

Source: Winnipeg Commodity Exchange (WCE)

Average Open Interest of Canola Futures in Winnipeg   In Contracts

Year	Jan.	Feb.	Mar.	Apr.	May	June	July	Aug.	Sept.	Oct.	Nov.	Dec.
1995	47,579	43,662	36,530	32,580	38,361	42,961	43,607	42,828	51,067	57,638	46,640	45,444
1996	42,646	43,808	45,126	47,989	54,228	52,176	49,387	40,619	42,242	52,273	53,121	54,323
1997	48,681	48,281	50,815	50,025	49,212	43,941	35,496	30,039	25,255	36,674	38,702	42,510
1998	35,864	46,678	49,161	48,683	56,163	60,285	57,627	51,462	53,919	56,651	51,426	60,663
1999	57,958	64,014	57,851	57,351	51,808	53,039	49,273	41,819	53,425	67,244	63,780	64,286
2000	59,057	65,545	65,296	66,253	65,855	59,673	46,813	51,367	59,342	72,618	64,862	65,170
2001	57,537	73,539	88,111	78,143	77,425	84,315	72,430	70,137	67,275	71,651	65,580	66,884
2002	57,821	56,443	53,321	56,830	50,924	38,901	48,329	54,286	53,630	50,379	56,896	57,983
2003	52,818	54,749	55,369	53,480	50,549	49,930	47,479	45,314	44,510	49,008	45,423	48,655
2004	54,524	57,944	71,624	77,357	69,783	59,012	50,669	51,009	49,659	53,855	65,215	68,719

Source: Winnipeg Commodity Exchange (WCE)

World Supply and Distribution of Canola and Products   In Thousands of Metric Tons

	Canola					Canola Meal					Canola Oil				
Year	Pro-duction	Exports	Imports	Crush	Ending Stocks	Pro-duction	Exports	Imports	Con-sumption	Ending Stocks	Pro-duction	Exports	Imports	Con-sumption	Ending Stocks
1997-8	33,108	6,902	6,757	31,204	1,081	18,838	4,581	4,417	18,742	442	11,425	3,024	2,685	11,030	446
1998-9	35,885	6,836	6,990	31,952	2,241	19,173	2,052	2,167	19,365	365	11,847	1,844	1,625	11,586	488
1999-00	42,483	8,207	8,170	37,138	4,204	22,083	2,315	2,251	21,972	384	13,988	1,738	1,736	13,744	690
2000-1	37,405	7,176	7,019	35,443	2,700	21,148	1,833	1,715	21,125	289	13,330	1,138	1,260	13,443	699
2001-2	36,037	4,729	4,911	33,470	2,842	20,023	1,488	1,405	19,926	303	12,959	1,045	1,112	13,064	661
2002-3[1]	32,508	4,121	4,009	31,248	1,974	18,718	1,585	1,540	18,707	269	12,017	914	987	12,144	607
2003-4[2]	39,428	5,414	5,172	36,539	1,866	21,903	2,382	2,193	21,745	238	14,085	1,323	1,259	14,067	561
2004-5[3]	43,027	5,910	5,632	39,447	2,930	23,589	2,015	1,825	23,348	289	15,168	1,389	1,316	15,092	564

[1] Preliminary.   [2] Estimate.   [3] Forecast.   *Source: Economic Research Service, U.S. Department of Agriculture (ERS-USDA); The Oil World*

Salient Statistics of Canola and Canola Oil in the United States   In Thousands of Metric Tons

	Canola							Canola Oil						
	Supply				Disappearance			Supply				Disappearance		
Year	Stocks June 1	Pro-duction	Imports	Total	Crush	Exports	Total[3]	Stocks June 1	Pro-duction	Imports	Total	Domestic	Exports	Total
1997-8	36	355	355	746	589	126	715	30	205	504	739	529	158	687
1998-9	19	710	310	1,039	698	246	944	52	250	503	805	603	123	726
1999-00	77	621	242	940	722	136	858	79	281	534	894	669	129	798
2000-1	50	909	217	1,176	773	220	993	96	292	545	933	797	85	882
2001-2	39	908	125	1,072	757	218	975	51	265	503	819	679	116	795
2002-3	68	697	197	962	575	287	862	24	226	445	695	587	73	660
2003-4[1]	72	686	243	1,001	630	304	934	35	249	555	839	671	126	797
2004-5[2]	40	613	350	1,003	701	219	920	42	255	553	850	714	95	809

[1] Preliminary.   [2] Forecast.   [3] Includes planting seed and residual.   *Source: Economic Research Service, U.S. Department of Agriculture*

Wholesale Price of Canola Oil in Midwest[2]   In Cents Per Pound

Year	Jan.	Feb.	Mar.	Apr.	May	June	July	Aug.	Sept.	Oct.	Nov.	Dec.	Average
1996	50.75	50.75	50.75	50.75	50.75	50.75	50.75	50.75	50.75	60.56	90.00	90.00	58.11
1997	90.00	90.00	90.00	90.00	90.00	90.00	90.00	90.00	90.00	82.00	82.00	82.00	88.00
1998	28.00	29.00	30.30	30.58	31.13	28.45	28.44	26.85	29.75	28.20	27.19	26.10	28.67
1999	25.31	21.44	20.69	21.50	20.38	20.58	19.33	19.75	19.25	18.44	18.19	17.95	20.23
2000	17.31	16.50	17.25	18.69	17.75	16.45	15.50	15.69	15.60	15.00	15.31	15.50	16.38
2001	14.81	15.19	16.69	16.69	18.00	19.25	22.50	21.80	19.94	19.00	20.56	21.88	18.86
2002	20.81	21.31	27.44	21.94	21.95	23.19	25.06	28.45	29.81	30.75	34.19	41.19	27.17
2003[1]	24.30	28.88	27.63	27.44	28.13	27.13	26.56	26.30	28.44				27.20

[1] Preliminary.   [2] Data prior to 1998 are for Refined (Denatured), in Tanks in New York
Source: Economic Research Service, U.S. Department of Agriculture (ERS-USDA)

Average Price of Canola in Vancouver   In Canadian Dollars Per Metric Ton

Year	Jan.	Feb.	Mar.	Apr.	May	June	July	Aug.	Sept.	Oct.	Nov.	Dec.	Average
1997	441.96	441.68	457.95	448.09	446.00	428.47	395.58	400.68	390.38	398.81	419.12	410.21	423.24
1998	416.48	428.88	434.68	441.44	450.56	443.11	404.86	387.05	389.34	400.40	412.17	417.41	418.87
1999	402.74	368.17	363.24	362.16	353.21	356.53	317.36	305.73	302.93	302.68	297.76	287.62	335.01
2000	286.09	277.92	280.97	287.34	284.59	274.12	265.32	262.24	269.17	265.32	267.75	278.59	274.95
2001	279.07	285.05	302.04	299.59	310.00	320.79	356.98	368.33	351.01	332.16	328.99	334.53	322.38
2002	329.23	328.38	329.39	316.74	318.67	330.21	369.42	401.78	408.43	413.64	436.25	418.74	366.74
2003	396.78	380.81	351.97	362.89	344.59	333.48	322.64	319.37	324.07	338.93	343.65	338.57	346.48
2004	345.51	370.53	402.02	395.92	384.09	378.62	360.93	349.57	341.29	288.64	275.37	265.15	346.47

Source: Winnipeg Commodity Exchange (WCE)

Average Wholesale Price of Canola Meal, 36% Pacific Northwest   In Dollars Per Short Ton

Crop Year	Oct.	Nov.	Dec.	Jan.	Feb.	Mar.	Apr.	May	June	July	Aug.	Sept.	Average
1997-8	----	----	----	----	----	----	----	----	----	----	----	----	131.15
1998-9	----	----	----	----	----	----	----	----	----	----	----	----	112.28
1999-00	----	----	----	----	----	----	----	----	----	----	----	----	117.07
2000-1	122.58	132.30	142.34	140.53	132.90	132.01	140.25	144.00	149.30	154.29	142.60	137.27	139.20
2001-2	142.85	142.44	129.48	135.34	137.33	150.15	146.60	141.90	142.10	153.40	149.10	149.30	143.33
2002-3	131.50	134.70	142.17	154.10	155.80	147.55	145.60	148.50	146.95	137.10	135.50	149.20	144.06
2003-4	169.65	187.19	181.35	201.07	205.50	228.65	214.40	200.03	189.00	192.09	146.99	145.55	188.46
2004-5[1]	133.39	138.81	135.13	129.21									134.14

[1] Preliminary.   *Source: Economic Research Service, U.S. Department of Agriculture (ERS-USDA)*

Cassava

Cassava is a perennial woody shrub with an edible root. Cassava, which is also called manioc, mandioca, or yucca, grows in tropical and subtropical areas of the world. Cassava has been known since the 1500s and originates in Latin America. The cassava's starchy roots are a major source of dietary energy for more than 500 million people. Cassava is the highest producer of carbohydrates among staple crops, and it ranks fourth in food crops in developing countries. The leaves of the cassava plant are also edible and are relatively rich in protein and vitamins A and B.

Cassava is drought-tolerant and needs less soil preparation and weeding than other crops. Because cassava can be stored in the ground for up to 3 years, it also serves as a reserve food when other crops fail. The cassava is propagated by cuttings of the woody stem, thereby resulting in a low multiplication rate compared to crops propagated by true seeds.

One problem with cassava is the poisonous cyanides, which need to be destroyed before consumption. The cyanide content differs with each variety of cassava, but higher cyanide is usually correlated to high yields. The cyanide content can be destroyed through heat and various processing methods such as grating, sun drying, and fermenting.

Cassava is the primary source of tapioca. Cassava is also eaten raw or boiled, and is processed into livestock feed, starch and glucose, flour, and pharmaceuticals. One species of cassava has been successfully grown for its rubber.

Prices – The price of tapioca (hard pellets, FOB Rotterdam) rose by 19% in the first quarter of 2004 to an 8-year high of $130 per metric ton from $110 per metric ton in 2003. The 2004 price was 55% higher than the trough of $82 in 2001.

Supply – World production of cassava in 2002, the latest full reporting year for that series, rose by +0.9% to 184.853 million metric tons from 183,289 million in 2001. The world's largest producers of cassava in 2002 were Nigeria (with 18.7% of world production), Brazil (12.5%), Thailand (9.1%), and Indonesia (9.0%).

Trade – World exports of tapioca in 2003 rose +33% to 4.717 million metric tons from 3,555 million in 2002. Thailand accounted for 85% of world exports in 2003, followed by Vietnam with 13% of world exports and Indonesia with 1%. The world's two main importers of tapioca in 2003 were China with 51% of world imports and the European Union with 40% of world imports.

World Cassava Production   In Thousands of Metric Tons

Year	Brazil	China	Ghana	India	Indo-nesia	Mozam-bique	Nigeria	Para-guay	Tan-zania	Thailand	Uganda	Congo	World Total
1995	25,423	3,501	6,612	5,929	15,442	4,178	31,404	3,054	5,969	17,388	2,224	17,500	165,436
1996	24,584	3,601	7,111	5,443	17,002	4,734	31,418	2,648	5,992	17,388	2,245	18,000	164,711
1997	24,305	3,651	7,000	5,868	15,134	5,337	30,409	3,155	5,700	18,084	2,291	16,973	164,373
1998	19,503	3,701	7,227	6,000	14,696	5,639	32,695	3,300	6,128	15,591	3,204	17,060	162,856
1999	20,864	3,751	7,845	6,700	16,438	5,353	32,697	3,694	7,182	16,507	4,875	16,500	171,918
2000	23,336	3,801	8,107	6,800	16,089	5,362	32,010	2,719	7,120	19,064	4,966	15,959	178,567
2001	22,479	3,851	8,966	6,900	17,055	5,400	32,586	3,568	6,884	18,396	5,265	15,436	183,289
2002[1]	23,108	3,851	9,731	6,900	16,723	5,400	34,476	4,142	6,888	16,870	5,300	14,929	184,853

[1] Estimate.   *Source: Food and Agriculture Organization of the United Nations (FAO-UN)*

Prices of Tapioca, Hard Pellets, F.O.B. Rotterdam   U.S. Dollars Per Tonne

Year	Jan.	Feb.	Mar.	Apr.	May	June	July	Aug.	Sept.	Oct.	Nov.	Dec.	Average
1996	167	160	155	158	163	154	149	154	146	139	140	133	152
1997	133	118	112	108	114	110	100	97	100	102	102	100	108
1998	96	100	98	104	106	104	105	106	112	122	124	109	107
1999	104	102	101	102	108	104	99	102	100	99	100	97	102
2000	94	90	88	92	85	88	88	81	78	74	76	79	84
2001	83	80	77	78	80	82	84	84	87	83	84	84	82
2002	86	82	82	84	87	91	96	97	95	93	93	89	90
2003	91	92	95	96	101	101	103	108	114	134	138	143	110
2004	138	132	121	118									127

Source: The Oil World

World Trade in Tapioca   In Thousands of Metric Tons

	Exports					Imports						
Year	China	Indonesia	Thailand	Viet Nam	Total World Exports	China	EC-12[2]	Japan	Rep. of Korea	United States	Former USSR	Total World Imports
1996	11	389	3,607	1	4,052	75	3,321	22	554	----	----	4,174
1997	11	247	4,155	68	4,519	242	3,413	15	585	----	----	4,605
1998	10	221	3,199	87	3,555	250	2,620	19	463	----	----	3,536
1999	10	340	4,341	117	4,857	381	3,781	18	212	----	----	4,501
2000	10	151	3,915	215	4,334	170	3,765	19	292	----	----	4,543
2001	10	177	4,494	409	5,140	1,950	2,728	20	445	----	----	5,288
2002	----	130	3,067	308	3,555	1,760	1,576	14	157	----	----	3,605
2003[1]	----	42	3,994	629	4,717	2,368	1,869	21	247	----	----	4,655

[1] Estimate.   [2] Intra-EU trade is excluded.   *Source: The Oil World*

Castor Beans

Castor bean plants are native to the Ethiopian region of tropical east Africa. The seeds of the castor bean are used to produce castor oil. The average castor bean seed contains 35% to 55% oil. The oil is removed from the bean seeds by either pressing or solvent extraction. Castor oil is used in many products. In the US, the paint and varnish industry is the single largest market for castor oil. Castor oil is also used for coating fabrics, insulation, cosmetics, skin emollients, hair oils, inks, nylon plastics, greases, and hydraulic fluids.

Ricin is found in all parts of the castor bean plant, but the most concentrated amounts are found in the cake by-product after oil extraction. Ricin is one of the most deadly, naturally occurring poisons known. Ricin received attention when it was used in a subway attack in Japan in 1995 and again when it was sent to a Congressional office in an envelope in February 2004. One non-deadly use for ricin is for medical research where it is being studied for use as a potential treatment for cancer.

Supply – World production of castor-seed beans in the 2003/04 marketing year rose by +12.6% to 1.080 million metric tons from the 16-year low of 959,000 metric tons in 2002/03. The world's largest producer of castor-seed beans by far is India with 62% of world production in 2003 at 670,000 metric tons. The second and third largest producers are China with 24% of world production (258,000 metric tons) and Brazil with 7% of world production (78,000 metric tons).

Demand – US consumption of castor oil in 2003/04 recovered by 12% to 23.546 million pounds from the multi-decade low of 20.971 million pounds in 2002/03. Still, US consumption of castor oil is down by about one-half from 1999/2000.

World Production of Castorseed Beans   In Thousands of Metric Tons

Crop Year	Brazil	China	Ecuador	India	Mexico	Paraguay	Pakistan	Philip-pines	Sudan	Tanzania	Thailand	Former U.S.S.R.	World Total
1997-8	97	180	4	829	2	16	5	4	1	3	11	2	1,189
1998-9	17	230	4	840	1	19	6	4	1	3	7	2	1,168
1999-00	33	250	4	910	1	8	3	4	1	3	7	2	1,261
2000-1	116	300	4	867	1	11	1	4	1	3	9	2	1,353
2001-2[1]	100	260	4	610	1	13	2	4	1	3	9	2	1,043
2002-3[2]	72	265	4	550	1	12	2	4	1	3	9	2	959
2003-4[3]	78	258	4	670	1	13	2	4	1	3	9	2	1,080

[1] Preliminary.   [2] Estimate.   [3] Forecast.   *Sources: Foreign Agricultural Service, U.S. Department of Agriculture (FAS-USDA); The Oil World*

Castor Oil Consumption[2] in the United States   In Thousands of Pounds

Year	Oct.	Nov.	Dec.	Jan.	Feb.	Mar.	Apr.	May	June	July	Aug.	Sept.	Total
1998-9	2,348	3,579	3,740	3,323	4,197	5,004	5,218	4,639	4,396	4,471	4,465	4,494	49,874
1999-00	4,281	3,917	4,682	3,819	4,328	5,346	4,135	3,341	4,268	3,884	4,257	4,573	50,831
2000-1	2,694	4,601	2,386	3,975	2,896	3,209	3,159	3,840	3,112	3,050	4,686	2,257	39,865
2001-2	4,127	2,346	1,650	3,012	3,703	3,129	3,062	3,096	1,243	2,992	2,872	2,867	34,099
2002-3	3,281	1,887	1,528	1,641	1,642	1,629	1,123	1,315	1,518	1,839	1,449	2,119	20,971
2003-4	2,072	1,836	1,779	1,526	1,251	2,241	2,396	2,250	1,905	1,542	2,382	2,366	23,546
2004-5[1]	2,155	1,391	1,581										20,508

[1] Preliminary.   [2] In inedible products (Resins, Plastics, etc.).   *Source: Bureau of the Census, U.S. Department of Commerce*

Castor Oil Stocks in the United States, on First of Month   In Thousands of Pounds

Year	Oct.	Nov.	Dec.	Jan.	Feb.	Mar.	Apr.	May	June	July	Aug.	Sept.
1998-9	40,018	46,809	36,881	35,668	31,961	22,252	13,771	11,950	5,568	13,952	34,956	25,944
1999-00	44,427	34,180	31,191	44,315	36,632	26,885	25,486	27,605	39,038	38,118	42,934	31,015
2000-1	32,585	35,858	30,058	24,728	32,566	35,186	24,808	51,808	57,910	48,415	40,279	59,461
2001-2	53,083	45,933	23,973	38,459	31,058	36,743	39,591	39,528	43,227	50,814	49,283	53,075
2002-3	41,322	37,282	33,195	32,983	25,926	20,551	22,460	15,337	23,212	24,138	32,110	27,827
2003-4	26,463	17,753	16,630	18,582	14,097	13,985	7,507	22,751	W	25,593	18,381	14,922
2004-5[1]	34,525	31,608	24,287	19,476								

[1] Preliminary.   *Source: Bureau of the Census, U.S. Department of Commerce*

Average Wholesale Price of Castor Oil No. 1, Brazilian Tanks in New York   In Cents Per Pound

Year	Jan.	Feb.	Mar.	Apr.	May	June	July	Aug.	Sept.	Oct.	Nov.	Dec.	Average
1997	41.50	41.50	41.50	41.50	41.50	41.50	41.50	41.50	41.50	41.50	41.50	41.50	41.50
1998	41.50	41.50	41.50	41.50	41.50	48.00	48.00	48.00	48.00	48.00	48.00	48.00	45.29
1999	48.00	48.00	48.00	48.00	48.00	48.00	48.00	48.00	48.00	48.00	48.00	48.00	48.00
2000	47.00	47.00	47.00	47.00	47.00	47.00	47.00	48.00	48.00	48.00	48.00	48.00	47.42
2001	48.00	48.00	48.00	48.00	48.00	48.00	48.00	48.00	48.00	48.00	47.50	47.50	47.92
2002	47.50	47.50	47.50	47.50	47.50	47.50	47.00	47.00	47.00	47.00	47.00	47.00	47.25
2003	47.00	47.00	47.00	47.00	47.00	47.00	47.00	47.00	47.00				47.00

Source: Foreign Agricultural Service, U.S. Department of Agriculture (FAS-USDA)

Cattle and Calves

The beef cycle begins with the cow-calf operation, which breeds the new calves. Most ranchers breed their herds of cows in summer, thus producing the new crop of calves in spring (the gestation period is about nine months). This allows the calves to be born during the milder weather of spring and provides the calves with ample forage through the summer and early autumn. The calves are weaned from the mother after 6-8 months and most are then moved into the "stocker" operation. The calves usually spend 6-10 months in the stocker operation, growing to near full-sized by foraging for summer grass or winter wheat. When the cattle reach 600-800 pounds, they are typically sent to a feedlot and become "feeder cattle". In the feedlot, the cattle are fed a special food mix to encourage rapid weight gain. The mix includes grain (corn, milo, or wheat), a protein supplement (soybean, cottonseed, or linseed meal), and roughage (alfalfa, silage, prairie hay, or an agricultural by-product such as sugar beet pulp). The animal is considered "finished" when it reaches full weight and is ready for slaughter, typically at around 1,200 pounds, which produces a dressed carcass of around 745 pounds. After reaching full weight, the cattle are sold for slaughter to a meat packing plant. Futures and options on live cattle and feeder cattle are traded at the Chicago Mercantile Exchange. Both the live and feeder cattle futures contracts trade in terms of cents per pound.

Prices – Live cattle prices in 2004 were generally strong, recovering from the plunge seen in December 2003 when a cow from a Washington state dairy farm was found to have mad cow disease. Live cattle prices ended 2004 at 89.85 cents per pound, up 16.5% yr/yr from 77.20 cents at the end of 2003. Live cattle prices in 2004 remained below the all-time record high of 104.25 cents per pound posted in November 2003. Live cattle prices were able to remain strong in 2004 mainly because of continued strong demand from US consumers, which was able to counteract the negative impact of the ban on US beef exports from Japan and other key Asian countries that remained in place through all through 2004. The US and Japan in 2004 reached a framework agreement to allow resumption of US beef exports to Japan of beef from cattle under 20 months old, but Japan dragged its feet on implementing that agreement and resumption of US beef exports wasn't expected to resume until mid or late 2005. Live cattle prices were also supported in 2004 by the fact that the US maintained its ban on live cattle imports from Canada all through 2004 (that ban was due to be lifted March 7, 2004).

Supply – The world cattle and buffalo figures (as of Jan 1) showed a small +0.5% increase in 2004 to 1.019 billion head, which is just slightly above the 4-decade low of 1.014 billion head seen in 2003. As of January 1, 2004 there were 94.882 million cattle and calves on US farms, down – 1.3% yr/yr and the lowest level since 1959. World production of beef and veal in 2004 rose +1.2% to 50.660 million metric tons (carcass weight equivalent). The world's largest beef producers are the US with 11.206 million metric tons of production in 2004, followed by the European Union (8.035 million metric tons), Brazil (7.830 million metric tons), and China (6.683 million metric tons). US commercial production of beef fell by –6.6% yr/yr in 2004 to 24.498 billion pounds, which was a 10-year low.

Demand – World consumption of beef and veal in 2004 rose slightly by +0.4% yr/yr to 49.206 million metric tons. US consumption of beef and veal in 2004 rose +2.0% yr/yr to 12.582 million metric tons. The other key consumers of beef are the European Union (8.175 million metric tons in 2004), China (6.648 million metric tons), and Brazil (6.415 million metric tons).

Trade – US imports and exports of live cattle fell sharply in 2004 due to mad cow disease in North America and various import and export bans. US imports of cattle in 2004 (through Q3) fell by –31.0% yr/yr to an annualized 1.209 million head, and US exports of cattle in 2004 (through Q3) plunged by –63.7% yr/yr to 36,439 head. By weight, US imports of beef in 2004 rose +18.1% yr/yr to 3.551 billion pounds, which was a record high. US exports of beef in 2004 plunged by –82.4% yr/yr to 443 million pounds, which was sharply below the 2.518 billion pound level seen before mad cow hit in December 2003 and largely shut down US beef exports. The key countries to which the US normally exports its beef are Japan, South Korea, Mexico, and Canada.

World Cattle and Buffalo Numbers as of January 1   In Thousands of Head

Year	Argentina	Australia	Brazil	China	Colombia	France	Germany	India	Mexico	Russia	Ukraine	United States	World Total (Mil. Head)
1996	53,569	26,500	149,228	104,000	18,478	20,662	15,890	296,462	28,140	39,700	17,558	103,548	1,048
1997	51,696	26,780	146,110	110,318	19,038	20,557	15,760	299,802	26,822	35,800	15,313	101,656	1,043
1998	49,238	26,710	144,670	121,757	19,507	20,154	15,227	303,030	25,628	31,500	12,579	99,744	1,043
1999	49,437	26,688	143,893	124,354	20,621	20,097	14,942	306,967	24,859	28,600	11,722	99,115	1,041
2000	49,832	27,588	146,272	126,983	21,700	20,197	14,657	312,572	23,715	27,000	10,627	98,198	1,045
2001	50,167	27,720	150,382	128,663	22,676	20,518	14,557	313,774	22,551	25,500	9,424	97,298	1,044
2002	50,369	27,870	156,314	128,242	23,757			317,000	21,296	24,510	9,433	96,723	1,051
2003	50,869	27,479	161,463	130,848				323,000	20,519	23,500	9,108	96,100	1,018
2004[1]	50,768	26,600	165,492	134,672				327,250	19,524	22,285	7,886	94,882	1,022
2005[2]	49,066	26,600	169,583	138,712				330,250	17,684	20,995	6,780	94,725	1,024

[1] Preliminary.   [2] Forecast.   *Source: Foreign Agricultural Service, U.S. Department of Agriculture (FAS-USDA)*

Cattle Supply and Distribution in the United States   In Thousands of Head

Year	Cattle & Calves on Farms January 1	Imports	Calves Born	Total Supply	Livestock Slaughter - Cattle and Calves					Total Slaughter	Deaths on Farms	Exports	Total Disap- pearance
					Commercial								
					Federally Inspected	Other[3]	All Commercial		Farm				
1995	102,755	2,786	40,264	145,805	36,272	798	37,069		225	37,294	4,382	95	41,771
1996	103,548	1,965	39,823	145,336	37,435	917	38,351		224	38,575	4,572	174	43,321
1997	101,656	2,046	38,961	142,663	37,101	792	37,893		218	38,111	4,676	282	43,069
1998	99,744	2,034	38,812	140,590	36,209	714	36,923		215	37,138	4,210	285	41,633
1999	99,115	1,945	38,796	139,856	36,737	695	37,432		210	37,642	4,114	329	42,085
2000	98,198	2,187	38,631	139,016	36,720	658	37,378		210	37,588	4,097	481	42,166
2001	97,277	2,437	38,280	137,994	35,752	625	36,377		200	36,577	4,209	678	41,464
2002	96,704	2,503	38,224	137,431	36,140	641	36,780		190	36,970	4,076	243	41,289
2003[1]	96,100	1,752	37,903	135,754	35,883	611	36,494		192	36,686		100	
2004[2]	94,888	1,375	37,625	133,888	32,981	585	33,566					30	

[1] Preliminary.   [2] Estimate.   [3] Wholesale and retail.   *Source: Economic Research Service, U.S. Department of Agriculture (ERS-USDA)*

Beef Supply and Utilization in the United States

Year/ Quarter	Beginning Stocks	Production		Imports	Total Supply	Exports	Ending Stocks	Total Disap- pearance	Per Capita Disappearance	
		Commercial	Total						Carcass Weight	Retail Weight
		Million Pounds							Pounds	
2000	314	26,777	28,244	3,031	31,259	2,468	402			69.5
I	314	6,653	6,967	720	7,687	540	369			17.2
II	367	6,699	7,066	820	7,886	565	374			17.5
III	380	6,914	7,294	775	8,069	625	378			18.0
IV	406	6,511	6,917	700	7,617	620	412			16.7
2001		26,107	26,107	3,164	29,268	2,269				66.2
I		6,182	6,182	785	6,967	569				16.1
II		6,502	6,502	839	7,341	509				16.8
III		6,723	6,723	848	7,571	583				17.0
IV		6,700	6,700	689	7,389	610				16.3
2002		27,090	27,090	3,218	30,308	2,447				67.6
I		6,377	6,377	737	7,114	572				16.2
II		6,833	6,833	934	7,767	601				17.5
III		7,097	7,097	839	7,936	662				17.3
IV		6,783	6,783	708	7,491	612				16.6
2003[1]		26,238	26,238	3,006	29,244	2,518				64.9
I		6,282	6,282	810	7,092	582				16.2
II		6,902	6,902	741	7,643	678				16.9
III		7,081	7,081	619	7,700	680				16.9
IV		5,973	5,973	836	6,809	578				15.0
2004[2]		24,544	24,544	3,679	28,223	461				66.0
I		5,834	5,834	873	6,707	36				16.0
II		6,254	6,254	929	7,183	120				16.9
III		6,360	6,360	940	7,300	138				16.9
IV		6,096	6,096	937	7,033	167				16.2

[1] Preliminary.   [2] Forecast.   *Source: Economic Research Service, U.S. Department of Agriculture (ERS-USDA)*

United States Cattle on Feed in 13 States   In Thousands of Head

Year/ Quarter	Number on Feed[3]	Placed on Feed	Marketings	Other Disappearance	Year/ Quarter	Number on Feed[3]	Placed on Feed	Marketings	Other Disappearance
2001	11,798	24,092	23,401	924	2003[1]	10,658	24,930	23,467	868
I	11,798	5,685	5,703	257	I	10,658	5,771	5,508	208
II	11,523	5,888	6,133	267	II	10,713	5,849	6,450	189
III	11,011	6,331	6,058	159	III	9,923	6,855	6,377	183
IV	11,125	6,188	5,507	241	IV	10,218	6,455	5,132	288
2002	11,565	23,576	23,637	846	2004[2]	11,253	23,259	22,281	917
I	11,565	5,952	5,709	221	I	11,253	5,168	5,433	230
II	11,587	5,374	6,243	211	II	10,748	5,609	5,999	246
III	10,507	6,262	6,176	141	III	10,117	6,204	5,649	175
IV	10,452	5,988	5,509	273	IV	10,497	6,278	5,200	266

[1] Preliminary.   [2] Estimate.   [3] Beginning of period.   *Source: Economic Research Service, U.S. Department of Agriculture (ERS-USDA)*

CATTLE AND CALVES

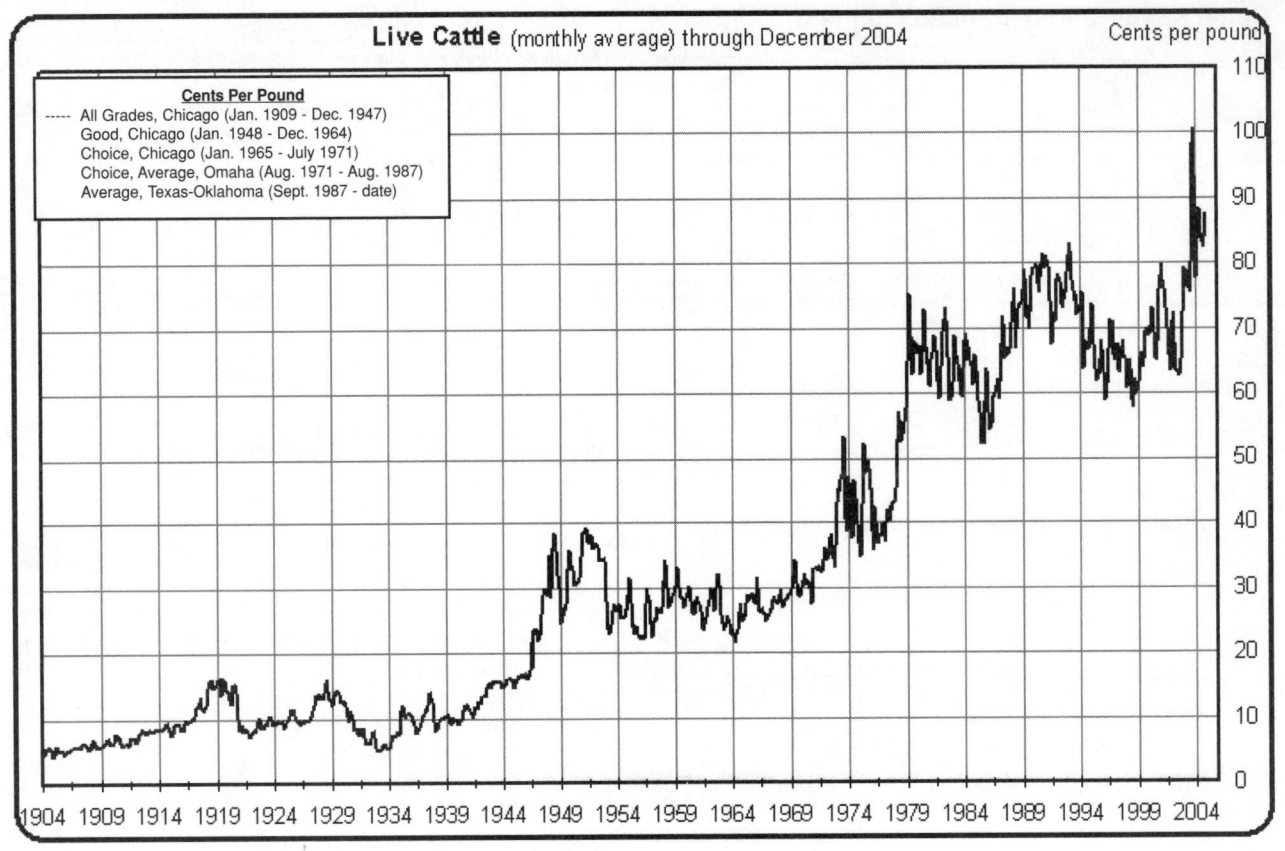

Live Cattle (monthly average) through December 2004 — Cents per pound

Cents Per Pound
----- All Grades, Chicago (Jan. 1909 - Dec. 1947)
Good, Chicago (Jan. 1948 - Dec. 1964)
Choice, Chicago (Jan. 1965 - July 1971)
Choice, Average, Omaha (Aug. 1971 - Aug. 1987)
Average, Texas-Oklahoma (Sept. 1987 - date)

United States Cattle on Feed, 1000+ Capacity Feedlots[2], on First of Month   In Thousands of Head

Year	Jan.	Feb.	Mar.	Apr.	May	June	July	Aug.	Sept.	Oct.	Nov.	Dec.
1995	8,031	8,119	8,227	8,328	8,233	8,182	7,734	7,391	7,189	7,722	8,420	8,685
1996	8,667	8,304	8,152	8,286	7,758	7,253	6,578	6,337	6,612	7,486	8,534	9,003
1997	8,943	8,813	8,769	8,904	8,484	8,231	7,679	7,536	7,850	8,558	9,390	9,718
1998	9,455	9,180	8,835	8,607	8,295	8,289	7,825	7,706	7,750	8,376	9,190	9,404
1999	9,021	8,917	8,878	8,899	8,583	8,547	8,183	7,889	8,185	8,793	9,789	10,020
2000	9,752	9,885	9,695	9,593	9,391	9,411	8,959	8,812	8,972	9,502	10,192	10,213
2001	11,798	11,941	11,695	11,523	11,170	11,245	11,011	10,891	10,855	11,125	11,863	11,891
2002	11,565	11,572	11,518	11,587	10,971	10,990	10,507	10,109	10,159	10,452	10,785	10,946
2003	10,658	10,700	10,546	10,713	10,535	10,539	9,923	9,590	9,839	10,218	11,043	11,335
2004[1]	11,253	11,138	10,977	10,748	10,360	10,625	10,117	9,853	9,973	10,497	11,334	11,334

[1] Preliminary.   [2] 7 States through 2000.   *Source: Economic Research Service, U.S. Department of Agriculture (ERS-USDA)*

United States Cattle Placed on Feed, 1000+ Capacity Feedlots[2]   In Thousands of Head

Year	Jan.	Feb.	Mar.	Apr.	May	June	July	Aug.	Sept.	Oct.	Nov.	Dec.	Total
1995	1,631	1,532	1,681	1,403	1,673	1,356	1,404	1,653	2,173	2,278	1,804	1,446	20,034
1996	1,312	1,441	1,666	1,150	1,242	1,068	1,483	1,965	2,267	2,536	1,953	1,423	19,506
1997	1,663	1,552	1,694	1,296	1,612	1,224	1,751	2,111	2,278	2,454	1,826	1,304	20,765
1998	1,492	1,290	1,421	1,358	1,740	1,314	1,677	1,773	2,254	2,396	1,732	1,250	19,697
1999	1,681	1,563	1,741	1,443	1,733	1,515	1,565	2,085	2,345	2,629	1,823	1,408	21,531
2000	1,931	1,606	1,736	1,470	1,998	1,413	1,674	2,091	2,286	2,387	1,678	1,440	21,710
2001	2,263	1,580	1,842	1,551	2,372	1,965	1,986	2,204	2,141	2,702	1,908	1,578	24,092
2002	2,179	1,810	1,963	1,463	2,267	1,644	1,840	2,228	2,194	2,396	1,982	1,610	23,576
2003	2,089	1,650	2,032	1,870	2,307	1,672	1,997	2,384	2,474	2,781	1,926	1,748	24,930
2004[1]	1,754	1,610	1,804	1,598	2,367	1,644	1,720	2,099	2,385	2,701	1,743	1,834	23,259

[1] Preliminary.   [2] 7 States through 2000.   *Source: Economic Research Service, U.S. Department of Agriculture (ERS-USDA)*

24

Live Cattle Futures - Chicago Mercantile Exchange
(weekly close) as of December 31, 2004
Cents per pound

United States Cattle Marketings, 1000+ Capacity Feedlots[2]   In Thousands of Head

Year	Jan.	Feb.	Mar.	Apr.	May	June	July	Aug.	Sept.	Oct.	Nov.	Dec.	Total
1995	1,484	1,372	1,513	1,437	1,667	1,754	1,698	1,815	1,594	1,529	1,478	1,412	18,753
1996	1,626	1,541	1,476	1,613	1,747	1,696	1,678	1,653	1,342	1,431	1,418	1,415	18,636
1997	1,728	1,554	1,497	1,648	1,785	1,732	1,852	1,755	1,528	1,545	1,429	1,499	19,552
1998	1,689	1,579	1,580	1,609	1,681	1,727	1,755	1,687	1,577	1,537	1,455	1,564	19,440
1999	1,738	1,560	1,668	1,681	1,696	1,835	1,816	1,747	1,682	1,570	1,530	1,601	20,124
2000	1,747	1,749	1,764	1,601	1,863	1,828	1,784	1,895	1,708	1,647	1,568	1,500	20,654
2001	2,042	1,745	1,916	1,815	2,196	2,122	2,047	2,186	1,825	1,896	1,800	1,811	23,401
2002	2,083	1,801	1,825	1,996	2,171	2,076	2,193	2,135	1,848	1,979	1,731	1,799	23,637
2003	1,972	1,733	1,803	1,985	2,238	2,227	2,270	2,075	2,032	1,855	1,537	1,740	23,467
2004[1]	1,775	1,692	1,966	1,889	2,023	2,082	1,926	1,923	1,800	1,798	1,625	1,777	22,276

[1] Preliminary.   [2] 7 States through 2000.   *Source: Economic Research Service, U.S. Department of Agriculture (ERS-USDA)*

Quarterly Trade of Live Cattle in the United States   In Head

	Imports					Exports				
Year	First Quarter	Second Quarter	Third Quarter	Fourth Quarter	Annual	First Quarter	Second Quarter	Third Quarter	Fourth Quarter	Annual
1995	868,694	804,686	488,515	624,350	2,786,245	26,597	18,441	19,794	29,716	94,548
1996	605,648	467,059	391,633	501,108	1,965,448	33,906	42,796	42,757	54,848	174,307
1997	494,637	500,052	423,838	627,825	2,046,352	63,217	58,153	81,095	79,879	282,344
1998	538,018	503,547	373,451	618,993	2,034,009	69,824	63,459	53,145	98,781	285,209
1999	549,847	424,182	313,211	657,836	1,945,076	51,830	59,195	47,049	171,245	329,319
2000	580,174	537,009	346,087	724,016	2,187,286	117,889	67,895	72,028	223,430	481,242
2001	700,239	612,645	444,637	679,194	2,436,715	111,549	75,152	297,069	194,683	678,453
2002	785,559	398,072	474,128	845,214	2,502,973	73,401	62,140	49,930	57,472	242,943
2003	630,303	408,833	142,780	569,669	1,751,585	38,246	34,145	10,953	16,926	100,270
2004[1]	309,712	315,800	281,020	468,621	1,375,153	4,091	20,955	2,216	2,709	29,971

[1] Preliminary.   *Source: Economic Research Service, U.S. Department of Agriculture (ERS-USDA)*

CATTLE AND CALVES

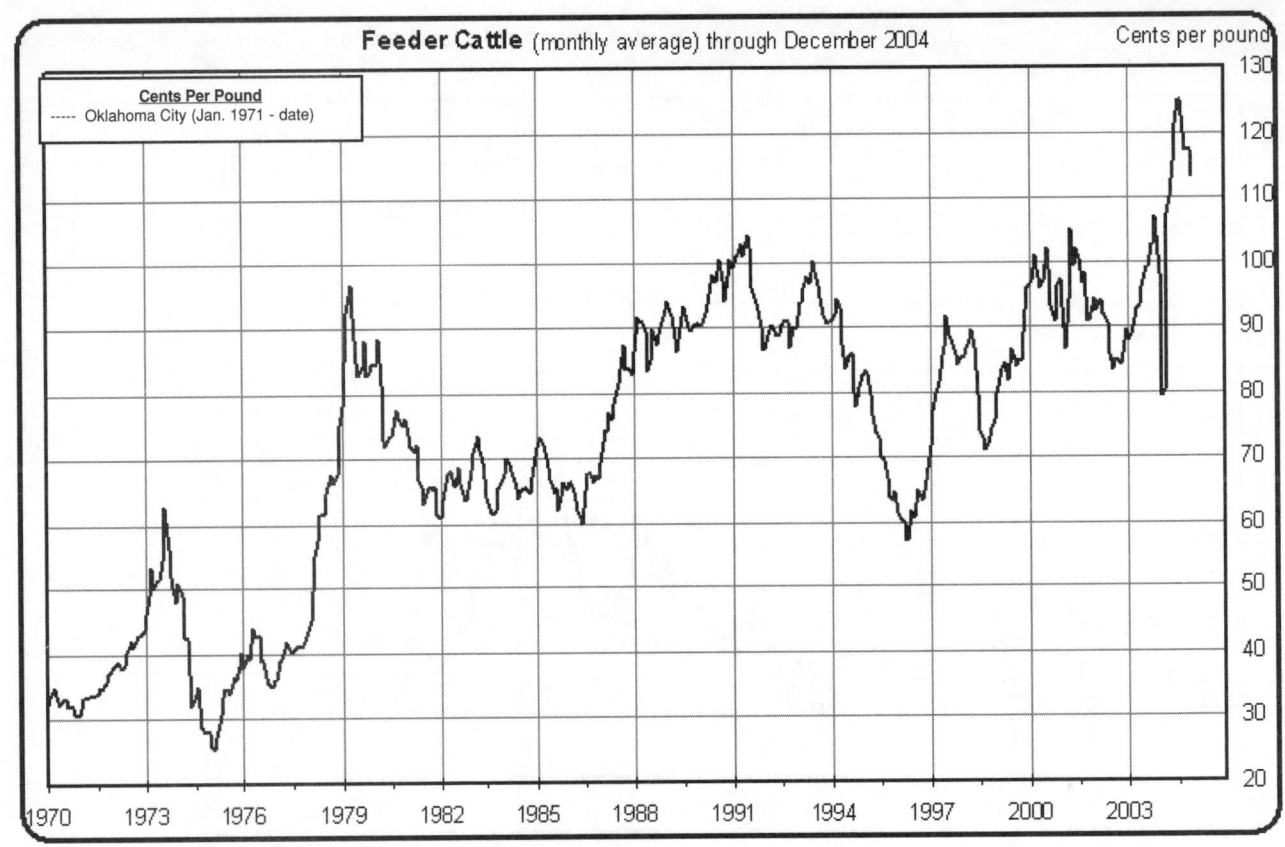

Feeder Cattle (monthly average) through December 2004   Cents per pound

Cents Per Pound
----- Oklahoma City (Jan. 1971 - date)

Average Slaughter Steer Price, Choice 2-4, Texas, 1100-1300 Lb.   In Dollars Per 100 Pounds

Year	Jan.	Feb.	Mar.	Apr.	May	June	July	Aug.	Sept.	Oct.	Nov.	Dec.	Average
1998	64.57	60.77	64.52	65.00	64.52	63.85	60.28	60.00	57.93	61.54	62.23	59.97	62.10
1999	61.46	63.17	64.75	65.34	65.00	66.15	64.51	65.29	66.05	69.63	70.28	69.01	65.89
2000	69.07	68.88	71.74	73.13	71.28	69.41	67.22	65.02	65.43	68.51	72.19	76.41	69.86
2001	78.79	79.40	79.44	76.50	74.93	72.64	70.71	69.07	68.75	66.30	63.60	63.62	71.98
2002	67.25	70.72	72.59	67.79	65.32	63.64	62.49	62.96	64.43	64.93	70.12	72.24	67.04
2003	77.18	78.77	77.52	79.24	79.50	76.73	76.89	81.74	90.59	105.50	101.88	90.75	84.69
2004	80.36	79.15	86.96	87.04	88.22	89.19	84.27	84.15	82.33	84.03	84.64	86.60	84.75

Source: Economic Research Service, U.S. Department of Agriculture (ERS-USDA)

Average Price of Feeder Steers in Oklahoma City   In Dollars Per 100 Pounds

Year	Jan.	Feb.	Mar.	Apr.	May	June	July	Aug.	Sept.	Oct.	Nov.	Dec.	Average
1998	85.58	86.53	87.87	89.46	86.84	79.54	74.13	72.72	71.13	71.85	74.24	75.71	79.63
1999	79.49	80.92	83.21	84.44	81.80	84.37	86.80	83.84	85.24	84.75	89.13	95.92	84.99
2000	96.49	97.21	101.16	99.01	95.88	97.01	102.11	99.05	93.41	90.84	96.19	97.40	97.15
2001	93.08	86.63	94.17	105.06	99.71	102.16	100.39	96.74	98.31	91.06	90.83	94.51	96.05
2002	92.43	93.66	94.06	91.76	90.78	85.68	83.29	85.19	84.71	84.23	85.69	89.43	88.41
2003	87.76	88.84	91.31	92.94	93.58	96.04	99.28	99.15	102.68	102.63	106.87	98.09	96.60
2004	79.35	80.18	107.35	109.99	115.40	121.10	124.63	124.65	116.97	116.96	117.13	113.01	110.56

Source: Economic Research Service, U.S. Department of Agriculture (ERS-USDA)

Federally Inspected Slaughter of Cattle in the United States   In Thousands of Head

Year	Jan.	Feb.	Mar.	Apr.	May	June	July	Aug.	Sept.	Oct.	Nov.	Dec.	Total
1998	2,977	2,691	2,838	2,872	2,906	3,050	2,987	2,987	2,938	2,991	2,717	2,834	34,787
1999	2,904	2,665	2,990	2,916	2,947	3,154	3,037	3,099	3,045	3,033	2,882	2,814	35,486
2000	2,878	2,883	3,078	2,735	3,128	3,191	2,918	3,211	2,984	3,082	2,879	2,665	35,631
2001	2,947	2,533	2,867	2,667	3,152	3,075	2,898	3,193	2,758	3,103	2,854	2,726	34,771
2002	2,999	2,564	2,688	2,899	3,098	3,017	3,141	3,163	2,816	3,205	2,812	2,719	35,120
2003	2,950	2,519	2,725	2,918	3,201	3,208	3,245	3,094	3,082	2,953	2,387	2,626	34,907
2004[1]	2,527	2,381	2,818	2,654	2,792	2,950	2,746	2,775	2,689	2,693	2,492	2,642	32,158

[1] Preliminary.   *Source: National Agricultural Statistics Board, U.S. Department of Agriculture (NASS-USDA)*

26

Feeder Cattle Futures - Chicago Mercantile Exchange
(weekly close) as of December 31, 2004

Average Open Interest of Live Cattle Futures in Chicago   In Contracts

Year	Jan.	Feb.	Mar.	Apr.	May	June	July	Aug.	Sept.	Oct.	Nov.	Dec.
1995	80,306	78,793	76,821	64,763	61,460	56,783	58,077	55,511	58,319	62,222	69,495	69,065
1996	72,870	83,064	91,348	97,315	97,911	96,320	96,547	93,557	92,804	88,467	88,062	87,305
1997	97,014	103,437	108,157	98,354	99,640	96,279	99,042	98,590	94,137	93,579	100,368	102,741
1998	105,559	102,036	101,264	88,257	88,167	87,493	86,776	86,874	95,013	102,636	108,263	106,156
1999	115,254	115,283	115,410	104,482	103,290	101,078	96,843	101,858	121,305	123,466	126,040	120,204
2000	128,918	123,980	123,925	122,596	117,834	106,196	116,266	120,526	123,945	123,517	131,773	132,239
2001	132,298	132,866	131,312	123,075	112,180	114,970	116,162	105,252	114,214	109,677	108,574	95,182
2002	93,589	91,566	98,176	98,343	98,846	91,129	93,541	92,966	109,651	111,338	121,671	116,588
2003	111,874	105,882	98,943	96,875	107,193	111,397	113,324	115,417	130,836	124,525	113,224	106,522
2004	98,752	99,491	112,449	124,930	128,727	126,481	114,656	109,588	104,928	109,832	112,709	123,478

Source: Chicago Mercantile Exchange (CME)

Volume of Trading of Live Cattle Futures Chicago   In Thousands of Contracts

Year	Jan.	Feb.	Mar.	Apr.	May	June	July	Aug.	Sept.	Oct.	Nov.	Dec.	Total
1995	289,710	259,210	391,721	287,194	285,686	290,224	245,250	266,793	233,402	220,130	246,655	241,130	3,257,105
1996	312,018	275,399	333,200	457,536	385,875	303,091	319,815	299,498	278,083	339,419	312,577	309,681	3,926,192
1997	361,620	352,173	312,113	331,948	285,885	303,369	387,526	324,943	316,822	374,632	238,003	330,608	3,919,642
1998	355,728	400,210	327,169	400,584	296,651	321,370	334,424	369,604	370,282	373,207	318,152	349,125	4,216,506
1999	298,814	342,572	338,076	320,457	296,512	342,854	287,557	266,544	371,735	345,269	375,960	253,198	3,839,548
2000	347,290	323,524	356,258	236,494	302,001	244,755	248,377	293,450	277,913	293,972	397,879	359,599	3,681,512
2001	511,050	357,474	385,581	302,829	348,294	289,093	318,564	324,614	340,969	403,101	403,009	294,695	4,279,273
2002	331,026	275,699	387,115	448,508	304,900	247,940	286,248	288,525	314,927	352,487	315,658	298,703	3,851,736
2003	378,862	343,931	334,007	306,713	391,477	311,239	449,966	319,677	473,218	469,405	324,732	332,862	4,436,089
2004	362,295	265,370	442,636	353,886	419,888	345,611	381,151	340,973	382,536	344,517	511,516	359,749	4,510,128

Source: Chicago Mercantile Exchange (CME)

CATTLE AND CALVES

Beef Steer-Corn Price Ratio in the United States

Year	Jan.	Feb.	Mar.	Apr.	May	June	July	Aug.	Sept.	Oct.	Nov.	Dec.	Average
1997	24.2	24.6	24.3	24.3	25.4	25.4	27.0	26.6	26.6	26.5	27.1	26.5	25.7
1998	25.8	24.8	25.2	27.5	28.3	28.3	27.9	31.6	32.2	32.1	32.3	30.0	28.8
1999	30.2	31.0	31.8	32.4	32.8	33.9	37.5	37.8	38.3	41.5	41.7	38.9	35.7
2000	37.5	35.9	36.2	37.0	34.7	37.4	42.9	44.7	42.6	40.5	39.7	39.0	39.0
2001	40.1	40.2	41.1	42.1	42.5	43.6	40.1	38.7	37.7	38.1	36.6	34.6	39.6
2002	36.1	38.1	38.2	37.0	35.3	34.0	31.2	28.3	27.4	29.3	31.5	32.3	33.2
2003	33.4	33.4	32.9	33.7	33.4	33.6	36.4	38.6	40.6	46.1	45.4	41.4	37.4
2004[2]	35.7	31.5	32.0	30.8	32.3	33.5	36.6	39.5	40.6	42.3	44.0	45.0	37.0

[1] Bushels of corn equal in value to 100 pounds of steers and heifers.   [2] Preliminary.   *Source: Economic Research Service, U.S. Department of Agriculture*

Farm Value, Income and Wholesale Prices of Cattle and Calves in the United States

	January 1		Gross Income From C & C[2]	At Ohama				Feeder Heifers at Oklahoma	Cows, Boning Utility	Cows, Commercial	Wholesale Prices, Central U.S.		
				Steers[3]		Heifers[4]							
	Per Head	Total		Choice	Select	Select	Choice	City[6]	Sioux Falls[6]	Sioux Falls	Choice 700-850 lb.	Select 700-850 lb.	Cow[6], Canner[7]
Year	Dollars	Million $	Million $					Dollars per 100 Pounds					
1998	603	60,193	33,720	60.07	56.17	55.17	59.23	67.89	36.19	38.93	98.42	92.20	61.49
1999	594	58,834	36,861	65.64	NA	NA	65.68	71.90	38.40	40.61	110.91	103.07	66.51
2000	683	67,099	41,078	69.52	NA	NA	69.55	82.23	41.71	44.45	117.45	108.83	72.57
2001	725	70,495	40,805	67.68	NA	NA	67.81	84.19	44.39	46.65	122.17	114.42	55.32
2002	747	72,284	38,302	66.39	NA	NA	67.39	76.70	40.47	39.63	113.59	107.66	NA
2003	728	69,949		82.37	NA	NA	82.06	85.88	49.74	46.62	143.20	130.07	NA
2004[1]	819	77,733						100.09	55.20	52.35	141.33	132.65	NA

[1] Preliminary.   [2] Excludes interfarm sales & Gov't. payments. Cash receipts from farm marketings + value of farm home consumption.   [3] 1,000 to 1,100 lb.   [4] 1,000 to 1,200 lb.   [5] 1992 to date are 700 to 750 lb., 1987 thru 1991 are 600 to 700 lb.   [6] All weights.   [7] & Cutter.
Source: Economic Research Service, U.S. Department of Agriculture (NASS-USDA)

Average Price Received by Farmers for Beef Cattle in the United States   In Dollars Per 100 Pounds

Year	Jan.	Feb.	Mar.	Apr.	May	June	July	Aug.	Sept.	Oct.	Nov.	Dec.	Average
1997	61.40	61.90	64.80	64.80	65.10	62.30	62.80	63.90	63.60	63.30	63.30	62.90	63.30
1998	62.50	60.40	61.30	63.00	63.00	61.80	58.40	57.40	56.10	58.00	58.10	56.80	59.70
1999	59.00	60.60	62.40	62.70	62.10	63.70	62.60	63.50	63.80	66.20	66.20	66.60	63.28
2000	67.80	67.60	69.80	71.30	69.40	68.50	67.50	65.50	65.30	66.70	69.10	71.90	68.37
2001	74.80	74.70	76.00	75.40	73.60	73.60	71.80	70.60	69.00	66.50	64.00	64.80	71.23
2002	67.10	70.00	70.60	67.30	65.10	64.00	63.70	64.40	64.50	64.60	67.30	70.40	66.58
2003	73.20	73.90	72.60	74.50	75.50	74.90	75.80	79.30	84.90	91.50	93.40	90.40	79.99
2004[1]	80.90	78.50	83.40	84.80	88.40	89.50	88.50	88.90	85.80	86.10	85.10	86.80	85.56

[1] Preliminary.   *Source: National Agricultural Statistics Service, U.S. Department of Agriculture (NASS-USDA)*

Average Price Received by Farmers for Calves in the United States   In Dollars Per 100 Pounds

Year	Jan.	Feb.	Mar.	Apr.	May	June	July	Aug.	Sept.	Oct.	Nov.	Dec.	Average
1997	68.10	74.90	80.00	82.20	84.30	85.40	86.90	88.00	86.90	84.30	82.90	83.30	82.30
1998	86.60	88.70	89.80	90.80	88.90	81.70	76.60	76.90	74.10	75.70	77.50	80.20	82.30
1999	83.20	86.90	87.30	88.20	87.60	89.00	89.20	89.60	90.90	91.90	93.00	98.60	89.62
2000	103.00	105.00	109.00	111.00	107.00	104.00	106.00	106.00	103.00	102.00	106.00	106.00	105.67
2001	108.00	109.00	112.00	112.00	111.00	110.00	108.00	106.00	107.00	99.70	96.70	101.00	106.70
2002	102.00	105.00	105.00	101.00	99.50	96.50	92.40	94.90	92.40	92.00	91.90	95.30	97.33
2003	96.80	97.20	96.70	98.90	100.00	101.00	102.00	106.00	109.00	112.00	111.00	112.00	103.55
2004[1]	110.00	111.00	115.00	117.00	121.00	125.00	131.00	131.00	129.00	126.00	124.00	122.00	121.83

[1] Preliminary.   *Source: National Agricultural Statistics Board, U.S. Department of Agriculture (NASS-USDA)*

Federally Inspected Slaughter of Calves and Vealers in the United States   In Thousands of Head

Year	Jan.	Feb.	Mar.	Apr.	May	June	July	Aug.	Sept.	Oct.	Nov.	Dec.	Total
1997	143	122	128	126	114	115	131	123	133	137	121	142	1,534
1998	125	111	125	107	99	115	131	122	132	121	109	127	1,422
1999	103	98	115	95	87	102	109	115	117	102	100	110	1,252
2000	91	92	97	75	86	91	92	98	91	95	91	90	1,088
2001	89	77	82	72	77	75	81	92	77	91	85	82	981
2002	86	71	76	80	76	74	94	94	87	98	88	96	1,019
2003	92	81	83	77	74	72	83	78	80	85	76	95	976
2004[1]	77	70	75	69	63	65	67	71	66	61	66	73	823

[1] Preliminary.   *Source: Crop Reporting Board, U.S. Department of Agriculture (CRB-USDA)*

Cement

Cement is made in a wide variety of compositions and is used in many different ways. The best-known cement is *Portland cement*, which is bound with sand and gravel to create concrete. Concrete is used to unite the surfaces of various materials and to coat surfaces to protect them from various chemicals. Portland cement is almost universally used for structural concrete. It is manufactured from lime-bearing materials, usually limestone, together with clays, blast-furnace slag containing alumina and silica or shale. The combination is usually approximately 60 percent lime, 19 percent silica, 8 percent alumina, 5 percent iron, 5 percent magnesia, and 3 percent sulfur trioxide. To slow the hardening process, gypsum is often added. In 1924, the name "Portland cement" was coined by Joseph Aspdin, a British cement maker, because of the resemblance between concrete made from his cement and Portland stone. The United States did not start producing Portland cement in any great quantity until the 20th century. Hydraulic cements are those that set and harden in water. Clinker cement is an intermediate product in cement manufacture. The production and consumption of cement is directly re-lated to the level of activity in the construction industry.

Prices – The average value (F.O.B. mill) of Portland cement in 2003 fell −1.3% yr/yr to $75.00 per ton. That was moderately below the record high value of $78.56 per ton seen in 2000.

Supply – World production of hydraulic cement in 2003, the latest reporting year, rose +6.0% yr/yr to a new record high of 1.950 billion metric tons. The world's largest hydraulic cement producers are China with 42% of world production in 2003, India (6%), US (5%), and Japan (4%). US production of Portland cement in 2003 rose +3.3% yr/yr to a new record high of 88.106 million tons. US shipments of finished Portland cement from mills in the US in 2004 (through November, annualized) rose +5.8% to a record high of 96.397 million metric tons.

Demand – US consumption of cement in 2003 rose +3.7% to 114.100 million tons, which was a new record high.

Trade – The US relied on imports for 20% of its cement consumption in 2003. The two main suppliers of cement to the US are Canada and Mexico. US exports of cement in 2003 rose +0.4% yr/yr to 837,000 tons.

World Production of Hydraulic Cement   In Thousands of Short Tons

Year	Brazil	China	France	Germany	India	Italy	Japan	Rep. of Korea	Russia	Spain	Turkey	United States	World Total
1996	34,597	491,190	19,514	31,533	75,000	33,327	94,492	58,434	27,800	25,157	35,214	80,818	1,493,000
1997	38,096	511,730	19,780	35,945	80,000	33,721	91,938	60,317	26,700	27,632	36,035	84,255	1,540,000
1998	39,942	536,000	19,500	36,610	85,000	35,512	81,328	46,091	26,000	33,080	38,200	85,522	1,540,000
1999	40,270	573,000	20,219	35,912	90,000	37,299	80,120	48,157	28,400	35,782	34,258	87,777	1,600,000
2000	39,208	597,000	20,137	34,727	95,000	38,925	81,097	51,255	32,400	38,115	35,825	89,510	1,660,000
2001	38,927	661,040	19,839	30,989	100,000	39,804	76,550	52,046	35,300	40,512	30,125	90,450	1,730,000
2002[1]	38,027	725,000	20,000	30,000	102,000	40,000	71,828	55,514	37,700	42,500	32,577	91,266	1,840,000
2003[2]	37,980	813,190	20,000	30,000	110,000	38,000	71,000	59,199	41,000	42,000	33,000	94,329	1,950,000

[1] Preliminary.   [2] Estimate.   *Source: U.S. Geological Survey (USGS)*

Salient Statistics of Cement in the United States

Year	Net Import Reliance as a % of Apparent Consumption	Production Portland	Production Others[3]	Production Total	Capacity Used at (Portland Mills) %	Shipments From Mills Total Mil. MT	Shipments From Mills Value[4] Mil. $	Average Value (F.O.B. Mill) $ per MT	Stocks at Mills Dec. 31	Exports	Apparent Consumption	Imports for Consumption[5] by Country Canada	Japan	Mexico	Spain	Total
		---- 1,000 Metric Tons ----				----- 1,000 Metric Tons -----						---- 1,000 Metric Tons ----				
1996	12	75,797	3,469	79,266	83.4	83,963	5,952	70.89	5,488	803	90,355	5,351	[6]	1,272	1,595	14,154
1997	14	78,948	3,634	82,582	84.7	90,359	6,637	73.46	5,784	791	96,018	5,350	----	995	1,845	17,596
1998	19	79,942	3,989	83,931	84.9	96,857	7,404	76.45	5,393	743	103,460	5,957	----	1,280	2,204	24,086
1999	23	81,577	4,375	85,952	83.6	103,271	8,083	78.27	6,367	694	108,862	5,511	----	1,286	1,900	29,351
2000	20	83,514	4,332	87,846	80.7	105,557	8,293	78.56	7,566	738	110,470	4,948	----	1,409	1,177	28,683
2001	21	84,450	4,450	88,900	79.1	112,510	8,600	76.50	6,600	746	112,810	5,110	----	1,645	651	25,861
2002[1]	19	85,283	4,449	89,732	78.7	108,500	8,250	76.00	7,680	834	110,020	5,181	----	1,228	327	24,169
2003[2]	20	88,106	4,737	92,843	77.9	111,000	8,340	75.00	6,610	837	114,100	5,601	----	891	355	23,242

[1] Preliminary.   [2] Estimate.   [3] Masonry, natural & pozzolan (slag-line).   [4] Value received F.O.B. mill, excluding cost of containers.   [5] Hydraulic & clinker cement for consumption.   [6] Less than 1/2 unit.   *Source: U.S. Geological Survey (USGS)*

Shipments of Finished Portland Cement from Mills in the United States   In Thousands of Metric Tons

Year	Jan.	Feb.	Mar.	Apr.	May	June	July	Aug.	Sept.	Oct.	Nov.	Dec.	Total
1998	4,552.0	4,559.7	5,867.4	7,009.7	7,420.2	8,095.1	8,295.6	7,963.3	8,089.5	8,404.6	6,640.5	6,059.4	82,956.8
1999	4,487.3	5,132.9	6,380.5	7,112.2	7,406.9	8,096.9	7,782.2	8,173.2	7,652.7	8,204.2	7,453.4	5,959.1	83,841.5
2000	4,765.5	5,343.1	7,196.9	6,930.2	8,448.2	8,391.5	7,843.8	8,982.3	7,860.8	8,474.2	6,587.0	4,865.5	84,980.3
2001	5,107.6	5,088.8	6,684.5	7,799.4	8,507.9	8,385.8	8,333.2	8,851.2	7,512.2	8,953.3	7,353.3	5,548.0	88,124.9
2002	5,554.3	5,369.3	6,133.9	7,859.7	8,291.4	8,135.6	8,466.9	8,676.2	7,909.7	8,326.1	6,956.3	5,293.4	86,972.9
2003	5,485.6	4,559.9	6,482.6	8,008.5	8,288.4	8,492.2	9,063.8	8,829.1	8,755.3	9,780.8	6,987.5	6,348.3	91,081.9
2004[1]	5,241.3	5,145.4	8,060.9	8,833.1	8,621.7	9,113.7	9,136.1	9,344.4	8,895.4	8,595.5	7,376.2		96,396.9

[1] Preliminary.   *Source: U.S. Geological Survey (USGS)*

Cheese

Since prehistoric times, humans have been making and eating cheese. Dating back as far as 6,000 BC, archaeologists have discovered that cheese had been made from cow and goat milk and stored in tall jars. The Romans turned cheese making into a culinary art, mixing sheep and goat milk and adding herbs and spices for flavoring. By 300 AD, cheese was being exported regularly to countries along the Mediterranean coast.

Cheese is made from the milk of cows and other mammals such as sheep, goats, buffalo, reindeer, camels, yaks, and mares. More than 400 varieties of cheese exist. There are three basic steps common to all cheese making. First, proteins in milk are transformed into curds, or solid lumps. Second, the curds are separated from the milky liquid (or whey) and shaped or pressed into molds. Finally, the shaped curds are ripened according to a variety of aging and curing techniques. Cheeses are usually grouped according to their moisture content into fresh, soft, semi-soft, hard, and very hard. Many classifications overlap due to texture changes with aging.

Cheese is a multi-billion-dollar a year industry in the US. Cheddar cheese is the most common natural cheese produced in the US, accounting for 35% of US production. Cheeses originating in America include Colby, cream cheese,

and Monterey Jack. Varieties other than American cheeses, mostly Italian, now have had a combined level of production that easily exceeds American cheeses.

Prices – Average monthly cheese prices at the Chicago Mercantile Exchange in 2004 (through October) rose sharply by 25.7% yr/yr to 165.03 cents per pound, which was a 23-year high. The record monthly average high of 167.20 cents per pound was posted in 1981.

Supply – World production of cheese in 2003 was unchanged at 12.647 million metric tons, which was a new record high. The US and Europe are the world's largest producers of cheese, and US production in 2003 accounted for 31% of world production. US production of cheese in 2004 (annualized through November) rose +2.5% to 8.812 billion pounds, which was a new record high.

Demand – US consumption of cheese in 2003 rose +1.1% to a new record high of 9.080 billion pounds. US per capita cheese consumption in 2001, the latest reporting year, fell to 29.60 pounds per person per year from the record of 29.80 pounds seen in 2000.

Trade – US imports of cheese in 2002 rose +6.8% yr/yr to 475 million pounds, which was a record high. US exports of cheese in 2002 rose +3.0% to 119 million pounds, which was a record high.

World Production of Cheese   In Thousands of Metric Tons

Year	Argentina	Australia	Brazil	Canada	Egypt	European Union	Japan	Mexico	Zealand	Russia	Ukraine	United States	World Total
1995	370	241	360	277	310	4,741	31	116	197	217	72	3,138	11,345
1996	390	268	385	289	325	4,841	33	110	230	173	60	3,274	11,705
1997	415	285	405	329	370	5,047	34	112	240	165	45	3,325	11,100
1998	407	305	421	330	380	5,291	35	127	266	170	52	3,398	11,518
1999	446	320	434	329	382	5,711	35	126	245	185	53	3,581	12,016
2000	445	373	445	328	380	5,861	34	134	297	220	67	3,746	12,499
2001	440	374	460	329	395	5,865	34	140	281	260	105	3,747	12,602
2002	370	413	470	350	410	5,993	36	145	312	340	129	3,877	13,019
2003[1]	325	368	460	342	450	6,117	35	126	301	335	169	3,900	13,049
2004[2]	345	391	470	326	455	6,292	35	130	313	330	200	4,020	13,373

[1] Preliminary.   [2] Estimate.   *Source: Foreign Agricultural Service, U.S. Department of Agriculture (FAS-USDA)*

Supply and Distribution of All Cheese in the United States   In Millions of Pounds

	Supply					Cheese 40-lb. Blocks Wisconsin Assembly Points cents/lb.	Distribution				Domestic Disappearance		
Year	Production Whole Milk[2]	Production All Cheese[3]	January 1 Commercial Stocks	Imports[4]	Total Supply		Exports & Shipments[5]	- Gov't - Dec. 31 Stocks	American Cheese Removed by USDA Programs	Total Disappearance	American Cheese Donated	Total	Per Capita
1994	2,974	6,735	466	335	7,536	131.50	49	.9	6.9	7,095	0	6,994	26.82
1995	3,131	6,917	437	340	7,695	132.80	65	.4	6.1	7,279	0	7,174	26.90
1996	3,281	7,218	412	338	7,968	146.80	72	.3	4.6	7,478	0	7,365	27.30
1997	3,286	7,330	487	312	8,130	132.40	83	.5	11.3	7,646	0	7,510	27.50
1998	3,315	7,492	481	371	8,344	158.10	81	.6	8.2	7,797	0	7,664	27.70
1999	3,533	7,894	518	436	8,847	142.28	85	1.0	4.6	8,219	0	8,086	29.00
2000	3,642	8,258	621	416	9,295	116.14	105	2.3	28.0	8,580	0	8,406	29.80
2001	3,544	8,261	706	445	9,412	144.93	115	4.0	3.9	8,744	0	8,586	30.00
2002	3,691	8,547	659	475	9,681	118.22	119	2.7	15.8	9,001	0	8,819	30.60
2003[1]	3,670	8,598	730	476	9,804	131.24	115	27.4	41.3	9,080			

[1] Preliminary.   [2] Whole milk American cheddar.   [3] All types of cheese except cottage, pot and baker's cheese.   [4] Imports for consumption.
[5] Commercial.   *Source: Economic Research Service, U.S. Department of Agriculture (ERS-USDA)*

Production of Cheese in the United States In Millions of Pounds

Year	American Whole Milk	American Part Skim	American Total	Swiss, Including Block	Munster	Brick	Limburger	Cream & Neufchatel Cheese	Italian Varieties	Blue Mond	All Other Varieties	Total of All Cheese[2]	Cottage Cheese Lowfat	Cottage Cheese Curd[3]	Cottage Cheese Creamed[4]
1994	2,974	24.7	2,999	221.2	113.6	12.2	.8	573.4	2,625.7	36.5	152.1	6,735	321.1	463.3	410.0
1995	3,131	24.0	3,155	221.7	109.1	10.4	.9	543.8	2,674.4	36.6	164.6	6,917	325.9	458.9	384.9
1996	3,281	NA	3,281	219.0	106.8	10.6	.7	574.7	2,812.4	38.3	106.7	7,218	329.9	448.3	360.4
1997	3,286	NA	3,286	207.6	100.2	8.5	.7	614.9	2,881.4	42.8	119.8	7,330	346.7	458.5	359.5
1998	3,315	NA	3,315	206.4	94.6	7.6	.9	621.3	3,004.7	5	166.0	7,492	361.2	465.8	366.8
1999	3,533	NA	3,533	221.0	80.3	8.1	.7	639.3	3,144.7	5	181.0	7,894	359.3	464.8	360.6
2000	3,642	NA	3,642	229.3	85.5	8.6	.6	687.4	3,288.9	5	219.7	8,258	363.7	461.0	371.5
2001	3,544	NA	3,544	245.5	82.2	8.7	.7	645.1	3,425.9	5	199.6	8,261	370.2	453.2	371.6
2002	3,691	NA	3,691	254.1	81.1	10.0	.7	686.2	3,470.0	5	229.8	8,547	374.3	436.6	374.2
2003[1]	3,670	NA	3,670	264.8	79.5	9.8	.7	676.8	3,522.0	5	241.2	8,598	380.0	448.3	385.2

[1] Preliminary. [2] Excludes full-skim cheddar and cottage cheese. [3] Includes cottage, pot, and baker's cheese with a butterfat content of less than 4%. [4] Includes cheese with a butterfat content of 4 to 19 %. [5] Included in All Other Varieties. *Source: Economic Research Service, U.S. Department of Agriculture ERS-USDA)*

Average Price of Cheese, 40-lb. Blocks, Chicago Mercantile Exchange[2] In Cents Per Pound

Year	Jan.	Feb.	Mar.	Apr.	May	June	July	Aug.	Sept.	Oct.	Nov.	Dec.	Average
1995	124.5	130.4	131.1	122.8	122.1	126.9	126.7	132.2	141.3	145.0	145.8	144.6	132.8
1996	139.3	139.3	140.9	145.1	151.8	151.5	158.2	167.6	145.5	162.3	133.9	126.0	146.8
1997	127.9	132.3	134.0	125.6	116.5	117.9	123.3	137.6	141.4	142.4	143.8	146.1	132.4
1998	144.5	144.7	138.8	129.7	123.0	151.3	162.6	166.9	171.0	183.5	188.7	192.5	158.1
1999	162.4	131.5	134.0	133.6	124.8	138.1	159.7	189.0	167.3	134.0	117.3	115.7	142.3
2000	114.6	111.6	112.2	110.7	110.6	120.0	125.2	125.5	133.4	109.4	107.5	113.0	116.1
2001	110.3	120.0	131.9	140.5	160.3	166.8	168.5	171.8	173.9	139.7	126.4	129.1	144.9
2002	132.4	120.8	121.3	124.5	120.1	113.0	108.9	115.8	120.4	119.5	108.9	113.1	118.2
2003	109.3	109.2	108.2	112.3	114.2	118.6	151.2	160.0	160.0	158.8	139.3	133.8	131.2
2004[1]	130.6	139.6	182.0	216.9	199.3	171.1	144.9	157.3	157.0	151.7	169.6	159.2	164.9

[1] Preliminary. [2] Data through December 2001 are for Wholesale Price of Cheese, 40-lb. Blocks, Wisconsin Assembly Points.
Source: Economic Research Service, U.S. Department of Agriculture (ERS-USDA)

Production[2] of Cheese in the United States In Millions of Pounds

Year	Jan.	Feb.	Mar.	Apr.	May	June	July	Aug.	Sept.	Oct.	Nov.	Dec.	Total
1995	559.3	523.3	596.0	559.6	595.3	579.2	556.5	550.8	571.3	588.6	584.7	618.4	6,883
1996	590.0	576.0	625.4	606.0	636.5	595.8	582.2	589.5	584.5	612.2	595.5	623.9	7,218
1997	598.1	577.1	638.0	598.5	642.0	623.4	613.2	596.5	604.3	615.5	594.5	627.9	7,329
1998	617.2	574.3	646.7	636.9	650.4	639.9	607.9	596.4	583.8	633.2	637.8	667.4	7,492
1999	631.6	591.7	698.2	663.8	668.9	664.4	641.3	642.6	637.6	666.5	683.4	704.2	7,894
2000	692.9	649.5	714.8	694.0	730.4	695.7	687.6	683.8	653.8	688.5	675.0	688.4	8,255
2001	680.3	625.3	713.7	670.2	706.8	678.5	676.0	660.0	641.8	682.1	691.2	703.1	8,129
2002	717.5	667.9	742.8	719.2	748.3	708.3	692.2	714.3	683.9	732.2	725.4	747.2	8,599
2003	714.8	648.6	730.3	718.8	737.0	712.3	718.3	700.1	708.7	740.0	710.0	758.9	8,598
2004[1]	735.9	704.3	779.6	756.8	748.4	717.3	707.9	714.0	716.1	748.1	748.2	772.4	8,849

[1] Preliminary. [2] Excludes cottage cheese. *Source: National Agricultural Statistics Service, U.S. Department of Agriculture (NASS-USDA)*

Cold Storage Holdings of All Varieties of Cheese in the United States, on First of Month Millions of Pounds

Year	Jan.	Feb.	Mar.	Apr.	May	June	July	Aug.	Sept.	Oct.	Nov.	Dec.
1995	436.9	449.7	448.7	458.8	466.1	465.8	473.6	482.4	458.1	428.5	418.7	393.6
1996	412.1	441.3	466.4	490.9	525.5	541.8	542.8	536.6	506.9	495.8	494.6	480.2
1997	487.0	501.5	494.6	517.0	555.4	584.3	604.8	604.9	582.3	543.7	505.0	474.4
1998	480.4	509.3	521.5	533.1	557.6	568.5	583.7	595.8	576.8	553.0	522.7	494.5
1999	517.2	622.4	635.9	645.1	688.7	741.3	728.4	748.7	694.7	651.3	622.0	591.7
2000	621.3	728.1	757.2	765.1	794.0	811.4	828.1	870.3	839.9	780.9	732.0	696.0
2001	707.8	709.9	723.9	711.6	711.8	712.1	739.2	752.6	721.2	708.7	672.2	631.3
2002	660.0	693.6	720.3	731.7	765.6	789.0	797.6	833.6	801.5	753.9	720.4	697.1
2003	730.1	761.2	770.0	771.3	781.1	791.0	800.1	809.0	794.2	762.2	722.4	695.5
2004[1]	724.4	756.9	766.8	759.5	769.8	806.8	841.7	869.6	811.5	790.7	756.2	704.3

Quantities are given in net weight. [1] Preliminary. *Source: National Agricultural Statistics Service, U.S. Department of Agriculture (NASS-USDA)*

Chromium

Chromium (symbol Cr) is a steel-gray, hard, and brittle, metallic element that can take on a high polish. Chromium and its compounds are toxic. Discovered in 1797 by Louis Vauquelin, chromium is named after the Greek word for color, *khroma*. Vauquelin also discovered that an emerald's green color is due to the presence of chromium. Many precious stones owe their color to the presence of chromium compounds.

Chromium is primarily found in chromite ore. The primary use of chromium is to form alloys with iron, nickel, or cobalt. Chromium improves hardness and resistance to corrosion and oxidation in iron, steel, and nonferrous alloys. It is a critical alloying ingredient in the production of stainless steel, making up 10% or more of the final composition. More than half of the chromium consumed is used in metallic products, and about one-third is used in refractories. Chromium is also used as a lustrous decorative plating agent, in pigments, leather processing, plating of metals, and catalysts.

Supply – World production of chromium in 2003 rose +9.2% yr/yr to 15.500 million metric tons, and was up sharply from the 7-year low of 12.100 million metric tons in 2001. The world's largest producers of chromium in 2003 were South Africa with 48% of world production, Kazakhstan with 19%, India with 14%, and Zimbabwe with 5%. India has emerged as a major producer of chromium in the past two decades. India's 2003 production level of 2.210 million metric tons was more than 6 times the level of 360,000 metric tons seen 20 years earlier. South Africa's production in 2003 rose to a record 7.405 million metric tons, double the levels seen as recently as the early-1990s. Kazakhstan's production in 2003 of 2.928 million was an 11-year high. Zimbabwe's chromium production in 2003 of 725,822 metric tons as moderately below the 3-decade high of 780,150 metric tons posted in 2001. Government stocks of chromium as of Dec 31, 2003 fell -25% yr/yr to 154,000 metric tons.

Demand – Based on the most recently available data, the metallurgical and chemical industry accounts for 94% of chromium usage in the US, with the remaining 6% used by the refractory industry.

Trade – The US relied on imports for 74% of its chromium consumption in 2003, up from the record low of 63% seen in 2002. That is well below the record high of 91% posted back in the 1970s. US chromium imports in 2003 rose 21% yr/yr to 317,000 metric tons. That is less than one-half of the record high of 640,000 metric tons posted in 1957. US exports of chromium in 2003 rose +60% yr/yr to 46,000 tons.

World Mine Production of Chromite   In Thousands of Metric Tons (Gross Weight)

Year	Albania	Brazil	Cuba	Finland	India	Iran	Kazakhstan	Madagascar	Philippines	South Africa	Turkey	Zimbabwe	World Total
1994	118	360	29	573	909	354	2,100	90	76	3,640	1,270	517	10,400
1995	160	448	31	598	1,540	371	2,420	106	111	5,090	2,080	707	14,000
1996	144	408	37	582	1,363	130	1,190	137	107	5,078	1,279	697	11,600
1997	106	301	44	589	1,363	169	1,796	140	88	6,162	1,703	640	13,600
1998	102	537	46	498	1,311	212	1,603	104	54	6,480	1,404	605	13,700
1999	71	458	52	597	1,473	255	2,406	----	20	6,817	770	653	14,200
2000	120	550	56	628	1,947	153	2,607	131	26	6,622	546	668	14,800
2001	86	418	50	575	1,678	105	2,046	24	27	5,502	390	780	12,100
2002[1]	91	284	46	566	2,699	80	2,369	11	24	6,436	314	749	14,200
2003[2]	90	391	50	549	2,210	120	2,928	45	24	7,405	229	726	15,500

[1] Preliminary.   [2] Estimate.   *Source: U.S. Geological Survey (USGS)*

Salient Statistics of Chromite in the United States   In Thousands of Metric Tons (Gross Weight)

Year	Net Import Reliance as a % of Apparent Consumption	Production of Ferro-chromium	Exports	Imports for Consumption	Reexports	Consumption by - Primary Conumer Groups - Total	Metallurgical & Chemical	Refractory	Government[5] Stocks, Dec. 31 -- Metallurgical & Chemical	Refractory	Total Stocks	- $ per Metric Ton - South Africa[3]	Turkish[4]
1994	75	67	31	272		322	302	20	250	17	266	60	110
1995	80	73	24	415		W	W	W	194	11	205	80	230
1996	79	37	47	361		W	W	W	165	8	173	80	230
1997	75	61	27	349		W	W	W	167	8	175	75	150
1998	80	W	55	383		W	W	W	W	W	159	68	145
1999	80	W	53	475		W	W	W	W	W	130	63	145
2000	78	W	86	453		W	W	W	396	241	637	60-65	140-150
2001	78	W	43	239		W	W	W	396	241	637	NA	NA
2002[1]	63	W	29	263		W	W	W	78	126	204	NA	NA
2003[2]	74	W	46	317		W	W	W	72	83	154	NA	NA

[1] Preliminary.   [2] Estimate.   [3] Cr_2O_3, 44% (Transvaal).   [4] 48% Cr_2O_3.   [5] Data through 1999 are for Consumer.   W = Withheld.
Source: U.S. Geological Survey (USGS)

Coal

Coal is a sedimentary rock composed primarily of carbon, hydrogen, and oxygen. Coal is a fossil fuel formed from ancient plants buried deep in the Earth's crust over 300 million years ago. Historians believe coal was first used commercially in China for smelting copper and for casting coins around 1,000 BC. Almost 92% of all coal consumed in the US is burned by electric power plants, and coal accounts for about 55% of total electricity output. Coal is also used in the manufacture of steel. The steel industry first converts coal into coke, then combines the coke with iron ore and limestone, and finally heats the mixture to produce iron. Other industries use coal to make fertilizers, solvents, medicine, pesticides, and synthetic fuels.

There are four types of mined coal: anthracite (used in high-grade steel production), bituminous (used for electric-ity generation and for making coke), sub-bituminous, and lignite (both used primarily for electricity generation).

Coal futures trade at the New York Mercantile Exchange (NYMEX). The contract trades in units of 1,550 tons and is priced in terms of dollars and cents per ton.

Supply – US production of bituminous coal in 2004 rose by +3.4% yr/yr to 1.108 billion short tons.

Demand – US consumption of coal in 2003, the latest reporting year for the series, rose by +2.7% to 1.094 billion tons, which was a new record high.

Trade – US exports of coal in 2003 rose +8.6% yr/yr to 43.014 million tons, and imports rose +48.4% yr/yr to 25.044 million tons. The key exporting destinations for the US are Canada and Europe.

World Production[3] of Coal (Monthly Average)   In Thousands of Metric Tons

Year	Australia	Canada	China	Czech-Rep.	Ger-many	India	Indo-nesia	Kazak-hstan	Poland	Russia	Ukraine	United Kingdom	United States
1995	15,921	3,216	113,394	1,431	4,905	22,785	3,460	6,626	11,349	14,743	6,796	4,420	78,091
1996	16,120	3,336	116,417	1,378	4,428	23,840	3,945	6,086	11,425	13,875	6,178	4,183	80,426
1997	17,235	3,435	114,402	1,339	4,267	24,764	4,340	6,268	11,427	13,317	6,293	4,041	82,398
1998	18,247	3,190	94,806	1,343	3,776	24,356	5,027	5,672	9,644	12,779	6,431	3,431	84,484
1999	18,751	3,043	80,200	1,193	3,657	25,004	5,892	4,644	9,301	13,799	6,804	3,090	83,191
2000	25,292	2,817	70,782	1,238	3,111	25,802	6,402	6,239	8,598	14,292	6,749	2,600	81,164
2001	27,409	2,845	80,040	1,261	2,406	26,563	7,554	6,355	8,658	15,507	6,908	2,677	84,771
2002	21,739	5,573	92,339	1,206	2,197	27,938	8,588	5,884	8,676	15,198	6,838	2,476	81,139
2003[1]	22,431	5,177	109,602	1,137	2,215	29,036	9,551	6,571	8,520	16,329	6,316	2,353	NA
2004[2]	23,250	5,489	124,321	1,116	2,310	30,890	9,120	6,646	8,362	17,210	5,428	1,704	NA

[1] Preliminary.   [2] Estimate.   [3] All grades of anthracite and bituminous coal, but excludes recovered slurries, lignite and brown coal..
NA = Not avaliable.   *Source: United Nations*

Production of Bituminous & Lignite Coal in the United States   In Thousands of Short Tons

Year	Alabama	Colorado	Illinois	Indiana	Kentucky	Montana	Ohio	Pennsyl-vania	Texas	Virginia	West Virginia	Wyoming	Total
1995	24,640	25,710	48,180	26,007	153,739	39,451	26,118	61,576	52,684	34,099	162,997	263,822	1,032,974
1996	24,637	24,886	46,656	29,670	152,425	37,891	28,572	67,942	55,164	35,590	170,433	278,440	1,063,856
1997	24,468	27,449	41,159	35,497	155,853	41,005	29,154	76,198	53,328	35,837	173,743	281,881	1,089,932
1998	23,224	30,825	38,182	36,297	145,609	42,092	28,600	76,519	53,578	34,059	175,794	313,983	1,109,768
1999	19,504	29,989	40,417	34,004	139,626	41,102	22,480	76,368	53,071	32,181	157,919	337,119	1,095,474
2000	19,324	29,137	33,444	27,965	130,688	38,352	22,269	74,619	49,498	32,834	158,257	338,900	1,073,612
2001	19,513	33,372	33,783	36,738	134,298	39,143	25,400	74,784	45,042	33,060	162,631	368,749	1,125,749
2002	19,062	35,103	33,358	35,513	124,388	37,386	21,157	67,104	45,247	30,126	150,222	373,161	1,092,916
2003[1]	20,207	35,831	31,760	35,512	113,126	36,994	22,009	63,792	47,517	31,771	139,755	376,270	1,071,753
2004[2]	22,230	40,403	32,782	35,688	113,807	39,015	22,950	64,852	45,544	32,355	149,794	395,930	1,111,438

[1] Preliminary.   [2] Estimate.   *Source: Energy Information Administration, U.S. Department of Energy (EIA-DOE)*

Production[2] of Bituminous Coal in the United States   In Thousands of Short Tons

Year	Jan.	Feb.	Mar.	Apr.	May	June	July	Aug.	Sept.	Oct.	Nov.	Dec.	Total
1995	88,351	83,893	93,020	80,092	83,291	84,210	79,511	88,035	89,052	90,573	86,779	81,292	1,032,974
1996	83,013	83,671	90,392	88,158	88,562	83,824	88,331	94,664	87,388	94,195	86,400	86,493	1,059,104
1997	92,425	88,028	92,265	87,909	94,296	86,382	88,666	89,319	92,298	94,562	83,344	94,913	1,085,254
1998	97,012	86,167	95,091	91,735	90,397	92,099	90,497	91,212	95,442	96,723	90,544	94,567	1,106,128
1999	90,928	92,015	98,672	88,630	84,436	89,734	87,759	92,600	92,248	89,146	90,885	92,450	1,089,503
2000	87,222	86,846	99,045	81,793	88,715	90,583	84,442	96,361	88,848	92,542	94,035	87,272	1,077,704
2001	96,721	86,802	99,176	89,954	94,840	92,657	89,037	99,048	88,985	99,529	93,736	88,234	1,118,719
2002	101,939	90,208	90,108	90,039	91,673	85,555	86,190	92,054	92,212	94,033	87,836	91,058	1,092,905
2003	92,649	82,130	88,976	89,202	90,435	88,348	88,301	89,355	90,344	93,928	84,155	94,154	1,071,977
2004[1]	93,182	86,306	94,489	91,644	87,124	94,739	91,806	94,729	93,045	93,059	92,047	95,934	1,108,104

[1] Preliminary.   [2] Includes small amount of lignite.   *Source: Energy Information Administration, U.S. Department of Energy (EIA-DOE)*

COAL

Production[2] of Pennsylvania Anthracite Coal In Thousands of Short Tons

Year	Jan.	Feb.	Mar.	Apr.	May	June	July	Aug.	Sept.	Oct.	Nov.	Dec.	Total
1995	304	304	372	332	335	353	307	396	428	445	388	347	4,682
1996	302	349	367	371	361	335	367	418	385	557	505	434	4,751
1997	351	366	492	374	351	390	407	423	415	448	384	415	4,678
1998	306	305	309	405	384	388	525	454	452	533	167	167	4,612
1999	355	369	389	354	459	402	343	436	479	414	407	406	4,808
2000	271	283	382	342	375	383	366	430	412	417	402	366	4,432
2001	302	275	323	283	300	297	328	358	318	375	349	173	3,681
2002	131	117	116	121	122	240	116	126	119	130	120	126	1,584
2003	108	98	98	115	114	107	97	95	101	130	111	116	1,290
2004[1]	197	183	209	115	105	222	192	199	205	181	190	160	2,158

[1] Preliminary.   [2] Represents production in Pennsylvania only.   *Source: Energy Information Administration, U.S. Department of Energy (EIA-DOE)*

Salient Statistics of Coal in the United States In Thousands of Short Tons

Year	Production	Imports	Consumption	Exports Brazil	Exports Canada	Exports Europe	Exports Asia	Exports Total	Total Ending Stocks[2]	Losses & Unaccounted For[3]
1994	1,033,504	7,584	951,461	5,482	9,193	35,825	17,957	71,359	169,358	-2,743
1995	1,032,974	7,201	962,039	6,351	9,427	48,620	19,095	88,547	169,083	-7,863
1996	1,063,856	7,126	1,005,573	6,540	12,029	47,193	17,980	90,473	151,627	-7,366
1997	1,089,932	7,487	1,030,453	7,455	14,975	41,331	14,498	83,545	140,374	-4,418
1998	1,117,535	8,724	1,038,972	6,475	19,901	33,773	12,311	77,295	164,602	-13,118
1999	1,100,431	9,089	1,038,648	4,442	19,826	22,508	9,157	58,476	188,590	-11,592
2000	1,073,612	12,513	1,084,094	4,536	18,769	24,969	6,702	58,489	140,282	-8,150
2001	1,127,689	19,787	1,060,146	4,574	17,633	20,821	3,246	48,666	181,912	-2,966
2002	1,094,283	16,875	1,066,355	3,538	16,686	15,574	1,735	39,601	192,127	-5,012
2003[1]	1,071,753	25,044	1,094,861	3,514	20,760	15,148	266	43,014	165,468	-14,419

[1] Preliminary.   [2] Producer & distributor and consumer stocks, excludes stocks held by retail dealers for consumption by the residential and commercial sector.   [3] Equals production plus imports minus the change in producer & distributor and consumer stocks minus consumption minus exports.
Source: Energy Information Administraion, U.S. Department of Energy (EIA-DOE)

Consumption and Stocks of Coal in the United States In Thousands of Short Tons

	Consumption Electric Utilities Anthracite	Bituminous	Lignite	Total	Industrial Coke Plants	Other Industrial[2]	Residential and Commercial	Total	Stocks, Dec. 31[3] Consumer Electric Utilities	Coke Plants	Other Industrials	Producers and Distributors
Year												
1994	1,123	737,102	79,045	838,354	31,740	75,179	6,013	951,286	126,897	2,657	6,585	33,219
1995	978	749,951	78,078	850,230	33,011	73,055	5,807	962,104	126,304	2,632	5,702	34,444
1996	1,009	795,252	78,421	896,921	31,706	71,689	6,006	1,006,321	114,623	2,667	5,688	28,648
1997	1,014	821,823	77,524	921,364	30,203	71,515	6,463	1,029,544	98,826	1,978	5,597	33,973
1998	867	832,094	77,906	936,619	28,189	67,439	4,856	1,037,103	120,501	2,026	5,545	36,530
1999	686	815,909	77,525	940,922	28,108	64,738	4,878	1,038,647	141,604	1,943	5,569	39,475
2000	NA	781,821	75,794	985,821	28,939	65,208	4,127	1,084,095	102,296	1,494	4,587	31,905
2001	NA	NA	NA	964,433	26,075	65,268	4,369	1,060,146	138,496	1,510	6,006	35,900
2002	NA	NA	NA	977,507	23,656	60,747	4,445	1,066,355	141,714	1,364	5,792	43,257
2003[1]	NA	NA	NA	1,004,283	24,248	61,150	4,445	1,094,126	121,371	905	4,718	36,781

[1] Preliminary.   [2] Including transportation.   [3] Excludes stocks held at retail dealers for consumption by the residential and commercial sector.
Source: Energy Information Administration, U.S. Department of Energy (EIA-DOE)

Average Prices of Coal in the United States In Dollars Per Short Ton

Year	End-Use-Sector Electric Utilities	Coke Plants	Other Industrial[2]	Imports[3]	Exports Steam	Metallurgical	Total Average[3]	Year	End-Use-Sector Electric Utilities	Coke Plants	Other Industrial[2]	Imports[3]	Exports Steam	Metallurgical	Total Average[3]
1994	28.03	46.56	32.55	30.21	34.34	42.77	39.93	1999	24.72	45.85	31.59	30.77	29.91	41.91	36.50
1995	27.01	47.34	32.42	34.13	34.51	44.30	40.27	2000	24.28	44.38	31.46	30.10	29.67	38.99	34.90
1996	26.45	47.33	32.32	33.78	34.09	45.49	40.76	2001	24.68	46.42	32.26	34.00	31.88	41.63	36.97
1997	26.16	47.36	32.41	34.32	32.45	45.47	40.55	2002	24.74	50.67	35.49	35.51	34.51	45.41	40.44
1998	25.64	46.06	32.30	32.18	30.27	44.53	38.89	2003[1]	25.29	50.63	34.17	31.45	26.94	44.55	35.98

[1] Preliminary.   [2] Manufacturing plants only.   [3] Based on the free alongside ship (F.A.S.) value.
Source: Energy Information Administration, U.S. Department of Energy (EIA-DOE)

Trends in Bituminous Coal, Lignite and Pennsylvania Anthracite in the U.S.   In Thousands of Short Tons

| | Bituminous Coal and Lignite | | | | Labor Productivity | | | Pennsylvania Anthracite | | | | | All Mines |
| | Production | | | | Under- | Surface | Average | Under- | Surface | Total | Miners[1] | Labor Product. | Labor Product. |
Year	Under-gound	Surface	Total	Miners[1] Employed	ground - Short Tons	Per Miner	Per Hour -	ground			Employed	Short Tons Miner/Hr.	Short Tons Miner/Hr.
1994	399,103	634,401	1,033,504	97,500	3.19	7.67	4.98	343	4,278	4,621	1,183	1.93	4.98
1995	396,249	636,725	1,032,974	90,252	3.39	8.48	5.38	428	4,254	4,682	1,069	2.08	5.38
1996	409,849	654,007	1,063,856	83,462	3.57	9.05	5.69	391	4,360	4,751	1,171	1.92	5.69
1997	420,657	669,274	1,089,932	81,516	3.83	9.46	6.04	419	4,259	4,678	1,287	1.76	6.04
1998	417,728	699,807	1,117,535	85,418	3.90	9.58	6.20	408	4,823	5,231	1,281	2.04	6.20
1999	391,790	708,642	1,100,431	78,723	3.99	10.39	6.61	377	4,376	4,753	1,326	1.76	6.61
2000	373,659	699,953	1,073,612	72,748	4.15	11.01	6.99	301	4,271	4,572	1,272	1.89	6.99
2001	380,627	745,308	1,127,689	77,088	4.02	10.60	6.82	341	1,143	1,484	955	.81	6.82
2002	357,385	735,910	1,094,283	75,466	3.98	10.38	6.80	305	998	1,303	872	.78	6.80
2003	352,785	717,870	1,071,753	71,023	4.04	10.76	6.95	282	977	1,259	820	.82	6.95

[1] Excludes miners employed at mines producing less than 10,000 tons.   *Source: Energy Information Administration, U.S. Department of Energy (EIA-DOE)*

Average Mine Prices of Coal in the United States   In Dollars Per Short Ton

| | Average Mine Price by Method | | | Average Mine Prices by Rank | | | | Bituminous & Lignite FOB Mines[2] | Anthracite FOB Mines[2] | All Coal CIF[3] Electric Utility Plants |
Year	Under-ground	Surface	Total	Lignite	Sub-bituminous	Bituminous	Anthracite[1]			
1994	26.39	15.02	19.41	10.77	8.37	25.68	36.07	25.68	36.07	28.03
1995	26.18	14.25	18.83	10.83	8.10	25.56	39.78	25.56	39.78	27.01
1996	25.96	13.82	18.50	10.92	7.87	25.17	36.78	25.17	36.78	26.45
1997	25.68	13.39	18.14	10.91	7.42	24.64	35.12	24.64	35.12	26.16
1998	25.64	12.92	17.67	10.80	6.96	24.87	42.91	24.87	42.91	25.64
1999	24.33	12.37	16.63	11.04	6.87	23.92	35.13	23.92	35.13	24.72
2000	23.84	12.26	16.44	11.41	7.12	24.15	40.90	24.15	40.90	24.28
2001	25.37	13.18	17.38	11.52	6.67	25.36	47.67	25.36	47.67	24.68
2002	26.68	13.65	17.98	11.07	7.34	26.57	47.78	26.57	47.78	24.74
2003	26.71	13.42	17.85	11.20	7.73	26.73	49.55	26.73	49.55	25.29

[1] Produced in Pennsylvania.   [2] FOB = free on board.   [3] CIF = cost, insurance and freight.   W = Withheld data.
Source: Energy Information Adminstration, U.S. Department of Energy (EIA-DOE)

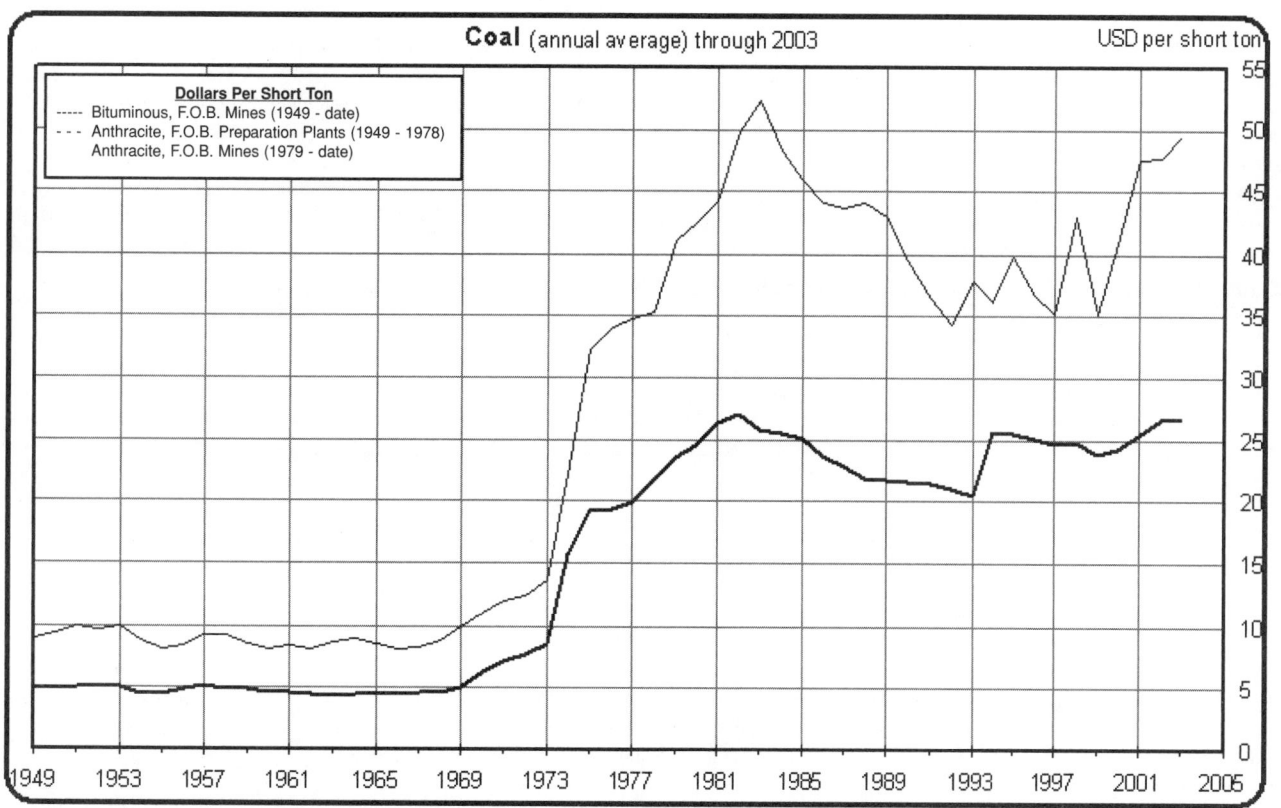

Coal (annual average) through 2003   USD per short ton

Dollars Per Short Ton
----- Bituminous, F.O.B. Mines (1949 - date)
- - - Anthracite, F.O.B. Preparation Plants (1949 - 1978)
    Anthracite, F.O.B. Mines (1979 - date)

Cobalt

Cobalt (symbol Co) is a lustrous, silvery-white, magnetic, metallic element used chiefly for making alloys. Cobalt was known in ancient times and used by the Persians in 2250 BC to color glass. The name *cobalt* comes from the German word *kobalt* or *kobold*, meaning evil spirit. Miners gave cobalt its name because it was poisonous and troublesome since it polluted and degraded other mined elements, like nickel. In the 1730s, George Brandt first isolated metallic cobalt and was able to show that cobalt was the source of the blue color in glasses. In 1780, it was recognized as an element. Cobalt is generally not found in nature as a free metal and is instead found in ores. Cobalt is generally produced as a by-product of nickel and copper mining.

Cobalt is used in a variety of applications: high temperature steel alloys; fasteners in gas turbine engines; magnets and magnetic recording media; drying agents for paints and pigments; and steel-belted radial tires. Cobalt-60, an important radioactive tracer and cancer-treatment agent, is an artificially produced radioactive isotope of cobalt.

Prices – The price of cobalt plunged in 2003 rose sharply by +53% to $10.60 per pound from $6.91 per pound in 2002. The 2003 price was still far below the record high of $29.21 per pound posted in 1995.

Supply – World production of cobalt in 2003 fell by -3.8% to 48,400 metric tons from the record high of 50,300 metric tons seen in 2002. The world's largest cobalt mine

producers are the Congo with 25% of world production in 2003, Zambia (23%), Australia (14%), and Canada (9%).

The United States does not specifically mine or refine cobalt although some cobalt is produced as a by-product of mining operations. Imports, stock releases, and secondary materials comprise the US cobalt supply. Secondary production includes extraction from super-alloy scrap, cemented carbide scrap, and spent catalysts. In the US, there are two domestic producers of extra-fine cobalt powder. One produced the powder from imported primary metal and the other from recycled materials. There are seven companies that produce cobalt compounds. US secondary production of cobalt in 2004 rose +16.8% yr/yr to 2,500 metric tons.

Demand – US consumption of cobalt in 2003 rose +1.4% yr/yr to 10,000 metric tons, which was below the record high of 11,800 metric tons seen in 2002. The largest use of cobalt by far was for super-alloys with 3,400 metric tons of consumption in 2003. Other smaller-scaled applications for cobalt include cutting and wear-resistant materials (662 metric tons), welding materials (632 metric tons), and magnetic alloys (339 metric tons).

Trade – US imports of cobalt in 2003 fell by -4.4% to 8,080 metric tons, well below the 19-year high of 9,410 metric tons seen in 2001. The US relies on imports for 76% of its cobalt consumption, which is down from the 99% level seen in the early 1970s.

World Mine Production of Cobalt   In Metric Tons (Cobalt Content)

Year	Australia	Bots-wana	Canada	Cuba	Finland (Refinery)	France (Refinery)	Japan (Refinery)	New Caledonia	Norway (Refinery)	Russia	Congo[3]	Zambia	World Total
1994	2,300	225	4,265	972	3,000	146	161	1,000	2,823	3,000	826	3,600	18,000
1995	2,500	271	5,339	1,591	3,610	161	227	1,100	2,804	3,500	1,647	5,908	24,500
1996	2,800	408	5,714	2,011	4,160	174	258	1,100	3,098	3,300	2,000	6,959	26,200
1997	3,000	334	5,709	2,358	5,000	159	264	1,000	3,417	3,300	3,500	6,037	27,400
1998	3,300	335	5,861	2,665	10,600	300	480	1,000	4,500	3,600	5,000	11,900	35,300
1999	4,100	331	5,323	2,537	10,000	300	480	1,100	4,500	3,900	7,000	5,640	32,700
2000	5,600	308	5,298	2,943	10,000	300	480	1,200	4,500	4,000	11,000	4,600	38,300
2001	6,200	325	5,326	3,411	10,000	300	480	1,400	4,500	4,600	15,000	8,000	47,800
2002[1]	6,700	269	5,148	3,124	10,000	300	480	1,400	4,500	4,600	14,500	10,000	50,300
2003[2]	6,900	362	4,304	3,000	10,000	600	600	1,400	4,600	4,800	12,000	11,300	48,400

[1] Preliminary.   [2] Estimate.   [3] Formerly Zaire.   *Source: U.S. Geological Survey (USGS)*

Salient Statistics of Cobalt in the United States   In Metric Tons (Cobalt Content)

Year	Net Import Reliance as a % of Apparent Consumption	Cobalt Secondary Production	Processors and Consumer Stocks Dec. 31	Imports for Consumption	Ground Coat Frit	Stainless & Heat Resisting	Catalysts	Super-alloys	Tool Steel	Magnetic Alloys	Pigments	Drier in Paints, etc.[3]	Cutting & Wear-Resistant Material	Welding Materials	Total Apparent Uses	Price $ Per Pound[4]
1994	81	1,570	914	6,780	W	41	871	2,810	84	698	198	809	723	312	8,730	24.66
1995	79	1,860	818	6,440	196	38	732	2,940	146	757	172	770	748	287	8,970	29.21
1996	76	2,280	770	6,710	391	38	652	3,360	95	719	191	733	722	347	9,380	25.50
1997	76	2,750	763	8,430	490	38	734	4,170	112	879	201	556	789	342	11,200	23.34
1998	73	3,080	750	7,670	W	38	W	4,060	96	771	W	W	844	421	11,500	21.43
1999	73	2,720	738	8,150	W	W	W	3,830	W	794	W	W	755	291	10,700	17.02
2000	74	2,550	820	8,770	W	W	W	4,070	W	625	W	W	760	867	11,600	15.16
2001	78	2,780	852	9,410	W	W	W	4,850	W	472	W	W	720	661	11,800	10.55
2002[1]	75	2,800	917	8,450	W	W	W	3,700	W	416	W	W	618	634	9,860	6.91
2003[2]	78	2,140	699	8,080	W	W	W	3,400	W	339	W	W	662	632	10,000	10.60

[1] Preliminary.   [2] Estimate.   [3] Or related usage.   [4] Annual spot for cathodes.   W = Withheld proprietary data.

Source: U.S. Geological Survey (USGS)

Cocoa

Cocoa is the common name for a powder derived from the fruit seeds of the cacao tree. The Spanish called cocoa "the food of the gods" when they found it in South America 500 years ago. Today, it remains a valued commodity. Dating back to the time of the Aztecs, cocoa was mainly used as a beverage. The processing of the cacao seeds, also known as cocoa beans, begins when the harvested fruit is fermented or cured into a pulpy state for three to nine days. The cocoa beans are then dried in the sun and cleaned in special machines before they are roasted to bring out the chocolate flavor. After roasting, they are put into a crushing machine and ground into cocoa powder. Cocoa has a high food value because it contains as much as 20 percent protein, 40 percent carbohydrate, and 40 percent fat. It is also mildly stimulating because of the presence of theobromine, an alkaloid that is closely related to caffeine. Roughly two-thirds of cocoa bean production is used to make chocolate and one-third to make cocoa powder.

Four major West African cocoa producers, the Ivory Coast, Ghana, Nigeria and Cameroon, together account for about two-thirds of world cocoa production. Outside of West Africa, the major producers of cocoa are Indonesia, Brazil, Malaysia, Ecuador, and the Dominican Republic. Cocoa producers like Ghana and Indonesia have been making efforts to increase cocoa production while producers like Malaysia have been switching to other crops. Ghana has had an ongoing problem with black pod disease and with smuggling of the crop into neighboring Ivory Coast. Brazil was once one of the largest producers of cocoa but has had problems with witches' broom disease. In West Africa, the main crop harvest starts in the September-October period and can be extended into the January-March period. Cocoa trees reach maturity in 5-6 years but can live to be 50 years old or more. During the course of a growing season, the cocoa tree will produce thousands of flowers but only a few will develop into cocoa pods.

Cocoa futures and options are traded at the CSCE Division of the New York Board of Trade (NYBOT) and on the London International Financial Futures and Options Exchange (LIFFE). The futures contracts call for the delivery of 10 metric tons of cocoa and the contract is priced in US dollars per metric ton.

Prices – Cocoa prices on the CSCE nearest-futures chart in 2004 consolidated near the middle of the range established by the sharp rally from the 3-decade low near $674

per metric ton posted in December 2000 to the 2-decade high of $2,420 posted in early 2003. Cocoa futures closed 2004 at $1547 per metric ton, up 2.1% from the $1515 close in 2003. Cocoa prices were supported in 2004 by the 9% drop in world cocoa production in 2004-05, which caused a 144,000 metric tons drop in stocks over the course of the year. The stocks/consumption ratio in 2004-05 fell to 40.2%, which was on the lower end of the range of 37.7% (1985-86) to 69.4% (1991-92) seen in the past 2 decades. Consumption in 2004 was strong and rose to a new record high. Cocoa prices were boosted in November 2004 when the Ivory Coast government broke the 18-month ceasefire with rebels in the north and also bombed a French military encampment in the north. The French retaliated by destroying virtually all the Ivory Coast's military aircraft, which led to angry mobs taking to the streets in Abidjan. Cocoa production and shipments temporarily dropped 25% due to that disruption. The cocoa markets in 2005 will key on world demand, the dollar, and the ability of the Ivory Coast to boost its production after the –8.4% drop in production in 2004-05.

Supply – The world cocoa crop in 2004-05 fell –8.6% yr/yr to 3.130 million metric tons from the record high of 3.423 million metric tons seen in 2003-04. The drop in production caused closings stocks in 2004-05 to fall –9.9% yr/yr to 1.308 million metric tons, and the stocks/consumption ratio to fall to the low level of 40.2%. World grindings in 2004-05 rose by +1.0% yr/yr to 3.251 million metric tons, which was a new record high. The world's largest cocoa producer by far is the Ivory Coast where production in 2004-05 fell –8.4% yr/yr to 1.270 million metric tons from the record high of 1.386 million metric tons in 2003-04. The Ivory Coast accounted for 40.6% of world cocoa production in 2004-05. Other major cocoa producers include Ghana with 19% of world production, and Indonesia with 13%.

Demand – World consumption of cocoa in 2003-04 rose +7.2% yr/yr to a new record high of 3.219 million metric tons. The world's largest cocoa consumers are the European Union with 36% of world consumption in 2003-04, followed by the US with 13% of world consumption.

Trade – US imports of cocoa and cocoa products in 2004 rose sharply by +11.9% yr/yr to 1.171 million metric tons, which was a new record high. That is 64% more than US cocoa imports of 715,000 metric tons seen in 1990.

World Supply and Demand Cocoa — In Thousands of Metric Tons

Crop Year Beginning October	Stocks Oct. 1	Net World Production[4]	Total Availability	Seasonal Grindings	Closing Stocks	Stock Change	Stock/ Consumption Ratio %
1995-6	1,372	2,941	4,313	2,655	1,636	264	61.6
1996-7	1,636	2,712	4,348	2,730	1,598	-39	58.5
1997-8	1,598	2,626	4,224	2,773	1,431	-167	51.6
1998-9	1,431	2,808	4,239	2,756	1,461	31	53.0
1999-00	1,461	3,049	4,510	2,988	1,499	38	50.2
2000-1	1,499	2,823	4,322	3,076	1,225	-274	39.8
2001-2	1,225	2,801	4,026	2,835	1,170	-55	41.3
2002-3[1]	1,170	3,131	4,301	3,004	1,273	104	42.4
2003-4[2]	1,273	3,423	4,696	3,219	1,452	179	45.1
2004-5[3]	1,452	3,130	4,582	3,251	1,308	-144	40.2

[1] Preliminary.   [2] Estimate.   [3] Forecast.   [4] Obtained by adjusting the gross world crop for a one percent loss in weight.

Source: ED&F Man Cocoa Ltd.

COCOA

World Production of Cocoa Beans   In Thousands of Metric Tons

Crop Year Beginning October	Brazil	Cameroon	Colombia	Dominican Republic	Ecuador	Ghana	Indonesia	Ivory Coast	Malaysia	Mexico	Nigeria	Papua New Guinea	World Total
1995-6	222	117	45	55	103	404	284	1,265	116	30	165	35	2,941
1996-7	183	121	39	47	101	323	327	1,130	102	35	160	28	2,712
1997-8	173	114	38	60	28	409	331	1,090	57	30	165	26	2,635
1998-9	138	123	39	22	72	398	396	1,175	79	25	200	35	2,808
1999-00	124	115	37	28	92	435	428	1,404	37	31	175	46	3,049
2000-1	163	133	42	37	81	395	412	1,185	29	33	177	39	2,823
2001-2	124	131	40	44	72	340	464	1,240	10	31	167	38	2,801
2002-3[1]	163	155	41	44	78	497	449	1,360	10	33	152	42	3,131
2003-4[2]	163	150	41	45	105	736	419	1,386	10	27	161	40	3,423
2004-5[3]	162	150	41	45	95	590	420	1,270	10	30	165	41	3,130

[1] Preliminary.   [2] Estimate.   [3] Forecast.   *Source: ED&F Man Cocoa Ltd*

World Consumption of Cocoa[4]   In Thousands of Metric Tons

Year	Canada	Brazil	European Union	Ghana	Indonesia	Cote d'Ivoire	Japan	Malaysia	Singapore	Turkey	United States	Russia	World Total
1994-5	35	174	1,072	64	52	108	39	101	59	15	331	75	2,483
1995-6	39	183	1,158	60	60	130	49	96	63	16	345	75	2,655
1996-7	35	180	1,130	68	72	145	53	103	61	16	394	74	2,730
1997-8	53	188	1,160	67	74	195	43	94	68	22	399	50	2,773
1998-9	42	191	1,125	65	83	210	47	109	63	22	406	48	2,756
1999-00	56	202	1,195	75	88	230	48	117	60	25	439	62	2,988
2000-1	58	195	1,197	80	91	285	49	121	59	39	445	67	3,076
2001-2[1]	56	173	1,103	79	108	265	50	93	62	39	393	69	2,835
2002-3[2]	57	196	1,121	70	115	290	64	129	71	49	400	60	3,004
2003-4[3]	59	202	1,161	95	115	295	58	190	65	50	415	58	3,219

[1] Preliminary.   [2] Estimate.   [3] Forecast.   [4] Figures represent the grindings of cocoa beans in each country.   NA = Not available.
Source: ED&F Man Cocoa Ltd

Imports of Cocoa Butter in Selected Countries   In Metric Tons

Year	Australia	Austria	Belgium	Canada	France	Germany	Italy	Japan	Netherlands	Sweden	Switzerland	United Kingdom	United States
1994	13,030	5,410	34,061	11,551	36,698	59,170	9,173	15,937	43,192	7,079	17,242	35,453	54,550
1995	12,150	7,425	26,185	11,146	40,245	69,928	12,027	12,898	38,300	7,078	17,835	30,654	57,210
1996	14,316	7,124	23,771	12,166	47,349	69,298	11,178	16,096	39,193	5,698	18,690	32,781	68,761
1997	14,896	6,922	34,222	16,782	46,516	71,094	9,706	16,609	29,023	6,937	19,058	37,021	87,687
1998	16,305	5,984	25,722	16,941	43,610	76,057	8,957	15,363	28,523	7,403	19,857	32,951	65,306
1999	22,573	5,363	42,278	17,323	49,722	70,323	8,281	17,824	35,602	6,884	21,278	39,648	80,475
2000	20,591	4,425	52,917	22,005	48,033	71,985	11,106	21,696	27,253	5,986	19,923	36,360	94,649
2001	20,634	3,814	51,576	23,307	51,029	80,839	11,764	21,663	36,643	6,350	18,901	40,668	80,808
2002	20,800	3,638	49,467	24,397	58,949	82,313	12,101	20,212	37,569	6,401	20,187	39,117	54,788
2003[1]	22,307	3,963	58,076	26,314	58,651	77,880	13,343	22,579	55,820	6,564	21,455	38,799	78,315

[1] Preliminary.   NA = Not available.   *Source: ED&F Man Cocoa Ltd*

Imports of Cocoa Liquor and Cocoa Powder in Selected Countries   In Metric Tons

Year	Cocoa Liqour France	Germany	Japan	Netherlands	United Kingdom	United States	Cocoa Powder Denmark	France	Germany	Italy	Japan	Netherlands	United States
1994	42,392	2,682	14,913	2,312	4,443	26,846	3,625	19,215	28,806	12,884	6,461	10,078	67,207
1995	46,570	5,083	6,822	1,832	5,030	19,192	3,229	17,081	32,247	15,265	6,310	10,048	66,075
1996	62,938	7,437	9,926	2,133	5,069	15,357	3,711	18,398	36,211	15,006	13,069	6,678	68,658
1997	61,148	10,299	8,401	1,393	5,860	17,850	4,189	19,555	35,069	15,872	8,941	4,424	71,024
1998	70,883	9,121	12,534	1,144	3,813	21,894	3,865	19,533	32,479	17,122	8,779	3,746	84,211
1999	74,721	13,833	1,421	25,639	4,396	12,823	3,676	19,342	33,404	16,464	9,779	8,405	84,975
2000	67,812	14,295	1,618	33,815	8,529	10,902	3,348	21,932	34,601	18,261	11,245	22,492	86,908
2001	67,500	17,548	1,553	41,913	10,289	17,940	4,014	25,736	32,621	20,164	11,949	30,149	113,593
2002	64,820	28,100	1,193	46,369	14,038	22,215	NA	24,445	36,583	19,201	10,299	26,021	95,499
2003[1]	71,337	31,391	1,764	NA	20,154	20,018	NA	31,933	32,805	18,573	12,895	35,275	99,977

[1] Preliminary.   NA = Not available.   *Source: ED&F Man Cocoa Ltd*

Imports of Cocoa and Products in the United States   In Thousands of Metric Tons

Year	Jan.	Feb.	Mar.	Apr.	May	June	July	Aug.	Sept.	Oct.	Nov.	Dec.	Total
1995	68	54	44	48	47	48	48	51	53	49	54	79	643
1996	90	87	90	80	55	49	62	53	53	60	60	86	821
1997	80	47	77	71	64	54	59	47	64	61	56	88	768
1998	86	105	90	71	55	65	65	62	72	63	54	77	865
1999	100	79	81	93	51	60	77	62	68	67	82	102	922
2000	111	128	101	91	70	67	70	70	86	76	59	69	999
2001	108	97	77	47	68	61	80	78	76	86	92	118	989
2002	87	74	73	61	76	72	87	98	61	66	90	72	916
2003	115	74	92	71	68	74	95	82	79	95	85	116	1,046
2004[1]	110	82	130	100	101	103	94	94	100	90	80	89	1,171

[1] Preliminary.   *Source: Foreign Agricultural Service, U.S. Department of Agriculture (FAS-USDA)*

Visible Stocks of Cocoa in Port of Hampton Road Warehouses[1], at End of Month   In Thousands of Bags

Year	Jan.	Feb.	Mar.	Apr.	May	June	July	Aug.	Sept.	Oct.	Nov.	Dec.
1995	2,152.7	2,098.6	2,195.7	2,212.3	2,120.2	2,016.0	1,919.8	1,786.6	1,713.1	1,598.2	1,463.9	1,470.3
1996	1,439.8	1,492.8	1,458.0	1,549.6	1,561.7	1,493.9	1,412.3	1,315.4	1,239.6	1,338.9	1,108.1	1,116.2
1997	1,128.3	1,132.1	1,133.0	1,094.0	1,010.5	970.2	872.4	840.1	727.3	763.9	695.7	704.8
1998	726.5	693.4	841.9	842.5	811.6	764.7	714.3	712.3	795.4	801.9	705.9	673.0
1999	661.6	693.2	642.5	579.7	536.9	500.7	489.0	472.7	473.4	451.8	438.9	421.2
2000	469.7	448.4	571.7	583.4	711.1	672.4	720.3	925.2	921.4	839.7	762.9	816.0
2001	741.9	657.4	632.0	607.7	577.3	518.8	498.2	487.5	475.2	506.8	509.0	511.4
2002	504.7	462.8	436.7	424.0	383.8	353.4	327.4	273.3	255.4	194.8	181.5	169.9
2003	149.9	121.7	103.1	102.3	80.5	71.9	69.2	67.7	56.9	53.0	49.6	49.3
2004	48.6	47.8	47.5	47.5	44.3	43.9	41.2	40.4	40.1	38.0	38.0	36.8

[1] Licensed and unlicensed warehouses approved by the CSCE.   *Source: New York Board of Trade (NYBOT)*

Visible Stocks of Cocoa in Philadelphia (Del. River) Warehouses[1], at End of Month   In Thousands of Bags

Year	Jan.	Feb.	Mar.	Apr.	May	June	July	Aug.	Sept.	Oct.	Nov.	Dec.
1995	807.5	1,034.3	1,038.9	1,020.2	963.7	924.3	860.7	759.2	852.2	727.0	666.0	735.6
1996	960.2	1,005.2	1,205.6	1,658.8	1,871.3	1,851.7	1,969.1	1,816.2	1,851.1	1,705.1	1,671.7	1,696.5
1997	1,753.0	1,634.4	1,579.6	1,641.0	1,578.7	1,625.9	1,696.2	1,637.6	1,530.9	1,491.8	1,414.2	1,394.0
1998	1,420.3	1,435.7	1,592.6	1,555.3	1,398.5	1,287.8	1,279.8	1,376.9	1,373.7	1,260.6	1,406.7	1,637.1
1999	1,763.0	1,832.8	1,982.7	2,217.8	2,019.4	1,999.6	2,084.6	2,133.4	2,144.1	2,015.5	1,774.4	1,608.5
2000	1,619.0	1,801.7	2,466.4	2,582.0	2,581.6	2,363.7	2,168.3	2,101.6	2,105.1	2,039.1	1,697.4	1,589.4
2001	1,844.0	2,082.3	2,173.3	1,960.0	1,785.9	1,610.4	1,391.6	1,543.0	1,391.3	1,131.4	1,303.2	1,682.1
2002	1,701.5	1,876.7	1,849.3	1,708.0	1,746.4	1,689.5	1,793.1	1,832.7	1,750.9	1,334.5	1,162.7	1,250.6
2003	1,347.2	1,422.0	1,327.9	1,326.5	1,217.2	1,202.3	1,229.2	1,123.7	930.6	798.9	723.7	806.0
2004	1,294.9	1,061.5	1,259.1	1,187.1	1,238.8	1,342.0	1,432.6	1,529.3	1,366.4	1,569.4	1,312.8	1,335.7

[1] Licensed and unlicensed warehouses approved by the CSCE.   *Source: New York Board of Trade (NYBOT)*

Visible Stocks of Cocoa in New York Warehouses[1], at End of Month   In Thousands of Bags

Year	Jan.	Feb.	Mar.	Apr.	May	June	July	Aug.	Sept.	Oct.	Nov.	Dec.
1995	560.5	634.5	559.2	539.4	510.4	561.1	579.3	595.4	459.9	598.7	679.7	598.7
1996	667.6	646.1	632.7	627.2	656.1	633.5	1,191.7	1,154.2	1,121.4	973.2	950.1	919.0
1997	984.7	981.3	945.0	1,250.0	1,574.4	1,524.7	1,512.8	1,348.0	1,217.3	1,073.7	1,020.0	980.4
1998	973.9	1,342.7	1,271.3	1,675.7	1,552.3	1,516.7	1,404.6	1,293.1	1,300.1	1,126.4	989.2	1,031.6
1999	1,085.0	1,089.3	1,083.1	1,134.1	1,139.4	1,114.3	1,093.5	974.5	941.9	821.7	847.5	1,573.1
2000	1,633.7	1,689.5	1,926.9	2,049.8	1,926.7	1,789.6	1,632.2	1,383.7	1,323.7	1,234.8	1,100.0	1,019.4
2001	1,005.6	1,173.8	1,119.6	1,024.9	967.5	906.6	776.2	758.5	657.6	687.4	750.8	1,196.2
2002	1,088.9	870.8	892.0	816.1	739.1	736.0	640.9	553.6	670.1	525.7	473.1	554.8
2003	614.6	625.4	593.7	612.9	515.1	476.1	423.6	388.2	483.4	301.9	391.3	342.9
2004	229.9	415.2	616.1	579.9	712.7	680.1	676.3	596.1	486.3	334.5	272.0	209.6

[1] Licensed and unlicensed warehouses approved by the CSCE.   *Source: New York Board of Trade (NYBOT)*

COCOA

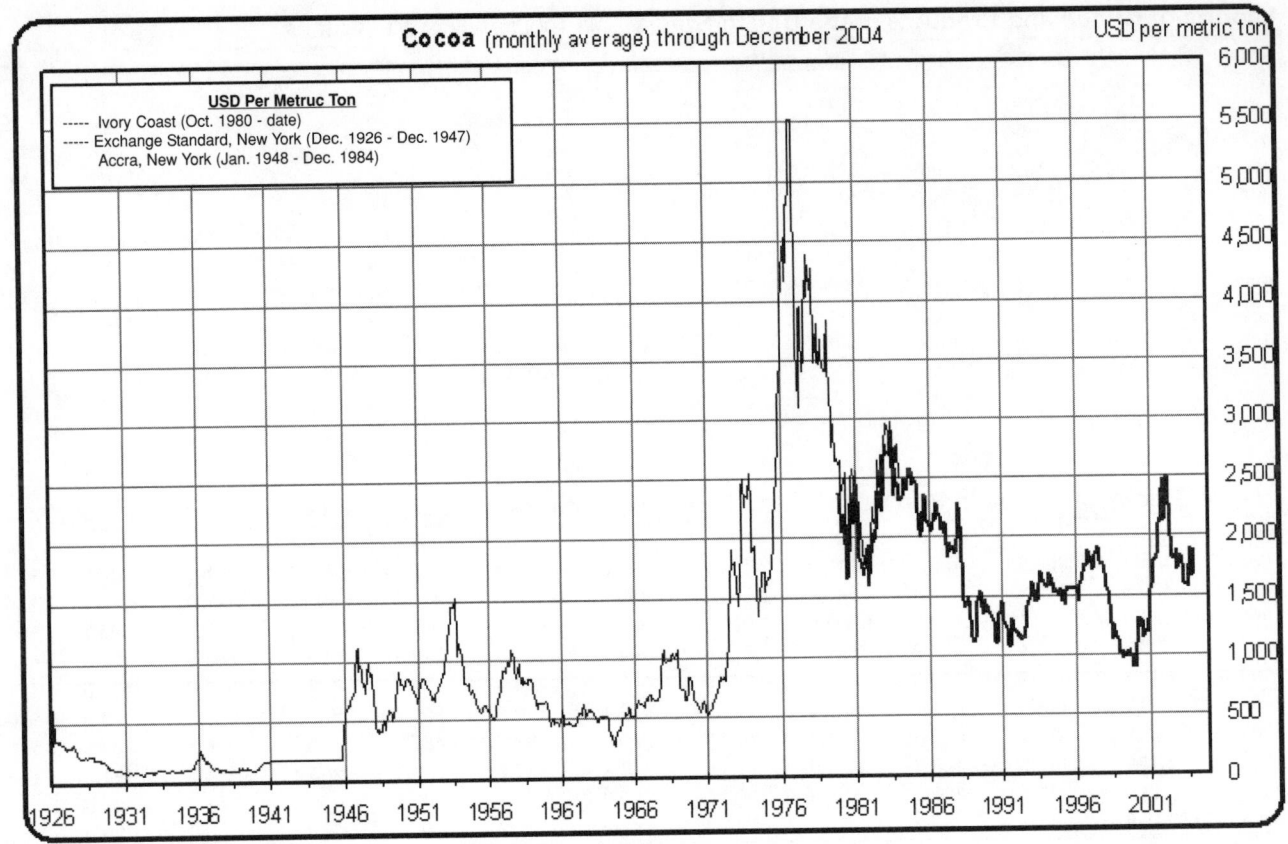

Cocoa (monthly average) through December 2004

USD per metric ton

USD Per Metruc Ton
----- Ivory Coast (Oct. 1980 - date)
----- Exchange Standard, New York (Dec. 1926 - Dec. 1947)
       Accra, New York (Jan. 1948 - Dec. 1984)

Average Cash Price of Cocoa, Ivory Coast in New York   In Dollars Per Metric Ton

Year	Jan.	Feb.	Mar.	Apr.	May	June	July	Aug.	Sept.	Oct.	Nov.	Dec.	Average
1995	1,653	1,685	1,651	1,629	1,594	1,590	1,522	1,553	1,510	1,516	1,562	1,482	1,579
1996	1,455	1,476	1,421	1,536	1,558	1,577	1,556	1,563	1,559	1,578	1,546	1,560	1,532
1997	1,517	1,452	1,591	1,628	1,624	1,748	1,736	1,743	1,864	1,832	1,770	1,819	1,694
1998	1,750	1,721	1,812	1,835	1,902	1,812	1,792	1,761	1,767	1,750	1,694	1,630	1,769
1999	1,565	1,498	1,415	1,276	1,144	1,263	1,209	1,154	1,156	1,133	1,037	1,027	1,240
2000	1,027	962	1,025	993	998	1,033	1,034	980	988	991	905	911	987
2001	1,093	1,299	1,290	1,244	1,281	1,146	1,152	1,200	1,183	1,288	1,439	1,543	1,263
2002	1,586	1,674	1,794	1,800	1,814	1,836	2,081	2,191	2,391	2,471	2,123	2,322	2,007
2003	2,483	2,506	2,258	2,232	1,996	1,818	1,803	1,843	1,877	1,713	1,737	1,832	2,008
2004	1,840	1,763	1,695	1,610	1,588	1,571	1,733	1,889	1,698	1,654	1,867	1,848	1,730

Source: Economic Research Service, U.S. Department of Agriculture (ERS-USDA)

Average Open Interest of Cocoa Futures in New York   In Contracts

Year	Jan.	Feb.	Mar.	Apr.	May	June	July	Aug.	Sept.	Oct.	Nov.	Dec.
1995	78,873	80,786	82,299	78,435	80,547	75,496	74,975	65,794	68,547	72,758	76,680	79,844
1996	90,478	93,533	98,049	95,390	96,346	88,232	80,873	77,134	77,942	79,572	77,139	78,592
1997	86,960	90,589	96,771	96,956	94,651	97,385	101,815	101,138	106,487	108,263	99,544	97,009
1998	90,574	82,205	78,022	73,237	79,294	74,347	74,295	73,975	71,978	74,139	74,127	73,480
1999	77,067	72,324	69,221	65,856	71,990	75,195	70,787	69,939	74,572	79,770	89,035	92,609
2000	100,540	110,316	106,056	102,382	113,239	111,948	112,864	117,260	123,463	138,523	139,141	138,266
2001	132,711	119,459	114,036	102,275	107,008	111,224	104,473	99,280	92,235	96,204	93,088	92,326
2002	97,563	98,169	96,336	98,851	103,746	100,701	107,080	102,441	107,294	107,880	82,236	82,844
2003	96,375	91,944	83,625	83,230	95,307	96,813	89,846	78,197	76,468	86,392	99,038	94,010
2004	88,879	84,078	99,918	100,429	108,150	99,476	103,350	111,318	101,998	119,033	117,876	118,769

Source: New York Board of Trade (NYBOT)

Volume of Trading of Cocoa Futures in New York   In Contracts

Year	Jan.	Feb.	Mar.	Apr.	May	June	July	Aug.	Sept.	Oct.	Nov.	Dec.	Total
1995	197,032	183,784	191,328	208,707	169,061	199,211	140,789	205,169	120,433	149,810	211,171	113,603	2,090,098
1996	177,720	226,701	213,189	242,988	164,749	183,544	159,070	164,719	107,634	167,227	185,226	128,809	2,121,576
1997	180,669	172,510	219,896	235,020	130,041	251,471	186,280	200,707	168,981	204,394	180,805	143,735	2,274,509
1998	175,844	145,311	171,333	192,120	143,602	183,719	131,642	156,737	115,066	125,320	155,280	114,606	1,810,580
1999	136,109	155,090	141,090	180,837	130,019	230,925	125,360	144,290	147,124	143,335	209,608	124,249	1,868,036
2000	156,812	231,562	232,803	186,837	147,072	267,470	124,906	191,849	111,740	174,216	186,515	98,266	2,110,048
2001	311,900	168,587	164,131	136,021	154,397	201,299	108,189	207,569	118,428	124,884	202,847	107,565	2,005,817
2002	155,699	187,550	129,833	217,590	160,364	220,289	176,450	209,249	138,394	207,310	162,982	114,270	2,079,980
2003	172,845	215,240	136,564	179,956	176,969	207,255	143,888	206,428	146,113	197,316	209,775	135,857	2,128,206
2004	174,684	180,693	181,667	244,946	174,452	238,201	219,018	260,025	146,090	150,443	290,227	128,604	2,389,050

Source: New York Board of Trade (NYBOT)

Coconut Oil and Copra

Coconut oil and copra come from the fruit of the coconut palm tree, which originated in Southeast Asia. Coconut oil has been used for thousands of years as cooking oil, and is still a staple in the diets of many people living in tropical areas. Until shortages of imported oil developed during WWII, Americans also used coconut oil for cooking.

Copra is the meaty inner lining of the coconut. It is an oil-rich pulp with a light, slightly sweet, nutty flavor. Copra is used mainly as a source of coconut oil and is also used shredded for baking. High-quality copra contains about 65% to 72% oil, and oil made from the copra is called crude coconut oil. Crude coconut oil is processed from copra by expeller press and solvent extraction. It is not considered fit for human consumption until it has been refined, which consists of neutralizing, bleaching and deodorizing it at high heat with a vacuum. The remaining oil cake obtained as a by-product is used for livestock feed.

Premium grade coconut oil, also called virgin coconut oil, is oil made from the first pressing without the addition of any chemicals. Premium grade coconut oil is more expensive than refined or crude oil because the producers use only selected raw materials and there is a lower production yield due to only one pressing.

Coconut oil accounts for approximately 20% of all vegetable oils used worldwide. Coconut oil is used in margarines, vegetable shortening, salad oils, confections, and in sports drinks to boost energy and enhance athletic performance. It is also used in the manufacture of soaps, deter-gents, shampoos, cosmetics, candles, glycerin and synthetic rubber. Coconut oil is very healthy, unless it is hydrogenated, and is easily digested.

Prices – The average monthly price of coconut oil (crude) in 2003 (through September, annualized) rose +14.3% to 25.07 cents per pound from the 13-year low of 21.94 cents posted in 2002. The record high of 60.21 cents per pound was posted in 1984.

Supply – World production of copra in 2004 fell -4.7% yr/yr to 5.031 million metric tons. That was well below the record high of 5.668 million metric tons posted in 2001. The world's largest producers of copra are the Philippines with 42% of world production, Indonesia with 24%, India with 14%, and Mexico with 4%. World production of coconut oil in the 2003-04 marketing year fell -0.2% yr/yr to 3.204 million metric tons, mildly below the record of 3.508 million posted in 2000.

Demand – Virtually all of world production of copra in 2003-04 went for crushing into coconut meal and oil (99%). World consumption of coconut oil in 2003-04 rose +0.3% yr/yr to 3.270 million metric tons, mildly below the record of 3.349 million metric tons in 2000-01.

Trade – Copra is generally crushed in the country of origin, meaning that less than 4% of copra is exported and the rest is exported in the form of coconut oil. World exports of coconut oil in 2003-04 fell -3.9% yr/yr to 1.906 million metric tons.

World Production of Copra   In Thousands of Metric Tons

Year	India	Indonesia	Ivory Coast	Malaysia	Mexico	Mozambique	New Guinea	Philippines	Sri Lanka	Thailand	Vanuatu	Vietnam	World Total
1995	655	1,080	72	66	217	74	125	2,500	113	103	30	208	5,544
1996	720	1,155	75	60	204	75	178	1,725	75	61	33	210	4,880
1997	720	1,300	45	60	217	76	159	2,210	67	61	34	96	5,363
1998	735	965	43	50	237	76	143	2,270	71	61	43	68	5,077
1999	718	860	36	48	199	73	146	1,250	68	65	30	72	3,874
2000	700	1,330	45	49	202	75	152	2,140	98	69	27	45	5,248
2001	710	1,180	45	49	198	75	70	2,790	95	69	24	50	5,668
2002[1]	713	1,290	45	50	203	75	71	2,065	70	61	10	52	5,004
2003[2]	690	1,250	45	51	183	72	85	2,390	75	65	20	53	5,281
2004[3]	700	1,230	45	51	200	75	87	2,100	85	70	28	54	5,031

[1] Preliminary.   [2] Estimate.   [3] Forecast.   Source: The Oil World

World Supply and Distribution of Coconut Oil   In Thousands of Metric Tons

	Production							Consumption						Ending Stocks		
Year	India	Indonesia	Malaysia	Philippines	Total	Exports	Imports	European Union	India	Indonesia	Philippines	United States	Total	Philippines	United States	Total
1994-5	383	638	36	1,564	3,312	1,775	1,760	660	384	492	309	491	3,325	99	74	430
1995-6	397	612	35	1,206	2,912	1,374	1,405	606	396	373	306	427	3,005	100	38	368
1996-7	424	756	35	1,257	3,150	1,726	1,658	688	432	213	339	504	3,067	92	68	384
1997-8	442	652	39	1,628	3,411	2,125	2,111	771	440	211	302	540	3,184	32	178	598
1998-9	431	458	51	783	2,369	1,040	1,136	578	446	110	295	461	2,744	58	69	319
1999-00	421	787	54	1,198	3,082	1,800	1,724	754	435	110	299	420	2,914	112	62	411
2000-1	431	700	48	1,731	3,508	2,177	2,180	729	450	277	348	437	3,349	60	118	572
2001-2[1]	421	773	45	1,441	3,249	1,865	1,887	689	450	280	372	516	3,341	60	103	503
2002-3[2]	422	752	41	1,428	3,209	1,984	1,945	746	461	264	354	371	3,262	53	99	411
2003-4[3]	419	736	47	1,428	3,204	1,906	1,918	725	450	282	346	384	3,270	50	76	357

[1] Preliminary.   [2] Estimate.   [3] Forecast.   Source: The Oil World

Supply and Distribution of Coconut Oil in the United States   In Millions of Pounds

	----- Rotterdam -----						---------- Disappearance ----------			------- Production of Coconut Oil (Refined) -------				
	Copra	Coconut	Imports											
	Tonne	Oil, CIF	For Con-	Stocks	Total		Total	Edible	Inedible		Oct.-	Jan.-	April-	July-
Year	--------- $ U.S. ---------		sumption	Oct. 1	Supply	Exports	Domestic	Products	Products	Total	Dec.	Mar.	June	Sept.
1994-5	432	656	1,100	163	1,263	18	1,082	247	694	546.8	137.5	142.7	144.3	122.3
1995-6	487	746	873	163	1,036	11	941	221	453	445.0	127.5	118.4	132.8	66.4
1996-7	452	693	1,188	83	1,271	11	1,111	120	471	324.2	77.0	61.5	101.5	84.2
1997-8	391	625	1,440	149	1,589	7	1,190	141	472	397.8	113.4	103.6	100.4	80.4
1998-9	468	748	791	392	1,183	11	1,021	144	380	363.2	89.6	82.9	99.3	91.4
1999-00	357	539	926	152	1,078	14	927	221	371	442.3	69.1	117.0	129.6	126.7
2000-1	208	323	1,100	136	1,236	8	968	237	297	534.9	135.7	128.3	146.9	124.0
2001-2	245	388	1,150	260	1,410	11	1,100	294	302	501.8	139.5	126.1	115.4	120.8
2002-3[1]	286	450	1,150	301	1,451	10	1,201	305	310	546.7	128.8	137.0	155.6	125.2
2003-4[2]	398	605	809	219	1,028	15	847	330	274	594.9	160.7	132.8	162.8	138.6

[1] Preliminary.   [2] Estimate.   *Source: Bureau of Census, U.S. Department of Commerce*

Consumption of Coconut Oil in End Products (Edible and Inedible) in the U.S.   In Millions of Pounds

Year	Jan.	Feb.	Mar.	Apr.	May	June	July	Aug.	Sept.	Oct.	Nov.	Dec.	Total
1995	78.2	79.5	86.5	81.0	79.7	82.0	76.5	71.4	61.6	62.1	59.8	59.9	878.0
1996	47.0	54.3	60.1	60.2	68.6	54.6	55.1	47.9	44.9	49.6	50.3	47.9	640.7
1997	44.1	44.8	52.8	46.1	41.9	49.4	49.9	48.3	66.9	53.4	43.9	48.0	589.5
1998	51.5	48.1	59.4	54.3	54.5	47.0	49.3	50.3	53.7	49.4	50.0	42.1	609.6
1999	39.9	44.7	50.8	43.0	41.4	45.4	36.9	33.3	46.2	41.5	43.6	38.8	505.5
2000	49.4	44.0	52.7	54.6	51.4	56.5	49.1	56.2	54.7	44.1	44.3	43.0	600.0
2001	49.3	40.6	45.5	42.5	48.3	43.3	46.5	45.6	48.4	50.3	44.4	45.5	550.2
2002	55.4	41.3	50.8	59.3	53.9	46.4	50.7	51.8	45.9	54.3	56.1	49.4	615.4
2003	51.2	49.3	56.8	50.6	52.3	46.7	48.9	49.6	50.3	47.8	41.8	38.5	583.7
2004[1]	50.0	51.7	58.5	54.6	48.5	55.6	52.9	55.1	48.9	48.2	64.3	51.7	640.0

[1] Preliminary.   *Source: Bureau of Census, U.S. Department of Commerce*

Stocks of Coconut Oil (Crude and Refined) in the U.S., on First of Month   In Millions of Pounds

Year	Jan.	Feb.	Mar.	Apr.	May	June	July	Aug.	Sept.	Oct.	Nov.	Dec.
1995	155.6	173.6	168.1	163.7	148.5	183.5	163.8	136.9	124.1	162.9	199.7	187.7
1996	164.7	229.1	200.4	217.7	173.6	175.9	171.5	116.7	113.8	84.0	78.6	65.0
1997	125.9	147.4	141.1	204.5	174.5	161.3	143.8	143.4	154.3	149.6	162.1	194.2
1998	274.2	332.4	344.5	337.4	318.8	300.6	366.3	424.6	434.4	392.6	431.8	447.3
1999	401.7	446.5	387.5	366.3	309.8	240.5	134.7	197.5	191.8	152.0	106.4	142.2
2000	93.6	123.6	100.1	99.6	102.3	104.0	137.7	163.6	161.4	136.4	178.1	161.6
2001	245.4	280.3	357.8	276.5	286.9	194.3	254.4	260.9	246.4	259.7	234.1	231.3
2002	245.9	238.8	249.6	251.3	233.5	231.6	303.3	301.6	245.8	226.5	273.8	264.1
2003	195.2	194.0	214.3	224.9	223.7	187.8	162.2	202.9	195.6	218.9	184.6	186.1
2004[1]	167.2	160.3	192.6	181.7	131.4	108.7	90.6	132.8	149.2	131.3	147.7	182.5

[1] Preliminary.   NA = Not available.   *Source: Bureau of Census, U.S. Department of Commerce*

Average Price of Coconut Oil (Crude) Tank Cars in New York   In Cents Per Pound

Year	Jan.	Feb.	Mar.	Apr.	May	June	July	Aug.	Sept.	Oct.	Nov.	Dec.	Average
1994	30.30	29.69	27.31	28.19	29.45	30.25	29.56	30.35	30.63	30.60	34.19	33.69	30.35
1995	32.50	32.00	31.13	31.00	30.50	35.00	37.90	35.63	35.00	36.00	37.88	33.69	34.02
1996	35.80	36.63	36.75	38.75	39.50	42.25	41.80	42.80	47.20	48.00	49.50	50.00	42.42
1997	44.20	44.00	42.88	42.50	42.50	35.00	36.50	36.50	37.00	37.25	37.25	37.25	39.40
1998	37.25	37.25	37.25	37.25	37.25	37.00	36.50	35.50	36.50	39.00	37.50	38.50	37.23
1999	35.38	35.00	34.00	34.06	38.25	42.13	39.83	36.08	46.00	46.00	46.00	46.00	39.89
2000	40.88	32.94	28.81	26.63	24.25	21.90	19.63	18.58	16.40	16.81	17.50	15.70	23.34
2001	26.00	24.00	22.75	22.50	21.00	21.00	24.00	26.50	26.50	26.50	24.50	24.50	24.15
2002	16.38	17.38	17.25	18.75	20.05	21.13	21.06	21.35	28.50	28.25	27.13	26.00	21.94
2003[1]	26.00	26.00	24.60	24.50	24.50	25.00	25.00	25.00	25.00				25.07

[1] Preliminary.   *Source: Economic Research Service, U.S. Department of Agriculture (ERS-USDA)*

Coffee

Coffee is one of the world's most important cash commodities. Coffee is the common name for any type of tree in the genus madder family. It is actually a tropical evergreen shrub that has the potential to grow 100 feet tall. The coffee tree grows in tropical regions between the Tropics of Cancer and Capricorn in areas with abundant rainfall, year-round warm temperatures averaging about 70 degrees Fahrenheit, and with no frost. In the US, the only areas that produce any significant amount of coffee are Puerto Rico and Hawaii. The coffee plant will produce its first full crop of beans at about 5 years old and then be productive for about 15 years. The average coffee tree produces enough beans to make about 1 to 1 ½ pounds of roasted coffee per year. It takes approximately 4,000 handpicked green coffee beans to make a pound of coffee. Wine was actually the first drink made from the coffee tree using the coffee cherries, honey, and water. In the 17th century, the first coffee house, also known as a "penny university" because of the price per cup, opened in London. The London Stock Exchange grew from one of these first coffee houses.

Coffee is generally classified into two types of beans: arabica and robusta. The most widely produced coffee is arabica, which makes up about 70 percent of total production. It grows mostly at high altitudes of 600 to 2,000 meters, with Brazil and Colombia being the largest producers. Arabic coffee is traded on the New York Board of Trade. The stronger of the two types is robusta. It is grown at lower altitudes with the largest producers being Indonesia, West Africa, Brazil, and Vietnam. Robusta coffee is traded on the LIFFE exchange.

Ninety percent of the world coffee trade is in green (unroasted) coffee beans. Seasonal factors have a significant influence on the price of coffee. There is no extreme peak in world production at any one time of the year, although coffee consumption declines by 12 percent or more below the year's average in the warm summer months. Therefore, coffee imports and roasts both tend to decline in spring and summer and pick up again in fall and winter.

The very low prices for coffee in 2000-03 created serious problems for coffee producers. When prices fall below the costs of production, there is little or no economic incentive to produce coffee. The result is that coffee trees are neglected or completely abandoned. When prices are low, producers cannot afford to hire the labor needed to maintain the trees and pick the crop at harvest. The result is that trees yield less due to reduced use of fertilizer and fewer employed coffee workers. One effect is a decline in the quality of the coffee that is produced. Higher quality Arabica coffee is often produced at higher altitudes, which entails higher costs. It is this coffee that is often abandoned. Although the pressure on producers is severe, the market eventually comes back into balance as supply declines in response to low prices.

Coffee prices are subject to upward spikes in June, July and August due to freeze scares in Brazil during the winter months in the Southern Hemisphere. The Brazilian coffee crop is harvested starting in May and extending for several weeks into what are the winter months in Brazil. A major freeze in Brazil occurs about every five years.

Coffee futures are traded on the Bolsa de Mercadorias & Futuros (BM&F), the Tokyo Grain Exchange (TGE), the London International Financial Futures and Options Exchange (LIFFE), and the CSCE Division of the New York Board of Trade (NYBOT). Options are traded on the BM&F, the LIFFE and the CSCE.

Prices – Coffee prices on the CSCE nearest-futures chart in 2004 rallied sharply, establishing a large 5-year rounded bottom pattern and posting a new 5-year high. Coffee futures traded in a depressed price range in 2001-03 but finally took a turn higher in 2004. Bullish fundamentals include (1) a steady increase in demand, and (2) falling production, which is expected to produce a world inventory drawdown of 5-7 mln bags in the 2004-05 marketing year. The International Coffee Organization expects coffee production in 2005-06 to fall -6% yr/yr to 107 million 60-kg bags. That would add to the -6% yr/yr drop in production in 2004-05 to 114 million bags. If the expected inventory drawdown occurs, that would take the stocks/use ratio down to a record low of 55% versus the 10-year average of 101.5%.

Brazil's upcoming 2005-06 coffee crop (harvested May-Sep 2005) is expected to fall to 31-33 million bags from 38.6 million bags in 2004-05 due to poor tending and the biennial tree cycle. Brazil's poor tending was caused in part by low coffee prices seen in 2000-03, which left little incentive and capital for tree tending. Brazil had a huge record crop of 51.600 million bags in 2002-03 before the declines in the past two years. Columbia's crop is less volatile and rose +0.8% yr/yr to 11.800 million bags in 2003-04. Vietnam's 2004-05 coffee crop (harvested through January 2005) is expected to fall sharply by around -20% from 11.8 million bags in 2003-04 because of an extended drought during the early stages of crop development. Vietnam has become a major coffee producer, boosting its production to a record high of 15.333 million bags in 2000-01 from only about 2 million bags in 1990.

Supply – World coffee production in the 2004-05 marketing year (July-June) rose +8.7% yr/yr to 119.020 million bags (1 bag equals 60 kilograms or about 132.3 pounds). The 2004-05 production level of 119.020 million bags was well below the record production year seen in 2002-03 of 124.179 million bags. The rise in production allowed ending stocks to rise +14.4% to 25.803 million bags, reversing some of the −24% yr/yr drop in stocks seen in 2003-04 to 22.551 million bags. Brazil is the world's largest coffee producer by far with 41.7 million bags of production in 2004-05, accounting for 35% of total world production. Other key producers include Vietnam with 12% of world production and Columbia with 10%.

Demand – World coffee consumption in 2004-05 rose +2.6% yr/yr to a new record high of 28.563 million bags. US coffee consumption rose to about 22.0 million bags in 2004.

Trade – World coffee exports in 2004-05 fell −2.3% yr/yr to 82.244 million bags, which was a 3-year low. The world's largest exporters of coffee are Brazil with 30% of world exports in 2004-05, Vietnam with 15%, and Columbia with 11%. The key countries from which the US imported coffee in 2004 were Brazil (which accounted for 20% of US imports), Columbia (17%), Mexico (7%), and Guatemala (7%).

World Supply and Distribution of Coffee   In Thousands of 60 Kilogram Bags (132.276 Lbs. Per Bag)

Crop Year	Beginning Stocks	Pro- duction	Imports	Supply	Total Exports	Bean Exports	Rst/Grn Exports	Soluble Exports	Domestic Use	Ending Stocks
1995-6	41,215	88,946	1,079	131,240	74,103	69,021	231	4,851	24,049	33,088
1996-7	33,088	103,786	1,091	137,965	84,509	79,918	196	4,395	24,361	29,095
1997-8	29,095	97,687	1,220	128,002	77,939	73,249	193	4,497	25,180	24,883
1998-9	24,883	108,453	1,435	135,271	85,133	80,855	269	4,009	25,738	24,400
1999-00	24,400	113,819	1,274	139,493	92,660	87,499	288	4,873	25,608	21,225
2000-1	21,225	118,170	1,484	140,879	90,966	84,882	289	5,795	26,315	23,598
2001-2	23,598	111,351	1,617	136,566	87,662	81,108	338	6,216	27,746	21,158
2002-3[1]	21,158	126,649	1,494	149,301	91,882	85,200	281	6,401	27,130	30,289
2003-4[2]	30,289	109,506	1,553	141,348	90,950	83,940	322	6,688	27,847	22,551
2004-5[3]	22,551	119,020	1,625	143,196	88,830	82,244	315	6,271	28,563	25,803

[1] Preliminary.   [2] Estimate.   [3] Forecast.   *Source: Foreign Agricultural Service, U.S. Department of Agriculture (FAS-USDA)*

World Production of Green Coffee   In Thousands of 60 Kilogram Bags (132.276 Lbs. Per Bag)

Crop Year	Brazil	Colombia	Costa Rica	El Salvador	Ethiopia	Guate- mala	India	Indo- nesia	Ivory Coast	Mexico	Uganda	Vietnam	World Total
1995-6	16,800	12,939	2,595	2,325	3,800	3,827	3,717	5,800	2,900	5,400	4,200	3,917	88,946
1996-7	28,000	10,779	2,376	2,498	3,800	4,141	3,417	7,900	5,333	5,300	4,297	5,750	103,788
1997-8	23,500	12,043	2,455	2,040	3,833	4,200	3,805	7,000	4,080	4,950	3,032	7,000	97,652
1998-9	35,600	10,868	2,459	1,860	3,867	4,300	4,415	6,950	2,217	5,010	3,640	7,500	108,453
1999-00	30,800	9,512	2,688	2,612	3,833	4,364	4,870	6,660	5,700	6,193	3,097	11,010	113,819
2000-1	34,100	10,500	2,502	1,624	3,683	4,564	5,020	6,495	5,100	4,800	3,205	15,333	118,170
2001-2	35,100	11,950	2,338	1,610	3,756	3,530	5,010	6,160	3,568	4,200	3,166	12,833	111,351
2002-3[1]	53,600	11,712	2,207	1,351	3,693	3,802	4,588	6,140	2,119	4,350	2,910	11,167	126,649
2003-4[2]	32,000	11,053	2,119	1,250	4,333	3,802	4,500	6,000	1,610	4,500	3,100	15,000	109,506
2004-5[3]	41,700	11,600	1,955	1,285	4,000	3,671	4,840	5,800	1,550	4,500	3,000	14,167	119,020

[1] Preliminary.   [2] Estimate.   [3] Forecast.   *Source: Foreign Agricultural Service, U.S. Department of Agriculture (FAS-USDA)*

World Exportable[4] Production of Green Coffee   In Thousands of 60 Kilogram Bags (132.276 Lbs. Per Bag)

Crop Year	Brazil	Colombia	Costa Rica	El Salvador	Ethiopia	Guate- mala	Indonesia	Ivory Coast	Kenya	Mexico	Uganda	Vietnam	World Total
1995-6	6,300	11,439	2,360	2,055	2,300	3,527	3,750	2,852	1,789	4,340	4,140	3,700	65,393
1996-7	17,000	9,279	2,130	2,268	2,300	3,856	5,820	5,282	1,115	4,450	4,217	5,463	79,817
1997-8	12,000	10,483	2,150	1,805	2,250	3,850	5,360	4,025	1,005	3,955	2,952	6,717	72,986
1998-9	23,100	9,418	2,154	1,633	2,234	3,900	5,350	2,159	1,125	4,050	3,580	7,200	83,162
1999-00	18,000	7,982	2,347	2,445	2,200	3,964	5,305	5,640	1,662	5,138	2,977	10,660	88,336
2000-1	21,000	8,970	2,157	1,473	2,016	4,139	5,160	5,038	841	3,822	3,085	14,916	92,010
2001-2	21,400	10,360	1,988	1,466	1,923	3,110	4,695	3,504	846	3,200	3,016	12,333	83,820
2002-3[1]	40,100	10,452	1,902	1,209	1,860	3,382	4,660	2,054	903	3,400	2,830	10,667	99,793
2003-4[2]	18,200	9,798	1,854	1,108	2,500	3,382	4,300	1,543	979	3,550	2,940	14,467	81,989
2004-5[3]	27,500	10,340	1,700	1,143	2,165	3,251	3,950	1,481	1,062	3,550	2,840	13,500	90,807

[1] Preliminary.   [2] Estimate.   [3] Forecast.   [4] Marketing year begins in October in some countries and April or July in others. Exportable production represents total harvested production minus estimated domestic consumption.   *Source: Foreign Agricultural Service, U.S. Department of Agriculture*

Coffee Imports in the United States   In Thousands of 60 Kilogram Bags (132.276 Lbs. Per Bag)

Year	Brazil	Colombia	Costa Rica	Dominican Republic	Ecuador	El Salvador	Ethiopia	Guate- mala	Indonesia	Mexico	Peru	Vene- zuela	Grand Total
1995	2,453	2,511	389	267	763	285	109	1,641	516	2,939	622	89	16,491
1996	2,042	3,050	483	257	677	402	137	1,750	1,251	3,822	441	446	18,721
1997	2,446	3,260	609	155	442	501	308	1,922	1,328	3,039	652	65	19,673
1998	2,804	3,510	776	165	377	501	184	1,565	1,274	2,589	774	146	20,101
1999	4,847	3,418	783	80	461	550	77	2,149	724	3,276	766	372	21,787
2000	2,747	3,191	780	73	177	1,209	91	2,380	693	3,725	868	32	22,840
2001	3,007	3,272	915	50	230	507	80	2,040	887	2,057	692	4	20,490
2002	5,060	3,596	987	51	145	470	74	1,626	759	2,034	842	170	20,631
2003	5,321	3,883	914	80	133	569	101	2,023	966	1,510	807	180	21,694
2004[1]	4,475	3,714	957	2	157	524	121	1,624	1,636	1,477	788	103	22,047

[1] Preliminary.   *Source: Bureau of Census, U.S. Department of Commerce*

COFFEE

Monthly Coffee Imports in the United States   In Thousands of 60 Kilogram Bags[2]

Year	Jan.	Feb.	Mar.	Apr.	May	June	July	Aug.	Sept.	Oct.	Nov.	Dec.	Total
1995	1,469	1,253	1,702	1,221	1,190	1,240	1,117	1,094	1,220	1,326	1,492	1,563	15,886
1996	1,824	1,657	1,753	1,395	1,444	1,236	1,329	1,341	1,364	1,279	1,485	1,828	17,936
1997	1,582	1,837	1,966	1,792	1,738	1,583	1,783	1,391	1,147	1,215	1,184	1,629	18,848
1998	1,747	1,893	1,827	1,587	1,540	1,412	1,386	1,478	1,369	1,499	1,423	1,837	18,998
1999	1,742	1,866	2,243	1,787	1,602	1,691	1,488	1,639	1,491	1,470	1,639	1,903	20,561
2000	2,189	2,092	2,416	2,003	2,199	1,960	1,912	1,815	1,598	1,583	1,546	1,527	22,840
2001	1,747	1,690	1,906	1,825	1,823	1,685	1,863	1,605	1,430	1,502	1,581	1,833	20,490
2002	1,652	1,364	1,613	1,697	1,672	1,547	1,802	1,794	1,850	1,877	1,807	1,958	20,631
2003	1,994	1,755	2,007	1,916	1,715	1,710	2,015	1,732	1,712	1,750	1,525	1,863	21,694
2004[1]	1,813	1,635	1,967	1,862	2,049	2,034	1,784	1,766	1,708	1,684	1,798	1,947	22,047

[1] Preliminary.   [2] 132.276 pounds per bag.   *Source: Bureau of the Census, U.S. Department of Commerce*

Average Price of Brazilian[1] Coffee in New York   In Cents Per Pound

Year	Jan.	Feb.	Mar.	Apr.	May	June	July	Aug.	Sept.	Oct.	Nov.	Dec.	Average
1995	162.81	161.07	171.48	166.54	161.72	145.22	139.68	149.54	130.26	127.23	125.33	110.46	145.95
1996	127.54	144.05	140.99	132.92	134.76	125.44	106.93	108.28	103.10	105.77	103.76	103.71	119.77
1997	127.28	160.21	179.75	183.73	209.62	184.21	158.52	158.25	167.77	152.12	149.07	171.12	166.80
1998	179.83	177.78	154.84	141.11	124.89	104.09	96.04	101.92	92.76	91.32	96.67	100.28	121.81
1999	99.43	91.72	88.90	86.14	96.29	91.69	78.13	76.67	70.43	78.74	98.41	109.47	88.84
2000	97.68	91.51	89.93	86.46	87.23	78.32	79.89	70.57	71.14	72.28	68.95	64.39	79.86
2001	62.38	62.50	60.35	55.11	57.19	51.86	46.43	46.49	42.42	38.63	42.28	41.60	50.60
2002	42.56	42.79	48.79	49.90	45.19	42.96	43.58	40.55	44.46	45.28	48.37	46.70	45.09
2003	49.14	48.54	43.77	48.71	51.06	47.11	49.64	52.88	55.19	53.51	54.15	56.92	50.89
2004	64.32	66.08	65.79	62.89	64.31	67.62	59.39	60.25	69.46	68.63	80.20	89.17	68.18

[1] And other Arabicas.   *Source: Coffee Publications, Inc.*

Average Monthly Retail [1] Price of Coffee in the United States   In Cents Per Pound

Year	Jan.	Feb.	Mar.	Apr.	May	June	July	Aug.	Sept.	Oct.	Nov.	Dec.	Average
1997	330.0	331.6	351.2	389.4	410.9	442.8	462.8	466.9	461.7	439.2	430.3	416.1	411.1
1998	402.5	397.3	403.3	395.9	387.8	378.6	377.1	370.4	362.0	350.3	348.2	344.6	376.5
1999	343.5	342.8	347.6	346.6	349.5	342.1	342.0	342.8	339.3	348.2	333.7	334.7	342.7
2000	365.4	367.7	363.3	358.4	353.1	343.1	344.6	344.4	333.9	331.7	324.3	321.2	345.9
2001	322.4	321.7	320.5	312.8	309.7	315.6	309.7	304.6	302.5	301.5	298.8	291.3	309.3
2002	293.6	294.6	285.9	297.6	301.1	293.8	297.7	292.9	292.1	287.2	288.2	283.8	292.4
2003	299.9	292.4	293.3	300.8	293.7	293.1	294.4	292.1	291.9	282.5	277.9	287.5	291.6
2004	289.2	285.6	293.2	290.8	283.1	275.0	287.8	287.8	287.4	284.0	277.8	277.6	284.9

[1] Roasted in 13.1 to 20 ounce cans.   *Source: Coffee Publications, Inc.*

Average Price of Colombian Mild Arabicas[1] in the United States   In Cents Per Pound

Year	Jan.	Feb.	Mar.	Apr.	May	June	July	Aug.	Sept.	Oct.	Nov.	Dec.	Average
1997	146.18	188.62	212.96	199.22	318.50	227.15	190.57	193.46	196.29	169.40	161.38	183.32	198.92
1998	184.21	190.59	166.07	158.17	146.33	135.83	125.03	129.45	117.56	115.01	121.74	123.96	142.83
1999	123.07	116.92	117.05	114.02	123.95	121.45	107.05	105.28	97.77	103.69	126.76	140.35	116.45
2000	130.13	124.73	119.51	112.67	110.31	100.30	101.67	91.87	89.98	90.25	84.01	75.81	102.60
2001	75.33	76.70	76.94	78.25	80.92	74.38	69.70	73.50	68.80	62.88	65.72	62.57	72.14
2002	63.46	65.64	71.16	70.17	63.44	60.86	59.60	58.98	62.49	66.54	72.83	67.92	65.26
2003	69.68	69.60	61.82	66.12	67.56	65.01	67.84	68.65	68.37	66.59	67.04	69.38	67.31
2004	76.61	79.34	80.12	77.08	80.61	85.62	78.27	78.85	85.71	85.52	95.63	106.48	84.15

[1] ICO monthly and composite indicator prices on the New York Market, 1979 ICA Agreement basis.   *Source: Coffee Publications, Inc.*

Average Price of Other Mild Arabicas[1] in the United States   In Cents Per Pound

Year	Jan.	Feb.	Mar.	Apr.	May	June	July	Aug.	Sept.	Oct.	Nov.	Dec.	Average
1997	131.83	167.20	193.82	204.43	264.50	212.55	186.52	185.17	184.38	161.45	154.15	174.25	185.02
1998	175.04	175.87	154.82	147.08	134.35	121.56	113.86	119.89	108.07	107.07	113.84	115.54	132.25
1999	110.99	103.24	103.23	99.69	109.10	104.21	90.85	87.64	81.06	92.22	112.74	123.56	101.54
2000	109.17	101.17	98.26	92.76	91.76	84.10	85.20	74.52	73.83	75.43	70.47	64.81	85.12
2001	64.98	67.00	65.88	65.68	68.94	63.79	58.47	59.68	57.71	56.23	58.96	55.63	61.91
2002	57.34	60.51	66.38	65.78	58.45	55.12	53.07	52.02	57.58	64.05	70.15	64.75	60.43
2003	65.22	67.60	61.66	65.35	66.47	61.34	62.32	63.60	65.50	62.58	62.36	65.01	64.08
2004	74.25	77.51	77.29	74.24	76.40	82.24	73.64	72.99	81.22	79.90	89.88	102.19	80.15

[1] ICO monthly and composite indicator prices on the New York Market, 1979 ICA Agreement basis.   *Source: Coffee Publications, Inc.*

Average Price of Robustas 1976[1] in the United States   In Cents Per Pound

Year	Jan.	Feb.	Mar.	Apr.	May	June	July	Aug.	Sept.	Oct.	Nov.	Dec.	Average
1997	67.66	76.65	81.31	78.48	95.74	91.94	82.52	76.92	77.43	76.90	78.20	84.65	80.70
1998	86.03	85.79	84.67	90.60	92.64	84.55	78.40	79.98	80.88	80.36	80.40	82.82	83.93
1999	81.65	77.68	72.70	68.89	68.28	66.20	62.28	63.80	60.44	59.25	64.10	66.40	67.64
2000	53.62	49.41	47.26	45.21	45.19	43.72	41.93	38.94	39.47	36.55	33.34	30.78	42.12
2001	31.00	31.96	30.96	28.59	29.71	29.33	27.59	25.86	23.79	21.26	22.03	23.57	27.14
2002	22.88	24.46	29.77	30.35	29.43	29.26	29.31	28.74	33.31	34.44	39.38	38.68	30.83
2003	42.75	42.35	38.26	38.68	38.90	35.33	36.71	37.92	38.76	37.32	36.05	37.59	38.39
2004	41.32	39.10	38.61	38.02	38.04	41.09	36.44	34.81	35.10	31.77	34.07	38.98	37.28

[1] ICO monthly and composite indicator prices on the New York Market, 1979 ICA Agreement basis.   *Source: Coffee Publications, Inc.*

Average Price of Composite 1979[1] in the United States   In Cents Per Pound

Year	Jan.	Feb.	Mar.	Apr.	May	June	July	Aug.	Sept.	Oct.	Nov.	Dec.	Average
1997	100.03	121.89	137.47	142.20	180.44	155.38	135.04	132.63	132.51	121.09	118.16	130.02	133.91
1998	130.61	130.78	119.93	119.66	114.23	103.84	97.32	101.25	95.82	95.01	98.26	100.73	108.95
1999	97.63	92.36	89.41	85.72	89.51	85.41	78.21	77.22	71.94	76.36	88.22	95.63	85.64
2000	82.15	76.15	73.49	69.53	69.23	64.56	64.09	57.59	57.31	56.40	52.18	48.27	64.25
2001	49.19	49.39	48.52	47.31	49.38	46.54	43.07	42.77	41.17	42.21	44.24	43.36	45.60
2002	43.46	44.30	49.49	50.19	47.30	45.56	44.70	42.79	47.96	50.79	54.69	51.68	47.74
2003	54.04	54.07	49.61	51.87	53.19	48.90	50.89	52.22	54.10	51.72	49.81	52.44	51.91
2004	58.69	59.87	60.80	58.80	59.91	64.28	58.46	56.98	61.47	61.10	67.74	77.72	62.15

[1] ICO monthly and composite indicator prices on the New York Market, 1979 ICA Agreement basis.   *Source: Coffee Publications, Inc.*

COFFEE

Average Open Interest of Coffee 'C' Futures in New York   In Contracts

Year	Jan.	Feb.	Mar.	Apr.	May	June	July	Aug.	Sept.	Oct.	Nov.	Dec.
1995	34,455	35,391	36,925	34,387	34,615	34,462	30,156	27,448	27,800	28,408	24,505	26,412
1996	28,430	28,224	28,127	28,793	28,394	25,096	26,188	25,799	23,929	26,202	27,599	27,201
1997	38,516	42,888	39,092	32,644	30,324	22,552	21,497	19,818	22,788	25,109	23,636	28,577
1998	30,042	30,539	30,211	32,617	36,345	36,651	37,531	30,074	30,429	32,940	31,677	32,816
1999	36,194	36,693	41,294	43,846	45,947	45,675	45,411	46,725	46,255	47,956	46,271	46,764
2000	47,829	50,620	50,565	53,662	49,692	50,293	45,513	40,177	40,133	42,906	43,187	45,086
2001	48,914	53,050	58,111	57,722	53,481	58,311	57,888	57,243	55,674	58,345	55,317	53,953
2002	57,897	66,825	66,798	66,207	66,289	68,994	69,197	69,635	70,079	73,753	73,431	69,343
2003	69,508	71,682	76,934	77,954	72,716	72,155	72,110	68,259	73,809	79,038	81,253	76,670
2004	92,388	103,966	102,281	98,430	96,738	102,276	89,446	88,021	83,001	78,047	83,360	107,832

Source: New York Board of Trade (NYBOT)

Volume of Trading of Coffee 'C' Futures in New York   In Contracts

Year	Jan.	Feb.	Mar.	Apr.	May	June	July	Aug.	Sept.	Oct.	Nov.	Dec.	Total
1995	169,250	191,352	213,326	156,191	163,248	186,550	162,562	161,076	165,337	152,959	157,240	123,923	2,003,014
1996	203,369	186,526	152,797	197,442	137,454	158,929	171,800	196,991	136,054	196,696	135,305	166,213	2,039,576
1997	242,719	280,014	267,369	223,330	219,214	186,227	135,664	136,807	142,610	151,171	145,610	163,446	2,294,181
1998	155,774	194,435	186,712	194,732	157,935	189,768	165,868	189,047	156,556	172,956	197,776	133,471	2,095,030
1999	216,810	201,670	252,841	243,630	237,968	243,164	187,019	232,817	151,724	270,013	244,258	177,309	2,659,223
2000	158,962	232,174	166,970	224,266	177,753	218,467	198,975	175,868	119,304	163,399	187,230	111,593	2,134,961
2001	189,977	221,775	167,466	236,757	182,621	220,708	134,809	250,151	100,443	153,739	229,495	111,430	2,199,371
2002	201,327	279,966	229,764	295,701	159,670	225,177	174,567	254,563	232,255	250,483	236,307	178,728	2,718,508
2003	205,420	283,317	169,611	334,188	255,935	270,424	237,210	278,746	332,473	309,930	314,182	219,595	3,211,031
2004	389,864	397,656	301,270	395,552	324,849	467,887	247,439	366,171	305,196	280,733	424,146	292,540	4,193,303

Source: New York Board of Trade (NYBOT)

Coffee 'C' Futures - New York Board of Trade   Cents per pound
(weekly close) as of December 31, 2004

Coke

Coke is the hard and porous residue left after certain types of bituminous coals are heated to high temperatures (up to 2,000 degrees Fahrenheit) for about 17 hours. It is blackish-gray and has a metallic luster. The residue is mostly carbon. Coke is used as a reducing agent in the smelting of pig iron and the production of steel. Petroleum coke is made from the heavy tar-like residue of the petroleum refining process. It is used primarily to generate electricity.

Supply – Coke production in the US in 2004 rose +5.0% yr/yr to 305.862 million barrels. That was a 3-decade high but was still well below the US production record of 369.305 million barrels posted back in 1957. US stocks at coke plants (Dec 31) in 2003 fell by –37% yr/yr to 380,000 tons.

Trade – US coke exports in 2003 fell sharply by –8.8% to 721,780 tons, and about one-half of those exports were to Canada. US coke imports in 2003 fell –14.9% yr/yr to 2.759 million tons. About one-half of the imports were from Japan.

Salient Statistics of Coke in the United States   In Thousands of Short Tons

| | Coke and Breeze Production at Coke Plants | | | | | | | Producer and Distributor Stocks | Exports | | Imports | |
| | By Census Division | | | | | | | | | | | |
Year	Middle Atlantic	East North Central	East South Central	Other	Total	Coke Total	Breeze Total	Consumption[2]	Dec. 31	Canada	Total	Japan	Total
1998	6,371	9,224	2,922	2,766	21,283	20,041	1,242	23,108	933	830	1,129	2,062	3,834
1999	5,869	10,115	2,821	2,448	21,253	20,016	1,237	22,423	852	686	898	2,012	3,224
2000	6,095	10,835	2,558	2,608	22,096	20,808	1,289	23,242	1,054	795	1,146	1,884	3,781
2001	W	10,272	1,979	7,893	20,144	18,949	1,195	20,202	981	793	1,069	1,508	2,340
2002	W	8,287	1,925	7,712	17,924	16,778	1,146	19,603	606	610	792	1,554	3,242
2003[1]	W	8,642	2,068	7,738	18,448	17,173	1,275	19,436	380	436	722	1,395	2,759

[1] Preliminary.   [2] Equal to production plus imports minus the change in producer and distributor stocks minus exports.
Source: Energy Information Administration, U.S. Department of Energy (EIA-DOE)

Production of Petroleum Coke in the United States   In Thousands of Barrels

Year	Jan.	Feb.	Mar.	Apr.	May	June	July	Aug.	Sept.	Oct.	Nov.	Dec.	Total
1998	20,929	18,968	21,998	21,834	21,790	20,856	21,790	22,469	21,526	21,234	20,837	22,258	256,489
1999	22,312	20,084	22,148	21,444	21,410	20,943	21,741	22,180	21,249	22,166	21,695	22,866	260,238
2000	21,502	20,017	21,654	21,161	21,785	22,095	23,321	22,835	22,455	22,121	22,628	24,262	265,836
2001	23,970	21,112	23,299	23,713	42,465	23,345	23,838	23,339	22,321	23,306	23,350	24,203	298,261
2002	24,543	22,849	23,529	23,850	24,713	23,305	24,556	23,939	23,465	22,527	23,497	24,913	285,686
2003	23,420	20,030	23,810	23,768	24,831	24,054	26,080	25,746	24,072	24,588	24,208	26,560	291,167
2004[1]	25,640	22,380	24,025	25,086	26,789	25,874	26,263	26,151	24,259	25,899	25,897	27,599	305,862

[1] Preliminary.   *Source: Energy Information Administration, U.S. Department of Energy (EIA-DOE)*

Coal Receipts and Average Prices at Coke Plants in the United States

| | Coal Receipts at Coke Plants | | | | | Average Price of Coal Receipts at Coke Plants | | | | |
| | By Census Division, In Thousands of Short Tons | | | | | By Census Division, In Dollars per Short Ton | | | | |
Year	Middle Atlantic	East North Central	East South Central	Other	Total	Middle Atlantic	East North Central	East South Central	Other	Total
1998	8,430	12,442	3,777	3,705	28,354	44.16	48.39	46.43	W	46.06
1999	7,784	13,524	3,571	3,276	28,155	44.33	47.74	45.28	W	45.85
2000	7,971	14,020	3,209	3,520	28,720	42.89	45.62	44.74	W	44.38
2001	W	13,084	2,678	10,622	26,384	W	47.53	47.69	W	46.42
2002	W	11,184	2,335	10,136	23,655	W	52.80	50.03	W	50.67
2003[1]	W	11,252	2,452	10,019	23,723	W	52.94	48.20	W	50.63

[1] Preliminary.   W = Withheld proprietary data.   *Source: Energy Information Administration, U.S. Department of Energy (EIA-DOE)*

Coal Carbonized and Coke and Breeze Stocks at Coke Plants in the U.S.   In Thousands of Short Tons

| | Coal Carbonized at Coke Plants | | | | | Stocks at Coke Plants, Dec. 31 | | | | | | |
| | By Census Division | | | | | By Census Division | | | | | | |
Year	Middle Atlantic	East North Central	East South Central	Other	Total	Middle Atlantic	East North Central	East South Central	Other	Total	Coke Total	Breeze Total
1998	8,401	12,311	3,736	3,741	28,189	160	526	176	215	1,077	933	144
1999	7,799	13,404	3,584	3,321	28,108	69	500	157	277	1,003	852	150
2000	8,129	13,971	3,290	3,549	28,939	148	628	166	255	1,197	1,054	143
2001	W	12,981	2,608	10,486	26,075	W	637	266	607	1,510	981	88
2002	W	11,154	2,319	10,183	23,656	W	424	155	169	748	606	141
2003[1]	W	11,410	2,541	10,297	24,248	W	233	135	144	512	380	132

[1] Preliminary.   W = Withheld proprietary data.   *Source: Energy Information Administration, U.S. Department of Energy (EIA-DOE)*

Copper

The word *copper* comes from name of the Mediterranean island Cyprus that was a primary source of the metal. Dating back more than 10,000 years, copper is the oldest metal used by humans. From the Pyramid of Cheops in Egypt, archeologists recovered a portion of a water plumbing system whose copper tubing was found in serviceable condition after more than 5,000 years.

Copper is one of the most widely used industrial metals because it is an excellent conductor of electricity, has strong corrosion-resistance properties, and is very ductile. It is also used to produce the alloys of brass (a copper-zinc alloy) and bronze (a copper-tin alloy), both of which are far harder and stronger than pure copper. Electrical uses of copper account for about 75% of total copper usage, and building construction is the single largest market (the average US home contains 400 pounds of copper). Copper is biostatic, meaning that bacteria will not grow on its surface, and it is therefore used in air-conditioning systems, food processing surfaces, and doorknobs to prevent the spread of disease.

Copper futures and options are traded on the London Metal Exchange (LME) and the COMEX Division of the New York Mercantile Exchange (Nymex). Copper futures are traded on the Shanghai Futures Exchange. The Nymex copper futures contract calls for the delivery of 25,000 pounds of Grade 1 electrolyte copper and is priced in terms of cents per pound.

Prices – Nymex copper futures prices rallied through most of 2004 and posted a 16-year high of $1.55 per pound in December 2004. That was only mildly below the record high on the nearest futures chart of $1.65 posted in December 1988. Copper futures closed 2004 at $1.487, up 43% yr/yr. Bullish factors for copper in 2004 included the weak dollar and very strong copper demand, particularly from China, which created a production deficit of about 750,000 metric tons for the year.

Supply – World production of copper in 2002, the latest reporting year, fell by –0.7% yr/yr to 13.600 million metric tons, which was slightly below the record high of 13.700 million metric tons seen in 2001. The world's largest copper producers are Chile with 33.7% of world production, Indonesia (8.5%), the US (8.4%), and Australia (6.5%). US production of refined copper in 2004 (annualized through September) fell –1.7% yr/yr to 1.285 million short tons, which was far below the record US production level of 2.490 million short tons seen in 1998.

Demand – US consumption of copper in 2002, the latest reporting year, fell –9.5% yr/yr to 2.370 million metric tons, which was the lowest level since 1993. The primary users of copper in the US by class of consumer are wire rod mills with 72% of usage in 2002, brass mills with 25% of usage, and nominal use of 1% or less by foundries, ingot makers, and chemical plants.

Trade – US exports of copper (annualized through August) rose sharply by 65.8% yr/yr to 154,560 metric tons in 2004, which was the highest level since 1996. US imports of copper in 2004 (annualized through August) fell –11.8% yr/yr to 778,350 metric tons, which was the lowest level of US copper imports since 1998.

World Mine Production of Copper (Content of Ore)   In Thousands of Metric Tons

Year	Australia	Canada[3]	Chile	China	Indonesia	Mexico	Peru	Poland	Russia[4]	South Africa	United States[3]	Zambia	World Total
1993	402.0	732.6	2,055.4	345	298.6	301.2	355.0	382.6	584	166.3	1,800	396.2	9,430
1994	415.6	616.8	2,219.9	396	322.2	294.7	395.9	378.0	573	160.1	1,820	373.2	9,490
1995	397.8	726.3	2,488.6	445	443.6	333.6	409.7	384.2	525	161.6	1,850	316.0	10,000
1996	547.3	688.4	3,115.8	439	507.5	340.7	484.2	421.9	523	152.6	1,920	334.0	11,000
1997	558.0	659.5	3,392.0	511	529.1	390.5	506.5	414.8	505	153.1	1,940	352.9	11,500
1998	607.0	705.8	3,686.8	504	780.8	384.6	483.3	436.2	500	166.0	1,860	315.0	12,100
1999	739.0	620.1	4,391.2	533	766.0	381.2	536.4	463.2	530	144.3	1,600	280.0	12,800
2000	829.0	633.9	4,602.4	613	1,012.1	364.6	553.9	454.1	570	137.1	1,440	249.1	13,200
2001[1]	869.0	633.5	4,739.0	605	1,081.0	371.1	722.0	474.0	600	141.9	1,340	312.0	13,700
2002[2]	883.0	600.2	4,581.0	585	1,160.0	329.6	843.2	502.8	695	129.6	1,140	330.0	13,600

[1] Preliminary.   [2] Estimate.   [3] Recoverable.   [4] Formerly part of the U.S.S.R.; data not reported separately until 1992.
Source: U.S. Geological Survey (USGS)

Commodity Exchange Inc. Warehouse Stocks of Copper, on First of Month   In Thousands of Short Tons

Year	Jan.	Feb.	Mar.	Apr.	May	June	July	Aug.	Sept.	Oct.	Nov.	Dec.
1995	27.0	18.7	17.7	9.0	11.5	7.0	13.1	16.7	16.5	11.2	6.1	5.4
1996	24.0	12.1	12.8	13.9	20.7	13.2	7.4	17.3	22.1	21.7	30.8	38.5
1997	29.5	19.0	24.8	43.6	49.5	43.0	46.3	30.0	46.5	61.5	67.8	79.8
1998	91.5	100.7	112.3	112.6	107.6	84.8	63.5	55.7	56.6	67.7	69.4	74.7
1999	93.9	101.8	112.3	123.1	132.6	131.7	133.7	120.2	108.8	97.5	90.9	90.9
2000	91.6	95.6	95.6	95.9	865.2	75.0	73.6	73.2	62.8	62.3	63.4	64.9
2001	64.7	79.3	90.0	105.1	126.5	150.9	165.1	176.1	186.8	199.6	211.0	236.5
2002	269.2	284.8	304.0	314.1	326.0	337.4	355.7	374.6	375.9	380.3	381.6	382.8
2003	399.3	395.2	373.7	362.7	351.2	336.7	320.5	310.6	303.9	299.0	294.4	288.1
2004	280.9	262.7	241.9	213.3	171.7	130.7	95.1	79.0	62.3	49.2	45.5	42.4

Source: New York Mercantile Exchange (NYMEX), COMEX division

Salient Statistics of Copper in the United States   In Thousands of Metric Tons

	--------------- New Copper Produced ---------------					------ Imports[5] ------		------ Exports ------			-- Stocks, Dec 31 --		Apparent		
	--- From Domestic Ores ---			From		Secon-			Ore,				Primary	Blister &	--- Consumption ---	
			Refin-	Foreign	Total	dary Re-	Unmanu-		Concen-			Producers	Material	Refined	Primary
Year	Mlnes	Smelters	eries	Ores[3]	New	covered[4]	factured	Refined	trate[6]	Refined[7]	COMEX	(Refined)	in Solution	Copper (Reported)	& Old Copper[8]
1993	1,800	1,270	1,210	89	1,790	543	637	343	227	217	67	153	146	2,360	2,510
1994	1,850	1,310	1,280	64	1,840	500	763	470	261	157	24	119	167	2,680	2,690
1995	1,850	1,250	1,300	91	1,930	443	825	429	239	217	22	163	171	2,530	2,540
1996	1,920	1,300	1,290	147	2,010	428	961	543	195	169	27	146	173	2,610	2,830
1997	1,940	1,440	1,370	113	2,070	498	999	632	127	93	83	314	180	2,790	2,940
1998	1,860	1,490	1,290	238	2,140	466	1,190	683	37	86	85	532	160	2,890	3,030
1999	1,600	1,090	1,110	196	1,890	381	1,280	837	63	25	83	565	138	2,980	3,130
2000	1,450	W	865	163	1,590	357	1,350	1,060	107	94	59	334	122	3,030	3,130
2001[1]	1,340	W	808	192	1,630	316	1,400	991	45	23	244	957	98	2,620	2,500
2002[2]	1,140	W	725	116	1,440	207	1,230	927	23	27	362	1,030	44	2,370	2,610

[1] Preliminary.   [2] Estimate.   [3] Also from matte, etc., refinery reports.   [4] From old scrap only.   [5] For consumption.   [6] Blister (copper content).   [7] Ingots, bars, etc.   [8] Old scrap only.   *Source: U.S. Geological Survey (USGS)*

Consumption of Refined Copper[3] in the United States   In Thousands of Metric Tons

| | ------------------------------- By-Products ------------------------------- | | | | | ---------------------------- By Class of Consumer ---------------------------- | | | | | | Total |
| | | Wire | Ingots & | Cakes | | | Wire Rod | Brass | Chemiacl | Ingot | | Miscel- | Con- |
Year	Cathodes	Bars	Ingot Bars	& Slabs	Billets	Other[4]	Mills	Mills	Plants	Makers	Foundries	laneous[5]	sumption
1993	2,130.0	W	37.7	55.5	W	136.0	1,819.1	503.0	0.9	2.2	10.2	27.6	2,360.0
1994	2,410.0	W	37.3	73.2	W	164.0	2,060.0	568.0	1.1	4.5	11.1	30.4	2,680.0
1995	2,250.0	W	31.3	75.9	W	181.0	1,950.0	533.0	1.1	7.7	15.6	31.4	2,530.0
1996	2,320.0	W	26.8	80.8	W	181.0	1,980.0	588.0	1.1	3.6	15.8	28.6	2,610.0
1997	2,490.0	W	29.4	81.1	W	194.0	2,140.0	597.0	1.0	4.2	16.6	29.9	2,790.0
1998	2,600.0	W	30.7	76.2	W	184.0	2,170.0	659.0	1.1	5.4	19.2	31.8	2,890.0
1999	2,710.0	W	24.4	79.3	W	166.0	2,230.0	691.0	1.2	4.5	21.2	29.8	2,980.0
2000	2,730.0	W	23.8	101.0	W	175.0	2,240.0	723.0	1.2	4.6	24.3	32.5	3,030.0
2001[1]	2,360.0	W	24.0	95.9	W	140.0	1,940.0	623.0	1.2	4.6	21.6	28.6	2,620.0
2002[2]	2,140.0	W	29.3	72.6	W	126.0	1,710.0	593.0	1.0	4.6	26.4	35.7	2,370.0

[1] Preliminary.   [2] Estimate.   [3] Primary & secondary.   [4] 1991 to date include Wirebars and Billets.   [5] Includes iron and steel plants, primary smelters producing alloys other than copper, consumers of copper powder and copper shot, and other manufacturers.   W - Withheld proprietary data.
Source: U.S. Geological Survey (USGS)

London Metals Exchange Warehouse Stocks of Copper, at End of Month   In Thousands of Metric Tons

Year	Jan.	Feb.	Mar.	Apr.	May	June	July	Aug.	Sept.	Oct.	Nov.	Dec.
1995	309.9	280.9	239.9	204.9	197.9	166.5	151.5	163.1	178.2	193.6	222.2	364.8
1996	355.1	348.4	322.3	303.9	309.7	263.0	227.6	275.5	240.7	122.1	96.1	119.6
1997	194.2	216.2	177.2	145.8	133.0	128.3	234.9	278.7	332.8	344.6	338.8	337.8
1998	365.7	376.0	339.5	262.3	261.8	249.3	260.9	307.7	414.2	460.6	511.9	590.1
1999	646.9	695.9	722.2	748.2	776.6	754.8	769.6	789.0	774.0	793.8	779.7	790.5
2000	807.3	824.1	755.4	697.8	605.7	553.4	487.8	449.2	401.5	380.9	349.4	357.4
2001	349.9	327.9	400.5	445.2	431.3	464.7	651.9	661.2	729.0	737.2	780.4	799.5
2002	855.5	910.9	950.9	973.8	958.3	892.1	893.6	896.6	870.6	863.2	862.8	855.9
2003	833.8	825.9	813.2	768.2	740.8	665.8	612.6	620.3	580.4	516.5	467.0	430.7
2004[1]	358.2	281.6	187.5	151.3	132.3	101.5	87.7	111.3	91.8	77.9	59.8	

[1] Preliminary.   *Source: American Bureau of Metal Statistics (ABMS)*

Copper Refined from Scrap in the United States   In Thousands of Metric Tons

Year	Jan.	Feb.	Mar.	Apr.	May	June	July	Aug.	Sept.	Oct.	Nov.	Dec.	Total
1995	30.9	30.6	36.0	32.7	33.7	28.2	18.7	25.1	25.4	25.0	26.2	24.4	319.0
1996	25.0	23.7	25.5	22.5	26.8	30.9	24.4	25.0	26.8	30.6	25.9	26.3	333.0
1997	35.9	30.0	36.4	32.6	35.4	30.8	26.4	28.4	34.3	36.5	24.6	29.3	383.0
1998	25.9	28.6	23.7	31.0	17.8	21.4	24.2	23.9	23.8	31.8	23.2	26.3	336.0
1999	20.1	21.8	23.7	17.6	16.2	17.5	21.2	18.2	21.3	21.0	17.7	20.0	230.0
2000	19.4	18.6	25.8	22.5	22.1	15.4	11.7	19.7	14.1	14.3	19.7	15.6	208.0
2001	15.4	14.2	15.2	13.4	12.8	13.2	13.9	13.5	12.3	10.2	6.4	5.7	154.0
2002	7.1	6.2	7.2	7.6	8.2	7.8	7.0	7.6	7.1	6.3	5.1	3.9	81.1
2003	5.8	3.9	5.7	3.9	4.1	4.9	4.9	3.9	4.2	4.5	4.1	4.1	53.8
2004[1]	4.2	3.9	4.3	4.4	4.2	4.5	4.1	3.9	4.7	4.5			51.1

[1] Preliminary.   *Source: U.S. Geological Survey (USGS)*

COPPER

Copper Futures - New York Mercantile Exchange
(weekly close) as of December 31, 2004
Cents per pound

Average Open Interest of Copper Futures in New York   In Contracts

Year	Jan.	Feb.	Mar.	Apr.	May	June	July	Aug.	Sept.	Oct.	Nov.	Dec.
1995	52,632	50,770	47,267	47,793	50,089	48,200	40,968	37,744	33,709	36,476	38,475	35,996
1996	47,771	45,706	42,732	46,771	47,284	52,558	56,564	56,549	55,408	58,124	61,031	55,807
1997	54,468	56,022	58,205	50,574	56,740	56,774	47,767	44,632	49,612	54,912	67,026	67,502
1998	69,607	72,302	67,154	68,670	65,033	66,002	63,271	61,116	60,520	62,944	67,984	76,846
1999	76,861	73,109	75,318	70,534	76,341	70,842	75,640	70,084	80,188	72,240	69,179	69,819
2000	82,289	73,778	68,026	75,520	69,531	63,786	71,389	79,565	83,546	73,609	74,161	70,349
2001	77,952	76,721	78,034	83,647	72,970	85,495	83,690	88,782	87,004	88,166	85,809	68,981
2002	72,823	79,806	79,156	75,229	74,350	80,981	82,661	102,056	99,225	99,470	89,213	79,218
2003	81,820	81,499	72,484	85,485	77,704	81,509	82,868	94,517	92,768	106,924	103,218	90,208
2004	91,726	88,136	77,158	71,705	65,531	64,879	65,310	71,096	81,162	85,421	81,928	88,822

Source: New York Mercantile Exchange (NYMEX), COMEX division

Volume of Trading of Copper Futures in New York   In Contracts

Year	Jan.	Feb.	Mar.	Apr.	May	June	July	Aug.	Sept.	Oct.	Nov.	Dec.	Total
1995	242,760	267,883	232,229	242,302	195,554	274,587	167,836	213,110	169,689	181,945	185,141	146,378	2,519,414
1996	184,431	173,689	157,553	210,836	200,469	255,172	150,445	174,351	166,537	250,420	227,800	160,216	2,311,919
1997	193,543	221,504	190,000	218,607	164,728	238,918	191,609	198,156	197,746	202,615	203,376	135,368	2,356,170
1998	172,133	223,117	197,652	264,061	175,956	217,316	202,596	213,541	196,355	195,255	250,986	174,642	2,483,610
1999	159,147	288,394	230,716	296,162	224,221	319,157	244,567	267,325	220,958	193,628	231,399	177,288	2,852,962
2000	220,488	276,374	195,668	261,971	232,971	241,854	187,453	283,328	171,080	243,342	266,051	197,544	2,778,124
2001	240,588	246,052	247,722	279,348	260,697	317,001	159,394	298,639	129,622	190,469	337,589	149,520	2,856,641
2002	217,598	233,704	164,747	254,259	218,091	267,201	263,395	303,642	195,637	232,731	276,492	179,789	2,807,286
2003	232,921	269,806	249,306	274,079	221,364	301,709	252,713	324,175	196,481	230,413	363,865	172,438	3,089,270
2004	213,536	385,848	265,312	340,236	203,906	280,882	208,415	310,299	212,082	245,011	317,220	207,878	3,190,625

Source: New York Mercantile Exchange (NYMEX), COMEX division

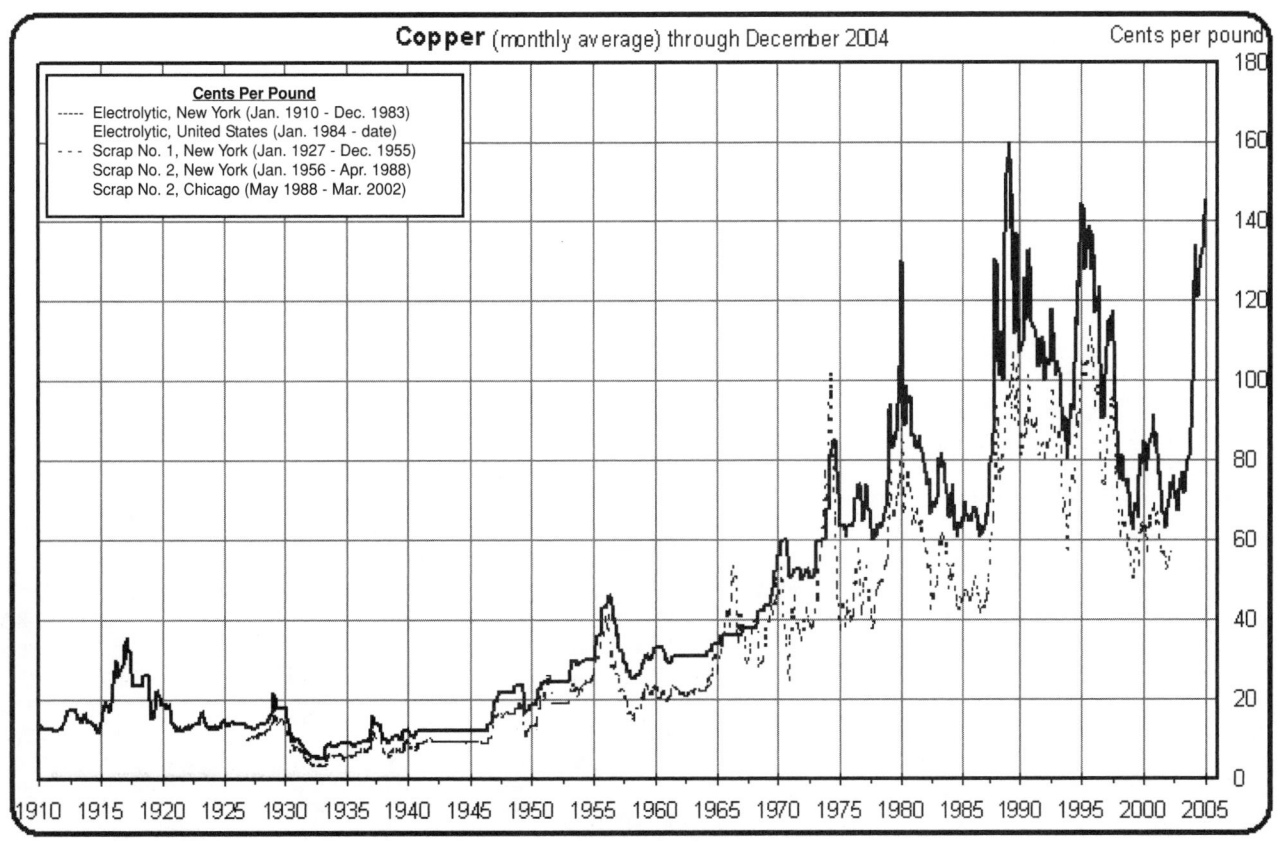

Copper (monthly average) through December 2004 — Cents per pound

Cents Per Pound
- - - - - Electrolytic, New York (Jan. 1910 - Dec. 1983)
Electrolytic, United States (Jan. 1984 - date)
- - - Scrap No. 1, New York (Jan. 1927 - Dec. 1955)
Scrap No. 2, New York (Jan. 1956 - Apr. 1988)
Scrap No. 2, Chicago (May 1988 - Mar. 2002)

Producers' Price of Electrolytic (Wirebar) Copper, Delivered to U.S. Destinations   In Cents Per Pound

Year	Jan.	Feb.	Mar.	Apr.	May	June	July	Aug.	Sept.	Oct.	Nov.	Dec.	Average
1995	151.91	146.00	151.14	146.00	139.80	149.51	150.00	149.77	144.14	140.00	148.48	143.78	146.74
1996	130.09	128.75	130.20	131.29	135.33	116.55	103.63	104.14	102.51	101.80	112.58	114.78	117.86
1997	120.29	121.02	126.50	121.70	127.25	129.57	121.94	114.11	107.14	105.08	99.53	91.39	115.55
1998	88.88	87.52	91.69	93.54	90.02	86.90	87.37	85.30	87.62	84.26	83.51	78.30	87.09
1999	77.07	75.96	74.50	78.79	81.07	77.23	88.02	87.88	92.89	91.26	91.10	93.35	84.09
2000	96.83	94.41	91.63	89.32	94.80	92.74	95.81	98.67	103.49	99.63	95.25	98.92	95.96
2001	95.70	94.01	92.07	88.27	88.85	84.58	81.44	79.34	77.41	75.21	78.13	79.83	84.57
2002	81.79	84.23	86.60	85.11	85.22	88.23	84.44	79.82	79.71	80.16	84.57	75.56	82.62
2003	78.62	80.21	78.87	75.60	78.56	80.44	81.55	83.51	85.34	91.50	96.47	103.72	84.53
2004	113.93	129.91	139.96	135.82	129.44	129.11	134.34	135.50	138.74	142.01	147.99	151.88	135.72

Source: American Metal Market (AMM)

Dealers' Buying Price of No. 2 Heavy Copper Scrap in Chicago   In Cents Per Pound

Year	Jan.	Feb.	Mar.	Apr.	May	June	July	Aug.	Sept.	Oct.	Nov.	Dec.	Average
1995	89.48	90.79	89.39	91.75	85.91	88.73	92.32	92.65	92.70	90.64	92.00	92.00	90.70
1996	87.17	82.90	83.24	83.29	82.95	71.48	61.43	62.00	62.00	63.00	64.84	66.00	72.53
1997	68.73	71.63	77.50	79.18	77.33	78.19	72.64	70.24	65.67	63.74	61.31	58.43	70.38
1998	53.26	52.58	53.09	54.00	52.60	49.64	48.00	47.71	46.00	44.00	40.00	40.00	48.41
1999	36.32	36.00	36.00	36.00	39.60	41.77	41.00	45.09	46.19	48.00	48.00	48.67	41.90
2000	50.00	50.00	50.00	49.15	49.00	49.00	49.30	52.65	54.60	55.00	52.65	51.00	51.04
2001	51.62	49.16	49.00	49.81	50.00	50.00	49.14	44.00	44.00	43.48	41.45	41.47	46.93
2002	41.00	41.00	41.00	41.00	41.00	41.00	41.00	41.00	41.00	41.00	41.00	41.00	41.00
2003	41.00	41.00	41.00	41.00	41.00	41.00	41.00	41.00	41.00	48.17	56.00	56.00	43.99
2004	56.65	69.00	69.00	69.32	76.00	76.00	76.64	90.00	90.00	90.00	90.00	90.00	78.55

Source: American Metal Market (AMM)

COPPER

Imports of Refined Copper into the United States   In Thousands of Metric Tons

Year	Jan.	Feb.	Mar.	Apr.	May	June	July	Aug.	Sept.	Oct.	Nov.	Dec.	Total
1995	34.9	30.0	37.1	36.9	36.5	37.9	31.5	31.8	28.7	38.7	44.4	40.3	429.0
1996	43.1	41.2	48.2	49.6	56.8	44.6	53.8	64.8	62.3	46.1	61.8	47.2	543.0
1997	55.4	48.0	43.6	43.6	61.0	42.0	53.1	73.3	53.8	55.0	53.4	42.0	632.0
1998	62.8	49.6	59.9	64.7	57.6	52.8	45.0	51.7	71.1	52.7	62.0	63.4	683.0
1999	64.7	53.2	68.1	59.9	62.3	63.8	73.0	84.5	90.3	81.0	59.0	77.5	837.0
2000	84.9	67.8	85.5	92.1	83.6	84.5	89.4	83.0	98.6	112.0	100.0	73.7	1,060.0
2001	105.0	91.6	90.1	94.4	70.3	72.7	61.7	66.3	83.5	71.0	110.0	74.4	991.0
2002	82.5	87.8	53.0	92.6	59.9	76.2	80.3	90.5	69.9	79.0	82.0	73.0	927.0
2003	60.7	87.8	69.9	78.5	72.7	62.3	74.0	78.1	81.7	82.0	73.2	61.1	882.0
2004[1]	55.4	48.8	70.7	59.3	70.8	51.3	83.9	78.7	91.7				814.1

[1] Preliminary.   *Source: U.S. Geological Survey (USGS)*

Exports of Refined Copper from the United States   In Thousands of Metric Tons

Year	Jan.	Feb.	Mar.	Apr.	May	June	July	Aug.	Sept.	Oct.	Nov.	Dec.	Total
1995	11.1	24.0	25.6	18.2	23.4	38.9	16.3	16.6	12.1	9.0	12.5	9.5	217.0
1996	13.7	16.5	12.7	12.3	10.8	10.7	15.7	17.7	14.5	16.4	12.8	16.0	170.0
1997	11.1	9.8	6.5	6.5	71.9	8.2	6.9	7.5	6.3	7.4	8.2	8.5	93.3
1998	6.2	12.1	12.2	7.5	7.8	6.4	7.5	6.4	5.8	5.0	3.6	6.2	86.2
1999	2.4	1.1	1.8	1.3	1.6	4.2	1.6	1.5	1.2	1.4	3.7	3.3	25.2
2000	1.6	5.3	22.0	12.2	18.1	12.8	6.7	4.4	2.9	4.3	1.2	2.1	93.6
2001	1.2	.9	.8	1.9	1.0	.8	1.7	2.6	1.2	4.6	5.3	.6	22.5
2002	.4	.7	3.2	.7	.8	6.8	7.7	2.6	1.3	.6	.5	1.5	26.6
2003	2.5	.8	1.5	.6	15.9	23.0	5.1	4.1	4.3	4.6	8.5	22.3	93.2
2004[1]	11.0	18.5	23.9	28.4	3.7	2.7	5.5	9.4	.6				138.1

[1] Preliminary.   *Source: U.S. Geological Survey (USGS)*

Stocks of Refined Copper in the United States, on First of Month   In Thousands of Short Tons

Year	Jan.	Feb.	Mar.	Apr.	May	June	July	Aug.	Sept.	Oct.	Nov.	Dec.
1995[2]	55.8	39.6	37.0	22.6	33.1	30.8	27.0	50.0	60.6	71.1	69.4	73.4
1996	120.0	131.4	125.5	123.1	126.3	107.9	102.8	106.2	104.7	68.0	76.0	77.5
1997	88.2	98.8	104.4	116.0	117.9	121.7	122.9	148.8	177.1	197.9	227.6	253.3
1998	281.5	282.2	312.7	315.7	304.5	308.6	306.2	319.0	334.1	367.4	407.2	444.6
1999	562.6	593.1	614.6	653.5	676.6	687.8	668.4	657.2	639.7	611.2	626.5	608.2
2000	619.2	620.8	619.5	582.9	537.0	508.8	467.8	418.0	397.7	394.3	379.1	344.2
2001	383.8	408.4	416.2	481.9	552.6	585.7	626.7	733.1	767.4	895.6	916.6	985.7
2002	1,045.1	1,096.2	1,132.4	1,155.3	1,175.0	1,158.8	1,126.7	1,132.2	1,123.0	1,123.7	1,110.5	1,109.0
2003	1,119.8	109.7	1,038.8	1,042.1	998.3	959.8	891.8	848.9	855.6	825.5	761.2	768.0
2004[1]	733.8	646.3	566.7	463.9	367.0	311.8	247.8	218.3	194.5	174.4	151.2	

Recoverable copper content.   [1] Preliminary.   [2] New reporting method beginning January 1995, includes Comex, London Metal Exchange, and Refiners. Beginning January 1999, includes Consumers.   *Source: American Bureau of Metal Statistics (ABMS)*

Stocks of Refined Copper Outside the United States, on First of Month   In Thousands of Short Tons

Year	Jan.	Feb.	Mar.	Apr.	May	June	July	Aug.	Sept.	Oct.	Nov.	Dec.
1995[2]	611.6	655.8	622.2	577.9	537.0	525.6	494.9	464.7	465.7	467.7	481.4	503.5
1996	560.2	566.0	552.5	517.5	498.7	563.9	507.9	476.6	544.4	499.5	391.8	362.0
1997	405.4	469.5	476.3	445.7	413.5	402.4	408.3	489.6	550.9	607.7	574.5	553.3
1998	580.8	512.4	487.3	438.1	371.1	368.0	335.7	324.0	387.2	468.0	506.9	509.0
1999	922.6	944.3	960.3	963.0	990.5	1,008.3	993.3	990.0	1,017.0	996.9	1,001.5	992.0
2000	983.8	1,034.9	1,040.7	1,011.4	988.6	880.9	866.0	857.3	837.0	826.7	784.1	764.8
2001	795.0	999.5	986.4	971.2	995.7	969.4	1,000.8	1,091.0	1,108.7	1,083.3	1,021.0	1,104.5
2002	1,241.3	1,273.5	1,291.5	1,370.4	1,391.1	1,399.4	1,289.0	1,342.6	1,369.1	1,321.1	1,219.7	1,224.5
2003	1,238.8	2,147.6	1,188.0	1,216.3	1,147.4	1,109.8	1,129.2	1,139.9	1,150.9	1,140.2	1,170.8	1,157.1
2004[1]	1,306.1	1,175.4	1,086.7	876.5	798.4	629.0	587.1	612.7	627.0	597.4	537.7	

Recoverable copper content.   [1] Preliminary.   [2] New reporting method beginning January 1995, includes London Metal Exchange and Refiners. Beginning January 1999, also includes Shanghai Metal Exchange, Consumers and Other.   *Source: American Bureau of Metal Statistics (ABMS)*

Production of Refined Copper in the United States   In Thousands of Short Tons

Year	Jan.	Feb.	Mar.	Apr.	May	June	July	Aug.	Sept.	Oct.	Nov.	Dec.	Total
1995	202.7	185.5	204.8	194.6	210.0	198.3	193.8	208.8	199.0	206.5	211.3	208.1	2,423
1996	210.8	197.6	209.7	212.4	213.5	193.4	206.1	199.5	198.8	223.1	199.3	212.0	2,476
1997	206.0	192.0	204.0	202.0	198.0	179.0	207.0	203.0	213.0	222.0	205.0	212.0	2,470
1998	214.0	204.0	216.0	209.0	197.0	188.0	197.0	203.0	201.0	217.0	207.0	217.0	2,490
1999	185.0	178.0	220.0	198.0	186.0	175.0	163.0	161.0	172.0	172.0	157.0	162.0	2,130
2000	157.0	149.0	173.0	144.0	161.0	146.0	134.0	149.0	141.0	140.0	147.0	154.0	1,800
2001	155.0	144.0	156.0	145.0	155.0	157.0	146.0	143.0	148.0	149.0	152.0	150.0	1,800
2002	134.0	117.0	124.0	129.0	134.0	128.0	130.0	124.0	120.0	129.0	120.0	119.0	1,508
2003	124.0	110.0	118.0	98.7	98.8	106.0	110.0	110.0	112.0	108.0	101.0	111.0	1,308
2004[1]	104.0	98.9	105.0	111.0	109.0	113.0	104.0	107.0	112.0	111.0			1,290

Recoverable copper content.   [1] Preliminary.   *Source: U.S. Geological Survey (USGS)*

Stocks of Refined Copper in the United States, on First of Month   In Thousands of Short Tons

Year	Jan.	Feb.	Mar.	Apr.	May	June	July	Aug.	Sept.	Oct.	Nov.	Dec.
1992	75.3	76.3	67.2	69.7	75.9	65.0	62.2	71.2	87.1	99.5	110.3	107.1
1993	135.4	152.7	144.3	132.3	146.0	153.6	137.1	151.0	128.4	117.2	124.6	107.1
1994	103.0	87.7	83.6	72.8	70.7	70.4	73.3	81.1	74.6	66.5	52.7	53.6
1995[2]	55.8	39.6	37.0	22.6	33.1	30.8	27.0	50.0	60.6	71.1	69.4	73.4
1996	120.0	131.4	125.5	123.1	126.3	107.9	102.8	106.2	104.7	68.0	76.0	77.5
1997	88.2	98.8	104.4	116.0	117.9	121.7	122.9	148.8	177.1	197.9	227.6	253.3
1998	281.5	282.2	312.7	315.7	304.5	308.6	306.2	319.0	334.1	367.4	407.2	444.6
1999	562.6	593.1	614.6	653.5	676.6	687.8	668.4	657.2	639.7	611.2	626.5	608.2
2000	619.2	620.8	619.5	582.9	537.0	508.8	467.8	418.0	397.7	394.3	379.1	344.2
2001[1]	383.8	408.4	416.2	481.9	552.6	585.7	626.7	733.1	767.4	895.6		

Recoverable copper content.   [1] Preliminary.   [2] New reporting method beginning January 1995, includes Comex, London Metal Exchange, and Refiners. Beginning January 1999, includes Consumers.   *Source: American Bureau of Metal Statistics (ABMS)*

Deliveries of Refined Copper to Fabricators in the United States   In Thousands of Short Tons

Year	Jan.	Feb.	Mar.	Apr.	May	June	July	Aug.	Sept.	Oct.	Nov.	Dec.	Total
1995[2]	233.8	209.2	239.1	200.9	230.0	210.5	187.1	208.8	202.9	224.7	222.4	175.5	2,545
1996	221.6	227.2	240.0	242.2	270.7	222.1	233.8	246.8	277.5	239.7	240.6	231.9	2,896
1997	246.3	234.5	240.6	247.4	254.9	228.1	241.1	258.2	252.3	259.2	256.0	236.6	2,959
1998	284.5	248.4	288.1	289.2	278.7	258.0	252.4	242.1	260.7	232.0	251.9	220.0	3,106
1999	199.6	202.8	235.0	221.4	206.3	201.9	188.0	186.8	193.7	182.3	182.4	175.2	2,375
2000	166.8	161.3	176.3	157.0	173.7	161.3	145.2	149.7	150.6	154.8	149.8	162.7	1,909
2001	166.1	150.8	167.4	148.4	167.6	165.2	162.7	154.0	151.6	160.7	154.7	147.5	1,897
2002	152.1	126.0	140.7	149.3	148.6	136.2	147.9	141.1	129.5	141.6	124.5	129.7	1,667
2003	136.4	123.4	124.6	106.6	107.7	117.0	127.1	120.6	125.8	127.9	114.4	133.8	1,465
2004[1]	126.4	131.1	137.6	137.7	130.9	143.5	133.3	132.9	136.8	127.4	129.6		1,601

Recoverable copper content.   [1] Preliminary.   [2] New reporting method beginning January 1995, includes crude copper deliveries.
Source: American Bureau of Metal Statistics (ABMS)

Deliveries of Refined Copper to Fabricators Outside the United States   In Thousands of Short Tons

Year	Jan.	Feb.	Mar.	Apr.	May	June	July	Aug.	Sept.	Oct.	Nov.	Dec.	Total
1990	419.9	466.3	436.7	392.9	408.3	466.7	303.7	373.5	370.8	448.9	469.1	420.7	4,972
1991	405.0	404.4	391.5	361.2	406.3	433.5	368.5	323.4	420.7	499.1	391.4	483.4	4,807
1992	453.7	408.9	441.8	416.4	413.4	432.4	410.4	364.7	432.6	403.5	406.1	461.3	5,045
1993	427.9	392.9	452.3	361.7	422.2	442.6	384.4	347.9	387.5	414.8	463.4	458.5	4,956
1994	399.8	429.5	481.2	466.5	468.9	428.1	387.9	369.2	423.5	448.9	457.1	436.0	5,197
1995[2]	758.5	810.1	892.8	882.2	853.0	867.3	863.7	814.1	803.4	835.1	796.6	726.2	9,903
1996	875.2	859.4	934.3	907.2	816.7	950.7	908.3	817.4	911.5	1,056.0	922.7	918.3	10,878
1997	862.2	889.7	977.9	1,007.1	991.1	982.7	897.8	873.9	886.2	1,009.0	980.4	966.6	11,349
1998	1,091.7	973.8	1,062.0	1,055.5	995.7	1,014.8	986.8	924.8	913.3	987.9	982.1	1,023.0	12,011
1999[1]	314.5	745.5											6,360

Recoverable copper content.   [1] Preliminary.   [2] New reporting method beginning January 1995, includes crude copper deliveries.
Source: American Bureau of Metal Statistics (ABMS)

55

Corn

Corn is a member of the grass family of plants and is a native grain of the American continents. Fossils of corn pollen that are over 80,000 years old have been found in lake sediment under Mexico City. Archaeological discoveries show that cultivated corn existed in the southwestern US for at least 3,000 years, indicating that the indigenous people of the region cultivated corn as a food crop long before the Europeans reached the New World. Corn is a hardy plant that grows in many different areas of the world. It can grow at altitudes as low as sea level and as high as 12,000 feet in the South American Andes Mountains. Corn can also grow in tropical climates that receive up to 400 inches of rainfall per year or in areas that receive only 12 inches of rainfall per year. Corn is used primarily as livestock feed in both the United States and the rest of the world. Other uses for corn are alcohol additives for gasoline, adhesives, corn oil for cooking and margarine, sweeteners, and as a food for humans. Corn is the largest crop in the US, both in terms of the value of the crop and of the acres planted.

The largest futures market for corn is at the Chicago Board of Trade. Corn futures also trade at the Bolsa de Mercadorias & Futuros (BM&F) in Brazil, the Budapest Commodity Exchange, the Marche a Terme International de France (MATIF), the Mercado a Termino de Buenos Aires in Argentina, the Kanmon Commodity Exchange (KCE) in Korea, and the Tokyo Grain Exchange (TGE). The CBOT futures contract calls for the delivery of 5000 bushels of No. 2 yellow corn at par contract price, No. 1 yellow at 1-1/2 cents per bushel over the contract price, or No. 3 yellow at 1-1/2 cents per bushel below the contract price.

Prices – Corn futures prices rallied early in 2004 mainly because of strong demand and a draw-down in stocks that occurred through the first half of 2004. Corn futures posted an 8-year high of $3.35-1/2 per bushel in April 2004 on the nearest-futures chart. However, corn prices then plunged through summer and autumn of 2004 as it became obvious that a bumper crop was on the way. In fact, the corn crop turned out to be massive at 11.807 billion bushels in 2004-05, which was a new US record and was up sharply by +17% yr/yr from the 2003-04 crop of 10.114 billion bushels. US farmers harvested 73.311 million acres of corn, which was the highest level since 1985-86. Moreover, the ideal growing conditions during the summer produced an incredibly high yield of a new record 160.2 bushels per acre. Demand for corn remained strong through 2004, particularly due to ethanol usage, but demand was not strong enough to offset such a massive crop. The USDA projected that the carry-over for 2004-05 (as of September 1, 2005) would more than double to 2.010 billion bushels from 958 million bushels in 2003-04, which would be the highest carry-over since 1993. Corn prices are likely to remain weak through 2005 as the market chews through the huge carry-over and as planted acres in spring 2005 hit a new record high due to soybean rust. There are estimates that US farmers may plant 3 million fewer acres of soybeans due to soybean rust disease, which moved into the US for the first time in autumn 2004. Most of that acreage is likely to be switched to corn, which currently has a higher profit margin in any case than soybeans.

Supply – World production of corn in the 2004-05 marketing year rose sharply by +12.8% yr/yr to 700.572 million metric tons, which was a new record high. The world's largest corn producers are the US with 43% of world production, China (18%), and Brazil (6%). Corn production in both China and Brazil has nearly doubled since 1980. Production in the US over that time frame has risen by about 50%. The world area harvested with corn in 2004-05 fell -1.4% yr/yr to 299.8 million hectares. That was only mildly above 292.6 million hectares in 2002-03, which was the smallest world area harvested with corn in at least the last four decades. World corn ending stocks in 2004-05 rose +21.0% to 160.1 million metric tons, recovering from the tight level of stocks of 132.3 million metric tons in 2003-04.

US corn production in the 2004-05 marketing year (Sep-Aug) rose sharply by +17% yr/yr to a record crop size of 11.807 billion bushels from 10.114 billion bushels in 2003-04. US farmers harvested 73.311 million acres of corn in 2004-05, which was the largest crop area since 1985-86. Corn yield in 2004-05 rose sharply to 160.2 bushels per acre from 142.2 bushels in 2003-04, and easily established a new record high. Carry-over stocks on September 1, 2004, going into the new 2004-05 marketing year, fell sharply to 958 million bushels from 1.087 billion bushels on September 1, 2003. The largest corn producing states in the US are Iowa with 19.2% of US production in 2004, Illinois (17.7%), Nebraska (11.3%), Minnesota (9.2%), and Indiana (7.9%). The value of the US corn crop in 2004-05 was $23.033 billion.

Demand – World consumption of corn in 2004-05 rose by +2.7% yr/yr to a new record high of 968.8 million metric tons, falling short of 2004-05 production of 996.6 million metric tons by 27.8 million metric tons. The distribution tables for corn show that the largest category of usage, aside from animal feed, is for ethanol production (alcohol fuel) with 1.425 billion bushels of usage in 2004-05, representing 51.4% of total non-feed usage. Corn usage for ethanol has nearly tripled just in the past 7 years, and that usage category is likely to grow due to the high prices of crude oil and gasoline. After ethanol, the largest non-feed usage categories are for high fructose corn syrup (HFCS) with 19.1% of US usage, corn starch (10.1%), glucose and dextrose sugars (7.9%), cereal and other corn products (6.8%), and alcoholic beverages (4.8%).

Trade – US exports of corn in 2003-04 rose sharply by +16.7% yr/yr to 47.579 million metric tons, but that was still far below the record high of 61.417 million metric tons posted in 1979-80. The largest destination countries for US corn exports are Japan, which accounted for 31.4% of US corn exports in 2003-04, Mexico (11.6%), Taiwan (9.9%), South Korea (8.3%), Egypt (6.5%), and Canada (4.2%).

World Production of Corn or Maize   In Thousands of Metric Tons

Crop Year	Argentina	Brazil	Canada	China	European Union	Egypt	India	Mexico	Romania	South Africa	United States	Ukraine	World Total
1995-6	11,100	32,480	7,271	112,000	12,394	9,530	8,454	17,780	9,923	10,171	187,970	8,537	517,352
1996-7	15,500	35,700	7,542	127,470	14,432	10,612	9,547	18,922	9,610	10,136	234,518	8,293	592,172
1997-8	19,360	30,100	7,180	104,309	16,754	10,852	10,005	17,368	12,680	7,693	233,864	9,564	575,363
1998-9	13,500	32,393	8,952	132,954	15,204	10,680	8,600	17,789	8,000	7,946	247,882	8,386	605,631
1999-00	17,200	31,641	9,161	128,086	45,229	5,678	11,470	19,240	10,500	11,455	239,549	1,737	606,674
2000-1	15,400	41,536	6,827	106,000	44,529	5,636	12,068	17,917	4,800	8,040	251,854	3,848	589,766
2001-2	14,700	35,501	8,389	114,088	50,142	6,160	13,510	20,400	7,000	10,050	241,377	3,641	598,777
2002-3[1]	15,500	44,500	8,999	121,300	49,360	6,000	11,100	19,280	7,300	9,675	227,767	4,180	601,424
2003-4[2]	13,500	42,000	9,600	115,830	39,930	6,150	14,720	21,800	6,500	9,700	256,278	6,850	621,182
2004-5[3]	17,000	42,000	8,850	126,000	52,475	6,200	14,000	21,000	12,000	9,700	299,917	8,800	700,572

[1] Preliminary.   [2] Estimate.   [3] Forecast.   *Source: Foreign Agricultural Service, U.S. Department of Agriculture (FAS-USDA)*

World Supply and Demand of Course Grains   In Millions of Metric Tons/Hectares

Crop Year Beginning Oct.1	Area Harvested	Yield	Pro-duction	World Trade	Total Con-sumption	Ending Stocks	Stocks as % of Con-sumption[3]
1995-6	314.8	2.54	800.9	88.2	835.5	161.4	19.3
1996-7	323.4	2.81	908.9	94.3	869.3	201.1	23.1
1997-8	311.2	2.83	881.1	85.8	867.0	215.1	24.8
1998-9	308.4	2.89	890.3	96.7	869.3	236.1	27.2
1999-00	299.8	2.92	876.8	104.8	881.8	230.5	26.1
2000-1	296.7	2.90	861.4	104.4	883.6	208.3	23.6
2001-2	300.8	2.96	891.2	102.6	904.9	194.6	21.5
2002-3	292.5	2.98	872.4	104.3	901.3	165.7	18.4
2003-4[1]	304.0	2.99	910.0	102.2	943.5	132.3	14.0
2004-5[2]	299.8	3.32	996.6	98.6	968.8	160.1	16.5

[1] Preliminary.   [2] Estimate.   [3] Represents the ratio of marketing year ending stocks to total consumption.   *Source: Foreign Agricultural Service, U.S. Department of Agriculture (FAS-USDA)*

Acreage and Supply of Corn in the United States   In Millions of Bushels

Crop Year Beginning Sept. 1	Planted	Harvested — For Grain	Harvested — For Silage	Yield Per Harvested Acre Bushels	Carry-over, Sept. 1 — On Farms	Carry-over, Sept. 1 — Off Farms	Supply — Beginning Stocks	Supply — Pro-duction	Supply — Imports	Supply — Total Supply
		In Thousands of Acres		Bushels						
1995-6	71,245	64,995	5,295	113.5	740.9	816.9	1,558	7,400	16	8,974
1996-7	79,229	72,644	5,607	127.1	196.6	229.3	426	9,233	13	9,672
1997-8	79,537	72,671	6,054	126.7	475.0	408.2	883	9,207	9	10,099
1998-9	80,165	72,589	5,913	134.4	640.0	667.8	1,308	9,759	19	11,088
1999-00	77,386	70,487	6,037	133.8	797.0	990.0	1,787	9,431	15	11,239
2000-1	79,551	72,440	6,082	136.9	793.0	924.5	1,718	9,915	7	11,693
2001-2	75,752	68,808	6,148	138.2	753.2	1,146.0	1,899	9,507	10	11,412
2002-3	78,894	69,330	7,122	129.3	586.8	1,009.6	1,596	8,967	14	10,578
2003-4[1]	78,603	70,944	6,583	142.2	484.9	601.8	1,087	10,089	14	11,190
2004-5[2]	80,930	73,632	6,103	160.4	438.0	520.1	958	11,807	15	12,780

[1] Preliminary.   [2] Estimate.   *Source: Economic Research Service, U.S. Department of Agriculture (ERS-USDA)*

Production of Corn (For Grain) in the United States, by State   In Million of Bushels

Year	Illinois	Indiana	Iowa	Kansas	Mich-igan	Minn-esota	Missouri	Nebraska	Ohio	South Dakota	Texas	Wis-consin	Total
1995	1,130.0	598.9	1,402.2	244.3	249.6	731.9	149.9	854.7	375.1	193.6	216.6	347.7	7,373.9
1996	1,468.8	670.4	1,711.2	357.2	211.5	868.8	340.4	1,179.8	310.8	365.0	198.2	333.0	9,232.6
1997	1,425.5	701.5	1,642.2	371.8	255.1	851.4	299.0	1,135.2	475.7	326.4	241.5	402.6	9,206.8
1998	1,473.5	760.4	1,769.0	419.0	227.6	1,032.8	285.0	1,239.8	470.9	429.6	185.0	404.2	9,758.7
1999	1,491.0	748.4	1,758.2	420.2	253.5	990.0	247.4	1,153.7	403.2	367.3	228.3	407.6	9,437.3
2000	1,668.6	815.9	1,740.0	416.0	244.3	957.0	396.1	1,014.3	485.1	431.2	235.6	363.0	9,968.4
2001	1,649.2	884.5	1,664.4	387.4	199.5	806.0	345.8	1,139.3	437.5	370.6	167.6	330.2	9,506.8
2002	1,471.5	631.6	1,931.6	301.6	234.0	1,051.9	283.5	940.8	264.3	308.8	202.3	391.5	8,966.8
2003	1,812.0	786.9	1,868.3	300.0	259.8	970.9	302.4	1,124.2	478.9	427.4	194.7	367.7	10,089.2
2004[1]	2,088.0	929.0	2,244.4	432.0	257.3	1,121.0	466.6	1,319.7	491.4	539.5	233.5	353.6	11,807.2

[1] Preliminary.   *Source: National Agricultural Statistics Service, U.S. Department of Agriculture (NASS-USDA)*

CORN

Supply and Disappearance of Corn in the United States   In Millions of Bushels

| Crop Year Beginning Sept. 1 | Supply | | | | Disappearance — Domestic Use | | | | Exports | Total Disappearance | Ending Inventory | | |
	Beginning Stocks	Production	Imports	Total Supply	Food, Alcohol & Industrial	Seed	Feed & Residual	Total			Gov't Owned[3]	Privately Owned[4]	Total
2000-1	1,718	9,915	6.8	11,639	1,938	19.3	5,842	7,799	1,941	9,740			1,899
Sept.-Nov.	1,718	9,915	1.3	11,634	466	0	2,131	2,598	507	3,104			8,530
Dec.-Feb.	8,530	----	.9	8,531	465	0	1,607	2,072	415	2,488			6,043
Mar.-May	6,043	----	3.1	6,046	496	18.7	1,153	1,667	455	2,122			3,924
June-Aug.	3,924	----	1.5	3,926	511	.6	951	1,462	564	2,026			1,899
2001-2	1,899	9,503	10.1	11,412	2,026	20.1	5,864	7,911	1,905	9,815			1,596
Sept.-Nov.	1,899	9,503	2.4	11,404	492	0	2,200	2,692	448	3,139			8,265
Dec.-Feb.	8,265	----	1.7	8,266	482	0	1,540	2,023	448	2,471			5,795
Mar.-May	5,795	----	4.2	5,799	521	18.6	1,166	1,706	497	2,203			3,597
June-Aug.	3,597	----	1.9	3,599	531	1.5	958	1,491	512	2,002			1,596
2002-3	1,596	8,967	14.4	10,578	2,320	20.1	5,558	7,899	1,593	9,491			1,087
Sept.-Nov.	1,596	8,967	3.4	10,567	549	0	1,986	2,535	393	2,929			7,638
Dec.-Feb.	7,638	----	4.1	7,642	563	0	1,547	2,110	400	2,510			5,132
Mar.-May	5,132	----	5.2	5,137	598	19.0	1,141	1,759	393	2,152			2,985
June-Aug.	2,985	----	1.8	2,987	610	1.1	884	1,494	406	1,900			1,087
2003-4[1]	1,087	10,114	14.0	11,190	2,537	20.0	5,798	8,355	1,897	10,232			958
Sept.-Nov.	1,087	10,114	2.5	11,178	589	0	2,166	2,755	470	3,225			7,954
Dec.-Feb.	7,954	----	3.0	7,957	609	0	1,578	2,187	499	2,686			5,271
Mar.-May	5,271	----	5.0	5,277	676	0	1,161	1,837	469	2,306			2,970
June-Aug.	2,970	----	3.0	2,973	664	0	892	1,556	459	2,015			958
2004-5[2]	958	11,807	15.0	12,780	2,795		6,075	8,870	1,900	10,770			2,010
Sept.-Nov.	958	11,807	2.0	12,767	639	0	2,182	2,821	497	3,318			9,449

[1] Preliminary.   [2] Estimate.   [3] Uncommitted inventory.   [4] Includes quantity under loan and farmer-owned reserve.
Source: Economic Research Service, U.S. Department of Agriculture (ERS-USDA)

Corn Production Estimates and Cash Price in the United States

| Year | Corn for Grain Production Estimates (In Thousands of Bushels) | | | | | St. Louis No. 2 Yellow | Omaha No. 2 Yellow | Gulf Ports No. 2 Yellow | Kansas City No. 2 White | Chicago No. 2 Yellow | Average Farm Price[2] | Value of Production (Million Dollars) |
	Aug. 1	Sept. 1	Oct. 1	Nov. 1	Final	Dollars Per Bushel						
1996-7	8,694,628	8,803,928	9,012,148	9,265,288	9,232,557	2.90	2.70	3.07	3.09	2.84	2.71	25,149
1997-8	9,275,870	9,267,655	9,311,705	9,359,485	9,206,832	2.60	2.36	2.78	2.93	2.56	2.43	22,352
1998-9	9,592,089	9,737,949	9,743,399	9,836,069	9,758,685	1.99	1.88	2.35	2.51	2.06	1.94	18,922
1999-00	9,560,919	9,380,947	9,466,977	9,537,137	9,430,612	2.02	1.80	2.23	1.98	1.97	1.82	17,104
2000-1	10,369,369	10,362,374	10,191,817	10,053,942	9,915,051	2.01	1.82	2.26	2.06	1.99	1.85	18,499
2001-2	9,266,397	9,238,356	9,429,543	9,545,513	9,506,840	2.15	1.95	2.35	2.20	2.13	1.98	18,888
2002-3	8,886,009	8,848,529	8,969,836	9,003,364	8,966,787	2.49	2.29	2.71	2.94	2.46	2.32	20,882
2003-4	10,064,452	9,944,418	10,207,141	10,277,932	10,089,222	2.43	2.43	2.94	2.68	2.56	2.50	24,477
2004-5[1]	10,923,099	10,960,710	11,613,226	11,740,920	11,807,217			2.44			2.10	23,033

[1] Preliminary.   [2] Season-average price based on monthly prices weighted by monthly marketings.   *Source: Economic Research Service, U..S. Department of Agriculture (ERS-USDA)*

Distribution of Corn in the United States   In Millions of Bushels

| Crop Year Beginning Sept. 1 | Food, Seed and Industrial Use | | | | | | | | Exports (Including Grain Equiv. of Products) | Domestic Disappearance | Total Utilization |
| | HFCS | Glucose & Dextrose | Starch | Alcohol | | Seed | Cereal & Other Products | Total | Livestock Feed[4] | | |
				Fuel	Beverage[3]						
1996-7	504	246	229	429	130	20.3	135	1,672	5,277	1,797.4	6,991	8,789
1997-8	513	229	246	481	133	20.4	182	1,784	5,482	1,504.4	7,287	8,791
1998-9	531	219	240	526	127	19.8	184	1,826	5,468	1,984.2	7,314	9,298
1999-00	540	222	251	566	130	20.3	185	1,893	5,665	1,936.6	7,578	9,515
2000-1	530	218	247	628	130	19.3	185	1,938	5,842	1,941.3	7,799	9,740
2001-2	541	217	246	706	131	20.1	186	2,026	5,864	1,904.8	7,911	9,815
2002-3	532	219	256	996	131	20.1	187	2,320	5,558	1,592.5	7,899	9,491
2003-4[1]	530	228	272	1,168	132	20.0	187	2,517	5,800	2,000.0	8,355	10,355
2004-5[2]	529	219	280	1,425	133		189	2,775				

[1] Preliminary.   [2] Estimate.   [3] Also includes nonfuel industrial alcohol.   [4] Feed and waste (residual, mostly feed).   *Source: Economic Research Service, U.S. Department of Agriculture (ERS-USDA)*

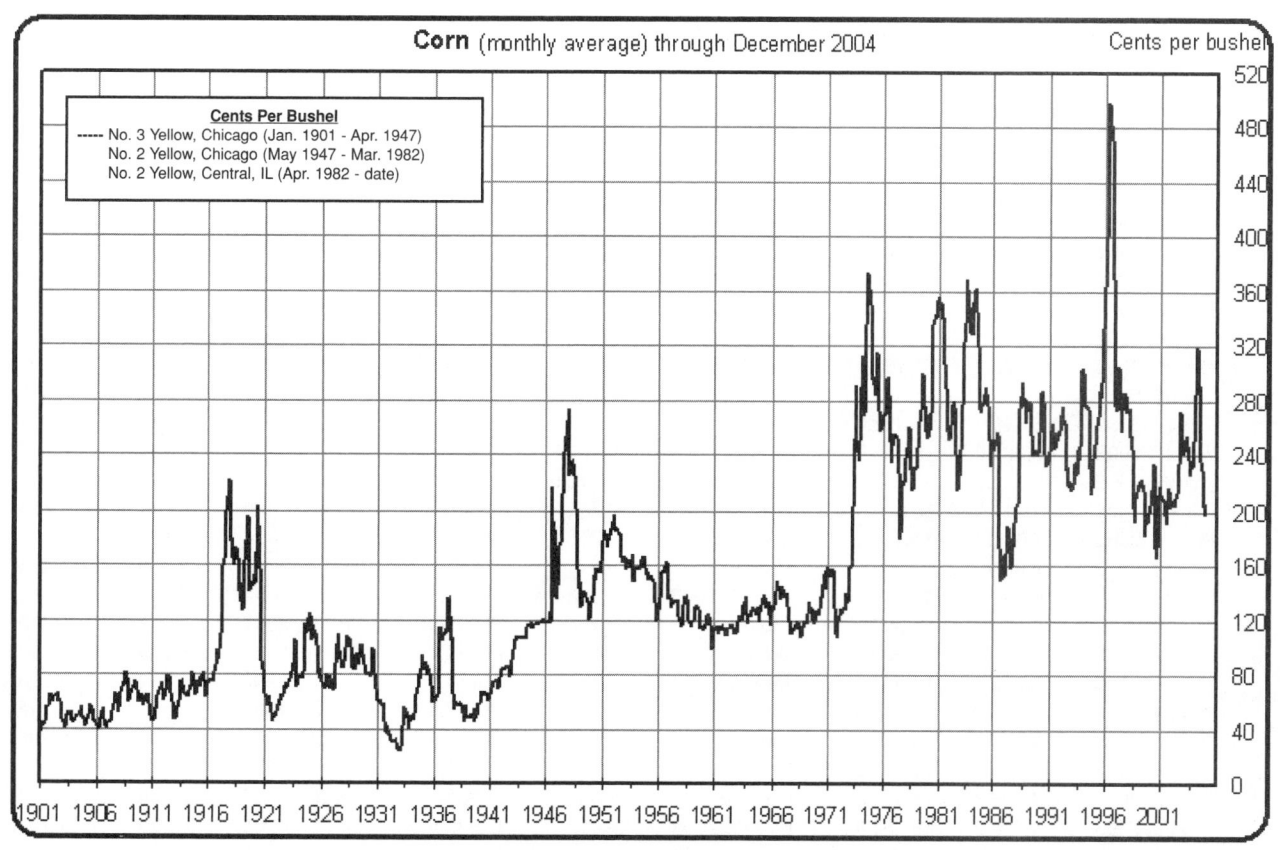

Corn (monthly average) through December 2004 — Cents per bushel

Cents Per Bushel
- - - No. 3 Yellow, Chicago (Jan. 1901 - Apr. 1947)
No. 2 Yellow, Chicago (May 1947 - Mar. 1982)
No. 2 Yellow, Central, IL (Apr. 1982 - date)

Average Cash Price of Corn, No. 2 Yellow in Central Illinois   In Dollars Per Bushel

Year	Sept.	Oct.	Nov.	Dec.	Jan.	Feb.	Mar.	Apr.	May	June	July	Aug.	Average
1995-6	2.83	3.12	3.22	3.36	3.53	3.71	3.92	4.47	4.86	4.74	4.70	4.48	3.91
1996-7	3.39	2.81	2.63	2.62	2.62	2.71	2.90	2.87	2.74	2.59	2.44	2.60	2.74
1997-8	2.61	2.66	2.70	2.60	2.60	2.58	2.59	2.41	2.37	2.29	2.16	1.86	2.45
1998-9	1.78	1.94	2.09	2.08	2.07	2.05	2.09	2.05	2.03	1.99	1.67	1.84	1.97
1999-00	1.81	1.72	1.82	1.84	1.95	2.03	2.08	2.09	2.15	1.83	1.53	1.49	1.86
2000-1	1.58	1.81	1.96	2.01	1.99	1.95	1.92	1.87	1.78	1.76	1.92	2.00	1.88
2001-2	1.94	1.84	1.90	1.97	1.95	1.92	1.92	1.89	1.96	2.04	2.22	2.50	2.00
2002-3	2.57	2.41	2.36	2.32	2.29	2.33	2.31	2.36	2.40	2.37	2.13	2.26	2.34
2003-4	2.25	2.11	2.26	2.38	2.52	2.73	2.89	3.03	2.90	2.76	2.26	2.17	2.52
2004-5[1]	1.98	1.77	1.79	1.87									1.85

[1] Preliminary.   *Source: Economic Research Service, U.S. Department of Agriculture (ERS-USDA)*

Average Cash Price of Corn, No. 2 Yellow at Gulf Ports[2]   In Dollars Per Bushel

Year	Sept.	Oct.	Nov.	Dec.	Jan.	Feb.	Mar.	Apr.	May	June	July	Aug.	Average
1995-6	3.32	3.57	3.63	3.76	4.00	4.18	4.34	4.80	5.17	4.99	5.07	4.73	4.30
1996-7	3.69	3.27	2.97	2.97	3.02	3.08	3.25	3.17	3.01	2.86	2.69	2.86	3.07
1997-8	2.88	3.05	2.98	2.89	2.90	2.88	2.89	2.71	2.69	2.64	2.55	2.24	2.78
1998-9	2.18	2.43	2.47	2.42	2.48	2.40	2.45	2.39	2.35	2.36	2.12	2.20	2.35
1999-00	2.21	2.17	2.17	2.21	2.36	2.42	2.42	2.43	2.43	2.13	1.91	1.91	2.23
2000-1	2.03	2.15	2.26	2.45	2.40	2.35	2.32	2.22	2.14	2.11	2.30	2.36	2.26
2001-2	2.27	2.19	2.28	2.35	2.34	2.30	2.28	2.21	2.29	2.37	2.53	2.79	2.35
2002-3	2.89	2.79	2.77	2.71	2.69	2.69	2.67	2.67	2.74	2.72	2.72	2.44	2.71
2003-4	2.63	2.65	2.75	2.84	2.95	3.12	3.26	3.39	3.28	3.13	2.65	2.64	2.94
2004-5[1]	2.48	2.48	2.38	2.43									2.44

[1] Preliminary.   [2] Barge delivered to Louisiana Gulf.   *Source: Economic Research Service, U.S. Department of Agriculture (ERS-USDA)*

CORN

Weekly Outstanding Export Sales and Cumulative Exports of U.S. Corn — In Thousands of Metric Tons

Marketing Year 2002/03 Week Ending	Out-standing Sales	Out-standing Sales	Marketing Year 2003/04 Week Ending	Out-standing Sales	Cumu-lative Exports	Marketing Year 2004/05 Week Ending	Out-standing Sales	Cumu-lative Exports
Sep 05, 2002	6,205.8	439.0	Sep 04, 2003	7,625.7	460.8	Sep 02, 2004	6,935.9	230.3
Sep 12, 2002	6,417.7	1,276.1	Sep 11, 2003	7,682.7	1,318.8	Sep 09, 2004	7,430.6	943.3
Sep 19, 2002	6,352.4	2,080.4	Sep 18, 2003	8,251.7	2,127.3	Sep 16, 2004	7,896.0	1,634.2
Sep 26, 2002	6,851.7	2,535.7	Sep 25, 2003	8,274.1	3,021.0	Sep 23, 2004	7,798.2	2,637.5
Oct 03, 2002	7,023.6	3,034.1	Oct 02, 2003	8,451.1	3,800.4	Sep 30, 2004	7,397.0	3,817.8
Oct 10, 2002	6,890.1	3,836.0	Oct 09, 2003	9,228.5	4,660.7	Oct 07, 2004	7,933.9	4,765.3
Oct 17, 2002	6,584.1	4,659.0	Oct 16, 2003	9,062.1	5,581.1	Oct 14, 2004	8,638.0	5,361.7
Oct 24, 2002	6,972.6	5,299.0	Oct 23, 2003	9,633.6	6,490.0	Oct 21, 2004	8,531.5	6,558.1
Oct 31, 2002	7,629.2	5,729.0	Oct 30, 2003	10,206.7	7,345.8	Oct 28, 2004	9,339.7	7,203.0
Nov 07, 2002	7,986.4	6,521.0	Nov 06, 2003	10,238.5	8,062.2	Nov 04, 2004	9,052.7	8,320.9
Nov 14, 2002	8,119.0	7,322.0	Nov 13, 2003	10,243.0	8,974.8	Nov 11, 2004	8,740.6	9,357.7
Nov 21, 2002	8,308.0	8,285.0	Nov 20, 2003	10,600.5	10,219.2	Nov 18, 2004	9,141.4	10,258.0
Nov 28, 2002	7,922.4	9,344.6	Nov 27, 2003	10,312.9	11,356.4	Nov 25, 2004	8,917.1	11,067.4
Dec 05, 2002	7,414.6	10,398.6	Dec 04, 2003	10,341.5	12,365.7	Dec 02, 2004	8,624.0	12,275.4
Dec 12, 2002	7,081.4	11,444.1	Dec 11, 2003	10,318.8	13,311.5	Dec 09, 2004	8,113.4	13,422.7
Dec 19, 2002	6,635.2	12,568.4	Dec 18, 2003	9,846.9	14,737.0	Dec 16, 2004	7,770.2	14,491.7
Dec 26, 2002	6,561.4	13,012.7	Dec 25, 2003	9,763.3	15,578.8	Dec 23, 2004	7,496.3	15,462.5
Jan 02, 2003	5,860.0	13,997.8	Jan 01, 2004	9,150.0	16,607.5	Dec 30, 2004	6,974.5	16,415.0
Jan 09, 2003	5,635.2	14,839.1	Jan 08, 2004	8,985.7	17,611.1	Jan 06, 2005	6,999.0	17,048.8
Jan 16, 2003	5,596.3	15,551.0	Jan 15, 2004	9,112.7	18,483.4	Jan 13, 2005	7,156.5	17,798.5
Jan 23, 2003	5,219.3	16,241.0	Jan 22, 2004	8,944.2	19,427.3	Jan 20, 2005	6,839.6	18,878.1
Jan 30, 2003	5,266.9	16,938.2	Jan 29, 2004	9,043.2	20,309.7	Jan 27, 2005	6,256.8	19,798.5
Feb 06, 2003	5,029.4	17,793.2	Feb 05, 2004	9,441.2	21,064.4	Feb 03, 2005	6,744.2	20,306.4
Feb 13, 2003	4,826.8	18,461.8	Feb 12, 2004	9,521.8	21,936.2	Feb 10, 2005	6,768.7	21,024.2
Feb 20, 2003	4,775.0	19,182.5	Feb 19, 2004	9,512.4	22,932.5	Feb 17, 2005	6,996.4	21,706.7
Feb 27, 2003	5,465.2	19,904.1	Feb 26, 2004	9,094.4	23,721.9	Feb 24, 2005		
Mar 06, 2003	5,631.2	20,443.5	Mar 04, 2004	8,330.2	25,059.6	Mar 03, 2005		
Mar 13, 2003	6,013.2	21,230.8	Mar 11, 2004	8,706.6	25,995.3	Mar 10, 2005		
Mar 20, 2003	6,065.8	21,879.7	Mar 18, 2004	8,829.1	27,065.3	Mar 17, 2005		
Mar 27, 2003	5,570.8	22,732.4	Mar 25, 2004	8,449.5	28,139.1	Mar 24, 2005		
Apr 03, 2003	5,457.6	23,705.6	Apr 01, 2004	9,050.5	28,853.9	Mar 31, 2005		
Apr 10, 2003	5,380.0	24,468.9	Apr 08, 2004	9,143.6	29,983.5	Apr 07, 2005		
Apr 17, 2003	5,151.7	25,282.5	Apr 15, 2004	9,657.2	30,619.0	Apr 14, 2005		
Apr 24, 2003	5,379.4	25,955.1	Apr 22, 2004	9,921.4	31,280.3	Apr 21, 2005		
May 01, 2003	5,430.7	26,483.3	Apr 29, 2004	10,214.9	32,080.6	Apr 28, 2005		
May 08, 2003	5,879.4	27,098.7	May 06, 2004	9,698.9	33,102.7	May 05, 2005		
May 15, 2003	5,804.4	27,922.9	May 13, 2004	9,781.1	33,754.7	May 12, 2005		
May 22, 2003	5,640.2	28,722.5	May 20, 2004	9,893.6	34,904.5	May 19, 2005		
May 29, 2003	5,289.2	29,607.5	May 27, 2004	9,449.6	35,759.1	May 26, 2005		
Jun 05, 2003	5,301.5	30,324.5	Jun 03, 2004	8,519.6	36,742.4	Jun 02, 2005		
Jun 12, 2003	5,177.8	31,190.7	Jun 10, 2004	8,093.5	37,762.9	Jun 09, 2005		
Jun 19, 2003	5,264.4	31,917.9	Jun 17, 2004	7,523.6	38,492.4	Jun 16, 2005		
Jun 26, 2003	5,116.9	32,833.5	Jun 24, 2004	7,533.2	39,292.9	Jun 23, 2005		
Jul 03, 2003	5,075.2	33,595.6	Jul 01, 2004	7,158.1	40,187.5	Jun 30, 2005		
Jul 10, 2003	4,839.2	34,308.6	Jul 08, 2004	6,791.2	41,212.1	Jul 07, 2005		
Jul 17, 2003	4,532.1	35,085.7	Jul 15, 2004	6,203.0	42,157.6	Jul 14, 2005		
Jul 24, 2003	4,237.6	35,927.7	Jul 22, 2004	5,775.4	42,963.9	Jul 21, 2005		
Jul 31, 2003	3,851.0	36,739.3	Jul 29, 2004	5,170.1	43,981.7	Jul 28, 2005		
Aug 07, 2003	3,684.2	37,238.1	Aug 05, 2004	4,677.7	44,747.1	Aug 04, 2005		
Aug 14, 2003	3,180.0	38,006.4	Aug 12, 2004	3,861.7	45,793.6	Aug 11, 2005		
Aug 21, 2003	2,653.1	38,727.9	Aug 19, 2004	3,019.1	46,769.6	Aug 18, 2005		
Aug 28, 2003	1,900.0	39,646.0	Aug 26, 2004	2,177.1	47,704.2	Aug 25, 2005		

Source: Foreign Agricultural Service, U.S. Department of Agriculture (FAS-USDA)

Average Price Received by Farmers for Corn in the United States   In Dollars Per Bushel

Year	Sept.	Oct.	Nov.	Dec.	Jan.	Feb.	Mar.	Apr.	May	June	July	Aug.	Average
1995-6	2.69	2.79	2.87	3.07	3.09	3.37	3.51	3.85	4.14	4.20	4.43	4.30	3.53
1996-7	3.55	2.89	2.66	2.63	2.69	2.65	2.79	2.80	2.69	2.56	2.42	2.50	2.74
1997-8	2.52	2.54	2.51	2.52	2.56	2.55	2.54	2.41	2.34	2.28	2.19	1.89	2.40
1998-9	1.83	1.91	1.93	2.00	2.06	2.05	2.06	2.04	1.99	1.97	1.74	1.75	1.94
1999-00	1.75	1.69	1.70	1.82	1.91	1.98	2.03	2.03	2.11	1.91	1.64	1.52	1.84
2000-1	1.61	1.74	1.86	1.97	1.98	1.96	1.96	1.89	1.82	1.76	1.87	1.90	1.86
2001-2	1.91	1.84	1.85	1.98	1.97	1.93	1.94	1.91	1.93	1.97	2.13	2.38	1.98
2002-3	2.47	2.34	2.28	2.32	2.33	2.34	2.33	2.34	2.38	2.34	2.17	2.15	2.32
2003-4	2.20	2.12	2.20	2.31	2.39	2.61	2.75	2.89	2.87	2.79	2.51	2.34	2.50
2004-5[1]	2.20	2.15	2.05	2.04	2.12	2.02							2.10

[1] Preliminary.   *Source: Economic Research Service, U.S. Department of Agriculture (ERS-USDA)*

Corn Price Support Data in the United States

Crop Year Beginning Sept. 1	National Average Loan Rate[3] --- Dollars Per Bushel ---	Target Price	Placed Under Loan	% of Pro-duction	Acquired by CCC	Owned by CCC Aug. 31	CCC Inventory As of Dec. 31 CCC Owned	CCC Inventory As of Dec. 31 Under CCC Loan	Quantity Pledged (Thousands of Bushels)	Face Amount (Thousands of Dollars)
					------------------------------- Millions of Bushels -------------------------------					
1993-4	1.72	2.75	618	9.8	0	45	54	812	13,697	26,052
1994-5	1.89	2.75	2,002	19.9	0	----	44	1,598	26,318	53,474
1995-6	1.89	2.75	970	13.1	0	----	42	579	677,115	1,232,669
1996-7	1.89	NA	561	6.1	0	----	30	756	970,590	1,764,291
1997-8	1.89	NA	1,132	12.3	19	----	2	81	1,129,915	2,062,308
1998-9	1.89	NA	823	8.4	0	----	15	----	1,129,915	2,062,308
1999-00	1.89	NA	----	----	----	----	26	----	1,420,878	2,590,443
2000-1	1.89	NA	----	----	----	----	36	----	1,393,947	2,562,172
2001-2[1]	1.89	NA					24		1,294,561	2,557,874
2002-3[2]	1.98	2.60					18			

[1] Preliminary.   [2] Estimate.   [3] Findley or announced loan rate.   *Source: National Agricultural Statistics Service, U.S. Department of Agriculture (NASS-USDA)*

U.S. Exports[1] of Corn (Including Seed), By Country of Destination   In Thousands of Metric Tons

Year Beginning Oct. 1	Algeria	Canada	Egypt	Irael	Japan	Mexico	Rep. of Korea	Russia	Saudi Arabia	Spain	Taiwan	Vene-zuela	Total
1994-5	798	1,108	2,342	658	16,030	3,165	8,866	9	864	2,337	6,150	886	58,596
1995-6	507	736	1,854	625	14,900	6,268	7,333	50	844	1,156	5,600	479	52,660
1996-7	862	879	2,364	556	15,425	3,141	5,404	88	1,025	1,080	5,609	730	46,638
1997-8	829	1,404	1,951	141	13,957	4,423	3,364	1	883	141	3,488	645	37,755
1998-9	947	898	2,954	395	15,375	5,576	6,659	405	1,175	92	4,538	1,329	51,949
1999-00	1,099	1,080	3,542	748	14,939	4,910	2,822	491	1,197	16	4,989	1,146	49,378
2000-1	1,180	2,797	4,116	621	14,091	5,928	3,109	26	1,003	0	4,894	1,152	48,192
2001-2	1,343	3,979	4,283	847	14,817	4,025	1,085	86	670	5	4,599	502	47,058
2002-3	1,009	3,811	2,904	313	14,384	5,220	272	0	222	0	4,139	651	40,780
2003-4[2]	1,158	1,995	3,088	1,154	14,921	5,527	3,946	39	219	5	4,714	669	47,579

[1] Excludes exports of corn by-products.   [2] Preliminary.   *Source: Economic Research Service, U.S. Department of Agriculture (ERS-USDA)*

Stocks of Corn (Shelled and Ear) in the United States   In Millions of Bushels

Year	On Farms Mar. 1	On Farms June 1	On Farms Sept. 1	On Farms Dec. 1	Off Farms Mar. 1	Off Farms June 1	Off Farms Sept. 1	Off Farms Dec. 1	Total Stocks Mar. 1	Total Stocks June 1	Total Stocks Sept. 1	Total Stocks Dec. 1
1995	3,502.0	2,072.0	740.9	3,960.0	2,089.7	1,342.9	816.9	2,145.8	5,591.7	3,414.9	1,557.8	6,105.8
1996	2,000.2	780.1	196.6	4,800.0	1,799.3	937.8	229.3	2,103.0	3,799.5	1,717.9	425.9	6,903.0
1997	2,870.0	1,501.0	475.0	4,822.0	1,624.1	995.6	408.2	2,424.8	4,494.1	2,496.6	883.2	7,246.8
1998	2,975.0	1,830.0	640.0	5,320.0	1,964.9	1,209.8	667.8	2,731.8	4,939.9	3,039.8	1,307.8	8,051.8
1999	3,570.0	2,257.0	797.0	5,195.0	2,128.4	1,359.2	990.0	2,844.4	5,698.4	3,616.2	1,787.0	8,039.4
2000	3,300.0	2,029.8	793.0	5,550.0	2,301.9	1,556.1	924.5	2,972.2	5,601.9	3,585.9	1,717.5	8,522.2
2001	3,600.0	2,230.8	753.2	5,275.0	2,443.0	1,693.2	1,146.0	2,989.7	6,043.0	3,924.0	1,899.1	8,264.7
2002	3,355.0	2,020.6	586.8	4,800.0	2,440.3	1,576.3	1,009.6	2,838.0	5,795.3	3,596.9	1,596.4	7,638.0
2003	2,940.0	1,620.2	484.9	5,286.0	2,191.9	1,364.7	601.8	2,667.8	5,131.9	2,984.9	1,086.7	7,953.8
2004[1]	3,030.0	1,540.0	438.0	6,144.0	2,241.5	1,430.1	520.1	3,304.8	5,271.5	2,970.1	958.1	9,448.8

[1] Preliminary.   *Source: National Agricultural Statistics Service, U.S. Department of Agriculture (NASS-USDA)*

CORN

Corn Futures - Chicago Board of Trade
(weekly close) as of December 31, 2004

Cents per bushel

Volume of Trading of Corn Futures in Chicago   In Thousands of Contracts

Year	Jan.	Feb.	Mar.	Apr.	May	June	July	Aug.	Sept.	Oct.	Nov.	Dec.	Total
1995	787.2	832.4	973.7	987.7	1,213.7	1,759.5	1,293.7	1,318.6	1,220.2	1,613.2	1,743.1	1,356.0	15,105.1
1996	1,992.2	1,819.6	1,607.6	2,655.2	2,085.2	1,545.1	1,590.5	1,144.6	1,183.4	1,435.7	1,514.7	1,046.3	19,620.2
1997	1,160.6	1,483.0	1,693.3	1,780.1	1,291.7	1,347.5	1,527.7	1,318.3	1,060.2	1,700.2	1,434.4	1,188.0	16,985.0
1998	1,250.2	1,276.5	1,432.8	1,620.3	1,148.5	1,771.0	1,415.3	1,231.4	1,126.3	1,319.3	1,217.2	986.6	15,795.5
1999	955.1	1,374.2	1,440.1	1,420.6	975.1	1,597.4	1,708.0	1,669.8	1,131.9	1,096.2	1,500.9	855.6	15,724.8
2000	1,502.2	1,580.9	1,713.1	1,386.3	1,789.7	1,830.7	1,178.3	1,291.8	1,057.4	1,256.1	1,612.8	986.1	17,185.4
2001	1,397.2	1,197.4	1,329.5	1,518.7	1,173.2	1,612.1	2,023.5	1,549.0	1,072.3	1,223.3	1,741.2	891.4	16,728.7
2002	996.3	1,449.6	944.7	1,498.0	1,434.5	1,851.5	1,958.4	2,158.7	1,635.4	1,523.3	1,801.4	880.5	18,132.4
2003	1,204.0	1,559.1	1,156.9	1,633.1	1,657.0	1,951.2	1,499.3	1,830.6	1,389.7	2,057.7	1,815.9	1,364.3	19,118.7
2004	2,025.7	2,367.0	2,190.9	2,870.9	1,855.3	2,538.6	1,740.5	1,883.0	1,446.9	1,476.4	2,473.3	1,169.6	24,038.2

Source: Chicago Board of Trade (CBT)

Average Open Interest of Corn Futures in Chicago   In Contracts

Year	Jan.	Feb.	Mar.	Apr.	May	June	July	Aug.	Sept.	Oct.	Nov.	Dec.
1995	292,090	311,372	336,433	355,443	368,381	427,744	413,839	418,450	439,170	473,698	490,970	487,977
1996	500,837	508,496	469,697	453,707	403,118	350,066	304,265	298,894	302,170	326,373	332,809	306,256
1997	305,779	347,392	382,261	351,852	290,649	274,760	267,531	281,194	307,415	378,453	379,045	331,386
1998	328,020	341,444	358,221	366,657	337,703	327,237	297,894	318,162	321,992	332,337	342,868	322,157
1999	357,682	363,153	357,126	343,624	338,467	323,658	329,460	315,858	316,247	410,955	461,037	389,187
2000	445,999	478,892	482,080	487,758	476,891	445,018	391,967	387,289	356,583	397,966	454,920	414,851
2001	454,326	469,027	440,548	455,718	424,386	423,840	389,898	387,710	370,315	419,447	462,930	416,593
2002	459,314	464,368	431,923	430,712	411,346	430,856	458,081	509,069	501,523	485,859	496,998	450,016
2003	455,967	469,611	445,343	411,983	406,987	385,775	384,561	383,590	356,181	420,680	470,165	447,455
2004	543,985	641,380	678,041	704,868	637,417	621,898	566,465	562,172	548,816	606,307	639,531	588,860

Source: Chicago Board of Trade (CBT)

Corn Oil

Corn oil is a bland, odorless oil produced by refining the crude corn oil that is mechanically extracted from the germ of the plant seed. High-oil corn, the most common type of corn used to make corn oil, typically has an oil content of 7% or higher compared to about 4% for normal corn. Corn oil is widely used as cooking oil, for making margarine and mayonnaise, and for making inedible products such as soap, paints, inks, varnishes, and cosmetics. For humans, studies have shown that that no vegetable oil is more effective than corn oil in lowering blood cholesterol levels.

Prices – The average monthly price of corn oil (wet mill price in Chicago) in the 2003-04 marketing year (Oct-Sep) rose +0.7% yr/yr to 28.36 cents per pound, which was well below the record high of 36.50 cents posted in 1973/74.

Seasonally, prices tend to be highest around March/April and lowest late in the calendar year.

Supply – US corn oil production in the 2003-04 marketing year rose by +8.0% yr/yr to 2.650 billion pounds, which was a new record high. Seasonally, production tends to peak around December and March and reaches a low in July. US stocks in the 2003-04 marketing year (Oct 1) rose +9.6% yr/yr to 114 million pounds.

Demand – US usage (domestic disappearance) in 2003-04 rose +11.5% to 1.804 billion pounds.

Exports – US corn oil exports in 2003-04 rose +1.1% to 900 million pounds. US corn oil imports in 2003-04 were unchanged at 65 million pounds, which tied the previous year's record.

Supply and Disappearance of Corn Oil in the United States   In Millions of Pounds

Crop Year Beginning Oct. 1	Stocks Oct. 1	Pro-duction	Imports	Total Supply	Baking and Frying Fats	Salad and Cooking Oil	Marg-arine	Total Edible Products	Domestic Disap-pearance	Exports	Total Disap-pearance
1997-8	129	2,335	28.1	2,492	W	375	W	492	1,272	1,118	2,390
1998-9	102	2,374	42.4	2,518	W	384	W	496	1,394	989	2,383
1999-00	135	2,501	17.5	2,654	W	800	W	953	1,417	970	2,387
2000-1	267	2,403	27.3	2,698	W	956	W	1,298	1,630	951	2,581
2001-2	117	2,461	61.0	2,639	W	W	W	950	1,363	1,172	2,535
2002-3[1]	104	2,453	65.0	2,622					1,618	890	2,508
2003-4[2]	114	2,650	65.0	2,829					1,804	900	2,704

[1] Preliminary.   [2] Estimate.   W = Withheld proprietary data.   *Source: Economic Research Service, U.S. Department of Agriculture (ERS-USDA)*

Production[2] of Crude Corn Oil in the United States   In Millions of Pounds

Year	Oct.	Nov.	Dec.	Jan.	Feb.	Mar.	Apr.	May	June	July	Aug.	Sept.	Total
1998-9	209.2	199.4	189.2	182.9	177.0	201.0	201.1	205.3	205.7	194.8	212.5	196.3	2,374
1999-00	204.3	212.3	218.6	214.8	199.0	214.9	210.5	213.6	204.3	226.4	225.3	201.9	2,546
2000-1	208.6	192.7	190.4	198.9	180.5	201.6	200.7	206.2	204.0	205.7	211.1	203.2	2,404
2001-2	196.0	203.3	206.5	200.1	183.8	187.1	189.4	219.8	227.3	220.2	217.0	211.0	2,462
2002-3	218.6	195.0	212.3	206.8	181.7	206.0	199.7	203.6	207.1	216.5	202.5	203.2	2,453
2003-4	209.1	196.5	193.2	201.0	182.9	195.8	200.0	197.7	210.7	204.3	205.2	200.1	2,397
2004-5[1]	208.8	187.1	191.0										2,348

[1] Preliminary.   [2] Not seasonally adjusted.   *Source: Bureau of the Census, U.S. Department of Commerce*

Consumption Corn Oil, in Refining, in the United States   In Millions of Pounds

Year	Oct.	Nov.	Dec.	Jan.	Feb.	Mar.	Apr.	May	June	July	Aug.	Sept.	Total
1998-9	106.6	104.4	105.0	82.0	W	102.0	94.6	101.7	104.3	90.1	97.0	103.5	1,190
1999-00	96.2	97.1	114.7	94.9	89.2	W	W	W	W	W	134.2	129.6	1,296
2000-1	136.2	112.2	129.3	106.7	122.6	118.7	111.9	140.4	W	W	W	W	1,467
2001-2	W	W	W	W	W	W	W	W	W	W	W	W	W
2002-3	W	W	W	W	W	W	W	W	W	W	W	W	W
2003-4	W	W	W	W	W	W	134.6	W	152.8	W	W	W	1,724
2004-5[1]	W	165.4	131.6										

[1] Preliminary.   W = Withheld proprietary data.   *Source: Bureau of Census, U.S. Department of Commerce*

Average Corn Oil Price, Wet Mill in Chicago   In Cents Per Pound

Year	Oct.	Nov.	Dec.	Jan.	Feb.	Mar.	Apr.	May	June	July	Aug.	Sept.	Average
1998-9	29.46	29.65	29.88	29.15	26.58	23.01	23.08	22.96	22.95	22.43	22.41	22.08	25.30
1999-00	21.97	21.96	21.68	20.81	20.06	19.28	18.32	16.63	14.57	13.55	13.03	11.85	17.81
2000-1	10.52	10.37	10.54	10.25	11.06	11.91	13.76	14.84	15.94	17.28	18.73	17.30	13.54
2001-2	17.18	18.30	22.45	20.54	18.35	18.37	17.70	17.00	17.60	19.10	21.72	21.40	19.14
2002-3	22.45	26.90	28.25	29.30	28.90	27.20	27.55	29.10	30.15	29.90	30.68	27.71	28.17
2003-4	26.99	27.56	28.73	29.26	30.16	30.56	30.36	30.34	28.36	27.33	25.61	25.07	28.36
2004-5[1]	23.10	24.24	26.67	27.41									25.36

[1] Preliminary.   *Source: Economic Research Service, U.S. Department of Agriculture (ERS-USDA)*

Cotton

Cotton is a natural vegetable fiber that comes from small trees and shrubs of a genus belonging to the mallow family, one of which is the common American Upland cotton plant. Cotton has been used in India for at least the last 5,000 years and probably much longer, and was also used by the ancient Chinese, Egyptians, and North and South Americans. Cotton was one of the earliest crops grown by European settlers in the US.

Cotton requires a long growing season, plenty of sunshine and water during the growing season, and then dry weather for harvesting. In the United States, the Cotton Belt stretches from northern Florida to North Carolina and westward to California. In the US, planting time varies from the beginning of February in Southern Texas to the beginning of June in the northern sections of the Cotton Belt. The flower bud of the plant blossoms and develops into an oval boll that splits open at maturity. At maturity, cotton is most vulnerable to damage from wind and rain. Approximately 95% of the cotton in the US is now harvested mechanically with spindle-type pickers or strippers and then sent off to cotton gins for processing. There it is dried, cleaned, separated, and packed into bales.

Cotton is used in a wide range of products from clothing to home furnishings to medical products. The value of cotton is determined according to the staple, grade, and character of each bale. Staple refers to short, medium, long, or extra-long fiber length, with medium staple accounting for about 70% of all US cotton. Grade refers to the color, brightness, and amount of foreign matter and is established by the US Department of Agriculture. Character refers to the fiber's diameter, strength, body, maturity (ratio of mature to immature fibers), uniformity, and smoothness. Cotton is the fifth leading cash crop in the US and is one of the nation's principal agricultural exports. The weight of cotton is typically measured in terms of a "bale," which is deemed to weigh 480 pounds.

Cotton futures and options are traded on the New York Cotton Exchange, a division of the New York Board of Trade. Cotton futures are also traded on the Bolsa de Mercadorias & Futuros (BM&F). Cotton yarn futures are traded on the Central Japan Commodity Exchange (CCOM) and the Osaka Mercantile Exchange (OME). The New York Cotton Exchange's futures contract calls for the delivery of 50,000 pounds net weight (approximately 100 bales) of No. 2 cotton with a quality rating of Strict Low Middling and a staple length of 1-and-2/32 inch. Delivery points include Texas (Galveston and Houston), New Orleans, Memphis, and Greenville/Spartanburg in South Carolina.

Prices – Cotton prices on the New York Board of Trade nearest futures chart posted an 8-year high of 84.80 cents per pounds in October 2003, but then fell sharply throughout 2004. The year's low of 42 cents was established in August. Cotton futures closed 2004 at 44.77 cents, down 40% from the 2003 close of 75.07 cents. The main bearish factor in 2004 was simply the record US cotton crop of 23.01 million bales, which stemmed from ideal weather and growing conditions. The favorable weather caused the US yield to soar to a remarkable 828 pounds per acre. The huge US crop caused a sharp increase in the US carryover stocks to 7.3 million bales, more than double the previous year's carryover of 3.51 million bales. The huge US crop helped push world cotton production sharply higher by +7.4% yr/yr to 94.5 million bales. World carryover stocks in 2004-05 rose sharply by 31% yr/yr to 46.74 million bales since world demand couldn't absorb all the new supply. Strong Chinese demand helped absorb at least some of the new supply, however. Chinese mill use was driven higher by a sharp 22% increase in Chinese textile exports to the US and a 12% increase to Europe, and by strong domestic retail sales of apparel.

Supply – World cotton production in 2003-04, the last full marketing year, rose +7.4% yr/yr to 94.495 million bales (480 pounds per bale). That was just 4% below the record world crop of 98.349 million bales seen in 2001-02. The world's largest cotton producers are China with 27% of world production in 2003-04, the US with 19%, India with 13%, and Pakistan with 9%. World beginning stocks in 2003-04 fell –20.9% yr/yr to 37.308 million bales, which was a 7-year low.

The US cotton crop in 2004-05 rose sharply by +26.0% yr/yr to a record high of 23.01 million bales. US farmers harvested 13.223 million acres of cotton in 2004-05, up 10.2% yr/yr, and slightly above the 10-year average of 13.1 million acres. The US cotton yield in 2004-05 was a record 828 pounds per acre, up sharply by 13.4% from 730 pounds in 2003-04. The leading US producing states of Upland cotton are Texas with 35.7% of US production in 2004, Mississippi (10.7%), Arkansas (9.6%), Georgia (8.4%), and California (8.2%). US production of cotton cloth has fallen sharply by almost half in the past decade due to the movement of the textile industry out of the US to low-wage foreign countries. Specifically, US production of cotton cloth fell –10.3% yr/yr to a record low of 2.600 billion square yards. That was about one-fourth of the 10.012 billion square yard production level seen in 1950.

Demand – World consumption of cotton in 2003-04 rose by +1.0% yr/yr to 98.452 million bales, which was a new record high. Consumption of cotton continues to move toward countries with low wages, where the raw cotton is used to produce textiles and other cotton products. The largest consumers of cotton in 2003-04 were China (31%), India (14%), and Pakistan (10%). US consumption of cotton by mills in 2003-04 fell –14.7% yr/yr to 6.200 million bales, and accounted for 32% of US production. The remaining 68% of US cotton production went for exports.

Trade – World exports of cotton in 2003-04 rose +10.1% yr/yr to 33.732 million bales, which was a new record high. The US is the world's largest cotton exporter by far and accounts for 36% of world cotton exports. Key world cotton importers include Turkey with 7.6% of total world imports in 2003-04, Indonesia with 7.3%, Mexico with 5.7%, and Russia with 5.4%. US cotton exports in 2003-04 rose sharply by +18.5% yr/yr to 2.996 billion bales, which was a new record high. The main destinations for US exports in 2003-04 were China (36%), Mexico (12%), Indonesia (7%), Taiwan (4%), and Thailand (3%).

Supply and Distribution of All Cotton in the United States   In Thousands of 480-Pound Bales

Crop Year Beginning Aug. 1	Acre Planted	Acre Harvested	Acre Yield	Supply Beginning Stocks[3]	Supply Pro-duction[4]	Supply Imports	Supply Total	Disappearance Mill Use	Disappearance Exports	Disappearance Total	Unac-counted	Ending Stocks	Farm Price[5]	"A" Index Price[6]	Value of Pro-duction
	1,000 Acres		Lbs./acre										Cents per Lb.		Million $
1995-6	16,931	16,007	537	2,650	17,900	408	20,958	10,604	7,675	18,322	-27	2,609	76.5	85.61	6,574.6
1996-7	14,653	12,888	705	2,609	18,942	403	21,954	11,126	6,865	17,991	8	3,971	70.5	78.66	6,408.1
1997-8	13,898	13,406	673	3,971	18,793	13	22,777	11,349	7,500	18,849	-41	3,887	66.2	72.11	5,975.6
1998-9	13,393	10,684	625	3,887	13,918	443	18,248	10,401	4,344	14,699	394	3,939	61.7	58.97	4,119.9
1999-00	14,874	13,425	607	3,939	16,968	97	21,004	10,240	6,750	16,944	145	3,915	46.8	52.85	3,809.6
2000-1	15,517	13,053	632	3,915	17,188	16	21,119	8,862	6,740	15,602	483	6,000	51.6	57.25	4,260.4
2001-2	15,769	13,828	705	6,000	20,303	21	26,324	7,696	11,000	18,696	-180	7,448	32.0	41.88	3,121.8
2002-3	13,958	12,417	665	7,448	17,209	67	24,724	7,273	11,900	19,173	-166	5,385	45.7	55.81	3,777.1
2003-4[1]	13,480	12,003	730	5,385	18,255	45	23,685	6,489	13,759	20,248	69	3,506	63.2	69.24	5,516.8
2004-5[2]	13,659	13,057	846	3,506	23,006	40	26,091	6,100	12,500	18,600	9	7,500			5,299.6

[1] Preliminary. [2] Estimate. [3] Excludes preseason ginnings (adjusted to 480-lb. bale net weight basis). [4] Includes preseason ginnings.
[5] Marketing year average price. [6] Average of 5 cheapest types of SLM 1 3/32 staple length cotton *offered on the European market.*
Source: Economic Research Service, U.S. Department of Agriculture (ERS-USDA)

World Production of All Cotton   In Thousands of 480-Pound Bales

Crop Year Beginning Aug. 1	Argen-tina	Brazil	China	Egypt	India	Iran	Mexico	Pakistan	Sudan	Turkey	United States	Uzbek-istan	World Total
1995-6	2,090	1,884	21,900	1,088	13,250	800	974	8,200	490	3,911	17,900	5,740	93,063
1996-7	1,493	1,405	19,300	1,568	13,918	825	1,078	7,323	485	3,600	18,942	4,813	89,894
1997-8	1,428	1,890	21,100	1,532	12,337	600	984	7,175	400	3,651	18,793	5,228	92,031
1998-9	918	2,391	20,700	1,050	12,883	638	1,039	6,300	210	3,860	13,918	4,600	85,358
1999-00	615	3,216	17,600	1,055	12,180	650	669	8,600	240	3,634	16,968	5,180	87,612
2000-1	758	4,312	20,300	920	10,931	735	394	8,200	340	3,600	17,188	4,400	88,785
2001-2	300	3,519	24,400	1,441	12,300	575	432	8,300	330	3,975	20,303	4,900	98,766
2002-3	290	3,890	22,600	1,310	10,600	460	205	7,800	375	4,179	17,209	4,600	88,309
2003-4[1]	515	5,850	22,300	920	13,800	520	357	7,750	310	4,100	18,255	4,100	94,923
2004-5[2]	750	5,850	29,000	1,350	15,200	550	550	11,500	500	4,250	23,006	5,000	116,717

[1] Preliminary. [2] Estimate. *Source: Foreign Agricultural Service, U.S. Department of Agriculture (FAS-USDA)*

World Stocks and Trade of Cotton   In Thousands of 480-Pound Bales

Crop Year Beginning Aug. 1	Beginning Stocks United States	Beginning Stocks Uzbek-istan	Beginning Stocks China	Beginning Stocks World Total	Imports Indo-nesia	Imports Mexico	Imports Russia	Imports Turkey	Imports World Total	Exports United States	Exports Uzbek-istan	Exports China	Exports World Total
1995-6	2,650	956	10,328	29,884	2,139	528	1,100	519	27,529	7,675	4,524	21	27,359
1996-7	2,609	1,304	15,852	36,614	2,147	894	1,000	1,355	28,763	6,865	4,550	10	26,494
1997-8	3,971	822	18,805	40,059	1,910	1,371	1,225	1,450	26,488	7,500	4,570	34	26,590
1998-9	3,887	635	22,555	43,684	2,323	1,422	850	1,139	25,248	4,298	3,812	681	23,649
1999-00	3,939	603	24,233	44,885	2,076	1,813	1,600	2,400	28,276	6,750	4,100	1,692	27,226
2000-1	3,915	838	18,958	41,672	2,650	1,865	1,650	1,758	26,479	6,740	3,400	448	26,464
2001-2	6,000	743	15,551	42,452	2,356	2,065	1,800	2,977	29,408	11,000	3,400	342	29,023
2002-3	7,448	1,093	13,808	47,190	2,228	2,300	1,650	2,265	30,460	11,900	3,500	751	30,629
2003-4[1]	5,385	993	8,884	38,223	2,150	1,856	1,475	2,370	33,922	13,759	2,950	173	33,087
2004-5[2]	3,506	898	7,843	35,547	2,300	1,600	1,475	2,350	33,557	12,700	3,400	150	33,283

[1] Preliminary. [2] Estimate. *Source: Foreign Agricultural Service, U.S. Department of Agriculture (FAS-USDA)*

World Consumption of All Cottons in Specified Countries   In Thousands of 480-Pound Bales

Year	Brazil	China	Egypt	France	Ger-many	India	Italy	Japan	Mexico	Pakistan	United States	Uzbek-istan	World Total
1995-6	3,759	19,400	1,010	484	606	11,977	1,539	1,529	1,100	7,200	10,647	873	86,040
1996-7	3,727	19,950	919	536	640	13,120	1,562	1,401	1,600	7,000	11,126	750	88,021
1997-8	3,626	19,150	1,033	505	650	12,675	1,612	1,400	2,000	7,187	11,349	850	87,157
1998-9	3,774	18,700	950	495	575	12,620	1,310	1,250	2,200	7,000	10,401	825	85,350
1999-00	4,236	21,300	800	500	565	13,547	1,400	1,320	2,400	7,650	10,194	850	91,812
2000-1	4,200	23,500	750	425	600	13,544	1,330	1,190	2,100	8,100	8,862	1,100	91,954
2001-2	3,800	26,250	650	390	525	13,275	1,250	1,050	2,200	8,500	7,696	1,150	94,511
2002-3	3,600	29,900	900	340	475	13,300	1,175	1,000	2,100	9,400	7,273	1,200	97,452
2003-4[1]	3,800	32,000	900	235	300	13,500	925	825	2,000	9,600	6,489	1,250	98,473
2004-5[2]	4,100	36,750	950	200	275	14,500	875	725	2,000	10,200	6,200	1,325	105,803

[1] Preliminary. [2] Estimate. *Source: Foreign Agricultural Service, U.S. Department of Agriculture (FAS-USDA)*

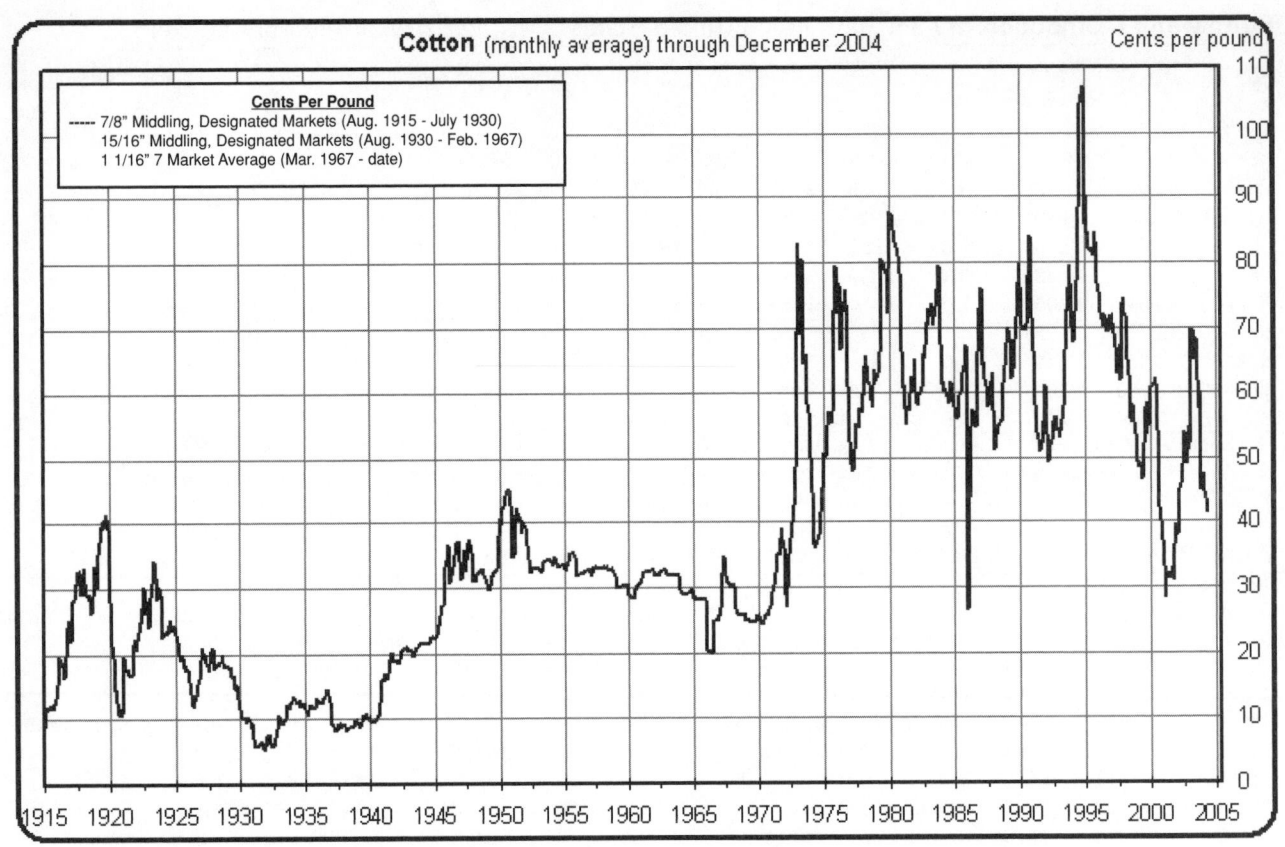

Average Spot Cotton Prices[2], C.I.F. Northern Europe   In U.S. Cents Per Pound

Crop Year Beginning Aug. 1	Argentina "C"[3] 1 1/16"	Australia M 1 3/32"	Cotlook Index A	Cotlook Index B	Egypt Giza[4] 81	Greece M 1 3/32"	Mexico[5] M 1 3/32"	Pakistan Sind/ Punjab[6]	Tanzania AR[7] Type 3	Turkey Izmir[8] 1 3/32"	U.S. Calif. ACALA SJV[9]	U.S. Memphis Terr.[10] M 1 3/32"	U.S. Orleans/ Texas[11] M 1 1/32"
1990-1	77.06	85.58	82.90	77.80	177.43	84.24	84.46	77.19	89.62	81.32	92.84	88.13	80.35
1991-2	55.08	65.97	63.05	58.50	128.10	65.90	68.19	58.14	68.90	74.66	74.47	66.35	63.41
1992-3	64.31	64.01	57.70	53.70	99.24	56.92	----	52.66	62.24	----	68.37	63.08	58.89
1993-4	80.20	72.81	70.60	67.30	88.35	58.81	----	54.42	69.83	59.80	77.55	72.80	69.78
1994-5	101.88	81.05	92.75	92.40	93.70	88.64	82.65	73.75	----	----	106.40	98.67	95.70
1995-6	82.98	93.75	85.61	81.06	----	84.95	94.94	81.86	96.20	90.38	103.49	94.71	90.37
1996-7	79.71	83.24	78.59	74.80	----	75.85	79.60	73.37	79.22	----	89.55	82.81	79.77
1997-8	69.96	77.49	72.19	70.69	----	72.03	81.70	72.93	84.04	----	85.11	78.12	74.74
1998-9	57.19	66.48	58.91	54.26	----	58.66	65.78	----	72.70	----	78.57	73.65	70.95
1999-00[1]	----	61.97	52.80	49.55	----	51.71	56.43	----	55.67	----	68.76	60.22	55.67

[1] Preliminary.   [2] Generally for prompt shipment.   [3] 1 1/32 prior to January 20, 1984; 1 1/16 since.   [4] Dendera until 1969/70; Giza 67 1969/70 until December 1983; Giza 69/75/81 until November 1990; Giza 81 since.   [5] S. Brazil Type 5, 1 1/32 prior to 1968-69; 1 1/16 until 1987/88; Brazilian Type 5/6, 1 1/16 since.   [6] Punjab until 1979/80; Sind SG until June 1984; Sind/Punjab SG until January 1985; Afzal 1 until January 1986; Afzal 1 1/32 since.   [7] No. 1 until 1978/79; No. 1/2 until February 1986; AR' Mwanza No. 3 until January 1992; AR' Type 3 since.   [8] Izmir ST 1 White 1 1/16 RG prior to 1981/82; 1 3/32 from 1981/82 until January 1987; Izmir/Antalya ST 1 White -3/32 RG since.   [9] SM 1 3/32 prior to 1975/76; SM 1 1/8 since.   [10] SM 1 1/16 prior to 1981/82; Middling 1 3/32 since.   [11] Middling 1 prior to 1988/89; Middling 1 1/32 since.   *Source: International Cotton Advisory Committee*

Average Producer Price Index of Gray Cotton Broadwovens   Index 1982 = 100

Year	Jan.	Feb.	Mar.	Apr.	May	June	July	Aug.	Sept.	Oct.	Nov.	Dec.	Average
1995	117.8	120.2	120.7	121.6	123.4	123.6	124.1	125.4	125.3	123.7	123.7	123.8	122.6
1996	123.6	123.7	122.0	122.0	121.1	120.7	120.7	119.9	119.7	120.4	120.0	120.4	121.2
1997	120.3	120.8	120.7	120.8	121.2	120.6	121.4	121.6	121.4	120.8	121.6	121.2	121.0
1998	122.8	122.0	122.1	121.5	121.8	120.8	120.0	119.1	118.8	118.1	117.3	117.8	120.2
1999	117.1	117.3	118.8	116.5	116.4	116.1	116.5	112.9	112.9	113.1	112.6	108.6	114.9
2000	112.1	111.1	106.9	108.2	108.6	107.7	108.3	108.8	110.1	110.2	112.3	112.3	109.7
2001	112.8	113.1	113.1	112.7	112.8	112.9	113.2	112.9	112.9	112.0	111.2	111.1	112.6
2002	110.7	109.9	110.1	108.1	107.3	108.0	106.9	107.0	106.9	105.9	105.7	106.2	107.7
2003	105.7	105.2	105.0	105.9	106.0	106.7	107.2	109.1	110.1	111.0	110.6	108.9	107.6
2004[1]	109.9	111.2	110.6	111.5	112.3	112.6	113.7	113.2	113.6	113.7	113.4	112.5	112.4

[1] Preliminary.   *Source: Bureau of Labor Statistics (0337-01), U.S. Department of Commerce*

Average Price of SLM 1 1/16",Cotton[2] at Designated US Mkts   In Cents Per Pound (Net Weight)

Year	Aug.	Sept.	Oct.	Nov.	Dec.	Jan.	Feb.	Mar.	Apr.	May	June	July	Average
1995-6	85.90	90.00	84.65	84.16	82.18	81.81	81.56	81.13	84.69	83.22	80.23	76.84	83.03
1996-7	76.15	75.24	72.21	70.12	71.98	70.53	70.53	71.12	69.09	69.30	71.03	71.83	71.59
1997-8	71.61	70.75	69.46	68.90	64.57	62.75	63.66	67.04	61.88	65.21	73.50	74.18	67.79
1998-9	71.87	71.75	67.61	64.95	59.88	56.20	55.46	58.17	57.01	55.54	53.74	49.23	60.12
1999-00	49.72	48.39	49.46	48.12	46.65	51.92	54.29	57.67	53.76	58.31	54.97	55.13	52.36
2000-1	59.33	60.62	60.54	62.16	61.04	56.66	54.10	47.22	42.19	40.02	37.38	37.48	51.56
2001-2	36.05	33.22	28.42	31.23	32.21	32.13	31.60	33.23	31.86	31.14	36.36	39.78	33.10
2002-3	39.20	37.91	39.62	44.98	46.38	48.60	51.35	53.82	53.38	48.94	50.92	54.45	47.46
2003-4	51.94	58.02	69.38	68.88	65.09	68.21	63.35	61.78	57.50	60.22	52.35	45.05	60.15
2004-5[1]	44.92	47.48	44.55	42.62	41.68	43.21							44.08

[1] Preliminary.   [2] Grade 41, leaf 4, staple 34, mike 35-36 and 43-49 , strength 23.5-26.4.   *Source: Agricultural Marketing Service,*
U.S. Department of Agriculture (AMS-USDA)

Average Spot Cotton, 1 3/32", Price (SLM) at Designated U.S. Markets   In Cents Per Pound (Net Weight)

Year	Aug.	Sept.	Oct.	Nov.	Dec.	Jan.	Feb.	Mar.	Apr.	May	June	July	Average
1995-6	88.31	92.71	87.06	86.43	84.25	84.32	84.04	83.65	87.25	85.90	82.71	78.86	85.46
1996-7	77.97	76.92	73.90	71.74	75.75	72.53	72.86	73.60	71.23	71.38	73.25	74.04	73.76
1997-8	73.69	72.64	71.13	70.35	66.30	64.55	65.78	69.25	64.31	67.66	76.02	76.63	69.86
1998-9	73.93	73.75	69.90	67.18	62.18	58.56	58.27	61.34	60.33	58.89	56.85	52.61	62.82
1999-00	52.90	51.27	52.43	51.51	49.73	55.02	57.38	61.02	57.52	63.09	59.28	58.80	55.83
2000-1	62.60	63.62	63.13	65.08	64.73	60.18	57.18	50.08	44.94	42.54	39.88	39.96	54.49
2001-2	38.88	36.11	31.55	34.03	34.82	34.55	34.08	36.04	34.84	34.03	39.31	42.86	35.93
2002-3	42.31	41.07	43.08	48.78	50.70	52.87	55.34	57.88	57.54	52.96	55.09	58.46	51.34
2003-4	55.87	61.76	73.27	72.63	68.90	71.96	67.34	66.42	63.11	65.97	57.99	51.11	64.69
2004-5[1]	50.45	52.55	49.45	47.23	46.41								49.22

[1] Preliminary.   *Source: Agricultural Marketing Service, U.S. Department of Agriculture (AMS-USDA)*

Average Spot Prices of U.S. Cotton[1], Base Quality (SLM) at Designated Markets   In Cents Per Pound

Crop Year Beginning Aug. 1	Dallas (East Tex.-Okl.)	Fresno (San Joaquin Valley)	Greenville (South-east)	Greenwood (South Delta)	Lubbock (West Texas)	Memphis (North Delta)	Phoenix Desert (South-west)	Average
1994-5	86.96	93.73	87.17	87.25	86.66	87.25	87.96	88.14
1995-6	80.89	87.40	83.86	83.76	80.64	83.76	80.90	83.03
1996-7	70.29	74.47	72.33	72.11	69.89	72.11	69.88	71.58
1997-8	65.93	71.79	68.60	68.36	65.88	68.36	65.63	67.79
1998-9	57.66	63.78	62.06	61.82	57.76	61.82	55.92	60.12
1999-00	50.49	56.67	53.81	53.34	50.12	53.34	48.79	52.36
2000-1	51.03	52.45	52.63	52.32	50.71	52.32	49.47	51.56
2001-2	32.59	34.64	33.02	33.24	32.39	33.24	32.60	33.10
2002-3	46.76	47.52	48.28	48.46	46.51	48.47	46.27	47.46
2003-4[2]	59.95	59.71	60.80	60.85	59.71	60.78	59.23	60.15

[1] Prices are for mixed lots, net weight, uncompressed in warehouse.   [2] Preliminary.
Source: Agricultural Marketing Service, U.S. Department of Agriculture (AMS-USDA)

Average Price[1] Received by Farmers for Upland Cotton in the United States   In Cents Per Pound

Year	Aug.	Sept.	Oct.	Nov.	Dec.	Jan.	Feb.	Mar.	Apr.	May	June	July	Average
1995-6	72.2	74.8	74.2	75.0	75.7	76.4	75.7	76.8	78.9	76.7	76.9	73.6	75.4
1996-7	71.9	71.6	71.5	69.7	69.3	67.9	68.1	69.3	67.6	68.3	67.1	67.5	69.3
1997-8	67.0	69.6	69.4	67.9	63.8	61.1	62.5	63.9	63.6	63.5	69.7	68.0	65.2
1998-9	66.0	66.2	65.9	64.6	60.6	58.1	55.6	55.1	55.6	55.0	54.6	53.8	60.2
1999-00	52.7	45.3	46.3	44.3	42.8	43.1	46.8	47.7	45.4	47.6	45.1	48.8	45.0
2000-1	51.4	50.6	55.5	58.0	57.8	52.1	48.5	41.1	42.6	40.9	39.2	38.9	49.8
2001-2	37.3	36.5	30.7	27.8	30.8	27.3	28.0	28.4	27.2	26.7	33.7	35.3	29.8
2002-3	33.0	35.2	39.4	43.0	44.3	45.5	46.5	48.6	45.4	45.9	45.5	46.3	43.2
2003-4	46.3	55.7	67.8	63.0	63.3	62.2	61.9	59.4	61.2	60.6	60.5	54.5	59.7
2004-5[2]	53.7	49.3	49.5	44.4	40.7	39.6	38.1						45.0

[1] Weighted average by sales.   [2] Preliminary.   *Source: Agricultural Marketing Service, U.S. Department of Agriculture (AMS-USDA)*

COTTON

Purchases Reported by Exchanges in Designated U.S. Spot Markets[1]   In Running Bales

Crop Year Beginning Aug. 1	Aug.	Sept.	Oct.	Nov.	Dec.	Jan.	Feb.	Mar.	Apr.	May	June	July	Market Total
1995-6	60,442	38,855	73,857	209,279	381,943	765,502	153,758	241,197	225,797	73,459	59,042	31,324	2,314,455
1996-7	62,884	73,925	148,337	477,331	613,430	696,494	412,095	242,606	72,234	130,163	201,557	93,205	3,224,261
1997-8	48,504	106,503	323,400	367,010	617,470	655,432	482,625	396,946	92,072	210,906	105,139	39,647	3,445,654
1998-9	27,193	52,066	114,998	229,743	498,082	414,832	191,872	236,762	71,993	63,335	62,192	64,092	2,027,160
1999-00	83,564	95,241	195,370	320,434	517,579	744,400	294,843	189,460	89,473	129,879	49,012	33,942	2,743,197
2000-1	63,607	69,083	143,938	323,891	288,242	217,755	215,318	191,667	274,185	193,774	152,905	167,647	2,302,012
2001-2	118,000	94,697	214,785	644,860	225,869	289,778	180,362	278,853	84,259	155,391	143,422	93,489	2,523,765
2002-3	43,047	49,671	194,020	204,564	369,838	481,730	432,055	169,064	170,951	213,679	149,780	86,830	2,565,229
2003-4	125,240	245,295	273,028	167,285	321,083	417,090	267,237	167,357	62,031	70,979	79,061	58,400	2,254,086
2004-5	135,568	46,749	91,390	263,999	369,597	402,504							2,619,614

[1] Seven markets.   Source: Agricultural Marketing Service, U.S. Department of Agriculture (AMS-USDA)

Production of Cotton (Upland and American-Pima) in the U.S.   In Thousands of 480-Pound Bales

Year	Upland Alabama	Arizona	Arkansas	California	Georgia	Louisiana	Mississippi	Missouri	North Carolina	South Carolina	Tennessee	Texas	Total American-Pima
1995	492	793	1,468	2,312	1,941	1,375	1,841	513	798	376	724	4,460	367.6
1996	789	778	1,636	2,390	2,079	1,286	1,876	591	1,002	455	675	4,345	528.5
1997	550	847	1,683	2,191	1,919	986	1,821	565	930	410	662	5,140	548.0
1998	553	608	1,209	1,146	1,542	641	1,444	350	1,026	350	546	3,600	442.3
1999	625	716	1,428	1,580	1,567	901	1,731	472	816	281	595	5,050	674.3
2000	543	791	1,425	2,210	1,663	911	1,711	540	1,429	379	710	3,940	389.1
2001	920	690	1,833	1,770	2,220	1,034	2,396	695	1,673	423	978	4,260	700.4
2002	570	613	1,669	1,460	1,578	739	1,935	610	806	131	818	5,040	678.3
2003[1]	820	550	1,804	1,495	2,110	1,027	2,120	700	1,037	326	890	4,330	432.3
2004[2]	820	680	2,085	1,770	1,800	885	2,370	820	1,350	390	990	7,500	736.0

[1] Preliminary.   [2] Forecasted.   Source: Agricultural Statistics Board, U.S. Department of Agriculture (ASB-USDA)

Cotton Production and Yield Estimates

Year	Forecast of Production (1,000 Bales of 480 Lbs.[1]) Aug. 1	Sept. 1	Oct. 1	Nov. 1	Dec. 1	Jan. 1	Actual Crop	Forecasts of Yield (Lbs. Per Harvested Acre) Aug. 1	Sept. 1	Oct. 1	Nov. 1	Dec. 1	Jan. 1	Actual Crop
1995	21,811	20,266	18,771	18,838	18,236	17,971	17,900	663	615	574	567	551	540	537
1996	18,577	17,900	18,189	18,594	18,738	18,951	18,942	686	661	673	698	704	709	705
1997	17,783	18,418	18,410	18,848	18,819	18,977	18,793	637	658	665	673	672	686	673
1998	14,263	13,563	13,288	13,231	13,452	----	13,918	640	614	616	612	621	----	625
1999	18,304	17,535	16,430	16,531	16,875	----	16,968	649	621	588	592	604	----	607
2000	19,159	18,315	17,485	17,510	17,399	----	17,188	648	622	620	622	619	----	632
2001	20,003	19,992	20,072	20,175	20,064	----	20,303	670	679	681	685	691	----	705
2002	18,439	18,134	18,070	17,815	17,375	----	17,209	675	675	674	665	648	----	665
2003	17,104	16,939	17,559	18,215	18,215	----	18,255	667	667	696	722	722	----	730
2004	20,183	20,895	21,545	22,545	22,815	----	23,006	727	758	782	818	828	----	846

[1] Net weight bales.   Source: Agricultural Statistics Board, U.S. Department of Agriculture (ASB-USDA)

Supply and Distribution of Upland Cotton in the United States   In Thousands of 480-Pound Bales

Crop Year Beginning Aug. 1	Area Planted (1,000 Acres)	Harvested (1,000 Acres)	Yield Lbs./Acre	Supply Beginning Stocks[3]	Production[4]	Imports	Total	Disappearance Mill Use	Exports	Total	Ending Stocks	Farm Price[5] Cents/Lb.
1995-6	16,717	15,796	533	2,588	17,532	400	20,520	10,538	7,375	17,913	2,543	75.4
1996-7	14,395	12,632	700	2,543	18,414	403	21,359	11,020	6,399	17,419	3,920	69.3
1997-8	13,648	13,157	666	3,920	18,245	13	22,178	11,234	7,060	18,294	3,822	65.2
1998-9	13,064	10,449	619	3,822	13,476	431	17,729	10,254	4,056	14,264	3,836	60.2
1999-00	14,584	13,138	595	3,836	16,294	53	20,183	10,055	6,303	16,358	3,665	45.0
2000-1	15,347	12,884	626	3,665	16,799	8	20,472	8,738	6,303	15,041	5,879	49.8
2001-2	15,499	13,560	694	5,879	19,603	6	25,488	7,592	10,603	18,195	7,120	29.8
2002-3	13,714	12,174	652	7,120	16,530	10	23,661	7,170	11,266	18,436	5,140	43.2
2003-4[1]	13,301	11,826	723	5,140	17,823	3	22,966	6,424	13,221	19,645	3,428	59.7
2004-5[2]	13,508	12,970	808	3,428	21,825	5	25,258	6,035	11,975	17,960	7,307	45.0

[1] Preliminary.   [2] Estimate.   [3] Excludes preseason ginnings (adjusted to 480-lb. bale net weight basis).   [4] Includes preseason ginnings.   [5] Marketing year average price.   Source: Economic Research Service, U.S. Department of Agriculture (ERS-USDA)

Cotton Futures - New York Board of Trade
(weekly close) as of December 31, 2004

Cents per pound

Average Open Interest of #2 Cotton Futures in New York — In Contracts

Year	Jan.	Feb.	Mar.	Apr.	May	June	July	Aug.	Sept.	Oct.	Nov.	Dec.
1995	71,353	75,100	79,090	71,488	71,714	68,159	65,656	69,653	69,528	65,768	38,475	35,996
1996	58,001	60,231	57,542	61,795	64,555	62,342	61,921	60,182	58,168	58,415	57,397	47,652
1997	59,909	65,392	72,130	76,779	73,464	70,296	73,893	79,309	87,134	92,430	89,150	87,120
1998	89,358	86,739	81,236	85,505	84,562	90,178	81,652	78,571	85,378	88,970	88,917	77,873
1999	79,598	75,794	62,857	60,384	61,470	66,789	68,975	65,690	63,976	60,369	63,746	61,474
2000	63,987	67,720	69,788	56,038	54,058	48,024	53,621	63,069	73,735	67,767	65,017	62,931
2001	71,849	73,383	71,389	70,407	66,680	64,032	61,183	65,257	65,496	59,777	56,896	58,156
2002	64,096	64,572	63,451	63,827	67,601	65,848	74,892	72,612	69,554	71,526	82,802	74,685
2003	83,775	89,852	91,336	78,658	73,146	69,137	62,565	62,781	80,348	108,981	97,809	79,627
2004	93,191	81,871	84,600	89,082	81,988	79,310	77,029	75,449	69,514	76,556	86,280	84,409

Source: New York Board of Trade (NYBOT)

Volume of Trading of #2 Cotton Futures in New York — In Contracts

Year	Jan.	Feb.	Mar.	Apr.	May	June	July	Aug.	Sept.	Oct.	Nov.	Dec.	Total
1995	223,073	290,600	286,098	219,187	214,052	185,276	183,171	199,050	191,534	196,676	195,601	141,116	2,525,434
1996	215,882	196,225	147,393	251,786	236,684	264,047	131,183	177,430	166,629	229,305	229,281	128,010	2,373,855
1997	201,610	253,475	302,609	258,851	175,227	314,406	234,718	202,008	212,966	216,771	266,800	197,839	2,837,280
1998	221,308	289,222	310,075	362,688	218,595	407,922	226,138	230,752	195,690	303,849	272,775	161,816	3,200,830
1999	179,049	244,300	209,127	250,622	157,552	260,649	187,631	178,236	175,282	193,552	298,531	120,120	2,454,651
2000	270,792	279,566	248,017	220,222	232,947	272,023	147,878	175,707	154,735	172,875	242,013	180,982	2,597,757
2001	267,930	270,876	237,356	215,903	175,808	214,513	132,065	118,685	98,947	152,702	258,847	116,033	2,259,665
2002	156,834	248,299	162,781	237,861	188,340	234,442	170,893	128,185	145,946	199,779	296,859	157,741	2,327,960
2003	202,615	267,234	217,791	325,627	249,314	271,822	164,027	127,080	283,988	422,132	356,052	148,310	3,035,992
2004	272,948	359,105	300,820	376,669	184,869	357,548	159,924	195,886	196,739	224,431	341,709	185,370	3,156,018

Source: New York Board of Trade (NYBOT)

COTTON

Daily Rate of Upland Cotton Mill Consumption[2] on Cotton-System Spinning Spindles in the U.S.
In Thousands of Running Bales

Crop Year Beginning Aug. 1	Aug.	Sept.	Oct.	Nov.	Dec.	Jan.	Feb.	Mar.	Apr.	May	June	July	Average
1995-6	38.8	39.4	37.6	38.1	37.9	37.5	38.1	39.5	39.4	39.6	40.5	39.8	38.9
1996-7	40.5	40.7	40.5	41.5	41.1	41.3	40.4	39.4	41.0	41.0	40.9	42.5	40.9
1997-8	40.7	42.4	42.0	42.4	43.9	41.8	41.7	41.1	40.5	40.8	40.0	41.5	41.6
1998-9	39.3	38.7	39.9	37.4	37.5	38.6	38.2	37.9	37.8	37.5	37.7	36.8	38.1
1999-00	36.1	36.4	37.3	37.2	37.6	36.8	37.5	37.6	37.5	37.0	38.1	36.5	37.1
2000-1	36.4	35.6	34.5	33.0	34.4	33.5	31.9	31.8	30.6	29.7	27.6	28.6	32.3
2001-2	28.8	28.1	27.5	26.3	27.1	27.1	27.5	27.9	27.4	28.4	29.3	30.6	28.0
2002-3	28.0	28.3	27.9	27.4	27.2	26.5	26.8	26.6	26.0	25.1	24.0	24.1	26.5
2003-4	23.3	22.8	22.7	23.1	22.5	23.6	22.7	23.0	22.3	22.7	22.8	23.4	22.9
2004-5[1]	23.8	23.4	22.8	23.3	23.5	22.5							23.2

[1] Preliminary.   [2] Not seasonally adjusted.   *Source: Bureau of the Census; U.S. Department of Commerce*

Consumption of American and Foreign Cotton in the United States   In Thousands of Running Bales

Year	Aug.	Sept.	Oct.	Nov.	Dec.	Jan.	Feb.	Mar.	Apr.	May	June	July	Total
1995-6	829	1,020	798	761	801	744	787	1,029	810	824	1,040	731	10,216
1996-7	847	1,028	829	816	858	810	819	1,014	834	840	1,044	781	10,519
1997-8	868	1,100	872	855	951	848	861	1,068	839	854	1,017	770	10,902
1998-9	835	1,013	834	758	796	979	795	983	777	793	970	678	10,210
1999-00	762	949	793	757	801	736	769	966	772	771	990	670	9,735
2000-1	766	929	741	663	749	661	657	837	641	628	727	510	8,510
2001-2	616	751	600	521	563	541	580	759	575	594	754	571	7,425
2002-3	574	733	585	545	598	671	556	708	541	523	616	456	7,106
2003-4	476	599	482	468	504	478	475	609	461	473	582	446	6,053
2004-5[1]	484	604	483	460	500	455							5,972

[1] Preliminary.   *Source: Bureau of the Census, U.S. Department of Commerce*

Exports of All Cotton[2] from the United States   In Thousands of Running Bales

Year	Aug.	Sept.	Oct.	Nov.	Dec.	Jan.	Feb.	Mar.	Apr.	May	June	July	Total
1995-6	315	245	452	733	1,230	1,262	1,295	777	576	343	263	183	7,675
1996-7	257	171	277	573	899	666	728	848	711	631	604	501	6,866
1997-8	458	299	400	581	774	734	777	888	669	477	574	571	7,202
1998-9	402	280	265	795	1,027	156	182	221	169	256	260	330	4,344
1999-00	254	146	167	455	654	658	736	978	708	659	508	479	6,402
2000-1	430	336	382	435	541	564	614	720	568	692	784	648	6,715
2001-2	612	824	678	649	927	964	1,042	1,225	999	842	1,067	679	10,505
2002-3	472	653	373	626	935	1,206	873	1,597	1,174	1,150	1,273	1,231	11,561
2003-4	810	555	446	758	1,116	1,194	1,238	1,869	1,453	1,117	1,576	1,021	13,154
2004-5[1]	760	374	422	632	1,087	1,179							8,907

[1] Preliminary.   *Source: Foreign Agricultural Service, U.S. Department of Agriculture (FAS-USDA)*

U.S. Exports of American Cotton to Countries of Destination   In Thousands of 480-Pound Bales

Crop Year Beginning Aug. 1	Canada	China	Hong Kong	Indo-nesia	Italy	Japan	Rep. of Korea	Mexico	Philip-pines	Taiwan	Thai-land	United Kingdom	Total
1994-5	253	2,257	347	925	83	1,061	951	558	173	441	352	89	9,401
1995-6	294	1,845	223	794	115	940	769	618	144	331	255	85	7,674
1996-7	253	1,756	129	594	46	630	568	733	84	197	255	66	6,862
1997-8	288	737	151	464	85	637	712	1,447	53	220	376	13	7,202
1998-9	281	71	245	229	29	406	381	1,359	59	82	249	6	4,298
1999-00	245	147	316	573	61	424	307	1,500	71	257	476	4	6,401
2000-1	322	124	287	558	52	355	489	1,760	42	237	367	1	6,740
2001-2	235	306	407	947	58	385	577	1,516	126	693	693	0	10,397
2002-3[1]	303	1,840	364	869	81	380	480	1,777	104	592	556	4	11,607
2003-4[2]	302	4,921	169	889	63	284	469	1,619	100	526	396	20	13,759

[1] Preliminary.   [2] Estimate.   *Source: Foreign Agricultural Service, U.S. Department of Agriculture (FAS-USDA)*

Cotton[1] Government Loan Program in the United States

Crop Year Beginning Aug. 1	Support Price -- Cents Per Lb. --	Target Price	Put Under Support Ths Bales	% of Production	Acquired ----- Ths. Bales -----	Owned July 31	Crop Year Beginning Aug. 1	Support Price -- Cents Per Lb. --	Target Price	Put Under Support Ths Bales	% of Production	Acquired ----- Ths. Bales -----	Owned July 31
1994-5	50.00	72.9	4,716	24.4	[3]	[3]	1999-00	51.92	NA	8,721	54.9	0	1
1995-6	51.92	72.9	3,478	19.8	0	0	2000-1	51.92	NA	8,837	52.6	89	5
1996-7	51.92	NA	3,340	18.1	0	0	2001-2	51.92	NA	13,655	69.7	257	2
1997-8	51.92	NA	4,281	23.5	0	0	2002-3[2]	52.00	74.2	12,740	77.1	44	106
1998-9	51.92	NA	4,724	36.8	31	3	2003-4[2]	52.00	74.2				

[1] Upland. [2] Preliminary. [3] Less than 500 bales. NA = Not applicable. Source: Economic Research Service, U.S. Department of Agriculture (ERS-USDA)

Production of Cotton Cloth[1] in the United States   In Millions of Square Yards

Year	First Quarter	Second Quarter	Third Quarter	Fourth Quarter	Total Year	Year	First Quarter	Second Quarter	Third Quarter	Fourth Quarter	Total Year
1995	1,169	1,137	1,090	1,093	4,488	2000	1,075	1,129	1,111	1,079	4,395
1996	1,182	1,230	1,198	1,187	4,796	2001	1,047	976	873	811	3,706
1997	1,211	1,276	1,283	1,309	5,078	2002	893	912	894	825	3,524
1998	1,226	1,167	1,218	1,142	4,753	2003	836	780	662	620	2,898
1999	1,170	1,164	1,078	1,039	4,451	2004[2]	648	644	657		2,600

[1] Cotton broadwoven goods over 12 inches in width. [2] Preliminary. Source: Bureau of Census, U.S. Department of Commerce

Cotton Ginnings[1] in the United States To: In Thousands of Running Bales

Crop Year	Aug. 1	Sept. 1	Sept. 15	Oct. 1	Oct. 15	Nov. 1	Nov. 15	Dec. 1	Dec. 15	Jan. 1	Jan. 15	Feb. 1	Total Crop
1995-6	17	433	898	2,455	4,795	8,430	11,262	14,199	16,101	17,011	17,292	17,416	17,469
1996-7	48	342	637	2,146	4,780	8,876	11,906	14,623	16,528	17,681	18,101	18,308	18,439
1997-8	2	359	683	1,210	3,752	7,930	11,601	14,735	16,662	17,613	18,013	18,170	18,301
1998-9	146	523	739	2,056	4,265	7,359	9,366	11,310	12,558	13,160	13,376	13,458	13,534
1999-00	81	561	1,018	2,690	4,885	8,263	11,006	13,379	14,992	15,965	16,322	16,468	16,528
2000-1	245	842	1,454	3,264	5,930	9,221	11,546	13,657	15,364	16,097	16,518	16,648	16,742
2001-2	99	609	802	2,072	4,616	8,806	12,558	15,564	17,606	18,759	19,268	19,532	19,771
2002-3	56	538	898	1,656	3,520	6,697	9,265	12,368	14,392	15,654	16,285	16,576	16,710
2003-4	29	567	958	2,001	3,819	7,393	10,507	13,466	15,678	16,883	17,409	17,601	17,709
2004-5[2]	48	563	1,157	2,222	4,772	8,757	12,007	14,722	17,241	18,993	20,283	21,212	

[1] Excluding linters. [2] Preliminary. Source: National Agricultural Statistics Service, U.S. Department of Agriculture (NASS-USDA)

Fiber Prices in the United States   In Cents Per Pound

Year	Cotton[1] Actual	Cotton[1] Raw[5] Equivalent	Rayon[2] Actual	Rayon[2] Raw[5] Equivalent	Polyester[3] Actual	Polyester[3] Raw[5] Equivalent	Price Ratios[4] in Percent Cotton/Rayon	Price Ratios[4] in Percent Cotton/Polyester
1996	86.24	95.83	118.00	122.92	81.10	84.48	.78	1.14
1997	76.29	84.77	115.00	119.79	69.50	72.40	.71	1.17
1998	74.21	82.45	110.25	114.84	62.50	65.11	.72	1.29
1999	61.45	68.28	98.92	103.04	51.67	53.82	.66	1.27
2000	64.06	71.17	97.58	101.65	57.08	59.46	70.00	119.10
2001	47.08	52.32	98.50	102.61	60.42	62.93	52.00	83.00
2002	45.56	50.63	97.83	101.91	61.17	63.72	50.00	79.00
2003	62.54	69.49	90.25	94.01	60.67	63.20	74.11	110.95
2004[6]	60.42	67.13	99.08	103.21	62.67	65.28	66.48	103.45
Jan.	75.42	83.80	87.00	90.63	60.00	62.50	92.50	134.10
Feb.	71.58	79.53	87.00	90.63	61.00	63.54	87.80	125.20
Mar.	70.65	78.50	87.00	90.63	61.00	63.54	86.60	123.50
Apr.	66.09	73.43	87.00	90.63	61.00	63.54	81.00	115.60
May	68.23	75.81	101.00	105.21	61.00	63.54	72.10	119.30
June	61.85	68.72	101.00	105.21	61.00	63.54	65.30	108.20
July	53.61	59.57	101.00	105.21	61.00	63.54	56.60	93.70
Aug.	51.88	57.64	101.00	105.21	63.00	65.63	54.80	87.80
Sept.	56.27	62.52	107.00	111.46	65.00	67.71	56.10	92.30
Oct.	51.45	57.17	110.00	114.58	65.00	67.71	49.90	84.40
Nov.	49.62	55.13	110.00	114.58	65.00	67.71	48.10	81.40
Dec.	48.38	53.76	110.00	114.58	68.00	70.83	46.90	75.90

[1] SLM-1 1/16 at group B Mill points, net weight. [2] 1.5 and 3.0 denier, regular rayon staples. [3] Reported average market price for 1.5 denier polyester staple for cotton blending. [4] Raw fiber equivalent. [5] Actual prices converted to estimated raw fiber equivalent as follows: cotton, divided by 0.90, rayon and polyester, divided by 0.96. [6] Preliminary. Source: Economic Research Service, U.S. Department of Agriculture (ERS-USDA)

Cottonseed and Products

Cottonseed is crushed to produce both oil and meal. Cottonseed oil is typically used for cooking oil and cottonseed meal is fed to livestock. Before the cottonseed is crushed for oil and meal, it is delinted of its linters. Linters are used for padding in furniture, absorbent cotton swabs, and for the manufacture of many cellulose products. The sediment left by cottonseed oil refining, called foots, provides fatty acids for industrial products. The value of cottonseeds represents a substantial 18% of a cotton producer's income.

Prices – The monthly average price of cottonseed oil in 2004 (through November) fell sharply by –20.1% yr/yr to 29.33 cents per pound, falling back from the 31-year high of 36.73 cents posted in 2003. The average monthly price of cottonseed meal in 2004 (through November) rose by +14.4% yr/yr to a 7-year high of $174.22 per ton.

Supply – World production of cottonseed in the 2003-04 marketing year rose +6.1% yr/yr to 35.512 million metric tons, which was well below the record high of 37.691 million metric tons posted in 1991-92. The world's largest cottonseed producers are China with 24% of world production, the US with 17%, India with 16%, and Pakistan with 10%. US production of cottonseed in the 2004-05 marketing year rose sharply by +25.2% yr/yr to 8.344 million tons, which was a new record high. US production of cottonseed oil in 2004-05 rose by +8.1% yr/yr to a 7-year high of 945 million pounds. US production of cottonseed cake and meal in the 2003-04 marketing year (Aug-July) rose by +4.3% yr/yr to 1.200 million tons.

Demand – US cottonseed crushed (consumed) in the US in the 2003-04 marketing year rose by +5.8% to 2.639 million tons, which was sharply below the levels above 4 million tons seen in the 1970s.

Trade – US exports of cottonseed in 2004-05 rose +6.8% to 379,000 metric tons, while imports were negligible at 75 metric tons.

World Production of Cottonseed   In Thousands of Metric Ton

Crop Year	Argentina	Australia	Brazil	China	Egypt	Greece	India	Mexico	Pakistan	Turkey	United States	Former USSR	World Total
1995-6	748	595	690	8,487	384	725	5,339	344	3,604	1,288	6,213	3,150	35,290
1996-7	564	859	568	7,481	560	540	5,890	421	3,189	1,220	6,480	2,707	34,557
1997-8	542	941	763	8,193	564	590	5,150	348	3,124	1,193	6,291	2,692	34,522
1998-9	337	1,012	961	8,012	379	665	5,420	369	2,990	1,282	4,867	2,580	32,868
1999-00	223	1,047	1,310	6,817	375	730	5,300	237	3,824	1,315	5,764	2,832	33,695
2000-1	257	1,062	1,720	7,868	340	720	4,800	128	3,651	1,289	5,838	2,530	34,021
2001-2	102	1,054	1,407	9,470	527	710	5,370	152	3,610	1,320	6,761	2,753	37,333
2002-3[1]	90	470	1,451	8,758	480	640	4,650	68	3,472	1,245	5,610	2,635	33,474
2003-4[2]	152	400	2,133	8,669	330	570	5,660	119	3,400	1,300	6,073	2,560	35,512

[1] Preliminary.   [2] Estimate.   *Source: The Oil World*

Salient Statistics of Cottonseed in the United States   In Thousands of Short Tons

Crop Year Beginning Aug. 1	Supply			Disappearance				Farm Price $/Ton	Value of Production Mil. $	Products Produced	
	Stocks	Production	Total Supply	Crush	Exports	Other	Total Disappearance			Oil Million Lbs.	Meal Thousand Sh. Tons
1996-7	517	7,144	7,681	3,860	116	3,182	7,158	126	914.6	1,310	1,807
1997-8	523	6,935	7,553	3,885	149	2,957	6,990	121	835.4	1,224	1,769
1998-9	563	5,365	6,135	2,719	68	2,955	5,742	129	687.2	832	1,232
1999-00	393	6,354	7,055	3,079	198	3,505	6,781	89	565.5	939	1,390
2000-1	274	6,436	7,084	2,753	235	3,669	6,657	105	675.7	847	1,338
2001-2	427	7,452	8,206	2,791	274	4,742	7,807	91	667.3	876	1,294
2002-3	400	6,184	6,687	2,495	370	3,477	6,341	101	616.4	725	1,115
2003-4[1]	347	6,665	7,013	2,643	355	3,595	6,592	117	779.0	874	1,244
2004-5[2]	421	8,411	8,857	2,900	410	5,050	8,360	105	874.3	945	1,350

[1] Preliminary.   [2] Estimate.   *Source: Economic Research Service, U.S. Department of Agriculture (ERS-USDA)*

Average Wholesale Price of Cottonseed Meal (41% Solvent)[2] in Memphis   In Dollars Per Short Ton

Year	Jan.	Feb.	Mar.	Apr.	May	June	July	Aug.	Sept.	Oct.	Nov.	Dec.	Average
1996	208.80	202.80	195.60	220.00	191.25	192.20	201.56	193.10	193.10	183.25	196.60	224.50	200.23
1997	207.20	183.75	189.10	189.10	193.75	190.30	170.75	176.25	192.00	189.10	189.10	190.50	188.41
1998	153.10	139.10	128.70	116.25	105.00	129.40	146.65	130.30	115.60	106.50	107.90	119.75	124.85
1999	110.60	101.25	106.90	110.90	108.75	114.50	115.00	100.65	111.92	111.83	112.00	124.20	110.71
2000	126.88	130.50	129.38	125.00	123.25	130.63	131.88	130.50	153.12	150.00	141.88	160.83	136.15
2001	184.00	148.75	138.13	140.00	137.50	126.88	129.69	130.63	131.25	131.25	128.13	134.17	138.37
2002	133.13	125.00	131.88	124.30	120.88	137.50	151.50	159.75	156.38	150.10	150.00	156.00	141.37
2003	157.38	143.60	142.40	142.40	131.75	131.50	143.00	151.70	153.20	163.50	182.50	185.00	152.33
2004[1]	188.00	193.00	205.10	219.67	203.00	185.40	177.50	156.20	142.75	126.75	119.00	117.00	169.45

[1] Preliminary.   *Source: Economic Research Service, U.S. Department of Agriculture (ERS-USDA)*

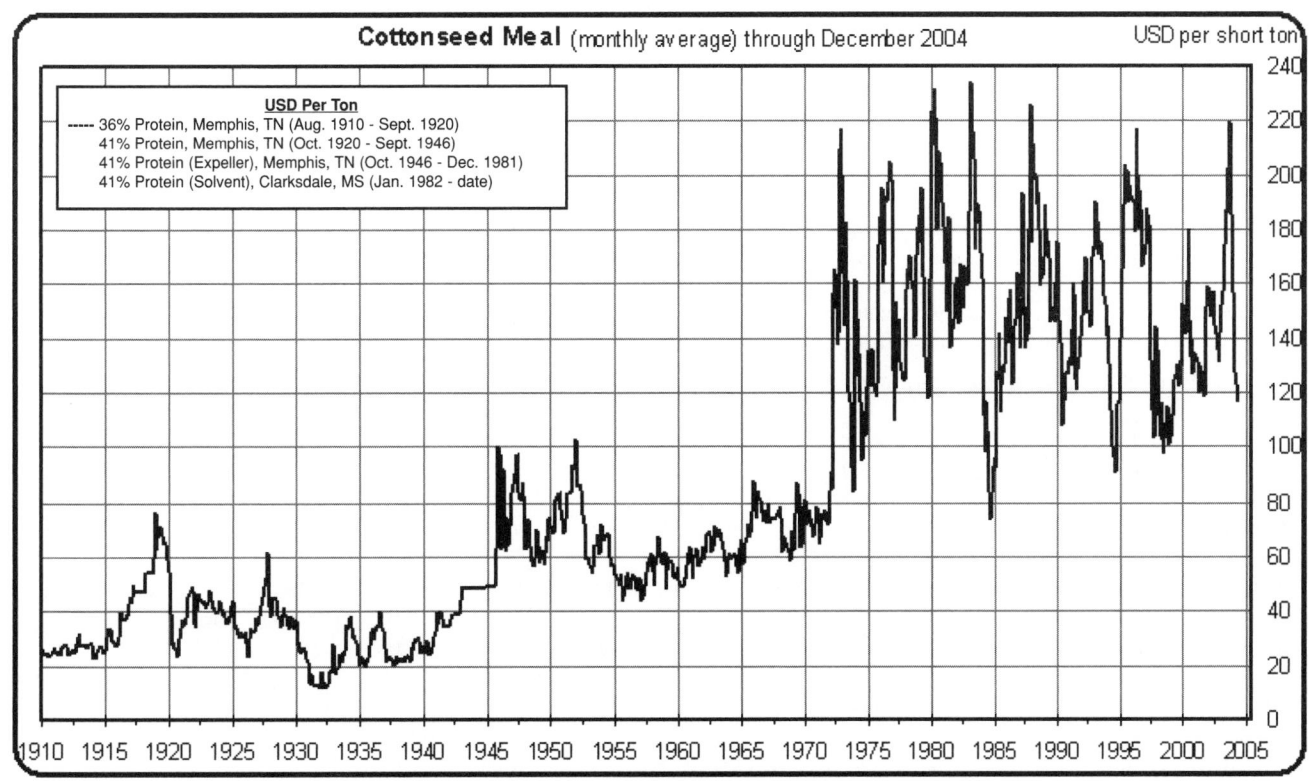

Cottonseed Meal (monthly average) through December 2004 — USD per short ton

USD Per Ton
----- 36% Protein, Memphis, TN (Aug. 1910 - Sept. 1920)
41% Protein, Memphis, TN (Oct. 1920 - Sept. 1946)
41% Protein (Expeller), Memphis, TN (Oct. 1946 - Dec. 1981)
41% Protein (Solvent), Clarksdale, MS (Jan. 1982 - date)

Supply and Distribution of Cottonseed Oil in the United States   In Millions of Pounds

Crop Year Beginning Oct. 1	Supply				Disappearance			Per Capita Cunsump. of Salad & Cook Oils - In Lbs. -	Utilization Food Uses			Prices	
	Stocks	Pro- duction	Imports	Total Supply	Domestic	Exports	Total		Short- ening	Salad & Cooking Oils	Total	U.S.[3] (Crude) ----- \$/Met. Ton -----	Rott[4] (Cif)
1998-9	79	832	48.2	958	772	111	882	28	170	262	457	633	632
1999-00	76	939	8.1	1,023	833	141	974	29	183	320	554	474	496
2000-1	49	847	0	896	673	131	804	35	178	205	426	352	428
2001-2	93	876	0	969	779	150	930		200	317	539	396	441
2002-3	40	725	21.0	786	640	111	750		172	W	427	832	920
2003-4[1]	36	874	0	910	690	110	801					688	814
2004-5[2]	109	915	0	1,024	834	110	944					518	

[1] Preliminary.   [2] Estimate.   [3] Valley Points FOB; Tank Cars.   [4] Rotterdam; US, PBSY, fob gulf.   W = Withheld proprietary data.
Source: Economic Research Service, U.S. Department of Agriculture (ERS-USDA)

Consumption of Crude Cottonseed Oil in Refining in the United States   In Millions of Pounds

Year	Oct.	Nov.	Dec.	Jan.	Feb.	Mar.	Apr.	May	June	July	Aug.	Sept.	Total
1998-9	52.9	49.6	50.2	46.6	48.9	50.7	36.4	28.3	28.4	30.5	46.2	43.5	512.3
1999-00	51.9	57.3	61.5	60.0	58.1	67.8	62.0	52.7	43.2	22.7	45.8	37.2	620.1
2000-1	56.9	53.7	56.7	67.4	61.6	59.5	38.1	46.0	51.4	42.8	49.6	29.8	613.6
2001-2	48.5	63.9	61.6	65.2	58.3	58.9	56.6	56.9	45.2	37.1	53.0	47.5	652.7
2002-3	48.5	59.5	56.0	66.8	55.8	57.1	59.2	49.7	42.4	31.9	38.7	34.9	600.5
2003-4	60.1	63.5	61.6	64.5	58.6	68.5	55.1	55.2	52.5	43.8	53.6	52.2	689.1
2004-5[1]	60.0	66.4	67.0										773.5

[1] Preliminary.   *Source: U.S. Bureau of Census, U.S. Department of Commerce*

Exports of Cottonseed Oil (Crude and Refined) from the United States   In Thousands of Pounds

Year	Jan.	Feb.	Mar.	Apr.	May	June	July	Aug.	Sept.	Oct.	Nov.	Dec.	Total
1998	24,003	15,077	16,150	22,874	20,791	22,994	15,348	14,392	8,818	11,056	7,610	11,447	190,560
1999	11,541	10,235	7,780	11,387	6,328	7,161	8,725	8,111	9,275	11,060	12,313	23,025	126,941
2000	10,627	9,447	13,181	8,258	7,402	7,550	11,546	10,642	16,467	13,263	11,652	8,898	128,934
2001	14,684	6,638	7,237	10,595	12,722	7,525	10,325	20,809	6,439	19,891	5,662	19,831	142,359
2002	12,905	17,550	12,137	8,319	21,013	9,444	7,863	8,727	6,831	12,698	11,105	10,761	139,352
2003	7,017	8,483	10,054	8,234	9,706	8,161	6,593	8,663	8,764	8,640	9,349	8,176	101,839
2004[1]	14,253	8,982	8,281	10,399	9,632	10,720	7,886	9,330	4,807	5,669	7,619	7,507	105,084

[1] Preliminary.   *Source: Economic Research Service, U.S. Department of Agriculture (ERS-USDA)*

COTTONSEED AND PRODUCTS

Cottonseed Crushed (Consumption) in the United States   In Thousands of Short Tons

Year	Aug.	Sept.	Oct.	Nov.	Dec.	Jan.	Feb.	Mar.	Apr.	May	June	July	Total
1996-7	229.2	225.0	331.7	355.1	352.6	381.0	362.8	362.2	334.4	351.3	280.8	294.0	3,860
1997-8	244.4	178.6	329.7	374.5	371.3	428.4	352.3	370.8	359.1	309.1	278.8	277.6	3,875
1998-9	246.0	174.9	272.7	254.3	262.7	282.2	259.5	280.2	205.5	172.0	159.9	149.2	2,719
1999-00	166.8	230.7	281.6	302.5	296.4	300.2	299.4	297.7	263.5	250.3	221.3	153.5	3,064
2000-1	170.8	141.1	265.9	252.3	241.5	295.2	268.7	261.9	186.0	228.3	241.9	199.2	2,753
2001-2	186.8	147.6	267.5	287.0	273.1	281.3	253.2	251.8	243.0	233.3	200.3	166.3	2,791
2002-3	195.1	131.4	207.8	242.5	236.6	274.5	224.5	230.4	241.5	203.6	179.4	127.4	2,495
2003-4	138.7	98.9	251.6	254.8	252.0	265.2	242.3	278.0	217.1	240.2	217.7	182.4	2,639
2004-5[1]	193.8	141.0	247.9	260.3	263.5								2,655

[1] Preliminary.   Source: Economic Research Service, U.S. Department of Agriculture (ERS-USDA)

Production of Cottonseed Cake and Meal in the United States   In Thousands of Short Tons

Year	Aug.	Sept.	Oct.	Nov.	Dec.	Jan.	Feb.	Mar.	Apr.	May	June	July	Total
1996-7	100.9	99.1	146.1	161.5	158.2	174.5	164.6	162.1	152.2	160.7	128.6	123.2	1,732
1997-8	128.2	92.1	147.8	168.7	178.2	194.4	158.5	170.4	162.3	141.8	128.8	124.0	1,795
1998-9	114.7	77.1	118.7	115.9	122.5	130.2	114.8	127.2	90.6	75.6	75.6	71.0	1,234
1999-00	82.1	107.5	132.1	140.8	138.3	135.3	137.7	140.2	120.0	109.4	109.3	79.5	1,432
2000-1	74.1	79.3	134.1	121.4	117.1	136.0	118.9	120.3	83.4	101.0	114.3	89.7	1,290
2001-2	83.9	70.8	118.5	126.5	118.2	129.0	112.5	115.0	109.2	107.9	96.3	73.7	1,261
2002-3	92.4	79.3	95.5	112.6	108.0	123.0	100.3	96.7	108.9	89.8	81.4	63.0	1,151
2003-4	74.9	59.5	112.3	111.0	112.5	113.9	105.1	123.4	94.2	104.7	97.7	91.0	1,200
2004-5[1]	95.3	82.5	105.4	110.4	118.7								1,229

[1] Preliminary.   Source: Bureau of Census, U.S. Department of Commerce

Production of Crude Cottonseed Oil[2] in the United States   In Millions of Pounds

Year	Aug.	Sept.	Oct.	Nov.	Dec.	Jan.	Feb.	Mar.	Apr.	May	June	July	Total
1996-7	70.3	69.4	98.9	114.8	115.9	123.9	114.8	114.7	103.7	109.8	86.9	85.9	1,209
1997-8	80.6	66.0	97.8	120.3	119.6	136.4	111.1	115.5	112.7	96.1	87.3	88.8	1,232
1998-9	77.8	59.6	78.3	80.0	80.6	84.0	80.2	86.7	64.4	53.4	52.4	45.9	843
1999-00	56.1	69.6	88.3	95.4	94.2	93.4	93.2	93.8	82.6	75.7	70.2	49.2	962
2000-1	55.1	52.1	84.3	76.8	73.5	85.9	78.4	76.4	53.9	66.8	66.6	55.7	826
2001-2	57.5	42.2	79.4	86.2	81.7	87.5	78.3	78.2	74.6	74.5	61.8	50.6	853
2002-3	60.2	53.7	62.8	72.1	67.9	80.8	65.6	66.7	71.0	59.9	52.8	39.9	753
2003-4	45.0	40.7	77.5	78.2	79.0	82.4	75.7	87.2	67.0	73.8	66.7	59.7	833
2004-5[1]	68.6	58.1	77.1	82.2	81.4								882

[1] Preliminary.   [2] Not seasonally adjusted.   Source: Bureau of Census, U.S. Department of Commerce

Production of Refined Cottonseed Oil in the United States   In Millions of Pounds

Year	Aug.	Sept.	Oct.	Nov.	Dec.	Jan.	Feb.	Mar.	Apr.	May	June	July	Total
1996-7	62.4	53.0	64.9	82.8	82.2	85.9	80.7	78.1	75.2	76.9	56.4	53.6	852
1997-8	57.4	38.1	48.3	71.0	74.8	82.2	73.1	68.2	69.8	55.2	50.3	53.0	741
1998-9	55.8	29.1	51.1	47.9	48.5	45.4	47.3	49.0	35.2	27.4	27.5	29.7	494
1999-00	44.8	42.4	50.4	55.6	59.5	58.3	56.7	65.8	60.0	51.0	41.9	22.0	608
2000-1	44.4	36.2	55.1	52.2	54.9	65.7	59.8	57.8	36.9	44.8	50.0	41.5	599
2001-2	49.4	29.6	48.2	63.6	61.3	64.9	58.0	58.5	56.2	56.7	45.2	36.8	628
2002-3	52.7	47.1	48.3	59.2	55.7	66.5	55.6	56.8	58.9	49.4	42.4	31.7	624
2003-4	38.5	34.6	59.8	63.5	61.4	64.3	58.4	68.3	55.1	55.1	52.4	43.8	655
2004-5[1]	53.4	52.0	59.7	66.1	66.9								716

[1] Preliminary.   Source: Bureau of the Census, U.S. Department of Commerce

Stocks of Cottonseed Oil (Crude and Refined) in the U.S., at End of Month   In Millions of Pounds

Year	Aug.	Sept.	Oct.	Nov.	Dec.	Jan.	Feb.	Mar.	Apr.	May	June	July
1996-7	101.2	94.1	97.5	102.5	106.0	120.9	133.7	137.5	131.7	116.1	103.4	85.9
1997-8	78.0	66.4	68.6	86.4	105.3	133.8	141.2	140.7	159.8	150.4	130.9	118.8
1998-9	97.3	78.6	89.1	110.0	85.5	109.5	113.3	125.3	126.0	112.0	100.7	83.7
1999-00	107.8	76.0	81.1	88.7	85.1	84.5	79.6	115.2	127.4	127.5	103.0	81.3
2000-1	59.9	49.0	66.5	75.2	95.0	109.5	134.4	139.9	133.5	123.5	126.8	114.0
2001-2	97.7	91.8	113.8	112.9	109.8	124.9	120.3	106.9	110.3	97.3	82.7	61.8
2002-3	46.1	39.7	32.8	40.2	38.0	46.1	58.8	72.2	83.3	84.2	91.4	64.0
2003-4	50.5	36.0	51.9	56.1	68.7	85.9	100.6	117.6	116.8	125.7	121.0	123.0
2004-5[1]	123.3	109.0	106.6	110.6	111.3							

[1] Preliminary.   Source: Bureau of Census, U.S. Department of Commerce

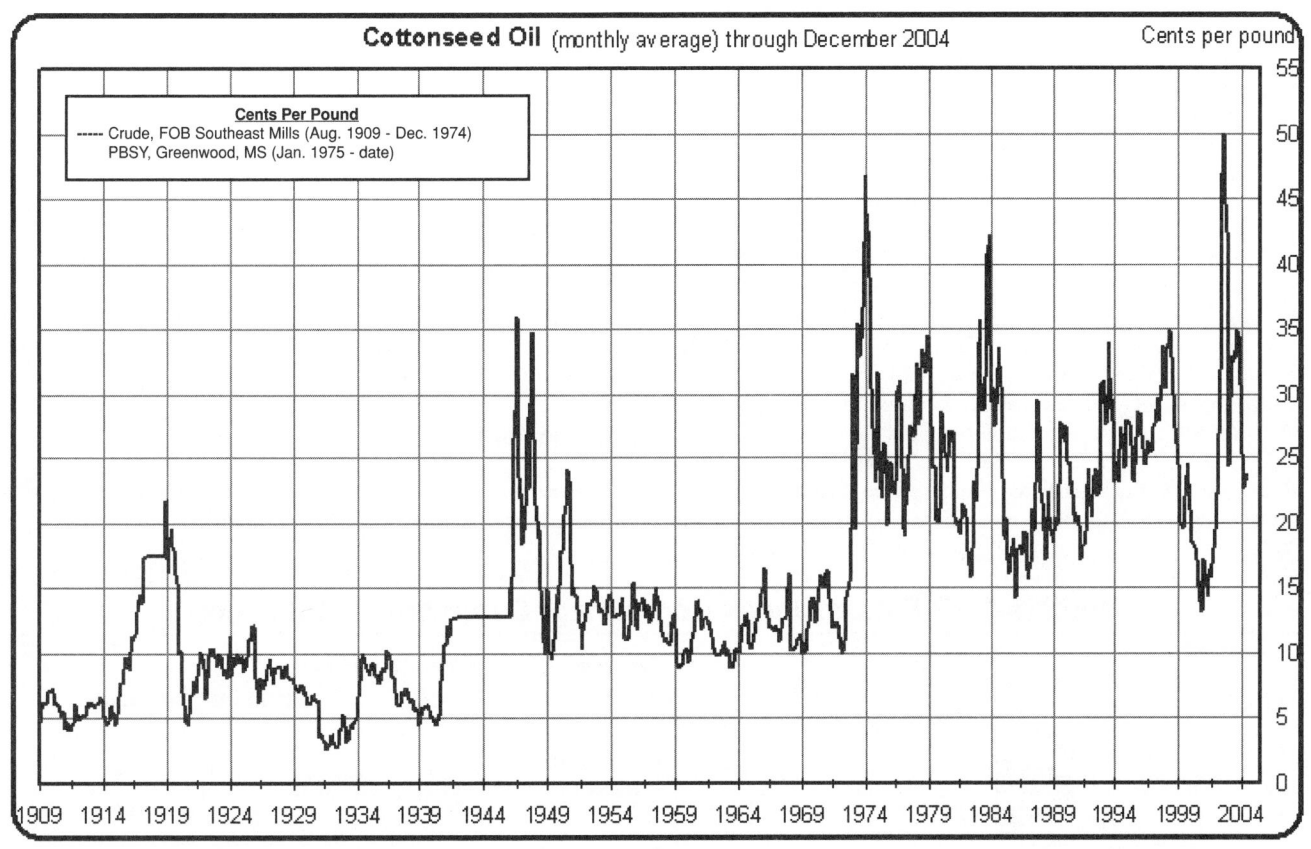

Cottonseed Oil (monthly average) through December 2004   Cents per pound

Cents Per Pound
----- Crude, FOB Southeast Mills (Aug. 1909 - Dec. 1974)
PBSY, Greenwood, MS (Jan. 1975 - date)

Average Price of Crude Cottonseed Oil, PBSY, Greenwood, MS. in Tank Cars   In Cents Per Pound

Year	Jan.	Feb.	Mar.	Apr.	May	June	July	Aug.	Sept.	Oct.	Nov.	Dec.	Average
1995	28.70	29.95	27.14	27.61	27.51	30.04	30.63	30.26	28.61	27.61	26.27	26.10	26.36
1996	24.45	24.35	24.25	26.77	28.46	27.94	28.25	27.81	26.13	24.55	24.28	24.29	25.96
1997	25.21	25.44	26.18	25.10	25.19	25.01	26.53	27.11	28.03	28.47	29.11	26.78	26.51
1998	27.69	29.37	30.46	32.47	33.13	30.22	29.40	30.11	33.26	33.99	34.16	33.40	31.47
1999	31.72	28.21	26.27	24.39	24.25	25.19	24.70	21.39	20.22	20.15	19.69	21.25	23.95
2000	21.98	22.65	23.70	24.57	22.97	21.54	21.03	20.17	18.52	18.16	17.83	17.25	20.86
2001	16.24	15.20	15.53	14.03	14.53	13.27	16.78	17.18	15.78	14.44	15.91	16.07	15.41
2002	16.38	15.89	16.77	16.98	17.95	19.48	21.30	22.32	22.32	26.84	36.90	46.89	23.34
2003	49.82	49.90	47.52	44.57	42.33	28.69	24.38	25.51	29.64	32.93	32.24	33.26	36.73
2004	32.76	34.21	34.91	34.47	32.57	30.72	27.83	25.29	23.29	22.74	23.88	23.81	28.87

Source: Economic Research Service, U.S. Department of Agriculture (ERS-USDA)

Exports of Cottonseed Oil to Important Countries from the United States   In Thousands of Metric Tons

Year	Canada	Dominican Republic	Egypt	Guate-mala	Japan	Mexico	Nether-lands	El Salvador	South Korea	Turkey	Vene-zuela	Total
1995	12.0	----	10.3	1.9	17.9	5.7	1.4	37.8	19.2	----	2.8	137.7
1996	23.2	.0	0	1.7	15.8	3.3	0	20.6	7.2	0	.0	96.0
1997	28.0	.0	0	.4	11.3	2.5	4.2	25.3	1.9	2.5		110.6
1998	37.6	.1	0	0	6.0	6.1	0	16.1	2.1	0	.0	86.9
1999	37.5	0	0	0	4.2	5.4	.5	.8	.0	0	0	57.0
2000	40.2	.0	0	0	7.6	7.9	.4	0	.1	0	0	58.5
2001	26.0	.0	0	.5	6.5	8.6	3.1	4.8	2.5	0	0	64.6
2002	36.4	0	3.0	0	5.4	6.9	0	1.8	4.7	.3	0	63.2
2003	33.6	0	0	0	3.5	7.2	0	.0	.7	0	0	46.2
2004[1]	26.3	0	0	0	11.5	8.7	0	0	.0	0	0	47.7

[1] Preliminary.   *Source: Foreign Agricultural Service, U.S. Department of Agriculture (FAS-USDA)*

Reuters-CRB Futures Index

The Reuters Commodity Research Bureau Futures Price Index was first calculated by Commodity Research Bureau, Inc. in 1957 and made its inaugural appearance in the 1958 CRB Commodity Year Book.

The Index originally consisted of two cash markets and 26 futures markets which were traded on exchanges in the U.S. and Canada. It included barley and flaxseed from the Winnipeg exchange; cocoa, coffee "B", copper, cotton, cottonseed oil, grease wool, hides, lead, potatoes, rubber, sugar #4, sugar #6, wool tops and zinc from New York exchanges; and corn, oats, wheat, rye, soybeans, soybean oil, soybean meal, lard, onions, and eggs from Chicago exchanges. In addition to those 26, the Index also included the spot New Orleans cotton and Minneapolis wheat markets.

Like the Bureau of Labor Statistics spot index, the Reuters-CRB Futures Price Index is calculated to produce an unweighted geometric mean of the individual commodity price relatives. In other words, a ratio of the current price to the base year average price. Currently, 1967 is the base year the Index is calculated against (1967=100).

The formula considers all future delivery contracts that expire on or before the end of the sixth calendar month from the current date, using up to a maximum of five contracts per commodity. However, a minimum of two contracts must be used to calculate the current price, even if the second contract is outside the six-month window. Contracts are excluded when in their delivery period.

The 2004 closing value of 283.90 was 11.21 percent higher than the 2003 close of 255.29. 12 of the 17 component commodities finished higher for the year.

Futures Markets

Futures and options on the Reuters-CRB Futures Price Index are traded on the New York Board of Trade (NYBOT).

Reuters-CRB Futures Index Component Commodities by Group

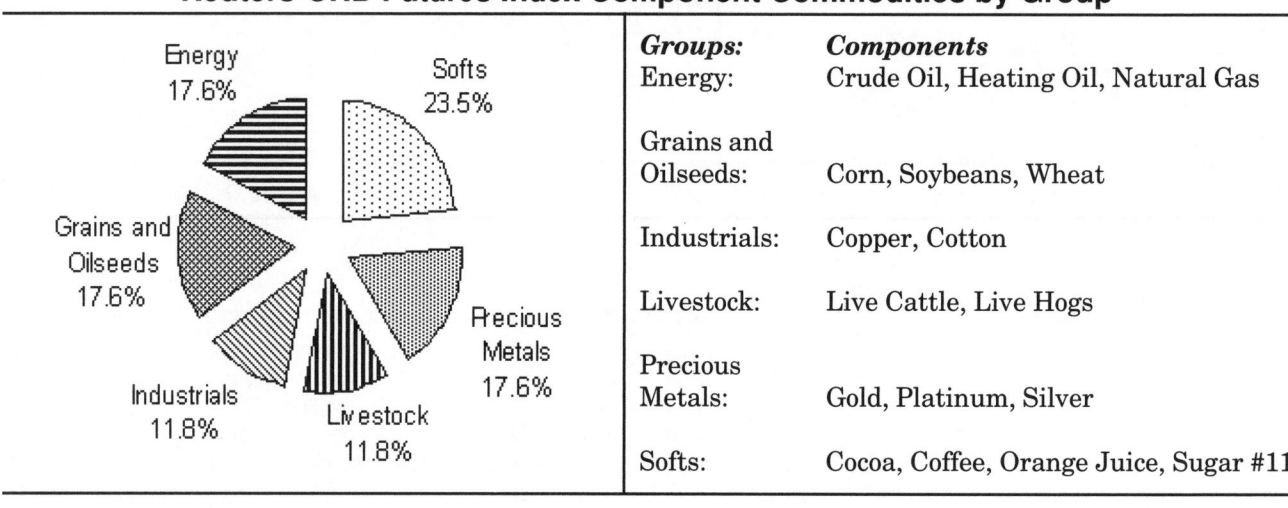

Groups:	Components
Energy:	Crude Oil, Heating Oil, Natural Gas
Grains and Oilseeds:	Corn, Soybeans, Wheat
Industrials:	Copper, Cotton
Livestock:	Live Cattle, Live Hogs
Precious Metals:	Gold, Platinum, Silver
Softs:	Cocoa, Coffee, Orange Juice, Sugar #11

The Reuters-CRB Futures Index is computed using a three-step process:

1) Each of the Index's 17 component commodities is arithmetically averaged using the prices for all of the designated contract months which expire on or before the end of the sixth calendar month from the current date, except that: a) no contract shall be included in the calculation while in delivery; b) there shall be a minimum of two contract months for each component commodity (adding contracts beyond the six month window if necessary); c) there shall be a maximum of five contract months for each commodity (dropping the most deferred contracts to remain at five, if necessary). The result is that the Index extends six to seven months into the future depending on where one is in the current month. For example, live cattle's average price on October 30, 1995 would be computed as follows:

$$\text{Cattle Average} = \frac{\text{Dec. '96} + \text{Feb. '97}}{2}$$

2) These 17 component averages are then geometrically averaged by multiplying all of the numbers together and taking the 17th root.

$$\text{Geometric Average} = \sqrt[17]{\text{Crude Avg.} * \text{Heating Oil Avg.} * \text{Sugar Avg.} ....}$$

3) The resulting average is divided by 30.7766, the 1967 base-year average for these 17 commodities. That result is then multiplied by an adjustment factor of .8486. This adjustment factor is necessitated by the nine revisions to the Index since its inception in 1957. Finally, that result is multiplied by 100 in order to convert the Index into percentage terms:

$$\text{Reuters-CRB Futures Index} = \frac{\text{Current Geometric Average}}{\text{1967 Geometric Avg. (30.7766)}} * .8486 * 100$$

Reuters-CRB Futures Index - New York Board of Trade
(weekly close) as of December 31, 2004

Reuters-CRB Futures Index
17 Futures Markets
Cattle (Live), Cocoa, Coffee, Copper, Corn, Cotton, Crude Oil, Gold (NY), Heating Oil #2, Hogs (Lean), Natural Gas, Orange Juice, Platinum, Silver (NY), Soybeans, Sugar #11 (World), Wheat (Chi.)

Average Open Interest of Reuters-CRB Futures Index in New York   In Contracts

Year	Jan.	Feb.	Mar.	Apr.	May	June	July	Aug.	Sept.	Oct.	Nov.	Dec.
1995	2,144	2,164	2,147	2,370	2,016	2,144	2,053	2,070	2,062	1,942	2,003	1,640
1996	1,934	1,826	1,753	2,355	1,881	1,890	1,562	1,345	1,596	1,853	1,861	1,866
1997	1,944	2,128	2,090	2,245	2,192	1,817	1,957	1,741	1,656	1,843	1,789	1,752
1998	1,679	1,557	1,626	1,509	1,641	1,895	1,832	1,719	1,839	2,162	2,639	2,787
1999	2,863	3,027	3,153	3,041	3,785	3,388	3,300	3,443	4,231	4,851	4,579	4,087
2000	3,487	3,525	3,271	3,117	3,155	2,737	2,104	1,640	1,551	1,632	1,544	1,438
2001	1,280	1,063	1,032	1,036	969	1,006	1,058	1,048	993	559	354	404
2002	422	514	458	384	400	412	489	399	583	646	684	710
2003	748	877	835	849	939	905	858	917	1,078	1,029	1,013	760
2004	838	870	942	704	357	305	413	412	539	600	581	604

Source: New York Board of Trade (NYBOT)

Volume of Trading of Reuters-CRB Futures Index in New York   In Contracts

Year	Jan.	Feb.	Mar.	Apr.	May	June	July	Aug.	Sept.	Oct.	Nov.	Dec.	Total
1995	6,151	5,545	5,763	7,955	7,877	7,573	6,875	10,094	7,376	5,030	5,865	5,309	81,413
1996	7,490	6,041	6,428	10,784	9,526	5,543	7,476	5,816	6,311	6,527	5,990	3,181	81,113
1997	6,645	4,942	5,245	8,600	8,156	7,776	6,248	7,685	4,537	4,588	3,468	3,592	71,482
1998	7,659	4,623	3,953	3,890	2,933	5,634	3,394	4,578	5,101	4,013	8,814	4,401	58,993
1999	7,606	7,766	7,556	7,808	4,986	8,404	4,378	12,053	6,660	8,063	9,497	3,932	88,709
2000	14,975	6,760	3,941	7,582	7,402	8,924	2,023	3,973	1,333	2,122	3,254	1,205	63,494
2001	2,428	1,823	1,310	2,062	930	1,965	880	2,021	625	1,263	843	728	16,878
2002	1,251	1,231	896	1,472	785	1,191	1,217	915	1,100	1,654	1,430	1,141	14,283
2003	2,289	2,154	1,826	1,634	1,514	2,106	1,632	1,350	1,712	2,123	2,502	2,314	23,156
2004	2,477	1,695	3,169	2,672	1,209	1,618	792	1,341	759	813	1,630	979	19,154

Source: New York Board of Trade (NYBOT)

Currencies

A currency rate involves the price of the base currency (e.g., the dollar) quoted in terms of another currency (e.g., the yen) or in terms of a basket of currencies (e.g., the dollar index). The world's major currencies have traded in a floating-rate exchange rate regime ever since the Bretton-Woods international payments system broke down in 1971 when President Nixon broke the dollar's peg to gold. The two key factors affecting a currency's value are central bank monetary policy and the trade balance. An easy monetary policy (low interest rates) is bearish for a currency because the central bank is aggressively pumping new currency reserves into the marketplace and because foreign investors are not attracted to the low interest rate returns available in the country. By contrast, a tight monetary policy (high interest rates) is bullish for a currency because of the tight supply of new currency reserves and attractive interest rate returns for foreign investors.

The other key factor driving currency values is the nation's current account balance. A current account *surplus* is bullish for a currency due to the net inflow of the currency, while a current account *deficit* is bearish for a currency due to the net outflow of the currency. Currency values are also affected by economic growth and investment opportunities in the country. A country with a strong economy and lucrative investment opportunities will typically have a strong currency because global companies and investors want to buy into that country's investment opportunities. Futures on major currencies and on cross-currency rates are primarily traded at the Chicago Mercantile Exchange.

Dollar – The sharp sell-off in the dollar that began in early 2002 continued through 2004. The dollar index in 2004 closed –7.0% yr/yr, adding to the declines of –14.7% seen in 2003 and –12.8% seen in 2002. The dollar index through the end of 2004 fell by a total of –33.6% to a 9-year low of 80.39 from the 18-year high of 121.01 seen in July 2001.

Bearish factors for the dollar included (1) the massive US current account deficit which totaled 5.7% of US GDP and created a huge outflow of dollars from the US, and (2) the US Federal Reserve's continued easy monetary policy in the first half of 2004 with a federal funds rate target of 1.00%. The US in 2004 ran a record US current account deficit near $660 billion, up sharply from $531 billion in 2003. That was equal to about 5.7% of US GDP. The massive US current account deficit meant that the US had to import about $1.8 billion of capital from overseas every calendar day in order to cover its trade and services deficit.

Bullish factors for the dollar that limited the dollar's declines included (1) the strong US economy (+4.4% GDP growth in 2004) which continued to attract overseas investment capital, and (2) rising US short-term interest rate differentials as the Federal Reserve raised its funds rate target by a total of 1.25 percentage points in the latter half of the year to 2.25%.

Euro – The euro in 2004 extended its rally against the dollar into a third year and posted a new record high of $1.37 in December 2004. The euro rallied by a total of 66% from the October 2000 low of 82.30 cents to the record high of $1.3666 in December 2004. Bullish factors for the euro mainly centered on Europe's current account surplus, which created demand for euros to purchase European goods and services. In addition, Asian central banks purchased euros to try to provide some diversification from their mostly dollar-based currency reserves. The European Central Bank's key refinancing rate remained at 2.00% all year, which meant it was above the Fed's federal funds rate target until late in the year after the Fed had tightened to 2.25% by year-end. On the bearish side for the euro, Europe continued to see problems including weak economic growth, ongoing structural problems related to heavy business regulation, a sclerotic labor market, and fiscal problems where Germany and France couldn't keep their budget deficits below the 3% Euro-zone budget deficit ceiling.

Yen – The dollar also showed weakness against the yen in 2004, but not to the extent of the weakness seen against the euro. The dollar/yen fell by 4.3% in 2004 and posted a new 5-year low. The dollar/yen fell by a total of 24.6% in the 3 years through 2004 from the 6-year high of 135.04 posted in January 2002. The yen in 2004 continued to find support from the large Japanese trade surplus. After its heavy intervention effort in 2003, the Bank of Japan in 2004 did not intervene to try to halt the yen's appreciation against the dollar.

British Pound – The British pound rallied sharply against the dollar in 2004 and posted a 12-year high. The British pound has rallied sharply against the dollar in the past 3 years by a total of 42.9%. The British pound continued to benefit in 2004 from general dollar weakness, the strong British economy, and higher British interest rate differentials with the UK base rate at 4.50% by year-end (i.e., 225 basis points above the US federal funds rate target of 2.25% at year-end).

Reuters-CRB Currencies Index   (1977=100)

Year	Jan.	Feb.	Mar.	Apr.	May	June	July	Aug.	Sept.	Oct.	Nov.	Dec.	Average
1995	139.31	140.54	147.85	152.52	150.20	150.85	150.58	145.41	143.89	146.33	145.21	143.83	146.38
1996	141.69	141.01	141.12	139.61	138.11	138.37	139.53	140.52	139.51	138.74	139.92	137.47	139.63
1997	134.61	130.30	129.56	128.71	130.83	131.75	130.14	126.84	128.02	129.07	129.58	126.93	129.70
1998	125.06	126.10	125.65	124.96	124.33	122.86	121.89	120.65	126.18	130.98	128.86	130.69	125.68
1999	130.97	128.48	126.37	125.74	125.32	124.63	124.08	126.89	128.89	130.66	128.24	127.71	127.33
2000	127.65	124.37	124.01	123.43	119.42	122.54	121.59	119.04	117.11	115.99	114.89	117.55	120.63
2001	118.42	116.58	114.25	113.01	112.24	110.92	111.29	114.02	115.20	114.04	112.69	112.01	113.72
2002	110.20	109.38	110.40	111.33	114.54	117.39	121.30	119.68	119.54	119.02	120.77	121.97	116.29
2003	125.37	126.36	126.61	126.42	132.07	133.04	130.30	128.77	130.93	135.96	136.23	140.44	131.04
2004	143.44	143.23	140.68	139.36	137.62	140.48	141.81	140.92	141.25	144.04	149.66	152.54	142.92

Average.   *Source: Reuters*

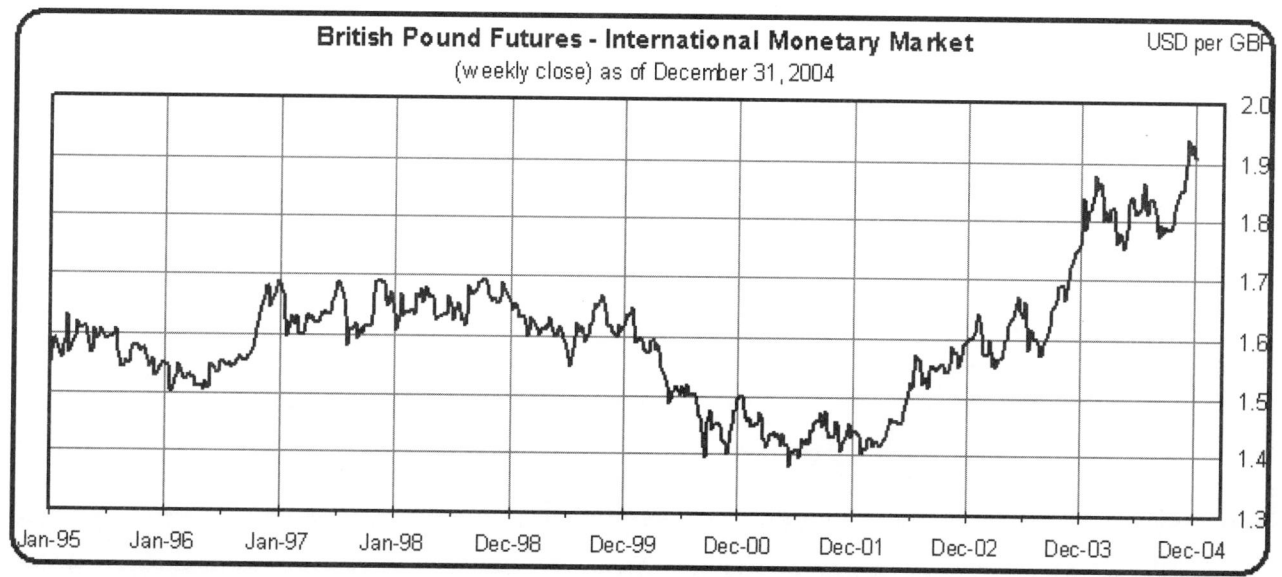

British Pound Futures - International Monetary Market
(weekly close) as of December 31, 2004
USD per GBP

U.S. Dollars per British Pound

Year	Jan.	Feb.	Mar.	Apr.	May	June	July	Aug.	Sept.	Oct.	Nov.	Dec.	Average
1995	1.5742	1.5727	1.6004	1.6087	1.5886	1.5960	1.5955	1.5668	1.5595	1.5782	1.5612	1.5411	1.5786
1996	1.5289	1.5376	1.5278	1.5159	1.5154	1.5417	1.5538	1.5501	1.5595	1.5863	1.6629	1.6660	1.5622
1997	1.6590	1.6258	1.6095	1.6285	1.6325	1.6457	1.6717	1.6044	1.6020	1.6331	1.6887	1.6606	1.6385
1998	1.6347	1.6402	1.6615	1.6720	1.6370	1.6509	1.6429	1.6355	1.6814	1.6933	1.6613	1.6713	1.6568
1999	1.6495	1.6269	1.6213	1.6085	1.6147	1.5957	1.5754	1.6051	1.6237	1.6570	1.6206	1.6131	1.6176
2000	1.6395	1.6007	1.5810	1.5807	1.5084	1.5102	1.5082	1.4885	1.4341	1.4509	1.4252	1.4657	1.5161
2001	1.4767	1.4522	1.4438	1.4350	1.4268	1.4025	1.4149	1.4376	1.4646	1.4520	1.4358	1.4422	1.4403
2002	1.4314	1.4233	1.4233	1.4434	1.4601	1.4849	1.5566	1.5375	1.5562	1.5576	1.5718	1.5882	1.5029
2003	1.6184	1.6077	1.5832	1.5751	1.6230	1.6606	1.6242	1.5942	1.6141	1.6778	1.6899	1.7536	1.6352
2004	1.8223	1.8675	1.8273	1.8050	1.7888	1.8292	1.8433	1.8195	1.7932	1.8069	1.8608	1.9298	1.8328

Average.   Source: FOREX

Volume of Trading of British Pound Futures in Chicago   In Contracts

Year	Jan.	Feb.	Mar.	Apr.	May	June	July	Aug.	Sept.	Oct.	Nov.	Dec.	Total
1995	295,416	263,900	351,089	124,103	195,292	264,635	133,691	219,644	271,815	129,859	191,694	334,952	2,776,090
1996	239,698	270,247	350,969	287,349	316,413	341,492	216,712	181,815	332,895	209,828	183,558	326,369	3,257,345
1997	240,280	168,714	289,352	185,273	236,648	279,338	265,125	194,612	234,092	202,058	144,975	286,099	2,726,566
1998	174,345	126,907	231,941	175,668	217,110	322,996	211,706	277,322	291,374	201,960	146,837	255,545	2,633,711
1999	182,398	151,829	350,218	205,348	285,044	332,107	250,328	178,203	275,899	177,921	163,232	181,470	2,733,997
2000	199,577	179,811	270,898	138,872	133,307	225,758	136,227	155,884	245,069	100,723	100,684	152,465	2,039,275
2001	125,643	126,230	198,749	126,975	166,262	248,926	164,219	183,572	197,117	178,944	161,367	187,388	2,065,392
2002	182,013	168,158	230,355	168,201	174,050	239,757	133,306	138,290	185,291	177,535	160,887	198,017	2,155,860
2003	158,326	161,822	217,383	158,137	164,674	288,625	214,871	163,548	284,467	212,596	206,163	364,543	2,595,155
2004	310,318	291,560	470,321	293,129	282,532	427,762	373,410	367,097	471,396	405,445	348,362	635,180	4,676,512

Source: International Monetary Market (IMM), division of the Chicago Mercantile Exchange (CME)

Average Open Interest of British Pound Futures in Chicago   In Contracts

Year	Jan.	Feb.	Mar.	Apr.	May	June	July	Aug.	Sept.	Oct.	Nov.	Dec.
1995	47,740	44,935	36,805	23,161	26,571	28,402	22,662	34,932	38,900	34,485	43,634	49,804
1996	40,315	50,106	52,349	54,954	52,573	61,461	55,080	50,862	53,868	51,934	62,128	47,652
1997	40,479	38,370	43,742	37,701	40,956	48,890	60,592	50,829	41,801	35,752	56,825	44,667
1998	33,616	31,282	38,712	41,256	47,303	55,511	39,156	49,645	63,756	53,458	54,004	53,578
1999	51,519	59,705	66,913	64,937	58,744	60,414	65,206	54,373	50,949	65,038	49,468	34,191
2000	37,192	45,329	51,645	41,488	51,965	43,009	30,766	36,320	42,781	30,978	34,627	32,913
2001	28,776	30,555	36,532	34,713	39,836	48,310	33,273	40,935	50,083	38,579	40,461	35,424
2002	26,450	31,023	30,474	39,952	46,178	47,355	38,138	31,320	31,513	29,599	40,901	36,671
2003	36,892	33,066	27,042	25,274	36,171	50,118	41,702	46,979	40,183	55,884	66,660	70,197
2004	61,694	68,173	51,968	43,830	45,843	53,615	68,262	71,503	60,274	66,565	87,487	86,572

Source: International Monetary Market (IMM), division of the Chicago Mercantile Exchange (CME)

CURRENCIES

Canadian Dollar Futures - International Monetary Market
(weekly close) as of December 31, 2004

Canadian Dollars per U.S. Dollar

Year	Jan.	Feb.	Mar.	Apr.	May	June	July	Aug.	Sept.	Oct.	Nov.	Dec.	Average
1995	1.4120	1.3995	1.4065	1.3749	1.3607	1.3772	1.3609	1.3550	1.3495	1.3449	1.3525	1.3685	1.3718
1996	1.3664	1.3753	1.3651	1.3591	1.3690	1.3649	1.3687	1.3717	1.3691	1.3501	1.3382	1.3621	1.3633
1997	1.3484	1.3555	1.3727	1.3947	1.3793	1.3844	1.3769	1.3894	1.3865	1.3863	1.4127	1.4272	1.3845
1998	1.4407	1.4335	1.4159	1.4294	1.4449	1.4647	1.4865	1.5344	1.5212	1.5430	1.5400	1.5429	1.4831
1999	1.5189	1.4971	1.5174	1.4868	1.4614	1.4691	1.4877	1.4921	1.4772	1.4767	1.4671	1.4713	1.4852
2000	1.4480	1.4499	1.4600	1.4681	1.4944	1.4762	1.4778	1.4819	1.4841	1.5119	1.5425	1.5219	1.4847
2001	1.5021	1.5227	1.5579	1.5581	1.5403	1.5238	1.5294	1.5384	1.5665	1.5708	1.5934	1.5793	1.5486
2002	1.5996	1.5961	1.5872	1.5814	1.5491	1.5312	1.5447	1.5685	1.5747	1.5783	1.5715	1.5588	1.5701
2003	1.5395	1.5119	1.4752	1.4567	1.3819	1.3520	1.3801	1.3948	1.3638	1.3226	1.3128	1.3121	1.4003
2004	1.2967	1.3292	1.3282	1.3410	1.3774	1.3582	1.3225	1.3127	1.2880	1.2476	1.1958	1.2177	1.3013

Average.   *Source: FOREX*

Volume of Trading of Canadian Dollar Futures in Chicago   In Contracts

Year	Jan.	Feb.	Mar.	Apr.	May	June	July	Aug.	Sept.	Oct.	Nov.	Dec.	Total
1995	126,828	138,251	188,703	91,458	119,567	148,314	128,002	131,981	261,402	213,286	97,156	174,511	1,819,459
1996	124,219	124,654	186,534	129,105	149,127	179,150	123,604	138,816	194,077	179,652	194,001	263,924	1,986,863
1997	189,879	127,310	295,170	151,141	230,733	276,764	146,870	187,149	262,260	268,428	130,528	322,879	2,589,111
1998	172,027	202,027	277,089	142,616	143,170	291,488	153,415	214,046	288,749	148,714	148,906	209,962	2,392,209
1999	170,975	173,034	279,945	203,427	164,352	309,740	216,066	186,031	263,380	167,703	165,587	277,211	2,577,451
2000	184,171	182,462	280,898	155,044	162,780	295,480	165,972	188,459	241,197	161,625	150,275	265,763	2,434,126
2001	194,738	201,075	317,860	188,203	228,359	350,967	221,558	235,883	265,096	214,085	218,108	287,335	2,923,267
2002	222,878	191,493	338,303	249,581	222,156	358,727	278,828	204,168	279,134	245,261	207,379	324,380	3,122,288
2003	270,811	256,672	475,496	289,192	353,096	494,150	331,345	266,189	393,329	285,682	294,352	509,304	4,219,618
2004	380,748	327,964	516,334	380,252	337,100	503,963	366,509	419,381	640,847	511,981	499,452	726,797	5,611,328

Source: International Monetary Market (IMM), division of the Chicago Mercantile Exchange (CME)

Average Open Interest of Canadian Dollar Futures in Chicago   In Contracts

Year	Jan.	Feb.	Mar.	Apr.	May	June	July	Aug.	Sept.	Oct.	Nov.	Dec.
1995	55,863	44,677	33,706	45,394	47,832	36,677	44,930	42,629	49,526	43,032	40,047	40,592
1996	31,028	37,674	38,551	41,411	46,470	37,141	37,522	42,063	44,014	68,674	82,817	72,586
1997	55,949	56,600	72,803	82,732	73,747	57,243	43,937	59,112	56,387	59,265	75,027	74,221
1998	63,300	67,862	61,528	58,938	64,859	74,027	71,313	75,193	60,863	51,967	61,318	50,271
1999	50,061	71,819	63,782	73,773	84,885	71,923	65,877	71,458	61,994	58,749	59,941	51,967
2000	66,374	64,528	58,621	60,389	76,444	69,033	67,198	65,370	65,779	81,995	77,746	65,452
2001	54,369	58,660	72,051	64,550	65,407	62,489	54,742	54,580	73,647	71,610	82,083	67,578
2002	68,927	72,132	70,484	68,120	81,574	86,250	74,347	63,116	63,605	57,031	60,648	71,852
2003	82,870	105,051	107,507	97,515	96,689	85,665	68,741	63,518	70,261	79,754	82,366	74,271
2004	74,577	64,032	61,981	72,750	84,356	68,458	73,164	83,483	97,486	112,648	110,035	81,976

Source: International Monetary Market (IMM), division of the Chicago Mercantile Exchange (CME)

Euro FX Futures - International Monetary Market
(weekly close) as of December 31, 2004

USD per EUR

Euro[1] per U.S. Dollar

Year	Jan.	Feb.	Mar.	Apr.	May	June	July	Aug.	Sept.	Oct.	Nov.	Dec.	Average
1995	1.2380	1.2536	1.3030	1.3292	1.3085	1.3196	1.3340	1.2939	1.2782	1.2987	1.2947	1.2757	1.2939
1996	1.2629	1.2543	1.2544	1.2430	1.2278	1.2386	1.2554	1.2686	1.2587	1.2532	1.2695	1.2416	1.2523
1997	1.2088	1.1592	1.1460	1.1396	1.1441	1.1309	1.0999	1.0694	1.0976	1.1190	1.1418	1.1114	1.1306
1998	1.0859	1.0896	1.0854	1.0931	1.1099	1.1015	1.0991	1.1041	1.1566	1.2015	1.1680	1.1746	1.1224
1999	1.1584	1.1202	1.0882	1.0700	1.0622	1.0385	1.0366	1.0603	1.0501	1.0705	1.0327	1.0117	1.0666
2000	1.0135	.9842	.9644	.9450	.9080	.9496	.9394	.9042	.8706	.8533	.8554	.9004	.9240
2001	.9380	.9208	.9085	.8931	.8747	.8536	.8616	.9023	.9123	.9062	.8882	.8913	.8959
2002	.8828	.8706	.8767	.8866	.9179	.9567	.9924	.9781	.9810	.9818	1.0020	1.0210	.9456
2003	1.0636	1.0778	1.0795	1.0875	1.1580	1.1670	1.1374	1.1154	1.1260	1.1701	1.1714	1.2314	1.1321
2004	1.2604	1.2633	1.2263	1.1999	1.2013	1.2147	1.2265	1.2192	1.2226	1.2504	1.3001	1.3415	1.2439

Average.   [1] Data through December 1998 are theoretical based on DEM * 1.95583.   *Source: FOREX*

Volume of Trading of Euro FX Futures in Chicago   In Thousands of Contracts

Year	Jan.	Feb.	Mar.	Apr.	May	June	July	Aug.	Sept.	Oct.	Nov.	Dec.	Total
1998	----	----	----	----	0.0	0	0	0	0	0	0	0.0	0.0
1999	69.0	96.6	288.4	157.6	183.7	276.4	259.7	258.1	422.8	302.5	303.1	383.0	3,000.8
2000	404.9	335.0	452.4	289.4	318.3	382.2	234.9	303.3	486.3	287.7	297.0	466.7	4,258.2
2001	453.5	373.2	556.4	368.3	407.7	585.3	425.1	494.7	533.9	533.6	545.0	781.1	6,057.8
2002	567.8	582.3	783.3	650.2	611.4	917.7	821.6	525.5	675.3	525.2	426.7	625.4	7,712.3
2003	610.6	749.2	977.9	785.5	902.7	1,103.8	866.2	824.5	1,112.4	1,069.6	958.9	1,232.6	11,193.9
2004	1,487.3	1,469.2	1,837.7	1,326.7	1,328.9	1,682.2	1,491.2	1,518.5	1,798.7	1,786.0	2,138.5	2,591.9	20,456.7

Source: International Monetary Market (IMM), division of the Chicago Mercantile Exchange (CME)

Average Open Interest of Euro FX Futures in Chicago   In Contracts

Year	Jan.	Feb.	Mar.	Apr.	May	June	July	Aug.	Sept.	Oct.	Nov.	Dec.
1998	----	----	----	----	1	1	1	1	1	0	7	7
1999	8,261	30,546	37,837	37,881	46,446	50,615	46,777	55,858	49,352	57,380	58,846	65,346
2000	63,124	68,413	61,180	59,110	67,644	63,361	57,723	69,561	77,617	73,314	79,577	92,730
2001	89,049	91,130	90,127	78,762	89,390	94,160	84,637	104,437	112,797	108,445	108,999	104,323
2002	100,258	108,955	113,075	112,413	136,660	135,364	112,462	101,992	99,365	85,462	103,156	108,602
2003	105,762	106,905	100,759	85,604	108,619	111,651	96,338	98,671	95,553	102,568	113,601	131,560
2004	125,879	133,690	115,712	112,361	138,193	120,281	140,430	160,315	121,180	136,959	202,074	175,374

Source: International Monetary Market (IMM), division of the Chicago Mercantile Exchange (CME)

CURRENCIES

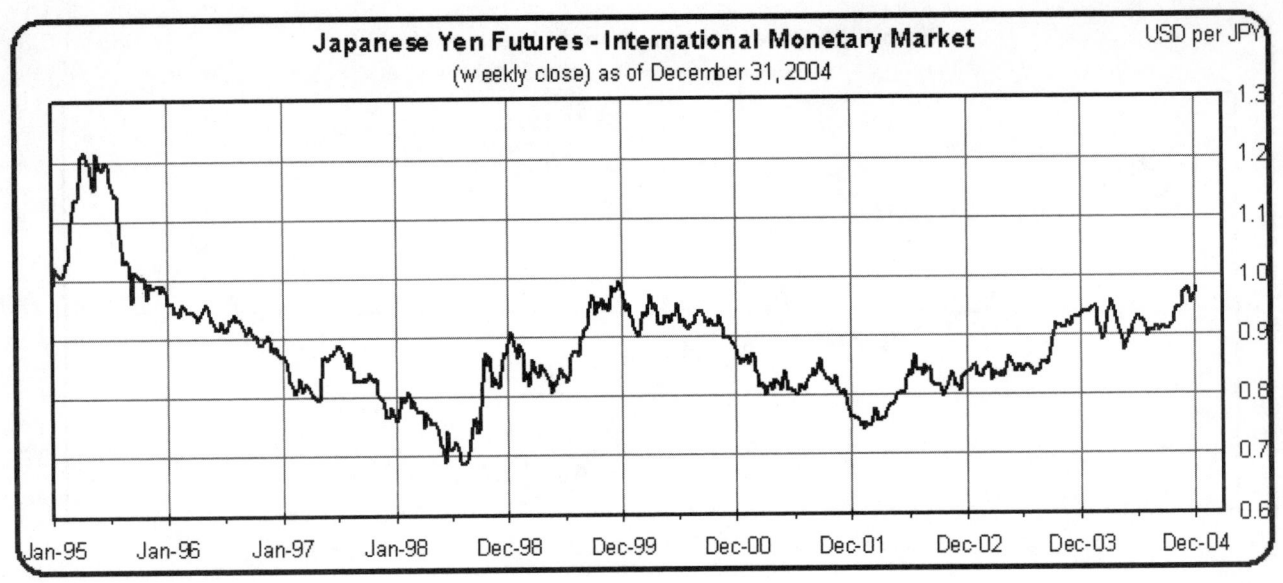

Japanese Yen Futures - International Monetary Market
(weekly close) as of December 31, 2004

USD per JPY

Japanese Yen per U.S. Dollar

Year	Jan.	Feb.	Mar.	Apr.	May	June	July	Aug.	Sept.	Oct.	Nov.	Dec.	Average
1995	99.67	98.14	90.40	83.59	84.96	84.55	87.22	94.72	100.49	100.76	101.93	101.84	94.02
1996	105.66	105.57	105.90	107.23	106.42	108.91	109.21	107.84	109.87	112.40	112.35	114.01	108.78
1997	117.93	122.90	122.72	125.66	118.93	114.25	115.30	117.90	120.85	121.06	125.35	129.62	121.04
1998	129.39	125.71	129.04	131.79	135.01	140.40	140.75	144.51	134.45	120.49	120.41	117.01	130.75
1999	113.23	116.62	119.49	119.73	121.88	120.69	119.38	113.16	107.00	105.94	104.62	102.64	113.70
2000	105.29	109.49	106.34	105.65	108.19	106.15	108.03	108.06	106.79	108.39	108.94	112.18	107.79
2001	116.83	116.17	121.44	123.64	121.66	122.38	124.45	121.29	118.64	121.35	122.39	127.72	121.50
2002	132.77	133.50	131.11	130.75	126.29	123.25	118.02	119.04	120.88	123.92	121.50	121.83	125.24
2003	118.76	119.39	118.76	119.81	117.37	118.31	118.64	118.61	114.94	109.51	109.17	107.70	115.91
2004	106.38	106.70	108.51	107.61	112.05	109.44	109.46	110.24	110.10	108.81	104.71	103.79	108.15

Average.   Source: FOREX

Volume of Trading of Japanese Yen Futures in Chicago   In Contracts

Year	Jan.	Feb.	Mar.	Apr.	May	June	July	Aug.	Sept.	Oct.	Nov.	Dec.	Total
1995	604,876	499,587	839,134	450,204	451,565	465,660	305,499	499,051	662,417	363,440	407,842	370,287	5,919,562
1996	431,105	412,270	473,070	415,810	438,466	566,723	461,813	328,638	549,694	343,145	388,033	482,170	5,290,937
1997	411,601	457,171	564,776	402,703	604,616	564,155	424,281	528,237	611,843	529,557	425,817	644,814	6,169,571
1998	557,789	500,854	636,600	480,331	453,351	1,017,003	515,927	590,808	895,764	551,920	386,306	467,196	7,053,849
1999	418,110	524,625	672,674	400,434	473,385	687,098	476,937	422,277	679,114	310,526	390,508	469,118	5,924,806
2000	433,899	299,111	569,748	250,482	265,785	427,445	248,759	285,889	367,085	213,903	222,692	405,187	3,989,985
2001	258,575	223,715	598,374	295,424	351,158	459,419	307,350	369,357	518,622	286,191	350,088	595,855	4,614,128
2002	415,702	417,497	630,832	391,668	318,478	461,712	301,232	234,168	499,210	349,451	255,356	535,807	4,811,113
2003	423,901	388,298	634,434	453,373	495,643	621,041	518,764	426,979	730,977	396,636	353,359	641,804	6,085,209
2004	410,080	484,880	741,789	516,382	415,513	685,842	487,487	490,689	807,607	629,603	650,503	1,074,947	7,395,322

Source: International Monetary Market (IMM), division of the Chicago Mercantile Exchange (CME)

Average Open Interest of Japanese Yen Futures in Chicago   In Contracts

Year	Jan.	Feb.	Mar.	Apr.	May	June	July	Aug.	Sept.	Oct.	Nov.	Dec.
1995	86,569	86,852	77,649	63,379	67,644	56,285	48,680	63,463	73,830	67,336	73,335	70,268
1996	80,645	78,915	71,643	76,655	73,832	85,398	77,941	73,535	86,723	76,620	72,130	67,301
1997	73,391	82,542	78,466	81,117	85,984	73,322	62,488	82,369	96,468	90,080	130,606	121,001
1998	95,338	101,448	97,183	97,389	106,139	132,732	113,084	145,241	108,808	88,991	89,108	79,262
1999	78,767	81,859	96,271	87,829	118,819	120,681	118,329	136,826	115,884	82,657	87,869	87,595
2000	93,785	125,318	95,034	75,631	80,840	68,359	60,966	79,195	64,845	64,648	68,719	100,713
2001	89,680	90,652	109,536	96,244	89,377	82,838	93,430	107,588	102,710	75,096	97,368	137,756
2002	129,917	123,735	95,535	72,358	88,905	88,324	77,168	71,683	79,980	80,104	74,584	99,643
2003	116,574	107,929	101,809	81,168	107,090	102,507	107,450	125,884	149,978	152,368	138,799	147,255
2004	156,929	156,416	120,848	117,483	108,078	105,505	106,280	110,234	93,780	127,644	181,093	172,526

Source: International Monetary Market (IMM), division of the Chicago Mercantile Exchange (CME)

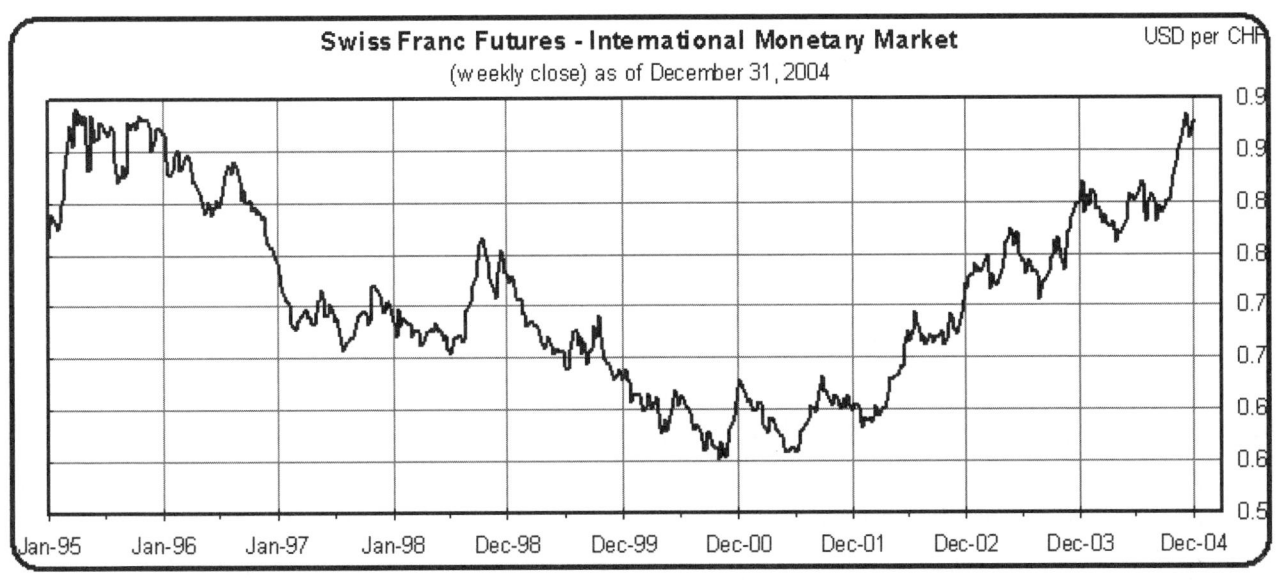

Swiss Franc Futures - International Monetary Market
(weekly close) as of December 31, 2004

Swiss Francs per U.S. Dollar

Year	Jan.	Feb.	Mar.	Apr.	May	June	July	Aug.	Sept.	Oct.	Nov.	Dec.	Average
1995	1.2865	1.2694	1.1691	1.1362	1.1678	1.1564	1.1542	1.1958	1.1868	1.1444	1.1440	1.1624	1.1811
1996	1.1810	1.1942	1.1945	1.2194	1.2546	1.2574	1.2324	1.2022	1.2333	1.2583	1.2757	1.3296	1.2361
1997	1.3925	1.4543	1.4622	1.4614	1.4298	1.4419	1.4810	1.5123	1.4702	1.4507	1.4057	1.4393	1.4501
1998	1.4756	1.4616	1.4896	1.5050	1.4782	1.4951	1.5126	1.4927	1.4002	1.3376	1.3856	1.3600	1.4495
1999	1.3856	1.4273	1.4656	1.4972	1.5078	1.5359	1.5472	1.5092	1.5251	1.4891	1.5541	1.5827	1.5022
2000	1.5888	1.6326	1.6624	1.6638	1.7151	1.6422	1.6503	1.7146	1.7564	1.7727	1.7772	1.6778	1.6878
2001	1.6296	1.6681	1.6903	1.7115	1.7525	1.7842	1.7564	1.6791	1.6338	1.6337	1.6501	1.6569	1.6872
2002	1.6710	1.6972	1.6741	1.6527	1.5868	1.5389	1.4731	1.4968	1.4929	1.4922	1.4647	1.4360	1.5564
2003	1.3748	1.3609	1.3617	1.3770	1.3091	1.3196	1.3597	1.3813	1.3741	1.3234	1.3314	1.2627	1.3446
2004	1.2425	1.2458	1.2773	1.2954	1.2818	1.2501	1.2458	1.2625	1.2624	1.2338	1.1702	1.1455	1.2428

Average.   *Source: FOREX*

Volume of Trading of Swiss Franc Futures in Chicago   In Contracts

Year	Jan.	Feb.	Mar.	Apr.	May	June	July	Aug.	Sept.	Oct.	Nov.	Dec.	Total
1995	441,183	439,121	579,510	321,736	402,216	374,352	249,013	353,817	417,160	328,248	311,200	289,039	4,506,595
1996	321,668	301,971	317,936	314,692	329,676	349,509	345,546	247,502	393,374	333,207	339,849	451,999	4,046,929
1997	360,482	316,346	436,807	343,582	432,533	389,458	316,105	305,189	394,103	429,683	220,959	344,886	4,290,133
1998	308,046	256,815	448,008	318,515	319,210	367,417	310,745	360,394	438,052	300,715	251,266	290,785	3,969,968
1999	294,598	262,128	416,987	284,021	323,252	384,664	351,105	311,835	482,425	407,570	287,172	304,493	4,110,250
2000	326,213	313,127	385,297	252,122	247,653	301,236	214,594	216,576	344,515	176,202	185,388	267,322	3,230,245
2001	193,487	203,006	280,280	168,700	191,601	325,961	257,565	229,380	261,837	227,481	238,232	297,281	2,874,811
2002	195,322	183,156	281,307	211,505	208,078	297,010	187,191	218,533	323,067	237,559	207,825	271,584	2,822,137
2003	236,109	289,893	412,709	256,871	277,835	384,893	314,997	252,056	349,889	237,163	283,751	300,492	3,596,658
2004	216,137	230,067	359,615	260,008	255,749	370,884	331,439	313,712	404,509	428,339	328,950	568,358	4,067,767

Source: International Monetary Market (IMM), division of the Chicago Mercantile Exchange (CME)

Average Open Interest of Swiss Franc Futures in Chicago   In Contracts

Year	Jan.	Feb.	Mar.	Apr.	May	June	July	Aug.	Sept.	Oct.	Nov.	Dec.
1995	39,726	44,364	39,358	30,270	30,586	26,766	23,121	30,267	34,228	34,889	38,033	44,741
1996	42,280	42,902	36,924	39,233	46,810	44,848	38,300	40,298	43,695	47,613	53,581	59,405
1997	51,652	54,114	51,121	45,725	48,651	42,530	55,279	58,098	49,296	43,585	51,822	48,560
1998	57,740	46,160	67,722	67,303	63,477	77,564	85,984	70,569	81,465	57,413	44,810	43,436
1999	39,434	58,279	66,250	66,530	73,322	75,322	66,603	71,060	60,214	65,020	67,936	64,507
2000	55,660	69,983	57,703	41,732	46,159	41,727	36,894	50,595	57,439	47,313	48,870	55,982
2001	50,121	44,405	46,470	41,641	53,265	60,943	53,687	60,986	61,689	48,962	53,445	46,771
2002	35,116	44,388	45,434	38,248	55,039	54,573	42,060	38,102	37,675	35,796	48,951	50,107
2003	56,268	57,099	50,008	37,451	53,642	49,688	41,489	50,677	52,641	54,259	62,584	60,475
2004	45,259	42,950	41,250	38,563	38,024	48,654	51,116	40,256	33,539	47,200	74,988	70,330

Source: International Monetary Market (IMM), division of the Chicago Mercantile Exchange (CME)

CURRENCIES

United States Merchandise Trade Balance[1]   In Millions of Dollars

Year	Jan.	Feb.	Mar.	Apr.	May	June	July	Aug.	Sept.	Oct.	Nov.	Dec.	Total
1995	-15,746	-14,221	-14,487	-16,051	-16,010	-15,862	-15,887	-13,415	-13,243	-13,108	-12,324	-12,600	-173,729
1996	-15,623	-12,911	-14,574	-15,897	-16,826	-14,839	-17,757	-16,759	-17,976	-15,320	-15,176	-17,695	-191,270
1997	-18,167	-16,780	-14,896	-16,505	-16,982	-15,610	-15,864	-16,909	-16,524	-16,270	-16,605	-16,962	-196,652
1998	-17,187	-18,331	-20,615	-20,860	-22,236	-20,404	-21,066	-22,291	-21,611	-20,990	-21,539	-21,059	-246,853
1999	-23,409	-25,233	-25,741	-25,851	-27,753	-30,381	-31,227	-30,518	-30,573	-31,576	-32,401	-32,255	-345,434
2000	-34,116	-34,708	-37,215	-36,934	-36,910	-37,827	-38,091	-36,839	-39,682	-40,205	-38,955	-39,360	-452,423
2001	-39,161	-34,648	-38,815	-37,270	-34,690	-35,760	-35,633	-34,458	-35,660	-35,034	-34,095	-31,534	-427,215
2002	-34,382	-36,951	-37,066	-39,348	-39,623	-40,390	-39,115	-41,730	-41,563	-40,112	-44,744	-47,873	-482,895
2003	-45,610	-44,794	-47,539	-46,179	-45,099	-44,255	-44,677	-44,393	-45,565	-46,176	-44,742	-48,523	-547,552
2004[2]	-49,688	-49,866	-51,501	-53,083	-51,570	-59,214	-54,857	-57,079	-55,080	-60,210	-63,476	-60,560	-666,184

[1] Not seasonally adjusted.   [2] Preliminary.   *Source: Bureau of Economic Analysis, U.S. Department of Commerce (BEA)*

Index of Real Trade-Weighted Dollar Exchange Rates for Total Agriculture[2]   2000 = 100

Year		Jan.	Feb.	Mar.	Apr.	May	June	July	Aug.	Sept.	Oct.	Nov.	Dec.
1997	U.S. Markets	85.7	87.7	88.0	88.2	86.6	86.4	87.5	89.1	89.1	90.0	93.7	96.8
	U.S. Competitors	66.4	69.6	70.6	71.4	70.7	72.1	74.9	77.6	76.0	75.0	75.1	78.5
1998	U.S. Markets	96.9	95.2	94.7	95.3	96.3	97.6	97.9	100.0	97.4	93.8	93.5	92.1
	U.S. Competitors	79.9	79.1	79.3	79.2	78.4	79.6	79.8	79.8	75.4	72.6	74.3	73.9
1999	U.S. Markets	92.5	94.5	95.4	95.5	96.2	96.6	97.1	95.6	94.8	94.1	94.5	94.3
	U.S. Competitors	75.6	79.2	81.5	82.7	83.1	85.5	86.0	84.7	85.7	84.4	87.4	88.6
2000	U.S. Markets	94.9	96.7	97.2	98.2	100.3	99.2	99.4	100.3	102.2	104.0	104.2	103.1
	U.S. Competitors	88.6	91.8	94.2	96.7	101.5	97.1	98.1	102.2	107.1	110.2	109.9	103.2
2001	U.S. Markets	103.3	105.1	107.2	107.6	108.1	109.1	108.9	107.1	107.5	107.4	107.9	108.4
	U.S. Competitors	99.8	103.4	105.4	107.2	109.6	112.6	111.1	105.9	105.8	106.1	107.3	105.5
2002	U.S. Markets	109.7	111.2	110.1	109.5	107.5	105.9	104.3	105.4	106.5	106.9	105.6	104.7
	U.S. Competitors	107.6	110.8	109.9	108.7	105.1	101.1	98.1	100.2	100.3	100.4	97.9	94.8
2003	U.S. Markets	103.1	103.5	103.5	102.2	98.7	99.0	100.5	101.4	99.8	97.2	96.7	94.7
	U.S. Competitors	90.3	89.4	89.1	87.0	80.4	80.3	83.0	85.1	83.7	79.5	78.8	74.6
2004[1]	U.S. Markets	93.4	93.7	95.0	96.4	97.8	97.0	96.7	96.6	95.6	94.3	91.4	89.8
	U.S. Competitors	72.1	72.2	74.9	77.4	77.8	77.1	76.2	76.5	75.7	73.5	70.2	68.2

[1] Preliminary.   [2] Real indexes adjust nominal exchange rates for differences in rates of inflation, to avoid the distortion caused by high-inflation countries. A higher value means the dollar has appreciated. Federal Reserve Board Index of trade-weighted value of the U.S. dollar against 10 major currencies. Weights are based on relative importance in world financial markets.   *Source: Economic Research Service, U.S. Department of Agriculture*

United States Balance on Current Account[1]   In Millions of Dollars

Year	First Quarter	Second Quarter	Third Quarter	Fourth Quarter	Annual
1995	-21,653	-31,022	-34,139	-22,664	-109,478
1996	-16,507	-29,230	-44,582	-29,888	-120,207
1997	-24,548	-28,196	-42,783	-40,452	-135,979
1998	-32,449	-50,433	-68,467	-58,208	-209,557
1999	-52,504	-71,384	-89,603	-83,331	-296,822
2000	-86,440	-99,684	-116,498	-110,821	-413,443
2001	-94,995	-98,248	-101,265	-91,193	-385,701
2002	-96,126	-118,496	-131,579	-127,743	-473,944
2003	-122,975	-135,194	-143,949	-128,550	-530,668
2004[2]	-131,503	-165,787	-178,369		-634,212

[1] Not seasonally adjusted.   [2] Preliminary.   *Source: Bureau of Economic Analysis, U.S. Department of Commerce (BEA)*

Merchandise Trade and Current Account Balances   In Billions of Dollars

Year	Merchandise Trade Balance					Current Account Balance				
	Canada	Germany	Japan	Switzerland	U.K.	Canada	Germany	Japan	Switzerland	U.K.
1995	18.9	15.9	74.8	16.2	-5.6	-4.4	-27.0	113.4	21.3	-14.3
1996	24.7	24.8	23.4	15.5	-5.3	3.4	-13.7	64.8	22.0	-10.9
1997	12.6	28.7	47.4	14.6	1.7	-8.2	-9.4	97.8	25.5	-1.6
1998	12.3	32.1	72.4	13.2	-14.1	-7.7	-12.3	119.5	25.9	-6.6
1999	24.2	17.0	69.4	14.9	-25.8	1.7	-24.0	114.3	30.3	-39.6
2000	41.6	7.7	68.0	14.1	-29.5	19.7	-25.3	118.8	31.7	-36.2
2001	41.1	37.0	26.2	10.9	-39.5	16.2	1.6	89.6	20.0	-32.2
2002	32.5	89.8	51.3	19.0	-46.9	14.4	41.5	111.7	23.6	-27.1
2003[1]	34.2	104.5	69.1	22.8	-53.5	17.1	54.8	135.3	42.6	-33.4
2004[2]	54.2	135.5	86.7	27.3	-74.7	34.5	89.1	164.5	46.0	-46.5

[1] Estimate.   [2] Projection.   *Source: Organization for Economic Cooperation and Development (OECD)*

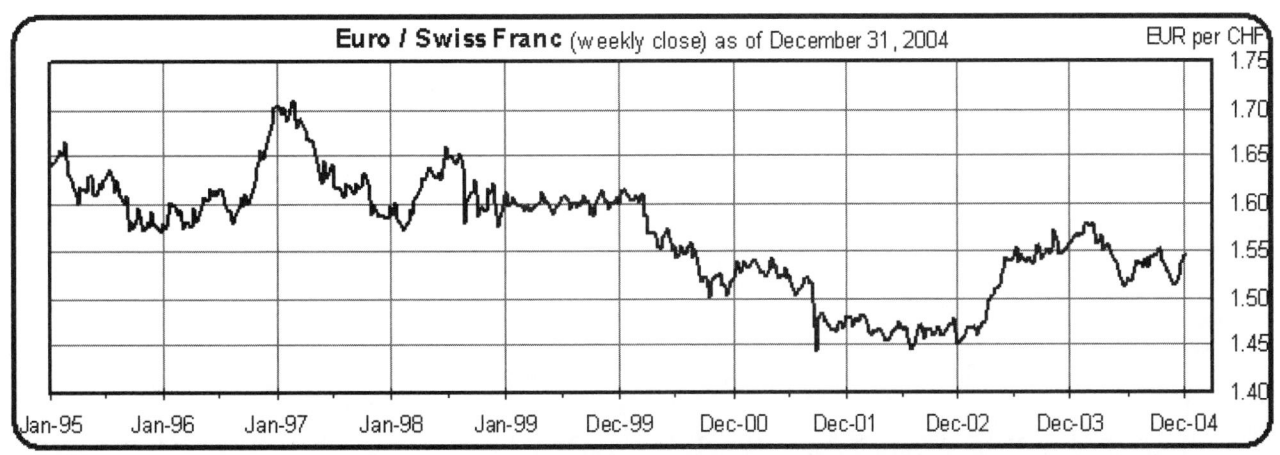

Euro / Swiss Franc (weekly close) as of December 31, 2004 — EUR per CHF

Euro / British Pound (weekly close) as of December 31, 2004 — EUR per GBP

Japanese Yen / British Pound (weekly close) as of December 31, 2004 — JPY per GBP

Euro / Japanese Yen (weekly close) as of December 31, 2004 — JPY per EUR

Diamonds

The diamond, which is the mineral form of carbon, is the hardest, strongest natural material known on earth. The name *diamond* is derived from *adamas*, the ancient Greek term meaning "invincible." Diamonds form deep within the Earth's crust and are typically billions of years old. Diamonds have also have been found in and near meteorites and their craters. Diamonds are considered precious gemstones but lower grade diamonds are used for industrial applications such as drilling, cutting, grinding and polishing.

Supply – World production of natural gem diamonds in 2003 rose sharply by +14.6% yr/yr to a record high of 80.900 million carats (one carat equals 1/5 gram or 200 milligrams). The world's largest producers of natural gem diamonds are Botswana with 28% of world production in 2003, Australia at 18%, Russia with 15%, Congo with 7%, and South Africa with 6%. World production of natural industrial diamonds in 2003 rose sharply by +9.4% yr/yr to 69.500 million carats. The main producer of synthetic diamonds is the US with 236.000 million carats of production in 2003, representing 44% of world production.

Trade – The US relied on net imports for 80% of its consumption of natural diamonds, which totaled 1.6 million carats in 2003.

World Production of Natural Gem Diamonds   In Thousands of Carats

Year	Angola	Australia	Botswana	Brazil	Central African Republic	China	Congo[3]	Ghana	Namibia	Russia	Sierra Leone	South Africa	World Total
1998	2,400	18,400	14,800	100	330	230	5,080	658	1,350	11,500	200	4,280	60,400
1999	3,360	13,403	17,200	900	311	230	4,120	546	1,630	11,500	7	4,000	60,600
2000	3,914	11,956	18,500	1,000	346	230	3,500	792	1,450	11,600	58	4,320	61,200
2001	4,653	11,779	19,800	700	337	235	3,640	936	1,487	11,600	167	4,470	64,500
2002[1]	4,520	15,142	21,300	500	311	235	4,400	770	1,350	11,500	147	4,350	70,600
2003[2]	4,770	14,900	22,800	500	300	235	5,400	800	1,650	12,000	214	5,070	80,900

[1] Preliminary.   [2] Estimate.   [3] Formerly Zaire.   *Source: U.S. Geological Survey (USGS)*

World Production of Natural Industrial Diamonds   In Thousands of Carats

Year	Angola	Australia	Botswana	Brazil	Central African Republic	China	Congo[3]	Ghana	Russia	Sierra Leone	South Africa	Venezuela	World Total
1998	364	22,500	5,000	----	200	900	21,000	165	11,600	50	6,420	17	68,700
1999	373	16,381	5,730	----	120	920	16,000	136	11,500	2	6,010	36	57,600
2000	435	14,612	6,160	----	115	920	14,200	198	11,600	19	6,470	80	55,300
2001	517	14,397	6,600	----	112	950	14,560	234	11,600	56	6,700	28	56,100
2002[1]	502	18,500	7,100	----	104	955	17,456	193	11,500	205	6,530	61	63,500
2003[2]	530	18,200	7,600	----	100	955	21,600	200	12,000	296	7,600	50	69,500

[1] Preliminary.   [2] Estimate.   [3] Formerly Zaire.   *Source: U.S. Geological Survey (USGS)*

World Production of Synthetic Diamonds   In Thousands of Carats

Year	Belarus	China	Czech Republic	France	Greece	Ireland	Japan	Russia	South Africa	Sweden	Ukraine	United States	World Total
1998	25,000	16,500	5,000	3,000	750	60,000	32,000	80,000	60,000	25,000	8,000	140,000	463,000
1999	25,000	16,500	3,000	3,000	750	60,000	32,000	80,000	----	25,000	8,000	161,000	420,000
2000	25,000	16,800	----	3,000	750	60,000	33,000	80,000	----	20,000	8,000	182,000	429,000
2001	25,000	17,000	----	3,000	----	60,000	33,000	80,000	60,000	20,000	8,000	202,000	508,000
2002[1]	25,000	17,000	----	3,000	----	60,000	34,000	80,000	60,000	20,000	8,000	222,000	529,000
2003[2]	25,000	17,000	----	3,000	----	60,000	34,000	80,000	60,000	20,000	8,000	236,000	543,000

[1] Preliminary.   [2] Estimate.   *Source: U.S. Geological Survey (USGS)*

Salient Statistics of Industrial Diamonds in the United States   In Millions of Carats

	Bort, Grit & Powder & Dust										Stones (Natural)				
	---- Natural and Synthetic ----														
	Production							Price Value of						Price Value of	Net Import Reliance
Year	Manufactured Diamond	Secondary	Imports for Consumption	Exports & Reexports	In Manufactured Products	Gov't Sales	Apparent Consumption	Imports $ Per Carat	Secondary Production	Imports for Consumption	Exports & Reexports	Gov't Sales	Apparent Consumption	Imports $ Per Carat	% of Consumption
1998	140.0	10.0	221.0	104.0	----	[3]	267.0	.44	.5	4.7	.8	.8	5.2	3.92	90
1999	208.0	10.0	208.0	98.0	----	[3]	328.0	.44	.4	3.1	.7	.6	3.4	4.61	88
2000	182.0	10.0	291.0	98.0	----	----	385.0	.39	[3]	2.5	1.6	1.0	2.2	5.31	86
2001	202.0	10.0	281.0	88.0	----	[3]	405.0	.31	[3]	2.5	1.0	.5	2.2	3.54	91
2002[1]	219.0	5.7	185.0	82.0	----	[3]	328.0	.34	[3]	2.1	1.1	.4	1.6	5.43	88
2003[2]	236.0	5.1	223.0	66.0	----	----	398.0	.29	[3]	1.6	.8	.3	1.4	2.46	80

[1] Preliminary.   [2] Estimate.   [3] Less than 1/2 unit.   *Source: U.S. Geological Survey (USGS)*

Eggs

Eggs are a low-priced protein source and are consumed worldwide. Each commercial chicken lays between 265-280 eggs per year. In the United States, the grade and size of eggs are regulated under the federal Egg Products Inspection Act (1970). The grades of eggs are AA, A, and B, and must have sound, whole shells and must be clean. The difference among the grades of eggs is internal and mostly reflects the freshness of the egg. Table eggs vary in color and can be determined by the color of the chicken's earlobe—white earlobes lay white eggs, reddish-brown earlobes lay brown eggs, etc. In the US, egg size is determined by the weight of a dozen eggs, not individual eggs, and range from Peewee to Jumbo. Store-bought eggs in the shell stay fresh for 3 to 5 weeks in a home refrigerator, according to the USDA.

Eggs are primarily used as a source of food, although eggs are also widely used for medical purposes. Fertile eggs, as a source of purified proteins, are used to produce many vaccines. Flu vaccines are produced by growing single strains of the flu virus in eggs, which are then extracted to make the vaccine. Eggs are also used in biotechnology to create new drugs. The hen's genetic make-up can be altered so the whites of the eggs are rich in tailored proteins that form the basis of medicines to fight cancer and other diseases. The US biotech company Viragen and the Roslin Institute in Edinburgh have produced eggs with 100 mg or more of the easily-extracted proteins used in new drugs to treat various illnesses including ovarian and breast cancers.

Prices – The average monthly price of all eggs received by farmers in the US fell by –5.0% yr/yr to 70.2 cents per dozen, which was down from the 14-year high of 73.8 cents posted in 2003.

Supply – World egg production in 2001, the latest reporting year, rose +2.1% yr/yr to 595.711 billion eggs. The world's largest egg producers are China with 49% of world production, the US with 11%, Japan with 5%, Russia with 4%, and Mexico with 4%. US egg production in 2004 (through November, annualized) rose +1.7% to 88.776 billion eggs, which was a new record high. The average number of hens and pullets on US farms in 2003 fell by –0.5% yr/yr to 337.262 million from the record high of 339.024 million in 2002.

Demand – US consumption of eggs in 2004 rose +0.7% yr/yr to a new record high of 6.205 billion eggs. That was a new record high and was up 60% from 10-years earlier, reflecting sharply higher egg consumption in the 2001-04 period due to the popularity of a low-carbohydrate diet since eggs are high in protein. US per capita egg consumption in 2004 rose +0.4% yr/yr 255.7 eggs per year per person. Per capita egg consumption was at a high of 277.2 eggs in 1970, fell sharply in the 1990s to a low of 174.9 in 1995, and then began rebounding in 1997 to current levels of over 250 eggs per year.

Trade – US imports of eggs in 2004 fell by –8.4% yr/yr to 12.0 million dozen eggs, falling from the 15-year high of 15.0 million posted in 2002. US export of eggs in 2004 rose by +3.9% yr/yr to 160.0 million dozen eggs, which was well below the export levels of more than 200 million seen in 1995-1998.

World Production of Eggs   In Millions of Eggs

Year	Brazil	China	France	Germany	Italy	Japan	Mexico	Russia	Spain	Ukraine	United Kingdom	United States	World Total[3]
1993	12,700	235,960	15,355	13,678	11,502	43,252	21,471	40,300	8,454	11,766	10,645	72,072	593,734
1994	13,460	281,010	16,370	13,960	11,599	43,047	25,896	37,400	9,670	10,145	10,620	74,136	643,045
1995	16,065	301,860	16,911	13,838	12,017	42,167	25,760	33,720	9,983	9,404	10,644	74,592	670,211
1996	15,932	253,680	16,500	13,922	11,923	42,786	26,045	31,500	8,952	8,763	10,668	76,536	631,846
1997	12,596	282,350	16,084	14,025	12,298	42,588	28,170	31,900	9,450	8,242	10,752	77,676	666,748
1998	13,636	307,760	16,900	14,164	12,433	42,117	29,898	33,000	9,084	8,269	10,812	79,896	695,281
1999	14,768	365,300	17,550	14,341	12,660	41,975	32,428	33,000	9,216	8,740	10,293	82,944	762,077
2000[1]	15,654	377,420	17,500	14,350	12,400	41,800	33,310	33,500	8,900	8,000	10,000	84,420	778,995
2001[2]	16,435	389,000	17,450	14,350	12,400	42,000	33,640	34,200	9,000	7,700	9,800	85,020	795,711

[1] Preliminary.   [2] Forecast.   [3] Selected countries.   *Source: Foreign Agricultural Service, U.S. Department of Agriculture (FAS-USDA)*

Salient Statistics of Eggs in the United States

	-- Hens & Pullets --		Rate of Lay Per Layer	-------- Eggs --------		Value of Production[5]	Total Egg Production				----- Consumption -----	
	On Farm Dec. 1[3]	Average Number During Year	During Year[4]	Total Produced	Price in Cents Per Dozen	Million Dollars		Imports[6]	Exports[6]	Used for Hatching	Total	Per Capita Eggs[6]
Year	----- Thousands -----		(Number)	------- Millions -------			-------------------------- Million Dozen --------------------------					(Number)
1996	303,754	297,958	256	76,281	74.9	4,776	6,367	5.4	253.1	863.8	5,242	234.6
1997	312,137	304,230	255	77,532	70.3	4,540	6,489	6.9	227.8	894.7	5,359	235.8
1998	321,718	312,035	255	79,754	66.8	4,439	6,658	5.8	218.8	921.8	5,522	240.2
1999	329,320	322,354	257	82,715	62.2	4,287	6,912	7.4	161.9	941.7	5,817	250.1
2000	332,410	327,985	257	84,386	61.8	4,346	7,034	8.4	171.1	940.2	5,927	252.1
2001	338,628	335,012	256	85,745	62.2	4,446	7,157	8.9	190.0	964.2	6,013	252.7
2002	339,827	339,024	257	87,252	58.9	4,281	7,268	15.0	174.0	961.3	6,148	255.9
2003[1]	340,979	338,393	259	87,473	73.1	5,315	7,273	13.3	146.2	959.4	6,177	254.7
2004[2]	344,278	342,279	260	89,131			7,424	13.5	166.5	987.2	6,283	256.5

[1] Preliminary.   [2] Forecast.   [3] All layers of laying age.   [4] Number of eggs produced during the year divided by the average number of all layers of laying age on hand during the year.   [5] Value of sales plus value of eggs consumed in households of producers.   [6] Shell-egg equivalent of eggs and egg products.   *Source: National Agricultural Statistics Service, U.S. Department of Agriculture (NASS-USDA)*

EGGS

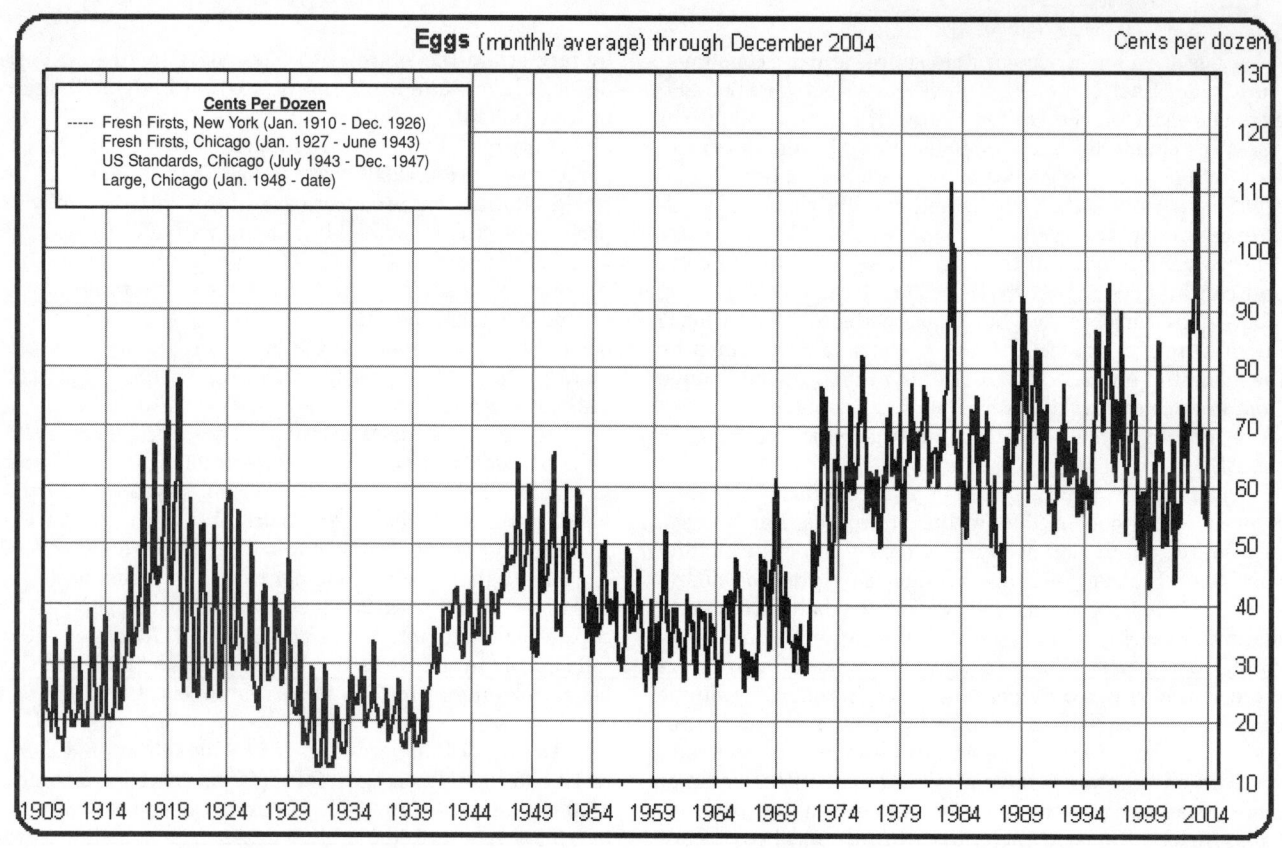

Eggs (monthly average) through December 2004 — Cents per dozen

Cents Per Dozen
----- Fresh Firsts, New York (Jan. 1910 - Dec. 1926)
Fresh Firsts, Chicago (Jan. 1927 - June 1943)
US Standards, Chicago (July 1943 - Dec. 1947)
Large, Chicago (Jan. 1948 - date)

Average Price Received by Farmers for All Eggs in the United States   In Cents Per Dozen

Year	Jan.	Feb.	Mar.	Apr.	May	June	July	Aug.	Sept.	Oct.	Nov.	Dec.	Average
1995	61.1	60.7	60.4	60.8	55.5	57.3	60.9	62.9	66.4	66.3	75.7	79.0	63.9
1996	78.2	75.7	79.1	75.8	69.3	70.7	69.8	73.7	75.8	73.5	82.0	87.9	76.0
1997	76.5	76.1	72.3	66.0	64.2	59.4	65.6	63.1	69.6	65.9	80.8	78.7	69.9
1998	74.3	64.9	69.9	63.7	54.9	59.6	58.2	65.0	63.3	66.3	72.8	75.5	65.7
1999	72.5	66.1	68.6	60.3	54.9	56.2	58.8	59.7	57.5	52.0	64.1	60.3	60.9
2000	57.8	67.8	56.9	64.7	52.0	61.8	56.5	66.4	59.2	66.8	72.0	80.7	63.6
2001	67.2	68.2	69.1	65.0	55.2	55.0	54.0	56.6	55.5	59.9	64.1	59.0	60.7
2002	62.3	55.9	68.5	52.2	50.5	62.1	60.8	66.4	57.1	56.0	70.7	62.8	60.4
2003	63.6	59.3	68.7	68.6	58.7	67.2	68.7	80.8	77.6	83.8	102.0	86.8	73.8
2004[1]	92.6	87.5	110.0	76.8	64.5	67.2	58.9	53.1	54.4	50.3	61.2	65.4	70.2

[1] Preliminary.   *Source: Economic Research Service, U.S. Department of Agriculture (NASS-USDA)*

Average Wholesale Price of Shell Eggs (Large) Delivered, Chicago   In Cents Per Dozen

Year	Jan.	Feb.	Mar.	Apr.	May	June	July	Aug.	Sept.	Oct.	Nov.	Dec.	Average
1995	58.55	58.24	60.22	59.87	52.50	56.84	68.10	65.93	71.10	71.34	83.93	86.35	66.08
1996	85.25	80.00	86.12	78.88	69.77	73.00	74.73	80.59	83.80	79.13	93.68	94.60	81.63
1997	79.77	75.18	77.25	68.55	64.40	61.02	74.66	66.07	74.26	68.39	89.87	82.68	73.51
1998	75.20	64.92	74.68	63.64	51.91	61.86	65.00	68.76	67.76	71.45	75.85	75.27	68.03
1999	72.34	62.13	67.85	52.74	51.35	47.86	58.40	59.30	52.86	48.38	59.26	56.38	57.40
2000	54.97	59.65	52.93	61.71	42.59	55.18	52.80	64.39	58.08	66.45	74.26	84.90	60.66
2001	68.52	64.45	69.00	66.12	50.61	49.81	52.83	55.46	50.21	57.41	62.50	58.05	58.75
2002	60.43	52.00	68.00	47.23	43.73	56.40	53.02	57.16	53.20	54.43	74.00	66.38	57.17
2003	69.57	65.39	71.05	68.83	59.10	68.76	72.39	88.26	86.21	92.07	113.16	101.09	79.66
2004	105.10	103.89	115.00	86.88	67.28	70.00	63.12	59.45	55.81	53.79	60.36	69.83	75.88

Source: National Agricultural Statistics Service, U.S. Department of Agriculture (NASS-USDA)

Total Egg Production in the United States   In Millions of Eggs

Year	Jan.	Feb.	Mar.	Apr.	May	June	July	Aug.	Sept.	Oct.	Nov.	Dec.	Total
1995	6,369	5,714	6,448	6,177	6,251	6,010	6,145	6,146	5,990	6,260	6,232	6,523	74,265
1996	6,398	5,954	6,495	6,243	6,340	6,169	6,440	6,447	6,235	6,495	6,409	6,696	76,321
1997	6,577	5,909	6,625	6,355	6,519	6,292	6,457	6,500	6,366	6,664	6,572	6,841	77,677
1998	6,766	6,109	6,869	6,603	6,665	6,456	6,720	6,694	6,480	6,791	6,723	7,047	79,923
1999	6,979	6,281	7,052	6,784	6,941	6,742	6,903	6,971	6,860	7,131	7,016	7,279	82,939
2000	7,157	6,648	7,234	7,013	7,104	6,801	7,061	7,104	6,854	7,130	7,027	7,287	84,420
2001	7,226	6,524	7,336	7,099	7,240	6,992	7,195	7,221	7,044	7,347	7,191	7,420	85,835
2002	7,264	6,581	7,417	7,105	7,297	7,126	7,347	7,356	7,147	7,412	7,226	7,451	86,729
2003[1]	7,390	6,665	7,424	7,187	7,327	7,105	7,403	7,367	7,112	7,439	7,326	7,554	87,299
2004[2]	7,386	6,901	7,547	7,358	7,513	7,289	7,557	7,538	7,344	7,659	7,482	7,728	89,302

[1] Preliminary.   [2] Estimate.   *Source: National Agricultural Statistics Service, U.S. Department of Agriculture (NASS-USDA)*

Per Capita Disappearance of Eggs[4] in the United States   In Number of Eggs

Year	First Quarter	Second Quarter	Third Quarter	Fourth Quarter	Total	Total Consumption (Million Dozen)	Year	First Quarter	Second Quarter	Third Quarter	Fourth Quarter	Total	Total Consumption (Million Dozen)
1994	45.0	43.0	43.9	46.0	177.9	3,864	2000	64.5	64.0	64.2	65.6	258.2	5,927
1995	44.0	43.1	42.7	45.0	174.9	3,834	2001	64.5	64.2	64.7	66.6	252.7	6,013
1996	44.5	42.1	43.4	45.0	175.0	3,893	2002	62.4	62.6	64.0	64.6	255.5	6,148
1997	59.0	59.3	59.7	62.1	240.1	3,894	2003[1]	62.6	63.0	63.8	65.3	254.7	6,177
1998	60.5	60.5	61.1	63.2	244.9	3,993	2004[2]	63.6	63.7	63.9	65.3	256.5	6,283
1999	62.7	62.8	63.8	66.2	255.7	4,070	2005[3]	63.2	63.9	63.9	65.4	256.4	6,343

[1] Preliminary.   [2] Estimate.   [3] Forecast   *Source: Economic Research Service, U.S. Department of Agriculture (ERS-USDA)*

Egg-Feed Ratio[1] in the United States

Year	Jan.	Feb.	Mar.	Apr.	May	June	July	Aug.	Sept.	Oct.	Nov.	Dec.	Average
1995	9.4	9.3	9.0	8.9	7.5	7.6	8.0	8.5	8.9	8.6	10.1	10.0	8.8
1996	9.8	8.7	9.1	7.9	6.5	6.7	6.3	6.9	8.1	9.3	11.3	12.5	8.6
1997	10.1	9.9	8.6	7.4	7.1	6.6	8.2	7.8	9.3	8.7	11.4	11.0	8.8
1998	10.1	8.3	9.4	8.5	6.7	8.0	7.9	10.8	10.7	11.3	12.6	12.8	9.7
1999	11.7	10.6	11.3	9.2	7.8	8.2	9.9	10.1	9.3	8.0	11.9	10.1	9.8
2000	8.9	11.3	8.0	9.9	6.4	9.5	9.2	12.9	10.3	12.2	13.1	15.0	10.6
2001	10.9	11.4	11.6	11.3	8.6	8.5	7.9	8.4	8.5	10.3	11.5	9.3	9.9
2002	10.2	8.4	11.6	7.4	6.7	9.5	7.5	7.9	7.1	6.6	10.5	8.9	8.5
2003	9.0	8.0	9.5	9.3	6.9	8.8	9.8	12.7	11.6	12.6	15.7	12.2	10.5
2004[2]	12.9	10.7	13.3	7.8	6.0	6.6	5.8	5.6	6.5	5.8	8.8	9.8	8.3

[1] Pounds of laying feed equivalent in value to one dozen eggs.   [2] Preliminary.   *Source: Economic Research Service, U.S. Department of Agriculture (ERS-USDA)*

Hens and Pullets of Laying Age (Layers) in the United States, on First of Month   In Thousands

Year	Jan.	Feb.	Mar.	Apr.	May	June	July	Aug.	Sept.	Oct.	Nov.	Dec.
1995	300,331	298,202	297,689	296,290	294,697	290,806	289,018	286,519	289,595	290,889	294,486	298,293
1996	299,261	298,320	298,348	298,029	295,123	293,740	294,044	296,612	296,911	298,433	299,910	303,754
1997	305,011	303,449	304,276	303,997	302,766	300,692	299,007	298,844	300,138	305,664	307,146	312,137
1998	311,593	312,111	314,322	313,833	309,945	309,235	309,049	308,747	309,706	312,807	316,840	321,718
1999	322,137	322,382	323,161	322,162	320,783	320,211	320,672	318,944	321,349	323,365	327,135	329,320
2000	328,307	328,767	330,876	330,807	327,597	325,012	324,843	326,240	325,212	327,219	329,092	332,410
2001	332,107	335,449	336,131	337,472	336,755	333,522	332,274	332,148	333,417	336,573	337,549	338,625
2002	339,423	338,465	337,478	337,376	336,131	335,547	335,236	335,717	336,561	337,923	338,350	339,827
2003	340,752	341,019	340,080	339,645	336,678	335,611	333,925	334,381	334,248	334,103	336,528	339,989
2004[1]	338,272	338,774	339,778	342,179	341,604	342,532	341,703	341,573	342,456	343,845	344,247	342,674

[1] Preliminary.   *Source: National Agricultural Statistics Service, U.S. Department of Agriculture (NASS-USDA)*

EGGS

Eggs Laid Per Hundred Layers in the United States   In Number of Eggs

Year	Jan.	Feb.	Mar.	Apr.	May	June	July	Aug.	Sept.	Oct.	Nov.	Dec.	Average
1995	2,130	1,919	2,173	2,092	2,137	2,075	2,137	2,135	2,065	2,140	2,108	2,183	2,108
1996	2,141	1,996	2,178	2,105	2,153	2,099	2,180	2,172	2,094	2,171	2,124	2,199	2,134
1997	2,161	1,943	2,176	2,093	2,156	2,093	2,155	2,165	2,096	2,172	2,122	2,193	2,127
1998	2,169	1,950	2,187	2,117	2,153	2,088	2,175	2,165	2,082	2,157	2,109	2,190	2,129
1999	2,165	1,946	2,185	2,110	2,166	2,104	2,158	2,177	2,128	2,192	2,138	2,214	2,140
2000	2,178	2,016	2,186	2,130	2,177	2,093	2,169	2,181	2,101	2,173	2,125	2,193	2,144
2001	2,165	1,943	2,178	2,106	2,160	2,100	2,166	2,170	2,103	2,180	2,130	2,188	2,132
2002	2,143	1,947	2,198	2,110	2,173	2,125	2,190	2,188	2,119	2,192	2,139	2,189	2,143
2003	2,168	1,957	2,184	2,125	2,180	2,122	2,215	2,203	2,128	2,218	2,166	2,223	2,157
2004[1]	2,182	2,033	2,209	2,148	2,192	2,126	2,206	2,197	2,134	2,220	2,170	2,234	2,171

[1] Preliminary.   Source: National Agricultural Statistics Service, U.S. Department of Agriculture (NASS-USDA)

Egg-Type Chicks Hatched by Commercial Hatcheries in the United States   In Thousands

Year	Jan.	Feb.	Mar.	Apr.	May	June	July	Aug.	Sept.	Oct.	Nov.	Dec.	Total
1995	32,374	32,743	36,019	35,078	37,540	34,996	29,572	31,442	33,586	33,383	29,129	30,639	396,501
1996	31,580	34,608	36,890	35,740	38,028	33,017	31,920	31,782	31,930	32,319	30,947	32,879	401,640
1997	33,752	35,655	37,347	38,842	39,020	36,796	33,772	33,061	37,118	35,262	28,122	35,796	424,543
1998	37,168	34,597	40,604	39,057	39,206	39,323	35,576	33,398	37,959	34,667	31,217	35,501	438,273
1999	35,242	36,367	41,172	42,285	40,726	41,439	34,275	35,518	39,287	39,044	32,802	33,564	451,721
2000	34,181	34,659	38,877	36,653	41,185	37,268	33,240	34,328	36,325	36,080	32,438	35,178	430,412
2001	36,728	37,836	41,015	42,789	42,655	40,822	38,651	34,987	37,140	35,825	32,355	31,870	452,673
2002	35,655	34,473	36,985	38,096	38,760	35,144	35,581	35,689	35,742	32,157	31,154	32,113	421,549
2003	33,521	30,510	36,775	37,804	37,631	36,602	35,566	33,199	35,763	34,812	30,241	33,645	416,069
2004[1]	35,350	32,078	37,530	37,514	38,631	38,066	34,127	36,024	36,750	35,971	38,421	37,035	437,497

[1] Preliminary.   Source: National Agricultural Statistics Service, U.S. Department of Agriculture (NASS-USDA)

Cold Storage Holdings of Frozen Eggs in the United States, on First of Month   In Millions of Pounds[2]

Year	Jan.	Feb.	Mar.	Apr.	May	June	July	Aug.	Sept.	Oct.	Nov.	Dec.
1995	19.5	19.5	18.3	18.5	17.3	18.1	22.9	20.6	18.0	16.2	14.4	12.5
1996	13.8	15.6	16.2	12.4	11.5	11.4	11.7	13.5	15.0	14.9	12.6	10.4
1997	10.2	11.0	11.5	8.5	8.5	8.2	8.3	8.9	11.1	10.8	10.9	10.3
1998	9.7	12.0	12.3	10.4	9.2	12.9	10.2	11.8	9.0	8.2	9.0	9.3
1999	11.0	11.0	10.8	9.2	9.4	9.7	11.3	11.1	8.8	9.5	9.0	8.5
2000	10.1	17.6	14.8	14.0	12.8	13.5	14.1	14.4	14.9	14.4	16.6	15.4
2001	15.0	16.9	15.5	14.6	15.9	15.8	14.4	16.7	17.8	17.7	15.5	13.9
2002	13.7	13.1	13.9	11.7	10.2	11.1	12.7	12.9	13.2	13.2	13.1	11.2
2003	13.5	15.3	17.1	17.0	15.7	17.7	18.0	18.6	18.0	16.6	16.9	14.9
2004[1]	18.0	21.3	21.1	19.2	20.9	20.6	18.3	16.7	17.3	18.7	17.9	17.3

[1] Preliminary.   [2] Converted on basis 39.5 pounds frozen eggs equals 1 case.   Source: National Agricultural Statistics Service, U.S. Department of Agriculture (NASS-USDA)

Electric Power

The modern electric utility industry began in the 1800s. In 1807, Humphry Davy constructed a practical battery and demonstrated both incandescent and arc light. In 1831, Michael Faraday built the first electric generator proving that rotary mechanical power could be converted into electric power. In 1879, Thomas Edison perfected a practical incandescent light bulb. The electric utility industry evolved from gas and electric carbon-arc commercial and street lighting systems. In 1882, in New York City, Thomas Edison's Pearl Street electricity generating station established the industry by displaying the four key elements of a modern electric utility system: reliable central generation, efficient distribution, successful end use, and a competitive price.

Electricity is measured in units called watts and watt-hours. Electricity must be used shortly after it is generated and cannot be stored to any significant degree. That means the power utilities must match the level of electricity generation to the level of demand in order to avoid wasteful over-production. The power industry has been deregulated to some degree in the past decade and now major utility companies sell power back and forth across major national grids in order to meet supply and demand needs. The quick changes in the supply-demand situation means that the price of electricity can be volatile.

Electricity futures trade at the New York Mercantile Exchange (NYMEX). The futures contract is a financially settled contract, which is priced based on electricity prices in the PJM western hub at 111 delivery points, mainly on the utility transmission systems of Pennsylvania Electric Co. and the Potomac Electric Co. The contract is priced in dollars and cents per megawatt hours.

Supply – US electricity production in 2004 (through September, annualized) rose +1.4% yr/yr to 2.562 trillion kilowatt-hours. That was well below the record high of 3.212 trillion kilowatt-hours in 1998 and indicated that recent electricity production has been reduced by more efficient production and distribution systems, and to some extent by electricity conservation by business and residential consumers. US electricity generation in 2003 required the use of 1.870 trillion cubic feet of natural gas (-17.2% yr/yr), 786 million short tons of coal (+2.4% yr/yr), and 107 million barrels of fuel oil (+21.0% yr/yr).

In terms of kilowatt-hours, coal is the most widely used source of electricity production, accounting for 59% of US electricity production in 2001, followed by nuclear (20%), natural gas (10%), hydro (7%), and fuel oil (3%). Alternative sources of fuel for electricity generation that are gaining favor include biomass, solar, wind, and fuel cells.

Demand – Residential use of electricity accounts for the largest single category of electricity demand with usage of 1.202 trillion kilowatt hours in 2001 accounting for 36% of overall usage. Business users together use more electricity than residential users, but business users are broken into the categories of commercial with 32% of usage and industrial with 29% of usage. Public authorities account for 3% of usage.

World Electricity Production (Monthly Average) In Millions of Kilowatt Hours

Year	Australia	Canada	China	Germany	India	Italy	Japan	Rep. of Korea	Russia	South Africa	Ukraine	United Kingdom	United States
1995	14,449	45,206	83,977	44,754	31,656	20,228	82,490	15,388	71,669	16,016	16,193	27,970	279,820
1996	14,806	46,307	90,109	46,277	32,991	20,340	84,113	17,125	70,600	16,096	15,166	27,191	287,250
1997	15,256	47,929	94,539	45,961	35,146	20,898	86,676	18,704	69,511	16,108	14,834	27,012	291,185
1998	14,737	45,259	97,183	46,367	37,379	21,659	76,763	17,942	68,930	17,119	14,402	27,914	301,489
1999	15,399	46,496	100,345	45,820	40,148	22,136	76,755	19,944	70,611	16,961	14,342	28,095	308,712
2000	15,712	48,563	109,426	46,417	41,725	22,986	78,391	22,200	73,117	17,557	14,287	28,484	316,662
2001	15,495	47,009	118,439	47,107	42,434	23,242	77,742	23,768	74,031	17,508	14,414	29,415	314,876
2002	15,646	48,227	133,513	45,375	44,141	23,638	77,139	25,500	74,078	18,142	14,477	29,220	293,174
2003[1]	15,564	46,911	153,229	NA	45,637	24,386	76,661	26,856	76,158	17,534	14,370	29,442	NA
2004[2]	16,182	47,176	171,218	NA	48,979	25,153	79,495	28,213	75,201	20,483	15,134	31,980	NA

[1] Preliminary. [2] Estimate. *Source: United Nations*

Installed Capacity, Capability & Peak Load of the U.S. Electric Utility Industry In Millions of Kilowatt Hours

	Installed Generating Capacity on December 31										Capability at Winter Peak Load	Non-Coincident Winter Peak Load	Capacity Margin Non-Coincident Peak Load (%)	Total Electric Utility Industry Generation	Annual Peak Load Factor (%)
		Type of Prime Mover				Type of Ownership				Power Districts, State Projects					
Year	Total Electric Utility Industry	Hydro	Gas, Turbine & Steam	Nuclear Power	Internal Combustion	Investor Owned	Cooperative	Subtotal Gov't	Municipal Utilities	Federal						
1990	735.1	87.2	531.1	108.0	8.7	568.8	26.3	139.9	40.1	65.4	34.4	696.8	484.0	20.4	2,808.2	60.4
1991	740.0	88.7	534.1	108.4	8.8	573.0	26.5	140.5	40.4	65.6	34.5	703.2	485.4	20.2	2,825.0	60.9
1992	741.7	89.7	534.5	107.9	9.6	572.9	26.0	142.7	41.6	66.1	35.0	707.8	493.0	21.1	2,797.2	61.1
1993	744.7	90.2	536.9	107.8	9.8	575.2	26.1	143.4	41.8	66.1	35.5	712.0	521.7	17.1	2,882.5	61.0
1994	746.0	90.3	537.9	107.9	9.9	574.8	26.4	144.7	42.0	66.3	36.4	715.1	518.3	16.7	2,910.7	61.2
1995	750.5	91.1	541.6	107.9	9.9	578.7	27.1	144.8	42.2	65.9	36.6	727.7	544.7	13.2	2,994.5	59.8
1996	756.5	91.0	546.6	109.0	9.9	582.2	27.2	147.1	43.0	67.2	36.9	740.5	545.1	14.9	3,073.1	61.0
1997	759.9	92.5	549.7	107.6	10.0	582.5	28.0	149.4	43.8	68.9	36.7	743.8	560.2	13.4	3,119.1	61.3
1998	728.3	91.2	522.1	104.8	10.2	531.3	32.5	164.5	50.5	68.7	45.3	835.3	652.4	12.0	3,212.2	62.0
1999[1]	678.0	89.8	476.3	102.3	9.6	483.7	34.6	159.6	50.2	68.7	40.7	848.9	656.3	10.3	3,173.7	61.2

[1] Preliminary. *Source: Edison Electric Institute (EEI)*

ELECTRIC POWER

Available Electricity and Energy Sales in the United States   In Billions of Kilowatt Hours

	------- Net Generation -------							------- Sales to Ultimate Customers -------							
	------- Electric Utility Industry -------															
Year	Total[2]	Hydro	Natural Gas	Coal	Fuel Oil	Nu-clear	Other Source[3]	Total	Total Million $	Total	Resi-den-tial	Inter-depart-mental	Com-mercial	Indust-rial	Street & Highway Lighting	Other Public Auth.	Rail ways & Rail-roads
1992	2,797	239.6	263.9	1,576	88.9	618.8	10.2	3,083	188,480	2,763	936	2.6	761.3	973	15.8	77.2	5.2
1993	2,883	265.1	258.9	1,639	99.5	610.3	9.6	3,197	198,220	2,861	995	2.7	794.6	977	18.1	69.7	5.4
1994	2,911	243.7	291.1	1,635	91.0	640.4	8.9	3,254	202,706	2,935	1,008	3.0	820.3	1,008	18.5	70.6	5.8
1995	2,995	293.7	307.3	1,653	60.8	673.4	6.4	3,353	207,717	3,013	1,043	2.1	862.7	1,013	17.9	69.9	5.5
1996	3,073	324.5	262.3	1,737	67.0	674.7	7.2	3,444	212,609	3,101	1,083	2.5	887.4	1,034	18.0	70.3	5.3
1997	3,119	333.5	283.1	1,789	77.1	629.4	7.5	3,492	215,334	3,146	1,076	2.6	928.6	1,037	19.7	75.6	5.3
1998	3,212	304.4	309.2	1,807	110.2	673.7	7.2	3,620	219,848	3,264	1,130	[4]	979.4	1,051	16.3	87.2	[4]
1999	3,174	293.9	296.4	1,768	86.9	725.0	3.7	3,695	219,896	3,312	1,145	[4]	1,002.0	1,058	15.9	107.0	[4]
2000	3,015	248.2	290.7	1,697	72.2	705.4	2.2	3,802	233,163	3,421	1,192	[4]	1,055.2	1,064	[4]	109.5	[4]
2001[1]	2,630	190.1	264.4	1,560	78.9	534.2	2.2	3,734	246,597	3,370	1,203	[4]	1,089.2	964	[4]	113.8	[4]

[1] Preliminary.   [2] Includes internal combustion.   [3] Includes electricity produced from geothermal, wood, waste, wind, solar, etc.   [4] Included in Other.
NA = Not available.   Source: Edison Electric Institute (EEI)

Electric Power Production by Electric Utilities in the United States   In Millions of Kilowatt Hours

Year	Jan.	Feb.	Mar.	Apr.	May	June	July	Aug.	Sept.	Oct.	Nov.	Dec.	Total
1995	253,077	228,127	233,675	217,381	236,381	256,083	292,827	304,709	245,574	234,409	234,117	258,170	2,994,529
1996	268,713	245,388	247,989	226,423	251,570	268,644	289,329	290,458	250,672	240,674	241,077	258,138	3,077,442
1997	273,410	233,907	244,659	230,512	243,143	266,588	304,628	294,557	266,649	253,267	243,726	267,477	3,122,523
1998	265,435	235,340	256,575	232,457	265,077	291,029	317,521	312,538	279,198	251,380	239,089	266,532	3,212,171
1999	275,230	239,825	258,678	238,969	255,266	281,233	318,745	307,835	261,347	243,212	235,129	258,205	3,173,674
2000	265,991	237,324	241,397	227,031	253,890	268,128	279,421	286,682	245,137	228,389	226,765	255,229	3,015,383
2001	236,467	199,802	211,942	197,499	215,508	233,622	253,400	258,901	214,236	204,307	192,518	211,742	2,629,944
2002	215,684	187,929	200,833	194,038	208,436	227,940	248,962	241,449	215,408	201,705	194,205	212,868	2,549,457
2003	217,338	189,944	193,305	181,914	200,634	212,297	234,888	234,675	201,966	192,198	189,362	213,758	2,462,279
2004[1]	221,046	197,938	191,994	181,951	206,623	219,090	234,462	226,877	208,447	196,692	190,431		2,482,419

[1] Preliminary.   Source: Energy Information Administration, U.S. Department of Energy (EIA-DOE)

Use of Fuels for Electric Generation in the United States

	---- Consumption of Fuel ----			Total Fuel in Coal Equivalent[3] (Thousand Short Tons)	Net Generation by Fuels[4] (Million Kilowatthour)	Pounds of Coal Per Kilowatthour (Pounds)	Cost of Fossil-fuel at Elec. Util. Cents/MBTU	Average Cost of Fuel Per Kiliowatthour (Cents)	Heat Rate BTU Per kilowatthour	Cost Per Million BTU Consumed (Cents)
Year	Coal (Thousand Short Tons)	Fuel Oil (Thousand Barels)[2]	Gas (Million Cubic Feet)							
1994	817,270	155,377	2,987,146	1,033,575	2,017,646	.999	152.6	1.59	10,425	152.6
1995	829,007	102,150	3,196,507	1,039,174	2,021,064	1.003	145.3	1.48	10,173	145.2
1996	874,681	113,274	2,732,107	1,063,755	2,066,666	1.007	151.9	1.55	10,176	151.9
1997	900,361	125,146	2,968,453	1,103,037	2,148,756	1.005	152.2	1.53	10,081	152.2
1998	910,867	178,614	3,258,054	1,147,317	2,226,860	.996	143.8	1.49	10,360	143.8
1999	894,120	143,830	3,113,419	1,113,614	2,150,989	1.012	144.1	1.48	10,301	144.1
2000	859,335	120,129	3,043,094				173.8			
2001	806,269	126,367	2,686,287				173.0			
2002[1]	767,803	88,595	2,259,684				151.5			
2003[1]	786,419	107,177	1,870,248							

[1] Preliminary.   [2] 42-gallon barrels.   [3] Coal equivalents are calculated on the basis of Btu instead of generation data.   [4] Excludes wood & waste fuels.
Source: Edison Electric Institute (EEI)

Fertilizer

Fertilizer is a natural or synthetic chemical substance, or mixture, that enriches soil to promote plant growth. The three primary nutrients that fertilizers provide are nitrogen, potassium, and phosphorus. In ancient times, and still today, many commonly used fertilizers contain one or more of the three primary ingredients: manure (containing nitrogen), bones (containing small amounts of nitrogen and large quantities of phosphorus), and wood ash (containing potassium).

At least fourteen different nutrients have been found essential for crops. These include three organic nutrients (carbon, hydrogen, and oxygen, which are taken directly from air and water), three primary chemical nutrients (nitrogen, phosphorus, and potassium), and three secondary chemical nutrients (magnesium, calcium, and sulfur). The others are micronutrients or trace elements and include iron, manganese, copper, zinc, boron, and molybdenum.

Prices – The average price of ammonia, a key source of ingredients for fertilizers, soared by 79% yr/yr in 2003 to a new record high of $245 per metric ton. The average price of phosphate rock in the US in 2002 rose by 3.3% yr/yr to $27.69 per metric ton. The average price of potash in the US in 2002 fell by –6.1% yr/yr to a 4-year low of $155.00 per metric ton from the record high of $165.00 posted in 2001.

Supply – World production of nitrogen (as contained in ammonia) in 2003 rose by +0.9% yr/yr to a new record high of 109.000 million metric tons. The world's largest producers of nitrogen in 2003 were China with 28% of world production, India (9%), the US (8%), and Russia (8%). US nitrogen production in 2003 fell -13.2% to a 3-decade low of 8.770 million metric tons.

World production of phosphate rock, basic slag and guano in 2003 rose +1.5% yr/yr to a 5-year high of 137.000 million metric tons. The world's largest producers of phosphate rock in 2003 were the US with 26% of world production, China (18%), Morocco (17%), and Russia (8%). US production in 2003 fell -0.8% y/y to 35.000 million metric tons, which was only 9% above the record low of 31.900 million in 2001.

World production of marketable potash rose by +8.0% yr/yr in 2003 to a 14-year high of 28.500 million metric tons. The world's largest producers of potash in 2003 were Canada with 32% of world production, Russia (17%), Belarus (15%), and Germany (13%). US production of potash in 2003 fell -8.3% yr/yr to a record low of 1.100 million metric tons.

Demand – US consumption of nitrogen in 2003 rose +16.4% yr/yr to 12.800 million metric tons, which was a record high. US consumption of phosphate rock in 2002 rose +5.9% to 37.400 million metric tons from the 16-year low of 35.300 million metric tons in 2001. US consumption of potash in 2002 was unchanged from 2001 at a 3-year low of 5.300 million metric tons.

Trade – US imports of nitrogen in 2003 rose +23% to 5.720 million metric tons and the US relied on imports for 42% of consumption. US imports of phosphate rock in 2002 rose +8.0% yr/yr to a record high of 2.700 million metric tons. US imports of potash rose +7.7% to 4.620 million metric tons in 2002, and imports accounted for 80% of US consumption.

World Production of Ammonia   In Thousands of Metric Tons of Contained Nitrogen

Year	Canada	China	France	Germany	India	Indo-nesia	Japan	Mexico	Nether-lands	Poland	Russia	United States	World Total
1995	3,773	22,600	1,470	2,518	8,287	3,336	1,584	1,992	2,580	1,726	7,900	13,000	100,000
1996	3,840	25,200	1,570	2,485	8,549	3,647	1,490	2,054	2,652	1,713	7,900	13,400	105,000
1997	4,081	24,700	1,757	2,471	9,328	3,770	1,509	1,448	2,478	1,824	7,150	13,300	103,000
1998	3,900	25,800	1,570	2,512	10,240	3,600	1,389	1,449	2,350	1,683	6,500	13,800	104,000
1999	4,135	28,300	1,580	2,406	10,376	3,450	1,385	1,003	2,430	1,474	7,633	12,900	107,000
2000	4,130	27,700	1,620	2,599	10,148	3,620	1,410	701	2,540	1,862	8,735	11,800	108,000
2001	3,439	28,200	1,380	2,522	10,081	3,655	1,318	548	1,990	1,735	8,690	9,120	105,000
2002[1]	3,594	30,100	1,172	2,560	9,827	4,200	1,188	537	2,050	1,311	8,600	10,100	108,000
2003[2]	3,646	30,200	1,153	2,803	9,708	4,250	1,054	440	1,750	1,906	9,100	8,770	109,000

[1] Preliminary.   [2] Estimate.   *Source: U.S. Geological Survey (USGS)*

Salient Statistics of Nitrogen[3] (Ammonia) in the United States   In Thousands of Metric Tons

Year	Net Import Reliance as a % of Apparent Consumption	Production[3] (Fixed) Fertilizer	Production[3] (Fixed) Non-fertilizer	Production[3] (Fixed) Total	Imports[4] (Fixed)	Nitrogen[5] Compounds Exports	Nitrogen[5] Compounds Produced	Nitrogen[5] Compounds Con-sumption	Stocks, Dec. 31- Ammonia	Stocks, Dec. 31- Fixed Nitrogen Com-pounds	Ammonia Con-sumption (Apparent)	Urea FOB Gulf[6] Coast	Urea FOB Corn Belt	Ammonium Nitrate: FOB Corn Belt	Ammonia FOB Gulf Coast
1996	19	11,500	1,720	13,220	3,390	435	11,502	11,100	881	1,390	16,400	188-190	197-210	160-170	190
1997	16	11,400	1,900	13,300	3,530	395	11,441	11,300	1,530	2,220	15,800	102-103	125-135	122-125	173
1998	19	11,800	1,950	13,800	3,460	614	11,712	11,300	1,050	1,270	17,100	82-85	110-125	110-115	121
1999	21	11,400	1,550	12,900	3,890	562	11,303	11,500	996	1,240	16,300	107-110	115-125	110-115	109
2000	21	10,300	1,510	11,800	3,880	662	10,272	12,500	1,120	1,400	14,900	158-161	175-180	140-150	169
2001	31	8,190	929	9,120	4,550	647	7,852	10,600	916	1,340	13,200	104-108	130-135	120-130	183
2002[1]	30	9,110	1,040	10,100	4,670	437	9,937	11,000	771	1,140	14,500	128-132	150-160	120-130	137
2003[2]	42	7,810	958	8,770	5,720	400	9,134	12,800	167	434	14,200	192-195	215-225	190-195	245

[1] Preliminary.   [2] Estimate.   [3] Anhydrous ammonia, synthetic.   [4] For consumption.   [5] Major downstream nitrogen compounds.   [6] *Granular.*

E = Net exporter.   *Source: U.S. Geological Survey (USGS)*

FERTILIZER

World Production of Phosphate Rock, Basic Slag & Guano   In Thousands of Metric Tons (Gross Weight)

Year	Brazil	China	Egypt	Israel	Jordan	Morocco	Russia	Senegal	Syria	Togo	Tunisia	United States	World Total
1994	3,937	24,100	632	3,961	4,217	19,764	8,000	1,587	1,203	2,149	5,699	41,100	127,000
1995	3,888	19,300	765	4,063	4,984	20,684	9,000	1,500	1,551	2,570	7,241	43,500	131,000
1996	3,823	21,000	808	3,839	5,355	20,855	8,300	1,340	2,189	2,731	7,167	45,400	135,000
1997	4,276	24,500	1,067	4,047	5,896	23,084	9,800	1,565	2,392	2,631	6,941	45,900	143,000
1998	4,421	25,000	1,076	4,067	5,925	23,587	10,100	1,478	2,496	2,250	7,901	44,200	144,000
1999	4,344	20,000	1,018	4,128	6,014	22,163	11,400	1,814	2,084	1,600	8,006	40,600	134,000
2000	4,725	19,400	1,096	4,110	5,526	21,463	11,100	1,739	2,166	1,400	8,339	38,600	132,000
2001	4,805	21,000	972	3,511	5,843	21,983	10,500	1,708	2,043	1,060	8,144	31,900	126,000
2002[1]	4,883	23,000	1,500	3,476	7,179	23,041	10,700	1,547	2,483	1,281	7,735	36,100	135,000
2003[2]	5,600	24,500	2,140	3,210	6,763	23,000	11,000	1,472	2,430	1,480	7,890	35,000	137,000

[1] Preliminary.   [2] Estimate.   *Source: U.S. Geological Survey (USGS)*

Salient Statistics of Phosphate Rock in the United States   In Thousands of Metric Tons

Year	Mine Production	Marketable Production	Value Million Dollars	Imports For Consumption	Exports	Apparent Consumption	Stocks, Dec. 31 (Producer)	Price - $ Avg. Per Metric Ton (FOB Mine)	Avg. Price of Florida & N. Carolina - $/Tonne - FOB Mine (-60% to +74%) - Domestic	Export	Average
1994	157,000	41,100	869	1,800	2,800	42,900	5,980	21.14	21.79	25.60	22.08
1995	165,000	43,500	947	1,800	2,760	42,700	5,710	21.75	21.29	28.35	21.75
1996	179,000	45,400	1,060	1,800	1,570	43,700	6,390	23.40	22.90	35.82	23.40
1997	166,000	45,900	1,080	1,830	335	43,600	7,910	24.50	24.40	34.80	24.50
1998	170,000	44,200	1,130	1,760	378	45,000	7,920	25.87	25.46	42.70	25.87
1999	161,000	40,600	1,240	2,170	272	43,500	6,920	31.49	30.56	41.96	31.49
2000	163,000	38,600	932	1,930	299	39,000	8,170	24.29	24.14	40.38	24.29
2001	130,000	31,900	856	2,500	9	35,300	7,510	26.81	26.82	W	26.81
2002[1]	154,000	36,100	993	2,700	62	37,400	8,860	27.69	27.69	W	27.69
2003[2]	153,000	35,000	946	2,400	64	38,800	7,540	26.95	26.95	W	26.95

[1] Preliminary.   [2] Estimate.   *Source: U.S. Geological Survey (USGS)*

World Production of Marketable Potash   In Thousands of Metric Tons (K_2O Equivalent)

Year	Belarus	Brazil	Canada	China	France	Germany	Israel	Jordan	Russia	Spain	United Kingdom	United States	World Total
1994	3,021	234	8,037	74	870	3,286	1,259	930	2,498	684	580	1,400	23,100
1995	3,211	215	9,066	80	799	3,278	1,330	1,075	2,800	760	582	1,480	24,800
1996	2,716	243	8,120	110	751	3,332	1,500	1,080	2,620	717	618	1,390	23,300
1997	3,247	280	8,989	115	725	3,423	1,488	850	3,400	639	565	1,400	25,200
1998	3,451	326	9,201	120	453	3,582	1,668	916	3,500	597	608	1,300	26,000
1999	4,553	348	8,475	260	345	3,543	1,700	1,080	4,200	656	495	1,200	27,300
2000	3,786	352	9,202	380	320	3,407	1,750	1,160	3,700	653	600	1,300	27,000
2001	3,700	319	8,224	385	244	3,550	1,770	1,180	4,300	471	532	1,200	26,300
2002[1]	3,800	337	8,189	450	130	3,450	1,920	1,170	4,400	407	540	1,200	26,400
2003[2]	4,230	340	9,200	500	----	3,600	1,960	1,230	4,740	510	620	1,100	28,500

[1] Preliminary.   [2] Estimate.   *Source: U.S. Geological Survey (USGS)*

Salient Statistics of Potash in the United States   In Thousands of Metric Tons (K_2O Equivalent)

Year	Net Import Reliance as a % of Consumption	Production	Sales by Producers	Value Million Dollars	Imports For Consumption	Exports	Apparent Consumption	Producer Stocks Dec. 31	Avg. Value Per Ton of Product ($)	Avg. Value of K_2O Equiv.	Avg. Price[3] $ Per Tonne
1994	76	1,400	1,470	284.0	4,800	464	5,810	234	95.93	193.50	125.34
1995	75	1,480	1,400	284.0	4,820	409	5,820	312	98.58	202.43	137.99
1996	77	1,390	1,430	299.0	4,940	481	5,890	265	101.08	208.57	134.07
1997	80	1,400	1,400	320.0	5,490	466	6,500	200	110.00	230.00	138.00
1998	80	1,300	1,300	330.0	4,780	477	5,600	300	115.00	250.00	145.00
1999	80	1,200	1,200	280.0	4,470	459	5,100	300	110.00	230.00	150.00
2000	70	1,300	1,200	290.0	4,600	367	5,600	ÑÑ	110.00	230.00	157.50
2001	80	1,200	1,100	260.0	4,540	366	5,300	ÑÑ	110.00	230.00	165.00
2002[1]	80	1,200	1,200	280.0	4,620	371	5,300	ÑÑ	110.00	230.00	155.00
2003[2]	80	1,100	1,200	280.0	4,720	329	5,400	ÑÑ	110.00	230.00	170.00

[1] Preliminary.   [2] Estimate.   [3] Unit of K_2O, standard 60% muriate F.O.B. mine.   *Source: U.S. Geological Survey (USGS)*

Fish

Fish are the primary source of protein for a large proportion of the world's population. The worldwide yearly harvest of all sea fish (including aquaculture) is between 85 and 130 million metric tons. There are approximately 20,000 species of fish, of which 9,000 are regularly caught. Only 22 fish species are harvested in large amounts. Ground-fish, which are fish that live near or on the ocean floor, account for about 10% of the world's fishery harvest, and include cod, haddock, pollock, flounder, halibut and sole. Large pelagic fish such as tuna, swordfish, marlin, and mahi-mahi, account for about 5% of world harvest. The fish eaten most often in the United States is canned tuna.

Rising global demand for fish has increased the pressure to harvest more fish to the point where all 17 of the world's major fishing areas have either reached or exceeded their limits. Atlantic stocks of cod, haddock and blue-fin tuna are all seriously depleted, while in the Pacific, anchovies, salmon and halibut are all over-fished. Aquaculture, or fish farming, reduces pressure on wild stocks and now accounts for nearly 20% of world harvest.

Supply – The US supply of fishery products rose +5.0% to 19.028 billion pounds in 2002 (the latest reporting year) from 18.119 billion pounds in 2001. The US domestic catch in 2002 fell by -1.0% to 9.397 billion pounds from 2001, and comprised 49% of US supply (down from 52% in 2001). Of the US domestic catch in 2002, 64.0% of the catch was finfish for human consumption, 12.7% was shellfish for human consumption, and 23.3% of the catch was a variety of fish for industrial use. The principal species of US fishery landings in 2002 were Pollock (with 3.349 billion pounds landed), Menhaden (1.751 billion pounds), Pacific Salmon (567 million pounds), Flounder (373 million pounds), and Sea Herring (214 million pounds).

More than 30% of the fish harvested are processed directly into fishmeal and fish oil. Fishmeal is used primarily in animal feed. Fish oil is used in both animal feed and human food products. World fishmeal production in the 2003/04 marketing year rose by 1.0% to 6.140 million metric tons. World production of fish oil in 2003 rose +4.0% to 979,000 metric tons. Peru and Chile are the world's largest producers of fishmeal and fish oil.

Trade – US imports of fishery products in 2002 rose to a 9-year high of 9.631 billion pounds, comprising 50.6% of total US supply.

Fishery Products -- Supply in the United States   In Millions of Pounds[2]

					---- Domestic Catch ----					---- Imports ----			
	Grand	- For Human Food -		For Industrial Use[4]	Total	% of Grand Total	- For Human Food -		For Industrial Use[4]	Total	% of Grand Total	- For Human Food -		For Industrial Use[4]
Year	Total	Finfish	Shellfish[3]				Finfish	Shellfish[3]				Finfish	Shellfish[3]	
1996	16,474	10,699	2,927	2,848	9,565	58.1	6,205	1,271	2,089	6,909	41.9	4,494	1,656	759
1997	17,133	10,580	3,160	3,393	9,843	57.5	5,969	1,277	2,598	7,290	42.5	4,612	1,883	795
1998	16,898	10,837	3,338	2,723	9,194	54.4	5,935	1,238	2,021	7,704	45.6	4,901	2,100	702
1999	17,378	10,831	3,630	2,916	9,339	53.7	5,490	1,341	2,507	8,039	46.3	5,341	2,289	409
2000	17,339	11,006	3,734	2,599	9,068	52.3	5,637	1,275	2,157	8,271	47.7	5,369	2,459	442
2001	18,119	11,330	3,977	2,812	9,492	52.4	6,162	1,152	2,178	8,627	47.6	5,168	2,825	634
2002[1]	19,028	11,770	4,237	3,022	9,397	49.4	6,013	1,192	2,193	9,631	50.6	5,757	3,045	829

[1] Preliminary.   [2] Live weight, except percent.   [3] For univalue and bivalues mollusks (conchs, clams, oysters, scallops, etc.) the weight of meats, excluding the shell is reported.   [4] Fish meal and sea herring.   *Source: Fisheries Statistics Division, U.S. Department of Commerce*

Fisheries -- Landings of Principal Species in the United States   In Millions of Pounds

	---- Fish ----									---- Shelfish ----				
Year	Cod, Atlantic	Flounder	Halibut	Herring, Sea	Man-haden	Pollock	Salmon, Pacific	Tuna	Whiting	Clams (Meats)	Crabs	Lobsters (American)	Oysters Scallops ------ (Meats) ------	Shrimp
1996	31	460	49	318	1,755	2,630	877	85	35	123	392	71	38 18	317
1997	29	566	70	348	2,028	2,522	568	83	34	114	430	84	40 15	290
1998	25	391	73	272	1,706	2,729	644	85	33	108	553	80	34 13	278
1999	21	331	80	267	1,989	2,336	815	58	31	112	458	87	27 27	304
2000	25	413	75	235	1,760	2,616	629	51	27	118	299	83	41 33	332
2001	33	352	78	300	1,741	3,188	723	52	28	123	272	74	33 47	324
2002[1]	29	373	82	214	1,751	3,349	567	49	18	130	308	82	34 53	317

[1] Preliminary.   *Source: National Marine Fisheries Service, U.S. Department of Commerce*

U.S. Fisheries: Quantity & Value of Domestic Catch & Consumption & World Fish Oil Production

	---- Disposition ----					For Human Food	For Industrial Products	Ex-vessel Value[3]	Average Price	Fish Per Capita Cunsumption	World[2] Fish Oil Production
Year	Fresh & Frozen	Canned	Cured	For Meal, Oil, Etc.	Total			- Million $ -	- Cents/Lb. -	- Pounds -	- 1,000 Tons -
	---- Millions of Pounds ----										
1996	7,054	678	93	1,740	9,565	7,474	2,091	3,487	36.5	NA	1,337
1997	6,873	648	108	2,213	9,842	7,244	2,598	3,448	35.0	NA	1,214
1998	6,870	516	129	1,679	9,194	7,173	2,021	3,128	34.0	NA	886
1999	6,416	712	133	2,078	9,339	6,832	2,507	3,467	37.1	NA	1,413
2000	6,657	530	119	1,763	9,069	6,912	2,157	3,550	39.1	NA	1,428
2001	7,085	536	123	1,748	9,492	7,314	2,178	3,228	34.0	NA	1,132
2002[1]	6,826	652	117	1,802	9,397	7,205	2,192	3,092	32.9	NA	942

[1] Preliminary.   [2] Crop years on a marketing year basis.   [3] At the Dock Prices.   *Source: Fisheries Statistics Division, U.S. Department of Commerce*

FISH

Imports of Seafood Products into the United States In Thousands of Pounds

| | Fresh | | | Frozen | | | | | | | Canned | Prepared |
| | Atlantic | Pacific | | | Atlantic | Pacific | | | | | | |
Year	Salmon	Salmon	Shrimp	Trout	Salmon	Salmon	Shrimp	Oysters[2]	Mussels[3]	Clams[4]	Salmon	Shrimp[5]
1996	116,606	43,962	----	4,552	10,752	8,514	507,823	14,222	21,241	6,596	4,182	74,648
1997	150,135	38,999	----	5,403	14,956	25,662	572,111	14,531	26,903	5,703	3,675	76,213
1998	190,131	38,486	----	5,670	19,092	17,134	599,466	18,049	34,099	6,541	3,430	95,942
1999	217,948	26,467	----	5,259	24,222	16,596	617,089	18,325	34,969	7,537	5,627	114,191
2000	257,218	19,908	----	7,083	32,089	12,866	621,231	20,810	43,141	8,074	8,893	139,526
2001	316,837	17,472	----	7,382	41,176	10,515	714,706	18,438	39,973	8,007	11,298	167,877
2002	356,164	23,210	----	9,887	56,883	18,317	730,002	19,084	45,695	7,457	16,378	216,439
2003[1]	349,474	22,462	----	9,023	64,999	26,658	878,124	22,257	43,236	8,752	25,177	234,084

[1] Preliminary. [2] Oysters fresh or prepared. [3] Mussels fresh or prepared. [4] Clams, fresh or prepared. [5] Shrimp, canned, breaded or prepared.
NA = Not available. Source: Bureau of the Census, U.S. Department of Commerce

Exports of Seafood Products into the United States In Thousands of Pounds

| | Fresh | | | Frozen | | | | | | | Canned | Prepared |
| | Atlantic | Pacific | | | Atlantic | Pacific | | | | | | |
Year	Salmon	Salmon	Shrimp	Trout	Salmon	Salmon	Shrimp	Oysters[2]	Mussels[3]	Clams[4]	Salmon	Shrimp[5]
1996	7,280	42,999	----	1,867	322	223,346	11,180	2,097	1,603	5,126	94,842	17,665
1997	7,504	25,529	----	1,709	322	152,516	11,967	2,890	1,157	4,916	81,407	14,826
1998	7,978	34,645	----	1,453	243	105,869	11,323	2,496	1,347	5,375	77,201	13,882
1999	10,717	40,683	----	1,697	182	157,278	13,607	2,727	1,861	5,240	113,556	13,153
2000	15,942	38,750	----	1,816	299	161,515	15,162	3,229	1,513	3,413	81,098	14,229
2001	18,417	20,651	----	1,077	84	167,933	13,905	3,915	1,485	3,939	109,109	13,640
2002	8,456	29,672	----	1,163	84	132,646	13,890	3,896	1,178	3,861	95,955	13,148
2003[1]	11,337	38,902	----	2,592	99	150,766	16,466	5,827	1,337	4,003	94,338	14,307

[1] Preliminary. [2] Oysters fresh or prepared. [3] Mussels fresh or prepared. [4] Clams, fresh or prepared. [5] Shrimp, canned, breaded or prepared.
NA = Not available. Source: Bureau of the Census, U.S. Department of Commerce

World Production of Fish Meal In Thousands of Metric Tons

Year	Chile	Spain	Denmark	EU-12	FSU-12	Iceland	Japan	Norway	Peru	South Africa	Thailand	United States	World Total
1996-7	1,209.9	86.1	334.6	555.5	206.3	272.5	363.5	259.7	2,150.5	52.6	384.4	366.1	6,992.7
1997-8	708.5	92.8	317.2	544.7	206.7	221.6	383.4	296.7	697.2	89.3	403.8	339.9	5,218.4
1998-9	823.4	86.1	319.1	542.7	147.1	240.6	388.5	352.6	1,597.4	76.2	398.0	389.9	6,341.6
1999-00	890.0	81.5	314.2	531.1	148.8	281.2	390.0	315.0	2,449.4	113.7	392.4	346.8	7,352.0
2000-1	731.0	88.0	311.9	534.4	137.4	284.0	350.0	238.8	2,144.2	97.8	385.0	337.1	6,797.1
2001-2[1]	766.0	90.0	308.2	535.8	147.2	309.9	323.0	222.9	1,688.1	115.7	390.0	349.8	6,437.9
2002-3[2]	818.7	92.0	238.9	473.4	147.4	269.9	328.0	193.5	1,335.3	130.0	400.0	320.6	6,079.9
2003-4[3]	780.0	94.0	270.0	512.5	147.6	273.0	334.0	150.0	1,380.0	130.0	410.0	330.0	6,140.0

[1] Preliminary. [2] Estimate. [3] Forecast. Source: The Oil World

World Production of Fish Oil In Thousands of Metric Tons

Year	Canada	Chile	China	Denmark	Iceland	Japan	Norway	Peru	South Africa	FSU-12	United States	World Total	Fish Oil CIF[4]
1996-7	4.8	192.6	9.0	138.0	143.2	47.6	86.4	413.3	4.1	41.0	119.8	1,289.0	502
1997-8	4.5	91.4	7.2	126.7	95.1	70.7	89.0	86.3	7.8	14.3	101.3	825.5	722
1998-9	3.3	176.8	28.8	135.2	92.1	72.8	99.2	376.5	6.8	14.5	141.6	1,277.3	408
1999-00	3.7	166.0	26.7	139.7	98.0	69.7	98.3	699.4	8.9	12.0	81.3	1,538.1	268
2000-1	4.1	142.9	26.3	121.3	99.0	65.0	66.4	400.8	7.9	11.1	123.3	1,218.2	375
2001-2[1]	4.3	140.2	28.0	108.7	85.0	63.8	61.2	162.2	10.0	11.0	103.9	932.0	593
2002-3[2]	4.5	134.0	30.0	104.9	123.0	61.4	49.2	200.1	9.0	11.3	81.3	972.2	560
2003-4[3]	4.6	136.0	32.0	115.0	98.0	61.0	41.2	215.0	10.0	11.0	95.0	985.1	

[1] Preliminary. [2] Estimate. [3] Forecast. [4] Any origin, N.W. Europe. NA = Not available. Source: The Oil World

Monthly Production of Catfish--Round Weight Processed, in the US In Thousands of Pounds (Live Weight)

Year	Jan.	Feb.	Mar.	Apr.	May	June	July	Aug.	Sept.	Oct.	Nov.	Dec.	Total
1997	42,409	45,067	48,431	45,721	43,409	42,282	43,376	44,154	43,472	46,275	40,137	40,216	524,949
1998	46,723	47,606	53,761	49,393	45,218	46,244	46,383	47,739	46,579	47,904	43,224	43,581	564,355
1999	48,723	48,891	56,310	46,830	47,703	48,445	50,074	50,372	50,414	52,407	48,118	48,341	596,628
2000	50,552	50,942	56,856	48,781	48,424	48,011	49,023	53,204	49,422	51,412	45,535	41,441	593,603
2001	46,999	50,257	57,766	52,478	51,736	47,883	47,829	51,690	49,699	52,264	44,670	43,837	597,108
2002	52,551	52,856	58,340	50,694	52,902	49,450	52,363	54,383	53,366	56,576	50,072	48,048	631,601
2003	55,523	55,461	65,007	57,105	58,424	52,441	54,089	54,153	51,885	57,652	51,246	48,518	661,504
2004[1]	53,849	54,173	60,272	53,896	52,324	50,155	51,055	53,295	51,329	52,396	49,536	48,170	630,450

[1] Preliminary. Source: Economic Research Service, U.S. Department of Agriculture (ERS-USDA)

Average Price Paid to Producers for Farm-Raised Catfish in the US   In Cents Per Pound (Live Weight)

Year	Jan.	Feb.	Mar.	Apr.	May	June	July	Aug.	Sept.	Oct.	Nov.	Dec.	Average
1997	73.0	73.0	73.0	73.0	73.0	72.0	71.0	70.0	69.0	69.0	69.0	69.0	71.2
1998	69.0	73.0	78.0	79.0	79.0	78.0	76.0	74.0	73.0	71.0	70.0	70.0	74.2
1999	70.3	71.4	73.2	75.6	77.7	77.5	76.8	74.3	72.8	71.6	71.3	71.6	73.7
2000	74.4	78.8	78.9	78.9	78.5	78.6	76.0	74.1	72.7	71.0	69.6	68.2	75.0
2001	69.3	69.6	69.7	69.4	68.7	66.9	65.6	62.4	61.0	59.6	56.6	55.4	64.5
2002	54.9	55.5	56.5	56.1	57.4	58.8	59.0	58.2	57.6	56.8	56.0	54.4	56.8
2003	52.9	54.4	58.5	63.0	61.8	58.6	56.4	55.2	56.0	56.7	61.0	62.9	58.1
2004[1]	66.8	70.3	72.3	72.8	72.0	68.9	68.2	68.3	68.3	69.5	68.9	69.0	69.6

[1] Preliminary.   Source: Economic Research Service, U.S. Department of Agriculture (ERS-USDA)

Sales of Fresh Catfish in the United States   In Thousands of Pounds

Year	Jan.	Feb.	Mar.	Apr.	May	June	July	Aug.	Sept.	Oct.	Nov.	Dec.	Total
Whole													
1999	3,650	3,957	4,467	3,459	3,492	3,380	3,471	3,271	3,583	3,561	3,209	3,313	42,813
2000	3,496	3,396	4,031	3,655	3,483	3,581	3,491	3,545	3,246	3,504	2,971	2,993	41,392
2001	3,516	3,242	4,260	3,644	3,271	3,166	3,233	3,204	3,174	3,294	2,865	2,803	39,672
2002	3,713	3,656	3,826	3,373	3,644	3,313	3,477	3,733	3,418	3,822	3,031	2,986	41,992
2003	3,833	3,785	4,339	3,643	3,692	3,266	3,553	3,510	3,233	3,231	2,798	2,693	41,576
2004[1]	3,205	3,266	3,808	3,001	2,853	2,707	2,875	3,002					37,076
Fillets[2]													
1999	4,581	5,030	5,768	4,897	4,918	4,707	4,846	5,002	4,550	4,811	4,171	4,142	57,423
2000	4,686	4,853	5,957	5,206	5,099	4,792	4,650	4,899	4,650	5,283	4,355	4,099	58,529
2001	4,884	6,112	6,751	5,709	5,587	5,122	5,191	5,313	5,264	5,273	4,463	4,489	64,158
2002	5,684	6,132	6,010	5,236	5,682	5,093	5,327	5,442	5,317	5,420	4,447	4,119	63,909
2003	5,362	5,158	6,715	5,700	6,364	5,737	5,984	6,013	5,308	6,082	5,187	4,710	68,320
2004[1]	5,964	6,455	6,815	5,887	5,688	5,500	5,559	5,483					71,027
Other[3]													
1999	1,243	1,614	1,724	1,153	1,227	1,126	1,305	1,495	1,354	1,676	1,299	1,227	16,443
2000	1,429	1,437	1,685	1,547	1,364	1,299	1,340	1,438	1,332	1,473	1,271	1,198	16,813
2001	1,443	1,292	2,156	1,309	1,282	1,298	1,375	1,436	1,449	1,430	1,223	1,252	16,945
2002	1,526	1,446	1,375	1,356	1,732	1,527	1,576	1,569	1,441	1,596	1,165	1,205	17,514
2003	1,668	1,532	1,599	1,458	1,472	1,319	1,425	1,366	1,473	1,361	1,138	1,134	16,945
2004[1]	1,435	1,518	1,567	1,426	1,299	1,248	1,181	1,173					16,271

[1] Preliminary.   [2] Includes regular, shank and strip fillets; excludes breaded products.   [3] Includes steaks, nuggets and all other products not reported.
Source: Economic Research Service, U.S. Department of Agriculture (ERS-USDA)

Prices of Fresh Catfish in the United States   In Dollars per Pound

Year	Jan.	Feb.	Mar.	Apr.	May	June	July	Aug.	Sept.	Oct.	Nov.	Dec.	Average
Whole													
1999	1.54	1.55	1.57	1.59	1.63	1.60	1.59	1.63	1.61	1.63	1.59	1.59	1.59
2000	1.63	1.67	1.69	1.70	1.68	1.63	1.65	1.70	1.67	1.64	1.62	1.58	1.66
2001	1.59	1.68	1.63	1.65	1.65	1.62	1.59	1.55	1.53	1.49	1.42	1.37	1.56
2002	1.36	1.35	1.30	1.34	1.36	1.37	1.35	1.32	1.32	1.28	1.24	1.25	1.32
2003	1.28	1.30	1.35	1.37	1.36	1.39	1.33	1.33	1.34	1.36	1.40	1.43	1.35
2004[1]	1.49	1.53	1.57	1.60	1.60	1.57	1.57	1.58					1.56
Fillets[2]													
1999	2.73	2.71	2.76	2.75	2.84	2.86	2.86	2.85	2.85	2.83	2.84	2.83	2.81
2000	2.82	2.87	2.89	2.88	2.88	2.90	2.90	2.88	2.85	2.83	2.83	2.81	2.86
2001	2.80	2.79	2.80	2.80	2.80	2.78	2.77	2.75	2.69	2.63	2.60	2.55	2.73
2002	2.52	2.49	2.49	2.51	2.53	2.55	2.55	2.54	2.54	2.52	2.49	2.47	2.52
2003	2.44	2.45	2.44	2.49	2.51	2.50	2.48	2.48	2.49	2.49	2.50	2.54	2.48
2004[1]	2.59	2.62	2.71	2.73	2.74	2.74	2.73	2.73					2.70
Other[3]													
1999	1.61	1.55	1.59	1.70	1.74	1.76	1.66	1.62	1.66	1.57	1.65	1.66	1.65
2000	1.66	1.69	1.69	1.66	1.71	1.71	1.72	1.69	1.62	1.68	1.71	1.68	1.69
2001	1.64	1.68	1.57	1.64	1.69	1.64	1.61	1.57	1.52	1.59	1.59	1.53	1.61
2002	1.53	1.57	1.54	1.51	1.45	1.51	1.51	1.50	1.54	1.48	1.55	1.46	1.51
2003	1.40	1.41	1.51	1.53	1.47	1.54	1.52	1.58	1.50	1.58	1.60	1.64	1.52
2004[1]	1.63	1.70	1.71	1.78	1.78	1.78	1.62	1.76					1.72

[1] Preliminary.   [2] Includes regular, shank and strip fillets; excludes breaded products.   [3] Includes steaks, nuggets and all other products not reported.
Source: Economic Research Service, U.S. Department of Agriculture (ERS-USDA)

Flaxseed and Linseed Oil

Flaxseed, also called linseed, is an ancient crop that was cultivated by the Babylonians around 3,000 BC. Flaxseed is used for fiber in textiles and to produce oil. Flaxseeds contain approximately 35% oil, of which 60% is omega-3 fatty acid. Flaxseed or linseed oil is obtained through either the expeller extraction or solvent extraction method. Manufacturers filter the processed oil to remove some impurities and then sell it as unrefined. Unrefined oil retains its full flavor, aroma, color, and naturally occurring nutrients. Flaxseed oil is used for cooking and as a dietary supplement as well as for animal feed. Industrial linseed oil is not for internal consumption due to possible poisonous additives and is used for making putty, sealants, linoleum, wood preservation, varnishes, and oil paints.

Flaxseed futures and options trade at the Winnipeg Commodity Exchange. The futures contract calls for the delivery of 20 metric tons of flaxseed. The contract is now priced in US dollars per metric ton.

Prices – The average monthly price received by US farmers for flaxseed in the 2004-05 marketing year (through December 2004) rose +22.2% yr/yr to $7.68 per bushel from $6.28 per bushel in the 2003-04 marketing year. The recent price was well below the record monthly average high of $9.66 posted in 1974-75.

Supply – World production of flaxseed in the 2003-04 marketing year rose +6.3% yr/yr to 2.222 million metric tons from the 11-year low of 2.090 million metric tons posted in 2002-03. The world's largest producer of flaxseed is Canada with 38% of world production in 2002-03, followed by China (21%), the US (12%), and India (10%). US production of flaxseed in 2003-04 fell by –17.0% yr/yr to 10.426 million bushels from the 26-year high of 12.569 million bushels posted in 2002-03. North Dakota is by far the largest producing state of flaxseed and accounted for 95.0% of flaxseed production in 2002, followed by Minnesota with 1.5% of production and South Dakota with 1.4% of production.

World production of linseed oil in 2003-04 rose by +3.0% yr/yr to 614,300 metric tons. The world's largest producers of linseed oil are China (with 20% of world production in 2003-04) the US (17%), and India (11%). US production of linseed oil in 2002-03 rose by +3.1% yr/yr to 201 million pounds.

Demand – US distribution of flaxseed in 2002-03 rose +5.7% yr/yr to 14.562 million bushels. The breakdown was 71% for crushing into meal and oil, 20% for exports, 6% for residual, and 3% for seed. US consumption of linseed oil (inedible products) in the 2003-04 marketing year fell -16.7% yr/yr to 79.078 million pounds.

Trade – US exports of flaxseed in 2002-03 rose sharply by +21.5% yr/yr to 2.900 million bushels. US imports of flaxseed in 2002-03 rose by +39.3% yr/yr to 2.650 million bushels.

World Production of Flaxseed   In Thousands of Metric Tons

Year	Argen-tina	Aust-ralia	Bang-ladesh	Canada	China	Egypt	France	Hungary	India	Rom-ania	United States	Former USSR	World Total
1994-5	152	6	48	960	511	18	44	4	325	7	74	110	2,474
1995-6	149	15	49	1,105	420	16	27	4	308	5	56	113	2,518
1996-7	72	7	46	851	480	17	29	4	319	5	41	86	2,300
1997-8	75	9	50	1,038	393	19	31	----	275	5	62	47	2,370
1998-9	85	10	50	1,210	523	24	29	1	265	3	170	55	2,828
1999-00	47	9	46	1,100	404	30	34	2	289	3	200	46	2,868
2000-1	22	9	48	775	520	30	38	1	240	1	273	76	2,358
2001-2[1]	16	9	50	770	420	26	28	1	240	2	291	82	2,159
2002-3[2]	11	6	50	750	463	19	44	1	200	2	301	69	2,090
2003-4[3]	26	8	50	840	460	22	32	2	230	2	265	85	2,222

[1] Preliminary.   [2] Estimate.   [3] Forecast.   *Source: The Oil World*

Supply and Distribution of Flaxseed in the United States   In Thousands of Bushels

Crop Year Beginning June 1	Planted	Harvested	Yield Per Acre (Bushels)	Beginning Stocks	Pro-duction	Imports	Total Supply	Seed	Crush	Exports	Residual	Total Distribution
	------- 1,000 Acres -------			----------- Supply -----------				------------- Distribution -------------			
1995-6	165	147	15.0	1,170	2,212	7,248	10,630	78	9,000	119	203	9,400
1996-7	96	92	17.4	1,230	1,602	8,390	11,222	122	10,000	144	503	10,769
1997-8	151	146	16.6	453	2,420	9,636	12,509	272	10,500	174	382	11,328
1998-9	336	329	20.4	1,181	6,708	5,992	13,881	313	10,600	476	333	11,723
1999-00	387	382	20.6	2,158	7,864	6,629	16,651	434	11,500	215	2,735	14,884
2000-1	536	517	20.8	1,767	10,730	2,850	15,347	474	12,000	1,015	572	14,039
2001-2	585	578	19.8	1,308	11,455	1,903	14,666	636	10,000	2,386	751	13,773
2002-3[1]	784	703	16.9	893	11,863	2,650	18,157	472	10,300	2,900	890	14,562
2003-4[2]	595	588	17.9		10,516							
2004-5[3]	523	516	20.3		10,471							

[1] Preliminary.   [2] Estimate.   [3] Forecast.   *Source: Economic Research Service, U.S. Department of Agriculture*

Production of Flaxseed in the United States, by States   In Thousands of Bushels

Crop Year	Minne-sota	North Dakota	South Dakota	Other States	Total	Crop Year	Minne-sota	North Dakota	South Dakota	Other States	Total
1995	171	1,725	260	55	2,211	2000	198	9,975	361	196	10,730
1996	60	1,386	126	30	1,602	2001	52	10,900	323	180	11,455
1997	96	1,997	252	75	2,420	2002	64	11,560	44	195	11,863
1998	432	5,817	294	165	6,708	2003	161	9,990	144	221	10,516
1999	300	6,867	357	340	7,864	2004[1]	51	9,943	135	342	10,471

[1] Preliminary.   *Source: National Agricultural Statistics Service, U.S. Department of Agriculture (NASS-USDA)*

Factory Shipments of Paints, Varnish and Lacquer in the United States   In Millions of Dollars

Year	First Quarter	Second Quarter	Third Quarter	Fourth Quarter	Total	Year	First Quarter	Second Quarter	Third Quarter	Fourth Quarter	Total
1995	3,330.3	3,838.0	3,814.5	3,423.4	14,406	2000	4,073.1	4,573.5	4,082.0	3,474.7	16,203
1996	3,438.6	4,161.9	3,954.9	3,428.9	14,984	2001	3,625.0	4,345.4	4,094.5	3,652.6	15,718
1997	3,515.2	4,023.4	3,924.1	3,323.0	14,786	2002	3,729.9	4,440.7	4,251.4	3,600.7	16,023
1998	3,600.7	4,216.4	4,063.9	3,804.4	15,685	2003	3,981.5	4,671.8	4,374.7	3,905.8	16,934
1999	3,926.2	4,452.2	4,216.5	3,925.7	16,521	2004[1]	3,972.6	4,624.5	4,508.7		17,474

[1] Preliminary.   *Source: Bureau of the Census, U.S. Department of Commerce*

Consumption of Linseed Oil (Inedible Products) in the United States   In Millions of Pounds

Year	July	Aug.	Sept.	Oct.	Nov.	Dec.	Jan.	Feb.	Mar.	Apr.	May	June	Total
1997-8	8.9	7.7	8.6	6.7	7.5	6.4	8.0	6.0	6.2	5.9	6.8	5.7	84.3
1998-9	7.2	6.8	6.4	5.6	4.6	6.6	5.9	4.7	6.8	6.4	5.6	7.9	74.6
1999-00	5.4	6.2	5.5	5.2	5.6	4.5	4.2	6.1	5.8	7.0	7.6	6.6	69.8
2000-1	6.5	7.2	7.3	7.5	6.5	5.7	8.0	6.7	7.7	7.6	9.3	9.4	89.3
2001-2	9.6	8.4	9.2	7.4	5.3	5.0	8.2	7.1	6.9	8.0	7.7	8.7	91.3
2002-3	11.7	9.6	10.0	7.0	5.7	7.3	6.8	6.4	8.7	8.5	6.6	6.7	94.9
2003-4	7.9	6.9	6.0	6.8	3.5	5.0	5.6	7.3	6.0	7.7	8.1	8.2	79.1
2004-5[1]	7.3	7.3	6.7	5.6	4.8	5.1							73.6

[1] Preliminary.   *Source: Bureau of the Census, U.S. Department of Commerce*

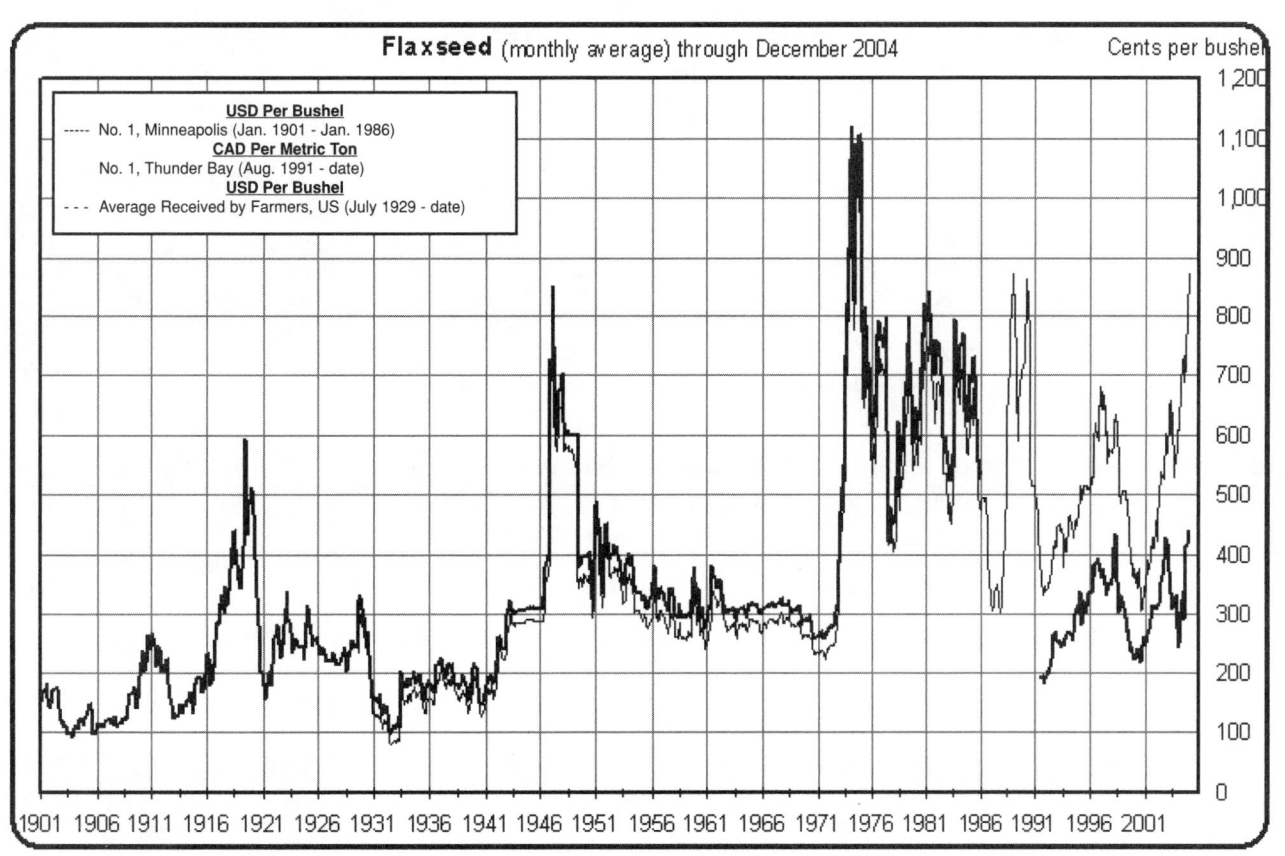

FLAXSEED AND LINSEED OIL

Supply and Distribution of Linseed Oil in the United States   In Millions of Pounds

Crop Year Beginning June 1	Supply			Disappearance			Average Price at Minneapolis Cents/Lb.
	Stocks June 1	Pro-duction	Total	Exports	Domestic	Total Disappearance	
1993-4	54	174	228	7	162	165	31.8
1994-5	63	172	235	24	166	190	33.7
1995-6	45	180	225	26	149	175	36.5
1996-7	50	200	250	66	149	215	36.0
1997-8	35	205	240	58	140	198	37.8
1998-9	35	207	249	63	138	201	37.5
1999-00	45	224	272	76	147	223	37.8
2000-1	49	234	293	100	150	250	36.0
2001-2[1]	43	195	238	90	103	193	36.0
2002-3[2]	45	201	246	92	109	201	33.0

[1] Preliminary.   [2] Forecast.   Source: Economic Research Service, U.S. Department of Agriculture (ERS-USDA)

World Production and Price of Linseed Oil   In Thousands of Metric Tons

Year	Argentina	Bang-ladesh	Belgium	China	Egypt	Germany	India	Japan	United Kingdom	United States	Former USSR	World Total	Rotterdam Ex-Tank $/Tonne
1994-5	46.8	13.0	35.2	137.4	8.2	104.0	91.4	29.2	41.4	81.7	10.6	697.5	657
1995-6	47.5	13.0	44.3	125.1	8.0	72.0	88.1	30.0	28.9	80.0	12.7	665.3	579
1996-7	17.1	12.5	52.1	142.5	9.6	52.2	90.0	31.0	34.1	97.9	16.5	676.7	560
1997-8	24.1	13.4	54.7	120.0	11.1	66.9	84.3	31.3	35.1	100.7	7.2	678.6	686
1998-9	24.5	13.6	59.2	150.0	15.2	74.1	80.1	26.5	34.3	107.6	10.7	731.2	575
1999-00	13.1	12.6	68.8	118.3	15.0	73.6	85.9	23.8	34.1	124.9	7.9	709.2	413
2000-1	6.2	12.9	75.2	134.5	23.0	63.4	74.7	21.1	17.0	114.7	16.4	670.1	378
2001-2	3.8	13.5	95.0	125.8	16.4	57.3	72.4	18.9	9.9	95.7	18.7	629.3	454
2002-3[1]	1.9	13.6	92.1	124.9	15.6	64.4	63.3	8.6	5.9	105.5	13.0	596.3	679
2003-4[2]	5.6	13.6	91.2	124.9	13.8	72.8	67.7	8.1	6.3	105.5	16.0	614.3	674

[1] Preliminary.   [2] Forecast.   Source: The Oil World

Average Price Received by Farmers for Flaxseed in the United States   In Dollars Per Bushel

Year	July	Aug.	Sept.	Oct.	Nov.	Dec.	Jan.	Feb.	Mar.	Apr.	May	June	Average
1995-6	5.11	5.21	5.11	5.11	5.17	5.03	5.26	5.21	5.28	5.31	6.13	5.90	5.32
1996-7	6.19	6.15	5.89	6.49	6.38	6.77	6.43	6.74	6.66	6.43	6.45	5.99	6.38
1997-8	6.07	5.53	5.72	5.81	5.71	5.72	5.82	6.27	6.26	6.23	6.33	6.17	5.97
1998-9	6.17	5.45	5.09	4.86	4.97	5.00	5.05	5.05	4.94	4.93	4.89	4.38	5.07
1999-00	4.40	3.86	4.00	3.76	3.66	3.61	3.75	3.43	3.70	3.66	3.77	3.64	3.77
2000-1	3.25	3.05	3.10	3.17	3.39	4.45	3.42	3.43	3.90	3.68	3.91	4.10	3.57
2001-2	4.28	4.09	4.10	4.21	4.33	4.55	4.22	4.75	4.75	4.80	5.02	5.29	4.53
2002-3	5.38	5.27	5.55	5.76	6.04	5.92	5.71	6.25	6.47	6.57	6.05	6.02	5.92
2003-4	6.38	5.30	5.43	5.77	6.02	6.15	6.08	6.39	6.52	6.98	7.11	7.25	6.28
2004-5[1]	7.33	6.90	7.19	7.36	8.70	8.42	8.90	10.50					8.16

[1] Preliminary.   Source: National Agricultural Statistics Service, U.S. Department of Agriculture (NASS-USDA)

Stocks of Linseed Oil (Crude and Refined) at Factories and Warehouses in the US   In Millions of Pounds

Year	July 1	Aug. 1	Sept. 1	Oct. 1	Nov. 1	Dec. 1	Jan. 1	Feb. 1	Mar. 1	Apr. 1	May 1	June 1
1995-6	39.5	44.6	37.4	46.0	48.0	44.5	45.3	58.9	64.0	62.0	60.6	47.2
1996-7	51.3	50.9	59.0	46.1	38.8	41.8	49.2	48.1	53.9	50.5	44.5	45.6
1997-8	39.9	35.2	40.3	33.3	38.6	40.3	46.9	60.8	55.8	63.1	54.6	49.4
1998-9	49.6	45.3	38.5	55.4	35.7	44.5	53.2	68.2	54.6	68.2	65.3	76.2
1999-00	68.7	65.5	68.9	74.0	92.4	69.6	72.0	69.5	65.7	53.9	49.1	44.2
2000-1	39.5	42.5	41.3	54.3	58.7	87.0	61.6	50.1	50.5	51.2	39.2	44.8
2001-2	29.1	30.2	22.6	38.4	32.4	29.9	33.4	36.6	26.8	33.4	32.3	31.1
2002-3	27.8	17.7	12.8	21.8	30.5	29.0	31.9	35.9	34.6	36.2	33.7	33.7
2003-4	30.2	27.2	22.3	78.5	42.0	35.0	40.0	43.4	37.6	32.9	24.5	19.9
2004-5[1]	15.1	15.8	8.0	13.0	17.1	26.9	31.3					

[1] Preliminary.   Source: Bureau of the Census, U.S. Department of Commerce

Flaxseed Futures - Winnipeg Commodity Exchange
(weekly close) as of December 31, 2004
CAD per metric ton

Wholesale Price of Raw Linseed Oil at Minneapolis in Tank Cars   In Cents Per Pound

Year	July	Aug.	Sept.	Oct.	Nov.	Dec.	Jan.	Feb.	Mar.	Apr.	May	June	Average
1994-5	30.31	32.00	32.00	33.50	35.00	35.00	35.00	35.00	35.00	35.00	35.00	35.00	33.98
1995-6	35.00	35.50	37.00	37.00	37.00	37.00	37.00	37.00	37.00	37.00	37.00	37.00	36.71
1996-7	37.00	37.20	37.50	37.00	33.75	32.12	36.00	36.00	36.00	36.00	36.00	36.00	35.88
1997-8	36.00	36.00	36.00	37.00	37.00	37.00	36.00	36.00	36.00	36.00	37.00	37.00	36.42
1998-9	37.00	37.00	37.00	37.00	37.00	37.00	36.00	36.00	36.00	36.00	36.00	36.00	36.50
1999-00	36.00	36.00	36.00	36.00	36.00	36.00	36.00	36.00	36.00	36.00	36.00	36.00	36.00
2000-1	36.00	36.00	36.00	36.00	36.00	36.00	36.00	36.00	36.00	36.00	36.00	32.00	35.67
2001-2	35.50	38.00	39.00	39.00	39.00	39.00	39.00	39.00	39.00	39.00	39.65	40.35	38.79
2002-3	40.00	38.00	41.00	31.75	41.00	41.00	41.00	41.00	41.00	41.00	41.19	41.75	39.97
2003-4[1]	41.75	41.75	42.00										41.83

[1] Preliminary.   *Source: Economic Research Service, U.S. Department of Agriculture (ERS-USDA)*

Average Open Interest of Flaxseed Futures in Winnipeg   In Contracts

Year	Jan.	Feb.	Mar.	Apr.	May	June	July	Aug.	Sept.	Oct.	Nov.	Dec.
1995	6,242	8,731	7,505	7,121	8,107	7,212	6,436	5,557	6,230	5,245	5,937	4,414
1996	6,059	6,056	4,402	5,192	6,970	4,435	3,102	2,989	3,257	3,438	4,326	5,119
1997	5,420	5,356	5,591	5,151	4,923	4,075	3,891	4,031	7,131	8,284	7,255	7,955
1998	10,059	10,190	9,707	8,540	6,480	6,874	6,030	6,767	7,421	7,221	7,564	5,828
1999	4,372	4,552	4,533	4,238	3,719	2,456	2,149	2,758	3,725	4,236	4,493	4,276
2000	4,365	4,907	5,588	6,218	5,066	3,696	3,152	3,585	3,936	4,666	4,922	4,914
2001	4,101	3,476	4,270	3,043	3,169	3,661	2,745	2,350	2,400	3,158	2,726	3,031
2002	2,225	1,981	1,921	1,787	1,270	935	612	699	776	704	424	249
2003	235	316	477	604	394	489	298	305	253	193	94	49
2004	38	23	15	0	0	0	0	0	179	15	214	578

Source: Winnipeg Commodity Exchange (WCE)

Volume of Trading of Flaxseed Futures in Winnipeg   In Contracts

Year	Jan.	Feb.	Mar.	Apr.	May	June	July	Aug.	Sept.	Oct.	Nov.	Dec.	Total
1995	10,707	15,819	10,676	15,315	12,569	9,235	6,579	5,922	11,790	11,051	15,064	7,798	132,525
1996	9,617	8,301	4,110	13,531	10,855	7,997	6,517	4,153	5,430	11,126	7,532	10,720	99,889
1997	7,640	6,486	7,123	10,912	6,256	7,851	7,662	7,081	20,967	23,418	20,049	15,311	140,756
1998	15,713	19,906	8,275	9,060	5,231	7,642	4,468	4,062	7,328	13,085	13,824	6,958	115,552
1999	4,855	8,922	4,383	8,460	5,241	5,891	4,863	2,833	5,852	12,078	7,710	7,345	78,433
2000	9,022	9,340	9,292	12,604	7,372	7,393	2,676	2,525	9,822	11,915	14,436	7,819	100,040
2001	8,232	6,428	6,928	7,117	6,514	6,745	4,344	2,620	5,242	7,291	4,689	6,326	72,476
2002	2,990	2,838	2,519	3,832	3,320	3,018	1,153	810	777	3,030	955	344	25,586
2003	333	724	412	368	452	738	343	96	491	273	183	25	4,438
2004	35	10	15	0	0	0	0	0	15	0	0	15	216

Source: Winnipeg Commodity Exchange (WCE)

Fruits

A fruit is any seed-bearing structure produced from a flowering plant. A widely used classification system divides fruit into fleshy or dry types. Fleshy fruits are juicy and include peaches, mangos, apples, and blueberries. Dry fruits include tree nuts such as almonds, walnuts, and pecans. Some foods that are commonly called vegetables, such as tomatoes, squash, peppers and eggplant, are technically fruits because they develop from the ovary of a flower.

Worldwide, over 430 million tons of fruit are produced each year and are grown everywhere except the Arctic and the Antarctic. The tropics, because of their abundant moisture and warm temperatures, produce the most diverse and abundant fruits. Mexico and Chile produce more than half of all the fresh and frozen fruit imported into the US. In the US, the top three fruits produced are oranges, grapes, and apples. Virtually all US production of almonds, pistachios, and walnuts occurs in California, which leads the US in tree nut production.

Prices – Fruit prices were fairly strong in 2003, the last reporting year, with the fresh fruit Consumer Price Index rising +3.3% to 279.1 and the processed fruit CPI index rising +2.3% to 114.1. Fruit prices generally rose in 2003: Red Delicious Apples (+3.4% to 98.0 cents per pound), bananas (+0.3% to 50.9 cents per pound), Anjou pears (-0.7% to 99.0 cents per pound), Thompson seedless grapes (+0.6% to $1.899 per pound), lemons (-5.3% to $1.317 per pound), grapefruits (+11.6% to 72.3 cents per pound), navel oranges (+0.3% to 83.8 cents per pound), and Valencia oranges (+1.7% to 55.5 cents per pound).

Supply – US commercial production of selected fruits in 2003, the last reporting year, fell -4.2% to 31.794 million short tons. By weight, oranges accounted for 36% of that US fruit production figure, followed by grapes at 21%, and apples at 14%. The value of US fruit production in 2003 rose +2.8% yr/yr to $13.191 billion.

Demand – US per capita fresh fruit consumption in 2003 rose +1.1% to 100.40 pounds per year, which was still below the record high of 101.58 pounds in 1998. The highest per capita consumption categories for non-citrus fruits in 2003 were bananas (26.16 pounds) and apples (16.51 pounds). Per capital consumption of citrus fruits was the highest for oranges (11.88 pounds), grapefruit (4.10 pounds) and lemons (3.32 pounds).

The utilization breakdown for 2003 shows that 39% of total US non-citrus fruit utilization went for fresh fruit, 22% for wine, 13% for dried fruit, 11% for canned fruit, 8% for juice, and 4% for frozen fruit. The value of utilized non-citrus fruit production in 2003 rose +4.3% yr/yr to $8.486 billion.

Commercial Production for Selected Fruits in the United States   In Thousands of Short Tons

Year	Apples	Cherries[2]	Cran-berries	Grapes	Grape-fruit	Lemons	Nect-arines	Oranges	Peaches	Pears	Pine-apples[3]	Prunes & Plums	Straw-berries	Tangelos	Tang-erines	Total All Fruits
1997	5,162	373	275	7,291	2,885	962	264	12,692	1,312	1,043	324	926	814	178	425	35,507
1998	5,823	371	272	5,820	2,593	897	224	13,670	1,190	990	332	559	819	128	360	34,590
1999	5,316	344	318	6,236	2,513	747	274	9,824	1,252	1,044	352	735	916	115	327	30,819
2000	5,291	352	286	7,688	2,763	840	267	12,997	1,276	993	354	902	950	99	458	36,115
2001	4,712	415	267	6,569	2,462	996	275	12,221	1,204	1,027	323	651	826	95	373	32,916
2002	4,262	212	285	7,339	2,424	801	300	12,374	1,268	890	320	736	942	97	420	33,173
2003[1]	4,307	362	309	6,573	2,063	1,026	273	11,545	1,260	928	315	812	1,041	105	382	31,794

[1] Preliminary.   [2] Sweet and tart.   [3] Utilized production.   *Source: Economic Research Service, U.S. Department of Agriculture (ERS-USDA)*

Utilized Production for Selected Fruits in the United States   In Thousands of Short Tons

Year	Utilized Production				Value of Production			
	Citrus[2]	Noncitrus	Tree Nuts[3]	Total	Citrus[2]	Noncitrus	Tree Nuts[3]	Total
	In Thousands of Short Tons				In Thousands of Dollars			
1997	17,270	18,400	1,210	36,880	2,582,767	8,189,821	2,093,697	12,866,285
1998	17,770	16,552	908	35,230	2,600,066	7,251,032	1,365,349	11,216,447
1999	13,633	17,347	1,288	32,267	2,431,179	8,077,404	1,505,926	12,014,509
2000	17,276	18,854	1,086	37,216	2,513,174	7,883,036	1,496,584	11,892,794
2001	16,216	16,740	1,304	34,260	2,319,917	7,918,636	1,513,063	11,751,616
2002	16,194	17,122	1,448	34,764	2,610,559	8,138,427	2,078,670	12,827,656
2003[1]	15,180	16,640	1,424	33,244	2,255,963	8,486,489	2,448,264	13,190,716

[1] Preliminary.   [2] Year harvest was completed.   [3] Tree nuts on an in-shell equivalent.
Source: Economic Research Service, U.S. Department of Agriculture (ERS-USDA)

Annual Average Retail Prices for Selected Fruits in the United States   In Dollars Per Pound

Year	Red Delicious Apples	Bananas	Anjou Pears	Thompson Seedless Grapes	Lemons	Grapefruit	Oranges Navel	Oranges Valencias
1997	.907	.487	.985	1.712	1.154	.520	.592	.682
1998	.943	.494	1.089	1.589	1.198	.599	.565	.657
1999	.897	.491	.950	1.841	1.236	.612	.843	.947
2000	.919	.501	.986	1.745	1.289	.610	.613	.610
2001	.868	.507	.966	1.850	1.265	.651	.722	.524
2002	.948	.508	.997	1.887	1.391	.648	.836	.565
2003[1]	.980	.509	.990	1.899	1.317	.723	.838	.575

[1] Estimate.   *Source: Economic Research Service, U.S. Department of Agriculture (ERS-USDA)*

FRUITS

Utilization of Noncitrus Fruit Production, and Value in the U.S.   1,000 Short Tons (Fresh Equivalent)

Year	Utilized Pro- duction	Fresh	Canned	Dried	Juice	Frozen	Wine	Other	Value of utilized Production $1,000
			------- Processed -------						
1994	17,339	6,710	2,090	2,816	1,886	665	2,711	228	6,268,176
1995	16,348	6,285	1,753	2,400	1,857	647	2,992	205	6,815,962
1996	16,103	6,313	1,873	2,275	1,582	604	3,043	180	7,265,788
1997	18,400	6,642	2,130	2,660	1,666	699	4,035	293	8,189,821
1998	16,552	6,514	1,845	1,911	1,786	711	3,315	198	7,251,032
1999	17,347	6,691	1,986	2,154	1,887	717	3,351	244	8,077,404
2000	18,854	7,015	1,812	3,023	1,712	691	4,130	191	7,883,036
2001	16,740	6,488	1,859	2,290	1,462	665	3,568	169	7,918,636
2002	17,122	6,549	1,727	2,582	1,251	591	3,999	138	8,138,427
2003[1]	16,640	6,543	1,755	2,218	1,299	674	3,618	223	8,486,489

[1] Preliminary.   *Source: Economic Research Service, U.S. Department of Agriculture (ERS-USDA)*

Average Price Indexes for Fruits in the United States

Year	Index of all Fruit and Nut Prices Received by Growers (1990-92=100)	Fresh Fruit	Dried Fruit	Canned Fruits and Juices	Frozen Fruits and Juices	Fresh Fruit	Processed Fruit
		------- Producer Price Index -------				---- Consumer Price Index ----	
		1982 = 100				1982-84 = 100	
1994	90	82.7	116.1	126.0	132.3	203.2	134.3
1995	97	85.6	116.1	129.4	136.7	200.3	137.0
1996	118	100.8	119.1	137.5	83.6	234.4	83.1
1997	110	99.4	123.3	138.4	148.2	236.3	148.5
1998	111	90.5	121.8	134.3	101.5	246.5	101.9
1999	115	103.6	122.9	137.0	106.1	266.3	105.4
2000	98	91.4	122.4	139.5	108.9	258.3	106.9
2001	109	97.7	120.3	143.3	111.9	265.1	109.0
2002	105	91.5	120.7	141.6	111.2	270.2	111.6
2003[1]	106	84.1	122.1	142.3	115.7	279.1	114.1

[1] Estimate.   *Source: Economic Research Service, U.S. Department of Agriculture (ERS-USDA)*

Fresh Fruit: Per Capita Consumption[1] in the United States   In Pounds

Year	Oranges	Tangerines and Tangelos	Lemons	Grapefruit	Total	Apples	Apricots	Avacados	Bananas	Cherries	Cran- berries
	----- Citrus Fruit -----					----- Noncitrus Fruit -----					
1994	12.94	2.09	2.66	6.07	24.74	19.36	.15	1.35	27.78	.52	.08
1995	11.83	1.99	2.84	6.00	23.84	18.69	.10	1.58	27.08	.29	.08
1996	12.58	2.15	2.86	5.85	24.58	18.67	.09	1.58	27.60	.40	.08
1997	13.91	2.52	2.76	6.18	26.52	18.09	.14	1.73	27.16	.60	.07
1998	14.61	2.17	2.46	5.94	26.58	18.98	.12	1.52	28.01	.52	.07
1999	8.38	2.30	2.61	5.75	20.37	18.50	.12	1.92	30.70	.63	.11
2000	11.74	2.86	2.44	5.09	23.51	17.46	.15	2.21	28.45	.60	.14
2001	11.88	2.72	2.96	4.85	23.90	15.60	.08	2.50	26.63	.77	.13
2002	11.73	2.55	3.33	4.63	23.34	15.99	.09	2.33	26.77	.70	.11
2003[2]	11.88	2.72	3.32	4.10	23.93	16.51	.13	2.55	26.16	.92	.10

[1] All data on calendar-year basis except for citrus fruits; apples, August; grapes and pears, July; grapefruit, September; lemons, August of prior year; all other citrus, November.   [2] Preliminary.   *Source: Economic Research Service, U.S. Department of Agriculture (ERS-USDA)*

Fresh Fruit: Per Capita Consumption[1] in the United States   In Pounds

Year	Grapes	Kiwifruit	Mangos	Nectarines & Peaches	Pears	Pine- apples	Papaya	Plums & Prunes	Straw- berries	Total Noncitrus	Total Fruit
	----- Noncitrus Fruit Continued -----										
1994	7.25	.57	.97	5.42	3.44	2.02	.30	1.60	4.05	75.13	99.87
1995	7.46	.55	1.12	5.33	3.36	1.91	.37	.93	4.06	73.23	97.07
1996	6.73	.54	1.34	4.38	3.05	1.90	.54	1.43	4.27	72.87	97.45
1997	7.76	.48	1.44	5.51	3.39	2.34	.47	1.51	4.05	75.03	101.55
1998	7.17	.55	1.49	4.69	3.43	2.75	.47	1.18	3.87	75.14	101.72
1999	7.97	.55	1.62	5.29	3.53	3.03	.62	1.28	4.52	80.70	101.07
2000	7.44	.56	1.75	5.30	3.39	3.22	.68	1.19	4.81	77.61	101.12
2001	7.38	.57	1.79	5.16	3.25	3.16	.78	1.33	4.17	73.64	97.54
2002	8.41	.49	1.97	5.23	3.06	3.82	.79	1.26	4.60	76.01	99.35
2003[2]	7.65	.37	2.06	5.17	3.04	4.40	.87	1.24	4.91	76.47	100.4

[1] All data on calendar-year basis except for citrus fruits; apples, August; grapes and pears, July; grapefruit, September; lemons, August of prior year; all other citrus, November.   [2] Preliminary.   *Source: Economic Research Service, U.S. Department of Agriculture (ERS-USDA)*

103

Gas

Natural gas is a fossil fuel that is colorless, shapeless, and odorless in its pure form. It is a mixture of hydrocarbon gases formed primarily of methane, but it can also include ethane, propane, butane, and pentane. Natural gas is combustible, clean burning, and gives off a great deal of energy. Around 500 BC, the Chinese discovered that the energy in natural gas could be harnessed. They passed it through crude bamboo-shoot pipes and then burned it to boil sea water to create potable fresh water. Around 1785, Britain became the first country to commercially use natural gas produced from coal for streetlights and indoor lights. In 1821, William Hart dug the first well specifically intended to obtain natural gas and he is generally regarded as the "father of natural gas" in America. There is a vast amount of natural gas estimated to still be in the ground in the US. Natural gas as a source of energy is significantly less expensive than electricity per Btu.

Natural gas futures and options are traded on the New York Mercantile Exchange (NYMEX). The NYMEX natural gas futures contract calls for the delivery of natural gas representing 10,000 million British thermal units (mmBtu) at the Henry Hub in Louisiana, which is the nexus of 16 intra-state and inter-state pipelines. The contract is priced in terms of dollars per mmBtu. NYMEX also has basic swap futures contracts available for 30 different natural gas pricing locations versus the benchmark Henry Hub location. Natural gas futures are also listed in London on the International Petroleum Exchange (IPE).

Prices – NYMEX natural gas futures on the nearest-futures chart in 2004 traded in a range of about $4.50-$7.50 per mmBtu early in the year, rallied to a 2-year high of $9.200 in November, and then fell back to close the year at $6.149. Natural gas remained below the record high of $11.90 per mmBtu posted in February 2003 tied to the US-Iraq war.

Supply – US recovery of natural gas in 2003 rose +1.1% to 24,243 billion cubic feet, which was just below the record high of 24,501 billion recovered in 2001. The top US producing states of natural gas are Texas with 26.4% of US production in 2003, Oklahoma with 8.3%, New Mexico with 7.7%, Wyoming with 7.5%, and Louisiana with 6.9%. The world's largest natural gas producers are Russia with 2,054,288 terajoules of production in 2004 and the US with 1,722,443 terajoules of production in 2002.

Demand – US delivered consumption of natural gas in 2003 fell -4.9% yr/yr to 20,192 billion cubic feet, of which 25% was delivered to residences, 16% to commercial establishments, 24% to electrical utility plants, and 35% to industrial establishments.

Trade – US imports (consumed) in 2003 fell -0.5% yr/yr to 3,996 billion cubic feet from the record high of 4,015 billion cubic feet imported in 2002. US exports of natural gas in 2003 rose +34.0% yr/yr to a record high of 692 billion cubic feet.

World Production of Natural Gas (Monthly Average Marketed Production[3])   (In Terajoule[4])

Year	Australia	Canada	China	Germany	Indonesia	India	Italy	Mexico	Netherlands	Romania	Russia	United Kingdom	United States
1995	96,912	511,447	58,261	55,714	203,633	72,796	63,371	93,473	209,229	50,401	1,891,583	246,818	1,683,674
1996	99,461	530,891	72,609	62,479	248,574	74,776	63,436	106,214	236,803	48,023	1,844,954	293,536	1,706,764
1997	99,077	537,295	81,954	61,804	248,585	84,892	61,173	109,568	209,526	41,547	1,771,467	299,503	1,711,134
1998	95,265	538,273	84,033	60,748	274,281	88,195	60,159	182,615	198,554	32,932	1,665,726	314,506	1,722,107
1999	92,440	569,819	79,523	62,651	282,485	91,468	56,616	182,610	186,672	38,952	1,807,313	345,040	1,704,788
2000	92,746	588,447	90,287	59,164	267,707	94,783	54,289	178,861	178,989	38,254	1,898,046	377,565	1,726,861
2001	96,523	550,463	98,431	60,463	258,122	91,063	48,008	171,940	192,180	40,422	1,887,953	370,237	1,759,236
2002	96,841	553,183	106,720	61,147	280,939	92,568	46,190	168,675	186,206	38,004	1,934,011	361,414	1,722,443
2003[1]	99,771	534,434	111,352	61,441	297,080	100,012	42,708	174,733	NA	37,231	2,016,895	358,798	NA
2004[2]	101,851	547,750	130,419	55,534	NA	97,900	40,632	177,769	NA	37,045	2,025,873	329,260	NA

[1] Preliminary.   [2] Estimate.   [3] Compares all gas collected & utilized as fuel or as a chemical industry raw material, including gas used in oilfields and/or gasfields as a fuel by producers.   [4] Terajoule = 10 to the 12th power Joule = approximately 10 to the 9th power BTU.   NA = Not available.
Source: United Nations

Marketed Production of Natural Gas in the United States, by States   (In Million Cubic Feet)

Year	Alaska	California	Colorado	Kansas	Louisiana	Michigan	Mississippi	New Mexico	Oklahoma	Texas	Wyoming	Total
1994	555,402	309,427	453,207	712,730	5,169,705	222,657	63,448	1,557,689	1,934,864	6,353,844	696,018	19,709,525
1995	469,550	279,555	523,084	721,436	5,108,366	238,203	95,533	1,625,837	1,811,734	6,330,048	673,775	19,506,474
1996	480,828	286,494	572,071	712,796	5,289,742	245,740	103,263	1,554,087	1,734,887	6,470,620	666,036	19,812,241
1997	468,311	285,690	637,375	687,215	1,505,014	305,950	107,300	1,558,633	1,703,888	5,167,334	738,368	19,866,093
1998	466,648	315,277	696,321	603,586	1,551,979	278,076	108,068	1,501,098	1,669,367	5,227,477	903,836	19,961,348
1999	462,967	382,715	722,738	553,419	1,566,916	277,364	111,021	1,511,671	1,594,002	5,054,486	971,230	19,804,848
2000	458,995	376,580	752,985	525,729	1,455,014	296,556	88,558	1,695,295	1,612,890	5,282,104	1,088,328	20,197,511
2001	471,440	377,824	817,206	480,145	1,502,086	275,036	107,541	1,689,125	1,615,384	5,282,723	1,363,879	20,570,295
2002	463,301	360,205	841,521	454,901	1,361,751	274,476	112,980	1,632,080	1,551,272	5,141,075	1,453,957	19,920,790
2003[1]	476,236	339,773	955,727	419,913	1,372,227	238,513	136,043	1,545,243	1,668,863	5,277,904	1,505,452	20,029,934

[1] Preliminary.   *Source: Energy Information Administration, U.S. Department of Energy (EIA-DOE)*

World Production of Natural Gas Plant Liquids   (Thousand Barrels per Day)

Year	Algeria	Canada	Mexico	Saudi Arabia	Russia	United States	Persian Gulf[2]	OAPEC[3]	OPEC[4]	World
1995	145	581	447	701	180	1,762	1,106	1,301	1,506	5,492
1996	150	596	423	697	185	1,830	1,082	1,295	1,501	5,585
1997	160	636	388	712	195	1,817	1,152	1,384	1,589	5,729
1998	155	651	424	755	220	1,759	1,225	1,449	1,662	5,883
1999	190	653	439	745	231	1,850	1,232	1,491	1,728	6,075
2000	230	699	438	750	232	1,911	1,298	1,623	1,843	6,333
2001	250	709	433	800	237	1,868	1,470	1,828	2,053	6,734
2002	270	698	408	1,000	246	1,880	1,698	2,080	2,308	7,042
2003	270	724	418	1,013	390	1,719	1,768	2,198	2,340	7,313
2004[1]	250	658	442	1,183	456	1,811	1,959	2,351	2,527	7,429

[1] Preliminary.   [2] Bahrain, Iran, Iraq, Kuwait, Qatar, Saudi Arabia and the United Arab Emirates.   [3] Organization of Arab Petroleum Exporting Countries.   [4] Organization of Pertroleum Exporting Countries.   Source: Energy Information Administration, U.S. Department of Energy (EIA-DOE)

Recoverable Reserves and Deliveries of Natural Gas in the United States   (in Billions of Cubic Feet)

Year	Gross Withdrawals	Recoverable Reserves of Natural Gas Dec. 31[2]	Residential	Commercial	Electric Utility Plants[3]	Industrial	Total Deliveries	Lease & Plant Fuel	Used as Pipeline Fuel	Heating Value BTU per Cubic Foot
1994	23,581	163,837	4,848	2,897	2,987	8,167	18,899	1,124	685	1,028
1995	23,744	165,146	4,850	3,034	3,197	8,580	19,660	1,220	700	1,027
1996	24,114	166,474	5,241	3,161	2,732	8,870	20,006	1,250	711	1,027
1997	24,213	167,223	4,984	3,215	4,065	8,511	20,782	1,203	751	1,026
1998	24,108	164,041	4,520	2,999	4,588	8,320	20,438	1,173	635	1,031
1999	23,823	167,406	4,726	3,045	4,820	8,079	20,681	1,079	645	1,027
2000	24,174	177,427	4,996	3,182	5,206	8,142	21,540	1,151	642	1,025
2001	24,501	183,460	4,771	3,023	5,342	7,344	20,495	1,119	624	1,028
2002	23,977	186,946	4,890	3,103	5,672	7,557	21,236	1,113	667	1,028
2003[1]	24,243	189,044	5,078	3,217	5,135	7,139	20,587	1,123	665	

[1] Preliminary.   [2] Estimated proved recoverable reserves of dry natural gas.   [3] Figures include gas other than natural (impossible to segregate); therefore, shown separately from other consumption.   Source: Energy Information Administration, U.S. Department of Energy (EIA-DOE)

Gas Utility Sales in the United States by Types and Class of Service   (In Trillions of BTUs)

Year	Total Utility Sales	Number of Customers (Millions)	Residential	Commercial	Industrial	Electric Generation	Other	Total	Residential	Commercial	industrial	Electric Generation	Other
1994	9,248	57.9	4,845	2,253	1,690	420	159	49,852	30,552	12,276	5,529	1,170	597
1995	9,221	58.7	4,803	2,281	1,591	328	218	46,436	28,742	11,573	4,816	836	549
1996	10,242	60.0	5,333	2,518	1,748	641	3	53,630	32,942	13,250	5,812	1,615	12
1997	9,722	61.0	5,056	2,341	1,593	728	4	54,876	34,187	13,203	5,556	1,912	18
1998	8,781	61.5	4,534	2,063	1,370	810	5	47,084	30,130	11,020	4,189	1,726	20
1999	8,975	60.8	4,622	2,067	1,553	729	5	47,202	30,095	10,731	4,715	1,641	21
2000	9,232	61.3	4,741	2,077	1,698	709	6	59,243	35,828	13,338	7,432	2,612	33
2001[1]	8,667	61.4	4,525	2,053	1,461	620	8	69,150	42,454	16,848	7,513	2,286	49
2002[2]	8,864	62.0	4,589	2,055	1,748	459	13	57,112	35,062	13,512	6,840	1,639	59

[1] Preliminary.   [2] Estimate.   Source: American Gas Association (AGA)

Salient Statistics of Natural Gas in the United States

Year	Marketed Production	Extraction Loss	Dry Production	Storage Withdrawals	Imports (Consumed)	Total Supply	Consumption	Exports	Added to Storage	Total Disposition	Wellhead Price	Imports	Exports	Residential	Commercial	Industrial	Electric Utilities
	In Billions of Cubic Feet										USD Per Thousand Cubic Feet						
1994	19,710	889	18,821	2,579	2,624	24,207	21,247	162	2,865	23,581	1.85	1.87	2.50	6.41	5.44	3.05	2.28
1995	19,506	908	18,599	3,025	2,841	24,837	22,207	154	2,610	23,744	1.55	1.49	2.39	6.06	5.05	2.71	2.02
1996	19,812	958	18,854	2,981	2,937	25,635	22,610	153	2,979	24,114	2.17	1.97	2.97	6.34	5.40	3.42	2.69
1997	19,866	964	18,902	2,894	2,994	25,502	22,737	157	2,870	24,213	2.32	2.17	3.02	6.94	5.80	3.59	2.78
1998	24,108	938	19,024	2,432	3,152	25,826	22,246	159	2,961	25,826	1.96	1.97	2.45	6.82	5.48	3.14	2.40
1999	23,823	973	18,832	2,808	3,586	25,699	22,405	163	2,636	25,699	2.19	2.24	2.61	6.69	5.33	3.12	2.62
2000	24,174	1,016	19,182	3,550	3,782	26,815	23,333	244	2,721	26,815	3.68	3.95	4.10	7.76	6.59	4.45	4.38
2001	24,501	954	19,616	2,344	3,977	26,697	22,239	373	3,510	26,697	4.00	4.43	4.19	9.63	8.43	5.24	4.61
2002[1]	23,941	957	18,928	3,180	4,015	26,767	23,007	516	2,713	26,767	2.95	3.14	3.41	7.89	6.63	4.02	3.68
2003[2]	24,056	876	19,036	3,166	3,996	27,063	22,375	692	3,360	27,063	4.88	5.17	5.57	9.52	8.29	5.81	5.54

[1] Preliminary.   [2] Estimate.   Source: Energy Information Administration, U.S. Department of Energy (EIA-DOE)

GAS

Average Open Interest of Natural Gas Futures in New York   In Contracts

Year	Jan.	Feb.	Mar.	Apr.	May	June	July	Aug.	Sept.	Oct.	Nov.	Dec.
1995	148,448	151,882	157,097	150,101	148,797	144,402	143,942	140,297	135,226	133,969	140,301	166,227
1996	155,024	150,521	149,809	159,132	147,616	156,959	151,913	135,191	138,657	144,944	147,854	151,498
1997	156,231	162,567	171,467	181,745	206,685	197,637	199,296	213,640	235,509	242,184	231,556	210,259
1998	192,652	198,853	203,402	251,344	255,837	264,517	255,878	273,350	275,868	252,827	236,292	240,832
1999	244,472	268,649	284,312	315,336	332,398	330,725	316,034	353,767	336,622	316,157	309,130	292,161
2000	262,845	266,826	295,176	313,739	342,455	347,353	330,604	339,025	373,654	369,448	389,363	377,470
2001	364,532	346,343	360,032	380,632	421,145	456,512	473,675	497,972	494,475	488,187	455,766	415,882
2002	458,924	491,215	527,765	559,413	556,277	526,016	494,133	437,285	419,532	413,312	393,953	391,424
2003	415,642	420,329	367,673	354,154	365,838	366,610	357,299	343,622	354,568	352,685	356,622	340,756
2004	322,762	312,475	322,366	338,786	382,160	366,135	373,853	378,787	393,477	392,626	383,712	387,605

Source: New York Mercantile Exchange (NYMEX)

Volume of Trading of Natural Gas Futures in New York   (In Thousands of Contracts)

Year	Jan.	Feb.	Mar.	Apr.	May	June	July	Aug.	Sept.	Oct.	Nov.	Dec.	Total
1995	733.0	557.8	676.1	524.5	621.3	622.5	641.8	745.6	548.3	664.4	763.0	988.5	8,086.7
1996	887.2	655.7	694.6	620.0	590.7	681.3	829.0	628.8	679.1	924.4	802.8	820.4	8,813.9
1997	922.8	693.6	664.7	836.3	945.4	803.7	812.9	1,313.8	1,377.1	1,394.0	1,104.8	1,054.6	11,923.6
1998	1,005.6	1,089.1	1,193.5	1,625.9	1,245.2	1,568.8	1,310.4	1,237.0	1,656.3	1,339.5	1,243.1	1,464.0	15,978.3
1999	1,296.7	1,158.6	1,788.5	1,655.8	1,465.3	1,474.2	1,865.8	1,892.1	1,978.6	1,676.5	1,552.3	1,360.7	19,165.1
2000	1,388.8	1,470.9	1,505.0	1,179.3	1,822.2	1,853.7	1,331.4	1,483.9	1,510.2	1,594.9	1,759.5	975.1	17,875.0
2001	1,044.4	1,044.6	1,131.7	1,144.8	1,632.5	1,536.9	1,350.3	1,510.9	901.1	1,639.7	1,891.7	1,639.6	16,468.4
2002	1,942.5	1,668.6	2,381.1	2,421.7	2,281.4	1,911.7	2,266.1	2,115.6	1,990.0	2,103.4	1,569.2	1,706.4	24,357.8
2003	2,134.4	1,909.1	1,362.4	1,321.3	1,521.7	1,584.8	1,543.7	1,315.3	1,503.7	1,948.9	1,376.6	1,515.2	19,037.1
2004	1,162.1	1,125.1	1,420.3	1,443.1	1,587.5	1,588.5	1,508.8	1,724.1	1,885.6	1,458.3	1,320.0	1,218.6	17,441.9

Source: New York Mercantile Exchange (NYMEX)

Average Price of Natural Gas at Henry Hub   In Dollars Per MMBtu

Year	Jan.	Feb.	Mar.	Apr.	May	June	July	Aug.	Sept.	Oct.	Nov.	Dec.	Average
1995	1.51	1.58	1.54	1.63	1.64	1.62	1.44	1.56	1.64	1.77	2.04	2.71	1.72
1996	2.93	4.82	2.95	2.23	2.24	2.49	2.48	2.03	1.84	2.37	3.03	3.91	2.78
1997	3.31	2.22	1.89	2.03	2.24	2.20	2.19	2.48	2.85	3.04	3.02	2.36	2.49
1998	2.10	2.22	2.24	2.43	2.14	2.17	2.17	1.85	2.02	1.89	2.10	1.72	2.09
1999	1.85	1.77	1.79	2.15	2.25	2.30	2.31	2.79	2.54	2.72	2.35	2.36	2.27
2000	2.42	2.65	2.79	3.03	3.58	4.28	3.96	4.41	5.11	5.02	5.54	8.95	4.31
2001	8.18	5.62	5.16	5.16	4.21	3.71	3.11	2.95	2.15	2.45	2.35	2.43	3.96
2002	2.25	2.31	3.03	3.42	3.49	3.22	2.98	3.09	3.55	4.12	4.04	4.75	3.35
2003	5.49	7.41	6.08	5.27	5.81	5.83	5.03	4.97	4.61	4.66	4.47	6.13	5.48
2004	6.17	5.39	5.38	5.71	6.30	6.29	5.93	5.44	5.11	6.39	6.15	6.64	5.91

Source: Energy Information Administration, U.S. Department of Energy (EIA-DOE)

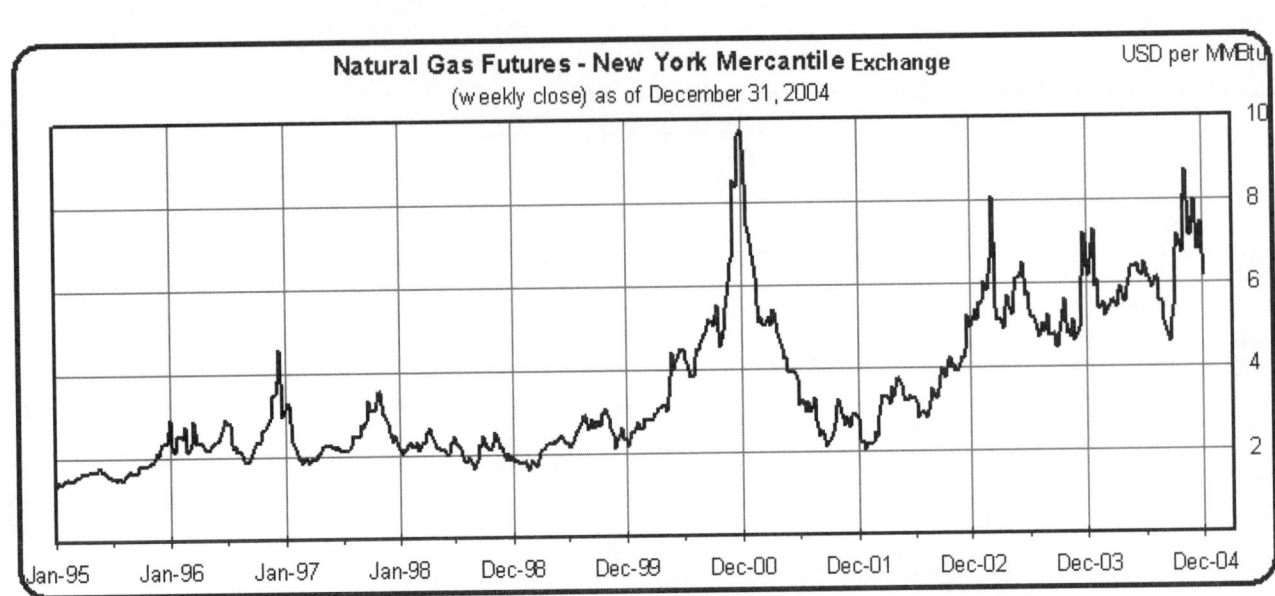

Natural Gas Futures - New York Mercantile Exchange (weekly close) as of December 31, 2004   USD per MMBtu

Gasoline

Gasoline is a complex mixture of hundreds of lighter liquid hydrocarbons and is used chiefly as a fuel for internal-combustion engines. Petroleum crude, or crude oil, is still the most economical source of gasoline with refineries turning more than half of every barrel of crude oil into gasoline. The three basic steps to all refining operations are the separation process (separating crude oil into various chemical components), conversion process (breaking the chemicals down into molecules called hydrocarbons), and treatment process (transforming and combining hydrocarbon molecules and other additives). Another process, called *hydro treating*, removes a significant amount of sulfur from finished gasoline as is currently required by the state of California.

Octane is a measure of a gasoline's ability to resist pinging or knocking noise from an engine. Most gasoline stations offer three octane grades of unleaded fuel—regular at 87 (R+M)/2, midgrade at 89 (R+M)/2, and premium at 93 (R+M)/2. Additional refining steps are needed to increase the octane, which increases the retail price. This does not make the gasoline any cleaner or better, but yields a different blend of hydrocarbons that burn more slowly.

In an attempt to improve air quality and reduce harmful emissions from internal combustion engines, Congress in 1990 amended the Clean Air Act to mandate the addition of ethanol to gasoline. Some 2 billion gallons of ethanol are now added to gasoline each year in the US. The most common blend is E10, which contains 10% ethanol and 90% gasoline. Auto manufacturers have approved that mixture for use in all US vehicles. Ethanol is an alcohol-based fuel produced by fermenting and distilling crops such as corn, barley, wheat and sugar.

Unleaded gasoline futures and options trade at the New York Mercantile Exchange (NYMEX). The NYMEX gasoline futures contract calls for the delivery of 1,000 barrels (42,000 gallons) of unleaded gasoline in the New York harbor and is priced in terms of dollars and cents per gallon.

Price – NYMEX gasoline futures prices rallied early in the year to a high of $1.47 per gallon in May, which was a record high going back to the beginning of futures trading in 1984. Gasoline prices range-traded until late in the year when prices sank back to close the year at $1.09 per gallon. The average monthly retail price of regular unleaded gasoline in 2004 (through October) rose +17.4% yr/yr to $1.87 per gallon, which was a record high. The average monthly retail price of unleaded premium motor gasoline in the US in 2004 (through October) rose by +15.5% to $2.05 per gallon, which was a new record high. The average monthly refiner price of finished aviation gasoline to end users in 2004 (through September) rose by +25.8% yr/yr to a record high of $1.88 per gallon.

Supply – US production of gasoline in 2004 (through November, annualized) rose +2.1% yr/yr to 8.678 million barrels per day, which was a new record high. Gasoline stocks in September 2004 were 135.9 million barrels, down from 144.8 million barrels in September 2003 and 157.4 million barrels in 2002.

Demand – US consumption of finished motor gasoline in 2004 (through November, annualized) rose +1.3% yr/yr to 9.054 million barrels per day, which was a new record high.

Average Spot Price of Unleaded Gasoline in New York   In Cents Per Gallon

Year	Jan.	Feb.	Mar.	Apr.	May	June	July	Aug.	Sept.	Oct.	Nov.	Dec.	Average
1995	50.99	51.43	50.74	61.01	64.76	59.47	51.45	53.45	56.10	48.89	51.15	53.44	54.41
1996	50.70	53.26	58.56	69.17	65.10	58.03	61.65	61.17	62.43	65.52	69.23	68.58	61.95
1997	67.64	62.49	61.28	58.59	62.08	55.17	58.58	70.42	62.17	58.35	55.60	51.75	60.34
1998	47.85	45.14	44.13	46.98	48.26	43.95	42.29	40.14	42.70	43.71	36.78	30.92	42.74
1999	34.24	31.81	42.33	50.11	48.86	48.65	58.35	63.89	69.37	62.63	69.57	70.55	54.20
2000	70.43	81.30	89.11	73.15	89.06	96.18	86.76	86.97	96.04	94.71	93.94	73.66	85.94
2001	83.32	82.56	78.18	94.95	92.37	71.85	68.31	77.18	75.00	59.79	51.34	51.85	73.89
2002	54.30	55.41	69.64	74.66	70.32	71.65	76.62	76.75	78.36	82.34	76.08	80.56	72.22
2003	87.56	99.62	95.51	80.08	76.16	80.65	87.17	100.42	90.41	87.12	87.33	88.37	88.37
2004	99.66	104.63	109.12	112.02	133.98	115.70	122.65	120.89	126.17	137.75	126.96	106.90	118.04

Source: Energy Information Administration, U.S. Department of Energy (EIA-DOE)

Average Open Interest of Unleaded Regular Gasoline Futures in New York   In Contracts

Year	Jan.	Feb.	Mar.	Apr.	May	June	July	Aug.	Sept.	Oct.	Nov.	Dec.
1995	61,015	67,631	65,201	76,323	76,269	69,676	64,379	58,426	62,089	58,782	57,902	70,098
1996	64,561	64,990	70,100	71,895	66,172	52,882	55,394	55,618	57,119	59,993	58,416	62,760
1997	68,188	84,693	92,520	97,619	90,407	78,492	83,082	103,538	103,250	94,602	92,852	103,497
1998	106,353	102,656	108,667	117,521	107,235	100,792	89,846	86,902	85,188	81,991	87,306	103,079
1999	105,532	113,683	111,449	110,531	107,644	102,927	113,619	120,468	120,328	111,758	109,428	96,652
2000	89,049	103,586	105,448	105,133	103,831	96,772	80,886	66,598	74,735	80,446	88,509	92,041
2001	117,540	126,762	124,631	124,162	111,576	103,058	101,249	92,156	87,841	102,414	115,699	126,634
2002	136,795	139,191	133,649	129,274	120,224	114,663	106,463	94,648	95,754	100,427	105,175	109,737
2003	117,558	124,288	113,380	98,627	96,405	93,285	95,433	99,394	85,457	90,007	95,002	105,919
2004	125,207	141,837	150,573	146,375	148,782	138,248	140,691	146,532	147,088	150,643	138,280	153,907

Source: New York Mercantile Exchange (NYMEX)

GASOLINE

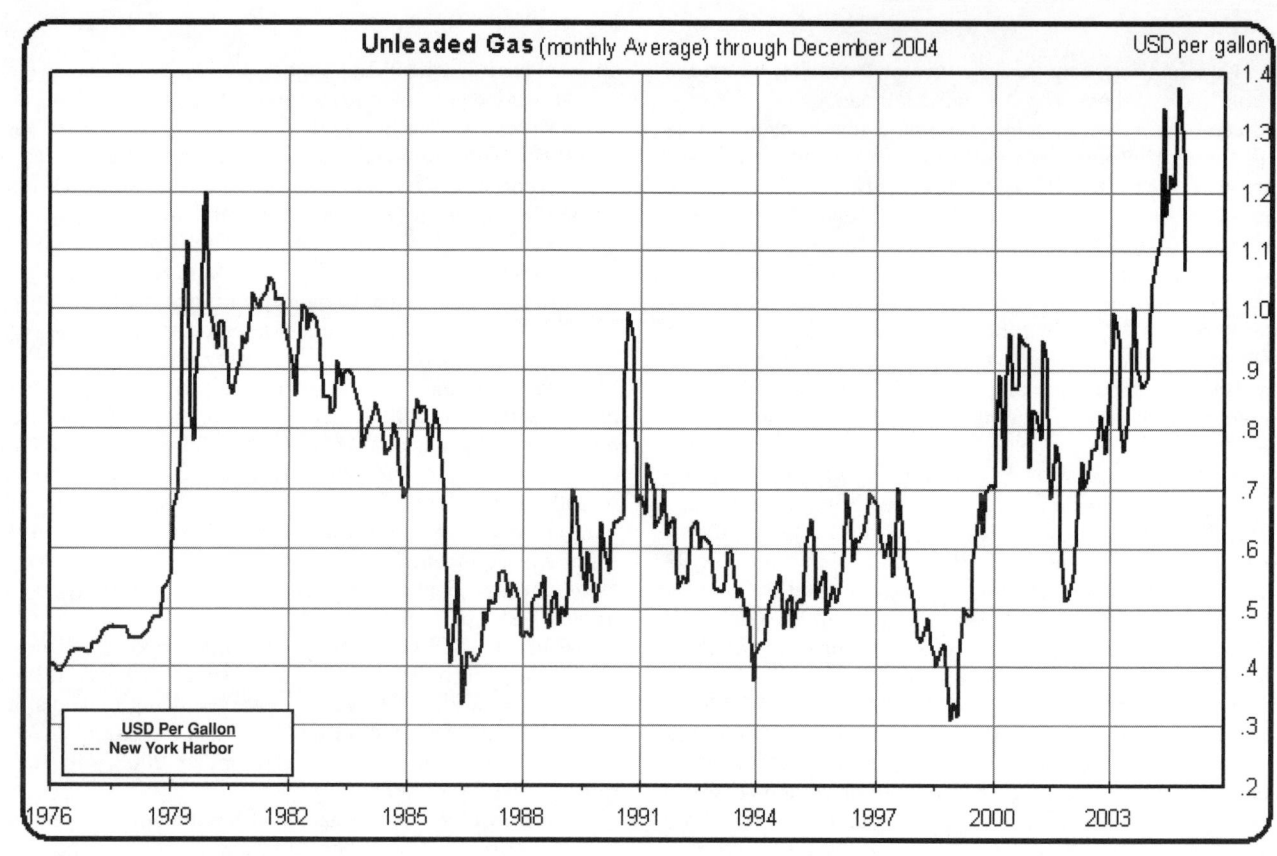

Unleaded Gas (monthly Average) through December 2004 — USD per gallon

USD Per Gallon
----- New York Harbor

Volume of Trading of Unleaded Regular Gasoline Futures in New York   In Thousands of Contracts

Year	Jan.	Feb.	Mar.	Apr.	May	June	July	Aug.	Sept.	Oct.	Nov.	Dec.	Total
1995	592.3	506.6	736.7	663.7	780.6	680.8	565.7	556.6	573.6	473.0	480.5	461.7	7,071.8
1996	543.8	449.5	570.3	676.2	623.3	468.0	533.8	463.8	469.0	527.6	487.6	499.3	6,312.3
1997	590.1	563.2	605.1	623.2	618.3	555.5	721.4	795.4	664.9	613.6	509.9	614.6	7,475.1
1998	613.6	612.3	766.4	789.3	681.1	753.1	680.6	592.0	654.2	670.2	577.8	601.7	7,992.3
1999	561.5	619.7	876.4	741.5	721.1	737.7	822.0	800.4	751.3	705.1	748.8	615.7	8,701.2
2000	693.6	721.9	921.6	730.0	927.5	838.5	650.6	677.2	641.2	635.7	612.1	595.1	8,645.2
2001	825.2	701.2	809.2	981.0	1,056.5	895.0	737.3	790.8	581.9	664.9	613.3	567.2	9,223.5
2002	795.0	744.7	942.7	1,019.3	985.2	834.5	967.8	893.6	867.6	1,105.0	865.9	958.4	10,979.7
2003	1,054.1	968.7	1,010.9	909.0	933.7	944.0	987.5	1,021.5	943.0	877.1	760.8	761.6	11,172.1
2004	956.1	998.7	1,169.2	1,169.0	1,203.8	1,194.5	1,027.0	1,177.7	1,052.9	983.7	849.0	995.9	12,777.5

Source: New York Mercantile Exchange (NYMEX)

Production of Finished Motor Gasoline in the United States   In Thousand Barrels per Day

Year	Jan.	Feb.	Mar.	Apr.	May	June	July	Aug.	Sept.	Oct.	Nov.	Dec.	Average
1995	7,303	7,243	7,168	7,529	7,678	7,843	7,747	7,642	7,785	7,544	7,739	7,821	7,588
1996	7,333	7,303	7,242	7,475	7,724	7,820	7,811	7,696	7,585	7,496	7,835	7,784	7,647
1997	7,308	7,315	7,322	7,822	8,056	8,180	7,947	8,048	8,147	8,039	7,984	8,143	7,870
1998	7,749	7,485	7,591	8,029	8,057	8,372	8,287	8,200	8,029	7,995	8,263	8,395	8,082
1999	7,886	7,607	7,531	8,138	8,207	8,402	8,280	8,183	8,187	8,266	8,142	8,471	8,111
2000	7,798	7,658	8,032	8,130	8,398	8,550	8,320	8,251	8,358	8,031	8,394	8,298	8,186
2001	7,888	7,822	8,011	8,450	8,651	8,637	8,481	8,277	8,381	8,446	8,366	8,301	8,312
2002	8,160	8,117	8,072	8,626	8,729	8,661	8,665	8,666	8,320	8,190	8,738	8,734	8,475
2003	7,991	8,023	7,942	8,470	8,702	8,723	8,663	8,774	8,556	8,613	8,771	8,756	8,501
2004[1]	8,339	8,282	8,429	8,820	8,932	8,903	8,801	8,828	8,482	8,783	8,744	8,982	8,694

[1] Preliminary.   *Source: Energy Information Administration, U.S. Department of Energy (EIA-DOE)*

Disposition of Finished Motor Gasoline, Total Product Supplied in the U.S.   In Thousand Barrels per Day

Year	Jan.	Feb.	Mar.	Apr.	May	June	July	Aug.	Sept.	Oct.	Nov.	Dec.	Average
1995	7,163	7,481	7,788	7,651	7,894	8,220	7,888	8,187	7,786	7,781	7,866	7,742	7,789
1996	7,254	7,552	7,729	7,869	7,998	8,089	8,135	8,216	7,641	8,038	7,875	7,775	7,891
1997	7,312	7,651	7,808	8,067	8,128	8,260	8,471	8,195	8,004	8,166	7,955	8,093	8,017
1998	7,590	7,755	7,956	8,137	8,070	8,437	8,659	8,500	8,308	8,405	8,136	8,401	8,253
1999	7,701	8,031	8,128	8,506	8,420	8,886	8,942	8,579	8,305	8,542	8,240	8,859	8,431
2000	7,653	8,291	8,305	8,375	8,661	8,824	8,642	8,921	8,518	8,417	8,384	8,670	8,472
2001	8,099	8,234	8,532	8,575	8,706	8,690	9,023	8,953	8,557	8,655	8,677	8,585	8,610
2002	8,227	8,607	8,655	8,766	9,078	9,140	9,143	9,313	8,687	8,814	8,829	8,893	8,848
2003	8,414	8,525	8,602	8,838	9,042	9,170	9,192	9,411	8,926	9,108	8,946	9,011	8,935
2004[1]	8,680	8,743	8,922	9,067	9,178	9,237	9,243	9,244	9,030	9,103	9,070	9,219	9,061

[1] Preliminary.   *Source: Energy Information Administration, U.S. Department of Energy (EIA-DOE)*

Stocks of Finished Gasoline[2] on Hand in the United States, at End of Month   In Millions of Barrels

Year	Jan.	Feb.	Mar.	Apr.	May	June	July	Aug.	Sept.	Oct.	Nov.	Dec.
1995	182.7	180.0	167.8	167.1	167.1	163.5	166.0	154.6	158.9	155.6	155.6	161.3
1996	168.7	168.4	158.3	159.8	161.8	163.8	163.7	154.9	161.3	149.1	150.7	157.0
1997	164.9	161.3	153.8	152.0	157.8	163.9	150.6	149.6	158.1	158.0	161.1	166.1
1998	175.3	172.8	166.4	168.3	174.9	177.7	172.5	168.8	164.7	160.0	167.5	172.0
1999	185.2	178.4	167.8	168.9	176.5	172.3	163.6	158.6	159.2	158.8	160.5	151.6
2000	165.3	156.4	157.1	160.6	162.2	164.5	164.6	151.0	154.2	147.4	156.7	153.0
2001	158.7	154.6	144.7	150.3	160.1	169.4	162.3	150.6	158.0	160.2	161.2	161.5
2002	169.7	165.5	159.8	167.0	168.3	167.6	164.8	157.3	157.4	148.2	158.0	161.9
2003	158.4	152.1	145.0	151.9	156.1	153.4	149.6	144.7	144.8	140.3	145.9	146.8
2004[1]	142.9	136.8	132.9	134.1	137.7	140.8	141.8	139.8	135.9	138.0	141.3	143.1

[1] Preliminary.   [2] Includes oxygenated and other finished.   *Source: Energy Information Administration, U.S. Department of Energy (EIA-DOE)*

Average Refiner Price of Finished Motor Gasoline to End Users[1] in the U.S.   In Cents Per Gallon

Year	Jan.	Feb.	Mar.	Apr.	May	June	July	Aug.	Sept.	Oct.	Nov.	Dec.	Average
1995	74.5	73.3	73.1	77.3	83.4	83.9	80.0	76.9	75.8	73.6	71.8	73.0	76.5
1996	74.6	74.8	79.8	88.1	92.7	90.3	87.5	84.9	84.4	84.4	86.7	85.9	84.7
1997	86.6	86.1	84.3	83.9	84.5	83.3	81.5	86.8	87.2	84.3	81.6	77.8	83.9
1998	73.3	69.0	65.6	67.4	71.0	70.4	69.4	66.7	65.4	66.4	64.0	60.0	67.3
1999	59.2	56.8	65.1	79.0	78.2	75.6	80.6	86.5	88.8	87.1	88.4	90.3	78.1
2000	91.7	98.7	113.1	108.7	110.3	121.3	117.3	110.3	117.5	115.5	113.5	106.3	110.6
2001	106.8	106.7	103.9	117.7	130.1	120.7	103.2	102.5	1,009.2	89.9	76.9	68.5	103.2
2002	70.6	71.8	87.2	100.4	99.9	99.1	100.3	100.1	100.1	104.0	101.2	98.1	94.7
2003	106.0	122.1	130.0	120.1	110.0	109.3	110.6	123.1	126.5	115.0	109.5	106.5	115.7
2004[2]	117.3	125.6	133.8	139.6	157.1	154.7	148.6	145.4	145.2	158.6	155.3		143.7

[1] Excludes aviation and taxes.   [2] Preliminary.   *Source: Energy Information Administration, U.S. Department of Energy (EIA-DOE)*

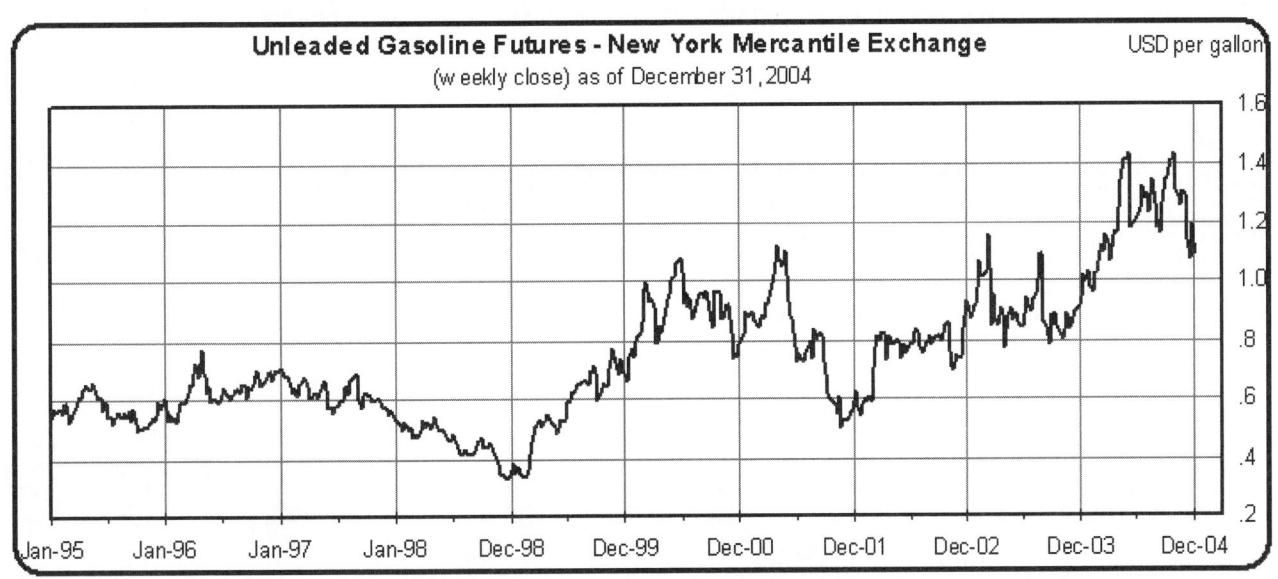

Unleaded Gasoline Futures - New York Mercantile Exchange   USD per gallon
(weekly close) as of December 31, 2004

GASOLINE

Average Retail Price of Unleaded Premium Motor Gasoline[2] in the United States   In Cents per Gallon

Year	Jan.	Feb.	Mar.	Apr.	May	June	July	Aug.	Sept.	Oct.	Nov.	Dec.	Average
1995	132.4	131.6	130.6	132.5	138.3	141.1	138.4	135.2	133.2	131.5	129.2	129.0	133.6
1996	131.7	131.1	134.8	143.1	150.7	148.1	145.3	142.1	141.7	140.8	142.8	143.8	141.3
1997	144.1	143.4	141.5	141.3	140.9	141.1	138.8	143.3	145.8	142.6	139.7	136.3	141.6
1998	131.9	127.1	122.9	123.7	127.5	127.9	126.8	124.4	123.0	123.6	122.5	118.7	125.0
1999	117.1	115.5	118.6	136.7	137.0	133.9	137.8	144.1	146.8	146.4	145.4	148.6	135.7
2000	148.6	155.1	172.3	169.8	168.2	178.6	177.3	168.9	176.4	174.4	173.8	167.9	169.3
2001	165.7	167.1	163.8	174.8	193.4	188.1	169.5	163.6	172.6	156.0	142.7	131.2	165.7
2002	132.3	133.0	145.0	162.2	162.5	160.8	160.7	162.0	161.9	164.3	164.3	158.9	157.8
2003	166.6	182.8	192.4	184.6	172.9	170.0	171.0	180.8	191.1	178.9	172.4	168.6	177.7
2004[1]	177.9	185.8	194.9	201.2	218.6	222.5	213.0	209.1	208.2	221.5	220.3	208.0	206.8

[1] Preliminary.   [2] Including taxes.   *Source: Energy Information Administration, U.S. Department of Energy (EIA-DOE)*

Average Retail Price of Unleaded Regular Motor Gasoline[2] in the United States   In Cents per Gallon

Year	Jan.	Feb.	Mar.	Apr.	May	June	July	Aug.	Sept.	Oct.	Nov.	Dec.	Average
1995	112.9	112.0	111.5	114.0	120.0	122.6	119.5	116.4	114.8	112.7	110.1	110.1	114.7
1996	112.9	112.4	116.2	125.1	132.3	129.9	127.2	124.0	123.4	122.7	125.0	126.0	123.1
1997	126.1	125.5	123.5	123.1	122.6	122.9	120.5	125.3	127.7	124.2	121.3	117.7	123.4
1998	113.1	108.2	104.1	105.2	109.2	109.4	107.9	105.2	103.3	104.2	102.8	98.6	105.9
1999	97.2	95.5	99.1	117.7	117.8	114.8	118.9	125.5	128.0	127.4	126.4	129.8	116.5
2000	130.1	136.9	154.1	150.6	149.8	161.7	159.3	151.0	158.2	155.9	155.5	148.9	151.0
2001	147.2	148.4	144.7	156.4	172.9	164.0	148.2	142.7	153.1	136.2	126.3	113.1	146.1
2002	113.9	113.0	124.1	140.7	142.1	140.4	141.2	142.3	142.2	144.9	144.8	139.4	135.8
2003	147.3	164.1	174.8	165.9	154.2	151.4	152.4	162.8	172.8	160.3	153.5	149.4	159.1
2004[1]	159.2	167.2	176.6	183.3	200.9	204.1	193.9	189.8	189.1	202.9	201.0	188.2	188.0

[1] Preliminary.   [2] Including taxes.   *Source: Energy Information Administration, U.S. Department of Energy (EIA-DOE)*

Average Retail Price of All-Types[2] Motor Gasoline[3] in the United States   In Cents per Gallon

Year	Jan.	Feb.	Mar.	Apr.	May	June	July	Aug.	Sept.	Oct.	Nov.	Dec.	Average
1995	119.0	118.1	117.3	119.7	125.6	128.1	125.2	122.2	120.6	118.5	116.1	116.0	120.5
1996	118.6	118.1	121.9	130.5	137.8	135.4	132.8	129.8	129.3	128.7	130.8	131.8	128.8
1997	131.8	131.2	129.3	128.8	128.4	128.6	126.3	131.0	133.4	130.0	127.1	123.6	129.1
1998	118.6	113.7	109.7	110.6	114.6	114.8	113.4	110.8	109.1	109.9	108.6	104.6	111.5
1999	103.1	101.4	104.8	123.2	123.3	120.4	124.4	130.9	133.4	132.9	131.9	135.3	122.1
2000	135.6	142.2	159.4	156.1	155.2	166.6	164.2	155.9	163.5	161.3	160.8	154.4	156.3
2001	152.5	153.8	150.3	161.7	181.2	173.1	156.5	150.9	160.9	144.2	132.4	120.0	153.1
2002	120.9	121.0	132.4	149.3	150.8	148.9	149.6	150.8	150.7	153.5	153.4	147.7	144.1
2003	155.7	168.6	179.1	170.4	158.7	155.8	156.7	167.1	177.1	164.6	157.8	153.8	163.8
2004[1]	163.5	171.5	180.9	187.5	205.0	208.3	198.2	194.1	193.4	207.2	205.3	192.6	192.3

[1] Preliminary.   [2] Also includes types of motor oil not shown separately.   [3] Including taxes.   *Source: Energy Information Administration, U.S. Department of Energy (EIA-DOE)*

Average Refiner Price of Finished Aviation Gasoline to End Users[2] in the U.S.   In Cents per Gallon

Year	Jan.	Feb.	Mar.	Apr.	May	June	July	Aug.	Sept.	Oct.	Nov.	Dec.	Average
1995	99.6	99.8	99.0	101.3	105.8	106.4	101.8	99.2	101.3	96.8	95.4	96.0	100.5
1996	97.6	100.6	105.0	111.2	114.4	113.5	113.7	114.4	114.3	115.0	115.1	115.3	111.6
1997	113.7	114.9	113.8	114.7	115.7	114.6	112.5	114.6	115.6	113.9	113.0	107.7	113.8
1998	104.3	101.1	98.2	98.6	99.9	99.0	98.4	95.9	94.1	95.1	93.2	88.5	97.2
1999	87.1	85.1	90.1	101.4	104.2	104.1	107.9	113.2	115.4	117.6	116.4	119.6	105.9
2000	118.7	119.5	129.1	124.3	126.8	139.8	142.6	NA	138.2	134.9	134.9	126.1	130.6
2001	128.5	129.2	124.5	134.9	150.9	145.1	134.6	136.3	142.4	125.3	119.4	115.8	132.3
2002	111.8	110.6	122.6	129.8	128.9	127.3	139.2	136.9	139.1	143.0	141.8	139.8	128.8
2003	139.7	W	W	W	139.8	145.1	151.9	162.2	158.9	150.8	W	146.6	149.4
2004[1]	W	W	W	177.4	194.9	193.2	187.0	185.8	189.2	W	W		187.9

[1] Preliminary.   [2] Excluding taxes.   W = Withheld.   *Source: Energy Information Administration, U.S. Department Energy (EIA-DOE)*

110

Gold

Gold is a dense, bright yellow metallic element with a high luster. Gold is an inactive substance and is unaffected by air, heat, moisture, and most solvents. Gold has been coveted for centuries for its unique blend of rarity, beauty, and near indestructibility. The Egyptians mined gold before 2,000 BC. The first known, pure gold coin was made on the orders of King Croesus of Lydia in the sixth century BC.

Gold is found in nature in quartz veins and secondary alluvial deposits as a free metal. Gold is produced from mines on every continent with the exception of Antarctica, where mining is forbidden. Because it is virtually indestructible, much of the gold that has ever been mined still exists above ground in one form or another. The largest producer of gold in the US by far is the state of Nevada, with Alaska and California running a distant second and third.

Gold is a vital industrial commodity. Pure gold is one of the most malleable and ductile of all the metals. It is a good conductor of heat and electricity. Gold melts at 1,064 degrees Celsius and boils at about 2,808 degrees Celsius. The prime industrial use of gold is in electronics. Another important sector is dental gold where it has been used for almost 3,000 years. Other applications for gold include decorative gold leaf, reflective glass, and jewelry.

In 1792, the United States first assigned a formal monetary role for gold when Congress put the nation's currency on a bimetallic standard, backing it with gold and silver. Under the gold standard, the US government was willing to exchange its paper currency for a set amount of gold, meaning the paper currency was backed by a physical asset with real value. However, President Nixon in 1971 severed the convertibility between the US dollar and gold, which led to the breakdown of the Bretton Woods international payments system. Since then, the prices of gold and of paper currencies have floated freely. US and other central banks now hold physical gold reserves primarily as a store of wealth.

Gold futures and options are traded at the New York Mercantile Exchange. Gold futures are traded on the Bolsa de Mercadorias and Futuros (BM&F) and on the Tokyo Commodity Exchange (TOCOM), the Chicago Board of Trade (CBOT) and the Korea Futures Exchange (KOFEX). The Nymex gold futures contract calls for the delivery of 100 troy ounces of gold (0.995 fineness), and the contract trades in terms of dollars and cents per troy ounce.

Prices – Nymex gold futures prices in 2004 extended the rally that began in 2001 and posted a new 16-year high of $456.50 in December 2004. That entire rally was driven primarily by the plunge in the dollar. Gold showed a very strong negative daily correlation of –0.92 with the dollar index in 2004, showing that when the dollar falls, gold rises, and vice versa. When the dollar falls in value relative to other currencies and real assets, the price of gold rises when quoted in terms of the weaker dollar. Gold was also driven higher in 2004 by the relatively strong US and global economy, which drove industrial and jewelry demand for gold.

Supply – World mine production of gold rose +0.4% yr/yr to 2.590 million kilograms in 2003, which was just below the record high of 2.600 million kilograms in 2001 (1 kilogram = 32.1507 troy ounces). The world's largest producers of gold are South Africa with 15% of world production in 2003, followed by Australia (11%), the US (11%), China (8%), Russia (7%), and Canada (5%). US gold mine production fell by –7.0% yr/yr in 2003 to 277,000 kilograms, which was the lowest production level since 1989. US refinery production of gold in 2003 rose by +0.5% yr/yr to 197,000 kilograms from domestic and foreign ore sources, and rose by +18.7% yr/yr to 92,700 kilograms from secondary scrap sources.

World monetary institutions and central banks holdings of gold fell by 3.52 million troy ounces to 909.58 million troy ounces in 2004 from 2003. The 2004 holdings equate to roughly $364 billion worth of gold, assuming a gold price of $400 per ounce. The amount of gold held by world monetary institutions and central banks has steadily fallen in the past 6 years and is near a post-war low as some of these institutions have sold gold to raise cash and reduce expensive storage costs.

Demand – US consumption of gold in 2003 rose +22.7% yr/yr to 200,000 kilograms, which was a 4-year high. The most recent data available from the early 1990's showed that 71% of gold demand came from jewelry and the arts, 22% from industrial uses, and 7% from dental uses.

Trade – US exports of gold in 2003 (excluding coinage) rose by +37.0% yr/yr to 352,000 kilograms. US imports of gold in 2003 for consumption rose +14.7% yr/yr to 240,000 kilograms, which was a 5-year high.

World Mine Production of Gold   In Kilograms (1 Kilogram = 32.1507 Troy Ounces)

Year	Australia	Brazil	Canada	Chile	China	Ghana	Indonesia	Papua N. Guinea	Russia	South Africa	United States	Uzbekistan	World Total
1994	256,188	72,397	146,428	38,786	132,000	43,478	42,600	59,286	146,600	580,201	327,000	65,000	2,250,000
1995	253,504	64,424	152,032	44,585	140,000	53,087	64,031	53,405	132,170	523,809	317,000	65,000	2,230,000
1996	289,530	60,011	166,378	53,174	145,000	49,211	83,564	51,119	123,300	496,846	326,000	72,000	2,290,000
1997	314,500	58,488	171,479	49,459	175,000	54,662	86,927	45,418	124,000	491,680	362,000	81,700	2,450,000
1998	310,070	49,567	165,599	44,980	178,000	72,541	124,018	61,641	114,900	465,100	366,000	80,000	2,500,000
1999	301,070	52,634	157,617	48,069	173,000	79,946	127,184	65,747	125,870	451,300	341,000	85,000	2,570,000
2000	296,410	50,393	156,207	54,143	180,000	72,100	124,596	74,540	143,000	430,800	353,000	85,000	2,590,000
2001	285,030	51,867	158,875	42,673	185,000	68,341	166,091	67,043	152,500	394,800	335,000	87,000	2,600,000
2002[1]	273,010	47,886	151,504	38,688	192,000	69,271	142,238	65,200	168,411	395,173	298,000	90,000	2,580,000
2003[2]	282,000	48,000	140,559	40,000	202,000	69,600	140,000	64,000	170,068	375,787	277,000	90,000	2,590,000

[1] Preliminary.   [2] Estimate.   *Source: U.S. Geological Survey (USGS)*

GOLD

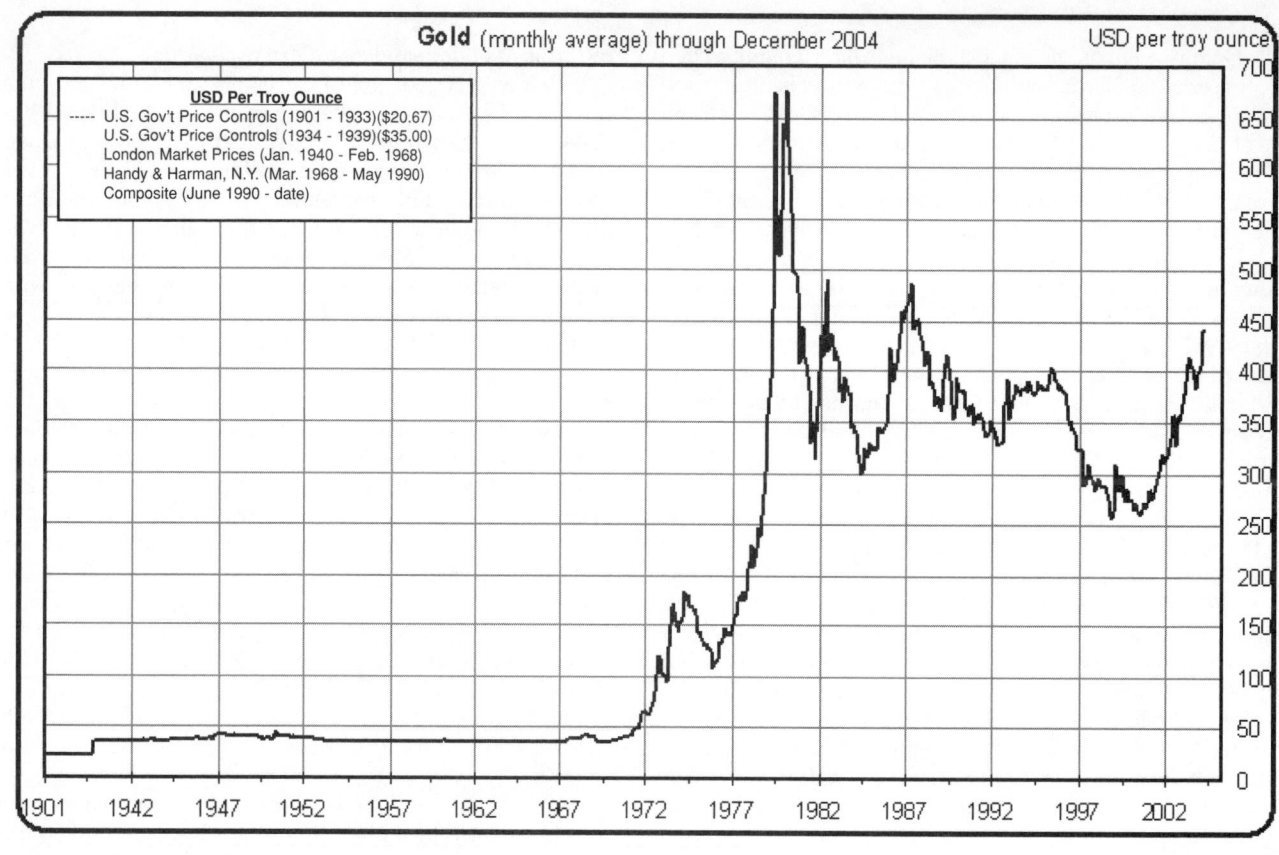

Gold (monthly average) through December 2004 — USD per troy ounce

USD Per Troy Ounce
----- U.S. Gov't Price Controls (1901 - 1933)($20.67)
U.S. Gov't Price Controls (1934 - 1939)($35.00)
London Market Prices (Jan. 1940 - Feb. 1968)
Handy & Harman, N.Y. (Mar. 1968 - May 1990)
Composite (June 1990 - date)

Salient Statistics of Gold in the United States   In Kilograms (1 Kilogram = 32.1507 Troy Ounces)

Year	Mine Production	Value Million $	Refinery Production Domestic & Foreign Ores	Secondary (Old Scrap)	Exports (Excluding Coinage)	Imports for Consumption	Stocks, Dec. 31 Treasury Department[3]	Futures Exchange	Industry	Official World Reserves[4]	Dental	Consumption Industrial[5]	Jewelry & Arts	Total
1994	327,000	4,050.0	241,000	148,000	471,000	114,000	8,142,000	49,100	32,700	34,800	5,430	17,013	53,700	76,100
1995	317,000	3,950.0	NA	NA	347,000	126,000	8,140,000	45,400	NA	34,600	NA	NA	NA	NA
1996	326,000	4,090.0	NA	NA	471,000	159,000	8,140,000	20,700	NA	34,400	NA	NA	NA	NA
1997	362,000	3,870.0	270,000	100,000	476,000	209,000	8,140,000	15,200	17,300	34,000	NA	NA	NA	137,000
1998	366,000	3,480.0	277,000	163,000	522,000	278,000	8,130,000	25,200	16,600	33,600	NA	NA	NA	219,000
1999	341,000	3,070.0	265,000	143,000	523,000	221,000	8,170,000	37,900	14,700	33,500	NA	NA	NA	245,000
2000	353,000	3,180.0	197,000	81,600	547,000	223,000	8,140,000	52,900	9,300	33,000	NA	NA	NA	183,000
2001	335,000	2,940.0	191,000	82,700	489,000	194,000	8,120,000	38,000	3,700	33,000	NA	NA	NA	179,000
2002[1]	298,000	2,980.0	196,000	78,100	257,000	217,000	8,140,000	63,900	3,500	32,200	NA	NA	NA	163,000
2003[2]	277,000	3,250.0	197,000	92,700	352,000	249,000	8,140,000	97,100	5,600	31,800	NA	NA	NA	200,000

[1] Preliminary.   [2] Estimate.   [3] Includes gold in Exchange Stabilization Fund.   [4] Held by market economy country central banks and governments andinternational monetary orgainzations.   [5] Including space and defense.   NA = Not available.   *Source: U.S. Geological Survey (USGS)*

Monthly Average Gold Price (Handy & Harman) in New York   In Dollars Per Troy Ounce

Year	Jan.	Feb.	Mar.	Apr.	May	June	July	Aug.	Sept.	Oct.	Nov.	Dec.	Average
1995	378.55	376.51	382.12	391.11	385.46	387.56	386.40	383.63	382.22	383.14	385.53	387.42	384.22
1996	399.59	404.73	396.21	392.96	391.98	385.58	383.69	387.43	382.97	381.07	378.46	369.02	387.81
1997	355.10	346.71	351.67	344.47	343.75	340.75	324.08	324.03	322.74	324.87	307.10	288.65	331.16
1998	289.18	297.49	295.90	308.40	299.39	292.31	292.79	283.76	289.01	295.92	293.89	291.29	294.12
1999	287.05	287.22	285.96	282.45	276.94	261.31	255.81	256.56	265.23	310.72	292.74	283.69	278.81
2000	284.26	299.60	286.39	279.75	275.10	285.73	281.01	274.44	273.53	270.00	266.05	271.68	278.96
2001	265.58	261.99	263.03	260.56	272.07	270.23	267.53	272.40	283.78	283.06	276.49	275.98	271.06
2002	281.47	295.40	294.06	302.68	314.08	321.81	313.51	310.18	319.49	316.56	319.14	333.21	310.13
2003	356.91	359.60	340.55	328.25	355.03	356.35	351.01	359.91	379.07	378.92	389.13	407.44	363.51
2004[1]	414.09	404.52	405.99	403.96	383.94	392.73	398.08	400.86	405.45	420.46	438.21	442.20	409.21

[1] Preliminary.   *Source: U.S. Geological Survey (USGS)*

Gold Futures - New York Mercantile Exchange
(weekly close) as of December 31, 2004

Average Open Interest of Gold in New York (NYMEX) In Thousands of Contracts

Year	Jan.	Feb.	Mar.	Apr.	May	June	July	Aug.	Sept.	Oct.	Nov.	Dec.
1995	184,549	170,972	168,651	191,667	173,805	174,075	175,727	176,135	185,128	185,854	170,674	141,751
1996	210,695	226,160	203,968	201,826	203,056	192,423	185,374	159,435	185,907	192,606	187,145	185,994
1997	199,710	190,524	167,595	157,176	160,512	170,640	207,352	198,099	201,267	188,365	212,757	188,558
1998	180,994	171,507	183,358	180,267	158,157	172,250	169,180	192,623	183,351	186,680	164,304	153,063
1999	179,726	185,345	178,456	198,202	193,978	207,122	205,687	193,023	206,186	216,034	189,433	156,754
2000	149,606	158,026	160,325	155,188	162,516	144,099	133,087	126,893	132,731	132,546	134,630	113,830
2001	134,401	142,673	126,558	120,111	118,426	116,788	114,098	116,687	125,907	125,639	114,238	111,622
2002	124,222	142,763	142,638	159,892	190,845	174,123	166,042	146,596	167,620	162,456	164,581	191,594
2003	221,495	210,247	186,656	176,033	191,459	198,808	199,741	224,694	284,906	258,238	275,346	277,183
2004	283,813	238,816	256,873	274,898	250,963	225,001	239,579	237,940	259,181	306,522	344,665	329,669

Source: New York Mercantile Exchange (NYMEX), COMEX division

Volume of Trading of Gold Futures in New York (NYMEX) In Thousands of Contracts

Year	Jan.	Feb.	Mar.	Apr.	May	June	July	Aug.	Sept.	Oct.	Nov.	Dec.	Total
1995	881.9	420.0	1,087.5	613.0	777.0	588.1	669.9	500.5	495.5	387.7	982.5	378.1	7,781.6
1996	1,384.7	987.5	943.6	647.1	858.5	582.1	749.8	541.9	541.9	528.5	795.2	458.8	8,694.5
1997	1,102.8	830.2	899.4	508.5	762.1	522.7	1,147.5	667.8	715.8	988.0	808.8	588.1	9,541.9
1998	1,078.2	534.2	877.2	698.1	845.2	718.7	712.4	680.0	851.7	769.6	705.6	519.0	8,990.1
1999	860.8	517.4	1,147.6	561.1	1,069.6	573.6	964.3	709.6	1,067.3	993.8	674.7	436.1	9,575.8
2000	616.4	833.5	767.7	362.2	701.5	625.5	532.5	374.4	403.2	424.9	625.7	349.0	6,643.5
2001	755.2	483.3	766.6	438.1	971.6	481.4	578.3	547.4	341.0	481.4	573.6	367.4	6,785.3
2002	733.6	613.2	717.7	559.8	1,089.6	775.5	998.9	585.8	621.8	669.0	844.8	808.5	9,018.2
2003	1,260.1	1,007.5	987.6	667.8	1,160.3	824.3	1,191.7	837.5	1,034.0	1,091.3	1,397.3	776.3	12,235.5
2004	1,581.3	962.6	1,649.5	1,202.9	1,344.8	960.6	1,405.0	953.0	944.9	1,067.2	1,864.7	1,053.2	14,989.6

Source: New York Mercantile Exchange (NYMEX), COMEX division

GOLD

Commodity Exchange, Inc. (COMEX) Depository Warehouse Stocks of Gold   In Thousands of Troy Ounces

Year	Jan. 1	Feb. 1	Mar. 1	Apr. 1	May 1	June 1	July 1	Aug. 1	Sept. 1	Oct. 1	Nov. 1	Dec. 1
1995	1,577.4	1,498.4	1,386.5	1,360.2	1,391.3	1,487.7	1,504.7	1,607.7	1,448.0	1,745.0	1,394.9	1,315.1
1996	1,459.8	1,868.5	1,412.0	1,428.7	1,335.4	1,710.6	1,263.0	1,273.0	1,401.5	1,283.3	1,060.0	1,103.7
1997	665.8	837.1	582.9	1,000.1	946.0	878.2	850.2	914.0	733.1	894.4	614.7	760.8
1998	488.4	445.9	480.9	719.8	658.5	1,077.3	1,054.7	1,092.3	911.3	958.4	827.1	819.3
1999	809.5	809.1	859.7	1,034.0	895.9	879.3	818.3	936.1	1,198.2	928.0	874.4	1,137.4
2000	1,219.4	1,392.9	1,373.9	1,968.1	1,966.7	1,900.6	1,890.1	2,012.6	1,961.1	1,918.1	1,865.5	1,863.6
2001	1,701.2	1,775.3	1,653.7	1,302.4	858.3	864.2	891.3	901.1	793.6	824.3	1,164.6	1,425.7
2002	1,220.3	1,186.7	1,285.7	1,322.3	1,372.3	1,764.1	1,850.7	1,835.6	1,915.0	1,892.4	1,994.9	2,046.5
2003	2,056.5	2,159.8	2,262.4	2,383.9	2,460.7	2,474.9	2,675.1	2,743.8	2,729.4	2,822.6	2,912.1	3,058.9
2004	3,122.2	3,324.0	3,476.9	3,677.1	4,142.0	4,391.8	4,399.6	4,657.0	4,880.1	5,122.4	5,334.7	5,374.3

Source: New York Mercantile Exchange (NYMEX), COMEX division

Central Gold Bank Reserves   In Millions of Troy Ounces

Year	Belgium	Canada	France	Germany	Italy	Japan	Netherlands	Switzerland	United Kingdom	United States	Industrial Total	Developing Oil	Developing Non-Oil	IMF[2]	Bank for Int'l Settlements	World Total
1992	25.0	9.9	81.9	95.2	66.7	24.2	43.9	83.3	18.6	261.8	877.4	42.0	100.3	103.4	6.8	1,129.9
1993	25.0	6.1	81.9	95.2	66.7	24.2	35.1	83.3	18.5	261.8	860.4	42.4	108.1	103.4	8.6	1,123.0
1994	25.0	3.9	81.9	95.2	66.7	24.2	34.8	83.3	18.4	261.7	856.9	42.4	106.6	103.4	7.0	1,116.2
1995	20.5	3.4	81.9	95.2	66.7	24.2	34.8	83.3	18.4	261.7	848.7	41.9	111.9	103.4	7.3	1,113.2
1996	15.3	3.1	81.9	95.2	66.7	24.2	34.8	83.3	18.4	261.7	840.1	42.5	115.5	103.4	6.6	1,108.2
1997	15.3	3.1	81.9	95.2	66.7	24.2	27.1	83.3	18.4	261.6	821.9	42.3	115.8	103.4	6.2	1,089.7
1998	9.5	2.5	102.4	119.0	83.4	24.2	33.8	83.3	23.0	261.6	809.0	41.6	115.7	103.4	6.4	1,076.1
1999	8.3	1.8	97.2	111.5	78.8	24.2	31.6	83.3	20.6	261.7	810.4	41.2	112.9	103.4	6.5	1,074.5
2000	8.3	1.2	97.3	111.5	78.8	24.6	29.3	78.8	16.5	261.6	796.5	41.6	112.0	103.4	6.5	1,060.1
2001[1]	8.0	1.2	97.0	112.0	79.0	24.6	29.0	74.6	13.4	261.6	791.3	42.3	111.3	103.4	6.5	1,054.7

[1] Preliminary.   [2] International Monetary Fund.   *Source: American Metal Market (AMM)*

Mine Production of Recoverable Gold in the United States   In Kilograms

Year	Arizona	California	Idaho	Montana	Nevada	Alaska	Colorado	South Dakota	New Mexico	Utah	Other States	Total
1994	2,050	30,100	3,610	12,600	214,000	5,660	4,420	W	W	W	33,560	306,000
1995	1,920	25,600	8,850	12,400	210,000	4,410	W	W	W	W	53,820	317,000
1996	1,740	23,800	7,410	9,110	213,000	5,020	W	W	W	W	57,920	318,000
1997	2,140	24,200	7,490	10,200	243,000	18,400	W	16,400	W	W	40,170	362,000
1998	1,840	18,700	W	8,200	273,000	18,300	W	12,100	W	W	33,860	366,000
1999	786	17,500	W	7,540	9,310	16,200	W	10,300	W	W	279,364	341,000
2000	442	17,200	W	9,310	268,000	15,600	W	8,230	W	W	34,218	353,000
2001	W	13,800	W	W	253,000	16,700	W	W	W	W	51,500	335,000
2002	W	9,180	W	W	240,000	W	W	W	W	W	48,820	298,000
2003[1]	W	4,270	W	W	227,000	W	W	W	W	W	45,730	277,000

[1] Preliminary.   W = Withheld proprietary data, included in Other States.   *Source: U.S. Geological Survey (USGS)*

Consumption of Gold, By End-Use in the United States   In Kilograms

	Jewelry and the Arts					Industrial				
Year	Gold-Filled & Other	Electro-plating	Karat Gold	Total	Dental	Gold-Filled & Other	Electro-plating	Karat Gold	Total	Grand Total
1987	9,256	3,133	58,635	71,024	6,944	21,010	12,343	1,892	35,245	113,319
1988	7,598	1,469	57,959	67,027	7,576	21,034	15,088	1,104	37,226	111,836
1989	7,364	1,283	60,877	69,524	7,927	15,723	20,684	1,215	37,621	115,078
1990	8,132	429	69,952	78,514	8,700	12,725	17,251	1,020	30,996	118,216
1991	3,848	373	79,875	84,096	8,485	8,102	12,624	1,068	21,793	114,375
1992	3,546	581	79,381	83,508	6,543	8,802	10,476	1,082	20,360	110,410
1993	3,530	373	61,700	65,600	6,170	9,470	9,090	1,100	19,700	91,400
1994[1]	3,650	369	49,700	53,700	5,430	7,450	9,470	96	17,000	76,100
1995[1]	NA	NA	NA	NA	NA	NA	NA	NA	NA	NA
1996[1]	NA	NA	NA	NA	NA	NA	NA	NA	NA	NA

[1] Preliminary.   *Source: U.S. Geological Survey (USGS)*

114

Gold in British Pound (weekly close) as of December 31, 2004   GBP per troy ounce

Gold in Euro (weekly close) as of December 31, 2004   EUR per troy ounce

Gold in Japanese Yen (weekly close) as of December 31, 2004   JPY per troy ounce

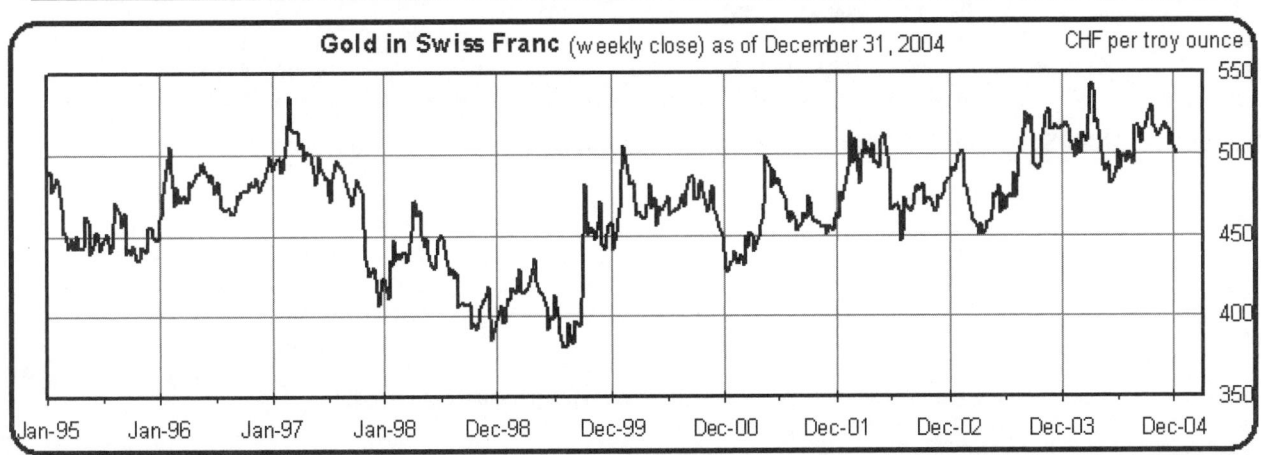

Gold in Swiss Franc (weekly close) as of December 31, 2004   CHF per troy ounce

Grain Sorghum

Grain sorghums include milo, kafir, durra, feterita, and kaoliang. Grain sorghums are tolerant of drought by going into dormancy during dry and hot conditions and then resuming growth as conditions improve. Grain sorghums are a staple food in China, India, and Africa but in the US they are mainly used as livestock feed. The two key US producing states are Texas and Kansas, each with about one-third of total US production. US sorghum production has become more popular with the breeding of dwarf grain sorghum hybrids which are only about 3 feet tall (versus up to 10 feet tall for wild sorghum) and are easier to harvest with a combine. The U.S. sorghum crop year begins September 1.

Prices – The monthly average price for sorghum grain received by US farmers in the 2003-04 marketing year (Sep-Aug) rose by +9.0% yr/yr to $4.42 per hundred pounds, which was an 8-year high going back to the record high of $5.70 posted in 1995-96. However, sorghum prices in the first four months of the 2004-05 marketing year (i.e., Sep-Dec 2004) fell sharply–27.9% to an average $3.19 per hundred pounds. The value of US grain sorghum production in 2003-04 was $966 million.

Supply – World production of sorghum in the 2003-04 marketing year rose by +5.2% to 54.720 million metric tons,

recovering from the 52.027 million metric ton crop in 2002-03, which was the smallest crop since 1968-69. US grain sorghum production in 2004-05 rose sharply by +14.7% yr/yr to 471.572 million bushels, which was a 3-year high. Sorghum acreage harvested in 2004-05 fell -15.9% to 6.559 million acres, which was the smallest sorghum acreage harvested since the 1950s. Yield was excellent in 2004-05 with 71.9 bushels per acre, which was the highest since 1994-95.

Demand – World utilization (consumption) of grain sorghum in the 2003-04 marketing year rose +0.7% to 54.022 million metric tons, recovering from the 53.638 million metric ton utilization level seen in 2002-03, which was the lowest since 1967-68.

Trade – World exports of sorghum in the 2003-04 marketing year rose +8.7% to 6.355 million metric tons, recovering from 5.849 million metric tons posted in 2002-03, which was the lowest since 1971-72. US exports in 2003-04 rose by +13.1% yr/yr to 5.334 million metric tons, and accounted for 84% of total world exports. Argentina is the world's other major exporter with 500 million metric tons of exports in 2003-04, accounting for 8% of world exports. Major world importers are Mexico with 49% of world imports and Japan with 24% of world imports.

World Supply and Demand Grain Sorghum   In Thousands of Metric Tons

Year	Argentina	Non-U.S.	U.S.	Total	Japan	Mexico	Unaccounted	Total	Total Production	China	Mexico	U.S.	Total	Non-U.S.	U.S.	Total
	Exports				Imports				Production	Utilization				Ending Stocks		
1999-00	920	1,660	6,484	8,144	2,206	4,890	54	8,144	59,044	3,319	11,200	8,628	60,364	3,225	1,661	4,886
2000-1	439	1,607	6,009	7,616	1,983	5,037	57	7,616	53,377	2,561	11,200	6,543	54,642	2,687	1,061	3,748
2001-2	419	980	6,142	7,122	1,776	4,837	202	7,033	57,958	2,700	10,750	6,427	56,922	3,235	1,549	4,784
2002-3[1]	639	1,028	4,681	5,709	1,562	3,384	36	5,510	52,570	2,825	9,900	4,939	53,501	2,760	1,093	3,853
2003-4[2]	200	1,431	5,093	6,524	1,434	3,026	13	6,568	57,950	2,950	9,800	5,594	56,996	3,955	852	4,807
2004-5[3]	400	1,105	4,445	5,550	1,400	3,500	145	5,410	56,478	2,800	10,300	6,477	56,181	3,619	1,485	5,104

[1] Preliminary.   [2] Estimate.   [3] Forecast.   *Source: Foreign Agricultural Service, U.S. Department of Agriculture (FAS-USDA)*

Salient Statistics of Grain Sorghum in the United States

Year	Acreage Planted[4] for All Purposes 1,000 Acres	Acreage Harvested 1,000 Acres	Production 1,000 Bushels	Yield Per Harvested Acre Bushels	Price in Cents Per Bushel	Value of Production Million $	Acreage Harvested 1,000 Acres	Production 1,000 Tons	Yield Per Harvested Acre	On Farms	Off Farms	On Farms	Off Farms
			For Grain				For Silage			Sorghum Grain Stocks			
										Dec. 1		June 1	
										1,000 Bushels			
1999-00	9,288	8,544	595,166	69.7	157	937.4	320	3,716	11.6	90,300	259,136	27,300	99,606
2000-1	9,195	7,726	470,526	60.9	189	847.1	278	2,932	10.5	74,300	187,681	19,000	57,411
2001-2	10,252	8,584	514,524	59.9	194	979.8	336	3,728	11.1	72,400	241,477	17,300	88,178
2002-3[1]	9,589	7,125	360,713	50.6	232	855.1	408	3,913	9.6	53,600	178,252	11,150	70,744
2003-4[2]	9,420	7,798	411,237	52.7	239	965.0	343	3,552	10.4	45,200	190,736	7,650	72,944
2004-5[3]	7,486	6,517	454,899	69.8	150-190	839.2	352	4,763	13.5	78,700	203,182		

[1] Preliminary.   [2] Estimate.   [3] Forecast.   NA = Not available.   *Source: Economic Research Service, U.S. Department of Agriculture (ERS-USDA)*

Production of All Sorghum for Grain in the United States, by States   In Thousands of Bushels

Year	Arkansas	Colorado	Illinois	Kansas	Louisiana	Mississippi	Missouri	Nebraska	New Mexico	Oklahoma	South Dakota	Texas	Total
1998	6,890	10,545	7,918	264,000	7,500	2,340	26,560	56,400	2,925	15,300	9,940	105,800	519,933
1999	9,750	8,610	9,215	258,400	19,270	4,872	22,010	42,770	7,425	18,000	4,640	185,850	595,166
2000	9,940	6,720	8,075	188,800	17,845	6,708	24,840	35,000	1,625	13,680	5,880	143,350	470,070
2001	14,620	9,460	8,085	232,500	17,850	7,134	20,680	35,700	6,300	15,120	8,850	130,000	514,524
2002	17,710	1,800	6,391	135,000	13,365	6,237	15,725	15,000	2,800	14,850	3,060	130,050	369,758
2003[1]	17,220	4,320	8,610	130,500	14,025	6,132	16,170	31,000	1,674	9,250	6,750	153,900	411,237

[1] Preliminary.   *Source: National Agricultural Statistics Service, U.S. Department of Agriculture (NASS-USDA)*

Grain Sorghum Quarterly Supply and Disappearance in the United States   In Millions of Bushels

Crop Year Beginning Sept. 1	Supply				Disappearance — Domestic Use						Ending Stocks		
	Beginning Stocks	Production	Imports	Total Supply	Food Alcohol & Industrial	Seed	Feed & Residual	Total	Export	Total	Gov't Owned[3]	Privately Owned[4]	Total Stocks
2001-2	42.0	515.0	0	556.0	45.0	0	208.0	495.0	242.0	737.0			61.0
Sept.-Nov.	42.0	515.0	0	556.0	15.0	0	164.0	242.0	63.0	305.0			314.0
Dec.-Feb.	314.0	----	0	314.0	15.0		26.0	120.0	78.0	198.0			194.0
Mar.-May	194.0	----	0	194.0	10.0		26.0	89.0	53.0	142.0			105.0
June-Aug.	105.0	----	0	105.0	5.0		-8.0	45.0	47.0	92.0			61.0
2002-3	61.0	361.0	0	422.0	24.0		170.0	379.0	184.0	563.0			43.0
Sept.-Nov.	61.0	361.0	0	422.0	5.0		134.0	190.0	51.0	241.0			232.0
Dec.-Feb.	232.0	----	0	232.0	5.0		18.0	69.0	46.0	115.0			163.0
Mar.-May	163.0	----	0	163.0	8.0		33.0	81.0	40.0	121.0			82.0
June-Aug.	82.0	----	0	82.0	6.0		-14.0	39.0	48.0	87.0			43.0
2003-4[1]	43.0	411.0	0	454.0	20.0		200.0	421.0	201.0	622.0			34.0
Sept.-Nov.	43.0	411.0	0	454.0	7.0		151.0	218.0	61.0	279.0			236.0
Dec.-Feb.	236.0	----	0	236.0	6.0		14.0	77.0	57.0	134.0			159.0
Mar.-May	159.0	----	0	159.0	7.0		25.0	78.0	47.0	125.0			81.0
June-Aug.	81.0	----	0	81.0	1.0		11.0	47.0	36.0	83.0			34.0
2004-5[2]	34.0	455.0	0	488.0	50.0		205.0	430.0	175.0	605.0			58.0
Sept.-Nov.	34.0	455.0	0	488.0	17.0		145.0	207.0	44.0	251.0			282.0

[1] Preliminary.   [2] Forecast.   [3] Uncommitted inventory.   [4] Includes quantity under loan & farmer-owned reserve.   *Source: Economic Research Service, U.S. Department of Agriculture (ERS-USDA)*

Average Price of Sorghum Grain, No. 2, Yellow in Kansas City   In Dollars Per Hundred Pounds (Cwt.)

Year	Sept.	Oct.	Nov.	Dec.	Jan.	Feb.	Mar.	Apr.	May	June	July	Aug.	Average
1997-8	4.13	4.36	4.30	4.26	4.33	4.36	4.40	4.10	4.09	4.03	4.03	3.74	4.18
1998-9	2.98	3.17	3.45	3.41	3.41	3.43	3.48	3.37	3.35	3.32	2.92	2.92	3.30
1999-00	2.97	2.71	2.75	2.87	3.20	3.28	3.51	3.53	3.75	3.18	2.71	2.76	3.10
2000-1	2.67	3.14	3.41	3.66	3.64	3.63	3.56	3.45	3.30	3.26	3.59	3.65	3.41
2001-2	3.55	3.38	3.44	3.59	3.61	3.55	3.58	3.47	3.44	3.57	3.97	4.60	3.65
2002-3	4.86	4.70	4.72	4.62	4.52	4.43	4.07	4.24	4.12	4.06	3.71	3.71	4.31
2003-4	4.15	4.18	4.50	4.61	4.71	4.88	5.18	5.37	4.94	4.67	3.92	3.75	4.57
2004-5[1]	3.45	3.21	3.17	3.21	3.13								3.23

[1] Preliminary.   *Source: Economic Research Service, U.S. Department of Agriculture (ERS-USDA)*

Exports of Grain Sorghum, by Country of Destination from the United States   In Metric Tons

Year Beginning Oct. 1	Canada	Ecuador	Ethiopia	Israel	Japan	Jordan	Mexico	South Africa	Spain	Sudan	Turkey	World Total
1997-8	5,076	0	49,999	82,583	1,451,123	0	3,287,628	0	203,896	0	94	5,164,844
1998-9	3,484	0	0	92,335	1,480,220	0	3,290,663	0	196,110	0	101	5,194,028
1999-00	4,061	0	21,940	167,816	1,045,253	0	4,773,760	12,857	178,829	0	0	6,297,344
2000-1	4,170	0	24,117	82,776	853,211	0	4,864,414	0	0	0	0	5,866,340
2001-2	4,912	0	0	25,082	1,233,799	0	4,695,814	37,272	8,193	0	0	6,014,304
2002-3[1]	5,921	91	48,000	65,725	1,059,424	0	3,150,014	43,918	266,892	5,880	0	4,690,875
2003-4[2]	7,956	210	54,320	105,170	882,028	0	2,837,863	156	267,691	11,430	0	4,663,210

[1] Preliminary.   [2] Estimate.   *Source: Economic Research Service, U.S. Department of Agriculture (ERS-USDA)*

Grain Sorghum Price Support Program and Market Prices in the United States

Year	Price Support Operations									No. 2 Yellow ($ Per Cwt.)			
	Price Support		Aquired by CCC	Owned by CCC at Year End	Basic Loan Rate	Target Price	Findley Loan Rate	Effective Base[3] Million Acres	Partici-pation Rate[4] % of Base	Kansas City	Texas High Plains	Los Angeles	Gulf Ports
	Quantity	% of Production											
	Million Cwt.				$ Per Bushel								
1996-7	11.4	2.6	----	----	[5]	NA	1.81	13.2	98.8	4.55	5.02	----	5.03
1997-8	9.8	2.8	.1	.1	[5]	NA	1.76	13.1	98.8	4.11	4.72	----	4.76
1998-9	12.0	4.1	.6	.2	[5]	NA	1.74	13.6	98.8	3.29	3.78	----	3.97
1999-00	9.6	2.9	1.0	----	[5]	NA	1.74	13.7	98.8	3.10	3.36	----	3.79
2000-1	8.6	3.3	.4	----	[5]	NA	1.71	13.6		3.41	3.94	----	4.22
2001-2[1]	9.6	3.3	.1	.1	[5]	NA	1.71	13.6		3.65	4.05	----	4.34
2002-3[2]	3.7	1.8	0	0	[5]	2.54	1.98	12.1		4.34	3.52	----	3.76

[1] Preliminary.   [2] Estimate.   [3] National effective crop acreage base as determined by ASCS.   [4] Percentage of effective base acres enrolled in acreage reduction programs.   [5] Beginning with the 1996-7 marketing year, target prices are no longer applicable.   Source: Economic Research Service, U.S. Department of Agriculture (ERS-USDA)

Hay

Hay is a catchall term for forage plants, typically grasses such as timothy and Sudan-grass, and legumes such as alfalfa and clover. Alfalfa and alfalfa mixtures account for nearly half of all hay production. Hay is generally used to make cured feed for livestock. Curing, which is the proper drying of hay, is necessary to prevent spoilage. Hay, when properly cured, contains about 20% moisture. If hay is dried excessively, however, there is a loss of protein, which makes it less effective as livestock feed. Hay is harvested in virtually all of the lower 48 states.

Prices – The average monthly price of hay received by US farmers rose by +5.8% yr/yr to $90.55 per ton in the first eight months of the 2004-05 marketing year (i.e., May 2004 through December 2004). The record high is $100.00 posted in 1997-98. The farm production value of hay produced in 2003-04 was $12.331 million.

Supply – US hay production in 2004-05 rose +5.6% yr/yr to 165.9 million tons, which was a record high. US farmers harvested 61.589 million acres of hay in 2004-05, down −2.8% yr/yr. The yield in 2004-05 was 2.69 tons per acre, which was a record high. US carryover (May 1) in 2004-05 rose +17.5% to 25.9 million tons.

The largest hay producing states in the US are Texas (with 7.9% of US hay production in 2003), California (5.9%), Missouri (5.2%), Nebraska (4.8%), South Dakota (4.6%), Iowa (3.5%), Minnesota (3.3%), Oklahoma (3.2%) and Idaho (3.2%).

Salient Statistics of All Hay in the United States

Crop Year Beginning May 1	Acres Harvested 1,000 Acres	Yield Per Acre Tons	Production	Carryover May 1	Disappearance	Supply Per Animal Unit	Disappearance Per Animal Unit	Animal Units Fed[3] Millions	Farm Price $ Per Ton	Farm Production Value Million $	Alfalfa (Certified)	Timothy	Red Clover	Sudan-Grass
			---- Millions of Tons ----			---- In Tons ----					---- Dollars Per Cwt. ----			
1999-00	63,220	2.53	159.7	24.8	155.7	2.52	2.12	73.3	76.9	11,014	287.00	78.80	178.00	52.20
2000-1	59,854	2.54	151.9	28.8	159.6	2.49	2.20	72.5	84.6	11,417	277.00	115.00	143.00	53.00
2001-2	63,521	2.47	156.8	21.1	155.4	2.46	2.15	72.2	96.5	12,597	278.00	105.00	132.00	53.00
2002-3	63,942	2.34	149.5	22.5	151.3	2.41	2.10	72.0	93.7	12,338	280.00	90.00	130.00	56.00
2003-4[1]	63,383	2.49	157.6	22.0	NA	2.54	NA	70.7	85.8	12,007	286.00	107.00	144.00	55.30
2004-5[2]	61,916	2.55	157.8	25.9					89.3	12,197	157.00	90.00	130.00	56.00

Retail Price Paid by Farmers for Seed, April 15

[1] Preliminary. [2] Estimate. [3] Roughage-consuming animal units fed annually. NA = Not available. *Source: Economic Research Service, U.S. Department of Agriculture (ERS-USDA)*

Production of All Hay in the United States, by States   In Thousands of Tons

Year	California	Idaho	Iowa	Minnesota	Missouri	New York	North Dakota	Ohio	Oklahoma	South Dakota	Texas	Wisconsin	Total
1999	8,782	5,132	5,970	7,130	7,225	7,700	5,511	3,060	5,000	9,440	13,135	7,510	159,707
2000	8,568	5,292	6,000	6,840	6,657	6,055	5,110	4,521	4,659	7,393	8,880	6,000	151,921
2001	8,915	4,938	5,565	6,195	7,853	7,578	5,065	4,275	4,025	9,150	10,837	4,790	156,764
2002	9,774	5,288	5,645	5,810	8,323	5,750	3,920	3,400	5,985	4,815	13,410	5,340	149,467
2003	9,485	4,950	5,515	5,245	8,122	7,600	4,598	3,974	5,304	7,210	12,388	4,380	157,585
2004[1]	9,000	5,350	6,240	5,895	9,420	6,143	3,666	3,232	6,030	6,870	12,295	4,880	157,774

[1] Preliminary. *Source: Agricultural Statistics Board, U.S. Department of Agriculture (ASB-USDA)*

Hay Production and Farm Stocks in the United States   In Thousands of Short Tons

Year	Alfalfa & Mixtures	All Others	All Hay	Corn for Silage[1]	Sorghum Silage[1]	Farm Stocks May 1	Farm Stocks Dec. 1
1999	84,385	75,322	159,707	95,633	3,716	24,662	109,115
2000	80,347	71,574	151,921	102,156	2,773	28,848	106,412
2001	80,327	76,437	156,764	102,077	3,728	21,106	110,384
2002	83,014	76,453	149,467	102,293	3,913	22,458	102,978
2003	76,276	81,312	157,585	107,378	3,552	22,013	111,027
2004[2]	75,383	82,391	157,774	107,336	4,763	25,947	114,294

[1] Not included in all tame hay. [2] Preliminary. *Source: Agricultural Statistics Board, U.S. Department of Agriculture (ASB-USDA)*

Mid-Month Price Received by Farmers for All Hay (Baled) in the United States   In Dollars Per Ton

Year	May	June	July	Aug.	Sept.	Oct.	Nov.	Dec.	Jan.	Feb.	Mar.	Apr.	Average[2]
1999-00	91.6	81.7	78.4	77.4	74.5	73.7	74.0	71.1	71.8	72.6	74.8	78.2	76.7
2000-1	91.0	82.5	80.2	80.5	83.0	84.9	84.0	84.9	85.2	86.8	87.2	94.8	85.4
2001-2	106.0	95.8	96.3	97.4	99.0	98.0	95.9	95.6	91.7	91.7	92.3	98.3	96.5
2002-3	103.0	95.8	93.6	92.4	93.0	93.8	93.2	91.1	91.4	91.4	92.8	92.9	93.7
2003-4	98.0	94.6	89.0	85.0	84.4	83.7	81.5	80.6	80.1	81.2	81.8	89.6	85.8
2004-5[1]	101.0	95.2	90.4	89.8	87.7	89.8	86.2	84.3	84.2	84.7			89.3

[1] Preliminary. [2] Marketing year average. *Source: Economic Research Service, U.S. Department of Agriculture (ERS-USDA)*

Heating Oil

Heating oil is a heavy fuel oil that is derived from crude oil. Heating oil is also known as No. 2 fuel oil and accounts for about 25% of the yield from a barrel of crude oil. That is the second largest "cut" after gasoline. The price to consumers of home heating oil is generally comprised of 42% for crude oil, 12% for refining costs, and 46% for marketing and distribution costs (Source: EIA's Petroleum Marketing Monthly, 2001). Generally, a $1 increase in the price of crude oil translates into a 2.5-cent per gallon rise in heating oil. Because of this, heating oil prices are highly correlated with crude oil prices, although heating oil prices are also subject to swift supply and demand shifts due to weather changes or refinery shutdowns.

The primary use for heating oil is for residential heating. In the US, approximately 8.1 million households use heating oil as their main heating fuel. Most of the demand for heating oil occurs from October through March. The Northeast region, which includes the New England and the Central Atlantic States, is most reliant on heating oil. This region consumes approximately 70% of US heating oil. However, demand for heating oil has been dropping as households switch to a more convenient heating source like natural gas. In fact, demand for heating oil is down by about 10 billion gallons/year from its peak use in 1976 (Source: American Petroleum Institute).

Refineries produce approximately 85% of US heating oil as part of the "distillate fuel oil" product family, which includes heating oil and diesel fuel. The remainder of US heating oil is imported from Canada, the Virgin Islands, and Venezuela.

Recently, a team of Purdue University researchers developed a way to make home heating oil from a mixture of soybean oil and conventional fuel oil. The oil blend is made by replacing 20% of the fuel oil with soybean oil, potentially saving 1.3 billion gallons of fuel oil per year. This soybean heating oil can be used in conventional furnaces without altering existing equipment. The soybean heating oil is relatively easy to produce and creates no sulfur emissions.

The "crack-spread" is the processing margin earned when refiners buy crude oil and refine it into heating oil and gasoline. The crack-spread ratio commonly used in the industry is the 3-2-1, which involves buying 1 heating oil contract and 2 gasoline futures contracts, and then selling 3 crude oil contracts. As long as the crack spread is positive, it is profitable for refiners to buy crude oil and refine it into products. The NYMEX has a crack-spread calculator on their web site at www.NYMEX.com.

Heating oil futures and options trade at the New York Mercantile Exchange (NYMEX). The heating oil futures contract calls for the delivery of 1,000 barrels of fungible No. 2 heating oil in the New York harbor. In London, gas/oil futures and options are traded on the International Petroleum Exchange (IPE).

Prices – NYMEX heating oil futures prices on the nearest-futures chart started the year around $1 per gallon but steadily rallied and posted a new record high of $1.6030 in October. Heating oil prices then backed off to close the year at $1.23.

Supply – US production of distillate fuel oil in 2004 (through November, annualized) rose by +2.3% yr/yr to 3.792 million barrels per day, which was a record high. Stocks of distillate fuel oil in October 2004, the latest reporting month, were 123.0 million barrels, down from 130.9 million barrels in October 2003. US production of residual fuel in 2004 (through November, annualized) fell by −2.4% yr/yr to 644,000 barrels per day, and was less than half the production levels of over 1 million barrels per day produced in the 1970s. US stocks of residual fuel oil as of July 2004 rose to 37.5 million barrels from 35.3 million barrels a year earlier.

Demand – US usage of distillate fuel oil in 2004 (through November, annualized) rose +3.3% yr/yr to 4.056 million barrels per day, which was a new record high. That figure includes both heating oil and diesel fuel usage.

Trade – US imports of distillate fuel oil in 2004 (through November, annualized) fell -4.0% to 320,000 barrels per day from the 3-decade high of 333,000 barrels per day seen in 2003. US exports of distillate fuel oil in 2004 (through November, annualized) fell by −3.0% yr/yr to 104,000 barrels per day, which was the lowest level since 97,000 barrels per day in 1989. US imports of residual fuel oil in 2003 rose +31.3% yr/yr to 327,000 barrels per day, which was less than a third of the levels above 1 million barrels per day seen back in the 1970s. US exports of residual fuel oil in 2003 rose +11.3% to 197,000 barrels per day, which was moderately below the record high of 226,000 barrels per day seen in 1991.

Average Price of #2 Heating Oil — In Cents Per Gallon

Year	Jan.	Feb.	Mar.	Apr.	May	June	July	Aug.	Sept.	Oct.	Nov.	Dec.	Average
1995	47.98	47.64	45.95	49.40	50.31	47.75	46.65	49.14	50.21	48.89	51.89	57.76	49.46
1996	55.64	61.24	65.19	67.90	57.59	51.56	55.58	60.42	67.61	72.34	70.13	72.13	63.11
1997	69.90	61.15	54.83	57.74	56.31	52.32	53.11	54.02	53.19	57.24	56.23	51.09	56.43
1998	46.59	44.26	42.12	42.97	41.07	37.88	36.24	34.48	40.15	38.29	35.59	31.38	39.25
1999	33.41	30.48	38.74	43.07	41.68	43.36	50.02	54.81	60.27	58.34	64.89	67.36	48.87
2000	91.32	94.37	77.29	75.32	75.88	78.32	78.14	89.13	98.87	97.46	102.70	94.08	87.74
2001	84.30	78.55	74.17	78.02	77.11	75.74	69.88	73.41	71.65	62.63	54.37	52.60	71.04
2002	53.52	54.03	63.52	66.60	66.54	64.50	67.79	69.81	77.25	76.55	72.14	81.70	67.83
2003	90.09	112.84	99.70	79.75	74.31	75.95	79.03	81.61	73.54	81.97	83.35	89.04	85.10
2004	97.91	91.19	90.88	91.87	101.65	99.41	109.42	116.86	125.73	148.55	138.16	127.32	111.58

Source: Energy Information Administration, U.S. Department of Energy (EIA-DOE)

HEATING OIL

Heating Oil Futures - New York Mercantile Exchange
(weekly close) as of December 31, 2004
USD per gallon

Average Open Interest of #2 Heating Oil Futures in New York   In Contracts

Year	Jan.	Feb.	Mar.	Apr.	May	June	July	Aug.	Sept.	Oct.	Nov.	Dec.
1995	128,664	112,508	118,700	121,974	115,501	122,163	136,722	140,214	149,934	152,244	139,232	138,596
1996	114,324	95,745	90,080	94,161	98,038	97,699	109,524	119,366	138,513	141,217	127,512	108,558
1997	100,333	105,223	122,149	139,981	135,523	141,864	151,403	149,243	151,407	141,008	126,528	145,153
1998	171,177	163,114	177,158	174,587	176,663	196,903	205,071	198,527	188,096	188,019	192,835	184,100
1999	167,686	160,388	166,472	172,127	170,842	168,307	182,383	188,726	192,883	179,040	165,334	146,997
2000	135,431	132,407	108,646	100,389	117,055	129,872	153,914	169,092	177,997	168,388	155,475	142,145
2001	138,980	127,219	120,899	127,395	130,328	141,436	149,577	145,605	145,692	155,540	162,392	153,850
2002	166,824	173,110	160,205	144,936	139,979	136,201	131,742	141,084	147,692	153,739	161,137	156,268
2003	178,932	174,224	134,616	111,706	118,822	124,675	127,273	146,821	150,893	156,142	145,857	145,555
2004	153,794	145,924	161,945	174,618	176,784	167,331	193,291	206,099	197,783	188,843	176,298	163,629

Source: New York Mercantile Exchange (NYMEX)

Volume of Trading of #2 Heating Oil Futures in New York   In Thousand of Contracts

Year	Jan.	Feb.	Mar.	Apr.	May	June	July	Aug.	Sept.	Oct.	Nov.	Dec.	Total
1995	779.8	608.7	716.0	622.8	729.8	618.8	612.7	563.6	714.2	650.8	659.5	990.1	8,266.8
1996	977.2	768.1	666.2	586.5	530.9	402.0	530.2	624.4	766.5	1,014.2	725.0	750.7	8,341.9
1997	794.4	719.0	588.6	710.1	592.0	679.4	679.6	694.7	828.3	742.7	619.3	722.9	8,371.0
1998	793.6	641.8	776.4	578.4	688.5	904.9	720.2	683.0	748.2	768.2	766.5	793.9	8,863.8
1999	738.9	662.3	973.3	706.3	768.1	802.7	770.4	707.9	720.1	819.6	818.6	712.7	9,200.7
2000	914.0	770.3	645.2	556.1	673.3	705.9	663.0	1,004.4	954.9	878.1	939.0	927.3	9,631.4
2001	914.4	650.7	758.0	728.6	722.8	849.9	712.9	745.8	694.0	853.8	835.5	798.1	9,264.5
2002	998.5	810.8	885.5	844.1	789.8	720.1	798.8	866.0	794.4	1,017.9	1,039.5	1,129.9	10,695.2
2003	1,340.1	1,158.9	965.9	757.7	811.6	802.9	849.9	891.3	1,118.5	1,095.5	817.3	971.8	11,581.7
2004	1,153.8	1,059.7	1,139.9	1,007.8	910.0	1,100.5	920.7	1,105.7	1,060.8	1,148.6	1,112.7	1,164.4	12,884.5

Source: New York Mercantile Exchange (NYMEX)

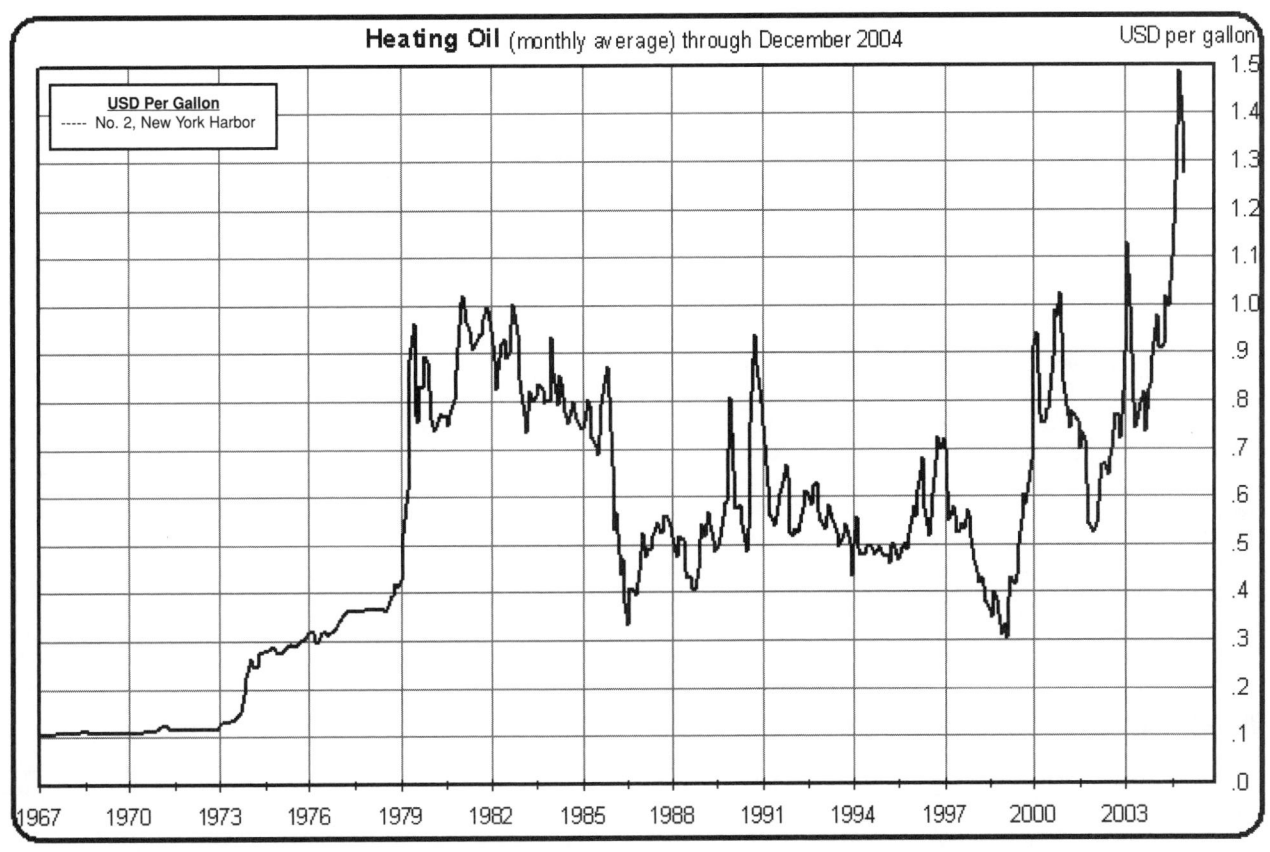

Stocks of Distillate and Residual Fuel in the United States, on First of Month   In Millions of Barrels

Year	Jan.	Feb.	Mar.	Apr.	May	June	July	Aug.	Sept.	Oct.	Nov.	Dec.	Residual Fuel ----- Oil Stocks ----- Jan. 1	July 1
1995	145.2	140.2	122.1	115.4	114.6	118.3	114.7	125.0	130.9	131.7	131.4	135.4	41.9	36.0
1996	130.2	113.8	97.3	89.7	90.1	95.7	101.6	106.8	110.3	115.0	114.7	121.8	36.8	34.8
1997	126.7	111.3	105.9	101.8	97.5	108.4	118.2	123.0	132.9	138.9	136.2	140.5	45.9	39.2
1998	139.0	133.1	127.9	124.4	125.7	136.8	139.1	148.8	150.5	152.5	147.5	154.6	40.4	39.8
1999	156.2	147.9	142.3	125.7	125.3	134.8	133.2	138.1	142.0	145.2	137.6	140.6	44.9	42.5
2000	124.1	106.7	105.2	96.0	100.1	105.4	106.4	112.9	111.0	115.3	116.5	121.1	35.8	37.0
2001	118.0	118.2	117.0	105.0	104.9	107.1	113.9	125.2	122.0	127.0	128.9	138.9	36.2	41.7
2002	144.5	137.8	130.0	123.0	122.6	127.4	130.9	133.4	130.6	126.9	121.4	124.4	41.0	32.7
2003	134.1	112.2	97.2	98.5	97.1	106.1	111.8	117.7	126.4	130.9	131.4	137.2	31.3	35.3
2004[1]	136.8	122.5	111.3	104.0	101.4	106.9	114.0	121.4	130.5	123.0	117.9	122.9	37.8	37.5

[1] Preliminary.   *Source: Energy Information Administration; U.S. Department of Energy (EIA-DOE)*

Production of Distillate Fuel Oil in the United States   In Thousand Barrels per Day

Year	Jan.	Feb.	Mar.	Apr.	May	June	July	Aug.	Sept.	Oct.	Nov.	Dec.	Average
1995	3,054	2,954	3,157	3,126	3,111	3,109	3,056	3,145	3,287	3,169	3,341	3,344	3,155
1996	3,110	3,145	3,110	3,305	3,258	3,291	3,139	3,295	3,403	3,626	3,665	3,558	3,325
1997	3,119	3,089	3,258	3,291	3,525	3,517	3,362	3,427	3,452	3,488	3,543	3,578	3,389
1998	3,323	3,280	3,397	3,468	3,560	3,520	3,569	3,482	3,399	3,215	3,438	3,431	3,424
1999	3,176	3,253	3,183	3,407	3,458	3,374	3,521	3,419	3,482	3,506	3,608	3,401	3,399
2000	3,123	3,348	3,342	3,533	3,650	3,481	3,520	3,678	3,844	3,774	3,785	3,872	3,580
2001	3,609	3,612	3,483	3,650	3,652	3,702	3,837	3,654	3,625	3,796	3,968	3,744	3,695
2002	3,508	3,498	3,360	3,647	3,709	3,679	3,561	3,538	3,536	3,380	3,768	3,922	3,592
2003	3,403	3,459	3,732	3,796	3,833	3,728	3,673	3,730	3,721	3,750	3,800	3,845	3,707
2004[1]	3,599	3,467	3,558	3,881	3,858	3,957	3,902	3,981	3,625	3,807	4,004	4,167	3,817

[1] Preliminary.   *Source: Energy Information Administration, U.S. Department of Energy (EIA-DOE)*

HEATING OIL

Imports of Distillate Fuel Oil in the United States   In Thousand Barrels per Day

Year	Jan.	Feb.	Mar.	Apr.	May	June	July	Aug.	Sept.	Oct.	Nov.	Dec.	Average
1997	293	246	245	256	220	219	223	202	210	213	161	232	227
1998	195	213	237	209	185	202	229	181	203	239	179	245	210
1999	304	322	248	213	261	238	234	273	249	216	265	188	250
2000	218	510	260	234	316	258	199	234	283	259	332	447	295
2001	789	635	348	288	310	302	209	212	317	253	244	241	344
2002	298	248	234	219	193	204	188	205	196	350	373	496	267
2003	325	503	460	246	287	337	299	375	352	281	241	305	333
2004[1]	362	501	432	244	273	305	300	311	270	242	318	291	321

[1] Preliminary.   *Source: Energy Information Administration, U.S. Department of Energy (EIA-DOE)*

Exports of Distillate Fuel Oil in the United States   In Thousand Barrels per Day

Year	Jan.	Feb.	Mar.	Apr.	May	June	July	Aug.	Sept.	Oct.	Nov.	Dec.	Average
1997	133	107	120	166	153	174	151	185	160	133	149	192	152
1998	131	120	135	168	227	152	124	105	133	139	110	108	138
1999	117	116	159	191	187	180	123	130	162	192	170	212	162
2000	132	112	211	178	127	149	132	253	194	255	191	135	173
2001	67	77	75	107	146	120	113	140	152	99	132	202	119
2002	109	279	67	68	74	93	44	119	127	96	114	171	112
2003	119	132	161	139	162	101	103	80	43	62	81	100	107
2004[1]	72	86	99	92	100	163	113	120	88	101	102	176	109

[1] Preliminary.   *Source: Energy Information Administration, U.S. Department of Energy (EIA-DOE)*

Disposition of Distillate Fuel Oil, Total Product Supplied in the U.S.   In Thousand Barrels per Day

Year	Jan.	Feb.	Mar.	Apr.	May	June	July	Aug.	Sept.	Oct.	Nov.	Dec.	Average
1997	133	107	120	166	153	174	151	185	160	133	149	192	152
1998	131	120	135	168	227	152	124	105	133	139	110	108	138
1999	117	116	159	191	187	180	123	130	162	192	170	212	162
2000	132	112	211	178	127	149	132	253	194	255	191	135	173
2001	67	77	75	107	146	120	113	140	152	99	132	202	119
2002	109	279	67	68	74	93	44	119	127	96	114	171	112
2003	119	132	161	139	162	101	103	80	43	62	81	100	107
2004[1]	72	86	99	92	100	163	113	120	88	101	102	176	109

[1] Preliminary.   *Source: Energy Information Administration, U.S. Department of Energy (EIA-DOE)*

Production of Residual Fuel Oil in the United States   In Thousands Barrels per Day

Year	Jan.	Feb.	Mar.	Apr.	May	June	July	Aug.	Sept.	Oct.	Nov.	Dec.	Average
1997	800	789	639	617	618	727	645	643	688	711	786	810	705
1998	765	672	790	857	766	739	778	782	749	676	753	805	762
1999	775	726	683	679	725	706	736	701	702	658	596	690	698
2000	640	627	649	620	640	679	741	760	702	747	778	768	696
2001	809	743	750	817	786	783	639	622	653	710	685	655	721
2002	625	613	617	601	582	540	566	583	607	593	648	641	601
2003	658	683	652	632	729	666	632	663	662	640	616	686	660
2004[1]	658	658	633	691	661	641	610	624	611	606	698	714	650

[1] Preliminary.   *Source: Energy Information Administration U.S. Department of Energy (EIA-DOE)*

Supply and Disposition of Residual Fuel Oil in the United States

Year	Supply — Total Production	Imports	Disposition — Stock Change	Exports	Product Supplied	Ending Stocks Million Barrels	Average Sales to End Users[3] Cents per Gallon
			Thousand Barrels Per Day				
1997	708	194	-15	120	797	40	42.3
1998	762	275	12	138	887	45	30.5
1999	698	237	-25	129	830	36	37.4
2000	696	352	1	139	909	36	60.2
2001	721	295	13	191	811	41	53.1
2002	601	249	-27	177	700	31	56.9
2003	660	327	18	197	772	38	69.8
2004[1]	650	371	12	205	804	42	

[1] Preliminary.   [2] Less than +500 barrels per day and greater than -500 barrels per day.   [3] Refiner price excluding taxes.

Source: Energy Information Administration, U.S. Department of Energy (EIA-DOE)

Hides and Leather

Hides and leather have been used since ancient times for boots, clothing, shields, armor, tents, bottles, buckets, and cups. Leather is produced through the tanning of hides, pelts, and skins of animals. The remains of leather have been found in the Middle East dated back at least 7,000 years.

Today, most leather is made of cowhide but it is also made from the hides of lamb, deer, ostrich, snakes, crocodiles, and even stingray. Cattle hides are the most valuable byproduct of the meat packing industry. US exports of cowhides bring more than $1 billion in foreign trade, and US finished leather production is worth about $4 billion.

Prices – The average monthly price of wholesale cattle hides (packer heavy native steers FOB Chicago) in 2004 (through October) fell -1.4% yr/yr to 82.85 cents per pound. That was well below the record high of 90.06 cents per pound posted in 1989.

Supply – World production of cattle and buffalo hides in 2001, the last reporting year for the series, rose by +0.6% yr/yr to 8.221 million metric tons. The world's largest producers of cattle and buffalo hides in 2001 were the US with 14% of world production, Brazil with 8% and Argentina with 5%. US new supply of cattle hides from domestic slaughter in 2003 fell -0.8% yr/yr to 35.454 million hides, which was far below the record high of 43.582 million hides posted in 1976.

US production of leather footwear has been dropping off sharply in recent years due to the movement of production offshore to lower cost producers. US production of leather footwear in 2003 fell -46% yr/yr to 22.3 million pairs and was a mere 4% of the 562.3 million pairs produced in 1970.

Demand – World consumption of cowhides and skins in 2000, the last reporting year for the series, rose +1.4% to 4,774 metric tons, which was a record high for the data series, which goes back to 1983. The world's largest consumers of cowhides and skins in 2000 were the US with 13.0% of world consumption, Italy (10.6%), Brazil (8.9%), Mexico, (6.0%), Argentina (6.0%), and South Korea (5.9%).

Trade – US net exports of cattle hides in 2002 fell -10.4% yr/yr to 19.484 million hides from the 13-year high of 21.750 million hides posted in 2001. The total value of US leather exports in 2002 fell -4.8% yr/yr to $1.162 billion. The largest destinations for US exports in 2003 were South Korea (which took 25% of US exports), Taiwan (10%), Mexico (7%), Italy (4%), and Thailand (4%). World imports of cowhides and skins in 2000 rose +2.8% yr/yr to a record high of 2,058 metric tons. The world's largest importers of cowhides and skins in 2000 were South Korea (with 13% of world imports in 2000), Italy (11%) and Taiwan (7%).

World Production of Cattle and Buffalo Hides   In Thousands of Metric Tons

Year	Argentina	Australia	Brazil	Canada	Colombia	France	Germany	Italy	Mexico	Russia	United Kingdom	United States	World Total
1993	357	212	461	76	81	162	198	150	161	315	96	921	6,835
1994	356	207	448	77	77	160	190	149	165	376	96	974	7,060
1995	347	207	475	79	81	159	176	150	170	376	107	1,011	7,658
1996	388	198	496	88	84	164	176	150	160	357	67	1,065	7,539
1997	384	211	515	91	81	163	176	148	161	294	67	1,174	7,872
1998	338	230	637	94	81	154	161	142	170	275	67	1,070	7,950
1999	364	230	667	99	86	151	160	145	170	229	64	1,099	8,061
2000	372	238	670	96	84	150	152	143	175	233	68	1,116	8,200
2001[1]	348	248	670	94	84	150	153	130	176	228	61	1,032	8,098
2002[2]	369	209	715	92	87	160	153	132	176	228	65	1,032	8,222

[1] Preliminary.   [2] Forecast.   Source: Food and Agricultural Organization of the United Nations (FAO-UN)

Salient Statistics of Hides and Leather in the United States   In Thousands of Equivalent Hides

	New Supply of Cattle Hides				Wholesale Prices		Production		Value of	Wholesale Leather			Footwear	
	Domestic Slaughter				Cents Per Pound					Indexes				
										Upper				
Year	Federally Inspected	Unin-spected[4]	Total Production	Net Exports	Heavy Native Cows[2]	Heavy Native Steers[3]	All U.S. Tanning	Cattle-hide	Leather Exports $1,000	Men	Women	Pro-duction[5]	Exports
	Thousands of Equivalent Hides						In 1,000 Equiv. Hides			1982 = 100		Million Pairs	
1994	33,483	713	34,196	16,259	94.99	87.4	18,842	18,117	811,951	144.7	127.2	163,000	22,505
1995	34,879	760	35,639	18,336	93.69	88.1	18,092	17,480	870,247	150.1	129.0	147,550	20,571
1996	36,583	177	36,760	18,626	92.15	87.6	18,769	18,135	950,510	152.4	132.1	127,315	23,726
1997	35,567	751	36,318	17,562	90.99	87.7	19,592	18,930	1,145,664	156.4	132.2	124,444	21,958
1998	34,787	677	35,464	15,937	75.45	76.4	20,297	19,706	1,289,547	158.0	132.4	108,536	19,009
1999	35,486	664	36,150	15,700	73.80	72.4	21,342	20,620	1,137,534	157.0	133.0	78,581	18,176
2000	35,631	615	36,246	19,670	83.41	80.2	17,332	16,746	1,125,957	157.2	133.6	58,870	20,157
2001	34,771	599	35,370	21,750	85.52	85.8	14,212	13,779	1,221,131	158.4	133.8	54,757	19,472
2002	35,120	614	35,735	19,484	85.73	82.3		16,403	1,161,943	158.8	133.5		21,582
2003[1]	34,863	590	35,454		88.34	83.8				161.4	132.1		

[1] Preliminary.   [2] Central U.S., heifers.   [3] F.O.B. Chicago.   [4] Includes farm slaughter; diseased & condemned animals & hides taken off fallen animals.   [5] Other than rubber.   Sources: Leather Industries of America (LIA); Bureau of Labor Statistics, U.S. Department of Commerce (BLS)

HIDES AND LEATHER

Production of All Footwear (Shoes, Sandals, Slippers, Athletic, Etc.) in the U.S.   In Millions of Pairs

Year	First Quarter	Second Quarter	Third Quarter	Fourth Quarter	Total	Year	First Quarter	Second Quarter	Third Quarter	Fourth Quarter	Total
1994	42.5	40.8	40.1	39.5	163.0	1999	26.7	26.1	24.5	21.7	78.6
1995	37.2	38.3	34.8	36.7	147.0	2000	----	----	----	----	68.7
1996	33.2	31.8	29.7	33.2	128.0	2001	----	----	----	----	54.8
1997	31.4	33.1	28.6	30.6	124.4	2002	----	----	----	----	41.1
1998	32.8	31.8	29.3	28.6	108.5	2003[1]	----	----	----	----	22.3

[1] Preliminary.   *Source: Bureau of the Census, U.S. Department of Commerce*

Average Factory Price[2] of Footwear in the United States   In Dollars Per Pair

Year	First Quarter	Second Quarter	Third Quarter	Fourth Quarter	Total	Year	First Quarter	Second Quarter	Third Quarter	Fourth Quarter	Total
1994	25.77	23.60	21.49	22.44	23.22	1999	23.33	22.70	19.90	19.50	21.19
1995	19.61	21.46	25.37	21.26	21.79	2000	----	----	----	----	24.14
1996	23.65	22.78	22.14	20.38	22.07	2001	----	----	----	----	25.66
1997	22.42	21.56	22.21	22.24	22.11	2002	----	----	----	----	24.12
1998	24.39	24.21	20.27	19.78	21.84	2003[1]	----	----	----	----	45.95

[1] Preliminary.   [2] Average value of factory shipments per pair.   *Source: Bureau of the Census, U.S. Department of Commerce*

Imports and Exports of All Cattle Hides in the United States   In Thousands of Hides

Year	Imports Total	Imports From Canada	Total	Canada	Italy	Japan	Rep. of Korea	Mexico	Portugal	Romania	Spain	Taiwan	Thailand
1995	2,165	1,656	20,095	952	332	3,246	8,283	899	111	63	215	3,017	781
1996	2,927	2,710	20,328	1,149	522	2,372	7,956	2,123	64	171	189	2,871	455
1997	1,496	1,405	19,195	1,320	469	1,802	7,470	2,501	55	0	148	2,866	323
1998	1,909	1,808	17,867	1,126	1,164	1,407	4,897	2,846	91	0	440	2,701	336
1999	1,906	1,742	17,621	829	738	1,252	6,038	2,723	46	0	262	2,863	343
2000	1,972	1,876	21,658	875	1,163	1,529	7,673	2,196	37	0	189	2,844	562
2001	1,721	1,615	23,471	716	920	1,343	7,602	1,647	54	0	159	2,751	888
2002	1,298	1,227	20,784	837	1,099	584	5,812	1,470	14	0	189	2,145	914
2003			19,139	530	779	483	4,784	1,257	6	0	63	1,982	788
2004[1]			18,820	343	417	468	4,230	1,419	4	0	16	1,842	688

(Imports — From Canada; U.S. Exports - by Country of Destination)

[1] Preliminary.   *Source: Leather Industries of America*

Imports of Bovine Hides and Skins by Selected Countries   In Metric Tons

Year	Brazil	Canada	Hong Kong	Italy	Japan	Mexico	Portugal	Rep. of Korea	Spain	Taiwan	Turkey	United States	World Total
1992	11	17	80	131	188	71	32	385	26	91	28	65	1,266
1993	21	26	81	141	188	71	39	372	35	94	37	57	1,426
1994	16	28	95	243	139	60	56	356	29	112	17	49	1,556
1995	33	35	100	250	152	30	43	342	42	112	43	57	1,715
1996	20	34	79	263	123	71	42	341	33	124	50	60	1,692
1997	13	39	64	254	114	96	37	323	44	140	68	60	1,985
1998	10	42	71	249	96	110	39	229	44	142	45	59	1,876
1999[1]	8	34	91	215	95	115	42	254	29	142	55	57	2,002
2000[2]	8	36	93	220	95	115	43	260	30	142	60	57	2,058

[1] Preliminary.   [2] Forecast.   *Source: Foreign Agricultural Service, U.S. Department of Agriculture (FAS-USDA)*

Exports of Bovine Hides and Skins by Selected Countries   In Metric Tons

Year	Australia	Brazil	Canada	Germany	Hong Kong	Italy	Nether- lands	New Zealand	Poland	Russia	United Kingdom	United States	World Total
1992	144	71	74	38	75	9	66	31	17	28	19	610	1,261
1993	142	76	87	40	76	7	35	21	5	150	25	581	1,374
1994	96	84	79	24	93	10	37	22	2	216	22	455	1,271
1995	85	148	90	34	100	10	47	22	2	195	22	510	1,351
1996	93	174	97	33	72	20	47	28	3	212	24	506	1,423
1997	115	216	97	35	60	16	48	27	3	210	25	473	1,475
1998	111	220	86	31	69	24	32	28	6	202	17	443	1,400
1999[1]	115	230	83	28	90	7	30	30	7	190	15	436	1,389
2000[2]	108	250	85	31	92	8	25	30	7	170	15	427	1,399

[1] Preliminary.   [2] Forecast.   *Source: Foreign Agricultural Service, U.S. Department of Agriculture (FAS-USDA)*

Hides (monthly average) through December 2004   Cents per pound

Cents Per Pound
----- Heavy Native Steers, Chicago (Jan. 1901 - date)
- - - Light Native Steers, Chicago (Jan. 1901 - Feb. 1966)

Utilization of Bovine Hides and Skins by Selected Countries   In Metric Tons

Year	Argentina	Brazil	Colombia	Germany	Italy	Japan	Mexico	Rep. of Korea	Spain	Taiwan	Turkey	United States	World Total
1991	308	396	98	143	435	253	225	400	119	101	78	491	4,009
1992	298	382	97	129	435	229	231	400	98	91	90	528	3,977
1993	302	510	94	100	435	226	232	385	98	94	95	554	4,322
1994	304	505	96	83	550	200	226	374	94	112	85	536	4,282
1995	300	493	89	79	570	191	200	355	98	112	100	523	4,365
1996	308	461	91	80	615	165	230	353	95	124	110	548	4,332
1997	332	387	89	101	570	150	251	347	106	140	120	572	4,609
1998	285	412	91	100	540	135	275	265	108	142	100	603	4,584
1999[1]	300	415	89	102	500	130	280	280	104	142	110	623	4,707
2000[2]	285	425	89	103	505	130	285	283	108	142	120	623	4,774

[1] Preliminary.   [2] Forecast.   *Source: Foreign Agricultural Service, U.S. Department of Agriculture (FAS-USDA)*

Wholesale Price of Hides (Packer Heavy Native Steers) F.O.B. Chicago   In Cents Per Pound

Year	Jan.	Feb.	Mar.	Apr.	May	June	July	Aug.	Sept.	Oct.	Nov.	Dec.	Average
1995	90.10	91.42	97.99	102.32	99.64	92.45	85.74	82.46	82.45	82.16	78.02	73.02	88.15
1996	73.67	75.11	77.96	84.58	87.56	82.51	89.45	96.06	98.91	101.51	94.60	90.65	87.71
1997	89.77	93.47	99.44	99.40	89.44	81.45	80.20	83.92	84.86	86.35	89.20	82.61	88.34
1998	66.88	77.33	82.61	83.72	85.05	83.13	81.17	81.11	75.23	67.95	67.53	68.26	76.66
1999	69.42	69.97	70.84	67.36	65.96	66.89	68.17	72.41	77.52	80.43	79.67	78.00	72.22
2000	75.92	76.29	77.86	78.83	79.24	75.18	77.25	81.64	85.60	84.89	84.41	85.31	80.20
2001	85.33	84.12	93.02	102.64	106.19	97.31	87.59	77.28	73.51	70.58	73.30	69.16	85.00
2002	68.23	72.39	80.41	83.21	84.32	86.72	84.43	85.77	85.84	85.75	83.35	85.18	82.13
2003	83.77	85.81	86.04	85.81	79.42	77.64	80.53	84.09	86.78	86.13	85.89	86.05	84.00
2004	85.17	81.79	82.89	79.15	80.16	82.43	85.11	84.54	85.05	82.23	81.42	78.02	82.33

Source: National Agricultural Statistics Service, U.S. Department of Agriculture (NASS-USDA)

Hogs

Hogs are generally bred twice a year in a continuous cycle designed to provide a steady flow of production. The gestation period for hogs is 3-1/2 months and the average litter size is 9 pigs. The pigs are weaned at 3-4 weeks of age. The pigs are then fed so as to maximize weight gain. The feed consists primarily of grains such as corn, barley, milo, oats, and wheat. Protein is added from oilseed meals. Hogs typically gain 3.1 pounds per pound of feed. The time from birth to slaughter is typically 6 months. Hogs are ready for slaughter at about 254 pounds, producing a dressed carcass weight of around 190 pounds and an average 88.6 pounds of lean meat. The lean meat consists of 21% ham, 20% loin, 14% belly, 3% spareribs, 7% Boston butt roast and blade steaks, and 10% picnic, with the remaining 25% going into jowl, lean trim, fat, miscellaneous cuts, and trimmings. Futures on lean hogs are traded at the Chicago Mercantile Exchange. The futures contract is settled in cash based on the CME Lean Hog Index price, meaning that no physical delivery of hogs occurs. The CME Lean Hog Index is based on the 2-day average net price of slaughtered hogs at the average lean percentage level.

Prices – Lean hog futures prices on the nearest futures chart rallied sharply in early 2004 to a 7-1/2 year high due to the shut-down of US beef exports when mad cow disease was found in the US in December 2003. Lean hog prices then traded in a wide and choppy range through the remainder of the year, closing 2004 up 43% yr/yr at 76.40 cents per pound. The average cash price of hogs (51-52% lean) in 2004 rose by +33% to $52.43 per hundred pounds.

Pork prices were strong in 2004 due to strong domestic demand and particularly strong export demand due to the shut down of US beef exports on mad cow disease. US exports of pork soared by +24% in 2004. At the same time, there wasn't much US herd expansion in 2004. The key for 2005 for hog prices will be the extent to which foreign pork demand drops off once US beef exports to Asia restart, which is expected around mid-year.

Supply – World pork production in 2004 rose +2.1% yr/yr to 90.858 million metric tons. The USDA is forecasting a further +0.8% rise in 2005 to 91.619 million metric tons. The world's largest pork producers are China with 52% of world production in 2004, the European Union (23%), and the US (10%). US pork production in 2004 rose +2.1% to 9.332 million metric tons, and is forecasted to rise by another +1.9% to 9.512 million metric tons in 2005. The number of hogs and pigs on US farms in 2004 (Jan 1) rose slightly by +0.1% to 60.501 million, which was the highest level since 1980. The federally-inspected hog slaughter in the US in 2004 (annualized through November) rose +2.0% to 101.675 million head.

Demand – World consumption of pork in 2004 rose by +2.1% yr/yr to 90.503 million metric tons. The USDA is forecasting a further +0.8% rise in world pork consumption in 2005 to 91.197 million metric tons. The US accounted for 9.9% of world pork consumption in 2004. US consumption of pork in 2004 rose by +1.5% to 8.950 million metric tons, and the USDA is forecasting a further +1.0% yr/yr rise in 2005 to 9.041 million metric tons.

Trade – World pork exports in 2004 rose +1.6% yr/yr to 4.182 million metric tons, and the USDA is forecasting a further +1.2% rise in 2005 to 4.223 million metric tons. The world's largest pork exporters are the European Union with 30% of world exports in 2004, Canada with 23%, the US with 22%, and Brazil with 14%. US pork exports in 2004 rose +20.4% yr/yr to 938,000 metric tons and the USDA is forecasting a further +2.2% rise in 2005 to 959,000 metric tons. World pork imports in 2004 rose +0.3% to 3.700 million metric tons, and the USDA is forecasting a further +2.1% rise in 2005 to 3.779 million metric tons. The world's largest pork importers are Japan, which accounted for 33% of world imports in 2004, the US (14%), Russia (14%), Mexico (11%), and Hong Kong (9%).

Salient Statistics of Pigs and Hogs in the United States

	Pig Crop						Value of Hogs		Hog	Quantity	Value	Hogs Slaughtered in Thousand Head				
	Spring[3]			Fall[4]			on Farms, Dec. 1		Marketings	Produced	of Pro-	Commercial				
	Sows Farrowed	Pig Crop	Pigs Per Litter	Sows Farrowed	Pig Crop	Pigs Per Litter	$ Per Head	Total Million $	Thousand Head	(Live Wt.) Mill. Lbs.	duction Mil. $	Federally Inspected	Other	Total	Farm	Total
Year	--- 1,000 Head ---			--- 1,000 Head ---												
1995	6,046	50,077	8.28	5,843	48,739	8.35	70.7	4,115	102,684	24,426	9,829	94,203	2,123	96,325	210	96,535
1996	5,648	47,887	8.46	5,449	46,571	8.55	94.0	5,281	101,852	23,267	12,013	90,534	1,860	92,394	175	92,569
1997	5,595	48,393	8.65	5,885	51,190	8.70	82.0	4,986	104,301	23,979	12,552	90,228	1,733	91,960	165	92,125
1998	6,015	52,469	8.73	6,047	52,536	8.69	44.0	2,766	117,240	25,715	8,674	99,285	1,745	101,029	165	101,194
1999	5,877	51,519	8.77	5,764	50,835	8.82	72.0	4,254	121,137	25,791	7,766	99,739	1,806	101,544	150	101,694
2000	5,683	50,087	8.81	5,727	50,660	8.85	77.0	4,542	118,418	25,717	10,791	96,436	1,540	97,976	130	98,106
2001	5,619	49,472	8.81	5,767	51,031	8.85	77.0	4,590	119,262	25,884	11,430	96,528	1,434	97,962	120	98,082
2002	5,776	50,858	8.81	5,716	50,820	8.89	71.0	4,231	124,013	26,274	8,691	98,915	1,348	100,263	115	100,378
2003[1]	5,655	50,029	8.85	5,773	51,462	8.91	67.0	4,018	124,106	26,334	9,729	99,685	1,233	100,931	114	101,045
2004[2]	5,706	50,737	8.89	5,740	51,568	8.98						102,359	1,096	103,454	114	103,568

[1] Preliminary.   [2] Estimate.   [3] December-May.   [4] June-November.   *Source: Economic Research Service, U.S. Department of Agriculture (ERS-USDA)*

World Hog Numbers in Specified Countries as of January 1   In Thousands of Head

Year	Brazil	Canada	China	Denmark	France	Germany	Philip-pines	Poland	Russia	Spain	Ukraine	United States	World Total
1996	32,068	11,588	441,692	115,959	9,900	6,461	11,100	9,023	22,630	10,510	13,144	58,201	791,301
1997	31,369	11,480	362,836	116,043	9,823	6,516	10,250	9,750	19,500	10,698	11,236	56,124	701,300
1998	31,427	11,985	400,348	118,450	9,904	7,096	10,520	10,210	16,579	7,967	9,479	61,158	741,044
1999	31,427	12,429	422,563	152,006	9,879	6,700	10,860	10,398	16,400	6,539	10,083	62,204	770,055
2000	31,860	12,904	430,198	156,534	9,805	7,000	10,781	10,764	16,100	7,243	10,073	59,335	777,122
2001	32,440	13,576	446,815	152,825	9,788	7,350	10,649	11,715	15,780	7,495	7,652	59,110	783,883
2002	32,710	14,367	457,430	152,473	9,612	7,856	10,569	11,816	16,570	7,165	8,317	59,722	796,947
2003	32,655	14,672	462,915	154,311	9,725	8,110	10,549	12,218	17,000	6,794	9,204	59,554	806,822
2004[1]	32,081	14,623	466,017	152,569	9,724	8,367	10,668	12,518	17,200	6,779	7,470	60,449	807,300
2005[2]	32,323	14,900	470,410	151,970	9,500	8,274	10,303	12,669	17,600	6,800	6,000	60,700	810,179

[1] Preliminary.   [2] Forecast.   *Source: Foreign Agricultural Service, U.S. Department of Agriculture (FAS-USDA)*

Hogs and Pigs on Farms in the United States on December 1   In Thousands of Head

Year	Georgia	Illinois	Indiana	Iowa	Kansas	Minne-sota	Missouri	Nebraska	North Carolina	Ohio	South Dakota	Wis-consin	Total
1995	900	4,800	4,000	13,400	1,230	4,950	1,100	4,050	8,200	1,800	1,450	900	58,264
1996	800	4,400	3,750	12,200	1,450	4,850	3,450	3,600	9,300	1,500	1,200	800	56,171
1997	520	4,700	3,950	14,600	1,530	5,700	3,550	3,500	9,600	1,700	1,400	740	61,158
1998	480	4,850	4,050	15,300	1,590	5,700	3,300	3,400	9,700	1,700	1,400	690	62,206
1999	480	4,050	3,250	15,400	1,460	5,500	3,150	3,000	9,500	1,480	1,260	570	59,342
2000	380	4,150	3,350	15,100	1,520	5,800	2,900	3,050	9,300	1,490	1,320	610	59,138
2001	315	4,250	3,200	15,400	1,570	5,800	3,000	2,900	9,800	1,430	1,290	540	59,804
2002	345	4,150	3,250	15,500	1,530	6,100	2,950	3,000	9,700	1,440	1,330	520	59,554
2003	295	4,000	3,100	15,900	1,650	6,500	2,950	2,900	10,000	1,520	1,280	480	60,444
2004[1]	275	4,000	3,150	16,100	1,720	6,500	2,900	2,850	9,800	1,450	1,330	430	60,501

[1] Preliminary.   *Source: National Agricultural Statistics Service, U.S. Department of Agriculture (NASS-USDA)*

Hog-Corn Price Ratio[1] in the United States

Year	Jan.	Feb.	Mar.	Apr.	May	June	July	Aug.	Sept.	Oct.	Nov.	Dec.	Average
1995	16.8	17.5	16.4	15.1	15.3	16.8	17.6	18.5	18.0	16.4	13.9	14.2	16.4
1996	13.8	13.8	13.9	12.9	13.7	13.4	13.2	13.9	15.4	19.3	20.5	21.1	15.4
1997	20.0	19.9	17.7	19.2	21.6	22.6	24.3	22.1	20.0	18.6	18.0	16.5	20.0
1998	14.1	14.1	13.7	14.8	18.1	18.6	16.8	18.6	16.1	14.6	9.7	7.3	14.7
1999	12.8	13.5	13.6	14.8	18.4	17.3	18.2	20.7	19.4	20.2	19.6	19.6	17.3
2000	19.3	20.2	20.5	23.3	22.9	25.6	29.5	28.8	25.8	23.8	19.8	20.2	23.3
2001	18.8	20.0	23.5	25.3	27.7	29.7	27.6	26.6	23.7	21.8	18.9	16.8	23.4
2002	19.1	19.9	18.6	16.6	17.2	18.2	18.4	13.4	10.7	13.2	12.2	13.1	15.9
2003	14.2	14.7	14.9	14.9	17.4	19.2	19.7	18.4	18.0	17.3	15.8	14.8	16.6
2004[2]	15.4	16.3	17.2	16.4	19.8	20.3	22.7	23.7	24.9	24.2	27.2	25.6	21.1

[1] Bushels of corn equal in value to 100 pounds of hog, live weight.   [2] Preliminary.   *Source: Economic Research Service, U.S. Department of Agriculture (ERS-USDA)*

Cold Storage Holdings of Frozen Pork[2] in the United States, on First of Month   In Millions of Pounds

Year	Jan.	Feb.	Mar.	Apr.	May	June	July	Aug.	Sept.	Oct.	Nov.	Dec.
1995	365.3	389.6	395.1	416.8	422.3	434.9	431.1	408.3	354.0	332.6	321.6	347.1
1996	334.8	382.2	385.5	352.9	385.5	381.3	351.8	322.7	322.9	340.3	333.3	316.4
1997	313.8	342.2	383.9	404.7	440.2	413.4	406.2	388.7	371.8	346.6	354.2	334.1
1998	346.4	446.1	464.5	458.8	487.0	477.4	426.8	414.6	392.6	388.9	411.9	443.4
1999	503.5	510.3	540.9	552.8	596.9	572.7	528.6	494.6	432.6	430.6	438.1	422.5
2000	415.4	481.4	523.5	534.7	532.1	537.9	495.5	478.5	455.6	439.5	438.6	445.6
2001	411.5	471.4	468.3	432.3	432.6	421.5	374.1	339.5	332.6	366.9	430.6	432.7
2002	465.0	503.9	510.9	531.5	567.7	548.0	497.8	472.2	464.4	480.2	489.8	463.9
2003	468.5	512.7	519.7	530.5	520.0	499.7	460.0	440.7	430.2	435.2	446.8	438.9
2004[1]	470.7	504.1	482.8	453.8	455.1	418.9	379.7	373.4	389.7	422.1	426.8	436.3

[1] Preliminary.   [2] Excludes lard.   *Source: Economic Research Service, U.S. Department of Agriculture (ERS-USDA)*

HOGS

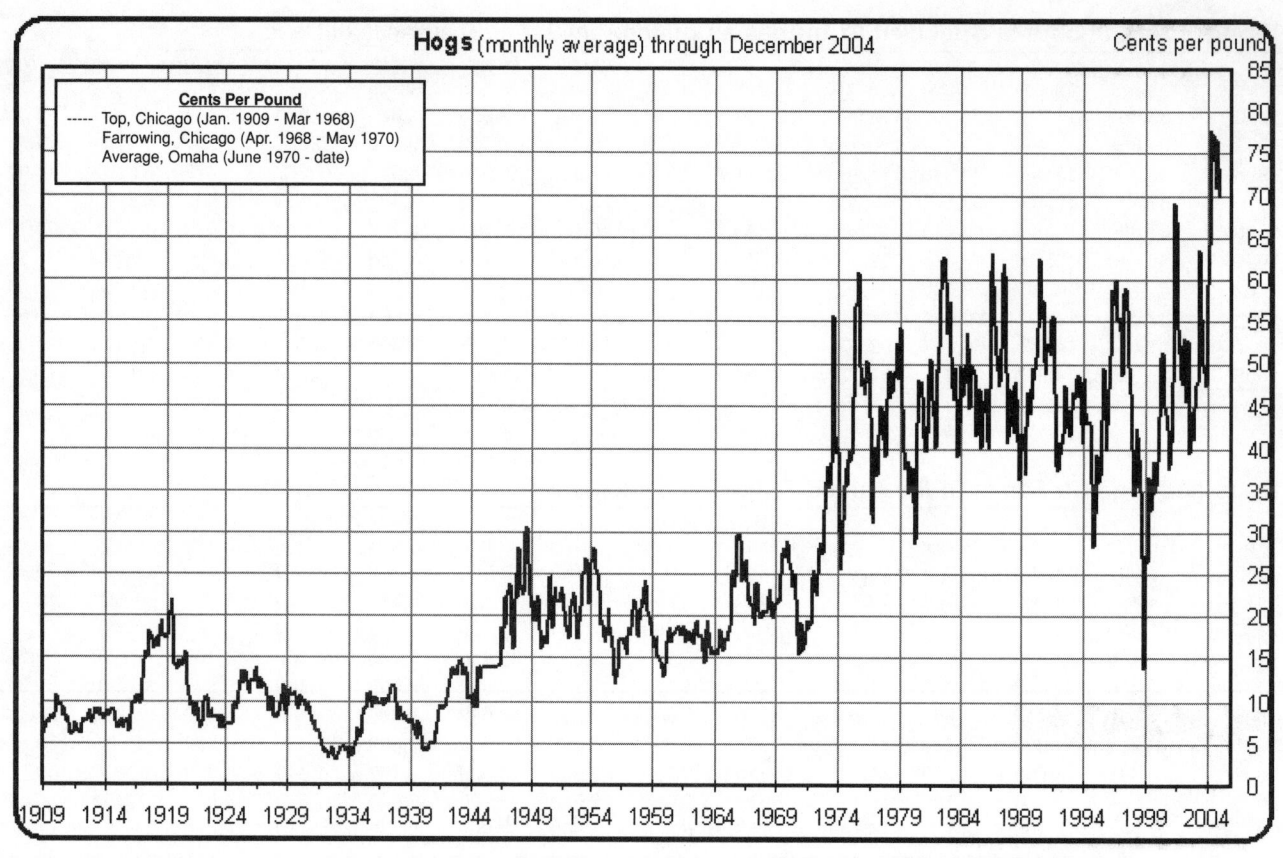

Hogs (monthly average) through December 2004   Cents per pound

Cents Per Pound
----- Top, Chicago (Jan. 1909 - Mar 1968)
Farrowing, Chicago (Apr. 1968 - May 1970)
Average, Omaha (June 1970 - date)

Average Price of Hogs, National Base 51-52% lean[2] In Dollars Per Hundred Pounds (Cwt.)

Year	Jan.	Feb.	Mar.	Apr.	May	June	July	Aug.	Sept.	Oct.	Nov.	Dec.	Average
1995	37.82	39.09	37.94	35.88	37.35	43.03	47.18	49.46	48.67	45.42	40.02	43.80	42.14
1996	42.39	46.93	49.06	50.88	58.29	56.45	59.47	60.49	54.60	55.41	54.42	55.47	53.66
1997	52.96	51.36	48.52	54.41	57.84	57.43	58.89	54.17	49.45	46.12	44.86	40.33	51.36
1998	35.60	34.53	37.22	37.22	45.51	45.32	39.85	37.98	32.00	29.60	19.95	16.62	34.28
1999	28.58	29.65	28.25	31.69	38.45	35.39	32.84	38.56	35.71	35.84	35.34	37.70	34.00
2000	38.32	41.58	43.52	49.59	50.21	51.48	50.45	45.35	43.49	43.09	37.84	41.40	44.69
2001	38.61	41.47	48.41	49.28	52.34	54.53	53.75	52.47	46.93	41.27	35.49	35.14	45.81
2002	40.16	40.65	37.47	32.97	34.64	37.32	40.53	34.00	26.98	31.69	29.99	32.35	34.90
2003	34.39	35.64	36.11	36.42	43.62	47.88	44.98	41.90	41.82	38.63	36.02	36.02	39.45
2004[1]	39.02	45.21	48.30	48.34	58.45	57.95	58.21	56.19	55.34	53.68	56.23	53.15	52.51

[1] Preliminary.   [2] Data Prior to January 1998 are for Sioux City.   *Source: Economic Research Service, U.S. Department of Agriculture (ERS-USDA)*

Average Price Received by Farmers for Hogs in the United States   In Cents Per Pound

Year	Jan.	Feb.	Mar.	Apr.	May	June	July	Aug.	Sept.	Oct.	Nov.	Dec.	Average
1995	36.8	39.1	37.8	35.6	37.1	42.2	46.3	48.6	48.4	45.7	39.9	43.5	41.8
1996	42.6	46.5	48.7	49.7	56.8	56.4	58.6	59.7	54.7	55.6	54.4	55.6	53.3
1997	53.8	52.8	49.4	53.8	58.2	57.8	58.9	55.3	50.4	47.3	45.1	41.6	52.0
1998	36.0	35.9	34.9	35.6	42.4	42.5	36.9	35.2	29.5	27.8	18.9	15.0	32.6
1999	26.5	27.7	28.0	30.1	36.6	34.1	31.6	36.2	33.9	34.2	33.4	35.6	32.3
2000	36.8	39.9	41.7	47.4	48.3	48.9	48.3	43.8	41.6	41.4	36.8	39.8	42.9
2001	37.2	39.2	45.9	47.8	50.4	52.2	51.7	50.8	45.2	40.2	35.0	33.3	44.1
2002	37.7	38.5	36.0	31.7	33.2	35.8	39.2	31.9	26.5	30.8	27.8	30.3	33.3
2003	33.0	34.3	34.7	34.8	41.3	45.0	42.7	39.6	39.7	36.7	34.7	34.2	37.6
2004[1]	36.8	42.6	47.2	47.4	56.8	56.6	57.1	55.4	54.8	52.1	55.7	52.3	51.2

[1] Preliminary.   *Source: Economic Research Service, U.S. Department of Agriculture (ERS-USDA)*

Quarterly Hogs and Pigs Report in the United States, 10 States   In Thousands of Head

Year[2]	Inventory[3]	Breeding[3]	Market[3]	Farrowings	Pig Crop	Year[2]	Inventory[3]	Breeding[3]	Market[3]	Farrowings	Pig Crop
1995	59,990	7,060	52,930	11,847	98,516	2000	59,342	6,234	53,109	11,410	100,747
I	59,990	7,060	52,930	2,886	23,851	I	59,342	6,234	53,109	2,798	24,522
II	58,465	6,998	51,467	3,170	26,373	II	57,782	6,190	51,593	2,885	25,565
III	59,560	7,180	52,380	2,976	24,813	III	59,117	6,234	52,884	2,889	25,548
IV	60,540	6,898	53,642	2,815	23,479	IV	59,495	6,246	53,250	2,838	25,112
1996	58,264	6,839	51,425	11,114	94,458	2001	59,138	6,270	52,868	11,385	100,503
I	58,264	6,839	51,425	2,735	23,054	I	59,138	6,270	52,868	2,748	23,963
II	55,741	6,701	49,040	2,930	24,833	II	57,524	6,232	51,292	2,870	25,509
III	56,038	6,682	49,356	2,718	23,244	III	58,603	6,186	52,417	2,878	25,539
IV	56,961	6,577	50,384	2,731	23,327	IV	59,777	6,158	53,619	2,889	25,492
1997	56,124	6,578	49,546	11,480	99,583	2002	59,804	6,209	53,594	11,492	101,677
I	56,141	6,667	49,474	2,684	23,164	I	59,804	6,209	53,594	2,835	24,857
II	55,049	6,637	48,412	2,911	25,229	II	59,256	6,230	53,026	2,941	26,001
III	57,366	6,789	50,577	2,946	25,696	III	60,391	6,208	54,183	2,883	25,725
IV	60,456	6,858	53,598	2,939	25,494	IV	60,753	6,051	54,702	2,833	25,094
1998	61,158	6,957	54,200	12,062	104,981	2003	59,554	6,058	53,496	11,429	101,491
I	61,158	6,957	54,200	2,929	25,480	I	59,554	6,058	53,496	2,769	24,400
II	60,163	6,942	53,220	3,086	26,989	II	58,183	6,027	52,156	2,886	25,629
III	62,213	6,958	55,254	3,054	26,634	III	59,602	6,026	53,576	2,918	25,974
IV	63,488	6,875	56,612	2,993	25,878	IV	61,009	5,938	55,071	2,856	25,488
1999	62,206	6,682	55,523	11,641	102,354	2004[1]	60,444	6,009	54,434	11,446	102,306
I	62,206	6,682	55,523	2,891	25,247	I	60,444	6,009	54,434	2,836	25,105
II	60,191	6,527	53,663	2,986	26,272	II	59,520	5,961	53,558	2,870	25,633
III	60,896	6,515	54,380	2,920	25,862	III	60,698	5,937	54,760	2,888	26,010
IV	60,776	6,301	54,474	2,844	24,973	IV	61,379	5,962	55,416	2,852	25,558

[1] Preliminary.   [2] Quarters are Dec. preceding year-Feb.(I), Mar.-May(II), June-Aug.(III) and Sept.-Nov.(IV).   [3] Beginning of period.
Source: National Agricultural Statistics Service, U.S. Department of Agriculture (NASS-USDA)

Federally Inspected Hog Slaughter in the United States   In Thousands of Head

Year	Jan.	Feb.	Mar.	Apr.	May	June	July	Aug.	Sept.	Oct.	Nov.	Dec.	Total
1995	7,882	7,157	8,628	7,379	8,012	7,731	6,918	8,083	7,752	8,358	8,424	7,881	94,203
1996	8,129	7,506	7,549	7,886	7,485	6,395	7,187	7,509	7,541	8,423	7,469	7,455	90,534
1997	7,610	6,836	7,437	7,590	6,971	6,859	7,169	7,197	7,872	8,625	7,601	8,461	90,228
1998	8,454	7,590	8,335	8,198	7,443	7,596	8,130	8,024	8,443	9,192	8,650	9,231	99,285
1999	8,373	7,746	8,945	8,386	7,303	8,176	7,778	8,256	8,501	8,806	8,750	8,719	99,739
2000	8,010	7,955	8,695	7,108	7,816	7,823	7,235	8,481	7,992	8,746	8,633	7,943	96,436
2001	8,521	7,491	8,207	7,722	7,836	7,368	7,333	8,247	7,687	9,210	8,610	8,298	96,528
2002	8,552	7,400	7,879	8,321	8,215	7,425	7,957	8,425	8,384	9,276	8,548	8,534	98,915
2003	8,680	7,587	8,069	8,238	7,715	7,665	8,008	7,951	8,466	9,547	8,506	9,254	99,685
2004[1]	8,704	7,805	8,942	8,567	7,494	8,415	8,008	8,616	8,897	8,882	8,881	9,150	102,359

[1] Preliminary.   *Source: National Agricultural Statistics Service, U.S. Department of Agriculture (NASS-USDA)*

Average Live Weight of all Hogs Slaughtered Under Federal Inspection   In Pounds Per Head

Year	Jan.	Feb.	Mar.	Apr.	May	June	July	Aug.	Sept.	Oct.	Nov.	Dec.	Average
1995	258	256	257	258	258	258	256	253	252	255	259	258	257
1996	257	254	255	255	255	256	251	250	250	255	258	257	254
1997	257	256	256	256	256	257	253	252	255	257	261	260	256
1998	259	258	257	257	256	255	252	252	253	257	262	261	257
1999	259	259	259	260	260	260	257	254	256	259	262	262	259
2000	262	262	263	263	264	263	260	258	260	263	266	265	262
2001	265	264	264	265	264	264	261	258	262	267	269	268	264
2002	268	267	267	268	267	266	261	259	261	264	268	268	265
2003	268	267	268	268	268	266	263	261	263	268	270	269	267
2004[1]	269	268	268	268	266	264	262	262	265	267	270	270	267

[1] Preliminary.   *Source: Economic Research Service, U.S. Department of Agriculture (ERS-USDA)*

HOGS

Lean Hog Futures - Chicago Mercantile Exchange   Cents per pound
(weekly close) as of December 31, 2004

Data through December 1996 contract are for Live Hogs * .74 Adjusted to correspond to the Lean Hogs contract.

Average Open Interest of Lean Hog[1] Futures in Chicago   In Contracts

Year	Jan.	Feb.	Mar.	Apr.	May	June	July	Aug.	Sept.	Oct.	Nov.	Dec.
1995	36,705	30,958	30,736	28,035	28,294	28,729	29,959	31,599	34,183	31,312	31,519	35,127
1996	35,253	34,823	38,730	42,900	41,916	36,620	35,616	32,541	32,591	34,329	33,148	32,163
1997	33,105	33,953	31,289	34,071	41,978	37,398	36,141	33,712	31,483	36,928	39,363	39,394
1998	45,908	42,241	38,965	33,610	34,257	32,456	32,085	31,199	34,165	34,051	42,224	45,241
1999	46,003	44,211	43,803	48,277	55,951	52,398	54,723	49,915	53,055	54,089	54,432	50,691
2000	49,209	54,094	57,472	68,535	64,938	54,208	45,730	38,233	38,802	38,254	40,075	45,141
2001	41,425	41,892	48,381	45,296	41,910	45,715	51,661	47,760	42,072	36,983	32,821	27,687
2002	28,720	31,662	33,056	33,472	33,161	28,719	29,338	32,030	36,136	35,245	42,852	43,974
2003	40,660	39,862	40,446	37,883	43,672	47,338	39,706	37,700	49,469	46,295	43,552	43,352
2004	46,380	55,058	63,889	77,756	80,271	81,370	79,860	84,840	86,092	86,423	94,336	98,326

[1] Data thru October 1995 are Live Hogs, November 1995 thru December 1996 are Live Hogs and Lean Hogs.
Source: Chicago Mercantile Exchange (CME)

Volume of Trading of Lean Hog[1] Futures in Chicago   In Contracts

Year	Jan.	Feb.	Mar.	Apr.	May	June	July	Aug.	Sept.	Oct.	Nov.	Dec.	Total[2]
1995	155,766	115,800	181,919	116,767	145,350	155,295	139,013	144,590	135,262	132,122	142,460	136,191	1,700.7
1996	177,299	138,002	150,117	216,476	208,696	177,359	185,872	157,540	158,077	203,789	170,586	152,098	2,095.9
1997	180,241	159,600	200,118	212,810	222,759	188,615	181,637	146,297	149,950	175,135	152,876	130,871	2,100.9
1998	180,241	182,698	174,752	132,952	155,737	167,767	185,427	157,973	164,964	173,163	218,950	241,767	2,136.3
1999	218,608	171,108	196,825	189,773	214,852	237,240	239,096	167,787	190,238	187,794	205,505	139,270	2,358.1
2000	175,399	186,352	231,532	158,765	218,222	235,036	172,725	145,849	146,240	142,240	153,043	146,404	2,111.8
2001	183,493	159,020	197,004	142,892	165,220	184,421	198,503	164,712	152,178	177,601	163,798	129,497	2,018.3
2002	145,266	120,994	168,929	196,956	163,816	158,074	166,064	140,154	174,797	167,065	165,039	164,106	1,931.3
2003	186,436	137,479	186,511	156,370	209,740	210,901	199,782	124,677	232,705	207,247	164,190	148,117	2,164.2
2004	212,420	170,270	249,205	211,501	295,271	304,279	315,197	215,233	356,295	242,204	376,823	255,488	3,204.2

[1] Data thru October 1995 are Live Hogs, November 1995 thru December 1996 are Live Hogs and Lean Hogs.   [2] In thousands of contracts.
Source: Chicago Mercantile Exchange (CME)

Honey

Honey is the thick, supersaturated sugar solution produced by bees to feed their larvae. It is composed of fructose, glucose and water in varying proportions and also contains several enzymes and oils. The color of honey varies due to the source of nectar and age of the honey. Light colored honeys are usually of higher quality than darker honeys. The average honeybee colony can produce more than 700 pounds of honey per year but only 10 percent is usually harvested by the beekeeper. The rest of the honey is consumed by the colony during the year. American per capita honey consumption is 1 pound per person per year. Honey is said to be humanity's oldest sweet, and beeswax the first plastic.

Honey is used in many ways, including direct human consumption, baking, and medicine. Honey has several healing properties. Its high sugar content nourishes injured tissues, thus enhancing faster healing time. Honey's phytochemicals create a form of hydrogen peroxide that cleans out the wound, and the thick consistency protects the wound from contact with air Honey has also proven superior to antibiotic ointments for reducing rates of infection in people with burns.

Prices – US average domestic honey prices in 2003 rose by 5.8% to 140.4 cents per pound from 2002, and more than doubled in the previous three years from the 9-year low of 59.7 cents in 2000. The value of US honey production in 2003 rose to a record $256 million from $228 million in 2002, and was nearly double the levels seen in 1999-2001.

Supply – World production of honey in 2002, the latest reporting year for the series, rose +1.2% to a record 1.270 million metric tons from 1.255 million metric tons in 2001. The world's largest producer of honey by far is China with 288,000 metric tons of production in 2002, representing about 20% of total world production.

US production of honey in 2003 rose by +5.5% to 181.1 million pounds from 171.7 million pounds in 2002, but remained sharply below the 10-year high of 220.3 million pounds posted in both 1998 and 2000. Stocks rose slightly by 3.4% to 40.7 million pounds in 2003 (Jan 1) from the 23-year low of 39.4 million pounds posted in 2002. Yield per colony remained depressed at 69.9 pounds per colony in 2003, versus the 75-85 pound range seen in the 1990s. The number of colonies, however, rose +0.6% to 2.590 million in 2003.

Trade – The US in 2002 imported much more honey than it produced, with imports in 2002 at 202.5 million pounds versus US domestic production in that year of 171.7 million pounds. US exports of honey are small and totaled only 7.3 million pounds in 2002, accounting for only 3.6% of US production.

World Production of Honey   In Metric Tons

Year	Argentina	Australia	Brazil	Canada	China	Germany	Japan	Mexico	Russia	United States	Total
1996	57,000	26,000	18,000	27,000	189,000	15,000	3,000	49,000	46,000	90,000	1,091,000
1997	70,000	27,000	18,000	31,000	215,000	15,000	3,000	54,000	49,000	89,000	1,148,000
1998	65,000	22,000	18,000	46,000	211,000	16,000	3,000	55,000	50,000	100,000	1,178,000
1999	93,000	19,000	20,000	37,000	236,000	20,000	3,000	55,000	51,000	94,000	1,234,000
2000	93,000	21,000	22,000	32,000	252,000	20,000	3,000	59,000	54,000	100,000	1,246,000
2001	80,000	22,000	22,000	35,000	255,000	26,000	3,000	59,000	53,000	84,000	1,255,000
2002[1]	85,000	22,000	22,000	33,000	258,000	22,000	3,000	55,000	55,000	90,000	1,270,000

[1] Preliminary.   Source: Foreign Agricultural Service, U.S. Department of Agriculture (FAS-USDA)

Salient Statistics of Honey in the United States   In Millions of Pounds

Year	Number of Colonies (1,000)	Yield Per Colony Pounds	Stocks Jan. 1	Total U.S. Production	Imports for Consumption	Domestic Disappearance	Exports	Total Supply	Placed Under Loan	CCC Take Over	Net Gov't Expenditure[3] Mil. $	Domestic Avg. Price All Honey - Cents Per Pound -	National Avg. Price Support - Cents Per Pound -	Per Capita Consumption Pounds
1999	2,688	76.4	79.4	205.3	182.5	----	11.1	----	----	----	----	60.1	----	----
2000	2,620	84.1	85.3	220.3	198.5	----	10.1	----	----	----	----	59.7	----	----
2001	2,506	74.0	64.6	185.5	144.8	----	7.4	----	----	----	----	70.4	----	----
2002	2,574	66.7	39.4	171.7	202.6	----	6.9	----	----	----	----	132.7	----	----
2003[1]	2,599	70.0	40.8	181.7	200.3	----	6.9	----	----	----	----	138.7	----	----
2004[2]	2,556	71.8	61.2	183.6								108.5		

[1] Preliminary.   [2] Forecast.   [3] Fiscal year.   Source: Economic Research Service, U.S. Department of Agriculture (ERS-USDA)

Production and Yield of Honey in the United States

	Production in Thousands of Pounds						Value of Production $1,000	Yield per Colony in Pounds					
Year	California	Florida	Minnesota	North Dakota	South Dakota	Total		California	Florida	Minnesota	North Dakota	South Dakota	Average
1999	30,300	23,256	11,890	26,775	23,296	205,250	126,075	60	102	82	105	104	76.4
2000	30,800	24,360	13,500	34,500	28,435	220,339	132,742	70	105	90	115	121	84.1
2001	27,625	22,000	10,935	26,880	15,275	185,461	132,225	65	100	81	96	65	74.0
2002	23,500	20,460	8,541	24,000	11,475	171,718	228,338	50	93	73	75	51	66.7
2003	32,160	14,910	9,960	29,580	15,050	181,727	253,106	67	71	83	87	70	70.0
2004[1]	17,550	20,090	10,125	30,420	22,575	183,582	201,790	45	98	75	78	105	71.8

[1] Preliminary.   Source: National Agricultural Statistics Service, U.S. Department of Agriculture (NASS-USDA)

Interest Rates, U.S.

US interest rates can be characterized in two main ways, by credit quality and maturity. Credit quality refers to the level of risk associated with a particular borrower. US Treasury securities, for example, carry the lowest risk. Maturity refers to the time at which the security matures and must be repaid. Treasury securities carry the full spectrum of maturities, from short-term cash management bills, to T-bills (4-weeks, 3-months, and 6-months), T-notes (2-year, 3-year, 5-year and 10-year), and 30-year T-bonds. The most active futures markets are the Treasury note and bond futures traded at the Chicago Board of Trade (CBOT) and the Eurodollar futures traded at the Chicago Mercantile Exchange (CME).

Prices – 10-year US Treasury note yields established the year's high and low early in 2004 and then traded basically sideways the remainder of the year. The 10-year T-note yield hit a low of 3.65% in March 2004 and a high of 4.90% in May 2004, finally closing the year at 4.22%, virtually unchanged from the 2003 close of 4.25%. The 5-year T-note yield followed the same basic pattern, trading in the range of 2.60% to 4.10% and closing the year at 3.61%, up 36 basis points from the 2003 close of 3.25%. The 30-year T-bond yield traded in the range of 4.62% (March 2004) to 5.59% (May 2004) and closed the year at 4.83%, down 24 basis points from 2003 close of 5.07%. The 3-month cash Eurodollar rate moved sideways early in 2004 near 1.10%, and then began a steady ascent starting in March, rising by 146 basis points to 2.56% by the end of the year.

Short-term interest rates started rising in spring 2004 when it became obvious that the Federal Reserve would have to start removing its emergency monetary policy which was originally put into place after the US economy struggled from the stock market bubble bursting in late 2000, the September 11, 2001 terrorist attacks, and the spate of corporate scandals seen in 2002 and 2003. The Fed had cut the funds rate target from 6.5% in 2000 to a low of 1.00% by June 2003. However, the Federal Reserve at its June 2004 meeting raised its federal funds target by 25 basis points to 1.25% and then raised the funds rate by 25 basis points at each of the subsequent four FOMC meetings in 2004, producing an overall rate hike of 125 basis points to 2.25% by the end of 2004. The Fed raised the funds rate by another 25 basis points at its February 2005 meeting to 2.50%. As of March 2005, the market was expecting another 125 basis points of tightening to a funds rate target of 3.75% by the end of 2005.

The Fed's tighter monetary policy had a one-to-one effect in pushing up the 3-month Eurodollar rate. However, T-note yields were able to remain low during the year despite the Fed's tighter monetary policy. Federal Reserve Chairman Greenspan referred to the low level of long-term interest rates in the face of a tighter monetary policy as a "conundrum" when he testified before a Congressional committee in February 2005. However, the market kept long-term interest rates at relatively low levels due to confidence that inflation would remain low. In addition, foreign central banks were heavy buyers of Treasury securities in 2004 as a means to invest their foreign exchange dollar reserves, which they acquired through large trade surpluses. Foreign central banks purchased an average of about 42% of the new Treasury securities sold in 2004.

U.S. Producer Price Index[2] for All Commodities   1982 = 100

Year	Jan.	Feb.	Mar.	Apr.	May	June	July	Aug.	Sept.	Oct.	Nov.	Dec.	Average
1995	122.9	123.5	123.9	124.6	124.9	125.3	125.3	125.1	125.2	125.3	125.4	125.7	124.8
1996	126.3	126.2	126.4	127.4	128.1	128.0	128.0	128.3	128.2	128.0	128.2	129.1	127.7
1997	129.7	128.5	127.3	127.0	127.4	127.2	126.9	127.2	127.5	127.8	127.9	126.8	127.6
1998	125.4	125.0	124.7	124.9	125.1	124.8	124.9	124.2	123.8	124.0	123.6	122.8	124.4
1999	122.9	122.3	122.6	123.6	124.7	125.2	125.7	126.9	128.0	127.7	128.3	127.8	125.5
2000	128.3	129.8	130.8	130.7	131.6	133.8	133.7	132.9	134.7	135.4	135.0	136.2	132.7
2001	140.0	137.4	135.9	136.4	136.8	135.5	133.4	133.4	133.3	130.3	129.8	128.1	134.2
2002	128.5	128.4	129.8	130.8	130.8	130.9	131.2	131.5	132.3	133.2	133.1	132.9	131.1
2003	135.3	137.6	141.2	136.8	136.7	138.0	137.7	138.0	138.5	139.3	138.9	139.5	138.1
2004[1]	141.4	142.1	143.1	144.8	146.8	147.2	147.4	148.0	147.7	149.8	151.3	150.1	146.6

[1] Preliminary.   [2] Not seasonally adjusted.   *Source: Bureau of Labor Statistics, U.S. Department of Commerce (BLS)*

U.S. Consumer Price Index[2] for All Urban Consumers   1982-84 = 100

Year	Jan.	Feb.	Mar.	Apr.	May	June	July	Aug.	Sept.	Oct.	Nov.	Dec.	Average
1995	150.3	150.9	151.4	151.9	152.2	152.5	152.5	152.9	153.2	153.7	153.6	153.5	152.4
1996	154.4	154.9	155.7	156.3	156.6	156.7	157.0	157.3	157.8	158.3	158.6	158.6	156.9
1997	159.1	159.6	160.0	160.2	160.1	160.3	160.5	160.8	161.2	161.6	161.5	161.3	160.5
1998	161.6	161.9	162.2	162.5	162.8	163.0	163.2	163.4	163.6	164.0	164.0	163.9	163.0
1999	164.3	164.5	165.0	166.2	166.2	166.2	166.7	167.1	167.9	168.2	168.3	168.3	166.6
2000	168.8	169.8	171.2	171.3	171.5	172.4	172.8	172.8	173.7	174.0	174.1	174.0	172.2
2001	175.1	175.8	176.2	176.9	177.7	178.0	177.5	177.5	178.3	177.7	177.4	176.7	177.1
2002	177.1	177.8	178.8	179.8	179.8	179.9	180.1	180.7	181.0	181.3	181.3	180.9	179.9
2003	181.7	183.1	184.2	183.8	183.5	183.7	183.9	184.6	185.2	185.0	184.5	184.3	184.0
2004[1]	185.2	186.2	187.4	188.0	189.1	189.7	189.4	189.5	189.9	190.9	191.0	190.3	188.9

[1] Preliminary.   [2] Not seasonally adjusted.   *Source: Bureau of Labor Statistics, U.S. Department of Commerce (BLS)*

3-Month Eurodollar Futures - International Monetary Market
(weekly close) as of December 31, 2004

Average Open Interest of 3-month Eurodollar Futures in Chicago   In Thousands of Contracts

Year	Jan.	Feb.	Mar.	Apr.	May	June	July	Aug.	Sept.	Oct.	Nov.	Dec.
1995	2,443.6	2,535.4	2,463.9	2,447.4	2,503.3	2,390.8	2,279.5	2,374.6	2,347.2	2,290.3	2,405.5	2,480.5
1996	2,519.4	2,638.6	2,511.4	2,483.5	2,571.8	2,590.1	2,504.4	2,485.5	2,392.4	2,349.7	2,378.2	2,225.7
1997	2,190.8	2,333.2	2,423.1	2,523.1	2,671.3	2,706.5	2,699.2	2,788.0	2,769.3	2,815.1	2,799.5	2,661.6
1998	2,713.4	2,821.5	2,797.9	2,892.6	3,089.0	3,093.9	3,027.7	3,223.0	3,359.9	3,303.4	3,297.4	3,000.1
1999	2,917.9	3,039.5	2,973.5	2,894.7	3,183.2	3,208.8	3,064.4	3,115.6	2,904.0	2,918.2	2,879.7	2,859.4
2000	2,971.3	3,261.4	3,138.7	3,156.6	3,331.7	3,272.1	3,160.3	3,225.7	3,181.8	3,067.2	3,201.1	3,349.7
2001	3,576.4	3,878.6	4,117.4	4,109.3	4,316.3	4,471.7	4,452.4	4,753.5	4,567.8	4,524.0	4,950.8	4,559.1
2002	4,592.0	4,937.0	4,727.9	4,411.6	4,421.0	4,295.5	4,123.7	4,482.4	4,243.4	4,237.9	4,553.7	4,072.5
2003	4,007.1	4,500.1	4,517.3	4,448.6	5,098.7	5,514.2	5,218.4	5,277.9	5,034.1	4,935.4	5,024.2	4,936.1
2004	5,128.0	5,624.1	5,640.5	5,602.2	6,060.0	6,117.3	6,026.7	6,236.3	5,992.8	5,968.9	6,527.8	6,706.7

Source: International Monetary Market (IOM), division of the Chicago Mercantile Exchange (CME)

Volume of Trading of 3-month Eurodollar Futures in Chicago   In Thousands of Contracts

Year	Jan.	Feb.	Mar.	Apr.	May	June	July	Aug.	Sept.	Oct.	Nov.	Dec.	Total
1995	10,341	10,429	9,549	6,069	9,897	10,105	6,670	7,013	7,171	6,478	6,055	5,952	95,730
1996	7,486	9,267	9,526	6,872	7,414	7,415	8,323	6,968	8,232	7,014	5,057	5,308	88,883
1997	7,903	6,918	8,936	9,352	8,447	8,050	7,292	9,295	7,635	12,570	6,314	7,058	99,770
1998	10,908	7,861	8,842	9,488	7,202	8,350	5,452	9,811	13,594	11,757	9,628	6,579	109,473
1999	7,471	7,675	8,719	7,347	8,957	9,650	7,746	8,898	7,629	7,501	6,223	5,604	93,418
2000	8,380	9,723	10,198	10,172	10,261	9,791	7,385	7,010	8,205	9,276	7,561	10,152	108,115
2001	17,515	12,908	15,479	15,192	15,691	14,310	12,673	14,948	16,776	14,139	21,150	13,234	184,015
2002	19,487	14,491	17,987	17,947	18,717	17,932	20,367	17,758	15,310	18,496	13,349	10,240	202,081
2003	13,534	12,315	18,275	15,393	19,403	21,163	18,733	18,724	18,817	20,004	15,432	16,978	208,771
2004	20,809	16,042	22,584	26,674	25,549	28,067	25,114	24,859	32,283	25,737	27,945	21,920	297,584

Source: International Monetary Market (IOM), division of the Chicago Mercantile Exchange (CME)

2-Year Treasury Note Futures - Chicago Board of Trade
(weekly close) as of December 31, 2004   Nominal Value

Prior to the March 2000 contract, prices are theoretical based on a 6% coupon.

Average Open Interest of 2-Year U.S. Treasury Note Futures in Chicago   In Contracts

Year	Jan.	Feb.	Mar.	Apr.	May	June	July	Aug.	Sept.	Oct.	Nov.	Dec.
1995	43,794	41,932	33,705	29,109	26,227	18,721	19,346	18,657	16,756	17,057	25,740	19,362
1996	20,194	26,865	21,125	17,494	16,606	17,547	15,758	16,849	17,792	17,730	19,247	20,309
1997	20,599	23,027	22,750	24,090	29,379	33,225	36,047	47,253	44,003	40,960	37,785	37,701
1998	39,649	40,462	40,840	40,899	46,833	47,241	44,701	48,888	47,030	37,245	38,222	40,303
1999	39,971	40,747	40,339	40,078	34,731	35,959	35,349	37,624	38,693	38,157	38,702	34,135
2000	34,325	43,026	44,512	43,772	49,033	51,216	55,806	53,449	47,912	53,338	60,894	77,860
2001	82,168	79,389	81,688	72,517	66,185	63,601	56,610	72,951	74,353	65,433	72,697	71,270
2002	86,505	103,331	103,568	87,850	102,040	105,931	99,383	107,955	110,434	108,089	115,503	113,618
2003	107,084	114,234	123,909	108,979	120,264	118,776	112,052	149,099	151,922	144,646	149,014	156,506
2004	161,948	195,229	186,836	172,374	198,864	210,667	191,740	207,103	216,394	205,549	221,643	248,517

Source: Chicago Board of Trade (CBT)

Volume of Trading of 2-Year U.S. Treasury Note Futures in Chicago   In Contracts

Year	Jan.	Feb.	Mar.	Apr.	May	June	July	Aug.	Sept.	Oct.	Nov.	Dec.	Total
1995	60,170	93,842	131,682	29,273	73,610	68,363	34,073	68,666	37,805	34,181	81,013	49,033	761,711
1996	38,710	98,916	51,861	28,135	60,097	46,049	37,971	61,838	58,688	25,530	69,046	61,006	637,847
1997	32,403	93,921	79,008	44,548	100,191	102,651	53,120	138,498	96,988	68,512	107,780	100,630	1,018,250
1998	77,139	104,312	107,051	52,038	140,903	123,312	59,360	177,445	160,102	93,117	140,650	72,923	1,308,352
1999	64,460	132,651	66,958	62,860	132,319	93,555	46,547	139,182	71,284	43,987	124,064	72,262	1,050,129
2000	51,539	159,339	97,880	76,889	160,157	105,192	43,017	180,980	107,353	97,403	287,602	126,469	1,493,820
2001	174,603	299,158	160,898	194,758	273,983	163,314	93,386	316,446	198,066	122,944	303,778	160,646	2,461,980
2002	195,004	332,884	290,410	159,242	376,968	242,925	177,001	376,991	253,009	174,779	387,153	232,287	3,198,653
2003	146,797	392,934	292,515	153,316	513,945	339,209	274,095	513,993	522,811	281,118	496,714	488,459	4,415,906
2004	310,401	829,814	630,037	462,388	872,216	788,845	406,716	1,009,935	1,014,541	678,045	1,393,333	1,058,503	9,454,774

Source: Chicago Board of Trade (CBT)

5-Year Treasury Note Futures - Chicago Board of Trade
(weekly close) as of December 31, 2004

Nominal Value

Prior to the March 2000 contract, prices are theoretical based on a 6% coupon.

Average Open Interest of 5-Year U.S. Treasury Note Futures in Chicago   In Contracts

Year	Jan.	Feb.	Mar.	Apr.	May	June	July	Aug.	Sept.	Oct.	Nov.	Dec.
1995	206,539	210,192	199,357	200,087	213,531	189,332	176,329	173,897	163,419	162,121	177,915	171,023
1996	163,026	184,523	200,253	191,690	179,951	177,370	174,484	179,599	154,764	138,246	155,820	154,764
1997	176,691	208,928	219,540	235,543	227,882	225,691	226,306	225,792	234,309	233,480	248,377	257,886
1998	257,094	270,048	282,327	277,540	274,145	257,193	264,756	389,118	382,855	383,809	353,399	326,860
1999	290,373	268,561	247,526	246,916	311,106	348,627	325,348	341,495	298,861	328,581	272,628	288,523
2000	387,008	475,464	420,789	417,929	428,239	379,628	402,658	405,087	372,779	373,698	381,432	380,248
2001	377,692	391,989	374,481	376,929	436,278	421,968	460,960	483,252	451,429	463,247	554,640	491,105
2002	507,207	576,204	585,576	632,211	656,402	594,924	554,875	652,799	655,029	662,475	720,688	692,750
2003	685,117	743,152	777,801	835,470	856,337	827,497	781,691	840,392	737,028	819,361	925,644	880,093
2004	874,173	1,008,121	987,152	1,042,998	1,145,368	1,118,543	1,217,335	1,322,524	1,168,141	1,099,420	1,290,661	1,318,746

Source: Chicago Board of Trade (CBT)

Volume of Trading of 5-Year U.S. Treasury Note Futures in Chicago   In Thousands of Contracts

Year	Jan.	Feb.	Mar.	Apr.	May	June	July	Aug.	Sept.	Oct.	Nov.	Dec.	Total
1995	988	1,296	1,387	783	1,291	1,403	829	1,100	1,009	770	996	785	12,637
1996	837	1,312	1,085	816	1,135	878	882	1,062	979	690	831	957	11,463
1997	928	1,157	1,271	984	1,191	1,144	761	1,245	1,244	1,314	1,068	1,183	13,489
1998	1,452	1,482	1,391	1,155	1,281	1,377	944	2,481	1,913	1,583	1,723	1,279	18,060
1999	1,120	1,554	1,337	1,115	1,906	1,544	1,166	2,164	1,034	1,245	1,607	1,193	16,984
2000	1,801	2,874	2,010	1,708	2,548	1,757	1,189	2,253	1,516	1,774	2,260	1,643	23,332
2001	2,423	2,592	2,281	2,063	3,222	2,264	1,702	2,697	2,617	2,526	4,053	2,684	31,122
2002	2,868	3,826	3,848	3,092	4,638	4,096	4,437	5,354	4,859	5,027	5,013	3,453	50,512
2003	4,436	5,178	5,534	4,624	7,268	6,166	6,463	7,090	7,454	6,364	6,885	6,286	73,746
2004	5,857	7,389	7,776	7,793	10,979	9,458	7,110	10,656	10,312	7,686	11,037	9,417	105,469

Source: Chicago Board of Trade (CBT)

INTEREST RATES, U.S.

10-Year Treasury Note Futures - Chicago Board of Trade
(weekly close) as of December 31, 2004

Nominal Value

Prior to the March 2000 contract, prices are theoretical based on a 6% coupon.

Average Open Interest of 10-year U.S. Treasury Note Futures in Chicago   In Contracts

Year	Jan.	Feb.	Mar.	Apr.	May	June	July	Aug.	Sept.	Oct.	Nov.	Dec.
1995	282,978	285,187	265,747	263,816	273,945	289,052	306,046	323,078	277,011	278,832	270,527	249,073
1996	260,374	297,850	285,501	319,234	331,032	293,416	302,330	326,391	291,208	284,581	313,298	303,702
1997	332,285	343,661	323,982	348,683	350,814	336,927	363,744	407,147	387,284	398,645	404,980	374,448
1998	430,335	507,986	474,916	494,417	533,214	513,369	512,173	604,862	555,268	482,928	508,299	503,533
1999	528,538	549,518	515,404	510,091	541,057	574,514	588,272	623,806	607,305	653,080	582,003	487,888
2000	595,180	653,822	571,932	615,618	621,361	583,900	608,358	602,068	547,582	564,606	555,189	508,888
2001	550,287	541,619	560,035	595,103	628,693	512,127	550,155	627,305	610,435	590,328	661,963	559,949
2002	572,937	643,864	679,635	699,051	806,458	792,956	877,642	958,338	888,696	970,176	938,028	751,575
2003	772,919	896,941	914,943	897,057	968,072	993,643	1,009,484	1,032,497	856,204	985,673	1,140,655	965,049
2004	1,145,871	1,320,644	1,312,896	1,347,662	1,392,428	1,300,251	1,348,191	1,456,605	1,503,596	1,626,867	1,767,443	1,641,994

Source: Chicago Board of Trade (CBT)

Volume of Trading of 10-year U.S. Treasury Note Futures in Chicago   In Thousands of Contracts

Year	Jan.	Feb.	Mar.	Apr.	May	June	July	Aug.	Sept.	Oct.	Nov.	Dec.	Total
1995	1,753	1,979	2,459	1,368	2,236	2,496	1,589	2,029	1,859	1,460	1,731	1,488	22,445
1996	1,649	2,313	2,076	1,632	2,211	1,716	1,556	1,866	1,810	1,495	1,905	1,711	21,940
1997	1,781	1,940	2,052	1,703	2,026	1,942	1,510	2,536	2,063	2,594	1,826	1,991	23,962
1998	2,394	2,749	2,817	2,342	2,696	2,682	1,704	3,632	3,560	2,883	2,912	2,112	32,483
1999	2,269	3,562	2,994	2,145	3,519	3,153	2,438	3,736	2,509	2,471	3,202	2,048	34,046
2000	3,557	4,975	3,750	3,530	4,712	3,706	2,581	4,460	3,780	3,824	4,514	3,313	46,701
2001	4,633	4,915	4,501	4,299	5,483	4,084	3,493	5,683	4,390	4,145	7,270	4,690	57,586
2002	5,540	6,407	6,521	5,463	8,309	7,548	8,981	10,590	8,529	11,199	9,679	7,020	95,786
2003	9,121	10,746	11,321	9,377	13,817	12,149	15,285	14,249	13,707	13,587	12,475	10,912	146,745
2004	13,608	14,569	16,984	16,478	17,786	15,184	12,954	17,419	18,468	16,622	21,006	15,039	196,119

Source: Chicago Board of Trade (CBT)

30-Year Treasury Bond Futures - Chicago Board of Trade
(weekly close) as of December 31, 2004

Nominal Value

Prior to the March 2000 contract, prices are theoretical based on a 6% coupon.

Average Open Interest of 30-year U.S. Treasury Bond Futures in Chicago   In Contracts

Year	Jan.	Feb.	Mar.	Apr.	May	June	July	Aug.	Sept.	Oct.	Nov.	Dec.
1995	384,356	389,908	369,989	367,964	399,500	421,234	438,267	381,237	361,394	395,346	447,409	426,384
1996	382,001	403,403	395,338	381,926	413,944	443,644	464,145	471,203	420,622	409,950	463,731	479,086
1997	497,539	545,775	509,573	493,511	554,418	480,669	530,011	608,474	624,231	723,321	719,186	737,703
1998	744,894	764,309	766,233	806,559	888,215	1,040,659	1,084,889	1,061,223	837,986	769,932	782,677	662,025
1999	657,180	801,115	664,131	618,453	717,453	674,225	672,983	748,974	647,816	621,816	637,656	561,919
2000	637,023	612,298	530,957	503,412	434,771	390,928	394,075	440,437	402,156	399,880	443,282	445,386
2001	413,244	479,165	519,987	509,558	503,194	455,799	458,613	531,098	525,972	567,177	602,647	478,418
2002	468,455	520,573	479,939	463,100	472,778	458,020	427,896	465,971	496,815	467,440	459,877	440,225
2003	420,797	506,910	487,277	449,286	566,887	596,186	554,632	521,928	423,995	443,177	489,185	471,848
2004	488,484	571,445	557,595	488,921	553,721	512,566	517,893	594,905	584,416	594,353	640,026	634,008

Source: Chicago Board of Trade (CBT)

Volume of Trading of 30-year U.S. Treasury Bond Futures in Chicago   In Thousands of Contracts

Year	Jan.	Feb.	Mar.	Apr.	May	June	July	Aug.	Sept.	Oct.	Nov.	Dec.	Total
1995	7,058	7,714	9,624	5,835	8,722	8,447	5,790	7,084	7,317	6,927	6,626	5,232	86,376
1996	7,529	8,781	7,199	6,011	7,932	6,521	6,422	6,626	6,926	6,772	7,298	6,708	84,725
1997	8,105	7,523	7,493	7,520	8,339	7,400	7,680	10,228	8,356	12,468	7,736	6,980	99,828
1998	9,595	9,368	9,764	8,517	9,054	10,209	8,071	12,025	11,159	10,698	8,155	5,609	112,224
1999	8,075	10,031	8,667	7,197	9,556	8,072	6,415	7,995	6,560	6,301	6,909	4,263	90,042
2000	7,966	8,157	5,379	5,282	5,973	4,459	3,080	4,710	4,529	4,460	5,073	3,682	62,751
2001	5,123	5,546	5,196	4,584	6,022	4,233	3,347	4,966	4,331	4,599	6,746	3,886	58,579
2002	4,133	4,721	4,505	3,933	5,191	4,722	5,158	5,667	4,534	5,190	4,723	3,606	56,082
2003	3,625	4,841	5,107	3,795	7,188	5,896	6,352	6,198	5,738	5,122	4,823	4,835	63,522
2004	5,025	5,763	6,688	5,983	6,464	5,557	4,540	6,344	7,639	5,659	7,374	5,914	72,949

Source: Chicago Board of Trade (CBT)

INTEREST RATES, U.S.

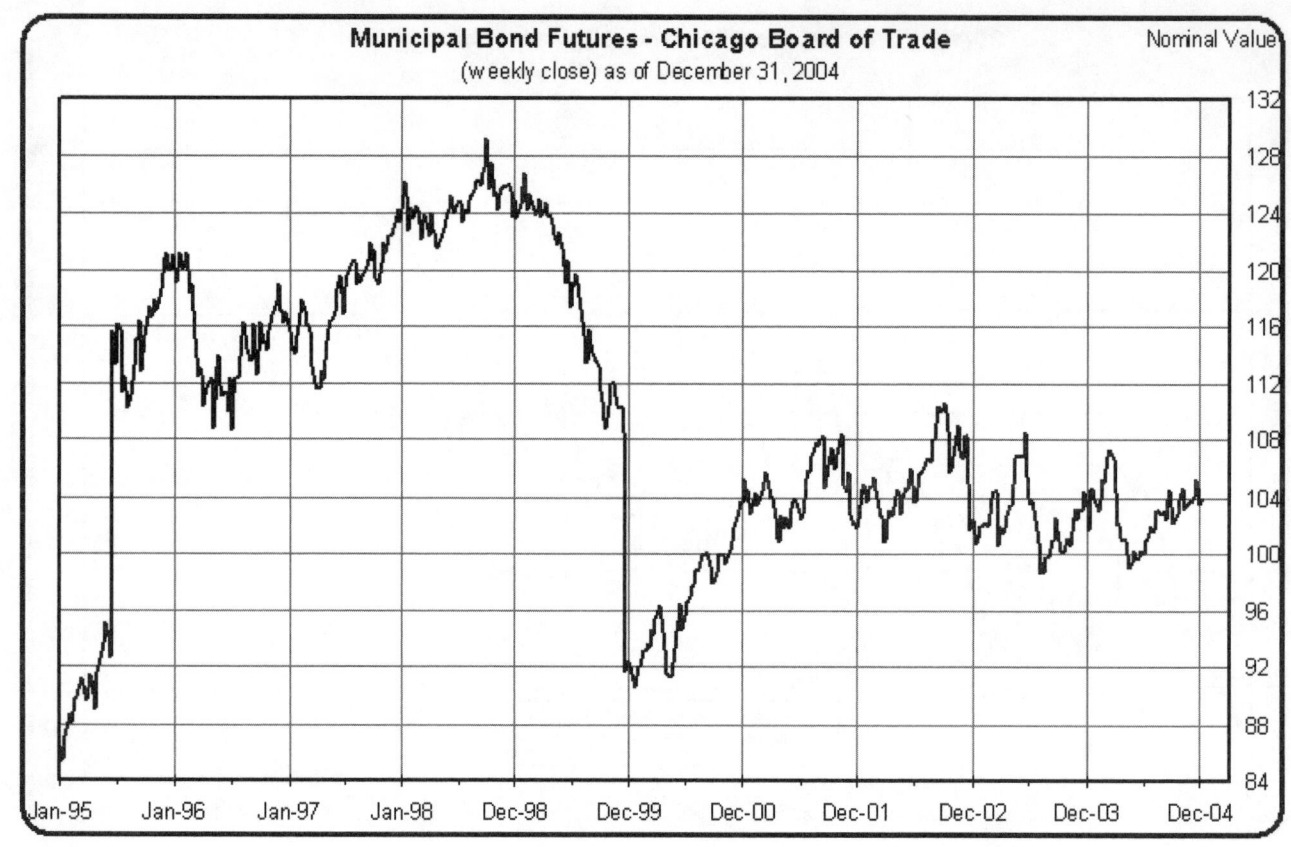

Municipal Bond Futures - Chicago Board of Trade
(weekly close) as of December 31, 2004

Nominal Value

U.S. Federal Funds Rate   In Percent

Year	Jan.	Feb.	Mar.	Apr.	May	June	July	Aug.	Sept.	Oct.	Nov.	Dec.	Average
1995	5.53	5.92	5.98	6.05	6.01	6.00	5.85	5.74	5.80	5.76	5.80	5.60	5.84
1996	5.56	5.22	5.31	5.22	5.56	5.27	5.40	5.22	5.30	5.24	5.31	5.29	5.30
1997	5.25	5.19	5.39	5.51	5.50	5.56	5.52	5.54	5.54	5.50	5.52	5.50	5.46
1998	5.56	5.51	5.49	5.45	5.49	5.56	5.54	5.55	5.51	5.07	4.83	4.68	5.35
1999	4.63	4.76	4.81	4.74	4.74	4.76	4.99	5.07	5.22	5.20	5.42	5.30	4.97
2000	5.46	5.73	5.85	6.02	6.27	6.53	6.54	6.50	6.52	6.51	6.51	6.40	6.24
2001	5.98	5.49	5.31	4.80	4.21	3.97	3.77	3.65	3.07	2.49	2.09	1.82	3.89
2002	1.73	1.74	1.73	1.75	1.75	1.75	1.73	1.74	1.75	1.75	1.34	1.24	1.67
2003	1.24	1.26	1.25	1.26	1.26	1.22	1.01	1.03	1.01	1.01	1.00	0.98	1.13
2004	1.00	1.01	1.00	1.00	1.00	1.03	1.26	1.43	1.61	1.76	1.93	2.16	1.35

Source: Bureau of Economic Analysis, U.S. Department of Commerce (BEA)

U.S. Municipal Bond Yield[1]   In Percent

Year	Jan.	Feb.	Mar.	Apr.	May	June	July	Aug.	Sept.	Oct.	Nov.	Dec.	Average
1995	6.53	6.22	6.10	6.02	5.95	5.84	5.92	6.06	5.91	5.80	5.64	5.45	5.95
1996	5.43	5.43	5.79	5.94	5.98	6.02	5.92	5.76	5.87	5.72	5.59	5.64	5.76
1997	5.72	5.63	5.76	5.88	5.70	5.53	5.35	5.41	5.39	5.38	5.33	5.19	5.52
1998	5.06	5.10	5.21	5.23	5.20	5.12	5.14	5.10	4.99	4.93	5.03	4.98	5.09
1999	5.02	5.03	5.10	5.08	5.18	5.37	5.36	5.58	5.69	5.92	5.86	5.95	5.43
2000	6.08	6.00	5.83	5.75	6.00	5.80	5.63	5.51	5.56	5.59	5.54	5.22	5.71
2001	5.10	5.18	5.13	5.27	5.29	5.20	5.20	5.03	5.09	5.05	5.04	5.25	5.15
2002	5.16	5.11	5.29	5.22	5.19	5.09	5.02	4.95	4.74	4.88	4.95	4.85	5.04
2003	4.90	4.81	4.76	4.74	4.41	4.33	4.74	5.10	4.92	4.89	4.73	4.65	4.75
2004	4.61	4.55	4.41	4.82	5.07	5.05	4.87	4.70	4.56	4.49	4.52	4.48	4.68

[1] 20-bond average.   *Source: Bureau of Economic Analysis, U.S. Department of Commerce (BEA)*

138

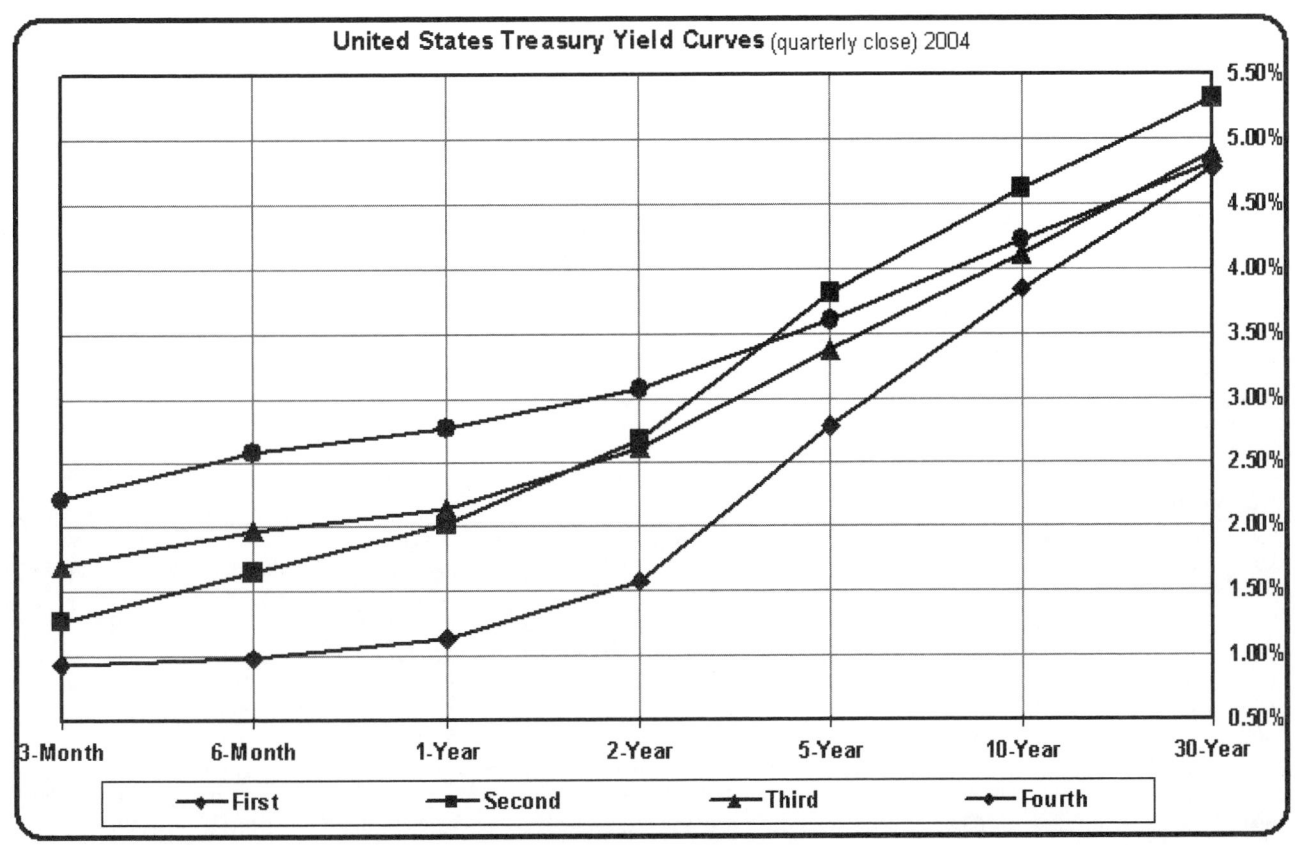

United States Treasury Yield Curves (quarterly close) 2004

U.S. Industrial Production Index[1]   1997 = 100

Year	Jan.	Feb.	Mar.	Apr.	May	June	July	Aug.	Sept.	Oct.	Nov.	Dec.	Average
1995	111.9	111.6	111.7	111.4	111.5	111.7	111.7	112.6	113.0	112.5	112.7	112.8	114.5
1996	112.4	113.8	113.2	114.3	114.8	115.5	115.5	115.8	116.0	116.2	120.6	120.9	119.5
1997	121.3	122.1	122.5	123.1	123.3	123.5	124.5	125.2	125.6	129.3	129.9	130.3	127.0
1998	130.3	130.2	130.7	131.3	131.9	130.6	130.5	132.4	131.9	134.1	133.8	133.8	132.4
1999	134.1	134.5	135.1	135.5	136.2	136.6	137.4	137.7	138.1	139.1	141.9	142.8	139.2
2000	143.6	144.3	145.2	146.3	147.2	147.9	147.6	148.7	148.8	146.3	145.8	145.1	145.7
2001	143.9	143.5	142.9	142.0	141.6	140.3	140.4	140.0	138.5	137.7	108.8	108.3	111.5
2002	109.0	109.2	109.6	110.1	110.4	110.8	111.6	111.3	111.2	111.0	111.2	110.6	111.0
2003	111.2	111.6	110.8	110.1	110.0	110.0	110.8	110.9	111.5	111.8	112.7	112.9	110.9
2004[2]	113.2	114.4	114.1	114.7	115.5	115.1	115.9	116.0	115.7	116.6	116.8	117.8	115.5

[1] Total Index of the Federal Reserve Index of Quantity Output, seasonally adjusted.   [2] Preliminary.
Source: Bureau of Economic Analysis, U.S. Department of Commerce (BEA)

U.S. Gross National Product, National Income, and Personal Income   In Billions of Constant Dollars[1]

	Gross Domestic Product					National Income					Personal Income				
Year	First Quarter	Second Quarter	Third Quarter	Fourth Quarter	Annual Average	First Quarter	Second Quarter	Third Quarter	Fourth Quarter	Annual Average	First Quarter	Second Quarter	Third Quarter	Fourth Quarter	Annual Average
1995	7,298	7,338	7,432	7,523	7,398	6,356	6,408	6,492	6,559	6,454	6,072	6,119	6,175	6,243	6,152
1996	7,624	7,777	7,866	8,000	7,817	6,677	6,797	6,877	7,010	6,840	6,371	6,491	6,566	6,655	6,521
1997	8,114	8,250	8,382	8,471	8,304	7,115	7,220	7,361	7,473	7,292	6,773	6,847	6,957	7,084	6,915
1998	8,587	8,658	8,790	8,954	8,747	7,573	7,688	7,823	7,927	7,753	7,247	7,376	7,486	7,583	7,423
1999	9,067	9,174	9,314	9,520	9,268	8,074	8,161	8,255	8,456	8,237	7,658	7,729	7,824	7,999	7,802
2000	9,629	9,823	9,862	9,954	9,817	8,681	8,750	8,858	8,892	8,795	8,266	8,372	8,514	8,566	8,430
2001	10,022	10,129	10,135	10,226	10,128	8,988	9,002	8,890	9,040	8,980	8,689	8,720	8,733	8,755	8,724
2002	10,338	10,446	10,547	10,618	10,487	9,137	9,222	9,242	9,301	9,225	8,804	8,897	8,896	8,919	8,879
2003	10,745	10,884	11,117	11,271	11,004	9,408	9,569	9,771	9,971	9,680	9,002	9,106	9,209	9,330	9,162
2004[2]	11,473	11,658	11,815		11,648	10,128	10,262	10,265		10,218	9,445	9,593	9,674		9,571

[1] Seasonally adjusted at annual rates.   [2] Preliminary.   *Source: Bureau of Economic Analysis, U.S. Department of Commerce (BEA)*

INTEREST RATES, U.S.

U.S. Money Supply M1[2]   In Billions of Dollars

Year	Jan.	Feb.	Mar.	Apr.	May	June	July	Aug.	Sept.	Oct.	Nov.	Dec.	Average
1995	1,151.1	1,147.0	1,146.5	1,149.1	1,144.7	1,143.9	1,144.9	1,145.1	1,140.9	1,136.4	1,133.2	1,126.9	1,142.5
1996	1,122.8	1,118.3	1,122.1	1,124.8	1,116.3	1,114.6	1,111.6	1,100.9	1,094.8	1,085.1	1,081.9	1,079.8	1,106.1
1997	1,080.0	1,077.5	1,071.0	1,062.6	1,062.9	1,065.1	1,065.3	1,073.8	1,066.7	1,065.1	1,069.1	1,072.2	1,069.3
1998	1,073.5	1,077.7	1,076.9	1,076.2	1,077.6	1,076.0	1,074.4	1,074.3	1,078.4	1,084.3	1,093.0	1,094.8	1,079.8
1999	1,096.3	1,096.7	1,097.3	1,101.1	1,102.2	1,098.7	1,097.9	1,097.9	1,095.6	1,101.2	1,110.2	1,122.4	1,101.5
2000	1,121.1	1,108.8	1,107.9	1,112.8	1,105.6	1,103.9	1,104.0	1,100.7	1,098.9	1,098.2	1,092.4	1,087.5	1,103.5
2001	1,095.6	1,099.8	1,106.8	1,111.0	1,115.8	1,123.5	1,136.1	1,146.6	1,200.0	1,161.7	1,167.3	1,179.1	1,136.9
2002	1,184.7	1,186.7	1,188.8	1,179.7	1,184.6	1,187.8	1,194.4	1,182.9	1,191.4	1,200.5	1,206.2	1,216.7	1,192.0
2003	1,221.2	1,235.8	1,238.3	1,245.0	1,259.1	1,269.4	1,273.1	1,282.4	1,282.7	1,283.6	1,285.1	1,292.8	1,264.0
2004[1]	1,289.9	1,307.7	1,320.9	1,321.3	1,324.8	1,332.6	1,325.5	1,343.4	1,347.9	1,347.7	1,362.7	1,361.9	1,332.2

[1] Preliminary.   [2] M1 -- The sum of currency held outside the vaults of depository institutions, Federal Reserve Banks, and the U.S. Treasury; travelers checks; and demand and other checkable deposits issued by financial institutions (except demand deposits due to the Treasury and depository institutions), minus cash items in process of collection and Federal Reserve float. Seasonally adjusted.
Source: Board of Governors of the Federal Reserve System

U.S. Money Supply M2[2]   In Billions of Dollars

Year	Jan.	Feb.	Mar.	Apr.	May	June	July	Aug.	Sept.	Oct.	Nov.	Dec.	Average
1995	3,503.3	3,500.4	3,501.9	3,509.8	3,533.4	3,560.0	3,578.5	3,600.6	3,611.6	3,623.7	3,632.0	3,640.9	3,566.4
1996	3,659.2	3,673.9	3,698.9	3,710.3	3,720.9	3,734.3	3,749.6	3,758.4	3,768.3	3,782.1	3,796.5	3,817.0	3,739.1
1997	3,831.0	3,841.9	3,857.0	3,873.4	3,886.5	3,904.4	3,923.9	3,952.8	3,972.2	3,989.8	4,011.0	4,032.0	3,923.0
1998	4,056.3	4,088.5	4,115.6	4,138.9	4,159.7	4,185.9	4,204.3	4,229.7	4,271.6	4,313.1	4,352.3	4,384.6	4,208.4
1999	4,406.7	4,433.8	4,444.1	4,474.7	4,493.9	4,515.2	4,539.6	4,560.6	4,576.3	4,594.8	4,620.8	4,650.2	4,525.9
2000	4,677.2	4,692.8	4,723.0	4,771.7	4,766.2	4,784.7	4,796.7	4,831.6	4,863.5	4,881.6	4,893.1	4,934.7	4,801.4
2001	4,990.1	5,028.3	5,087.0	5,146.9	5,149.6	5,188.5	5,218.4	5,251.8	5,361.1	5,357.4	5,402.5	5,452.4	5,219.5
2002	5,481.2	5,508.3	5,516.1	5,517.8	5,545.0	5,566.1	5,610.5	5,650.6	5,677.0	5,728.1	5,773.5	5,803.7	5,614.8
2003	5,836.8	5,872.8	5,888.8	5,924.0	5,971.5	6,012.7	6,057.8	6,103.9	6,085.8	6,077.7	6,072.8	6,076.6	5,998.4
2004[1]	6,089.3	6,128.1	6,166.8	6,204.3	6,262.6	6,274.7	6,277.5	6,298.0	6,333.0	6,357.8	6,394.2	6,417.0	6,266.9

[1] Preliminary.   [2] M2 -- M1 plus savings deposits (including money market deposit accounts) and small-denomination (less than $100,000) time deposits issued by financial institutions; and shares in retail money market mutual funds (funds with initial investments of less than $50,000), net of retirement accounts. Seasonally adjusted.   *Source: Board of Governors of the Federal Reserve System*

U.S. Money Supply M3[2]   In Billions of Dollars

Year	Jan.	Feb.	Mar.	Apr.	May	June	July	Aug.	Sept.	Oct.	Nov.	Dec.	Average
1995	4,393.4	4,394.4	4,415.5	4,436.0	4,476.1	4,515.8	4,541.2	4,576.5	4,595.8	4,613.7	4,625.2	4,636.0	4,518.3
1996	4,670.1	4,698.5	4,734.5	4,752.4	4,788.7	4,811.9	4,838.1	4,858.2	4,884.9	4,926.1	4,946.0	4,985.4	4,824.5
1997	5,013.2	5,041.7	5,080.2	5,119.8	5,147.1	5,177.4	5,235.8	5,291.4	5,332.3	5,376.3	5,417.1	5,460.5	5,224.4
1998	5,508.9	5,541.3	5,611.6	5,647.3	5,687.0	5,728.5	5,750.0	5,815.1	5,882.1	5,953.7	6,010.2	6,051.9	5,765.6
1999	6,080.8	6,129.5	6,133.6	6,172.3	6,201.1	6,237.7	6,268.9	6,299.0	6,322.9	6,378.4	6,464.3	6,552.0	6,270.0
2000	6,605.8	6,637.1	6,704.8	6,765.7	6,777.8	6,826.1	6,877.1	6,947.1	7,005.5	7,028.9	7,040.5	7,120.3	6,861.4
2001	7,238.2	7,304.8	7,369.5	7,502.1	7,560.3	7,639.9	7,684.3	7,687.8	7,845.8	7,889.7	7,966.6	8,034.8	7,643.6
2002	8,063.7	8,107.8	8,116.1	8,137.6	8,171.4	8,185.8	8,236.5	8,294.4	8,333.9	8,372.1	8,497.4	8,571.5	8,257.3
2003	8,589.2	8,625.7	8,642.8	8,673.0	8,723.5	8,777.3	8,870.2	8,901.8	8,897.9	8,893.5	8,875.0	8,876.7	8,778.9
2004[1]	8,935.8	9,000.4	9,077.7	9,144.0	9,233.2	9,273.9	9,277.8	9,310.5	9,358.7	9,365.4	9,392.9	9,438.8	9,234.1

[1] Preliminary.   [2] M3 -- M2 plus large-denomination ($100,000 or more) time deposits; repurchase agreements issued by depository institutions; Eurodollar deposits, specifically, dollar-denominated deposits due to nonbank U.S. addresses held at foreign offices of U.S. banks worldwide and all banking offices in Canada and the United Kingdom; and institutional money market mutual funds (funds with initial investments of $50,000 or more). Seasonally adjusted.   *Source: Board of Governors of the Federal Reserve System*

U.S. Money Supply MZM[2]   In Billions of Dollars

Year	Jan.	Feb.	Mar.	Apr.	May	June	July	Aug.	Sept.	Oct.	Nov.	Dec.	Average
1995	2,887.4	2,861.5	2,848.9	2,846.3	2,863.5	2,891.8	2,910.6	2,931.0	2,942.9	2,955.3	2,963.2	2,973.1	2,906.3
1996	2,995.9	3,017.0	3,048.2	3,061.4	3,075.0	3,093.2	3,112.9	3,123.2	3,135.0	3,148.0	3,166.0	3,192.1	3,097.3
1997	3,207.4	3,224.1	3,245.9	3,262.0	3,275.6	3,296.4	3,322.2	3,356.5	3,384.4	3,406.9	3,430.2	3,459.4	3,322.6
1998	3,491.0	3,527.8	3,564.0	3,603.0	3,638.6	3,677.0	3,704.7	3,745.6	3,804.2	3,866.9	3,925.2	3,972.4	3,710.0
1999	4,004.2	4,049.1	4,061.6	4,106.4	4,135.2	4,164.5	4,189.1	4,218.1	4,234.5	4,257.4	4,293.7	4,332.1	4,170.5
2000	4,366.1	4,375.0	4,412.9	4,458.5	4,455.6	4,472.9	4,502.2	4,547.4	4,597.0	4,613.4	4,626.0	4,680.1	4,508.9
2001	4,768.4	4,867.4	4,953.5	5,052.0	5,106.4	5,186.2	5,241.1	5,271.3	5,443.9	5,506.3	5,585.2	5,674.0	5,221.3
2002	5,706.8	5,753.2	5,770.7	5,789.8	5,826.1	5,848.4	5,894.3	5,932.2	5,956.8	5,973.8	6,090.8	6,159.0	5,891.8
2003	6,169.8	6,199.6	6,205.1	6,227.9	6,263.6	6,315.5	6,412.2	6,442.1	6,438.5	6,414.3	6,394.9	6,385.1	6,322.4
2004[1]	6,397.8	6,429.4	6,478.0	6,526.0	6,590.6	6,602.4	6,589.0	6,602.6	6,629.5	6,627.7	6,651.2	6,670.3	6,566.2

[1] Preliminary.   [2] MZM (money, zero maturity) -- M2 minus small-denomination time deposits, plus institutional money market mutual funds (that is, those included in M3 but excluded from M2). The label MZM was coined by William Poole (1991); the aggregate itself was proposed earlier by Motley (1988).   Seasonally adjusted.   *Source: Board of Governors of the Federal Reserve System*

Prime Rate and Discount Rate
(monthly close) through December 2004

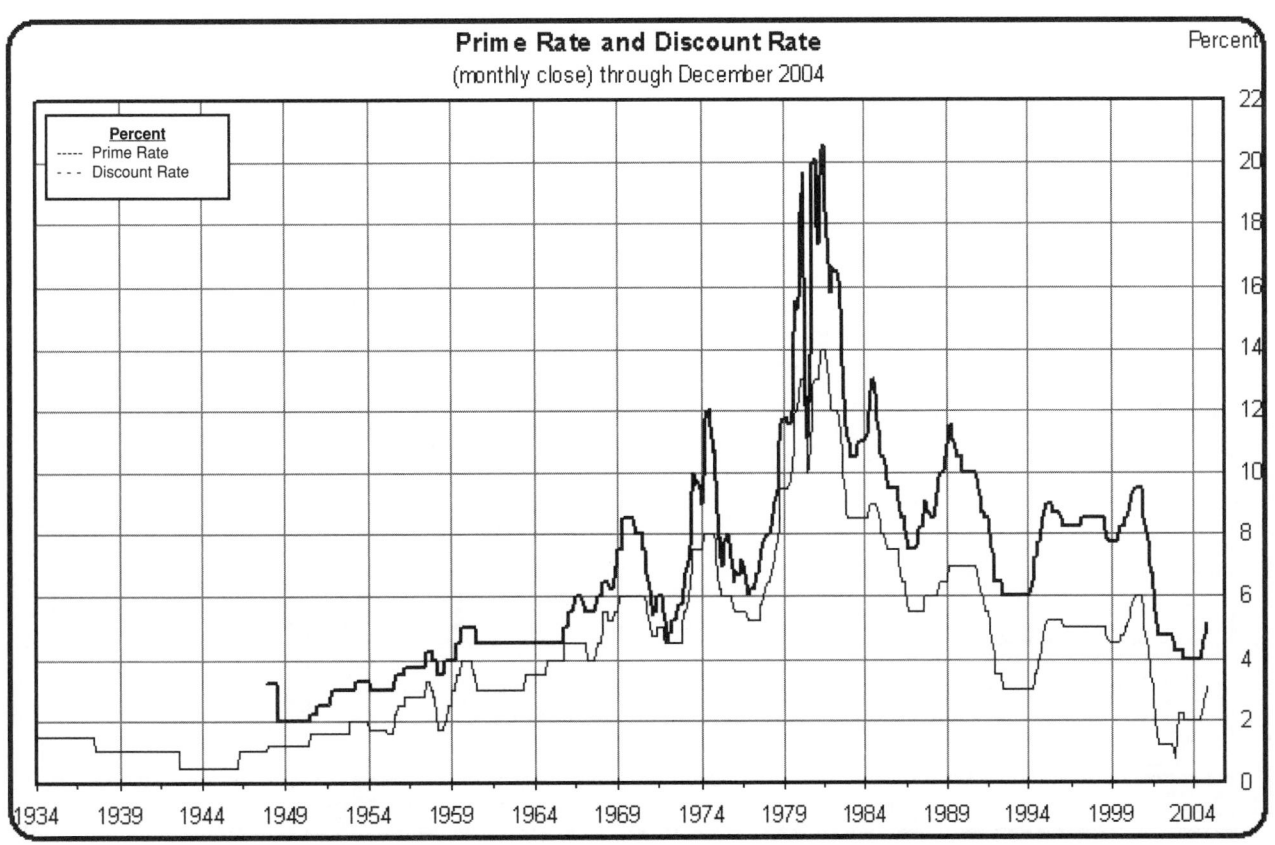

Municipal Bonds and Corporate AAA Bond Yields
(monthly average) through December 2004

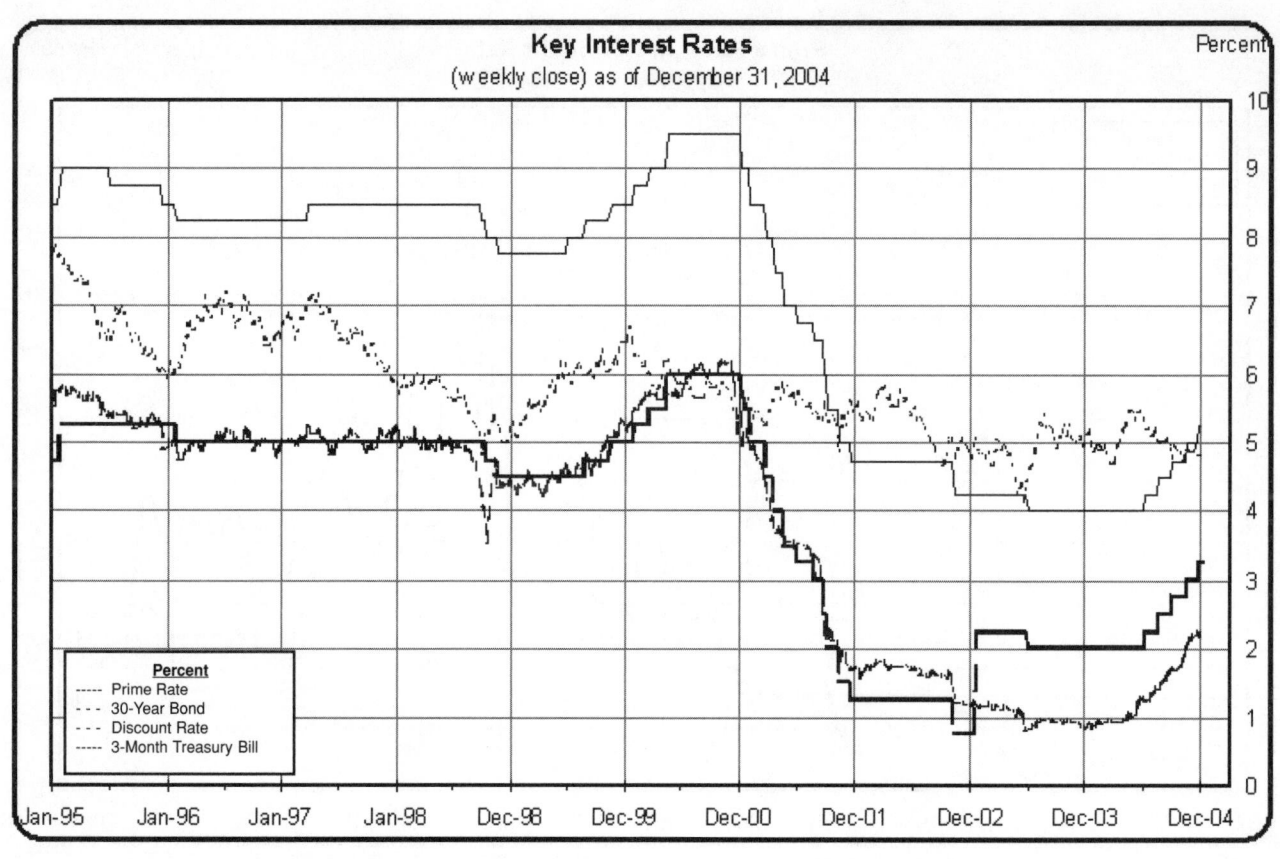

Key Interest Rates
(weekly close) as of December 31, 2004

Percent

Percent
- - - - Prime Rate
- - - - 30-Year Bond
- - - Discount Rate
- - - - 3-Month Treasury Bill

5-Year Treasury Note Yield
(monthly average) through December 2004

Percent

Interest Rates, Worldwide

Interest rate futures contracts are widely traded throughout the world. The most popular futures contracts are generally 10-year government bonds and the 3-month interest rate contracts. In Europe, futures on German interest rates are traded at the all-electronic Eurex Exchange in Frankfurt. Futures on UK interest rates are traded at the Liffe Exchange in London. Futures on Canadian interest rates are traded at the Montreal Exchange. Futures on Japanese interest rates are traded at the Singapore Exchange (Simex) and at the Tokyo Stock Exchange. A variety of other interest rate futures contracts are traded throughout the rest of the world (please see the front of this Yearbook for a complete list).

Euro-Zone – The Eurex 10-year Euro Bund futures contract showed weakness during the spring of 2004 but then rallied sharply through the remainder of the year and closed sharply higher on the year at 118.59, up from 113.12 at the end of 2003. The German 10-year government bond yield traded between 4.0-4.5% in the first half of 2004, but then fell as low as 3.70% by the end of 2004. The 3-month Euribor rate in 2004 remained locked just above the European Central Bank's 2-week refinancing rate, which remained unchanged at 2.00% all during 2004. The ECB cut its 2-week refi rate by a total of 275 basis points after the world recession started in 2000, i.e., from 4.75% in 2000 to 2.00% by mid-2003. The refi rate remained at 2.00% from mid-2003 through all through 2004 and into early 2005. The markets in early 2004 thought the ECB would have to raise its key interest rate later in the year, particularly given that the US Federal Reserve in 2004 ended up raising interest rates by 125 basis points. However, it turned out that the ECB left its monetary policy unchanged all year due to weak economic growth and the damage to exports caused by the strong euro. Euro-Zone GDP remained weak between +1.6% and +2.2% in 2004, dampened by the strong euro and by Europe's general structural problems. Meanwhile, the European unemployment rate remained very high all year in the range of 8.8%-9.0%, also keeping the pressure on the ECB to maintain an easy monetary policy to stimulate the economy and curb unemployment. The tame inflation picture meant there was no real pressure on the ECB to raise interest rates. The Euro-Zone CPI in 2004 averaged about +2.2%, which was just slightly above the ECB's ceiling of 2%. The Euro-Zone CPI remained under control despite the surge in oil prices during 2004 because of the strong euro (which pushed down import prices) and weak economic demand.

UK – The Liffe 10-year Gilt futures contract showed some weakness early in the year but then rallied steadily in the second half of the year to close with moderate gains on the year. The 10-year gilt yield posted a 2-1/2 year high of 5.15% in May but then fell back through the remainder of the year to close at the year's low of 4.56%. The 3-month UK Libor rate in early 2004 continued the rise that began in June 2003 and reached a 3-1/2 year high by August, but then moved sideways the remainder of the year. That rate movement tracked Bank of England's monetary policy. The BOE raised the base rate from the 3.50% level seen in July-September 2003 to 4.75% by August 2004, for an overall rate hike of 125 basis points. The BOE then left the base rate unchanged through the remainder of 2004. The BOE raised interest rates in response to strong GDP growth and very strong UK consumer credit growth early in the year.

Canada – The Canadian 10-year T-note futures contract traded at the Montreal Exchange showed some weakness during spring 2004 but then rallied the remainder of the year. The 10-year Canadian bond yield posted the year's high of 4.83% in June 2004 but then fell steadily during the remainder of the year to close at 4.31%, which was a multi-decade low. The 3-month Canadian Libor rate hit the year's low of 2.10% in March but then rose to 2.73% by October, moving sideways the remainder of the year to close at 2.65%. The Bank of Canada starting in mid-2003 cut its benchmark rate from 3.25% in spring 2003 to 2.00% by spring 2004. However, the Bank of Canada then raised its benchmark rate by 50 basis points in August and September 2004 to 2.50%, where it finished the year 25 basis points above the Fed's year-end funds rate target of 2.25%. Canada's GDP rebounded sharply from a 3-year low of +0.7% yr/yr in August 2003 to a 2-year high of +4.6% by August 2004, finally trailing off late in the year to end 2004 at +3.0%.

Japan – The 10-year JGB futures contract at the Simex showed weakness in March 2004 and hit the year's low, but then rallied through the remainder of 2004 to close little changed on the year. The 10-year JGB yield moved sharply higher from its record low of 0.54% in May 2003 to a 4-year high of 1.86% in July 2004, falling back through the remainder of the year to close the year at 1.44%. Meanwhile, the 3-month Japanese Libor rate remained locked below 0.10% where it has been since mid-2001. The Bank of Japan maintained its zero interest rate monetary policy all through 2004 as it continued to hope for a respite from the lost-decade of growth that followed the real estate and stock market bubble seen in the late-1980s. While there was some optimism that Japan might finally see a sustained economic rebound in 2004, the Japanese economy in fact showed negative GDP growth in the last three quarters of 2004, meaning the Japanese economy had slipped back into recession. The strength in the yen versus the dollar was one of the factors holding back the Japanese economy, along with the continued inability of the Japanese banking system to return to health. The Japanese stock market failed to show much strength during 2004, as concern continued about the weak economy and weak earnings. The main positive factor for Japan was strong growth in neighboring China, which provided a key export market for Japanese goods.

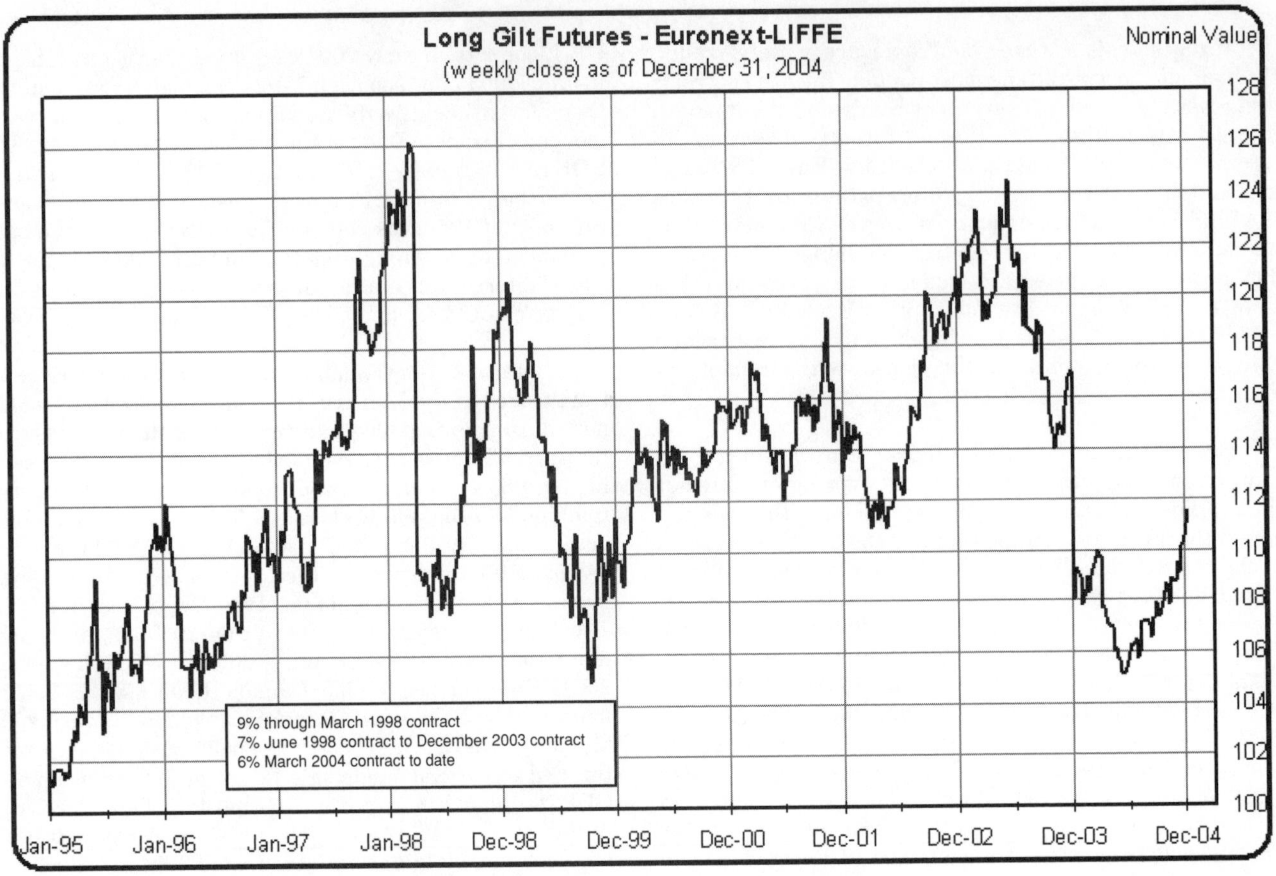
Long Gilt Futures - Euronext-LIFFE
(weekly close) as of December 31, 2004
Nominal Value
128
126
124
122
120
118
116
114
112
110
108
106
104
102
100
9% through March 1998 contract
7% June 1998 contract to December 2003 contract
6% March 2004 contract to date
Jan-95
Jan-96
Jan-97
Jan-98
Dec-98
Dec-99
Dec-00
Dec-01
Dec-02
Dec-03
Dec-04

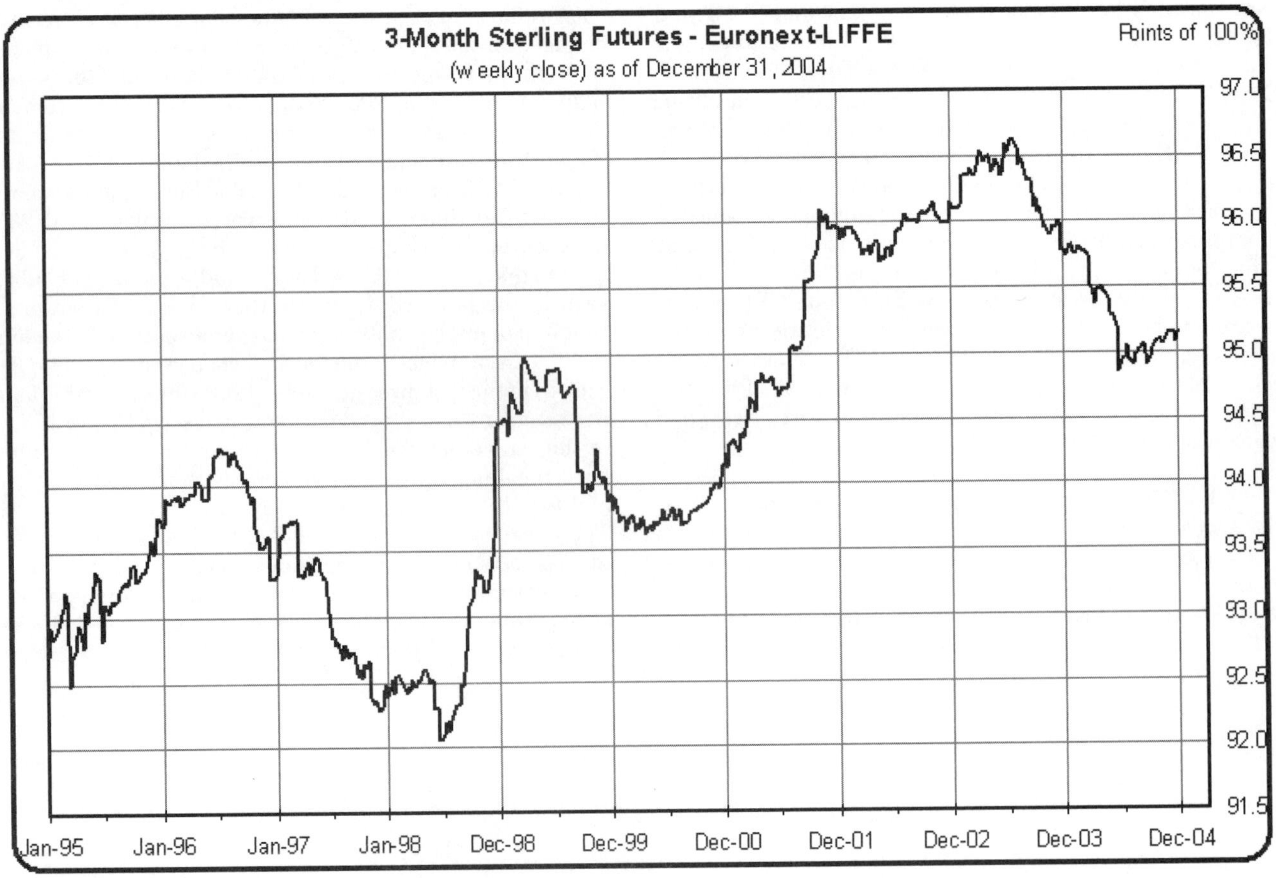
3-Month Sterling Futures - Euronext-LIFFE
(weekly close) as of December 31, 2004
Points of 100%
97.0
96.5
96.0
95.5
95.0
94.5
94.0
93.5
93.0
92.5
92.0
91.5
Jan-95
Jan-96
Jan-97
Jan-98
Dec-98
Dec-99
Dec-00
Dec-01
Dec-02
Dec-03
Dec-04

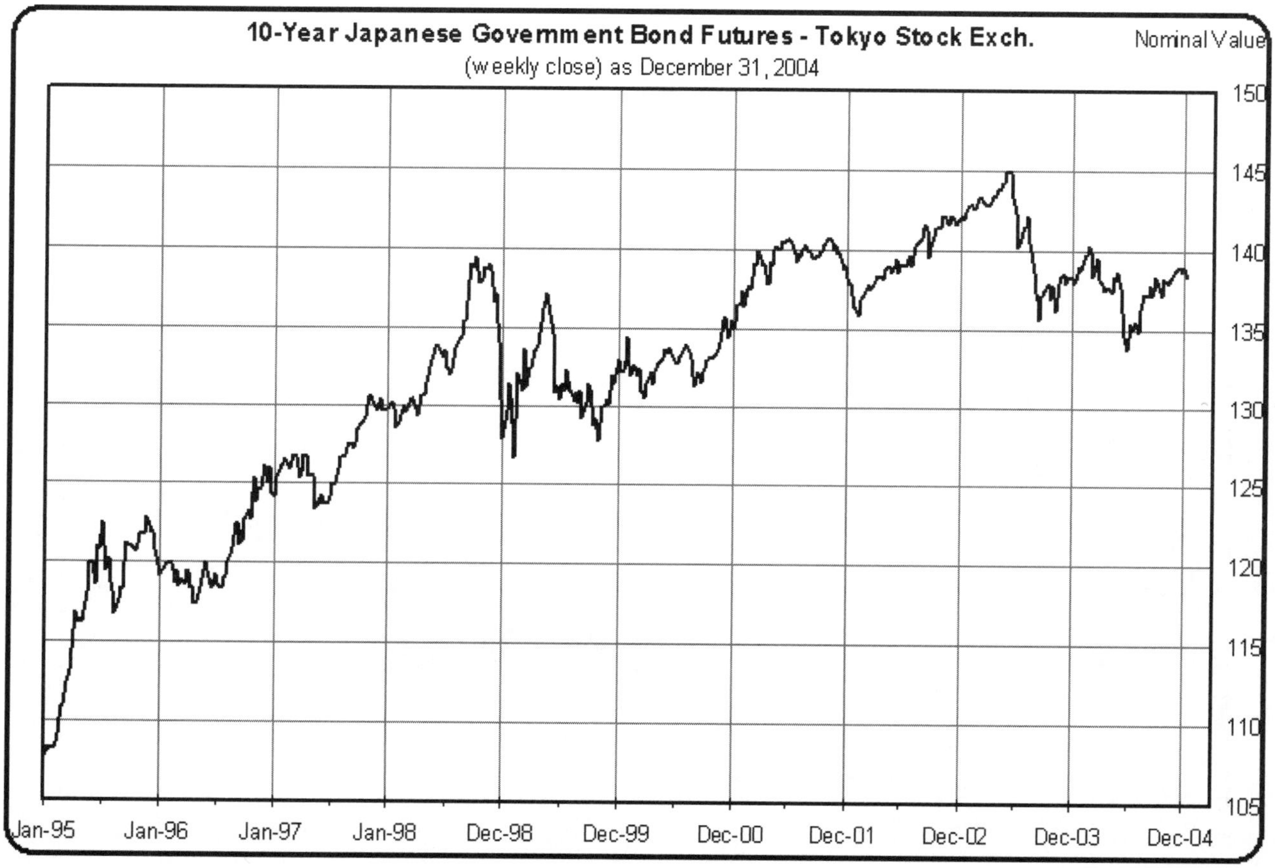
10-Year Japanese Government Bond Futures - Tokyo Stock Exch.
(weekly close) as December 31, 2004
Nominal Value
150
145
140
135
130
125
120
115
110
105
Jan-95
Jan-96
Jan-97
Jan-98
Dec-98
Dec-99
Dec-00
Dec-01
Dec-02
Dec-03
Dec-04

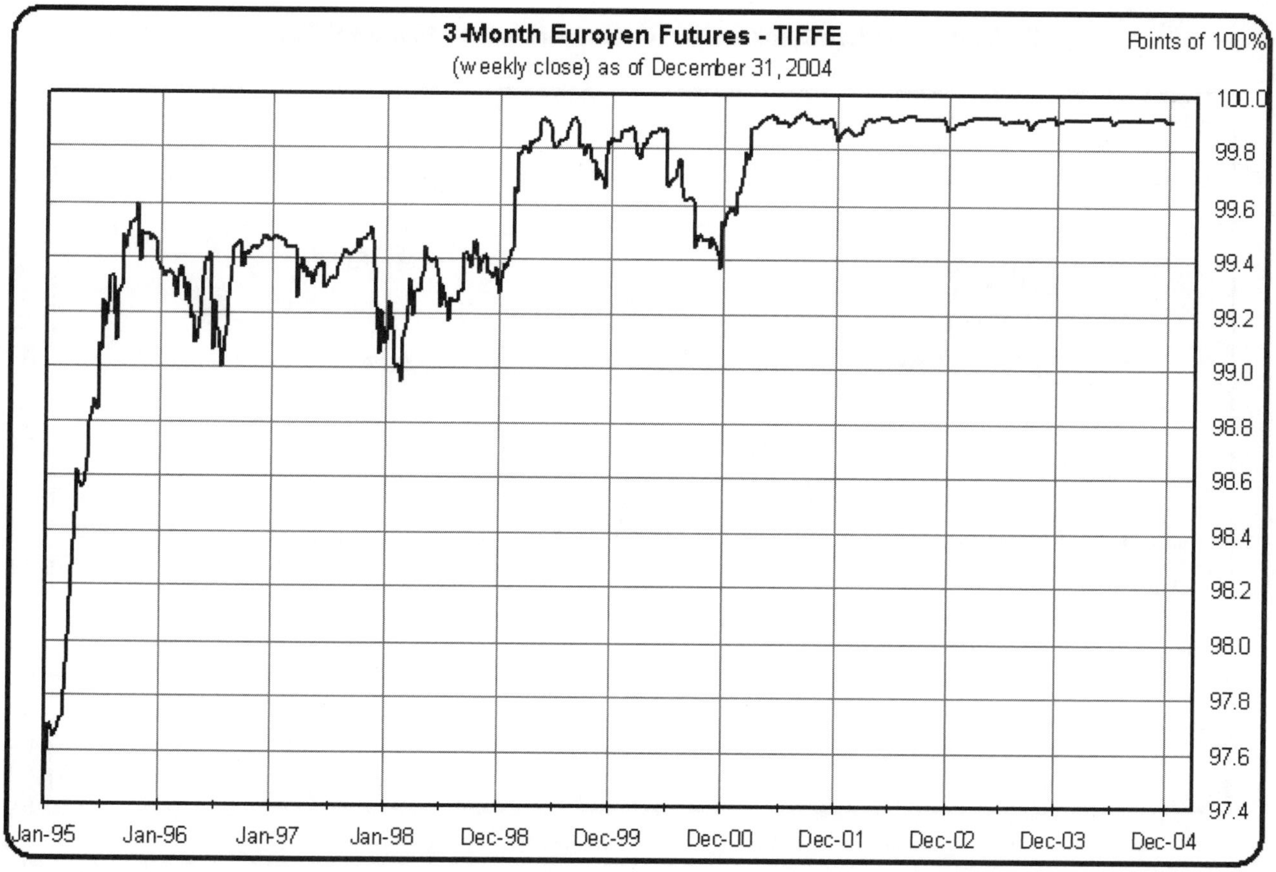
3-Month Euroyen Futures - TIFFE
(weekly close) as of December 31, 2004
Points of 100%
100.0
99.8
99.6
99.4
99.2
99.0
98.8
98.6
98.4
98.2
98.0
97.8
97.6
97.4
Jan-95
Jan-96
Jan-97
Jan-98
Dec-98
Dec-99
Dec-00
Dec-01
Dec-02
Dec-03
Dec-04

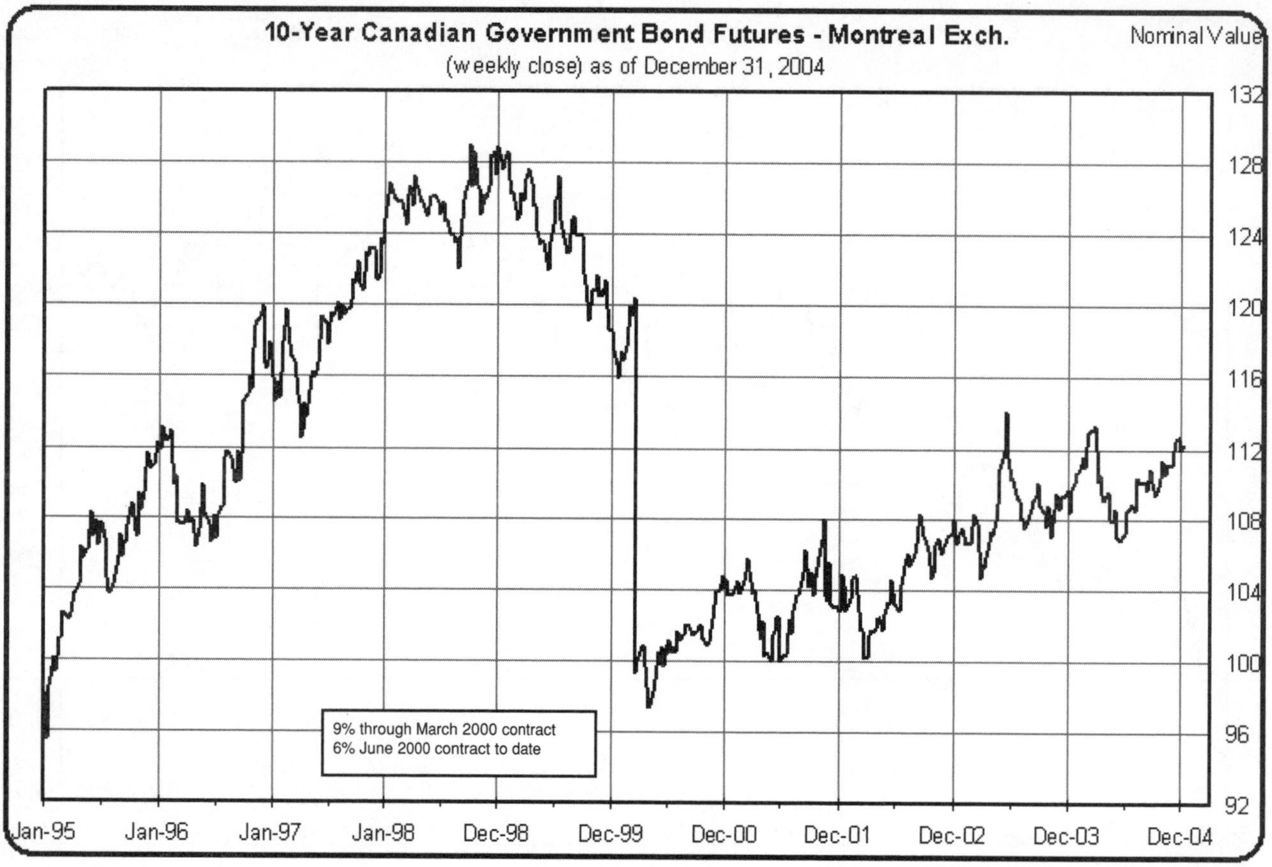
10-Year Canadian Government Bond Futures - Montreal Exch.
(weekly close) as of December 31, 2004
Nominal Value
9% through March 2000 contract
6% June 2000 contract to date
132
128
124
120
116
112
108
104
100
96
92
Jan-95
Jan-96
Jan-97
Jan-98
Dec-98
Dec-99
Dec-00
Dec-01
Dec-02
Dec-03
Dec-04

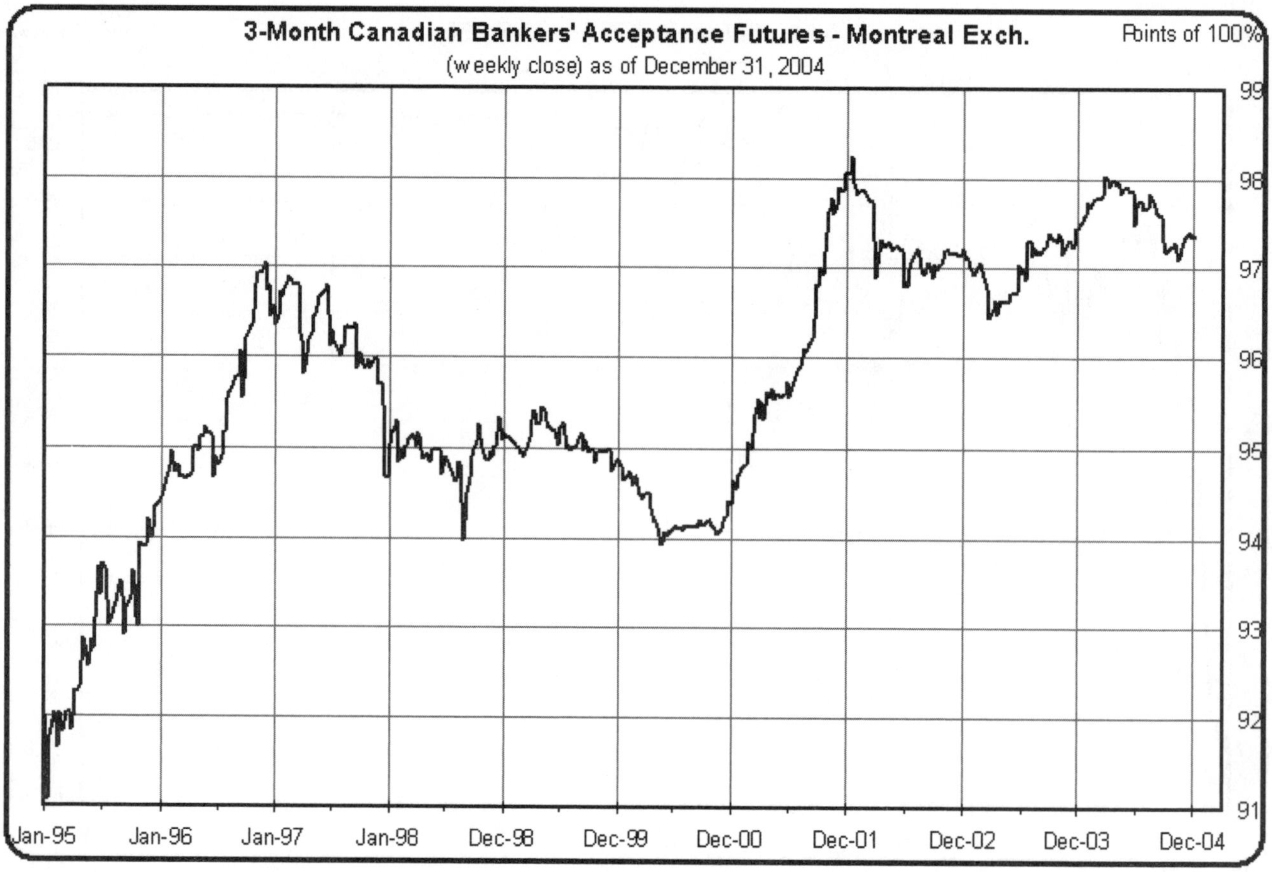
3-Month Canadian Bankers' Acceptance Futures - Montreal Exch.
(weekly close) as of December 31, 2004
Points of 100%
99
98
97
96
95
94
93
92
91
Jan-95
Jan-96
Jan-97
Jan-98
Dec-98
Dec-99
Dec-00
Dec-01
Dec-02
Dec-03
Dec-04

Australia -- Economic Statistics   Percentage Change from Previous Period

Year	Real GDP	Nominal GDP	Real Private Consumption	Real Public Consumption	Grossed Fixed Investment	Real Total Domestic Demand	Real Exports of Goods & Services	Real Imports of Goods & Services	Consumer Prices[1]	Unemployment Rate
1997	3.7	5.4	4.0	2.6	9.3	3.2	11.5	10.5	.3	8.3
1998	5.4	5.7	4.5	3.5	8.3	6.9	-.2	6.0	.9	7.8
1999	4.3	4.9	4.9	2.2	6.4	5.2	4.7	9.3	1.5	6.9
2000	3.3	7.7	3.1	4.8	.6	2.1	10.9	7.5	4.5	6.3
2001	2.7	6.1	2.9	.6	-1.9	1.3	1.8	-4.2	4.4	6.8
2002	3.6	6.5	4.0	3.8	15.7	6.2	.3	11.9	3.0	6.4
2003	3.3	6.1	4.1	3.8	8.2	6.1	-2.6	11.0	2.8	6.0
2004[2]	3.6	7.3	5.4	3.2	6.1	4.9	6.4	13.5	2.3	5.6
2005[3]	3.8	6.4	3.6	3.1	4.4	3.8	8.3	7.6	2.4	5.5

[1] National accounts inplicit private consumption deflator.   [2] Estimate.   [3] Projection.   Source: Organization for Economic Co-operation and Development (OECD)

Canada -- Economic Statistics   Percentage Change from Previous Period

Year	Real GDP	Nominal GDP	Real Private Consumption	Real Public Consumption	Grossed Fixed Investment	Real Total Domestic Demand	Real Exports of Goods & Services	Real Imports of Goods & Services	Consumer Prices[1]	Unemployment Rate
1997	4.2	5.5	4.6	-1.0	15.2	6.2	8.3	14.2	1.6	9.1
1998	4.1	3.7	2.8	3.2	2.4	2.5	9.1	5.1	1.0	8.3
1999	5.5	7.4	3.8	2.1	7.3	4.3	10.7	7.8	1.7	7.6
2000	5.2	9.6	4.0	3.1	4.7	4.8	8.9	8.1	2.7	6.8
2001	1.8	2.9	2.7	3.7	4.1	1.2	-2.8	-5.0	2.5	7.2
2002	3.4	4.5	3.4	2.8	2.4	3.7	1.1	1.4	2.2	7.6
2003	2.0	5.3	3.1	3.8	4.9	4.6	-2.4	3.8	2.8	7.6
2004[2]	3.0	6.5	3.3	2.8	6.2	3.0	7.7	8.4	1.9	7.2
2005[3]	3.3	6.2	3.2	3.1	5.3	3.9	6.8	9.1	2.0	7.1

[1] National accounts inplicit private consumption deflator.   [2] Estimate.   [3] Projection.   Source: Organization for Economic Co-operation and Development (OECD)

France -- Economic Statistics   Percentage Change from Previous Period

Year	Real GDP	Nominal GDP	Real Private Consumption	Real Public Consumption	Grossed Fixed Investment	Real Total Domestic Demand	Real Exports of Goods & Services	Real Imports of Goods & Services	Consumer Prices[1]	Unemployment Rate
1997	1.9	3.2	.2	2.1	-.2	.7	12.0	7.2	1.3	12.1
1998	3.6	4.4	3.6	-.1	7.2	4.2	8.4	11.5	.7	11.5
1999	3.2	3.7	3.5	1.5	8.3	3.7	4.2	6.1	.6	10.7
2000	4.2	5.0	2.9	3.0	8.4	4.5	13.4	15.2	1.8	9.4
2001	2.1	3.8	2.8	2.9	2.1	2.0	1.9	1.6	1.8	8.7
2002	1.1	3.6	1.8	4.6	-1.8	1.5	1.7	3.3	1.9	9.0
2003	.5	2.0	1.7	2.5	.1	1.4	-2.6	.3	2.2	9.7
2004[2]	2.1	4.0	2.3	2.3	3.5	3.2	3.4	7.7	2.3	9.8
2005[3]	2.0	3.8	2.2	1.7	3.1	2.5	6.0	7.7	1.8	9.7

[1] National accounts inplicit private consumption deflator.   [2] Estimate.   [3] Projection.   Source: Organization for Economic Co-operation and Development (OECD)

Germany -- Economic Statistics   Percentage Change from Previous Period

Year	Real GDP	Nominal GDP	Real Private Consumption	Real Public Consumption	Grossed Fixed Investment	Real Total Domestic Demand	Real Exports of Goods & Services	Real Imports of Goods & Services	Consumer Prices[1]	Unemployment Rate
1997	1.5	2.2	.7	.3	.7	.6	11.4	8.4	1.5	9.2
1998	1.7	2.8	1.7	1.9	2.3	2.2	6.4	8.6	.6	8.7
1999	1.9	2.4	3.6	.8	3.8	2.7	5.1	8.1	.6	8.0
2000	3.1	2.8	2.2	1.1	3.4	2.1	14.2	11.1	1.4	7.3
2001	1.0	2.3	1.8	1.0	-4.0	-.6	6.1	1.4	1.9	7.4
2002	.1	1.6	-.7	1.9	-6.3	-1.9	4.1	-1.6	1.3	8.2
2003	-.1	1.0	.0	.1	-2.2	.5	1.8	3.9	1.0	9.1
2004[2]	1.2	2.1	-.7	.1	-2.0	.3	8.1	6.4	1.7	9.2
2005[3]	1.4	2.2	.8	.0	.6	.9	5.7	4.9	1.3	9.3

[1] National accounts inplicit private consumption deflator.   [2] Estimate.   [3] Projection.

Source: Organization for Economic Co-operation and Development (OECD)

INTEREST RATES, WORLDWIDE

Italy -- Economic Statistics   Percentage Change from Previous Period

Year	Real GDP	Nominal GDP	Real Private Consump-tion	Real Public Consump-tion	Grossed Fixed Invest-ment	Real Total Domestic Demand	Real Exports of Goods & Services	Real Imports of Goods & Services	Consumer Prices[1]	Unem-ployment Rate
1997	2.0	4.5	3.2	.2	2.1	2.7	6.4	10.1	1.9	11.8
1998	1.7	4.5	3.2	.2	3.8	3.1	3.4	8.9	2.0	11.9
1999	1.7	3.3	2.6	1.3	5.1	3.2	.1	5.6	1.7	11.5
2000	3.2	5.4	2.8	1.7	7.3	2.4	9.7	7.1	2.6	10.7
2001	1.7	4.4	.8	3.9	1.6	1.4	1.6	.5	2.3	9.6
2002	.4	3.4	.4	1.9	1.3	1.3	-3.4	-.2	2.6	9.1
2003	.4	3.3	1.2	2.2	-2.1	1.3	-3.9	-.6	2.8	8.8
2004[2]	1.3	4.1	1.3	.7	3.8	1.2	4.5	4.3	2.1	8.1
2005[3]	1.7	3.8	1.5	.6	4.9	2.1	6.1	7.5	2.5	7.5

[1] National accounts implicit private consumption deflator.   [2] Estimate.   [3] Projection.   *Source: Organization for Economic Co-operation and Development (OECD)*

Japan -- Economic Statistics   Percentage Change from Previous Period

Year	Real GDP	Nominal GDP	Real Private Consump-tion	Real Public Consump-tion	Grossed Fixed Invest-ment	Real Total Domestic Demand	Real Exports of Goods & Services	Real Imports of Goods & Services	Consumer Prices[1]	Unem-ployment Rate
1997	1.9	2.1	.9	1.0	.9	.9	11.4	1.0	1.7	3.4
1998	-1.1	-1.2	-.1	2.0	-3.9	-1.5	-2.4	-6.6	.7	4.1
1999	.1	-1.4	.2	4.6	-.9	.2	1.5	3.3	-.3	4.7
2000	2.8	.8	1.0	4.9	2.7	2.4	12.4	9.2	-.7	4.7
2001	.4	-1.1	1.7	3.0	-1.1	1.2	-6.1	.1	-.7	5.0
2002	-.3	-1.4	1.0	2.4	-6.1	-1.0	8.0	1.9	-.9	5.4
2003	2.5	-.1	.8	1.0	3.2	1.8	10.1	5.0	-.3	5.3
2004[2]	4.0	1.6	3.4	1.9	2.8	3.2	14.4	9.9	-.1	4.8
2005[3]	2.1	.9	2.2	2.1	1.2	1.9	7.4	7.1	.1	4.5

[1] National accounts implicit private consumption deflator.   [2] Estimate.   [3] Projection.   *Source: Organization for Economic Co-operation and Development (OECD)*

Switzerland -- Economic Statistics   Percentage Change from Previous Period

Year	Real GDP	Nominal GDP	Real Private Consump-tion	Real Public Consump-tion	Grossed Fixed Invest-ment	Real Total Domestic Demand	Real Exports of Goods & Services	Real Imports of Goods & Services	Consumer Prices[1]	Unem-ployment Rate
1997	1.9	1.8	1.5	-.1	2.0	.5	11.1	8.3	.5	4.0
1998	2.8	2.5	2.4	-.9	6.5	4.0	3.9	7.5	.0	3.4
1999	1.3	2.0	2.3	.3	1.2	.3	6.5	4.3	.8	2.9
2000	3.6	4.4	2.3	2.6	4.3	2.1	12.2	9.6	1.6	2.5
2001	1.0	1.7	2.0	4.2	-3.1	2.3	.2	3.2	1.0	2.5
2002	.3	2.0	.3	3.2	.3	-.8	-.2	-2.8	.6	3.1
2003	-.4	.5	.5	1.4	-.3	.2	.0	1.4	.6	4.0
2004[2]	1.9	3.0	1.8	1.0	5.0	2.0	4.1	4.7	.8	4.0
2005[3]	1.9	3.0	1.6	.2	4.2	2.2	5.1	6.1	1.2	3.6

[1] National accounts implicit private consumption deflator.   [2] Estimate.   [3] Projection.   *Source: Organization for Economic Co-operation and Development (OECD)*

United Kingdom -- Economic Statistics   Percentage Change from Previous Period

Year	Real GDP	Nominal GDP	Real Private Consump-tion	Real Public Consump-tion	Grossed Fixed Invest-ment	Real Total Domestic Demand	Real Exports of Goods & Services	Real Imports of Goods & Services	Consumer Prices[1]	Unem-ployment Rate
1997	3.3	6.2	3.6	-.4	6.8	3.5	8.4	9.8	1.8	7.0
1998	3.1	6.0	3.9	1.2	12.7	4.8	2.8	9.3	1.6	6.2
1999	2.9	5.2	4.4	3.5	1.6	3.9	4.3	7.9	1.3	6.0
2000	3.9	5.2	4.6	2.3	3.6	3.8	9.4	9.1	.8	5.5
2001	2.3	4.6	2.9	2.6	2.6	2.9	2.9	4.9	1.2	5.1
2002	1.8	5.0	3.3	3.8	2.7	2.9	.1	4.1	1.3	5.2
2003	2.2	5.3	2.3	3.5	2.2	2.5	.1	1.3	1.4	5.0
2004[2]	3.2	5.4	3.0	3.8	6.5	3.8	2.6	4.7	1.3	4.7
2005[3]	2.6	4.8	1.8	1.9	5.3	2.4	7.9	6.5	1.7	4.7

[1] National accounts implicit private consumption deflator.   [2] Estimate.   [3] Projection.   *Source: Organization for Economic Co-operation and Development (OECD)*

Iron and Steel

Iron (symbol Fe) is a soft, malleable, and ductile metallic element. Next to aluminum, iron is the most abundant of all metals. Pure iron melts at about 1535 degrees Celsius and boils at 2750 degrees Celsius. Archaeologists in Egypt discovered the earliest iron implements dating back to about 3000 BC, and iron ornaments were used even earlier.

Steel is an alloy of iron and carbon, often with an admixture of other elements. The physical properties of various types of steel and steel alloys depend primarily on the amount of carbon present and how it is distributed in the iron. Steel is marketed in a variety of sizes and shapes, such as rods, pipes, railroad rails, tees, channels, and I-beams. Steel mills roll and form heated ingots into the required shapes. The working of steel improves the quality of the steel by refining its crystalline structure and making the metal tougher. There are five classifications of steel: carbon steels, alloy steels, high-strength low-alloy steels, stainless steel, and tool steels.

Prices – Steel prices in 2004 rallied sharply due to strong demand from China and the weak dollar. The average wholesale price of No. 1 heavy melting steel scrap rallied sharply by 93% to an average monthly price of $220.28 per metric ton from $114.03 in 2003, and prices in 2004 were nearly triple the cyclical low of $74.17 seen in the recessionary year of 2001.

Supply – World production of iron ore in 2003 rose by +5.8% to 1.164 billion metric tons, which was a new record high. The world's largest producers of iron ore are China with 22.4% of world production in 2003), Brazil (18.2%), and Australia (16.1%). The US accounted for only 4.0% of world iron ore production in 2003. World production of raw steel (ingots and castings) in 2003 rose +6.2% to 962 million metric tons, with the largest producers being China (with 22.9% of world production), Japan (11.5%), and the US (9.7%).

US production of steel ingots in 2004 rose by 8% to about 108.7 million short tons from 100.442 million in 2003. US production of pig iron (excluding ferro-alloys) rose by 5% in 2004 to about 45.0 million short tons from 42.856 million in 2003.

Demand – US consumption of ferrous scrap and pig iron fell –8.9% yr/yr in 2003 to 102.900 million metric tons, which was the lowest level since 1986. The largest consumers of ferrous scrap and pig iron were the manufacturers of pig iron and steel ingots and castings with 92% of consumption at 94.500 million metric tons in 2003. Iron foundries and miscellaneous users accounted for 5% of consumption, and manufacturers of steel castings (scrap) accounted for 3% of consumption.

Trade – The US imported 12.6 million metric tons of iron ore in 2003, up slightly by +0.8% yr/yr from 12.6 million metric tons in 2002. The bulk of US iron ore imports came from Canada (6.970 million metric tons) and Brazil (4.980 million metric tons).

World Production of Raw Steel (Ingots and Castings)   In Thousands of Metric Tons

Year	Brazil	Canada	China	France	Germany	Italy	Japan	Rep. of Korea	Russia	Ukraine	United Kingdom	United States	World Total
1994	25,747	13,897	92,613	18,031	40,837	26,151	98,295	33,745	48,812	24,081	17,286	91,244	725,107
1995	25,076	14,415	95,360	18,100	42,051	27,766	101,640	36,772	51,589	22,309	17,604	95,191	752,260
1996	25,237	14,735	101,237	17,633	39,793	23,910	98,801	38,903	49,253	22,332	17,992	95,535	749,992
1997	26,153	15,554	108,911	19,767	45,007	25,842	104,545	42,554	48,502	25,629	18,489	98,486	798,892
1998	25,800	15,930	115,590	20,126	44,046	25,798	93,548	39,896	43,822	23,461	17,066	98,600	770,000
1999	24,600	16,300	124,260	20,211	42,056	24,964	94,192	41,042	51,524	27,390	16,634	97,400	790,000
2000	27,865	15,900	128,500	21,002	46,376	26,544	106,444	43,107	59,098	31,780	15,022	102,000	850,000
2001	26,718	16,300	151,630	19,431	44,775	26,483	102,866	43,852	59,030	33,110	13,610	90,000	852,000
2002[1]	29,605	16,300	182,370	20,524	44,999	25,930	107,745	45,390	59,777	34,538	11,718	91,600	906,000
2003[2]	29,600	16,300	220,120	20,000	45,000	26,000	110,511	46,306	62,710	36,900	12,000	93,700	962,000

[1] Preliminary.   [2] Estimate.   *Source: U.S. Geological Survey (USGS)*

Average Wholesale Prices of Iron and Steel in the United States

	No. 1 Heavy Melting Steel Scrap		Hot Rolled Sheet[2]	Sheet Bars		Hot Rolled Strip	Carbon Steel Plates	Cold Rolled Strip	Galvanized Sheets	Railroad Steel Scrap[3]	Used Steel Cans[4]
	Pittsburg	Chicago		Hot Rolled	Cold Finished						
Year	---- $ Per Gross Ton ----			------------------------------------- Cents Per Pound -------------------------------------						------ $ Per Gross Ton ------	
1995	142.34	143.17	25.32	----	25.70	24.88	29.98	39.40	34.47	169.00	126.32
1996	137.28	136.07	23.94	----	26.46	25.00	31.58	----	35.05	169.00	121.27
1997	133.38	139.40	18.12	----	25.65	----	32.00	----	28.62	169.00	108.13
1998	110.10	118.76	15.57	----	25.50	----	22.50	----	24.11	164.29	109.44
1999	97.86	102.49	14.74	----	23.50	----	14.00	----	21.20	150.00	68.94
2000	103.73	96.07	15.67	----	23.08	----	15.69	----	21.38	150.00	82.23
2001	79.34	74.17	11.71	----	22.76	----	12.94	----	16.41	----	68.52
2002	101.06	89.92	16.46	----	23.26	----	----	----	22.00	----	66.71
2003	128.32	113.82	14.80	----	25.15	----	----	----	20.08	----	116.21
2004[1]	221.05	220.13	30.84	----	38.67	----	----	----	36.69	----	192.80

[1] Preliminary.   [2] 10 gauge; thru 1992, list prices; 1993 to date, market prices.   [3] Specialties scrap.   [4] *Consumer buying prices.*

NA = Not available.   *Source: American Metal Market (AMM)*

IRON AND STEEL

Salient Statistics of Steel in the United States   In Thousands of Short Tons

Year	Pig Iron Production	Producer Price Index for Steel Mill Products (1982=100)	Raw Steel Production By Type of Furnace Basic Oxygen	Open Hearth	Electric[2]	Stainless	Carbon	Alloy	Total	Net Shipments Steel Mill Products	Total Steel Products Exports	Imports
1995	56,097	120.1	62,523	----	42,407	2,265	92,656	10,009	104,930	97,494	8,157	27,270
1996	54,485	115.7	60,433	----	44,876	2,061	93,649	9,599	105,309	100,878	6,168	32,115
1997	54,679	116.4	61,053	----	47,508	2,382	95,933	10,246	108,561	105,858	7,369	34,389
1998	53,164	113.8	59,686	----	49,067	2,214	97,054	9,484	108,752	102,420	5,520	41,520
1999	51,002	105.3	57,722	----	49,673	2,086	98,694	5,421	107,395	106,201	5,426	35,731
2000	52,787	108.4	59,485	----	52,756	2,104	102,141	5,379	111,903	109,050	6,529	37,957
2001	46,424	101.3	52,204	----	47,118	1,836	92,946	4,666	99,322	99,448	6,144	30,080
2002	44,341	104.8	50,114	----	51,564	1,894	92,518	4,779	101,679	99,191	6,009	32,686
2003	43,122	109.5	50,942	----	48,751	1,952	98,772	4,901	99,693	105,625	8,220	23,125
2004[1]	44,731	147.0	50,613	----	58,456	2,073	105,161	4,851	109,069	112,085	7,933	35,808

[1] Preliminary. [2] Includes crucible steels. *Sources: American Iron & Steel Institute (AISI); U.S. Geological Survey (USGS)*

Production of Steel Ingots, Rate of Capability Utilization[1] in the United States   In Percent

Year	Jan.	Feb.	Mar.	Apr.	May	June	July	Aug.	Sept.	Oct.	Nov.	Dec.	Average
1995	93.8	95.6	96.0	92.9	91.6	90.1	86.8	88.3	93.6	90.3	92.1	90.2	91.7
1996	92.2	92.6	93.8	90.5	89.7	91.3	86.6	87.1	87.7	88.0	87.0	87.9	89.5
1997	85.3	89.3	89.6	89.2	87.9	87.0	85.1	86.4	91.2	86.9	89.6	86.3	89.4
1998	90.0	95.2	93.1	92.5	89.1	86.1	83.0	86.4	83.0	81.0	74.4	74.8	85.7
1999	77.2	79.5	81.7	81.8	81.7	79.7	79.4	82.8	82.3	88.2	89.1	88.5	82.7
2000	89.7	89.4	91.2	92.0	91.3	89.6	85.3	83.5	82.7	81.0	75.1	72.0	85.2
2001	77.6	82.3	81.8	82.9	81.5	81.6	79.8	80.4	80.5	77.5	73.5	65.9	78.8
2002	84.5	88.4	86.7	90.3	89.4	92.5	86.8	91.0	94.0	90.8	86.8	83.9	88.8
2003	83.1	87.3	85.0	87.8	81.1	86.2	78.9	78.3	80.7	82.8	82.8	81.9	83.0
2004[2]	88.0	90.9	93.8	93.3	92.9	94.4	93.5	95.0	97.3	97.5	94.8	91.5	93.6

[1] Based on tonnage capability to produce raw steel for a full order book. [2] Preliminary. *Sources: American Iron and Steel Institute (AISI); U.S. Geological Survey (USGS)*

Production of Steel Ingots in the United States   In Thousands of Short Tons

Year	Jan.	Feb.	Mar.	Apr.	May	June	July	Aug.	Sept.	Oct.	Nov.	Dec.	Total
1995	8,918	8,211	9,131	8,548	8,696	8,286	8,308	8,455	8,668	8,685	8,574	8,678	103,142
1996	8,981	8,438	9,136	8,588	8,798	8,661	8,585	8,627	8,407	8,702	8,276	8,689	104,356
1997	8,735	8,266	9,175	8,882	9,048	8,662	8,692	8,818	9,006	9,128	9,116	9,071	107,488
1998	9,510	9,087	9,839	9,524	9,483	8,863	8,832	9,194	8,548	8,681	7,710	8,013	107,643
1999	8,422	7,837	8,854	8,643	8,914	8,413	8,619	8,993	8,650	9,574	9,357	9,604	105,882
2000	9,838	9,170	10,009	9,843	10,097	9,592	9,411	9,213	8,830	8,978	8,054	7,982	111,015
2001	8,475	8,122	8,932	8,685	8,832	8,550	8,459	8,525	8,263	8,125	7,226	6,695	98,889
2002	8,050	7,609	8,261	8,214	8,401	8,414	8,510	8,918	8,916	9,015	8,340	8,329	100,976
2003	8,617	8,175	8,817	8,692	8,047	8,534	8,163	8,096	8,026	8,514	8,347	8,414	100,442
2004[1]	8,656	8,400	9,268	8,901	9,163	9,006	9,164	9,314	9,234	9,551	8,989	8,660	108,305

[1] Preliminary. *Source: American Iron and Steel Institute (AISI)*

Shipments of Steel Products[1] by Market Classifications in the United States   In Thousands of Short Tons

Year	Appliances Utensils & Cutlery	Auto- motive	Con- tainers, Packaging & Shipping Materials	Cons- truction Including Maint.	Con- tractors Products	Electrical Equip- ment	Export	Machinery, Industrial Equipment & Tools	Oil and Gas	Rail Trans- portaion	Steel for Converting & Pro- cessing[2]	Steel Service Center & Dis- tributors	All Other[3]	Total Ship- ments
1995	1,589	14,622	4,139	11,761	3,337	2,397	4,442	2,310	2,643	1,373	10,440	23,751	14,690	97,494
1996	1,713	14,665	4,101	15,561	[5]	2,401	2,328	2,410	3,254	1,400	10,245	27,124	15,676	100,878
1997	1,635	15,251	4,163	15,885	[5]	2,434	2,610	2,355	3,811	1,410	11,263	27,800	17,241	105,858
1998	1,729	15,842	3,829	15,289	[5]	2,255	2,556	2,147	2,649	1,657	9,975	27,751	16,741	102,420
1999	1,712	15,639	3,768	14,685	[5]	2,260	2,292	1,547	1,544	876	7,599	21,439	32,840	106,201
2000	1,530	14,697	3,684	14,763	[5]	2,039	2,752	1,513	2,268	994	7,753	22,537	35,093	109,624
2001	1,675	12,767	3,193	16,339	[5]	1,694	2,281	1,210	2,134	720	7,462	23,887	26,086	99,448
2002	1,734	12,562	3,251	15,729	[5]	1,336	1,844	1,137	1,658	751	7,201	22,828	29,160	99,191
2003	1,891	11,937	2,949	14,403	[5]	1,200	2,572	1,108	1,800	799	6,798	24,266	35,905	105,628
2004[4]	1,919	12,527	2,978	15,114	[5]	1,139	2,426	1,332	2,043	957	7,295	25,385	38,969	112,085

[1] All grades including carbon, alloy and stainless steel. [2] Net total after deducting shipments to reporting companines for conversion or resale.

[3] Includes agricultural; bolts, nuts rivets & screws; forgings (other than automotive); shipbuilding & marine equipment; aircraft; mining, quarrying & lumbering; other domestic & commercial equipment machinery; ordnance & other direct military; and shipments of non-reporting companies.

[4] Preliminary. *Source: American Iron and Steel Institute (AISI)*

150

Net Shipments of Steel Products[1] in the United States   In Thousands of Short Tons

Year	Cold Finished Bars	Rails & Accessories	Wire Drawn	Tin Mill Products	Plates (Cut & Coils)	Sheet & Strip Galv. (Hot Dipped)	Hot Rolled Bars	Pipe & Tubing	Structural Shapes & Steel Piling	Reinforcing Bars	Hot Rolled Sheets	Cold Rolled Sheets	Carbon	Alloy	Stainless
1995	1,782	630	654	3,942	9,043	11,329	6,902	5,437	6,278	5,048	16,978	12,347	90,485	5,115	1,894
1996	1,685	722	652	4,108	8,672	11,456	6,999	5,895	6,140	5,762	17,466	14,089	93,019	5,948	1,912
1997	1,809	875	619	4,057	8,855	12,439	8,153	6,548	6,029	6,188	18,221	13,322	97,509	6,282	2,067
1998	1,780	938	725	3,714	8,864	13,481	8,189	5,409	5,595	5,909	15,715	13,185	94,536	5,847	2,037
1999	1,775	646	611	3,771	8,200	14,870	8,078	4,772	5,995	6,183	17,740	13,874	98,694	5,421	2,086
2000	1,756	783	579	3,742	8,898	14,917	7,901	5,385	7,402	6,893	19,236	14,802	102,141	5,379	2,104
2001	1,369	630	481	3,202	8,349	14,310	7,032	5,377	6,789	6,976	18,866	12,352	92,314	4,789	1,837
2002	1,404	789	733	3,419	8,769	14,944	6,581	4,809	6,729	6,359	19,243	12,673	92,518	4,779	1,894
2003	1,426	739	684	3,513	9,230	15,221	6,486	4,597	7,437	7,970	22,218	13,485	98,772	4,901	1,952
2004[2]	1,520	843	428	3,247	10,740	16,306	7,181	5,328	7,812	8,274	23,106	14,762	105,161	4,851	2,073

[1] All grades, including carbon, alloy and stainless steel.   [2] Preliminary.   *Source: American Iron and Steel Institute (AISI)*

World Production of Pig Iron (Excludes Ferro-Alloys)   In Thousands of Metric Tons

Year	Belgium	Brazil	China	France	Germany	India	Italy	Japan	Russia	Ukraine	United Kingdom	United States	World Total
1994	8,974	25,177	97,410	13,293	29,923	17,808	11,157	73,776	36,116	21,200	11,943	49,400	544,000
1995	9,199	25,090	105,293	12,860	29,828	18,626	11,684	74,905	39,762	20,000	12,238	50,900	536,000
1996	8,628	23,978	107,225	12,108	30,012	19,864	10,347	74,597	36,061	18,143	12,830	49,400	549,000
1997	8,077	25,336	115,110	13,424	30,939	19,898	11,348	78,519	37,327	20,561	13,057	49,600	577,000
1998	8,730	25,111	118,600	13,603	30,162	20,194	10,704	74,981	34,827	20,840	12,574	48,200	572,000
1999	8,472	25,060	125,390	13,854	27,931	20,139	10,509	74,520	40,854	21,937	12,399	46,300	578,000
2000	8,472	27,723	131,010	13,621	30,846	21,321	11,223	81,071	44,618	25,700	10,891	47,900	616,000
2001	7,732	27,781	155,540	12,004	29,184	21,900	10,650	78,836	44,980	26,400	9,861	42,100	624,000
2002[1]	8,053	29,600	170,850	13,217	29,419	24,315	9,736	80,979	46,060	27,560	8,579	40,200	651,000
2003[2]	8,000	29,600	202,310	13,000	30,000	25,000	10,000	82,091	48,368	29,570	8,500	40,600	691,000

[1] Preliminary.   [2] Estimate.   *Source: U.S. Geological Survey (USGS)*

Production of Pig Iron (Excludes Ferro-Alloys) in the United States   In Thousands of Short Tons

Year	Jan.	Feb.	Mar.	Apr.	May	June	July	Aug.	Sept.	Oct.	Nov.	Dec.	Total
1995	4,820	4,453	4,916	4,568	4,674	4,499	4,576	4,688	4,727	4,687	4,738	4,762	56,115
1996	4,811	4,476	4,813	4,430	4,556	4,578	4,524	4,498	4,404	4,443	4,307	4,523	54,485
1997	4,489	4,243	4,713	4,440	4,690	4,452	4,420	4,443	4,605	4,662	4,717	4,861	54,680
1998	4,955	4,433	4,881	4,600	4,731	4,299	4,418	4,502	4,170	4,212	3,837	4,119	53,174
1999	4,140	3,802	4,257	4,157	4,352	4,045	4,204	4,280	4,167	4,572	4,447	4,722	51,145
2000	4,571	4,325	4,793	4,741	4,887	4,577	4,454	4,387	4,262	4,138	3,675	3,781	52,591
2001	3,808	3,691	4,255	4,183	4,278	4,143	4,048	4,121	3,920	3,837	3,202	2,965	46,451
2002	3,493	3,308	3,616	3,480	3,584	3,612	3,854	3,983	4,006	4,018	3,710	3,677	44,341
2003	3,832	3,631	3,906	3,810	3,381	3,569	3,395	3,253	3,289	3,527	3,530	3,733	42,856
2004[1]	3,682	3,524	4,018	3,749	3,670	3,633	3,590	3,839	3,818	3,940	3,668	3,389	44,520

[1] Preliminary.   *Source: American Iron and Steel Institute*

Salient Statistics of Ferrous Scrap and Pig Iron in the United States   In Thousands of Metric Tons

| | Consumption: Ferrous Scrap & Pig Iron Charged To | | | | | | | | | | | | Stocks -- Dec. 31 | | | |
| | Mfg. of Pig Iron & Steel Ingots & Castings | | | Iron Foundries & Misc. Users | | | Mfg. of Steel Castings (Scrap) | All Uses | | | Imports of Scrap[2] | Exports of Scrap[3] | Ferrous Scrap & Pig Iron at Consumers | | |
Year	Scrap	Pig Iron	Total	Scrap	Pig Iron	Total		Ferrous Scrap	Pig Iron	Grand Total			Scrap	Pig Iron	Total Stocks
1994	53,801	50,257	104,057	14,000	1,000	15,000	2,000	70,000	51,000	121,000	1,740	8,813	4,100	400	4,500
1995	56,000	51,000	107,000	13,000	1,100	14,100	2,000	72,000	52,000	124,000	2,090	10,400	4,200	620	4,820
1996	56,000	50,000	106,000	13,000	1,100	14,100	2,700	72,000	52,000	124,000	2,600	8,440	5,200	600	5,800
1997	58,000	51,000	109,000	13,000	1,200	14,200	1,800	73,000	52,000	125,000	2,870	8,930	5,500	510	6,010
1998	58,000	49,000	107,000	13,000	1,200	14,200	2,000	73,000	50,000	123,000	3,060	5,570	5,300	570	5,870
1999	56,000	48,000	104,000	13,000	1,100	14,100	1,900	71,000	49,000	120,000	3,360	5,000	5,450	724	6,174
2000	59,000	49,000	108,000	13,000	1,200	14,200	2,200	74,000	50,000	124,000	3,040	5,230	5,300	930	6,230
2001	57,000	47,000	104,000	12,000	1,100	13,100	2,200	71,000	48,000	119,000	2,390	6,750	4,920	787	5,707
2002	56,000	42,000	98,000	11,000	1,500	12,500	1,800	69,000	44,000	113,000	2,840	8,200	4,890	753	5,643
2003[1]	54,800	39,700	94,500	4,460	655	5,115	2,680	61,900	41,000	102,900	3,160	9,770	4,270	467	4,737

[1] Preliminary.   [2] Includes tinplate and terneplate.   [3] Excludes used rails for rerolling and other uses and ships, boats, and other vessels for scrapping.
Source: U.S. Geological Survey (USGS)

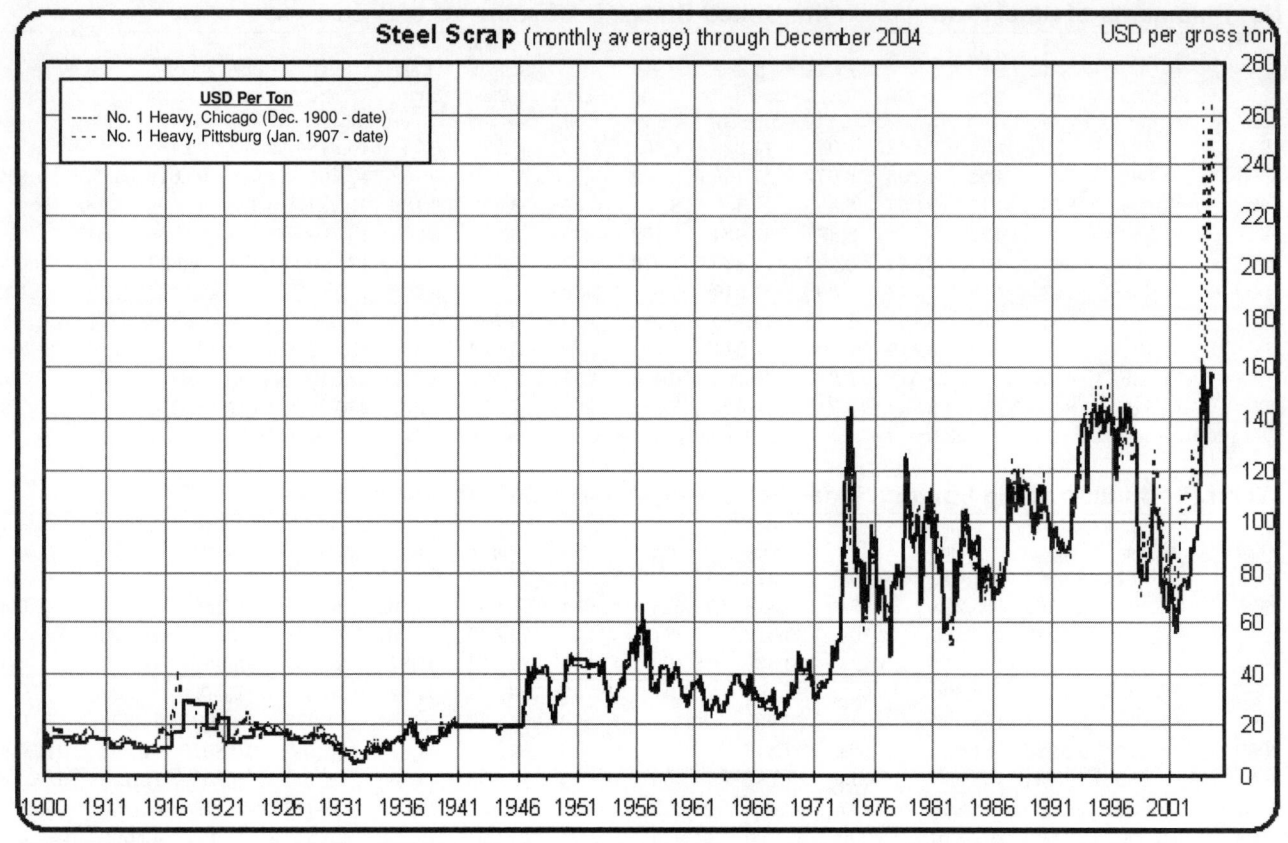

Steel Scrap (monthly average) through December 2004   USD per gross ton

USD Per Ton
----- No. 1 Heavy, Chicago (Dec. 1900 - date)
- - - No. 1 Heavy, Pittsburg (Jan. 1907 - date)

Consumption of Pig Iron in the U.S., by Type of Furnace or Equipment   In Thousands of Metric Tons

Year	Open Hearth	Electric	Cupola	Basic Oxygen Process	Air & Other Furnace	Direct Casting	Total
1994	----	1,700	520	49,138	4	39	51,401
1995	----	1,700	500	50,000	W	72	52,272
1996	----	2,200	530	49,000	W	42	52,000
1997	----	2,400	400	50,000	W	41	52,000
1998	----	4,000	590	46,000	W	36	50,000
1999	----	3,100	520	45,000	W	36	49,000
2000	----	2,900	530	47,000	W	35	50,000
2001	----	2,700	500	45,000	W	36	48,000
2002[1]	----	3,200	520	40,000	W	36	44,000
2003[2]	----	2,310	792	37,900	W	36	41,000

[1] Preliminary.   [2] Estimate.   W = Withheld.   *Source: U.S. Geological Survey (USGS)*

Wholesale Price of No. 1 Heavy Melting Steel Scrap in Chicago   In Dollars Per Metric Ton

Year	Jan.	Feb.	Mar.	Apr.	May	June	July	Aug.	Sept.	Oct.	Nov.	Dec.	Average
1995	152.05	147.50	140.20	141.50	144.50	141.64	141.50	149.76	144.90	141.50	136.50	136.50	143.17
1996	143.41	144.50	139.50	139.50	142.50	139.50	134.50	136.95	140.35	130.89	120.76	120.50	136.07
1997	131.14	143.50	139.70	132.59	136.50	136.50	143.50	146.50	139.60	139.63	142.50	142.50	139.51
1998	144.29	140.39	135.50	133.50	135.30	135.50	131.50	120.88	107.79	85.64	78.71	76.68	118.81
1999	89.66	101.50	90.89	90.50	100.00	104.32	100.98	105.95	106.50	106.50	113.40	120.17	102.49
2000	120.50	111.10	110.50	108.15	101.50	94.59	92.50	92.50	92.50	82.59	72.80	74.20	96.07
2001	83.55	74.50	74.50	74.50	73.23	72.50	75.93	76.50	76.50	72.54	67.50	67.50	74.17
2002	70.21	75.03	75.50	85.05	93.09	97.10	97.50	97.50	100.50	98.85	93.50	93.50	89.78
2003	96.93	101.97	105.07	105.50	101.69	96.88	101.05	116.79	122.02	122.50	138.22	159.74	114.03
2004	187.75	219.92	250.85	224.55	181.90	180.00	222.50	249.32	217.38	237.62	248.00	223.57	220.28

Source: American Metal Market (AMM)

World Production of Iron Ore[3]   In Thousands of Metric Tons (Gross Weight)

Year	Australia	Brazil	Canada	China	India	Maur- itania	Russia	South Africa	Sweden	Ukraine	United States	Vene- zuela	World Total
1994	128,493	177,331	37,703	240,200	60,473	11,440	73,300	30,489	19,663	51,300	58,454	18,318	991,858
1995	142,936	183,839	38,560	249,350	65,173	11,610	78,300	31,946	19,058	50,400	62,501	18,955	1,034,539
1996	147,100	174,157	34,400	249,550	66,657	11,360	72,100	30,830	21,020	47,600	62,083	18,480	1,018,436
1997	157,766	184,970	37,277	268,000	69,453	11,700	70,900	33,225	21,893	53,000	62,971	18,503	1,070,000
1998	155,731	197,500	37,808	247,000	72,532	11,400	72,343	32,948	20,930	50,758	62,931	16,553	1,050,000
1999	154,268	194,000	33,900	237,000	70,220	10,400	81,311	29,508	18,558	47,769	57,749	14,051	1,016,289
2000	167,935	212,576	35,427	223,000	75,950	11,345	86,630	33,707	20,557	55,883	63,089	17,353	1,078,251
2001	181,553	210,000	26,981	220,000	79,200	10,302	82,500	34,757	19,486	54,650	46,192	16,902	1,050,568
2002[1]	182,704	212,000	30,969	231,000	94,300	9,600	84,236	36,484	20,300	58,900	51,570	16,684	1,100,089
2003[2]	187,219	212,000	31,000	261,000	105,500	10,100	91,760	38,086	21,500	62,498	46,447	17,954	1,163,770

[1] Preliminary.   [2] Estimate.   [3] Iron ore, iron ore concentrates and iron ore agglomerates.   Source: U.S. Geological Survey (USGS)

Salient Statistics of Iron Ore[3] in the United States   In Thousands of Metric Tons

Year	Net Import Reliance as a % of Apparent Con- sumption	Production Total	Production Lake Superior	Production Other Regions	Ship- ments	Value Million $ (at Mine)	Average Value $ at Mine Per Ton	Stocks -- Dec. 31 Mines	Stocks Con suming Plants	Stocks Lake Erie Docks	Imports	Exports	Con- sumption	Value Million $ Imports
1994	18	58,215	57,848	367	57,600	1,410.0	24.49	2,790	16,300	2,230	17,500	4,980	80,200	499.0
1995	14	60,898	60,462	435	61,100	1,700.0	28.00	4,240	17,100	2,140	17,600	5,270	83,100	491.0
1996	14	62,132	61,748	383	62,200	1,750.0	28.07	4,650	18,800	2,260	18,400	6,260	79,600	556.0
1997	14	63,000	62,600	327	62,800	1,860.0	29.60	4,860	20,200	2,890	18,500	6,340	79,500	551.0
1998	17	62,900	62,591	327	63,200	1,970.0	31.14	6,020	20,500	4,080	16,900	6,000	78,200	517.0
1999	17	57,700	57,410	NA	58,500	1,550.0	26.47	5,710	17,900	2,770	14,300	6,120	75,100	399.0
2000	19	63,100	62,983	NA	61,000	1,560.0	25.57	9,150	16,800	2,860	15,700	6,150	76,500	420.0
2001	15	46,200	46,100	NA	50,600	1,210.0	23.87	3,800	12,300	1,960	10,700	5,610	67,300	293.0
2002[1]	11	51,600	51,500	NA	51,500	1,340.0	26.04	4,090	12,400	1,820	12,500	6,750	59,100	313.0
2003[2]	11	46,400	NA	NA	44,500	1,200.0	26.86	4,910	10,900	1,630	12,600	6,770	60,600	328.0

[1] Preliminary.   [2] Estimate.   [3] Usable iron ore exclusive of ore containing 5% or more manganese and includes byproduct ore.
NA = Not available.   Source: U.S. Geological Survey (USGS)

U.S. Imports (for Consumption) of Iron Ore[2]   In Thousands of Metric Tons

Year	Australia	Brazil	Canada	Chile	Maur- itania	Peru	Sweden	Vene- zuela	Total
1994	675	3,610	10,073	134	124	2	45	2,778	17,466
1995	570	4,810	9,050	57	317	54	47	2,500	17,600
1996	511	5,170	9,800	164	275	43	48	2,140	18,400
1997	742	4,970	10,000	228	----	252	149	2,090	18,600
1998	807	5,980	8,520	48	----	126	373	970	16,900
1999	694	5,540	6,860	69	----	63	421	327	14,300
2000	755	6,090	7,990	135	----	40	250	349	15,700
2001	576	4,260	4,530	711	----	71	70	87	10,700
2002	567	5,750	5,540	319	----	86	44	49	12,500
2003[1]	128	4,980	6,970	296	----	77	88	21	12,600

[1] Preliminary.   [2] Including agglomerates.   Source: U.S. Geological Survey (USGS)

Total[1] Iron Ore Stocks in the United States, at End of Month   In Thousands of Metric Tons

Year	Jan.	Feb.	Mar.	Apr.	May	June	July	Aug.	Sept.	Oct.	Nov.	Dec.
1995	20,316	19,361	18,193	18,293	19,371	20,905	22,336	23,632	23,414	24,389	24,123	23,576
1996	22,277	20,744	19,779	20,104	23,426	21,822	22,445	23,663	24,116	24,866	25,465	25,701
1997	25,913	25,262	24,745	24,812	25,001	25,620	26,076	26,971	27,562	28,029	28,053	27,912
1998	27,977	26,317	24,039	25,251	25,576	26,197	27,605	29,037	30,301	30,095	30,199	30,624
1999	29,631	28,463	28,614	28,292	29,151	29,021	28,857	27,840	26,506	25,528	25,290	26,371
2000	24,885	24,810	23,556	23,714	24,032	24,613	24,993	26,278	26,815	27,530	27,987	28,779
2001	27,583	26,076	24,570	23,800	23,600	21,664	21,010	20,440	20,050	19,660	18,690	18,000
2002	16,980	15,970	14,660	14,920	15,680	16,090	16,120	16,080	15,520	15,790	16,740	17,410
2003	17,640	19,790	21,100	18,560	17,690	17,880	17,950	18,360	17,220	17,140	17,440	16,460
2004[2]	16,600	19,970	21,380	20,760	20,780	19,680	18,270	17,100	16,070	16,560	16,300	15,590

[1] All stocks at mines, furnace yards and at U.S. docks.   [2] Preliminary.   Source: U.S. Geological Survey (USGS)

Lard

Lard is the layer of fat found along the back and underneath the skin of a hog. The hog's fat is purified by washing it with water, melting it under constant heat, and straining it several times. Lard is an important byproduct of the meatpacking industry. It is valued highly as cooking oil because there is very little smoke when it is heated. However, demand for lard in cooking is declining because of the trend toward healthier eating. Lard is also used for medicinal purposes such as ointments, plasters, liniments, and occasionally as a laxative for children. Lard production is directly proportional to commercial hog production, meaning the largest producers of hogs are the largest producers of lard.

Prices – The average monthly wholesale price of lard in 2004 (through November) rose by +27.7% to 26.33 cents per pound, which was the highest level since 28.69 cents in 1984. The record price of 29.654 cents was seen in 1975.

Supply – World production of lard in the 2003-04 marketing year rose by +2.7% yr/yr to 7.276 million metric tons, which was a record high. The world's largest lard producers are China (with 43% of world production), United States (7%), Germany (6%), former USSR (5%), Poland (4%), Spain (4%), and Brazil (4%). US production of lard in 2002-03 rose +2.4% yr/yr to 1.083 billion pounds.

Demand – US consumption of lard in 2004 (through October, annualized) rose +1.4% to 273.251 million pounds. That was only mildly above the record low of 269.486 million pounds. The current level of consumption is less than one-fifth of consumption seen in 1971 of 1.574 billion pounds.

Exports – US exports of lard in 2002-03 fell by –18.4% yr/yr to 84.0 million pounds, and accounted for 7.8% of US production.

World Production of Lard   In Thousands of Metric Tons

Year	Brazil	Canada	China	France	Germany	Italy	Japan	Poland	Romania	Spain	United States	Former USSR	World Total
1995-6	194.3	83.0	2,136.6	154.6	405.6	198.5	76.3	284.9	105.1	206.5	449.3	385.0	5,860.4
1996-7	197.4	83.1	2,400.2	157.3	396.5	197.6	74.1	259.4	99.1	211.8	437.0	351.5	6,065.0
1997-8	214.3	91.5	2,624.8	162.3	413.4	194.0	67.9	266.4	96.9	238.5	478.9	339.7	6,406.1
1998-9	234.3	99.3	2,665.5	167.4	444.5	201.3	66.4	270.1	92.9	258.1	501.7	337.4	6,597.9
1999-00	250.5	107.5	2,771.4	164.7	423.5	200.9	65.1	254.7	81.1	262.0	491.6	344.2	6,675.1
2000-1	262.1	112.6	2,832.1	155.7	415.2	195.9	62.3	240.1	72.7	264.9	488.6	338.4	6,686.5
2001-2[1]	270.3	118.1	2,918.6	157.4	422.3	199.3	61.8	257.0	69.5	266.9	508.1	351.3	6,881.6
2002-3[2]	277.8	119.7	3,019.2	156.7	433.2	204.8	59.3	282.0	69.0	290.9	510.0	361.7	7,088.0
2003-4[3]	284.8	121.7	3,134.8	157.5	433.5	212.6	58.5	286.2	68.9	296.7	530.0	370.4	7,276.4

[1] Preliminary. [2] Estimate. [3] Forecast. *Source: The Oil World*

Supply and Distribution of Lard in the United States   In Millions of Pounds

	Supply				Disappearance					
Year	Production	Stocks Oct. 1	Total Supply	Domestic	Baking & Frying Fats	Margarine[3]	Exports	Total Disappearance	Direct Use	Per Capita (Lbs.)
1994-5	1,052.4	34.4	1,089.0	924.4	332.2	43.0	140.4	1,064.7	561.9	3.4
1995-6	1,012.6	24.3	1,038.8	921.8	295.9	33.0	94.3	1,016.1	593.0	3.5
1996-7	979.0	22.7	1,002.9	879.6	262.0	15.0	103.3	982.9	602.4	3.5
1997-8	1,064.7	19.9	1,086.7	924.6	285.0	17.0	121.8	1,046.4	623.3	3.4
1998-9	1,106.1	40.4	1,148.4	987.6	250.0	26.0	139.9	1,127.5	654.0	3.6
1999-00	1,091.0	20.8	1,097.8	917.8	234.0	14.0	155.0	1,072.8	675.0	3.5
2000-1	1,058.0	27.0	1,087.0	895.0	NA	5.0	174.0	1,069.0	644.0	2.3
2001-2[1]	1,058.0	18.0	1,080.0	963.0	NA	14.0	103.0	1,066.0	661.0	2.3
2002-3[2]	1,083.0		1,109.0	1,012.0			84.0	1,096.0	706.0	2.4

[1] Preliminary. [2] Forecast. [3] Includes edible tallow. NA = not avaliable. *Source: Economic Research Service, U.S. Department of Agriculture (ERS-USDA)*

Consumption of Lard (Edible and Inedible) in the United States   In Millions of Pounds

Year	Jan.	Feb.	Mar.	Apr.	May	June	July	Aug.	Sept.	Oct.	Nov.	Dec.	Total
1996	30.5	35.4	36.7	46.9	36.8	31.4	32.6	33.9	30.9	34.5	34.7	33.6	417.9
1997	26.5	30.5	31.0	36.5	39.9	36.2	36.1	35.0	37.4	39.0	41.5	40.4	429.8
1998	34.1	29.9	31.1	29.6	28.5	35.9	33.0	33.0	37.1	37.7	38.9	33.9	402.7
1999	34.6	30.2	28.8	31.1	30.5	32.9	28.9	33.0	29.2	31.2	31.3	30.3	372.1
2000	27.3	25.7	29.1	23.3	30.3	27.6	24.4	31.3	31.1	32.6	29.6	31.7	343.9
2001	27.8	22.2	28.3	24.5	22.5	23.3	21.8	27.1	23.2	27.9	26.7	24.4	299.8
2002	26.4	26.1	21.8	26.7	24.8	21.2	22.9	26.4	23.6	26.4	28.1	28.7	303.2
2003	22.6	22.3	23.4	21.4	23.3	24.0	23.0	21.4	22.5	24.3	20.2	21.0	269.5
2004[1]	22.9	25.8	25.9	23.9	23.5	22.0	19.1	19.7	21.3	22.4	21.9	19.5	267.6

[1] Preliminary. *Source: Bureau of the Census, U.S. Department of Commerce*

Average Wholesale Price of Lard, Loose, Tank Cars, in Chicago   In Cents Per Pound

Year	Jan.	Feb.	Mar.	Apr.	May	June	July	Aug.	Sept.	Oct.	Nov.	Dec.	Average
1995	21.21	21.13	19.25	18.34	18.25	19.02	20.25	21.30	21.48	20.90	21.38	21.35	20.32
1996	20.52	18.17	18.01	18.67	20.47	22.61	24.55	26.30	27.09	23.11	19.70	22.17	21.78
1997	24.93	25.47	24.69	20.82	20.94	22.68	23.83	23.95	23.14	23.41	23.97	22.85	23.39
1998	19.09	16.03	17.36	17.64	18.66	19.38	17.93	18.65	16.58	17.39	17.60	16.27	17.72
1999	16.89	13.91	11.98	13.12	13.43	12.98	11.87	13.89	17.44	20.55	17.74	16.12	14.99
2000	15.66	12.38	11.99	11.96	12.68	12.64	10.32	10.35	11.14	13.04	12.06	12.14	12.20
2001	13.57	11.92	11.07	12.09	11.84	13.38	18.05	24.11	22.00	13.04	13.18	14.92	14.93
2002	12.69	12.50	13.07	12.42	11.38	14.64	14.60	15.00	15.21	14.39	16.28	18.42	14.22
2003	18.61	17.11	16.85	16.72	17.29	18.90	18.93	20.08	23.98	27.50	26.40	25.18	20.63
2004	26.50	25.83	23.77	22.58	21.31	22.50	27.53	32.06	32.38	27.95	27.26	26.50	26.35

Source: Economic Research Service, U.S. Department of Agriculture (ERS-USDA)

United States Cold Storage Holdings of all Lard[1], on First of Month   In Millions of Pounds

Year	Jan.	Feb.	Mar.	Apr.	May	June	July	Aug.	Sept.	Oct.	Nov.	Dec.
1995	40.6	50.3	46.4	43.0	36.8	27.1	25.8	22.1	30.2	24.3	19.9	21.6
1996	38.4	38.6	25.8	28.8	21.5	23.2	23.7	30.5	20.7	22.7	20.1	18.8
1997	18.9	16.3	18.5	19.2	18.9	18.7	23.0	23.2	21.5	19.9	21.3	19.7
1998	22.2	30.1	38.3	42.5	41.6	47.6	43.7	44.8	38.8	40.4	34.8	26.3
1999	28.4	30.4	30.6	34.0	27.1	39.9	30.7	25.5	29.4	20.8	19.1	22.8
2000	26.7	27.8	29.2	30.1	20.2	22.5	18.9	19.3	17.3	17.4	16.3	16.8
2001	16.0	14.9	14.9	17.9	13.7	13.1	10.3	12.4	11.8	13.6	13.0	11.7
2002	13.2	18.0	16.4	16.5	20.3	22.4	18.9	18.3	12.0	10.5	14.6	11.3
2003	10.5	14.0	19.6	18.7	16.5	13.5	11.9	9.7	8.4	9.3	10.1	12.4
2004[2]	13.3	19.8	18.6	20.3	20.5	15.0	12.9	10.8	10.3	11.8	11.4	13.2

[1] Stocks in factories and warehouses (except that in hands of retailers).   [2] Preliminary.   *Source: Bureau of the Census, U.S. Department of Commerce*

Lead

Lead (symbol Pb) is a dense, toxic, bluish-gray metallic element, and is the heaviest stable element. Lead was one of the first known metals. The ancients used lead in face powders, rouges, mascaras, paints, condiments, wine preservatives, and water supply plumbing. The Romans were slowly poisoned from lead because of its diverse daily usage.

Lead is usually found in ore with zinc, silver, and most often copper. The most common lead ore is galena, containing 86.6% lead. Cerussite and angleside are other common varieties of lead. More than half of the lead currently used comes from recycling.

Lead is used in building construction, bullets and shot, tank and pipe lining, storage batteries, and electric cable sheathing. Lead is used extensively as a protective shielding for radioactive material (e.g., X-ray apparatus) because of its high density and nuclear properties. Lead is also part of solder, pewter, and fusible alloys.

Lead futures and options trade at the London Metal Exchange (LME). The LME lead futures contract calls for the delivery of 25 metric tons of at least 99.970% purity lead ingots (pigs). The contract is priced in US dollars per metric ton. Lead first started trading on the LME in 1903.

Prices – Lead prices more than doubled in the rally that began in mid-2003 and continued through 2004. Cash lead prices hit a new high for the rally of about $1050 per metric ton at the very end of 2004. Bullish factors included strong demand for base metals, tight supplies, and the weak dollar.

Supply – World smelter production of lead (both primary and secondary) in 2003 rose +2.9% yr/yr to 6.820 mil-lion metric tons and easily posted a new record production level. The world's largest smelter producers of lead (both primary and secondary) are China with 23% of world production in 2003, followed by the US with 20%, Germany with 5%, and the UK with 5%.

US mine production of recoverable lead rose +2.0% yr/yr to 449,000 metric tons in 2003, recovering from 2002's 6-year low of 440,000 metric tons. Missouri was responsible for 96% of US production, with the remainder produced mainly by Idaho and Montana. Lead recovered from scrap in the US (secondary production) rose +3.3% yr/yr in 2003 (through October, annualized) to 1.150 million metric tons, which was a new record high and highlighted lead scrap recovery efforts in the US. That is more than twice the amount of lead produced in the US from mines (primary production). The value of US refined lead production in 2003 fell to $236.0 million, which was a 9-year low and was well below the record high of $668 million posted back in 1979.

Demand – US lead consumption in 2004 (through October, annualized) fell by -4.9% to 1.417 million metric tons, which was a 9-year low. The record level of US lead consumption was 1.680 million metric tons posted in 1999.

Trade – The US relied on imports for 11% of its lead consumption in 2003. US imports of lead pigs and bars in 2004 fell –16.7% yr/yr to a 12-year low of 175,000 metric tons. US lead exports in 2003 were comprised by ore concentrate (253,000 metric tons), scrap (92,800 metric tons), unwrought lead (92,100 metric tons), and wrought lead (30,500 metric tons).

World Smelter (Primary and Secondary) Production of Lead   In Thousands of Metric Tons

Year	Aus-tralia[3]	Belgium[4]	Canada[3]	China[2]	France	Germany	Italy	Japan	Mexico[3]	Spain	United Kingdom[3]	United States	World Total
1994	237.0	123.5	251.6	467.9	260.5	331.7	205.9	292.2	171.0	140.0	352.5	1,280	5,360
1995	241.0	122.0	281.4	608.0	296.7	311.2	180.4	287.6	176.0	80.0	320.7	1,390	5,590
1996	228.0	125.0	309.4	706.0	302.8	238.1	209.8	287.4	160.0	86.0	345.6	1,400	5,630
1997	238.0	110.8	271.4	707.0	302.3	329.2	211.6	296.8	178.0	74.9	391.0	1,450	5,880
1998	206.0	91.5	265.5	757.0	318.0	380.2	199.3	302.1	173.0	90.0	348.9	1,450	5,970
1999	272.8	103.2	266.4	918.0	279.0	373.6	215.3	293.4	221.1	96.0	348.1	1,460	6,280
2000	251.8	118.0	284.8	1,100.0	258.0	415.0	235.0	311.7	253.2	120.0	337.2	1,470	6,660
2001	303.0	96.0	230.9	1,200.0	238.0	374.0	203.0	302.4	253.5	98.0	366.0	1,390	6,580
2002[1]	211.0	88.0	251.3	1,330.0	204.0	390.0	205.0	285.8	237.2	116.0	370.0	1,380	6,630
2003[2]	350.0	65.0	272.0	1,580.0	100.0	357.0	214.0	295.3	250.0	102.0	340.0	1,390	6,820

[1] Preliminary.   [2] Estimate.   [3] Refonded & bullion.   [4] Includes scrap.   *Source: U.S. Geological Survey (USGS)*

Consumption of Lead in the United States, by Products   In Metric Tons

Year	Ammun-ition	Bearing Metals	Pipes, Traps & Bends[2]	Cable Covering	Calking Lead	Casting Metals	Other Metal Products[3]	Total Other Oxides[4]	Sheet Lead	Solder	Storage Battery — Grids, Post, etc.	Oxides	Brass and Bronze	Total Consumption
1994	62,400	5,560	3,370	16,000	764	18,900	5,330	62,700	21,500	12,200	797,000	425,000	6,320	1,450,000
1995	70,900	6,490	2,210	5,640	935	18,100	5,220	61,700	27,900	16,200	711,000	618,000	5,260	1,560,000
1996	52,100	4,350	1,810	W	767	18,900	5,220	62,100	19,400	9,020	635,000	706,000	5,460	1,540,000
1997	52,400	2,490	1,860	4,930	1,390	34,000	7,570	67,000	19,100	9,580	634,000	761,000	4,410	1,620,000
1998	52,800	2,210	3,130	4,630	1,350	32,600	8,160	53,400	15,500	10,900	685,000	742,000	3,460	1,630,000
1999	58,300	1,570	2,020	2,410	971	34,300	7,130	58,200	15,400	13,100	765,000	707,000	3,940	1,680,000
2000	63,700	1,490	2,010	W	1,140	35,100	25,800	52,400	23,800	11,500	796,000	690,000	3,670	1,720,000
2001	53,600	837	2,370	W	927	31,800	17,100	43,900	22,400	6,120	655,000	694,000	2,590	1,550,000
2002	57,600	406	2,250	W	1,060	34,800	24,200	51,900	25,600	6,450	554,000	641,000	2,730	1,440,000
2003[1]	48,800	406	1,670	W	822	31,700	22,800	35,700	24,200	6,310	523,000	642,000	2,810	1,390,000

[1] Preliminary.   [2] Including building.   [3] Including terne metal, type metal, and lead consumerd in foil, collapsible tubes, annealing, plating, galvanizing and fishing weights.   [4] Includes paints, glass and ceramic products, and other pigments and chemicals.   W = Withheld proprietary data.

Source: U.S. Geological Survey (USGS)

Salient Statistics of Lead in the United States   In Thousands of Metric Tons

Year	Net Import Reliance as a % of Apparent Consumption	Production of Refined Lead From Domestic Ores[3]	Production of Refined Lead From Foreign Ores[3]	Production Total Primary	Total Value of Refined Million $	Secondary Lead Recovered As Soft Lead	Secondary Lead Recovered In Antimonial Lead	Secondary Lead Recovered In Other Alloys	Total	Total Value of Secondary Million $	Stocks, Dec. 31 Primary	Stocks, Dec. 31 Consumer[4]	Average Price New York	Average Price London[5]
1994	19	328.0	23.4	351.4	288.0	527.0	371.0	16.1	931.0	763.0	9.3	68.8	37.17	24.83
1995	17	374.0	W	374.0	348.0	584.0	400.0	19.2	1,020.0	951.0	14.2	79.4	42.28	28.08
1996	17	326.0	W	326.0	351.0	625.0	420.0	9.2	1,070.0	1,150.0	8.1	72.1	48.83	31.22
1997	14	343.0	W	343.0	352.0	663.0	411.0	14.2	1,110.0	1,130.0	11.9	89.1	46.54	28.29
1998	21	337.0	W	337.0	336.0	667.0	417.0	16.1	1,120.0	1,110.0	10.9	77.9	45.27	23.96
1999	20	350.0	W	350.0	337.0	635.0	444.0	18.1	1,110.0	1,070.0	12.3	78.7	43.72	22.78
2000	24	341.0	W	341.0	328.0	651.0	428.0	36.8	1,130.0	1,090.0	18.6	106.0	43.57	20.57
2001	20	290.0	W	290.0	279.0	734.0	291.0	75.9	1,100.0	1,060.0	W	100.0	43.64	21.58
2002[1]	18	262.0	W	262.0	252.0	754.0	289.0	72.8	1,120.0	1,070.0	W	111.0	43.56	20.52
2003[2]	11	245.0	W	245.0	236.0	829.0	303.0	15.6	1,150.0	1,110.0	W	107.0	43.76	23.34

[1] Preliminary.   [2] Estimate.   [3] And base bullion.   [4] Also at secondary smelters.   [5] LME data in dollars per metric ton beginning July 1993.
W = Withheld Proprietary data.   E = Net exporter.   Source: U.S. Geological Survey (USGS)

United States Foreign Trade of Lead   In Thousands of Metric Tons

Year	Exports Ore Concentrate	Exports Unwrought Lead[3]	Exports Wrought Lead[4]	Exports Scrap	Exports Ash & Residues	Imports for Consumption Ores, Flue Dust or Fume & Mattes	Imports for Consumption Base Bullion	Imports for Consumption Pigs & Bars	Imports for Consumption Reclaimed Scrap, etc.	Imports for Consumption Value Million $	General Imports From Ore, Flue Dust & Matte Australia	General Imports From Ore, Flue Dust & Matte Canada	General Imports From Ore, Flue Dust & Matte Peru	General Imports From Pigs & Bars Canada	General Imports From Pigs & Bars Mexico	General Imports From Pigs & Bars Peru
1994	38.7	48.2	5.3	88.1	20.6	0.5	0.6	230.8	0.1	146.6	0.5	0.2	----	159.0	31.9	25.6
1995	65.5	48.2	9.0	105.0	8.0	2.6	0.0	264.0	0.1	191.7	1.5	----	0.1	182.0	54.3	22.1
1996	59.7	44.0	16.7	85.3	19.4	6.6	0.0	268.0	0.2	217.0	----	4.4	----	192.0	56.9	17.1
1997	42.2	37.4	15.9	88.4	16.8	17.8	0.0	265.0	0.1	200.3	----	0.8	3.4	186.0	70.4	6.4
1998	72.4	24.1	15.4	99.2	9.0	32.7	0.5	267.0	[6]	191.9	2.4	6.5	18.5	181.0	63.6	11.4
1999	93.5	23.4	13.9	117.0	1.4	12.3	0.1	311.0	----	196.5	0.1	1.2	8.8	198.0	27.2	6.9
2000	117.0	21.4	27.2	71.6	11.3	31.2	0.1	356.0	0.0	217.1	----	[6]	10.8	216.0	18.4	1.8
2001	181.0	17.0	17.7	108.0	14.2	2.2	----	271.0	10.2	166.8	----	----	----	167.0	12.4	2.3
2002[1]	241.0	31.4	11.7	106.0	----	0.0	----	210.0	2.6	124.9	----	----	----	172.0	7.5	----
2003[2]	253.0	92.1	30.5	92.8	----	----	----	175.0	4.2	112.6	----	----	----	167.0	8.3	----

[1] Preliminary.   [2] Estimate.   [3] And lead alloys.   [4] Blocks, pigs, etc.   [6] Less than 1/2 unit.   Source: U.S. Geological Survey (USGS)

Annual Mine Production of Recoverable Lead in the United States   In Metric Tons

Year	Total	Idaho	Missouri	Montana	Other States	Missouri's % of Total
1994	363,443	W	290,738	9,940	63,100	80%
1995	386,000	W	359,000	8,350	18,200	93%
1996	426,000	W	397,000	7,970	21,200	93%
1997	448,000	W	412,000	9,230	26,600	92%
1998	481,000	W	439,000	7,310	35,100	91%
1999	503,000	W	464,000	7,950	31,200	92%
2000	449,000	W	410,000	W	38,700	91%
2001	454,000	W	423,000	W	30,900	93%
2002[1]	440,000	W	428,000	W	12,300	97%
2003[2]	449,000	W	432,000	W	17,200	96%

[1] Preliminary.   [2] Estimate.   W = Withheld, included in Other States.   NA = Not Avaliable.   Source: U.S. Geological Survey (USGS)

Mine Production of Recoverable Lead in the United States   In Thousands of Metric Tons

Year	Jan.	Feb.	Mar.	Apr.	May	June	July	Aug.	Sept.	Oct.	Nov.	Dec.	Total
1995	29.6	30.3	35.2	28.9	32.7	34.8	32.5	33.5	29.9	34.1	31.6	32.1	385.0
1996	36.9	36.4	35.6	35.9	37.5	33.8	35.6	34.1	26.9	35.2	33.6	35.7	426.0
1997	36.7	36.7	37.2	38.6	38.6	35.1	33.4	33.7	34.4	35.4	31.7	32.8	448.0
1998	37.4	35.4	37.8	37.3	35.7	34.7	34.3	35.6	36.1	40.3	37.8	39.2	449.0
1999	41.2	42.1	44.4	43.1	41.7	42.6	47.2	43.6	41.5	41.2	37.8	38.1	505.0
2000	35.1	36.7	43.0	37.5	37.4	37.8	33.0	36.8	36.8	32.4	38.8	36.9	447.0
2001	42.9	37.8	39.4	33.7	35.0	32.2	38.2	39.6	32.4	39.5	32.1	35.4	450.0
2002	39.5	35.5	41.2	36.1	39.3	36.1	35.0	39.6	33.2	34.8	34.1	34.2	438.6
2003	33.7	34.9	38.5	36.2	38.8	39.2	41.3	38.0	38.3	37.2	34.0	33.9	444.0
2004[1]	33.4	32.8	33.5	35.1	31.2	33.1	33.8	36.9	36.9	36.2			411.5

[1] Preliminary.   Source: U.S. Geological Survey (USGS)

LEAD

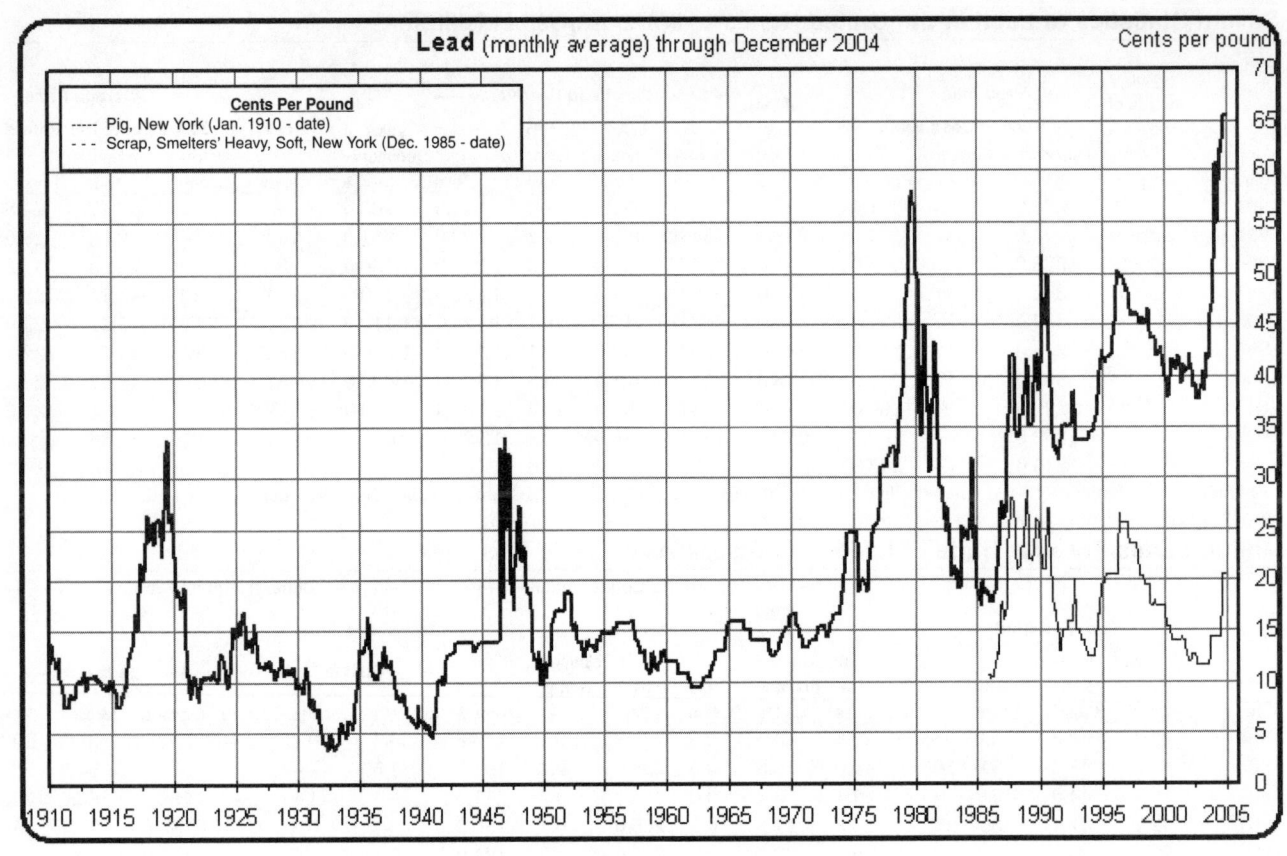

Lead (monthly average) through December 2004   Cents per pound

Cents Per Pound
----- Pig, New York (Jan. 1910 - date)
- - - Scrap, Smelters' Heavy, Soft, New York (Dec. 1985 - date)

Average Price of Pig Lead, U.S. Primary Producers (Common Corroding)[1] In Cents Per Pound

Year	Jan.	Feb.	Mar.	Apr.	May	June	July	Aug.	Sept.	Oct.	Nov.	Dec.	Average
1995	44.00	44.00	42.00	42.00	42.00	42.00	42.00	43.65	44.00	44.00	46.10	48.00	43.65
1996	48.00	49.50	50.96	52.00	52.00	52.00	50.29	49.18	50.00	50.00	50.00	50.00	50.33
1997	50.00	50.00	48.70	48.00	48.00	48.00	48.00	48.00	48.00	48.00	48.00	48.00	48.39
1998	48.00	48.00	48.00	48.00	48.00	48.00	48.00	48.00	48.00	48.00	45.47	45.00	47.54
1999	45.00	45.00	45.00	45.00	45.00	45.00	45.00	45.00	45.00	45.00	45.00	45.00	45.00
2000	45.00	45.00	45.00	45.00	45.00	45.00	45.00	45.00	45.00	45.00	45.00	45.00	45.00
2001	45.00	45.00	45.00	45.00	45.00	45.00	45.00	45.00	45.00	45.00	45.00	45.00	45.00
2002	45.00	45.00	45.00	45.00	45.00	45.00	45.00	45.00	45.00	45.00	45.00	45.00	45.00
2003	23.14	24.65	23.81	23.13	24.56	24.77	26.93	26.05	27.23	30.16	32.09	35.46	26.83
2004	38.48	44.79	45.30	39.93	42.44	45.16	48.20	47.46	48.08	48.01	49.54	49.75	45.60

[1] New York Delivery. Source: American Metal Market (AMM)

Refiners Production[1] of Lead in the United States In Metric Tons

Year	Jan.	Feb.	Mar.	Apr.	May	June	July	Aug.	Sept.	Oct.	Nov.	Dec.	Total
1995	32,100	29,100	32,600	32,300	32,600	28,300	31,000	29,300	30,600	34,200	30,100	31,500	374,000
1996	34,700	30,400	30,900	28,600	27,500	21,700	25,500	24,700	25,400	25,300	26,100	25,500	326,000
1997	28,800	28,500	31,900	30,400	30,800	28,700	25,900	28,000	21,600	30,500	29,000	28,700	343,000
1998	29,200	25,900	30,000	29,700	29,500	20,300	28,900	NA	NA	NA	NA	NA	337,000
1999	NA	NA	NA	NA	NA	NA	NA	NA	NA	NA	NA	NA	350,000
2000	NA	NA	NA	NA	NA	NA	NA	NA	NA	NA	NA	NA	341,000
2001	NA	NA	NA	NA	NA	NA	NA	NA	NA	NA	NA	NA	290,000
2002	NA	NA	NA	NA	NA	NA	NA	NA	NA	NA	NA	NA	262,000
2003	NA	NA	NA	NA	NA	NA	NA	NA	NA	NA	NA	NA	245,000
2004[2]	NA	NA	NA	NA	NA	NA	NA	NA	NA	NA	NA		

[1] Represents refined lead produced from domestic ores by primary smelters plus small amounts of secondary material passing through these smelters. Includes GSA metal purchased for remelt. [2] Preliminary. *Source: U.S. Geological Survey (USGS)*

Total Stocks of Lead[1] in the United States at Refiners, at End of Month   In Metric Tons

Year	Jan.	Feb.	Mar.	Apr.	May	June	July	Aug.	Sept.	Oct.	Nov.	Dec.
1995	8,200	9,750	11,500	14,500	16,700	16,200	21,300	14,000	12,800	9,820	9,830	14,200
1996	15,000	15,000	15,000	15,000	15,000	19,600	19,900	14,200	12,200	7,060	7,830	8,160
1997	8,460	11,800	21,400	19,900	15,000	10,900	6,530	7,790	5,370	7,310	8,710	11,900
1998	13,000	15,900	18,700	20,900	11,400	11,400	13,700	NA	NA	NA	NA	10,900
1999	NA	NA	NA	NA	NA	NA	NA	NA	NA	NA	NA	12,300
2000	NA	NA	NA	NA	NA	NA	NA	NA	NA	NA	NA	18,600
2001	NA	NA	NA	NA	NA	NA	NA	NA	NA	NA	NA	NA
2002	NA	NA	NA	NA	NA	NA	NA	NA	NA	NA	NA	NA
2003	NA	NA	NA	NA	NA	NA	NA	NA	NA	NA	NA	NA
2004[2]	NA	NA	NA	NA	NA	NA	NA	NA	NA	NA	NA	

[1] Primary refineries.   [2] Preliminary.   Source: U.S. Geological Survey (USGS)

Total[1] Lead Consumption in the United States   In Thousands of Metric Tons

Year	Jan.	Feb.	Mar.	Apr.	May	June	July	Aug.	Sept.	Oct.	Nov.	Dec.	Total
1995	119.0	119.0	119.0	109.0	110.0	113.0	115.0	105.0	115.0	116.0	118.0	116.0	1,370
1996	107.0	100.0	106.0	111.0	113.0	106.0	104.0	146.0	140.0	147.0	163.0	143.0	1,530
1997	139.0	138.0	138.0	140.0	137.0	141.0	116.0	119.0	122.0	123.0	117.0	117.0	1,600
1998	116.0	115.0	119.0	128.0	127.0	129.0	128.0	128.0	129.0	129.0	134.0	125.0	1,550
1999	128.0	129.0	130.0	127.0	128.0	130.0	137.0	136.0	141.0	136.0	140.0	133.0	1,680
2000	139.0	139.0	139.0	139.0	140.0	140.0	135.0	141.0	139.0	139.0	136.0	132.0	1,660
2001	145.0	135.0	133.0	130.0	138.0	136.0	135.0	136.0	142.0	146.0	138.0	138.0	1,652
2002	132.0	131.0	133.0	142.0	142.0	144.0	143.0	145.0	141.0	145.0	142.0	133.0	1,673
2003	134.0	129.0	126.0	120.0	121.0	121.0	121.0	122.0	123.0	127.0	122.0	125.0	1,491
2004[2]	119.0	118.0	119.0	119.0	117.0	119.0	118.0	118.0	117.0	117.0			1,417

[1] Represents total consumption of primary & secondary lead as metal, in chemicals, or in alloys.   [2] Preliminary.   Source: U.S. Geological Survey (USGS)

Lead Recovered from Scrap in the United States   In Thousands of Metric Tons (Lead Content)

Year	Jan.	Feb.	Mar.	Apr.	May	June	July	Aug.	Sept.	Oct.	Nov.	Dec.	Total
1995	82.5	80.8	84.4	72.8	73.7	72.5	79.9	71.5	82.3	80.0	82.3	82.1	945.0
1996	75.7	76.2	84.2	83.7	84.7	80.7	81.2	89.0	92.1	98.8	97.3	93.2	1,100.0
1997	88.0	89.8	91.7	86.0	88.2	85.7	86.7	94.7	97.3	96.2	95.2	91.7	1,110.0
1998	95.0	92.0	92.6	94.1	92.5	89.7	89.3	95.7	94.4	95.0	95.1	90.7	1,110.0
1999	89.5	89.1	88.9	91.0	90.2	91.1	81.3	91.9	91.6	93.5	91.4	93.1	1,110.0
2000	91.0	88.0	91.1	91.4	90.5	91.3	88.6	95.1	94.0	96.0	95.4	93.7	1,110.0
2001	90.3	90.4	86.7	92.6	93.7	93.6	90.4	95.1	93.9	96.7	94.6	94.6	1,112.6
2002	89.3	82.3	88.2	93.1	93.9	93.6	88.0	96.1	93.3	97.5	95.0	95.7	1,106.0
2003	95.7	83.6	86.2	85.1	94.0	94.8	95.7	93.9	93.3	102.0	93.7	95.2	1,113.2
2004[1]	94.0	94.2	96.3	97.9	94.4	96.6	97.4	96.3	94.8	96.8			1,150.4

[1] Preliminary.   Source: U.S. Geological Survey (USGS)

Domestic Shipments[1] of Lead in the United States, by Refiners   In Thousands of Short Tons

Year	Jan.	Feb.	Mar.	Apr.	May	June	July	Aug.	Sept.	Oct.	Nov.	Dec.	Total
1988	33.5	29.5	39.2	33.0	41.4	44.7	32.0	34.7	33.7	43.0	38.5	35.5	438.7
1989	29.3	28.5	32.2	35.7	45.1	36.4	32.8	41.5	40.0	44.2	40.2	31.1	437.1
1990	39.3	33.9	39.1	33.5	38.4	32.9	32.6	38.9	36.6	38.9	37.9	31.7	433.7
1991	35.4	33.8	34.3	39.8	33.9	26.0	31.8	37.9	35.1	35.7	28.7	26.7	399.2
1992	31.3	23.9	30.4	26.3	25.6	27.2	27.3	28.7	26.3	28.5	26.3	21.7	323.5
1993	24.6	23.6	32.5	30.0	31.3	35.1	28.9	34.0	35.5	35.5	31.7	33.5	376.2
1994	35.9	32.8	35.2	32.7	34.7	36.7	31.6	33.4	34.8	34.3	34.0	33.3	409.3
1995	36.5	30.3	35.1	31.1	33.7	31.9	28.6	40.3	34.9	40.9	33.2	29.8	406.4
1996	37.2	32.4	29.5	30.2	29.4	26.7	27.7	33.5	30.1	33.5	28.1	27.6	366.0
1997[2]	31.5	27.8	24.7	35.2	39.2	36.1	33.4	29.4	26.4	31.5	30.4	28.1	377.8

[1] Includes GSA metal.   [2] Preliminary.   Source: American Metal Market (AMM)

Lumber & Plywood

Humans have utilized lumber for construction for thousands of years, but due to the heaviness of timber and the manual methods of harvesting, large-scale lumbering didn't occur until the mechanical advances of the Industrial Revolution. Lumber is produced from both hardwood and softwood. Hardwood lumber comes from deciduous trees that have broad leaves. Most hardwood lumber is used for miscellaneous industrial applications, primarily wood pallets, and includes oak, gum, maple, and ash. Hardwood species with beautiful colors and patterns are used for such high-grade products as furniture, flooring, paneling, and cabinets and include black walnut, black cherry, and red oak. Wood from cone-bearing trees is called softwood, regardless of its actual hardness. Most lumber from the US is softwood. Softwoods, such as southern yellow pine, Douglas fir, ponderosa pine, and true firs, are primarily used as structural lumber such as 2x4's and 2x6's, poles, paper and cardboard.

Plywood consists of several thin layers of veneer bonded together with adhesives. The veneer sheets are layered so that the grain of one sheet is perpendicular to that of the next, which makes plywood exceptionally strong for its weight. Most plywood has from three to nine layers of wood. Plywood manufacturers use both hard and soft woods, although hardwoods serve primarily for appearance and are not as strong as those made from softwoods. Plywood is primarily used in construction, particularly for floors, roofs, walls, and doors. Homebuilding and remodeling account for two-thirds of US lumber consumption. The price of lumber and plywood is highly correlated with the strength of the US home-building market.

The forest and wood products industry is dominated by Weyerhaeuser Company (ticker symbol WY), which has about $20 billion in annual sales. Weyerhaeuser is a forest products conglomerate that engages not only in growing and harvesting timber, but also in the production and distribution of forest products, real estate development, and construction of single-family homes. Forest products include wood products, pulp and paper, and containerboard. The timberland segment of the business manages 7.2 million acres of company-owned land and 800,000 acres of leased commercial forestlands in North America. The company's Canadian division has renewable, long-term licenses on about 35 million acres of forestland in five Canadian provinces. In order to maximize its long-term yield from its acreage, Weyerhaeuser engages in a number of forest management activities such as extensive planting, suppression of non-merchantable species, thinning, fertilization, and operational pruning.

Lumber futures and options are traded on the Chicago Mercantile Exchange (CME). The CME's lumber futures contract calls for the delivery of 111,000 board feet (one 73 foot rail car) of random length 8 to 12 foot 2 x 4s, the type used in construction. The contract is priced in terms of dollars per thousand board feet.

Prices – CME lumber futures prices rallied early in the 2004 and posted an 8-year high of $464.00 in May 2004, but then saw a steep sell-off in autumn that took prices down to the year's low of $286.70 in October. Lumber futures closed the year at $356.40. Lumber futures posted their record high of $493.50 in March 1993.

Supply – The US leads the world in the production of industrial round wood with 405.159 million cubic meters of production in 2003 (unchanged yr/yr), followed by Canada with 197.714 million cubic meters (+0.1% yr/yr), and Russia with 121.800 million cubic meters (+2.7% yr/yr). The US also leads the world in the production of plywood with 14.870 million cubic meters of production in 2003 (-2.9% yr/yr), followed by Canada with 2.483 million cubic meters (+0.3% yr/yr), and Russia with 1.960 million cubic meters (+7.6% yr/yr). US softwood lumber production in 2004 (through September, annualized) rose +7.6% yr/yr to 38.432 billion board feet. That was a 9-year high but was well below the record high of 48.177 billion board feet seen in 1988.

Demand – US consumption of softwood lumber in 2003, the last full reporting year, rose by +11.7% yr/yr to 56.585 billion board feet, which was a new record high.

Trade – US total lumber imports in 2003, the last full reporting year, rose +1.1% to 22.022 billion board feet, which was a record high. US imports of hardwood in 2003 rose by +7.3% to 793 million board feet. US imports of softwood in 2003 rose by +1.0% to 21.188 billion board feet. The leading softwood import was spruce with 855 million board feet of imports in 2003, followed by cedar at 536 million board feet.

Total US exports of lumber in 2003 rose +2.7% yr/yr to 2.376 billion board feet, which was well below exports of more than 3 billion board feet seen in the early 1990s. US exports of hardwood in 2003 rose by +1.4% yr/yr to 1.236 billion board feet. US exports of softwood in 2003 rose by +12.9% yr/yr to 957 million board feet. The largest types of US softwood exports are southern pine with 132 million board feet of exports, Ponderosa white pine (100 million board feet), and Douglas Fir (96 million board feet). The world's largest exporter of plywood is Russia with 1.201 million cubic meters of exports in 2003, followed by Finland with 1.172 million cubic meters, and Canada with 1.018 million cubic meters.

World Production of Industrial Roundwood by Selected Countries   In Thousands of Cubic Meters

Year	Austria	Canada	Czech Repulic	Finland	France	Germany	Poland	Romania	Russia	Spain	Sweden	Turkey	United States
1994	11,701	177,346	11,172	44,644	32,442	36,018	16,711	9,640	83,650	12,990	52,100	9,211	410,781
1995	11,346	183,027	11,716	46,124	33,561	36,914	19,240	10,015	83,050	12,997	59,800	10,745	408,948
1996	11,812	177,943	11,882	42,178	30,643	34,538	18,824	9,441	73,005	12,433	52,500	10,229	406,625
1997	11,902	183,531	12,881	47,757	32,162	35,488	20,097	9,837	67,508	12,433	56,400	9,773	416,092
1998	10,858	173,901	13,171	49,541	32,718	36,441	21,793	8,629	77,400	13,164	54,700	9,979	422,034
1999	10,988	190,988	13,363	49,593	33,237	35,063	22,842	9,484	94,600	13,160	52,800	10,065	423,298
2000	10,416	197,357	13,501	50,147	43,440	51,088	24,489	10,116	105,800	12,721	57,400	10,429	420,619
2001	10,562	184,689	13,364	47,727	37,471	36,502	23,375	9,806	117,800	13,276	57,300	9,976	403,212
2002[1]	11,810	191,522	13,534	48,529	32,736	37,755	24,995	12,092	118,600	13,850	60,700	11,191	404,958
2003[2]	13,719	191,714	13,960	49,246	33,950	37,755	26,485	11,562	121,800	14,075	61,400	10,729	405,159

[1] Preliminary.   [2] Estimate.   NA = Not available.   *Source: Food and Agriculture Organization of the United Nations (FAO-UN)*

Lumber Production and Consumption in the United States   In Millions of Board Feet

| Year | Production | | | | | | Domestic Consumption | | | | | | |
	California Redwood	Inland Region	Southern Pine	West Coast	Other Softwood	Total Softwood	Inland Region	California Redwood	Southern Pine	West Coast	Other Softwood	Softwood Imports	Total Softwood
1996	1,371	7,079	15,262	7,745	1,809	33,266	7,073	1,363	15,112	6,821	1,301	18,214	49,883
1997	1,511	7,383	16,113	7,772	1,888	34,667	7,180	1,499	15,993	7,012	1,179	18,002	50,863
1998	1,391	7,298	16,151	7,797	2,040	34,677	7,256	1,409	15,788	7,502	1,567	18,686	52,209
1999	1,325	7,580	16,922	8,625	2,153	36,605	7,445	1,358	16,525	8,115	1,641	19,178	54,262
2000	1,320	7,078	16,672	8,782	2,115	35,967	6,926	1,257	16,374	8,300	1,629	19,449	53,934
2001	1,121	6,563	16,094	8,764	2,035	34,577	6,490	1,132	15,937	8,471	1,724	20,075	53,828
2002	1,035	6,760	16,686	9,244	2,106	35,831	6,643	1,056	16,571	8,966	1,833	20,986	56,054
2003	866	6,645	16,858	9,706	2,129	36,204	6,635	869	16,758	9,393	1,720	21,188	56,565
I	194	1,752	3,986	2,370	518	8,820	1,678	209	3,898	2,200	391	4,725	13,102
II	216	1,656	4,390	2,397	541	9,200	1,737	227	4,337	2,336	431	5,622	14,691
III	234	1,675	4,313	2,496	545	9,263	1,706	243	4,348	2,455	453	5,511	14,716
IV	222	1,562	4,169	2,443	525	8,921	1,514	190	4,175	2,402	445	5,330	14,056
2004[1] I	261	1,593	4,421	2,674	560	9,509	1,534	221	4,370	2,509	464	5,214	14,313
II	234	1,615	4,600	2,841	581	9,871	1,639	255	4,664	2,811	518	6,656	16,543
III	268	1,801	4,260	2,795	570	9,694	1,746	280	4,464	2,793	510	6,758	16,552

[1] Preliminary.   NA = Not available.   *Source: American Forest & Paper Association (AFPA)*

U.S. Housing Starts: Seasonally Adjusted Annual Rate   In Thousands of Units

Year	Jan.	Feb.	Mar.	Apr.	May	June	July	Aug.	Sept.	Oct.	Nov.	Dec.	Average
1995	1,407	1,316	1,249	1,267	1,314	1,281	1,461	1,416	1,369	1,369	1,452	1,431	1,361
1996	1,467	1,491	1,424	1,516	1,504	1,467	1,472	1,557	1,475	1,392	1,489	1,370	1,469
1997	1,355	1,486	1,457	1,492	1,442	1,494	1,437	1,390	1,546	1,520	1,510	1,566	1,475
1998	1,525	1,584	1,567	1,540	1,536	1,641	1,698	1,614	1,582	1,715	1,660	1,792	1,621
1999	1,748	1,670	1,710	1,553	1,611	1,559	1,669	1,648	1,635	1,608	1,648	1,708	1,647
2000	1,636	1,737	1,604	1,626	1,575	1,559	1,463	1,541	1,507	1,549	1,551	1,532	1,573
2001	1,600	1,625	1,590	1,649	1,605	1,636	1,670	1,567	1,562	1,540	1,602	1,568	1,601
2002	1,698	1,829	1,642	1,592	1,764	1,717	1,655	1,633	1,804	1,648	1,753	1,788	1,710
2003	1,856	1,657	1,728	1,637	1,748	1,850	1,893	1,835	1,922	1,983	2,054	2,067	1,853
2004[1]	1,934	1,895	2,000	1,963	1,979	1,817	1,985	2,018	1,905	2,065	1,805	2,063	1,952

[1] Preliminary.   Total Privately owned.   Source: American Forest & Paper Association (AF&PA)

Stocks (Gross) of Softwood Lumber in the United States, on First of Month   In Millions of Board Feet

Year	Jan.	Feb.	Mar.	Apr.	May	June	July	Aug.	Sept.	Oct.	Nov.	Dec.
1995	4,403	4,336	4,344	4,653	4,352	4,663	4,508	4,323	4,342	4,359	4,361	4,335
1996	4,293	4,435	4,459	4,357	4,251	4,153	4,156	4,038	3,918	3,965	3,939	3,906
1997	3,973	4,019	4,113	4,067	3,963	4,017	3,915	3,871	3,875	3,927	3,925	3,865
1998	3,884	3,970	4,048	4,062	4,158	4,084	NA	NA	NA	NA	NA	NA
1999	3,519	3,595	3,688	3,726	3,698	3,581	3,512	3,485	3,533	3,491	3,562	3,536
2000	3,639	3,704	3,811	3,887	3,960	2,738	3,902	3,936	3,878	3,848	3,957	3,875
2001	3,919	3,864	4,013	3,951	4,095	3,955	NA	3,961	3,938	4,076	4,100	4,248
2002	4,784	3,735	3,826	3,756	3,273	3,316	3,242	3,230	3,136	3,098	3,173	3,127
2003	3,175	3,177	3,202	3,249	3,308	3,211	3,075	3,085	3,081	3,158	3,076	3,055
2004[1]	2,904	2,904	2,904	2,873	2,966	2,966	2,966	2,966	3,030	3,030	3,031	

[1] Preliminary.   NA = Not available.   *Source: American Forest & Paper Association (AFPA)*

Lumber (Softwood)[2] Production in the United States   In Millions of Board Feet

Year	Jan.	Feb.	Mar.	Apr.	May	June	July	Aug.	Sept.	Oct.	Nov.	Dec.	Total
1995	4,084	3,577	3,931	3,675	3,805	3,897	3,641	3,866	3,757	4,105	3,549	3,297	45,184
1996	2,600	2,606	2,757	2,903	2,833	2,819	2,942	3,077	2,858	3,179	2,758	2,424	33,756
1997	3,012	2,791	2,866	3,149	2,890	3,027	3,097	2,889	2,905	3,094	2,536	2,487	34,743
1998	2,767	2,760	2,928	3,084	2,647	3,051	3,079	2,930	2,953	3,167	2,667	2,754	34,787
1999	2,783	2,921	3,190	3,227	3,071	3,318	3,115	3,054	2,992	3,096	2,954	2,795	36,516
2000	3,020	3,128	3,474	3,058	3,276	3,249	2,730	2,971	2,839	3,041	2,761	2,342	35,889
2001	2,832	2,457	2,918	2,928	NA	3,032	2,812	3,240	2,743	3,188	2,740	2,372	34,104
2002	3,019	2,761	3,074	3,284	3,126	3,200	3,104	3,128	2,862	3,386	2,599	2,482	36,025
2003	2,971	2,801	2,937	2,994	2,931	3,109	3,088	2,981	3,052	3,335	2,793	2,740	35,732
2004[1]	3,037	2,978	3,380	3,434	3,021	3,329	3,227	3,271	3,147	3,321	3,067		38,413

[1] Preliminary.   [2] Data prior to 1996 are Softwood and Hardwood.   *Source: American Forest & Paper Association (AFPA)*

LUMBER & PLYWOOD

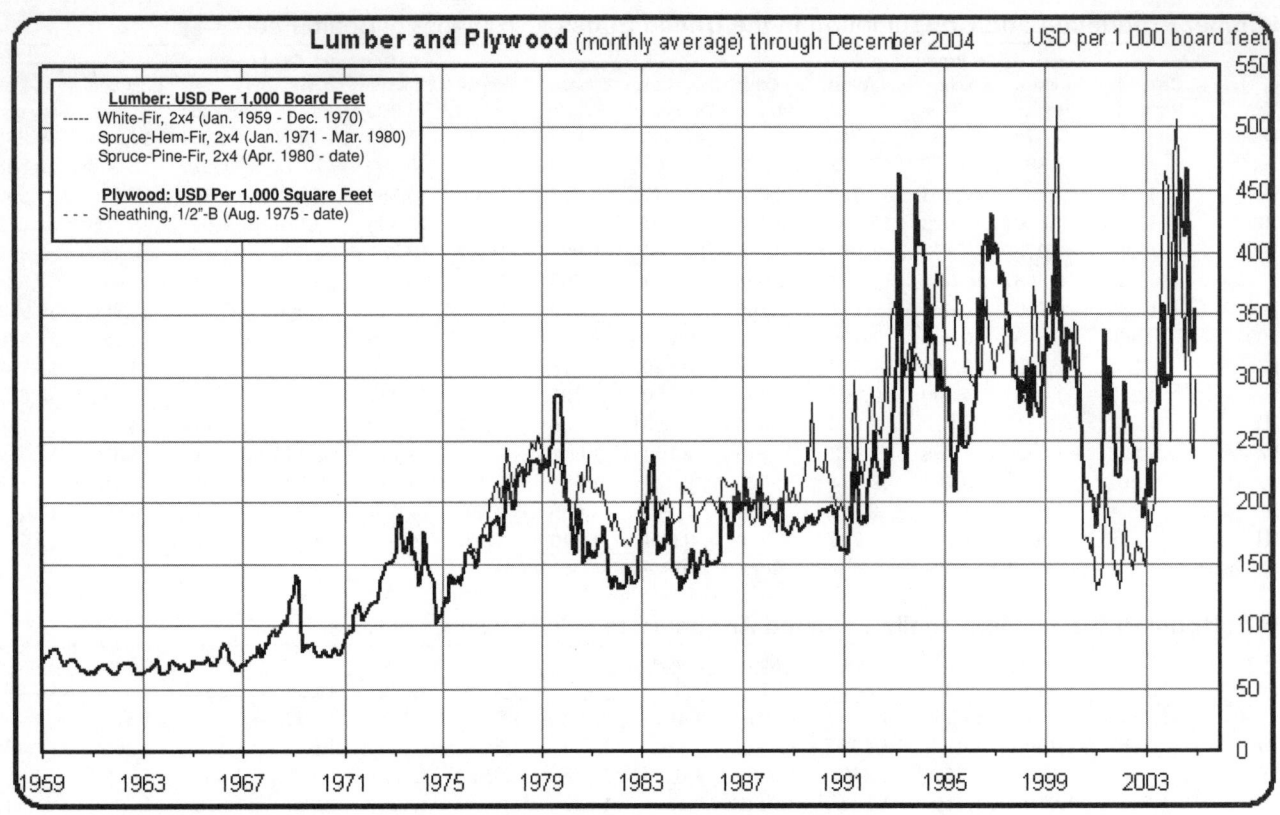

Lumber and Plywood (monthly average) through December 2004   USD per 1,000 board feet

Legend:
Lumber: USD Per 1,000 Board Feet
- - - - White-Fir, 2x4 (Jan. 1959 - Dec. 1970)
Spruce-Hem-Fir, 2x4 (Jan. 1971 - Mar. 1980)
Spruce-Pine-Fir, 2x4 (Apr. 1980 - date)

Plywood: USD Per 1,000 Square Feet
- - - Sheathing, 1/2"-B (Aug. 1975 - date)

Lumber (Softwood)[2] Shipments in the United States   In Millions of Board Feet

Year	Jan.	Feb.	Mar.	Apr.	May	June	July	Aug.	Sept.	Oct.	Nov.	Dec.	Total
1995	3,971	3,584	3,855	3,831	3,765	4,026	3,826	3,870	3,760	4,055	3,478	3,367	45,388
1996	2,460	2,581	2,863	3,002	2,934	2,813	3,058	3,196	2,813	3,206	2,792	2,353	34,071
1997	2,966	2,697	2,890	3,253	2,834	3,126	3,139	2,885	2,852	3,096	2,598	2,461	34,797
1998	2,685	2,685	2,863	3,019	2,684	3,175	3,132	2,963	2,948	3,205	2,703	2,865	34,927
1999	2,689	2,829	3,177	3,227	3,071	3,383	3,141	3,004	3,037	3,021	2,944	2,691	36,214
2000	2,953	3,039	3,394	2,974	3,292	3,309	2,686	3,027	2,871	2,931	2,752	2,444	35,672
2001	2,859	2,372	2,981	2,974	NA	2,961	2,936	3,279	2,644	3,166	2,732	2,396	34,145
2002	3,032	2,815	3,049	3,212	3,064	3,260	3,234	3,111	2,858	3,299	2,675	2,501	36,110
2003	3,018	2,742	2,843	3,134	2,969	3,173	3,209	3,137	3,030	3,413	2,787	2,722	36,177
2004[1]	3,067	2,840	3,262	3,582	3,061	3,385	3,485	3,372	3,086	3,345	3,120		38,842

[1] Preliminary.   [2] Data prior to 1996 are Softwood and Hardwood.   *Source: American Forest & Paper Association (AFPA)*

Imports and Exports of Lumber in the United States, by Type   In Millions of Board Feet

									Exports[2]					
			Imports[2]							Softwood				
		Software									Ponderosa/			
		Douglas					Total	Total	Douglas		White	Southern	Total	Total
Year	Cedar	Fir	Hemlock	Pine	Spruce	Total	Hardwood	Lumber	Fir	Hemlock	Pine	Pine	Total Hardwood	Lumber
1995	768	395	258	97	2,828	17,395	380	17,787	638	227	107	335	1,988	1,101	3,193
1996	727	264	257	133	1,989	18,214	397	18,641	685	195	97	315	1,935	1,141	3,173
1997	586	264	250	314	1,040	18,014	465	18,506	436	105	122	299	1,820	1,281	3,189
1998	514	417	268	363	849	18,686	589	19,306	252	39	113	279	1,265	1,119	2,601
1999	591	426	259	449	803	19,178	708	19,903	249	54	140	326	1,431	1,242	2,867
2000	694	455	184	450	812	19,449	795	20,268	232	46	116	298	1,355	1,319	2,822
2001	667	471	199	365	838	20,075	645	20,737	168	26	86	232	968	1,222	2,351
2002	648	385	69	445	1,046	20,986	739	21,774	111	19	83	205	848	1,219	2,313
2003	536	355	53	473	855	21,188	793	22,022	96	18	100	132	957	1,236	2,376
2004[1] I	143	102	13	274	220	5,214	222	5,438	24	8	25	36	214	347	612
II	180	138	14	161	320	6,656	256	6,919	22	3	22	36	197	952	1,209
III	172	164	21	125	289	6,758	249	7,015	23	3	21	38	198	861	1,108

[1] Preliminary.   [2] Includes sawed timber, board planks & scantlings, flooring, box shook and railroad ties.

Source: American Forest & Paper Association (AFPA)

Lumber Futures - Chicago Mercantile Exchange
(weekly close) as of December 31, 2004

USD per 1,000 board feet

Average Open Interest of Random Lumber[1] Futures in Chicago   In Contracts

Year	Jan.	Feb.	Mar.	Apr.	May	June	July	Aug.	Sept.	Oct.	Nov.	Dec.
1995	1,757	1,923	2,142	2,509	2,742	3,252	2,896	2,918	2,809	3,039	2,626	2,940
1996	3,378	4,040	3,752	4,395	5,666	4,972	3,280	5,243	4,743	4,797	4,341	3,691
1997	3,745	3,211	3,048	3,337	2,895	3,137	2,767	3,119	3,267	4,006	3,606	4,068
1998	4,249	3,332	3,394	4,102	4,353	4,773	4,048	4,081	3,466	4,295	3,434	3,893
1999	4,864	5,497	4,698	4,456	4,927	6,405	6,263	4,882	3,457	3,704	2,963	2,868
2000	3,004	3,131	2,728	3,175	3,171	3,218	3,064	3,638	3,845	4,277	4,208	4,405
2001	4,605	4,494	3,654	3,644	3,867	3,733	2,612	2,949	2,148	2,102	2,173	2,416
2002	2,106	2,382	2,441	2,011	1,502	2,136	1,879	2,265	2,654	2,974	3,315	3,249
2003	3,238	3,222	2,521	2,804	2,937	3,188	2,370	2,827	3,492	3,033	1,824	1,887
2004	2,884	3,996	3,790	5,414	5,436	5,042	5,123	6,216	4,667	3,826	3,489	3,539

[1] July 1995 thru March 1996, Lumber and Random Lumber.   *Source: Chicago Mercantile Exchange (CME)*

Volume of Trading of Random Lumber[1] Futures in Chicago   In Contracts

Year	Jan.	Feb.	Mar.	Apr.	May	June	July	Aug.	Sept.	Oct.	Nov.	Dec.	Total
1995	12,150	12,909	15,088	12,139	14,536	20,126	13,766	16,919	15,718	18,981	15,551	14,803	182,686
1996	22,954	19,960	20,956	27,094	28,271	26,100	19,302	27,792	31,982	32,042	25,236	22,525	304,214
1997	28,561	20,946	21,071	24,624	18,248	24,797	20,308	18,503	21,736	24,416	15,131	21,977	260,318
1998	19,556	20,339	20,881	24,673	20,519	24,112	21,763	20,453	19,412	19,578	22,002	16,559	249,847
1999	25,962	22,184	28,151	22,618	23,835	30,410	30,791	25,683	24,177	18,125	20,802	15,118	287,856
2000	19,871	19,486	18,936	16,136	21,003	18,057	16,636	16,563	19,037	17,155	20,706	17,582	221,168
2001	21,567	15,076	24,561	22,458	23,681	18,878	15,210	16,440	12,882	11,608	11,989	12,490	206,840
2002	15,328	13,239	16,401	13,910	12,427	11,950	12,046	10,154	13,518	13,442	15,828	16,180	164,423
2003	24,241	17,533	17,027	11,573	20,132	21,840	21,097	22,418	22,891	19,387	12,480	13,272	223,891
2004	17,921	17,713	22,544	25,743	19,951	17,190	22,672	20,902	24,238	17,111	17,271	19,617	242,873

[1] July 1995 thru March 1996, Lumber and Random Lumber.   *Source: Chicago Mercantile Exchange (CME)*

163

LUMBER & PLYWOOD

Production of Plywood by Selected Countries   In Thousands of Cubic Meters

Year	Austria	Canada	Finland	France	Germany	Italy	Japan	Poland	Romania	Russia	Spain	Sweden	United States
1996	150	2,114	824	536	512	402	4,421	173	98	666	210	132	18,554
1997	150	2,128	908	539	448	414	NA	226	87	884	210	123	17,554
1998	150	2,049	992	541	428	420	NA	178	76	1,102	382	114	17,468
1999	155	2,228	1,076	546	364	450	NA	223	65	1,324	382	105	17,551
2000	155	2,244	1,096	558	357	450	NA	261	72	1,484	380	110	17,271
2001	186	2,326	1,140	509	321	418	NA	242	79	1,590	380	106	15,417
2002[1]	186	2,476	1,240	459	285	450	NA	261	90	1,821	360	87	15,307
2003[2]	186	2,483	1,300	419	245	445	NA	268	94	1,960	370	75	14,870

[1] Preliminary.   [2] Estimate.   NA = Not available.   *Source: Food and Agricultural Organization of the United Nations (FAO-UN)*

Imports of Plywood by Selected Countries   In Thousands of Cubic Meters

Year	Austria	Belgium	Canada	Denmark	France	Germany	Italy	Japan	Netherlands	Sweden	Switzerland	United Kingdom	United States
1996	99	586	239	168	347	975	295	5,314	260	150	129	965	1,406
1997	110	684	256	226	353	1,095	312	5,326	394	148	138	967	1,592
1998	121	539	273	302	359	1,105	378	NA	528	147	143	969	1,964
1999	136	530	222	222	365	1,021	367	NA	558	152	150	972	2,494
2000	151	534	230	247	348	1,149	422	NA	594	178	153	1,041	2,385
2001	138	526	520	250	358	1,088	425	NA	600	157	143	1,145	3,010
2002[1]	163	505	489	254	349	973	558	NA	547	152	128	1,139	3,890
2003[2]	184	573	357	663	361	1,061	551	NA	522	161	128	1,056	4,249

[1] Preliminary.   [2] Estimate.   NA = Not available.   *Source: Food and Agricultural Organization of the United Nations (FAO-UN)*

Exports of Plywood by Selected Countries   In Thousands of Cubic Meters

Year	Austria	Baltic States	Belgium	Canada	Finland	France	Germany	Italy	Netherlands	Poland	Russia	Spain	United States
1996	163	187	88	360	618	180	135	117	80	76	382	77	1,135
1997	172	198	101	557	725	201	152	125	68	95	559	77	984
1998	180	NA	371	755	832	222	166	139	56	93	736	331	833
1999	192	NA	403	956	939	243	160	139	51	95	913	220	712
2000	246	NA	380	941	1,006	231	210	146	55	109	974	152	673
2001	286	NA	378	1,030	1,009	200	232	125	57	128	1,032	86	530
2002[1]	247	NA	371	1,055	1,117	189	167	204	58	138	1,157	82	523
2003[2]	259	NA	438	1,018	1,172	187	183	195	42	149	1,201	84	512

[1] Preliminary.   [2] Estimate.   NA = Not available.   *Source: Food and Agricultural Organization of the United Nations (FAO-UN)*

Imports of Industrial Roundwood by Selected Countries   In Thousands of Cubic Meters

Year	Austria	Belgium	Canada	Finland	France	Germany	Italy	Norway	Poland	Portugal	Spain	Sweden	United States
1996	4,451	2,391	6,088	6,575	1,601	1,263	4,936	2,476	393	1,065	1,902	5,018	524
1997	5,277	2,823	6,685	6,734	1,806	1,770	4,504	2,855	288	1,679	2,116	7,655	582
1998	5,113	2,823	6,955	9,235	1,980	2,255	5,223	3,494	371	2,122	4,136	9,172	970
1999	7,093	3,393	6,157	10,160	2,154	2,722	4,952	3,037	590	1,432	3,228	10,280	1,855
2000	8,451	3,992	6,507	9,875	2,012	3,549	5,805	3,315	732	1,340	3,771	11,721	2,453
2001	7,493	4,505	7,557	11,869	1,994	3,493	5,211	2,772	882	1,109	4,128	9,505	2,430
2002[1]	7,435	2,653	7,524	12,586	1,993	2,623	4,703	2,561	726	1,067	3,374	9,705	3,594
2003[2]	7,630	2,754	6,459	12,868	2,223	2,444	4,358	2,605	663	1,067	3,295	9,021	2,551

[1] Preliminary.   [2] Estimate.   *Source: Food and Agricultural Organization of the United Nations (FAO-UN)*

Exports of Industrial Roundwood by Selected Countries   In Thousands of Cubic Meters

Year	Canada	Czech Republic	Estonia	France	Germany	Hungary	Latvia	Lithuania	Russia	Slovakia	Sweden	Switzerland	United States
1996	955	2,687	1,898	2,227	2,992	555	1,467	952	15,915	529	1,621	979	11,937
1997	701	2,657	2,915	2,282	4,032	701	2,124	765	17,845	850	1,393	1,147	10,864
1998	2,029	2,497	3,792	2,857	4,871	1,204	2,760	792	19,972	714	1,420	1,006	12,290
1999	2,213	2,626	3,903	3,093	4,552	1,079	2,953	938	27,600	1,193	1,315	1,220	11,739
2000	2,903	1,857	4,257	5,522	5,558	1,282	4,190	1,200	30,835	1,550	1,431	3,754	11,952
2001	3,835	2,276	3,482	5,116	4,906	1,227	3,990	1,314	31,693	1,550	1,303	3,149	11,412
2002[1]	4,952	2,302	3,132	4,244	4,907	1,210	4,225	1,420	36,800	1,187	1,755	1,970	11,068
2003[2]	4,894	2,955	3,029	3,959	4,115	1,366	3,922	1,353	37,430	1,034	1,520	1,970	10,288

[1] Preliminary.   [2] Estimate.   *Source: Food and Agricultural Organization of the United Nations (FAO-UN)*

Magnesium

Magnesium (symbol Mg) is a silvery-white, light, and fairly tough, metallic element and is relatively stable. Magnesium is one of the alkaline earth metals. Magnesium is the eighth most abundant element in the earth's crust and the third most plentiful element found in seawater. Magnesium is ductile and malleable when heated, and with the exception of beryllium, is the lightest metal that remains stable under ordinary conditions. First isolated by the British chemist Sir Humphrey Davy in 1808, magnesium today is obtained mainly by electrolysis of fused magnesium chloride.

Magnesium compounds, primarily magnesium oxide, are used in the refractory material that line the furnaces used to produce iron and steel, nonferrous metals, glass, and cement. Magnesium oxide and other compounds are also used in the chemical, agricultural, and construction industries. Magnesium's principal use is as an alloying addition for aluminum. These aluminum-magnesium alloys are used primarily in beverage cans. Due to their lightness and considerable tensile strength, the alloys are also used in structural components in airplanes and automobiles.

Prices – The price of magnesium in 2003 fell to the range of $1.10-1.17 per pound from $1.10-1.22 in 2002. The 2003 level was a 23-year low and was well below the record high of $1.93-2.25 seen in 1995.

Supply – World primary production of magnesium in 2003 rose sharply by +12.9% yr/yr to a new record high of 508,000 metric tons. The world's largest primary produc-ers of magnesium are China with 340,000 metric tons of production in 2003, the US with production of 106,000 metric tons (in the latest data available for 1998), Russia with 52,000 metric tons, and Canada with 60,000 metric tons. China's production has more than quadrupled over the past 5 years from 70,500 metric tons in 1998 to 340,000 metric tons in 2003.

The largest secondary producer of magnesium by far is the US with 87% of world production (as of the latest data available in 2001), followed by Japan with 10% of world secondary production. US secondary production of magnesium in 2001 was about two-thirds that of US primary production.

Demand – Total US consumption of magnesium in 2003 fell -1.8% to 50,000 metric tons. US consumption of magnesium for structural products in 2003 rose +2.6% yr/yr to 52,055 metric tons. Of the structural product consumption category, 94% was for castings and the remaining 6% was for wrought products. US consumption of magnesium for aluminum alloys fell -3.2% yr/yr in 2003 to 33,800 metric tons. The consumption category for magnesium of "other uses" rose by +1.3% yr/yr in 2003 to 16,200 metric tons.

Trade – US exports of magnesium in 2003 fell -19.7% yr/yr to 20,400 metric tons, which was only slightly above the 27-year low of 19,600 metric tons seen in 2001. US imports of magnesium in 2003 fell -5.2% yr/yr to a 5-year low of 83,400 metric tons.

World Production of Magnesium (Primary and Secondary)   In Metric Tons

				Primary Production						Secondary Production			
Year	Brazil	Canada	China	France	Norway	Russia	United States	World Total	Japan	United Kingdom	United States	Former USSR	World Total
1994	9,700	28,900	24,000	12,280	27,635	35,400	128,000	282,000	19,009	1,000	62,100	5,000	88,700
1995	9,700	48,100	93,600	14,450	28,000	37,500	142,000	395,000	11,767	1,000	65,100	6,000	85,500
1996	9,000	54,000	73,100	14,000	37,800	35,000	133,000	378,000	8,175	1,000	71,200	6,000	88,000
1997	9,000	57,700	75,990	13,740	34,200	39,500	125,000	384,000	10,934	1,000	77,600	NA	91,100
1998	9,000	77,100	70,500	14,000	35,400	41,500	106,000	396,000	7,807	1,000	77,100	NA	87,500
1999	8,000	73,700	120,000	16,200	40,800	45,000	W	341,000	7,732	500	86,100	NA	96,000
2000	5,700	85,700	190,000	16,500	41,400	45,000	W	428,000	7,900	500	82,300	NA	92,300
2001	5,500	83,400	200,000	4,000	36,000	48,000	W	429,000	7,800	500	65,800	NA	75,700
2002[1]	6,000	80,000	250,000	----	10,000	50,000	W	450,000	----	----	----	----	----
2003[2]	6,000	60,000	340,000	----	----	52,000	W	508,000	----	----	----	----	----

[1] Preliminary.   [2] Estimate.   W = Withheld proprietary data.   *Source: U.S. Geological Survey (USGS)*

Salient Statistics of Magnesium in the United States   In Metric Tons

		Production							Domestic Consumption of Primary Magnesium				
	Primary	Secondary				Imports	Stocks	$ Price	Castings	Wrought	Total	Aluminum	Other	
Year	(Ingot)	New Scrap	Old Scrap	Total	Total Exports[3]	for Consumption	Dec. 31[4]	Per Pound[5]	Structural Products			Alloys	Uses[6]	Total
1994	128,000	32,500	29,600	62,100	45,200	29,100	20,030	1.63	15,676	7,690	23,366	61,100	27,900	89,000
1995	142,000	35,400	29,800	65,100	38,300	34,800	21,193	1.93-2.25	15,231	8,510	23,741	60,200	25,100	85,300
1996	133,000	41,100	30,100	71,200	40,500	46,600	25,000	1.70-1.80	16,400	8,080	24,480	52,300	25,500	77,800
1997	125,000	47,000	30,500	77,600	40,500	65,100	23,000	1.60-1.70	20,643	6,840	27,400	50,000	23,000	73,000
1998	106,000	45,200	31,800	77,100	35,400	82,500	27,000	1.52-1.62	27,057	7,100	34,157	52,000	20,900	72,900
1999	W	52,000	34,200	86,100	29,100	90,700	W	1.40-1.55	49,181	9,380	58,561	57,800	14,900	72,700
2000	W	52,200	30,100	82,300	23,800	91,400	W	1.23-1.30	29,457	2,120	31,577	55,400	17,400	72,800
2001	W	38,600	27,200	65,800	19,600	68,500	W	1.21-1.28	44,712	3,280	47,992	35,000	12,700	47,700
2002[1]	W	47,100	26,400	73,600	25,400	88,000	W	1.10-1.22	46,362	4,350	50,712	34,900	16,000	50,900
2003[2]	W	44,700	25,100	69,800	20,400	83,400	W	1.10-1.17	48,865	3,190	52,055	33,800	16,200	50,000

[1] Preliminary.   [2] Estimate.   [3] Metal & alloys in crude form & scrap.   [4] Estimate of Industry Stocks, metal.   [5] Magnesium ingots (99.8%), f.o.b. Valasco, Texas.   [6] Distributive or sacrificial purposes.   W = Withheld proprietary data.   *Source: U.S. Geological Survey (USGS)*

Manganese

Manganese (symbol Mn) is a silvery-white, very brittle, metallic element used primarily in making alloys. Manganese was first distinguished as an element and isolated in 1774 by Johan Gottlieb Gahn. Manganese dissolves in acid and corrodes in moist air.

Manganese is found in the earth's crust in the form of ores such as rhodochrosite, franklinite, psilomelane, and manganite. Pyrolusite is the principal ore of manganese. Pure manganese is produced by igniting pyrolusite with aluminum powder or by electrolyzing manganese sulfate.

Manganese is used primarily in the steel industry for creating alloys, the most important ones being ferromanganese and spiegeleisen. In steel, manganese improves forging and rolling qualities, strength, toughness, stiffness, wear resistance, and hardness. Manganese is also used in plant fertilizers, animal feed, pigments, and dry cell batteries.

Prices – The average monthly price of ferromanganese (high carbon, FOB plant) rose very sharply by 172% yr/yr in 2004 (through November) to a new record high of $1,355.90 per gross ton. That was sharply above the 17-year low of $447.44 per gross ton posted as recently as 2001.

Supply – World production of manganese ore in 2003 rose by +4.5% to 23.2 million metric tons, which was a 7-year high. That was well above the record low of 17.8 million metric tons posted in 1999. The world's largest producers of manganese ore are China with 17% of world production in 2003, South Africa with 15%, Ukraine with 11%, Australia with 11%, and Brazil with 11%. China's production in 2003 fell -11.1% yr/yr to 4.0 million metric tons, and that was down sharply from its record production level of 7.6 million metric tons in 1996.

Demand – US consumption of manganese ore in 2003 rose +10.6% to 398,000 metric tons, recovering from the record low of 360,000 metric tons in 2002. US consumption of ferromanganese in 2003 fell -2.0% yr/yr to a record low of 248,000 metric tons, which was less than a third of US consumption of 908,000 metric tons in 1970.

Trade – The US still relies on imports for 100% of its manganese consumption, as it has since 1985. US imports of manganese ore for consumption in 2003 fell -18.7% yr/yr to 347,000 metric tons. US imports of ferromanganese for consumption in 2003 fell -13.5% yr/yr to a 3-decade low of 238,000 metric tons. US imports of silico-manganese in 2003 rose +8.1% yr/yr to 267,000 metric tons. The primary sources of US imports of manganese ore in 2003 were Gabon with 123,000 metric tons of imports, South Africa (36,900 metric tons), and Australia (12,900 metric tons).

World Production of Manganese Ore   In Thousands of Metric Tons (Gross Weight)

Year	Aus-tralia[2] 37-53[4]	Brazil 30-50	China 30	Gabon 50-53	Georgia 29-30	Ghana 30-50	Hungary[3] 30-33	India 10-54	Mexico 27-50	Morocco 50-53	South Africa 30-48+	Ukraine 29-30	World Total
1994	1,920	2,199	3,570	1,436	150	270	55	1,632	307	31	2,851	2,979	18,000
1995	2,180	2,398	6,900	1,930	100	217	----	1,764	472	----	3,199	3,200	23,300
1996	2,109	2,506	7,600	1,983	97	448	----	1,797	485	----	3,240	3,070	24,300
1997	2,136	2,124	6,000	1,904	----	437	----	1,596	534	----	3,121	3,040	21,900
1998	1,500	1,940	5,300	2,092	----	537	----	1,557	510	----	3,044	2,226	19,900
1999	1,892	1,656	3,190	1,908	----	639	----	1,500	459	----	3,122	1,985	17,800
2000	1,614	1,925	3,500	1,743	----	896	----	1,550	435	----	3,635	2,741	19,600
2001	2,069	1,863	4,300	1,791	----	1,077	----	1,600	277	----	3,266	2,700	20,800
2002	2,187	2,529	4,500	1,856	----	1,136	----	1,700	233	----	3,322	2,470	22,200
2003[1]	2,555	2,600	4,000	2,000	----	1,200	----	1,650	310	----	3,501	2,591	23,200

[1] Preliminary.   [2] Metallurgical Ore.   [3] Concentrate.   [4] Ranges of percentage of manganese.   *Source: U.S. Geological Survey (USGS)*

Salient Statistics of Manganese in the United States   In Thousands of Metric Tons (Gross Weight)

Year	Net Import Reliance as a % of Apparent Consumption	Manganese Ore (35% or More Manganese) Imports for Consumption	Exports	Consumption	Stocks, Dec. 31[3]	Ferromanganese Imports for Consumption	Exports	Consumption	Avg. Price Mn. Metallurgical Ore $ Lg. Ton Unit[4]	Silicomanganese Exports	Imports
1994	100	331	15	449	269	336	11	347	2.40	6.8	273.0
1995	100	394	15	486	309	310	11	348	2.40	7.8	305.0
1996	100	478	32	478	319	374	10	326	2.55	5.3	323.0
1997	100	355	84	510	241	304	12	337	2.44	5.4	306.0
1998	100	332	8	499	163	339	14	290	2.40	6.7	346.0
1999	100	460	4	479	172	312	12	281	2.26	3.7	301.0
2000	100	447	10	486	226	312	8	300	2.39	1.9	378.0
2001	100	358	9	425	138	251	9	266	2.44	3.6	269.0
2002[1]	100	427	15	360	151	275	9	253	2.30	0.5	247.0
2003[2]	100	347	18	398	156	238	11	248	2.41	0.6	267.0

[1] Preliminary.   [2] Estimate.   [3] Including bonded warehouses; excludes Gov't stocks; also excludes small tonnages of dealers' stocks.   [4] 46-48% Mn, C.I.F. U.S. Ports.   *Source: U.S. Geological Survey (USGS)*

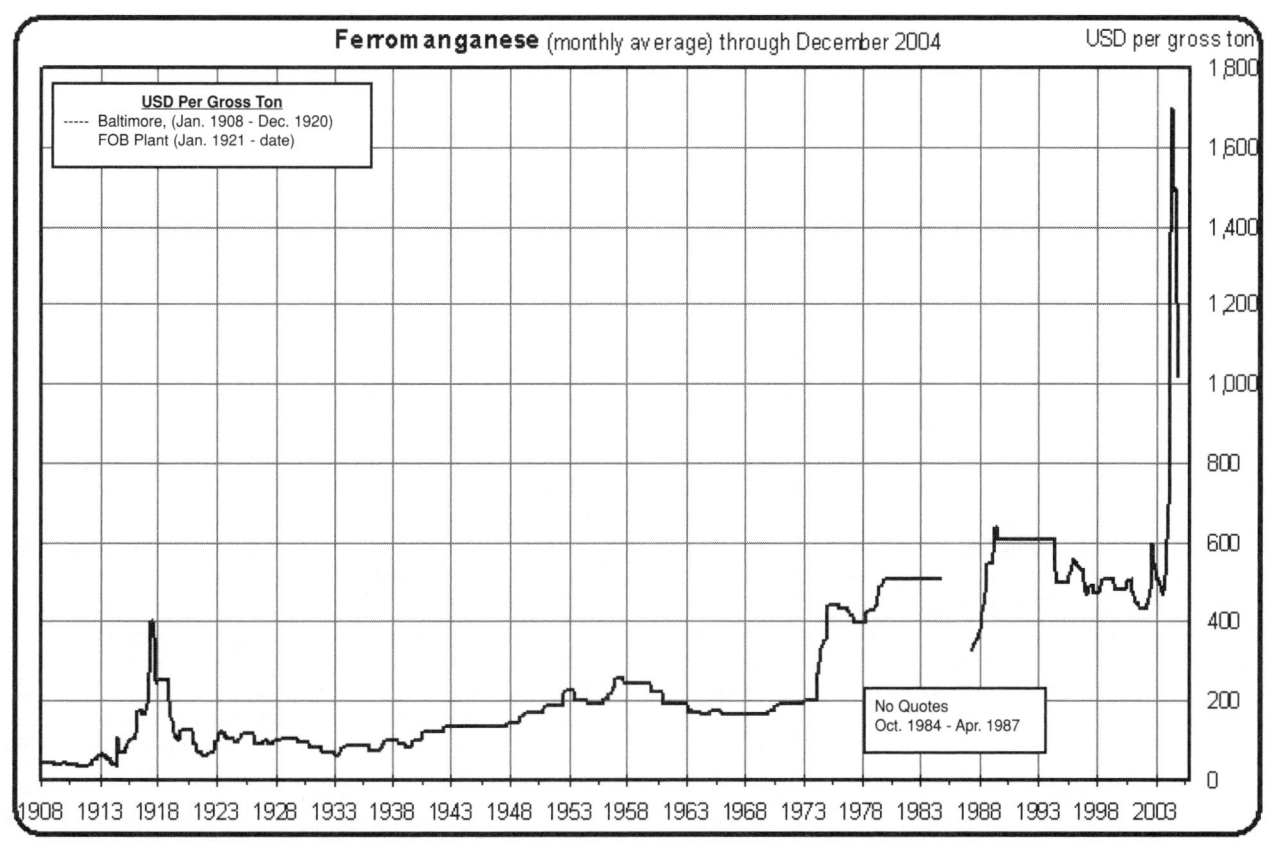

Imports[3] of Manganese Ore (20% or More Mn) in the United States   In Metric Tons (Mn Content)

Year	Australia	Brazil	Gabon	Mexico	Morocco	South Africa	Total	Customs Value Thous. $
1994	23,200	4,530	112,000	13,700	56	7,780	161,000	29,800
1995	31,600	7,080	104,000	23,600	37	13,100	187,000	33,300
1996	48,900	5,640	140,000	16,100	9	20,800	231,000	42,400
1997	16,400	9,100	99,400	30,100	37	----	156,000	30,800
1998	18,700	12,100	94,900	14,600	----	13,800	160,000	27,800
1999	23,500	1	142,000	9,130	----	39,100	224,000	37,200
2000	18,100	3,250	188,000	3,250	----	----	219,000	32,100
2001	18,000	3,480	158,000	1,720	----	17,400	199,000	28,000
2002[1]	18,400	12,900	140,000	1,100	----	41,800	214,000	29,200
2003[2]	12,900	7	123,000	1,520	----	36,900	175,000	27,000

[1] Preliminary.   [2] Estimate.   [3] Imports for consumption.   *Source: U.S. Geological Survey (USGS)*

Average Price of Ferromanganese   In Dollars Per Gross Ton

Year	Jan.	Feb.	Mar.	Apr.	May	June	July	Aug.	Sept.	Oct.	Nov.	Dec.	Average
1995	500.00	500.00	500.00	500.00	500.00	500.00	500.00	518.75	525.00	525.00	542.50	560.00	514.27
1996	560.00	552.50	550.00	550.00	541.00	535.00	533.13	527.50	527.50	527.50	501.25	477.50	531.91
1997	477.50	467.50	470.00	482.50	490.00	490.00	490.00	492.50	475.00	475.00	475.00	475.00	480.00
1998	175.00	175.00	175.00	190.00	190.00	510.00	510.00	510.00	510.00	510.00	510.00	510.00	497.92
1999	510.00	510.00	510.00	510.00	510.00	498.75	482.50	482.50	482.50	482.50	482.50	482.50	495.21
2000	482.50	482.50	482.50	482.50	482.50	482.50	501.63	505.00	509.00	510.00	510.00	477.50	492.40
2001	473.93	467.89	460.00	454.29	450.00	450.00	446.90	444.57	430.79	430.00	430.00	430.00	447.44
2002	430.00	430.00	437.14	447.73	449.55	456.75	481.82	556.14	597.00	589.67	552.89	518.93	495.64
2003	509.52	510.00	502.38	497.61	492.50	481.79	477.27	470.00	478.57	497.83	516.67	559.76	499.49
2004	610.00	790.00	1,382.61	1,700.00	1,700.00	1,674.43	1,490.34	1,488.64	1,500.00	1,371.43	1,207.50	1,019.52	1,327.87

Domestic standard, high carbon, FOB plant, carloads.   *Source: American Metal Market (AMM)*

Meats

US commercial red meat includes beef, veal, lamb, and pork. Red meat is a good source of iron, vitamin B12, and protein, and eliminating it from the diet can lead to iron and zinc deficiencies. Today, red meat is far leaner than it was 30 years ago due to newer breeds of livestock that carry less fat. The leanest cuts of beef include tenderloin, sirloin, and flank. The leanest cuts of pork include pork tenderloin, loin chops, and rib chops.

The USDA (United States Department of Agriculture) grades various cuts of meat. "Prime" is the highest USDA grade for beef, veal, and lamb. "Choice" is the grade designation below Prime for beef, veal, and lamb. "Commercial" and "Cutter" grades are two of the lower designations for beef, usually sold as ground meat, sausage, and canned meat. "Canner" is the lowest USDA grade designation for beef and is used primarily in canned meats not sold at retail.

Supply – World meat production in 2004 rose +1.0% to a new record high of 138.350 million metric tons. China is by far the world's largest meat producer with 51.198 million metric tons of production in 2004 (+2.2% yr/yr), accounting for 37% of world production. Other major world meat producers include the US with 15% of world production, Europe, and Brazil.

US production of meat in 2004 fell by –2.2% yr/yr to 45.672 billion pounds, which was well below the record high of 47.305 billion pounds produced in 2002. US production of beef in 2004 fell -3.4% yr/yr to 25.505 billion pounds, which was moderately below the record of 27.192 billion pounds in 2002. Beef accounted for 55.8% of all US meat production. US production of pork in 2004 fell -0.6% yr/yr to 19.772 billion pounds from the record high production level of 19.890 billion pounds in 2003. Pork accounts for 43.3% of US meat production. Veal accounts for only 0.4% of US meat production, and lamb and mutton account for only 0.4% of US meat production.

Demand – US per capita meat consumption in 2004 fell to a record low of 115.0 pounds per person per year, reflecting a trend towards eating more chicken and fish and the availability of meat substitutes. Per capita beef consumption fell to a record low of 62.0 pounds per person per year, which was about one-half the record high of 127.5 pounds seen in 1976. Per capita pork consumption in 2004 fell to 51.0 pounds per person per year, which was only slightly above the record low of 50.0 pounds posted in 2001.

Trade – World red meat exports in 2004 rose +8.3% to 6.934 million metric tons, which was well below the record of 10.065 million metric tons posted in 1999. The world's largest red meat exporters are Brazil with 20% of world exports in 2004, Australia with 19%, and the US with 17%.

World Total Meat Production[3]   In Thousands of Metric Tons

Year	Argentina	Australia	Brazil	Canada	China[4]	France	Germany	Italy	Mexico	Russia	United Kingdom	United States	World Total
1997	3,033	2,914	7,590	2,332	42,500	4,046	5,053	2,632	2,875	4,086	2,183	19,667	128,993
1998	2,648	2,973	7,830	2,544	45,982	4,065	5,244	2,595	2,852	3,775	2,367	20,541	135,368
1999	2,890	2,940	8,105	2,802	47,670	4,086	5,532	2,707	2,999	3,544	2,238	20,994	138,510
2000	2,928	2,986	8,530	2,886	48,292	3,966	5,331	2,692	3,045	3,494	2,134	20,991	139,351
2001	2,640	2,428	9,125	2,981	47,333	3,740	5,195	2,475	2,990	3,320	1,642	20,674	132,769
2002	2,700	2,496	9,805	3,148	49,112				3,015	3,370		21,356	137,685
2003	2,800	2,493	9,945	3,072	51,491				3,050	3,380		21,095	139,037
2004[1]	2,900	2,400	10,415	3,350	53,853				3,300	3,350		20,538	141,518
2005[2]	2,730	2,385	10,862	3,435	54,610				3,245	3,340		20,754	142,901

[1] Preliminary.   [2] Forecast.   [3] Data through 2000, includes beef, veal, pork, sheep and goat meat. Beginning 2001, excludes sheep and goat.
[4] Predominately pork production.   Source: Foreign Agricultural Service, U.S. Department of Agriculture (FAS-USDA)

Production and Consumption of Red Meats in The United States

	Beef			Veal			Lamb & Mutton			Pork (Excluding Lard)			All Meats		
	Commercial Production	Consumption Total	Per Capita	Commercial Production	Consumption Total	Per Capita	Commercial Production	Consumption Total	Per Capita	Commercial Production	Consumption Total	Per Capita	Commercial Production	Consumption Total	Per Capita
Year	-- Million Pounds --		Lbs.[4]	- Million Pounds -		Lbs.[4]	- Million Pounds -		Lbs.[4]	-- Million Pounds --		Lbs.[4]	-- Million Pounds --		Lbs.[4]
1997	25,490	25,611	95.9	334	333	1.2	260	332	1.1	17,274	16,823	61.4	43,358	43,099	159.6
1998	25,760	26,305	93.3	262	265	1.0	251	360	1.0	19,011	18,309	65.3	45,284	45,239	160.6
1999	26,493	26,936	68.0	235	235	1.0	248	358	1.0	19,308	18,954	53.0	46,284	46,483	122.0
2000	26,888	27,338	68.0	225	225	1.0	234	354	1.0	18,952	18,643	51.0	46,299	46,560	121.0
2001	26,212	27,026	66.0	205	204	1.0	227	368	1.0	19,160	18,492	50.0	45,804	46,089	118.0
2002	27,192	27,878	68.0	205	204	1.0	223	381	1.0	19,685	19,147	52.0	47,305	47,610	121.0
2003[1]	26,339	26,999	65.0	202	204	1.0	203	367	1.0	19,966	19,435	52.0	46,710	47,005	118.0
2004[2]	24,524	27,505	66.0	182	183	1.0	198	380	1.0	20,544	19,597	52.0	45,448	47,665	119.0
2005[3]	24,876	27,966	66.0	184	183	1.0	201	396	1.0	20,821	19,881	52.0	46,082	48,426	120.0

[1] Preliminary.   [2] Estimate.   [3] Forecast.   [4] Data through 1998, are for Carcass weight. Beginning 1998, data are for Retail-weight basis.
Source: Economic Research Service, U.S. Department of Agriculture (ERS-USDA)

Total Red Meat Imports[3] (Carcass Weight Equivalent) of Principal Countries   In Thousands of Metric Tons

Year	Canada	France	Germany	Hong Kong	Italy	Japan	Rep. of Korea	Nether- lands	Russia	Singa- pore	United Kingdom	United States	Total
1996	270	44	139	195	61	1,993	271	31	1,584	38	276	1,249	6,452
1997	303	47	132	217	64	1,767	303	56	1,951	36	293	1,383	6,707
1998	296	44	125	267	57	1,783	191	32	1,429	31	255	1,557	7,771
1999	319	53	135	284	61	1,939	398	25	1,705	39	256	1,729	8,859
2000	331	53	138	318	61	2,067	498	21	1,033	38	260	1,865	8,606
2001	390	19	72	331	56	2,023	369	32	1,210	32	164	1,866	8,096
2002	398			346		1,840	586		1,460			1,945	8,898
2003	364			383		1,943	598		1,270			1,901	8,733
2004[1]	195			399		1,829	400		1,150			2,133	8,293
2005[2]	190			420		1,861	483		1,150			2,166	8,572

[1] Preliminary.   [2] Forecast.   [3] Data through 2000, includes beef, veal, pork, sheep and goat meat. Beginning 2001, excludes sheep and goat.
Source: Foreign Agricultural Service, U.S. Department of Agriculture (FAS-USDA)

Total Red Meat Exports[3] (Carcass Weight Equivalent) of Principal Countries   In Thousands of Metric Tons

Year	Argentina	Australia	Brazil	Canada	China	Denmark	France	India	Ireland	Nether- lands	New Zealand	United States	World Total
1996	498	1,311	304	703	280	387	290	220	305	195	861	1,294	8,361
1997	460	1,465	314	802	267	531	282	231	271	202	979	1,446	9,003
1998	304	1,596	411	860	242	490	214	263	308	150	977	1,546	9,168
1999	360	1,672	573	1,046	141	594	333	236	369	209	892	1,677	10,052
2000	358	1,762	654	1,183	133	590	222	360	284	214	905	1,705	9,856
2001	169	1,466	1,085	1,302	199	555	185	370	77	147	516	1,737	9,008
2002	348	1,444	1,471	1,474	260		417				505	1,841	10,065
2003	386	1,338	1,778	1,359	325		439				578	1,922	10,477
2004[1]	540	1,360	2,040	1,500	375		540				600	1,140	10,355
2005[2]	600	1,360	2,200	1,550	450		625				605	1,231	10,797

[1] Preliminary.   [2] Forecast.   [3] Data through 2000, includes beef, veal, pork, sheep and goat meat. Beginning 2001, excludes sheep and goat.
Source: Foreign Agricultural Service, U.S. Department of Agriculture (FAS-USDA)

United States Meat Imports by Type of Product   In Metric Tons

Year	Beef and Veal Fresh	Beef and Veal Frozen	Beef and Veal Other Prepared or Preserved	Lamb, Mutton and Goat, Except Canned	Pork Fresh and Chilled	Pork Frozen	Pork Other Prepared or Preserved	Variety Meats, Fresh, hilled and Frozen	Other Livestock Meats NSE	Total
1994	179,121	535,328	74,704	23,276	130,648	78,378	94,013	27,511	13,012	1,155,990
1995	175,540	466,378	65,399	29,844	133,101	61,286	79,155	26,081	12,539	1,049,324
1996	227,874	412,805	66,719	33,009	125,220	58,336	72,650	32,579	13,744	1,042,934
1997	262,985	469,949	63,181	37,848	126,061	65,000	72,903	44,317	14,215	1,156,457
1998	295,820	527,063	68,884	51,630	146,965	70,227	76,230	47,031	13,058	1,296,907
1999	337,899	542,524	82,669	50,209	188,556	77,638	84,207	51,640	13,625	1,428,966
2000	336,117	608,737	73,750	59,968	229,395	91,446	92,672	57,388	14,281	1,563,753
2001	368,529	618,897	73,713	66,785	240,275	84,687	83,724	62,541	16,723	1,615,873
2002[1]	400,484	586,500	84,640	73,863	276,639	90,423	87,876	55,384	19,401	1,675,210

[1] Preliminary.   NSE = Not specified elsewhere.   *Source: Foreign Agricultural Service, U.S. Department of Agriculture (FAS-USDA)*

United States Meat Exports by Type of Product   In Metric Tons

Year	Beef and Veal Fresh and Chilled	Beef and Veal Frozen	Beef and Veal Prepared and Preserved	Lamb and Mutton, Fresh or Frozen	Pork Fresh and Chilled	Pork Frozen	Pork Prepared and Preserved	Variety Meats, Fresh, Chilled or Frozen	Other Meats	Total
1994	242,391	275,067	13,419	3,766	80,609	68,805	27,960	395,048	301,112	1,408,176
1995	262,381	319,416	13,651	2,511	100,235	127,835	35,766	466,213	353,207	1,681,215
1996	273,276	324,329	14,577	2,478	101,975	166,058	38,481	495,343	434,759	1,851,276
1997	316,534	359,460	15,227	2,545	134,684	151,121	38,301	469,789	435,258	1,922,918
1998	346,403	352,050	17,966	2,528	147,006	209,134	43,789	495,643	423,980	2,038,500
1999	370,184	414,458	19,323	2,219	160,910	225,492	47,898	524,325	455,561	2,220,369
2000	395,588	417,538	21,791	2,184	208,055	185,241	44,836	604,738	503,942	2,380,912
2001	393,105	362,972	23,932	2,770	227,807	247,461	52,788	685,063	513,969	2,509,866
2002[1]	407,600	393,836	27,232	3,042	235,548	231,274	83,167	592,185	619,491	2,593,375

[1] Preliminary.   *Source: Foreign Agricultural Service, U.S. Department of Agriculture (FAS-USDA)*

MEATS

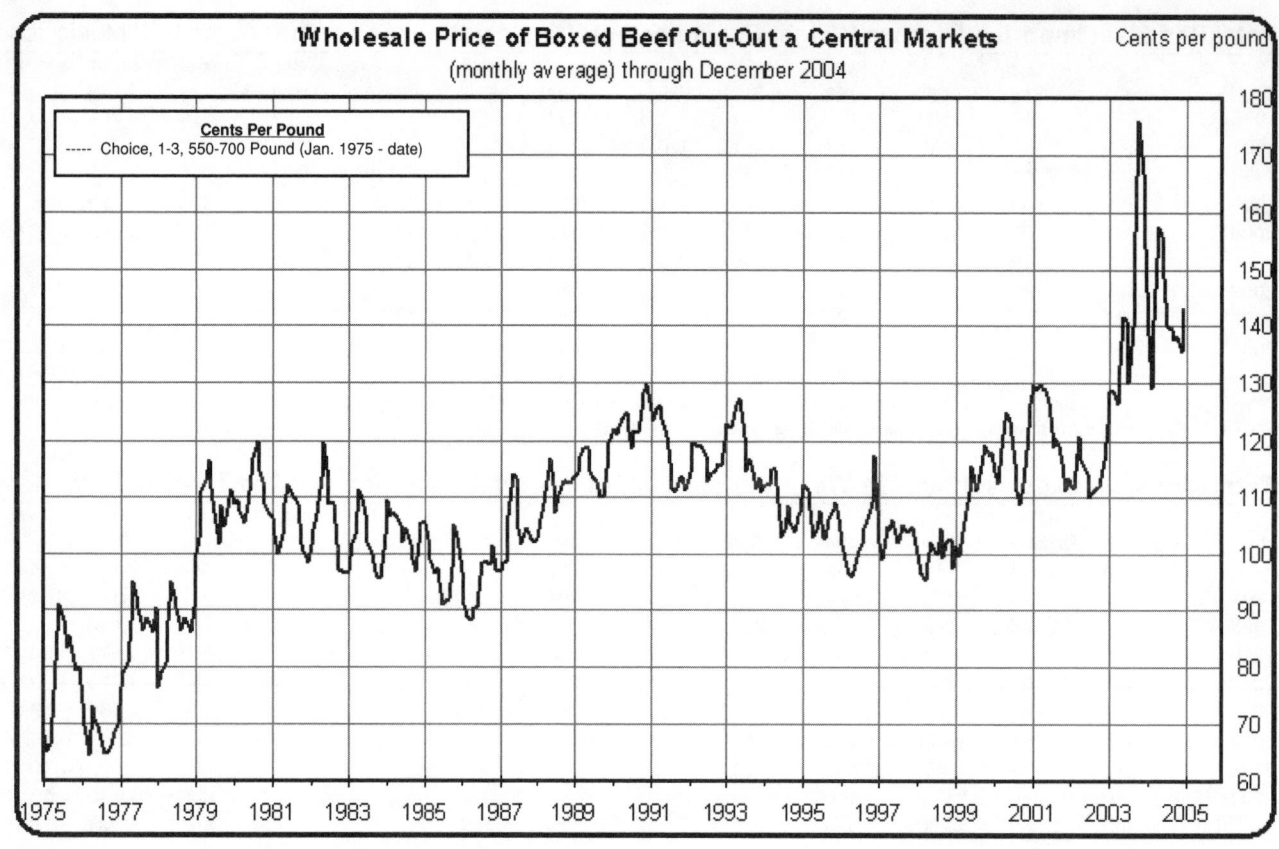

Wholesale Price of Boxed Beef Cut-Out a Central Markets
(monthly average) through December 2004

Cents per pound

Cents Per Pound
----- Choice, 1-3, 550-700 Pound (Jan. 1975 - date)

Exports and Imports of Meats in the United States (Carcass Weight Equivalent)[3]   In Millions of Pounds

	Exports				Imports			
Year	Beef and Veal	Lamb and Mutton	Pork[3]	All Meat	Beef and Veal	Lamb and Mutton	Pork[3]	All Meat
1995	1,821	6	787	2,614	2,103	64	664	2,832
1996	1,877	6	970	2,853	2,073	72	620	2,764
1997	2,136	5	1,044	3,185	2,343	83	634	3,061
1998	2,171	6	1,230	3,407	2,643	112	705	3,461
1999	2,412	5	1,277	3,694	2,873	112	827	3,813
2000	2,468	5	1,287	3,760	3,032	130	967	4,128
2001	2,269	7	1,560	3,836	3,164	146	951	4,260
2002	2,447	7	1,611	4,065	3,218	162	1,070	4,450
2003[1]	2,574	5	1,707	4,287	2,920	164	1,193	4,277
2004[2]	220	6	1,765	1,990	3,330	163	1,235	4,728

[1] Preliminary.   [2] Estimate.   [3] Includes meat content of minor meats and of mixed products.   *Source: Economic Research Service, U.S. Department of Agriculture (FAS-USDA)*

Average Wholesale Prices of Meats in the United States   In Cents Per Pound

	Composite Retail Price		Wholesale Value[4]		Net Farm Value of Pork[5]	Cow Beef Canner & Cutter, Central US	Boxed Beef Cut-out, Choice 1-3, Central US, 550-700 Lbs.	Pork Carcass Cut-out, US No. 2	Lamb Carcass, Choice-Prime, East Coast, 55-65 Lbs.	Pork Loins, Central US, 14-18 Lbs.	Skinned Ham, Central US, 20-26 Lbs.	Pork Bellies, Central US, 12-14 Lbs.
Year	of Beef, Choice, Grade 3	of Pork[3]	Beef	Pork								
1996	280.23	233.71	158.10	123.20	99.40	58.18	103.09	72.39	177.58	118.49	72.41	69.97
1997	279.53	244.97	158.20	123.10	95.30	64.30	103.26	70.87	178.67	108.89	69.99	73.91
1998	277.12	242.69	153.80	97.30	61.20	61.33	99.86	53.08	156.75	101.63	53.07	52.38
1999	287.76	241.44	171.55	99.00	60.40	66.51	111.06	53.45	170.29	100.38	51.35	57.12
2000	306.42	258.20	182.27	114.50	79.40	72.57	117.51	64.07	177.78	117.13	60.85	77.46
2001	337.73	269.39	192.12	117.80	81.30	79.50	122.61	66.83	148.96	116.97	64.86	78.61
2002	331.53	265.75	180.02	100.70	61.90	NA	114.42	53.49	151.28	97.98	47.52	69.91
2003[1]	374.62	265.82	222.90	107.40	69.60	NA	143.58	58.87	185.21	100.96	45.48	86.42
2004[2]	406.53	279.16			NA		142.15	73.53	189.08	117.14	64.98	99.35

[1] Preliminary.   [2] Estimate.   [3] Sold as retail cuts (ham, bacon, loin, etc.).   [4] Quantity equivalent to 1 pound of retail cuts.   [5] Portion of gross farm value minus farm by-product allowance.   *Source: Economic Research Service, U.S. Department of Agriculture (ERS-USDA)*

Average Wholesale Price of Boxed Beef Cut-Out[1], Choice, at Central Markets   In Cents Per Pound

Year	Jan.	Feb.	Mar.	Apr.	May	June	July	Aug.	Sept.	Oct.	Nov.	Dec.	Average
1995	112.17	111.12	107.87	103.03	104.21	107.65	103.03	102.55	105.82	107.77	108.88	106.08	106.68
1996	101.71	98.86	96.36	96.01	96.90	100.70	101.53	104.43	105.93	109.10	117.53	108.03	103.09
1997	101.90	98.98	104.87	104.17	105.97	101.83	102.38	105.14	104.06	103.72	104.63	101.50	103.26
1998	100.26	96.27	95.34	98.32	102.09	100.38	99.96	104.28	99.28	102.08	102.61	97.49	99.86
1999	101.37	99.37	103.62	107.55	110.89	115.39	111.14	114.00	115.13	119.21	117.38	117.71	111.05
2000	114.74	112.59	118.42	123.45	124.88	123.30	115.85	111.20	108.68	112.58	118.05	126.41	117.51
2001	129.78	128.87	129.58	128.93	129.03	126.82	118.93	120.20	119.30	115.93	110.95	113.04	122.61
2002	111.99	111.53	120.54	116.61	115.14	114.06	109.88	110.93	111.83	111.64	116.41	122.45	114.42
2003	128.59	128.77	126.35	133.03	141.44	141.16	130.13	139.91	156.64	176.06	167.15	153.71	143.58
2004[2]	138.60	129.29	141.34	157.53	155.70	148.54	140.27	139.33	137.82	138.45	135.64	143.31	142.15

[1] Choice 1-3, 550-700 pounds.   [2] Preliminary.   *Source: Economic Research Service, U.S. Department of Agriculture (ERS-USDA)*

Production (Commercial) of All Red Meats in the United States   In Millions of Pounds (Carcass Weight)

Year	Jan.	Feb.	Mar.	Apr.	May	June	July	Aug.	Sept.	Oct.	Nov.	Dec.	Total
1995	3,560	3,210	3,751	3,304	3,758	3,798	3,424	3,860	3,697	3,795	3,748	3,553	43,458
1996	3,823	3,519	3,512	3,690	3,767	3,439	3,585	3,707	3,396	3,827	3,435	3,432	43,132
1997	3,735	3,278	3,444	3,592	3,571	3,492	3,657	3,619	3,665	4,005	3,453	3,715	43,226
1998	3,836	3,476	3,726	3,701	3,582	3,732	3,781	3,770	3,827	4,033	3,725	3,945	45,134
1999	3,833	3,535	4,016	3,824	3,604	3,940	3,781	3,913	3,933	4,002	3,895	3,862	46,138
2000	3,784	3,767	4,044	3,460	3,878	3,941	3,644	4,113	3,861	4,096	3,919	3,619	46,126
2001	3,935	3,761	3,761	3,506	3,881	3,758	3,643	4,060	3,664	4,264	3,970	3,813	46,016
2002	4,081	3,501	3,677	3,902	4,018	3,813	4,016	4,141	3,873	4,382	3,908	3,859	47,171
2003	4,075	3,496	3,705	3,845	3,944	3,948	4,046	3,913	4,007	4,155	3,524	3,876	46,534
2004[1]	3,713	3,404	3,944	3,713	3,597	3,928	3,708	3,878	3,905	3,921	3,770	3,931	45,412

[1] Preliminary.   *Source: Economic Research Service, U.S. Department of Agriculture (ERS-USDA)*

Cold Storage Holdings of All[2] Meats in the United States, on First of Month   In Millions of Pounds

Year	Jan.	Feb.	Mar.	Apr.	May	June	July	Aug.	Sept.	Oct.	Nov.	Dec.
1995	802.0	838.7	833.8	834.0	852.7	831.2	820.8	803.6	733.4	711.3	732.3	757.0
1996	749.7	779.5	781.6	729.3	748.6	716.2	687.9	642.7	657.4	678.4	655.5	627.1
1997	621.3	655.9	669.9	719.5	752.5	719.7	742.9	726.3	731.5	728.2	739.1	741.0
1998	722.4	802.8	825.8	816.3	849.3	814.3	771.0	747.2	728.2	738.8	794.9	794.1
1999	821.0	833.0	863.1	883.5	936.4	901.2	843.9	810.4	834.9	746.3	780.3	750.5
2000	748.3	853.1	913.9	934.3	951.3	963.5	926.7	896.2	881.0	871.1	868.0	883.0
2001	836.2	907.8	852.6	787.9	771.4	772.5	742.2	717.4	732.6	775.3	849.0	880.9
2002	946.8	982.6	970.7	961.9	996.6	973.0	918.0	912.6	950.7	997.8	1,038.9	997.7
2003	1,011.5	1,015.2	978.2	951.9	926.8	901.5	847.5	825.0	817.3	832.1	836.9	828.1
2004[1]	879.0	953.7	932.5	885.8	890.2	835.3	804.0	814.3	849.5	894.4	892.9	912.6

[1] Preliminary.   [2] Includes beef and veal, mutton and lamb, pork and products, rendered pork fat, and miscellaneous meats. Excludes lard.
Source: Economic Research Service, U.S. Department of Agriculture (ERS-USDA)

Cold Storage Holdings of Frozen Beef in the United States, on First of Month   In Millions of Pounds

Year	Jan. 1	Feb. 1	Mar. 1	Apr. 1	May 1	June 1	July 1	Aug. 1	Sept. 1	Oct. 1	Nov. 1	Dec. 1
1995	411.2	420.3	407.7	385.4	392.2	359.1	352.3	359.3	344.9	347.7	381.6	381.4
1996	389.6	367.9	362.6	347.3	335.6	307.4	306.7	291.1	305.2	312.2	295.9	288.1
1997	284.9	290.3	261.7	290.4	285.4	278.7	305.6	302.8	324.6	349.1	351.6	378.2
1998	350.2	331.1	334.9	329.7	335.5	310.2	316.5	303.0	306.7	323.1	358.2	328.2
1999	296.4	301.1	300.1	309.2	316.8	306.7	293.1	292.7	377.9	294.4	322.5	308.9
2000	314.2	350.9	369.0	378.2	396.1	401.1	405.1	391.5	398.8	405.7	404.4	411.8
2001	401.7	410.9	360.2	332.6	315.3	325.1	340.8	351.4	373.2	382.8	395.1	427.6
2002	460.7	455.5	439.0	410.5	405.7	401.8	396.9	416.5	461.8	494.9	525.2	512.6
2003	524.6	482.4	441.9	403.1	389.7	385.1	371.5	368.2	371.0	379.8	375.2	373.8
2004[1]	395.1	434.4	435.0	416.8	421.2	402.8	411.3	427.0	446.0	457.2	452.6	463.3

[1] Preliminary.   *Source: Economic Research Service, U.S. Department of Agriculture (ERS-USDA)*

Mercury

Mercury (symbol Hg) was known to the ancient Hindus and Chinese, and was also found in Egyptian tombs dating back to 1500 BC. The ancient Greeks used Mercury in ointments, and the Romans used it in cosmetics. Alchemists thought mercury turned into gold when it hardened.

Mercury, also called quicksilver, is a heavy, silvery, toxic, transitional metal. Mercury is the only common metal that is liquid at room temperatures. When subjected to a pressure of 7,640 atmospheres (7.7 million millibars), mercury becomes a solid. Mercury dissolves in nitric or concentrated sulfuric acid, but is resistant to alkalis. It is a poor conductor of heat. Mercury has superconductivity when cooled to sufficiently low temperatures. It has a freezing point of about –39 degrees Celsius and a boiling point of about 357 degrees Celsius.

Mercury is found in its pure form or combined in small amounts with silvers, but is found most often in the ore cinnabar, a mineral consisting of mercuric sulfide. By heating the cinnabar ore in air until the mercuric sulfide breaks down, pure mercury metal is produced. Mercury forms alloys called amalgams with all common metals except iron and platinum. Most mercury is used for the manufacture of industrial chemicals and for electrical and electronic applications. Other uses for mercury include its use in gold recovery from ores, barometers, diffusion pumps, laboratory instruments, mercury-vapor lamps, pesticides, batteries, and catalysts. A decline in mercury production and usage since the 1970s reflects a trend for using mercury substitutes due to its toxicity.

Prices – The average monthly price of mercury in 2004 rose sharply by 103% yr/yr to a 23-year high of $373.46 per flask (34.5 kilograms). That was nearly three times the 13-year low of $131.14 posted in 1991.

Supply – World mine production of mercury in 2003 rose +1.3% yr/yr to a 5-year high of 1,530 metric tons. However, that was far below the record high of 10,364 metric tons posted in 1971. The world's largest miners of mercury are China with 40% of world production, followed by Algeria with 20%, Kyrgyzstan with 20%, and Spain with 10%. China's production soared to 610 metric tons in 2003, which is more than triple the record low of 190 metric tons seen in 2001, but well below its record of 1,200 metric tons posted in 1989.

Demand – The breakdown of domestic consumption of mercury by particular categories is no longer available, but the data as of 1997 showed that chlorine and caustic soda accounted for 46% of US mercury consumption, followed by wiring devices and switches (17%), dental equipment (12%), electrical lighting (8%), and measuring control instruments (7%). Substitutes for mercury include lithium and composite ceramic materials.

Trade – US foreign trade in mercury is small. US imports of mercury in 2003 fell sharply by -78% yr/yr to 46 metric tons from the 7-year high of 209 metric tons seen in 2002. US imports were mostly from Chile and Peru. US exports of mercury in 2003 rose sharply by 43% to 287 metric tons, which was a 9-year high.

World Mine Production of Mercury   In Metric Tons (1 tonne = 29.008216 flasks)

Year	Algeria	China	Finland	Kyrgyz-stan	Mexico	Spain	Tajik-istan	Turkey	Ukraine	United States	World Total
1995	292	780	90	380	15	1,497	50	----	40	W	3,190
1996	368	510	88	584	15	862	45	----	30	W	2,560
1997	447	830	63	550	15	389	40	----	25	W	2,410
1998	224	230	54	250	15	675	35	----	20	NA	1,580
1999	240	200	40	300	15	433	35	----	NA	NA	1,310
2000	216	200	76	257	15	500	40	----	NA	NA	1,360
2001	321	190	71	300	15	500	40	----	----	NA	1,500
2002[1]	307	435	70	300	15	300	20	----	----	NA	1,510
2003[2]	300	610	65	300	15	150	30	----	----	NA	1,530

[1] Preliminary.   [2] Estimate.   W = Withheld to avoid disclosing company proprietary data.   NA = Not available.   *Source: U.S. Geological Survey (USGS)*

Salient Statistics of Mercury in the United States   In Metric Tons

Year	Producing Mines	Secondary Production — Industrial	Secondary Production — Govern-ment[3]	Secondary Production — NDS[4] Shipments	Consumer & Dealer Stocks, Dec. 31	Industrial Demand	Exports	Imports
1995	8	534	----	----	321	436	179	377
1996	6	446	----	----	446	372	45	340
1997	5	389	----	----	203	346	134	164
1998	NA	NA	----	----	NA	NA	63	128
1999	NA	NA	----	----	NA	NA	181	62
2000	NA	NA	----	----	NA	NA	182	103
2001	NA	NA	----	----	NA	NA	108	100
2002[1]	NA	NA	----	----	NA	NA	201	209
2003[2]	NA	NA	----	----	NA	NA	287	46

[1] Preliminary.   [2] Estimate.   [3] Secondary mercury shipped from the Department of Energy.   [4] National Defense Stockpile.   NA = Not available.
Source: U.S. Geological Survey (USGS)

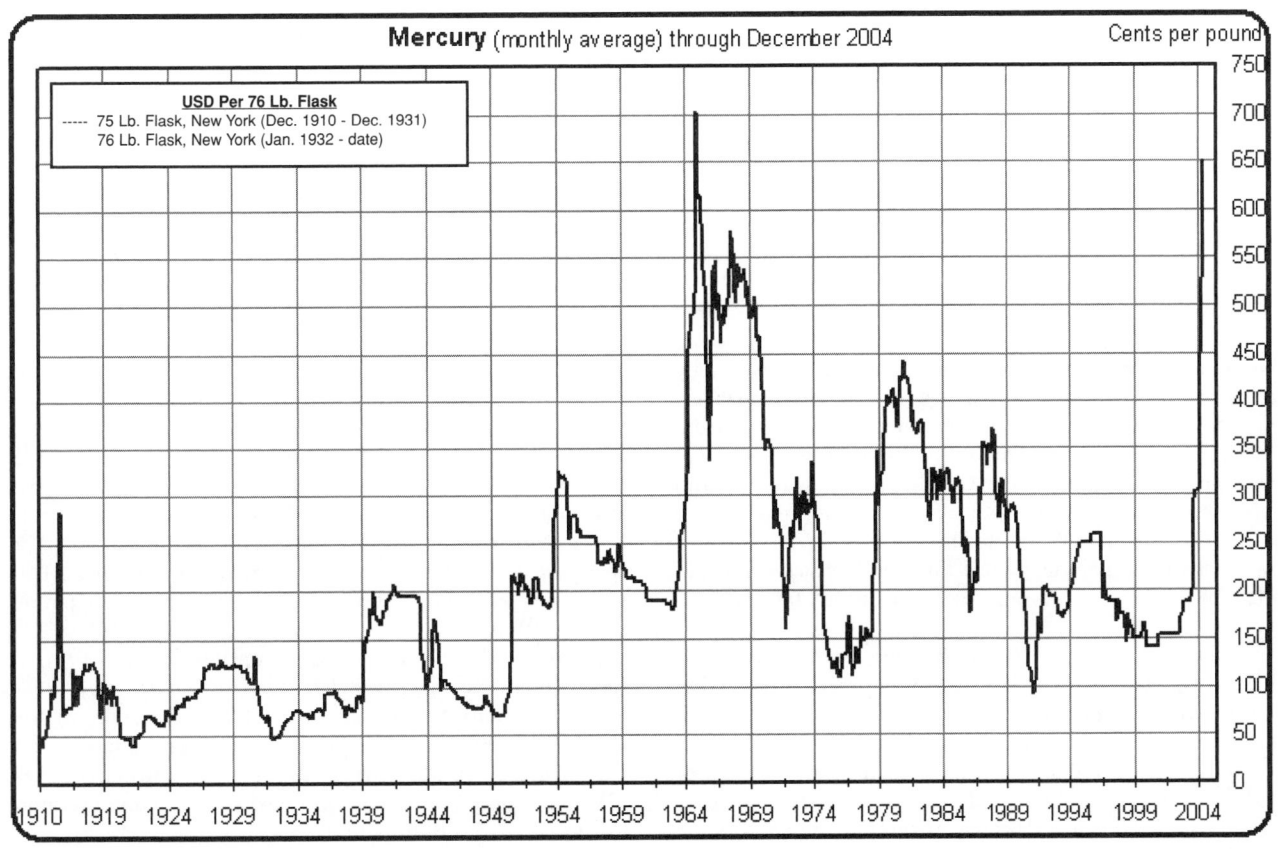

Average Price of Mercury in New York   In Dollars Per Flask of 76 Pounds (34.5 Kilograms)

Year	Jan.	Feb.	Mar.	Apr.	May	June	July	Aug.	Sept.	Oct.	Nov.	Dec.	Average
1995	235.00	240.00	241.30	250.00	250.00	250.00	250.00	250.00	250.00	250.00	250.00	250.00	247.19
1996	250.00	250.00	261.67	268.33	265.00	265.00	265.00	265.00	265.00	265.00	262.63	235.48	259.84
1997	233.98	232.76	228.88	228.64	220.00	199.05	200.00	198.10	190.83	198.83	191.47	187.00	209.13
1998	187.00	187.00	187.00	187.00	187.00	181.55	175.00	175.00	175.00	175.00	175.00	175.00	180.55
1999	175.00	152.63	150.00	150.00	150.00	150.00	150.00	150.00	150.00	150.00	150.00	150.00	152.09
2000	150.00	157.88	167.50	167.50	167.50	158.23	142.00	142.00	142.00	142.00	142.00	142.00	151.90
2001	142.00	142.00	142.00	142.00	142.00	143.71	154.00	154.00	154.00	154.00	154.00	154.00	148.12
2002	154.00	154.00	154.00	154.00	154.00	154.00	154.00	154.00	154.00	154.00	154.00	154.00	154.00
2003	165.43	175.00	175.00	175.00	185.23	187.50	187.50	187.50	187.50	187.50	195.63	200.00	184.07
2004	200.00	256.25	297.61	305.00	305.00	305.00	305.00	305.00	417.05	485.12	649.24	650.00	373.36

Source: American Metal Market (AMM)

Mercury Consumed in the United States   In Metric Tons

Year	Batteries[3]	Chlorine & Caustic Soda	Catalysts, Misc.	Dental Equip.	Electrical Lighting[3]	General Lab Use	Measuring Contraol Instrument	Paints	Wiring Devices & Switches[3]	Other Uses	Total
1988	448	354	86	53	31	26	77	197	176	55	1,503
1989	250	379	40	39	31	18	87	192	141	32	1,212
1990	106	247	29	44	33	32	108	14	70	38	720
1991	18	184	26	41	39	30	90	6	71	49	554
1992	13	209	20	42	55	28	80	-----	82	92	621
1993	10	180	18	35	38	26	65	-----	83	103	558
1994	6	135	25	24	27	24	53	-----	79	110	483
1995	-----	154	-----	32	30	-----	43	-----	84	93	436
1996[1]	-----	136	-----	31	29	-----	41	-----	49	86	372
1997[2]	-----	160	-----	40	29	-----	24	-----	57	36	346

[1] Preliminary.   [2] Estimate.   W = Withheld proprietary data.   *Source: U.S. Geological Survey (USGS)*

Milk

Evidence of man's use of animal milk as food was discovered in a temple in the Euphrates Valley near Babylon, dating back to 3,000 BC. Humans drink the milk produced from a variety of domesticated mammals, including cows, goats, sheep, camels, reindeer, buffaloes, and llama. In India, half of all milk consumed is from water buffalo. Camels' milk spoils slower than other types of milk in the hot desert. But the vast majority of milk used for commercial production and consumption comes from cows.

Milk directly from a cow in its natural form is called raw milk. Raw milk is processed by spinning it in a centrifuge, homogenizing it to create a consistent texture (i.e., by forcing hot milk under high pressure through small nozzles), and then sterilizing it through pasteurization (i.e., heating to a high temperature for a specified length of time to destroy pathogenic bacteria). Condensed, powdered, and evaporated milk are produced by evaporating some or all of the water content. Whole milk contains 3.5% milk fat. Lower-fat milks include 2% low-fat milk, 1% low-fat milk, and skim milk which has only 1/2 gram of milk fat per serving.

The Chicago Mercantile Exchange has three different milk futures contracts: Milk Class III which is milk used in the manufacturing of cheese, Milk Class IV which is milk used in the production of butter and all dried milk products, and Nonfat Dry Milk which is used in commercial or consumer cooking or to reconstitute nonfat milk by the consumer. The Milk Class III contract has the largest volume and open interest.

Prices – The average monthly price received by farmers of all milk sold to plants in 2004 rose sharply by +28.2% yr/yr to a record high of $16.04 per hundred pounds. The average monthly price received by farmers for fluid grade milk in 2004 rose +28.1% yr/yr to a record high of $16.05. The average monthly price received by farmers for manufacturing grade milk in 2004 rose +31.0% to a record high of $15.42 per hundred pounds.

Supply – The world's largest milk producers are India with 87.000 million metric tons of production in 2004, the US with 77.760 million metric tons of production, and Russia with 32.700 million metric tons of production. US milk production in 2004 (through November, annualized) rose +0.8% yr/yr to 171.595 billion pounds, which was a new record high. The number of dairy cows on US farms has fallen sharply in the past 3 decades from the 12 million level seen in 1970. In 2003, there were 9.084 million dairy cows on US farms, which was a new record low. Dairy farmers have been able to increase milk production even with fewer cows because of a dramatic increase in milk yield per cow. In 2004, the average cow produced a record 19,002 pounds of milk per year, nearly double the 9,751 pounds seen in 1970.

Demand – Per capita consumption of milk in the US has fallen in the past several decades and fell to a new record low of 206 pounds per year in 2002, down sharply by 26% from 277 pounds in 1977. The utilization breakdown shows the largest manufacturing usage categories are cheese (61.088 billion pounds of milk used in 2001) and creamery butter (27.675 billion pounds).

Trade – US imports of milk in 2003 fell -4.1% yr/yr to 4.895 billion pounds, which was moderately below the record of 5.716 billion pounds posted in 2001.

World Fluid Milk Production (Cow's Milk) In Thousands of Metric Tons

Year	Brazil	France	Germany	India	Italy	Nether-lands	New Zealand	Poland	Russia	Ukraine	United Kingdom	United States	World Total
1997	20,600	24,893	28,702	34,500	10,818	10,922	11,500	12,010	34,100	13,650	14,857	70,802	370,052
1998	21,630	24,793	28,378	35,500	10,736	11,000	11,640	12,530	33,000	13,800	14,218	71,334	373,627
1999	21,700	24,892	28,400	36,000	10,444	11,174	11,070	12,099	32,000	13,140	14,584	73,750	380,277
2000	22,134	24,890	28,400	36,250	10,350	10,800	12,235	11,830	31,900	12,400	14,200	75,929	386,769
2001	22,300	24,890	28,400	36,400	10,350	10,500	13,162	11,924	33,000	13,169	14,300	74,994	391,409
2002	22,635			36,200			13,925	11,880	33,500	13,860		77,140	402,266
2003[1]	22,860			36,500			14,346	11,996	33,000	13,400		77,253	406,582
2004[2]	23,100			37,500			15,000	12,200	32,200	13,280		77,525	411,330

[1] Preliminary. [2] Forecast. *Source: Foreign Agricultural Service, U.S. Department of Agriculture (FAS-USDA)*

Salient Statistics of Milk in the United States In Millions of Pounds

	Number of Milk Cows on Farms[3] (Thousands)	Production Per Cow[4] (Pounds)	Production Total[4]	Supply Beginning Stocks[5]	Supply Imports	Supply Total Supply	Utilization Exports[5]	Utilization Domestic Fed to Calves	Utilization Domestic Humans	Utilization Total Use	Average Farm Price Received Per Cwt. All Milk, Wholesale	Average Farm Price Received Per Cwt. Milk, Eligible for Fluid Market	Average Farm Price Received Per Cwt. Milk, Manufacturing Grade	Per Capita Consumption[6] (Fluid Milk in Lbs.)
Year														
1998	9,154	17,189	157,348	4,900	4,600	166,848	1,408	1,162	157,352	159,922	15.43	15.47	14.36	213
1999	9,156	17,772	162,716	5,300	4,700	172,716	1,303	1,109	163,316	165,728	14.37	14.43	13.78	213
2000	9,206	18,202	167,658	6,186	4,445	178,289	----	1,107	----	----	12.33	12.38	10.54	210
2001	9,114	18,158	165,497	7,010	5,716	178,223		1,036			14.98	14.99	14.78	208
2002	9,139	18,608	170,063	7,259	5,103	182,425		959			12.10	12.10	10.92	206
2003[1]	9,084	18,749	170,312	9,889	5,040	185,241		963			12.52	12.53	11.77	
2004[2]	9,010	18,958	170,805	8,331	5,215	184,351					16.03	16.04	15.43	

[1] Preliminary. [2] Estimate. [3] Average number on farms during year including dry cows, excluding heifers not yet fresh. [4] Excludes milk sucked by calves. [5] Government and commercial. [6] Product pounds of commercial sales and on farm consumption. *Source: Economic Research Service, U.S. Department of Agriculture (ERS-USDA)*

Utilization of Milk in the United States   In Millions of Pounds (Milk Equivalent)

Year	Butter from Whey Cream	Creamery Butter[2]	Cheese[3]	Cottage Cheese (Creamed)	Canned Milk[4]	Bulk Condensed Whole Milk Unsweet-ened	Bulk Condensed Whole Milk Sweet-ened	Dry Whole Milk Products	Ice Cream[5]	Other Frozen Dairy Products	Other Manu-factured Por-ducts[6]	Used on Farms Farm-Churned Butter	Total
1997	4,966	25,714	55,719	NA	1,208	227	314	898	2,112	13,859	686	256	1,394
1998	5,094	26,211	56,827	NA	1,017	222	186	1,050	2,151	14,301	697	244	1,406
1999	5,392	28,657	60,154	NA	1,037	216	171	868	2,305	14,370	682	219	1,328
2000	5,538	28,059	62,257	NA	965	180	163	815	2,218	14,447	700	196	1,303
2001	5,612	27,557	61,804	NA	991	170	163	303	2,220	14,395	701	170	1,181
2002[1]	5,791	30,250	64,504	NA	1,259	135	178	348	2,320	14,373	706	161	1,141

[1] Preliminary.   [2] Excludes whey butter.   [3] American and other.   [4] Includes evaporated and sweetened condensed.   [5] Milk equivalent of butter and condensed milk used in ice cream.   [6] Whole milk equivalent of dry cream, malted milk powder, part-skim milk, dry or concentrated ice cream mix, dehydrated butterfat and other miscellaneous products using milkfat.   *Source: National Agricultural Statistics Service, U.S. Department of Agriculture (NASS-USDA)*

Milk-Feed Price Ratio[1] in the United States   In Pounds

Year	Jan.	Feb.	Mar.	Apr.	May	June	July	Aug.	Sept.	Oct.	Nov.	Dec.	Average
1997	2.44	2.35	2.27	2.14	2.07	2.12	2.24	2.35	2.44	2.63	2.73	2.80	2.38
1998	2.75	2.77	2.73	2.70	2.58	2.89	3.00	3.60	3.98	4.18	4.22	4.27	3.31
1999	4.09	3.67	3.57	2.97	2.89	3.17	3.61	3.85	4.09	3.96	3.87	3.24	3.58
2000	3.07	2.94	2.91	2.84	2.63	2.96	3.29	3.38	3.34	3.12	3.03	3.04	3.05
2001	3.08	3.03	3.24	3.29	3.41	3.74	3.60	3.62	3.75	3.55	3.29	2.99	3.38
2002	3.03	3.00	2.89	2.81	2.64	2.54	2.34	2.27	2.30	2.46	2.44	2.44	2.60
2003	2.40	2.35	2.27	2.25	2.19	2.21	2.60	2.89	3.16	3.23	3.05	2.89	2.62
2004[2]	2.70	2.60	2.80	3.13	3.17	3.12	2.95	2.98	3.25	3.29	3.57	3.66	3.10

[1] Pounds of 16% protein mixed dairy feed equal in value to one pound of whole milk.   [2] Preliminary.   *Source: Economic Research Service, U.S. Department of Agriculture (ERS-USDA)*

Milk Production[1] in the United States   In Millions of Pounds

Year	Jan.	Feb.	Mar.	Apr.	May	June	July	Aug.	Sept.	Oct.	Nov.	Dec.	Total
1998	13,282	12,188	13,694	13,510	14,015	13,296	13,162	12,942	12,415	12,956	12,611	13,370	157,441
1999	13,628	12,607	14,270	13,938	14,458	13,633	13,444	13,357	12,970	13,412	13,140	13,854	162,711
2000	14,263	13,606	14,761	14,390	14,791	14,008	14,117	13,798	13,246	13,708	13,212	13,758	167,658
2001	13,998	12,894	14,375	14,078	14,646	13,957	13,877	13,564	13,129	13,611	13,305	13,902	165,332
2002	14,304	13,229	14,864	14,580	15,118	14,317	14,196	14,128	13,467	13,866	13,478	14,211	170,063
2003	14,584	13,441	15,044	14,634	15,003	14,328	14,263	14,015	13,468	13,898	13,470	14,164	170,312
2004[2]	14,402	13,595	14,762	14,519	15,012	14,293	14,405	14,215	13,619	14,070	13,610	14,303	170,805

[1] Excludes milk sucked by calves.   [2] Preliminary.   *Source: Economic Research Service, U.S. Department of Agriculture (ERS-USDA)*

Average Price Received by U.S. Farmers for All Milk (Sold to Plants)   In Dollars Per Hundred Pounds (Cwt.)

Year	Jan.	Feb.	Mar.	Apr.	May	June	July	Aug.	Sept.	Oct.	Nov.	Dec.	Average
1998	14.70	14.70	14.40	14.00	13.30	14.10	14.20	15.50	16.70	17.70	17.80	18.00	15.43
1999	17.40	15.50	15.00	12.60	12.70	13.10	13.80	15.10	15.70	14.90	14.40	12.20	14.37
2000	12.00	11.80	11.90	11.90	12.00	12.30	12.60	12.50	12.90	12.50	12.60	13.00	12.33
2001	13.20	13.00	13.90	14.60	15.50	16.20	16.20	16.50	17.10	15.60	14.40	13.50	14.98
2002	13.40	13.10	12.70	12.50	12.10	11.50	11.10	11.30	11.60	12.10	11.90	11.90	12.10
2003	11.70	11.40	11.00	11.00	11.00	11.00	12.10	13.30	14.50	15.00	14.40	13.80	12.52
2004[1]	13.20	13.60	15.40	18.20	19.40	18.20	16.00	15.00	15.40	15.50	16.10	16.40	16.03

[1] Preliminary.   *Source: Economic Research Service, U.S. Department of Agriculture (ERS-USDA)*

Average Farm Price of Milk Eligible for Fluid Market   In Dollars Per Hundred Pounds (Cwt.)

Year	Jan.	Feb.	Mar.	Apr.	May	June	July	Aug.	Sept.	Oct.	Nov.	Dec.	Average
1998	14.70	14.80	14.50	14.00	13.30	14.10	14.20	15.50	16.80	17.80	17.80	18.10	15.47
1999	17.50	15.60	15.10	12.60	12.80	13.20	13.90	15.00	15.70	15.00	14.50	12.30	14.43
2000	12.00	11.90	12.00	11.90	12.10	12.30	12.60	12.50	13.00	12.60	12.60	13.10	12.38
2001	13.20	13.10	13.90	14.60	15.50	16.20	16.20	16.50	17.10	15.60	14.50	13.50	14.99
2002	13.40	13.10	12.70	12.50	12.10	11.50	11.10	11.30	11.60	12.10	11.90	11.90	12.10
2003	11.80	11.40	11.00	11.00	11.00	11.00	12.10	13.30	14.50	15.00	14.40	13.80	12.53
2004[1]	13.20	13.60	15.40	18.20	19.40	18.30	16.00	15.00	15.40	15.50	16.10	16.40	16.04

[1] Preliminary.   *Source: Economic Research Service, U.S. Department of Agriculture (ERS-USDA)*

Molasses

Molasses is a dark-brown, heavy liquid obtained as a by-product of sugar processing. Sugarcane accounts for about 80% of molasses production, while sugar beets account for about 20% of production. In the sugar refining process, blackstrap molasses is produced by third and final separation process. Blackstrap molasses is used worldwide mostly as a feed supplement for livestock. Other uses for molasses include cooking or baking and the production of alcohol. Molasses, for example, is a key ingredient in pumpernickel bread. Molasses is also a key ingredient in some brands of rum. Molasses was a very popular sweetener during the American Colonial days through World War I because it was cheaper than sugar.

Prices – The price of molasses rose in 2004 due to the sharp rally in sugar prices during the year. World sugar futures prices at the New York Board of Trade rose from a 2-1/2 year low of 5.27 cents per pound in February 2004 to a 3-year high of 9.37 cents per pound in August 2004. Molasses and sugar prices have shown a fairly high correlation of 0.64 over the past 3 decades because molasses is a by-product of sugar production. The wholesale price of blackstrap molasses (cane) at Orleans averaged $58.67 per ton in 2004 (through August), up +1.7% from $57.71 per ton in 2003. That was well below the 8-year high of $67.95 posted in 2001.

Supply – The production of molasses is highly correlated with the production of sugar, and by extension sugarcane and sugar beets. World production of sugarcane in 2002-03 rose +1.3% yr/yr to 1.288 billion metric tons. The world's largest producers of sugarcane are Brazil with 28% of world production in 2002-03, followed by India with 22% of world production. US production of sugarcane amounts to 2.5% of world production. World production of sugar beets in 2002-03 rose +7.5% yr/yr to 246.5 million metric tons. The world's largest producers of sugar beets are France with 14% of world production in 2002-03, Germany with 11%, and the US with 10%.

World Production of Sugarcane, by Selected Countries   In Thousands of Metric Tons

Crop Year	Australia	Brazil	China	Cuba	India	Indonesia	Mexico	Pakistan	Philippines	South Africa	Thailand	United States	World Total
1995-6	37,438	303,699	70,279	36,000	271,230	31,427	42,562	47,168	26,000	16,714	50,597	27,938	1,172,160
1996-7	35,889	325,929	71,260	41,300	282,900	29,486	43,352	45,230	27,000	20,951	58,977	26,727	1,226,666
1997-8	38,463	337,195	83,012	38,900	277,250	27,764	45,220	41,998	26,813	22,155	56,394	28,751	1,253,052
1998-9	39,531	345,255	87,204	32,800	262,090	27,180	48,895	53,104	26,287	22,930	50,332	31,486	1,259,659
1999-00	38,534	333,848	78,108	34,000	295,730	24,000	46,880	55,191	23,780	21,223	50,332	32,023	1,266,330
2000-1	38,165	327,705	69,299	36,400	299,230	23,900	44,150	46,333	24,491	23,876	59,436	32,762	1,255,801
2001-2[1]	31,228	345,942	77,966	32,100	299,210	25,185	47,275	43,606	24,962	21,157	60,013	31,377	1,271,484
2002-3[2]	32,260	360,556	82,278	32,100	279,000	23,400	46,000	48,042	25,835	22,349	62,350	32,597	1,288,403

[1] Preliminary.   [2] Estimate.   *Source: Food and Agriculture Organization of the United Nations (FAO-UN)*

World Production of Sugarbeet, by Selected Countries   In Thousands of Metric Tons

Year	Belgium-Luxembourg	China	France	Germany	Italy	Poland	Russia	Spain	Turkey	Ukraine	United Kingdom	United States	World Total
1995-6	6,051	13,984	30,571	26,077	13,188	13,309	19,072	7,438	11,171	29,650	8,431	25,460	264,852
1996-7	6,125	16,726	31,211	26,064	12,250	17,846	16,166	8,236	14,543	23,009	10,420	24,204	265,925
1997-8	6,545	14,970	34,372	25,769	13,803	15,886	13,880	8,530	18,553	17,663	11,084	27,112	268,248
1998-9	5,366	14,466	31,156	26,787	13,382	15,171	10,798	8,866	22,283	15,523	10,002	29,483	263,165
1999-00	7,112	8,639	32,919	27,578	14,505	12,564	15,227	8,162	16,854	14,064	10,584	30,318	260,331
2000-1	5,311	8,073	31,121	27,870	11,569	13,134	14,054	7,930	18,821	13,199	9,079	29,521	244,819
2001-2[1]	5,614	10,889	26,841	24,730	11,107	11,364	14,556	6,775	12,633	15,575	8,335	23,373	229,292
2002-3[2]	5,898	11,562	33,331	26,786	11,500	11,652	15,500	7,877	13,000	14,400	9,435	24,993	246,476

[1] Preliminary.   [2] Estimate.   *Source: Food and Agriculture Organization of the United Nations (FAO-UN)*

U.S. Annual Average Prices of Molasses, by Types (F.O.B. Tank Car or Truck)   In Dollars Per Short Ton[2]

Year	Blackstrap							Beet Molasses	
	New Orleans	South Florida	Baltimore	Upper Mississippi	Savannah	California Ports[3]	Houston	Montana, Wyoming & Nebraska	Red River Valley[4]
1997	58.14	68.00	76.84	90.69	77.51	83.38	62.13	----	----
1998	46.35	59.92	63.37	78.00	68.75	69.30	48.85	----	----
1999	33.77	49.15	51.06	65.50	56.63	58.32	36.30	----	----
2000	44.64	58.34	61.73	71.66	65.42	71.78	48.94	----	----
2001	67.97	76.79	90.12	85.45	83.30	92.82	72.33	----	----
2002	64.57	74.23	87.02	84.01	87.50	84.81	68.76	----	----
2003	57.67	66.72	81.11	78.78	81.18	78.61	62.92	----	----
2004[1]	58.67	66.06					69.43	----	----

[1] Preliminary.   [2] To convert dollars per short ton to cents per gallon divide by 171.   [3] Los Angeles and Stockton.   [4] North Dakota and Minnesota.
Source: Agricultural Marketing Service, U.S. Department of Agriculture (AMS-USDA)

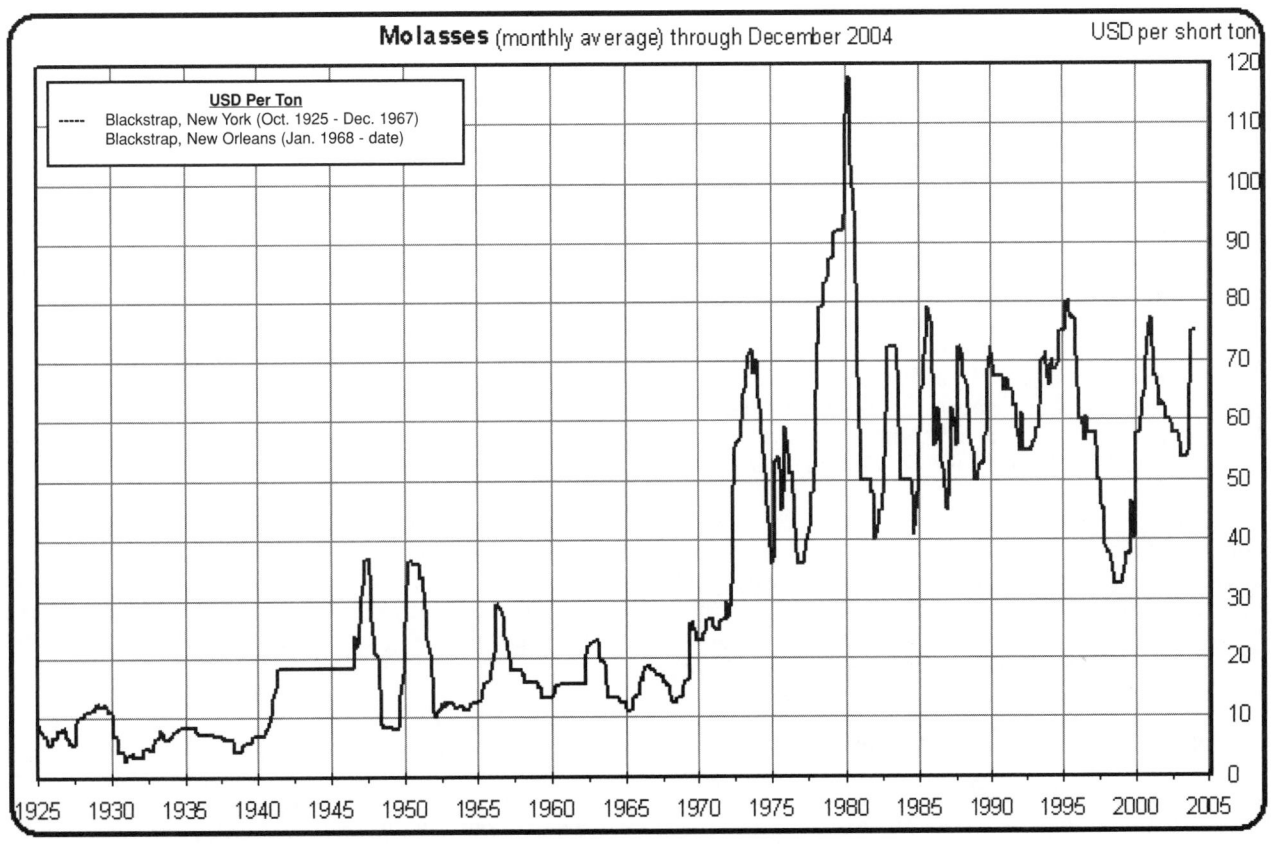

Salient Statistics of Molasses[3] in the United States   In Metric Tons

Year	Hawaii	Production Mainland Refiners Mainland Hills[4]	Black-strap	Beet	Puerto Rico	In Ship-ments From Hawaii	Total Imports	Inedible Imports From Brazil	Dominican Republic	Mexico	Mainland Exports[5]	Production of Edible Total Molasses U.S. Supply	(1,000 Gallons)
1992	182,849	782,566	123,000	950,312	25,097	183,657	1,115,863	0	127,500	117,722	282,098	2,873,300	1,460
1993	187,915	831,661	113,000	692,465	22,802	190,371	1,040,858	0	163,180	47,596	255,907	2,612,448	1,480
1994	180,884	824,453	114,000	1,200,000	18,531	151,172	1,556,640	0	121,320	197,753	277,098	3,459,167	1,500
1995	146,000	886,826	114,000	1,040,000	16,156	146,000	1,048,726	0	132,983	172,177	274,868	2,960,684	1,500
1996	NA	NA	NA	NA		NA	NA				NA	NA	NA
1997		900,000	100,000	1,200,000		100,000	1,583,755				300,000	3,583,755	NA
1998	NA	NA	NA	NA		NA	NA				NA	NA	NA
1999[1]	NA	NA	NA	NA		NA	NA				NA	NA	NA
2000[2]	NA	NA	NA	NA		NA	NA				NA	NA	NA

[1] Preliminary. [2] Estimate. [3] Feed and industrial molasses. [4] Includes high-test molasses from frozen cane. [5] Excluding exports from Hawaii and Puerto Rico. NA = Not available. *Source: Agricultural Marketing Service, U.S. Department of Agriculture (AMS-USDA)*

Wholesale Price of Blackstrap Molasses (Cane) at New Orleans   In Dollars Per Short Ton

Year	Jan.	Feb.	Mar.	Apr.	May	June	July	Aug.	Sept.	Oct.	Nov.	Dec.	Average
1995	69.00	70.31	68.75	68.75	68.75	69.38	74.25	75.00	75.00	75.00	75.00	75.00	72.00
1996	80.00	80.00	80.00	78.00	77.50	77.50	77.50	77.50	75.00	70.00	65.63	60.75	74.88
1997	60.00	60.00	59.00	56.56	56.88	60.31	57.50	45.00	45.00	37.50	37.50	37.50	46.35
1998	57.50	55.63	51.00	50.00	50.00	46.00	45.00	45.00	45.00	37.50	37.50	37.50	46.35
1999	37.50	36.25	35.00	34.38	32.50	32.50	32.50	32.50	32.50	32.50	33.75	33.75	33.80
2000	35.25	36.11	37.50	37.50	37.50	37.12	42.75	46.25	40.35	57.50	57.50	57.50	43.57
2001	57.50	57.50	59.38	60.25	63.75	66.25	70.75	73.75	76.25	77.50	77.50	75.00	67.95
2002	72.50	70.60	67.50	67.50	64.40	62.50	63.50	62.50	62.50	62.50	60.00	60.00	64.67
2003	60.00	60.00	60.00	58.75	57.50	57.50	57.50	57.50	57.50	56.25	56.25	53.75	57.71
2004[1]	53.75	53.75	53.75	53.75	54.69	66.00	66.00	75.00	75.00	75.00	75.00	75.00	64.72

[1] Preliminary. *Source: Agricultural Marketing Service, U.S. Department of Agriculture (AMS-USDA)*

Molybdenum

Molybdenum (symbol Mo) is a silvery-white, hard, malleable, metallic element. Molybdenum melts at about 2610 degrees Celsius and boils at about 4640 degrees Celsius. Swedish chemist Carl Wilhelm Scheele discovered molybdenum in 1778.

Molybdenum occurs in nature in the form of molybdenite and wulfenite. Contributing to the growth of plants, it is an important trace element in soils. Approximately 70% of the world supply of molybdenum is obtained as a by-product of copper mining. Molybdenum is chiefly used as an alloy to strengthen steel and resist corrosion. It is used for structural work, aircraft parts, and forged automobile parts because it withstands high temperatures and pressures and adds strength. Other uses include lubricants, a refractory metal in chemical applications, electron tubing, and a catalyst.

Prices – The average monthly US merchant price of molybdic oxide in 2004 (though December) rallied sharply by 171% yr/yr to a record high of $14.52 per pound. That was more than 6 times the decade low of $2.37 seen in 2001.

Supply – World production of molybdenum in 2003 rose by +3.3% yr/yr to 125,000 metric tons, showing a mild recovery from the 9-year low of 121,000 metric tons seen in 2002. The world's largest producers of molybdenum are the US with 27% of world production in 2003, China with 25%, and Chile with 24%.

US production of molybdenum concentrate in 2003 rose +4.7% yr/yr to 33,500 metric tons, recovering from the 20-year low of 32,000 metric tons posted in 2002. US production of molybdenum primary products in 2003 rose +12.4% to 11,800 metric tons, with 11,000 metric tons of that production in molybdic oxide and 760 metric tons in molybdenum metal powder.

Demand – US consumption of molybdenum concentrate in 2003 rose sharply by +29.7% yr/yr to 27,500 metric tons, recovering from the 9-year low of 21,200 metric tons posted in 2002. US consumption of molybdenum concentrate has more than doubled over the last 10 years. US consumption of molybdenum primary products rose by +2.6% yr/yr in 2003 to 15,700 metric tons, recovering mildly from the 16-year low of 15,300 posted in 2002.

Trade – US imports of molybdenum concentrate for consumption in 2003 rose +10.2% yr/yr to 5,190 metric tons, recovering from the 9-year low of 4,710 metric tons posted in 2002.

World Mine Production of Molybdenum — In Metric Tons (Contained Molybdenum)

Year	Bulgaria	Canada[3]	Chile	China	Iran	Kazakhstan	Mexico	Mongolia	Peru	Russia	United States	Uzbekisten	World Total
1997	----	8,223	21,339	33,300	600	100	4,842	2,000	3,835	2,000	60,100	500	139,000
1998	----	8,469	25,297	30,000	1,400	100	5,949	2,000	4,344	2,000	53,343	500	136,000
1999	----	6,250	27,309	29,700	1,600	155	7,961	1,910	5,470	2,400	42,400	500	129,000
2000	----	7,457	33,187	28,800	1,600	215	6,886	1,335	7,190	2,400	40,900	500	134,000
2001	----	8,556	33,492	28,200	1,500	225	5,518	1,514	9,500	2,600	37,600	500	133,000
2002[1]	----	7,521	29,466	29,300	1,400	230	3,428	1,590	8,616	2,900	32,000	500	121,000
2003[2]	----	7,500	30,000	30,600	1,400	230	3,523	1,600	9,632	2,900	33,500	500	125,000

[1] Preliminary. [2] Estimate. [3] Shipments. *Source: U.S. Geological Survey (USGS)*

Salient Statistics of Molybdenum in the United States — In Metric Tons (Contained Molybdenum)

| | Concentrate | | | | | | | Primary Products[4] | | | | | | |
| | | Shipments | | | | | | | Net Production | | Shipments | | | |
Year	Production	Total (Includes Exports)	Value Million $	For Exports	Consumption	Imports For Consumption	Stocks, Dec. 31[3]	Grand Total	Molybdic Oxide[5]	Molybdic Metal Powder	Price Average Value $ / Kg.[6]	To Domestic Destinations	Oxide for Exports (Groos Weight)	Consumption	Producer Stocks, Dec. 31
1997	60,100	32,100	406.0	20,000	24,300	6,330	3,660	25,900	22,700	2,000	9.46	25,900	1,240	20,000	6,500
1998	53,300	52,100	200.0	----	35,900	6,570	6,270	33,900	31,600	2,270	5.90	38,000	1,100	18,800	7,780
1999	42,400	42,800	251.0	----	34,500	6,390	4,580	19,200	17,400	1,880	5.90	39,000	1,130	18,700	5,340
2000	40,900	40,400	210.0	----	33,800	6,120	4,030	19,700	17,500	2,190	5.64	34,600	1,190	18,300	5,360
2001	37,600	37,000	192.0	----	33,300	6,010	4,210	15,700	14,900	771	5.20	32,600	940	15,800	5,600
2002[1]	32,000	32,300	232.0	----	21,200	4,710	3,870	10,500	10,000	513	8.27	27,500	1,670	15,300	4,300
2003[2]	33,500	33,600	324.0	----	27,500	5,190	2,520	11,800	11,000	760	11.57	30,100	2,580	15,700	2,760

[1] Preliminary. [2] Estimate. [3] At mines & at plants making molybdenum products. [4] Comprises ferromolybdenum, molybdic oxide, & molybdenum salts & metal. [5] Includes molybdic oxide briquets, molybdic acid, molybdenum trioxide, all other. [6] U.S. producer price per kilogram of molybdenum oxide contained in technical-grade molybdic oxide. W = Withheld proprietary data. *Source: U.S. Geological Survey (USGS)*

US Merchant Price of Molybdic Oxide — In Dollars Per Pound

Year	Jan.	Feb.	Mar.	Apr.	May	June	July	Aug.	Sept.	Oct.	Nov.	Dec.	Average
1998	4.10	4.10	4.17	4.51	4.05	4.00	4.00	4.00	4.00	4.00	4.00	4.00	4.08
1999	3.53	2.73	2.73	2.73	2.73	2.73	2.73	2.73	2.73	2.73	2.73	2.73	2.79
2000	2.86	3.55	3.40	2.55	2.55	2.55	2.55	2.64	2.70	2.70	2.70	2.39	2.74
2001	2.38	2.38	2.38	2.38	2.38	2.38	2.38	2.38	2.38	2.40	2.33	2.33	2.37
2002	2.33	2.33	2.33	2.75	2.99	6.93	5.32	4.75	4.73	4.70	3.82	3.48	3.87
2003	3.63	3.74	4.62	5.20	5.20	5.77	5.86	5.60	5.84	6.25	6.25	6.25	5.35
2004	7.63	8.15	8.93	13.11	14.00	15.03	15.75	16.70	18.27	19.50	22.66	27.50	15.60

Source: American Metal Market (AMM)

Nickel

Nickel (symbol Ni) is a hard, malleable, ductile metal that has a silvery tinge that can take on a high polish. Nickel is somewhat ferromagnetic and is a fair conductor of heat and electricity. Nickel is primarily used in the production of stainless steel and other corrosion-resistant alloys. Nickel is used in coins to replace silver, in rechargeable batteries, and in electronic circuitry. Nickel plating techniques, like electro-less coating or single-slurry coating, are employed in such applications as turbine blades, helicopter rotors, extrusion dies, and rolled steel strip.

Nickel futures and options trade at the London Metal Exchange (LME). The nickel futures contract calls for the delivery of 6 metric tons of primary nickel with at least 99.80% purity in the form of full plate, cut cathodes, pellets or briquettes. The contract is priced in terms of US dollars per metric ton.

Prices – Nickel prices in 2002 and 2003 staged a very sharp rally where prices roughly quadrupled from a low of $4,500 in late 2001 to a high of nearly $18,000 per metric ton at the end of 2003. Nickel prices in 2004 whipsawed below the high of $18,000 in a wide range between about $10,500 and $16,500. Strong demand and the weak dollar kept nickel prices at relatively high levels in 2004.

Supply – World mine production of nickel in 2002, the latest reporting year for the data series, was unchanged from the record of 1.340 million metric tons posted in 2001. That is approximately double the production seen in 1970. The world's largest mine producers of nickel in 2002 were Russia (with 23% of world production), Australia (16%), Canada (13%), Indonesia (9%), and New Caledonia (7%). In 2002, US secondary nickel production fell -1.0% to 99,790 metric tons from the record high of 100,800 metric tons in 2001.

Demand – US consumption of nickel in 2002 rose +1.6% to 191,000 metric tons and matched the record high production level of 191,000 metric tons posted in 1997. The primary US nickel consumption use is for stainless and heat-resisting steels, which accounted for 68% of US consumption in 2002. Other consumption uses were nickel alloys (7.3%), electro-plating anodes (6.4%), super alloys (6.3%), copper base alloys (3.0%), alloy steels (2.1%), cast irons (0.3%), and chemicals (0.2%).

Trade – The US relied on imports for 48% of its nickel consumption in 2002, down from 56% in 2001. US imports of primary and secondary nickel in 2002 fell -10.1% to a 10-year low of 130,110 metric tons. US exports of primary and secondary nickel in 2002 fell -19.5% to 49,920 metric tons, which was well below the record high of 58,050 metric tons posted in 2000.

World Mine Production of Nickel   In Metric Tons (Contained Nickel)

Year	Australia[3]	Botswana	Brazil	Canada	China	Dominican Republic	Greece	Indonesia	New Caledonia	Phillip-pines	Russia	South Africa	World Total
1996	113,134	21,910	25,245	192,649	43,800	45,168	21,600	87,911	122,486	14,539	230,000	33,861	1,060,000
1997	123,372	19,860	31,936	190,529	46,600	49,152	18,419	71,127	136,467	18,137	280,000	34,830	1,140,000
1998	143,513	21,700	36,764	208,201	48,700	40,311	16,985	74,063	125,319	23,713	290,000	36,679	1,180,000
1999	119,226	33,733	41,522	186,236	49,500	39,997	16,050	89,111	110,062	20,689	300,000	36,202	1,160,000
2000	165,700	20,286	45,317	190,793	50,300	39,943	19,535	98,200	128,789	17,388	315,000	36,616	1,270,000
2001[1]	197,000	18,585	47,097	194,058	51,500	39,120	20,830	102,000	117,554	27,359	325,000	36,443	1,340,000
2002[2]	211,000	20,005	45,029	178,338	54,500	38,859	22,670	122,000	99,650	26,532	310,000	38,546	1,340,000

[1] Preliminary.   [2] Estimate.   [3] Content of nickel sulfate and concentrates.   *Source: U.S. Geological Survey (USGS)*

Salient Statistics of Nickel in the United States   In Metric Tons (Contained Nickel)

Year	Net Import Reliance as a % of Apparent Consumption	Production Plant[4]	Secondary[5]	Alloy Sheets	Cast Irons	Copper Base Alloys	Electro-plating Anodes	Nickel Alloys	Stainless & Heat Resisting Steels	Super Alloys	Chemicals	Apparent Consumption	Stocks, Dec. 31 At Consumers' Plants	Stocks, Dec. 31 At Producer Plants	Primary & Secondary Nickel Exports	Primary & Secondary Nickel Imports	Avg. Price LME $/Lb.
1996	59	15,100	59,300	6,240	563	7,300	16,200	19,700	94,000	12,600	5,310	183,000	12,900	13,300	46,700	150,060	3.40
1997	56	16,000	68,400	9,290	654	6,530	15,900	19,400	105,000	19,000	3,720	191,000	16,070	12,600	56,600	158,000	3.14
1998	64	4,290	63,100	9,590	908	7,470	16,400	17,500	93,000	18,600	1,970	186,000	15,960	13,100	43,540	156,500	2.10
1999	63	NA	71,000	8,100	495	10,500	15,400	15,200	102,000	18,900	1,580	190,000	10,050	12,700	38,840	148,480	2.73
2000	58	NA	83,900	7,700	198	9,940	15,700	18,200	108,000	19,400	991	189,000	14,260	12,300	58,050	166,700	3.92
2001[2]	56	NA	100,800	7,590	886	7,190	12,500	17,900	121,000	18,400	1,630	188,000	13,910	12,600	57,050	144,760	2.70
2002[3]	43	NA	99,790	3,980	531	5,720	12,300	13,900	129,000	12,100	367	191,000	12,710	6,150	45,920	130,110	3.07

[1] Exclusive of scrap.   [2] Preliminary.   [3] Estimate.   [4] Smelter & refinery.   [5] From purchased scrap (ferrous & nonferrous).   W = Withheld proprietary data.   NA = Not avaliable.   *Source: U.S. Geological Survey (USGS)*

Average Price of Nickel[1] in the United States   In Cents Per Pound

Year	Jan.	Feb.	Mar.	Apr.	May	June	July	Aug.	Sept.	Oct.	Nov.	Dec.	Average
2000	403.00	456.00	493.00	469.00	474.00	346.00	399.00	385.00	413.00	380.00	360.00	358.00	411.33
2001	344.00	336.00	316.00	296.00	339.00	343.00	295.00	278.00	252.00	243.00	253.00	266.00	296.75
2002	266.00	266.00	266.00	266.00	295.00	331.00	341.00	342.00	332.00	321.00	354.00	363.00	311.92
2003	376.67	416.01	408.76	391.72	409.63	439.13	438.50	464.67	492.62	540.81	583.21	674.78	469.71
2004	734.25	725.15	659.93	625.29	542.52	648.94	715.77	656.11	640.61	689.95	673.15	656.37	664.00

[1] Plating material, briquettes.   *Source: American Metal Market (AMM)*

Oats

Oats are seeds or grains of a genus of plants that thrive in cool, moist climates. There are about 25 species of oats that grow worldwide in the cooler temperate regions. The oldest known cultivated oats were found inside caves in Switzerland and are believed to be from the Bronze Age. Oats are usually sown in early spring and harvested in mid to late summer, but in southern regions of the northern hemisphere, they may be sown in the fall. Oats are used in many processed foods such as flour, livestock feed, and furfural, a chemical used as a solvent in various refining industries. The oat crop year begins in June and ends in May. Oat futures and options are traded on the Chicago Board of Trade (CBOT) and the Winnipeg Commodity Exchange (WCE).

Prices – Oat prices on the CBOT weekly nearest futures chart started the year at $1.52 per bushel, showed some strength through March to post the year's high of $1.85, sank into the summer to hit the year's low of $1.20 and then recovered through the remainder of the year. Oat futures closed 2004 just mildly higher on the year at $1.56. Regarding cash prices, the average monthly price received by farmers for oats in the US in the first 7 months of the 2004-05 marketing year (i.e., June to December 2004) fell –5.6% yr/yr to $1.44 per bushel.

Supply – World oat production in 2004-05 fell –2.3% yr/yr to 26.060 million metric tons, which was only mildly above the record low of 24.000 million metric tons posted in 1999-00. World oat production in the past decade has dropped very sharply from levels above 40 million metric tons in the 1960s through the 1980s. The world's largest oat producers are the European Union with 34% of world production in 2004-05, the former USSR with 21%, Canada with 14%, the US with 7%, and Australia with 4%.

US oat production in the 2004-05 marketing year fell sharply by –19.7% yr/yr to 115.935 million bushels, which was a new record low. US oat production in the past decade has fallen sharply from levels mostly above 1 billion bushels seen from the early 1900s through the 1960s. US farmers harvested only 1.792 million acres of oats in 2004-05, which was a record low and was far below the levels above 30 million acres seen from the early 1900s through the 1950s. The oat yield in 2004-05 was 64.7 bushels per acre, which was only slightly below the record of 65.0 bushels seen in 2003-04. Oat stocks in the US as of September 1, 2004 were 116.254 million bushels, which was down from the year-earlier level of 131.737 million bushels. The largest US oat-producing states are the northern states of Minnesota (with 12.1% of US production in 2004), North Dakota (12.0%), South Dakota (12.0%), and Wisconsin (11.8%).

Demand – US usage of oats in 2004-05 fell –3.6% yr/yr to 212.0 million bushels. Based on the last complete set of data in 2001, feed and residual accounts for 66% of oat usage, 27% for food, alcohol and residual, 6% for feed, and 1% for exports.

Trade – US exports of oats were nominal at only 3.0 million bushels in 2004-05. US imports of oats in 2004-05 fell –5.6% yr/yr to a 9-year low of 85.0 million bushels.

World Production of Oats   In Thousands of Metric Tons

Year	Argentina	Australia	Canada	China	France	Germany	Italy	Poland	Sweden	Turkey	United States	Ex-USSR	World Total
1995-6	260	1,875	2,858	640	617	1,421	301	1,495	947	275	2,338	10,843	28,663
1996-7	310	1,653	4,361	600	622	1,606	350	1,581	1,200	275	2,224	10,430	30,637
1997-8	517	1,634	3,485	400	564	1,599	311	1,630	1,275	280	2,428	11,560	30,903
1998-9	383	1,798	3,958	650	658	1,279	280	1,460	1,136	310	2,409	6,490	25,911
1999-00	555	1,118	3,641	600	550	1,340	350	1,446	1,200	290	2,114	4,400	24,080
2000-1	645	1,050	3,389	600	460	1,090	460	1,070	1,150	314	2,165	6,000	26,047
2001-2	645	1,434	2,691	600	490	1,150	310	1,305	960	265	1,707	7,700	27,053
2002-3[1]	500	957	2,911	600	770	1,020	330	1,490	1,180	290	1,684	5,700	25,845
2003-4[2]	400	1,965	3,691	600	560	1,200	300	1,180	1,090	285	2,096	5,200	26,686
2004-5[3]	400	1,100	3,685	600		1,200	330	1,400	920	290	1,683	5,500	26,060

[1] Preliminary.   [2] Estimate.   [3] Forecast.   *Source: Foreign Agricultural Service, U.S. Department of Agriculture (FAS-USDA)*

Official Oats Crop Production Reports in the United States   In Thousands of Bushels

Year	July 1	Aug. 1	Sept. 1	Oct. 1	Dec. 1	Final	Year	July 1	Aug. 1	Sept. 1	Oct. 1	Dec. 1	Final
1993	262,860	249,830	249,830	208,138	----	206,770	1999	----	162,096	----	----	----	146,218
1994	248,151	247,753	247,753	229,717	----	229,008	2000	151,380	152,745	----	----	----	149,545
1995	181,508	186,167	186,167	----	----	162,027	2001	132,150	135,445	----	----	----	117,024
1996	154,968	157,663	----	----	----	153,245	2002	147,584	142,580	----	----	----	116,002
1997	182,672	187,127	----	----	----	167,246	2003	147,895	151,345	----	----	----	144,383
1998	183,201	177,211	----	----	----	165,981	2004[1]	121,860	127,950	----	----	----	115,935

[1] Preliminary.   *Source: National Agricultural Statistics Service, U.S. Department of Agriculture (NASS-USDA)*

Oat Stocks in the United States   In Thousands of Bushels

	On Farms				Off Farms				Total Stocks			
Year	Mar. 1	June 1	Sept. 1	Dec. 1	Mar. 1	June 1	Sept. 1	Dec. 1	Mar. 1	June 1	Sept. 1	Dec. 1
1995	78,400	46,750	107,200	87,200	70,575	53,848	72,967	65,804	148,975	100,598	180,167	153,004
1996	57,350	32,600	93,400	80,650	55,268	33,708	38,716	45,218	112,618	66,308	132,116	125,868
1997	56,200	33,100	107,950	83,200	39,362	33,576	48,972	61,051	95,562	66,676	156,922	144,251
1998	58,800	34,500	110,300	81,500	52,418	39,498	51,502	61,835	111,218	73,998	161,802	143,335
1999	61,700	40,700	97,300	79,800	50,850	40,678	51,151	53,872	112,550	81,378	148,451	133,672
2000	53,300	36,000	101,200	86,900	48,500	40,031	49,177	57,237	101,800	76,031	150,377	144,137
2001	55,800	32,050	74,800	58,100	54,128	40,677	41,592	56,117	109,928	72,727	116,392	114,217
2002	40,200	28,650	70,500	52,500	53,158	34,552	41,212	51,284	93,358	63,202	111,712	103,784
2003	35,000	20,600	82,100	64,400	47,879	29,233	49,637	54,900	82,879	49,833	131,737	119,300
2004[1]	45,600	27,500	74,300	60,400	49,414	37,348	41,458	44,563	95,014	64,848	115,758	104,963

[1] Preliminary.   *Source: National Agricultural Statistics Service, U.S. Department of Agriculture (NASS-USDA)*

Supply and Utilizationof Oats in the United States   In Millions of Bushels

	Acreage		Yield Per	Pro-		Total	Feed &	Food, Alcohol &			Total	Ending	Farm	Findley Loan	Target
	Planted	Harvested	Acre	duction	Imports	Supply	Residual	Industrial	Seed	Exports	Use	Stocks	Price	Rate	Price
Year	1,000 acres		(Bushels)	In Millions of Bushels									Dollars Per Bushel		
1995-6	6,225	2,952	54.6	161.1	80.5	342.2	194.9	67.0	12.0	2.1	275.9	66.3	1.67	.97	1.45
1996-7	4,638	2,655	57.7	153.2	97.5	317.1	171.7	63.0	13.1	2.5	250.4	66.7	1.96	1.03	NA
1997-8	5,068	2,813	59.5	167.2	98.4	332.3	184.6	59.0	12.6	2.1	258.3	74.0	1.60	1.11	NA
1998-9	4,892	2,755	60.2	166.0	108.0	347.7	195.6	57.0	12.0	1.7	266.3	81.4	1.10	1.11	NA
1999-00	4,668	2,445	59.6	145.6	99.0	326.0	180.0	56.8	11.2	1.8	250.0	76.0	1.12	1.13	NA
2000-1	4,473	2,325	64.2	149.5	106.0	332.0	189.0	57.0	11.0	1.7	259.0	73.0	1.10	1.16	NA
2001-2	4,403	1,905	61.4	117.0	96.0	286.0	148.0	59.0	13.0	2.8	223.0	63.0	1.59	1.21	NA
2002-3	4,995	2,058	56.4	116.0	95.0	274.0	150.0			2.6	224.0	50.0	1.81	1.35	1.40
2003-4[1]	4,597	2,220	65.0	144.4	90.0	285.0	144.0			2.5	220.0	65.0	1.48	1.35	1.40
2004-5[2]	4,085	1,792	64.7	115.9	85.0	266.0	135.0			3.0	212.0	54.0	1.35-1.45	1.33	1.44

[1] Preliminary.   [2] Forecast.   NA = Not available.   *Source: Economic Research Service, U.S. Department of Agriculture (ERS-USDA)*

Production of Oats in the United States, by States   In Thousands of Bushels

Year	Illinois	Iowa	Michigan	Minnesota	Nebraska	New York	North Dakota	Ohio	Penn-sylvania	South Dakota	Texas	Wisconsin	Total
1995	5,360	14,625	5,130	18,000	4,500	5,310	21,600	6,900	9,440	11,500	5,040	18,700	162,027
1996	4,620	12,920	3,600	15,120	7,455	3,850	19,000	5,130	7,560	21,600	3,400	17,400	153,245
1997	5,550	16,790	4,880	17,400	5,850	5,850	18,700	6,660	8,990	14,850	6,760	20,160	167,246
1998	3,920	10,915	4,800	19,530	5,320	6,510	25,200	6,500	8,480	20,100	6,890	18,300	165,981
1999	4,260	11,375	4,875	17,700	4,650	4,760	16,830	7,000	7,975	12,800	4,840	18,600	146,218
2000	4,015	12,060	4,800	22,320	1,890	3,900	19,845	6,840	8,265	13,420	4,300	19,040	149,165
2001	3,200	9,100	3,520	12,600	3,660	5,520	14,880	6,205	7,475	7,800	7,200	12,480	117,024
2002	3,285	13,300	4,160	14,840	2,365	4,160	12,600	3,355	7,015	5,400	6,160	15,000	116,002
2003	4,450	10,790	5,250	18,815	6,570	4,410	21,240	3,960	6,490	15,640	6,300	15,410	144,383
2004[1]	2,450	10,080	4,420	13,300	3,740	3,250	14,080	3,150	6,050	13,940	6,400	13,650	115,935

[1] Preliminary.   *Source: National Agricultural Statistics Service, U.S. Department of Agriculture (NASS-USDA)*

Average Cash Price of No. 2 Heavy White Oats in Toledo   In Dollars Per Bushel

Year	June	July	Aug.	Sept.	Oct.	Nov.	Dec.	Jan.	Feb.	Mar.	Apr.	May	Average
1995-6	1.65	1.76	1.83	1.90	1.76	1.91	2.21	2.14	2.06	2.17	2.32	2.05	1.98
1996-7	NQ	2.45	2.34	2.19	2.02	1.96	1.96	1.99	2.16	2.26	2.12	2.08	2.14
1997-8	2.12	1.79	1.84	1.80	1.77	NQ	NQ	NQ	NQ	NQ	NQ	NQ	1.86
1998-9	NQ	NQ	NQ	NQ	NQ	NQ	NQ	NQ	NQ	NQ	NQ	NQ	NQ
1999-00	NQ	NQ	NQ	NQ	NQ	NQ	NQ	NQ	NQ	NQ	NQ	NQ	NQ
2000-1	NQ	NQ	NQ	NQ	NQ	NQ	NQ	NQ	NQ	NQ	NQ	NQ	NQ
2001-2	NQ	NQ	NQ	NQ	NQ	NQ	NQ	NQ	NQ	NQ	NQ	NQ	NQ
2002-3	NQ	NQ	NQ	NQ	NQ	NQ	NQ	NQ	NQ	NQ	NQ	NQ	NQ
2003-4	NQ	NQ	NQ	NQ	NQ	NQ	NQ	NQ	NQ	NQ	NQ	NQ	NQ
2004-5[1]	NQ	NQ	NQ	NQ	NQ	NQ	NQ						

[1] Preliminary.   NQ = No quotes.   *Source: Economic Research Service, U.S. Department of Agriculture (ERS-USDA)*

OATS

Oat Futures - Chicago Board of Trade
(weekly close) as of December 31, 2004
Cents per bushel

Volume of Trading in Oats Futures in Chicago   In Contracts

Year	Jan.	Feb.	Mar.	Apr.	May	June	July	Aug.	Sept.	Oct.	Nov.	Dec.	Total
1995	13,512	37,014	29,490	45,536	34,116	107,082	29,862	45,677	31,676	38,641	52,321	47,005	511,932
1996	61,451	52,079	34,608	77,395	47,161	34,498	38,960	33,316	30,801	37,579	37,856	16,154	501,858
1997	34,238	51,608	39,607	41,988	27,028	29,632	25,473	26,486	21,241	42,630	38,187	19,214	397,332
1998	21,150	51,247	25,551	65,381	23,490	55,376	29,870	42,156	27,131	31,426	51,172	18,924	442,874
1999	23,747	35,706	43,671	44,974	22,399	40,722	35,812	27,928	17,893	16,155	42,029	20,370	371,406
2000	27,073	43,332	29,707	31,653	38,647	50,461	30,885	42,814	21,846	21,476	48,890	15,406	402,190
2001	26,377	38,040	24,903	41,482	20,516	41,926	50,440	22,883	31,252	50,580	53,578	38,877	440,854
2002	41,516	46,435	30,662	51,889	32,386	39,229	35,217	29,647	23,968	32,847	35,412	15,932	415,140
2003	26,149	31,892	27,766	26,022	20,442	24,113	23,230	21,562	26,658	33,621	30,273	27,170	318,898
2004	33,743	34,605	55,216	49,746	38,951	35,356	25,451	31,023	32,322	25,443	33,942	20,650	416,448

Source: Chicago Board of Trade (CBT)

Average Open Interest of Oats in Chicago   In Contracts

Year	Jan.	Feb.	Mar.	Apr.	May	June	July	Aug.	Sept.	Oct.	Nov.	Dec.
1995	13,133	13,231	13,000	15,426	16,054	13,611	11,019	11,348	11,012	11,970	12,542	13,003
1996	13,253	14,095	14,231	14,497	13,897	11,697	11,336	11,803	11,457	11,918	11,150	8,550
1997	8,088	9,650	12,649	11,024	9,830	9,395	8,131	8,606	8,618	10,953	11,816	10,964
1998	12,782	15,368	16,553	17,748	17,441	16,437	14,255	15,052	14,771	16,263	18,466	17,048
1999	17,126	17,019	16,677	15,398	13,491	12,705	11,927	11,670	9,802	10,638	12,754	12,360
2000	15,343	17,521	17,719	18,183	176,686	16,178	15,550	15,225	13,176	13,985	14,377	14,119
2001	14,093	15,060	14,873	14,962	14,875	13,695	11,861	11,707	10,059	12,111	14,453	12,142
2002	12,640	13,137	11,833	10,976	9,047	10,381	10,230	10,970	9,881	9,550	9,134	6,008
2003	6,929	6,715	5,945	6,135	5,833	5,640	5,811	5,958	6,261	6,194	6,268	5,122
2004	6,284	6,314	10,018	12,988	11,903	11,339	10,293	9,153	6,669	7,010	7,753	6,724

Source: Chicago Board of Trade (CBT)

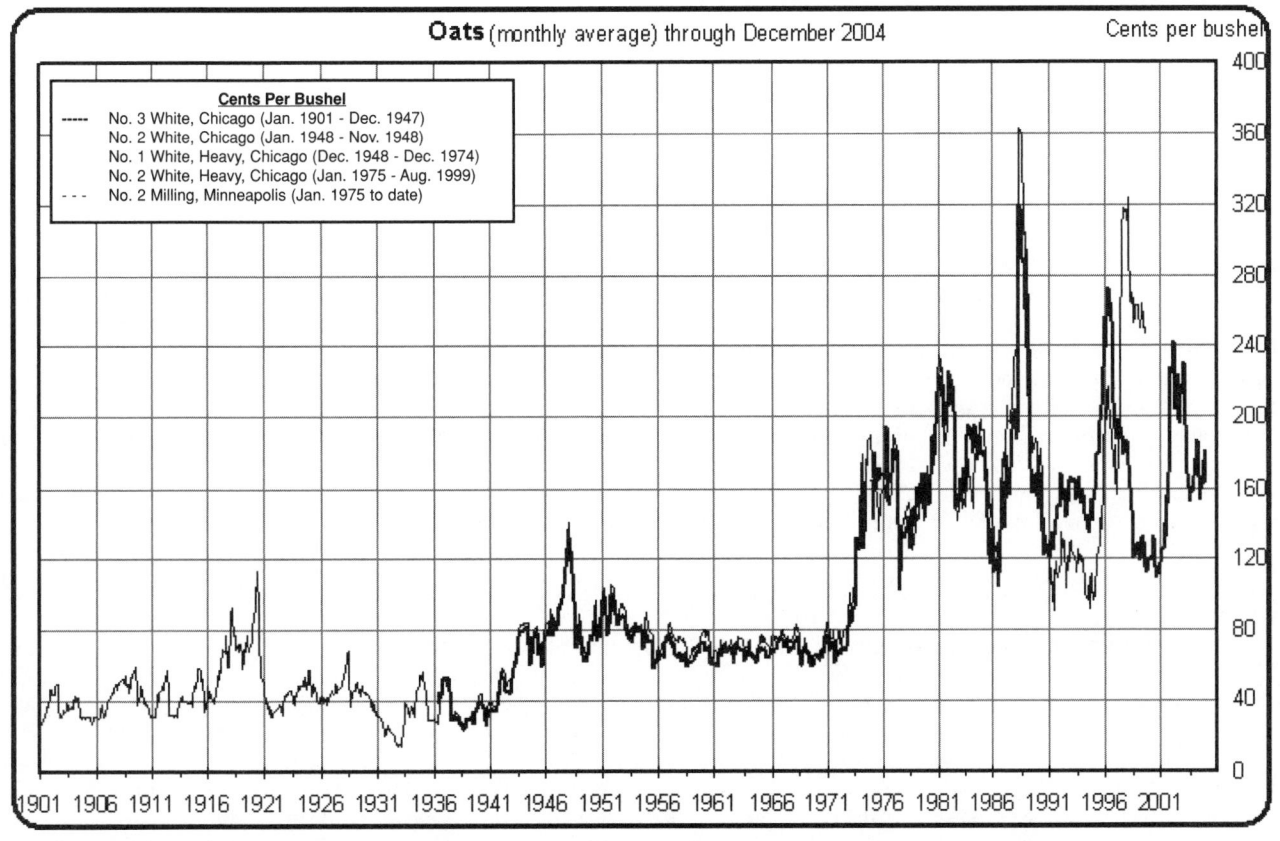

Average Cash Price of No. 2 Heavy White Oats in Minneapolis   In Dollars Per Bushel

Year	June	July	Aug.	Sept.	Oct.	Nov.	Dec.	Jan.	Feb.	Mar.	Apr.	May	Average
1995-6	1.73	1.92	1.96	2.04	2.11	2.63	2.50	2.40	2.31	2.47	2.56	2.68	2.28
1996-7	2.11	2.48	2.36	2.08	2.06	1.87	1.86	1.89	1.94	1.99	1.88	1.81	2.03
1997-8	1.89	1.76	1.80	1.78	1.75	1.65	1.71	1.68	1.59	1.65	1.54	1.58	1.70
1998-9	1.52	1.42	1.21	1.30	1.29	1.32	1.31	1.33	1.26	1.35	1.36	1.39	1.34
1999-00	1.34	1.25	1.20	1.17	1.20	1.20	1.28	1.21	1.19	1.34	1.45	NQ	1.26
2000-1	.73	.72	.69	.68	.70	.72	.70	.70	.75	.77	.80	.82	.73
2001-2	.83	.95	1.08	1.04	1.29	1.41	1.48	1.41	1.47	1.51	1.31	1.29	1.26
2002-3	1.40	1.24	1.23	1.36	1.36	1.33	1.36	1.44	1.28	1.28	1.22	1.08	1.30
2003-4	1.05	NQ	.98	1.01	1.00	.99	1.04	.99	1.14	1.08	1.22	1.08	1.05
2004-5[1]	1.04	.96	.99	1.11	1.01	1.04	1.13	1.18					1.06

[1] Preliminary.   NQ = No quote.   *Source: Economic Research Service, U.S. Department of Agriculture (ERS-USDA)*

Average Price Received by U.S. Farmers for Oats   In Dollars Per Bushel

Year	June	July	Aug.	Sept.	Oct.	Nov.	Dec.	Jan.	Feb.	Mar.	Apr.	May	Average
1995-6	1.38	1.52	1.48	1.43	1.50	1.72	1.91	1.93	1.96	2.04	2.13	2.48	1.46
1996-7	2.17	2.13	2.00	1.83	1.84	1.85	1.72	1.83	1.81	1.91	1.87	1.86	1.96
1997-8	1.81	1.68	1.57	1.47	1.62	1.66	1.57	1.60	1.60	1.64	1.61	1.53	1.61
1998-9	1.39	1.19	1.02	1.07	1.09	1.10	1.19	1.20	1.20	1.20	1.18	1.31	1.18
1999-00	1.22	1.08	.97	1.08	1.06	1.12	1.18	1.20	1.27	1.28	1.35	1.31	1.18
2000-1	1.24	1.07	.93	.95	1.08	1.22	1.14	1.21	1.28	1.24	1.28	1.28	1.16
2001-2	1.38	1.33	1.25	1.39	1.64	1.79	1.92	1.93	1.91	1.99	1.99	1.99	1.71
2002-3	1.95	1.69	1.67	1.80	1.80	1.91	1.95	2.04	2.11	2.08	1.98	1.95	1.91
2003-4	1.83	1.46	1.39	1.39	1.44	1.29	1.58	1.48	1.58	1.62	1.62	1.70	1.53
2004-5[1]	1.61	1.37	1.33	1.44	1.45	1.49	1.56	1.64	1.58				1.50

[1] Preliminary.   *Source: National Agricultural Statistics Service, U.S. Department of Agriculture (NASS-USDA)*

Olive Oil

Olive oil is derived from the fruit of the olive tree and originated in the Mediterranean area. Olives designated for oil are picked before ripening in the fall. Olive picking is usually done by hand. The olives are then weighed and washed in cold water. The olives, along with their oil-rich pits, are then crushed and kneaded until a homogeneous paste is formed. The paste is spread by hand onto metal plates, which are then stacked and pressed hydraulically to yield a liquid. The liquid is then centrifuged to separate the oil. It takes 1,300 to 2,000 olives to produce 1 quart of olive oil. The best olive oil is still produced from the first pressing, which is usually performed within 24 to 72 hours after harvest and is called *extra virgin* olive oil.

Supply – World production of olive oil (pressed oil) in the marketing year 2003/04 rose +10.2% to 2.915 million metric tons, which was a new record high. The world's largest producers of olive oil in 2003/04 were Spain (with 50%

of world production), Italy (15%), Greece (13%), Turkey (2%), and Syria (4%). Production levels in various countries are highly volatile from year-to-year depending on various weather and crop conditions.

Demand – World consumption of olive oil in the 2003/04 marketing year rose +3.1% to a new record high of 2.875 million metric tons. The US is the world's largest consumer of olive oil with 7.6% of world consumption in 2003/04. US consumption of olive oil reached a record 219,600 metric tons in 2003/04 and was about four times the consumption level seen 20 years earlier.

Trade – World olive oil imports in 2003/04 rose +5.7% to 571,500 metric tons. The US was the world's largest importer in 2003/04 with 230,300 metric tons, representing 40% of world imports. The world's largest exporters are Italy (with 31% of world exports), Spain (26%), Tunisia (16%), and Turkey (5%).

World Production of Olive Oil (Pressed Oil) In Thousands of Metric Tons

Year	Algeria	Argentina	Greece	Italy	Jordan	Libya	Morocco	Portugal	Spain	Syria	Tunisia	Turkey	World Total
1996-7	46.0	12.0	469.8	317.0	25.5	10.0	121.0	48.8	1,027.5	138.0	288.5	222.0	2,771.6
1997-8	6.5	8.5	405.0	585.0	16.0	6.0	75.0	45.5	1,212.0	78.0	99.0	45.0	2,615.5
1998-9	54.5	7.0	511.0	427.2	23.5	8.0	71.0	40.3	804.0	129.0	231.0	188.0	2,537.1
1999-00	33.5	11.5	454.0	670.0	7.0	7.0	45.0	58.3	694.1	88.0	225.0	61.0	2,412.4
2000-1	26.5	3.0	467.0	508.0	29.5	4.0	39.5	28.5	1,040.0	183.0	141.0	197.5	2,731.7
2001-2[1]	25.5	10.0	388.3	500.0	16.0	7.0	66.0	36.7	1,468.0	104.0	40.0	71.0	2,780.1
2002-3[2]	16.5	11.0	449.0	620.0	28.0	6.5	48.5	31.9	928.0	184.5	76.0	172.0	2,647.8
2003-4[3]	40.0	22.0	368.0	450.0	11.5	6.5	89.0	41.0	1,460.0	121.5	193.0	65.0	2,914.5

[1] Preliminary. [2] Estimate. [3] Forecast. *Source: The Oil World*

World Imports and Exports of Olive Oil (Pressed Oil) In Thousands of Metric Tons

| | ----- Imports ----- | | | | | | | ----- Exports ----- | | | | | |
Year	Australia	Brazil	Italy	Japan	Spain	United States	World Total	Greece	Italy	Spain	Tunisia	Turkey	World Total
1996-7	19.0	26.3	108.1	24.3	35.2	148.1	461.8	9.3	136.8	72.0	101.4	46.6	460.5
1997-8	17.7	28.9	89.4	35.5	28.0	161.0	467.8	9.3	140.2	82.0	126.8	42.2	469.4
1998-9	23.7	23.5	150.4	28.1	76.8	169.9	573.5	6.3	141.6	70.9	172.5	99.0	572.9
1999-00	24.2	25.6	105.2	27.2	23.4	189.3	507.1	9.4	180.0	97.2	122.4	25.8	502.1
2000-1	29.5	24.7	110.5	29.6	13.3	212.5	553.4	6.7	198.1	100.7	101.0	77.5	561.5
2001-2[1]	26.4	24.0	51.4	31.2	6.6	218.1	495.3	9.9	204.9	120.3	33.0	35.8	487.8
2002-3[2]	32.0	21.1	71.0	31.4	16.6	220.1	540.5	11.2	205.1	123.8	40.9	54.1	543.5
2003-4[3]	33.0	23.3	80.5	33.0	12.8	230.3	571.5	7.6	179.5	147.2	88.7	27.9	571.8

[1] Preliminary. [2] Estimate. [3] Forecast. *Source: The Oil World*

World Consumption and Ending Stocks of Olive Oil (Pressed Oil) In Thousands of Metric Tons

| | ----- Consumption ----- | | | | | | | ----- Ending Stocks ----- | | | | | |
Year	Brazil	Morocco	Syria	Tunisia	Turkey	United States	World Total	Greece	Italy	Spain	Syria	Turkey	World Total
1996-7	26.3	57.2	103.9	89.1	83.4	130.9	2,246.3	115.0	47.4	273.0	50.0	115.0	846.7
1997-8	28.9	61.3	106.9	61.0	82.9	154.8	2,406.9	118.3	204.1	533.1	24.0	35.0	1,053.7
1998-9	23.5	62.5	107.8	64.8	74.3	160.9	2,538.0	132.0	120.8	554.0	46.0	50.0	1,033.2
1999-00	25.6	55.7	99.0	63.3	76.3	180.1	2,610.7	143.0	177.5	320.0	36.6	9.9	839.9
2000-1	24.7	46.6	122.4	65.3	79.9	205.5	2,744.9	126.0	134.4	289.5	87.2	50.0	818.6
2001-2[1]	24.0	60.4	108.1	34.4	75.2	211.5	2,726.8	131.0	78.0	488.0	70.7	12.0	879.4
2002-3[2]	21.1	64.5	129.1	32.9	83.4	219.3	2,789.3	138.0	167.0	207.0	98.0	47.0	734.8
2003-4[3]	23.3	84.1	131.3	68.8	73.4	219.6	2,875.0	108.0	79.0	397.0	58.0	11.0	774.0

[1] Preliminary. [2] Estimate. [3] Forecast. *Source: The Oil World*

Onions

Onions are the bulbs of plants in the lily family. Onions can be eaten raw, cooked, pickled, used as a flavoring or seasoning, or dehydrated. Onions rank in the top 10 vegetables produced in the US in terms of dollar value. Since 1629, onions have been cultivated in the US, but are believed to be indigenous to Asia.

The two main types of onions produced in the US are yellow and white onions. Yellow varieties comprise approximately 75% of all onions grown for bulb production in the US. Onions that are planted as a winter crop in warm areas are milder in taste and odor than onions planted during the summer in cooler regions.

Prices – Onion prices in 2004 averaged a record $15.13 per hundred pounds, up from $15.00 in 2003. Onion prices were strong in early 2004 and reached a high of $21.30 in February but then trailed off to $9.42 by December due to ideal summer growing conditions in the US.

Supply – US production in 2004 rose sharply by 9.0% to a record 7.633 billion pounds. The farm value of the US production crop in 2003 was $940 million, up from $765 million in 2002. US farmers harvested 166,950 acres in 2004, up 3% from 2003. The yield per acre in 2004 was a record high of 45,700 pounds per acre.

Demand – US per capita consumption of onions in 2003 rose to 19.5 pounds from 19.3 pounds in 2002.

Trade – US exports of fresh onions in 2002 totaled 637 million pounds, and imports were not far behind at 595 million pounds.

Salient Statistics of Onions in the United States

Crop Year	Harvested Acres	Yield Per Acre	Pro- duction 1,000 Cwt.	Price Per Cwt.	Farm Value $1,000	Jan. 1 Pack Frozen	Annual Pack Frozen	Imports Canned	Exports (Fresh)	Imports (Fresh)	Per Capita[3] Utilization -- Lbs., Farm Weight -- All	Fresh
						---------- In Millions of Pounds ----------						
1999	175,500	424	75,032	9.78	641,278	40.3	310.5	5.2	660.1	576.9	20.8	18.5
2000	167,070	432	72,948	11.30	735,939	58.3	226.2	5.0	763.5	476.9	20.4	18.9
2001	164,990	419	69,961	11.40	680,350	54.9	142.6	5.0	708.2	632.6	19.5	18.5
2002	162,720	429	69,844	12.10	764,994	36.9	387.1	7.1	637.2	595.4	20.4	19.3
2003[1]	160,090	437	70,025	14.50	982,362	39.5	309.6	10.3	678.5	646.3	20.3	18.9
2004[2]	166,950	457	76,326	11.80	863,295	38.6					20.5	19.1

[1] Preliminary.   [2] Forecast.   [3] Includes fresh and processing.   *Source: Economic Research Service, U.S. Department of Agiculture (ERS-USDA)*

Production of Onions in the United States   In Thousands of Hundredweight (Cwt.)

Year	Arizona	California	Texas	Total (All)	California	Colorado	Idaho	Michigan	Minne- sota	New Mexico	New York	Oregon (Malheur)	Texas	Total (All)	Grand Total
	------------------ Spring ------------------				--- Summer ---										
1999	1,635	3,212	3,620	11,222	16,965	5,438	5,530	1,080	118	----	3,528	8,643	----	62,340	73,562
2000	1,376	3,089	4,185	11,812	16,154	4,083	4,810	945	19	----	4,674	6,960	----	59,909	71,721
2001	1,290	2,666	4,615	11,136	12,069	4,140	4,992	999	73	----	4,224	7,006	----	56,517	67,653
2002	690	2,708	4,725	9,561	11,562	4,400	6,272	897	78	----	2,829	7,800	----	60,283	69,844
2003	750	3,038	3,520	9,496	12,474	3,696	5,880	1,152	65	----	3,808	7,198	----	60,529	70,025
2004[1]	800	3,317	3,500	11,387	11,825	5,175	7,560	1,110	45	----	4,800	7,800	----	64,939	76,326

[1] Preliminary.   *Source: Agricultural Statistics Board, U.S. Department of Agiculture (ASB-USDA)*

Cold Storage Stocks of Frozen Onions in the United States, on First of Month   In Thousands of Pounds

Year	Jan.	Feb.	Mar.	Apr.	May	June	July	Aug.	Sept.	Oct.	Nov.	Dec.
1999	24,596	24,665	27,280	27,972	33,113	35,809	35,605	33,171	31,675	31,338	35,573	41,677
2000	41,236	40,730	44,029	45,874	52,691	55,340	53,537	42,910	40,792	34,318	37,408	39,909
2001	40,420	39,722	39,407	36,925	36,503	38,705	38,275	29,993	28,912	26,133	27,726	28,987
2002	29,893	33,646	34,851	35,477	40,789	41,066	40,762	33,370	36,895	36,120	39,796	39,310
2003	39,480	39,764	43,624	37,569	35,625	35,617	36,529	35,590	35,907	33,844	38,693	39,467
2004[1]	38,632	32,515	34,080	36,724	39,364	41,525	37,288	34,845	34,888	35,826	38,423	39,789

[1] Preliminary.   *Source: National Agricultural Statistics Service, U.S. Department of Agiculture (NASS-USDA)*

Average Price Received by Growers for Onions in the United States   In Dollars Per Hundred Pounds (Cwt.)

Year	Jan.	Feb.	Mar.	Apr.	May	June	July	Aug.	Sept.	Oct.	Nov.	Dec.	Season Average
1999	16.10	13.10	10.00	14.60	13.00	15.00	15.70	13.10	10.10	8.18	7.47	6.95	9.78
2000	5.86	4.86	4.38	10.00	12.50	12.10	13.30	12.10	10.60	10.10	10.70	11.10	11.30
2001	11.40	10.60	10.70	12.80	15.50	15.30	15.50	12.30	10.70	9.20	7.41	9.35	11.40
2002	9.48	8.27	6.92	16.20	16.10	15.60	15.10	12.20	10.00	9.61	9.79	11.50	12.10
2003	12.30	14.90	21.80	39.30	32.00	22.10	16.70	13.80	12.20	12.60	13.90	12.70	14.50
2004[1]	18.20	21.30	12.80	17.50	19.60	18.00	15.00	17.50	11.80	11.00	9.47	9.04	11.80

[1] Preliminary.   *Source: Economic Research Service, U.S. Department of Agiculture (ERS-USDA)*

Oranges and Orange Juice

The orange tree is a semi-tropical, non-deciduous tree, and the fruit is technically a hesperidium, a kind of berry. The orange originated in India and was called *na rangi* in Sanskrit. The original fruit was bitter compared to modern varieties. The three major varieties of oranges include the sweet orange, the sour orange, and the mandarin orange (or tangerine). In the US, only sweet oranges are grown commercially. Those include Hamlin, Jaffa, navel, Pineapple, blood orange, and Valencia. Sour oranges are mainly used in marmalade and in liqueurs such as triple sec and curacao.

Frozen Concentrated Orange Juice (FCOJ) was developed in 1945, which led to oranges becoming the main fruit crop in the US. The world's largest producer of orange juice is Brazil, followed by Florida. Two to four medium-sized oranges will produce about 1 cup of juice, and modern mechanical extractors can remove the juice from 400 to 700 oranges per minute. Before juice extraction, orange oil is recovered from the peel. Orange oil is used to produce flavors, perfumes, wood furniture conditioners, and cleaning agents. Approximately 50% of the orange weight is juice, the remainder is peel, pulp, and seeds, which are dried to produce nutritious cattle feed.

Frozen concentrated orange juice future and options are traded on the NYCE division of the New York Board of Trade (NYBOT). The NYCE orange juice futures contract calls for the delivery of 15,000 pounds of orange solids and is priced in terms of cents per pound.

Prices – NYCE orange juice futures in 2004 initially continued with the bear market trend that had been in place since 1990. The decline in 2003 and early 2004 was due to plenty of supply combined with lower demand due to the popularity of low-carb diets. Orange juice prices in May 2004 hit lows not seen since the 1970s. However, orange juice prices then rallied sharply in late summer and autumn after four major hurricanes hit the southeastern US and caused substantial damage to the Florida orange crop. The Florida orange crop in 2004-05 plunged by 33% yr/yr to 162 million 90-pound boxes, which was the smallest Florida orange crop since 1991-92. The US orange crop fell –25% yr/yr to 9.65 million tons.

Supply – World production of oranges in the 2003-04 marketing year rose +9.7% yr/yr to 50.175 million metric tons. The world's largest producers of oranges are Brazil with 37% of world production, followed by the US (23%), and Mexico (8%). US production of oranges in 2003-04 rose +10.9% yr/yr to 296 million boxes. Florida's production rose +19.2% yr/yr to 242 million boxes, while California's production fell –16.1% yr/yr to 52.000 million boxes. Florida produced 82% of US oranges in 2003-04.

World Production of Oranges   In Thousands of Metric Tons

Year	Argentina	Australia	Brazil	Egypt	Greece	Italy	Mexico	Morocco	South Africa	Spain	Turkey	United States	World Total
1994-5	712	416	16,520	1,513	926	1,800	3,570	657	770	2,697	920	10,474	43,664
1995-6	703	416	16,973	1,555	838	1,800	3,590	1,013	930	2,573	842	10,453	44,526
1996-7	841	556	18,972	1,613	946	2,100	3,917	774	895	2,200	890	11,618	48,438
1997-8	921	448	15,912	1,350	987	2,100	3,331	1,131	961	2,744	740	12,495	46,282
1998-9	660	515	18,360	1,442	795	1,422	2,903	900	1,048	2,442	970	8,989	43,961
1999-00	789	624	17,136	1,637	1,040	1,750	3,385	845	1,119	2,828	1,100	11,875	48,286
2000-1	913	437	14,729	1,610	976	1,800	3,885	693	1,119	2,688	1,070	11,139	44,588
2001-2[1]	780	633	18,360	1,696	1,076	1,724	4,020	720	1,263	2,822	1,250	11,290	49,853
2002-3[2]	700	410	15,382	1,734	1,145	1,723	3,734	800	1,265	2,867	1,250	10,510	45,756
2003-4[3]	730	550	18,523	1,742	550	1,677	4,000	730	1,260	3,091	1,250	11,751	50,175

[1] Preliminary.   [2] Estimate.   [3] Forecast.   NA = Not available.   *Source: Foreign Agricultural Service, U.S. Department of Agriculture (FAS-USDA)*

Salient Statistics of Oranges & Orange Juice in the United States

Year	California	Florida	Total U.S.	Farm Price $ Per Box	Farm Value Million $	Frozen Concentrates	Chilled Products	Total Processed	Yield Per Box Gallons[5]	Carry-in	Pack	Total Supply	Total Season Movement
	----- Production[4] -----					---- Florida Crop Processed ----				Frozen Concentrated Orange Juice - Florida			
	----- Million Boxes -----					-------- Million Boxes --------				----- In Millions of Gallons (42 Deg. Brix) -----			
1994-5	56.0	205.5	263.6	6.08	1,624.1	144.7	54.8	199.8	1.5	58.6	274.2	332.8	290.4
1995-6	58.0	203.3	263.9	6.85	1,821.6	132.9	64.5	197.7	1.5	42.4	284.5	326.9	285.7
1996-7	64.0	226.2	293.0	6.16	1,836.7	153.8	65.7	220.4	1.6	41.2	289.6	342.9	273.9
1997-8	69.0	244.0	315.5	6.13	1,965.4	160.9	74.8	236.6	1.6	69.7	290.2	359.9	263.8
1998-9	36.0	186.0	224.6	7.41	1,687.9	97.2	80.1	175.1	1.6	104.7	216.9	321.6	209.1
1999-00	64.0	233.0	299.8	5.56	1,666.1	134.2	90.1	226.7	1.5	105.2	254.0	359.2	239.7
2000-1	54.5	223.3	280.9	5.88	1,682.8	124.1	89.6	215.9	1.6	112.6	245.2	357.8	226.0
2001-2[1]	51.5	230.0	283.8	6.37	1,846.2	136.0	85.9	223.2	1.6	128.3	253.2	381.5	249.9
2002-3[2]	62.0	203.0	267.0	5.79	1,564.7	102.1	92.5	196.0	1.5	120.2	203.3	323.5	200.1
2003-4[3]	52.0	242.0	296.1	5.40	1,645.9	139.7	93.4	233.8	1.6	124.0	249.7	373.7	213.8

[1] Preliminary.   [2] Estimate.   [3] Forecast.   [4] Fruit ripened on trees, but destroyed prior to picking not included.   [5] 42 deg. Brix equivalent.
Source: Economic Research Service, U.S. Department of Agriculture (ERS-USDA); Florida Department of Citrus

Frozen Concentrate Orange Juice - New York Board of Trade
(weekly close) as December 31, 2004

Average Open Interest of Frozen Concentrated Orange Juice Futures in New York   In Contracts

Year	Jan.	Feb.	Mar.	Apr.	May	June	July	Aug.	Sept.	Oct.	Nov.	Dec.
1995	27,439	25,885	26,407	30,172	27,057	26,844	23,537	17,881	20,918	22,460	26,303	24,202
1996	22,943	21,670	25,232	23,788	21,724	20,934	20,159	19,834	18,029	18,000	22,513	26,405
1997	29,171	26,929	26,331	28,955	29,868	33,639	31,799	34,339	36,057	40,365	41,811	46,169
1998	38,885	37,893	36,843	33,146	35,749	32,608	25,503	26,394	28,017	26,506	21,984	24,562
1999	25,917	28,965	28,707	31,199	26,669	28,362	28,087	30,021	28,922	27,498	26,893	25,887
2000	23,727	24,647	19,684	22,475	23,456	27,087	27,386	30,272	30,090	32,328	30,192	30,757
2001	28,852	28,011	28,073	27,794	24,199	24,428	22,591	22,073	17,789	18,026	21,506	19,275
2002	15,716	16,593	18,515	22,328	23,498	26,581	28,137	33,206	27,323	23,758	22,651	23,461
2003	25,080	26,588	22,707	21,466	20,634	23,794	25,467	26,518	27,788	30,767	31,575	36,336
2004	36,079	35,325	32,806	36,112	34,704	42,299	39,970	38,259	39,877	38,990	33,342	36,072

Source: New York Board of Trade (NYBOT)

Volume of Trading of Frozen Concentrated Orange Juice Futures in New York   In Contracts

Year	Jan.	Feb.	Mar.	Apr.	May	June	July	Aug.	Sept.	Oct.	Nov.	Dec.	Total
1995	50,875	66,370	51,292	78,288	32,607	80,165	41,357	67,528	38,781	64,904	45,688	71,077	688,932
1996	59,666	82,057	46,272	65,752	62,247	44,827	40,884	58,346	44,239	40,680	39,291	70,676	654,937
1997	84,982	89,875	66,340	82,772	62,890	78,690	47,242	118,286	55,081	108,413	100,941	134,349	1,029,861
1998	96,020	81,554	66,235	101,651	70,909	79,319	48,844	85,544	81,187	98,639	29,541	75,171	914,614
1999	64,149	92,868	40,027	92,522	49,180	78,627	48,177	99,531	49,323	71,914	42,532	68,734	797,584
2000	45,680	78,532	33,617	71,024	50,475	80,372	46,548	67,312	38,485	64,831	45,966	89,362	712,204
2001	46,655	66,561	27,994	63,012	38,447	66,773	40,870	64,860	22,246	68,364	23,376	48,338	577,496
2002	31,709	50,898	30,316	58,644	37,283	52,238	45,316	78,111	36,053	71,635	24,111	61,443	577,757
2003	45,945	63,224	23,926	70,846	35,791	64,209	27,056	73,792	40,782	87,055	42,084	78,005	652,715
2004	52,908	86,600	41,941	99,532	45,741	123,815	105,220	118,021	65,655	89,064	56,502	85,438	970,437

Source: New York Board of Trade (NYBOT)

ORANGES AND ORANGE JUICE

Cold Storage Stocks of Orange Juice Concentrate in the U.S., on First of Month   In Millions of Pounds

Year	Jan.	Feb.	Mar.	Apr.	May	June	July	Aug.	Sept.	Oct.	Nov.	Dec.
1995	1,353.1	1,704.0	1,685.1	1,773.3	1,864.6	1,833.8	1,631.6	1,424.1	1,233.7	1,038.3	830.3	897.7
1996	1,050.6	1,295.4	1,353.0	1,322.3	1,443.9	1,596.9	1,535.0	1,423.6	1,238.6	965.6	732.7	691.0
1997	1,069.4	1,522.6	1,677.6	1,752.9	1,993.4	2,176.0	1,977.7	1,761.8	1,571.8	1,287.8	1,140.9	1,214.4
1998	1,503.4	1,945.9	2,029.7	2,025.0	2,487.0	2,627.5	2,457.7	2,249.0	2,025.1	1,803.9	1,470.7	1,540.2
1999	1,791.9	1,999.4	2,204.2	2,191.3	2,485.7	2,115.6	1,969.7	1,823.0	1,618.5	1,443.4	1,182.0	1,102.7
2000	1,330.7	1,540.6	1,632.7	1,857.9	1,812.5	1,965.6	2,037.9	1,843.7	1,457.7	1,346.6	1,169.4	1,202.0
2001	1,382.0	1,610.8	1,825.1	1,735.5	1,872.2	2,061.8	2,035.6	1,913.2	1,691.1	1,537.7	1,398.9	1,406.7
2002	1,571.7	1,721.3	1,770.9	1,794.4	1,886.0	1,982.8	1,934.0	1,870.9	1,680.9	1,543.6	1,409.6	1,471.2
2003	1,673.6	1,851.9	1,833.4	1,856.6	1,936.8	2,102.6	2,021.2	1,848.9	1,672.2	1,529.9	1,335.6	1,428.5
2004[1]	1,585.8	1,613.0	1,904.8	1,951.1	2,054.3	2,262.0	2,221.5	2,102.3	1,931.0	1,735.8	1,603.2	1,471.9

[1] Preliminary.   *Source: Agricultural Statistics Board, U.S. Department of Agriculture (ASB-USDA)*

Producer Price Index of Frozen Orange Juice Concentrate   1982 = 100

Year	Jan.	Feb.	Mar.	Apr.	May	June	July	Aug.	Sept.	Oct.	Nov.	Dec.	Average
1995	107.4	105.4	107.6	107.6	109.1	109.1	109.1	105.3	101.0	101.6	106.1	107.3	106.4
1996	109.4	112.5	117.2	119.5	119.5	119.5	115.3	113.6	113.6	112.8	112.8	108.8	114.5
1997	106.9	106.9	106.0	107.6	107.7	107.3	105.3	105.8	102.7	101.4	95.0	94.2	103.9
1998	94.9	101.2	104.1	103.2	108.8	109.1	109.5	109.6	109.5	110.2	119.1	121.2	108.4
1999	119.7	118.6	118.0	115.5	113.3	113.2	112.5	111.3	112.4	112.5	113.1	112.4	114.4
2000	110.0	108.9	108.0	107.1	106.9	106.6	105.4	104.8	101.5	100.4	99.8	99.1	104.9
2001	98.9	99.2	98.3	96.8	96.8	97.4	97.3	97.2	97.3	97.3	99.6	102.5	98.2
2002	103.0	102.9	103.1	102.9	102.8	103.2	103.2	103.5	107.4	107.4	109.7	110.2	104.9
2003	110.2	110.2	110.7	110.4	108.5	109.4	109.1	108.9	107.1	106.6	105.1	103.0	108.3
2004[1]	103.4	103.2	102.7	101.6	101.6	101.6	98.9	98.9	98.6	98.9	103.3	103.3	101.3

[1] Preliminary.   *Source: Bureau of Labor Statistics, U.S. Department of Labor (BLS)*

Average Price of Oranges (Equivalent On-Tree) Received by Growers in the U.S.   In Dollars Per Box

Year	Jan.	Feb.	Mar.	Apr.	May	June	July	Aug.	Sept.	Oct.	Nov.	Dec.	Average
1995	3.43	3.59	4.22	4.61	4.90	5.63	7.44	7.30	7.26	7.90	3.57	3.55	5.28
1996	3.97	4.39	5.20	6.11	6.63	6.72	6.97	8.15	13.70	10.94	4.17	3.52	6.71
1997	3.59	3.67	4.82	4.68	4.74	4.62	6.48	7.45	7.15	4.48	3.09	3.14	4.83
1998	3.14	3.55	5.05	5.44	5.70	6.05	6.77	5.56	5.64	5.98	5.03	4.82	5.23
1999	4.52	4.99	5.90	5.96	6.48	8.04	8.58	6.66	9.96	9.50	4.70	3.42	6.56
2000	3.35	3.18	3.24	4.20	4.39	4.34	2.45	0.35	0.29	1.43	3.20	2.95	2.78
2001	2.85	3.20	4.93	4.84	4.64	4.47	4.63	5.01	6.20	4.99	2.90	3.20	4.32
2002	3.75	4.05	4.64	4.65	4.47	4.00	4.06	6.61	5.33	5.18	3.11	3.23	4.42
2003	3.00	3.14	4.17	4.43	4.43	4.41	3.91	4.27	2.80	2.78	2.32	2.55	3.52
2004[1]	2.45	3.02	3.37	3.62	3.62	3.94	9.81	8.05	13.68	20.91	7.41	2.62	6.88

[1] Preliminary.   *Source: Economic Research Service, U.S. Department of Agriculture (ERS-USDA)*

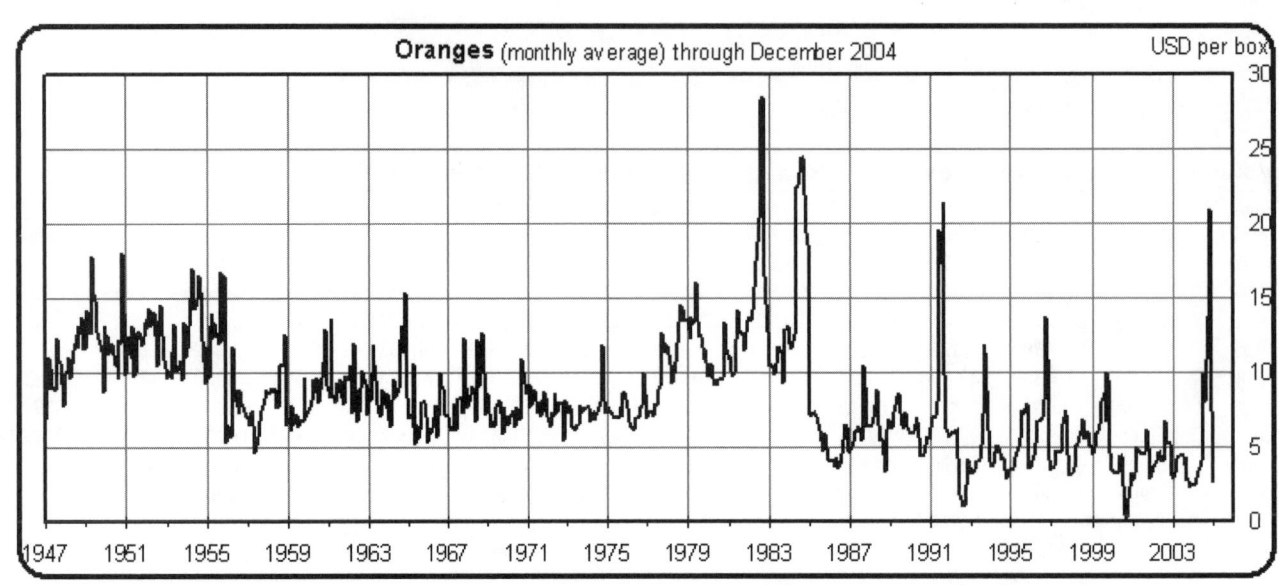

Oranges (monthly average) through December 2004   USD per box

Palm Oil

Palm oil is an edible vegetable oil produced from the flesh of the fruit of the oil palm tree. The oil palm tree is a tropical palm tree that is a native of the west coast of Africa and is different from the coconut palm tree. The fruit of the oil palm tree is reddish, about the size of a large plum, and grows in large bunches. A single seed, the palm kernel, is contained in each fruit. Oil is extracted from both the pulp of the fruit (becoming palm oil) and the kernel (palm kernel oil). About 1 metric ton of palm kernel oil is obtained for every 10 metric tons of palm oil.

Palm oil is commercially used in soap, ointments, cosmetics, detergents, and machinery lubricants. It is also used worldwide as cooking oil, shortening, and margarine. Palm kernel oil is a lighter oil and is used exclusively for food use. Crude palm oil and crude palm kernel oil are traded on the Kuala Lumpur Commodity Exchange.

Prices – The monthly average wholesale price of palm oil (CIF, bulk, US ports) in 2004 (through September, annualized) rose sharply by +36.2% yr/yr to 31.76 cents per pound. That was just mildly below the record high of 34.08 cents posted in 1984.

Supply – World production of palm oil in the 2003-04 marketing year rose by +3.3% to 28.425 million metric tons. World palm oil production has grown by nearly 15 times from the production level of 1.922 million metric tons seen back in 1970. Malaysia and Indonesia are the world's two major global producers of palm oil. Malaysian production in 2003-04 fell -1.5% to 12.979 million metric tons and Malaysian production accounted for 46% of global production. Indonesian production rose +9.2% to 11.040 million metric tons in 2003-04 and Indonesian production accounted for 39% of world production. Other minor global producers include Nigeria with 2.8% of world production, Thailand (2.3%), and Papua New Guinea with (1.2%).

Demand – US total disappearance of palm oil in 2002-03 fell -14.3% yr/yr to 185,000 metric tons from 215,900 metric tons (which was the highest level since 1986-87).

Trade – World palm oil exports in 2003-04 rose by 3.6% to 22.294 million metric tons, which was a new record high. The world's largest exporters are Malaysia with a 54% share of world exports, followed by Indonesia with a 35% share. The world's largest importers are India with a 17% share of world imports, followed by China (15%), the Netherlands (5%), UK (3%), and Germany (3%).

World Production of Palm Oil   In Thousands of Metric Tons

Crop Year	Brazil	Cameroon	Colombia	Costa Rica	Ecuador	Ghana	Indonesia	Ivory Coast	Malaysia	Nigeria	Papua/N Guinea	Thailand	World Total
1994-5	85	125	391	88	194	74	4,144	282	7,771	661	223	346	15,073
1995-6	90	130	393	93	220	79	4,587	277	8,264	667	236	369	16,152
1996-7	90	161	440	97	200	83	5,078	258	9,000	678	248	438	17,569
1997-8	88	140	439	108	205	107	5,320	270	8,509	688	206	469	17,305
1998-9	91	133	466	117	247	110	6,011	265	9,759	713	257	540	19,501
1999-00	105	136	513	136	228	109	6,855	283	10,492	735	300	533	21,270
2000-1	109	138	561	147	226	108	7,775	211	11,940	763	334	601	23,806
2001-2[1]	115	143	517	146	238	108	9,060	241	11,856	774	338	606	25,069
2002-3[2]	128	142	537	153	246	111	10,110	240	13,180	782	310	630	27,525
2003-4[3]	134	148	560	159	249	110	11,040	251	12,979	789	344	663	28,425

[1] Preliminary.   [2] Estimate.   [3] Forecast.   *Source: The Oil World*

World Trade of Palm Oil   In Thousands of Metric Tons

Crop Year	Imports							Exports					
	China	Germany	India	Netherlands	Pakistan	United Kingdom	World Total	Hong Kong	Indonesia	Malaysia	Papua/N Guinea	Singapore	World Total
1994-5	1,786	412	480	443	1,215	462	10,674	145	1,904	6,728	178	829	10,573
1995-6	1,178	446	970	544	1,166	500	10,558	160	2,082	6,896	191	829	10,582
1996-7	1,851	498	1,300	649	1,020	516	11,751	145	2,419	7,794	203	829	11,974
1997-8	1,490	370	1,684	670	1,210	457	11,971	120	2,459	7,847	207	253	11,795
1998-9	1,433	406	2,762	738	1,053	528	12,977	113	3,219	8,482	248	289	13,246
1999-00	1,474	431	3,482	780	1,086	558	14,792	130	3,898	9,051	292	251	14,675
2000-1	2,147	497	3,856	907	1,191	610	17,390	180	4,577	10,707	334	228	17,247
2001-2[1]	2,600	592	3,233	1,101	1,333	721	18,699	302	6,094	10,758	332	217	18,855
2002-3[2]	3,167	570	4,035	1,132	1,392	776	21,546	209	7,027	12,183	329	253	21,526
2003-4[3]	3,360	615	3,720	1,135	1,385	755	22,227	228	7,860	12,050	341	235	22,294

[1] Preliminary.   [2] Estimate.   [3] Forecast.   *Source: The Oil World*

PALM OIL

Supply and Distribution of Palm Oil in the United States   In Thousands of Metric Tons

Year Beginning Oct. 1	Stocks Oct. 1	Imports	Total Supply	Consumption Edible Products	Consumption Inedible Products	Consumption Total End Products	Total Disappearance	Exports	U.S. Import Value[4]	Malaysia, F.O.B., RBD	Palm Kernal Oil, Malaysia, C.I.F. Rotterdam
				------ In Millions of Pounds ------					---------- U.S. $ Per Metric Ton ----------		
1994-5	16.4	98.7	115.1	38.1	113.6	151.7	101.8	5.9	538	647	680
1995-6	7.4	106.9	114.3	6.7	103.9	110.6	91.1	9.2	511	545	729
1996-7	14.0	146.4	160.4	W	91.8	W	134.8	4.2	432	544	680
1997-8	21.4	128.0	149.4	W	93.8	W	128.8	4.4	464	640	653
1998-9	16.1	128.8	144.9	W	72.4	W	118.6	5.2	----	514	708
1999-00	21.1	156.6	177.7	W	55.0	W	148.5	3.4	----	338	533
2000-1	25.7	175.5	201.2	W	36.0	W	167.7	6.0	----	272	313
2001-2[1]	27.5	218.7	246.2	W	22.6	75.1	215.9	6.2	----	359	379
2002-3[2]	26.0	189.3	215.3	W	W	76.7	182.8	8.1	----	428	439
2003-4[3]	49.5	265.0	314.5	51.9	37.5	67.9	249.0	9.3	----	517	598

[1] Preliminary.   [2] Estimate.   [3] Forecast.   [4] Market value in the foreign country, excluding import duties, ocean freight and marine insurance.
Sources: The Oil World; Economic Research Service, U.S. Department of Agriculture (ERS-USDA)

Average Wholesale Palm Oil Prices, CIF, Bulk, U.S. Ports   In Cents Per Pound

Year	Jan.	Feb.	Mar.	Apr.	May	June	July	Aug.	Sept.	Oct.	Nov.	Dec.	Average
1994	21.91	21.67	21.72	23.08	26.27	28.94	27.44	30.18	32.15	31.93	34.95	36.83	28.09
1995	34.26	33.82	36.18	35.56	32.80	33.06	33.68	32.59	30.86	31.45	31.96	30.00	33.02
1996	27.08	26.52	26.33	27.52	28.57	25.43	24.78	24.46	27.24	26.13	26.95	27.45	26.54
1997	28.68	29.25	28.00	28.18	28.93	27.25	26.17	25.55	25.37	27.33	27.28	25.05	27.25
1998	29.30	29.59	30.53	32.10	31.11	31.42	32.33	33.14	33.14	33.06	33.30	34.00	31.92
1999	31.06	28.58	25.52	25.52	24.50	21.30	18.15	18.70	21.00	20.00	20.00	20.00	22.86
2000	18.65	17.66	17.73	18.21	18.12	16.52	16.85	16.23	15.90	13.19	13.56	12.75	16.28
2001	18.05	18.05	13.50	13.50	12.50	13.00	15.50	18.00	16.75	15.60	16.85	17.45	15.73
2002	17.75	17.06	17.30	17.75	18.85	21.44	20.50	21.85	32.00	31.75	31.75	31.75	23.31
2003	31.75	31.75	31.35	31.25	31.25	31.75	32.25	32.25	32.25				31.76

Source: Economic Research Service, U.S. Department of Agriculture (ERS-USDA)

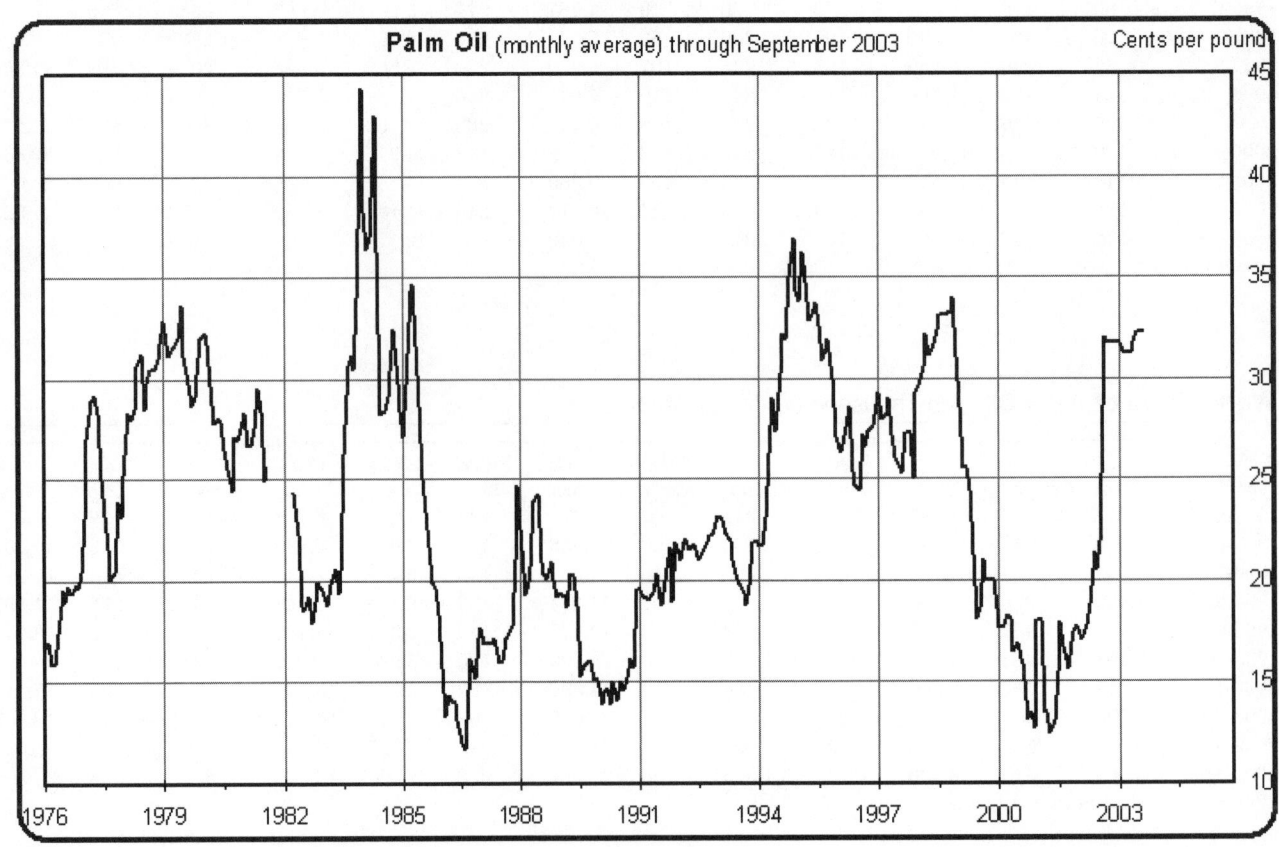

Palm Oil (monthly average) through September 2003   Cents per pound

Paper

The earliest known paper that is still in existence was made from cotton rags around 150 AD. Around 800 AD, paper made its appearance in Egypt but was not manufactured there until 900 AD. The Moors introduced the use of paper to Europe, and around 1150, the first papermaking mill was established in Spain, followed by England in 1495, and the US in 1690.

During the 17th and 18th centuries, the increased usage of paper created a shortage of cotton rags, which were the only source for papermaking. The solution to this problem lead to the introduction of the ground-wood process of pulp making in 1840 and the first chemical pulp process 10 years later.

Today, the paper and paperboard industries, including newsprint, are sensitive to the economic cycle. As the economy strengthens, paper use increases, and vice versa.

Prices – The average monthly index price for paper-board in 2004 (through November) rose +4.2% yr/yr to 169.6, recovering from the 5-year low of 162.7 posted in 2003. The average monthly producer price index of standard news-print paper in 2004 (through November) rose sharply by +10.1% to 123.4, continuing the upward rebound from the 18-year low of 105.7 posted in 2002.

Supply – US production of paper and paperboard in 2002 rose slightly by +0.9% yr/yr to 81.792 million metric tons from the 8-year low of 81.438 million posted in 2001. The US is the world's largest producer of paper and paper-board by far, followed by Canada with 20.226 million metric tons and Germany with 18.526 million metric tons.

US production of newsprint rose by +0.9% yr/yr to 433,200 metric tons per month in 2004, recovering from the 2-decade low of 429,000 metric tons in 2003. US production of newsprint is second, next to Canada, which had production of 684,300 metric tons per month in 2004.

Production of Paper and Paperboard by Selected Countries — In Thousands of Metric Tons

Year	Austria	Canada	Finland	France	Germany	Italy	Nether-lands	Norway	Russia	Spain	Sweden	United Kingdom	United States
1998	4,009	18,875	12,703	9,161	16,311	8,254	3,180	2,260	3,595	3,545	9,879	6,477	86,469
1999	4,142	20,280	12,947	9,603	16,742	8,568	3,256	2,241	4,535	4,435	10,071	6,576	88,670
2000	4,386	20,921	13,509	10,006	18,182	9,129	3,332	2,300	5,310	4,765	10,786	6,868	86,252
2001	4,250	19,834	12,502	9,625	17,879	8,926	3,174	2,220	5,625	5,131	10,534	6,467	81,249
2002	4,419	20,226	12,789	9,809	18,526	9,316	3,346	2,114	5,978	5,365	10,724	6,481	81,879
2003[1]	4,565	20,100	13,058	9,939	19,310	9,373	3,339	2,186	6,349	5,437	11,062	6,489	80,800

[1] Preliminary.   Source: Food and Agriculture Organization of the United Nations (FAO-UN)

Production of Newsprint by Selected Countries (Monthly Average) — In Thousands of Metric Tons

Year	Australia	Brazil	Canada	China	Finland	France	Germany	India	Japan	Rep. of Korea	Russia	Sweden	United States
1998	33.9	22.7	718.6	70.8	123.6	75.7	135.8	28.8	272.0	141.7	116.2	206.5	541.7
1999	31.8	20.2	767.0	93.4	124.2	79.2	136.9	32.4	274.6	144.8	135.0	209.0	543.0
2000	32.7	22.2	768.0	121.0	116.1	86.6	150.5	48.9	284.9	151.5	141.5	211.5	547.5
2001	32.3	19.2	697.8	127.4	108.0	86.0	170.5	53.0	288.7	136.6	144.3	205.3	480.8
2002	34.0	20.9	705.0	156.0	88.7	82.0	173.5	49.6	299.7	137.9	NA	202.0	437.4
2003[1]	35.2	14.0	708.3	170.9	78.9	60.0	178.1	58.2	292.9	133.3	NA	210.7	429.2
2004[2]	34.5	11.7	684.3	229.7	59.8	93.0	187.1	56.7	307.9	146.1	163.7	220.7	433.2

[1] Preliminary.   [2] Estimate.   Source: United Nations

Index Price of Paperboard   1982 = 100

Year	Jan.	Feb.	Mar.	Apr.	May	June	July	Aug.	Sept.	Oct.	Nov.	Dec.	Average
1998	155.9	156.1	156.0	155.2	154.2	153.7	152.2	150.9	149.0	146.9	144.7	143.6	151.6
1999	142.2	142.3	146.4	148.1	149.3	149.5	154.5	158.6	161.0	162.1	162.2	162.3	153.2
2000	163.1	163.6	173.6	176.6	180.4	180.3	180.9	181.2	180.9	180.4	180.2	179.5	176.7
2001	179.4	176.6	175.8	175.2	174.1	172.4	172.3	169.8	169.0	167.1	166.8	167.0	172.1
2002	165.0	164.0	162.6	162.8	161.1	161.1	161.8	165.8	166.7	167.1	167.3	166.6	164.3
2003	166.8	166.5	164.4	163.5	163.6	163.4	162.5	162.5	160.5	159.9	159.6	159.7	162.7
2004[1]	157.8	157.4	157.5	162.2	165.5	170.0	175.2	178.5	180.2	179.7	180.0	179.4	170.3

[1] Preliminary.   Source: Bureau of Labor Statistics, U.S. Department of Commerce (BLS) (0914)

Producer Price Index of Standard Newsprint   1982 = 100

Year	Jan.	Feb.	Mar.	Apr.	May	June	July	Aug.	Sept.	Oct.	Nov.	Dec.	Average
1998	142.2	142.5	141.8	142.3	140.0	140.3	143.4	143.1	144.6	147.6	147.6	145.0	143.4
1999	143.0	135.9	128.1	125.0	117.8	117.7	110.3	111.7	111.4	NA	NA	NA	122.3
2000	117.2	116.8	116.5	118.3	123.1	127.1	127.6	130.7	131.5	139.4	141.2	140.5	127.5
2001	140.6	141.4	143.0	150.9	146.8	148.5	146.6	142.4	134.5	130.1	121.6	117.3	138.6
2002	113.6	106.2	106.5	105.7	98.9	100.5	101.0	101.8	104.7	112.2	109.6	107.9	105.7
2003	106.1	107.4	106.3	110.2	112.6	112.5	111.0	114.3	116.8	118.1	114.6	115.0	112.1
2004[1]	116.5	116.7	118.8	122.4	125.0	126.0	125.6	125.7	125.4	125.9	129.6	134.2	124.3

[1] Preliminary.   NA = Not available.   Source: Bureau of Labor Statistics, U.S. Department of Commerce (BLS) (0913-02)

Peanuts and Peanut Oil

Peanuts are the edible seeds of a plant from the pea family. Although called a nut, the peanut is actually a legume. Ancient South American Inca Indians were the first to grind peanuts to make peanut butter. Peanuts originated in Brazil and were later brought to the US via Africa. The first major use of peanuts was as feed for pigs. It wasn't until the Civil War that peanuts were used as human food when both Northern and Southern troops used the peanut as a food source during hard times. In 1903, Dr. George Washington Carver, a talented botanist who is considered the "father of commercial peanuts," introduced peanuts as a rotation crop in cotton-growing areas. Carver discovered over 300 uses for the peanut including shaving cream, leather dye, coffee, ink, cheese, and shampoo.

Peanuts come in many varieties, but there are four basic types grown in the US: Runner, Spanish, Valencia, and Virginia. Over half of Runner peanuts are used to make peanut butter. Spanish peanuts are primarily used to make candies and peanut oil. Valencia peanuts are the sweetest of the four types. Virginia peanuts are mainly roasted and sold in and out of the shell.

Peanut oil is extracted from shelled and crushed peanuts through hydraulic pressing, expelled pressing, or solvent extraction. Crude peanut oil is used as a flavoring agent, salad oil, and cooking oil. Refined, bleached and deodorized peanut oil is used for cooking and in margarines and shortenings. The by-product called press cake is used for cattle feed along with the tops of the plants after the pods are removed. The dry shells can be burned as fuel.

Prices – The average monthly price received by farmers for peanuts (in the shell) in the first 5 months of the 2004-05 marketing year (i.e., Aug-Dec 2004) rose by +6.0% to 20.3 cents per pound, which was a 4-year high. The record high is 34.7 cents posted in 1990-91. The average monthly price of peanut oil in the 2003-04 marketing year rose +16.8% yr/yr to 59.75 cents per pound, which was a new record high. The average monthly price of peanut meal (50% Southeast Mills) rose by +40.6% yr/yr in 2003-04 to a 6-year high of $178.92 per short ton.

Supply – World peanut production in 2003-04 rose by +10.4% yr/yr to 33.450 million metric tons, which was just below the record high of 33.630 million metric tons posted in 2001-02. The world's largest peanut producers are China with 45% of world production, India with 22%, US with 6%, and Nigeria with 5%. US peanut production in the 2004-05 marketing year rose by +1.4% to 4.201 billion pounds, which was a 10-year high but was well below the record high of 4.927 billion pounds posted in 1991-92.

US farmers harvested 1.388 million acres of peanuts in 2004-05, up +5.8% yr/yr and above the 22-year low of 1.292 million acres seen in 2002-03. US peanut yield in 2004-05 fell -4.2% yr/yr to 3,027 pounds per acre from the record high of 3,159 pounds seen in 2003-04. The largest peanut producing states in the US are Georgia (with 44% of US production in 2004), Texas (18%), Alabama (13%), North Carolina (9%), and Florida (8%). US peanut oil production in 2004 (through October, annualized) fell by –38.4% to 141.533 million pounds, the lowest level since 108.200 million pounds in 1984.

Demand – US disposition of peanuts in 2003-04 fell by –4.5% yr/yr to 3.817 billion pounds. Of that disposition, 60% of the peanuts went for food, 17% for crushing into peanut oil, 13% for exports, and 10% for seed, loss and residual. The most popular type of peanut grown in the US is the Runner peanut with 87% of US production in 2003-04, followed by the Virginia peanut with 11% of production, and the Spanish peanut with 2% of production. Peanut butter is a primary use for all three types of peanuts and accounts for 55% of Runner peanut usage, 49% of Virginia peanut usage, and 22% of Spanish peanut usage. Snack peanuts is also a key usage category and accounts for 48% of Virginia peanut usage, 39% of Spanish peanut usage, and 23% of Runner peanuts usage. Candy accounts for 39% of Spanish peanut usage, 22% of Runner peanut usage, and 13% of Virginia peanut usage.

Trade – US exports of peanuts in 2003-04 rose by +2.0% yr/yr to 500 million pounds. US imports of peanuts fell by –13.3% yr/yr in 2003-04 to 65 million pounds.

World Production of Peanuts (in the Shell) In Thousands of Metric Tons

Year	Argentina	Burma	China	India	Indonesia	Nigeria	Senegal	South Africa	Sudan	Thailand	United States	Zaire	World Total
1995-6	660	501	10,200	7,400	1,055	800	827	193	370	147	1,570	585	27,665
1996-7	401	593	10,140	9,024	985	950	646	140	370	147	1,661	570	29,059
1997-8	897	559	9,648	7,580	990	1,250	506	97	370	130	1,605	400	27,561
1998-9	486	540	11,886	7,450	930	1,430	541	138	370	135	1,798	410	29,955
1999-00	600	562	12,639	5,500	1,020	1,450	764	165	370	137	1,737	400	29,330
2000-1	564	634	14,437	5,700	1,040	1,470	1,003	186	370	135	1,481	380	31,425
2001-2	517	731	14,415	7,600	1,033	1,490	903	120	370	129	1,940	370	33,872
2002-3	316	700	14,818	5,200	1,086	1,510	260	60	370	129	1,506	360	30,445
2003-4[1]	324	710	13,420	7,700	1,130	1,510	445	81	370	120	1,880	410	32,291
2004-5[2]	400	715	15,800	7,500	1,190	1,520	450	81	370	130	1,933		34,741

[1] Preliminary. [2] Estimate. *Source: Foreign Agricultural Service, U.S. Department of Agriculture (FAS-USDA)*

Salient Statistics of Peanuts in the United States

Crop Year	Agreage Planted ----- 1,000 Acres -----	Acreage Harvested for Nuts	Average Yield Per Acre In Lbs.	Pro-duction 1,000 Lbs.	Season Farm Price Cents/Lb.	Farm Value Million Dollars	---- Thousand Pounds (Year Beginning August 1) ----- Exports Unshelled	Exports Shelled	Imports Unshelled	Imports Shelled
1995-6	1,537.5	1,517.0	2,282	3,461,475	29.3	1,013.3	826,000	564,021	153,000	108,303
1996-7	1,401.5	1,380.0	2,653	3,661,205	28.1	1,029.8	668,000	440,438	127,000	95,041
1997-8	1,434.0	1,413.8	2,503	3,539,380	28.3	1,002.7	682,000	455,264	141,000	101,792
1998-9	1,521.0	1,467.0	2,702	3,963,440	28.4	1,125.9	562,000	----	155,000	----
1999-00	1,534.5	1,436.0	2,667	3,829,490	25.4	971.6	727,000	----	178,000	----
2000-1	1,536.8	1,336.0	2,444	3,265,505	27.4	896.1	527,000	----	216,000	----
2001-2	1,541.2	1,411.9	3,029	4,276,704	23.4	1,000.5	713,000	----	203,000	----
2002-3	1,353.0	1,291.7	2,571	3,321,040	18.2	599.7	490,000	----	75,000	----
2003-4[1]	1,344.0	1,312.0	3,159	4,144,150	19.3	799.4	500,000	----	65,000	----
2004-5[2]	1,430.0	1,394.0	3,057	4,261,700	19.6	834.4	500,000	----	65,000	----

[1] Preliminary.   [2] Estimate.   *Source: Economic Research Service, U.S. Department of Agriculture (ERS-USDA)*

Supply and Disposition of Peanuts (Farmer's Stock Basis) & Support Program in the United States

Crop Year	Supply Pro-duction	Supply Imports	Supply Stocks Aug. 1	Supply Total	Disposition Exports	Disposition Crushed for Oil	Disposition Seed, Loss & Residual	Disposition Food	Disposition Total Disap-pearance	Support Price	Addi-tional	Amount Put Under Support Quantity Mil. Lbs.	Amount Put Under Support % of Pro-duction
1995-6	3,461	153	1,198	4,812	826	999	238	1,993	4,054	33.92	6.6	818	24.0
1996-7	3,661	127	758	4,546	668	692	363	2,029	3,750	30.50	6.6	320	8.7
1997-8	3,539	141	795	4,475	682	544	303	2,099	3,627	30.50	6.6	417	11.8
1998-9	3,963	155	848	4,966	562	460	374	2,153	3,574	30.50	8.8	----	----
1999-00	3,829	178	1,392	5,399	727	713	493	2,233	4,166	30.50	8.8	----	----
2000-1	3,266	216	1,233	4,715	527	548	364	2,179	3,618	30.50	6.6	----	----
2001-2	4,277	203	1,097	5,576	713	693	483	2,211	4,100	30.50	6.6	----	----
2002-3[1]	3,320	75	1,476	4,872	490	857	422	2,228	3,997	NA	NA	----	----
2003-4[2]	4,144	65	875	4,892	500	656	378	2,283	3,817	NA	NA	----	----

[1] Preliminary.   [2] Estimate.   *Source: Economic Research Service, U.S. Department of Agriculture (ERS-USDA)*

Production of Peanuts (Harvested for Nuts) in the United States, by States   In Thousands of Pounds

Year	Alabama	Florida	Georgia	New Mexico	North Carolina	Okla homa	South Carolina	Texas	Virgina	Total
1995	483,360	193,590	1,414,880	43,000	347,040	201,880	30,800	540,000	206,925	3,461,475
1996	449,805	236,160	1,433,770	37,950	367,500	195,210	32,550	689,000	219,260	3,661,205
1997	372,490	228,060	1,333,830	46,710	329,640	184,800	30,450	822,150	191,250	3,539,380
1998	432,415	233,100	1,511,655	62,040	397,155	159,750	28,175	917,900	221,250	3,963,440
1999	448,050	260,380	1,400,800	61,600	298,840	189,600	25,300	926,800	218,120	3,829,490
2000	271,180	213,710	1,328,400	54,990	338,250	120,600	29,500	698,500	210,375	3,265,505
2001	532,325	250,100	1,711,620	67,044	356,475	197,890	30,600	895,900	234,750	4,276,704
2002	379,800	197,800	1,313,000	54,000	210,000	159,600	19,140	868,000	119,700	3,321,040
2003	508,750	345,000	1,863,000	45,900	320,000	98,000	57,800	810,000	95,700	4,144,150
2004[1]	557,200	364,000	1,830,000	59,500	357,000	102,300	112,200	775,500	104,000	4,261,700

[1] Preliminary.   *Source: Agricultural Statistics Board, U.S. Department of Agriculture (ASB-USDA)*

Supply and Reported Uses of Shelled Peanuts and Products in the United States In Thousands of Pounds

Crop Year Beginning Aug. 1	Shelled Peanuts Stocks, Aug. 1 Edible	Shelled Peanuts Stocks, Aug. 1 Oil Stock[2]	Shelled Peanuts Production Edible	Shelled Peanuts Production Oil Stock[2]	Candy[3]	Snacks[4]	Sandwich Spread	Butter[5]	Other Products	Total	Shelled Peanuts Crushed[6]	Crude Oil Pro-duction	Cake & Meal Pro-duction
1995-6	752,814	58,188	1,253,451	491,818	350,663	277,089	----	728,076	32,015	1,387,843	751,281	320,909	420,919
1996-7	370,431	126,318	1,692,581	305,674	360,846	290,102	----	727,531	33,825	1,412,304	520,413	220,877	294,590
1997-8	498,954	41,000	1,694,016	290,882	351,017	306,908	----	760,230	35,471	1,453,626	409,249	175,853	228,276
1998-9	580,370	14,091	2,227,037	310,459	380,177	349,806	----	744,706	22,131	1,496,820	345,825	145,254	192,425
1999-00	855,572	16,587	2,157,828	448,875	354,953	394,121	----	772,104	20,227	1,541,405	536,164	228,839	291,491
2000-1	707,672	14,463	1,939,736	337,324	355,610	361,516	----	753,239	19,998	1,490,363	411,558	178,523	230,099
2001-2	680,850	16,648	2,090,776	485,092	349,729	360,916	----	818,927	17,284	1,546,856	521,173	230,791	296,874
2002-3	504,186	24,231	1,983,016	611,627	354,232	344,913	----	828,529	24,379	1,552,053	644,194	285,685	356,888
2003-4[1]	603,529	17,686	2,439,231	394,748	359,197	418,726	----	901,621	15,890	1,695,434	446,245	172,977	226,995

[1] Preliminary.   [2] Includes straight run oil stock peanuts.   [3] Includes peanut butter made by manufacturers for own use in candy.   [4] Formerly titled Salted Peanuts.   [5] Includes peanut butter made by manufacturers for own use in cookies and sandwiches, but excludes peanut butter used in candy.
[6] All crushings regardless of grade.   *Source: National Agricultural Statistics Service, U.S. Department of Agriculture (NASS-USDA)*

PEANUTS AND PEANUT OIL

Shelled Peanuts (Raw Basis) Used in Primary Products, by Type   In Thousands of Pounds

| | Virginia | | | | Runner | | | | Spanish | | | |
Year	Candy[2]	Snack Peanuts	Peanut Butter[3]	Total	Candy[2]	Snack Peanuts	Peanut Butter[3]	Total	Candy[2]	Snack Peanuts	Peanut Butter[3]	Total
1995-6	25,176	93,041	71,310	203,183	304,285	169,142	634,350	1,123,719	21,202	14,906	22,416	60,941
1996-7	24,158	91,882	64,274	193,166	318,924	176,851	634,387	1,149,347	17,764	21,369	28,870	69,791
1997-8	48,428	80,309	59,228	182,100	302,791	206,718	676,839	1,206,946	19,798	19,581	24,163	64,580
1998-9	36,178	99,401	57,864	196,935	321,838	234,486	670,705	1,244,748	22,161	15,919	16,137	55,137
1999-00	23,173	100,384	73,926	200,804	315,467	278,440	690,564	1,300,393	16,313	15,297	7,614	40,208
2000-1	19,101	100,650	102,050	225,072	320,304	247,739	643,229	1,227,156	16,205	13,127	7,960	38,135
2001-2	26,640	97,046	106,573	233,356	303,668	250,079	702,454	1,269,776	19,421	13,791	9,900	43,724
2002-3	26,930	75,100	77,018	183,226	312,192	257,259	734,844	1,323,846	15,110	12,555	16,667	44,981
2003-4[1]	23,593	67,925	88,101	181,298	321,766	336,964	805,764	1,478,341	13,838	13,837	7,756	35,795

[1] Preliminary.   [2] Includes peanut butter made by manufacturers for own use in candy.   [3] Includes peanut butter made by manufacturers for own use in cookies and sandwiches, but excludes peanut butter used in candy.   Source: National Agricultural Statistics Service, U.S. Department of Agriculture (NASS-USDA)

Production, Consumption, Stocks and Foreign Trade of Peanut Oil in the U.S.   In Millions of Pounds

| Crop Year Beginning Aug. 1 | Production | | Consumption | | Stocks Dec. 31 | | Imports for Con- sumption | Exports |
	Crude	Refined	In Refining	In End Products	Crude	Refined		
1996-7	233.9	133.5	138.9	138.4	85.6	2.8	1.6	35.1
1997-8	144.3	104.0	111.6	121.6	42.6	3.0	6.6	8.8
1998-9	172.9	118.3	123.7	180.1	47.2	3.8	30.3	4.3
1999-00	262.9	195.9	238.9	260.4	19.7	1.7	9.6	5.8
2000-1	222.1	206.3	258.9	277.3	23.1	1.9	19.5	5.5
2001-2	278.5	179.1	291.9	282.5	8.2	1.7		
2002-3	267.7	166.3	W	277.6	52.9	3.5		
2003-4[1]	180.7	115.8	W	203.8	23.0	1.8		
2004-5[2]	120.4	83.1	W	240.3	40.3	2.4		

[1] Preliminary.   [2] Forecast.   Source: Bureau of the Census, U.S. Department of Commerce

Production of Crude Peanut Oil in the United States   In Millions of Pounds

Year	Jan.	Feb.	Mar.	Apr.	May	June	July	Aug.	Sept.	Oct.	Nov.	Dec.	Total
1995	27.9	28.6	42.7	36.9	39.2	29.2	26.9	26.3	17.4	13.2	19.5	24.3	332.0
1996	29.2	31.9	36.8	36.8	36.7	33.3	31.4	31.5	27.1	21.1	20.6	21.8	358.2
1997	19.9	16.1	18.8	17.9	13.3	15.9	9.9	12.1	6.1	12.2	11.6	14.0	167.7
1998	16.0	14.5	14.3	13.0	10.8	10.0	9.5	6.3	5.8	6.9	13.6	13.9	134.5
1999	16.2	18.2	15.8	18.2	16.4	20.7	20.8	17.8	16.3	13.5	22.6	22.7	219.2
2000	35.2	32.1	27.4	31.9	30.4	28.0	24.1	28.8	21.5	25.4	16.4	15.2	316.3
2001	17.3	15.7	20.1	15.3	12.4	19.1	16.3	16.7	12.9	17.1	13.8	25.6	202.4
2002	24.8	25.5	32.8	28.5	33.8	24.3	22.6	27.7	27.2	26.5	24.9	20.2	319.0
2003	21.7	16.6	19.4	20.5	20.0	23.2	19.8	17.3	18.3	24.1	15.6	13.2	229.6
2004[1]	12.6	15.7	13.0	14.7	11.8	13.7	10.7	9.8	5.8	10.0	11.9	12.6	142.4

[1] Preliminary.   Source: Bureau of the Census, U.S. Department of Commerce

Average Price of Peanut Meal 50% Southeast Mills   In Dollars Per Short Ton

Year	Oct.	Nov.	Dec.	Jan.	Feb.	Mar.	Apr.	May	June	July	Aug.	Sept.	Average
1995-6	132.50	175.00	204.00	220.00	215.00	210.00	210.00	212.00	210.00	224.25	227.00	192.80	202.70
1996-7	170.00	146.13	172.67	221.00	228.13	225.00	233.75	222.00	235.00	220.00	213.00	210.00	232.00
1997-8	210.00	210.00	210.00	210.00	210.00	210.00	210.00	210.00	210.00	210.00	207.50	205.00	209.60
1998-9	161.00	100.00	103.75	105.00	102.50	91.25	94.50	93.75	100.00	100.00	105.00	102.50	104.94
1999-00	98.00	103.00	103.00	104.00	104.75	110.00	115.00	115.00	119.60	118.00	118.00	118.00	108.15
2000-1	118.00	118.00	118.00	142.50	120.00	118.00	110.75	112.50	NA	123.50	130.50	126.25	121.64
2001-2	115.00	111.25	100.00	102.50	100.00	105.00	110.00	105.00	NA	130.00	135.00	136.88	113.69
2002-3	NA	130.00	122.50	118.50	114.25	124.00	125.00	135.00	135.00	135.75	130.00	130.00	127.27
2003-4	147.10	161.00	163.25	163.35	168.75	200.40	226.00	237.50	204.00	199.33	143.33	133.00	178.92
2004-5[1]	100.38	99.25	93.50	93.25									96.60

[1] Preliminary.   NA = Not available.   Source: Agricultural Marketing Service, U.S. Department of Agriculture (AMS-USDA)

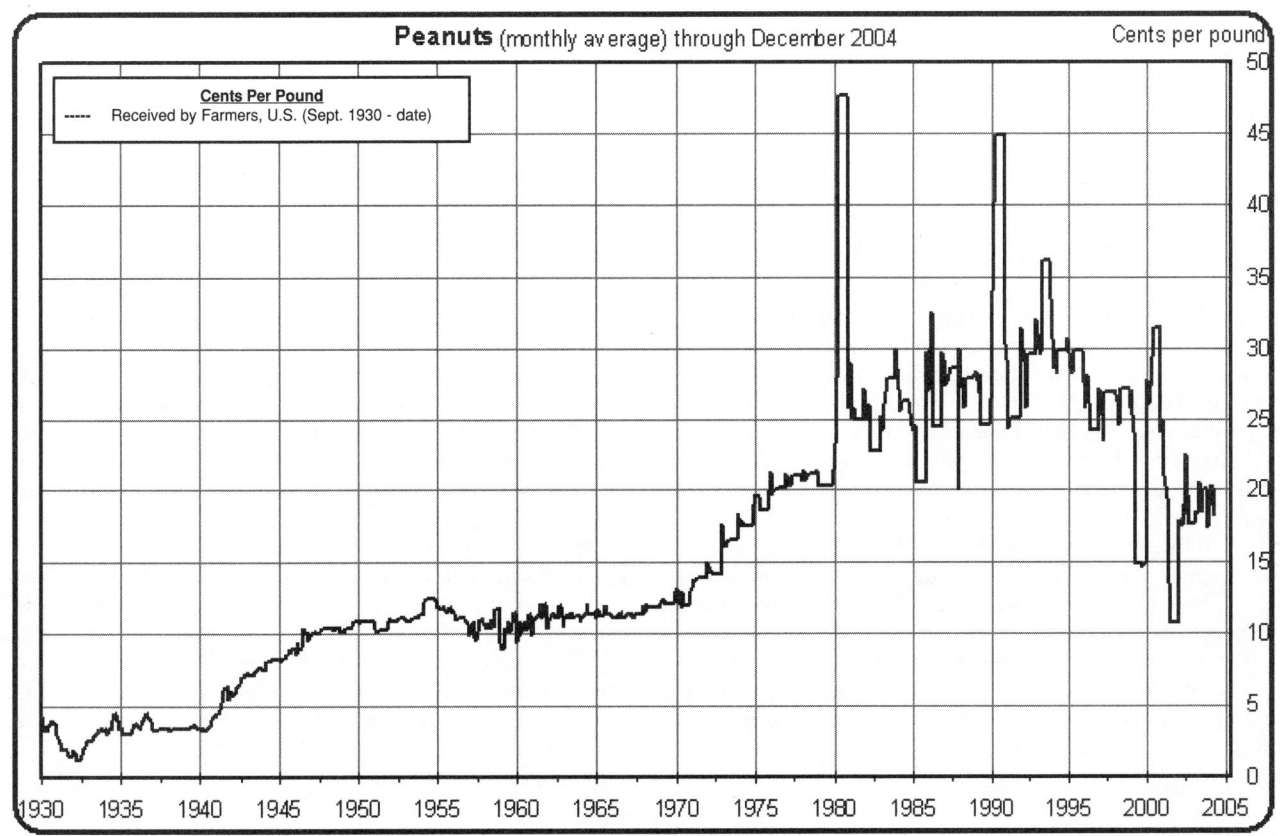

Peanuts (monthly average) through December 2004   Cents per pound

Cents Per Pound
----- Received by Farmers, U.S. (Sept. 1930 - date)

Average Price Received by Producers for Peanuts (in the Shell) in the U.S.   In Cents Per Pound

Year	Aug.	Sept.	Oct.	Nov.	Dec.	Jan.	Feb.	Mar.	Apr.	May	June	July	Average[1]
1995-6	30.6	29.7	28.6	29.5	28.3	29.8	NQ	NQ	NQ	NQ	NQ	NQ	29.4
1996-7	NQ	27.6	25.8	27.1	28.1	24.3	NQ	NQ	NQ	NQ	NQ	NQ	26.6
1997-8	23.3	27.1	25.4	25.0	30.7	24.7	NQ	NQ	NQ	NQ	NQ	NQ	26.0
1998-9	NQ	26.8	26.3	24.6	27.2	NQ	NQ	NQ	NQ	NQ	NQ	NQ	26.2
1999-00	25.7	27.0	25.4	24.1	21.8	14.9	NQ	NQ	NQ	NQ	NQ	NQ	23.2
2000-1	NQ	27.7	26.5	26.1	27.3	31.4	NQ	NQ	NQ	NQ	NQ	NQ	27.8
2001-2	24.1	24.9	22.8	21.0	19.5	13.5	10.7	NQ	NQ	NQ	NQ	NQ	19.5
2002-3	NQ	17.9	17.9	18.0	17.5	19.1	19.6	22.6	18.4	19.6	17.7	NQ	18.8
2003-4	NQ	18.3	18.5	18.4	19.6	20.6	18.9	18.5	20.1	20.0	19.9	17.4	19.1
2004-5[2]	19.0	19.2	20.3	20.2	18.3	18.9	18.9						19.3

[1] Weighted average by sales.   [2] Preliminarly.   NQ = No quote.   *Source: National Agricultural Statistics Service,*
U.S. Department of Agriculture (NASS-USDA)

Average Price of Domestic Crude Peanut Oil (in Tanks) F.O.B. Southeast Mills   In Cents Per Pound

Year	Oct.	Nov.	Dec.	Jan.	Feb.	Mar.	Apr.	May	June	July	Aug.	Sept.	Average
1995-6	42.50	41.63	39.20	37.25	36.00	36.60	39.25	42.80	43.00	43.00	42.60	40.80	40.39
1996-7	41.50	39.20	40.75	43.50	43.88	44.75	45.00	46.20	47.88	48.06	48.00	47.25	44.66
1997-8	49.63	51.00	51.25	51.60	51.00	51.00	50.00	47.20	45.50	44.00	43.75	43.88	48.32
1998-9	45.40	45.00	44.25	44.00	39.75	34.75	35.20	35.00	37.75	39.00	38.75	38.00	39.74
1999-00	40.40	41.00	35.40	33.00	32.50	31.60	33.00	36.25	36.00	35.63	35.00	34.90	35.39
2000-1	34.63	35.50	36.40	37.25	37.00	35.90	34.00	33.00	33.00	33.00	34.00	34.00	34.81
2001-2	36.25	37.00	37.00	35.00	28.00	27.50	27.00	27.00	30.00	34.00	35.20	36.25	32.52
2002-3	NA	42.00	43.67	45.75	46.00	47.00	50.25	52.75	56.60	58.25	60.00	60.67	51.18
2003-4	61.60	63.25	64.50	65.00	61.67	60.00	60.00	56.50	NA	56.00	53.75	55.00	59.75
2004-5[1]	55.00	55.00	55.67	56.00									55.42

[1] Preliminary.   *Source: Agricultural Marketing Service, U.S. Department of Agriculture (AMS-USDA)*

Pepper

The pepper plant is a perennial climbing shrub that originated in India and Sri Lanka. Pepper is considered the world's most important spice and has been used to flavor foods for over 3,000 years. Pepper was once considered so valuable that it was used to ransom Rome from Attila the Hun. Black pepper alone accounts for nearly 35% of the world's spice trade. Unlike many other popular herbs and spices, pepper can only be cultivated in tropical climates. The pepper plant produces a berry called a peppercorn. Both black and white pepper are obtained from the same plant. The colors of pepper are determined by the maturity of the berry at harvest and by different processing methods.

Black pepper is picked when the berries are still green and immature. The peppercorns are then dried in the sun until they turn black. White pepper is picked when the berries are fully ripe and bright red. The red peppercorns are then soaked, washed to remove the skin of the berry, and dried to produce a white to yellowish-white peppercorn. Black pepper has a slightly hotter flavor and stronger aroma than white pepper. Piperine, an alkaloid of pyridine, is the active ingredient in pepper that makes it hot.

Black pepper oil is obtained from crushed berries using solvent extraction. Black pepper oil is used in the treatment of pain, chills, flu, muscular aches, and in some perfumes. It is also helpful in promoting digestion in the colon.

The world's key pepper varieties are known by their place of origin. Popular types of pepper include Lampong Black and Muntok White from Indonesia, Brazilian black, and Malabar Black and Tellicherry from India.

Prices – The average monthly price for black pepper in 2003 fell sharply by –7.0% to 86.5 cents per pound, which was only one-third of the record high of 254.5 cents seen in 1999. The average monthly price for white pepper in 2003, by contrast, rose sharply by +16.6% to 140.6 cents per pound, but was still less than one-half of the record of 356.5 cents seen in 1998.

Trade – The world's largest exporters of pepper in 2002 were Vietnam (with 76,600 metric tons of exports), Indonesia (63,214 metric tons), Brazil (38,280 metric tons), Malaysia (22,840 metric tons), and India (21,066 metric tons).

US imports of black pepper in 2000, the latest reporting year for the series, fell -8.6% to 43,479 metric tons from 47,591 metric tons in 1999, which was a record high. The primary source of US imports of black pepper was Indonesia, which accounted for 36% of US imports, followed by India with 25%, Brazil with 18%, and Malaysia with 10%.

US imports of white pepper in 2000 rose +7.7% to a record high of 7,311 metric tons. The primary source of US imports of white pepper was Indonesia, which accounted for 87% of US imports, followed by 3% shares each from Singapore, Malaysia and China.

World Exports of Pepper (Black and White) and Prices in the United States   In Metric Tons

| | | | | | | | | | New York Spot Prices (Cents Per Pound) | | | | |
| | | | | | | | | | Indonesian | | | Indian | |
Year	Brazil	India	Indo-nesia	Mada-gascar	Malay-sia	Mexico	Sri Lanka	Vietnam	Lampong Black	Muntok White	Brazilian Black	Malabar Black	Telli-cherry[2]
1993	26,254	47,677	27,684	2,001	16,737	2,430	5,032	20,138	62.5	114.6	62.3	62.3	84.0
1994	22,231	36,536	36,036	2,066	23,275	2,615	1,850	16,000	95.3	151.9	95.0	95.0	110.7
1995	22,158	25,270	57,781	1,274	14,869	3,085	2,082	17,900	116.8	182.3	116.8	116.8	150.9
1996	24,178	47,211	36,849	1,570	28,124	4,200	2,612	25,300	114.8	178.9	114.8	114.8	140.0
1997	13,962	35,403	33,386	894	29,000	4,210	3,485	24,713	206.7	304.6	206.7	206.7	225.8
1998	17,249	32,859	38,723	339	18,717	3,365	5,493	15,000	239.5	356.5	239.5	239.5	286.6
1999	19,617	35,635	36,293	619	21,804	4,026	3,754	34,800	254.5	334.9	254.5	254.5	296.3
2000	20,469	19,125	47,502	588	23,684	4,534	4,855	36,400	228.1	227.1	228.1	228.1	282.6
2001	36,975	19,641	53,432	635	25,537	4,658	2,161	57,000	116.2	132.6	116.2	116.2	179.3
2002[1]	38,230	21,066	63,214	880	22,840	4,344	7,915	76,600	92.9	120.5	92.9	92.9	127.8

[1] Preliminary.   [2] Extra bold.   Source: Foreign Agricultural Service, U.S. Department of Agriculture (FAS-USDA)

United States Imports of Unground Pepper from Specified Countries   In Metric Tons

| | Black Pepper | | | | | | | White Pepper | | | | | |
Year	Brazil	India	Indo-nesia	Malay-sia	Singa-pore	Sri Lanka	Total	Brazil	China	Indo-nesia	Malay-sia	Singa-pore	Total
1991	15,069	2,308	11,330	8,154	391	396	38,860	2	7	4,938	37	96	5,174
1992	6,601	9,892	20,768	2,073	52	310	40,590	51	2	5,089	29	261	5,544
1993	4,580	21,985	7,666	209	----	539	35,969	322	114	4,304	137	363	5,481
1994	8,215	21,097	11,877	829	90	386	43,011	312	756	3,974	228	302	6,102
1995	3,165	10,836	19,630	268	30	327	34,465	414	280	4,037	164	211	5,266
1996	4,267	18,350	17,213	1,084	101	411	41,602	519	54	4,370	150	391	5,765
1997	4,328	23,404	13,610	2,203	678	285	45,319	75	522	3,755	199	750	5,751
1998	5,806	15,540	13,045	422	185	578	36,508	32	108	4,571	195	203	5,393
1999	7,093	24,931	8,429	2,392	525	441	47,591	32	451	5,202	420	342	6,789
2000[1]	7,853	10,981	15,713	4,148	306	516	43,479	15	210	6,345	185	215	7,311

[1] Preliminary.   Source: Foreign Agricultural Service, U.S. Department of Agriculture (FAS-USDA)

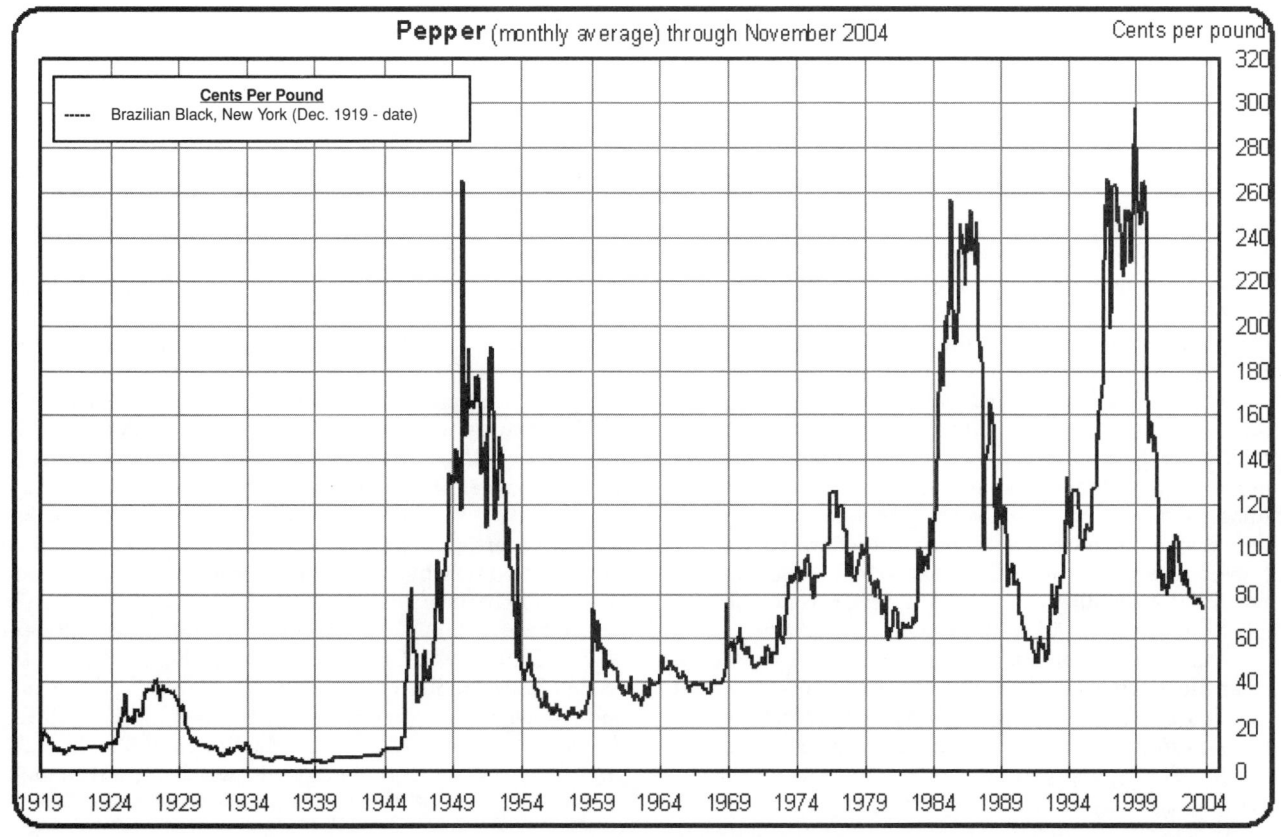

Pepper (monthly average) through November 2004 — Cents per pound

Average Black Pepper in New York (Brazilian)   In Cents Per Pound

Year	Jan.	Feb.	Mar.	Apr.	May	June	July	Aug.	Sept.	Oct.	Nov.	Dec.	Average
1995	111.0	110.0	114.2	124.8	127.3	126.0	127.0	126.3	118.2	113.5	104.8	99.0	116.8
1996	99.3	103.3	109.2	108.3	111.2	109.5	108.0	119.8	126.5	127.5	127.6	128.0	114.8
1997	138.6	151.8	149.0	161.8	173.4	193.8	229.5	255.0	251.3	264.8	266.3	245.0	206.7
1998	199.4	205.5	243.8	262.8	262.8	247.5	253.0	253.8	246.3	243.0	231.3	225.0	239.5
1999	222.5	225.8	252.5	248.0	252.5	250.0	229.0	249.3	263.8	282.0	297.5	281.0	254.5
2000	260.0	256.3	246.0	260.0	265.0	265.0	263.8	252.5	205.0	167.5	147.5	149.0	228.1
2001	157.5	146.3	144.0	150.0	143.8	123.0	97.3	87.0	90.0	89.3	81.6	85.3	116.2
2002	85.0	80.0	81.4	100.5	101.0	92.0	84.8	86.8	93.5	103.5	106.0	100.8	92.9
2003	93.8	89.0	88.5	85.5	83.8	89.0	90.0	86.6	83.5	81.6	80.0	78.0	85.8
2004	78.0	75.5	75.5	75.4	77.3	78.0	76.8	75.0	75.0	74.2	73.3		75.8

Source: Foreign Agricultural Service, U.S. Department of Agriculture (FAS-USDA)

Average White Pepper in New York (Indonesian)[1]   In Cents Per Pound

Year	Jan.	Feb.	Mar.	Apr.	May	June	July	Aug.	Sept.	Oct.	Nov.	Dec.	Average
1995	179.5	175.8	168.0	181.3	195.0	184.2	187.5	190.8	191.0	182.0	178.5	174.2	182.3
1996	174.5	177.5	181.6	179.5	172.6	164.8	154.0	169.6	181.5	193.5	191.8	205.8	178.9
1997	256.0	264.5	255.0	250.0	241.0	248.8	280.3	324.0	332.5	362.0	433.8	407.5	304.6
1998	348.0	346.3	362.5	390.0	393.0	358.8	354.0	356.3	348.8	340.0	340.0	340.0	356.5
1999	361.3	355.0	365.0	355.0	352.5	335.0	310.0	313.8	325.0	327.0	316.3	303.0	334.9
2000	295.0	293.8	264.0	253.8	246.3	242.0	226.3	227.5	205.0	171.3	150.0	150.0	227.1
2001	159.0	151.3	144.0	133.8	130.0	127.0	122.5	129.6	128.0	125.5	120.0	120.0	132.6
2002	111.3	100.3	95.6	108.8	108.0	105.0	104.5	118.8	130.0	154.0	157.5	153.0	120.6
2003	152.4	148.8	150.0	150.0	142.6	133.0	133.0	138.2	137.5	133.6	127.5	125.0	139.3
2004	118.0	118.0	125.8	130.0	130.0	125.0	127.0	120.5	119.0	113.8	109.5		121.5

[1] Muntok White.   *Source: Foreign Agricultural Service, U.S. Department of Agriculture (FAS-USDA)*

Petroleum

Crude oil is petroleum that is acquired directly from the ground. Crude oil was formed millions of years ago from the remains of tiny aquatic plants and animals that lived in ancient seas. Ancient societies such as the Persians, 10th century Sumatrans, and pre-Columbian Indians believed that crude oil had medicinal benefits. Around 4,000 BC in Mesopotamia, bitumen, a tarry crude, was used as caulking for ships, as a setting for jewels and mosaics, and as an adhesive to secure weapon handles. The walls of Babylon and the famed pyramids were held together with bitumen, and Egyptians used it for embalming. During the 19th century in America, an oil find was often met with dismay. Pioneers who dug wells to find water or brine, were disappointed when they struck oil. It wasn't until 1854, with the invention of the kerosene lamp, that the first large-scale demand for petroleum emerged. Crude oil is a relatively abundant commodity. The world has produced approximately 650 billion barrels of oil, but another trillion barrels of proved reserves have yet to be extracted. Crude oil was the world's first trillion-dollar industry and accounts for the single largest product in world trade.

Futures and options on crude oil trade at the New York Mercantile Exchange (Nymex) and at the International Petroleum Exchange in London (IPE). The Nymex trades two main types of crude oil: light sweet crude oil and Brent crude oil. The light sweet futures contract calls for the delivery of 1,000 barrels of crude oil in Cushing, Oklahoma. Light sweet crude is preferred by refiners because of its low sulfur content and relatively high yield of high-value products such as gasoline, diesel fuel, heating oil, and jet fuel. The Brent blend crude is based on a light, sweet North Sea crude oil. Brent blend crude production is approximately 500,000 barrels per day, and is shipped from Sullom Voe in the Shetland Islands.

Prices – NYMEX crude oil prices on the weekly nearest-futures chart in 2004 continued the rally that started in 2002 and posted a record high of $55.67 in October 2004. Oil prices settled back later in 2004 to close the year up +24.4% at $43.45. Bullish factors for crude in 2004 centered mainly on the weak dollar and on increased demand, particularly from China. World demand as of January 2005 was estimated at 83.4 million bpd, up 4.5% from 6 months earlier. In addition, Hurricane Ivan hit the Gulf of Mexico on September 16, 2004 and severely damaged oil platform pipelines in the Gulf of Mexico, causing production from the Gulf of Mexico to drop by some 25% for several months. OPEC (including Iraq) during 2004 ramped up its production to a 25-year high of 30.460 million barrels per day (bpd) in September 2004 to curb the Ivan-related surge in oil prices, but then OPEC started cutting back production near the end of 2004 as oil prices fell in response to Gulf of Mexico production coming back on line. OPEC production, excluding Iraq, in January 2005 was 27.620 million barrels per day, above its 27.0 million barrel per day ceiling, but down 2.4% from the peak of 28.290 bpd seen in October 2004. OPEC produces about one-third of world demand for oil. At its meeting on Jan 30, OPEC dropped its former $22-28 target for a basket of OPEC crude oil as largely irrelevant.

Supply – World crude oil production in 2003, the latest full reporting year, rose +3.6% yr/yr to 69.252 million barrels per day, which was a new record high. The world's largest oil producers are Saudi Arabia (with 12.8% of world production in 2003), Russia (11.7%), the United States (8.2%), Iran (5.5%), China (4.9%), and Mexico (4.9%). US crude oil production in 2003 fell –1.1% yr/yr to 5.681 million barrels per day, which was the lowest level in at least the last 3 decades. Alaskan production in 2003 fell –1.0% yr/yr to 974,000 barrels per day, and was less than one-half of the peak level of 2.107 million barrels per day seen in 1988.

Demand – US demand for crude oil in 2003 rose +2.4% yr/yr to 15.304 million barrels per day, which was a new record high. Most of that demand went for US refinery production into products such as gasoline and diesel fuel, aviation fuel, heating oil, kerosene, asphalt, and lubricants.

Trade – The US is highly dependent on imports of crude oil to meet its energy needs. US imports in 2003, the latest full reporting year, rose +5.7% yr/yr to 9.665 million barrels per day, which was a new record high. US imports of petroleum products in 2003 rose +8.7% to 2.599 million barrels per day, imports of distillate fuel oil rose +24.7% yr/yr to 333,000 barrels per day, and imports of residual fuel oil rose +31.3% yr/yr to 327,000 barrels per day.

World Production of Crude Petroleum   In Thousands of Barrels Per Day

Year	Canada	China	Indo-nesia	Iran	Kuwait	Mexico	Nigeria	Russia	Saudi Arabia	United Kingdom	United States	Vene-zuela	World Total
1995	1,805	2,990	1,503	3,643	2,057	2,618	1,993	5,995	8,231	2,489	6,560	2,750	62,335
1996	1,837	3,131	1,547	3,686	2,062	2,855	2,188	5,850	8,218	2,568	6,465	3,053	63,711
1997	1,893	3,200	1,520	3,664	2,083	3,023	2,317	5,920	8,562	2,517	6,452	3,315	65,690
1998	1,981	3,198	1,518	3,634	2,085	3,070	2,153	2,854	8,389	2,616	6,252	3,167	66,921
1999	1,907	3,206	1,472	3,557	1,898	2,906	2,130	6,079	7,833	2,684	5,881	2,826	65,848
2000	1,977	3,249	1,423	3,696	2,079	3,012	2,165	6,479	8,404	2,275	5,822	3,155	68,342
2001	2,029	3,300	1,340	3,724	1,998	3,157	2,256	6,917	8,031	2,282	5,801	3,010	67,942
2002	2,171	3,390	1,267	3,444	1,894	3,177	2,118	7,408	7,634	2,292	5,746	2,604	66,842
2003[1]	2,306	3,409	1,171	3,779	2,178	3,371	2,241	8,132	8,848	2,093	5,681	2,335	69,188
2004[2]	2,398	3,485	1,113	4,001	2,376	3,383	2,509	8,805	9,101	1,845	5,430	2,557	72,501

Includes lease condensate.   [1] Preliminary.   [2] Estimate.   *Source: Energy Information Administration, U.S. Department of Energy (EIA-DOE)*

Refiner Sales Prices of Residual Fuel Oil   In Cents Per Gallon

Year	Jan.	Feb.	Mar.	Apr.	May	June	July	Aug.	Sept.	Oct.	Nov.	Dec.	Average
1999	27.5	21.8	27.2	30.9	34.6	35.0	38.6	44.8	49.8	47.3	48.5	50.3	38.2
2000	55.3	59.2	53.2	52.3	58.9	65.8	65.1	61.5	71.9	73.7	71.3	66.6	62.7
2001	64.5	61.9	57.2	57.3	58.2	53.0	50.0	50.4	51.2	44.8	40.5	40.0	51.7
2002	51.8	52.2	53.5	59.4	63.5	61.4	63.2	67.4	67.8	72.7	73.6	73.9	64.0
2003	86.6	97.2	98.1	77.3	74.9	71.9	74.5	75.4	72.0	70.7	76.7	79.3	80.4
2004[1]	84.4	80.7	76.3	75.8	79.1	78.7	76.3	79.8	88.3	88.3	93.8		82.0

Sulfur 1% or less, excluding taxes.   [1] Preliminary.   *Source: Energy Information Administration, U.S. Department of Energy (EIA-DOE)*

Refiner Sales Prices of No. 2 Fuel Oil   In Cents Per Gallon

Year	Jan.	Feb.	Mar.	Apr.	May	June	July	Aug.	Sept.	Oct.	Nov.	Dec.	Average
1999	36.3	33.1	39.8	44.7	43.8	44.7	51.2	56.2	60.9	61.0	66.2	67.8	49.3
2000	84.1	92.4	79.6	76.4	78.4	80.3	81.0	88.3	100.9	98.8	100.4	94.1	88.6
2001	90.3	82.5	76.3	79.2	82.7	79.3	72.8	77.0	79.0	68.5	60.6	56.6	75.6
2002	57.6	57.8	64.5	68.3	68.4	66.0	68.9	71.3	78.3	79.6	74.8	80.8	69.4
2003	90.0	108.6	105.3	83.0	75.8	76.9	78.9	83.6	77.3	84.2	84.2	88.6	88.1
2004[1]	97.0	93.0	93.6	95.5	102.9	101.9	109.4	118.8	126.8	147.7	139.3		111.4

Excluding taxes.   [1] Preliminary.   *Source: Energy Information Administration, U.S. Department of Energy (EIA-DOE)*

Refiner Sales Prices of No. 2 Diesel Fuel   In Cents Per Gallon

Year	Jan.	Feb.	Mar.	Apr.	May	June	July	Aug.	Sept.	Oct.	Nov.	Dec.	Average
1999	36.2	35.1	43.2	48.8	47.9	50.4	56.4	61.6	64.9	65.0	69.9	70.5	54.6
2000	77.7	85.2	85.1	79.9	81.4	82.4	83.6	92.1	105.0	104.0	103.2	93.8	89.8
2001	90.7	85.8	78.1	82.6	89.8	85.3	75.5	80.8	84.1	71.4	61.6	54.7	78.4
2002	54.6	56.7	66.6	70.9	70.6	68.2	71.0	75.7	83.4	85.7	78.9	82.0	72.4
2003	89.2	107.8	102.5	86.4	79.2	81.0	83.7	88.8	80.7	87.0	86.5	89.2	88.3
2004[1]	96.2	96.8	101.0	107.6	112.4	107.2	115.6	124.4	133.1	153.1	142.4		117.3

Excluding taxes.   [1] Preliminary.   *Source: Energy Information Administration, U.S. Department of Energy (EIA-DOE)*

Refiner Sales Prices of Kerosine-Type Jet Fuel   In Cents Per Gallon

Year	Jan.	Feb.	Mar.	Apr.	May	June	July	Aug.	Sept.	Oct.	Nov.	Dec.	Average
1999	37.3	35.2	39.5	46.6	46.8	48.6	53.7	59.1	62.7	63.8	66.5	72.1	53.3
2000	80.4	83.6	83.4	77.4	77.9	79.9	83.6	87.9	105.1	104.4	105.1	99.0	88.0
2001	88.2	86.8	80.5	79.5	83.5	82.6	75.9	77.6	80.7	68.5	61.9	55.3	76.3
2002	57.2	57.1	63.9	69.1	69.6	67.8	71.4	73.8	81.5	84.5	75.1	79.9	71.6
2003	89.8	103.1	102.4	82.3	75.1	76.9	81.3	86.2	80.8	83.7	86.5	90.7	87.1
2004[1]	99.7	100.0	101.4	103.3	115.1	108.5	115.6	126.9	132.5	154.9	145.4		118.5

Excluding taxes.   [1] Preliminary.   *Source: Energy Information Administration, U.S. Department of Energy (EIA-DOE)*

Refiner Sales Prices of Propane   In Cents Per Gallon

Year	Jan.	Feb.	Mar.	Apr.	May	June	July	Aug.	Sept.	Oct.	Nov.	Dec.	Average
1999	26.5	26.1	26.8	28.7	29.1	29.1	34.7	38.3	42.6	43.7	42.6	41.8	34.2
2000	49.4	60.2	52.9	48.8	49.3	53.9	54.8	60.3	65.9	64.3	63.3	76.7	59.5
2001	86.4	66.9	60.1	58.6	56.2	48.7	43.6	45.6	46.4	46.1	41.6	38.1	54.1
2002	37.4	36.4	39.7	41.6	40.8	37.9	37.5	41.5	47.1	48.9	49.4	53.3	43.1
2003	60.5	72.7	69.2	53.8	54.3	57.1	55.9	58.6	56.7	59.7	58.7	64.8	60.7
2004[1]	71.7	70.1	61.9	60.4	65.6	66.1	72.1	83.0	80.4	88.6	88.3		73.5

Consumer Grade, Excluding taxes.   [1] Preliminary.   *Source: Energy Information Administration, U.S. Department of Energy (EIA-DOE)*

Supply and Disposition of Crude Oil in the United States   In Thousands of Barrels Per Day

	Supply						Stock	Disposition		Ending Stocks		
Yearly Average	-- Field Production --		Imports			Unaccounted for Crude Oil	Withdrawal[3]		Refinery Inputs	Exports			Other Primary
	Total Domestic	Alaskan	Total	SPR[2]	Other		SPR[2]	Other			Total	SPR[2]	
	In Thousands of Barrels Per Day										In Millions of Barrels		
1997	6,452	1,296	8,225	0	8,225	145	-7	57	14,662	108	868	563	305
1998	6,252	1,175	8,706	0	8,706	115	22	52	14,889	110	895	571	324
1999	5,881	1,050	8,731	8	8,722	191	-11	-107	14,804	118	852	567	284
2000	5,822	970	9,071	8	9,062	155	-73	3	15,067	50	826	541	286
2001	5,801	963	9,328	11	9,318	117	26	73	15,128	20	862	550	312
2002	5,746	984	9,140	16	9,124	110	134	-94	14,947	9	877	599	278
2003	5,681	974	9,665	0	9,665	54	108	-24	15,304	12	907	638	269
2004[1]	5,430	908	10,038	0	10,038	189	102	50	15,479	27	962	676	286

[1] Preliminary.   [2] Strategic Petroleum Reserve.   [3] A negative number indicates a decrease in stocks and a positive number indicates an increase.
Source: Energy Information Administration, U.S. Department of Energy (EIA-DOE)

PETROLEUM

Crude Petroleum Refinery Operations Ratio[1] in the United States   In Percent of Capacity

Year	Jan.	Feb.	Mar.	Apr.	May	June	July	Aug.	Sept.	Oct.	Nov.	Dec.	Average
1995	89.6	87.9	86.7	90.5	94.0	95.6	94.0	94.0	95.6	90.5	92.1	93.3	92.0
1996	90.6	89.1	90.6	93.7	94.4	95.4	93.9	95.0	95.5	94.6	94.7	94.3	93.5
1997	89.3	87.3	90.7	92.6	97.3	97.7	97.1	98.6	99.7	96.7	95.6	97.2	95.0
1998	93.3	91.3	94.4	96.4	97.1	98.9	99.2	99.8	95.0	89.7	94.7	95.1	95.4
1999	90.4	90.0	90.9	94.6	93.9	93.5	94.9	95.5	94.1	91.1	92.0	90.4	92.7
2000	85.7	86.4	89.8	92.6	94.7	96.2	96.9	95.9	94.3	92.4	92.7	94.0	92.6
2001	90.2	90.5	89.4	94.9	96.4	95.6	93.9	93.3	92.2	92.0	92.2	90.2	92.6
2002	87.7	86.6	87.9	93.0	91.5	93.1	93.5	92.9	90.4	87.5	92.6	91.1	90.7
2003	87.2	87.3	90.5	94.0	95.8	94.5	94.0	94.9	93.0	92.4	93.5	92.9	92.5
2004[2]	89.2	88.8	88.6	92.7	96.0	95.0	96.9	97.1	90.1	90.2	94.4	95.0	92.8

[1] Based on the ration of the daily average crude runs to stills to the rated capacity of refineries per day.   [2] Preliminary.
Source: Energy Information Administration, U.S. Department of Energy (EIA-DOE)

Crude Oil Refinery Inputs in the United States   In Thousands of Barrels Per Day

Year	Jan.	Feb.	Mar.	Apr.	May	June	July	Aug.	Sept.	Oct.	Nov.	Dec.	Average
1995	13,604	13,365	13,480	13,817	14,303	14,553	14,403	14,276	14,402	13,598	13,833	14,011	13,973
1996	13,708	13,529	13,755	14,263	14,401	14,535	14,319	14,423	14,483	14,276	14,276	14,194	14,195
1997	13,632	13,425	14,047	14,283	15,083	15,139	14,958	15,217	15,297	14,790	14,654	14,898	14,662
1998	14,313	14,034	14,590	14,961	15,104	15,368	15,496	15,660	14,854	14,001	14,769	14,832	14,889
1999	14,442	14,309	14,498	15,094	14,973	14,959	15,237	15,299	15,107	14,589	14,704	14,410	14,804
2000	13,779	14,028	14,613	15,053	15,494	15,643	15,819	15,640	15,407	15,029	15,023	15,232	15,067
2001	14,789	14,813	14,649	15,536	15,763	15,650	15,369	15,259	15,005	15,002	15,001	14,688	15,128
2002	14,487	14,306	14,526	15,325	15,301	15,397	15,430	15,338	14,861	14,303	15,155	14,900	14,947
2003	14,338	14,381	14,933	15,575	15,910	15,620	15,546	15,693	15,446	15,342	15,455	15,345	15,304
2004[1]	14,816	14,711	14,802	15,546	15,962	16,244	16,140	16,142	14,980	14,954	15,668	15,751	15,476

[1] Preliminary.   *Source: Energy Information Administration, U.S. Department of Energy (EIA-DOE)*

Production of Major Refined Petroleum Products in Continental United States   In Millions of Barrels

Year	Asphalt	Aviation Gasoline	Fuel Oil Distillate	Fuel Oil Residual	Gasoline	Jet Fuel	Kero-sene	Natural Gas Plant Liquids	Lubri-cants	Liquified Gasses Total	Liquified Gasses at L.P.G[2]	Liquified Gasses at L.P.G[3]
1995	170.4	7.8	1,151.7	287.6	2,722	516.8	19.2	643.2	63.7	759.9	521.1	238.8
1996	167.8	7.3	1,213.6	265.5	2,769	554.5	22.8	669.8	63.3	789.1	546.7	242.5
1997	177.0	7.2	1,238.0	258.3	2,826	567.3	23.9	663.3	65.9	799.4	547.3	252.2
1998	179.7	7.3	1,248.6	278.0	2,865	554.6	28.6	639.9	67.2	771.2	526.3	244.9
1999	184.3	7.5	1,240.8	254.8	2,896	571.3	24.4	675.1	66.8	811.0	564.5	246.5
2000	180.6	6.2	1,189.9	234.3	2,664	536.6	20.4	649.4	60.9	788.0	545.5	242.5
2001	177.3	6.5	1,348.4	262.8	2,913	558.2	26.7	680.3	64.1	810.1	569.1	241.0
2002	179.9	6.4	1,309.8	218.8	2,983	552.3	20.8	686.5	63.3	822.5	576.8	245.7
2003	181.0	5.8	1,355.5	241.8	2,992	543.1	20.4	626.7	60.6	766.1	526.4	239.6
2004[1]	185.6	6.2	1,397.6	238.0	3,013	566.3	23.2	662.7	62.0	797.2	561.3	235.9

[1] Preliminary.   [2] Gas processing plants.   [3] Refineries.   *Source: Energy Information Administration, U.S. Department of Energy (EIA-DOE)*

Stocks of Petroleum and Products in the United States on January 1   In Millions of Barrels

Year	Crude Petroleum	Strategic Reserve	Refined Products Total	Asphalt	Aviation Gasoline	Fuel Oil Distillate	Fuel Oil Residual	Finished Gasoline	Jet Fuel	Kero-sene	Liquified Gases[2]	Lubri-cants	Motor Gasoline Total	Motor Gasoline Finished[3]
1996	895.0	591.6	401.2	22.5	2.3	130.2	37.2	161.3	40.0	7.2	93.1	13.0	206	161
1997	849.7	565.8	452.6	20.5	2.3	126.7	45.9	157.0	39.9	7.0	86.2	12.7	202	157
1998	868.1	563.4	451.6	22.1	1.7	138.4	40.5	166.4	44.0	7.3	89.5	12.9	213	166
1999	894.9	571.4	407.1	21.4	1.8	156.1	44.9	171.8	44.7	6.9	115.1	13.2	219	172
2000	851.7	567.2	407.1	16.9	1.6	125.5	35.8	154.1	40.5	4.9	89.3	11.8	196	154
2001	826.2	540.7	415.7	25.0	1.3	118.0	36.2	153.0	44.5	4.1	82.5	12.1	207	153
2002	862.2	550.2	445.6	20.6	1.5	144.5	41.0	161.5	42.0	5.4	120.9	13.8	214	161
2003	876.7	599.1	425.1	21.3	1.4	134.1	31.3	161.9	39.2	5.5	105.7	12.0	199	162
2004	906.3	638.4	413.1	19.3	1.2	136.8	37.8	146.8	38.7	5.6	94.4	10.0		147
2005[1]	961.9	675.6	405.6	22.1	1.3	126.0	42.4	143.1	40.2	4.9	111.0	10.4		143

[1] Preliminary.   [2] Includes ethane & ethylene at plants and refineries.   [3] Includes oxygenated.   *Source: Energy Information Administration, U.S. Department of Energy (EIA-DOE)*

Stocks of Crude Petroleum in the United States, on First of Month   In Millions of Barrels

Year	Jan.	Feb.	Mar.	Apr.	May	June	July	Aug.	Sept.	Oct.	Nov.	Dec.
1995	922.2	920.8	931.0	929.4	924.1	919.6	907.3	899.5	897.5	902.8	910.6	894.9
1996	894.9	894.7	892.9	888.8	889.7	889.7	898.9	891.3	890.8	875.8	881.5	869.1
1997	849.7	865.9	862.1	877.6	883.9	890.5	885.3	873.0	864.2	866.6	879.3	886.9
1998	868.1	884.3	885.7	899.8	914.6	916.1	896.4	902.6	893.5	873.0	897.4	906.2
1999	894.4	896.6	897.4	908.0	902.3	914.8	902.8	906.0	889.1	878.0	875.7	866.2
2000	851.6	852.4	855.2	866.5	873.2	864.1	859.5	852.6	858.7	848.2	842.4	833.9
2001	826.2	836.0	824.2	850.8	873.0	871.7	851.5	856.6	851.6	854.1	858.4	859.5
2002	862.2	874.9	887.4	895.0	891.3	898.3	894.1	882.8	878.5	857.8	881.1	884.0
2003	876.7	872.2	869.6	879.7	889.8	886.7	891.7	895.6	896.0	908.9	924.6	913.9
2004[1]	906.4	912.6	923.6	945.8	957.2	962.9	966.9	961.1	949.3	944.8	958.7	964.4

[1] Preliminary.   *Source: Energy Information Administration; U.S. Department of Energy (EIA-DOE)*

Production of Crude Petroleum in the United States   In Thousands of Barrels Per Day

Year	Jan.	Feb.	Mar.	Apr.	May	June	July	Aug.	Sept.	Oct.	Nov.	Dec.	Average
1995	6,682	6,794	6,600	6,604	6,629	6,579	6,449	6,447	6,416	6,421	6,585	6,530	6,560
1996	6,495	6,577	6,571	6,444	6,394	6,458	6,338	6,360	6,482	6,481	6,476	6,506	6,465
1997	6,402	6,514	6,452	6,441	6,474	6,442	6,409	6,347	6,486	6,467	6,459	6,531	6,452
1998	6,541	6,476	6,408	6,483	6,347	6,267	6,194	6,203	5,789	6,143	6,140	6,043	6,252
1999	5,963	5,966	5,883	5,887	5,875	5,760	5,798	5,780	5,804	5,947	5,960	5,959	5,881
2000	5,784	5,852	5,918	5,854	5,847	5,823	5,739	5,789	5,758	5,809	5,833	5,855	5,822
2001	5,799	5,780	5,880	5,863	5,829	5,766	5,749	5,725	5,709	5,746	5,881	5,887	5,801
2002	5,848	5,871	5,883	5,859	5,924	5,915	5,770	5,811	5,411	5,363	5,597	5,699	5,746
2003	5,785	5,791	5,817	5,774	5,733	5,701	5,526	5,595	5,683	5,635	5,560	5,579	5,681
2004[1]	5,644	5,584	5,622	5,568	5,612	5,403	5,404	5,280	5,091	5,112	5,397	5,448	5,430

[1] Preliminary.   *Source: Energy Information Administration, U.S. Department of Energy (EIA-DOE)*

U.S. Foreign Trade of Petroleum and Products   In Thousands of Barrels Per Day

	----- Exports -----			---- Imports ----					----- Exports -----			---- Imports ----			
		Petro-leum		Petro-leum	Distillate	Residual	Net			Petro-leum		Petro-leum	Distillate	Residual	Net
Year	Total[2]	Products	Crude	Products	Fuel Oil	Fuel Oil	Imports[3]	Year	Total[2]	Products	Crude	Products	Fuel Oil	Fuel Oil	Imports[3]
1985	781	577	3,201	1,866	200	510	4,286	1995	949	855	7,230	1,605	193	187	7,886
1986	785	631	4,178	2,045	247	669	5,439	1996	981	871	7,508	1,971	230	248	8,498
1987	764	613	4,674	2,004	255	565	5,914	1997	1,003	896	8,225	1,936	228	194	9,158
1988	815	661	5,107	2,295	302	644	6,587	1998	945	835	8,706	2,002	210	275	9,764
1989	859	717	5,843	2,217	306	629	7,202	1999	940	822	8,731	2,122	250	237	9,912
1990	857	748	5,894	2,123	278	504	7,161	2000	1,040	990	9,071	2,389	295	352	10,419
1991	1,001	885	5,782	1,844	205	453	6,626	2001	971	951	9,328	2,543	344	295	10,900
1992	950	861	6,083	1,805	216	375	6,938	2002	984	975	9,140	2,390	267	249	10,546
1993	1,003	904	6,787	1,833	184	373	7,618	2003	1,027	1,014	9,665	2,599	333	327	11,238
1994	942	843	7,063	1,933	203	314	8,054	2004[1]	1,048	1,021	10,038	2,861	320	371	11,851

[1] Preliminary.   [2] Includes crude oil.   [3] Equals imports minus exports.   *Source: Energy Information Administration, U.S. Department of Energy (EIA-DOE)*

Domestic First Purchase Price of Crude Petroleum at Wells[1]   In Dollars Per Barrel

Year	Jan.	Feb.	Mar.	Apr.	May	June	July	Aug.	Sept.	Oct.	Nov.	Dec.	Average
1995	14.00	14.69	14.68	15.84	15.85	15.02	14.01	14.13	14.49	13.68	14.03	15.02	14.62
1996	15.43	15.54	17.63	19.58	17.94	16.94	17.63	18.29	19.93	21.09	20.20	21.34	18.46
1997	21.76	19.38	17.85	16.64	17.24	15.90	15.91	16.21	16.44	17.68	16.84	15.06	17.23
1998	13.48	12.16	11.53	11.64	11.49	10.00	10.46	10.18	11.28	11.32	9.65	8.05	10.87
1999	8.57	8.60	10.76	12.82	13.92	14.39	16.12	17.58	20.03	19.71	21.35	22.55	15.56
2000	23.53	25.48	26.19	23.20	25.58	27.62	26.81	27.91	29.72	29.65	30.36	24.46	26.72
2001	24.58	25.27	23.02	23.41	24.06	23.43	22.94	23.08	22.37	18.73	16.49	15.54	21.84
2002	15.89	16.92	20.04	22.14	23.51	22.59	23.51	24.76	26.08	25.29	23.38	25.29	22.51
2003	28.35	31.85	30.09	25.46	24.96	26.83	27.53	27.94	25.23	26.52	27.21	28.54	27.54
2004[2]	30.35	31.21	32.86	33.23	36.07	34.53	36.54	40.10	40.52	46.28	42.99		36.79

[1] Buyers posted prices.   [2] Preliminary.   *Source: Energy Information Administration, U.S. Department of Energy (EIA-DOE)*

Light Crude Oil Futures - New York Mercantile Exchange
(weekly close) as of December 31, 2004

Volume of Trading of Crude Oil Futures in New York   In Thousands of Contracts

Year	Jan.	Feb.	Mar.	Apr.	May	June	July	Aug.	Sept.	Oct.	Nov.	Dec.	Total
1995	2,133	1,657	2,290	2,220	2,409	2,172	1,749	1,794	1,968	1,835	1,739	1,647	23,614
1996	2,260	1,928	2,399	2,490	2,161	1,602	1,732	1,657	1,913	2,098	1,643	1,604	23,488
1997	1,950	1,974	2,087	2,034	2,135	2,099	2,221	2,054	2,028	2,574	1,770	1,847	24,771
1998	2,468	2,208	2,903	2,451	2,604	3,079	2,375	2,067	2,618	2,592	2,553	2,577	30,496
1999	2,534	2,326	3,768	3,167	3,038	3,307	3,471	3,355	3,388	3,571	3,465	2,470	37,860
2000	3,139	3,077	3,380	2,579	3,002	3,232	2,750	3,149	3,712	3,418	2,824	2,620	36,883
2001	3,035	2,855	3,449	3,312	3,469	3,572	3,170	3,316	2,773	2,913	3,210	2,455	37,531
2002	3,481	3,150	3,790	4,315	4,317	3,429	3,466	3,883	3,939	4,397	3,478	4,034	45,679
2003	4,553	4,039	4,151	3,355	3,329	3,534	3,401	3,732	3,826	4,248	3,624	3,646	45,437
2004	4,118	3,887	4,495	4,326	4,250	4,633	4,063	4,987	4,711	4,794	4,510	4,108	52,883

Source: New York Mercantile Exchange (NYMEX)

Average Open Interest of Crude Oil Futures in New York   In Contracts

Year	Jan.	Feb.	Mar.	Apr.	May	June	July	Aug.	Sept.	Oct.	Nov.	Dec.
1995	373,798	379,329	353,805	364,929	350,826	346,051	357,718	343,636	342,360	334,170	329,786	348,954
1996	389,935	400,236	427,306	460,841	424,994	376,164	367,405	364,458	395,358	410,387	385,415	368,331
1997	365,522	384,737	408,751	409,719	401,663	397,245	411,292	424,529	405,389	419,821	404,597	424,333
1998	424,810	445,167	468,438	463,961	450,611	467,998	476,516	486,499	486,047	481,657	487,175	501,591
1999	501,655	524,677	581,072	611,727	594,032	582,058	601,212	584,962	622,257	595,743	564,488	531,567
2000	512,049	519,090	513,359	467,259	453,042	462,476	432,571	416,934	461,298	478,242	479,008	438,118
2001	432,892	437,188	432,627	419,904	442,950	462,321	451,005	461,851	434,967	430,774	435,178	436,332
2002	448,063	454,154	497,405	488,061	512,413	474,087	457,033	454,219	505,530	528,548	482,227	531,078
2003	608,254	640,979	568,526	495,456	478,886	494,078	517,539	542,573	507,191	532,024	550,369	580,586
2004	647,658	656,889	673,520	690,021	722,494	705,104	692,850	705,577	684,819	716,973	705,218	676,250

Source: New York Mercantile Exchange (NYMEX)

Plastics

Plastics are moldable, chemically fabricated materials produced mostly from fossil fuels, such as oil, coal, or natural gas. The word plastic is derived from the Greek *plastikos*, meaning "to mold," and the Latin *plasticus*, meaning "capable of molding." Leo Baekeland created the first commercially successful thermosetting synthetic resin in 1909. More than 50 families of plastics have since been produced.

All plastics can be divided into either thermoplastics or thermosetting plastics. The difference is the way in which they respond to heat. Thermoplastics can be repeatedly softened by heat and hardened by cooling. Thermosetting plastics harden permanently after being heated once.

Prices – Plastics prices in 2004 showed the second consecutive year of strong gains following the recessionary lows seen in 2001 and 2002. Specifically, the average monthly producer price index of plastic resins and materials in the US in 2004 (through November) rose +9.5% yr/yr to 146.1, rebounding farther from the 5-year low of 130.7 posted in 2002. The average monthly producer price index of thermoplastic resins in the US in 2004 (through November) rose +9.7% yr/yr to 160.7, rebounding farther from the 5-year low of 129.1 posted in 2002. The average monthly producer price index of styrene plastic materials (also a thermoplastic) in the US in 2003 (the last available data year) rose +21.2% to 115.7 from the 24-year low of 95.5 posted in 2002. The average monthly producer price index of thermosetting

resins in the US in 2004 (through November) rose +8.3% yr/yr to a record high of 167.1.

Supply – Total US plastics production in 2003 fell -0.5% yr/yr to 107.669 billion pounds, down from the record of 108.262 billion pounds seen in 2002. US plastics production has more than doubled in the past two decades.

By sector, the thermoplastics sector is by far the largest, with 2003 production falling -0.8% yr/yr to 86.971 billion pounds and accounting for 80% of total US plastic production. Production in the thermosetting plastic sector (polyester unsaturated, phenolic, and epoxy) fell -1.8% yr/yr in 2003 to 7.754 billion pounds and accounted for 7% of total US plastics production. The category of "other plastics" rose +1.7% to 13.844 billion pounds and accounted for 13% of total US plastics production.

Demand – The breakdown by market for the usage of plastic resins shows that the largest single consumption category is "packaging" with 27.464 billion pounds of usage in 2003, accounting for 34% of total US consumption. After packaging, the largest categories are "building and construction" (18% of US consumption), and "commercial and industrial" (18%).

Trade – US exports of plastics in 2003 fell -10.3% yr/yr to 9.009 billion pounds, and were well below the record high of 10.048 billion pounds seen in 2002. US exports accounted for 11% of US supply disappearance in 2003.

Plastics Production by Resin in the United States   In Millions of Pounds

| | Thermosets | | | | -- Thermoplastics -- | | | | | | | | | | | |
Year	Polyester Unsat- urated	Phenlic	Epoxy	Total Thermo- sets	Thermo- plastic Polyester	Polyvinyl Chloride	Poly- styrene	Poly- propylene	Nylon	Low Density Polye- thylene[1]	High Density Polye- thylene	Total Thermo- plastics	Total Selected Plastics	Other Plastics	Total Plastics
1994	1,468	3,229	601	7,513	3,196	11,712	5,848	9,539	943	12,600	11,117	56,794	64,307	11,664	75,971
1995	1,577	3,204	632	7,519	3,785	12,295	5,656	10,890	1,020	12,886	11,211	59,331	66,850	11,834	78,684
1996	1,557	3,476	662	8,129	4,031	13,220	6,065	11,991	1,103	14,145	12,373	64,526	72,655	11,640	84,295
1997	1,621	3,734	654	8,647	4,260	14,084	6,380	13,320	1,222	14,579	12,557	67,872	76,519	12,287	88,806
1998	1,713	3,940	639	9,163	4,423	14,502	6,237	13,825	1,285	14,805	12,924	71,209	78,659	13,026	91,685
1999	2,985	4,388	657	8,030	6,735	14,912	7,075	15,493	1,349	15,807	13,864	78,457	86,487	13,467	99,954
2000	3,149	3,965	669	7,783	7,239	14,364	6,676	15,583	1,395	19,588	16,439	84,553	92,336	13,604	105,940
2001	3,021	3,894	597	7,512	6,972	14,626	6,223	16,135	1,159	18,389	15,195	81,726	89,238	12,720	101,958
2002	3,197	4,076	620	7,893	7,480	15,250	6,768	17,084	1,284	19,515	16,190	86,762	94,655	13,607	108,262
2003	3,152	4,015	587	7,754	7,950	14,938	6,478	17,497	1,306	18,915	15,906	86,071	93,825	13,844	107,669

[1] Includes LDPE and LLDPE.   *Source: American Plastics Council (APC)*

Total Resin Sales and Captive Use by Important Markets   In Millions of Pounds (Dry Weight Basis)

Year	Adhesive, Inks & Coatings	Building & Con- struction	Consumer & Indust- rial	Electrical & Elec- tronics	Exports	Furniture & Fur- nishings	Industrial & Mach- inary	Pack- aging	Trans- portation	Other	Total
1994	1,789	14,715	9,266	3,325	6,889	3,118	836	19,551	3,795	7,515	70,799
1995	1,795	13,551	8,921	2,872	7,162	3,189	805	17,107	3,376	7,421	66,200
1996	1,833	15,413	9,662	3,022	7,997	3,468	965	18,691	3,469	8,701	73,221
1997	1,713	11,418	10,357	2,806	8,647	3,099	729	19,135	3,411	8,640	69,955
1998	1,758	12,077	11,031	2,816	8,208	3,293	710	19,396	3,588	9,211	71,994
1999	1,753	13,793	11,645	3,036	8,424	2,885	802	21,210	3,632	10,189	77,123
2000	1,167	14,439	13,495	2,787	9,771	3,572	1,084	23,933	4,389	3,003	77,640
2001	1,143	13,988	13,409	2,501	9,295	3,226	968	25,948	4,207	2,705	77,390
2002	1,165	14,729	14,091	3,037	10,048	3,507	998	27,728	4,738	2,283	82,324
2003	1,170	14,495	14,194	2,862	9,009	3,361	962	27,464	4,732	2,021	80,270

Source: American Plastics Council (APC)

PLASTICS

Average Producer Price Index of Plastic Resins and Materials (066) in the United States (1982 = 100)

Year	Jan.	Feb.	Mar.	Apr.	May	June	July	Aug.	Sept.	Oct.	Nov.	Dec.	Average
1995	142.5	144.1	145.9	148.5	149.0	148.9	147.0	144.8	142.7	139.2	135.8	132.2	143.4
1996	129.9	128.4	128.4	127.7	130.6	132.1	133.2	135.2	137.9	138.0	138.0	137.7	133.1
1997	137.0	137.5	138.7	138.9	139.1	139.6	139.3	137.4	136.0	135.9	134.6	133.9	137.3
1998	134.0	132.2	131.0	130.7	128.8	126.8	125.0	123.7	119.6	118.6	117.1	115.9	125.3
1999	115.9	115.8	117.3	118.6	122.1	123.1	127.9	130.0	133.8	135.6	135.8	134.3	125.8
2000	133.2	135.7	139.4	143.7	147.4	147.8	146.4	146.3	142.4	140.7	138.8	137.3	141.6
2001	137.8	139.3	141.4	141.9	139.9	137.6	135.1	131.3	126.8	128.3	126.6	123.9	134.2
2002	122.0	121.3	123.1	125.4	128.0	130.1	135.3	136.4	136.7	138.2	137.0	135.3	130.7
2003	137.2	141.8	149.6	153.2	152.4	149.2	144.9	143.6	144.9	146.2	145.8	144.0	146.1
2004[1]	146.2	150.4	151.4	154.8	156.5	159.6	161.1	164.9	167.9	171.1	178.2	186.2	162.4

[1] Preliminary.   *Source: Bureau of Labor Statistics, U.S. Department of Commerce (BLS)*

Average Producer Price Index of Thermoplastic Resins (0662) in the United States (1982 = 100)

Year	Jan.	Feb.	Mar.	Apr.	May	June	July	Aug.	Sept.	Oct.	Nov.	Dec.	Average
1995	143.1	145.0	147.1	150.3	151.0	151.2	148.7	146.2	143.7	139.6	135.5	131.1	144.4
1996	128.4	126.7	126.8	125.9	129.4	131.1	132.5	134.8	137.8	137.9	137.9	137.6	132.2
1997	136.7	137.3	138.6	138.8	139.0	139.7	139.3	137.0	135.5	135.3	133.8	133.0	137.0
1998	133.0	130.7	129.5	129.2	127.0	124.7	122.5	121.0	116.4	115.3	113.7	112.2	122.9
1999	112.3	112.5	114.4	116.1	120.4	121.6	127.5	129.9	134.5	136.7	137.0	135.2	124.9
2000	133.8	136.0	140.4	145.2	149.3	149.6	147.6	147.4	142.7	140.3	137.9	136.0	142.2
2001	136.3	138.0	140.2	140.8	138.4	135.7	133.1	128.6	123.4	125.7	123.9	120.8	132.1
2002	118.4	117.8	120.3	123.8	126.2	128.6	135.0	135.9	136.2	137.6	136.1	133.8	129.1
2003	136.3	142.2	151.4	155.8	153.6	149.5	144.3	142.8	144.7	146.3	146.2	143.9	146.4
2004[1]	146.7	151.9	152.6	156.4	157.5	160.9	162.3	165.5	167.7	171.4	177.8	187.6	163.2

[1] Preliminary.   *Source: Bureau of Labor Statistics, U.S. Department of Commerce (BLS)*

Average Producer Price Index of Styrene Plastics Materials (0662-06) in the United States (1982 = 100)

Year	Jan.	Feb.	Mar.	Apr.	May	June	July	Aug.	Sept.	Oct.	Nov.	Dec.	Average
1995	129.0	127.0	132.5	134.7	135.9	137.5	135.1	133.2	132.1	130.1	127.9	126.1	131.8
1996	125.7	123.5	125.0	118.3	120.1	122.7	123.4	123.3	123.6	122.8	122.0	120.9	122.6
1997	120.6	123.1	123.0	121.6	121.6	121.6	122.7	117.7	118.0	116.5	113.5	113.7	119.5
1998	113.3	113.9	115.5	114.9	114.1	112.8	111.3	111.2	107.6	107.9	107.1	106.3	111.3
1999	103.5	102.4	103.5	104.7	103.0	102.3	103.1	101.5	101.4	99.8	99.4	100.5	102.1
2000	103.0	104.3	110.5	113.0	116.2	116.9	118.5	116.5	115.0	114.1	112.1	110.4	112.5
2001	110.5	109.2	107.9	108.0	101.8	99.9	97.6	95.7	87.3	89.4	90.0	85.4	98.6
2002	85.7	85.8	87.9	88.5	90.4	91.7	93.7	100.6	100.5	108.9	108.1	103.9	95.5
2003[1]	102.9	110.2	119.5	127.2	126.7	119.1	118.0	113.3	112.8	113.6	113.7	111.6	115.7
2004[1]	NA	NA	NA	NA	NA	NA	NA	NA	NA	NA	NA	NA	NA

[1] Preliminary.   *Source: Bureau of Labor Statistics, U.S. Department of Commerce (BLS)*

Average Producer Price Index of Thermosetting Resins (0663) in the United States (1982 = 100)

Year	Jan.	Feb.	Mar.	Apr.	May	June	July	Aug.	Sept.	Oct.	Nov.	Dec.	Average
1995	144.3	145.1	145.4	145.2	144.7	143.5	144.0	143.5	142.9	142.3	142.4	142.1	143.8
1996	141.8	141.9	141.2	141.3	141.4	141.2	140.6	141.5	141.7	142.0	142.0	142.2	141.6
1997	142.1	142.3	142.7	143.1	143.2	143.0	142.8	142.9	143.0	143.1	142.9	142.9	142.8
1998	143.6	144.0	143.2	142.9	142.6	142.7	142.5	142.2	141.2	140.9	140.1	140.3	142.2
1999	139.9	138.1	137.7	137.4	136.9	136.5	136.2	136.5	136.5	136.5	136.3	136.2	137.0
2000	136.8	141.1	141.3	142.8	144.9	146.0	147.6	147.8	147.5	149.5	150.3	151.0	145.6
2001	152.1	152.9	154.5	154.4	154.2	154.2	152.3	151.3	150.4	148.2	146.3	146.1	151.4
2002	146.2	144.6	143.8	141.2	144.1	145.5	145.8	147.6	148.4	150.3	150.3	150.6	146.5
2003	150.4	149.7	151.7	152.0	156.8	157.9	157.1	156.4	155.7	155.6	153.8	153.8	154.2
2004[1]	154.0	154.2	155.9	158.3	162.2	164.3	166.4	173.2	179.8	181.2	191.6	192.4	169.5

[1] Preliminary.   *Source: Bureau of Labor Statistics, U.S. Department of Commerce (BLS)*

204

Platinum-Group Metals

Platinum is a relatively rare, chemically inert metallic element that is more valuable than gold. Platinum is a grayish-white metal that has a high fusing point, is malleable and ductile, and has a high electrical resistance. Chemically, platinum is relatively inert and resists attack by air, water, single acids, and ordinary reagents. Weighing almost twice as much as gold, platinum is the heaviest of the precious metals. Platinum is the most important of the six-metal group, which also includes ruthenium, rhodium, palladium, osmium, and iridium. The word "platinum" is derived from the Spanish word *platina* meaning silver.

Platinum is one of the world's rarest metals with new mine production totaling only about 5 million troy ounces a year. All the platinum mined to date would fit in the average-size living room. Platinum is mined all over the world with supplies concentrated in South Africa. South Africa accounts for nearly 80% of world supply, followed by Russia, and North America.

Because platinum will never tarnish, lose its rich white luster, or even wear down after many years, it is prized by the jewelry industry. The international jewelry industry is the largest consumer sector for platinum, accounting for 51% of total platinum demand. In Europe and the US, the normal purity of platinum is 95%. Ten tons of ore must be mined and a five-month process is needed to produce one ounce of pure platinum.

The second major consumer sector for platinum is for auto catalysts, with 21% of total platinum demand. Catalysts in autos are used to convert most of vehicle emissions into less harmful carbon dioxide, nitrogen, and water vapor. Platinum is also used in the production of hard disk drive coatings, fiber optic cables, infra-red detectors, fertilizers, explosives, petrol additives, platinum-tipped spark plugs, glassmaking equipment, biodegradable elements for household detergents, dental restorations, and in anti-cancer drugs.

Palladium is very similar to platinum and is part of the same general metals group. Palladium is mined with platinum, but it is somewhat more common because it is also a by-product of nickel mining. The primary use for palladium is in the use of automotive catalysts, with that sector accounting for about 63% of total palladium demand. Other uses for palladium include electronic equipment (21%), dental alloys (12%), and jewelry (4%).

Rhodium, another member of the platinum group, is also used in the automotive industry in pollution control devices. To some extent palladium has replaced rhodium. Iridium is used to process catalysts and it has also found use in some auto catalysts. Iridium and ruthenium are used in the production of polyvinyl chloride. As the prices of these metals change, there is some substitution. Therefore, strength of platinum prices relative to palladium should lead to the substitution of palladium for platinum in catalytic converters.

Platinum futures and options and palladium futures are traded on the New York Mercantile Exchange (NYMEX). Platinum and palladium futures are traded on the Tokyo Commodity Exchange (TOCOM). The NYMEX platinum futures contract calls for the delivery of 50 troy ounces of platinum (0.9995 fineness) and the contract trades in terms of dollars and cents per troy ounce. The NYMEX palladium futures contract calls for the delivery of 50 troy ounces of palladium (0.9995 fineness) and the contract is priced in terms of dollars and cents per troy ounce.

Prices – NYMEX platinum futures prices started out 2004 at $811.30 per ounce and then extended the rally seen in 2003 to a 2-1/3 year high of $954.00 in April. Platinum prices took a sharp tumble in late April, and then traded mildly higher in a narrow range the remainder of the year to close 2004 at $863.70. NYMEX palladium futures prices rallied sharply in early 2004 to post a new 2-1/3 year high of $344.70 in April, and then likewise fell sharply in late April. Palladium prices then weakened further during the year to close 2004 at a 1-1/2 year low of $185.25.

Supply – World mine production of platinum in 2003, the latest reporting year, rose by 10.8% yr/yr to 205,000 kilograms, which was a record high production level. South Africa is the world's largest producer of platinum by far with 74% of world production in 2003, followed by Russia (18%), Canada (4%) and the US (2%). World mine production of palladium in 2003 rose +5.8% to 182,000 kilograms, which was a record high production level. The world's largest palladium producers are Russia with 41% of world production in 2003, South Africa with 40%, the US with 8%, and Canada with 6%. World production of platinum group metals other than platinum and palladium in 2003 rose +14.5% yr/yr to 65,700 kilograms, which was a record high. South Africa accounted for 76% of that production and Russia accounted for 22%.

US mine production of platinum in 2003 fell by –5.0% yr/yr to 4,170 kilograms from the record high of 4,390 kilograms posted in 2002. US mine production of palladium in 2003 fell by –5.4% yr/yr to 14,000 kilograms from the record high of 14,800 kilograms posted in 2002. US refinery production of scrap platinum and palladium in 2003 rose by +5.9% to 22,130 kilograms, which was just above the record low of 20,900 kilograms in 2002.

Demand – The total of platinum-group metals sold to consuming industries in the US in 2002 fell -21.2% yr/yr to 92,834 kilograms from the record high of 117,692 kilograms seen in 2001. The two main US industries that use platinum are the auto industry, which accounts for more than 60% of US platinum usage, and the jewelry industry, which accounts for about one-quarter of US platinum usage.

Trade – US imports of refined platinum and palladium for consumption rose +0.6% yr/yr to 223,653 kilograms, which was mildly above the 8-year low of 222,356 kilograms seen in 2002. US exports of refined platinum and palladium fell -36.4% yr/yr to 45,124 kilograms, which was a 7-year low. The US relied on imports for 96% of its platinum and palladium consumption in 2003.

PLATINUM-GROUP METALS

World Mine Production of Platinum   In Kilograms

Year	Australia	Canada	Colombia[3]	Finland	Japan	Russia	Serbia/ Montenegro	South Africa	United States	Zimbabwe	World Total
1995	100	5,945	973	60	730	27,000	10	102,000	1,590	7	139,000
1996	100	5,155	672	62	816	25,000	10	105,000	1,840	100	139,000
1997	300	4,813	406	60	693	30,000	10	115,861	2,610	345	155,000
1998	150	5,640	411	500	533	30,000	10	116,483	3,240	2,730	160,000
1999	90	5,663	448	500	737	32,000	5	121,304	2,920	479	164,000
2000	171	6,302	339	441	782	34,000	5	114,459	3,110	505	160,000
2001	174	7,410	674	510	791	35,000	5	130,307	3,610	519	179,000
2002[1]	200	7,400	661	508	762	35,000	5	133,796	4,390	2,306	185,000
2003[2]	225	7,400	700	500	750	36,000	5	151,022	4,170	4,400	205,000

[1] Preliminary.   [2] Estimate.   [3] Placer platinum.   *Source: U.S. Geological Survey (USGS)*

World Mine Production of Palladium and Other Group Metals   In Kilograms

	Palladium										Other Group Metals		
Year	Australia	Canada	Finland	Japan	Russia	Serbia/ Montenegro	South Africa	United States	Zimbabwe	World Total	Russia	South Africa	World Total
1995	400	9,319	95	2,174	85,000	50	51,000	5,260	17	153,000	3,600	29,797	34,200
1996	400	8,082	182	2,182	80,000	50	52,600	6,100	120	150,000	3,500	30,363	34,800
1997	400	7,545	180	1,899	70,000	50	55,675	8,430	245	144,000	13,500	25,068	39,200
1998	800	8,905	150	4,151	70,000	50	56,608	10,600	1,855	153,000	13,500	26,862	41,300
1999	816	8,939	150	5,354	67,000	25	58,164	9,800	342	151,000	13,400	37,011	51,200
2000	812	9,949		4,712	71,000	25	55,818	10,300	366	153,000	14,100	36,493	51,400
2001	828	11,700		4,805	72,000	25	62,601	12,100	371	164,000	14,500	35,839	51,100
2002[1]	810	11,500		5,618	73,000	25	64,244	14,800	1,943	172,000	14,500	41,721	57,400
2003[2]	820	11,500		5,600	74,000	20	72,758	14,000	3,170	182,000	14,600	49,594	65,700

[1] Preliminary.   [2] Estimate.   *Source: U.S. Geological Survey (USGS)*

Platinum-Group Metals Sold to Consuming Industries in the United States   In Kilograms

	Automotive		Chemical		Electrical		Dental & Medical		Jewelry & Decorative		Petroleum		All Platinum-Group Metals			
Year	Platinum	Other[3]	Platinum	Other[3]	Platinum	Other[3]	Platinum	Other[3]	Platinum	Other[3]	Platinum	Other[3]	Platinum	Palladium	Other[3]	Total
1995	27,990	12,440	2,022	2,395	4,510	18,225	778	6,158	1,337	1,431	3,421	871	43,524	45,188	----	88,712
1996	28,550	19,282	2,115	2,457	4,541	17,665	778	6,285	1,493	1,493	3,514	902	44,489	45,157	----	89,646
1997	28,923	20,402	2,239	2,426	4,945	19,997	840	6,376	2,115	1,617	3,390	871	46,184	50,227	----	96,411
1998	29,483	26,528	2,301	2,488	5,194	20,215	902	6,376	2,333	1,617	3,390	809	47,396	61,827	----	109,223
1999	31,100	29,390	2,364	2,519	5,443	21,148	933	6,065	3,110	1,679	3,514	778	50,310	65,248	----	115,558
2000	32,344	31,100	2,457	2,139	5,691	19,282	964	3,732	3,670	1,400	3,639	660	52,808	61,889	----	114,697
2001	33,411	34,832	2,644	715	5,909	17,354	995	3,670	4,043	1,431	4,199	715	55,399	62,293	----	117,692
2002[1]	17,727	19,904	3,110	2,333	3,577	6,998	1,244	6,531	9,641	----	1,400	----	33,899	29,079	----	62,978
2003[2]	27,368	40,741	2,955	2,177	3,888	7,464	778	7,153	10,108	----	1,400	----	42,296	50,538	----	92,834

[1] Preliminary.   [2] Estimate.   [3] Includes Palladium, iridium, osmium, rhodium, and ruthenium.   *Sources: U.S. Geological Survey (USGS); American Metal Market (AMM)*

Salient Statistics of Platinum and Allied Metals[3] in the United States   In Kilograms

Year	Net Import Reliance as a % of Apparent Consumption	Mine Production Platinum	Mine Production Palladium	Refinery Production (Secondary)	Total Refined	Refiner, Importer & Dealer Stocks as of Dec. 31 Platinum	Palladium	Other[4]	Total	Imports for Consumption Refined	Total	Exports Refined	Total	Apparent Consumption
1995	----	1,590	5,260	NA	NA	----	----	----	----	214,143	220,613	41,825	50,575	----
1996	84	1,840	6,100	NA	NA	----	----	----	----	248,860	255,880	39,709	48,836	----
1997	84	2,610	8,430	NA	NA	14,100	39,300	920	54,320	253,114	258,424	67,656	81,249	----
1998	94	3,240	10,600	NA	NA	13,700	38,800	920	53,420	297,101	303,351	52,716	73,162	----
1999	----	2,920	9,800	23,300	23,300	7,060	28,200	784	36,044	337,973	----	64,165	----	----
2000	83	3,110	10,300	23,780	23,780	5,190	19,000	784	24,974	316,633	----	84,087	----	----
2001	66	3,610	12,100	24,790	24,790	3,680	16,300	784	20,764	267,957	----	67,334	----	----
2002[1]	93	4,390	14,800	20,900	20,900	649	5,870	784	7,303	222,356	----	70,943	----	----
2003[2]	96	4,170	14,000	22,130	22,130	649	1,170	562	2,381	223,653	----	45,124	----	----

[1] Preliminary.   [2] Estimate.   [3] Includes platinum, palladium, iridium, osmium, rhodium, and ruthenium.   [4] Includes iridium, osmium, rhodium, and ruthenium.   W = Withheld proprietary data.   *Source: U.S. Geological Survey (USGS)*

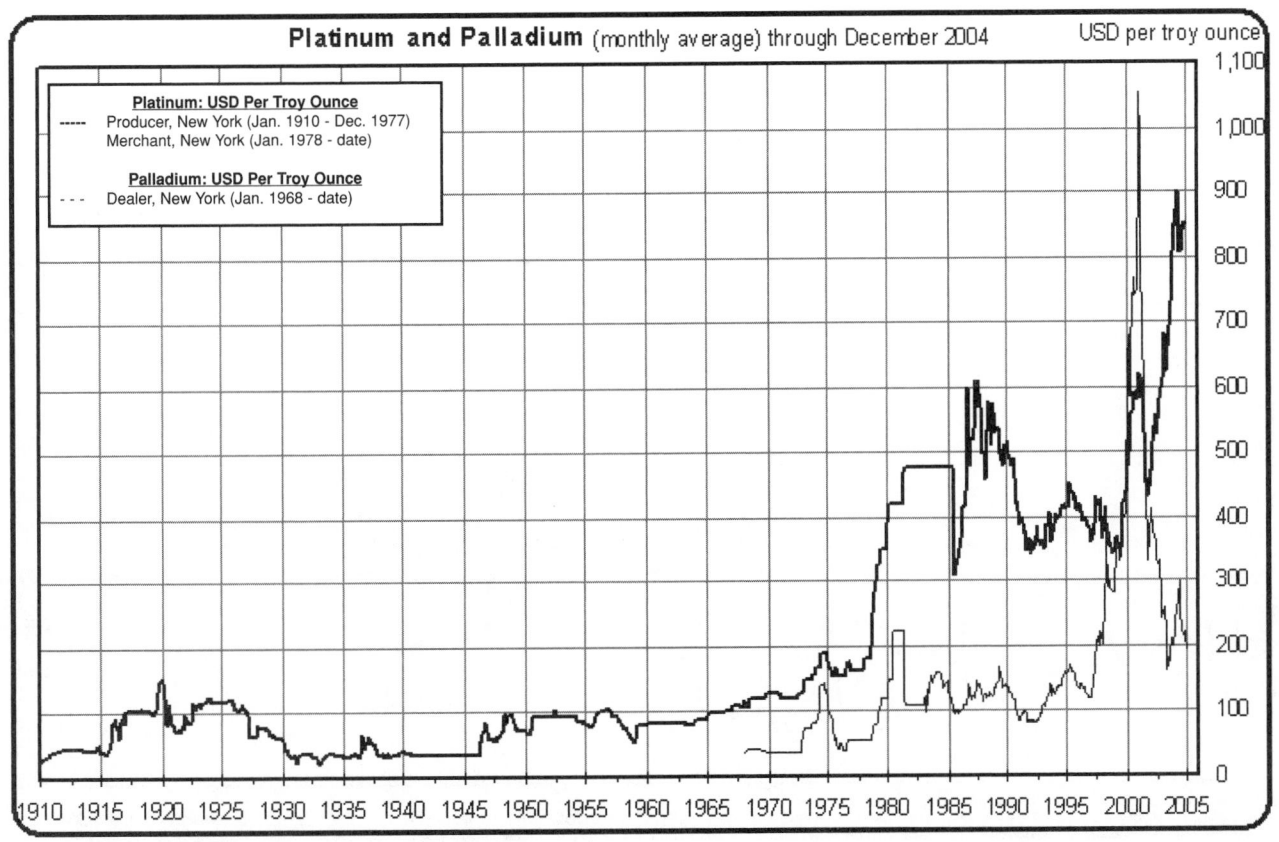

Average Merchant's Price of Platinum in the United States   In Dollars Per Troy Ounce

Year	Jan.	Feb.	Mar.	Apr.	May	June	July	Aug.	Sept.	Oct.	Nov.	Dec.	Average
1995	414.27	415.22	415.37	446.24	439.02	436.58	435.21	425.61	430.31	414.49	413.55	410.17	424.67
1996	416.59	421.45	412.39	405.71	402.86	393.18	392.00	400.97	391.43	385.53	383.92	372.97	398.24
1997	360.13	362.35	382.82	371.18	385.20	427.12	409.93	423.48	424.00	428.59	396.68	369.55	395.42
1998	375.30	390.56	396.18	412.82	392.60	357.38	379.34	372.24	361.40	347.27	348.42	352.76	373.85
1999	353.53	361.55	370.80	357.30	354.75	357.75	350.30	352.24	365.62	421.52	436.48	438.00	376.44
2000	432.95	517.02	478.28	493.53	519.57	557.45	558.53	572.76	592.53	576.91	592.73	608.28	541.49
2001	623.43	453.56	566.67	589.63	611.07	588.91	643.88	457.37	453.50	437.43	427.25	450.24	531.93
2002	471.52	470.68	511.95	539.20	533.66	554.70	526.32	545.48	556.05	580.11	588.15	594.89	539.39
2003	629.52	681.79	675.00	624.48	649.43	661.43	682.02	692.48	705.33	732.65	760.08	807.10	691.78
2004[1]	851.28	846.33	900.26	880.14	807.28	807.55	809.60	848.43	847.88	841.43	853.81	850.89	845.41

[1] Preliminary.   *Source: American Metal Market (AMM)*

Average Dealer[1] Price of Palladium in the United States   In Dollars Per Troy Ounce

Year	Jan.	Feb.	Mar.	Apr.	May	June	July	Aug.	Sept.	Oct.	Nov.	Dec.	Average
1995	156.67	157.53	161.18	170.91	160.87	158.59	156.27	138.81	143.76	137.36	135.57	132.37	150.83
1996	130.47	138.77	138.77	137.10	132.83	129.70	132.69	128.12	122.55	118.35	118.21	117.91	128.79
1997	121.48	134.26	151.13	152.75	167.52	203.62	176.84	210.90	190.17	206.52	209.93	200.70	177.15
1998	222.55	237.25	258.01	310.81	353.58	284.34	307.53	287.48	283.88	277.89	281.82	306.73	284.32
1999	317.28	351.38	351.78	358.83	330.70	339.84	333.17	341.64	358.55	387.05	400.38	420.17	357.50
2000	447.45	607.33	687.72	580.00	574.89	640.80	686.63	759.63	731.15	734.91	778.73	887.33	676.55
2001	1054.10	984.37	792.68	699.15	663.41	619.67	525.90	459.83	444.47	340.52	333.14	405.95	610.27
2002	412.62	377.79	377.15	372.50	360.00	339.20	325.41	327.55	330.50	319.09	289.20	243.57	339.55
2003	258.19	255.68	226.38	164.76	168.90	181.76	174.91	185.76	213.24	204.17	200.17	200.86	202.90
2004[2]	221.00	237.95	272.43	299.52	249.55	231.86	222.95	217.36	213.95	220.43	216.00	193.09	233.01

[1] Based on wholesale quantities, prompt delivery.   [2] Preliminary.   *Source: U.S. Geological Survey (USGS)*

PLATINUM-GROUP METALS

Platinum Futures - New York Mercantile Exchange
(weekly close) as of December 31, 2004
USD Per Troy Ounce

Volume of Trading of Platinum Futures in New York   In Contracts

Year	Jan.	Feb.	Mar.	Apr.	May	June	July	Aug.	Sept.	Oct.	Nov.	Dec.	Total
1995	61,400	38,594	131,294	69,892	60,382	75,353	53,422	62,451	98,837	55,919	56,339	82,810	846,693
1996	80,545	70,260	86,258	54,151	47,929	88,806	53,312	53,654	90,140	47,116	41,970	88,327	802,468
1997	60,515	83,325	86,242	57,719	67,000	72,481	37,836	36,391	62,462	46,188	28,913	58,625	698,597
1998	38,198	35,538	65,871	36,169	36,208	47,464	35,223	27,505	58,302	44,381	42,658	60,752	528,629
1999	37,700	53,698	68,350	36,900	26,507	75,444	57,536	36,115	102,196	30,637	32,176	40,009	597,268
2000	33,226	31,352	35,013	28,057	22,741	47,197	16,527	14,739	36,643	12,122	12,662	30,645	320,924
2001	19,278	12,885	31,617	14,961	15,714	23,245	14,494	12,477	17,040	9,957	11,401	22,890	205,969
2002	12,848	13,807	24,434	11,066	12,294	27,176	14,198	18,583	29,762	11,834	9,878	33,891	219,771
2003	15,545	15,157	38,170	13,472	18,968	30,961	10,852	11,878	37,686	19,275	14,040	42,301	268,305
2004	16,337	15,574	42,249	29,228	13,125	28,495	15,598	18,180	34,076	24,393	18,606	39,834	295,695

Source: New York Mercantile Exchange (NYMEX)

Average Open Interest of Platinum Futures in New York   In Contracts

Year	Jan.	Feb.	Mar.	Apr.	May	June	July	Aug.	Sept.	Oct.	Nov.	Dec.
1995	23,285	23,058	23,470	23,657	20,984	21,533	20,801	25,288	23,489	24,498	22,137	21,534
1996	23,130	21,535	23,156	25,081	26,343	27,720	25,861	25,455	28,511	28,305	27,423	29,143
1997	25,890	26,092	22,364	16,568	18,933	18,440	13,280	14,180	13,639	13,466	12,396	13,501
1998	10,791	10,932	13,220	13,559	12,048	11,471	10,607	9,733	11,950	14,601	15,709	13,289
1999	12,311	14,481	16,493	11,471	12,256	12,436	14,703	13,777	15,014	14,892	13,402	12,017
2000	10,858	10,952	9,218	8,484	9,057	10,585	9,566	9,731	9,716	8,106	8,163	8,507
2001	8,449	7,311	6,855	6,715	7,436	5,751	6,210	5,996	5,646	5,395	6,102	6,033
2002	6,587	6,213	7,121	6,823	6,031	6,901	5,516	6,405	6,930	7,211	7,406	8,388
2003	8,694	8,132	8,034	6,322	6,599	6,847	7,450	8,556	8,794	8,489	9,421	9,373
2004	8,210	7,379	8,879	7,698	5,555	5,590	5,376	6,282	6,091	6,092	7,208	7,184

Source: New York Mercantile Exchange (NYMEX)

Palladium Futures - New York Mercantile Exchange
(weekly close) as of December 31, 2004

USD Per Troy Ounce

Volume of Trading of Palladium Futures in New York   In Contracts

Year	Jan.	Feb.	Mar.	Apr.	May	June	July	Aug.	Sept.	Oct.	Nov.	Dec.	Total
1995	10,684	17,092	21,001	12,775	17,413	9,615	11,816	18,948	9,754	9,320	16,662	11,633	166,713
1996	13,725	33,519	11,931	16,416	27,467	8,989	9,896	23,740	10,721	8,149	28,870	12,187	205,610
1997	13,908	43,160	22,796	21,604	36,422	17,647	18,097	18,751	8,331	13,094	13,143	11,763	238,716
1998	11,506	17,786	18,678	14,042	17,942	7,370	4,241	8,737	6,214	4,962	12,839	6,933	131,250
1999	3,092	11,614	4,082	7,097	8,890	3,411	5,053	6,868	5,826	3,722	10,670	5,069	75,394
2000	4,584	13,976	2,803	1,833	7,034	2,622	3,120	5,169	2,523	2,460	3,041	1,601	50,766
2001	2,171	6,090	1,397	1,121	3,325	1,013	1,173	3,221	523	1,255	3,261	1,375	25,925
2002	1,275	3,372	1,538	1,527	6,126	2,166	2,154	8,971	1,452	1,710	8,118	2,644	41,053
2003	4,200	7,266	3,256	3,971	8,420	3,430	4,221	15,645	8,152	7,587	18,323	11,142	95,613
2004	17,093	41,036	20,508	30,214	27,343	11,433	7,606	28,895	10,690	15,036	41,269	16,429	267,552

Source: New York Mercantile Exchange (NYMEX)

Average Open Interest of Palladium Futures in New York   In Contracts

Year	Jan.	Feb.	Mar.	Apr.	May	June	July	Aug.	Sept.	Oct.	Nov.	Dec.
1995	7,484	7,579	7,102	7,231	6,519	6,413	6,739	6,852	5,950	6,120	6,486	6,090
1996	6,365	7,539	6,682	7,099	8,713	8,143	7,977	8,805	8,129	7,971	8,227	7,727
1997	8,291	10,946	10,528	9,759	9,947	7,072	5,538	4,973	3,822	4,282	4,291	4,030
1998	4,062	4,873	5,220	5,369	4,371	4,219	4,166	3,488	2,959	3,048	2,938	2,700
1999	2,846	3,234	2,957	3,015	2,796	2,757	2,823	2,496	2,755	3,210	3,301	3,045
2000	3,129	3,101	2,367	2,359	2,628	2,015	2,118	1,974	1,757	1,905	1,859	1,837
2001	1,828	1,666	1,525	1,577	1,613	1,385	1,420	1,318	1,383	1,286	1,477	1,244
2002	1,217	1,208	1,042	1,199	1,554	1,806	2,103	2,298	1,878	1,976	1,977	2,025
2003	2,000	2,039	1,948	1,997	2,315	2,609	2,680	3,605	5,184	5,533	6,096	6,737
2004	9,119	11,878	11,465	11,039	8,828	7,861	8,055	8,688	8,933	9,965	11,192	12,188

Source: New York Mercantile Exchange (NYMEX)

Pork Bellies

Pork bellies are the cut of meat from a hog from which bacon is produced. A hog has two belly slabs, generally weighing 8-18 pounds, depending on the hog's commercial slaughter weight. Slaughter weights average around 255 pounds, equal to a dressed carcass weight of about 190 pounds. Bellies account for about 12% of a hog's live weight, but represent a larger 14% of the total cutout value of the realized pork products. Pork bellies can be frozen and stored for up to a year before processing. The pork belly futures contract at the Chicago Mercantile Exchange calls for the physical delivery of 40,000 pounds of frozen pork bellies, which have been slaughtered at USDA federally inspected slaughtering plants. Each deliverable belly typically weighs 12-14 pounds each.

There are definite seasonal patterns in pork belly prices. Bellies are storable and the movement into cold storage builds early in the calendar year, peaking about mid-year. Net withdrawals from storage then carry stocks to a low around October. The cycle then starts again. Retail bacon demand also follows a time worn trend, peaking in the summer and tapering off to a low during the winter months. While demand patterns would suggest the highest prices in the summer and the lowest in the winter, just the opposite is not unusual. Such contra-seasonal price moves can be partially attributed to supply logistics, notably the availability of frozen storage stocks deliverable against futures at CME exchange-approved warehouses. When stocks prove either too large or small, the underlying demand variables for bacon can be relegated to the backburner as a market-moving factor. The fact that no contract months are traded between August and the following February adds to the late fall futures price distortion.

Belly prices (cash and futures) are sensitive to the inventory in cold storage and to the weekly net movement in and out of storage, which affords some insight to demand, although a better measure is the weekly quantity of bellies being sliced into bacon. Higher retail prices tend to encourage placing more supply into storage because of lower retail bacon demand. Bacon is not a necessary foodstuff so demand can be buoyed by favorable consumer disposable income. However, dietary standards have changed dramatically in recent years and do not favor the consumption of high fat and salt content food, like bacon. In addition, alternatives to pork bacon have emerged in recent years such as turkey bacon, which has lower fat and calorie content.

Prices – Pork bellies futures prices on the nearest futures chart rallied sharply in early 2004 along with live hog prices and posted a record high of 126 cents per pound. Pork belly prices settled back through the remainder of the year but still remained relatively strong from an historical perspective. The average monthly price of cash pork bellies (Midwest) rose by +16.2% in 2004 (through November) to a record 100.40 cents per pound. The average retail price of bacon in 2004 (through October) rose by +5.4% to a record high of $3.37 per pound.

Supply – Frozen pork belly storage stocks were relatively strong in 2004 and averaged 37.184 million pounds, up 12.4% from 2003. As of December 2004, there were 34.002 million pounds of pork bellies in storage.

Average Retail Price of Bacon, Sliced   In Dollars Per Pound

Year	Jan.	Feb.	Mar.	Apr.	May	June	July	Aug.	Sept.	Oct.	Nov.	Dec.	Average
1995	1.93	1.93	1.91	1.89	1.92	1.90	1.91	1.97	2.04	2.12	2.16	2.17	1.99
1996	2.14	2.20	2.20	2.24	2.35	2.49	2.54	2.68	2.81	2.72	2.66	2.64	2.47
1997	2.66	2.65	2.66	2.66	2.63	2.69	2.72	2.76	2.75	2.73	2.67	2.61	2.68
1998	2.64	2.62	2.54	2.44	2.44	2.46	2.52	2.51	2.58	2.57	2.62	2.58	2.54
1999	2.52	2.52	2.51	2.45	2.47	2.50	2.50	2.93	2.58	2.57	2.66	2.75	2.58
2000	2.75	2.87	2.93	2.95	3.01	3.13	3.17	3.20	3.21	3.07	3.05	3.03	3.03
2001	2.99	3.07	3.16	3.11	3.26	3.25	3.32	3.47	3.49	3.34	3.30	3.30	3.25
2002	3.27	3.32	3.27	3.26	3.18	3.19	3.23	3.29	3.16	3.24	3.21	3.24	3.24
2003	3.20	3.28	3.22	3.29	3.09	3.14	3.16	3.23	3.22	3.16	3.23	3.18	3.20
2004[1]	3.16	3.19	3.13	3.20	3.33	3.42	3.47	3.62	3.59	3.61	3.44	3.37	3.38

[1] Preliminary.   Source: Economic Research Service, U.S. Department of Agriculture (ERS-USDA)

Frozen Pork Belly Storage Stocks in the United States, on First of Month   In Thousands of Pounds

Year	Jan.	Feb.	Mar.	Apr.	May	June	July	Aug.	Sept.	Oct.	Nov.	Dec.
1995	61,073	62,776	64,228	78,975	78,539	77,919	67,607	47,055	17,435	6,255	13,478	37,092
1996	47,587	46,498	46,381	47,655	57,174	63,522	56,767	28,533	18,996	12,702	16,206	30,943
1997	37,930	38,030	44,277	54,767	54,015	55,274	52,274	33,657	18,346	11,148	14,408	25,365
1998	44,763	55,249	55,368	54,441	58,600	59,462	52,010	31,433	14,786	9,452	16,440	41,711
1999	72,657	82,605	93,323	106,194	109,521	108,257	93,383	69,675	34,814	19,273	22,489	26,170
2000	40,300	43,802	49,983	60,527	63,461	68,292	60,097	50,515	33,005	21,341	20,589	38,674
2001	47,099	50,145	47,154	45,440	43,878	46,029	39,552	24,996	12,754	8,960	28,216	36,297
2002	44,301	50,849	57,569	60,721	63,293	62,269	51,019	29,925	14,250	9,452	10,354	18,059
2003	28,254	35,354	38,278	42,971	48,542	45,870	43,504	32,075	17,900	10,180	21,135	33,073
2004[1]	49,017	63,095	57,123	50,126	48,363	41,366	37,185	23,383	15,230	11,344	15,970	33,955

[1] Preliminary.   Source: National Agricultural Statistics Service, U.S. Department of Agriculture (NASS-USDA)

Weekly Pork Belly Storage Movement

	Stocks[1] In Thousands of Pounds					Stocks[1] In Thousands of Pounds			
Week Ending	In	Out	On Hand	Net Move-ment	Week Ending	In	Out	On Hand	Net Move-ment
Jan 04, 2003	2,260	-344	15,961	1,916	Jan 03, 2004	2,906	-253	28,248	2,653
Jan 11, 2003	2,316	-82	18,195	2,234	Jan 10, 2004	3,596	-250	31,594	3,346
Jan 18, 2003	1,189	-251	19,133	938	Jan 17, 2004	2,364	-294	34,009	2,070
Jan 25, 2003	1,033	-381	19,755	622	Jan 24, 2004	1,675	-78	35,606	1,597
Feb 01, 2003	486	-239	19,969	247	Jan 31, 2004	1,433	-453	36,586	980
Feb 08, 2003	617	-134	20,485	483	Feb 07, 2004	716	-1,641	35,561	-925
Feb 15, 2003	345	-187	20,622	158	Feb 14, 2004	242	-804	35,099	-562
Feb 22, 2003	626	-48	21,221	278	Feb 21, 2004	221	-1,059	34,261	-838
Mar 01, 2003	1,004	-142	22,083	862	Feb 28, 2004	14	-951	33,324	-937
Mar 08, 2003	1,299	-172	23,210	1,127	Mar 06, 2004	89	-879	32,533	-790
Mar 15, 2003	860	-408	23,662	452	Mar 13, 2004	860	-408	23,662	452
Mar 22, 2003	125	-186	23,601	-61	Mar 20, 2004	0	-804	31,218	-804
Mar 29, 2003	245	-42	23,805	203	Mar 27, 2004	78	-797	30,499	-719
Apr 05, 2003	316	-205	23,916	111	Apr 03, 2004	747	-1,367	29,879	-620
Apr 12, 2003	440	-370	23,986	70	Apr 10, 2004	203	-757	29,325	-554
Apr 19, 2003	1,719	-127	25,578	1,592	Apr 17, 2004	726	-828	29,223	-102
Apr 26, 2003	1,905	-166	27,317	1,738	Apr 24, 2004	851	-161	29,913	690
May 03, 2003	279	-157	27,439	122	May 01, 2004	239	-901	29,251	-662
May 10, 2003	75	-634	26,880	-559	May 08, 2004	1,084	-549	29,786	536
May 17, 2003	40	-770	26,150	-730	May 15, 2004	1,440	-1,910	29,316	-470
May 24, 2003	637	-882	25,905	-245	May 22, 2004	NA	-2,128	27,187	-2,128
May 31, 2003	56	-955	25,006	-899	May 29, 2004	306	-893	27,828	-587
Jun 07, 2003	102	-890	24,218	-788	Jun 05, 2004	295	-2,158	25,964	-1,863
Jun 14, 2003	251	-643	23,826	-392	Jun 12, 2004	1,160	-871	26,254	289
Jun 21, 2003	345	-568	23,603	-223	Jun 19, 2004	367	-1,442	25,179	-1,075
Jun 28, 2003	168	-735	23,036	-567	Jun 26, 2004	1,245	-1,070	25,354	175
Jul 05, 2003	51	-771	23,316	-710	Jul 03, 2004	146	-1,536	23,964	-1,390
Jul 12, 2003	2,770	-2,218	25,868	3,552	Jul 10, 2004	939	-1,856	20,650	-917
Jul 19, 2003	50	-2,890	24,761	-2,840	Jul 17, 2004	370	-2,505	18,515	-2,135
Jul 26, 2003	159	-3,455	21,465	-3,296	Jul 24, 2004	859	-2,486	16,888	-1,627
Aug 02, 2003	106	-2,701	18,870	-2,595	Jul 31, 2004	103	-2,163	14,828	-2,060
Aug 09, 2003	65	-2,778	16,157	-2,713	Aug 07, 2004	484	-2,321	12,458	-1,837
Aug 16, 2003	124	-2,496	13,785	-2,372	Aug 14, 2004	59	-1,495	11,022	-1,436
Aug 23, 2003	184	-2,385	11,584	-2,201	Aug 21, 2004	229	-2,029	9,222	-1,800
Aug 30, 2003	155	-2,520	9,219	-2,365	Aug 28, 2004	229	-2,029	9,222	-1,800
Sep 06, 2003	82	-2,635	6,667	-2,553	Sep 04, 2004	193	-1,102	8,313	-909
Sep 13, 2003	242	-1,613	5,296	-1,371	Sep 11, 2004	134	-1,092	7,356	-958
Sep 20, 2003	116	-1,063	4,349	-947	Sep 18, 2004	85	-848	6,593	-763
Sep 27, 2003	53	-881	3,520	-828	Sep 25, 2004	156	-711	6,038	-555
Oct 04, 2003	145	-198	3,467	-53	Oct 02, 2004	325	-391	5,972	-66
Oct 11, 2003	297	-302	3,462	-5	Oct 09, 2004	286	-283	5,975	3
Oct 18, 2003	1,840	-62	5,240	1,778	Oct 16, 2004	17	-279	5,713	-262
Oct 25, 2003	3,446	-40	8,646	3,406	Oct 23, 2004	1,152	-537	6,327	615
Nov 01, 2003	2,074	-138	10,582	1,936	Oct 30, 2004	3,082	-279	9,131	2,803
Nov 08, 2003	1,811	-130	12,263	1,681	Nov 06, 2004	2,424	-150	11,405	2,274
Nov 15, 2003	1,534	-158	13,668	1,376	Nov 13, 2004	2,389	-366	13,427	2,023
Nov 22, 2003	2,243	-80	15,832	2,163	Nov 20, 2004	3,466	-1,072	15,821	2,394
Nov 29, 2003	2,308	-41	18,099	2,267	Nov 27, 2004	5,023	-24	20,820	4,999
Dec 06, 2003	1,828	-40	19,887	1,788	Dec 04, 2004	6,416	-128	27,108	6,288
Dec 13, 2003	1,736	-40	21,658	1,696	Dec 11, 2004	3,105	-2,347	27,866	758
Dec 20, 2003	1,359	-123	22,898	1,236	Dec 18, 2004	6,112	-123	33,855	5,989
Dec 27, 2003	2,816	-119	25,595	2,697	Dec 25, 2004	5,403	-3,634	35,625	1,769

[1] 60 Chicago and Outside Combined Chicago Mercantile Exchange approved warehouses.   *Source: Chicago Mercantile Exchange (CME)*

Pork Belly Futures - Chicago Mercantile Exchange
(weekly close) as of December 31, 2004

Cents Per Pound

Average Open Interest of Pork Belly Futures in Chicago   In Contracts

Year	Jan.	Feb.	Mar.	Apr.	May	June	July	Aug.	Sept.	Oct.	Nov.	Dec.
1995	10,294	9,080	7,809	7,367	8,017	7,036	5,666	4,271	6,246	7,007	7,103	7,282
1996	7,094	8,028	10,521	10,753	10,018	8,136	6,432	6,296	6,056	6,395	6,050	6,480
1997	7,504	7,930	7,260	7,165	8,950	7,203	5,905	4,791	5,242	7,520	8,302	9,009
1998	9,187	9,145	9,082	7,825	6,786	5,406	4,185	3,493	2,933	3,841	4,987	7,085
1999	7,217	6,192	4,623	5,113	6,030	6,639	5,003	2,415	2,320	3,206	4,011	4,868
2000	5,872	6,011	6,320	6,563	5,836	5,306	3,650	1,877	1,860	2,093	2,409	2,610
2001	2,719	2,908	2,935	3,138	2,808	2,354	2,526	2,579	2,695	2,321	2,441	2,451
2002	2,574	2,768	2,879	3,271	3,224	2,821	1,885	986	1,116	1,329	2,020	2,548
2003	2,842	2,805	2,915	3,082	3,383	3,410	2,858	1,632	1,899	1,885	2,075	2,484
2004	2,431	3,213	3,491	3,998	3,880	3,158	2,675	1,473	1,399	1,200	1,491	1,900

Source: Chicago Mercantile Exchange (CME)

Volume of Trading of Pork Belly Futures in Chicago   In Contracts

Year	Jan.	Feb.	Mar.	Apr.	May	June	July	Aug.	Sept.	Oct.	Nov.	Dec.	Total
1995	62,994	54,330	59,324	43,501	49,453	53,571	45,869	36,623	31,112	35,444	47,061	42,631	561,913
1996	48,563	56,623	61,669	61,703	61,868	55,337	55,121	45,399	39,182	48,973	42,709	35,502	612,649
1997	60,761	53,604	56,750	76,072	62,190	54,043	55,043	36,153	31,154	44,277	31,663	33,609	595,319
1998	41,894	50,105	47,249	61,910	36,058	48,913	41,133	33,832	24,006	30,538	30,093	35,521	481,252
1999	39,925	36,293	33,322	31,558	31,321	45,030	36,513	23,536	16,544	20,392	28,920	24,955	368,309
2000	37,650	38,943	39,061	31,464	40,311	31,229	25,051	17,875	10,711	11,854	11,737	13,690	309,576
2001	15,861	16,200	16,675	18,274	18,708	16,989	20,187	18,823	12,719	12,905	15,984	13,034	196,359
2002	16,495	16,650	14,279	17,758	13,648	15,764	16,773	7,490	6,857	8,107	8,659	9,574	152,054
2003	13,635	13,956	13,137	18,279	18,112	16,993	19,540	9,967	7,909	10,235	8,542	11,024	161,329
2004	11,519	14,738	17,699	18,412	17,366	15,136	16,012	10,518	9,410	5,713	7,643	7,783	151,949

Source: Chicago Mercantile Exchange (CME)

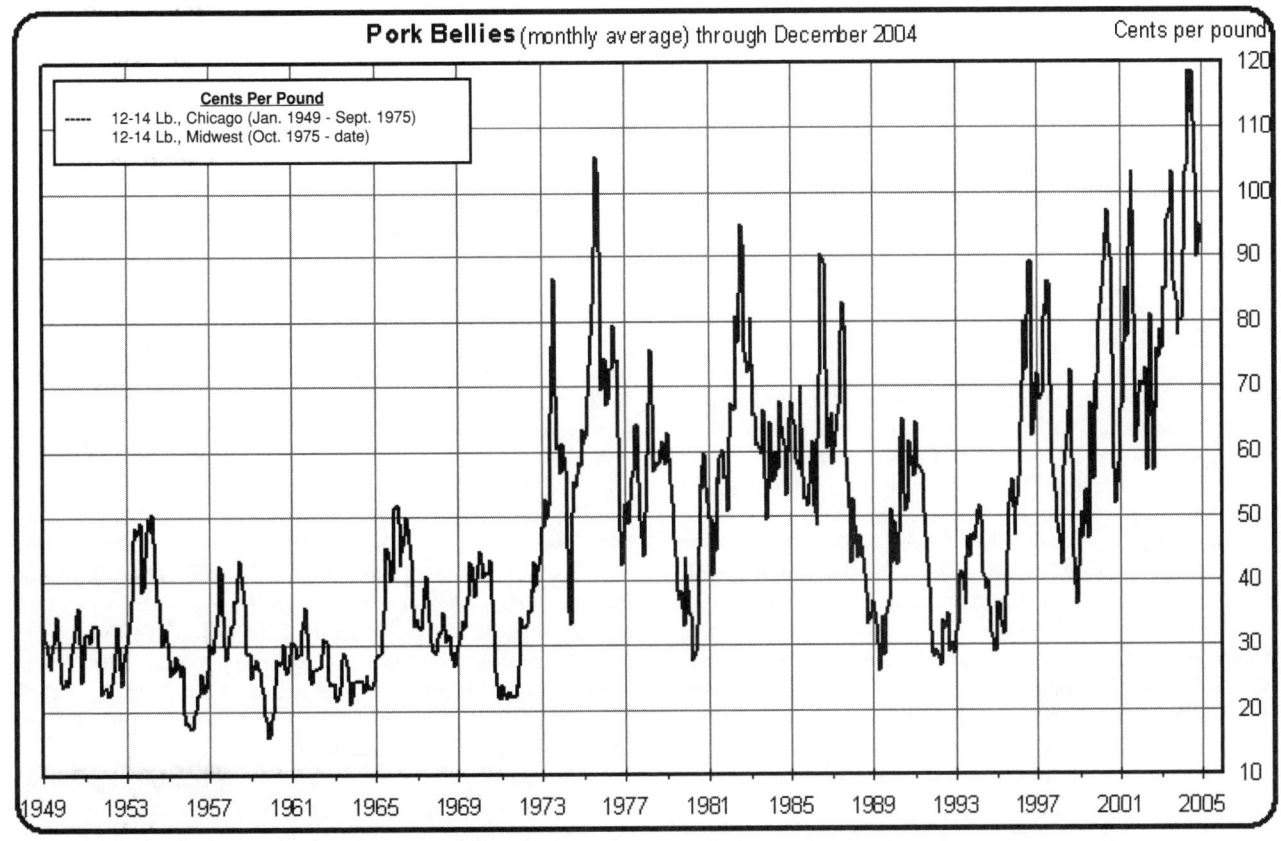

Pork Bellies (monthly average) through December 2004

Cents per pound

Cents Per Pound
----- 12-14 Lb., Chicago (Jan. 1949 - Sept. 1975)
12-14 Lb., Midwest (Oct. 1975 - date)

Average Price of Pork Bellies (12-14 lbs.), Central U.S.   In Cents Per Pound

Year	Jan.	Feb.	Mar.	Apr.	May	June	July	Aug.	Sept.	Oct.	Nov.	Dec.	Average
1995	36.03	35.80	36.30	33.83	31.70	37.94	43.10	52.42	54.43	56.20	47.28	51.45	43.04
1996	52.33	56.33	64.50	69.86	79.50	72.64	89.49	88.40	68.12	63.07	65.27	70.07	69.97
1997	72.04	68.42	59.05	80.54	82.58	80.68	86.70	85.43	72.25	57.97	53.77	47.52	70.58
1998	43.00	45.89	42.28	54.65	57.87	63.10	68.46	72.99	57.49	42.05	39.13	36.31	51.94
1999	48.80	50.76	46.51	49.23	53.76	53.41	47.78	67.29	57.87	70.83	67.81	71.37	57.12
2000	80.45	82.40	85.00	93.70	97.85	91.99	90.38	75.64	63.94	57.83	51.97	58.36	77.46
2001	66.61	66.68	78.04	85.80	77.91	91.50	102.42	98.39	81.91	61.30	63.68	69.13	78.61
2002	70.87	70.75	72.55	63.48	58.65	65.90	81.06	67.98	57.05	76.24	75.50	78.92	69.91
2003	78.02	79.54	85.80	84.94	96.58	97.05	102.37	85.65	83.15	84.46	78.53	81.00	86.42
2004[1]	79.78	90.76	103.67	109.15	117.53	113.00	118.22	99.92	92.00	88.90	91.50	87.81	99.35

[1] Preliminary.   *Source: Economic Research Service, U.S. Department of Agriculture (ERS-USDA)*

Average Price of Pork Loins (12-14 lbs.)[2] Central, U.S.   In Cents Per Pound

Year	Jan.	Feb.	Mar.	Apr.	May	June	July	Aug.	Sept.	Oct.	Nov.	Dec.	Average
1995	96.94	102.20	95.30	93.33	103.50	118.81	124.65	127.98	117.63	108.23	93.94	110.39	107.74
1996	110.00	116.43	120.49	119.70	131.61	115.73	126.16	118.18	112.28	115.40	115.39	120.45	118.49
1997	112.50	109.50	106.58	117.16	125.68	116.28	122.53	119.28	112.07	99.68	85.99	79.44	108.89
1998	76.50	103.03	104.56	102.51	130.64	113.13	106.51	105.90	97.23	99.63	79.90	72.49	99.34
1999	105.82	92.35	83.47	99.35	107.44	97.62	105.72	111.55	104.99	98.98	94.64	102.75	100.39
2000	99.29	110.66	110.06	127.48	115.38	132.53	131.73	120.45	119.22	119.90	104.19	114.68	117.13
2001	110.80	114.32	128.53	117.98	130.72	132.33	126.41	121.22	116.21	108.69	97.87	98.50	116.97
2002	106.95	105.73	100.08	94.13	101.71	104.80	108.64	97.85	87.17	93.04	82.60	93.03	97.98
2003	91.83	95.75	92.43	96.90	108.93	126.51	102.50	104.85	111.38	97.71	89.06	93.72	100.96
2004[1]	111.98	117.30	110.00	115.48	140.65	130.30	121.36	116.93	119.22	110.00	102.92	109.50	117.14

[1] Preliminary.   *Source: Economic Research Service, U.S. Department of Agriculture (ERS-USDA)*

Potatoes

The potato is a member of the nightshade family. The leaves of the potato plant are poisonous and a potato will begin to turn green if left too long in the light. This green skin contains solanine, a substance that can cause the potato to taste bitter and even cause illness in humans. In Peru, the Inca Indians were the first to cultivate potatoes around 200 BC. The Indians developed potato crops because their staple diet of corn would not grow above an altitude of 3,350 meters. In 1536, after conquering the Incas, the Spanish Conquistadors brought potatoes back to Europe. At first, Europeans did not accept the potato because it was not mentioned in the Bible and was therefore considered an "evil" food. But after Marie Antoinette wore a crown of potato flowers, it finally became a popular food. In 1897, during the Alaskan Klondike gold rush, potatoes were so valued for their vitamin C content that miners traded gold for potatoes. The potato became the first vegetable to be grown in outer space in October 1995.

The potato is a highly nutritious, fat-free, cholesterol-free and sodium-free food, and is an important dietary staple in over 130 countries. A medium-sized potato contains only 100 calories. Potatoes are an excellent source of Vitamin C and provide B vitamins as well as potassium, copper, magnesium, and iron. According to the US Department of Agriculture, "a diet of whole milk and potatoes would supply almost all of the food elements necessary for the maintenance of the human body."

Potatoes are one of the largest vegetable crops grown in the US, and are grown in all fifty states. The US ranks about 4th in world potato production. The top three types of potatoes grown extensively in the US are white, red, and Russets (Russets account for about two-thirds the US crop). Potatoes in the US are harvested in all four seasons, but the vast majority of the crop is harvested in fall. Potatoes harvested in the winter, spring and summer are used mainly to supplement fresh supplies of fall-harvested potatoes and are also important to the processing industries. The four principal categories for US potato exports are frozen, potato chips, fresh, and dehydrated. Fries account for approximately 95% of US frozen potato exports.

Prices – The average monthly price received for potatoes by US farmers in 2004 fell by -5.9% to $5.80 per hundred pounds, which was well below the 15-year high of $6.99 posted in 2001. Bearish factors included favorable summer growing conditions and the emphasis on lower carbohydrate diets.

Supply – The total potato crop in 2004 fell by -2.0% to 45.917 billion pounds, which was well below the record high of 51.362 billion pounds posted in 2000. The fall crop in 2004 fell by -0.2% to 40.982 billion pounds, accounting for 91% of the total crop. Stocks of the fall crop (as of Dec 1) were estimated at a 4-year high of 27.160 billion pounds. In 2004, the spring crop fell sharply by -21.9% to 1.908 billion pounds, the summer crop fell -1.5% to 1.849 billion pounds, and the winter crop rose by +19.6% to 482 million pounds.

The largest producing states for the fall 2004 crop were Idaho (with 32.2% of the crop), Washington (22.9%), Wisconsin (7.5%), North Dakota (6.5%), and Colorado (5.6%). For the spring crop, the largest producing states were California (with 34.9% of the crop) and Florida (29.4%).

Farmers harvested 1.170 million acres in 2004, down -6.3% from 2003 and the lowest acreage planting since 1980. The yield per harvested acre in 2004 rose by +4.9% to a new record high of 38,600 pounds per acre.

Demand – Total utilization of potatoes in 2003 fell slightly by –0.1% yr/yr to 45.781 billion pounds. The breakdown shows that the largest consumption category for potatoes is table stock with 29.6% of total consumption, followed by frozen French fries (27.6%), chips and shoestrings (11.5%), and dehydration (10.6%). US per capita consumption of potatoes in 2004 fell slightly by –0.4% to 134.6 pounds, which was well below the record high of 145.0 pounds seen in 1996.

Trade – US exports of potatoes in 2003, the latest reporting year for the series, fell sharply by -14.9% to 589.756 million pounds. US exports hit a record high of 693.196 million pounds in 2003. US imports rose +2.2% to 634.971 million pounds. The US record high for imports of 737.223 million pounds was posted in 1998.

Salient Statistics of Potatoes in the United States

Crop Year	Acreage Planted (1,000 Acres)	Acreage Harvested (1,000 Acres)	Yield Per Harvested Acre Cwt.	Total Production (In Thousands of Cwt.)	Seed & Feed	Shrinkage & Loss	Sold[2]	Farm Price $/Cwt.	Production[3] (Million $)	Sales (Million $)	Stocks on Jan. 1 1,000 Cwt.	(Fresh) Domestic Exports (Millions of Lbs.)	Imports (Millions of Lbs.)	Per Capita Fresh (In Pounds)	Per Capita Total (In Pounds)
1995	1,398	1,372	323	443,606	5,745	29,530	408,331	6.77	2,992	2,762	223,550	583,938	458,926	49.2	136.9
1996	1,455	1,426	350	499,254	6,221	41,222	451,190	4.91	2,425	2,220	261,320	564,010	690,768	49.9	145.0
1997	1,384	1,354	345	467,091	5,475	32,183	429,433	5.64	2,623	2,421	246,550	670,270	512,321	48.5	141.4
1998	1,417	1,388	343	475,771	5,766	35,454	434,551	5.56	2,635	2,416	246,230	650,918	737,223	47.0	138.1
1999	1,377	1,332	359	478,216	5,569	35,531	437,116	5.77	2,746	2,522	239,910	599,066	610,538	48.0	136.5
2000	1,384	1,348	381	513,621	5,288	43,688	464,645	5.08	2,591	2,360	275,270	676,577	502,706	47.3	138.7
2001	1,247	1,221	358	437,673	5,387	31,208	401,293	6.99	3,058	2,805	224,680	636,176	487,889	46.4	138.0
2002	1,300	1,266	362	458,171	5,622	30,905	421,644	6.67	3,045	2,812	231,690	693,196	621,475	44.5	132.2
2003	1,273	1,249	367	457,814	5,541	35,296	416,977	5.89	2,686	2,458	233,880	589,756	634,971		
2004[1]	1,194	1,168	391	456,362				5.62	2,564						

[1] Preliminary. [2] For all purposes, including food, seed processing & livestock feed. [3] Farm weight basis, excluding canned and frozen potatoes.
[4] Calendar Year. *Source: Economic Research Service, U.S. Department of Agriculture (ERS-USDA)*

214

Cold Storage Stocks of All Frozen Potatoes in the United States, on First of Month   In Millions of Pounds

Year	Jan.	Feb.	Mar.	Apr.	May	June	July	Aug.	Sept.	Oct.	Nov.	Dec.
1995	1,096.6	1,156.0	1,179.9	1,169.0	1,138.0	1,125.4	1,116.5	992.4	992.6	1,145.3	1,225.6	1,174.5
1996	1,123.7	1,147.2	1,172.5	1,164.6	1,112.1	1,076.4	1,059.7	907.1	957.8	1,124.9	1,225.2	1,146.3
1997	1,098.4	1,111.5	1,180.1	1,177.1	1,195.8	1,213.3	1,271.4	1,214.3	1,130.8	1,270.0	1,354.7	1,313.5
1998	1,163.5	1,147.2	1,235.7	1,278.3	1,225.1	1,282.8	1,316.5	1,234.7	1,204.5	1,266.8	1,341.0	1,290.5
1999	1,151.3	1,219.7	1,272.9	1,278.8	1,236.2	1,255.5	1,234.1	1,142.3	1,169.8	1,235.5	1,307.8	1,254.5
2000	1,165.4	1,140.9	1,270.1	1,283.4	1,239.4	1,250.4	1,186.3	1,180.3	1,185.7	1,291.5	1,351.5	1,285.9
2001	1,189.7	1,228.6	1,254.7	1,220.9	1,280.4	1,270.3	1,355.0	1,282.6	1,197.5	1,323.8	1,338.5	1,297.4
2002	1,239.8	1,274.2	1,271.5	1,271.4	1,222.7	1,182.3	1,223.5	1,106.6	1,040.6	1,141.4	1,252.2	1,214.4
2003	1,131.2	1,173.1	1,211.0	1,217.4	1,150.5	1,106.6	1,181.8	1,130.4	1,070.4	1,151.7	1,248.0	1,232.8
2004[1]	1,120.4	1,167.3	1,207.4	1,192.5	1,158.7	1,185.9	1,127.5	1,117.1	1,127.0	1,178.7	1,275.8	1,219.3

[1] Preliminary.   *Source: Agricultural Statistics Board, U.S. Department of Agriculture (ASB-USDA)*

Potato Crop Production Estimates, Stocks and Disappearance in the United States   In Millions of Cwt.

	Crop Production Estimates						Total Storage Stocks[2]					Fall Crop — 1,000 Cwt.				
	Total Crop			Fall Crop			Following Year					Pro-	Disap-pearance	Dec. 1	Average Price	Value of Sales
Year	Oct. 1	Nov. 1	Dec. 1	Oct. 1	Nov. 1	Dec. 1	Jan. 1	Feb. 1	Mar. 1	Apr. 1	May 1	duction	(Sold)	Stocks	$/Cwt.	$ 1,000
1995	----	444.8	----	----	402.4	256.7	223.6	189.4	156.0	115.9	75.9	394,785	370,679	256,710	6.43	2,372,983
1996	----	491.5	----	----	447.9	295.1	261.3	226.1	189.2	147.6	103.2	443,704	408,247	295,100	4.35	1,772,037
1997	----	459.4	----	----	417.5	278.8	246.6	212.6	175.9	134.2	92.8	413,513	387,089	278,830	5.20	2,011,004
1998	----	471.0	----	----	429.0	280.9	246.2	209.6	173.7	131.2	87.9	423,170	392,922	280,910	5.07	1,994,030
1999	----	481.5	----	----	435.6	275.1	239.9	207.2	169.6	128.4	86.9	420,567	390,210	275,100	5.29	2,064,564
2000	----	509.4	----	----	463.4	310.3	275.3	234.3	197.7	153.5	109.2	467,504	420,279	310,300	4.55	1,910,833
2001	----	441.8	----	----	400.7	258.8	224.7	192.1	158.6	120.0	81.2	393,631	358,812	258,750	6.54	2,349,036
2002	----	459.7	----	----	415.0	264.5	231.5	199.0	165.2	125.8	83.0	413,581	378,796	264,485	5.89	2,232,627
2003	----	459.2	----	----	413.5	267.9	233.6	200.2	166.3	126.1	85.0	410,588	371,755	267,900	5.23	1,943,986
2004[1]	----	450.2	----	----	407.8	271.8	238.2	201.2	168.4			410,023		271,800		

[1] Preliminary.   [2] Held by growers and local dealers in the fall producing areas.   *Source: Agricultural Statistics Board, U.S. Department of Agriculture*

Production of Potatoes by Seasonal Groups in the United States   In Thousands of Cwt.

	Winter	Spring			Summer			Fall								
Year	Total	Cali-fornia	Florida	Total	New Mexico	Virginia	Total	Colo-rado	Idaho	Maine	Minne-sota	North Dakota	Oregon	Washing-ton	Wis-consin	Total
1995	2,473	6,230	7,830	20,193	1,344	2,040	17,931	23,808	132,657	17,160	20,790	25,410	24,788	80,850	26,000	403,009
1996	3,273	7,538	7,765	22,417	1,404	1,463	19,176	29,175	142,800	21,175	24,600	28,820	30,124	94,990	33,150	454,388
1997	3,431	8,073	7,150	22,299	1,248	1,268	18,171	24,993	140,314	19,080	20,440	22,000	27,319	88,160	30,175	423,190
1998	2,980	6,198	7,358	21,121	962	1,380	18,933	25,360	138,000	18,060	21,170	28,670	26,229	93,225	30,895	432,737
1999	4,070	7,600	8,820	25,327	1,247	1,050	18,972	25,762	133,330	17,813	18,020	26,400	28,020	95,200	34,000	429,847
2000	4,960	7,426	6,343	21,921	1,050	1,292	19,236	27,972	152,320	17,920	21,240	26,950	30,683	105,000	33,800	467,504
2001	4,115	6,045	7,970	21,814	770	1,386	18,209	21,357	120,200	16,430	18,425	26,400	20,730	94,400	31,955	393,631
2002	4,206	7,695	7,883	22,452	736	1,386	17,932	27,885	133,385	16,960	18,810	23,460	24,936	92,340	30,750	413,581
2003	4,027	8,360	8,008	24,433	532	1,550	18,766	23,652	123,180	17,030	22,330	27,440	20,991	93,150	32,800	410,588
2004[1]	4,818	8,313	7,678	22,663	340	1,200	18,858	23,148	131,970	19,220	18,920	26,765	19,775	93,810	30,450	410,023

[1] Preliminary.   *Source: Agricultural Statistics Board, U.S. Department of Agriculture (ASB-USDA)*

Utilization of Potatoes in the United States   In Thousands of Cwt.

	Sales											Non-Sales			
		For Processing							Other Sales			Used on			
Crop Year	Table Stock	Chips, Shoe-strings	For Dehyd-ration	Frozen French Fries	Other Frozen Products	Canned Potatoes	Other Canned Products[2]	Starch & Flour	Live-stock Feed	Seed	Total Sales	Farms Where Grown	Shrink-age & Loss	Total Non-Sales	Total
1994	133,989	49,299	41,381	136,531	26,362	2,503	3,006	2,176	4,147	24,616	424,010	4,732	37,166	43,044	467,054
1995	124,875	47,284	45,065	129,029	27,073	3,342	2,385	1,668	3,224	25,769	409,714	4,792	29,630	35,385	445,099
1996	131,446	48,305	54,261	145,489	28,972	2,785	2,167	1,956	12,073	24,341	451,795	4,797	41,238	47,459	499,254
1997	131,670	48,130	48,389	131,628	33,397	2,822	2,675	1,311	3,603	25,808	429,433	4,167	32,183	37,658	467,091
1998	125,413	51,471	55,522	142,932	24,964	2,730	1,964	1,585	3,111	24,859	434,551	4,358	35,454	41,220	475,771
1999	134,130	52,916	50,831	140,196	23,593	3,311	2,394	1,310	3,141	25,294	437,116	4,415	35,531	41,100	478,216
2000	139,590	52,405	54,332	146,869	26,723	2,368	2,709	1,966	14,265	23,345	464,572	3,792	43,685	48,972	513,544
2001	122,552	54,080	40,759	126,711	23,598	2,590	1,722	1,015	3,496	24,537	401,060	4,088	31,227	36,613	437,673
2002	131,889	51,640	51,357	124,875	28,951	2,744	2,089	1,050	3,044	24,005	421,644	4,144	30,905	36,527	458,171
2003[1]	135,368	52,754	48,418	126,515	23,870	3,003	1,804	879	2,005	22,361	416,977	3,999	35,296	40,837	457,814

[1] Preliminary.   [2] Hash, stews and soups.   *Source: Agricultural Statistics Board, U.S. Department of Agriculture (ASB-USDA)*

POTATOES

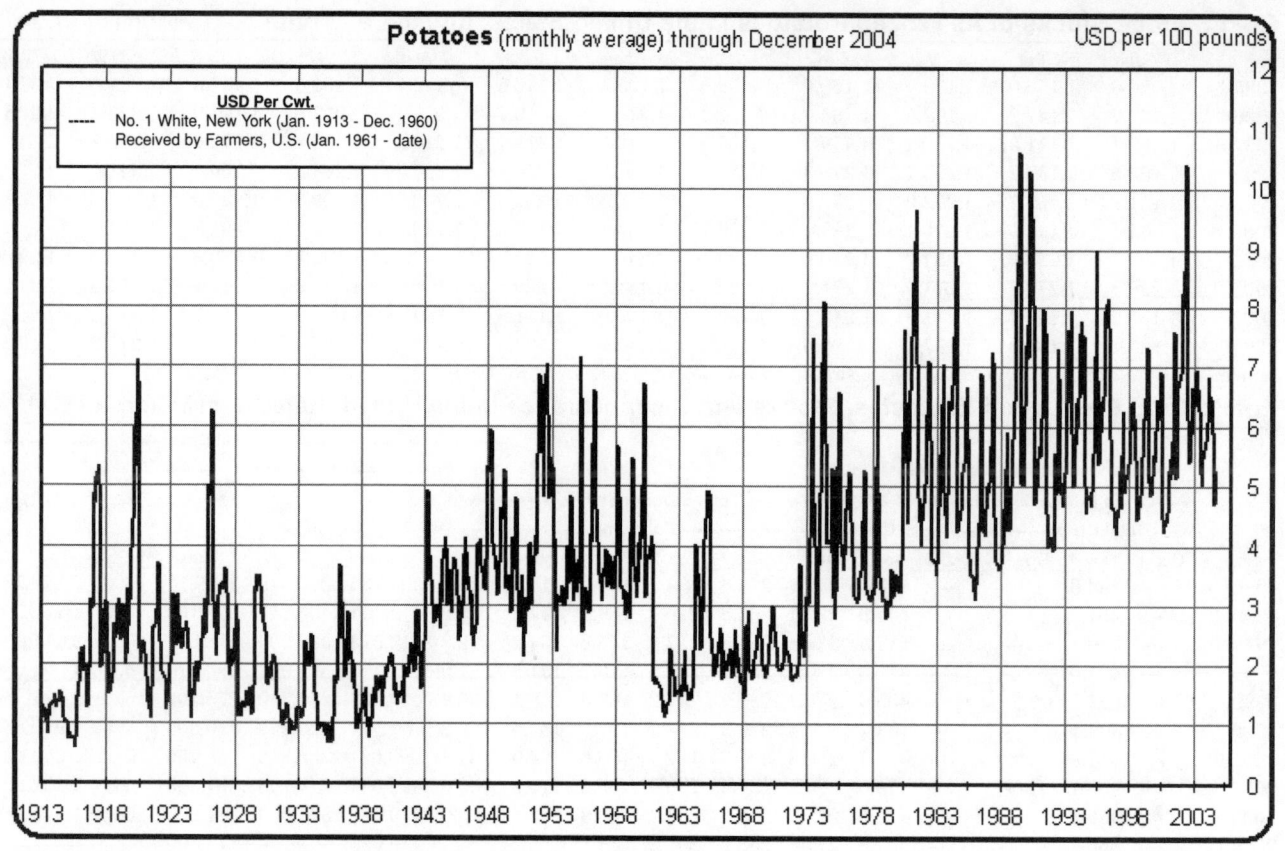

Per Capita Utilization of Potatoes in the United States   In Pounds (Farm Weight)

Year	Total	Fresh	Freezing	Chips & Shoe-string	Dehy-drating	Canning	Total
				--- Processing ---			
1995	136.9	49.2	56.2	16.4	13.2	1.9	87.7
1996	145.0	49.9	60.2	16.4	16.7	1.8	95.1
1997	141.4	48.5	59.3	15.9	15.9	1.8	92.9
1998	138.1	47.0	58.2	14.8	16.6	1.5	91.1
1999	136.5	48.0	58.5	15.9	12.3	1.8	88.5
2000	138.8	47.3	57.9	16.0	15.9	1.7	91.5
2001	138.2	46.4	57.9	17.6	14.7	1.6	91.8
2002	132.3	44.6	55.1	16.4	14.8	1.4	87.7
2003[1]	138.7	47.2	57.2	17.3	15.5	1.5	91.5
2004[2]	136.0	45.6	56.6	17.1	15.2	1.5	90.4

[1] Preliminary.   [2] Forecast.   Source: Agricultural Statistics Board, U.S. Department of Agriculture (ASB-USDA)

Average Price Received by Farmers for Potatoes in the United States   In Dollars Per Cwt.

Year	Jan.	Feb.	Mar.	Apr.	May	June	July	Aug.	Sept.	Oct.	Nov.	Dec.	Season Average
1995	4.83	4.97	5.37	5.41	5.86	7.12	8.75	6.64	5.76	6.30	6.39	6.33	6.75
1996	6.65	6.92	7.51	7.82	8.09	8.16	7.79	5.58	4.92	4.75	4.44	4.28	4.91
1997	4.22	4.56	4.64	4.67	5.31	5.67	5.66	6.31	5.08	4.93	5.12	5.36	5.64
1998	5.40	5.94	6.41	6.27	6.45	6.16	5.81	5.46	4.97	4.47	4.86	5.30	5.56
1999	5.50	5.75	6.12	6.50	6.13	6.54	7.35	6.02	5.09	4.86	5.52	5.44	5.77
2000	5.68	5.92	6.26	6.46	6.31	6.14	6.93	5.56	4.49	4.27	4.31	4.48	5.08
2001	4.56	5.26	5.12	5.47	5.24	5.75	6.46	7.61	6.04	5.15	5.96	6.66	6.99
2002	6.90	7.34	8.26	8.00	8.62	9.39	10.40	8.00	6.14	5.44	6.38	6.67	6.67
2003	6.67	6.33	6.87	6.94	6.96	6.68	6.30	5.75	5.24	5.03	5.46	5.77	5.89
2004[1]	5.75	5.87	6.09	6.84	6.54	6.49	5.91	5.94	5.27	4.73	5.04	5.27	5.62

[1] Preliminary.   Source: Agricultural Statistics Board, U.S. Department of Agriculture (ASB-USDA)

Potatoes Processed[1] in the United States, Eight States   In Thousands of Cwt.

States	Storage Season	to Dec. 1	to Jan. 1	to Feb. 1	to Mar. 1	to Apr. 1	to May 1	to June 1	Entire Season
Idaho and	1996-7	31,060	38,210	45,420	54,640	62,570	70,720	----	96,970
Oregon-	1997-8	26,880	33,950	41,050	49,470	57,620	65,750	----	91,450
Malheur	1998-9	27,510	34,700	42,670	51,210	60,040	68,550	76,410	92,860
Co	1999-00	27,970	34,490	40,790	49,220	57,820	66,080	74,110	88,210
	2000-1	29,290	35,720	43,470	50,580	58,910	66,760	75,270	93,460
	2001-2	20,940	27,330	33,620	40,860	47,710	54,150	61,200	73,390
	2002-3	28,380	34,860	41,200	48,600	56,240	63,840	71,280	85,390
	2003-4	24,310	30,730	36,260	43,640	49,570	53,680	63,770	77,530
	2004-5	24,360	30,840	36,820	44,610				
Maine[2]	1996-7	1,790	2,115	2,820	3,280	3,820	4,420	----	6,495
	1997-8	1,250	1,720	2,265	2,735	3,355	3,900	----	5,870
	1998-9	1,430	1,935	2,530	2,985	3,595	4,180	4,705	5,945
	1999-00	1,270	1,700	2,385	3,070	3,765	4,560	5,150	6,670
	2000-1	1,845	2,475	3,105	3,695	4,225	4,760	5,340	7,015
	2001-2	1,975	2,440	3,110	3,700	4,285	4,775	5,515	7,195
	2002-3	2,230	2,715	3,345	3,905	4,505	5,225	5,905	7,835
	2003-4	1,590	2,085	2,720	3,420	4,095	4,740	5,400	7,270
	2004-5	1,555	1,985	2,615	3,150				
Wash. &	1996-7	31,670	36,660	41,700	48,740	55,570	62,320	----	80,970
Oregon-	1997-8	28,580	33,990	38,690	46,400	53,720	59,780	----	76,930
Other	1998-9	33,630	38,890	45,650	53,290	60,930	67,180	74,190	83,730
	1999-00	33,320	39,620	45,500	53,350	61,080	67,230	74,840	83,210
	2000-1	34,770	40,970	47,720	55,250	62,860	69,850	78,010	91,130
	2001-2	29,320	35,310	40,540	47,910	54,970	61,360	69,400	77,180
	2002-3	33,680	39,490	44,190	51,920	58,710	64,300	71,480	79,110
	2003-4	32,670	38,520	43,610	51,210	58,500	64,160	72,350	79,800
	2004-5	32,305	38,130	43,570	50,730				
Other	1996-7	13,720	17,000	20,645	24,085	27,650	30,830	----	43,100
States[3]	1997-8	11,645	13,960	17,115	19,905	23,515	26,365	----	37,842
	1998-9	11,570	14,465	18,030	20,850	24,850	28,190	31,365	39,865
	1999-00	12,455	15,035	17,950	20,855	24,305	27,220	30,410	36,435
	2000-1	12,665	16,215	18,975	22,095	25,410	28,695	31,765	39,020
	2001-2	13,170	14,925	19,000	22,115	24,655	27,815	30,460	37,740
	2002-3	12,675	15,530	18,735	21,780	24,810	27,405	30,655	38,700
	2003-4	13,835	16,505	19,590	22,685	25,920	29,480	32,845	42,160
	2004-5	12,525	15,035	18,005	20,945				
Total	1996-7	78,240	93,985	110,585	130,745	149,610	168,290	----	227,535
	1997-8	68,355	83,620	99,120	118,510	138,210	155,795	----	212,092
	1998-9	74,140	89,990	108,880	128,335	149,415	168,100	186,670	222,400
	1999-00	75,015	90,845	106,625	126,495	146,970	165,090	184,510	214,525
	2000-1	78,570	95,380	113,270	131,620	151,405	170,065	190,385	230,625
	2001-2	65,405	80,005	96,270	114,585	131,620	148,100	166,575	195,505
	2002-3	76,965	92,595	107,470	126,205	144,265	160,770	179,320	211,035
	2003-4	72,405	87,840	102,180	120,955	138,085	154,760	174,365	206,760
	2004-5	70,745	85,990	101,010	119,435				
Dehydrated[4]	2001-2	----	----	----	----	----	----	----	38,581
	2002-3	15,675	19,660	23,710	27,950	31,915	36,105	40,455	48,940
	2003-4	14,250	18,440	22,050	26,090	30,290	34,630	39,070	47,750
	2004-5	13,365	17,015	19,995	23,735				

[1] Total quantity received and used for processing regardless of the State in which the potatoes were produced. Amount excludes quantities used for potato chips in Maine, Michigan and Wisconsin.   [2] Includes Maine grown potatoes only.   [3] Colorado, Minnesota, Nevada, North Dakota and Wisconsin.   [4] Dehydrated products except starch and flour. Included in above totals. Includes CO, ID, NV, ND, OR, WA, and WI.   *Source: National Agricultural Statistics Service, U.S. Department of Agriculture (NASS-USDA)*

Rayon and Other Synthetic Fibers

World Cellulosic Fiber Production   In Thousands of Metric Tons

Year	Brazil	Bulgaria	China	CIS	Czech Republic	India	Indo-nesia	Japan	Mexico	Taiwan	Thailand	United States	World Total
1995	53.1	----	435.0	----	35.0	262.1	----	212.7	----	139.6	----	226.0	2,423
1996	34.4	4.7	432.0	92.4	31.4	251.9	179.6	198.2	13.6	144.7	61.0	213.1	2,270
1997	36.4	4.2	450.0	108.7	27.3	242.4	212.9	184.1	14.8	148.4	60.2	208.1	2,314
1998	29.2	13.1	451.5	99.6	26.9	264.4	222.0	164.5	15.5	142.6	45.7	165.5	2,227
1999	34.6	13.5	472.1	88.0	17.6	248.5	195.6	135.5	13.5	143.7	55.3	134.7	2,074
2000	36.2	15.0	552.3	83.7	7.1	297.5	207.0	126.2	14.8	141.5	65.0	158.8	2,215
2001	28.7	12.2	608.6	64.4	7.6	251.9	205.0	107.1	22.6	127.4	65.0	103.0	2,083
2002	34.2	5.6	682.1	72.9	7.3	285.7	214.0	68.1	16.8	114.2	71.1	82.7	2,121
2003[1]	47.2	5.2	800.2	78.8	9.1	283.0	224.0	68.3	14.8	121.5	73.8	79.7	2,260
2004[2]	49.5	6.0	983.0	104.8	9.2	360.9	250.0	96.6	20.0	145.2	75.0	94.0	2,748

[1] Preliminary.   [2] Producing capacity.   Source: Fiber Economics Bureau, Inc. (FEB)

World Noncellulosic Fiber Production (Except Olefin)   In Thousands of Metric Tons

Year	Brazil	China	India	Indo-nesia	Japan	Korea	Mexico	Pakistan	Taiwan	Thailand	Turkey	United States[3]	World Total
1995	227.4	2,283.7	738.0	----	1,400.0	1,858.2	516.6	----	2,410.5	----	----	3,238.9	18,377
1996	229.6	2,729.6	916.4	779.6	1,399.0	2,025.2	584.6	312.8	2,561.0	533.0	478.5	3,284.1	19,765
1997	248.3	3,527.2	1,240.7	956.1	1,433.6	2,403.3	612.7	322.7	2,932.4	575.4	500.7	3,420.0	22,396
1998	268.6	4,406.8	1,361.3	881.5	1,363.6	2,446.0	591.1	427.8	3,111.5	542.6	529.8	3,222.7	23,254
1999	292.6	5,235.1	1,493.3	1,037.8	1,299.7	2,592.8	571.2	478.0	2,927.7	694.2	613.5	3,169.5	24,885
2000	311.1	6,158.4	1,568.4	1,142.7	1,307.9	2,659.0	586.8	503.9	3,122.9	769.5	744.5	3,149.2	26,219
2001	288.8	7,322.9	1,570.2	1,190.6	1,239.5	2,471.9	536.4	528.4	2,977.5	784.5	669.2	2,687.6	26,382
2002	293.1	8,849.4	1,695.3	1,132.8	1,129.1	2,455.7	509.6	581.7	3,089.3	852.6	728.1	2,805.0	28,008
2003[1]	314.2	10,441.1	1,792.0	1,143.3	1,030.3	2,418.0	457.6	579.6	3,045.9	872.5	766.9	2,693.2	29,498
2004[2]	387.7	14,170.0	2,342.3	1,420.0	1,432.1	2,847.8	632.5	763.5	3,474.1	1,078.1	946.2	3,259.2	37,759

[1] Preliminary.   [2] Producing capacity.   [3] Beginning 1995; data for USA and Canada.   Source: Fiber Economics Bureau, Inc. (FEB)

World Production of Synthetic Fibers   In Thousands of Metric Tons

| | Noncellulosic Fiber Production (Except Olefin) | | | | | | | Glass Fiber Production | | | | | | Cigarette |
| | By Fibers | | | | World Total | | | | | | | | | |
Year	Acrylic & Mod-acrylic	Nylon & Aramid	Polyester	Other Fibers[3]	Yarn & Monofil-aments	Staple, Tow & Fiberfill	Total	Europe	Japan	Americas	United States	China	Ex-USSR	Total	Tow Pro-duction
1995	2,446	3,740	11,945	247	9,684	8,693	18,377	567	318	96	981	85	55	2,308	550
1996	2,604	3,858	13,047	256	10,529	9,236	19,765	585	316	94	996	98	25	2,387	584
1997	2,706	4,028	15,406	256	12,093	10,303	22,396	610	328	100	1,007	75	27	2,431	582
1998	2,656	3,792	16,539	268	12,959	10,295	23,254	660	300	96	1,018	60	30	2,416	551
1999	2,513	3,800	17,879	294	13,660	10,825	24,485	674	300	96	1,126	60	30	2,538	544
2000	2,634	4,117	19,155	313	14,771	11,448	26,219	728	280	96	1,143	60	28	2,580	570
2001	2,562	3,784	19,563	335	14,968	11,276	26,243	701	273	93	1,016	67	32	2,431	590
2002	2,713	3,946	21,023	350	16,005	12,027	28,032	718	251	96	1,222	90	34	2,661	596
2003[1]	2,678	3,992	22,258	424	16,879	12,473	29,352	724	250	100	1,307	120	37	2,790	595
2004[2]	3,054	5,106	28,815	545	22,254	15,266	37,520	740	250	104	1,363	150	40	2,903	-----

[1] Preliminary.   [2] Producing capacity.   [3] Alginate, azion, spandex, saran, etc.   Source: Fiber Economics Bureau, Inc. (FEB)

Artificial (Cellulosic) Fiber Distribution in the United States   In Millions of Pounds

| | Yarn & Monofilament | | | | | Staple & Tow | | | | | Glass |
| | Producers' Shipments | | | | Domestic Con-sumption | Producers' Shipments | | | | Domestic Con-sumption | Fiber Ship-ments |
Year	Domestic	Exports	Total	Imports		Domestic	Exports	Total	Imports		
1995	169.3	7.8	177.1	34.0	203.3	259.8	28.7	288.5	40.8	300.6	2,163.0
1996	168.9	6.3	175.2	39.3	208.2	225.4	20.0	245.4	35.3	260.7	2,196.0
1997	145.9	4.1	150.0	42.9	188.8	205.3	60.1	265.4	51.6	256.9	2,275.0
1998	111.2	3.5	114.7	38.1	149.3	184.4	31.4	215.8	47.4	231.8	----
1999	111.0	3.0	114.0	28.2	139.3	168.8	29.9	198.7	47.5	216.3	----
2000	109.9	5.1	115.0	23.2	133.1	162.3	69.3	231.5	37.5	199.7	----
2001	81.3	6.7	88.0	14.5	95.8	117.2	35.5	152.7	33.9	151.2	----
2002	66.3	2.3	68.6	12.7	79.0	91.1	12.6	103.7	56.2	147.4	----
2003[1]	57.0	2.0	59.0	11.7	68.7	86.7	13.1	99.8	44.5	131.2	----

[1] Preliminary.   Source: Fiber Economice Bureau, Inc. (FEB)

Man-Made Fiber Production in the United States   In Millions of Pounds

Year	-- Artificial (Cellulosic) Fibers -- -- Rayon & Acetate -- Filament Yarn & Monofilament	Staple & Tow	Total Cellulosic	Synthetic (Noncellulosic) Fibers — Yarn & Monofilament — Nylon	Polyester	Olefin	Total Yarn	— Staple & Tow — Nylon	Polyester	Acrylic & Mod-acrylic	Olefin	Total Staple	Total Noncellulosic	Total Manufactured Fibers	Total Glass Fiber
1995	208	290	498	1,829	1,597	1,870	5,296	874	2,290	432	521	4,117	9,413	9,948	2,282
1996	219	245	464	1,917	1,571	1,951	5,438	883	2,260	465	610	4,217	9,655	9,979	2,326
1997[1]	187	266	453	2,039	1,644	2,058	5,740	797	2,446	461	623	4,327	10,067	10,465	2,408
1998	144	216	360	1,887	1,541	2,212	5,640	799	2,357	346	712	4,214	9,853	10,314	2,490
1999	115	199	314	1,896	1,595	2,278	5,769	787	2,291	316	797	4,192	9,960	10,263	2,570
2000	114	232	345	1,947	1,509	2,406	5,860	733	2,405	339	816	4,293	10,153	10,236	2,738
2001	----	153	153	1,642	1,188	2,238	5,067	606	2,040	280	721	3,646	8,713	----	2,638
2002	----	104	104	1,772	1,218	2,235	5,225	681	2,050	260	749	3,740	8,964	----	2,759
2003[1]	----	100	100	1,762	1,145	2,292	5,198	697	1,886	220	680	3,483	8,681	----	2,789
2004[2]	----	----	----	1,837	1,166	2,348	5,351	680	2,064	220	676	3,640	8,992	----	2,789

[1] Preliminary.   [2] Estimate.   Source: Fiber Economics Bureau, Inc. (FEB)

Domestic Distribution of Synethic (Noncellulosic) Fibers in the United States   In Millions of Pounds

Year	Yarn & Monofilament — Producers' Shipments — Domestic Nylon	Polyester	Olefin	Total	Exports	Total	Imports	Domestic Consumption	Staple & Tow — Producers' Shipments — Domestic Nylon	Polyester	Acrylic & Mod-acrylic	Olefin	Total	Exports	Total	Imports	Domestic Consumption
1995	1,741	1,440	1,870	5,052	259	5,311	394	5,445	829	2,100	266	458	3,653	399	4,052	625	4,278
1996	1,801	1,429	1,954	5,184	251	5,435	482	5,666	844	2,016	288	515	3,662	465	4,128	608	4,270
1997	1,877	1,528	2,015	5,421	239	5,659	589	6,010	757	2,250	289	542	3,837	392	4,229	673	4,510
1998	1,790	1,426	2,167	5,383	218	5,601	637	6,020	763	2,105	267	596	3,732	340	4,072	777	4,509
1999	1,765	1,463	2,251	5,480	244	5,724	719	6,199	756	2,138	233	726	3,852	338	4,190	788	4,640
2000	1,795	1,353	2,371	5,519	250	5,769	790	6,309	674	2,174	244	757	3,849	327	4,176	727	4,576
2001	1,606	1,189	2,200	4,995	155	5,150	697	5,692	607	1,881	169	673	3,330	308	3,638	757	4,087
2002	1,668	1,113	2,192	4,973	189	5,162	765	5,737	637	1,823	170	723	3,353	353	3,706	875	4,227
2003[1]	1,666	1,051	2,260	4,977	179	5,156	766	5,743	673	1,688	167	635	3,162	246	3,409	829	3,991

[1] Preliminary.   Source: Fiber Economice Bureau, Inc. (FEB)

Mill Consumption of Fiber & Products and Per Capita Consumption in the U.S.   In Millions of Pounds

Year	Cellulosic Fibers Yarn & Monofilament	Staple & Tow	Net Waste	Total Cellulosic	Noncellulosic Fibers Noncellulosic	Net Waste	Total Noncellulosic	Total Manufactured Fibers[2]	Cotton	Wool	Other Fibers[3]	Grand Total	Per Capita[4] Mill Consumption (Lbs.) Man-made Fibers[2]	Cotton	Wool	Other Fibers[3]	Total All Fibers
1995	203	301	3.9	508	9,723	76	9,799	10,307	5,110	162	65.6	15,633	43.1	29.4	1.4	2.5	76.3
1996	208	261	4.0	473	9,936	100	10,036	10,509	5,340	164	46.0	16,059	43.5	29.7	1.3	1.8	76.3
1997	189	257	2.5	448	10,520	103	10,623	11,071	5,448	164	42.8	16,726	45.7	31.9	1.3	2.0	80.9
1998	149	232	1.4	383	10,529	165	10,694	11,077	5,225	126	44.3	16,472	46.4	33.7	1.3	1.8	83.1
1999	139	216	1.6	357	10,839	177	11,016	11,373	4,996	85	40.4	16,495	48.0	34.5	1.1	1.9	85.5
2000	133	200	1.9	335	10,884	190	11,075	11,409	4,754	83	38.5	16,285	48.5	34.9	1.3	2.1	86.8
2001	96	151	2.4	249	9,779	193	9,972	10,221	3,983	89	30.3	14,324	44.3	33.0	1.4	1.6	80.3
2002	79	147	1.8	228	9,974	190	10,164	10,392	3,609	53	29.0	14,084	47.0	34.4	1.3	1.9	84.6
2003[1]	69	131	1.2	201	9,735	177	9,911	10,112	3,153	49	15.0	13,329	48.1	35.1	1.3	2.4	86.9

[1] Preliminary.   [2] Excludes Glass Fiber.   [3] Includes silk, linen, jute and sisal & others.   [4] Mill consumption plus inports less exports of semimanufactured and unmanufactured products.   Source: Fiber Economics Bureau, Inc. (FEB)

Producer Price Index of Grey Synthetic Broadwovens   (1982 = 100)

Year	Jan.	Feb.	Mar.	Apr.	May	June	July	Aug.	Sept.	Oct.	Nov.	Dec.	Average
1989	114.3	112.0	112.2	112.2	112.1	113.1	114.7	115.0	115.0	115.8	115.9	115.3	114.0
1990	115.6	115.7	115.6	115.7	115.5	115.6	115.7	115.2	115.3	115.6	115.8	116.1	115.6
1991	115.7	114.7	114.4	114.1	114.3	113.9	114.8	116.4	116.5	116.5	116.8	118.2	115.5
1992	119.0	119.9	120.3	120.9	121.8	122.0	122.6	122.0	121.7	120.8	119.4	119.9	120.9
1993	119.6	119.1	119.1	119.2	117.1	118.4	118.0	118.0	116.9	117.3	115.2	114.5	117.7
1994	113.5	112.8	112.9	113.2	113.2	113.3	113.1	113.3	114.1	111.8	112.9	113.8	113.2
1995	114.8	116.8	116.7	116.3	116.6	117.1	115.4	114.8	116.9	116.4	114.7	116.2	116.1
1996	114.3	114.1	116.9	117.9	116.8	115.7	116.1	117.1	116.9	117.2	116.6	117.0	116.4
1997	117.9	118.3	118.3	117.9	118.4	119.0	118.8	118.5	119.4	118.7	117.6	119.6	118.5
1998[1]	120.1	120.4	119.7	120.2	119.8	119.7	118.0	118.1	116.7	114.2	115.1	115.0	118.1

[1] Preliminary.   Source: Bureau of Labor Statistics, U.S. Department of Commerce (BLS) (0337-03)

Rice

Rice is a grain that is cultivated on every continent except Antarctica and is the primary food for half the people in the world. Rice cultivation probably originated as early as 10,000 BC in Asia. Rice is grown at varying altitudes (sea level to about 3,000 meters), in varying climates (tropical to temperate), and on dry to flooded land. The growth duration of rice plants is 3-6 months, depending on variety and growing conditions. Rice is harvested by hand in developing countries or by combines in industrialized countries. Asian countries produce about 90% of rice grown worldwide. Rough rice futures and options are traded on the Chicago Board of Trade (CBOT).

Prices – Rough rice prices on the CBOT nearest futures chart in early 2004 extended the rally that started in 2002 and posted a 7-1/2 year high of $11.32 per 100 pounds (cwt or hundredweight) in May 2004. Rough rise prices fell sharply in July and then range-traded the remainder of the year, finally closing the year at $7.18. Regarding cash prices, the average monthly price of rice received by farmers in the US in the first 5 months of the 2004-05 marketing year (i.e., August through December 2004) rose by +5.1% yr/yr to a 6-year high of $7.92 per hundred pounds (cwt.).

Supply – World rice production in the 2003-04 marketing year rose +2.5% to 390.433 million metric tons, recovering somewhat from 380.846 million in 2002-03 which was the lowest since 1980-81. The world's largest rice producers are China with 30% of world production in 2003-04, India with 23% of world production, Indonesia with 9%, Bangladesh with 7%, Vietnam with 5%, and Thailand with 5%. US production of rice in 2004-05 rose +14.3% yr/yr to 227.7 million Cwt. (hundred pounds), which was a new record high.

Demand – World utilization of rice in 2003-04 rose +0.7% yr/yr to 414.106 million metric tons, which was a new record high. US rice consumption in 2004-05 rose +4.3% yr/yr to 119.0 million Cwt. (hundred pounds), which was mildly below the record high of 123.3 million Cwt. posted in 2001-02.

Trade – World exports of rice in 2003-04 fell -9.7% yr/yr to 24.712 million metric tons, which was mildly below the record high of 27.888 million metric tons posted in 2001-02. The world's largest rice exporters are Thailand with 33% of world exports, Vietnam with 16%, the US with 12%, China with 8%, and India with 8%. US rice imports in 2004-05 fell by –7.1% yr/yr to 14.5 million Cwt. (hundred pounds), falling back from the record of 15.6 million Cwt. seen in 2003-04. US rice exports in 2004-05 rose by +1.3% yr/yr to 105.0 Cwt., which was well below the record of 124.6 million Cwt. posted in 2002-03.

World Rice Supply and Distribution   In Thousands of Metric Tons

| | | | Imports | | | | | Utilization | | | Ending Stocks | | |
Year	Brazil	Indonesia	European Union	Iran	Nigeria	Saudi Arabia	Total	China	India	Total	China	India	Total
1999-00	602	1,500	1,117	1,100	950	750	20,311	133,763	82,670	395,030	98,500	17,716	146,421
2000-1	654	1,500	1,204	765	1,250	992	21,847	134,356	75,851	391,843	94,103	25,051	150,522
2001-2	625	3,500	1,138	964	1,906	1,053	25,985	134,581	87,351	409,119	82,169	24,480	139,425
2002-3[1]	1,117	2,750	1,198	900	1,897	938	26,184	134,800	80,740	404,618	67,224	11,000	110,266
2003-4[2]	650	700	1,020	950	1,600	1,150	24,223	135,400	84,350	412,001	44,561	10,900	85,502
2004-5[3]	750	1,000	1,000	950	1,350	1,500	24,525	135,700	82,400	412,009	34,661	8,900	71,811

[1] Preliminary.   [2] Estimate.   [3] Forecast.   *Source: Foreign Agricultural Service, U.S. Department of Agriculture (FAS-USDA)*

World Production of Rough Rice   In Thousands of Metric Tons

Year	Bangladesh	Brazil	Burma	China	India	Indonesia	Japan	Rep. of Korea	Pakistan	Philippines	Thailand	Vietnam	World Total
1999-00	34,602	11,424	17,000	198,480	134,563	51,899	11,470	7,066	7,735	11,957	25,000	31,706	607,880
2000-1	37,633	10,196	18,571	187,909	127,319	51,500	11,863	7,197	7,204	12,515	25,844	31,020	592,414
2001-2	36,469	10,393	18,000	177,580	139,634	51,101	11,321	7,407	5,824	13,000	26,514	31,873	593,061
2002-3[1]	37,784	10,368	18,600	174,543	109,061	51,800	11,111	6,687	6,719	13,000	26,058	32,617	562,711
2003-4[2]	39,232	12,806	18,500	160,660	130,513	54,301	9,740	6,015	7,351	13,846	27,289	33,285	580,298
2004-5[3]	38,254	11,618	17,500	180,000	124,512	54,250	10,920	6,757	7,501	14,154	26,364	32,576	592,525

[1] Preliminary.   [2] Estimate.   [3] Forecast.   *Source: Foreign Agricultural Service, U.S. Department of Agriculture (FAS-USDA)*

World Exports of Rice (Milled Basis)   In Thousands of Metric Tons

Year	Argentina	Australia	Burma	China	European Union	Guyana	India	Pakistan	Thailand	Uruguay	Vietnam	United States	World Total
1999-00	417	610	159	2,951	364	252	1,400	2,104	6,549	685	3,370	2,804	22,837
2000-1	378	617	670	1,847	286	167	1,685	2,429	7,521	736	3,528	2,590	24,077
2001-2	134	247	1,002	1,963	336	175	6,300	1,628	7,245	475	3,245	2,954	26,548
2002-3[1]	175	150	388	2,583	250	150	5,440	1,992	7,552	615	3,795	3,860	28,617
2003-4[2]	225	275	125	825	225	175	2,750	1,775	10,000	625	4,200	3,331	26,139
2004-5[3]	415	275	300	800	250	175	2,600	2,000	8,250	775	3,900	3,334	24,370

[1] Preliminary.   [2] Estimate.   [3] Forecast.   *Source: Foreign Agricultural Service, U.S. Department of Agriculture (FAS-USDA)*

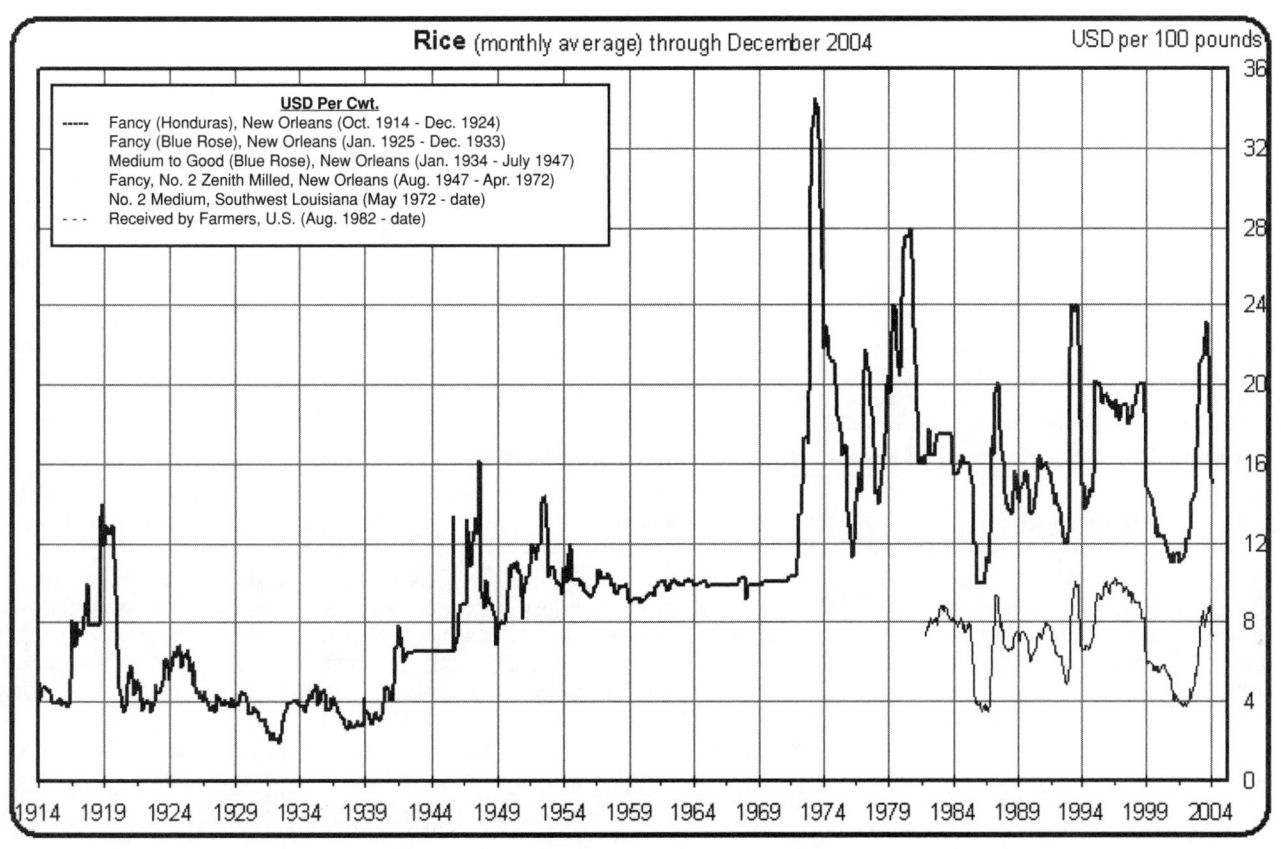

Rice (monthly average) through December 2004 — USD per 100 pounds

USD Per Cwt.
- - - - Fancy (Honduras), New Orleans (Oct. 1914 - Dec. 1924)
Fancy (Blue Rose), New Orleans (Jan. 1925 - Dec. 1933)
Medium to Good (Blue Rose), New Orleans (Jan. 1934 - July 1947)
Fancy, No. 2 Zenith Milled, New Orleans (Aug. 1947 - Apr. 1972)
No. 2 Medium, Southwest Louisiana (May 1972 - date)
- - - Received by Farmers, U.S. (Aug. 1982 - date)

Average Wholesale Price of Rice No. 2 (Medium)[1] Southwest Louisiana   In Dollars Per Cwt. Bagged

Year	Aug.	Sept.	Oct.	Nov.	Dec.	Jan.	Feb.	Mar.	Apr.	May	June	July	Average
1995-6	15.44	17.50	20.25	20.13	20.00	20.00	19.88	19.25	19.13	19.38	19.40	19.50	19.15
1996-7	19.50	19.50	19.25	19.25	19.00	18.81	19.19	19.25	19.25	19.25	18.40	19.00	19.14
1997-8	18.25	18.35	18.63	19.00	19.00	19.00	19.00	18.20	18.00	18.13	18.50	18.50	18.55
1998-9	18.35	18.75	19.00	19.00	20.00	20.00	20.00	20.00	20.00	20.00	20.00	20.00	19.59
1999-00	18.60	17.50	14.88	14.70	14.67	14.35	14.00	13.83	13.75	13.40	12.50	12.63	14.57
2000-1	13.00	12.34	12.48	12.41	12.38	12.38	12.25	12.00	11.82	11.53	11.25	11.25	12.09
2001-2	11.06	11.50	11.50	11.50	11.08	11.50	11.50	11.44	11.03	11.13	11.13	11.13	11.29
2002-3	11.13	11.50	12.25	12.25	12.25	12.63	13.50	14.05	14.25	14.44	14.50	14.88	13.13
2003-4	16.75	17.70	19.00	19.75	21.08	21.38	22.25	22.47	22.50	23.25	21.60	21.50	20.77
2004-5[2]	18.60	15.69	15.25	15.13	15.13								15.96

[1] U.S. No. 2 -- broken not to exceed 4%.   [2] Preliminary.   *Source: Economic Research Service, U.S. Department of Agriculture (ERS-USDA)*

Average Price Received by Farmers for Rice (Rough) in the United States   In Dollars Per Cwt.

Year	Aug.	Sept.	Oct.	Nov.	Dec.	Jan.	Feb.	Mar.	Apr.	May	June	July	Average[2]
1995-6	7.64	7.95	8.77	9.12	9.36	9.33	9.10	9.31	9.34	9.69	9.74	9.68	9.15
1996-7	10.10	10.00	9.66	9.41	9.82	9.95	10.10	10.20	10.30	10.20	9.90	10.00	9.96
1997-8	9.94	9.92	10.00	9.82	9.77	9.57	9.75	9.67	9.40	9.38	9.58	9.58	9.70
1998-9	9.01	9.42	9.31	9.02	9.10	9.09	9.02	8.93	8.49	8.21	8.25	8.26	8.89
1999-00	6.91	6.17	5.91	5.96	6.01	5.98	5.82	5.64	5.75	5.62	5.69	5.59	5.93
2000-1	5.72	5.53	5.57	5.72	5.69	5.86	5.72	5.66	5.68	5.40	5.14	5.32	5.61
2001-2	5.10	4.78	4.36	4.08	4.07	4.30	4.16	3.99	3.94	3.98	3.92	3.81	4.21
2002-3	3.71	3.94	3.69	3.70	4.13	4.66	4.24	4.31	4.61	4.84	5.43	5.31	4.38
2003-4	5.47	6.18	6.44	6.99	7.57	8.57	8.23	8.01	8.13	8.27	8.69	8.79	7.61
2004-5[1]	8.85	8.38	7.59	7.39	7.43	7.16	6.83						7.66

[1] Preliminary.   [2] Weighted average by sales.   *Source: Economic Research Service, U.S. Department of Agriculture (ERS-USDA)*

RICE

Salient Statistics of Rice, Rough & Milled (Rough Equivalent) in the United States   In Millions of Cwt.

Crop Year Beginning Aug. 1	Supply				Disappearance						Total Disap-pearance	Government Support Program					
					Domestic							CCC Stocks July 31	Put Under Price Support	Loan Rate ($ Per Cwt.)			
														Rough[3]			
	Stocks Aug. 1	Pro-duction	Imports	Total Supply	Food	Brewers	Seed	Total	Resi-dual	Exports				Long	Medium	All Classes	Milled Long
1999-00	22.1	206.0	10.1	238.2	90.1	16.0	3.8	121.9	6.5	88.8	210.7	0	107.6	6.67	6.12	6.50	10.66
2000-1	27.5	190.9	10.9	229.2	113.4	[4]	4.1	117.5	[4]	83.2	200.7	0	----	6.66	6.12	6.50	10.71
2001-2	28.5	215.3	13.2	256.9	119.3	[4]	4.0	123.3	[4]	94.7	218.0	0	----	6.67	6.09	6.50	10.69
2002-3	39.0	211.0	14.8	264.8	109.7	[4]	3.7	113.4	[4]	124.6	238.0	0	----	6.66	6.06	6.50	10.66
2003-4[1]	26.8	199.9	15.6	242.2	110.7	[4]	4.1	114.9	[4]	103.7	218.6	0	----	6.64	6.09	6.50	10.65
2004-5[2]	23.7	230.8	13.5	268.0	119.0	[4]	4.0	123.0	[4]	105.0	228.0	0	----	6.66	6.04	6.50	10.61

[1] Preliminary.   [2] Forecast.   [3] Loan rate for each class of rice is the sum of the whole kernels' loan rate weighted by its milling yield (average 56%) and the broken kernels' loan rate weighted by its milling yield (average 12%).   [4] Included in food.
Source: Economic Research Service, U.S. Department of Agriculture (ERS-USDA)

Acreage, Yield, Production and Prices of Rice in the United States

Crop Year	Acreage Harvested (1,000 Acres)		Yield Per Harvested Acre (In Lbs.)		Production 1,000 Cwt.			Value of Pro-duction $1,000	Wholesale Prices ($ Per Cwt.)		Milled Rice, Average C.I.F. at Rotterdam		
	Southern States	California	United States	California	United States	Southern States	California	United States		Arkan-sas[2]	Hous-ton[3]	U.S. No. 2[4]	Thai "A"[5]	Thai "B"[5]
												$ Per Metric Ton		
1999-00	3,007	505	3,512	7,270	5,866	169,337	36,690	206,027	1,231,207	15.01	15.33	272	----	278
2000-1	2,491	548	3,039	7,940	6,281	147,351	43,521	190,872	1,049,961	11.75	14.92	274	----	234
2001-2	2,843	471	3,314	8,170	6,496	176,780	38,490	215,270	925,055	10.57	12.88	208	----	225
2002-3	2,679	528	3,207	8,140	6,578	167,971	42,989	210,960	979,628	11.91	11.76	221	----	NA
2003-4	2,490	507	2,997	7,700	6,670	160,861	39,036	199,897	1,628,948	19.40	17.60	362	----	NA
2004-5[1]	2,735	590	3,325	8,600	6,942	180,059	50,759	230,818	1,676,020	14.79	18.39			

[1] Preliminary.   [2] F.O.B. mills, Arkansas, medium.   [3] Houston, Texas (long grain).   [4] Milled, 4%, container, FAS.   [5] SWR, 100%, bulk.
NA = Not available.   *Source: Economic Research Service, U.S. Department of Agriculture (ERS-USDA)*

U.S. Exports of Milled Rice, by Country of Destination   In Thousands of Metric Tons

Year Beginning October	Canada	Haiti	Iran	Ivory Coast	Jamaica	Mexico	Nether-lands	Peru	Saudi Arabia	South Africa	Switzer-land	United Kingdom	Total
1998-9	174.9	219.9	----	13.9	17.4	353.7	44.0	103.9	113.0	77.9	25.0	110.3	3,076
1999-00	181.1	221.0	----	21.1	38.2	525.8	60.6	19.5	164.8	70.6	30.2	141.9	3,307
2000-1	182.4	212.3	----	22.2	32.0	516.0	50.8	1.0	156.3	65.9	33.2	104.0	3,058
2001-2	174.5	247.1	----	25.0	28.7	740.4	52.9	11.2	97.0	67.3	18.0	106.0	3,536
2002-3	168.6	324.8	10.3	65.8	60.7	740.6	71.7	23.8	97.6	73.1	26.2	126.4	4,469
2003-4[1]	205.2	242.2	----	32.7	50.9	734.6	30.4	3.5	89.8	.0	10.7	99.5	3,713

[1] Preliminary.   *Source: Economic Research Service, U.S. Department of Agriculture (ERS-USDA)*

U.S. Rice Exports by Export Program   In Thousands of Metric Tons

Fiscal Year	PL 480	Section 416	CCC Credit Pro-grams[2]	CCC African Relief Exports	EEP[3]	Export Pro-grams[4]	Exports Outside Specified Export Programs	Total U.S. Rice Exports	% Export Programs as a Share of Total Exports
1999	542	0	192	0	0	287	2,479	3,066	19
2000	209	147	225	0	0	393	2,914	3,307	12
2001	144	30	----	0	0	231	2,828	3,059	8
2002	241	56	----	0	0	356	3,181	3,537	10
2003	263	0	----	0	0	309	4,161	4,470	7
2004[1]	129	0	----	0	0	223	3,491	3,714	6

[1] Preliminary.   [2] May not completely reflect exports made under these programs.   [3] Sales not shipments.   [4] adjusted for estimated overlap between CCC export credit and EEP shipments.   *Source: Economice Research Service, U.S. Department of Agriculture (ERS-USDA)*

Production of Rice (Rough) in the United States, by Type and Variety   In Thousands of Cwt.

Year	Long Grain	Medium Grain	Short Grain	Total	Year	Long Grain	Medium Grain	Short Grain	Total
1995	121,730	51,241	900	173,871	2000	128,756	59,514	2,602	190,872
1996	113,629	56,901	1,069	171,599	2001	167,555	46,105	1,610	215,270
1997	124,485	57,091	1,416	182,992	2002	157,243	52,201	1,516	210,960
1998	139,328	43,404	1,711	184,443	2003	149,011	48,180	2,706	199,897
1999	151,863	50,540	3,624	206,027	2004[1]	168,901	58,689	3,228	230,818

[1] Preliminary.   *Source: National Agricultural Statistics Service, U.S. Department of Agriculture (NASS-USDA)*

Rubber

Rubber is a natural or synthetic substance characterized by elasticity, water repellence, and electrical resistance. Pre-Columbian Native South Americans discovered many uses for rubber such as containers, balls, shoes, and waterproofing for fabrics such as coats and capes. The Spaniards tried to duplicate these products for many years but were unsuccessful. The first commercial application of rubber began in 1791 when Samuel Peal patented a method of waterproofing cloth by treating it with a solution of rubber and turpentine. In 1839, Charles Goodyear revolutionized the rubber industry with his discovery of a process called vulcanization, which involves combining rubber and sulfur and heating the mixture.

Natural rubber is obtained from latex, a milky white fluid, from the Hevea Brasiliensis tree. The latex is gathered by cutting a chevron shape through the bark of the rubber tree. The latex is collected in a small cup, with approximately 1 fluid ounce per cutting. The cuttings are usually done every other day until the cuttings reach the ground. The tree is then allowed to renew itself before a new tapping is started. The collected latex is strained, diluted with water, and treated with acid to bind the rubber particles together. The rubber is then pressed between rollers to consolidate the rubber into slabs or thin sheets and is air-dried or smoke-dried for shipment.

During World War II, natural rubber supplies from the Far East were cut off, and the rubber shortage accelerated the development of synthetic rubber in the US. Synthetic rubber is produced by chemical reactions, condensation or polymerization, of certain unsaturated hydrocarbons. Synthetic rubber is made of raw material derived from petroleum, coal, oil, natural gas, and acetylene and is almost identical to natural rubber in chemical and physical properties.

Natural rubber and Rubber Index futures are traded on the Osaka Mercantile Exchange (OME). The OME's natural rubber contract is based on the RSS3 ribbed smoked sheet No. 3. The OME's Rubber Index Futures Contract is based on a composite of 8 component grades from 6 rubber markets in the world. Rubber futures are also traded on the Shanghai Futures Exchange (SHFE) and the Tokyo Commodity Exchange (TOCOM).

Prices – The average monthly price for spot crude rubber (No.1 smoked sheets, ribbed, plantation rubber), basis in New York, rose slightly in 2004 by +0.2% to 49.25 cents per pound, which was a 7-year high. A 3-decade low of 33.88 cents was seen as recently as 2001 during that recessionary year.

Supply – World production of rubber in 2001, the latest full reporting year for the series, rose 5.5% to 7.130 million metric tons from 6.760 million metric tons in 2000. The world's largest producers of rubber in 2001 were Thailand with 32.0% of world production, Indonesia (22.1%), India (8.9%), Malaysia (7.7%), China (6.3%), and Vietnam (4.4%). In 2001, world production of synthetic rubber fell by –3.5% to 10.490 million metric tons. The world's largest producers of synthetic rubber in 2001 were the US with 19.7% of world production, Japan (14.0%), Russia (8.8%), and Germany (7.9%).

US production of synthetic rubber in 2002 was set to rebound upward to about 2.2 million metric tons from the 8-year low of 2.064 million metric tons posted in 2001. US production of car and truck tires in 2001 fell to 255.700 million tires from 276.765 million tires in 2000.

Demand – World consumption of natural and synthetic rubber in 2001 fell by –3.7% to 7.070 million metric tons from 7.340 million metric tons in 2000. The largest consumers of natural and synthetic rubber in 2001 were the US with 14% of consumption, Japan with 10%, and France and Germany with a combined 7.5%.

US consumption of natural rubber in 2002 was set to rebound upward from the 9-year low of 974,000 metric tons posted in 2001. US consumption of synthetic rubber in 2002 was on track to increase to at least 1.9 million metric tons from the 11-year low of 1.840 million metric tons in 2001.

Trade – World exports of natural rubber in 2001, the latest full reporting year for the series, rose +2.4% to a record 5.070 million metric tons. The world's largest exporters of natural rubber in 2001 were Thailand with 40% of world exports and Indonesia with 29% of world exports. Together, Thailand and Indonesia accounted for 69% of world exports.

US imports of natural rubber in 2002 were on track to rise to 1.09 million metric tons from the 8-year low of 972,000 posted in 2001. US exports of synthetic rubber in 2002 were set to rise to about 875,000 metric tons from 844,400 metric tons in 2001, which would be only moderately below the record export figure of 886,000 seen in 2000 before the world recession hit.

U.S. Imports of Natural Rubber (Includes Latex & Guayule)   In Thousands of Metric Tons

Year	Jan.	Feb.	Mar.	Apr.	May	June	July	Aug.	Sept.	Oct.	Nov.	Dec.	Total
1993	95.3	79.9	93.9	86.3	74.1	81.2	83.6	77.8	69.2	73.4	86.0	86.9	987.6
1994	87.5	74.7	102.6	78.9	88.3	77.8	66.7	85.0	78.8	89.3	70.0	76.0	975.6
1995	81.7	86.9	102.3	90.2	94.1	93.4	78.0	81.0	81.5	89.2	79.1	68.7	1,026.1
1996	105.4	86.1	82.2	90.6	65.1	70.4	79.0	81.0	82.1	113.6	73.5	85.0	1,014.0
1997	94.2	92.0	93.9	88.2	93.0	65.1	76.8	90.1	87.5	86.8	87.6	89.0	1,044.2
1998	104.4	76.6	102.8	81.0	98.0	92.9	96.4	100.8	123.2	104.8	84.5	111.4	1,176.8
1999	91.8	90.7	93.4	101.6	84.8	80.0	76.6	112.2	88.7	127.5	83.1	85.9	1,116.3
2000	127.4	88.2	114.1	107.9	114.9	120.1	65.9	96.2	79.2	96.2	92.2	89.3	1,191.6
2001	85.2	69.1	93.9	80.0	74.9	63.8	101.1	109.2	69.9	92.4	69.2	63.4	972.1
2002[1]	104.8	71.2	79.2	90.8	106.1	92.2							1,088.6

[1] Preliminary.   *Source: International Rubber Study Group (IRSG)*

RUBBER

World Production[1] of Rubber   In Thousands of Metric Tons

				Natural								Synthetic		
Year	China	India	Indo-nesia	Malaysia	Sri Lanka	Thailand	Vietnam	World Total	Ger-many	Japan	United States	Russia[3]	World Total
1992	309.3	383.0	1,387.0	1,173.2	106.1	1,531.0	114.0	5,440	544.7	1,389.9	2,300.0	1,610.5	9,300
1993	326.1	428.1	1,300.5	1,074.3	104.2	1,553.4	114.0	5,310	569.7	1,309.8	2,180.0	1,102.5	8,600
1994	374.0	464.0	1,358.5	1,100.6	105.3	1,717.9	156.0	5,720	621.6	1,349.0	2,390.0	631.9	8,870
1995	424.0	499.6	1,454.5	1,089.3	105.7	1,804.8	155.0	6,070	480.0	1,497.6	2,530.0	836.9	9,480
1996	430.0	540.1	1,527.0	1,082.5	112.5	1,970.4	220.0	6,440	548.1	1,519.9	2,486.0	775.1	9,760
1997	444.0	580.3	1,504.8	971.1	105.8	2,032.7	212.0	6,470	555.1	1,591.5	2,589.0	724.9	10,080
1998	450.0	591.1	1,714.0	885.7	95.7	2,075.9	218.0	6,850	619.0	1,520.1	2,600.0	621.0	9,880
1999	460.0	620.1	1,599.2	768.9	96.6	2,154.6	230.0	6,810	720.1	1,576.7	2,354.0	737.0	10,390
2000	445.0	629.0	1,501.1	615.4	87.6	2,346.4	291.0	6,760	849.2	1,591.7	2,395.4	837.1	10,870
2001[2]	451.0	631.5	1,576.5	547.0	86.2	2,283.9	317.0	7,130	828.4	1,465.5	2,064.4	919.2	10,490

[1] Including rubber in the form of latex.   [2] Preliminary.   [3] Formerly part of the U.S.S.R., data reported separately until 1992.
Source: International Rubber Study Group (IRSG)

World Consumption of Natural and Synthetic Rubber   In Thousands of Metric Tons

			Natural							Synthetic			
Year	Brazil	France	Ger-many	Japan	United Kingdom	United States	World Total	France	Ger-many	Japan	United Kingdom	United States	World Total
1992	123.4	179.0	212.8	685.4	124.5	910.2	5,320	365.4	506.0	1,080.6	231.0	1,959.6	9,360
1993	131.7	168.5	174.9	631.0	119.0	966.7	5,430	314.7	488.0	1,022.0	211.0	2,001.0	8,630
1994	144.7	179.8	186.4	639.8	135.0	1,001.7	5,650	400.1	512.2	1,026.2	220.0	2,117.6	8,820
1995	155.2	176.0	211.7	692.0	118.0	1,003.9	5,950	430.2	426.4	1,085.0	226.0	2,172.0	9,270
1996	160.7	182.2	193.0	714.5	111.0	1,001.7	6,110	436.1	497.0	1,124.5	230.0	2,186.6	9,590
1997	161.0	192.3	214.0	713.0	119.0	1,044.1	6,470	416.2	509.0	1,163.0	235.0	2,322.7	10,010
1998	185.3	223.0	247.0	707.3	139.0	1,157.4	6,570	451.4	582.0	1,115.7	177.0	2,354.4	9,870
1999	177.6	252.7	226.0	734.2	130.0	1,116.3	6,650	434.3	565.0	1,132.9	189.0	2,217.5	10,280
2000	226.8	308.6	250.0	751.8	133.0	1,194.8	7,340	481.5	632.0	1,137.5	188.0	2,190.3	10,830
2001[1]	217.8	282.0	246.0	729.2	107.0	974.1	7,070	464.5	612.0	1,085.1	167.0	1,839.5	10,340

[1] Preliminary.   *Source: International Rubber Study Group (IRSG)*

World Stocks[1] of Natural & Synthetic Rubber (by Countries) on January 1   In Thousands of Metric Tons

			In Producing Countries							In Consuming Countries (Reported Stocks)			
Year	Total Synthetic	Africa	Indo-nesia	Malaysia	Sri Lanka	Thai-land	Vietnam	Total Natural	Brazil	India	Japan	United States	Total
1993	1,004	19.6	110	187.2	16.0	89.0	12.0	560	17.0	90.9	82.9	108.0	442
1994	949	21.6	110	159.2	17.2	115.6	12.0	570	25.0	96.4	85.4	71.3	410
1995	915	17.0	110	187.0	16.5	96.5	19.0	480	17.0	94.1	72.9	45.2	363
1996	988	21.0	110	175.6	17.0	113.0	20.0	490	13.0	127.4	77.1	67.1	414
1997	1,057	20.5	70	190.3	17.6	147.7	28.0	510	13.0	123.4	86.8	79.3	427
1998	1,081	25.5	40	209.5	17.9	159.4	28.0	510	13.0	157.0	87.2	57.2	385
1999	1,116	27.6	30	234.2	18.6	209.5	36.0	750	13.0	194.0	58.0	70.4	406
2000	1,103	27.9	33	236.6	18.6	250.9	16.0	880	34.0	215.1	79.1	46.0	443
2001	1,196	28.7	48	212.7	18.7	188.6	22.0	630	40.0	203.3	95.2	44.6	452
2002[1]	1,189	31.0	45	191.6	19.0	213.0	31.0	650	42.0	225.5	46.9	42.6	429

[1] Preliminary.   *Source: International Rubber Study Group (IRSG)*

Net Exports of Natural Rubber from Producing Areas   In Thousands of Metric Tons

Year	Cam-bodia	Guat-emala	Indo-nesia	Liberia	Malaysia	Nigeria	Sri Lanka	Thai-land	Vietnam	Other Africa[2]	Other Asia[3]	World Total
1992	20.0	15.7	1,268.1	30.0	939.1	70.4	78.6	1,412.9	80.9	135.0	25.9	4,010
1993	21.0	16.9	1,214.3	45.0	769.8	79.7	69.6	1,396.8	96.7	136.0	32.6	3,880
1994	32.0	22.3	1,244.8	10.0	782.1	49.6	69.1	1,605.0	135.5	145.0	28.9	4,250
1995	30.0	23.2	1,323.8	13.0	777.5	99.2	68.2	1,635.5	138.1	140.0	31.1	4,340
1996	31.0	29.2	1,434.3	30.0	709.7	48.8	72.1	1,763.0	194.5	166.7	65.3	4,380
1997	32.0	28.3	1,403.8	67.2	586.8	53.0	61.4	1,837.1	194.2	186.1	58.6	4,580
1998	33.0	25.2	1,641.2	75.0	424.9	74.0	41.4	1,839.4	190.6	182.2	62.8	4,720
1999	34.0	26.7	1,494.6	100.0	435.5	38.0	42.7	1,886.3	230.0	196.5	59.6	4,660
2000	35.0	30.0	1,379.6	105.0	196.4	36.0	32.6	2,166.2	269.0	202.9	54.9	4,950
2001[1]	35.0	32.0	1,453.1	109.0	162.1	30.0	32.0	2,006.4	292.0	208.1	69.5	5,070

[1] Preliminary.   [2] Includes Cameroon, Cote d'Ivoire, Gabon, Ghana and Zaire.   [3] Includes Myanmar, Papua New Guinea and the Philippines.
Source: International Rubber Study Group (IRSG)

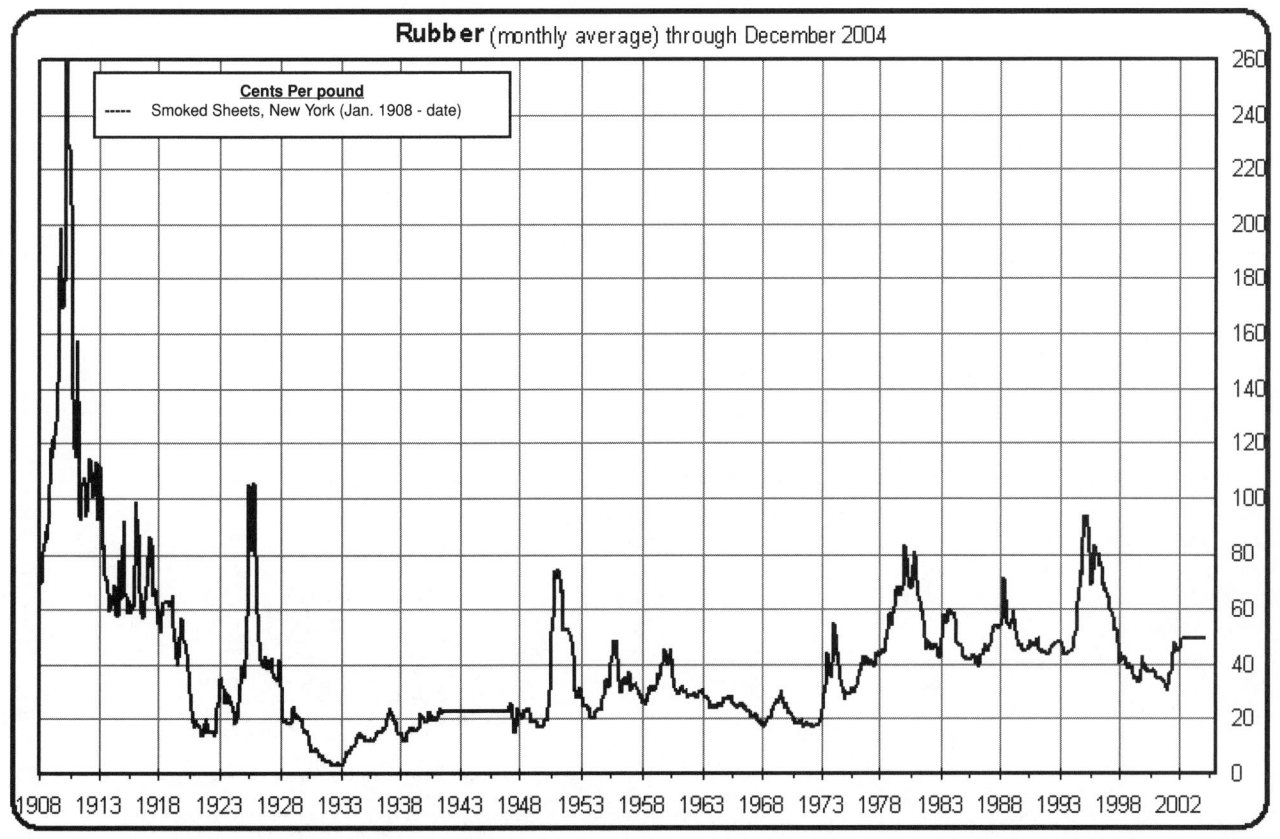

Rubber (monthly average) through December 2004

Cents Per pound
----- Smoked Sheets, New York (Jan. 1908 - date)

Average Spot Crude Rubber Prices (Smoked Sheets[1]) in New York   In Cents Per Pound

Year	Jan.	Feb.	Mar.	Apr.	May	June	July	Aug.	Sept.	Oct.	Nov.	Dec.	Average
1994	44.92	46.11	49.62	50.83	51.43	55.13	62.49	66.35	67.15	73.51	71.76	77.35	59.72
1995	85.68	92.61	94.15	93.43	89.50	80.57	72.13	68.54	70.70	73.59	83.19	83.39	82.29
1996	80.25	79.90	79.76	75.08	76.99	75.10	71.03	69.13	68.75	66.32	66.32	66.14	72.90
1997	65.06	64.76	63.53	59.97	57.71	57.30	51.96	52.45	51.89	51.36	47.99	40.53	55.38
1998	40.21	43.96	41.70	41.23	42.65	41.28	40.03	38.58	38.62	40.26	39.96	38.20	40.56
1999	38.99	38.58	36.34	34.98	35.75	34.64	33.60	33.63	34.45	37.58	42.57	38.88	36.67
2000	38.16	40.36	38.17	37.80	37.76	37.07	36.65	37.90	37.35	37.61	37.02	36.90	37.73
2001	35.98	35.66	34.78	34.50	34.80	35.00	34.80	34.48	33.07	31.98	31.14	30.35	33.88
2002	32.21	34.45	36.50	36.38	36.93	43.53	44.32	45.20	47.90	45.70	44.97	45.39	41.12
2003	47.95	49.25	49.25	49.25	49.25	49.25	49.25	49.25	49.25	49.25	49.25	49.25	49.14

[1] No. 1, ribbed, plantation rubber.   *Source: International Rubber Study Group (IRSG)*

Natural Rubber Prices in London   In Euro[1] Per Metric Ton

Year	Jan.	Feb.	Mar.	Apr.	May	June	July	Aug.	Sept.	Oct.	Nov.	Dec.	Average
Buyers' Price RSS 1 (CIF)													
1999	495.8	463.3	430.0	414.4	442.4	435.7	410.2	404.5	419.9	455.4	509.8	484.7	446.4
2000	462.0	518.2	487.6	496.0	500.5	501.8	494.5	529.5	526.2	537.4	518.4	502.4	506.2
2001	490.5	494.0	477.3	479.9	498.8	509.5	493.3	471.3	443.9	440.2	430.3	409.1	469.8
2002	461.8	502.5	522.1	511.9	518.9								503.4
Buyers' Prices RSS 3 (CIF)													
1999	466.4	451.6	417.9	394.0	418.8	425.3	391.1	384.8	398.6	439.0	489.5	453.3	427.1
2000	440.0	498.5	464.8	481.0	483.0	479.3	472.0	509.5	507.3	519.9	498.4	477.9	486.0
2001	464.2	467.3	450.2	455.6	482.5	497.3	477.3	450.7	423.6	418.3	411.4	389.4	449.0
2002	444.2	486.5	511.3	500.2	515.4	959.9	893.4	932.2	981.1				691.6
Sellers' Prices SMR 20 (CIF)													
1999	414.4	411.9	380.5	375.0	396.9	393.5	373.8	388.8	417.0	453.1	518.8	480.0	415.8
2000	471.9	504.4	472.5	466.3	465.0	447.5	435.0	477.0	478.1	486.3	487.0	483.8	472.9
2001	468.8	461.3	433.8	411.9	414.5	418.8	416.3	422.5	400.0	400.0	406.3	397.5	421.0
2002	428.0	461.3	510.6	500.6	503.5	921.3	864.6	898.5	978.9				674.1

[1] Data prior to June 2002 are in British Pound per metric ton.   *Source: International Rubber Study Group (IRSG)*

RUBBER

Consumption of Natural Rubber in the United States   In Thousands of Metric Tons

Year	Jan.	Feb.	Mar.	Apr.	May	June	July	Aug.	Sept.	Oct.	Nov.	Dec.	Total
1993	96.3	76.0	93.4	93.4	67.9	76.8	77.3	84.9	72.0	73.6	82.9	72.2	966.7
1994	92.8	84.9	93.1	82.7	89.6	84.6	76.2	87.8	74.8	90.1	66.4	78.7	1,001.7
1995	70.5	75.8	98.4	90.3	92.2	93.3	85.0	82.7	83.1	89.9	81.4	61.3	1,003.9
1996	102.5	85.8	81.2	87.9	65.6	76.7	81.9	88.1	83.3	108.4	72.1	68.2	1,001.7
1997	94.2	92.0	93.9	88.2	93.0	65.1	76.8	90.1	87.5	86.8	87.5	89.0	1,044.1
1998	104.4	76.6	102.7	81.0	98.0	92.9	96.4	91.7	119.1	104.8	78.4	111.4	1,157.4
1999	92.0	92.0	93.0	88.0	88.0	88.0	92.0	92.0	92.0	100.0	100.0	100.0	1,116.3
2000	110.0	110.0	110.0	114.0	114.0	114.0	80.0	80.0	80.0	93.0	93.0	93.0	1,194.8
2001	85.5	69.4	94.1	80.2	75.1	64.1	101.2	109.3	70.0	92.4	69.4	63.4	974.1
2002[1]	104.9	71.3	79.2	90.4	106.4	92.3	108.7						1,119.8

[1] Preliminary.   Source: International Rubber Study Group (IRSG)

Stocks of Natural Rubber in the United States, on First of Month   In Thousands of Metric Tons

Year	Jan.	Feb.	Mar.	Apr.	May	June	July	Aug.	Sept.	Oct.	Nov.	Dec.
1993	108.0	49.4	53.3	53.7	46.7	52.9	57.3	63.6	56.5	53.7	53.4	56.5
1994	71.3	65.9	55.7	65.2	61.4	60.0	53.2	43.8	41.0	45.0	44.2	47.8
1995	45.2	56.4	67.5	71.4	71.2	72.6	73.0	66.0	64.4	62.8	62.1	59.8
1996	67.1	70.0	70.3	71.2	73.9	73.4	67.1	64.2	57.2	56.0	61.1	62.4
1997	79.3	74.2	74.2	76.9	77.5	62.2	55.2	53.6	52.1	51.2	52.4	55.2
1998	57.2	61.2	65.5	63.5	60.9	66.7	53.6	57.9	54.7	58.3	58.9	66.5
1999	70.4	68.0	66.0	64.0	62.0	60.0	58.0	56.0	54.0	52.0	50.0	48.0
2000	46.0	63.4	41.6	45.7	39.6	40.5	46.6	32.5	48.7	47.9	51.1	50.3
2001	46.6	44.3	44.0	43.8	43.6	43.4	43.1	43.0	42.9	42.8	42.8	42.6
2002[1]	42.6	42.5	42.4	42.4	42.8	42.5	42.4	42.3				

[1] Preliminary.   Source: International Rubber Study Group (IRSG)

Stocks of Synthetic Rubber in the United States, on First of Month   In Thousands of Metric Tons

Year	Jan.	Feb.	Mar.	Apr.	May	June	July	Aug.	Sept.	Oct.	Nov.	Dec.
1993	406.9	345.9	345.7	346.0	340.5	351.8	342.1	341.6	333.6	326.4	319.9	321.4
1994	331.1	313.3	313.3	307.9	306.0	314.2	302.5	323.2	318.5	304.6	299.4	299.5
1995	305.4	307.4	302.8	293.5	319.4	315.6	325.9	349.2	355.7	354.6	347.0	351.5
1996	366.2	355.3	342.0	354.8	365.4	360.0	367.0	377.3	366.0	362.8	354.1	370.6
1997	400.5	400.4	408.4	412.7	411.9	403.5	393.1	376.9	378.4	364.4	365.2	377.7
1998	377.7	382.2	375.7	379.5	387.5	402.8	394.6	406.8	394.2	398.7	395.7	396.5
1999	409.3	404.0	404.0	406.0	399.0	420.0	410.0	419.0	413.0	390.0	391.0	389.0
2000	406.0	416.0	413.0	402.0	405.0	416.0	409.0	418.0	400.0	412.0	407.0	419.0
2001	443.0	451.0	467.0	4,559.0	448.0	433.0	426.0	420.0	394.0	400.0	394.0	379.0
2002[1]	392.0	377.0	379.0	393.0	398.0	384.0	385.0					

[1] Preliminary.   Source: International Rubber Study Group (IRSG)

Production of Synthetic Rubber in the United States   In Thousands of Metric Tons

Year	Jan.	Feb.	Mar.	Apr.	May	June	July	Aug.	Sept.	Oct.	Nov.	Dec.	Total
1993	120.0	160.0	220.0	190.0	200.0	180.0	190.0	180.0	180.0	180.0	190.0	180.0	2,180
1994	180.0	180.0	210.0	200.0	210.0	200.0	200.0	210.0	190.0	210.0	200.0	200.0	2,390
1995	220.0	200.0	210.0	210.0	240.0	220.0	210.0	230.0	210.0	200.0	200.0	190.0	2,530
1996	200.0	190.0	220.0	210.0	200.0	210.0	200.0	210.0	200.0	210.0	220.0	216.0	2,486
1997	220.0	200.0	220.0	230.0	220.0	200.0	220.0	220.0	230.0	210.0	210.0	203.0	2,589
1998	230.0	200.0	230.0	220.0	240.0	210.0	220.0	210.0	230.0	210.0	200.0	210.0	2,610
1999	200.0	181.0	209.0	195.0	205.0	190.0	199.0	192.0	180.0	204.0	197.0	202.0	2,354
2000	202.0	202.0	214.0	193.0	216.0	202.0	198.0	187.0	193.0	197.0	194.0	184.0	2,382
2001	203.0	188.6	184.3	172.1	175.5	162.3	166.7	164.7	174.3	178.6	155.1	139.2	2,064
2002[1]	176.1	171.9	192.3	190.6	187.5	185.0							2,207

[1] Preliminary.   Source: International Rubber Study Group (IRSG)

Consumption of Synthetic Rubber in the United States   In Thousands of Metric Tons

Year	Jan.	Feb.	Mar.	Apr.	May	June	July	Aug.	Sept.	Oct.	Nov.	Dec.	Total
1993	161.3	154.4	189.4	172.8	164.5	173.6	166.0	173.9	162.0	169.4	162.3	151.4	2,001
1994	177.7	160.8	191.8	173.0	173.5	187.5	164.9	187.1	176.0	178.8	175.7	170.8	2,118
1995	188.6	182.2	194.3	179.1	212.7	188.7	160.0	190.7	182.4	178.1	169.7	145.5	2,172
1996	188.0	173.7	186.9	176.8	184.9	178.5	177.0	197.3	182.9	201.0	177.8	165.5	2,187
1997	191.7	181.4	190.0	187.9	192.2	187.7	205.9	208.0	204.2	203.0	181.9	188.8	2,323
1998	196.5	192.5	214.8	194.4	199.8	201.4	192.0	204.5	202.2	200.3	181.2	174.8	2,354
1999	164.0	166.0	195.0	178.0	170.0	186.0	177.0	176.0	191.0	171.0	178.0	161.0	2,113
2000	173.0	185.0	202.0	178.0	194.0	196.0	177.0	189.0	172.0	182.0	168.0	147.0	2,163
2001	170.8	149.6	166.8	153.3	159.8	148.6	156.4	173.0	145.7	162.7	140.8	112.0	1,840
2002[1]	155.5	146.8	153.0	165.8	173.4	160.4	161.5						1,914

[1] Preliminary.   Source: International Rubber Study Group (IRSG)

U.S. Exports of Synthetic Rubber   In Thousands of Metric Tons

Year	Jan.	Feb.	Mar.	Apr.	May	June	July	Aug.	Sept.	Oct.	Nov.	Dec.	Total
1993	47.1	34.1	57.7	47.4	52.4	46.9	46.9	43.8	48.8	46.6	49.0	41.9	562.6
1994	48.8	46.4	55.4	57.0	52.4	49.6	50.2	62.8	60.7	59.9	56.9	55.0	655.1
1995	54.9	51.6	62.7	55.6	58.6	58.6	50.0	54.9	53.0	60.4	53.9	52.6	666.8
1996	61.1	57.7	64.0	68.0	48.2	66.8	62.3	57.1	63.9	65.2	58.6	58.6	731.5
1997	63.1	58.2	57.5	74.2	66.9	61.6	64.1	70.0	65.6	65.6	63.0	58.7	768.5
1998	61.1	60.8	62.8	59.8	66.9	61.8	60.1	64.4	63.7	62.3	59.2	59.2	742.1
1999	57.6	63.3	65.0	70.5	64.7	66.0	61.5	68.2	65.1	79.0	70.2	65.7	796.8
2000	64.3	73.4	83.8	70.2	73.2	72.3	72.4	78.6	78.6	75.2	73.3	70.7	886.0
2001	74.6	67.3	76.4	78.2	75.1	69.6	70.6	71.6	68.1	70.7	62.4	59.4	844.4
2002[1]	67.9	71.6	69.5	74.9	78.5	73.6	74.5						875.1

[1] Preliminary.   Source: International Rubber Study Group (IRSG)

Production of Tyres (Car and Truck) in the United States   In Thousands of Units

Year	First Quarter	Second Quarter	Third Quarter	Fourth Quarter	Total	Year	First Quarter	Second Quarter	Third Quarter	Fourth Quarter	Total
1985	54,460	49,385	46,468	46,610	196,923	1994	63,586	63,331	57,018	59,442	243,696
1986	49,240	45,687	46,855	48,507	190,289	1995	63,800	63,800	63,800	63,754	255,521
1987	51,205	50,210	49,723	51,839	202,978	1996	64,000	64,000	64,000	63,700	255,723
1988	54,677	52,986	51,195	52,493	211,351	1997	----	----	----	----	263,860
1989	56,716	56,626	50,086	49,444	212,870	1998	----	----	----	----	270,905
1990	55,915	53,856	51,163	49,729	210,663	1999	----	----	----	----	267,652
1991	51,296	52,796	49,183	51,115	202,391	2000	----	----	----	----	276,765
1992	57,890	57,319	57,554	57,487	230,250	2001[1]	65,367	62,809	62,366	56,106	255,700
1993	61,809	60,752	57,702	57,184	237,447	2002[2]	62,937	64,362			

[1] Preliminary.   [2] Estimate.   Source: International Rubber Study Group IRSG)

U.S. Foreign Trade of Tyres (Car and Truck)   In Thousands of Units

Year	Imports					Exports				
	First Quarter	Second Quarter	Third Quarter	Fourth Quarter	Total	First Quarter	Second Quarter	Third Quarter	Fourth Quarter	Total
1992	10,760	12,496	11,850	12,285	47,391	6,243	6,475	7,125	6,646	26,489
1993	11,519	13,045	12,688	13,036	50,288	7,266	6,930	7,163	7,133	28,492
1994	13,809	15,352	14,906	14,774	58,841	7,444	8,035	7,945	8,678	32,102
1995	14,883	14,977	13,762	12,718	56,340	8,438	8,502	8,478	9,174	34,592
1996	13,163	13,864	12,543	13,186	52,756	8,244	10,013	8,672	9,401	36,330
1997	13,359	14,487	15,314	16,064	59,434	9,466	11,386	10,456	11,085	42,452
1998	17,046	17,728	18,016	19,346	72,124	12,840	10,678	10,018	10,372	43,923
1999	19,471	22,295	22,194	23,784	87,768	9,874	9,580	10,480	10,537	40,945
2000[1]	24,200	24,698	23,561	22,123	94,019	11,200	10,200	10,200	10,100	44,164
2001[2]	19,563	22,251	22,072	20,956	84,842	10,087	10,362	11,004	10,691	42,144

[1] Preliminary.   [2] Estimate.   Source: International Rubber Study Group (IRSG)

Rye

Rye is a cereal grain and a member of the grass family. Hardy varieties of rye have been developed for winter planting. Rye is most widely grown in northern Europe and Asia. In the US, rye is used as an animal feed and as an ingredient in bread and some whiskeys. Bread using rye was developed in northern Europe in the Middle Ages where bakers developed a dark, hearty bread consisting of rye, oat and barley flours. Those were crops that grew more readily in the wet and damp climate of northern Europe, as opposed to wheat which fares better in the warmer and drier climates in central Europe. Modern rye bread is made with a mixture of white and rye flours. Coarsely ground rye flour is also used in pumpernickel bread and helps provide the dark color and course texture, along with molasses. The major producing states are North and South Dakota, Oklahoma, and Georgia. The crop year runs from June to May.

Supply – World rye production in 2004-05 rose sharply by +24.0% yr/yr to 17.415 million metric tons, recovering from the record low of 14.041 million metric tons seen in 2003-04. The world's largest producers of rye are the European Union with 58% of world production in 2004-05, followed by Russia with 19%, Belarus with 9%, and the Ukraine with 8%. US production of rye accounted for only 1.3% of world production in 2004-05.

US production of rye in 2004-05 fell –0.2% to 8.615 million bushels. That was far below the production levels above 20 million bushels seen from the late 1800s through the 1960s. US production of rye fell off in the 1970s, and fell to a record low of 6.971 million bushels in 2001-02. US acreage harvested with rye in 2004-05 rose +0.3% to 320,000 acres, which was only modestly above the record low of 281,000 acres in 2002-03. US farmers in the late 1800s through the 1960s typically harvested more than 1 million acres of rye, showing how domestic planting of rye has dropped off sharply in the past several decades. Rye yield in 2004-50 fell –0.7% to 26.9 bushels per acre, which was below the record high of 33.1 bushels per acre posted in 1984-85. Modern rye production yields are more than double the levels in the teens seen prior to the 1960s when yields started to rise.

Demand – Total US domestic usage of rye in 2003-04 rose +2.3% yr/yr to a 4-year high of 13.000 million bushels. The breakdown of domestic usage shows that 25% of rye in 2003-04 was used for food, 23% by industry, 23% as seed, and 29% as feed and residual.

Trade – World exports of rye in the 2004-05 marketing year fell –9.6% yr/yr to a 7-year low of 928,000 metric tons. US imports of rye in 2003-04 fell –33.3% yr/yr to 4.000 million bushels, which was a 3-year low and was well below the record of 6.000 million bushels seen in 2002-03. US exports of rye in 2003-04 were negligible but rose +20.0% yr/yr to 300,000 bushels.

World Production of Rye   In Thousands of Metric Tons

Year	Argentina	Australia	Belarus	Canada	Union	Kazakh-stan	Romania	Russia	Switzer land	Turkey	Ukraine	United States	World Total
1995-6	40	20	2,143	310	6,134	84	45	4,100	42	255	1,208	256	21,939
1996-7	36	20	1,794	309	5,680	29	48	5,900	46	245	1,100	227	22,049
1997-8	62	20	1,788	320	6,021	60	50	7,500	46	235	1,348	207	24,131
1998-9	66	20	1,384	408	6,345	20	45	3,300	20	232	1,140	309	20,081
1999-00	116	20	929	387	11,413	20	50	4,800	20	233	919	280	19,284
2000-1	125	20	1,360	260	10,203	50	50	5,450	20	260	966	213	19,072
2001-2	81	20	1,294	228	11,891	75	50	6,600	20	220	1,822	175	22,574
2002-3[1]	80	20	1,600	134	9,174	50	50	7,150	20	255	1,511	165	20,302
2003-4[2]	70	20	1,200	327	6,931	50	50	4,200	20	240	625	219	14,041
2004-5[3]	70	20	1,500	420	10,035	50	50	3,300	20	240	1,400	219	17,415

[1] Preliminary.   [2] Estimate.   [3] Forecast.   Source: Foreign Agricultural Service, U.S. Department of Agriculture (FAS-USDA)

World Imports and Exports of Rye   In Thousands of Metric Tons

Crop Year	Imports							Exports					
	European Union	Japan	Rep. of Korea	Turkey	Russia	United States	World Total	Belarus	Canada	European Union	Russia	United States	World Total
1995-6	1	332	928	2	128	96	1,742	2	113	1,768	100	1	2,241
1996-7	2	267	242	----	185	110	1,262	8	158	1,046	21	1	1,388
1997-8		323	4	----	2	141	676	----	142	487	1	2	651
1998-9	4	391	175	----	306	84	1,470	----	68	939	----	1	1,443
1999-00	368	397	476	183	464	87	2,276	----	87	2,085	----	7	2,387
2000-1	486	337	57	----	193	82	1,224	50	91	1,288	----	10	1,440
2001-2	433	335	121	20	7	126	1,150	30	66	730	4	5	1,129
2002-3[1]	513	414	31	14	----	156	1,344	110	53	748	291	3	1,493
2003-4[2]	76	341	114	43	6	84	805	60	171	626	156	2	1,026
2004-5[3]	100	350	100	15	100	76	796	100	125	550	----	3	928

[1] Preliminary.   [2] Estimate.   [3] Forecast.   Source: Foreign Agricultural Service, U.S. Department of Agriculture (FAS-USDA)

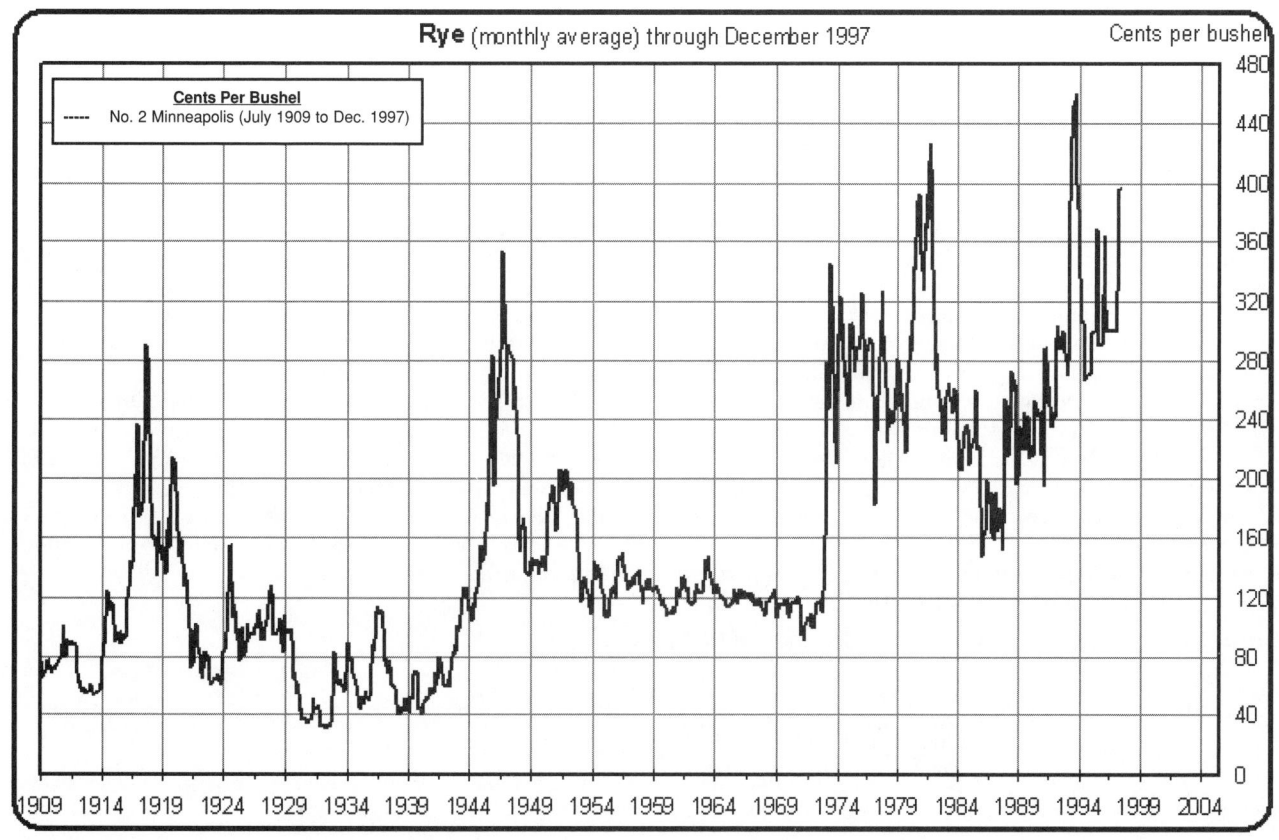

Production of Rye in the United States   In Thousands of Bushels

Year	Georgia	Kansas	Michigan	Minnesota	Nebraska	North Dakota	Oklahoma	Penns- ylvania	South Carolina	South Dakota	Texas	Wisconsin	Total
1995	1,155	400	544	609	480	726	810	330	440	1,650	380	480	10,064
1996	1,820	150	351	480	323	528	975	216	520	1,476	190	384	8,936
1997	1,430	300	450	400	240	513	1,080	400	250	728	330	432	8,132
1998	1,050	375	420	837	288	2,562	1,540	495	400	1,400	400	360	12,161
1999	1,050	300	756	775	405	1,517	1,045	600	500	1,012	450	384	11,038
2000	1,170	2	2	2	2	704	1,470	2	2	546	2	2	8,386
2001	875	2	2	2	2	340	1,150	2	2	350	2	2	6,971
2002	560	2	2	2	2	210	1,300	2	2	270	2	2	6,488
2003	800	2	2	2	2	750	1,540	2	2	672	2	2	8,634
2004[1]	600	2	2	2	2	780	1,980	2	2	649	2	2	8,615

[1] Preliminary.   [2] Estimates not published beginning in 2000.   Source: Agricultural Statistics Board, U.S. Department of Agriculture (ASB-USDA)

Salient Statistics of Rye in the United States   In Thousands of Bushels

Crop Year Beginning June 1	Supply				Disappearance						Acreage		Yield Per Harvested Acre Bushels
	Stocks June 1	Pro- duction	Imports	Total Supply	Food	Industry	Seed	Feed & Residual	Total	Exports	Total Disap- pearance	Planted	Harvested for Grain	
											----- 1,000 Acres -----			
1995-6	1,451	10,064	3,760	15,275	3,318	2,000	3,000	6,018	14,336	41	14,377	1,602	385	26.1
1996-7	898	8,936	4,327	14,161	3,459	2,000	3,000	4,916	13,375	32	13,407	1,457	345	25.9
1997-8	754	8,132	5,562	14,448	3,298	3,000	2,000	5,306	13,604	80	13,684	1,400	316	25.7
1998-9	764	12,161	3,322	16,247	3,639	3,000	3,000	4,392	14,031	33	14,064	1,566	418	29.1
1999-00	2,449	11,038	3,424	16,911	3,300	3,000	3,000	5,736	15,036	286	15,322	1,582	383	28.8
2000-1	1,589	8,386	3,230	13,205	3,300	3,000	3,000	2,307	11,607	390	11,997	1,329	296	28.3
2001-2	1,190	6,971	4,945	13,106	3,300	3,000	3,000	3,045	12,345	193	12,538	1,328	255	27.3
2002-3[1]	568	6,488	6,000	13,056	3,300	3,000	3,000	3,405	12,705	250	12,955	1,355	263	24.8
2003-4[2]	445	8,634	4,000	13,079	3,300	3,000	3,000	3,700	13,000	300	13,300	1,348	319	27.1
2004-5[3]		8,615										1,380	320	26.9

[1] Preliminary.   [2] Estimate.   [3] Forecast   Source: Economic Research Service, U.S. Department of Agriculture (ERS-USDA)

Salt

Salt, also known as sodium chloride, is a chemical compound that is an essential element in the diet of humans, animals, and even many plants. Since prehistoric times, salt has been used to preserve foods and was commonly used in the religious rites of the Greeks, Romans, Hebrews, and Christians. Salt, in the form of salt cakes, served as money in ancient Ethiopia and Tibet. As long ago as 1450 BC, Egyptian art shows records of salt production.

The simplest method of obtaining salt is through the evaporation of salt water from areas near oceans or seas. In most regions, rock salt is obtained from underground mining or by wells sunk into deposits. Salt is soluble in water, is slightly soluble in alcohol, but is insoluble in concentrated hydrochloric acid. In its crystalline form, salt is transparent and colorless, shining with an ice-like luster.

Prices – Salt prices in 2003 (vacuum and open pan, FOB mine) rose +3.5% yr/yr to $124.24 per ton, which was a new record high.

Supply – World production of salt in 2003, the last full reporting year, rose +1.0% yr/yr to 210.0 million metric tons.

That was well below the record high of 221.0 million metric tons posted in 1997. The world's largest salt producers are the US with 21% of world production in 2003, China (15%), Germany (8%), India (7%), and Canada (6%). US salt production in 2003 rose +8.4% yr/yr to 43.700 million metric tons, recovering from the 10-year low of 40.300 million metric tons posted in 2002.

Demand – US consumption of salt in 2003 rose +18.0% to 53.200 million metric tons, recovering from the 10-year low of 45.100 million metric tons seen in 2002. The 2003 level was only mildly below the record high of 54.000 million metric tons seen in 2001.

Trade – The US relied on imports for 20% of its salt consumption in 2004, down from 23% in 2003. US imports of salt for consumption in 2003 rose +58.1% yr/yr to 12.900 million metric tons, which matched the record high seen in 2001. US exports of salt in 2003 rose +4.2% to 718,000 metric tons, and the bulk of those exports (585,000 metric tons) going to Canada.

World Production of All Salt   In Thousands of Metric Tons

Year	Australia	Canada	China	France	Germany	India	Italy	Mexico	Poland	Spain	United Kingdom	United States	World Total
1996	7,905	12,248	29,035	7,860	15,907	14,466	3,541	8,508	4,163	4,000	6,610	42,300	204,000
1997	8,883	13,264	30,830	7,085	15,787	14,251	3,510	7,933	3,859	4,000	6,600	41,500	221,000
1998	9,033	13,296	22,420	7,000	15,700	11,964	3,600	8,412	4,005	3,500	6,600	41,300	200,000
1999	9,888	12,686	28,124	7,000	15,700	14,453	3,600	8,236	1,623	3,200	5,800	45,000	207,000
2000	8,778	12,164	31,280	7,000	15,700	14,453	3,600	8,884	1,576	3,200	5,800	45,600	209,000
2001	9,536	13,725	34,105	7,000	15,700	14,503	3,600	8,501	1,484	3,200	5,800	44,800	214,000
2002[1]	9,887	12,313	36,024	7,000	15,700	14,503	3,600	7,802	1,566	3,200	5,800	40,300	208,000
2003[2]	9,800	13,350	32,424	7,000	15,700	15,003	3,600	8,000	1,500	3,200	5,800	43,700	210,000

[1] Preliminary.   [2] Estimate.   *Source: U.S. Geological Survey (USGS)*

Salient Statistics of the Salt Industry in the United States   In Thousands of Metric Tons

Year	Net Import Reliance as a % of Apparent Consumption	Average Value FOB Mine Vacuum & Open Pan $ Per Ton	Production Total	Production Open & Vacuum Pan	Production Solar	Production Rock	Production Brine	Sold or Used Producers Open & Vacuum Pan	Sold or Used Producers Rock Salt	Sold or Used Producers Brine	Total Salt	Value[3] Million $	Imports for Consumption	Exports Total	Exports To Canada	Apparent Consumption
1996	19	120.54	42,200	3,920	3,270	13,500	21,500	3,900	14,500	21,500	42,900	1,060.0	10,600	869	710	52,600
1997	17	119.61	41,400	3,980	3,170	12,900	21,400	3,990	12,200	21,400	40,600	993.0	9,160	748	624	49,000
1998	17	114.93	41,200	4,040	3,190	12,900	21,100	4,040	12,700	21,100	40,800	986.0	8,770	731	533	48,800
1999	16	112.49	44,900	4,190	3,580	14,400	22,700	4,190	14,700	22,700	44,400	1,110.0	8,870	892	730	52,400
2000	15	113.95	45,600	4,200	3,810	15,000	22,500	4,190	13,600	22,500	43,300	1,040.0	8,960	642	500	51,600
2001	17	120.02	44,800	4,120	3,310	17,000	20,400	4,090	14,600	20,400	42,200	1,110.0	12,900	1,120	984	54,000
2002[1]	18	120.02	40,300	4,100	3,390	13,500	19,300	4,070	11,400	19,300	37,700	1,010.0	8,160	689	585	45,100
2003[2]	23	124.24	43,700	4,070	3,330	16,300	20,000	4,010	14,100	20,000	41,100	1,130.0	12,900	718	585	53,200

[1] Preliminary.   [2] Estimate.   [3] Values are f.o.b. mine or refinery & do not include cost of cooperage or containers.   *Source: U.S. Geological Survey*

Salt Sold or Used by Producers in the U.S. by Classes & Consumers or Uses   In Thousands of Metric Tons

Year	Chemical[2]	Tanning Leather	Textile & Dyeing	Meat Packers	Canning	Baking	Agricultural Distribution	Feed Dealers	Feed Manufacturers	Rubber	Oil	Paper & Pulp	Metal Processing	Water Treatment	Grocery Stores	Water Conditioning Distrib.	Ice Control and/or Stabilization
1996	22,400	83	288	407	336	169	661	1,150	403	71	2,430	122	199	534	855	719	17,700
1997	22,400	78	273	416	334	167	307	1,110	683	68	2,440	107	177	471	800	624	15,000
1998	22,000	93	250	440	275	219	362	1,190	536	68	2,320	115	170	531	807	598	9,490
1999	22,400	103	235	405	225	234	254	1,210	533	72	2,430	112	153	899	831	600	15,300
2000	22,400	82	209	402	220	234	262	1,240	540	71	2,510	106	112	589	823	568	19,700
2001	20,100	87	172	411	213	242	280	1,170	533	61	2,260	100	124	512	824	560	16,800
2002	19,500	79	154	395	230	215	245	1,040	507	61	2,010	93	118	662	781	525	13,300
2003[1]	20,100	71	151	374	231	210	215	1,090	460	67	2,210	88	126	777	802	537	18,500

[1] Preliminary.   [2] Chloralkali producers and other chemical.   *Source: U.S. Geological Survey (USGS)*

Sheep & Lambs

Sheep and lambs are raised for both their wool and meat. In countries that have high wool production, there is also demand for sheep and lamb meat due to the easy availability. Production levels have declined in New Zealand and Australia, but that has been counteracted by a substantial increase in China.

Prices – The average monthly price received by farmers for lambs in the US in 2004 (through November) rose by +8.5% to 102.09 cents per pound, recovering further from the 10-year low of 67.61 cents seen in 2001. The average monthly price received by US farmers for sheep in 2004 (through November) rose by +8.7% to 38.85 cents per pound, recovering further from the 12-year low of 29.03 cents in 2002. The average monthly wholesale price of slaughter lambs (choice) at San Angelo, Texas in 2004 (through November) rose by 5.3% to a new record high of 96.55 cents per pound.

Supply – World sheep and goat numbers in 2001 rose +0.7% to an 8-year high of 898.132 million. The world's largest producers of sheep and goats are China with 31% of world production in 2001, India (20%), Australia (13%), and New Zealand (5%).

The number of sheep and lambs on US farms in 2004 (Jan 1) fell -3.3% to a record low of 6.090 million head, illustrating the downward trend in US sheep production. The US states with the most sheep and lambs were Texas (with 18% of the US total), California (11%), Wyoming (7%), South Dakota (6%), and Colorado (6%).

World Sheep and Goat Numbers in Specified Countries on January 1   In Thousands of Head

Year	Argentina	Australia	China	India	Kazak-hstan	New Zealand	Romania	Russia	South Africa	Spain	Turkey	United Kingdom	World Total
1992	25,706	161,073	206,210	161,084	34,556	55,162	13,879	55,255	36,076	24,625	44,700	28,932	931,903
1993	24,500	140,542	207,329	162,155	34,420	52,568	12,079	51,368	35,770	24,615	44,600	29,493	900,400
1994	23,500	120,900	217,314	169,569	34,208	50,298	12,276	43,700	33,800	23,872	44,000	29,333	881,258
1995	21,626	121,100	240,528	171,626	25,132	50,135	12,119	34,500	33,385	23,058	43,000	29,484	874,912
1996	17,956	121,200	279,535	173,519	19,600	48,816	11,086	28,336	35,145	21,322	42,400	28,797	897,009
1997	17,295	120,228	236,961	175,976	13,742	47,394	10,317	23,519	35,830	23,981	41,100	28,256	842,179
1998	15,232	117,494	255,055	178,462	10,896	46,970	9,747	20,697	36,821	24,857	39,500	30,027	853,061
1999	13,953	117,091	268,143	180,130	9,556	46,150	9,167	18,213	34,910	24,199	37,300	31,080	897,310
2000[1]	13,800	117,191	271,130	180,885	9,000	45,800	8,700	15,698	35,000	23,700	34,400	30,800	891,751
2001[2]	14,100	118,321	280,420	181,440	8,700	46,000	8,500	15,700	35,220	23,600	31,000	30,600	898,132

[1] Preliminary.   [2] Forecast.   Source: Foreign Agricultural Service, U.S. Department of Agriculture (FAS-USDA)

Salient Statistics of Sheep & Lambs in the United States (Average Live Weight)   In Thousands of Head

| | -- Inventory, Jan. 1 -- | | | | --- Marketings[3] --- | | | Slaughter | | | | Production (Live Weight) | Farm Value Jan. 1 | |
Year	Without New Crop Lambs	With New Crop Lambs	Lamb Crop	Total Supply	Sheep	Lambs	Farm	Commercial	Total[4]	Net Exports	Total Disappearance	Mil. Lbs.	All Million $	$ Per Head
1996	8,465	8,465	5,361	13,826	1,024	6,023	65	4,184	4,249	272	5,426	565.7	732.2	86.5
1997	8,024	8,024	5,356	13,380	1,011	5,709	62	3,907	3,969	1,361	6,162	591.3	761.7	96.0
1998	7,825	7,825	5,013	12,838	977	5,510	57	3,804	3,861	618	5,260	555.7	797.8	102.0
1999	7,215	7,215	4,733	11,948	790	5,208	65	3,701	3,766	393	4,922	533.6	637.6	88.0
2000	7,032	7,032	4,622	11,654	788	4,827	67	3,460	3,527	329	4,554	508.9	668.8	95.0
2001	6,965	6,965	4,495	11,460	711	4,795	68	3,222	3,290	299	4,303	495.6	694.5	100.0
2002	6,685	6,685	4,357	11,042	855	4,794	66	3,286	3,352	266	4,380	485.1	618.1	94.0
2003[1]	6,300	6,300	4,140	10,440	827	4,368	68	2,979	3,047	105	3,804	468.4	656.6	104.0
2004[2]	6,105	6,090	4,096	10,186									721.3	118.0

[1] Preliminary.   [2] Estimate.   [3] Excludes interfarm sales.   [4] Includes all commercial and farm.   Source: Economic Research Service, U.S. Department of Agriculture (ERS-USDA)

Sheep and Lambs[3] on Farms in the United States on January 1   In Thousands of Head

Year	California	Colorado	Idaho	Iowa	Minnesota	Montana	New Mexico	Ohio	South Dakota	Texas	Utah	Wyoming	Total
1997	960	575	285	285	180	432	235	130	450	1,400	375	720	7,937
1998	800	575	285	265	165	415	290	135	420	1,530	420	710	7,825
1999	810	440	265	260	175	380	275	125	420	1,350	400	630	7,215
2000	800	440	275	265	165	370	290	134	420	1,200	400	570	7,032
2001	840	420	275	270	170	360	255	142	420	1,150	390	530	6,965
2002	800	370	260	250	160	335	230	140	400	1,130	365	480	6,685
2003	730	380	260	255	145	310	175	150	380	1,040	310	460	6,300
2004[1]	680	360	260	250	140	300	160	140	370	1,100	265	430	6,105
2005[2]	670	365	270	245	145	305	145	142	375	1,070	270	450	6,135

[1] Preliminary.   [2] Estimate.   [3] Includes sheep & lambs on feed for market and stock sheep & lambs.   Source: Economic Research Service, U.S. Department of Agriculture (ERS-USDA)

SHEEP & LAMBS

Average Wholesale Price of Slaughter Lambs (Choice) at San Angelo Texas   In Dollars Per Cwt.

Year	Jan.	Feb.	Mar.	Apr.	May	June	July	Aug.	Sept.	Oct.	Nov.	Dec.	Average
1996	74.44	85.63	84.07	83.10	86.17	97.50	92.67	83.75	84.40	82.58	80.00	88.88	85.27
1997	94.63	100.81	97.50	95.50	83.17	83.25	78.94	90.25	85.45	82.75	80.33	83.52	88.01
1998	74.38	74.31	71.50	63.00	73.00	91.21	82.21	82.05	69.50	67.20	63.33	71.44	73.59
1999	69.31	67.88	68.54	70.50	82.70	81.06	77.29	81.17	77.00	74.81	78.00	83.29	75.96
2000	73.71	76.83	78.17	78.25	89.65	78.30	84.17	82.20	82.00	77.50	76.70	75.33	79.40
2001	81.25	87.00	82.63	83.30	86.07	75.21	69.82	54.47	56.50	57.67	59.00	71.60	72.04
2002	65.85	70.00	64.00	65.15	64.06	68.75	75.83	74.35	73.69	76.20	83.00	86.88	72.31
2003	89.25	90.25	96.25	88.13	95.75	97.25	87.88	85.81	91.44	91.31	91.00	96.17	91.71
2004[1]	99.44	99.94	102.50	92.31	97.50	101.37	97.50	91.12	92.25	91.75	95.58	99.12	96.70

[1] Preliminary.   *Source: Economic Research Service, U.S. Department of Agriculture (ERS-USDA)*

Federally Inspected Slaughter of Sheep & Lambs in the United States   In Thousands of Head

Year	Jan.	Feb.	Mar.	Apr.	May	June	July	Aug.	Sept.	Oct.	Nov.	Dec.	Total
1996	352	353	403	374	313	271	313	315	313	365	324	336	4,032
1997	294	317	386	321	308	293	295	288	310	324	299	337	3,771
1998	301	300	377	367	270	283	269	263	295	312	290	344	3,671
1999	260	291	411	295	260	259	253	283	294	293	317	341	3,557
2000	271	284	334	330	248	247	229	269	257	266	286	287	3,308
2001	258	236	316	275	227	221	229	258	230	274	273	266	3,065
2002	244	244	311	263	267	216	241	246	259	284	255	262	3,092
2003	227	211	252	280	209	216	225	226	241	251	223	246	2,805
2004[1]	207	199	295	238	175	220	207	219	231	228	228	229	2,676

[1] Preliminary.   *Source: Economic Research Service, U.S. Department of Agriculture (ERS-USDA)*

Cold Storage Holdings of Lamb and Mutton in the U.S., on First of Month   In Thousands of Pounds

Year	Jan.	Feb.	Mar.	Apr.	May	June	July	Aug.	Sept.	Oct.	Nov.	Dec.
1996	7,606	9,794	13,017	12,247	13,649	12,187	13,726	13,164	14,645	11,249	10,494	9,788
1997	8,899	9,473	9,862	11,163	13,027	15,220	16,594	18,535	19,383	16,119	16,894	16,534
1998	13,741	13,920	15,284	16,226	16,306	16,666	16,040	16,188	14,530	12,253	12,558	11,914
1999	11,721	10,452	12,134	12,374	13,146	12,313	12,459	11,975	12,240	9,815	9,210	9,446
2000	8,740	10,394	10,335	11,437	13,345	13,137	13,984	13,557	14,042	12,867	12,195	12,486
2001	13,455	13,833	13,141	13,729	13,551	14,586	15,443	15,744	15,266	13,979	13,238	11,336
2002	11,905	13,110	11,269	10,528	13,172	12,938	13,553	14,215	14,458	11,961	12,004	9,255
2003	7,124	6,232	4,063	3,900	5,016	5,838	5,427	5,929	5,855	6,210	4,485	4,883
2004[1]	3,795	3,671	3,355	3,164	3,251	3,504	3,872	3,376	3,878	4,179	4,166	3,715

[1] Preliminary.   *Source: Economic Research Service, U.S. Department of Agriculture (ERS-USDA)*

Average Price Received by Farmers for Sheep in the United States   In Dollars Per Cwt.

Year	Jan.	Feb.	Mar.	Apr.	May	June	July	Aug.	Sept.	Oct.	Nov.	Dec.	Average
1996	34.40	33.80	34.00	27.30	25.30	26.60	30.50	29.10	30.20	28.80	29.80	34.20	30.33
1997	41.80	41.30	42.50	37.50	34.00	36.60	39.40	38.40	33.90	35.80	38.90	37.70	38.15
1998	42.00	39.60	41.00	34.40	30.30	30.20	29.40	28.30	26.80	26.10	26.40	30.10	32.05
1999	32.40	30.20	32.70	31.80	31.50	28.90	32.00	29.80	29.20	26.40	30.20	33.40	30.71
2000	36.80	39.50	38.80	35.00	30.50	30.00	34.20	30.70	30.30	29.50	33.60	36.20	33.76
2001	43.30	47.50	46.60	36.90	36.30	31.70	34.10	32.20	29.90	27.20	27.10	34.00	35.57
2002	36.20	34.30	31.80	26.00	25.30	23.50	25.60	25.60	24.50	25.60	31.30	38.70	29.03
2003	41.30	44.00	40.90	31.10	31.30	29.40	28.60	29.20	32.50	35.00	40.50	45.10	35.74
2004[1]	43.80	40.80	36.70	37.10	36.50	32.10	37.40	38.50	41.80	40.70	41.50	44.80	39.31

[1] Preliminary.   *Source: Economic Research Service, U.S. Department of Agriculture (ERS-USDA)*

Average Price Received by Farmers for Lambs in the United States   In Dollars Per Cwt.

Year	Jan.	Feb.	Mar.	Apr.	May	June	July	Aug.	Sept.	Oct.	Nov.	Dec.	Average
1996	76.10	84.30	86.60	85.90	90.30	100.70	98.30	89.10	88.50	87.00	84.60	88.20	88.30
1997	94.60	99.80	99.70	96.40	90.80	86.50	81.10	92.70	90.20	87.20	83.10	83.90	90.50
1998	78.40	75.00	70.10	66.00	63.00	88.90	81.30	80.10	71.80	67.60	62.60	64.70	72.46
1999	68.20	67.20	67.40	67.40	82.80	81.30	77.00	80.30	75.30	72.60	76.30	77.60	74.45
2000	70.90	72.00	80.20	82.60	96.40	89.70	87.00	83.60	80.80	76.80	71.50	71.80	80.28
2001	74.10	80.10	84.00	84.30	80.00	71.60	64.30	54.80	52.50	51.40	52.80	61.40	67.61
2002	65.50	67.80	66.70	64.70	64.40	72.90	75.60	75.30	76.30	79.60	84.00	87.20	73.33
2003	92.00	92.40	97.10	93.70	97.60	89.30	89.40	88.60	95.10	96.80	99.70	97.70	94.12
2004[1]	104.00	106.00	104.00	100.00	103.00	105.00	102.00	97.80	101.00	98.20	101.00	102.00	102.00

[1] Preliminary.   *Source: Economic Research Service, U.S. Department of Agriculture (ERS-USDA)*

Silk

Silk is a fine, tough, elastic fiber produced by caterpillars, commonly called silkworms. Silk is one of the oldest known textile fibers. Chinese tradition credits Lady Hsi-Ling-Shih, wife of the Emperor Huang Ti, with the discovery of the silkworm and the invention of the first silk reel. Dating to around 3000 BC, a group of ribbons, threads, and woven fragments was found in China. Also found, along the lower Yangzi River, were 7,000 year-old spinning tools, silk thread, and fabric fragments.

Silk filament was first woven into cloth in Ancient China. The Chinese successfully guarded this secret until 300AD, when Japan, and later India, learned the secret. In 550 AD, two Nestorian monks were sent to China to steal mulberry seeds and silkworm eggs, which they hid in their walking staffs, and then brought back to Rome. By the 17th century, France was the silk center of the West. Unfortunately, the silkworm did not flourish in the English climate, nor has it ever flourished in the US.

Sericulture is the term for the raising of silkworms. The blind, flightless moth, Bombyx mori, lays more than 500 tiny eggs. After hatching, the tiny worms eat chopped mulberry leaves continuously until they are ready to spin their cocoons. After gathering the complete cocoons, the first step in silk manufacturing is to kill the insects inside the cocoons with heat. The cocoons are then placed in boiling water to loosen the gummy substance, sericin, holding the filament together. The filament is unwound, and then rewound in a process called reeling. Each cocoon's silk filament is between 600 and 900 meters long. Four different types of silk thread may be produced: organzine, crepe, tram, and thrown singles. During the last 30 years, in spite of the use of man-made fibers, world silk production has doubled.

Raw silk is traded on the Kansai Agricultural Commodities Exchange (KANEX) in Japan. Dried cocoons are traded on the Chuba Commodity Exchange (CCE). Raw silk and dried cocoons are traded on the Yokohama Commodity Exchange.

Supply – World production of silk in 2002, the latest reporting year, rose +0.8% to 132,000 metric tons, which was a record high and was sharply above the 12-year low of 85,000 posted in 1997. China is the world's largest producer of silk by far with 71% of world production in 2002. Other key producers include India with 11% of world production, Vietnam (9%), and Turkmenistan (3%).

Trade – The world's largest exporters of silk are China with 58% of world exports in 2002, Brazil with 1.1% and North Korea with 0.6%. The world's largest importers of silk in 2002 were India (with 35% of world imports), Italy (13%), Japan (11%), and South Korea (8%).

World Production of Raw Silk   In Metric Tons

Year	Brazil	China	India	Iran	Japan	North Korea	South Korea	Kyrgyzstan	Thailand	Turkmenistan	Uzbekistan	Viet Nam	World Total
1993	2,450	76,801	14,168	480	4,254	4,600	683	1,000	1,500	500	2,000	550	109,790
1994	2,450	84,001	14,500	600	2,400	4,700	700	1,000	1,600	500	2,000	600	115,796
1995	2,450	80,001	15,000	600	2,400	4,700	700	1,000	1,600	500	2,000	650	112,350
1996	2,000	51,000	16,000	1,000	3,000	5,000	----	1,000	1,000	5,000	2,000	1,000	88,000
1997	2,000	51,000	16,000	1,000	2,000	4,000	----	1,000	1,000	5,000	2,000	1,000	85,000
1998	2,000	68,000	16,000	1,000	1,000	5,000	----	1,000	1,000	5,000	2,000	1,000	102,000
1999	2,000	70,000	16,000	1,000	1,000	5,000	----	1,000	1,000	5,000	1,000	1,000	98,000
2000	2,000	78,000	15,000	1,000	1,000	5,000	----	1,000	1,000	5,000	1,000	3,000	107,000
2001[1]	2,000	94,000	15,000	1,000	1,000	----	----	1,000	2,000	5,000	1,000	10,000	131,000
2002[2]	1,000	94,000	15,000	1,000	1,000	----	----	----	2,000	4,000	1,000	12,000	132,000

[1] Preliminary.   [2] Estimate.   Source: Food and Agricultural Organization of the United Nations (FAO-UN)

World Trade of Silk by Selected Countries   In Metric Tons

	Imports							Exports					
Year	France	Hong Kong	India	Italy	Japan	South Korea	World Total	Brazil	China	Hong Kong	Japan	North Korea	World Total
1993	1,001	5,475	4,977	5,634	5,982	4,494	36,086	1,495	15,652	7,204	904	1,200	35,634
1994	1,047	6,165	5,750	9,235	5,772	4,128	44,136	1,739	21,004	6,149	1,265	1,400	41,998
1995	663	4,775	4,276	5,612	4,331	3,513	37,854	966	16,788	5,176	925	1,000	40,633
1996	675	3,978	2,980	4,400	6,098	3,737	37,615	1,071	15,791	4,165	946	1,000	38,587
1997	582	4,320	2,437	5,482	4,229	2,796	45,817	905	14,384	4,501	936	1,000	37,233
1998	592	2,030	2,846	4,088	3,357	1,510	31,908	780	12,250	2,105	612	180	29,611
1999	579	1,258	5,120	4,985	3,792	2,265	35,352	408	16,251	1,153	227	130	35,041
2000	481	866	4,732	5,906	4,020	1,843	32,279	370	17,520	936	239	120	35,033
2001	452	256	6,929	4,506	2,823	1,628	26,384	232	14,485	259	124	90	27,364
2002[1]	706	51	9,266	3,498	2,853	2,108	26,726	331	17,842	128	116	170	30,756

[1] Preliminary.   Source: Food and Agricultural Organization of the United Nations (FAO-UN)

Silver

Silver is a white, lustrous metallic element that conducts heat and electricity better than any other metal. In ancient times, many silver deposits were on or near the earth's surface. Before 2,500 BC, silver mines were worked in Asia Minor. Around 700 BC, ancient Greeks stamped a turtle on their first silver coins. Silver assumed a key role in the US monetary system in 1792 when Congress based the currency on the silver dollar, but then discontinued the use of silver in coinage in 1965. Today Mexico is the only country that uses silver in its circulating coinage.

Silver is the most malleable and ductile of all metals, with the exception of gold. Silver melts at about 962 degrees Celsius and boils at about 2212 degrees Celsius. Silver is not very chemically active, although tarnishing occurs when sulfur and sulfides attack silver, forming silver sulfide on the surface of the metal. Because silver is too soft in its pure form, a hardening agent, usually copper, is mixed into the silver. Copper is usually used as the hardening agent because it does not discolor the silver. The term "sterling silver" refers to silver that contains at least 925 parts of silver per thousand (92.5%) to 75 parts of copper (7.5%).

Silver is usually found combined with other elements in minerals and ores. In the US, silver is mined in conjunction with lead, copper, and zinc. In the US, Nevada, Idaho, Alaska, and Arizona are the leading silver-producing states. For industrial purposes, silver is used for photography, electrical appliances, glass, and as an antibacterial agent for the health industry.

Silver futures and options are traded on the Comex division of the New York Mercantile Exchange, the Chicago Board of Trade (CBOT), and the London Metal Exchange (LME). Silver futures are traded on the Tokyo Commodity Exchange (TOCOM). The Nymex silver futures contract calls for the delivery of 5,000 troy ounces of silver (0.999 fineness) and is priced in terms of dollars and cents per troy ounce.

Prices – Nymex silver futures prices showed a temporary upward spike in early 2004 to a new 16-year high of $8.50 per troy ounce, and then showed a more sustained advance through most of the rest of the year. Silver futures closed 2004 at $6.837, up 14.6% yr/yr from the 2003 close of $5.965. The average monthly price of cash silver (Handy & Harman in NY) rose +36.3% yr/yr to $6.69 in 2004. The highest month-end price ever reached for cash silver was $38 per troy ounce back in January 1980. Bullish factors for silver during 2004 included the ongoing weakness in the dollar and increased industrial demand with stronger US and world GDP growth. During 2004, silver showed a fairly close daily correlation with gold of 0.74, and a moderate negative correlation with the dollar index of –0.49.

Supply – World mine production of silver in 2003, the latest full reporting year, fell –0.5%% yr/yr to 18,700 metric tons from the record high of 18,800 metric tons seen in 2002. The world's largest silver producers are Peru with 15% of world production in 2003, Mexico (14%), China (13%), Australia (10%), and the US (7%). US production of refined silver in 2004 (through November, annualized) plunged by –21.5% yr/yr to a 7-year low of 4,109 metric tons.

Demand – US consumption of silver in 2001, the latest reporting year, fell 6.8% yr/yr to 187.4 million troy ounces from the record level of consumption of 201.1 million seen in 2000. The largest demand for silver usage by far comes from photographic materials with 54.4% of total usage, followed by electrical contacts and conductors (15.7%), brazing alloys and solders (4.5%), catalysts (3.3%), batteries (2.8%), jewelry (2.6%), sterling ware (2.5%), silver plate (2.1%), and mirrors (1.3%). The world's largest consuming nation of silver for industrial purposes is the US with 20.2% of world consumption in 2002, followed by India and Japan (both at 14.7%), and Italy (6.5%).

Trade – US exports of refined silver in 2003 fell –75.8% yr/yr to 6.816 million troy ounces, which was far below the record high of 99.022 million troy ounces seen in 1997. The main destinations for US silver exports are the UK with 3.086 million troy ounces of exports in 2003, Switzerland (630,000 troy ounces), Canada (524,000 million troy ounces), and Japan (17,000 troy ounces). US imports of silver ore and concentrates fell to 82,000 troy ounces in 2003. US imports of refined silver bullion rose +3.4% yr/yr to 136.316 million troy ounces in 2003. The bulk of those imports came from Mexico (62.050 million troy ounces) and Canada (41.795 million troy ounces).

World Mine Production of Silver — In Thousands of Kilograms In Metric Tons

Year	Australia	Bolivia	Canada[3]	Chile	China	Kazak-hstan	Mexico	Peru	Poland	Russia	Sweden	United States	World Total[2]
1994	1,045	352	768	983	810	506	2,215	1,768	1,064	600	276	1,490	14,000
1995	939	425	1,285	1,041	910	489	2,324	1,929	1,001	600	268	1,560	14,900
1996	1,013	384	1,309	1,047	1,140	468	2,528	1,970	935	400	272	1,570	15,100
1997	1,106	387	1,224	1,091	1,300	690	2,679	2,090	1,038	400	304	2,180	16,500
1998	1,474	404	1,196	1,340	1,300	726	2,686	2,025	1,108	350	299	2,060	17,200
1999	1,720	422	1,174	1,381	1,320	905	2,467	2,231	1,100	375	284	1,950	17,100
2000	2,060	434	1,212	1,242	1,600	927	2,620	2,145	1,148	370	329	1,980	17,800
2001	2,100	408	1,265	1,349	1,910	982	2,760	2,353	1,194	380	306	1,740	18,500
2002[1]	2,077	450	1,408	1,210	2,200	893	2,747	2,687	1,229	400	299	1,350	18,800
2003[2]	1,872	451	1,309	1,250	2,500	827	2,569	2,775	1,200	700	306	1,240	18,700

[1] Preliminary. [2] Estimate. [3] Shipments. *Source: U.S. Geological Survey (USGS)*

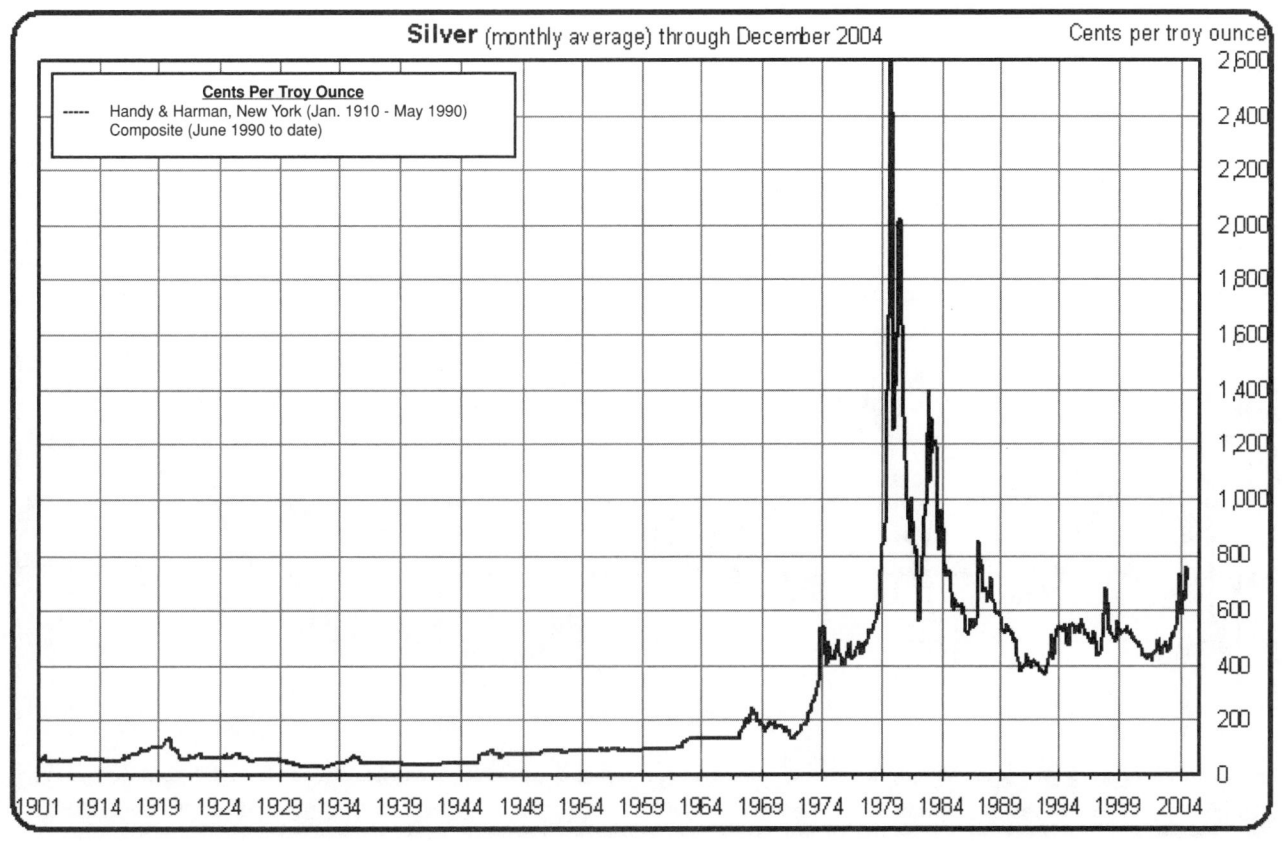

Silver (monthly average) through December 2004   Cents per troy ounce

Cents Per Troy Ounce
----- Handy & Harman, New York (Jan. 1910 - May 1990)
Composite (June 1990 to date)

Average Price of Silver in New York (Handy & Harman)   In Cents Per Troy Ounce (.999 Fine)

Year	Jan.	Feb.	Mar.	Apr.	May	June	July	Aug.	Sept.	Oct.	Nov.	Dec.	Average
1995	476.36	469.53	464.83	552.42	555.25	535.27	517.58	539.59	540.78	534.48	529.30	514.75	519.18
1996	547.03	562.75	551.38	540.14	536.02	513.58	502.95	510.50	501.57	492.76	481.69	480.14	518.34
1997	483.70	508.76	519.88	476.41	475.80	474.60	435.96	451.36	472.69	501.15	507.30	571.53	489.07
1998	584.58	672.61	617.18	628.86	558.65	526.05	546.82	516.45	502.67	500.18	498.39	476.85	552.68
1999	511.61	554.55	519.85	509.21	529.83	507.73	522.81	529.36	527.86	541.67	519.20	521.95	524.75
2000	523.47	529.65	510.15	510.37	504.30	505.20	501.82	492.76	494.50	488.14	471.93	466.40	499.89
2001	470.19	457.34	439.93	439.25	443.59	436.79	425.45	420.72	441.09	441.87	412.35	437.98	438.88
2002	450.17	444.79	457.00	460.50	473.55	492.13	494.57	456.16	458.93	442.28	453.87	465.78	462.39
2003	485.62	468.11	454.74	453.40	475.29	455.62	486.48	502.90	520.62	503.91	520.64	565.33	491.06
2004	637.13	647.71	729.48	708.57	589.19	588.38	637.55	670.98	641.93	717.55	751.43	712.43	669.36

Source: American Metal Market (AMM)

Average Price of Silver in London (Spot Fix)   In Pence Per Troy Ounce (.999 Fine)

Year	Jan.	Feb.	Mar.	Apr.	May	June	July	Aug.	Sept.	Oct.	Nov.	Dec.	Average
1995	302.80	300.36	290.35	341.95	248.74	336.31	323.80	343.72	348.99	340.29	339.90	336.05	329.44
1996	359.20	367.64	362.03	392.85	354.25	334.68	325.81	330.93	322.98	310.78	290.51	289.77	336.79
1997	287.63	311.95	323.99	293.08	291.43	289.16	272.73	280.36	295.67	308.69	300.76	348.90	300.36
1998	359.62	416.55	375.76	378.77	339.42	319.05	331.87	317.74	297.40	295.41	298.72	291.77	335.17
1999	312.69	340.46	320.27	315.12	326.80	315.51	328.86	327.98	322.20	326.42	317.53	319.87	322.75
2000	316.08	327.90	320.87	319.61	330.53	331.24	329.35	327.80	340.75	332.24	327.71	317.47	326.94
2001	315.87	312.57	304.50	304.36	310.19	309.54	300.97	277.97	297.93	289.21	286.92	306.25	302.43
2002	315.08	310.55	318.27	316.61	322.58	329.32	316.07	295.93	292.38	282.49	286.93	291.52	306.48
2003	297.21	289.23	287.39	285.06	292.05	272.79	295.53	313.01	320.30	298.01	306.53	320.48	298.13
2004	347.36	339.49	395.67	391.14	327.03	320.36	342.32	368.78	356.35	392.94	402.52	368.43	362.70

Source: American Metal Market (AMM)

SILVER

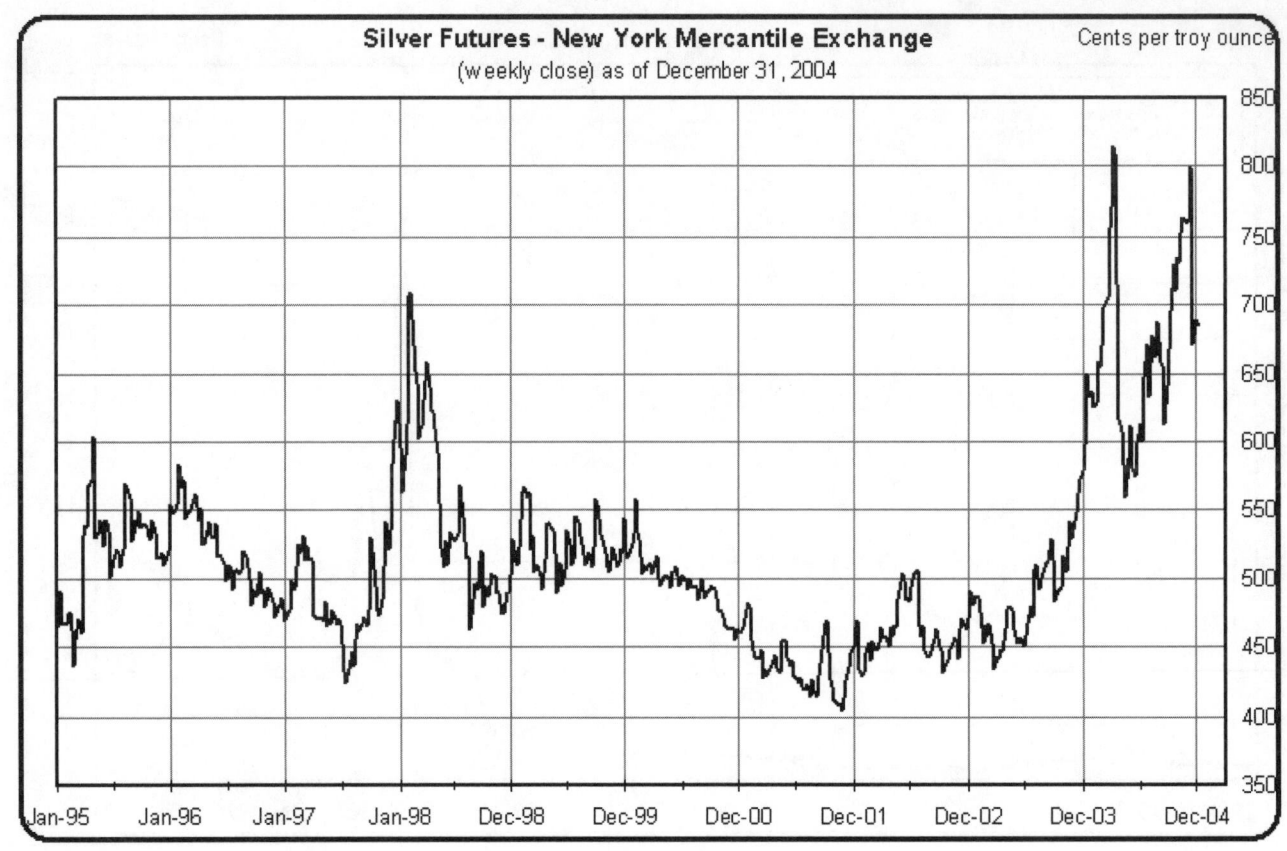

Average Open Interest of Silver Futures in New York (COMEX)   In Contracts

Year	Jan.	Feb.	Mar.	Apr.	May	June	July	Aug.	Sept.	Oct.	Nov.	Dec.
1995	132,158	139,806	132,317	129,063	112,723	108,941	101,842	111,251	95,433	101,763	105,453	95,551
1996	99,316	107,667	92,186	101,011	99,529	110,247	105,627	103,618	93,448	95,809	93,238	83,879
1997	91,385	94,539	90,531	97,434	87,510	90,145	96,777	89,250	79,344	100,464	96,695	93,761
1998	95,717	108,284	91,730	83,045	79,451	91,563	78,353	82,530	74,848	74,451	76,440	78,716
1999	77,946	97,593	82,435	82,824	78,745	78,943	78,151	86,601	77,490	86,577	80,564	70,275
2000	76,187	81,398	75,765	76,213	75,001	76,466	75,199	91,083	73,441	78,222	83,142	73,644
2001	69,408	72,798	74,337	71,589	67,328	67,429	75,019	75,830	65,533	66,530	74,228	66,903
2002	67,442	65,355	67,405	76,158	82,525	100,837	94,731	82,349	80,511	89,094	85,434	78,174
2003	98,561	94,472	84,485	87,445	85,232	80,001	91,544	108,118	110,423	92,216	101,303	103,007
2004	109,860	113,764	117,848	113,172	90,493	87,201	89,062	97,844	85,245	108,762	121,221	107,136

Source: New York Mercantile Exchange (NYMEX), COMEX Division

Volume of Trading of Silver Futures in New York (COMEX)   In Contracts

Year	Jan.	Feb.	Mar.	Apr.	May	June	July	Aug.	Sept.	Oct.	Nov.	Dec.	Total
1995	390,453	501,454	541,807	592,620	500,522	476,481	280,651	655,854	344,182	272,362	447,095	179,755	5,183,236
1996	415,801	583,767	368,175	547,629	334,973	549,631	296,905	460,686	316,366	321,781	415,441	259,653	4,870,808
1997	401,995	530,514	360,871	493,999	280,536	472,306	340,245	425,471	335,400	430,397	488,024	333,762	4,893,520
1998	352,688	550,800	368,127	360,130	310,130	393,971	278,774	367,257	283,475	280,066	319,216	229,982	4,094,616
1999	315,165	550,271	355,559	424,822	274,002	373,662	288,480	422,653	328,907	318,256	344,289	161,434	4,157,500
2000	258,053	425,910	231,336	318,752	216,938	407,455	175,235	370,739	146,007	149,252	303,673	113,667	3,117,017
2001	175,026	302,035	155,658	252,486	204,552	281,846	112,956	267,711	160,329	210,266	266,077	180,256	2,569,198
2002	265,773	271,293	163,898	325,889	243,475	389,798	281,214	296,579	164,537	209,249	292,861	230,998	3,135,564
2003	291,120	409,737	216,660	315,240	251,096	352,729	407,931	442,762	335,508	373,493	464,244	250,835	4,111,355
2004	385,058	544,939	408,447	671,204	278,703	425,501	316,264	427,973	281,737	364,158	541,366	360,775	5,006,125

Source: New York Mercantile Exchange (NYMEX), COMEX division

Mine Production of Recoverable Silver in the United States   In Metric Tons

Year	Arizona	California	Colorado	Idaho	Missouri	Montana	Nevada	New Mexico	South Dakota	Washington	Other States	Total
1998	211	11	W	447	W	W	670	W	2	1	723	2,060
1999	183	8	W	416	W	W	597	W	W	W	748	1,950
2000	W	8	3	W	W	W	734	W	W	2	1,240	1,980
2001	W	8	3	W	W	W	544	W	W	W	1,180	1,740
2002	W	3	W	W	W	W	424	W	W	W	927	1,350
2003[1]	W	1	W	W	W	W	322	W	W	W	916	1,240

[1] Preliminary.   W = Withheld proprietary data; included in Other States.   *Source: U.S. Geological Survey (USGS)*

Consumption of Silver in the United States, by End Use   In Millions of Troy Ounces

Year	Brazing Alloy & Solders	Catalysts	Batteries	Mirrors	Electrical Contacts-Conductors	Photo-graphic Materials	Silver-plate	Jewerly	Sterling Ware	Total Net Industrial Con-sumption	Coinage	Total Con-sumption
1992	7.1	3.8	3.1	1.2	18.3	64.4	2.9	3.0	3.9	118.9	8.1	127.0
1993	7.2	4.0	3.3	1.3	18.8	65.0	3.0	3.3	4.0	121.1	8.9	130.0
1994	7.5	4.2	3.6	1.5	19.5	71.0	3.1	3.7	4.2	130.1	8.1	138.2
1995	7.7	4.9	4.1	1.7	20.9	72.9	3.5	4.1	4.4	136.2	7.5	143.7
1996	8.2	5.5	4.5	2.1	22.3	78.3	3.9	4.4	4.8	146.7	5.0	151.7
1997	8.9	5.7	4.8	2.4	26.5	84.6	4.1	4.9	5.1	160.5	5.3	165.8
1998	9.3	5.9	4.9	2.6	28.4	91.0	4.5	5.5	5.7	172.3	5.6	177.9
1999	9.1	5.9	5.0	2.6	29.2	96.0	4.4	5.7	5.8	178.5	10.0	188.5
2000	8.6	6.3	5.2	2.6	32.7	104.0	4.5	6.1	5.6	191.1	10.0	201.1
2001[1]	8.5	6.1	5.3	2.5	29.5	102.0	4.0	4.9	4.6	NA	NA	187.4

[1] Preliminary.   *Source: The Silver Institute*

Commodity Exchange, Inc. (COMEX) Warehouse of Stocks of Silver   In Thousands of Troy Ounces

Year	Jan. 1	Feb. 1	Mar. 1	Apr. 1	May 1	June 1	July 1	Aug. 1	Sept. 1	Oct. 1	Nov. 1	Dec. 1
1995	260,708	264,045	235,114	211,028	189,668	184,570	181,269	175,764	156,544	156,529	156,110	156,932
1996	159,695	143,426	151,336	139,059	141,789	150,141	168,079	155,441	151,283	141,673	129,911	148,451
1997	204,051	195,450	193,381	191,676	189,498	201,682	184,691	169,079	164,296	138,775	133,470	128,252
1998	110,437	103,778	89,458	86,926	89,715	89,628	85,911	79,136	78,681	73,142	74,260	76,818
1999	75,807	75,108	78,135	79,605	78,819	77,512	73,514	77,592	79,606	79,391	79,155	78,416
2000	75,945	73,948	93,782	104,259	102,589	99,285	102,713	102,291	97,879	99,552	95,749	95,717
2001	93,983	93,195	98,659	96,694	95,745	96,090	98,700	100,494	102,770	101,538	103,982	105,235
2002	104,547	102,395	100,983	102,540	104,526	107,766	105,938	105,563	108,090	107,495	107,440	107,090
2003	107,394	107,610	109,153	108,521	108,168	105,092	107,222	105,406	104,862	106,283	118,238	124,498
2004	124,271	124,181	123,195	122,087	122,687	118,442	118,369	116,253	109,311	107,789	104,624	102,831

Source: New York Mercantile Exchange (NYMEX), COMEX Division

Production[2] of Refined Silver in the United States, from All Sources   In Metric Tons

Year	Jan.	Feb.	Mar.	Apr.	May	June	July	Aug.	Sept.	Oct.	Nov.	Dec.	Total
1995	279	273	340	281	381	355	331	404	364	340	384	351	4,083
1996	373	299	332	321	327	316	354	314	333	344	304	403	4,020
1997	343	262	296	331	250	326	292	344	331	281	340	382	3,778
1998	338	486	426	372	377	374	394	324	463	443	469	447	4,860
1999	424	420	441	356	368	394	404	316	354	371	364	396	4,608
2000	436	1,177	551	399	431	390	361	402	400	469	386	401	5,780
2001	405	343	405	360	360	331	395	380	338	403	442	383	4,545
2002	544	387	465	532	509	398	398	419	473	437	394	485	5,441
2003	483	426	320	412	357	431	430	373	361	809	363	471	5,235
2004[1]	407	418	460	337	361	178	175	351	433	255	392		4,109

[1] Preliminary.   [2] Includes U.S. mine production of recoverable silver plus imports of refined silver.   *Source: U.S. Geological Survey (USGS)*

SILVER

U.S. Exports of Refined Silver to Selected Countries   In Thousands of Troy Ounces

Year	Canada	France	Ger-many	Hong Kong	Japan	Singa-pore	South Korea	Switzer-land	United Arab Emirates	United Kingdom	Uruguay	Other Countries	World Total
1994	3,138	[2]	8	456	10,385	16	2,701	14	4,823	4,212	1,489	14	27,889
1995	1,665	431	[2]	[2]	5,819	2,209	2,932	1,177	10,288	63,980	939	5	90,462
1996	489	[2]	2	646	4,662	3,601	383	2,413	15,850	35,366	624	40	93,346
1997	1,861	[2]	2	797	6,044	[2]	547	5,369	16,750	62,693	402	57	99,022
1998	669	2,205	347	45	585	210	----	604	3,569	62,693	688	38	80,375
1999	2,180	2	1	----	585	37	31	624	4,244	7,716	180	5	19,804
2000	1,906	22	2	----	3,504	1	----	727	----	3,311	109	1	12,217
2001	1,598	----	----	11	1,202	2	----	354	----	20,029	105	10,472	30,960
2002	466	----	1	4	466	10	----	727	----	14,532	----	12,937	28,196
2003[1]	524	----	----	3	17	2	16	630	----	3,086	----	3,083	6,816

[1] Preliminary.   [2] Included in other countries, if any.   *Source: American Bureau of Metal Statistics, Inc. (ABMS)*

U.S. Imports of Silver From Selected Countries   In Thousands of Troy Ounces

Year	Canada	Mexico	Other Countries	Total	Canada	Chile	Mexico	Peru	Uruguay	Other Countries	Total
1994	369	3,805	97	4,271	28,678	1,923	22,135	12,663	[2]	742	66,141
1995	338	6,655	243	7,236	27,649	2,003	31,957	13,728	[2]	9,197	84,534
1996	256	4,662	----	4,918	35,365	1,874	30,285	12,153	[2]	3,122	82,799
1997	7	4,437	90	4,533	29,385	608	28,774	8,873	----	518	68,158
1998	24	5,851	427	6,301	34,722	813	41,152	9,388	----	3,945	90,020
1999	11	334	2	347	43,403	1,048	33,115	5,433	----	2,521	85,519
2000	46	----	----	46	38,902	225	44,689	2,787	----	35,899	122,502
2001	243	----	----	243	44,046	2,054	41,152	5,498	----	1,771	94,521
2002	149	1,813	----	1,961	48,868	2,331	67,837	6,430	----	6,350	131,815
2003[1]	82	----	----	82	41,795	1,987	62,050	18,261	----	12,223	136,316

[1] Preliminary.   [2] Included in other countries, if any.   *Source: American Bureau of Metal Statistics, Inc. (ABMS)*

World Silver Consumption[1]   In Millions of Troy Ounces

Year	Canada	France	Ger-many	India	Italy	Japan	Mexico	United Kingdom	United States	World Total	Austria	Canada	France	Ger-many	Mexico	United States	World Total	Grand Total
1994	1.6	27.2	45.7	93.9	51.6	108.4	14.6	30.4	140.4	722.4	.5	1.5	1.0	7.1	13.0	9.5	43.8	766.2
1995	2.0	30.0	43.6	101.3	49.5	112.7	16.9	31.6	148.7	752.7	.5	.7	1.2	2.4	.6	9.0	24.7	777.4
1996	2.0	26.9	41.0	122.2	51.7	112.1	20.3	33.8	155.0	785.8	.5	.7	.3	4.6	.5	7.1	23.3	809.1
1997	2.2	28.3	42.3	122.9	56.1	119.9	23.3	34.9	166.3	828.2	.4	.6	.3	3.7	.4	6.5	28.5	856.7
1998	2.3	28.4	38.4	114.7	55.9	112.8	21.7	38.6	162.9	801.5	.3	1.1	.3	10.0	.2	7.0	27.8	829.3
1999	2.1	26.6	35.1	121.5	61.8	122.5	21.3	39.3	175.5	840.6	.3	1.4	.3	7.0	.4	10.7	29.2	869.8
2000	2.0	28.8	31.8	131.0	65.1	135.0	16.6	42.7	181.8	877.2	.3	1.0	.4	9.5	.6	13.4	32.8	910.0
2001	2.0	28.7	32.4	154.0	58.2	119.3	15.9	46.0	157.5	839.6	.3	.9	.4	8.7	1.1	12.3	31.1	870.7
2002	2.1	27.1	29.4	122.5	56.0	118.7	17.0	43.2	162.9	813.0	.4	1.0	.5	7.5	1.1	14.2	32.8	845.8
2003[2]	2.2	25.6	29.4	122.5	55.0	115.9	18.7	44.4	162.7	823.9	.4	.3	.5	11.3	1.0	12.5	35.3	859.1

Industrial Uses columns: Canada, France, Germany, India, Italy, Japan, Mexico, United Kingdom, United States, World Total. Coinage columns: Austria, Canada, France, Germany, Mexico, United States, World Total.

[1] Non-communist areas only.   [2] Preliminary.   *Source: The Silver Institute*

Soybean Meal

Soybean meal is produced through processing and separating soybeans into oil and meal components. By weight, soybean meal accounts for about 35% of the weight of raw soybeans (at 13% moisture). If the soybeans are of particularly good quality, then the processor can get more meal weight by including more hulls in the meal while still meeting the 48% protein minimum. Soybean meal can be further processed into soy flour and isolated soy protein, but the bulk of soybean meal is used as animal feed for poultry, hogs and cattle. Soybean meal accounts for about two-thirds of the world's high-protein animal feed, followed by cottonseed and rapeseed meal, which together account for less than 20%. Soybean meal consumption has been moving to record highs in recent years. The soybean meal marketing year begins in October and ends in September. Soybean meal futures and options are traded on the Chicago Board of Trade (CBOT). The CBOT soybean meal futures contract calls for the delivery of 100 tons of soybean meal produced by conditioning ground soybeans and reducing the oil content of the conditioned product and having a minimum of 48.0% protein, minimum of 0.5% fat, maximum of 3.5% fiber, and maximum of 12.0% moisture.

Soybean crush – The term soybean "crush" refers to both the physical processing of soybeans and also to the dollar-value premium received for processing soybeans into their component products of meal and oil. The conventional model says that processing 60 pounds (one bushel) of soybeans produces 11 pounds of soybean oil, 44 pounds of 48% protein soybean meal, 3 pounds of hulls, and 1 pound of waste. The Gross Processing Margin (GPM) or crush equals (0.22 times Soybean Meal Prices in dollars per ton) + (11 times Soybean Oil prices in cents/pound) – Soybean prices in \$/bushel. A higher crush value will occur when the price of the meal and oil products are strong relative to soybeans, e.g., because of supply disruptions or because of an increase in demand for the products. When the crush value is high, companies will have a strong incentive to buy raw soybeans and boost the output of the products. That supply increase should eventually bring the crush value back into line with the long-term equilibrium.

Prices – Soybean meal futures prices at the Chicago Board of Trade in 2004 extended the rally that started in 2003 and moved sharply higher to a record high of \$378.50 per ton in July, but then quickly gave back all the gains in late-July and through September. Soybean meal prices finally closed the year at \$162.60, down 33% on the year. Regarding cash prices, the average price of soybean meal (48% solvent) in Decatur, Illinois in the first two months of the 2004-05 marketing year (i.e., October and November 2004) averaged \$154.64 per short ton, down sharply by –39.6% yr/yr from the 8-year high of \$256.05 per ton posted in 2003-04.

Supply – World soybean meal production in 2004-05 rose +8.9% yr/yr to 141.075 million metric tons, which was a new record high. The world's largest soybean meal producers are the US with 25% of world production in 2004-05, Brazil with 18%, China with 16%, and the European Union with 9%. US production of soybean meal in 2004-05 rose +8.1% yr/yr to 39.274 million short tons, which was mildly below the record high of 40.292 million short tons seen in 2001-02. US soybean meal stocks in 2004-05 (Oct 1) fell –4.1% yr/yr to a 7-year low of 211,000 short tons.

Demand – World consumption of soybean meal in 2004-05 rose +8.4% to 140.116 million metric tons, which was a new record high. The US accounted for 22% of that consumption and the European Union accounted for 26%. US consumption of soybean meal in 2004-05 rose +5.1% yr/yr to 30.754 million metric tons, which was a new record high.

Trade – World exports of soybean meal in 2004-05 rose +8.4% to 48.330 million metric tons, which was a new record high. Brazil accounted for 35% of world exports in 2004-05 and the US accounted for 11%. World imports of soybean meal in 2004-05 rose +6.4% yr/yr to 47.759 million metric tons, which was a new record high. US exports of soybean meal in 2004-05 rose +31.2% yr/yr to 5.700 million short tons, recovering from the 3-decade low of 4.344 million short tons seen in 2003-04. US imports of soybean meal in 2004-05 fell –38.9% yr/yr to 165,000 short tons from the record high of 270,000 short tons seen in 2003-04.

World Supply and Distribution of Soybean Meal   In Thousands of Metric Tons

Year Beginning Oct. 1	Production					Exports			Imports		Consumption			Ending Stocks		
	Brazil	China	EU	United States	Total	Brazil	United States	Total	EU	Total	EU	United States	Total	Brazil	United States	Total
1995-6	17,057	6,051	11,220	29,508	89,253	11,941	5,446	30,176	12,999	29,719	23,719	24,140	88,962	973	193	4,262
1996-7	15,737	5,963	11,428	31,035	90,446	10,660	6,344	30,095	11,420	30,733	22,340	24,785	91,571	835	191	3,775
1997-8	15,677	6,717	12,126	34,633	98,151	9,588	8,464	32,962	13,640	33,755	24,562	26,213	98,796	975	198	3,923
1998-9	16,642	10,023	12,354	34,285	107,071	9,830	6,461	34,861	16,425	35,261	27,258	27,812	106,240	1,190	300	5,154
1999-00	16,571	11,975	11,213	34,102	107,372	9,932	6,652	34,292	17,806	34,760	28,991	27,529	108,849	903	266	4,145
2000-1	17,863	15,050	13,073	35,730	116,434	10,679	6,988	35,498	18,327	36,499	31,212	28,706	117,815	721	348	3,765
2001-2	19,407	16,300	13,855	36,552	125,104	11,975	6,811	40,434	20,881	41,334	34,187	30,001	125,623	745	218	4,146
2002-3	21,353	21,000	12,883	34,650	129,990	13,750	5,461	42,250	21,642	43,174	34,359	29,358	131,298	644	200	3,762
2003-4[1]	22,781	20,190	11,350	32,953	129,581	14,761	3,941	44,600	22,500	44,894	33,569	29,266	129,281	1,624	191	4,356
2004-5[2]	25,289	22,400	11,930	35,811	141,075	17,006	5,171	48,330	24,500	47,759	36,115	30,754	140,116	1,700	227	4,744

[1] Preliminary.   [2] Forecast.   Source: Foreign Agricultural Service, U.S. Department of Agriculture (FAS-USDA)

SOYBEAN MEAL

Average Open Interest of Soybean Meal Futures in Chicago   In Contracts

Year	Jan.	Feb.	Mar.	Apr.	May	June	July	Aug.	Sept.	Oct.	Nov.	Dec.
1995	97,661	101,253	101,846	99,898	90,237	86,090	83,712	74,233	79,450	85,290	103,824	110,193
1996	95,903	90,010	87,468	101,204	91,453	88,641	77,961	80,727	93,373	88,969	90,007	84,399
1997	86,204	97,618	107,763	111,413	113,848	110,780	114,372	108,923	111,447	118,409	125,201	116,760
1998	114,243	122,979	131,390	137,251	136,212	136,216	126,108	139,239	140,904	141,426	134,095	122,788
1999	123,041	130,473	121,435	112,155	104,176	108,134	116,464	121,202	120,462	112,426	117,523	104,246
2000	115,285	124,822	120,157	123,957	123,691	112,425	105,230	94,469	105,240	103,263	120,164	127,529
2001	111,880	108,047	107,253	116,888	119,644	135,046	134,982	129,536	123,644	121,845	145,996	147,576
2002	146,674	137,425	134,880	130,138	132,376	143,956	142,728	132,996	137,799	131,249	137,836	140,902
2003	154,821	168,036	157,670	163,532	163,096	154,985	152,121	146,582	153,505	169,709	170,707	176,191
2004	183,462	186,137	185,647	175,069	162,284	149,584	135,675	134,987	133,045	137,447	152,846	147,296

Source: Chicago Board of Trade (CBT)

Volume of Trading of Soybean Meal Futures in Chicago   In Contracts

Year	Jan.	Feb.	Mar.	Apr.	May	June	July	Aug.	Sept.	Oct.	Nov.	Dec.	Total[1]
1995	283,623	307,477	404,387	410,860	532,694	479,589	610,833	491,775	481,949	449,009	523,440	625,606	5,601.2
1996	496,414	442,937	435,764	655,984	439,212	442,370	507,240	490,349	425,850	581,126	491,917	452,139	5,861.3
1997	479,001	481,841	509,515	576,564	581,886	569,760	579,748	452,188	531,299	589,542	561,133	512,471	6,424.9
1998	458,519	454,310	449,806	592,614	499,468	749,765	675,104	536,650	504,088	553,224	521,231	559,067	6,553.8
1999	420,240	509,348	476,104	477,102	390,527	646,806	710,110	597,026	568,859	511,503	572,194	447,078	6,326.9
2000	455,335	537,527	556,010	467,698	566,607	606,190	488,172	469,017	484,617	483,174	690,313	513,328	6,318.0
2001	530,193	431,822	470,608	485,106	584,352	625,089	709,973	630,909	491,398	652,931	659,328	472,063	6,743.8
2002	610,275	398,294	424,684	618,880	567,221	664,687	806,395	673,705	581,155	613,701	657,822	557,688	7,174.5
2003	639,628	551,401	527,723	676,739	599,614	749,844	772,104	692,778	677,194	896,429	700,676	674,315	8,158.4
2004	648,690	767,052	740,696	819,600	795,793	821,580	873,226	638,941	547,282	559,711	703,500	653,172	8,569.2

[1] In thousands of contracts.   *Source: Chicago Board of Trade (CBT)*

SOYBEAN MEAL

Supply and Distribution of Soybean Meal in the United States   In Thousands of Short Tons

Year Beginning Oct. 1	For Stocks Oct. 1	Pro- duction	Total Supply	Domestic	Exports	Total	Decatur 48% Protein Solvent	Decatur 44% Protein Solvent	Brazil FOB 45-46% Protein	Rotter- dam CIF
1995-6	223	32,527	32,826	26,611	6,002	32,613	236.00	260	256	256
1996-7	212	34,211	34,525	27,321	6,994	34,316	270.90	289	289	278
1997-8	210	38,176	38,442	28,894	9,330	38,224	185.28	204	201	197
1998-9	218	37,797	38,114	30,662	7,122	37,784	138.55	153	150	150
1999-00	330	37,591	37,970	30,346	7,331	37,677	167.70	185	182	180
2000-1	293	39,385	39,729	31,643	7,703	39,346	173.60	191	187	188
2001-2	383	40,292	40,818	33,070	7,508	40,578	167.73	180	174	174
2002-3[1]	240	38,194	38,600	32,361	6,019	38,380	181.57	200	163	197
2003-4[2]	220	36,324	36,815	32,260	4,344	36,604	256.05	282	211	273
2004-5[3]	211	39,274	39,650	33,700	5,700	39,400	150-165	176	155	215

[1] Preliminary.   [2] Estimate.   [3] Forecast.   Source: Economic Research Service, U.S. Department of Agriculture (ERS-USDA)

U.S. Exports of Soybean Cake & Meal by Country of Destination   In Thousands of Metric Tons

Year	Algeria	Australia	Canada	Dominican Republic	Italy	Japan	Mexico	Nether- lands	Philip- pines	Russia	Spain	Vene- zuela	Total
1995	216.7	190.6	809.9	219.8	95.4	247.4	425.8	879.3	593.6	11.5	212.8	181.5	6,370
1996	203.4	157.5	698.8	260.7	96.1	234.1	374.1	501.3	423.4	5.8	51.9	274.9	6,133
1997	250.8	136.7	662.9	261.5	295.8	288.1	220.1	508.5	483.2	8.3	345.0	337.1	7,309
1998	263.2	135.7	791.8	221.8	227.7	267.1	198.6	298.2	758.7	----	296.9	447.1	8,230
1999	213.2	167.1	796.7	309.9	60.9	209.6	425.4	231.5	825.5	289.4	77.7	359.6	6,839
2000	202.0	167.7	827.2	357.4	19.0	219.7	264.5	94.6	851.8	90.1	96.5	248.1	6,462
2001	178.8	157.5	1,050.6	364.9	132.8	279.1	419.8	241.1	689.0	102.2	132.4	137.8	7,426
2002	219.2	243.7	1,133.6	358.8	34.4	116.0	506.5	107.4	756.2	112.8	79.7	60.3	6,672
2003	184.7	364.3	1,079.2	317.5	0.3	258.7	741.9	84.0	238.2	47.1	5.6	190.1	5,653
2004[1]	105.8	117.0	1,362.6	118.0	0.6	147.7	856.2	125.6	288.3	3.2	48.4	193.4	4,826

[1] Preliminary.   Source: The Oil World

Production of Soybean Cake & Meal[2] in the United States   In Thousands of Short Tons

Year	Oct.	Nov.	Dec.	Jan.	Feb.	Mar.	Apr.	May	June	July	Aug.	Sept.	Total	Yield in lbs.
1995-6	2,893.2	2,948.9	2,972.3	2,945.2	2,652.1	2,757.5	2,683.1	2,534.6	2,566.2	2,656.3	2,513.4	2,404.1	32,527	47.69
1996-7	2,992.8	3,151.8	3,263.8	3,251.7	2,966.8	3,089.1	2,709.1	2,618.1	2,573.2	2,517.4	2,465.2	2,611.0	34,211	47.36
1997-8	3,344.0	3,390.6	3,624.2	3,592.1	3,279.2	3,484.0	3,172.5	2,956.7	2,795.2	2,941.5	2,665.6	2,930.7	37,176	47.41
1998-9	3,365.1	3,368.4	3,422.4	3,214.4	3,027.7	3,302.7	3,044.2	3,024.4	2,844.0	3,011.9	3,003.5	3,167.8	37,797	47.25
1999-00	3,573.4	3,400.4	3,413.5	3,332.8	2,998.2	3,123.6	2,906.1	2,882.5	2,845.4	3,118.8	2,906.8	3,089.7	37,591	47.76
2000-1	3,573.9	3,432.8	3,399.4	3,521.6	3,083.0	3,412.5	3,152.3	3,181.0	3,091.6	3,256.6	3,203.6	3,076.8	39,385	48.06
2001-2	3,534.4	3,538.7	3,655.3	3,703.1	3,313.2	3,589.7	3,315.7	3,344.2	3,194.1	3,085.4	3,106.7	2,911.3	40,292	44.27
2002-3	3,499.3	3,424.7	3,526.8	3,358.4	3,048.4	3,360.1	2,994.7	3,072.4	2,873.4	3,064.4	2,966.6	3,023.5	38,213	43.90
2003-4	3,462.1	3,465.9	3,483.7	3,479.3	3,144.9	3,092.4	2,682.4	2,792.4	2,616.2	2,752.2	2,480.2	2,872.6	36,324	
2004-5[1]	3,696.4	3,584.2	3,567.9										43,394	

[1] Preliminary.   [2] At oil mills; including millfeed and lecithin.   Sources: Economic Research Service, U.S. Department of Agriculture (ERS-USDA)

Stocks (at Oil Mills)[2] of Soybean Cake & Meal in the U.S., on First of Month   In Thousands of Short Tons

Year	Oct.	Nov.	Dec.	Jan.	Feb.	Mar.	Apr.	May	June	July	Aug.	Sept.
1995-6	223.4	196.9	241.3	394.8	302.2	229.9	369.3	382.1	306.8	406.2	298.8	218.3
1996-7	212.4	200.2	291.8	254.4	263.0	198.5	322.6	280.1	256.5	317.3	303.2	257.4
1997-8	206.6	218.2	412.2	262.0	269.3	280.7	238.0	210.4	290.2	193.1	205.3	187.2
1998-9	218.1	271.9	352.3	313.9	380.5	436.4	341.0	316.0	447.7	284.2	394.8	279.4
1999-00	330.2	467.6	460.2	436.5	489.8	482.5	350.2	441.2	325.0	260.2	305.8	225.9
2000-1	292.9	317.4	343.8	423.7	333.9	325.8	309.1	313.3	286.9	341.3	338.1	273.9
2001-2	383.3	305.5	302.9	393.7	289.7	272.0	336.5	253.8	212.7	343.3	202.4	256.5
2002-3	240.0	285.2	371.7	337.0	299.1	259.5	335.7	263.5	311.8	271.6	228.4	266.9
2003-4	219.9	317.8	432.4	280.7	328.9	415.8	375.0	338.6	465.5	314.9	344.6	196.3
2004-5[1]	210.7	357.7	286.8									

[1] Preliminary.   [2] Including millfeed and lecithin.   Source: Economic Research Service, U.S. Department of Agriculture (ERS-USDA)

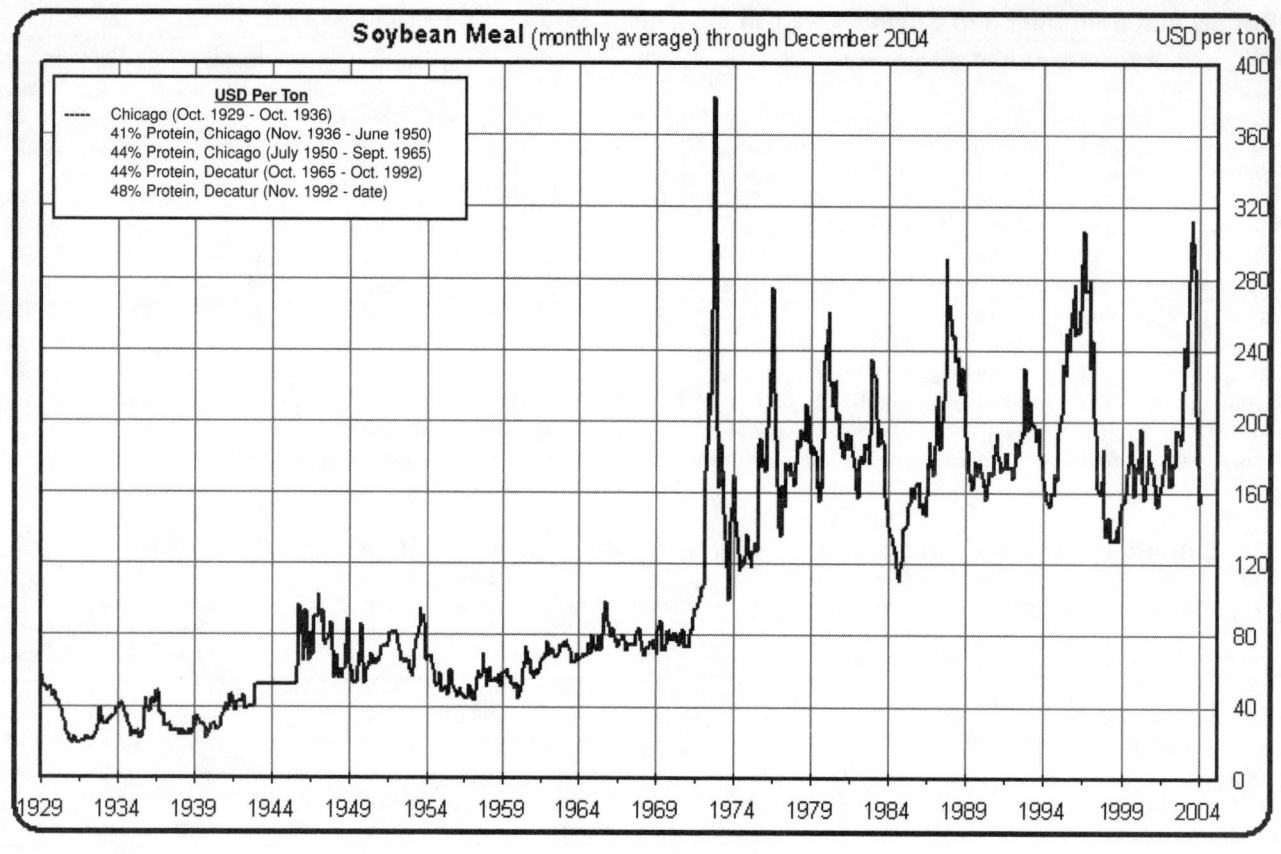

Average Price of Soybean Meal (44% Solvent) in Decatur Illinois   In Dollars Per Short Ton -- Bulk

Year	Oct.	Nov.	Dec.	Jan.	Feb.	Mar.	Apr.	May	June	July	Aug.	Sept.	Average
1992-3	168.6	170.9	176.4	175.6	167.5	172.4	175.6	181.7	181.3	217.6	206.9	186.5	181.8
1993-4	180.6	195.7	192.5	185.9	184.4	182.0	176.4	191.1	183.0	168.1	165.6	162.5	180.7
1994-5	156.4	150.9	145.4	145.1	149.4	145.7	151.0	148.1	149.1	160.1	157.5	171.8	152.5
1995-6	183.4	194.1	213.6	220.5	216.7	215.7	237.9	232.3	227.9	242.3	251.1	265.5	225.1
1996-7	238.0	242.7	240.9	240.7	253.6	270.4	277.7	296.0	275.9	261.5	261.6	265.7	260.4
1997-8	216.0	231.6	214.9	193.1	182.1	165.3	152.8	150.3	157.8	173.3	135.7	126.9	175.0
1998-9	129.4	139.3	139.6	131.0	124.4	127.2	128.6	127.0	131.7	125.7	135.9	144.1	132.0
1999-00	147.2	148.1	145.4	155.0	163.6	166.6	168.1	180.1	170.2	156.8	151.4	166.9	160.0
2000-1	166.0	173.7	187.9	175.6	158.3	149.1	149.7	155.6	163.1	183.9	170.6	163.5	166.4
2001-2	157.7	157.2	146.6	Disc.	Disc.	Disc.	Disc.	Disc.	Disc.	Disc.	Disc.	Disc.	153.8

Source: Economic Research Service, U.S. Department of Agriculture (ERS-USDA)

Average Price of Soybean Meal (48% Solvent) in Decatur Illinois   In Dollars Per Short Ton -- Bulk

Year	Oct.	Nov.	Dec.	Jan.	Feb.	Mar.	Apr.	May	June	July	Aug.	Sept.	Average
1995-6	193.90	204.10	223.60	232.00	228.30	226.57	249.30	244.30	238.80	252.50	261.20	276.40	235.90
1996-7	248.50	251.50	250.60	249.20	262.40	280.50	288.60	306.40	287.90	273.60	273.30	278.30	270.90
1997-8	229.30	245.30	222.50	202.85	192.75	174.20	162.50	160.00	168.55	183.40	146.25	135.80	185.28
1998-9	135.70	144.45	146.40	138.80	132.30	133.00	134.50	133.20	139.10	132.70	141.70	150.65	138.54
1999-00	153.57	154.70	154.00	163.41	170.85	175.50	177.53	189.34	177.45	163.38	157.48	174.60	167.65
2000-1	171.52	179.95	195.65	183.17	166.08	156.32	158.48	165.14	172.60	184.43	178.46	171.67	173.62
2001-2	165.45	166.10	154.18	158.01	153.11	160.49	161.57	164.28	170.33	187.45	186.25	185.45	167.72
2002-3	168.20	163.20	163.60	167.40	176.80	175.40	182.10	195.40	191.90	187.30	189.70	217.95	181.58
2003-4	225.20	242.00	231.54	252.15	257.39	301.14	311.83	300.69	285.81	284.05	205.34	175.51	256.05
2004-5	155.37	153.90	161.60	167.34									159.55

Source: Economic Research Service, U.S. Department of Agriculture (ERS-USDA)

Soybean Oil

Soybean oil is the natural oil extracted from whole soybeans. Typically, about 19% of a soybean's weight can be extracted as crude soybean oil. The oil content of U.S. soybeans correlates directly with the temperatures and amount of sunshine during the soybean pod-filling stages. Edible products produced with soybean oil include cooking and salad oils, shortening, and margarine. Soybean oil is the most widely used cooking oil in the US. It accounts for 80% of margarine production and for more than 75% of total US consumer vegetable fat and oil consumption. Soy oil is cholesterol-free and high in polyunsaturated fat. Soy oil is also used to produce inedible products such as paints, varnish, resins, and plastics. Of the edible vegetable oils, soy oil is the world's largest at about 32%, followed by palm oil and rapeseed oil. Soybean oil futures and options are traded on the Chicago Board of Trade (CBOT).

Prices – Soybean oil futures prices at the Chicago Board of Trade in early 2004 continued the rally seen in 2003 and moved sharply higher to post a new 2-decade high of 35.18 cents per pound in March. However, soybean oil futures then plunged through mid-year to post a new 1-1/2 year low and close the year at 20.61 cents, down 26% on the year. Regarding cash prices, the average monthly price of crude domestic soybean oil (in tank cars) in Decatur (F.O.B.)

fell -23.0% yr/yr to 23.08 cents per pound from the 21-year high of 29.97 cents posted in 2003-04.

Supply – World production of soybean oil in 2004-05 rose +8.7% yr/yr to a new record high of 32.647 million metric tons, which was roughly five times the level of 6.511 million metric tons seen in 1970-71. The US accounts for 26% of world soybean oil production, while Brazil accounts for 19%, and the European Union accounts for 8%. US production of soybean oil in 2004-05 rose +9.9% yr/yr to 18.770 billion pounds, which was just below the record high of 18.898 billion pounds seen in 2001-02.

Demand – World consumption of soybean oil in 2004-05 rose +6.5% yr/yr to a record high of 31.832 million metric tons. The US accounted for 25% of world consumption in 2004-05, while Brazil accounted for 10%, the European Union for 7%, and India for 7%. US consumption of soybean oil in 2004-05 rose +2.6% to 17.300 billion pounds, which was a record high.

Trade – World exports of soybean oil in 2004-05 rose +8.5% yr/yr to 9.753 million metric tons, which was a record high. US exports of soybean oil in 2004-05 rose +39.0% yr/yr to 1.300 billion pounds, which was well below the record of 3.079 billion pounds seen in 1997-98.

World Supply and Demand of Soybean Oil   In Thousands of Metric Tons

Year Beginning Oct. 1	Production Brazil	Production European Union	Production United States	Production Total	Exports Brazil	Exports United States	Exports Total	Imports India	Imports Total	Consumption Brazil	Consumption European Union	Consumption India	Consumption United States	Consumption Total	Stocks[3] United States	Stocks[3] Total
1995-6	4,078	2,529	6,913	20,218	1,600	450	4,873	60	4,693	2,574	2,031	772	6,108	19,622	914	2,672
1996-7	3,762	2,582	7,145	20,521	1,268	922	5,563	49	5,287	2,639	1,784	706	6,471	20,488	690	2,429
1997-8	3,748	2,746	8,229	22,432	1,191	1,397	6,551	236	6,211	2,757	1,706	1,095	6,922	22,157	627	2,364
1998-9	3,979	2,753	8,202	24,530	1,381	1,076	7,473	833	7,287	2,898	1,694	1,805	7,101	24,509	689	2,199
1999-00	3,962	2,504	8,085	24,589	1,150	624	6,438	790	6,300	2,937	1,639	1,582	7,283	24,079	904	2,571
2000-1	4,273	2,961	8,355	26,707	1,530	636	7,155	1,400	7,002	3,029	2,133	2,020	7,401	26,415	1,255	2,710
2001-2	4,640	3,136	8,572	28,832	1,775	1,143	8,441	1,550	8,034	3,032	2,260	2,387	7,635	28,570	1,070	2,565
2002-3	5,105	2,894	8,360	30,295	2,267	1,027	9,212	1,255	8,562	2,985	2,237	1,946	7,748	30,339	676	1,871
2003-4[1]	5,636	2,550	7,748	30,044	2,719	424	8,985	759	8,509	2,954	1,973	1,782	7,651	29,890	488	1,549
2004-5[2]	6,025	2,688	8,509	32,647	2,956	590	9,753	1,050	9,125	3,059	2,093	2,099	7,847	31,832	608	1,736

[1] Preliminary.   [2] Forecast.   [3] End of season.   *Source: Foreign Agricultural Service, U.S. Department of Agriculture (FAS-USDA)*

Supply and Distribution of Soybean Oil in the United States   In Millions of Pounds

Year Beginning Oct. 1	Production	Imports	Stocks Oct. 1	Exports	Total Domestic	Food Shortening	Food Margarine	Food Cooking & Salad Oils	Food Other Edible	Total Food	Non-Food Paint & Varnish	Non-Food Resins & Plastics	Total Non-Food	Total Disappearance
1995-6	15,240	95	1,137	992	13,465	4,702	1,699	5,317	159	11,877	48	119	297	14,457
1996-7	15,752	53	2,015	2,033	14,267	4,578	1,667	6,119	68	12,432	51	132	333	16,300
1997-8	18,143	60	1,520	3,079	15,262	4,688	1,623	6,188	78	12,576	49	128	490	18,341
1998-9	18,078	83	1,382	2,372	15,651	4,842	1,589	6,191	120	12,743	37	117	576	18,023
1999-00	17,825	83	1,520	1,376	16,057	7,153	1,481	7,075	132	15,841	65	96	586	17,433
2000-1	18,420	73	1,995	1,401	16,210	8,044	1,294	7,310	125	16,772	60	86	535	17,611
2001-2	18,898	46	2,767	2,519	16,833	8,572	1,242	7,880	125	17,818	60	85	519	19,352
2002-3	18,430	46	2,359	2,261	17,083	8,393	1,179	7,912	119	17,604	64	88	520	19,344
2003-4[1]	17,080	306	1,491	935	16,866						71	100	623	17,801
2004-5[2]	18,770	105	1,076	1,300	17,300						70	85	644	18,600

[1] Preliminary .   [2] Forecast.   *Source: Economic Research Service, U.S. Department of Agriculture (ERS-USDA)*

SOYBEAN OIL

Stocks of Crude Soybean Oil in the United States, at End of Month   In Millions of Pounds

Crop Year	Oct.	Nov.	Dec.	Jan.	Feb.	Mar.	Apr.	May	June	July	Aug.	Sept.
1999-00	1,378.3	1,422.9	1,516.5	1,742.4	1,829.7	1,847.2	1,847.5	1,760.3	1,802.9	1,903.7	1,831.3	1,773.4
2000-1	1,873.6	1,961.8	2,035.0	2,140.0	2,262.4	2,304.1	2,321.7	2,455.2	2,587.4	2,718.3	2,698.2	2,692.4
2001-2	2,553.4	2,606.0	2,658.1	2,815.7	2,686.6	2,741.9	2,661.2	2,757.5	2,529.3	2,350.9	2,338.2	2,176.7
2002-3	2,097.1	2,114.3	2,197.2	2,186.9	2,062.5	2,028.7	1,916.0	1,843.0	1,706.4	1,595.1	1,458.4	1,282.4
2003-4	1,236.8	1,329.7	1,390.1	1,737.3	1,797.5	1,675.7	1,452.3	1,410.3	1,296.4	1,198.0	1,001.8	887.7
2004-5[1]	1,019.5	1,013.1	1,111.2									

[1] Preliminary.   Source: Bureau of the Census, U.S. Department of Commerce

Stocks of Refined Soybean Oil in the United States, at End of Month   In Millions of Pounds

Crop Year	Oct.	Nov.	Dec.	Jan.	Feb.	Mar.	Apr.	May	June	July	Aug.	Sept.
1999-00	238.1	240.7	250.0	271.3	270.1	245.6	251.8	231.6	225.5	216.7	186.3	222.0
2000-1	187.2	205.7	263.1	239.3	211.5	199.9	184.1	200.9	189.3	177.2	171.7	184.8
2001-2	171.4	181.4	210.0	222.9	209.8	210.8	195.6	185.7	206.5	178.7	183.5	183.2
2002-3	197.1	212.0	202.3	209.8	209.5	215.9	204.1	210.8	222.1	199.1	196.0	208.3
2003-4	175.0	200.8	189.9	208.3	190.5	180.2	191.9	241.2	217.7	214.0	178.8	187.8
2004-5[1]	235.8	178.4	198.2									

[1] Preliminary.   Source: Bureau of the Census, U.S. Department of Commerce

U.S. Exports of Soybean Oil[1], by Country of Destination   In Metric Tons

Year Beginning Oct. 1	Canada	Ecuador	Ethiopia	Haiti	India	Mexico	Morocco	Pakistan	Panama	Peru	Turkey	Venezuela	Total
1995-6	43,912	1,155	4,426	15,041	20,841	46,644	0	0	9,512	35,999	1,960	1,877	449,876
1996-7	58,756	6,587	19,492	36,436	26,675	81,902	46,682	0	3,623	37,726	6,952	517	922,336
1997-8	26,711	10,897	4,175	14,191	38,610	102,950	30,493	0	13,591	49,426	2,452	654	1,396,755
1998-9	11,316	4,858	2,933	44,957	71,685	99,112	43,346	0	1,369	62,085	8,497	1,464	1,075,699
1999-00	22,715	0	13,627	25,214	23,413	118,079	14,091	0	299	66,686	15,680	414	623,651
2000-1	54,909	9,849	5,224	5,793	54,062	72,456	0	62,999	4,558	60,606	0	577	635,493
2001-2	87,047	0	2,225	9,452	88,529	161,760	39,439	59,999	12,616	37,677	85,199	635	1,142,755
2002-3	124,667	0	11,997	1,997	42,727	188,993	26,517	38,215	2,241	20,349	26,500	311	1,026,638
2003-4[2]	96,109	10	3,665	1,298	14,561	97,099	15,518	17	2,834	25,097	0	169	424,212

[1] Crude & Refined oil combined as such.   [2] Preliminary.   Source: Economic Research Service, U.S. Department of Agriculture (ERS-USDA)

Production of Crude Soybean Oil in the United States   In Millions of Pounds

Year	Oct.	Nov.	Dec.	Jan.	Feb.	Mar.	Apr.	May	June	July	Aug.	Sept.	Total
1996-7	1,401	1,430	1,473	1,474	1,348	1,413	1,254	1,216	1,196	1,176	1,141	1,231	15,752
1997-8	1,591	1,580	1,689	1,684	1,558	1,655	1,526	1,418	1,337	1,410	1,286	1,410	18,143
1998-9	1,598	1,598	1,611	1,528	1,439	1,587	1,453	1,450	1,383	1,451	1,452	1,528	18,078
1999-00	1,687	1,597	1,599	1,580	1,417	1,482	1,368	1,396	1,360	1,486	1,388	1,466	17,825
2000-1	1,673	1,591	1,579	1,642	1,436	1,602	1,485	1,479	1,449	1,526	1,506	1,453	18,420
2001-2	1,680	1,629	1,696	1,707	1,544	1,662	1,551	1,574	1,506	1,461	1,475	1,414	18,898
2002-3	1,693	1,632	1,696	1,613	1,474	1,633	1,448	1,492	1,391	1,482	1,440	1,445	18,438
2003-4	1,631	1,611	1,605	1,619	1,462	1,461	1,260	1,315	1,236	1,304	1,186	1,391	17,080
2004-5[1]	1,764	1,688	1,682										20,537

[1] Preliminary.   Source: Economic Research Service, U.S. Department of Agriculture (ERS-USDA)

Production of Refined Soybean Oil in the United States   In Millions of Pounds

Year	Oct.	Nov.	Dec.	Jan.	Feb.	Mar.	Apr.	May	June	July	Aug.	Sept.	Total
1996-7	1,111.7	1,064.1	1,025.7	969.8	931.5	1,057.1	1,023.7	1,026.2	984.8	1,019.1	1,094.3	1,072.5	12,381
1997-8	1,173.9	1,156.3	1,110.1	1,092.6	1,047.4	1,148.2	1,094.8	1,140.7	1,053.1	1,083.9	1,173.4	1,114.5	13,389
1998-9	1,200.6	1,108.8	1,042.2	1,016.7	976.7	1,138.2	1,073.2	1,087.7	1,060.7	1,058.6	1,122.6	1,116.2	13,002
1999-00	1,201.1	1,195.2	1,150.4	1,056.9	1,045.1	1,173.7	1,109.6	1,141.4	1,063.8	1,080.2	1,176.0	1,177.7	13,571
2000-1	1,260.3	1,159.7	1,093.4	1,107.5	1,166.8	1,211.3	1,170.0	1,234.1	1,204.6	1,222.8	1,317.4	1,201.2	14,349
2001-2	1,383.2	1,363.5	1,266.9	1,231.8	1,183.9	1,330.0	1,270.5	1,297.9	1,287.7	1,272.8	1,308.4	1,362.4	15,559
2002-3	1,451.2	1,367.2	1,262.2	1,224.5	1,181.0	1,308.2	1,238.6	1,378.8	1,316.1	1,293.8	1,290.5	1,334.8	15,647
2003-4	1,393.0	1,350.9	1,226.6	1,205.6	1,196.0	1,330.6	1,210.3	1,267.4	1,195.9	1,246.8	1,268.8	1,306.3	15,198
2004-5[1]	1,377.6	1,331.1	1,245.0										15,815

[1] Preliminary.   Source: Bureau of the Census, U.S. Department of Commerce

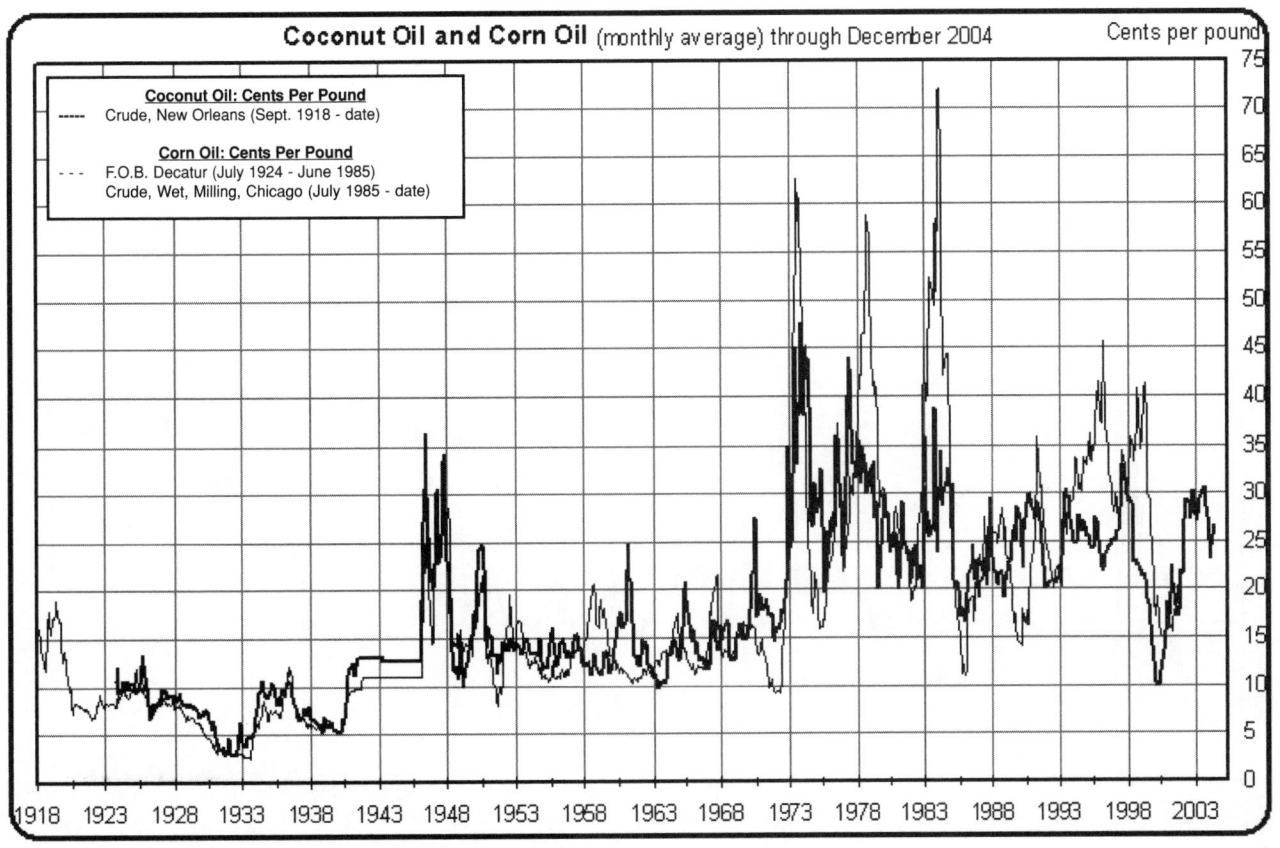

Coconut Oil and Corn Oil (monthly average) through December 2004   Cents per pound

Coconut Oil: Cents Per Pound
----- Crude, New Orleans (Sept. 1918 - date)

Corn Oil: Cents Per Pound
- - - F.O.B. Decatur (July 1924 - June 1985)
Crude, Wet, Milling, Chicago (July 1985 - date)

Consumption of Soybean Oil in End Products in the United States   In Millions of Pounds

Year	Jan.	Feb.	Mar.	Apr.	May	June	July	Aug.	Sept.	Oct.	Nov.	Dec.	Total
1995	991.1	950.0	1,093.8	1,006.2	1,077.3	1,020.8	948.7	1,046.1	1,042.3	1,092.0	1,067.7	1,002.6	12,339
1996	964.9	927.4	1,026.4	999.8	1,020.6	946.2	959.9	1,123.3	1,042.8	1,137.1	1,080.9	1,093.1	12,322
1997	1,086.0	979.7	1,104.9	1,060.4	1,034.1	995.2	991.4	1,126.1	1,067.8	1,128.5	1,100.0	1,087.8	12,762
1998	1,045.8	1,020.2	1,129.7	1,066.5	1,101.6	1,070.1	1,062.2	1,123.4	1,122.0	1,231.5	1,150.2	1,057.0	13,180
1999	1,031.5	979.0	1,156.1	1,087.7	1,091.9	1,079.5	1,082.9	1,185.0	1,185.7	1,183.0	1,199.3	1,135.6	13,397
2000	1,096.6	1,050.5	1,217.9	1,158.9	1,183.6	1,102.9	1,121.1	1,226.4	1,163.6	1,306.1	1,139.7	1,079.6	13,847
2001	1,065.9	1,151.7	1,308.8	1,202.4	1,224.2	1,261.6	1,307.6	1,557.5	1,411.0	1,687.3	1,624.0	1,485.8	16,288
2002	1,461.5	1,395.3	1,568.0	1,505.1	1,549.7	1,492.4	1,490.5	1,545.5	1,543.7	1,710.2	1,587.2	1,458.8	18,308
2003	1,418.1	1,347.4	1,490.0	1,494.9	1,552.6	1,493.1	1,509.5	1,483.5	1,577.7	1,660.7	1,544.2	1,451.4	18,023
2004[1]	1,388.1	1,417.6	1,555.2	1,468.0	1,506.7	1,421.1	1,429.2	1,473.6	1,483.2	1,558.3	1,533.7	1,368.9	17,604

[1] Preliminary.   *Source: Bureau of the Census, U.S. Department of Commerce*

U.S. Exports of Soybean Oil (Crude and Refined)   In Millions of Pounds

Year	Jan.	Feb.	Mar.	Apr.	May	June	July	Aug.	Sept.	Oct.	Nov.	Dec.	Total
1995	217.4	367.6	564.2	236.2	90.8	160.4	91.0	109.4	79.4	69.3	205.4	95.9	2,287
1996	189.1	97.0	68.0	75.3	63.9	16.1	27.1	28.0	56.7	121.0	303.8	213.3	1,259
1997	190.7	239.2	301.1	84.9	28.9	44.9	144.1	212.9	152.1	217.2	424.0	199.7	2,240
1998	449.4	387.6	268.6	191.1	148.1	204.7	161.8	316.0	108.9	189.6	343.5	376.7	3,146
1999	246.1	231.1	130.8	230.8	91.3	135.0	111.7	91.2	196.2	209.1	114.9	157.6	1,946
2000	103.0	146.1	161.3	91.5	48.3	109.8	105.8	57.0	69.0	43.9	115.2	261.6	1,313
2001	130.4	184.5	142.4	105.8	51.2	109.9	89.1	96.3	70.6	233.9	138.6	164.8	1,518
2002	249.7	446.8	233.2	233.8	87.0	345.8	180.7	95.4	109.8	113.6	194.9	210.2	2,501
2003	295.1	299.8	276.7	227.0	109.6	96.7	234.5	96.9	105.9	152.5	111.3	135.2	2,141
2004[1]	71.1	62.9	73.2	39.0	43.8	39.5	54.0	67.9	86.8	59.9	182.3	238.5	1,019

[1] Preliminary.   *Source: Economic Research Service, U.S. Department of Agriculture (ERS-USDA)*

SOYBEAN OIL

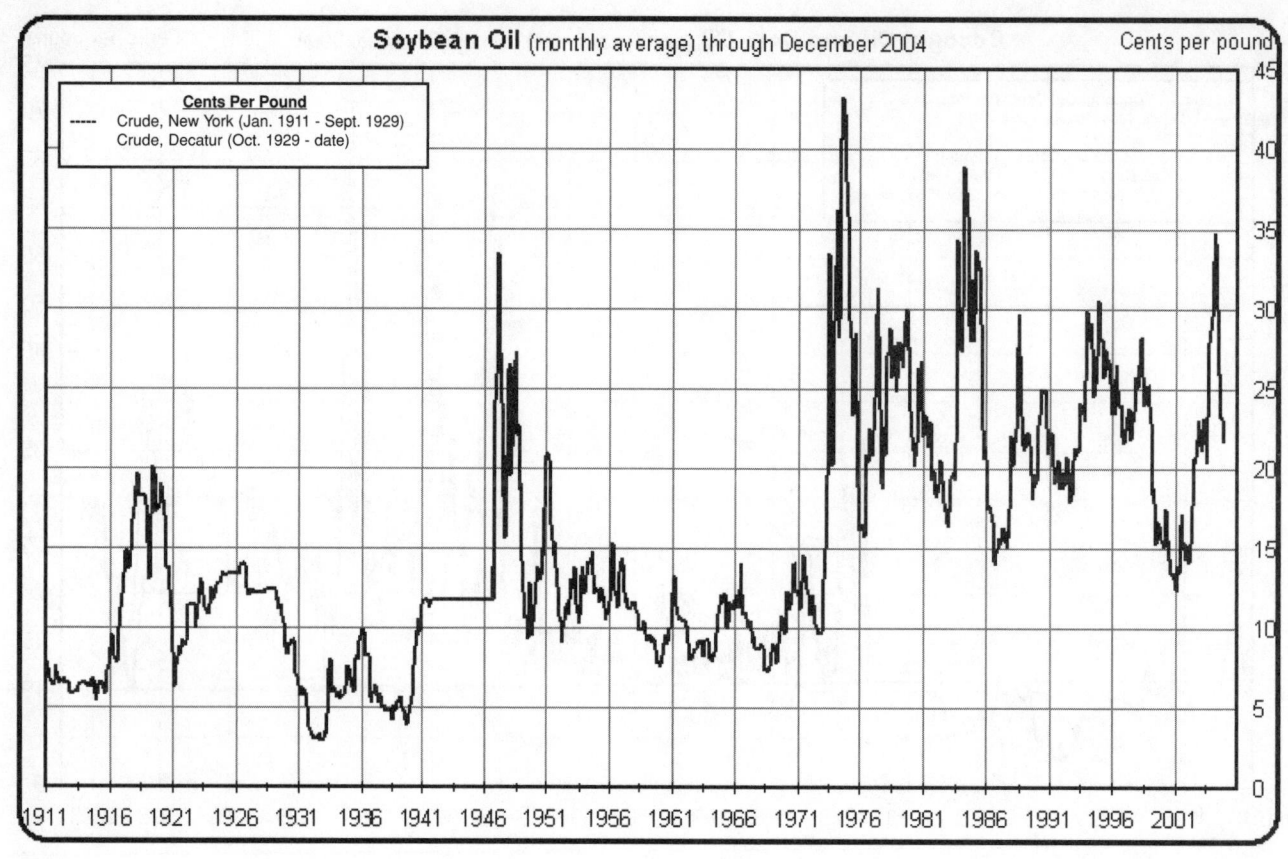

Soybean Oil (monthly average) through December 2004   Cents per pound

Cents Per Pound
----- Crude, New York (Jan. 1911 - Sept. 1929)
Crude, Decatur (Oct. 1929 - date)

Stocks of Soybean Oil (Crude & Refined) at Factories and Warehouses in the U.S.   In Millions of Pounds

Year	Oct. 1	Nov. 1	Dec. 1	Jan. 1	Feb. 1	Mar. 1	Apr. 1	May 1	June 1	July 1	Aug. 1	Sept. 1
1995-6	1,136.7	1,195.9	1,132.0	1,408.9	1,512.6	1,521.5	1,653.5	1,747.4	1,758.9	1,888.5	2,156.5	2,091.4
1996-7	2,015.4	1,992.9	1,898.4	2,027.1	2,172.3	2,203.2	2,171.3	2,163.8	2,143.2	2,137.9	1,978.1	1,699.9
1997-8	1,520.2	1,525.6	1,525.5	1,679.6	1,787.9	1,711.2	1,762.6	1,857.6	1,857.0	1,712.6	1,779.1	1,453.2
1998-9	1,382.4	1,416.8	1,406.5	1,312.9	1,505.6	1,607.6	1,716.2	1,640.5	1,767.3	1,647.4	1,671.2	1,630.8
1999-00	1,519.6	1,616.4	1,663.6	1,791.1	2,013.7	2,099.8	2,092.7	2,099.2	1,991.9	2,028.3	2,120.4	2,018.1
2000-1	1,995.3	2,060.8	2,167.5	2,298.0	2,379.7	2,474.0	2,504.0	2,505.8	2,656.1	2,776.7	2,895.5	2,869.9
2001-2	2,877.2	2,724.9	2,787.4	2,868.1	3,038.5	2,896.4	2,952.7	2,856.8	2,943.2	2,735.9	2,529.7	2,521.7
2002-3	2,358.6	2,280.1	2,326.1	2,398.0	2,395.7	2,271.9	2,244.6	2,120.2	2,053.9	1,928.5	1,794.2	1,654.4
2003-4	1,490.6	1,411.8	1,530.4	1,579.9	1,945.6	1,988.0	1,855.9	1,644.1	1,651.6	1,514.0	1,412.0	1,180.6
2004-5[1]	1,075.6	1,255.3	1,191.5									

[1] Preliminary.   Source: Economic Research Service, U.S. Department of Agriculture (ERS-USDA)

Average Price of Crude Domestic Soybean Oil (in Tank Cars) F.O.B. Decatur   In Cents Per Pound

Year	Oct.	Nov.	Dec.	Jan.	Feb.	Mar.	Apr.	May	June	July	Aug.	Sept.	Average
1995-6	26.56	25.41	24.76	23.69	23.65	23.60	25.82	26.50	24.95	24.10	23.99	23.92	24.70
1996-7	21.95	21.80	21.60	22.45	22.41	23.29	23.17	23.68	22.97	21.89	22.06	22.88	22.50
1997-8	24.31	25.73	25.08	25.09	26.51	27.09	28.10	28.28	25.83	24.88	23.99	25.13	25.84
1998-9	25.20	25.20	24.00	22.90	20.00	19.50	18.80	17.85	16.50	15.30	16.50	16.80	19.88
1999-00	16.08	15.63	15.30	15.63	15.09	16.21	17.52	16.75	15.65	14.70	14.34	14.24	15.60
2000-1	13.50	13.37	13.12	12.53	12.38	13.90	13.53	13.53	14.21	16.49	17.08	15.46	14.09
2001-2	14.38	15.23	15.10	14.82	14.15	14.75	15.31	15.98	17.69	19.12	20.61	20.32	16.46
2002-3	20.75	23.00	22.60	21.50	21.20	21.56	22.40	23.17	22.90	21.80	20.40	23.20	22.04
2003-4	27.40	27.76	29.54	30.34	33.05	34.66	34.19	32.68	30.07	28.05	25.98	25.87	29.97
2004-5[1]	23.23	22.95	21.79	20.47									22.11

[1] Preliminary.   Source: Economic Research Service, U.S. Department of Agriculture (ERS-USDA)

Soybean Oil Futures - Chicago Board of Trade
(weekly close) as of December 31, 2004

Cents per pound

Average Open Interest of Soybean Oil Futures in Chicago   In Contracts

Year	Jan.	Feb.	Mar.	Apr.	May	June	July	Aug.	Sept.	Oct.	Nov.	Dec.
1995	101,171	103,856	97,715	87,300	76,175	75,171	81,650	77,064	70,410	71,652	85,241	84,138
1996	87,214	85,611	87,859	95,954	95,422	86,366	81,440	80,090	83,211	98,514	97,496	86,119
1997	89,112	89,348	102,388	101,191	101,544	104,433	105,346	95,282	94,521	107,471	119,877	106,406
1998	105,798	121,657	142,100	160,004	159,248	139,934	117,487	112,177	115,879	115,260	110,386	104,738
1999	115,407	131,875	136,967	133,404	131,993	147,749	157,999	147,280	146,239	155,768	163,439	144,798
2000	131,948	135,196	143,699	155,114	134,093	140,582	134,392	135,506	136,590	135,584	142,712	134,873
2001	134,677	133,497	123,770	128,360	142,877	151,713	162,395	166,318	159,467	164,521	167,803	154,589
2002	149,103	158,157	149,913	136,198	128,707	129,480	135,762	143,144	146,759	139,626	169,978	155,871
2003	143,607	140,272	131,323	142,123	147,584	143,218	147,610	157,066	141,596	161,556	183,747	191,176
2004	198,361	212,204	186,745	159,478	141,772	136,887	135,649	142,574	132,936	147,046	154,316	151,778

Source: Chicago Board of Trade (CBT)

Volume of Trading of Soybean Oil Futures in Chicago   In Contracts

Year	Jan.	Feb.	Mar.	Apr.	May	June	July	Aug.	Sept.	Oct.	Nov.	Dec.	Total[1]
1995	424,387	363,695	464,413	355,884	457,682	418,182	377,355	330,507	303,893	317,201	431,711	366,426	4,611.3
1996	354,602	355,220	375,237	443,408	376,716	423,089	512,563	449,014	425,850	414,018	396,233	454,327	4,980.3
1997	473,290	381,921	503,998	445,848	389,741	439,626	442,846	375,122	417,970	413,722	489,541	511,369	5,285.0
1998	443,562	556,982	497,887	673,091	624,518	648,098	629,642	491,155	558,032	383,844	450,073	540,379	6,498.3
1999	367,303	555,097	520,622	463,236	350,850	489,184	516,205	552,198	523,376	395,243	497,090	433,491	5,663.9
2000	424,232	451,677	483,212	438,526	451,162	533,376	422,418	456,195	436,841	378,419	507,044	386,801	5,369.9
2001	327,570	458,445	416,718	443,454	403,110	541,194	751,299	612,349	447,390	550,995	579,460	502,341	6,034.3
2002	474,824	497,396	468,878	496,990	526,918	588,386	701,455	648,853	529,442	549,942	705,373	628,026	6,816.5
2003	522,939	540,645	473,694	618,483	520,043	740,549	761,460	594,687	636,469	733,405	656,464	618,502	7,417.3
2004	521,293	722,580	736,173	760,153	631,157	642,917	657,542	549,538	565,439	552,890	654,338	599,294	7,593.3

[1] In thousands of contracts.   *Source: Chicago Board of Trade (CBT)*

Soybeans

Soybean is the common name for the annual leguminous plant and its seed. The soybean is a member of the oilseed family and is not considered a grain. The soybean seeds are contained in pods and are nearly spherical in shape. The seeds are usually light yellow in color. The seeds contain 20% oil and 40% protein. Soybeans were an ancient food crop in China, Japan, and Korea and were only introduced to the US in the early 1800s. Today, soybeans are the second largest crop produced in the US behind corn. Soybean production in the US is concentrated in the Midwest and the lower Mississippi Valley. Soybean crops in the US are planted in May or June and are harvested in autumn. Soybean plants usually reach maturity 100-150 days after planting depending on growing conditions.

Soybeans are used to produce a wide variety of food products. The key value of soybeans lies in the relatively high protein content, which makes it an excellent source of protein without many of the negative factors of animal meat. Popular soy-based food products include whole soybeans (roasted for snacks or used in sauces, stews and soups), soy oil for cooking and baking, soy flour, protein concentrates, isolated soy protein (which contains up to 92% protein), soy milk and baby formula (as an alternative to dairy products), soy yogurt, soy cheese, soy nut butter, soy sprouts, tofu and tofu products (soybean curd), soy sauce (which is produced by a fermentation process), and meat alternatives (hamburgers, breakfast sausage, etc).

The primary market for soybean futures is at the Chicago Board of Trade. The CBOT's soybean contract calls for the delivery of 5,000 bushels of No. 2 yellow soybeans (at contract par), No. 1 yellow soybeans (at 6 cents per bushel above the contract price), or No. 3 yellow soybeans (at a 6 cents under the contract price). Soybean futures are also traded at exchanges in Brazil, Argentina, China, and Tokyo.

Prices – Soybean prices in early 2004 extended the 2003 rally, which was driven by the poor soybean crop seen in 2003-04 and strong demand. That combination drove the September 1, 2004 carry-over down to 112.5 million bushels, the smallest carry-over since 1973-74. Soybean prices on the nearest-futures chart surged to a 16-year high of $10.64 per bushel in April 2004. However, the summer 2004 growing season in the US was highly favorable for soybeans with cool weather and plenty of moisture. That prompted a record crop for 2004-05 of 3.141 million bushels, up +30% yr/yr. The projected carry-over for 2004-05 soared to 440 million bushels, the highest since the 1980s, since demand couldn't keep up with supply. Soybean prices plunged during summer and autumn 2004 as the size of the crop became obvious. As of early 2005, the market focus was on when demand would be able to chew through the big 2004 production surplus. In addition, the focus was also on farmer planting intentions for spring 2005 because of the fact that soybean rust moved into the US for the first time in autumn 2004. Scientists believe that Hurricane Ivan blew the spores from South America north into the lower Mississippi Valley states. Although soybean rust can be controlled by spraying fungicides, some farmers will simply decided to avoid the extra costs and risks and plant other crops instead, thus reducing soybean acres in 2005.

Supply – World soybean production during the 2004-05 marketing year (Sep-Aug) rose +21.6%% yr/yr to 230.768 million metric tons, which was a new record high. World soybean production has more than doubled from the 81 million metric ton level seen in 1980. The world's largest soybean producers are the US with 37% of world production in 2004-05, Brazil (28%), Argentina (17%), China (8%), and India (3%). China's soybean production has roughly doubled since 1980. Brazil's production has risen by roughly 4 times since 1980.

US soybean production in 2004-05 rose sharply by +30% yr/yr to 3.141 billion bushels, which was a new record high US production level. U.S. farmers harvested a record high 73.990 million acres of soybeans in 2004-05, up from 72.476 million acres in 2003-04. The average yield of 42.6 bushels per acre in 2004-05 was easily a new record high. The farm value of US soybean production in 2003-04 was $17.465 billion. US ending stocks at the beginning of the 2004-05 marketing year (September 1, 2004) fell to 112.5 million bushels, which was a 3-decade low for the carry-over into the new marketing year. The largest soybean producing states in the US are Iowa with 15.8% of US production in 2004-05, Illinois (15.6%), Indiana (9.1%), Minnesota (7.8%), Nebraska (7.2%), Missouri (7.2%), and Ohio (6.6%).

Demand – The distribution tables for US soybeans for the 2004-05 marketing year show that 59% of US soybean usage went for crushing, 36% for exports, and 6% for seed and residual. The quantity of soybeans that went for crushing rose +7.5% yr/yr in 2004-05 to 1.645 billion bushels. The world soybean crush rose +1.6% yr/yr in 2004-05 to 170.400 million metric tons, which was a new record high and was more than double the level seen in 1980.

Trade – World exports of soybeans in 2004-05 rose +13.6% yr/yr to 62.736 million metric tons, which was a new record high. The world's largest soybean exporters are the US with 44% of world exports in 2004-05 and Brazil with 36% of world production. The other main exporter is Argentina with 12% of world exports. US soybean exports in 2004-05 rose +14.1% yr/yr to 27.488 million metric tons, which was well below the record of 29.204 million metric tons seen in 2001-02. Brazil's soybean exports have more than quadrupled in the past decade and in 2004-05 rose +35.6% yr/yr to a new record high of 22.303 million metric tons. The world's largest importers of soybeans in 2004-05 were China with 35% of world imports, Europe with 26%, Japan with 8%, and Mexico with 7%. China's imports in 2004-05 rose +35.4% yr/yr to a record high of 22.000 million metric tons from negligible levels prior to 1994.

World Production of Soybeans   In Thousands of Metric Tons

Crop Year[4]	Argen-tina	Bolivia	Brazil	Canada	China	India	Indo-nesia	Mexico	Para-guay	Thai-land	United States	Russia	World Total
1995-6	12,430	900	24,150	2,293	13,500	4,476	1,517	190	2,408	368	59,174	290	125,033
1996-7	11,200	1,040	27,300	2,165	13,220	4,100	1,460	61	2,771	360	64,780	279	132,349
1997-8	19,500	1,071	32,500	2,738	14,728	5,350	1,306	189	2,988	338	73,176	280	158,188
1998-9	20,000	960	31,300	2,737	15,152	6,000	1,300	143	2,980	335	74,598	297	160,038
1999-00	21,200	1,240	34,700	2,776	14,290	5,200	1,300	123	2,911	330	72,224	334	160,682
2000-1	27,800	1,030	39,500	2,703	15,400	5,250	1,020	103	3,502	312	75,055	342	175,928
2001-2	30,000	1,240	43,500	1,635	15,410	5,400	870	66	3,547	270	78,672	350	185,123
2002-3[1]	35,500	1,650	52,000	2,336	16,510	4,000	780	89	4,500	250	75,010	423	197,079
2003-4[2]	34,000	1,950	52,600	2,263	15,400	6,800	820	125	4,000	220	66,778	393	189,810
2004-5[3]	39,000	1,950	64,500	3,050	18,000	7,000	840	125	5,000	270	85,484	450	230,768

[1] Preliminary.   [2] Estimate.   [3] Forecast.   [4] Spilt year includes Northern Hemisphere crops harvested in the late months of the first year shown combined with Southern Hemisphere crops harvested in the early months of the following year.   *Sources: Oil World; Foreign Agricultural Service, U.S. Department of Agriculture (FAS-USDA)*

World Crushings and Ending Stocks of Soybeans   In Thousands of Metric Tons

Year	Argen-tina	Brazil	China	European Union	India	Japan	Mexico	Taiwan	United States	World Total	Brazil	United States	World Total
				Crushings								Ending Stocks	
1995-6	10,285	21,703	7,470	14,091	4,046	3,700	2,436	2,356	37,273	112,464	5,962	4,993	17,582
1996-7	11,050	20,023	7,500	14,381	3,650	3,810	2,690	2,362	39,080	114,070	4,199	3,588	14,567
1997-8	12,886	19,946	8,450	15,278	4,770	3,720	3,600	2,043	43,464	123,520	7,796	5,438	25,869
1998-9	17,507	21,174	12,607	15,344	5,400	3,700	3,950	1,874	43,262	135,027	8,032	9,484	27,527
1999-00	17,075	21,084	15,070	13,994	4,400	3,750	4,100	2,098	42,927	135,546	9,352	7,897	28,574
2000-1	17,300	22,742	18,900	16,598	4,525	3,775	4,450	2,134	44,625	146,843	9,431	6,743	31,862
2001-2	20,859	24,693	20,250	17,531	4,629	3,885	4,610	2,187	46,259	158,014	12,108	5,663	33,225
2002-3[1]	23,527	27,168	26,540	16,259	3,420	4,012	4,336	2,151	43,948	164,831	15,932	4,853	40,667
2003-4[2]	25,039	29,331	25,439	14,323	5,534	3,663	3,895	2,047	41,631	164,430	16,804	3,059	38,862
2004-5[3]	26,200	32,442	28,250	15,100	5,940	3,885	4,490	2,060	45,178	178,715	23,456	11,843	60,805

[1] Preliminary.   [2] Estimate.   [3] Forecast.   *Sources: Oil World; Foreign Agricultural Service, U.S. Department of Agriculture (FAS-USDA)*

World Imports and Exports of Soybeans   In Thousands of Metric Tons

Year	China	European Union	Japan	Rep. of Korea	Mexico	Taiwan	World Total	Argen-tina	Brazil	Canada	Paraguay	United States	World Total
			Imports							Exports			
1995-6	795	14,525	4,776	1,422	2,401	2,646	32,380	2,087	3,458	599	1,587	23,108	31,628
1996-7	2,274	14,572	5,043	1,620	2,720	2,632	35,625	750	8,424	478	2,150	24,110	36,757
1997-8	2,940	15,137	4,873	1,349	3,502	2,387	38,463	3,230	8,760	769	2,293	23,760	39,684
1998-9	3,850	14,859	4,807	1,400	3,766	2,124	38,775	3,233	8,931	876	2,299	21,898	38,007
1999-00	10,100	14,129	4,907	1,606	4,039	2,408	45,673	4,131	11,101	949	2,025	26,537	45,461
2000-1	13,245	17,448	4,767	1,389	4,381	2,330	53,042	7,415	15,469	747	2,509	27,103	53,793
2001-2	10,385	18,369	5,023	1,434	4,510	2,578	54,219	6,005	15,000	495	2,386	28,948	53,596
2002-3[1]	21,417	16,824	5,087	1,516	4,230	2,351	62,647	8,713	19,734	700	3,200	28,423	61,693
2003-4[2]	16,933	14,791	4,688	1,368	3,800	2,218	54,336	6,710	19,816	880	2,265	24,089	55,204
2004-5[3]	22,000	15,859	5,000	1,550	4,400	2,320	62,219	7,665	22,303	950	2,750	27,488	62,736

[1] Preliminary.   [2] Estimate.   [3] Forecast.   *Sources: Oil World; Foreign Agricultural Service, U.S. Department of Agriculture (FAS-USDA)*

Supply and Distribution of Soybeans in the United States   In Millions of Bushels

Crop Year Beginning Sept. 1	Farms	Mills, Elevators[3]	Total	Pro-duction	Total Supply	Crushings	Exports	Seed, Feed & Residual	Total Distri-bution
	Stocks, Sept. 1	Supply				Distribution			
1995-6	105.1	229.7	334.8	2,174.3	2,513.5	1,370.0	849.0	111.0	2,330.0
1996-7	59.5	123.9	183.5	2,380.3	2,572.6	1,436.0	886.0	118.0	2,440.0
1997-8	43.6	88.2	131.8	2,688.8	2,825.6	1,597.0	874.0	155.0	2,626.0
1998-9	84.3	115.5	199.8	2,741.0	2,945.0	1,590.0	805.0	202.0	2,597.0
1999-00	145.0	203.5	348.5	2,653.8	3,006.0	1,578.0	973.0	165.0	2,716.0
2000-1	112.5	177.7	290.2	2,757.8	3,052.0	1,640.0	996.0	168.0	2,804.0
2001-2	83.5	164.2	247.7	2,890.7	3,141.0	1,700.0	1,064.0	169.0	2,933.0
2002-3	62.7	145.3	208.0	2,756.1	2,969.0	1,615.0	1,044.0	131.0	2,791.0
2003-4[1]	58.0	120.3	178.3	2,453.7	2,638.0	1,530.0	884.0	111.0	2,525.0
2004-5[2]	29.4	83.0	112.4	3,141.0	3,258.0	1,655.0	1,010.0	153.0	2,818.0

[1] Preliminary.   [2] Estimate.   [3] Also warehouses.   *Source: Economic Research Service, U.S. Department of Agriculture (ERS-USDA)*

SOYBEANS

Salient Statistics & Official Crop Production Reports of Soybeans in the U.S.   In Millions of Bushels

Year	Acreage Planted ---- 1,000 Acres ----	Acreage Harvested ---- 1,000 Acres ----	Yield Per Acre (Bu.)	Farm Price ($ / Bu.)	Farm Value (Million Dollars)	Yield of Oil	Yield of Meal	Crop Production Reports In Thousands of Bushels Aug. 1	Sept. 1	Oct. 1	Nov. 1	Dec. 1	Final
1995-6	62,575	61,624	35.3	6.72	14,611	11.15	47.69	2,245,901	2,284,551	2,190,661	2,182,991	----	2,176,814
1996-7	64,205	63,409	37.6	7.35	17,495	10.91	47.36	2,299,675	2,269,505	2,346,220	2,402,610	----	2,380,274
1997-8	70,005	69,110	38.9	6.47	17,396	11.25	47.41	2,744,451	2,745,891	2,721,843	2,736,115	----	2,688,750
1998-9	72,025	70,441	38.9	4.93	13,513	11.30	47.25	2,824,744	2,908,604	2,768,919	2,762,609	----	2,741,014
1999-00	73,730	72,446	36.6	4.63	12,287	11.34	47.76	2,869,519	2,778,392	2,696,272	2,672,972	----	2,653,758
2000-1	74,266	72,408	38.1	4.54	12,548	11.24	48.06	2,988,669	2,899,571	2,822,821	2,777,036	----	2,757,810
2001-2	74,075	72,975	39.6	4.38	12,606	11.14	44.27	2,867,474	2,833,511	2,907,042	2,922,914	----	2,890,682
2002-3	73,963	72,497	38.0	5.64	15,253	11.39	43.90	2,628,387	2,655,819	2,653,798	2,689,691	----	2,756,147
2003-4[1]	73,404	72,476	33.9	7.94	18,014			2,862,039	2,642,644	2,468,390	2,451,759	----	2,453,665
2004-5[2]	75,208	73,958	42.5	5.53	16,098			2,876,627	2,835,989	3,106,861	3,150,441	----	3,140,996

[1] Preliminary.   [2] Forecast.   *Source: National Agricultural Statistics Service, U.S. Department of Agriculture (NASS-USDA)*

Stocks of Soybeans in the United States   In Thousands of Bushels

Year	On Farms Mar. 1	Jun. 1	Sept. 1	Dec. 1	Off Farms[1] Mar. 1	Jun. 1	Sept. 1	Dec. 1	Total Stocks Mar. 1	Jun. 1	Sept. 1	Dec. 1
1995	635,300	348,800	105,130	861,500	734,898	443,072	229,684	971,929	1,370,198	791,872	334,814	1,833,429
1996	512,000	234,100	59,523	935,100	678,356	388,701	123,935	889,984	1,190,356	622,801	183,458	1,825,084
1997	514,000	216,000	43,600	1,048,000	541,754	283,890	88,233	951,417	1,055,754	499,890	131,833	1,999,417
1998	637,000	318,000	84,300	1,187,000	565,922	275,654	115,499	999,440	1,202,922	593,654	199,799	2,186,440
1999	815,000	458,000	145,000	1,150,000	642,338	390,573	203,482	1,032,666	1,457,338	848,573	348,482	2,182,666
2000	730,000	370,000	112,500	1,217,000	665,986	404,425	177,662	1,022,791	1,395,986	774,425	290,162	2,239,791
2001	780,000	365,000	83,500	1,240,000	623,908	343,180	164,247	1,035,713	1,403,908	708,180	247,747	2,275,713
2002	687,000	301,200	62,700	1,170,000	648,987	383,721	145,320	943,641	1,335,987	684,921	208,020	2,113,641
2003	636,500	272,500	58,000	820,000	565,528	329,862	120,329	868,653	1,201,028	602,362	178,329	1,688,653
2004	355,900	110,000	29,400	1,300,000	549,947	300,604	83,014	1,004,880	905,847	410,604	112,414	2,304,880

[1] Includes stocks at mills, elevators, warehouses, terminals and processors.   NA = Not avaliable.   *Source: National Agricultural Statistics Service, U.S. Department of Agriculture (NASS-USDA)*

Commercial Stocks of Soybeans in the United States, on First of Month   In Millions of Bushels

Year	Jan.	Feb.	Mar.	Apr.	May	June	July	Aug.	Sept.	Oct.	Nov.	Dec.
1995	80.7	72.5	67.8	63.5	51.8	50.8	44.3	35.7	33.6	23.0	60.8	61.7
1996	57.2	57.2	59.2	54.7	56.2	44.9	36.9	32.7	12.0	5.3	55.2	50.6
1997	32.6	28.8	22.9	26.0	29.2	24.7	14.3	12.8	6.3	4.5	50.2	49.4
1998	35.3	31.2	22.9	18.4	14.5	14.2	10.2	9.7	8.7	18.6	43.5	40.6
1999	39.1	31.5	29.0	28.7	25.0	18.9	16.1	17.3	14.1	19.5	46.9	42.3
2000	34.1	28.3	30.0	23.9	23.8	20.6	17.0	12.3	8.6	15.5	38.2	37.9
2001	34.5	28.8	25.2	22.5	16.3	15.0	12.9	13.4	11.9	9.6	34.7	38.2
2002	29.6	27.0	22.2	21.0	18.4	15.4	14.4	10.2	4.6	8.4	26.9	28.4
2003	25.9	13.2	13.9	12.8	9.7	9.4	11.7	7.6	4.5	7.0	33.0	36.7
2004	35.5	26.2	26.0	19.4	15.7	13.5	8.0	5.9	4.4	10.8	31.1	32.9

Source: Livestock Division, U.S. Department of Agriculture (LD-USDA)

Stocks of Soybeans at Mills in the United States, on First of Month   In Millions of Bushels

Year	Sept.	Oct.	Nov.	Dec.	Jan.	Feb.	Mar.	Apr.	May	June	July	Aug.
1993-4	42.0	28.0	108.6	114.9	120.9	126.1	118.5	119.7	98.7	97.8	90.0	63.5
1994-5	47.9	46.8	114.1	124.3	108.0	114.7	114.3	112.6	94.1	81.2	69.1	55.1
1995-6	52.8	54.2	125.6	129.1	120.0	123.3	121.9	110.6	104.2	92.5	70.4	57.4
1996-7	40.7	23.4	101.1	117.4	106.0	112.6	122.2	104.9	89.2	78.2	64.0	43.6
1997-8	28.3	37.0	126.4	124.3	110.3	98.7	93.4	72.0	56.9	41.0	42.5	44.1
1998-9	32.8	66.5	175.0	154.3	131.0	109.6	102.5	93.7	80.5	56.9	55.5	48.1
1999-00	41.7	70.8	162.9	144.7	144.2	140.3	137.8	129.6	98.7	78.7	78.4	52.1
2000-1	52.1	56.8	179.4	166.8	137.8	143.3	127.0	120.6	94.9	86.1	79.3	69.0
2001-2	69.0	41.3	152.8	137.1	121.4	129.6	128.2	112.9	104.2	88.2	67.9	65.4
2002-3[1]	46.4	36.3	114.5	113.5	106.0	109.2	103.5	91.5	91.6	76.1	64.9	55.6

[1] Preliminary.   *Source: Economic Research Service, U.S. Department of Agriculture (ERS-USDA)*

Production of Soybeans for Beans in the United States, by State   In Millions of Bushels

Crop Year	Arkansas	Illinois	Indiana	Iowa	Kentucky	Michigan	Minnesota	Mississippi	Missouri	Nebraska	Ohio	Tennessee	Total
1995-6	88.4	378.3	196.7	407.4	41.4	59.6	234.9	37.8	132.8	101.0	153.1	34.6	2,176.8
1996-7	112.0	398.9	203.7	415.8	44.8	46.7	224.2	54.3	149.9	135.5	157.2	38.5	2,380.3
1997-8	109.8	427.9	230.6	478.4	42.1	71.6	255.5	64.2	174.6	143.8	191.0	40.8	2,688.8
1998-9	85.0	464.2	231.0	496.8	36.0	73.7	285.6	48.0	170.0	165.0	193.2	35.1	2,741.0
1999-00	92.4	443.1	216.5	478.4	24.4	77.6	289.8	44.7	147.1	180.6	162.0	22.8	2,653.8
2000-1	80.3	459.8	252.1	464.6	45.2	73.1	293.2	34.8	175.0	173.9	186.5	28.8	2,757.8
2001-2	91.2	477.9	273.9	480.5	48.8	63.9	266.4	37.0	186.2	223.0	187.8	35.4	2,890.7
2002-3	96.5	453.7	239.5	499.2	42.6	78.5	308.9	43.8	170.0	176.3	151.0	34.7	2,756.1
2003-4	111.3	379.6	204.1	342.9	53.9	54.7	238.4	55.8	146.0	182.3	164.8	47.0	2,453.7
2004-5[1]	124.4	500.0	287.0	497.4	57.2	75.2	236.2	62.3	223.2	220.9	207.7	48.4	3,141.0

[1] Preliminary.   *Source: Agricultural Statistics Board, U.S. Department of Agriculture (ASB-USDA)*

United States Exports of Soybeans   In Millions of Bushels

Year	Sept.	Oct.	Nov.	Dec.	Jan.	Feb.	Mar.	Apr.	May	June	July	Aug.	Total
1993-4	30.1	73.6	72.4	73.9	71.0	67.8	53.6	34.8	27.5	26.7	17.1	40.7	589.1
1994-5	42.3	99.9	78.5	104.2	89.3	91.4	83.1	80.7	45.2	35.5	41.2	46.7	838.1
1995-6	70.7	77.4	65.5	89.6	106.2	82.9	93.5	52.9	42.1	51.8	46.0	52.6	851.2
1996-7	41.6	95.8	152.4	121.6	106.5	105.7	68.2	58.8	43.0	32.4	23.2	36.5	885.9
1997-8	42.6	174.3	150.4	121.2	91.1	94.8	56.9	36.7	27.3	24.7	27.9	26.6	874.3
1998-9	27.9	135.6	106.3	90.4	84.3	66.8	72.4	52.5	37.8	36.4	36.7	57.5	804.7
1999-00	69.4	122.8	104.5	109.1	104.0	103.1	109.7	50.6	45.6	46.0	50.3	58.4	973.4
2000-1	51.4	141.4	123.0	106.6	103.3	126.5	135.2	52.8	39.8	39.5	33.1	43.4	995.9
2001-2	31.7	158.9	158.0	133.2	157.2	132.0	63.8	46.0	45.6	43.2	56.0	38.0	1,063.7
2002-3[1]	30.9	136.7	152.8	114.7	157.0	154.0	91.5	66.4	38.6	30.8	39.0	32.7	1,045.0

[1] Preliminary.   *Source: Economic Research Service, U.S. Department of Agriculture (ERS-USDA)*

Spread Between Value of Products and Soybean Price in the United States   In Cents Per Bushel

Year	Sept.	Oct.	Nov.	Dec.	Jan.	Feb.	Mar.	Apr.	May	June	July	Aug.	Average
1993-4	95	108	105	92	93	99	88	85	89	88	94	118	96
1994-5	117	134	114	107	104	103	85	72	58	74	62	65	91
1995-6	68	82	58	64	53	48	53	67	44	50	52	47	57
1996-7	84	92	105	92	74	74	62	54	82	67	94	123	83
1997-8	177	96	108	87	57	51	35	33	33	29	53	43	67
1998-9	53	53	38	40	33	30	35	37	34	36	47	45	40
1999-00	48	61	64	58	75	61	70	70	80	81	69	62	66
2000-1	81	76	77	89	85	59	65	72	67	81	96	92	78
2001-2	102	108	106	83	86	65	65	65	57	63	64	89	79
2002-3	77	73	52	60	53	52	61	53	62	59	72	74	62

Source: Economic Research Service, U.S. Department of Agriculture (ERS-USDA)

Soybean Crushed (Factory Consumption) in the United States   In Millions of Bushels

Year	Sept.	Oct.	Nov.	Dec.	Jan.	Feb.	Mar.	Apr.	May	June	July	Aug.	Total
1993-4	98.4	113.7	114.4	114.1	110.7	103.3	113.3	105.6	103.0	97.2	101.0	101.0	1,276
1994-5	105.9	119.3	122.5	128.5	127.3	116.5	128.1	119.4	114.2	105.6	108.4	109.5	1,405
1995-6	107.4	120.6	123.4	125.1	122.8	111.2	115.5	112.1	106.3	107.5	111.9	105.7	1,370
1996-7	100.9	127.0	133.1	138.1	137.3	125.1	130.1	114.8	110.7	108.9	106.1	103.8	1,436
1997-8	110.8	142.2	142.8	153.1	151.8	138.3	147.0	134.0	123.9	117.5	123.8	111.9	1,597
1998-9	123.9	142.4	143.0	144.6	136.4	127.6	140.0	128.4	128.0	121.2	127.3	126.9	1,590
1999-00	133.8	150.2	142.8	143.0	139.2	125.4	130.4	121.5	121.0	117.9	130.2	122.2	1,578
2000-1	128.9	149.1	143.1	142.3	146.7	128.9	141.8	131.1	132.7	128.0	133.6	133.5	1,640
2001-2	128.2	150.2	149.1	153.4	155.1	139.0	149.8	139.2	140.6	134.6	129.8	130.6	1,700
2002-3[1]	122.3	149.5	145.7	150.2	142.7	129.2	142.7	127.0	130.5	121.4	129.3	125.1	1,615

One Bushel = 60 Pounds.   [1] Preliminary.   *Source: Economic Research Service, U.S. Department of Agriculture (ERS-USDA)*

SOYBEANS

Soybean Futures - Chicago Board of Trade
(weekly close) as of December 31, 2004

Cents per bushel

Average Open Interest of Soybean Futures in Chicago   In Contracts

Year	Jan.	Feb.	Mar.	Apr.	May	June	July	Aug.	Sept.	Oct.	Nov.	Dec.
1995	138,345	138,794	137,843	138,624	133,533	143,119	143,671	135,584	144,409	167,200	174,775	194,021
1996	198,731	199,150	192,927	207,284	191,989	179,548	180,817	182,324	196,361	178,872	155,937	152,966
1997	157,728	176,242	189,352	188,617	186,792	159,720	141,658	133,732	150,606	172,098	148,760	150,201
1998	135,340	142,778	147,900	152,732	143,994	149,563	133,532	140,236	158,627	163,759	143,814	146,463
1999	152,757	166,003	162,690	166,565	164,777	163,663	157,433	134,105	146,087	174,583	164,306	153,693
2000	149,468	172,494	174,465	195,189	193,500	167,678	140,894	126,952	149,074	183,734	168,023	177,324
2001	160,730	164,017	148,190	156,781	137,227	153,190	181,194	165,630	167,677	195,366	175,522	173,116
2002	156,898	169,242	169,882	164,388	156,548	188,692	220,758	201,494	201,808	210,033	208,099	213,868
2003	201,536	217,680	226,421	251,314	230,325	222,185	190,206	190,533	232,030	265,088	241,320	252,874
2004	258,708	267,482	263,737	262,919	222,310	199,108	172,194	171,791	190,006	242,654	228,700	241,904

Source: Chicago Board of Trade (CBT)

Volume of Trading of Soybean Futures in Chicago   In Thousands of Contracts

Year	Jan.	Feb.	Mar.	Apr.	May	June	July	Aug.	Sept.	Oct.	Nov.	Dec.	Total
1995	614.0	572.0	799.6	698.3	949.4	1,050.8	1,196.7	817.0	800.2	1,127.8	840.4	1,145.4	10,612
1996	1,302.6	1,122.9	1,009.4	1,683.2	1,149.3	989.5	1,295.9	989.8	1,050.2	1,002.7	1,695.6	940.1	14,231
1997	1,119.8	1,254.2	1,405.9	1,585.5	1,391.1	1,355.6	1,217.4	835.0	852.3	1,505.8	1,010.7	1,006.6	14,540
1998	875.7	971.2	935.9	1,116.2	973.6	1,378.8	1,286.3	884.5	864.4	1,264.6	867.0	1,012.9	12,431
1999	871.1	1,025.3	1,440.1	963.5	823.6	1,149.5	1,502.5	1,669.8	903.0	1,158.6	839.4	872.3	12,482
2000	1,071.9	1,099.3	1,191.6	1,079.1	1,321.6	1,302.0	883.4	801.4	860.9	1,188.8	932.5	895.3	12,628
2001	935.0	947.4	843.1	916.3	909.5	1,155.6	1,508.1	1,122.0	648.7	1,356.1	964.7	844.1	12,150
2002	1,078.8	899.9	1,065.7	1,238.6	1,048.3	1,311.8	1,762.2	1,346.4	1,002.9	1,486.1	1,070.9	1,163.5	14,475
2003	1,267.3	1,222.9	997.1	1,588.9	1,368.2	1,723.4	1,385.7	1,193.5	1,308.5	2,416.3	1,535.4	1,538.5	17,546
2004	1,509.7	1,879.6	1,957.2	2,036.2	1,593.2	1,601.7	1,551.3	1,107.6	1,052.8	1,635.3	1,395.3	1,526.1	18,846

Source: Chicago Board of Trade

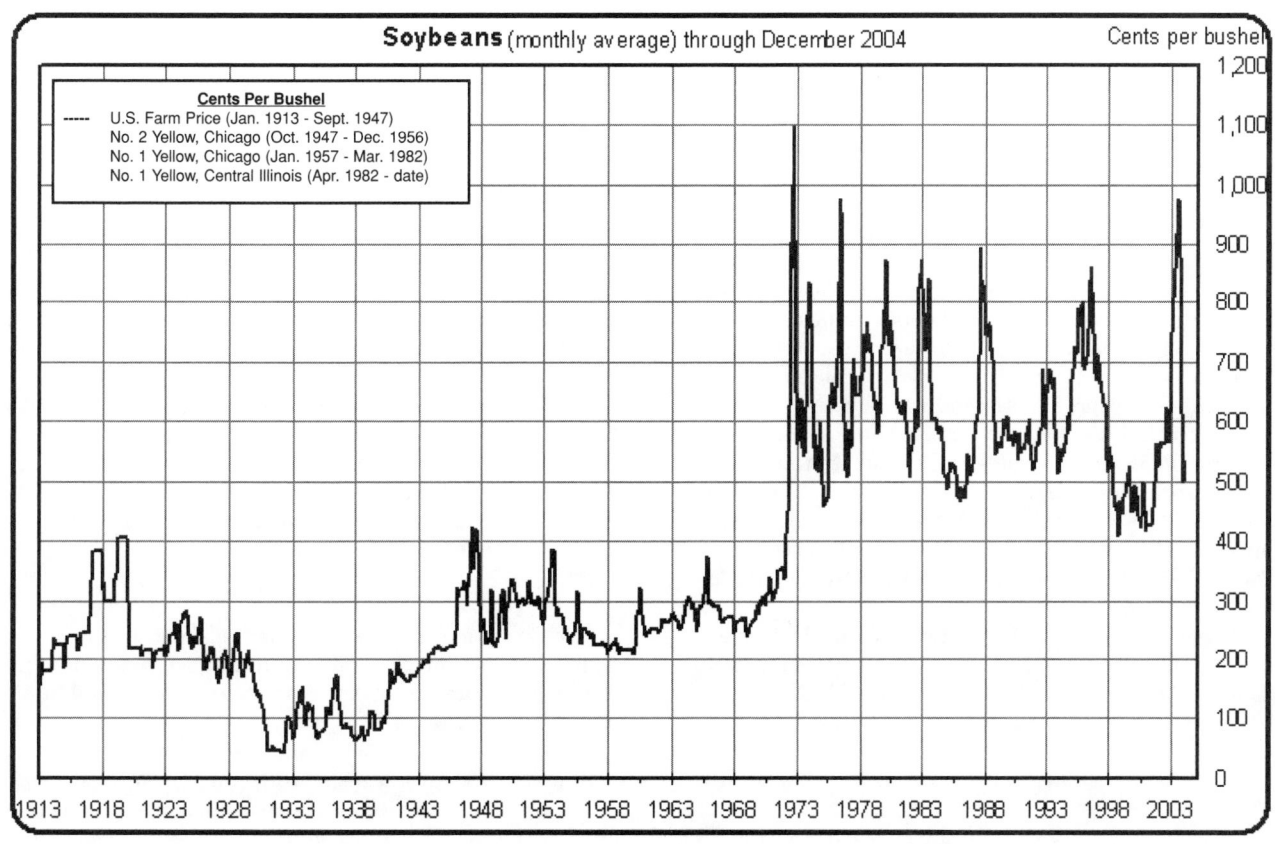

Average Cash Price of No. 1 Yellow Soybeans at Illinois Processor   In Cents Per Bushel

Year	Sept.	Oct.	Nov.	Dec.	Jan.	Feb.	Mar.	Apr.	May	June	July	Aug.	Average
1993-4	643	606	664	694	701	686	692	670	689	685	603	576	659
1994-5	557	531	566	567	558	560	574	578	580	577	623	602	573
1995-6	632	656	686	717	737	730	726	791	808	778	795	816	739
1996-7	820	711	704	708	737	769	833	854	878	837	769	741	780
1997-8	703	684	727	699	679	680	662	649	649	640	642	556	664
1998-9	533	536	572	558	532	490	475	480	468	462	425	465	500
1999-00	485	470	464	460	473	500	513	529	542	510	474	463	490
2000-1	484	468	483	506	477	457	451	441	457	474	517	510	477
2001-2	469	430	441	438	437	440	464	471	492	519	575	567	479
2002-3[1]	579	541	575	566	570	590	580	611	640	635	601	589	590

[1] Preliminary.   *Source: Economic Research Service, U.S. Department of Agriculture (ERS-USDA)*

Average Price Received by Farmers for Soybeans in the United States   In Dollars Per Bushel

Year	Sept.	Oct.	Nov.	Dec.	Jan.	Feb.	Mar.	Apr.	May	June	July	Aug.	Average
1995-6	5.98	6.15	6.40	6.76	6.77	7.01	7.00	7.43	7.69	7.41	7.62	7.82	6.72
1996-7	7.79	6.94	6.90	6.91	7.13	7.38	7.97	8.23	8.40	8.16	7.52	7.25	7.35
1997-8	6.72	6.50	6.85	6.71	6.69	6.57	6.40	6.26	6.26	6.16	6.14	5.43	6.47
1998-9	5.25	5.18	5.40	5.37	5.32	4.80	4.61	4.63	4.51	4.44	4.20	4.39	4.93
1999-00	4.57	4.48	4.45	4.43	4.62	4.79	4.91	5.00	5.19	4.93	4.53	4.45	4.63
2000-1	4.59	4.45	4.55	4.78	4.68	4.46	4.39	4.22	4.33	4.46	4.79	4.85	4.54
2001-2	4.53	4.09	4.16	4.20	4.22	4.22	4.38	4.47	4.64	4.88	5.35	5.53	4.38
2002-3	5.39	5.20	5.46	5.46	5.51	5.55	5.59	5.82	6.07	6.09	5.82	5.68	5.64
2003-4	6.06	6.60	7.05	7.17	7.35	8.28	9.27	9.62	9.57	9.05	8.46	6.83	7.94
2004-5[1]	5.84	5.56	5.36	5.45	5.57	5.39							5.53

[1] Preliminary.   *Source: Economic Research Service, U.S. Department of Agriculture (ERS-USDA)*

Stock Index Futures, U.S.

A stock index simply represents a basket of underlying stocks. Indices can be either price-weighted or capitalization-weighted. In a price-weighted index, such as the Dow Jones Industrials Average, the prices of each of the stocks are simply added up and divided by a divisor, meaning that stocks with higher prices have a higher weighting in the index value. In a capitalization-weighted index, such as the Standard and Poor's 500 index, the weighting of each stock corresponds to the size of the company as determined by its capitalization (i.e., the total dollar value of its stock). Stock indices cover a variety of different sectors. For example, the Dow Jones Industrials Average contains 30 blue-chip stocks that represent the industrial sector. The S&P 500 index includes 500 of the largest blue-chip US companies. The NYSE index includes all the stocks that trade at the New York Stock Exchange. The Nasdaq 100 includes the largest 100 companies that trade on the Nasdaq Exchange. The most popular US stock index futures contract is the S&P 500 at the Chicago Mercantile Exchange (CME).

Prices – The US stock market traded sideways early in 2004 and posted a 1-year low in August. However, a strong rally then emerged that took the S&P 500 to a new 3-1/2 year high. The S&P 500 in 2004 closed up +9.0%, adding to the +26.4% gain seen in 2003. By the end of 2004, the S&P 500 had shown an overall 58.4% rally from the bear market low seen in October 2002. However, it would take a further rally of 28% from the 2004 close for the S&P 500 to match its record high posted back in March 2000. The Dow Jones Industrials index rallied only +3.1% in 2004. The Nasdaq Composite index in 2004 rose by +8.6%. The small and mid-cap stocks performed much better than the large-cap stocks in 2004. The Russell 2000 small-cap index closed the year up +17.0% and showed a +5.2% annual gain through 2004, much better than the comparable 5-year annual return of –3.8% for the S&P 500.

The stock market in early 2004 paused and consolidated as the market regained its balance after the sharp rally in 2003 from the bear market lows. However, stock prices took off in the latter half of 2004 as it became clear that earnings would be stronger than expected. Earnings in Q3-2004 were relatively strong at +16.8%, coming on top of the +21.3% gain seen in the previous year in Q3-2003, according to Thomson First Call. Earnings in Q4-2004 were also strong at +19.9%, well above expectations of +15.5% as the quarter began. For all of 2004, earnings growth was very strong at +20.2%, adding to the +18.4% gain seen in 2003. The back-to-back earnings growth near 20% in 2003 and 2004 was much stronger than the long-term average of +7.0%.

The stock market in 2004 benefited from the ideal combination of low interest rates and a strong economy that allowed corporate earnings to grow sharply. The main threat to the stock market in 2004 was oil prices, but the surge in oil prices never took a big bite out of economic growth. The weak dollar was also a negative factor, but foreign investors nevertheless seemed content to continue to plow money into US stocks. The stock market in late 2004 also benefited from the reelection of President Bush given his stock-friendly initiatives such as cutting capital gains and dividend taxes, and his push for private retirement accounts.

Dow Jones Industrial Average (30 Stocks)

Year	Jan.	Feb.	Mar.	Apr.	May	June	July	Aug.	Sept.	Oct.	Nov.	Dec.	Average
1995	3,872.5	3,953.7	4,062.8	4,230.7	4,391.6	4,510.8	4,684.8	4,639.3	4,746.8	4,760.5	4,935.8	5,136.1	4,493.8
1996	5,179.4	5,518.7	5,612.2	5,579.9	5,616.7	5,671.5	5,496.3	5,685.5	5,804.0	5,995.1	6,318.4	6,435.9	5,742.8
1997	6,707.0	6,917.5	6,901.1	6,657.5	7,242.4	7,599.6	7,990.7	7,948.4	7,866.6	7,875.8	7,677.4	7,909.8	7,441.1
1998	7,808.4	8,323.6	8,709.5	9,037.4	9,080.1	8,873.0	9,097.1	8,478.5	7,909.8	8,164.3	9,005.8	9,018.7	8,625.5
1999	9,345.9	9,323.0	9,753.6	10,443.5	10,853.9	10,704.0	11,052.2	10,935.5	10,714.0	10,396.9	10,809.8	11,246.4	10,464.9
2000	11,281.3	10,541.9	10,483.4	10,944.4	10,580.3	10,582.9	10,663.0	11,014.5	10,967.9	10,441.0	10,666.1	10,652.4	10,734.9
2001	10,682.7	10,774.6	10,081.3	10,234.5	11,005.0	10,767.2	10,444.5	10,314.7	9,042.6	9,220.8	9,721.8	9,979.9	10,189.1
2002	9,923.8	9,891.1	10,501.0	10,165.2	10,080.5	9,492.4	8,616.5	8,685.5	8,160.2	8,048.1	8,625.7	8,526.7	9,226.4
2003	8,474.4	7,916.2	7,977.7	8,332.1	8,623.4	9,098.1	9,154.5	9,284.8	9,492.5	9,683.6	9,762.2	10,124.7	8,993.7
2004	10,540.1	10,601.5	10,323.7	10,419.9	10,083.8	10,364.9	10,152.1	10,032.8	10,204.6	10,001.6	10,411.8	10,673.4	10,317.5

Average. *Source: New York Stock Exchange (NYSE)*

Dow Jones Transportation Average (20 Stocks)

Year	Jan.	Feb.	Mar.	Apr.	May	June	July	Aug.	Sept.	Oct.	Nov.	Dec.	Average
1995	1,515.8	1,547.2	1,584.6	1,648.9	1,646.2	1,699.3	1,852.1	1,883.9	1,961.4	1,922.9	2,008.3	2,029.5	1,775.0
1996	1,932.7	2,030.0	2,136.0	2,180.0	2,229.1	2,213.4	2,053.1	2,060.4	2,050.8	2,100.1	2,224.3	2,273.9	2,123.7
1997	2,295.0	2,341.4	2,427.8	2,464.0	2,635.1	2,711.4	2,858.0	2,925.8	3,086.0	3,239.9	3,155.7	3,233.5	2,781.1
1998	3,275.8	3,456.8	3,521.5	3,586.5	3,401.9	3,373.2	3,459.3	3,021.1	2,763.0	2,647.8	2,953.4	3,027.6	3,207.3
1999	3,172.0	3,188.3	3,296.4	3,477.7	3,628.2	3,396.1	3,423.7	3,207.0	3,006.2	2,928.7	2,988.7	2,902.1	3,217.9
2000	2,812.2	2,483.4	2,534.5	2,823.9	2,813.2	2,717.2	2,822.3	2,835.6	2,641.5	2,491.0	2,792.3	2,822.9	2,715.8
2001	3,029.9	3,010.2	2,792.5	2,776.6	2,908.2	2,770.4	2,887.3	2,852.1	2,344.8	2,217.3	2,404.6	2,603.0	2,716.4
2002	2,735.3	2,719.1	2,942.9	2,776.0	2,734.8	2,702.2	2,432.1	2,318.5	2,216.0	2,216.6	2,321.6	2,331.7	2,537.2
2003	2,297.3	2,102.5	2,094.6	2,278.7	2,429.9	2,459.6	2,554.5	2,617.3	2,744.7	2,841.3	2,920.0	2,969.3	2,525.8
2004	3,021.0	2,889.4	2,838.3	2,941.1	2,877.1	3,069.0	3,099.8	3,065.8	3,205.1	3,372.6	3,589.4	3,750.0	3,143.2

Average. *Source: New York Stock Exchange (NYSE)*

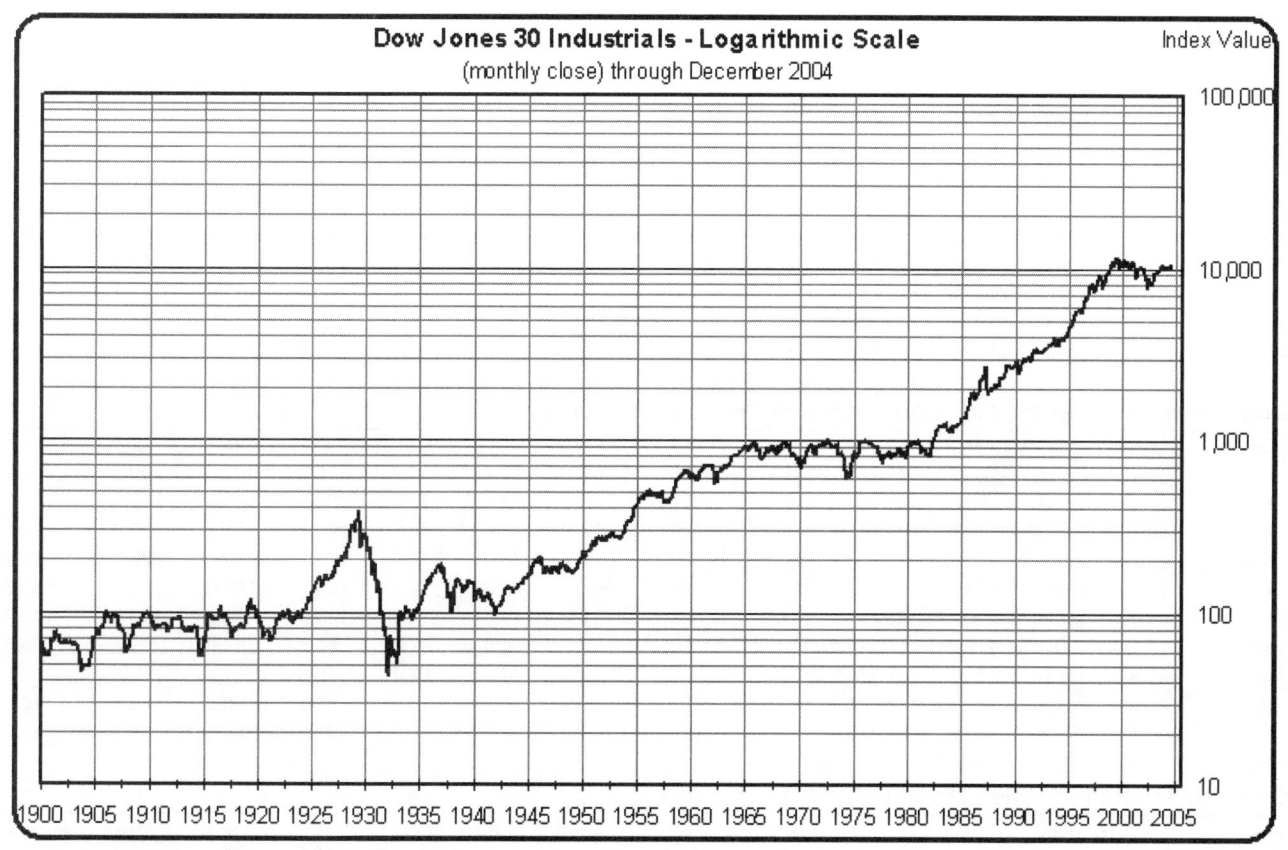

Dow Jones Industrial Average (30 Stocks)

Year	Jan.	Feb.	Mar.	Apr.	May	June	July	Aug.	Sept.	Oct.	Nov.	Dec.	Average
1995	3,872.5	3,953.7	4,062.8	4,230.7	4,391.6	4,510.8	4,684.8	4,639.3	4,746.8	4,760.5	4,935.8	5,136.1	4,493.8
1996	5,179.4	5,518.7	5,612.2	5,579.9	5,616.7	5,671.5	5,496.3	5,685.5	5,804.0	5,995.1	6,318.4	6,435.9	5,742.8
1997	6,707.0	6,917.5	6,901.1	6,657.5	7,242.4	7,599.6	7,990.7	7,948.4	7,866.6	7,875.8	7,677.4	7,909.8	7,441.1
1998	7,808.4	8,323.6	8,709.5	9,037.4	9,080.1	8,873.0	9,097.1	8,478.5	7,909.8	8,164.3	9,005.8	9,018.7	8,625.5
1999	9,345.9	9,323.0	9,753.6	10,443.5	10,853.9	10,704.0	11,052.2	10,935.5	10,714.0	10,396.9	10,809.8	11,246.4	10,464.9
2000	11,281.3	10,541.9	10,483.4	10,944.4	10,580.3	10,582.9	10,663.0	11,014.5	10,967.9	10,441.0	10,666.1	10,652.4	10,734.9
2001	10,682.7	10,774.6	10,081.3	10,234.5	11,005.0	10,767.2	10,444.5	10,314.7	9,042.6	9,220.8	9,721.8	9,979.9	10,189.1
2002	9,923.8	9,891.1	10,501.0	10,165.2	10,080.5	9,492.4	8,616.5	8,685.5	8,160.2	8,048.1	8,625.7	8,526.7	9,226.4
2003	8,474.4	7,916.2	7,977.7	8,332.1	8,623.4	9,098.1	9,154.5	9,284.8	9,492.5	9,683.6	9,762.2	10,124.7	8,993.7
2004	10,540.1	10,601.5	10,323.7	10,419.9	10,083.8	10,364.9	10,152.1	10,032.8	10,204.6	10,001.6	10,411.8	10,673.4	10,317.5

Average.   *Source: New York Stock Exchange (NYSE)*

Standard & Poor's 500 Composite Price Index

Year	Jan.	Feb.	Mar.	Apr.	May	June	July	Aug.	Sept.	Oct.	Nov.	Dec.	Average
1995	465.3	481.9	493.2	507.9	523.8	539.4	557.4	559.1	578.8	582.9	595.5	614.6	541.6
1996	614.4	649.5	647.1	547.2	661.2	668.5	644.1	662.7	674.9	701.5	735.7	743.3	662.5
1997	766.1	798.4	792.2	763.9	833.1	876.3	925.3	927.7	937.0	951.2	938.9	962.4	872.7
1998	963.4	1,023.7	1,076.8	1,112.2	1,108.4	1,108.4	1,156.6	1,074.6	1,020.7	1,032.5	1,144.5	1,190.0	1,084.3
1999	1,248.7	1,246.6	1,281.7	1,334.8	1,332.1	1,322.6	1,381.0	1,327.5	1,318.2	1,300.0	1,391.0	1,428.7	1,326.1
2000	1,425.6	1,388.9	1,442.2	1,461.4	1,418.5	1,462.0	1,473.0	1,485.5	1,468.0	1,390.1	1,375.0	1,330.9	1,426.8
2001	1,335.6	1,305.8	1,185.9	1,189.8	1,270.4	1,238.8	1,204.5	1,178.5	1,047.6	1,076.6	1,129.7	1,144.9	1,192.3
2002	1,140.2	1,100.7	1,153.8	1,112.0	1,079.3	1,014.1	903.6	912.6	867.8	854.6	909.9	899.2	995.6
2003	895.8	837.6	846.6	890.0	936.0	988.0	992.5	989.5	1,019.4	1,038.7	1,049.9	1,080.6	963.7
2004	1,132.5	1,143.4	1,124.0	1,133.1	1,102.8	1,132.8	1,105.9	1,088.9	1,117.7	1,118.1	1,168.9	1,199.2	1,130.6

Average.   *Source: Index and Option Market (IOM), division of the Chicago Mercantile Exchange (CME)*

STOCK INDEX FUTURES, U.S.

Composite Index of Leading Indicators   (1992 = 100)

Year	Jan.	Feb.	Mar.	Apr.	May	June	July	Aug.	Sept.	Oct.	Nov.	Dec.	Average
1995	101.5	101.1	100.7	100.6	100.4	100.5	100.7	101.0	101.1	100.9	100.9	101.2	100.9
1996	100.5	101.4	101.6	101.8	102.1	102.3	102.3	102.4	102.5	102.5	102.5	102.6	102.0
1997	102.8	103.3	103.4	103.3	103.6	103.6	103.9	104.0	104.3	104.4	104.7	104.6	103.8
1998	104.8	105.2	105.4	105.4	105.4	105.2	105.6	105.6	105.6	105.7	106.2	106.4	105.5
1999	104.5	104.7	104.8	104.7	105.0	105.3	105.6	105.5	105.4	105.5	105.7	110.3	105.6
2000	110.7	110.3	110.5	110.5	110.5	110.4	109.8	109.9	109.9	109.5	109.2	108.8	110.0
2001	108.9	109.0	108.7	108.6	109.3	109.5	109.8	109.7	109.1	109.2	110.1	110.5	109.4
2002	111.0	111.0	111.0	110.8	111.4	111.2	111.0	110.9	110.4	110.4	111.0	111.1	110.9
2003	111.0	110.6	110.4	110.5	111.6	112.0	112.8	113.2	113.3	113.9	114.2	114.3	112.3
2004[1]	114.7	114.8	115.7	115.8	116.3	116.2	116.0	115.6	115.3	114.9	115.2	115.4	115.5

[1] Preliminary.   *Source: The Conference Board (TCB) Copyrighted.*

Consumer Confidence, The Conference Board   (1985 = 100)

Year	Jan.	Feb.	Mar.	Apr.	May	June	July	Aug.	Sept.	Oct.	Nov.	Dec.	Average
1995	101.4	99.4	100.2	104.6	102.0	94.6	101.4	102.4	97.3	96.3	101.6	99.2	100.0
1996	88.4	98.0	98.4	104.8	103.5	100.1	107.0	112.0	111.8	107.3	109.5	114.2	104.6
1997	118.7	118.9	118.5	118.5	127.9	129.9	126.3	127.6	130.2	123.4	128.1	136.2	125.4
1998	128.3	137.4	133.8	137.2	136.3	138.2	137.2	133.1	126.4	119.3	126.4	126.7	131.7
1999	128.9	133.1	134.0	135.5	137.7	139.0	136.2	136.0	134.2	130.5	137.0	141.7	135.3
2000	144.7	140.8	137.1	137.7	144.7	139.2	143.0	140.8	142.5	135.8	132.6	128.6	139.0
2001	115.7	109.3	116.9	109.9	116.1	118.9	116.3	114.0	97.0	85.3	84.9	94.6	106.6
2002	97.8	95.0	110.7	108.5	110.3	106.3	97.4	94.5	93.7	79.6	84.9	80.7	96.6
2003	78.8	64.8	61.4	81.0	83.6	83.5	77.0	81.7	77.0	81.7	92.5	94.8	79.8
2004[1]	97.7	88.5	88.5	93.0	93.1	102.8	105.7	98.7	96.7	92.9	92.6	102.3	96.0

[1] Preliminary.   *Source: The Conference Board (TCB) Copyrighted.*

Capacity Utilization Rates (Total Industry)   In Percent

Year	Jan.	Feb.	Mar.	Apr.	May	June	July	Aug.	Sept.	Oct.	Nov.	Dec.	Average
1995	84.8	84.5	84.2	83.8	83.7	83.6	82.8	83.6	83.6	83.0	82.9	82.9	83.6
1996	81.9	82.6	82.0	82.3	82.5	82.8	82.3	82.5	82.6	82.3	82.7	82.8	82.4
1997	82.7	83.5	83.4	83.4	83.3	83.3	83.4	83.8	84.0	84.2	84.3	84.1	83.6
1998	84.0	83.7	83.5	83.5	83.4	82.6	81.9	83.2	82.6	82.9	82.3	82.0	83.0
1999	82.2	82.1	82.2	82.1	82.3	82.1	82.3	82.6	82.1	82.7	82.8	83.2	82.4
2000	82.5	82.5	82.7	82.9	83.2	82.9	82.2	81.7	81.7	81.1	80.7	80.3	82.0
2001	79.3	78.6	78.1	77.8	77.2	76.6	76.1	75.9	75.4	75.0	74.5	74.4	76.6
2002	74.8	74.6	74.9	75.1	75.3	75.8	75.7	75.7	75.7	75.4	75.5	75.2	75.3
2003	75.4	75.5	75.2	74.6	74.7	74.9	75.4	75.3	75.8	76.0	76.7	76.8	75.5
2004[1]	76.9	77.7	77.4	77.7	78.2	77.8	78.3	78.3	78.0	78.5	78.6	79.2	78.1

[1] Preliminary.   *Source: Bureau of Economic Analysis, U.S. Department of Commerce (BEA)*

Manufacturers New Orders, Durable Goods   In Billions of Constant Dollars

Year	Jan.	Feb.	Mar.	Apr.	May	June	July	Aug.	Sept.	Oct.	Nov.	Dec.	Average
1995	153.42	151.82	151.72	146.32	149.74	148.21	147.45	152.12	156.78	154.37	154.09	158.89	154.10
1996	158.86	155.10	157.67	156.01	162.59	162.67	168.25	162.76	170.45	170.59	169.34	166.02	163.48
1997	171.73	174.80	170.02	173.13	177.05	176.93	175.82	181.08	181.15	181.33	189.71	181.44	177.03
1998	184.33	183.87	184.17	187.35	181.58	182.22	186.22	190.39	193.18	189.33	190.21	197.11	194.42
1999	211.18	203.31	209.39	204.68	206.78	207.27	216.02	218.02	214.83	212.77	215.34	229.47	209.76
2000	225.14	221.12	230.44	217.17	232.76	254.20	220.74	227.27	232.41	217.30	221.14	220.90	220.55
2001	197.36	205.41	209.56	198.11	201.86	196.99	196.53	194.41	174.92	199.09	187.14	188.34	195.44
2002	190.08	194.99	191.78	192.65	193.48	184.76	200.59	198.62	189.66	192.67	190.66	190.01	192.80
2003	194.21	192.26	194.57	190.00	189.13	194.23	197.39	197.18	201.29	208.82	203.42	206.56	197.41
2004[1]	201.03	208.36	219.67	212.63	209.43	211.13	214.65	212.97	214.60	211.65	214.08		211.84

[1] Preliminary.   *Source: Bureau of Economic Analysis, U.S. Department of Commerce (BEA)*

Corporate Profits After Tax -- Quarterly   In Billions of Dollars

Year	First Quarter	Second Quarter	Third Quarter	Fourth Quarter	Average	Year	First Quarter	Second Quarter	Third Quarter	Fourth Quarter	Average
1993	347.4	364.8	371.8	399.6	370.9	1999	593.2	592.9	582.1	602.5	592.7
1994	354.8	407.4	423.7	440.4	406.6	2000	551.8	560.5	551.5	547.2	552.8
1995	446.4	467.4	494.2	504.1	478.0	2001	556.2	565.2	516.9	614.4	563.2
1996	504.0	518.4	526.2	544.3	523.2	2002	669.3	685.0	687.9	720.6	690.7
1997	599.1	619.4	641.5	629.6	622.4	2003	688.0	761.7	818.4	876.8	786.2
1998	562.9	547.6	554.2	548.6	553.3	2004[1]	909.1	902.7	864.7		892.2

[1] Preliminary.   *Source: Bureau of Economic Analysis, U.S. Department of Commerce (BEA)*

Change in Manufacturing and Trade Inventories   In Billions of Dollars

Year	Jan.	Feb.	Mar.	Apr.	May	June	July	Aug.	Sept.	Oct.	Nov.	Dec.	Average
1995	127.4	78.5	100.6	97.6	54.4	48.1	42.9	50.6	51.4	61.8	24.1	-39.7	58.5
1996	66.2	14.2	-27.7	61.5	-8.4	80.3	123.6	-272.1	90.6	143.4	86.1	72.0	19.9
1997	107.0	103.4	76.3	56.2	25.2	76.8	20.9	19.1	91.5	55.2	43.1	28.2	47.1
1998	27.8	86.1	85.7	38.5	5.5	11.4	-91.6	47.9	67.6	36.3	51.0		34.0
1999	10.4	36.8	66.7	31.2	44.4	61.6	67.2	42.5	58.0	50.4	121.1	70.9	50.6
2000	69.5	59.5	17.5	38.8	82.8	129.5	8.7	87.4	10.1	77.7	26.4	5.8	63.7
2001	1.7	-40.5	-73.0	-36.6	-38.9	-105.1	-68.2	-34.2	-75.3	-200.6	-139.2	-78.7	-65.2
2002	-0.9	-31.5	-47.8	-20.1	33.6	27.8	78.5	3.5	-106.8	18.5	33.0	-86.0	17.6
2003	-118.4	-60.3	-18.3	0.1	111.8	89.5	24.1	-39.4	78.7	54.4	57.5	45.7	21.8
2004[1]	23.1	116.7	106.2	103.2	98.0	159.9	146.3	106.3	-0.3	66.3			92.6

[1] Preliminary.   *Source: Bureau of Economic Analysis, U.S. Department of Commerce (BEA)*

Productivity: Index of Output per Hour, All Persons, Nonfarm Business -- Quarterly   (1992 = 100)

Year	First Quarter	Second Quarter	Third Quarter	Fourth Quarter	Average	Year	First Quarter	Second Quarter	Third Quarter	Fourth Quarter	Average
1993	100.4	99.8	100.2	100.9	100.3	1999	111.3	111.5	112.3	114.2	112.3
1994	101.6	101.5	101.1	101.9	101.5	2000	113.7	115.8	115.5	116.6	115.4
1995	101.7	101.7	102.0	102.8	102.1	2001	116.5	118.1	118.5	120.4	118.4
1996	103.7	104.8	105.1	105.4	104.8	2002	122.4	122.8	124.1	124.6	123.5
1997	104.9	106.2	107.2	107.5	106.5	2003	125.8	127.8	130.6	131.7	129.0
1998	108.4	108.7	109.8	110.4	109.3	2004[1]	132.8	134.1	134.7	135.0	134.2

[1] Preliminary.   *Source: Bureau of Economic Analysis, U.S. Department of Commerce (BEA)*

Civilian Unemployment Rate

Year	Jan.	Feb.	Mar.	Apr.	May	June	July	Aug.	Sept.	Oct.	Nov.	Dec.	Average
1995	5.6	5.5	5.4	5.7	5.6	5.6	5.7	5.7	5.7	5.5	5.6	5.6	5.6
1996	5.7	5.5	5.5	5.5	5.5	5.3	5.4	5.2	5.2	5.2	5.3	5.3	5.4
1997	5.4	5.3	5.2	4.9	4.8	5.0	4.9	4.9	4.9	4.8	4.6	4.7	5.0
1998	4.6	4.6	4.7	4.3	4.4	4.5	4.5	4.5	4.5	4.5	4.4	4.3	4.5
1999	4.3	4.4	4.2	4.3	4.2	4.3	4.3	4.2	4.2	4.1	4.1	4.1	4.2
2000	4.0	4.1	4.1	3.9	4.1	4.0	4.0	4.1	3.9	3.9	4.0	4.0	4.0
2001	4.2	4.2	4.3	4.5	4.4	4.5	4.5	4.9	4.9	5.4	5.7	5.8	4.8
2002	5.6	5.5	5.7	6.0	5.8	5.9	5.9	5.7	5.6	5.7	6.0	6.0	5.8
2003	5.7	5.8	5.8	6.0	6.1	6.4	6.2	6.1	6.1	6.0	5.9	5.7	6.0
2004[1]	5.6	5.6	5.7	5.6	5.6	5.6	5.5	5.4	5.4	5.5	5.4	5.4	5.5

[1] Preliminary.   *Source: Bureau of Economic Analysis, U.S. Department of Commerce (BEA)*

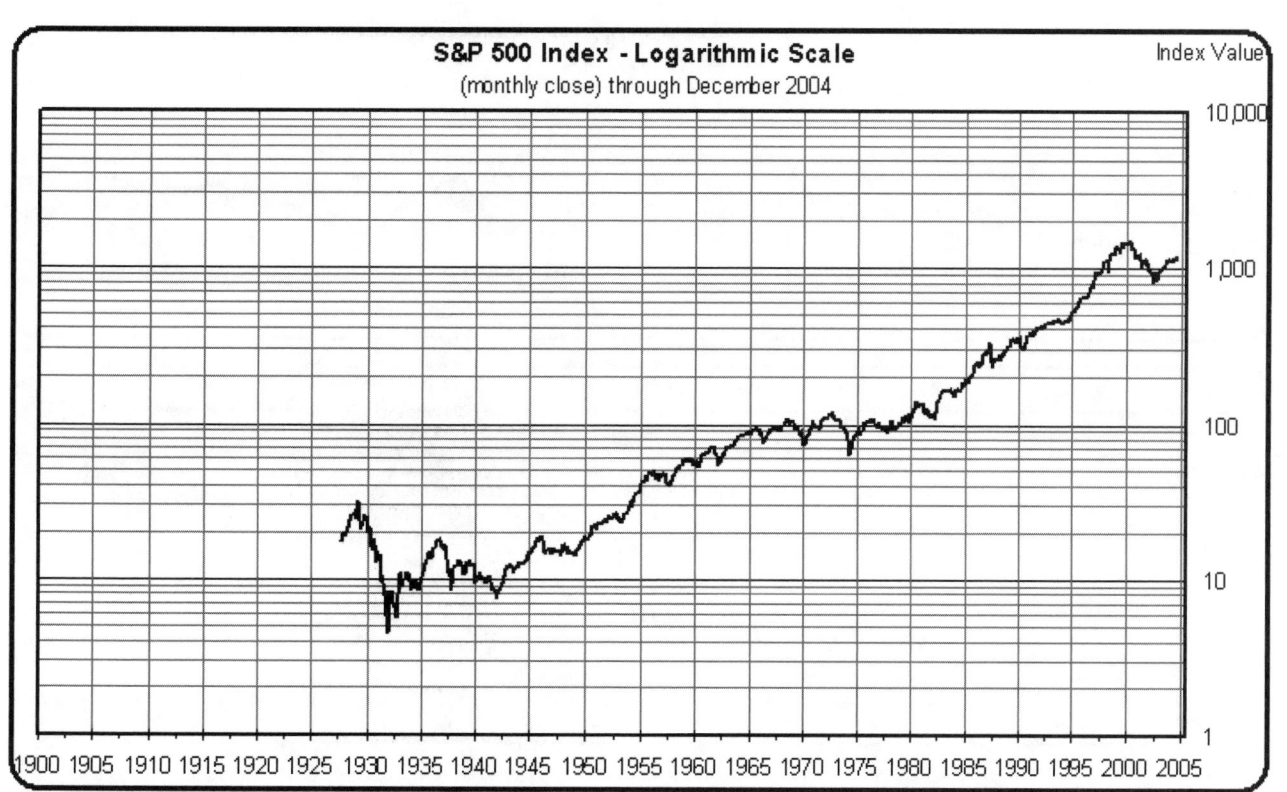

S&P 500 Index - Logarithmic Scale
(monthly close) through December 2004

STOCK INDEX FUTURES, U.S.

Dow Jones 30 Industrials Index (weekly close) as of December 31, 2004

S&P 500 Index (weekly close) as of December 31, 2004

NASDAQ 100 Index (weekly close) as of December 31, 2004

Value Line 'A' Index (weekly close) as of December 31, 2004

Volume of Trading of S&P 500 Stock Index Futures in Chicago   In Thousands of Contracts

Year	Jan.	Feb.	Mar.	Apr.	May	June	July	Aug.	Sept.	Oct.	Nov.	Dec.	Total
1995	2,703	2,733	4,449	2,473	3,497	3,732	2,565	3,018	3,701	3,250	2,966	3,452	38,539
1996	3,520	3,872	4,011	2,722	3,456	3,530	3,215	2,577	3,739	3,298	2,916	3,751	40,607
1997	3,371	2,857	4,163	3,608	3,203	3,955	2,617	2,848	3,556	3,136	1,994	2,982	38,290
1998	2,270	1,878	3,018	2,237	2,253	3,524	2,139	3,019	3,802	2,598	1,831	2,835	31,404
1999	1,994	2,145	3,018	1,960	2,007	2,768	1,756	2,200	3,017	2,150	1,675	2,322	27,013
2000	1,911	1,917	2,956	1,651	1,685	2,226	1,079	1,358	2,149	1,681	1,636	2,212	22,461
2001	1,552	1,631	2,781	1,624	1,653	2,154	1,320	1,598	2,571	1,798	1,692	2,124	22,498
2002	1,459	1,677	2,251	1,473	1,585	2,721	2,206	1,615	2,943	1,931	1,374	2,465	23,700
2003	1,443	1,343	2,900	1,257	1,416	2,782	1,223	1,079	2,412	1,118	921	2,281	20,175
2004	945	839	2,487	880	938	2,136	837	965	2,076	866	1,105	2,101	16,176

Source: Index and Option Market (IOM), division of the Chicago Mercantile Exchange (CME)

Average Open Interest of S&P 500 Stock Index Futures in Chicago   In Contracts

Year	Jan.	Feb.	Mar.	Apr.	May	June	July	Aug.	Sept.	Oct.	Nov.	Dec.
1995	427,004	442,628	445,584	420,104	443,296	453,364	420,024	422,608	417,812	402,794	441,780	447,528
1996	406,400	428,058	419,688	368,620	399,070	407,914	369,248	382,266	413,944	374,726	416,102	448,382
1997	393,086	396,528	417,542	377,100	392,034	417,006	372,274	392,812	423,449	391,922	402,044	417,717
1998	394,410	408,851	417,721	365,746	371,732	412,739	370,410	385,820	434,838	405,395	421,928	435,907
1999	399,093	406,516	410,164	381,402	391,035	400,503	372,455	385,809	408,176	394,316	408,751	416,425
2000	369,295	374,365	400,089	379,651	383,677	409,448	380,118	391,867	416,600	413,912	447,245	498,049
2001	488,284	495,621	517,666	498,594	490,148	505,063	485,839	501,281	556,737	529,730	550,201	551,175
2002	495,352	519,023	542,358	513,048	542,839	592,888	594,727	621,558	644,806	607,848	631,224	647,022
2003	596,064	619,738	658,749	622,917	643,030	691,003	611,564	611,578	631,509	582,111	589,392	633,997
2004	612,911	614,843	624,209	595,593	587,717	604,154	586,760	597,581	632,050	636,566	686,531	714,420

Source: Index and Option Market (IOM), division of the Chicago Mercantile Exchange (CME)

Volume of Trading of S&P 400 Midcap Stock Index Futures in Chicago   In Contracts

Year	Jan.	Feb.	Mar.	Apr.	May	June	July	Aug.	Sept.	Oct.	Nov.	Dec.	Total
1995	12,097	13,983	36,531	8,674	11,263	31,526	10,076	15,921	42,147	18,905	20,464	46,907	268,494
1996	25,322	21,781	46,382	13,417	19,190	33,720	20,338	17,112	37,149	12,510	12,459	36,798	296,178
1997	13,698	14,968	33,860	16,993	15,463	33,287	12,162	14,923	39,164	18,063	10,776	43,242	266,599
1998	13,622	12,896	42,781	15,623	17,023	38,656	15,345	19,967	44,913	23,591	16,713	48,870	310,000
1999	18,752	20,938	43,395	27,664	16,574	42,709	17,790	18,188	39,723	18,341	19,974	42,073	326,121
2000	16,918	15,298	45,942	23,892	19,863	42,514	12,140	12,515	42,658	21,701	25,334	59,265	338,040
2001	21,527	19,884	58,286	18,061	19,258	50,331	22,029	23,805	50,706	23,741	19,591	51,641	378,860
2002	22,322	22,814	43,819	23,019	22,484	51,775	30,607	23,075	52,375	25,593	21,262	48,105	387,250
2003	18,827	18,392	44,454	15,841	15,194	40,603	15,153	12,082	43,112	15,253	13,109	50,797	302,817
2004	13,647	10,361	46,214	13,921	13,078	153,311	12,602	13,582	36,701	7,923	9,824	36,971	368,135

Source: Index and Option Market (IOM), division of the Chicago Mercantile Exchange (CME)

Average Open Interest of S&P 400 Midcap Stock Index Futures in Chicago   In Contracts

Year	Jan.	Feb.	Mar.	Apr.	May	June	July	Aug.	Sept.	Oct.	Nov.	Dec.
1995	13,787	13,355	11,130	9,275	9,329	9,929	11,198	11,708	13,107	11,702	12,341	12,863
1996	11,088	10,474	11,375	8,700	9,254	10,403	9,763	10,867	11,168	9,641	10,596	11,107
1997	11,215	11,825	11,258	9,721	10,807	10,877	11,292	12,346	13,505	11,595	11,874	13,329
1998	12,688	13,319	14,363	14,130	13,352	13,940	12,964	13,589	14,893	16,645	16,768	17,569
1999	16,191	16,309	14,573	12,154	12,705	14,422	14,263	13,496	13,182	12,699	13,933	14,902
2000	12,810	13,119	13,965	12,495	13,355	14,040	12,957	13,162	15,026	16,143	16,510	17,479
2001	15,246	15,461	17,235	16,953	15,623	16,606	16,334	16,132	16,718	15,109	15,307	15,337
2002	13,691	14,109	14,954	14,340	16,402	16,611	15,121	16,213	17,006	14,695	15,394	16,432
2003	13,793	13,498	14,530	13,120	13,353	13,986	13,123	13,029	13,726	14,014	15,465	17,446
2004	15,911	15,988	16,554	15,870	15,819	17,148	13,939	13,600	14,213	13,339	14,046	14,755

Source: Index and Option Market (IOM), division of the Chicago Mercantile Exchange (CME)

STOCK INDEX FUTURES, U.S.

Volume of Trading of NASDAQ 100 Index Futures in Chicago   In Contracts

Year	Jan.	Feb.	Mar.	Apr.	May	June	July	Aug.	Sept.	Oct.	Nov.	Dec.	Total
1998	65,660	60,471	96,694	68,574	70,704	111,933	106,791	107,509	97,099	100,156	71,441	107,995	1,065,027
1999	111,120	132,436	169,368	181,776	172,840	226,193	164,822	176,429	242,149	209,007	218,672	317,418	2,322,230
2000	349,813	366,408	575,942	503,064	460,085	432,062	296,944	310,549	445,334	490,863	400,412	464,454	5,095,930
2001	422,811	416,445	650,488	498,026	487,334	542,305	369,731	369,845	474,133	516,469	391,042	434,690	5,573,319
2002	380,076	367,561	436,495	378,294	443,579	529,496	454,630	334,242	466,898	367,750	315,925	428,341	4,903,287
2003	360,307	301,454	487,916	301,395	330,640	519,597	350,514	251,058	488,363	322,898	259,960	447,119	4,421,221
2004	271,404	268,590	591,556	321,242	297,320	427,805	286,693	245,050	433,251	286,048	226,853	356,171	4,011,983

Source: Index and Option Market (IOM), division of the Chicago Mercantile Exchange (CME)

Average Open Interest of NASDAQ 100 Index Futures in Chicago   In Contracts

Year	Jan.	Feb.	Mar.	Apr.	May	June	July	Aug.	Sept.	Oct.	Nov.	Dec.
1998	6,918	8,184	9,314	7,652	8,833	11,128	9,991	9,507	9,233	8,187	9,176	10,838
1999	10,669	14,766	19,786	21,286	23,028	26,938	21,646	22,765	21,808	19,946	23,429	27,876
2000	27,242	34,555	37,795	36,512	37,578	35,314	29,974	32,922	34,754	35,559	44,022	48,757
2001	46,582	49,495	59,916	56,328	49,337	54,394	50,854	55,234	61,665	51,977	61,196	67,769
2002	49,992	52,883	52,617	51,157	65,219	73,151	60,625	67,760	84,317	72,229	77,451	76,660
2003	71,219	79,905	87,252	71,636	77,717	88,914	80,002	83,940	91,685	75,191	85,651	86,480
2004	73,805	74,892	89,874	81,220	80,905	83,282	69,818	71,711	84,355	74,161	83,675	87,172

Source: Index and Option Market (IOM), division of the Chicago Mercantile Exchange (CME)

Volume of Trading of Dow Jones Industrials Index Futures in Chicago   In Contracts

Year	Jan.	Feb.	Mar.	Apr.	May	June	July	Aug.	Sept.	Oct.	Nov.	Dec.	Total
1998	260,628	244,907	293,651	284,515	259,720	358,647	298,254	366,874	381,320	344,732	224,397	246,441	3,564,086
1999	284,341	262,932	341,744	365,209	364,417	365,429	279,381	342,753	386,373	378,531	266,183	257,805	3,895,098
2000	322,046	340,377	472,179	321,026	284,005	270,374	215,234	211,612	277,620	319,636	267,051	268,010	3,569,170
2001	275,814	310,088	594,326	411,767	377,620	389,919	320,335	410,927	573,479	520,885	375,793	329,898	4,890,851
2002	409,009	472,893	538,804	467,571	456,210	616,754	811,518	539,507	639,154	699,005	427,235	407,665	6,485,325
2003	452,579	426,198	559,372	428,972	410,967	473,432	368,277	286,508	367,845	218,394	157,726	266,032	4,416,302
2004	224,713	207,423	362,668	203,745	208,229	246,564	183,469	149,931	230,829	169,627	152,412	237,528	2,577,138

Source: Chicago Board of Trade (CBT)

Average Open Interest of Dow Jones Industrials Index Futures in Chicago   In Contracts

Year	Jan.	Feb.	Mar.	Apr.	May	June	July	Aug.	Sept.	Oct.	Nov.	Dec.
1998	14,853	15,558	14,421	13,846	14,464	16,226	15,707	17,586	18,569	17,416	17,795	17,597
1999	16,794	19,401	19,807	20,492	25,890	22,198	21,556	25,333	23,977	24,847	22,342	17,299
2000	13,713	16,331	20,443	18,157	19,253	17,394	14,367	15,748	14,840	15,087	19,113	20,966
2001	21,830	23,423	28,340	32,497	33,767	29,357	26,792	33,015	35,451	31,997	30,598	27,018
2002	23,862	35,588	37,582	28,714	32,810	34,482	32,412	32,272	34,665	31,923	34,045	31,892
2003	27,032	30,429	34,371	31,160	34,936	36,352	36,773	43,974	41,747	34,066	37,835	39,727
2004	34,656	44,306	50,172	44,494	45,304	46,641	42,790	42,042	45,940	41,250	43,662	53,469

Source: Chicago Board of Trade (CBT)

Volume of Trading of E-mini NASDAQ 100 Index Futures in Chicago   In Thousands of Contracts

Year	Jan.	Feb.	Mar.	Apr.	May	June	July	Aug.	Sept.	Oct.	Nov.	Dec.	Total
1999	----	----	----	----	----	29	62	83	90	105	113	193	675
2000	304	382	604	628	745	762	756	883	1,508	1,589	1,446	1,512	11,118
2001	1,845	1,942	2,603	2,873	2,908	2,969	2,529	2,568	2,387	3,935	3,151	2,595	32,304
2002	3,719	3,649	3,652	4,227	4,625	4,713	5,789	4,225	4,337	6,252	4,812	4,490	54,491
2003	5,200	4,620	5,749	5,132	5,075	6,323	6,369	4,816	7,095	6,601	5,254	5,655	67,889
2004	6,157	5,640	8,011	6,387	6,749	5,646	7,139	6,123	6,476	7,322	5,844	5,675	77,169

Source: Index and Option Market (IOM), division of the Chicago Mercantile Exchange (CME)

Average Open Interest of E-mini NASDAQ 100 Index Futures in Chicago   In Contracts

Year	Jan.	Feb.	Mar.	Apr.	May	June	July	Aug.	Sept.	Oct.	Nov.	Dec.
1999	----	----	----	----	----	894	2,410	4,320	3,867	3,037	5,051	8,685
2000	8,582	9,250	11,117	15,625	23,465	26,095	23,863	31,506	30,956	33,123	58,709	54,420
2001	45,370	65,061	79,962	78,094	90,822	95,236	90,803	131,259	132,349	75,686	115,350	124,023
2002	78,070	94,150	98,159	100,849	153,348	176,394	130,337	171,043	162,133	110,952	154,104	155,987
2003	169,160	227,905	258,023	196,739	240,759	257,390	262,564	316,032	287,936	214,659	279,379	244,333
2004	205,078	251,011	251,486	257,573	304,034	261,067	213,080	256,749	299,794	279,170	374,750	384,492

Source: Chicago Board of Trade (CBT)

Volume of Trading of E-mini S&P 500 Index Futures in Chicago   In Thousands of Contracts

Year	Jan.	Feb.	Mar.	Apr.	May	June	July	Aug.	Sept.	Oct.	Nov.	Dec.	Total
1998	269	221	285	298	285	371	380	569	430	519	431	492	4,551
1999	576	636	775	602	843	868	887	1,065	1,144	1,237	1,072	964	10,669
2000	1,306	1,388	1,489	1,462	1,676	1,550	1,403	1,439	1,683	2,109	1,843	1,673	19,021
2001	2,226	2,231	3,191	3,067	2,931	2,905	2,925	3,478	3,601	5,255	4,021	3,289	39,119
2002	4,933	5,337	5,609	7,165	7,564	9,772	14,277	11,200	11,765	17,175	11,054	9,892	115,742
2003	13,584	12,631	15,820	13,520	12,846	15,040	14,854	10,860	15,354	14,558	11,002	11,108	161,177
2004	13,087	11,355	18,033	14,993	15,889	12,428	14,361	12,921	12,755	14,636	13,705	13,039	167,203

Source: Index and Option Market (IOM), division of the Chicago Mercantile Exchange (CME)

Average Open Interest of E-mini S&P 500 Index Futures in Chicago   In Contracts

Year	Jan.	Feb.	Mar.	Apr.	May	June	July	Aug.	Sept.	Oct.	Nov.	Dec.
1998	8,986	15,144	17,540	12,134	16,341	16,337	8,600	29,003	14,201	13,003	15,376	15,842
1999	16,215	24,969	20,971	44,037	20,790	22,077	16,960	25,551	24,960	25,056	30,013	26,544
2000	17,180	25,282	29,645	28,738	38,257	39,918	33,696	45,619	42,442	49,468	66,143	63,052
2001	55,514	68,516	79,934	91,866	110,788	91,638	97,093	126,197	152,253	134,662	224,754	178,681
2002	86,278	120,099	139,965	156,392	225,593	246,288	291,654	349,037	319,341	312,885	418,964	385,220
2003	265,170	356,616	490,037	567,591	741,790	718,511	399,502	492,470	513,398	460,938	467,668	525,310
2004	510,518	576,446	643,118	545,385	579,876	645,794	603,841	697,956	693,529	708,359	979,884	969,343

Source: Index and Option Market (IOM), division of the Chicago Mercantile Exchange (CME)

Volume of Trading of NYSE Composite Stock Index Futures[1] in New York   In Contracts

Year	Jan.	Feb.	Mar.	Apr.	May	June	July	Aug.	Sept.	Oct.	Nov.	Dec.	Total
1998	39,823	33,856	46,307	36,316	35,765	47,905	61,862	93,694	73,646	50,314	27,106	50,457	597,051
1999	30,430	31,482	49,055	29,219	26,201	27,103	15,653	22,556	28,433	23,058	16,528	17,848	317,566
2000	15,324	16,603	21,235	14,394	10,637	11,210	4,307	5,574	5,085	6,145	5,170	9,974	125,658
2001	5,490	4,307	19,300	6,594	4,091	10,353	23,855	32,182	23,399	22,276	19,231	34,661	205,739
2002	20,273	21,056	26,949	27,801	24,166	22,325	21,873	14,561	13,193	10,821	5,897	7,564	216,479
2003	3,917	5,622	9,210	7,718	2,794	4,366	628	553	1,940	408	726	3,282	41,164
2004	3,427	1,127	2,532	159	56	1,705	76	412	1,766	46	915	2,457	14,678

[1] Data thru Feb 2003 are Old Index ($500), Mar 2003 thru Sep 2003 are Old ($500) and New Index ($50).   *Source: New York Futures Exchange (NYFE)*

Average Open Interest of NYSE Composite Stock Index Futures[1] in New York   In Contracts

Year	Jan.	Feb.	Mar.	Apr.	May	June	July	Aug.	Sept.	Oct.	Nov.	Dec.
1998	4,803	5,216	5,252	4,754	4,888	5,990	10,154	12,249	10,574	8,554	7,977	9,806
1999	8,299	8,661	5,457	4,050	4,169	3,849	3,419	3,882	3,730	3,958	4,447	4,260
2000	3,653	3,715	3,747	3,285	2,533	2,597	2,452	2,793	2,463	1,690	1,943	2,406
2001	2,387	2,648	3,510	3,694	2,929	2,408	5,271	5,802	5,451	6,448	6,884	6,617
2002	4,341	4,215	5,147	4,141	3,605	3,178	5,157	5,772	3,649	1,567	2,209	2,065
2003	1,255	1,496	1,898	1,670	1,391	1,294	936	1,009	1,106	533	604	752
2004	1,180	1,230	999	733	758	734	696	717	703	656	837	739

[1] Data thru Feb 2003 are Old Index ($500), Mar 2003 thru Sep 2003 are Old ($500) and New Index ($50).   *Source: New York Futures Exchange (NYFE)*

Volume of Trading of Mini-Value Line Stock Index Futures in Kansas City   In Contracts

Year	Jan.	Feb.	Mar.	Apr.	May	June	July	Aug.	Sept.	Oct.	Nov.	Dec.	Total
1998	7,086	4,989	6,893	6,590	7,307	7,537	5,067	8,700	7,170	5,959	3,894	4,978	76,170
1999	2,938	3,241	4,800	3,958	1,915	3,546	1,792	1,739	2,184	1,908	1,225	1,547	30,793
2000	1,397	1,097	1,468	1,054	1,280	811	698	642	1,003	1,328	1,526	1,460	13,764
2001	1,248	1,470	2,441	1,650	902	1,325	1,183	1,071	1,982	1,591	1,104	1,387	17,354
2002	1,513	1,237	1,598	1,283	1,794	1,511	1,878	1,113	974	1,472	1,467	1,530	17,370
2003	376	181	721	264	90	88	46	153	80	94	94	204	2,391
2004	130	134	159	175	63	215	77	33	126	76	67	174	1,429

Source: Kansas City Board of Trade (KCBT)

Average Open Interest of Mini-Value Line Stock Index Futures in Kansas City   In Contracts

Year	Jan.	Feb.	Mar.	Apr.	May	June	July	Aug.	Sept.	Oct.	Nov.	Dec.
1998	1,739	1,442	1,433	1,498	1,549	1,390	697	839	667	696	914	780
1999	746	738	699	725	900	967	515	503	381	314	300	283
2000	273	284	246	135	155	148	155	216	179	182	181	185
2001	233	333	377	233	275	285	283	268	222	125	249	368
2002	299	348	367	372	359	229	142	161	100	127	300	417
2003	376	328	169	89	45	33	26	33	48	36	40	46
2004	47	64	49	48	47	56	61	56	40	15	22	32

Source: Kansas City Board of Trade (KCBT)

Stock Index Futures, Worldwide

World stocks – World stock markets in 2004 put in another strong year and the 2000-02 bear market drifted farther back into history. The MSCI World Index, a benchmark for large companies based in 23 developed countries, rallied by +15.2% in 2004, adding to the +33.8% gain seen in 2003. That 2-year gain followed the three consecutive years of declines in 2002 (-19.5%), 2001 (-16.5%), and 2000 (-12.9%). That three-year decline in 2000-2002 was the longest string of losses in the MSCI World Index since the introduction of the index in 1970. Still, it would take a further 12.1% rally from the 2004 close for the MSCI World Index to match its record high of 3772.66 posted back in March 2000.

The world stock markets traded sideways in early 2004 on a consolidation of the gains seen in 2003. World stocks then rallied sharply starting in August through the remainder of the year. Bullish factors centered on continued strong earnings growth combined with low interest rates. The US Federal Reserve raised its federal funds rate by a total of 125 basis points to 2.25% in 2004, but that was still a very low level from an historical standpoint and still represented a stimulative monetary policy. The European Central Bank kept its refinancing rate at a very low 2.00% all year. The Bank of Japan maintained its zero interest rate monetary policy all year. Oil prices rose sharply in 2004 but that was not enough to derail optimism in the world equity markets. China continued to provide a sharp boost to world economic growth in 2004, and China's insatiable demand also boosted the earnings of many global companies that sell products within China.

Small-Capitalization Stocks – World small-cap stocks did better than the large-cap stocks in 2004 and easily rallied to a new record high. The small-caps performed well mainly because earnings growth in small-cap companies was roughly twice as strong as large-caps. The MSCI World Small-Cap Index, which tracks companies with market caps between $200 million and $1.5 billion, rallied 22.6% in 2004, beating the MSCI World Index's return of +15.2% by 7.4 percentage points. In 2003, the MSCI World Small-Cap index rallied +55.5% and beat the MSCI World Index's return of 33.2% by 22.3 percentage points. During the 2002-04 bull market, the MSCI World Small-Cap index showed an overall rally of 112% from the October 2002 low to the 2004 high.

World Industry Groups – The Morgan Stanley Industry Sectors performed as follows in terms of ranking: Energy +25.3%, Utilities +24.3%, Industrials +17.5%, Materials +15.7%, Financials +14.8%, Telecom +14.7%, Consumer Discretionary +13.6%, Consumer Staples +9.9%, Health Care +4.7%, and Information Technology +2.1%. The world energy, industrial and cyclical stocks did well in 2004, boosted by strong energy and commodity prices and by the strong business cycle. Consumer Discretionary and Consumer Staples did relatively well as consumer spending remained strong. The worst-performing sector was Information Technology with only a +2.1% gain. The IT sector continued to suffer from a continued post-bubble hang-over and from newer concerns that the IT industry is maturing and consolidating and that the days of stratospheric growth are over.

Emerging markets – Emerging stock markets did very well again in 2003 as the bull market encouraged investors to reach for riskier and potentially more rewarding stocks.

The stronger world economy put the emerging countries on a more solid footing, particularly emerging countries that export oil or commodities, or that produce cheap-labor products that are becoming more attractive in the global marketplace as trade barriers fall. The MSCI Emerging Markets Free Index, which tracks companies based in 26 emerging countries, rallied 22.4% in 2004, beating the MSCI World Index gain of +15.2% by 7.2 percentage points. In 2003, the MSCI Emerging Markets index gain of +51.6% beat the MSCI World index gain of +33.8% by a hefty 17.8 percentage points.

G7 – The G7 industrialized countries in 2004 saw stock market gains that were far exceeded by most emerging market countries, where greater growth opportunities lie. Of the G7 countries, the ranked stock market gains are as follows: Italy MIB +14.9%, Canada Toronto Composite +12.5%, US S&P 500 +9.0%, Japan Nikkei 225 +7.6%, UK FTSE 100 +7.5%, France CAC40 +7.4%, and German DAX index +7.3%.

North America – In North America, Mexico's stock market smartly beat both the US and Canadian stock markets. The Mexican Bolsa index closed 2004 up +46.9%, beating the S&P 500 gain in the US of +9.0% and the Toronto Exchange Composite index gain of +12.5%.

Latin America – In Latin America in 2004, there were some very impressive gains for the second straight year: Peru's Lima General Index +52.4%, Venezuela's Stock Market Index +34.9%, Argentina's Merval Index +28.3%, Chile's Stock Market Select Index +21.0%, and Brazil's Bovespa Index +17.8%.

Europe – Europe put in another year of weak relative performance with the Dow Jones Stoxx 50 index closing only +4.3% higher on the year. European stocks were weighed down by weak European economic growth and the strong euro, which hurt corporate earnings. There were strong gains seen in the Italian MIB of +14.9% and the Spanish IBEX 35 of +17.4%. However, the big three in Europe showed middling gains: UK (+7.5%), France (+7.4%), and Germany (+7.3%).

Asia – Asia saw strong stock market gains, which were boosted by the extremely strong demand from China for various imported goods. The Morgan Stanley Far East Index showed a sharp gain of +16.7%. However, the Japanese Nikkei index rose only +7.6% in 2004, held back by continued weak Japanese economic growth during the year, which actually turned negative in the last three quarters of 2004. The strongest gains in Asia were seen in Indonesia's Jakarta Composite Index +44.6%, Vietnam Stock index +39.3%, Pakistan 100 Index +39.1%, Philippines Composite index +26.4%, New Zealand's Exchange 50 index +25.1%, Australia's All-Ordinaries index +22.6%, Singapore Straights Times index +17.1%, Malaysia's Kuala Lumpur Composite index +14.3%, Hong Kong Hang Seng +13.2%, India's Mumbai Sensex 30 index +13.1%, and South Korea's Composite index +10.5%. There were single-digit gains in Japan's Nikkei 225 of +7.6% and Taiwan's TAIEX index of +4.2%. The Thailand Stock Exchange index fell –13.5%, and China's Shanghai Composite index fell –15.4% (the MSCI China index fell –0.7% in 2004). China's stock market was hurt in 2004 by the government's attempts to slow the economy and by profit-taking after the rally seen in the past 1-1/2 years.

STOCK INDEX FUTURES, WORLDWIDE

Comparison of International Stock Price Indexes   (1990 = 100)

Year	Jan.	Feb.	Mar.	Apr.	May	June	July	Aug.	Sept.	Oct.	Nov.	Dec.	Average
United States													
1998	294.7	315.4	331.2	334.2	327.9	340.8	336.9	287.7	305.7	330.2	349.8	369.5	327.0
1999	384.6	372.2	386.7	401.3	391.3	412.6	399.4	396.9	385.6	409.7	417.5	441.6	400.0
2000	419.2	410.7	450.5	436.6	427.0	437.2	430.1	456.2	431.8	429.7	395.3	396.9	426.8
2001	410.6	372.7	348.8	375.6	377.5	368.0	364.1	340.7	312.9	318.6	342.5	345.1	356.4
2002	339.7	332.7	344.9	323.7	320.8	297.5	274.0	275.4	245.1	266.2	281.4	264.5	297.2
2003	257.2	252.8	255.0	275.6	289.6	292.9	297.7	303.0	299.4	315.8	318.1	334.2	290.9
2004[1]	340.0	344.2	338.5	332.8	336.9	342.9	331.2	331.9	335.0	339.7	352.8	364.3	340.9
Canada													
1998	195.8	207.3	220.9	224.0	221.9	215.3	202.6	161.7	164.0	181.5	185.4	189.6	197.5
1999	196.7	184.5	192.9	205.0	200.0	204.9	207.0	203.8	203.4	212.1	219.9	245.9	206.3
2000	247.9	266.8	276.6	273.2	270.4	298.0	304.2	328.8	303.3	281.8	257.8	261.1	280.8
2001	272.5	236.1	222.4	232.3	238.6	226.1	224.8	216.3	199.9	201.3	217.1	224.7	226.0
2002	223.6	223.2	229.5	224.0	223.8	208.9	193.1	193.3	180.7	182.7	192.1	193.3	205.7
2003	192.0	191.6	185.4	192.5	200.5	204.1	212.2	219.5	216.9	227.2	229.7	240.3	209.3
2004[1]	249.1	256.9	251.0	241.0	246.0	249.8	247.2	244.9	253.4	259.3	264.0	270.3	252.7
France													
1998	174.5	188.3	213.3	213.5	222.4	231.3	229.8	200.9	176.0	193.8	211.5	216.9	206.0
1999	233.9	225.2	231.0	242.4	239.4	249.6	241.1	252.5	252.6	269.0	293.9	327.8	254.9
2000	311.4	340.6	345.9	353.2	353.6	354.7	360.0	364.5	344.8	352.0	326.2	326.1	344.4
2001	330.0	295.3	285.0	310.3	300.1	287.5	279.8	258.0	224.4	238.9	246.3	254.5	275.8
2002	245.5	245.6	257.9	245.5	235.2	214.5	187.9	185.2	152.8	173.3	183.0	168.6	207.9
2003	161.6	151.5	144.1	162.5	164.6	169.7	176.6	182.2	172.5	185.6	188.4	195.8	171.3
2004[1]	200.2	205.0	199.5	202.2	201.9	205.4	200.7	197.8	200.3	204.0	206.5	210.2	202.8
Germany													
1998	204.9	217.5	234.9	302.0	329.3	348.7	347.3	285.8	264.6	276.2	297.0	295.8	299.1
1999	305.1	290.4	288.8	318.9	299.8	318.0	301.6	311.6	304.5	326.7	348.6	411.4	318.8
2000	404.2	452.0	449.3	438.4	420.4	407.9	425.1	426.7	401.9	418.5	376.8	380.4	416.8
2001	401.8	367.1	344.7	370.4	362.0	358.2	346.5	306.8	254.7	269.6	295.0	305.1	331.8
2002	302.0	297.9	319.1	298.1	284.9	259.1	218.8	219.5	163.7	186.4	196.3	171.0	243.1
2003	162.5	150.6	143.3	173.9	176.4	190.4	206.2	206.0	192.6	216.2	221.5	234.4	189.5
2004[1]	240.0	237.6	228.0	235.6	231.9	239.6	230.3	223.8	230.2	234.1	243.9	251.6	235.6
Italy													
1998	184.0	194.3	239.3	220.9	236.1	222.1	240.5	208.1	184.6	194.1	223.7	231.5	214.9
1999	231.7	234.1	245.4	245.9	237.1	237.5	221.5	230.4	231.0	226.5	241.3	282.8	238.8
2000	276.8	330.7	308.7	303.1	307.1	309.0	308.5	320.5	307.2	318.8	316.3	298.3	308.8
2001	303.3	276.4	267.4	278.1	266.1	254.1	249.1	237.9	197.7	208.7	220.9	223.1	248.6
2002	223.6	220.8	233.9	227.6	214.5	196.7	182.7	183.2	157.1	170.0	185.9	170.0	197.2
2003	162.6	166.3	157.2	173.3	180.5	181.1	181.6	184.4	181.5	189.0	196.3	195.6	179.1
2004[1]	201.3	203.3	199.4	204.9	200.5	206.5	202.1	199.1	206.4	212.2	218.6	229.6	207.0
Japan													
1998	57.7	58.4	57.3	54.3	54.4	54.9	56.8	48.9	46.5	47.1	51.6	48.0	53.0
1999	50.3	49.8	54.9	57.9	55.9	60.8	62.0	60.5	61.1	62.2	64.4	65.7	58.8
2000	67.8	69.2	70.6	62.4	56.7	60.4	54.6	58.5	54.6	50.4	50.8	47.8	58.7
2001	48.0	44.7	45.1	48.3	46.0	45.0	41.1	37.2	33.9	36.0	37.1	36.6	41.6
2002	34.7	36.7	38.2	39.9	40.8	36.8	34.3	33.4	32.6	30.0	32.0	29.8	34.9
2003	28.9	29.0	27.7	27.2	29.2	31.5	33.2	35.9	35.5	35.5	35.0	37.0	32.1
2004[1]	37.4	38.3	40.6	40.8	39.0	41.1	39.3	38.4	37.5	37.4	37.8	39.9	39.0
United Kingdom													
1998	234.3	247.9	257.0	257.6	258.9	253.4	252.6	225.5	216.6	231.4	242.7	247.0	243.7
1999	249.0	261.0	267.4	279.8	266.9	272.2	270.2	271.5	261.1	268.3	285.2	299.5	271.0
2000	274.9	276.2	287.3	277.3	278.7	279.9	282.9	296.3	279.8	284.4	272.1	275.6	280.5
2001	279.9	264.9	250.5	265.0	259.7	252.0	246.1	239.3	216.2	222.9	232.2	233.1	246.8
2002	230.6	227.9	236.2	232.1	228.7	209.1	189.4	189.0	166.4	179.1	185.0	174.9	204.0
2003	159.1	162.5	160.3	174.7	181.9	182.1	189.0	190.7	187.3	196.3	198.3	203.9	182.2
2004[1]	202.0	207.2	202.9	206.7	203.4	205.9	202.5	204.5	209.8	212.2	216.6	222.7	208.0

[1] Preliminary.   Not Seasonally Adjusted.   *Source: Economic and Statistics Administration, U.S. Department of Commerce (ESA)*

Toronto 300 Stock Index (weekly close) as of December 31, 2004

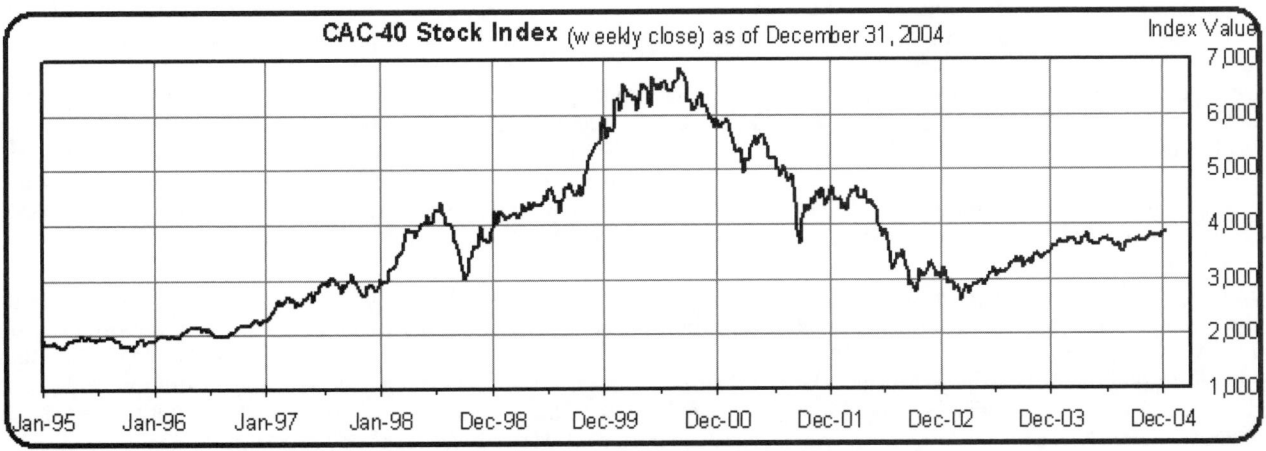

CAC-40 Stock Index (weekly close) as of December 31, 2004

Hang Seng Stock Index (weekly close) as of December 31, 2004

Nikkei 225 Stock Index (weekly close) as of December 31, 2004

Sugar

The white crystalline substance called sugar is the organic chemical compound sucrose, one of several related compounds all known as sugars. These include glucose, dextrose, fructose, and lactose. All sugars are members of the larger group of compounds called carbohydrates and are characterized by a sweet taste. Sucrose is considered a double sugar because it is composed of one molecule of glucose and one molecule of fructose. While sucrose is common in many plants, it occurs in the highest concentration in sugarcane (Saccharum officinarum) and sugar beets (Beta vulgaris). Sugarcane is about 7 to 18 percent sugar by weight while sugar beets are 8 to 22 percent.

Sugarcane is a member of the grass family and is a perennial. Sugarcane is cultivated in tropical and subtropical regions around the world roughly between the Tropics of Cancer and Capricorn. It grows best in hot, wet climates where there is heavy rainfall followed by a dry season. The largest cane producers are Florida, Louisiana, Texas, and Hawaii. On a commercial basis sugarcane is not grown from seeds but from cuttings or pieces of the stalk.

Sugar beets, which are produced in temperate or colder climates, are annuals grown from seeds. Sugar beets do best with moderate temperatures and evenly distributed rainfall. The beets are planted in the spring and harvested in the fall. The sugar is contained in the root of the beet but the sugars from beets and cane are identical. Sugar beet production takes place mostly in Europe, the US, China, and Japan. The largest sugar beet producing states are Minnesota, Idaho, North Dakota, and Michigan. Sugar beets are refined to yield white sugar and very little raw sugar is produced.

Sugar beets and sugarcane are produced in over 100 countries around the world. Of all the sugar produced, about 25 percent is processed from sugar beets and the remainder from sugar cane. The trend has been that production of sugar from cane is increasing relative to that produced from beets. The significance of this in that sugarcane is a perennial plant while the sugar beet is an annual, and due to the longer production cycle, sugarcane production and the sugar processed from that cane, may not be quite as responsive to changes in price.

Sugar futures are traded on the Bolsa de Mercadorias & Futuros (BM&F), Kansai Commodities Exchange (KANEX), the Tokyo Grain Exchange (TGE), the London International Financial Futures and Options Exchange (LIFFE), and the CSCE Division of the New York Board of Trade (NYBOT). Options are traded on the BM&F, the TGE, the LIFFE and the NYBOT.

Raw sugar is traded on the CSCE Division of the New York Board of Trade while white sugar is traded on the London International Financial Futures Exchange (LIFFE). The most actively traded contract is the No. 11 (World) sugar contract at the CSCE. The No. 11 contract calls for the delivery of 112,000 pounds (50 long tons) of raw cane centrifugal sugar from any of 28 foreign countries of origin and the United States. The CSCE also trades the No. 14 sugar contract (Domestic), which calls for the delivery of raw cen-

trifugal cane sugar in the United States. Futures on white sugar are traded on the London International Financial Futures Exchange and call for the delivery of 50 metric tons of white beet sugar, cane crystal sugar, or refined sugar of any origin from the crop current at the time of delivery.

Prices – World sugar prices on the CSCE No.11 sugar nearest-futures chart rallied sharply during 2004, from the year's low of 5.27 cents per pound in February 2004 to a 3-1/2 year high of 9.37 cents in October 2004. The underlying fundamental picture in 2004 was bullish for sugar due to: (1) strong import demand from India (the world's top sugar consumer) where drought and disease cut India's 2004-05 crop by 30% yr/yr and is expected to cut the 2005-06 crop by another 12% yr/yr, (2) supply problems elsewhere in Asia (China is expected to import some 1.5 million metric tons, +25% yr/yr in 2005, and Thailand's crop is expected to fall 11% in 2004-05 and 2005-06 combined, and (3) strong demand for sugarcane in Brazil for ethanol which is now taking more than 50% of the crop. Due to the combination of strong demand and reduced supply, the USDA is forecasting that ending stocks will fall –8.9% yr/yr in 2004-05 to 36.545 million metric tons, and fall another –13.2% yr/yr to 31.738 million metric tons in 2005-06.

Supply – The USDA is forecasting that world production of centrifugal (raw) sugar in the 2005-06 marketing year (Oct 1 to Sep 30) will be unchanged at 141.687 million metric tons, following the –4.8% yr/yr drop in 2004-05 to 141.732 million metric tons and the +10.8% yr/yr rise in 2003-04 to a record high of 148.874 million metric tons. The world's largest sugar producers are Brazil with 19% of world production in 2004-05, the European Union with 12%, and India with 11%. US centrifugal sugar production in 2004-05 rose +2.6% to 7.843 million metric tons. World ending stocks in 2004-05 fell –8.9% to 36.545 metric tons and are forecasted to fall further by –13.2% in 2005-06 to 31.738 million metric tons. The stocks/consumption ratio fell to 26.3% in 2004-05 and is forecasted to fall further to 22.6% in 2005-06, which would be the tightest level since 1995-96. US production in 2004-05 of cane sugar fell –14.3% to 3.390 million short tons, and beet sugar production rose +0.7% yr/yr to 4.727 million short tons.

Demand – World domestic consumption of centrifugal (raw) sugar in 2004-05 rose by +0.6% yr/yr to 139.311 million metric tons, and is forecast by the USDA to rise another +1.0% in 2005-06 to 140.455 million metric tons. US domestic disappearance (consumption) of sugar in 2004-05 rose by +1.4% yr/yr to 9.815 million short tons. The latest available figures show US per capita sugar consumption at 60.9 pounds per year, which is only about two-thirds of the levels seen in the early 1970s.

Exports – World exports of centrifugal sugar in 2004-05 fell –0.5% yr/yr to 45.595 million metric tons, which was just below the record high of 45.828 million metric tons posted in 2003-04. The world's largest sugar exporter is Brazil, which exported 15.240 million metric tons of sugar in 2004-05, accounting for 33% of world exports. The next largest exporters are Thailand with 11% or world exports, the European Union with 10%, and Australia with 9%.

World Production, Supply & Stocks/Consumption Ratio of Sugar   In 1000's of Metric Tons (Raw Value)

Marketing Year	Beginning Stocks	Production	Imports	Total Supply	Exports	Domestic Consumption	Ending Stocks	Stocks/ Consumption Percentage
1995-6	21,660	118,021	32,313	171,994	30,658	115,307	26,029	22.6
1996-7	25,785	123,728	33,228	182,741	35,039	117,432	30,270	25.8
1997-8	30,266	122,964	33,821	187,051	37,295	120,362	29,394	24.4
1998-9	29,394	125,402	33,596	188,392	37,446	122,690	28,256	23.0
1999-00	28,256	131,071	36,200	195,527	37,420	124,757	33,350	26.7
2000-1	33,248	136,435	36,035	205,718	41,503	127,241	36,974	29.1
2001-2	36,974	130,662	38,763	206,399	37,699	129,842	38,858	29.9
2002-3	38,858	134,386	37,960	211,204	41,179	134,457	35,568	26.5
2003-4[1]	35,568	148,874	39,731	224,173	45,828	138,217	40,128	29.0
2004-5[2]	40,128	141,732	39,391	221,251	45,595	139,111	36,545	26.3

[1] Preliminary.   [2] Forecast.   *Source: Foreign Agricultural Service, U.S. Department of Agriculture (FAS-USDA)*

World Production of Sugar (Centrifugal Sugar-Raw Value)   In Thousands of Metric Tons

Year	Australia	Brazil	China	Cuba	European Union	India	Indonesia	Mexico	Pakistan	Thailand	United States	Ukraine	World Total
1995-6	5,196	12,500	6,299	3,300	16,761	16,410	2,450	4,556	3,212	5,448	7,191	3,600	118,021
1996-7	5,049	13,700	6,686	4,400	17,234	18,225	2,090	4,642	2,643	6,223	6,686	3,800	123,728
1997-8	5,659	14,650	7,789	4,200	18,221	14,616	2,094	4,818	2,560	6,013	6,536	2,935	122,964
1998-9	5,567	15,700	8,631	3,200	19,305	14,592	2,190	5,486	3,805	4,245	7,276	2,032	125,402
1999-00	4,997	18,300	8,969	3,760	17,818	17,436	1,492	4,982	3,791	5,386	7,597	2,000	131,071
2000-1	5,448	20,100	7,525	4,060	19,498	20,219	1,690	4,979	2,595	5,721	8,203	1,720	136,435
2001-2	4,162	17,100	6,849	3,500	18,519	20,480	1,800	5,220	2,648	5,107	7,956	1,687	130,662
2002-3	4,662	20,400	8,305	3,600	16,153	20,475	1,725	5,169	3,453	6,397	7,167	1,790	134,386
2003-4[1]	5,461	23,810	11,380	2,250	18,671	22,140	1,755	5,229	3,944	7,286	7,644	1,550	148,874
2004-5[2]	4,994	26,400	10,730	2,300	16,506	15,450	1,730	5,330	4,047	7,010	7,843	1,580	141,732

[1] Preliminary.   [2] Estimate.   *Source: Foreign Agricultural Service, U.S. Department of Agriculture (FAS-USDA)*

World Stocks of Centrifugal Sugar at Beginning of Marketing Year   In Thousands of Metric Tons (Raw Value)

Year	Australia	Brazil	China	Cuba	European Union	India	Indonesia	Iran	Mexico	Philippines	Russia	United States	World Total
1995-6	125	455	1,168	420	3,004	2,776	414	135	1,421	412	1,520	1,213	21,660
1996-7	152	710	3,215	647	1,794	5,990	365	270	1,587	100	875	1,126	25,785
1997-8	101	510	2,684	567	2,006	8,455	474	425	1,403	511	1,035	1,354	30,266
1998-9	228	860	2,784	484	2,535	6,979	559	485	1,055	345	705	1,350	29,394
1999-00	253	560	2,515	568	3,001	5,850	520	365	991	183	1,105	1,523	28,256
2000-1	183	1,010	2,548	488	3,107	7,374	908	405	941	454	2,650	1,487	33,248
2001-2	518	710	1,851	438	3,730	10,710	1,330	207	1,063	330	3,000	2,013	36,974
2002-3	634	860	1,004	302	3,420	11,985	1,415	197	1,548	322	3,100	1,978	38,858
2003-4[1]	507	210	869	382	2,717	11,670	1,385	148	1,172	239	2,130	1,386	35,568
2004-5[2]	662	270	2,021	82	3,732	12,430	1,340	380	1,194	277	1,050	1,510	40,128

[1] Preliminary.   [2] Estimate.   *Source: Foreign Agricultural Service, U.S. Department of Agriculture (FAS-USDA)*

Centrifugal Sugar (Raw Value) Imported into Selected Countries   In Thousands of Metric Tons

Year	Algeria	Canada	China	European Union	Iran	Japan	Rep. of Korea	Malaysia	Morocco	Nigeria	Russia	United States	World Total
1995-6	895	1,090	4,110	2,137	301	1,065	1,703	1,345	1,030	490	2,700	1,664	32,313
1996-7	920	1,156	1,775	1,813	919	1,065	1,673	1,411	1,120	542	3,200	2,536	33,228
1997-8	925	1,062	1,014	1,808	1,091	1,230	1,608	1,497	1,166	555	3,600	2,517	33,821
1998-9	925	1,056	420	1,829	921	970	1,592	1,424	1,065	660	4,210	1,962	33,596
1999-00	940	1,129	543	1,867	1,702	1,085	1,542	1,403	1,188	700	5,400	1,655	36,200
2000-1	900	1,207	687	1,786	1,949	960	1,650	1,514	1,256	825	5,170	1,484	36,035
2001-2	975	1,211	1,083	1,839	1,591	1,000	1,486	1,574	1,325	714	5,650	1,443	38,763
2002-3	1,020	1,235	1,375	2,025	1,600	1,000	1,407	1,590	1,385	775	4,850	1,393	37,960
2003-4[1]	1,410	1,378	842	2,036	1,600	950	1,483	1,590	1,406	1,000	4,000	1,569	39,731
2004-5[2]	1,350	1,364	1,220	2,065	1,500	600	1,442	1,600	1,500	1,150	3,670	1,598	39,391

[1] Preliminary.   [2] Estimate.   *Source: Foreign Agricultural Service, U.S. Department of Agriculture (FAS-USDA)*

SUGAR

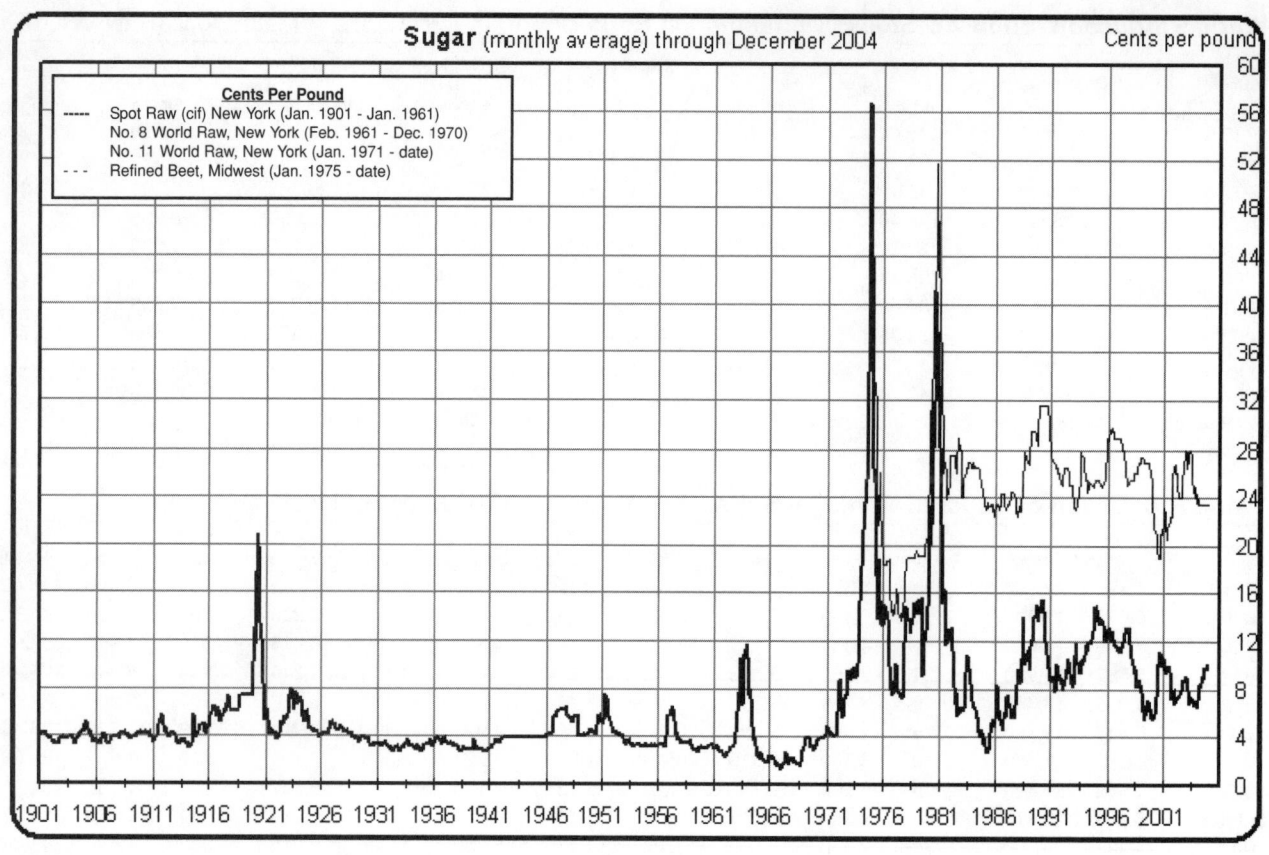

Sugar (monthly average) through December 2004   Cents per pound

Cents Per Pound
- Spot Raw (cif) New York (Jan. 1901 - Jan. 1961)
- No. 8 World Raw, New York (Feb. 1961 - Dec. 1970)
- No. 11 World Raw, New York (Jan. 1971 - date)
- Refined Beet, Midwest (Jan. 1975 - date)

Centrifugal Sugar (Raw Value) Exported From Selected Countries   In Thousands of Metric Tons

Year	Australia	Brazil	Colombia	Cuba	Dominican Republic	European Union	India	Guatemala	Mauritius	South Africa	Swaziland	Thailand	Total
1995-6	4,321	4,300	523	2,603	295	5,449	931	40	508	369	296	3,809	30,658
1996-7	4,242	5,800	694	3,830	325	4,631	923	940	560	399	307	4,537	35,039
1997-8	4,564	5,800	821	3,598	364	5,228	1,075	422	645	1,056	293	4,194	37,295
1998-9	4,554	7,200	1,020	2,426	270	6,361	1,361	21	560	1,160	267	2,839	37,446
1999-00	4,076	8,750	960	3,120	191	5,329	1,086	10	649	1,355	283	3,352	37,420
2000-1	4,123	11,300	959	3,400	185	6,138	1,140	25	426	1,410	284	4,147	41,503
2001-2	3,056	7,700	965	2,980	185	6,607	1,190	1,360	544	1,580	287	3,394	37,699
2002-3	3,594	11,600	1,085	2,900	185	4,793	1,310	1,130	526	1,235	208	4,157	41,179
2003-4[1]	4,114	14,000	1,306	2,150	185	5,281	1,335	1,410	567	1,296	278	5,280	45,828
2004-5[2]	3,950	15,240	1,300	2,400	185	4,616	1,335	300	590	1,071	285	5,160	45,595

[1] Preliminary.   [2] Estimate.   *Source: Foreign Agricultural Service, U.S. Department of Agriculture (FAS-USDA)*

Average Wholesale Price of Refined Beet Sugar[1]--Midwest Market   In Cents Per Pound

Year	Jan.	Feb.	Mar.	Apr.	May	June	July	Aug.	Sept.	Oct.	Nov.	Dec.	Average
1995	25.50	25.50	25.50	25.50	25.13	25.10	24.75	24.75	25.50	25.75	28.13	28.85	25.83
1996	28.69	29.00	29.50	29.50	29.70	29.50	29.50	29.00	29.00	29.00	29.00	29.00	29.20
1997	29.00	29.00	28.13	28.00	28.00	27.50	27.00	26.65	26.38	24.90	25.00	25.50	27.09
1998	25.50	25.50	25.50	25.50	26.00	26.00	26.00	26.00	26.50	26.90	27.00	27.00	26.12
1999	27.20	27.13	27.00	27.00	27.00	27.00	27.00	27.00	27.00	26.00	26.00	25.20	26.71
2000	23.38	22.25	21.50	21.00	19.75	19.00	19.00	19.00	20.70	21.25	21.00	21.80	20.80
2001	23.13	22.75	22.00	20.50	21.38	21.90	22.50	22.50	24.63	25.75	26.20	26.50	23.31
2002	26.75	26.00	25.95	24.63	24.50	24.00	24.00	25.40	26.25	26.75	27.40	27.88	25.79
2003	27.80	26.50	27.13	27.63	28.00	28.00	27.63	25.50	24.00	24.70	23.94	23.63	26.21
2004[2]	23.70	23.50	23.50	23.50	23.50	23.50	23.50	23.50	23.50	23.50	23.38	23.20	23.48

[1] These are f.o.b. basis prices in bulk, not delivered prices.   [2] Preliminary.   *Source: Economic Research Service, U.S. Department of Agriculture (ERS)*

Average Price of World Raw Sugar[1]   In Cents Per Pound

Year	Jan.	Feb.	Mar.	Apr.	May	June	July	Aug.	Sept.	Oct.	Nov.	Dec.	Average
1995	14.87	14.43	14.58	13.63	13.49	13.99	13.46	13.75	12.72	11.94	11.96	12.40	13.44
1996	12.57	12.97	13.07	12.43	11.94	12.54	12.83	12.33	11.87	11.65	11.29	11.38	12.24
1997	11.13	11.06	11.17	11.50	11.54	12.02	12.13	12.54	12.65	12.86	13.19	12.90	12.06
1998	11.71	11.06	10.66	10.27	10.17	9.33	9.70	9.50	8.21	8.24	8.73	8.59	9.68
1999	8.40	7.05	6.11	5.44	5.83	6.67	6.11	6.39	6.98	6.90	6.54	6.00	6.54
2000	5.64	5.51	5.54	6.48	7.33	8.72	10.18	11.14	10.35	10.96	10.02	10.23	8.51
2001	10.63	10.26	9.64	9.27	9.96	9.80	9.48	8.77	8.60	7.15	7.80	8.02	9.12
2002	7.96	6.81	7.27	7.12	7.33	7.07	8.02	7.86	8.54	8.84	8.87	8.81	7.88
2003	8.56	9.14	8.50	7.92	7.41	6.85	7.18	7.30	6.70	6.74	6.83	6.95	7.51
2004[2]	6.42	7.01	8.23	8.21	8.08	8.41	9.19	8.99	9.10	9.84	9.65	10.19	8.61

[1] Contract No. 11, f.o.b. stowed Caribbean port, including Brazil, bulk spot price.   [2] Preliminary.   *Source: Economic Research Service, U.S. Department of Agriculture (ERS-USDA)*

Average Price of Raw Sugar in New York (C.I.F., Duty/Free Paid, Contract #12/#14)   In Cents Per Pound

Year	Jan.	Feb.	Mar.	Apr.	May	June	July	Aug.	Sept.	Oct.	Nov.	Dec.	Average
1995	22.65	22.69	22.46	22.76	23.10	23.09	24.47	23.18	23.21	22.67	22.60	22.63	22.96
1996	22.39	22.68	22.57	22.71	22.62	22.48	21.80	22.51	22.38	22.37	22.12	22.14	22.40
1997	21.88	22.07	21.81	21.79	21.70	21.62	22.04	22.21	22.30	22.27	21.90	21.93	21.96
1998	21.85	21.79	21.74	22.14	22.31	22.42	22.66	22.19	21.92	21.67	21.83	22.19	22.06
1999	22.41	22.38	22.55	22.57	22.65	22.61	22.61	21.24	20.10	19.50	17.45	17.87	21.16
2000	17.70	17.24	18.46	19.43	19.12	19.31	17.64	18.12	18.97	21.15	21.39	20.56	19.09
2001	20.81	21.18	21.40	21.51	21.19	21.04	20.64	21.10	20.87	20.90	21.19	21.43	21.11
2002	21.03	20.69	19.92	19.73	19.52	19.93	20.86	20.91	21.65	21.94	22.22	22.03	20.87
2003	21.62	21.91	22.14	21.87	21.80	21.62	21.32	21.26	21.34	20.92	20.91	20.37	21.42
2004[1]	20.54	20.57	20.86	20.88	20.69	20.03	20.14	20.10	20.47	20.31	20.40	20.55	20.46

[1] Preliminary.   *Source: Economic Research Service, U.S. Department of Agriculture (ERS-USDA)*

Supply and Utilization of Sugar (Cane and Beet) in the United States   In 1,000's of Short Tons (Raw Value)

	Supply									Utilization				
	Production			Offshore Receipts							Net Changes in Invisible Stocks	Refining Loss Adjustment	Domestic Disappearance		
Year	Cane	Beet	Total	Foreign	Terri-tories	Total	Beginning Stocks	Total Supply	Total Use	Exports			In Poly-hydric Alcohol[4]	Total	Per Capita Pounds
1996-7	3,191	4,013	7,204	2,774	0	2,774	1,492	11,471	9,983	211	30	0	21	9,564	65.2
1997-8	3,632	4,389	8,021	2,163	0	2,163	1,488	11,672	9,992	179	-1	0	20	9,672	64.9
1998-9	3,945	4,421	8,366	1,823	0	1,823	1,679	11,868	10,238	230	-67	0	24	9,873	64.9
1999-00	4,076	4,974	9,050	1,636	0	1,636	1,639	12,325	10,090	124	-126	0	32	9,993	66.3
2000-1	4,089	4,680	8,769	1,590	0	1,590	2,216	12,575	10,396	141	123	0	33	10,000	65.5
2001-2	3,985	3,915	7,900	1,535	0	1,535	2,180	11,615	10,087	137	-24	0	33	9,785	64.5
2002-3[1]	3,964	4,462	8,426	1,730	0	1,730	1,528	11,684	10,014	142	161	0	24	9,504	63.2
2003-4[2]	3,957	4,692	8,649	1,750	0	1,750	1,670	12,070	10,173	288	23	0	41	9,678	60.9
2004-5[3]	3,390	4,727	8,117	1,639	0	1,639	1,897	11,653	10,180	200	0	0	40	9,815	NA

[1] Preliminary.   [2] Estimate.   [3] Forecast.   [4] Includes feed use.   Source: Economic Research Service, U.S. Department of Agriculture (ERS-USDA)

Sugar Cane for Sugar & Seed and Production of Cane Sugar and Molasses in the United States

		Yield of Cane Per	Production			Sugar Yield Per	Farm Price	Farm Value		Sugar Production				Molasses Made	
	Acreage Harvested 1,000	Harvested Acre	for Sugar	for Seed	Total	Acre	$ Per	of Cane Used for Sugar	of Cane Used for Sugar & Seed	Raw Value		Refined Basis 1,000			
Year	Acres	Net Tons	1,000 Tons			Short Tons	Ton	1,000 Dollars		Total 1,000 Tons	Per Ton of Cane in Lbs.	Tons	Edible	Total[3]	
													1,000 Gallons		
1996	888.9	33.1	27,687	1,777	29,464	----	28.3	784,113	833,297	----	----	----	----	----	
1997	914.0	34.7	30,003	1,706	31,709	----	28.1	842,840	890,257	----	----	----	----	----	
1998	947.1	36.6	32,743	1,964	34,707	----	27.3	893,049	944,562	----	----	----	----	----	
1999	993.3	35.5	33,577	1,722	35,299	----	25.6	859,175	901,900	----	----	----	----	----	
2000	1,023.3	35.0	34,291	1,823	36,114	----	26.1	895,917	941,791	----	----	----	----	----	
2001	1,027.8	33.7	32,775	1,812	34,587	----	29.0	951,813	1,003,046	----	----	----	----	----	
2002	1,023.2	34.7	33,903	1,650	35,553	----	28.4	961,896	1,007,142	----	----	----	----	----	
2003[1]	992.3	34.1	31,942	1,916	33,858	----	29.5		998,269	----	----	----	----	----	
2004[2]	952.1	30.8	27,713	1,582	29,295	----				----	----	----	----	----	

[1] Preliminary.   [2] Estimate.   [3] Excludes edible molasses.   *Source: Economic Research Service, U.S. Department of Agriculture (ERS-USDA)*

269

SUGAR

U.S. Sugar Beets, Beet Sugar, Pulp & Molasses Produced from Beets and Raw Sugar Spot Prices

Year of Harvest	Acreage Planted (1,000 Acres)	Acreage Harvested (1,000 Acres)	Yield Per Harvested Acre Ton	Production 1,000 Tons	Sugar Yield Per Acre Sh. Tons	Price[3] Dollars	Farm Value $1,000	Sugar Production Equivalent Raw Value[4] (1,000 Short Tons)	Refined Basis	Raw Sugar Prices World Refined #5	CSCE #11 World	CSCE N.Y. Duty Paid	Wholesale List Price HFCS (42%) Midwest
1995	1,445	1,420	19.8	28,065	2.78	38.10	1,070,663	3,944	----	17.99	13.44	22.96	15.63
1996	1,368	1,323	20.2	26,680	3.06	45.40	1,211,001	3,900	----	16.64	12.24	22.40	14.46
1997	1,459	1,428	20.9	29,886	3.00	38.80	1,160,029	----	----	14.33	12.06	21.96	10.70
1998	1,498	1,451	22.4	32,499	----	36.40	1,181,494	----	----	11.59	9.68	22.06	10.58
1999	1,561	1,527	21.9	33,420	----	37.20	1,242,895	----	----	9.10	6.54	21.16	11.71
2000	1,564	1,373	23.7	32,541	----	34.20	1,113,030	----	----	9.97	8.51	19.09	11.32
2001	1,371	1,243	20.7	25,764	----	39.80	1,025,306	----	----	11.29	9.12	21.11	11.90
2002	1,427	1,361	20.4	27,707	----	39.60	1,097,329	----	----	10.35	7.88	20.87	13.05
2003[1]	1,365	1,348	22.7	30,583	----	41.40	1,270,026	----	----	9.74	7.51	21.42	13.24
2004[2]	1,346	1,307	22.9	29,932	----			----	----	10.87	8.61	20.46	13.20

[1] Preliminary.　[2] Estimate.　[3] Includes support payments, but excludes Government sugar beet payments.　[4] Refined sugar multiplied by factor of 1.07.　[5] F.O.B. Europe.　*Source: Economic Research Service, U.S. Department of Agriculture (ERS-USDA)*

Sugar Deliveries and Stocks in the United States   In Thousands of Short Tons (Raw Value)

Year	Quota Allocation	Actual Imports	Deliveries by Primary Distributors: Cane Sugar Refineries	Beet Sugar Factories	Importers of Direct Consumption Sugar	Mainland Cane Sugar Mills[3]	Total Deliveries	Total Domestic Consumption	Stocks, Jan. 1: Cane Sugar Refineries[4]	Beet Sugar Factories	CCC	Refiners' Raw	Mainland Cane Mills	Total
1995	2,413.1	2,308.0	4,808	4,486	44	15	9,337	9,451	185	1,594	6	448	906	3,139
1996	2,339.1	2,276.9	5,539	3,923	33	14	9,496	9,619	195	1,383	0	334	996	2,909
1997	1,791.3	1,733.3	5,553	3,997	27	----	9,578	9,755	196	1,520	0	323	1,156	3,195
1998	1,289.7	1,254.2	5,349	4,313	24	----	9,686	9,854	212	1,535	0	322	1,308	3,377
1999	----	----	5,419	4,536	41	----	9,996	10,167	255	1,499	0	332	1,335	3,421
2000	----	----	5,508	4,433	36	----	9,977	10,091	208	1,554	0	356	1,737	3,855
2001	----	----	5,172	4,680	58	----	9,911	10,075	262	1,500	767	274	1,533	4,337
2002	----	----	5,407	4,291	109	----	9,808	9,994	288	1,472	634	351	1,781	4,525
2003[1]	----	----	5,232	4,219	60	----	9,511	9,713	298	1,300	246	299	1,289	3,432
2004[2]	----	----	4,993	4,674	75	----	9,742	9,922	326	1,817	0	286	1,659	4,088

[1] Preliminary.　[2] Estimate.　[3] Sugar for direct consumption only.　[4] Refined.　*Source: Economic Research Service, U.S. Department of Agriculture (ERS-USDA)*

Sugar, Refined--Deliveries to End User in the United States   In Thousands of Short Tons

Year	Bakery & Cereal Products	Beverages	Confectionery[2]	Hotels, Restaurant & Institutions	Ice Cream & Dairy Products	Canned, Bottled & Frozen Foods	All Other Food Uses	Retail Grocers[3]	Wholesale Grocers[4]	Non-food Uses	Non-industrial Uses	Industrial Uses	Total Deliveries
1995	1,905	169	1,372	103	452	279	863	1,236	2,173	64	3,701	5,103	8,804
1996	1,993	196	1,335	80	445	318	849	1,263	2,241	66	3,759	5,202	8,962
1997	2,161	158	1,350	78	436	308	793	1,281	2,283	66	3,828	5,272	9,100
1998	2,301	165	1,336	79	438	331	907	1,230	2,223	76	3,761	5,556	9,317
1999	2,312	179	1,361	72	499	346	862	1,263	2,257	71	3,804	5,630	9,434
2000	2,264	168	1,328	71	499	330	817	1,242	2,241	85	3,893	5,491	9,383
2001	2,273	158	1,316	59	484	310	800	1,255	2,250	74	3,927	5,414	9,341
2002	2,069	189	1,221	53	530	297	727	1,322	2,374	99	4,122	5,132	9,253
2003	2,043	209	1,086	51	534	298	616	1,266	2,550	98	4,214	4,886	9,100
2004[1]	2,178	240	1,124	77	603	314	700	1,271	2,517	91	4,122	5,251	9,373

[1] Preliminary.　[2] And related products.　[3] Chain stores, supermarkets.　[4] Jobbers, sugar dealers.　*Source: Economic Research Service, U.S. Department of Agriculture (ERS-USDA)*

Deliveries[1] of All Sugar by Primary Distributors in the U.S., by Quarters   In Thousands of Short Tons

Year	First Quarter	Second Quarter	Third Quarter	Fourth Quarter	Total	Year	First Quarter	Second Quarter	Third Quarter	Fourth Quarter	Total
1993	2,039	2,172	2,432	2,277	8,420	1999	2,208	2,553	2,655	2,580	9,996
1994	2,121	2,265	2,532	2,260	8,646	2000	2,318	2,484	2,611	2,564	9,977
1995	2,105	2,311	2,542	2,379	8,801	2001	2,370	2,486	2,580	2,474	9,911
1996	2,191	2,355	2,519	2,430	8,964	2002	2,227	2,439	2,645	2,497	9,808
1997	2,143	2,401	2,591	2,443	9,100	2003	2,183	2,360	2,464	2,504	9,511
1998	2,233	2,428	2,565	2,458	9,213	2004[2]	2,286	2,368	2,520	2,568	9,742

Raw Value.　[1] Includes for domestic consumption and for export.　[2] Preliminary.　*Source: Economic Research Service, U.S. Department of Agriculture (ERS-USDA)*

Sugar #11 Futures - New York Board of Trade
(weekly close) as of December 31, 2004
Cents per pound

Average Open Interest of World Sugar No. 11 Futures in New York   In Contracts

Year	Jan.	Feb.	Mar.	Apr.	May	June	July	Aug.	Sept.	Oct.	Nov.	Dec.
1995	186,893	167,451	149,027	152,600	127,978	121,877	114,027	119,787	114,069	119,561	140,008	157,779
1996	156,047	159,563	150,093	142,773	137,897	148,447	144,527	153,845	153,202	144,830	150,866	150,573
1997	155,156	147,198	143,623	166,143	150,480	175,139	165,884	197,331	187,477	158,065	200,486	201,922
1998	206,100	212,072	183,472	182,770	171,555	186,978	149,536	152,754	155,076	138,762	139,896	148,983
1999	165,717	176,465	168,624	188,324	196,864	177,266	142,416	151,621	189,606	161,760	167,549	175,125
2000	191,464	199,031	193,554	187,810	201,756	200,973	172,361	171,808	160,809	154,101	148,035	145,760
2001	157,478	158,192	158,448	167,555	131,640	126,426	112,483	128,181	139,915	146,058	163,358	170,710
2002	184,096	205,138	194,541	187,415	157,738	158,276	149,202	170,667	202,144	207,456	207,598	217,904
2003	244,036	265,758	220,971	192,497	170,867	184,257	180,898	196,857	195,200	185,917	200,605	207,995
2004	246,347	269,863	268,250	275,423	267,362	282,842	300,961	309,436	292,917	322,079	304,462	332,803

Source: New York Board of Trade (NYBOT)

Volume of Trading of World Sugar No. 11 Futures in New York   In Contracts

Year	Jan.	Feb.	Mar.	Apr.	May	June	July	Aug.	Sept.	Oct.	Nov.	Dec.	Total
1995	591,861	489,274	472,519	478,757	352,000	485,131	298,756	402,358	360,086	246,584	278,906	254,850	4,711,082
1996	550,780	544,514	341,940	526,255	384,302	496,745	279,707	290,732	562,082	264,290	203,921	306,584	4,751,852
1997	436,935	493,199	268,343	618,176	308,563	575,264	400,150	427,082	580,551	440,208	323,286	413,214	5,284,971
1998	601,378	688,036	431,818	551,628	364,203	686,997	294,354	370,179	527,270	303,951	358,096	346,201	5,524,111
1999	683,891	543,477	452,485	688,181	361,895	762,271	346,534	408,289	657,572	344,434	405,495	256,775	5,911,299
2000	422,527	609,793	501,115	617,633	523,939	717,700	376,769	420,611	622,350	507,562	371,824	242,027	5,933,850
2001	410,492	545,538	380,640	567,921	426,987	515,561	356,483	419,123	447,349	348,896	413,965	317,374	5,150,329
2002	568,789	629,533	417,314	693,589	412,150	610,338	529,509	381,027	756,038	402,811	432,100	340,558	6,173,756
2003	566,040	797,616	443,842	729,453	489,195	719,819	535,892	545,886	760,213	475,322	403,091	674,355	7,140,724
2004	513,562	1,018,664	1,181,124	993,743	617,324	1,100,639	614,596	679,522	1,248,663	626,476	539,501	632,736	9,766,550

Source: New York Board of Trade (NYBOT)

Sulfur

Sulfur (symbol S) is an odorless, tasteless, light yellow, nonmetallic element. As early as 2000 BC, Egyptians used sulfur compounds to bleach fabric. The Chinese used sulfur as an essential component when they developed gunpowder in the 13th century.

Sulfur is widely found in both its free and combined states. Free sulfur is found mixed with gypsum and pumice stone in volcanic regions. Sulfur dioxide is an air pollutant released from the combustion of fossil fuels. The most important use of sulfur is the production of sulfur compounds. Sulfur is used in skin ointments, matches, dyes, gunpowder, and phosphoric acid.

Supply – World production of sulfur (all forms) in 2003 rose +2.1% yr/yr to 61.800 million metric tons, which was a new record high. The world's largest producers of sulfur are the US with 16% of world production, Canada (15%), Russia (11%), and China (10%). US production of sulfur rose by +3.6% yr/yr in 2003 to 9.600 million metric tons, recovering from the 3-decade low of 9.270 million metric tons seen in 2002.

Demand – US consumption of sulfur in all forms rose by +5.3% in 2003 to 12.000 million metric tons, recovering further from the 17-year low of 10.900 million metric tons seen in 2001. US consumption of elemental sulfur rose by +5.8% in 2003 to 11.000 million metric tons, recovering further from the 3-decade low of 9.520 million metric tons seen in 2001. US consumption of sulfuric acid rose +20.5% yr/yr in 2003 to 10.100 million metric tons.

Trade – US exports of recovered sulfur in 2003 rose +8.0% yr/yr to 742,000 metric tons, recovering further from the 10-year low of 675,000 metric tons seen in 2001. US imports of recovered sulfur in 2003 rose by +12.1% yr/yr to 2.870 million metric tons, which was a new record high.

World Production of Sulfur (All Forms)   In Thousands of Metric Tons

Year	Canada	China	France	Germany	Iraq	Japan	Mexico	Poland	Russia	Saudi Arabia	Spain	United States	World Total
1996	9,490	7,260	1,090	1,110	475	3,150	1,280	1,982	3,800	2,300	943	11,800	55,200
1997	9,480	7,670	1,060	1,160	450	3,391	1,340	1,985	3,750	1,750	967	12,000	56,900
1998	9,694	6,170	1,110	1,180	450	3,428	1,387	1,675	4,651	2,050	993	11,700	57,400
1999	9,815	5,770	1,100	2,358	----	3,462	1,334	1,524	5,265	1,940	955	11,500	58,500
2000	9,788	5,560	1,110	2,401	----	3,486	1,325	1,831	5,900	2,101	708	10,500	59,700
2001	9,744	5,380	1,100	2,494	----	3,773	1,450	1,352	6,250	2,350	668	9,470	60,400
2002[1]	8,925	5,730	1,000	2,499	----	3,216	1,452	1,220	6,350	2,360	685	9,270	60,500
2003[2]	9,030	6,090	1,000	2,358	----	3,310	1,610	1,180	6,600	2,400	706	9,600	61,800

[1] Preliminary.　[2] Estimate.　*Source: U.S. Geological Survey (USGS)*

Salient Statistics of Sulfur in the United States   In Thousands of Metric Tons (Sulfur Content)

	Production of										Sales Value of Shipments		
	Elemental Sulfur				By-product Sulfuric Acid	Other Sulfuric Acid Compounds	Pro-duction (All Forms)	Imports Sulfuric Acid[4]	Exports Sulfuric Acid[4]	Producer Stocks Dec. 31[5]	Apparent Con-sumption (All Forms)	F.O.B. Mine/Plant	
	Native - Sulfur[3]	Recovered											
Year	Frasch	Petroleum & Coke	Natural Gas	Total								Frasch Recovered $ Per Metric Ton	Average
1996	2,900	5,370	2,100	7,480	1,430	----	11,800	2,070	117	646	13,600	W　W	34.11
1997	2,820	5,230	2,420	7,650	1,550	----	12,000	2,010	118	761	13,900	W　W	36.06
1998	1,800	6,060	2,160	8,220	1,610	----	11,700	2,040	155	283	14,200	W　W	29.14
1999	1,780	6,210	2,010	8,220	1,320	----	11,500	1,370	155	451	13,800	W　W	37.81
2000	900	6,360	2,020	8,380	1,030	----	10,500	1,420	191	208	12,700	----　----	24.73
2001	----	6,480	2,000	8,490	982	----	9,470	1,410	210	232	10,900	----　----	10.01
2002[1]	----	6,750	1,760	8,500	772	----	9,270	1,060	147	181	11,400	----　----	11.84
2003[2]	----	6,970	1,950	8,920	683	----	9,600	908	205	206	12,000	----　----	28.71

[1] Preliminary.　[2] Estimate.　[3] Or sulfur ore; Withheld included in natural gas.　[4] Basis 100% H2SO4, sulfur equivalent.　[5] Frasch & recovered.
[6] Data 1996 to date includes Frasch.　W = Withheld proprietary data.　*Source: U.S. Geological Survey (USGS)*

Sulfur Consumption & Foreign Trade of the United States   In Thousands of Metric Tons (Sulfur Content)

	Consumption			Sulfuric Acid Sold or Used, by End Use[2]						Foreign Trade				
	Native Sulfur Frasch	Re-covered Sulfur	Total Elemental Form	Total Sulfuric Acid	Pulpmills & Paper Product	Inorganic Chem-icals[3]	Synthetic Rubber & Plastic	Pho-sphatic Fertilizers	Petro-leum Refining[4]	Exports		Imports		
Year										Frasch	Re-covered	Value 1,000 $	Frasch Re-covered	Value 1,000 $
1996	W	11,500	11,500	10,900	343	152	270	7,380	525	----	855	51,700	---- 1,960	70,200
1997	W	11,800	11,800	10,700	334	232	85	7,000	610	----	703	36,000	---- 2,060	64,900
1998	W	11,900	11,900	10,600	134	174	69	7,590	632	----	889	35,400	---- 2,270	58,400
1999	W	11,700	11,700	10,400	138	174	68	7,770	508	----	685	35,800	---- 2,580	51,600
2000	W	11,100	11,100	9,620	136	152	68	7,110	497	----	762	53,700	---- 2,330	39,400
2001	W	9,520	9,520	9,530	194	158	68	6,840	591	----	675	48,800	---- 1,730	22,100
2002	W	10,400	10,400	8,380	122	27	66	6,660	90	----	687	40,000	---- 2,560	26,800
2003[1]	W	11,000	11,000	10,100	225	71	82	6,660	140	----	742	46,100	---- 2,870	70,600

[1] Preliminary.　[2] Sulfur equivalent.　[3] Including inorganic pigments, paints & allied products, and other inorganic chemicals & products.
[4] Including other petroleum and coal products.　W = Withheld proprietary data.　NA = Not available.　*Source: U.S. Geological Survey (USGS)*

Sunflowerseed, Meal and Oil

Sunflowers are native to South and North America, but are now grown almost worldwide. Sunflowerseed oil accounts for approximately 14% of the world production of seed oils. Sunflower varieties that are commercially grown contain from 39% to 49% oil in the seed. Sunflower crops produce about 50 bushels of seed per acre on average, which yields approximately 50 gallons of oil.

Sunflowerseed oil accounts for around 80% of the value of the sunflower crop. Refined sunflowerseed oil is edible and used primarily as a salad and cooking oil and in margarine. Crude sunflowerseed oil is used industrially for making soaps, candles, varnishes, and detergents. Sunflowerseed oil contains 93% of the energy of US No. 2 diesel fuel and is being explored as a potential alternate fuel source in diesel engines. Sunflower meal is used in livestock feed and when fed to poultry, increases the yield of eggs. Sunflower seeds are also used for birdfeed and as a snack for humans.

Prices – The average monthly price received by US farmers for sunflower seeds in the first four months of the 2004-05 marketing year (i.e., September through December 2004) was $13.05 per hundred pounds. That was an 11-year high and was up +3.7% from $12.58 in the 2003-04 marketing year.

Supply – World sunflowerseed production in the 2003-04 marketing year rose +10.8% yr/yr to 26.320 million metric tons, which was only mildly below the record high of 27.403 million metric tons posted in 1998-99. The world's largest sunflowerseed producers are the former USSR with 38% of world production, Argentina with 12%, China with 7%, and France with 6%. The US accounted for 4.6% of world production in 2003-04.

US production of sunflowerseeds in 2004-05 fell by –10.1% yr/yr to 1.086 million metric tons, which was far below the record production level of 3.309 million metric tons posted in 1979-80. US farmers harvested 1.780 million acres of sunflowers in 2004-05. That was down –19.0% yr/yr and was the smallest area harvested since 1.775 million acres in 1987-88.

Demand – Total US disappearance of sunflowerseeds in 2003-04 rose +24.2% yr/yr to 1.411 million metric tons, of which 44% went to non-oil and seed use, 43% to crushing for oil and meal, and 13% to exports.

Trade – World sunflowerseed exports in 2003-04 rose +26.7% yr/yr to a 5-year high of 3.235 million metric tons. The world's largest exporters are the former USSR which accounted for 43% of world exports in 2003-04 and Hungary which accounted for 15% of world exports. US exports of 116,000 metric tons accounted for only 3.6% of world exports in 2003-04.

World Production of Sunflowerseed   In Thousands of Metric Tons

Crop Year	Argen-tina	Bulgaria	China	France	Hungary	India	Romania	South Africa	Spain	Turkey	United States	Ex-USSR	World Total
1994-5	5,900	595	1,370	2,050	665	1,204	767	450	979	600	2,193	4,356	23,342
1995-6	5,600	650	1,270	1,900	730	1,400	933	755	575	750	1,819	7,368	25,720
1996-7	5,450	527	1,333	1,996	905	1,250	1,096	560	1,178	670	1,614	5,316	24,410
1997-8	5,630	438	1,176	1,995	540	890	869	585	1,373	672	1,668	5,442	23,452
1998-9	7,180	524	1,465	1,713	718	944	1,073	1,109	1,097	850	2,392	5,762	27,405
1999-00	5,760	660	1,765	1,868	793	801	1,301	531	579	820	1,969	7,394	26,846
2000-1	2,970	423	1,954	1,833	484	730	721	638	848	630	1,608	7,820	23,140
2001-2	3,730	405	1,750	1,584	632	726	824	929	871	530	1,551	5,462	21,591
2002-3[1]	3,340	523	1,900	1,497	777	1,060	1,003	643	757	820	1,112	7,832	23,762
2003-4[2]	3,200	660	1,800	1,494	975	1,160	1,310	586	769	560	1,209	9,870	26,320

[1] Preliminary.   [2] Forecast.   Source: Economic Research Service, U.S. Department of Agriculture (ERS-USDA)

World Imports and Exports of Sunflowerseed   In Thousands of Metric Tons

Crop Year	Imports						Exports						
	France	Germany	Nether-lands	Spain	Turkey	World Total	Argen-tina	France	Hungary	Ex-USSR	United States	Uraguay	World Total
1994-5	109	279	543	472	550	3,287	884	628	260	708	287	----	3,173
1995-6	300	366	617	681	500	3,972	550	480	249	1,750	224	----	3,647
1996-7	338	406	496	296	532	3,343	65	78	212	2,422	117	91	3,310
1997-8	208	278	439	312	554	3,049	504	64	104	1,744	265	60	3,049
1998-9	395	364	477	576	766	3,995	940	29	152	1,944	291	106	4,050
1999-00	130	261	650	443	486	3,174	265	27	236	1,420	168	28	3,088
2000-1	176	300	477	369	322	2,782	94	11	191	1,872	153	21	2,759
2001-2	46	146	341	200	164	1,656	342	25	234	225	176	130	1,705
2002-3[1]	74	214	465	232	287	2,473	232	4	478	624	122	223	2,553
2003-4[2]	335	220	463	270	565	3,300	55	3	490	1,405	116	108	3,235

[1] Preliminary.   [2] Forecast.   Source: Economic Research Service, U.S. Department of Agriculture (ERS-USDA)

SUNFLOWERSEED, MEAL AND OIL

Sunflowerseed Statistics in the United States   In Thousands of Metric Tons

Crop Year Beginning Sept. 1	Harvested Acres 1,000	Harvested Yield Per Cwt.	Farm Price $ Per Metric Ton	Value of Production Million $	Supply Stocks, Sept. 1	Supply Production	Supply Imports	Supply Total	Disappearance Crush	Disappearance Exports	Disappearance Non-oil Use & Seed	Disappearance Total
1997-8	2,792	13.17	256	426.5	196	1,668	29	1,893	1,061	189	551	1,801
1998-9	3,492	15.10	225	559.0	92	2,392	34	2,518	1,178	260	849	2,287
1999-00	3,441	12.62	166	326.9	231	1,969	41	2,241	1,139	205	666	2,010
2000-1	2,647	13.39	152	244.2	231	1,608	66	1,905	923	201	625	1,749
2001-2	2,555	13.38	215	326.0	156	1,551	76	1,783	760	235	679	1,674
2002-3	2,167	11.31	220-250	294.6	109	1,112	98	1,319	319	166	635	1,120
2003-4[1]	2,197	12.13		316.2	199	1,209	90	1,498	627	170	538	1,335
2004-5[2]	1,711	11.97		268.4	163	929	97	1,189	454	140	519	1,113

[1] Preliminary.   [2] Forecast.   Source: Economic Research Service, U.S. Department of Agriculture (ERS-USDA)

World Production of Sunflowerseed Oil and Meal   In Thousands of Metric Tons

Year	Sunflowerseed Oil Argentina	France	Spain	Turkey	Ex-USSR	World Total	Sunflowerseed Meal Argentina	France	Spain	Turkey	United States	Ex-USSR	World Total
1996-7	2,159	689	550	503	1,229	9,109	2,260	838	639	561	456	1,235	10,804
1997-8	2,166	543	617	544	1,258	8,440	2,300	697	717	607	507	1,306	10,056
1998-9	2,356	591	612	628	1,467	9,264	2,426	759	711	701	624	1,477	10,962
1999-00	2,143	614	527	520	2,222	9,549	2,111	749	613	583	555	2,207	10,977
2000-1	1,463	645	503	400	2,382	8,689	1,441	797	585	449	464	2,318	10,007
2001-2	1,308	471	444	299	2,074	7,450	1,268	604	516	336	364	2,095	8,636
2002-3[1]	1,368	489	454	402	2,909	8,608	1,342	601	527	452	173	2,832	9,743
2003-4[2]	1,346	569	456	464	3,326	9,477	1,317	718	530	522	283	3,295	10,762

[1] Preliminary.   [2] Forecast.   Source: Economic Research Service, U.S. Department of Agriculture (ERS-USDA)

Sunflower Oil Statistics in the United States   In Thousands of Metric Tons

Crop Year Beginning Oct. 1	Supply Stocks, Oct. 1	Supply Production	Supply Imports	Total	Disappearance Exports	Disappearance Domestic	Total	Minneapolis, Crude $ Per Metric Ton
1997-8	42	435	3	480	370	83	480	608
1998-9	27	534	2	563	363	145	563	446
1999-00	55	474	2	531	286	174	531	364
2000-1	71	396	4	471	247	162	471	357
2001-2	62	305	16	383	205	168	383	529
2002-3	10	138	28	176	52	112	176	496-562
2003-4[1]	12	270	12	294	107	169	294	
2004-5[2]	18	197	5	220	50	156	220	

[1] Preliminary.   [2] Forecast.   Source: Economic Research Service, U.S. Department of Agriculture (ERS-USDA)

Sunflower Meal Statistics in the United States   In Thousands of Metric Tons

Crop Year Beginning Oct. 1	Supply Stocks, Oct. 1	Supply Production	Supply Imports	Total	Disappearance Exports	Disappearance Domestic	Total	28% Protein $ Per Metric Ton
1997-8	5	494	----	499	13	481	499	90
1998-9	5	617	----	622	41	576	622	72
1999-00	5	549	----	554	21	528	554	83
2000-1	5	458	----	463	8	450	463	100
2001-2	5	358	26	389	26	358	389	96
2002-3	5	172	63	240	3	232	240	95
2003-4[1]	5	308	20	333	12	316	333	102-132
2004-5[2]	5	227		232	9	218	232	

[1] Preliminary.   [2] Forecast.   Source: Economic Research Service, U.S. Department of Agriculture (ERS-USDA)

Average Price Received by Farmers for Sunflower[2] in the United States   In Dollars Per Hundred Pounds

Year	Sept.	Oct.	Nov.	Dec.	Jan.	Feb.	Mar.	Apr.	May	June	July	Aug.	Average
1999-00	8.76	6.99	6.87	7.52	7.34	8.72	8.53	7.93	9.63	8.09	8.16	7.82	8.03
2000-1	6.31	5.76	6.20	6.49	6.92	7.29	7.46	7.67	7.99	8.40	8.71	9.48	7.39
2001-2	8.64	8.19	9.10	9.71	9.52	10.00	10.20	10.50	10.50	11.80	13.80	12.90	10.41
2002-3	13.10	12.00	12.00	12.30	12.10	12.50	12.50	12.30	12.20	12.00	11.60	10.90	12.13
2003-4	10.40	11.40	11.50	11.70	12.10	12.80	13.60	13.50	13.70	13.40	13.30	13.60	12.58
2004-5[1]	12.90	12.40	13.00	13.50	13.70	13.60							13.18

[1] Preliminary.   [2] KS, MN, ND and SD average.   Source: Economic Research Service, U.S. Department of Agriculture (ERS-USDA)

Tall Oil

Tall oil is a product of the paper and pulping industry. Crude tall oil is the major byproduct of the kraft or sulfate processing of pinewood. Crude tall oil starts as tall oil soap which is separated from recovered black liquor in the kraft pulping process. The tall oil soap is acidified to yield crude tall oil. The resulting tall oil is then fractionated to produce fatty acids, rosin, and pitch. Crude tall oil contains 40-50 percent fatty acids such as oleic and linoleic acids; 5-10 percent sterols, alcohols, and other neutral components. The demand is for the tall oil rosin and fatty acids which are used to produce adhesives, coatings, and ink resins. The products find use in lubricants, soaps, linoleum, flotation and waterproofing agents, paints, varnishes, and drying oils.

Since tall oil and its production are derived from the paper and pulping industry, the amount of tall oil produced is related in part to the pulp industry and in part to the U.S. economy.

Consumption of Tall Oil in Inedible Products in the United States   In Millions of Pounds

Year	Jan.	Feb.	Mar.	Apr.	May	June	July	Aug.	Sept.	Oct.	Nov.	Dec.	Total
1996	93.1	103.4	89.2	104.1	100.5	96.6	85.4	100.7	94.9	111.5	101.4	98.8	1,180
1997	111.5	89.0	91.0	99.5	97.0	105.8	103.7	94.4	84.7	87.2	87.3	88.4	1,139
1998	86.7	114.4	113.2	120.0	108.0	101.8	117.2	114.8	120.3	111.6	119.0	121.0	1,348
1999	99.4	115.1	111.0	114.0	99.9	109.2	119.1	113.0	103.9	108.4	106.4	102.2	1,302
2000	91.7	88.1	106.4	97.5	90.9	98.8	91.8	106.6	94.9	93.7	89.4	96.2	1,146
2001	97.7	96.4	104.4	101.6	105.1	100.7	99.9	98.3	102.4	81.4	87.7	74.4	1,150
2002	93.4	132.9	115.0	121.3	109.3	121.6	128.5	130.2	121.5	141.9	115.5	118.6	1,450
2003	136.1	119.9	136.9	126.3	121.7	121.9	119.3	111.6	131.4	124.1	104.9	120.1	1,474
2004[1]	126.8	109.4	136.1	123.7	135.7	160.5	166.9	140.8	125.3	124.6	129.4	129.5	1,609

[1] Preliminary.   *Source: Bureau of the Census, U.S. Department of Commerce*

Production of Crude Tall Oil in the United States   In Millions of Pounds

Year	Oct.	Nov.	Dec.	Jan.	Feb.	Mar.	Apr.	May	June	July	Aug.	Sept.	Total
1996-7	119.2	113.9	114.5	119.9	125.1	125.1	118.5	116.6	116.4	135.0	132.9	130.8	1,337.2
1997-8	122.7	115.4	135.4	137.7	126.6	127.5	132.3	131.2	131.1	132.0	120.2	121.1	1,540.6
1998-9	118.4	113.4	119.3	118.0	115.2	134.6	121.0	103.8	100.7	103.2	103.5	113.6	1,364.8
1999-00	93.8	101.6	107.8	101.3	104.6	115.2	95.4	91.8	99.5	94.5	97.0	86.5	1,202.6
2000-1	92.3	91.6	81.4	94.9	83.7	103.7	99.7	99.9	95.1	94.1	105.4	93.0	1,134.8
2001-2	99.1	100.7	86.5	101.8	93.7	105.5	104.2	96.0	88.5	94.7	103.6	91.4	1,165.6
2002-3	102.5	87.3	101.8	108.7	89.8	111.5	108.3	99.6	91.8	109.2	100.8	97.1	1,208.6
2003-4	102.1	87.9	109.0	113.7	96.1	112.1	102.8	106.8	99.2	94.4	108.9	104.1	1,236.9
2004-5[1]	88.1	93.7	100.6										1,129.5

[1] Preliminary.   *Source: Bureau of the Census, U.S. Department of Commerce*

Stocks of Crude Tall Oil in the United States, on First of Month   In Millions of Pounds

Year	Oct.	Nov.	Dec.	Jan.	Feb.	Mar.	Apr.	May	June	July	Aug.	Sept.
1996-7	172.3	192.1	167.4	182.4	173.0	196.0	200.8	220.6	187.3	237.5	248.5	242.2
1997-8	208.6	187.9	209.7	202.1	202.8	219.4	256.8	254.1	239.1	259.1	278.4	245.2
1998-9	268.7	219.8	200.3	197.5	164.8	156.9	163.3	177.5	183.0	180.7	183.6	152.7
1999-00	146.8	130.9	135.3	121.5	131.8	153.5	136.6	138.5	154.6	130.5	136.7	117.1
2000-1	110.5	102.4	105.4	117.0	118.9	118.2	134.4	139.6	171.7	132.0	160.5	145.4
2001-2	132.7	125.6	142.1	127.9	135.8	155.2	165.6	177.4	190.7	175.4	161.8	155.1
2002-3	160.2	154.1	155.7	160.5	176.0	167.4	156.3	173.4	163.7	180.3	199.3	209.5
2003-4	210.7	207.3	203.0	210.2	209.6	216.3	205.3	207.1	194.1	190.5	196.1	162.2
2004-5[1]	174.1	140.3	124.4	101.2								

[1] Preliminary.   *Source: Bureau of the Census, U.S. Department of Commerce*

Stocks of Refined Tall Oil in the United States, on First of Month   In Millions of Pounds

Year	Oct.	Nov.	Dec.	Jan.	Feb.	Mar.	Apr.	May	June	July	Aug.	Sept.
1996-7	8.3	7.0	7.5	8.9	6.5	26.5	17.4	31.7	20.9	32.0	13.2	16.6
1997-8	32.3	25.6	34.9	21.4	30.4	17.0	14.2	13.0	13.1	15.1	14.7	15.3
1998-9	15.1	14.9	17.0	12.5	14.8	9.9	7.2	7.6	7.2	7.3	6.3	7.0
1999-00	7.5	7.0	8.5	9.1	9.8	11.0	9.8	13.7	10.4	7.8	11.9	8.2
2000-1	9.6	9.0	9.9	10.2	10.7	12.5	11.8	13.9	12.6	19.5	13.4	21.6
2001-2	22.4	17.2	17.1	19.9	20.7	20.9	21.5	22.7	20.9	18.6	18.4	16.0
2002-3	13.3	16.5	18.7	20.1	20.1	18.6	20.4	19.7	15.8	14.5	13.5	13.9
2003-4	13.1	20.1	19.6	19.9	19.2	13.7	14.3	12.7	16.3	14.2	16.6	17.7
2004-5[1]	14.8	16.6	16.9	17.6								

[1] Preliminary.   *Source: Bureau of the Census, U.S. Department of Commerce*

Tallow and Greases

Tallow and grease are derived from processing (rendering) the fat of cattle. Tallow is used to produce both edible and inedible products. Edible tallow products include margarine, cooking oil, and baking products. Inedible tallow products include soap, candles, and lubricants. Production of tallow and greases is directly related to the number of cattle produced. Those countries that are the leading cattle producers are also the largest producers of tallow. The American Fats and Oils Association provides specifications for a variety of different types of tallow and grease, including edible tallow, lard (edible), top white tallow, all beef packer tallow, extra fancy tallow, fancy tallow, bleachable fancy tallow, prime tallow, choice white grease, and yellow grease. The specifications include such characteristics as the melting point, color, density, moisture content, insoluble impurities, and others.

Prices – The monthly average price of tallow (inedible, No. 1 Packers-Prime, delivered Chicago) in 2004 (through October) was unchanged from 2003 at 18.29 cents per pound. That was mildly below the record high of 21.60 cents posted in 1979. The wholesale price of edible tallow in 2004 rose slightly to 20.4 cents per pound from 20.3 cents in 2003, and remained well below the record high of 30.3 cents posted in 1981.

Supply – World production of tallow and greases (edible and inedible) in 2000, the latest available reporting year, fell by –3.2% yr/yr to 8.312 million metric tons from the record high of 8.584 million metric tons posted in 1999. The world's largest producer of tallow and greases by far is the US with 43% of world production, followed by Australia with 6%, Brazil with 6%, Russia with 4%, and Canada with 4%.

U.S. production of edible tallow in 2002 rose +6.8% yr/yr to 1.969 billion pounds, which was a new record high. US production of inedible tallow and greases in 2004 fell by –1.4% yr/yr to 6.161 billion pounds, which was well below the record high of 7.156 billion pounds posted in 2002.

Demand – US consumption of inedible tallow and greases in 2004 rose +4.3% yr/yr to 2.538 billion pounds, of which virtually all went to animal feed. US consumption of edible tallow fell -1.9% yr/yr to 1.482 billion pounds, which was mildly below the record high of 1.593 billion pounds posted in 2000. US per capita consumption of tallow was unchanged at 4.5 pounds per person per year in 2003 from 2002, which was well below the record high of 6.4 pounds posted in 1985.

Trade – US exports of inedible tallow and grease in 2004 rose +15.4% yr/yr to 354 million pounds, and accounted for 5.5% of total US supply. US exports of edible tallow rose +40.4% yr/yr to 511 million pounds, and accounted for 25% of US supply.

World Production of Tallow and Greases (Edible and Inedible)   In Thousands of Metric Tons

Year	Argentina	Australia	Brazil	Canada	France	Germany	Rep. of Korea	Netherlands	New Zealand	Russia	United Kingdom	United States	World Total
1991	285	530	340	193	185	270	85	150	132	386	230	3,180	6,968
1992	268	472	336	212	275	197	121	150	134	352	225	3,309	7,077
1993	260	526	429	209	240	178	115	163	145	706	212	3,650	8,492
1994	250	446	435	213	206	167	120	159	135	437	215	3,851	8,258
1995	248	423	46	217	220	166	118	158	147	377	230	3,756	8,312
1996	240	397	467	242	220	168	198	161	155	400	165	3,581	8,184
1997	265	456	460	250	220	167	209	200	161	340	160	3,467	8,342
1998	220	560	467	265	220	166	235	190	150	340	170	3,694	8,374
1999[1]	235	565	480	285	220	165	230	168	135	330	180	3,855	8,584
2000[2]	230	540	505	290	220	165	230	192	142	310	195	3,562	8,312

[1] Preliminary.   [2] Forecast.   *Source: Foreign Agricultural Service, U.S. Department of Agriculture (FAS-USDA)*

Salient Statistics of Tallow and Greases (Inedible) in the United States   In Millions of Pounds

Year	Supply Production	Supply Stocks, Jan. 1	Supply Total	Exports	Consumption Soap	Consumption Feed	Consumption Total	Wholesale Prices, Cents/Lb. Edible, (Loose) Chicago	Wholesale Prices, Cents/Lb. Inedible, No. 1 Chicago
1995	6,481	350	6,831	2,486	264	2,071	2,334	21.4	19.2
1996	6,242	373	6,615	1,807	245	2,389	2,634	22.0	20.1
1997	6,249	266	6,515	775	245	2,401	2,646	23.5	20.8
1998	6,644	339	6,983	1,041	228	2,533	2,761	19.1	17.5
1999	7,079	437	7,516	877	229	2,847	3,076	15.1	13.0
2000	7,035	405	7,440	791	146	2,727	2,849	11.6	10.0
2001	6,870	347	7,217	616	107	2,834	2,843	13.7	12.0
2002	7,156	327	7,482	384	W	2,886	2,886	14.8	13.5
2003[1]	6,246	240	6,486	307	W	2,434	2,434	20.3	18.3
2004[2]	6,250	282	6,532	347	W	2,535	2,535	19.8	18.0

[1] Preliminary.   [2] Estimate.   *Sources: Economic Research Service, U.S. Department of Agriculture (ERS-USDA); Bureau of the Census, U.S. Department of Commerce*

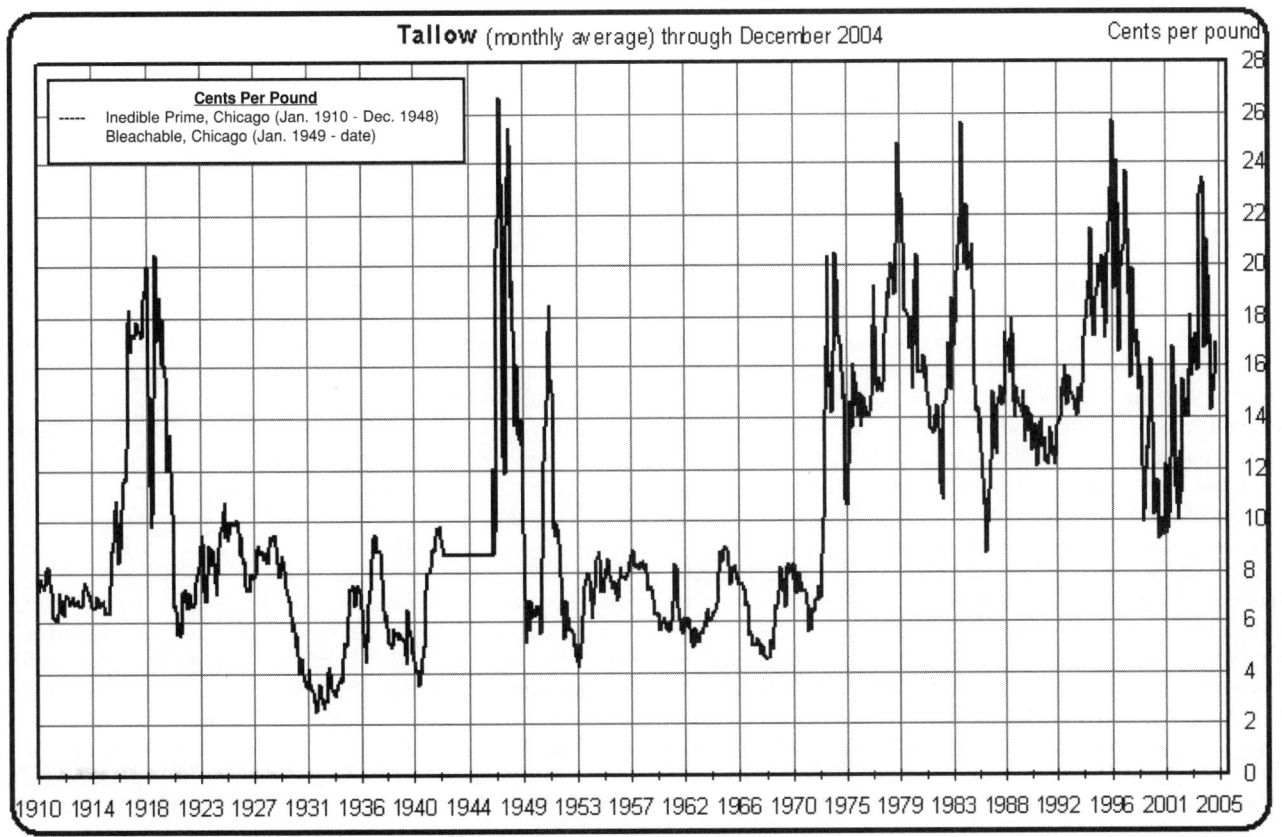

Tallow (monthly average) through December 2004 — Cents per pound

Cents Per Pound
----- Inedible Prime, Chicago (Jan. 1910 - Dec. 1948)
Bleachable, Chicago (Jan. 1949 - date)

Supply and Disappearance of Edible Tallow in the United States   In Millions of Pounds, Rendered Basis

| Year | Supply | | | Disappearance | | | | | Per Capita (Lbs.) |
	Stocks Jan. 1	Production	Total	Domestic	Exports	Total	Diret Use	Baking or Frying Fats	
1993	33	1,425	1,470	1,127	310	1,437	412	404	4.4
1994	33	1,510	1,606	1,275	295	1,570	639	405	4.9
1995	36	1,536	1,590	1,268	279	1,548	533	374	4.9
1996	43	1,520	1,568	1,317	218	1,535	602	320	5.0
1997	33	1,416	1,455	1,223	185	1,408	585	312	4.6
1998	47	1,537	1,586	1,301	246	1,547	868	259	4.8
1999	39	1,729	1,775	1,425	317	1,742	998	262	5.2
2000	33	1,840	1,881	1,593	248	1,841	1,137	283	5.8
2001[1]	40	1,844	1,915	1,511	364	1,875	978	NA	4.5
2002[2]	40	1,969	2,018	1,482	511	1,993	968	NA	4.5

[1] Preliminary.   [2] Forecast.   *Sources: Economic Research Service, U.S. Department of Agriculture (ERS-USDA); Bureau of the Census, U.S. Department of Commerce*

Wholesale Price of Tallow, Inedible, No. 1 Packers (Prime), Delivered, Chicago   In Cents Per Pound

Year	Jan.	Feb.	Mar.	Apr.	May	June	July	Aug.	Sept.	Oct.	Nov.	Dec.	Average
1995	21.75	18.86	18.00	17.75	17.50	17.89	19.61	19.81	19.53	19.46	19.75	20.08	19.17
1996	19.45	17.00	17.03	17.54	19.37	19.50	20.98	22.40	25.98	21.05	19.65	21.63	20.13
1997	23.40	22.88	19.35	17.39	18.09	19.64	19.65	20.10	20.88	22.13	22.88	22.60	20.75
1998	18.20	16.88	17.58	17.70	20.35	19.63	17.31	17.57	16.69	16.98	16.90	16.70	17.71
1999	16.30	12.53	11.18	11.38	10.40	11.49	11.50	11.69	14.38	16.37	14.95	13.88	13.00
2000	11.89	10.14	10.67	10.21	11.60	10.74	9.19	9.48	10.07	10.05	9.35	11.23	10.39
2001	12.17	9.46	9.62	10.26	10.19	12.35	15.44	16.83	13.75	11.24	10.60	12.34	12.02
2002	10.00	10.54	12.64	11.06	11.59	15.47	14.80	14.00	14.23	13.98	15.91	18.08	13.53
2003	17.13	15.65	16.60	16.54	16.48	17.30	16.08	15.85	18.70	22.78	23.37	23.08	18.30
2004[1]	23.23	16.72	17.80	21.05	18.01	18.08	19.55	16.92	17.20	14.33	15.61	16.97	17.96

[1] Preliminary.   *Sources: Economic Research Service, U.S. Department of Agriculture (ERS-USDA)*

Tea

Tea is the common name for a family of mostly woody flowering plants. The tea family contains about 600 species placed in 28 genera and they are distributed throughout the tropical and subtropical areas, with most species occurring in eastern Asia and South America. The tea plant is native to Southeast Asia. There are more than 3,000 varieties of tea, each with its own distinct character, and each is generally named for the area in which it is grown. Tea may have been consumed in China as long ago as 2700 BC and certainly since 1000 BC. In 2737 BC, the Chinese Emperor Shen Nung, according to Chinese mythology, was a scholar and herbalist. While his servant boiled drinking water, a leaf from the wild tea tree he was sitting under dropped into the water and Shen Nung decided to try the brew. Today, half the world's population drinks tea. Tea is the world's most popular beverage next to water.

Tea is a healthful drink and contains antioxidants, fluoride, niacin, folic acid, and as much vitamin C as a lemon. The average 5 oz. cup of brewed tea contains approximately 40 to 60 milligrams of caffeine (compared to 80 to 115 mg in brewed coffee). Decaffeinated tea has been available since the 1980s. Herbal tea contains no true tea leaves but is actually brewed from a collection of herbs and spices.

Tea grows mainly between the tropic of Cancer and the tropic of Capricorn, requiring 40 to 50 inches of rain per year and a temperature ideally between 50 to 86 degrees Fahrenheit. In order to rejuvenate the bush and keep it at a convenient height for the pickers to access, the bushes must be pruned every four to five years. A tea bush can produce tea for 50 to 70 years, but after 50 years, the yield is reduced.

The two key factors in determining different varieties of tea are the production process (sorting, withering, rolling, fermentation, and drying methods) and the growing conditions (geographical region, growing altitude, and soil type). Black tea, often referred to as fully fermented tea, is produced by allowing picked tea leaves to wither and ferment for up to 24 hours. After fermenting, the leaves are fired, which stops oxidation. Green tea, or unfermented tea, is produced by immediately and completely drying the leaves and omitting the oxidization process, thus allowing the tea to remain green in color.

Supply – World production of tea in 2002, the latest full reporting year for the series, rose +4.0% to 3.100 million metric tons, which was a record high. The world's largest producers of tea in 2002 were India (with 25.0% of world production), China (25%), Sri Lanka (10%), Kenya (9%), Turkey (5%), and Indonesia (5%).

Trade – US tea imports in 2003 rose +3.1% to 177,211 metric tons, which was a record high. World tea imports in 2002 rose by +3.7% to 1.436 million metric tons. The world's largest tea importers in 2002 were Russia (with 12% of total world imports), the United Kingdom (11%), Pakistan (7%), and the US (7%). The world's largest exporters in 2002 were Sri Lanka (with 21% of world exports), China (19%), India (13%), Kenya (7%), Indonesia (7%), Vietnam (6%), and Argentina (4%).

World Tea Production, in Major Producing Countries — In Thousands of Metric Tons

Year	Argentina	Bangladesh	China	India	Indonesia	Iran	Japan	Kenya	Malawi	Sri Lanka	Turkey	Ex-USSR[2]	World Total
1996	47.0	48.0	617.0	780.0	166.0	62.0	89.0	257.0	37.0	258.0	115.0	42.0	2,710
1997	54.0	53.0	637.0	811.0	149.0	69.0	91.0	221.0	44.0	277.0	140.0	39.0	2,791
1998	57.0	51.0	688.0	870.0	166.0	60.0	83.0	294.0	40.0	280.0	178.0	52.0	3,040
1999	56.0	56.0	697.0	870.0	161.0	80.0	88.0	249.0	48.0	284.0	178.0	65.0	3,078
2000	53.0	46.0	704.0	835.0	162.0	50.0	85.0	236.0	45.0	306.0	139.0	27.0	2,947
2001	63.0	52.0	722.0	848.0	163.0	51.0	85.0	217.0	37.0	295.0	143.0	25.0	2,980
2002[1]	63.0	52.0	760.0	826.0	163.0	51.0	85.0	287.0	38.0	310.0	150.0	23.0	3,100

[1] Preliminary. [2] Mostly Georgia and Azerbaijan. *Sources: Foreign Agricultural Service, U.S. Department of Agriculture (FAS-USDA); Food and Agriculture Organization of the United Nations (FAO-UN)*

World Tea Exports from Producing Countries — In Metric Tons

Year	Argentina	Bangladesh	Brazil	China	India	Indonesia	Kenya	Malawi	P. New Guinea	Sri Lanka	Vietnam	Zimbabwe	World Total
1996	35,042	20,981	3,891	173,145	138,360	101,532	260,819	36,700	9,300	218,714	20,800	11,540	1,234,708
1997	56,806	21,740	3,404	205,381	191,472	66,843	199,224	39,824	6,500	267,726	32,901	13,057	1,315,534
1998	58,987	25,049	3,208	219,325	201,798	67,219	263,685	40,518	6,600	270,938	33,000	11,076	1,415,223
1999	52,144	21,494	2,914	202,681	177,507	97,847	245,716	30,000	8,200	268,330	37,300	15,722	1,372,179
2000	50,000	11,000	3,714	230,696	200,868	105,581	217,282	69,600	8,500	287,005	55,600	16,916	1,489,215
2001[1]	58,110	6,400	4,082	252,204	177,603	99,797	207,244	32,200	8,800	293,524	67,900	6,162	1,446,783
2002[2]	57,643	3,964	3,979	254,875	181,617	100,185	88,311	36,631	5,200	290,500	74,800	18,855	1,360,111

[1] Preliminary. [2] Estimate. *Source: Food and Agriculture Organization of the United Nations (FAO-UN)*

Imports of Tea in the United States — In Metric Tons

Year	Jan.	Feb.	Mar.	Apr.	May	June	July	Aug.	Sept.	Oct.	Nov.	Dec.	Total
1999	11,017	9,796	14,737	15,041	17,271	17,007	14,794	15,743	9,468	11,935	10,628	10,604	158,040
2000	10,831	13,475	18,217	15,929	19,861	18,367	14,396	13,008	10,725	10,873	11,662	10,611	167,952
2001	14,596	11,917	15,237	16,772	15,802	16,426	16,041	14,415	11,917	14,072	14,548	11,150	172,893
2002	14,785	14,237	16,029	17,326	18,747	15,158	15,189	11,977	9,777	14,384	12,148	12,073	171,829
2003	15,051	13,519	15,651	17,810	18,863	15,089	15,290	13,778	11,240	16,417	11,439	13,054	177,201
2004[1]	15,072	14,737	18,357	19,288	18,810	18,784	16,512	14,114	14,524	13,851	14,867	14,706	193,620

[1] Preliminary. *Source: Foreign Agricultural Service, U.S. Department of Agriculture (FAS-USDA)*

Tin

Tin (symbol Sn) is a silvery-white, lustrous gray metallic element. Tin is soft, pliable and has a highly crystalline structure. When a tin bar is bent or broken, a crackling sound called a "tin cry" is produced due to the breaking of the tin crystals. People have been using tin for at least 5,500 years. Tin has been found in the tombs of ancient Egyptians. In ancient times, tin and lead were considered different forms of the same metal. Tin was exported to Europe in large quantities from Cornwall, England, during the Roman period, from approximately 2100 BC to 1500 BC. Cornwall was one of the world's leading sources of tin for much of its known history and into the late 1800s.

The principal ore of tin is the mineral cassiterite, which is found in Malaya, Bolivia, Indonesia, Thailand, and Nigeria. About 80% of the world's tin deposits occur in unconsolidated placer deposits in riverbeds and valleys, or on the sea floor, with only about 20% occurring as primary hard-rock lodes. Tin deposits are generally small and are almost always found closely allied to the granite from which it originates. Tin is also recovered as a by-product of mining tungsten, tantalum, and lead. After extraction, tin ore is ground and washed to remove impurities, roasted to oxidize the sulfides of iron and copper, washed a second time, and then reduced by carbon in a reverberatory furnace. Electrolysis may also be used to purify tin.

Pure tin, rarely used by itself, was used as currency in the form of tin blocks and was considered legal tender for taxes in Phuket, Thailand, until 1932. Tin is used in the manufacture of coatings for steel containers used to preserve food and beverages. Tin is also used in solder alloys, electroplating, ceramics, and in plastic. The world's major tin research and development laboratory, ITRI Ltd, is funded by companies that produce and consume tin. The focus of the research efforts have been on possible new uses for tin that would take advantage of tin's relative non-toxicity to replace other metals in various products. Some of the replacements could be lead-free solders, antimony-free flame-retardant chemicals, and lead-free shotgun pellets. No tin is currently mined in the U.S.

Tin futures and options trade on the London Metal Exchange (LME). Tin has traded on the LME since 1877 and the standard tin contract began in 1912. The futures contract calls for the delivery of 5 metric tons of tin ingots of at least 99.85% purity. The contract trades in terms of US dollars per metric ton.

Prices – The average monthly price of tin (straights) in 2004 rose sharply by +61.0% to $5.33 per pound, which was the highest yearly price since 1985. The 2004 price of $5.33 was nearly twice the 2-decade low of $2.83 per pound seen as recently as 2002. The average monthly price of ex-dock tin in New York in 2004 rose sharply by +75.8% to $4.07 per pound from 2003, and was more than double the 21-year low of $1.99 per pound posted in 2001.

Supply – World mine production of tin in 2003 fell by 13.3% yr/yr to an 8-year low of 209,000. The world's largest mine producers of tin are Indonesia with 34% of world production in 2003, China with 24%, and Peru with 19%. World smelter production of tin fell -0.4% in 2003 to 279,000 metric tons, which was mildly below the record high of 300.000 million metric tons produced in 2001. The world's largest producers of smelted tin are China with 36% of world production in 2003, Indonesia with 23%, and Malaysia with 7%. The US does not mine tin, and therefore supply consists only of scrap and imports. US tin recovery in 2003 was unchanged at 7,750 metric tons, which was a record low.

Demand – US consumption of tin (pig) in 2004 (through July) rose to an annualized 46,159 metric tons from the 7-year low of 45,840 metric tons posted in 2003. The breakdown of US consumption of tin by finished products in 2003 shows that the largest consuming industry of tin is solder (with 28% of consumption), followed by chemicals (23%), tin plate (21%), and bronze and brass (7%).

Trade – The US relied on imports for 91% of its tin consumption in 2003. US imports of unwrought tin metal in 2003 fell -12.1% to 37,100 metric tons, which was a 7-year low. The largest sources of US imports in 2003 were Bolivia (with 5,720 metric tons of imports), China (4,340 metric tons), Indonesia (3,070 metric tons), and Brazil (3,000 metric tons). US exports of tin in 2003 rose +25.5% to 3,690 metric tons from 2002.

World Mine Production of Tin — In Metric Tons (Contained Tin)

Year	Australia	Bolivia	Brazil	China	Indo-nesia	Malaysia	Nigeria	Peru	Portugal	Russia	Thailand	United Kingdom	World Total
1994	7,495	16,169	16,619	54,100	30,610	6,458	278	20,275	4,332	10,460	3,926	1,922	178,000
1995	8,656	14,419	17,317	61,900	46,058	6,402	357	22,331	4,627	9,000	2,201	1,973	201,000
1996	8,828	14,802	19,617	69,600	52,304	5,174	139	27,004	4,637	8,000	1,300	2,103	220,000
1997	10,169	12,898	19,065	67,500	55,175	5,065	150	27,952	2,667	7,500	746	2,396	217,000
1998	10,204	11,308	14,238	70,100	53,959	5,754	200	49,574	3,100	4,500	1,656	376	231,000
1999	10,011	12,417	13,202	80,100	47,754	7,339	3,300	59,191	2,200	2,500	2,712	----	246,000
2000	9,146	12,464	13,773	99,400	51,629	6,307	2,760	70,901	1,200	2,500	1,930	----	277,000
2001	9,602	12,298	14,200	95,000	61,862	4,972	2,870	69,696	1,200	2,000	1,950	----	281,000
2002[1]	6,268	15,242	14,200	62,000	88,142	4,215	2,800	38,815	1,000	1,300	1,130	----	241,000
2003[2]	6,500	15,000	14,200	50,000	70,000	3,359	2,000	38,800	1,000	2,000	817	----	209,000

[1] Preliminary.   [2] Estimate.   *Source: U.S. Geological Survey (USGS)*

TIN

World Smelter Production of Primary Tin   In Metric Tons

Year	Australia	Bolivia	Brazil	China	Indo-nesia	Japan	Malaysia	Mexico	Russia	South Africa	Spain	Thailand	World Total
1994	315	15,285	20,400	67,800	31,100	706	37,990	768	11,500	43	500	7,759	216,000
1995	570	17,709	16,787	67,700	38,628	630	39,433	770	9,500	----	500	8,243	223,000
1996	460	16,733	18,361	71,500	39,000	524	38,051	1,234	9,000	----	150	10,981	211,000
1997	605	16,853	17,525	67,700	52,658	507	34,822	1,188	6,700	----	150	11,986	241,000
1998	655	11,102	14,900	79,300	53,401	500	27,201	1,078	3,000	----	100	15,353	247,000
1999	600	11,166	12,787	90,800	49,105	568	28,913	1,262	4,500	----	50	17,306	267,000
2000	775	9,353	13,825	112,000	46,432	593	26,228	1,204	4,800	----	----	17,076	288,000
2001	1,171	11,292	13,800	105,000	53,470	668	30,417	1,789	4,569	----	----	22,387	300,000
2002	611	10,976	11,675	82,000	67,455	659	30,887	1,756	4,615	----	----	17,548	280,000
2003[1]	600	11,000	11,700	100,000	65,000	662	18,000	1,800	5,500	----	----	12,000	279,000

[1] Preliminary.   Source: U.S. Geological Survey (USGS)

United States Foreign Trade of Tin   In Metric Tons

		Concentrates[2] (Ore)			Imports for Consumption								
								Unwrought Tin Metal					
Year	Exports (Metal)	Total All Ore	Bolivia	Peru	Total All Metal	Bolivia	Brazil	China	Indo-nesia	Malaysia	Singa-pore	Thailand	United Kingdom
1994	2,560	-----	-----	-----	32,400	7,260	9,990	3,230	6,620	1,390	142	-----	666
1995	2,790	-----	-----	-----	33,200	6,630	8,070	5,610	7,230	3,810	40	-----	97
1996	3,670	-----	-----	-----	30,200	6,290	9,460	2,760	7,550	965	120	-----	243
1997	4,660	57	-----	-----	40,600	6,680	8,610	4,710	7,610	1,640	120	600	20
1998	5,020	-----	-----	-----	44,000	5,160	4,710	9,870	7,880	1,870	822	540	790
1999	6,770	-----	-----	-----	47,500	3,850	4,700	13,900	7,930	944	60	20	60
2000	6,640	-----	-----	-----	44,900	6,330	5,860	10,200	5,320	214	20	-----	514
2001	4,350	-----	-----	-----	37,500	6,040	5,510	6,360	3,880	674	145	-----	118
2002	2,940	-----	-----	-----	42,200	6,150	4,840	7,600	3,340	122	-----	-----	2
2003[1]	3,690	-----	-----	-----	37,100	5,720	3,000	4,340	3,070	490	-----	-----	143

[1] Preliminary.   [2] Tin content.   Source: U.S. Geological Survey (USGS)

Consumption (Total) of Tin (Pig) in the United States   In Metric Tons

Year	Jan.	Feb.	Mar.	Apr.	May	June	July	Aug.	Sept.	Oct.	Nov.	Dec.	Total
1995	3,500	3,600	3,680	3,726	3,877	3,833	3,544	3,895	3,825	3,823	3,735	3,770	44,808
1996	3,862	3,938	3,940	3,878	3,894	3,976	3,926	3,996	3,687	3,779	3,908	3,730	48,800
1997	4,953	4,025	4,023	4,067	3,999	4,079	3,936	3,912	4,050	4,098	3,964	4,250	44,350
1998	4,410	4,493	4,445	4,508	4,388	4,483	4,273	4,300	4,404	4,402	4,348	4,268	52,720
1999	4,660	4,667	4,790	4,790	4,760	4,700	4,254	4,396	4,340	4,316	4,275	4,227	55,100
2000	4,362	4,466	4,430	4,377	4,466	4,470	4,398	4,476	4,397	4,460	4,244	4,157	47,040
2001	4,252	4,185	4,095	4,141	4,148	4,128	4,055	4,163	4,153	4,197	4,129	3,974	49,620
2002	3,965	3,866	3,868	3,819	4,087	3,887	3,887	3,842	3,835	3,966	3,822	3,811	46,655
2003	3,814	3,808	3,851	3,891	3,701	3,814	3,841	3,850	3,803	3,816	3,764	3,887	45,840
2004[1]	3,851	3,632	3,887	3,837	3,874	4,001	3,844	3,871	3,850	3,870	3,927		46,303

[1] Preliminary.   Source: U.S. Geological Survey (USGS)

Tin Stocks (Pig-Industrial) in the United States, on First of Month   In Metric Tons

Year	Jan.	Feb.	Mar.	Apr.	May	June	July	Aug.	Sept.	Oct.	Nov.	Dec.
1995	2,741	3,931	3,850	2,780	3,000	3,080	3,210	3,910	3,800	3,880	4,380	4,290
1996	4,580	6,000	5,200	4,390	4,880	5,590	5,760	5,640	4,790	4,580	4,810	6,810
1997	4,670	5,100	5,610	5,600	5,070	5,270	5,180	5,650	5,590	5,420	5,290	5,590
1998	6,100	5,570	5,390	5,840	6,170	5,940	5,830	5,580	6,660	6,270	5,880	5,710
1999	5,620	8,120	7,770	7,760	7,760	7,510	7,750	7,560	7,870	7,790	8,390	8,800
2000	8,300	8,330	7,960	7,580	7,810	7,930	8,090	8,240	7,820	8,210	7,200	7,970
2001	8,140	8,330	8,360	8,460	8,270	8,640	8,760	8,760	8,920	9,030	7,630	7,470
2002	7,700	7,320	7,020	6,990	6,870	6,600	6,540	6,590	6,670	7,130	6,880	6,950
2003	7,280	6,980	6,690	6,640	6,390	6,400	6,380	6,420	6,250	6,180	6,190	6,340
2004[1]	6,520	6,010	6,130	6,280	5,850	6,000	5,900	6,290	6,110	6,030	5,900	6,350

[1] Preliminary.   Source: U.S. Geological Survey (USGS)

Average Price of Ex-Dock Tin in New York[1]   In Cents Per Pound

Year	Jan.	Feb.	Mar.	Apr.	May	June	July	Aug.	Sept.	Oct.	Nov.	Dec.	Average
1995	374.77	260.25	266.45	288.00	283.62	314.33	316.06	331.64	304.12	297.77	304.47	300.28	303.48
1996	299.55	297.45	296.68	308.49	306.71	296.20	298.47	291.30	292.13	285.11	285.87	280.61	294.88
1997	281.91	281.34	281.51	274.36	274.23	267.31	261.03	259.85	262.56	266.77	268.33	262.61	270.15
1998	249.39	252.65	262.36	271.65	279.50	284.27	268.87	270.98	260.79	259.17	261.82	251.75	264.43
1999	244.46	251.04	255.13	256.97	269.42	253.64	251.09	251.32	256.38	260.70	278.24	274.51	258.73
2000	283.63	271.70	263.42	259.59	259.70	260.16	257.77	255.92	262.54	254.56	253.64	252.19	261.24
2001	249.32	246.91	243.14	238.33	238.53	231.14	210.17	188.42	179.53	181.38	194.77	195.90	216.46
2002	189.23	183.23	187.65	195.36	201.95	208.01	211.51	188.36	193.79	206.67	205.94	206.63	199.15
2003	201.53	217.98	219.58	217.90	225.40	223.69	225.81	229.58	233.59	248.22	252.93	285.40	231.80
2004	305.34	313.55	357.66	418.57	449.29	438.72	439.24	437.68	438.91	436.80	439.24	414.16	407.43

Source: American Metal Market (AMM)

Average Price of Tin (Straights) in New York   In Cents Per Pound

Year	Jan.	Feb.	Mar.	Apr.	May	June	July	Aug.	Sept.	Oct.	Nov.	Dec.	Average
1995	415.05	379.08	378.61	395.99	399.17	433.75	438.04	458.66	423.71	417.23	425.41	419.75	415.37
1996	418.68	415.65	414.71	429.34	427.24	413.65	416.63	409.12	407.79	400.25	400.65	394.46	412.35
1997	396.18	395.50	395.64	386.52	386.58	377.83	369.97	369.01	372.45	377.39	378.00	371.35	381.37
1998	356.97	359.76	370.96	381.99	392.16	397.36	377.72	380.02	368.89	366.87	370.49	357.69	373.41
1999	348.77	356.50	361.11	363.01	372.62	359.05	359.96	357.35	366.06	370.68	392.04	288.77	357.99
2000	400.90	384.13	372.50	368.42	370.13	370.81	366.49	364.65	375.25	363.54	362.94	360.68	371.70
2001	356.37	352.87	348.19	341.59	340.61	329.68	302.57	276.55	263.17	264.88	281.23	279.46	311.43
2002	271.59	263.91	270.54	280.98	288.74	296.02	299.39	269.30	277.60	293.79	292.40	292.95	283.10
2003	304.44	312.32	314.52	312.26	321.92	319.67	322.10	327.16	332.21	350.90	356.46	396.46	330.87
2004	422.33	433.50	485.99	557.29	575.39	570.99	565.68	568.14	572.72	573.79	577.07	550.97	537.82

Source: U.S. Geological Survey (USGS)

281

Tin Plate Production & Tin Recovered in the United States   In Metric Tons

	------ Tin Content of Tinplate Produced ------				----------------------------- Tin Recovered from Scrap by Form of Recovery -----------------------------								
	-------- Tinplate (All Forms) --------												
	Tinplate Waste		Tin Content	Tin Per Tonne of Plate	Tin	Bronze		Type		Anti-monial	Chemical Com-		Grand
Year	---- Gross Weight ----		(Tonne)	(Kilograms)	Metal	& Brass	Solder	Metal	Babbitt	Lead	pounds	Misc.[2]	Total
1994	188,921	1,528,303	9,396	6.1	NA	NA	NA	NA	NA	NA	NA	NA	NA
1995	205,000	1,660,000	9,600	5.8	W	11,200	W	39	W	335	W	W	11,600
1996	181,100	1,551,000	9,617	6.2	W	11,400	W	37	34	171	W	W	11,600
1997	157,000	2,010,000	9,300	4.6	W	12,200	W	W	W	149	W	W	12,300
1998	W	1,700,000	8,900	5.2	NA	NA	NA	NA	NA	NA	NA	NA	NA
1999	W	1,750,000	9,080	5.2	NA	NA	NA	NA	NA	NA	NA	NA	NA
2000	119,000	1,320,000	8,800	6.7	NA	NA	NA	NA	NA	NA	NA	NA	NA
2001	97,800	2,000,000	7,800	3.9	NA	NA	NA	NA	NA	NA	NA	NA	NA
2002	45,900	2,450,000	7,750	3.2	NA	NA	NA	NA	NA	NA	NA	NA	NA
2003[1]	W	2,500,000	7,750	3.1	NA	NA	NA	NA	NA	NA	NA	NA	NA

[1] Preliminary.   [2] Includes foil, terne metal, cable lead, and items indicated by symbol W.   W = Withheld Proprietary data.
Source: U.S. Geological Survey (USGS)

Consumption of Primary and Secondary Tin in the United States   In Metric Tons

| | Net Import Reliance as a % of Apparent | Industry Stocks | -------------------------- Net Receipts -------------------------- | | | | Available | Stocks Dec. 31 (Total Available Less Total | Total | Consumed in Manu-facturing |
Year	Consumption	Jan. 1[2]	Primary	Secondary	Scrap	Total	Supply	Processed)	Processed	Products
1994	83	9,540	35,400	4,210	4,940	44,500	54,100	11,600	42,500	42,200
1995	84	8,480	39,400	5,020	6,240	50,600	59,100	13,000	46,100	46,000
1996	83	9,300	39,200	2,750	6,140	48,100	57,300	12,500	44,900	44,700
1997	85	9,180	39,000	2,360	6,010	47,300	56,500	11,900	44,600	44,400
1998	85	9,280	39,900	2,490	6,240	48,600	57,900	12,000	45,800	45,700
1999	85	9,290	40,500	2,790	6,360	49,700	58,900	11,900	47,000	46,900
2000	86	8,910	41,400	2,990	6,050	50,400	59,300	12,200	47,100	47,000
2001	88	8,830	34,500	2,180	4,770	41,400	50,200	8,220	42,000	41,900
2002	79	8,500	34,200	1,610	4,230	40,100	48,600	8,550	40,000	39,800
2003[1]	91	7,940	32,400	1,370	3,420	37,200	45,200	7,540	37,600	37,400

[1] Preliminary.   [2] Includes tin in transit in the U.S.   *Source: U.S. Geological Survey (USGS)*

Consumption of Tin in the United States, by Finished Products   In Metric Tons (Contained Tin)

Year	Tinplate[2]	Solder	Babbitt	Bronze & Brass	Tinning	Chem-icals[3]	Tin Powder	Bar Tin & Anodes	White Metal	Other	Total	Primary	Secondary
1994	9,480	15,100	831	3,080	1,230	5,740	625	1,190	992	3,990	42,200	33,700	8,530
1995	9,670	17,700	871	2,830	1,110	7,060	W	1,200	965	4,550	46,000	35,200	10,800
1996	9,340	15,600	851	2,760	2,050	7,520	573	1,150	1,340	3,230	44,700	36,500	8,180
1997	9,350	15,900	909	3,160	1,210	8,170	W	684	754	3,980	44,400	36,200	8,250
1998	8,900	16,900	1,020	3,610	1,100	8,180	W	704	778	4,260	45,700	37,100	8,620
1999	9,150	18,700	1,610	3,410	905	8,220	W	721	943	3,220	46,900	38,000	8,890
2000	8,800	18,800	1,660	3,360	1,200	8,040	W	714	1,260	3,210	47,000	38,100	8,940
2001	7,800	17,000	770	3,430	1,070	7,590	W	570	1,390	2,230	41,900	34,200	7,630
2002	7,750	13,800	1,310	3,040	679	8,400	W	617	1,320	2,920	39,800	34,000	5,830
2003[1]	7,790	10,600	2,570	2,600	833	8,720	W	849	1,220	2,180	37,400	32,900	4,490

[1] Preliminary.   [2] Includes small quantity of secondary pig tin and tin acquired in chemicals.   [3] Including tin oxide.   W = Withheld proprietary data.
Source: U.S. Geological Survey (USGS)

Titanium

Titanium (symbol Ti) is a silver-white, metallic element used primarily to make light, strong alloys. It ranks ninth in abundance among the elements in the crust of the earth but is never found in the pure state. It occurs as an oxide in various minerals. It was first discovered in 1791 by Rev. William Gregor and was first isolated as a basic element in 1910. Titanium was named after the mythological Greek god Titan for its strength.

Titanium is extremely brittle when cold, but is malleable and ductile at a low red heat, and thus easily fabricated. Due to its strength, low weight, and resistance to corrosion, titanium is used in metallic alloys and as a substitute for aluminum. It is used extensively in the aerospace industry, in desalinization plants, construction, medical implants, paints, pigments, and lacquers.

Prices – The price of the mineral ilmenite, a primary source of titanium, traded in the range of $80-100 per metric ton in 2003 versus $85-100 in 2002. The price of titanium metal sponge traded in the range of $2.72-3.95 per pound in 2003 versus $3.64 in 2002. The price of titanium dioxide pigments (Anatase) traded in the range of 85-90 cents per pound in 2003 versus 85-95 cents per pound in 2002.

Supply – World production of titanium ilmenite concentrates in 2003 rose +6.1% to 5.910 million metric tons, which was a record high. The world's largest producers of titanium ilmenite concentrates are Australia with 35% of world production in 2003, China with 14%, Norway with 14%, Ukraine with 11%, and India with 9%.

World production of titanium rutile concentrates in 2003 fell -8.6% yr/yr to 374,000 metric tons, which was well below the record high of 545,000 metric tons seen in 1994. The world's largest producers are Australia with 36% of world production in 2003, followed by South Africa with 32% and the Ukraine with 16%.

Demand – US consumption of titanium dioxide pigment in 2003 fell -3.6% yr/yr to 1.070 million metric tons, which was a 7-year low. US consumption of ilmenite in 2003 was unchanged at 1.300 million metric tons, which was a 5-year high. US consumption of rutile in 2003 rose +0.4% yr/yr to 489,000 metric tons, recovering further from the 5-year low of 483,000 metric tons seen in 2001.

Trade – US imports of titanium dioxide pigment in 2003 rose +3.9% to a new record high of 240,000 metric tons. US imports of ilmenite in 2003 fell -4.3% yr/yr to 10-year low of 804,000 metric tons. US imports of rutile in 2003 rose +9.5% yr/yr to 427,000 metric tons, recovering further from the 7-year low of 325,000 metric tons in 2001.

Average Prices of Titanium in the United States

Year	Ilmenite F.O.B. Australian Ports	Slag, 85% TiO2 F.O.B. Richards Bay, South Africa	Rutile Large Lots Bulk, F.O.B. U.S. East Coast	Rutile Bagged F.O.B. Australian Ports	Average Price of Grade A Titanium Sponge, F.O.B. Shipping Point	Titanium Metal Sponge	Titanium Dioxide Pigments, F.O.B. U.S. Plants	
	---- Dollars Per Metric Ton ----				---- Dollars Per Pound ----			
1994	74-80	334	410-430	450-480	3.96	3.75-4.25	.94-.96	.92-.94
1995	81-85	349	550-650	650-800	4.06	4.25-4.50	.92-.96	.99-1.03
1996	82-92	353	525-600	700-800	----	4.25-4.50	1.06-1.08	1.08-1.10
1997	68-81	391	500-550	650-710	----	4.25-4.50	1.01-1.03	1.04-1.06
1998	72-77	386	470-530	570-620	----	4.25-4.50	.96-.98	.97-.99
1999	90-103	406	435-510	500-530	----	3.70-4.80	.92-.94	.99-1.02
2000	83-105	425	470-500	480-570	----	3.95	.92-.94	.99-1.02
2001	90-110	419	450-500	475-565	----	3.58	.92-.94	1.00-1.09
2002[1]	85-100	445	430-470	400-540	----	3.64	.85-.95	.85-.95
2003[2]	80-100	401	415-445	430-540	----	2.72-3.95	.85-.95	.85-.90

[1] Preliminary. [2] Estimate. NA = Not available. *Source: U.S. Geological Survey (USGS)*

Salient Statistics of Titanium in the United States   In Metric Tons

Year	Titanium Dioxide Pigment Production	Imports[3]	Apparent Consumption	Ilmenite Imports[3]	Ilmenite Consumption	Titanium Slag Imports[3]	Titanium Slag Consumption	Rutile[4] Imports[3]	Rutile Consumption	Ores & Concentrates	Scrap	Dioxide & Pigments	Ingots, Billets, Etc.
1994	1,250,000	176,000	1,090,000	808,000	W	472,000	583,000	332,000	510,000	19,000	4,120	313,000	1,559
1995	1,250,000	183,000	1,130,000	861,000	1,410,000	388,000	582,000	318,000	480,000	32,300	3,420	306,000	2,560
1996	1,230,000	167,000	1,070,000	939,000	1,400,000	421,000	----	324,000	398,000	15,500	3,410	292,000	3,130
1997	1,340,000	194,000	1,130,000	952,000	1,520,000	430,000	----	336,000	489,000	23,800	5,500	362,000	3,860
1998	1,330,000	200,000	1,140,000	1,010,000	1,300,000	626,000	----	387,000	421,000	59,700	7,010	356,000	3,780
1999	1,350,000	225,000	1,160,000	1,070,000	1,280,000	678,000	----	344,000	494,000	9,380	8,130	344,000	3,390
2000	1,400,000	218,000	1,150,000	918,000	1,250,000	533,000	----	438,000	537,000	18,900	5,060	423,000	2,980
2001	1,330,000	209,000	1,100,000	1,060,000	1,180,000	594,000	----	325,000	483,000	7,800	7,500	349,000	3,260
2002[1]	1,410,000	231,000	1,110,000	840,000	1,300,000	445,000	----	390,000	487,000	3,810	6,000	485,000	3,460
2003[2]	1,420,000	240,000	1,070,000	804,000	1,300,000	409,000	----	427,000	489,000	10,300	5,320	518,000	3,960

[1] Preliminary. [2] Estimate. [3] For consumption. [4] Natural and synthetic. W = Withheld proprietary data. *Source: U.S. Geological Survey (USGS)*

TITANIUM

World Production of Titanium Illmenite Concentrates   In Thousands of Metric Tons

Year	Australia[2]	Brazil	China	Egypt	India	Malaysia	Norway	Ukraine	United States	Vietnam	World Total	-- Titaniferous Slag[3] -- Canada	South Africa
1994	1,817	97	155	----	300	117	826	530	W	32	3,970	764	744
1995	2,011	102	160	----	290	152	833	359	W	50	4,010	815	990
1996	2,061	98	165	124	330	245	747	500	W	50	4,380	825	1,000
1997	2,265	97	170	125	332	168	750	500	W	50	4,470	850	1,100
1998	2,433	103	175	125	378	125	590	507	W	80	4,560	950	1,100
1999	2,008	96	180	130	378	128	600	537	W	91	4,150	950	1,168
2000	2,173	123	250	125	380	125	750	577	400	174	5,080	950	1,057
2001	2,047	111	300	125	430	130	750	650	500	180	4,220	950	1,090
2002	1,956	174	750	125	460	106	750	670	400	180	5,570	900	1,150
2003[1]	2,067	180	800	125	500	95	800	670	500	180	5,910	875	1,100

[1] Preliminary.   [2] Includes leucoxene.   [3] Approximately 10% of total production is ilmenite. Beginning in 1988, 25% of Norway's ilmenite production was used to produce slag containing 75% TiO2.   W = Withheld proprietary data.   *Source: U.S. Geological Survey (USGS)*

World Production of Titanium Rutile Concentrates   In Metric Tons

Year	Australia	Brazil	India	Sierre Leone	South Africa	Sri Lanka	Thailand	Ukraine	World Total
1994	233,000	1,911	14,000	137,000	78,000	2,410	49	80,000	545,000
1995	195,000	1,985	14,000	----	90,000	2,697	----	112,000	416,000
1996	180,000	2,018	15,000	----	115,000	3,532	----	50,000	366,000
1997	233,000	1,742	14,000	----	123,000	2,970	----	50,000	425,000
1998	238,000	1,800	16,000	----	130,000	1,930	----	50,000	438,000
1999	179,000	4,300	16,000	----	100,000	----	----	49,000	348,000
2000	208,000	3,162	17,000	----	100,000	----	----	58,600	387,000
2001	206,000	1,791	19,000	----	90,000	----	----	60,000	377,000
2002	218,000	2,645	18,000	----	100,000	----	----	70,000	409,000
2003[1]	173,000	2,650	18,000	----	120,000	----	----	60,000	374,000

[1] Preliminary.   NA = Not available.   *Source: U.S. Geological Survey (USGS)*

World Production of Titanium Sponge Metal & U.S. Consumption of Titanium Concentrates

Year	Production of Titanium (In Metric Tons) Sponge Metal[2] China	Japan	Russia	United Kingdom	United States	Total	-- U.S. Consumption of Titanium Concentrates, by Products (In Metric Tons) -- Ilmenite (TiO$_2$ Content) Pigments	Misc.	Total	Rutile (TiO$_2$ Content) Welding Rod Coatings	Pigments	Misc.	Total
1994	2,000	14,400	12,000	----	29,510	33,000	W	637	W	W	460,000	18,500	478,500
1995	2,000	16,000	12,000	----	W	35,000	1,010,000	[3]	1,010,000	W	417,000	22,300	439,300
1996	2,000	21,100	18,000	----	W	51,000	1,010,000	[3]	1,010,000	W	341,000	24,200	365,000
1997	2,000	24,100	20,000	----	W	58,000	1,410,000	[3]	1,410,000	W	406,000	27,600	434,000
1998	----	----	----	----	----	----	1,290,000	14,000	1,300,000	W	384,000	37,300	421,000
1999	----	----	----	----	----	----	1,270,000	13,400	1,280,000	----	469,000	25,800	494,000
2000	----	----	----	----	----	----	1,240,000	13,900	1,250,000	----	513,000	24,100	537,000
2001	----	----	----	----	----	----	1,160,000	15,400	1,180,000	----	455,000	28,500	483,000
2002	----	----	----	----	----	----	1,280,000	16,000	1,300,000	----	464,000	22,900	487,000
2003[1]	----	----	----	----	----	----	1,280,000	16,700	1,300,000	----	466,000	22,500	489,000

[1] Preliminary.   [2] Unconsolidated metal in various forms.   [3] Included in Pigments.   NA = Not available.   W = Withheld proprietary data.
Source: U.S. Geological Survey (USGS)

284

Tobacco

Tobacco is a member of the nightshade family. It is commercially grown for its leaves and stems, which are rolled into cigars, shredded for use in cigarettes and pipes, processed for chewing, or ground into snuff. Christopher Columbus introduced tobacco cultivation and use to Spain after observing natives from the Americas smoking loosely rolled tobacco-stuffed tobacco leaves.

Tobacco is cured, or dried, after harvesting and then aged to improve its flavor. The four common methods of curing are: air cured, fire cured, sun cured, and flue cured. Flue curing is the fastest method of curing and requires only about a week compared with up to 10 weeks for other methods. Cured tobacco is tied into small bundles of about 20 leaves and aged one to three years.

Virginia tobacco is by far the most popular type used in pipe tobacco since it is the mildest of all blending tobaccos. Approximately 60% of the US tobacco crop is from Virginia. Burley tobacco is the next most popular tobacco. It is air-cured, burns slowly and provides a relatively cool smoke. Other tobacco varieties include Perique, Kentucky, Oriental, and Latakia.

Prices – Tobacco prices (Types 11-37) half way through the 2004/05 marketing year (July-June) rallied to an average of $1.89 per pound from $1.77 in 2003/04. That is just below the record high of $1.90 posted in 2001/02.

Supply – World production of tobacco in 2004 rose by +6.7% yr/yr to 6.648 million metric tons, rebounding upward from the 18-year low of 6.232 million metric tons seen in 2003. The world's largest producers of tobacco are China with 36% of world production, followed at a distance by Brazil (with 13% of world production), India (10%), and the US (6%). US production in 2004 rose by +5.4% yr/yr to 397,347 metric tons, where it was down by roughly half from the 2-decade high of 810,154 metric tons posted in 1997.

Tobacco in the US is primarily grown in the Mid-Atlantic States, which account for the vast majority of US production. Specifically, the largest tobacco producing states in the US are North Carolina (with 40% of US production in 2004), Kentucky (26%), Tennessee (8%), South Carolina (7%), and Georgia (5%).

Flue-cured tobacco (type 11-14) is the most popular tobacco type grown in the US and US production in 2004 rose sharply by +12.0% to 511.700 million pounds from 2003. The second most popular type is burley tobacco (type 31), which saw US production in 2004 rise +7.0% to 301.450 million pounds.

US production of tobacco in 2004 rose +10.0% to 883 million pounds, which is half of the 2-decade high of 1.787 billion pounds posted in 1997. US farmers have sharply reduced the planting acreage for tobacco. Harvested tobacco acreage rose slightly by +0.6% to 413,600 acres, but that was only slightly above the record low of 411,200 acres harvested in 2003, and was far below the 22-year high of 836,200 posted in 1997. Yields have been fairly constant and have averaged about 2,100 pounds per acre in the past 10 years. The farm value of the US tobacco crop in 2003 fell by -6.7% to $1.574 billion, which was the lowest crop value since 1973.

US marketings of flue-cured tobacco (Types 11-14) in the 2004-05 marketing year rose by +0.8% yr/yr to 511.7 million pounds. US marketings of burley tobacco (Type 31) in the 2004-05 marketing year rose by +11.0% yr/yr to 301.5 million pounds, and was down by more than half from the 11-year high of 628.2 million pounds posted in 1997-98.

US production of cigarettes in 2004 fell by –1.0% to 495.0 billion cigarettes, which was down sharply from the record high of 754.5 million posted in 1996. US production of cigars rose by +5.2% yr/yr to 4.017 billion in 2003, which was the highest level since 1977. US production of chewing tobacco in 2004 fell by -6.5% to 40.5 million pounds, which was a record low.

Demand – US per capita consumption of tobacco products in 2004 fell by -0.8% to a record low of 3.89 pounds per person per year. That is less than half of the record high of 9.68 pounds, which occurred at the beginning of the series in 1970. Per capita cigarette consumption in 2004 fell -2.5% to 1,791 cigarettes per person per year, which was a record low. Per capita consumption of cigars in 2004 fell -6.8% to 37.51 cigars per person per year, which was well below the 2-decade high of 40.5 cigars posted in 2002. Per capita consumption of loose smoking tobacco in 2004 fell -9.1% yr/yr to a record low of 0.10 pounds.

Trade – US tobacco exports in 2004 rose +3.5% yr/yr to 354.0 million pounds, rebounding further from the record low of 325.8.8 million pounds seen in 2002. Meanwhile, US tobacco imports in 2004 fell –10.9% yr/yr to 561.7 million pounds from the 11-year high of 630.1 million pounds see in 2003. The US exported 125.0 billion cigarettes and 190 million cigars in 2004.

World Production of Leaf Tobacco   In Metric Tons

Year	Brazil	Canada	China	Greece	India	Indo-nesia	Italy	Japan	Pakistan	Turkey	United States	Zim-babwe	World Total
1995	398,000	79,287	2,404,700	131,875	587,100	171,400	124,492	78,212	80,917	204,900	575,380	209,042	6,452,451
1996	439,000	65,320	3,234,000	131,000	562,750	177,000	130,590	66,031	80,760	229,400	688,258	207,767	7,467,560
1997	576,600	71,110	3,234,000	132,450	623,700	17,500	140,634	68,504	86,279	310,850	810,154	192,144	7,882,078
1998	447,000	69,300	2,365,000	132,200	633,200	148,980	132,030	63,959	92,728	260,750	671,257	223,977	7,214,471
1999	595,000	64,864	2,469,300	129,700	648,600	156,882	130,762	64,727	103,430	250,484	586,355	198,967	7,263,347
2000	589,000	48,271	2,552,000	126,700	661,600	185,121	129,937	60,803	104,096	250,495	453,600	245,214	7,240,343
2001	542,400	53,112	2,349,627	126,000	585,600	172,200	131,761	60,565	82,854	207,261	449,510	207,253	6,769,761
2002	674,000	49,015	2,447,000	123,000	650,000	170,000	125,811	58,174	92,880	151,722	398,707	169,844	6,620,190
2003[1]	636,700	42,683	2,257,000	124,000	660,000	169,000	122,235	50,662	86,411	163,482	376,935	84,022	6,231,737
2004[2]	890,500	39,870	2,369,100	124,000	665,000	169,000	120,900	50,000	95,600	153,750	397,347	60,750	6,648,077

[1] Preliminary.   [2] Estimate.   *Source: Foreign Agricultural Service, U.S. Department of Agriculture (FAS-USDA)*

TOBACCO

Production and Consumption of Tobacco Products in the United States

| | Cigar-ettes | Cigars[3] | \-\-\-\- Chewing Tobacco \-\-\-\- | | | | Smoking Tobacco | Snuff[4] | Cigar-ettes | Cigars[3] | Cigar-ettes | Cigars[3] | Smoking Tobacco | Chewing Tobacco | Total Products |
| | | | Plug | Twist | Loose-leaf | Total | | | | | | | | | |
Year	- Billions -	- Millions -	\-\-\- In Millions of Pounds \-\-\-						\-\- Number \-\-		In Pounds				
1995	746.5	2,040	4.1	1.1	57.4	62.6	12.2	60.2	2,505	27.5	4.22	.45	.13	.67	4.67
1996	754.5	2,413	3.9	1.1	56.0	61.1	12.0	61.5	2,482	32.7	4.20	.54	.12	.43	4.70
1997	719.6	2,324	3.5	1.0	53.7	58.1	11.4	64.3	2,423	36.9	4.10	.61	.12	.41	4.55
1998	679.7	2,751	3.1	1.0	49.2	53.3	11.7	65.5	2,320	38.0	3.70	.62	.12	.37	4.49
1999	606.6	2,938	2.8	0.9	47.2	50.9	14.7	67.0	2,136	39.5	3.60	.65	.14	.35	4.32
2000	594.6	2,825	2.6	0.8	46.0	49.4	13.6	69.5	2,092	38.1	3.50	.63	.15	.33	4.14
2001	562.4	3,743	2.4	0.8	43.9	47.0	12.7	70.9	2,026	40.5	3.40	.66	.15	.31	4.11
2002	532.0	3,819	2.2	0.8	41.5	44.5	15.5	72.7	1,979	40.1	3.50	.66	.15	.29	4.23
2003[1]	500.0	4,017	1.8	0.7	40.8	43.3	17.8	75.6	1,837	40.3	3.20	.53	.11	.25	3.92
2004[2]	495.0	NA	1.7	0.7	38.2	40.5	16.7	79.5	1,791	37.5	3.20	.62	.10	.24	3.89

[1] Preliminary. [2] Estimate. [3] Large cigars and cigarillos. [4] Includes loose-leaf. [5] Consumption of tax-paid tobacco products. Unstemmed processing weight. [6] 18 years and older. Source: Economic Research Service, U.S. Department of Agriculture (ERS)

Production of Tobacco in the United States, by States   In Thousands of Pounds

Year	Florida	Georgia	Indiana	Kentucky	Mary-land	North Carolina	Ohio	Penn-sylvania	South Carolina	Tenn-essee	Virginia	Wis-consin	Total
1995	17,676	84,000	13,601	328,581	11,475	484,599	15,015	15,685	105,000	92,907	81,269	6,220	1,268,538
1996	20,100	113,620	14,972	395,542	10,000	585,542	12,640	16,817	117,810	109,888	103,543	5,162	1,518,704
1997	19,053	89,225	18,690	497,928	12,000	731,199	22,230	17,020	126,360	114,292	117,576	5,690	1,787,399
1998	17,102	90,200	17,000	443,628	9,100	551,730	17,934	15,720	92,250	111,100	95,898	4,230	1,479,867
1999	15,312	64,020	11,700	408,492	9,100	448,980	17,052	11,170	78,000	122,601	88,855	2,818	1,292,692
2000	11,475	68,820	7,980	283,065	8,265	406,500	13,200	10,170	81,260	95,958	56,613	2,255	1,052,999
2001	11,700	64,206	9,450	254,653	3,300	386,920	11,956	6,166	78,400	86,893	63,415	3,619	991,223
2002	11,960	53,000	7,800	222,991	1,800	347,920	9,625	6,815	59,475	71,331	64,407	3,817	871,122
2003	11,000	59,400	8,190	225,042	1,595	299,995	8,745	7,880	63,000	65,632	38,818	4,255	802,654
2004[1]	9,800	46,690	8,610	234,500	1,870	351,630	10,976	8,100	60,750	67,970	67,787	3,585	883,171

[1] Preliminary. Source: Agricultural Statistics Board, U.S. Department of Agriculture (ASB-USDA)

Salient Statistics of Tobacco in the United States

Year	Acres Harvested 1,000 Acres	Yield Per Acre Pounds	Pro-duction Million Pounds	Farm Price Cents/Lb.	Farm Value Million $	Tobacco (July - June) Exports[2]	Imports[3]	Cigar-ettes	U.S. Exports of Cigars & Cheroots	All Tobacco	Smoking Tobacco[4]	All Tobacco	Fire Cured[6]	Cigar Filler[7]	Mary-land
						- Million Pounds -		\-\-\- Millions \-\-\-		In Millions of Pounds					
1995	663.1	1,913	1,269	182.0	2,305	432.6	623.3	231,100	94	462	91.8	2,541	80.5	20.5	9.7
1996	733.1	2,072	1,519	188.2	2,854	533.1	717.2	243,900	67	486	110.4	2,225	80.2	17.9	11.7
1997	836.2	2,137	1,787	180.2	3,217	450.1	565.8	217,000	86	487	118.2	2,031	83.3	13.2	15.0
1998	717.7	2,061	1,480	182.8	2,701	461.9	529.6	201,300	93	467	142.5	2,250	84.8	13.0	18.7
1999	647.2	1,997	1,293	182.8	2,356	394.7	480.2	151,400	84	423	151.1	2,301	86.7	11.4	20.6
2000	472.4	2,229	1,053	191.0	2,002	351.4	457.8	148,300	113	397	136.1	2,388	87.8	9.5	16.0
2001	432.3	2,293	991	195.7	1,940	386.7	568.0	133,900	124	411	118.2	1,893	93.8	12.1	13.4
2002	427.3	2,039	871	193.6	1,687	325.8	549.7	127,400	123	338	144.0	1,738	99.5	12.3	9.7
2003	411.2	1,952	803	196.7	1,579	342.1	630.1	121,500	155	343	121.2	1,584	100.5	10.7	8.2
2004[1]	409.1	2,159	883	198.4	1,752	354.0	561.7	125,000	190	361	45.4	1,283	101.5	9.7	7.2

Column group headers: Stocks of Tobacco[5] — Various Types

[1] Preliminary. [2] Domestic. [3] For consumption. [4] In bulk. [5] Flue-cured and cigar wrapper, year beginning July 1; for all other types, October 1. [6] Kentucky-Tennessee types 22-23. [7] Types 41-46. Source: Economic Research Service, U.S. Department of Agriculture (ERS-USDA)

Tobacco Production in the United States, by Types   In Thousands of Pounds (Farm-Sale Weight)

Year	11-14	21	22	23	31	32	35-36	37	41	41-61	51	54	55	61
1995	746,616	1,540	26,609	11,041	436,343	17,935	8,488	79	9,225	19,887	2,441	4,513	1,707	2,001
1996	908,345	1,738	29,461	13,029	520,483	16,545	8,550	112	10,272	20,441	2,901	3,610	1,552	2,106
1997	1,047,438	1,968	27,952	12,342	648,633	18,240	8,196	119	10,780	22,511	3,637	4,194	1,496	2,404
1998	812,797	2,340	25,922	11,573	582,336	15,370	9,663	122	9,450	19,744	3,633	3,270	960	2,431
1999	656,752	2,672	24,773	10,630	555,185	14,350	11,640	155	5,920	16,535	4,169	2,252	566	3,628
2000	598,915	2,548	34,167	14,920	362,788	13,395	15,896	165	5,040	10,205	1,070	1,825	430	1,840
2001	579,091	2,202	30,720	12,377	334,066	5,346	13,949	154	4,120	13,318	3,822	3,042	577	1,757
2002	514,385	1,471	23,292	10,145	293,537	4,205	10,570	116	4,410	13,401	4,021	3,151	666	1,153
2003	456,690	839	23,504	10,165	281,698	4,195	11,230	84	5,280	14,249	3,386	3,472	783	1,328
2004[1]	516,420	1,368	24,800	10,636	298,811	5,830	11,584	119	4,140	13,603	3,983	2,805	780	1,895

[1] Preliminary. Source: Agricultural Statistics Board, U.S. Department of Agriculture (ASB-USDA)

U.S. Exports of Unmanufactured Tobacco   In Millions of Pounds (Declared Weight)

Year	Australia	Belgium-Luxem.	Denmark	France	Germany	Italy	Japan	Nether-lands	Sweden	Switzer-land	Thailand	United Kingdom	Total
1995	4.8	17.9	14.6	3.9	70.7	14.8	106.9	39.2	3.0	14.4	19.0	14.2	461.8
1996	5.6	39.7	15.1	3.2	60.1	17.3	88.7	40.4	3.7	14.9	15.9	34.4	485.5
1997	4.2	38.9	15.5	7.0	72.2	18.3	80.5	30.2	5.2	11.4	21.6	18.2	487.4
1998	5.0	25.2	14.8	6.6	84.6	13.6	85.3	43.9	2.6	10.3	14.2	15.6	466.3
1999	3.2	18.3	14.9	5.6	71.9	15.1	60.3	64.5	3.9	16.1	6.8	9.0	417.5
2000	3.6	23.2	15.7	5.5	86.1	15.8	63.6	19.7	3.5	9.5	7.3	7.3	402.4
2001	3.4	49.7	12.2	11.5	94.8	6.2	51.6	21.6	3.6	14.4	7.7	1.6	409.7
2002	4.5	29.4	13.6	10.3	59.5	8.6	49.6	10.3	1.2	27.3	12.6	6.0	338.0
2003	6.3	61.7	13.5	8.8	55.8	7.6	42.4	9.8	1.6	34.8	3.6	4.8	343.3
2004[1]	3.6	27.4	10.2	16.3	53.5	6.6	34.6	15.8	NA	9.4	8.5	4.0	361.0

[1] Preliminary.   Source: Economic Research Service, U.S. Department of Agriculture (ERS-USDA)

U.S. Salient Statistics for Flue-Cured Tobacco (Types 11-14) in the United States   In Millions of Pounds

Crop Year	Acres Harvested 1,000	Yield Per Acre Pounds	Mar-ketings	Stocks July 1	Total Supply	Exports	Domestic Disap-pearance	Total Disap-pearance	Farm Price Cents/Lb.	Placed Under Gov't Loan Million Lb.	Price Support Level Cents/Lb.	Loan Stocks Nov. 30	Loan Stocks Uncom-mitted
1995-6	386.2	1,933	854	1,187	2,041	345	531	875	179.4	12.0	159.7	157.6	62.3
1996-7	422.2	2,151	897	1,166	2,063	391	555	947	183.4	1.8	160.1	181.0	.0
1997-8	458.3	2,285	1,014	1,117	2,130	336	541	877	172.0	195.5	162.1	145.3	.0
1998-9	368.8	2,204	815	1,253	2,068	341	492	834	175.5	82.4	162.8	311.5	182.7
1999-00	303.8	2,162	654	2,162	2,816	262	437	699	173.7	136.4	163.2	318.3	144.9
2000-1	250.0	2,396	564	1,189	1,754	238	479	717	179.3	27.4	164.0	256.9	135.9
2001-2	238.1	2,432	544	1,036	1,581	276	389	665	185.7	15.0	166.0	93.2	65.0
2002-3	245.6	2,094	565	916	1,481	220	423	643	182.5	24.8	165.6	17.8	12.8
2003-4[1]	233.4	1,957	508	838	1,345	216	333	523	185.1	59.8	166.3	70.6	68.7
2004-5[2]	231.0	2,215	512	823	1,335	200	412	612	186.2		169.0	108.2	128.5

[1] Preliminary.   [2] Estimate.   Source: Economic Research Service, U.S. Department of Agriculture (ERS-USDA)

Salient Statistics for Burley Tobacco (Type 31) in the United States   In Millions of Pounds

Crop Year	Acres Harvested 1,000	Yield Per Acre Pounds	Mar-ketings	Stocks Oct. 1	Total Supply	Exports	Domestic Disap-pearance	Total Disap-pearance	Farm Price Cents/Lb.	Gross Sales[3]	Price Support Level Cents/Lb.	Loan Stocks Nov. 30	Loan Stocks Uncom-mitted
1995-6	234.2	1,863	483	959	1,441	165	386	551	185.5	341.6	172.5	212.5	50.8
1996-7	268.3	1,940	516	890	1,407	209	446	656	192.2	422.6	173.7	216.8	27.1
1997-8	335.3	1,934	628	751	1,379	168	379	548	188.5	337.9	176.0	105.6	38.5
1998-9	307.1	1,896	590	832	1,422	169	349	520	190.3	431.6	177.8	183.8	142.2
1999-00	303.6	1,829	551	901	1,453	139	273	413	182.9	356.6	178.9	226.6	186.7
2000-1	193.8	1,957	315	1,040	1,355	142	524	666	196.3	169.7	180.5	420.7	336.5
2001-2	167.6	2,033	344	689	1,033	140	245	385	197.3	258.5	182.6	119.3	74.8
2002-3	157.7	1,861	300	648	948	149	221	370	197.4	217.7	183.5	124.2	46.1
2003-4[1]	152.3	1,850	272	578	850	174	136	310	197.7	197.3	184.9	91.7	26.5
2004-5[2]	156.3	1,929	302	527	829	140	211	351	198.8	202.3	187.3	115.1	8.5

[1] Preliminary.   [2] Estimate.   [3] Before Christmas holidays.   Source: Economic Research Service, U.S. Department of Agriculture (ERS-USDA)

Exports of Tobacco from the United States (Quantity and Value)   In Metric Tons

Year	Flue-Cured	Value 1,000 USD	Burley	Value 1,000 USD	Total	Value 1,000 USD	Manu-factured	Value 1,000 USD
1995	123,040	866,208	47,129	365,206	209,481	1,399,863	77,135	5,221,487
1996	112,797	786,473	52,202	380,012	222,316	1,390,311	83,383	5,238,340
1997	116,457	832,381	56,803	454,849	221,510	1,553,314	85,734	4,956,392
1998	110,435	776,640	50,167	409,773	211,930	1,458,877	NA	4,517,500
1999	86,838	611,054	49,398	404,564	191,975	1,311,643	NA	3,232,862
2000	84,980	606,145	36,649	306,883	179,892	1,204,085	NA	4,012,711
2001	89,242	653,795	41,254	352,256	186,300	1,268,839	NA	2,734,378
2002	72,838	531,455	39,083	326,580	153,427	1,049,709	NA	1,950,188
2003[1]	70,323	517,702	41,555	344,191	155,724	1,038,073	NA	1,843,923
2004[2]	66,686	487,475	58,092	368,569	163,769	1,044,373	NA	1,566,930

[1] Preliminary.   [2] Forecast.   NA = Not available.   Source: Foreign Agricultural Service, U.S. Department of Agriculture (FAS-USDA)

Tung Oil

Tung oil is a yellow drying oil produced from the seed of the tung tree. The seeds or nuts of the tung tree are harvested and pressed to yield tung oil. Tung oil is used mostly as an industrial lubricant and drying agent, and is the most powerful drying agent known. It is also used in paints and varnishes, soaps, inks, and electrical insulators. Tung oil is poisonous, containing glycerol esters of unsaturated fats. The oil is also used as a substitute for linseed oil in paints, varnishes, and linoleum, and as a waterproofing agent.

Prices – The price of tung oil in 2003 (through September) rose sharply by +66% yr/yr to 72.51 cents per pound, recovering from the 14-year low of 43.77 cents per pound seen in 2002.

Demand – US consumption of tung oil has fallen sharply over the past decade. In 2004 (through October), US consumption fell -9.7% yr/yr to 3.828 million pounds. The 2004 consumption level was only 18% of that seen in 1996, which was a 15-year high of 21.645 million pounds.

Trade – World imports of tung oil fell -7.6% yr/yr in 2003 to 27,484 metric tons. US imports of tung oil in 2002 rose 2.9% to 4,287 metric tons. The world's largest importers of tung oil are South Korea with 23% of world imports, the US with 16%, Japan with 7%, and the Netherlands with 6%. The world's largest exporter of tung oil by far is China with 19,509 metric tons of exports in 2003, accounting for 75% of total world exports.

World Tung Oil Trade   In Metric Tons

							Imports		Exports				
Year	Germany	Hong Kong	Japan	Nether-lands	South Korea	Taiwan	United States	World Total	Argen-tina	China	Hong Kong	Para-guay	World Total
1997	733	1,404	6,807	1,702	6,345	5,931	6,264	38,013	3,976	30,012	991	4,260	41,851
1998	601	1,101	3,813	2,738	4,410	5,730	3,880	31,672	2,205	21,743	552	2,161	28,643
1999	1,002	470	2,455	2,488	3,560	6,699	5,822	31,528	1,425	24,172	560	2,303	30,890
2000	885	416	2,225	2,156	4,900	4,346	3,554	28,273	1,870	24,213	494	2,799	30,649
2001	582	36	1,647	1,904	3,390	2,113	4,429	23,594	1,061	17,615	108	1,974	21,991
2002[1]	325	702	1,930	1,793	6,968	5,185	4,166	29,760	916	23,334	589	4,390	30,351
2003[2]	303	306	2,023	1,687	6,396	3,974	4,287	27,484	2,299	19,509	323	2,479	25,985

[1] Preliminary.   [2] Estimate.   *Source: The Oil World*

Consumption of Tung Oil in Inedible Products in the United States   In Thousands of Pounds

Year	Jan.	Feb.	Mar.	Apr.	May	June	July	Aug.	Sept.	Oct.	Nov.	Dec.	Total
1998	935	1,146	1,342	1,103	1,536	1,255	1,248	1,172	1,214	1,216	1,037	1,112	14,316
1999	862	797	967	1,071	2,137	1,140	1,519	1,043	1,012	933	962	937	13,380
2000	1,065	1,083	1,064	1,193	1,159	1,176	1,107	1,224	733	711	700	648	11,863
2001	1,044	842	533	366	281	431	253	430	399	411	243	235	5,468
2002	427	476	583	410	471	454	428	877	695	978	862	886	7,547
2003	685	276	508	317	322	233	270	349	406	269	376	228	4,239
2004[1]	428	400	350	402	264	324	338	310	186	186	101	109	3,398

[1] Preliminary.   *Source: Bureau of the Census, U.S. Department of Commerce*

Stocks of Tung Oil at Factories & Warehouses in the U.S., on First of Month   In Thousands of Pounds

Year	Jan.	Feb.	Mar.	Apr.	May	June	July	Aug.	Sept.	Oct.	Nov.	Dec.
1998	2,484	3,116	4,548	3,949	3,357	3,300	2,435	2,409	3,578	2,523	2,501	2,272
1999	2,010	3,427	5,427	3,740	3,078	2,788	2,710	2,346	2,047	1,959	1,359	1,002
2000	691	910	611	2,555	2,254	1,982	1,658	1,381	1,262	1,217	1,011	827
2001	685	2,438	2,181	2,131	1,881	1,727	1,578	1,168	1,046	714	W	W
2002	W	W	W	W	1,341	1,206	885	516	483	551	560	478
2003	490	W	858	763	722	790	398	W	W	W	W	W
2004[1]	W	W	W	519	229	209	226	137	91	161	121	117

[1] Preliminary.   W = Withheld proprietary data.   *Source: Bureau of the Census, U.S. Department of Commerce*

Average Price of Tung Oil (Imported, Drums) F.O.B. in New York   In Cents Per Pound

Year	Jan.	Feb.	Mar.	Apr.	May	June	July	Aug.	Sept.	Oct.	Nov.	Dec.	Average
1997	74.00	92.00	92.00	103.00	103.00	103.00	103.00	108.00	110.00	110.00	110.00	110.00	101.50
1998	110.00	110.00	110.00	110.00	100.00	100.00	100.00	100.00	100.00	100.00	100.00	100.00	103.33
1999	100.00	100.00	100.00	100.00	100.00	74.00	74.00	74.00	74.00	74.00	74.00	74.00	84.83
2000	59.00	59.00	59.00	59.00	59.00	59.00	59.00	59.00	59.00	59.00	59.00	59.00	59.00
2001	60.50	62.00	62.00	62.00	62.00	62.00	62.00	62.00	62.00	62.00	60.50	60.50	61.63
2002	60.50	44.50	44.50	42.00	40.00	40.00	40.00	40.00	40.00	43.75	45.00	45.00	43.77
2003[1]	45.00	45.00	52.80	84.75	85.00	85.00	85.00	85.00	85.00				72.51

[1] Preliminary.   *Source: Economic Research Service, U.S. Department of Agriculture (ERS-USDA)*

Tungsten

Tungsten (symbol W) is a grayish-white, lustrous, metallic element. The atomic symbol for tungsten is W because of its former name of Wolfram. Tungsten has the highest melting point of any metal at about 3410 degrees Celsius and boils at about 5660 degrees Celsius. In 1781, the Swedish chemist Carl Wilhelm Scheele discovered tungsten.

Tungsten is never found in nature but is instead found in the minerals wolframit, scheelite, huebnertite, and ferberite. Tungsten has excellent corrosion resistance qualities and is resistant to most mineral acids. Tungsten is used as filaments in incandescent lamps, electron and television tubes, alloys of steel, spark plugs, electrical contact points, cutting tools, and in the chemical and tanning industries.

Prices – The average monthly price of tungsten at US ports in 2004 rose sharply by +33.7% yr/yr to $83.78 per short ton, which was a 3-year high and was only mildly below the 2-decade high of $87.72 per ton posted in 2001.

Supply – World concentrate production of tungsten in 2003 rose by 5.6% yr/yr to 62,100 metric tons, which was a new record high. The world's largest producer of tungsten by far is China with 52,000 metric tons of production in 2003 representing 84% of total world production.

Trade – The US in 2003 relied on imports for 69% of its tungsten consumption, down from 70% in 2002. US imports for consumption in 2003 rose +14.7% yr/yr to 4,690 metric tons, which was a 5-year high. US exports in 2003 were negligible at 20 metric tons.

World Concentrate Production of Tungsten   In Metric Tons (Contained Tungsten[3])

Year	Austria	Bolivia	Brazil	Burma	Canada	China	Mongolia	North Korea	Portugal	Russia	Rwanda	Thailand	World Total
1996	1,413	582	99	334	----	26,500	17	900	776	3,000	49	37	34,700
1997	1,400	513	40	272	----	25,000	26	900	1,036	3,000	33	30	33,200
1998	1,423	497	----	178	----	30,000	35	500	831	3,000	109	35	37,000
1999	1,610	334	13	87	----	31,100	27	500	434	3,500	41	30	37,700
2000	1,600	382	18	74	----	37,000	52	500	743	3,500	108	30	44,000
2001	1,237	533	22	48	----	38,500	63	500	698	3,500	142	53	45,300
2002[1]	1,400	400	24	30	2,550	49,500	35	600	693	3,400	153	30	58,800
2003[2]	1,400	442	25	30	2,750	52,000	40	600	700	3,900	150	30	62,100

[1] Preliminary.   [2] Estimate.   [3] Conversion Factors: WO3 to W, multiply by 0.7931; 60% WO3 to W, multiply by 0.4758.
Source: U.S. Geological Survey (USGS)

Salient Statistics of Tungsten in the United States   In Metric Tons (Contained Tungsten)

Year	Net Import Reliance as a % of Apparent Consumption	Total Consumption	Tool	Stainless & Heat Assisting	Alloy Steel[3]	Super-alloys	Cutting & Wear Resistant Materials	Products Made from Metal Powder	Miscellaneous	Chemical and Ceramic	Exports	Imports for Consumption	Consumers	Producers
1996	89	5,260	434	107	177	371	5,960	687	0	97	18	4,190	569	44
1997	84	6,590	361	151	277	366	6,280	828	151	123	12	4,850	658	44
1998	78	3,210	[4]	532	219	333	6,640	1,270	532	97	10	4,750	603	W
1999	81	2,100	W	486	189	306	5,910	1,860	----	93	26	2,870	376	W
2000	68	W	W	408	W	498	5,960	W	----	89	70	2,370	W	W
2001	59	W	W	389	W	599	5,650	W	----	80	220	2,680	W	W
2002[1]	70	W	W	313	W	426	4,820	W	----	133	94	4,090	W	W
2003[2]	69	W	W	312	W	W	5,210	W	----	129	20	4,690	W	W

Column groupings: "Consumption of Tungsten Products by End Uses" spans Tool through Chemical and Ceramic; "Steel" spans Tool, Stainless & Heat Assisting, Alloy Steel; "Stocks at End of Year — Concentrates" spans Consumers and Producers.

[1] Preliminary.   [2] Estimate.   [3] Other than tool.   [4] Included with stainless & heat assisting.   W = Withheld proprietary data; included with Miscellaneous.   *Source: U.S. Geological Survey*

Average Price of Tungsten at U.S. Ports (Including Duty)   In Dollars Per Short Ton

Year	Jan.	Feb.	Mar.	Apr.	May	June	July	Aug.	Sept.	Oct.	Nov.	Dec.	Average
1998	64.00	64.00	64.00	64.00	64.00	62.44	57.00	57.00	57.00	57.00	54.43	49.88	57.19
1999	49.50	49.50	49.50	49.50	48.57	48.75	49.16	50.88	51.50	54.44	54.75	54.75	52.00
2000	53.75	53.75	53.75	53.29	50.50	50.50	51.88	53.50	69.00	74.00	76.00	78.92	64.67
2001	83.50	86.00	90.00	93.00	96.15	96.50	93.88	92.88	91.00	89.89	83.84	79.57	87.72
2002	----	70.00	70.00	70.00	70.00	68.13	57.88	59.88	60.25	60.25	60.25	60.25	64.26
2003	60.25	61.55	63.00	63.00	63.00	63.00	63.00	63.00	63.00	63.00	63.00	63.00	62.65
2004	63.00	63.00	66.83	89.77	92.50	92.50	88.95	86.09	87.00	89.86	92.00	93.83	83.78

U.S. Spot Quotations, 65% WO3, Basis C.I.F.   *Source: U.S. Geological Survey (USGS)*

Turkeys

During the past three decades, the turkey industry has experienced tremendous growth in the US. Turkey production has more than tripled since 1970, with a current value of over $7 billion. Turkey was not a popular dish in Europe until a roast turkey was eaten on June 27, 1570, at the wedding feast of Charles XI of France and Elizabeth of Austria. The King was so impressed with the birds that the turkey subsequently became a popular dish at banquets held by French nobility.

The most popular turkey product continues to be the whole bird, with heavy demand at Thanksgiving and Christmas. The primary breeders maintain and develop the quality stock, concentrating on growth and conformation in males and fecundity in females, as well as characteristics important to general health and welfare. Turkey producers include large companies that produce turkeys all year round, and relatively small companies and farmers who produce turkeys primarily for the seasonal Thanksgiving market.

Prices – The average monthly price received by farmers for turkeys in the US in 2004 rose sharply by +17.7% yr/yr to 42.2 cents per pound, but remained mildly below the record high of 43.5 cents per pound posted in 1996. The monthly average retail price of turkeys (whole frozen) in the US in 2004 (through October) rose +2.5% yr/yr to 110.9

cents per pound, which was a new record high. Turkey prices have nearly tripled from the low 40-cent area seen in the early 1970s.

Supply – World production of turkeys in 2003 rose by +0.8% yr/yr to 4.937 million metric tons, which was a new record high. World production of turkeys has grown by more than two and one-half times since 1980 when production was 2.090 million metric tons. The US is the largest producer of turkeys by far with 2.541 million metric tons of production in 2003, representing 52% of world production. The value of US turkey production in 2003 was $2.720 billion.

Demand – World consumption of turkeys in 2003 rose +0.9% to 4.718 million metric tons, which was just below the record high of 4.744 million metric tons posted in 2001. US turkey consumption of 2.319 million metric tons in 2003 accounted for 49% of world consumption.

US per capita consumption of turkeys in 2004 (through the third quarter) fell -1.7% yr/yr to 17.1 pounds per person per year. US per capital consumption of turkeys has been in the range of 17-18 pounds since 1990, but the USDA is currently projecting that per capita consumption will drop below 17 pounds in 2005 (to 16.7 pounds) for the first time since 1989.

Production and Consumption of Turkey Meat, by Selected Countries — In Thousands of Metric Tons (RTC)

	Production							Consumption						
Year	Brazil	Canada	European Union	Mexico	Russia	United States	World Total	Brazil	Canada	European Union	Mexico	Russia	United States	World Total
1996	92	146	----	11	20	2,450	4,552	79	133	----	105	128	2,225	4,421
1997	101	142	1,638	11	12	2,455	4,587	78	134	1,486	124	163	2,141	4,387
1998	107	139	1,700	11	9	2,366	4,571	87	139	1,526	127	156	2,214	4,519
1999	115	139	2,100	12	8	2,372	4,839	89	136	1,890	136	169	2,224	4,807
2000	137	152	2,019	12	7	2,419	4,844	93	137	1,818	146	170	2,223	4,753
2001	165	149	2,098	13	7	2,490	4,934	96	135	1,931	157	171	2,269	4,827
2002	182	147	2,102	13	9	2,557	5,018	92	143	1,910	154	174	2,316	4,837
2003	200	148	2,024	14	12	2,529	4,935	89	138	1,914	170	126	2,300	4,789
2004[1]	220	147	2,030	17	15	2,414	4,852	92	136	1,930	183	85	2,257	4,733
2005[2]	250	147	2,020	17	17	2,496	4,956	95	133	1,935	189	97	2,281	4,779

[1] Preliminary. [2] Forecast. *Source: Foreign Agricultural Service, U.S. Department of Agriculture (FAS-USDA)*

Salient Statistics of Turkeys in the United States

	Poults Placed[3]	Number Raised[4]	Liveweight Produced	Liveweight Price	Value of Production	Ready-to-Cook Basis Production	Beginning Stocks	Exports	Consumption Total	Per Capita	Costs Feed	Costs Total	Wholesale Ready-to-Cook Production Costs	Wholesale Ready-to-Cook 3-Region Weighted Average Price[5]
Year	In Thousands	In Thousands	Mil. Lbs.	Cents/Lb.	Million $	In Millions of Pounds	In Millions of Pounds	In Millions of Pounds	In Millions of Pounds	Lbs.	Liveweight Basis	Liveweight Basis		
1994	317,468	286,585	6,540.3	40.4	2,643.1	4,937	249	280	4,652	17.7	24.00	37.70	63.40	65.90
1995	320,882	292,356	6,761.3	41.0	2,769.4	5,069	254	348	4,705	17.6	21.90	35.60	60.80	66.20
1996	325,375	302,713	7,222.8	43.3	3,124.5	5,401	271	438	4,907	18.2	31.60	45.30	72.90	66.80
1997	305,612	301,251	7,225.1	39.9	2,884.4	5,412	328	606	4,720	17.3	28.20	41.90	68.70	63.80
1998	297,798	285,204	7,050.9	38.0	2,683.5	5,215	415	446	4,880	17.7	22.96	36.66	62.12	62.15
1999	297,387	270,494	6,886.4	40.8	2,806.6	5,231	304	378	4,905	17.6	19.00	32.70	57.17	67.81
2000	298,094	269,969	6,942.8	40.7	2,828.5	5,334	254	445	4,903	17.4	19.98	33.68	58.40	68.06
2001	301,721	272,059	7,154.8	39.0	2,796.8	5,489	241	487	5,004	17.5	20.55	34.25	59.11	63.63
2002[1]	296,877	275,477	7,494.9	36.5	2,732.5	5,638	241	439	5,108	17.7	20.85	34.55	59.48	61.09
2003[2]	289,542	274,348	7,549.3	36.0	2,720.2	5,576	333	484	5,074	17.4	22.59	36.29	61.66	60.41

[1] Preliminary. [2] Estimate. [3] Poults placed for slaughter by hatcheries. [4] Turkeys place August 1-July 31. [5] Regions include central, eastern and western. Central region receives twice the weight of the other regions in calculating the average. *Source: Economic Research Service, U.S. Department of Agriculture (ERS-USDA)*

Turkey-Feed Price Ratio in the United States   In Pounds[2]

Year	Jan.	Feb.	Mar.	Apr.	May	June	July	Aug.	Sept.	Oct.	Nov.	Dec.	Average
1995	6.8	6.4	6.5	6.4	6.3	6.3	6.0	6.3	6.4	6.4	6.5	5.7	6.3
1996	5.3	5.2	5.1	4.8	4.6	4.9	4.9	4.8	5.3	6.2	6.4	6.1	5.3
1997	5.4	5.1	5.0	5.1	5.3	5.6	6.0	5.9	6.1	6.2	6.2	5.8	5.7
1998	5.4	5.2	5.4	5.7	5.8	6.1	6.5	7.6	8.1	8.3	8.2	7.5	6.7
1999	6.5	7.1	7.5	7.8	8.2	8.7	9.7	9.5	9.6	10.0	9.9	9.2	8.6
2000	7.6	7.2	7.6	7.9	7.8	8.5	9.5	10.0	10.1	10.0	9.8	8.1	8.7
2001	7.3	7.5	7.7	8.0	8.1	8.3	7.9	7.8	8.3	9.6	9.6	8.1	8.2
2002	7.2	7.2	6.8	6.8	7.3	7.3	6.9	6.3	6.0	6.1	6.5	6.4	6.7
2003	5.7	5.7	5.9	5.9	5.7	5.8	5.9	5.7	6.0	6.3	6.3	5.7	5.9
2004[1]	5.1	4.6	4.5	4.6	4.8	5.2	5.9	7.0	7.9	8.4	8.8	8.3	6.3

[1] Preliminary.   [2] Pounds of feed equal in value to one pound of turkey, liveweight.   *Source: Economic Research Service, U.S. Department of Agriculture (ERS-USDA)*

Average Price Received by Farmers for Turkeys in the United States (Liveweight)   In Cents Per Pound

Year	Jan.	Feb.	Mar.	Apr.	May	June	July	Aug.	Sept.	Oct.	Nov.	Dec.	Average
1995	39.3	37.2	38.3	38.3	38.4	39.3	39.6	41.9	43.6	45.2	47.3	44.0	41.0
1996	40.9	42.4	41.8	42.2	43.2	44.4	45.0	44.3	44.2	45.1	45.5	43.2	43.5
1997	38.6	36.4	37.8	39.7	41.3	41.6	41.1	41.0	41.1	41.0	41.9	38.7	40.0
1998	35.5	34.0	34.6	35.7	35.5	35.9	37.5	38.6	40.2	42.7	43.8	40.3	37.9
1999	34.8	35.7	37.0	38.7	39.4	41.3	42.0	43.0	44.3	45.3	45.3	42.2	40.8
2000	36.4	35.7	38.2	40.0	40.8	41.8	42.2	43.2	44.8	46.1	47.1	40.5	41.4
2001	36.6	36.3	37.1	37.6	38.2	38.3	38.5	38.7	40.5	44.2	44.5	38.7	39.1
2002	34.1	34.1	32.9	32.9	35.8	37.2	38.6	38.2	37.2	37.2	39.8	38.7	36.4
2003	34.6	34.5	35.1	35.6	34.9	34.9	33.6	32.7	36.2	39.1	41.2	38.2	35.9
2004[1]	34.9	35.0	36.6	38.7	40.4	42.0	43.6	45.4	46.5	48.4	49.0	46.2	42.2

[1] Preliminary.   *Source: Economic Research Service, U.S. Department of Agriculture (ERS-USDA)*

Average Wholesale Price of Turkeys[1] (Hens, 8-16 Lbs.) in New York   In Cents Per Pound

Year	Jan.	Feb.	Mar.	Apr.	May	June	July	Aug.	Sept.	Oct.	Nov.	Dec.	Average
1995	60.71	58.54	60.04	60.05	60.57	62.76	64.78	68.52	72.92	76.73	80.31	70.35	66.36
1996	64.60	64.65	65.07	64.82	65.39	65.85	65.66	64.94	64.16	69.09	73.58	70.05	66.49
1997	59.71	57.84	59.30	62.93	66.64	68.60	68.59	68.20	67.89	67.33	70.07	62.18	64.94
1998	55.65	54.04	55.49	55.49	58.68	58.14	58.68	63.17	65.65	71.52	72.95	69.00	61.54
1999	57.67	58.84	61.69	63.02	65.55	68.89	71.62	73.57	76.28	79.30	78.99	72.39	68.98
2000	61.58	61.84	65.35	67.38	69.18	70.36	71.55	73.61	76.53	78.74	79.58	70.31	70.50
2001	61.50	61.18	62.38	63.45	65.65	66.00	66.10	66.38	68.81	72.86	73.48	67.71	66.29
2002	60.86	60.03	59.00	59.52	63.52	65.68	66.52	66.56	67.15	67.75	69.79	66.96	64.45
2003	61.04	61.13	61.24	61.43	60.36	60.12	58.18	57.74	61.52	66.08	69.33	66.85	62.09
2004[2]	62.13	61.61	62.62	64.52	66.41	68.95	71.21	73.32	74.69	76.89	78.29	76.05	69.72

[1] Ready-to-cook.   [2] Preliminary.   *Source: Economic Research Service, U.S. Department of Agriculture (ERS-USDA)*

Certified Federally Inspected Turkey Slaughter in the U.S. (RTC Weights)   In Millions of Pounds

Year	Jan.	Feb.	Mar.	Apr.	May	June	July	Aug.	Sept.	Oct.	Nov.	Dec.	Total
1995	386.3	368.9	433.1	369.6	441.4	478.4	409.1	447.3	419.5	480.2	463.0	394.4	5,091
1996	412.4	426.5	422.3	430.9	483.0	454.7	484.8	476.6	440.9	518.1	465.9	406.1	5,422
1997	439.7	389.5	399.6	448.8	465.8	481.4	488.8	453.0	457.6	510.0	450.6	457.9	5,443
1998	430.5	407.7	437.8	444.0	419.1	454.2	456.0	409.9	425.3	470.5	459.5	428.2	5,243
1999	408.9	361.0	428.8	435.8	438.6	452.4	434.7	464.3	451.3	468.7	487.6	425.4	5,257
2000	396.9	412.4	466.2	413.5	489.2	479.4	422.8	481.6	423.0	494.7	478.2	396.5	5,354
2001	458.3	405.9	458.7	425.1	485.1	460.7	465.1	481.7	409.2	536.2	477.7	413.2	5,477
2002	477.2	442.1	447.8	487.2	496.7	448.0	474.7	475.9	439.4	519.0	488.2	457.9	5,654
2003	473.6	427.1	464.6	471.1	475.8	478.0	483.9	449.3	453.6	522.8	450.3	436.1	5,586
2004[1]	435.5	389.0	466.6	445.2	445.1	462.8	455.4	462.2	451.2	461.5	479.6	434.4	5,389

[1] Preliminary.   *Source: Economic Research Service, U.S. Department of Agriculture (ERS-USDA)*

TURKEYS

Per Capita Consumption of Turkeys in the United States   In Pounds

Year	First Quarter	Second Quarter	Third Quarter	Fourth Quarter	Total	Year	First Quarter	Second Quarter	Third Quarter	Fourth Quarter	Total
1994	3.6	3.9	4.4	6.2	17.8	2000	3.7	4.2	4.4	5.5	17.8
1995	3.6	3.9	4.2	6.2	17.9	2001	3.9	3.8	4.3	5.6	17.5
1996	3.7	3.9	4.6	6.2	18.5	2002	3.5	3.9	4.4	5.9	17.7
1997	3.5	4.0	4.2	6.0	17.6	2003	3.6	3.9	4.6	5.3	17.4
1998	3.9	3.9	4.2	6.0	18.1	2004[1]	3.6	4.0	4.5	5.0	17.1
1999	3.8	3.8	4.4	5.8	18.0	2005[2]	3.4	3.8	4.0	5.4	17.0

[1] Preliminary.   [2] Estimate.   Source: Economic Research Service, U.S. Department of Agriculture (ERS-USDA)

Storage Stocks of Turkeys (Frozen) in the United States on First of Month   In Millions of Pounds

Year	Jan.	Feb.	Mar.	Apr.	May	June	July	Aug.	Sept.	Oct.	Nov.	Dec.
1995	254.4	312.9	359.5	432.1	466.2	536.3	598.8	651.1	678.2	686.0	644.2	270.1
1996	271.3	339.2	423.1	445.4	514.5	587.4	679.7	718.2	723.2	721.0	658.3	347.8
1997	328.0	401.0	446.4	496.5	543.3	611.8	667.9	714.3	742.0	770.7	736.6	438.6
1998	415.1	497.6	512.7	527.0	579.7	614.1	656.5	701.8	706.8	699.5	658.7	310.4
1999	304.3	363.8	375.6	374.9	455.4	494.3	556.1	599.0	580.3	596.4	494.5	252.3
2000	254.3	319.4	353.9	391.4	416.9	480.3	506.8	524.0	524.9	528.1	473.9	261.1
2001	241.3	291.4	333.5	355.8	392.6	456.0	506.7	534.2	545.3	542.0	497.9	260.0
2002	240.5	327.1	413.2	457.6	515.2	578.2	644.1	706.2	685.6	672.4	624.9	334.3
2003	333.0	451.9	492.7	549.3	573.5	658.8	718.2	722.5	706.5	647.5	582.7	350.7
2004[1]	354.0	420.5	471.7	504.6	548.8	571.1	595.7	599.6	600.2	527.4	478.2	294.9

[1] Preliminary.   Source: Economic Research Service, U.S. Department of Agriculture (ERS-USDA)

Average Retail[2] Price of Turkeys (Whole frozen) in the United States   In Cents Per Pound

Year	Jan.	Feb.	Mar.	Apr.	May	June	July	Aug.	Sept.	Oct.	Nov.	Dec.	Average
1995	69.5	67.1	68.5	68.6	70.1	72.5	74.2	77.8	81.6	84.9	86.5	77.5	74.9
1996	103.5	104.7	106.9	101.4	104.3	104.1	104.4	108.6	106.5	107.4	98.1	102.0	104.3
1997	106.3	106.7	104.7	103.2	104.5	107.8	107.4	109.2	108.9	106.2	97.6	98.2	105.1
1998	103.4	100.1	99.6	97.2	95.7	99.1	100.8	102.4	105.2	102.5	93.4	95.4	99.6
1999	96.9	100.1	98.4	93.6	97.5	100.5	103.1	101.5	101.8	102.5	96.4	97.6	99.2
2000	101.3	102.5	101.5	99.7	102.9	106.5	109.5	104.5	104.4	106.7	98.1	99.4	103.1
2001	108.8	112.5	112.7	109.7	109.4	110.9	111.0	113.5	116.2	114.6	98.0	99.5	109.7
2002	102.2	105.1	106.6	104.0	102.5	107.3	108.0	106.8	106.6	111.7	103.8	98.8	105.3
2003	106.6	105.8	105.5	100.1	106.0	110.6	113.4	116.2	116.7	111.2	100.6	105.4	108.2
2004[1]	108.4	109.4	113.4	108.4	109.0	111.7	112.9	114.2	108.8	112.3	99.6	100.3	109.0

[1] Preliminary.   [2] Data prior to 1996 are prices to selected retailers.   Source: Economic Research Service, U.S. Department of Agriculture (ERS-USDA)

Average Retail-to-Consumer Price Spread of Turkeys (Whole) in the United States   In Cents Per Pound

Year	Jan.	Feb.	Mar.	Apr.	May	June	July	Aug.	Sept.	Oct.	Nov.	Dec.	Average
1995	28.5	32.0	33.7	32.1	32.7	32.8	30.8	28.2	27.0	20.1	10.6	21.2	27.5
1996	30.4	30.7	33.6	28.0	29.3	28.0	27.9	32.1	30.3	28.9	18.0	26.6	28.7
1997	38.3	40.7	37.5	32.0	29.6	32.0	32.0	34.5	34.3	31.9	20.0	26.9	32.5
1998	38.8	37.2	35.2	31.2	29.4	30.7	29.6	29.0	29.3	21.3	10.3	19.0	28.4
1999	29.9	32.7	28.6	21.3	22.5	22.6	23.2	29.1	18.5	17.6	12.0	19.6	23.1
2000	32.1	33.9	29.1	25.9	27.6	29.5	30.9	23.7	21.1	21.7	13.4	23.1	26.0
2001	39.5	43.3	42.5	39.1	37.7	38.7	38.6	40.5	41.0	35.6	18.7	27.0	36.9
2002	34.2	37.9	40.7	38.3	32.9	35.9	35.9	34.9	35.4	40.2	29.8	24.6	35.1
2003	38.4	37.6	36.8	31.2	38.1	42.9	47.1	50.0	47.2	37.8	25.1	33.2	38.8
2004[1]	39.4	40.4	42.5	35.0	33.5	33.9	33.3	32.5	25.7	26.9	14.0	17.9	31.3

[1] Preliminary.   Source: Economic Research Service, U.S. Department of Agriculture (ERS-USDA)

Uranium

Uranium (symbol U) is a chemically reactive, radioactive, steel-gray, metallic element and is the main fuel used in nuclear reactors. Uranium is the heaviest of all the natural elements. Traces of uranium have been found in archeological artifacts dating back to 79 AD. Uranium was discovered in pitchblende by German chemist Martin Heinrich Klaproth, in 1789. Klaproth named it uranium after the recently discovered planet Uranus. French physicist Antoine Henri Becquerel discovered the radioactive properties of uranium in 1896 when he produced an image on a photographic plate covered with a light-absorbing substance. Following Becquerel's experiments, investigations of radioactivity led to the discovery of radium and to new concepts of atomic organization.

The principal use for uranium is fuel in nuclear power plants. Demand for uranium concentrates is directly linked to the level of electricity generated by nuclear power plants. Uranium ores are widely distributed throughout the world and are primarily found in Canada, DRC (formerly Zaire), and the US. Uranium is obtained from primary mine production and secondary sources. Two Canadian companies are the primary producers of uranium from deposits in the Athabasca Basin of northern Saskatchewan. Specifically, the companies Cameco accounted for 19% of global mine production in 2000 and Cogema Resources accounted for 15% of world production. Secondary sources of uranium include excess inventories from utilities and other fuel cycle participants, used reactor fuel, and dismantled Russian nuclear weapons.

Prices – The average price of delivered uranium in 2002 rose by +2.1% yr/yr to $10.36 per pound from $10.15 in 2001. The 2001 price of $10.15 was a record low for the data series that goes back to 1981. The price of delivered uranium in 2002 of $10.36 was roughly one-third of the price of $30 per pound and above seen in the 1980s through 1986 when the price started falling.

Supply – World production of uranium oxide (U308) concentrate in 2001 rose +9.0% yr/yr to a 10-year high of 47,395 short tons from 43,475 short tons in 2000. The world's two largest uranium producers are Canada with 16,270 short tons of production in 2001, representing 34% of world production, and Australia with 10,035 short tons of production in 2001, representing 21% of world production. Smaller producers include Niger (with 8.0% of world production), Namibia (6.1%), the US (2.8%), South Africa (2.4%), the Ukraine (2.2%), China (1.4%), the Czech Republic and Slovakia (1.3%), and France (0.4%).

US uranium production in 2001 fell 30% yr/yr to a record low of 1,315 short tons from 1,890 short tons in 2000. US production reached a peak of 21,850 short tons in 1980 and production has since fallen steadily to the record low in 2001, which was only 6% of the record level of production.

Trade – US imports of uranium in 2003 rose +0.7% yr/yr to a record high of 53.044 million pounds. The US is being forced to import more uranium as domestic production steadily declines. US exports of uranium fell -14.3% yr/yr to 13.187 million pounds, which was still well above the 7-year low of 8.510 million pounds posted in 1999.

World Production of Uranium Oxide (U₃O₈) Concentrate — In Short Tons (Uranium Content)

Year	Australia	Canada	China	Czech Rep. & Slovakia	France	Gabon	Germany	Namibia	Niger	South Africa	United States	Ex-USSR	World Total
1994	3,050	11,950	----	----	1,700	750	----	2,500	3,800	2,250	1,950	----	41,750
1995	4,900	13,600	----	----	1,250	800	----	2,600	3,750	1,850	3,050	----	43,050
1996	6,450	15,250	----	----	1,200	750	----	3,150	4,300	2,200	3,150	----	46,650
1997	7,150	15,650	----	----	940	600	----	3,770	4,500	1,065	2,900	----	46,550
1998	6,350	14,200	----	----	660	950	----	3,590	4,850	1,250	2,435	----	44,110
1999	7,875	10,680	----	----	450	380	----	3,495	3,790	1,195	2,325	----	39,640
2000	9,830	13,875	655	795	525	----	45	2,430	3,270	1,305	1,890	655	43,475
2001	10,035	16,270	650	595	195	----	----	2,910	3,795	1,135	1,315	1,050	47,395
2002[1]	10,857	17,153	W	0	----	W	W	1,082	W	764	6,206	W	52,709
2003[2]	9,326	17,050	W	W	----	0	0	1,034	0	1,438	10,200	W	56,552

[1] Preliminary. [2] Estimate. *Source: American Bureau of Metal Statistics, Inc. (ABMS)*

Commercial and U.S. Government Stocks of Uranium, End of Year — In Millions of Pounds U₃O₈ Equivalent

Year	Utility Natural Uranium	Utility Enriched Uranium[1]	Domestic Supplier Natural Uranium	Domestic Supplier Enriched Uranium[1]	Total Commercial Stocks	DOE Owned & USEC Held Natural Uranium	DOE Owned & USEC Held Enriched Uranium[1]
1994	42.4	23.0	17.4	4.1	86.9	57.2	28.0
1995	41.2	17.5	13.2	.5	72.5	82.0	28.8
1996	42.2	23.9	13.0	1.0	80.0	83.2	25.3
1997	47.1	18.8	10.3	30.1	106.2	53.2	----
1998	42.1	23.7	35.0	35.7	136.5	24.5	----
1999	44.8	13.5	29.5	39.4	127.1	53.1	----
2000	36.0	18.9	12.6	43.8	111.3	53.1	----
2001	34.4	21.2	9.2	39.0	103.8	53.1	----
2002	31.0	22.4	15.0	32.9	102.1	51.8	----
2003	22.7	23.0	W	W	85.2	W	W

[1] Includes amount reported as UF₆ at enrichment suppliers.   DOE = Department of Energy   USEC = U.S. Energy Commission
Source: Energy Information Administration, U.S. Department of Energy (EIA-DOE)

URANIUM

Reported Average Price Settlements for Purchases by U.S. Utilities and Domestic Suppliers   In $/Pound

Year of Delivery	Contract Price	Market Price[1]	Price & Cost Floor	Total	Contract & Market	Year of Delivery	Contract Price	Market Price[1]	Price & Cost Floor	Total	Contract & Market
	Averages of Reported Prices						*Averages of Reported Prices*				
1994	10.68	9.76	20.03	10.57	10.63	1999	12.72	9.52	14.75	11.16	12.57
1995	10.58	10.19	17.86	12.05	10.79	2000	12.31	9.11	----	11.04	----
1996	13.40	13.66	16.13	14.91	13.72	2001	11.72	8.04	----	10.15	----
1997	13.33	11.20	14.52	12.11	13.13	2002	10.73	9.79	----	10.36	----
1998	12.53	9.33	13.50	10.31	12.37	2003	----	----	----	10.81	----

[1] No floor.   Note: Price excludes uranium delivered *under litigation settlements. Price is given in year-of-delivery dollars.*
Source: *Energy Information Administration, U.S. Department of Energy (EIA-DOE)*

Uranium Industry Statistics in the United States   In Millions of Pounds U$_3$O$_8$

Year	Production Mine	Production Concentrate	Concentrate Shipments	Employment Exploration	Employment Mining	Employment Milling	Employment Processing	Employment Total	Deliveries to U.S. Utilities[1]	Average Price Delivered Uranium $/Lb. U$_3O_8$	Imports	Avg. Price Delivered Uranium Imports $/Lb. U$_3O_8$	Exports
1994	2.5	3.352	6.319	41	157	105	149	980	38.3	10.40	36.6	8.95	17.7
1995	3.5	6.000	5.500	27	226	121	161	1,107	43.4	11.25	41.3	10.20	9.8
1996	4.7	6.300	6.000	27	333	155	175	1,118	47.3	14.12	45.4	13.15	11.5
1997	4.7	5.600	5.800	30	413	175	175	1,097	42.0	12.88	43.0	11.81	17.0
1998	4.8	4.700	4.900	30	518	160	203	1,120	42.7	12.14	43.7	11.19	15.1
1999	4.5	4.600	5.500	7	310	201	132	848	47.9	11.63	47.6	10.55	8.5
2000	3.1	4.000	3.200	1	157	106	137	627	51.8	11.04	44.9	9.84	13.6
2001	2.6	2.600	2.200	0	81	42	122	423	55.4	10.15	46.7	9.51	11.7
2002	2.4	2.300	3.800	W	W	104	100	426	52.7	10.36	52.7	10.05	15.4
2003	2.2	2.000	1.600	W	W	W	W	321			53.0	10.59	13.2

[1] From suppliers under domestic purchases.   Source: *Energy Information Administration, U.S. Department of Energy (EIA-DOE)*

Month-End Uranium (U$_3$O$_8$) Transaction Values[1]   In Dollars Per Pound

Year	Jan.	Feb.	Mar.	Apr.	May	June	July	Aug.	Sept.	Oct.	Nov.	Dec.	Average
1995	8.30	8.45	8.65	8.78	9.18	9.48	9.50	9.83	9.83	9.83	9.95	10.05	9.32
1996	10.20	10.48	10.93	11.70	13.03	13.25	14.93	15.18	15.40	15.53	15.48	15.38	13.45
1997	15.33	15.08	14.85	14.75	14.43	10.95	10.68	10.45	10.55	10.48	10.43	10.53	12.37
1998	10.63	10.63	10.60	10.05	10.00	9.80	9.80	9.73	9.55	9.35	9.25	9.05	9.87
1999	9.03	9.08	9.20	9.20	9.53	9.48	9.48	9.40	9.35	9.23	9.18	9.13	9.27
2000	9.03	8.70	8.55	8.50	8.40	8.18	8.13	7.98	7.88	7.40	7.15	6.80	8.06
2001	6.78	6.83	6.83	7.25	7.38	7.45	7.83	7.95	9.00	9.47	9.44	9.50	7.97
2002	9.58	9.72	9.90	9.76	9.90	9.90	9.88	9.85	9.79	9.85	9.86	9.97	9.83
2003	10.20	10.10	10.10	10.16	10.84	10.90	10.90	11.13	11.47	12.32	13.18	13.98	11.27
2004	14.85	15.47	16.50	17.52	17.75	17.86	17.90	17.90	18.60	20.80	20.20	20.50	17.99

[1] Transaction value is a weighed average price of recent natural uranium sales transactions, based on prices paid on transactions closed within the previous three-month period for which delivery is scheduled within one year of the transaction date; at least 10 transactions involving a sum total of at least 2 million pounds of U$_3$O$_8$ equivalent.   Source: *American Metal Market (AMM)*

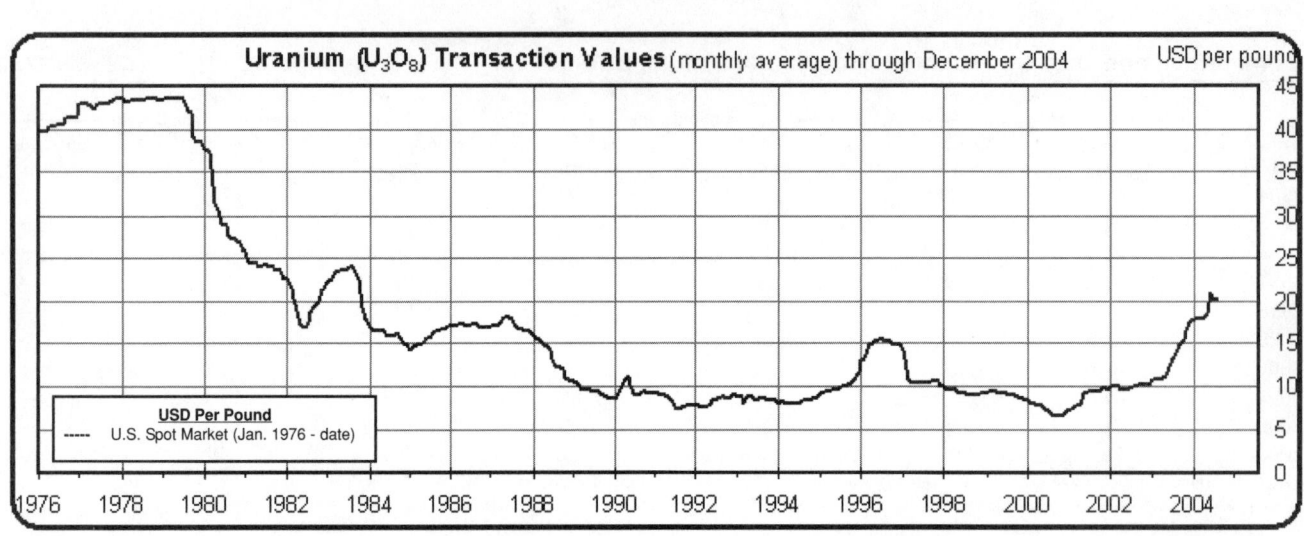

Uranium (U$_3$O$_8$) Transaction Values (monthly average) through December 2004   USD per pound

USD Per Pound
----- U.S. Spot Market (Jan. 1976 - date)

Vanadium

Vanadium (symbol V) is a silvery-white, soft, ductile, metallic element. Discovered in 1801, but mistaken for chromium, vanadium was rediscovered in 1830 by Swedish chemist Nils Sefstrom, who named the element in honor of the Scandinavian goddess Vanadis.

Never found in the pure state, vanadium is found in about 65 different minerals such as carnotite, roscoelite, vanadinite, and patronite, as well as in phosphate rock, certain iron ores, some crude oils, and meteorites. Vanadium is one of the hardest of all metals. It melts at about 1890 degrees Celsius and boils at about 3380 degrees Celsius.

Vanadium has good structural strength and is used as an alloying agent with iron, steel, and titanium. It is used in aerospace applications, transmission gears, photography, as a reducing agent, and as a drying agent in various paints.

Prices – The price of vanadium in 2003 rose to the range of $1.50-$2.80 per pound from the decade-low of $1.25-$1.70 per pound posted in 2002.

Supply – Virtually all (99%) of vanadium is produced from ores, concentrates, and slag, with the remainder coming from petroleum residues, ash, and spent catalysts. World production of vanadium in 2003 fell -8.1% yr/yr to 40,600 metric tons. That was moderately below the record high production level of 45,800 posted in 1996.

The world's largest producer of vanadium is South Africa with 17,700 metric tons of production in 2003 representing 44% of world production. The two other major producers are China with 33% of world production and Russia with 21% of world production. Production in Russia and South Africa has been relatively stable in recent years, while China's production grew sharply in the late 1990s. China's production level of 13,200 metric tons in 2003 was below the record high of 15,500 metric tons posted in 1998, but was more than double the levels seen in the early 1990s. Japan is the only significant producer of vanadium from petroleum residues, ash, and spent catalysts with 245 metric tons of production in each of the last 9 years.

Trade – The US exports very little vanadium. US imports of vanadium were mainly in the form of ore, slag and residues with 2,220 metric tons of imports in 2003, up 19% yr/yr. Other key import categories of vanadium were ferrovanadium (1,690 metric tons, -33% yr/yr), vanadium pentoxide, anhydride (679 metric tons, +67% yr/yr), and oxides and hydroxides (74 metric tons, +12% yr/yr).

World Production of Vanadium   In Metric Tons (Contained Vanadium)

| | | | From Ores, Concentrates and Slag | | | | | | From Petroleum Residues, Ash, Spent Catalysts | | | |
| | | | Republic of South Africa | | | | | | | | | |
Year	China[3]	Russia	Content of Pentoxide & Vanadate Products	Content of Vanadiferous Slag Products	Total	Total[4]	Japan[5]	United States[6]	Total	World Total
1994	5,400	11,900	6,050	9,600	16,350	34,700	252	2,740	2,990	37,700
1995	13,700	11,000	6,500	9,000	16,297	42,100	245	1,990	2,240	44,400
1996	14,000	11,000	----	----	14,770	40,900	245	3,730	3,980	45,800
1997	15,000	9,000	----	----	15,590	40,700	245	----	245	40,900
1998	15,500	7,000	----	----	18,868	42,500	245	----	245	42,700
1999	10,400	7,000	----	----	17,612	36,000	245	----	245	36,300
2000	12,000	7,000	----	----	18,021	40,700	245	----	245	41,000
2001	12,000	8,000	----	----	18,184	43,900	245	----	245	41,000
2002[1]	13,200	8,000	----	----	25,227	50,500	245	----	245	44,200
2003[2]	13,200	8,500	----	----	17,700	40,400	245	----	245	40,600

[1] Preliminary.   [2] Estimate.   [3] In vanadiferous slag product.   [4] Excludes U.S. production.   [5] In vanadium pentoxide product.
[6] In vanadium pentoxide and ferrovanadium products.   *Source: U.S. Geological Survey(USGS)*

Salient Statistics of Vanadium in the United States   In Metric Tons (Contained Vanadium)

| | Con-sumer & Producer Stocks, Dec. 31 | Vanadium Consumption by Uses in the U.S. | | | | | | | | Exports | | | | Imports | | | |
| | | Tool Steel | Cast Irons | High Strength, Low Alloy | Stainless & Heat Re-sisting | Super-alloys | Carbon | Full Alloy | Total | Average $ Per Lb. V₂O₅ | Vanadium Pent-oxide, Anhydride | Oxides & Hydr-oxides | Ferro-Vana-dium | Ores, Vanadium Slag, Re-sidues | Vanadium Pent-oxide, Anhydride | Oxides & Hydr-oxides | Ferro-Vana-dium |
Year																	
1994	1,110	424	31	979	26	16	1,680	777	4,290	1.55	335	1,050	374	1,900	294	3	1,910
1995	1,100	443	40	1,070	32	20	1,870	833	4,640	4.63	229	1,010	340	2,530	547	36	1,950
1996	1,070	433	W	890	22	16	1,820	1,030	4,200	3.11	241	2,670	479	2,270	485	11	1,880
1997	1,000	481	W	944	20	24	1,800	908	4,730	7.40-11.00	614	385	446	2,950	711	126	1,840
1998	336	269	W	950	42	20	1,650	891	4,380	5.25-15.50	681	232	579	2,400	847	33	1,620
1999	348	344	W	865	W	14	1,050	861	3,620	4.35-6.25	747	70	213	1,650	208	----	1,930
2000	303	225	W	944	W	17	1,090	773	3,030	3.85-6.60	653	100	172	1,890	902	21	2,510
2001	251	146	W	797	W	18	1,030	689	2,660	3.60-4.50	670	385	70	1,670	600	57	2,550
2002[1]	221	270	W	900	W	12	731	748	2,690	1.25-1.70	453	443	142	1,870	406	66	2,520
2003[2]	237	143	W	924	W	10	783	799	2,710	1.50-2.80	791	438	424	2,220	679	74	1,690

[1] Preliminary.   [2] Estimate.   W = Withheld proprietary data.   *Source: U.S. Geological Survey (USGS)*

Vegetables

Vegetables are the edible products of herbaceous plants, which are plants with soft stems. Vegetables are grouped according to the edible part of each plant including leaves (e.g., lettuce), stalks (celery), roots (carrot), tubers (potato), bulbs (onion), fruits (tomato), seeds (pea), and flowers (broccoli). Each of these groups contributes to the human diet in its own way. Fleshy roots are high in energy value and good sources of the vitamin B group, seeds are relatively high in carbohydrates and proteins, while leaves, stalks, and fruits are excellent sources of minerals, vitamins, water, and roughage. Vegetables are an important food for the maintenance of health and prevention of disease. Higher intakes of vegetables have been shown to lower the risks of cancer and coronary heart disease.

Vegetables are best consumed fresh in their raw state in order to derive the maximum benefits from their nutrients. While canned and frozen vegetables are often thought to be inferior to fresh vegetables, they are sometimes nutritionally superior to fresh produce because they are usually processed immediately after harvest when nutrient content is at its peak. When cooking vegetables, aluminum utensils should not be used, because aluminum is a soft metal that is affected by food acids and alkalis. Scientific evidence shows that tiny particles of aluminum from foods cooked in aluminum utensils enter the stomach and can injure the sensitive lining of the stomach.

Prices – The monthly average index of fresh vegetable prices received by growers in the US in 2004 (through November) fell by -6.7% to141.9 from the record high of 152.0 posted in 2003. That reversed the majority of the sharp +10.4% increase seen in 2003.

Demand – The leading vegetable in terms of US per capita consumption in 2003 was the potato with 135.1 pounds of consumption. Runner-up vegetables were tomatoes (88.9 pounds), sweet lettuce (31.0 pounds), corn (27.1 pounds), and onions (18.8 pounds). Total US per capita vegetable consumption in 2003 was 443.9 pounds, up +1.7% from 2002. That is up 25% from 356.2 pounds in 1980.

Index of Prices Received by Growers for Commercial Vegetables[1] in the United States

Year	Jan.	Feb.	Mar.	Apr.	May	June	July	Aug.	Sept.	Oct.	Nov.	Dec.	Average
1999	105	112	121	130	118	110	104	106	105	97	98	116	110
2000	98	86	107	135	131	117	119	129	143	125	144	115	121
2001	121	147	138	137	144	120	125	145	134	103	109	171	133
2002	158	192	272	120	115	109	115	121	119	105	110	104	137
2003	113	113	123	131	140	157	121	140	146	144	158	170	138
2004[2]	137	155	118	136	119	113	125	138	136	165	178	126	137

Not seasonally adjusted. 1990-92=100. [1] Includes fresh and processing vegetables. [2] Preliminary. *Source: National Agricultural Statistics Service, U.S. Department of Agriculture (NASS-USDA)*

Index of Prices Received by Growers for Fresh Vegetables (0113-02) in the United States

Year	Jan.	Feb.	Mar.	Apr.	May	June	July	Aug.	Sept.	Oct.	Nov.	Dec.	Average
1999	131.9	93.1	117.4	144.4	111.3	125.8	103.4	113.7	117.5	101.6	100.9	151.6	117.7
2000	111.3	100.5	122.3	126.8	152.0	128.1	127.2	136.7	155.9	165.0	173.9	120.3	135.0
2001	147.0	168.6	178.7	145.6	144.9	129.4	109.7	127.2	132.3	112.3	105.9	121.0	135.2
2002	146.1	188.7	242.5	101.7	107.2	123.2	127.1	125.4	116.7	126.9	127.4	119.0	137.7
2003	147.8	127.5	153.0	167.7	165.0	138.8	133.3	136.6	164.7	156.9	148.4	184.7	152.0
2004[1]	143.8	125.9	140.3	133.1	132.9	101.0	102.8	128.3	141.6	200.3	211.1	143.7	142.1

Not seasonally adjusted. 1990-92=100. [1] Preliminary. *Source: National Agricultural Statistics Service, U.S. Department of Agriculture (NASS)*

Producer Price Index of Canned[1] Processed Vegetables (0244) in the United States   1982 = 100

Year	Jan.	Feb.	Mar.	Apr.	May	June	July	Aug.	Sept.	Oct.	Nov.	Dec.	Average
1999	120.6	120.6	120.9	120.9	121.0	121.0	120.8	120.9	120.7	120.7	121.3	121.3	120.9
2000	121.3	120.8	121.2	120.9	121.2	121.5	121.1	120.9	121.1	121.6	121.7	121.3	121.2
2001	121.4	121.4	121.3	121.3	121.4	121.9	124.1	124.9	125.3	126.5	128.0	128.1	123.8
2002	128.3	128.2	128.0	128.2	128.3	128.0	127.7	129.4	128.7	129.5	129.1	129.1	128.5
2003	128.8	129.0	128.9	129.3	129.4	129.3	129.4	129.1	130.0	130.7	131.1	131.3	129.7
2004[2]	131.5	131.7	131.9	131.9	131.7	132.8	133.0	133.3	133.1	134.7	135.6	135.8	133.1

Not seasonally adjusted. [1] Includes canned vegetables and juices, including hominy and mushrooms. [2] Preliminary. *Source: Bureau of Labor Statistics, U.S. Department of Labor (BLS)*

Producer Price Index of Frozen Processed Vegetables (0245) in the United States   1982 = 100

Year	Jan.	Feb.	Mar.	Apr.	May	June	July	Aug.	Sept.	Oct.	Nov.	Dec.	
1999	125.8	126.6	125.6	126.7	125.9	126.0	126.8	126.1	126.0	126.4	125.5	125.3	126.1
2000	125.4	126.2	125.7	126.3	126.3	124.9	125.9	126.4	126.2	126.9	126.1	126.2	126.0
2001	127.6	128.5	127.7	128.7	128.4	127.7	128.9	128.8	128.8	130.0	129.2	129.1	128.6
2002	130.0	131.1	130.1	131.2	130.7	129.7	131.4	131.3	131.5	132.2	131.9	132.6	131.1
2003	133.4	134.1	133.3	134.0	134.1	133.9	134.9	134.2	134.2	135.2	135.1	135.0	134.3
2004[1]	135.1	136.0	135.3	135.3	134.3	134.7	135.4	135.8	136.2	137.3	136.9	136.7	135.8

Not seasonally adjusted. [1] Preliminary. *Source: Bureau of Labor Statistics, U.S. Department of Labor (BLS)*

Per Capita Use of Selected Commercially Produced Fresh and Processing Vegetables in the U.S.
In Pounds, farm weight basis

Crop	1994	1995	1996	1997	1998	1999	2000	2001	2002	2003[9]	2004[10]
Asparagus, All	0.9	1.0	0.9	1.0	1.0	1.2	1.3	1.2	1.2	1.4	1.4
Fresh	0.6	0.6	0.6	0.7	0.7	0.9	1.0	0.9	1.0	1.1	1.1
Canning	0.2	0.3	0.2	0.2	0.2	0.2	0.2	0.2	0.2	0.2	0.2
Freezing	0.1	0.1	0.1	0.1	0.1	0.1	0.1	0.1	0.1	0.1	0.1
Snap beans, All	7.2	6.8	7.2	6.7	7.4	7.6	7.9	7.8	7.2	7.5	7.4
Fresh	1.5	1.6	1.5	1.3	1.6	1.9	2.0	2.2	2.1	2.0	2.1
Canning	3.8	3.5	3.8	3.6	3.8	3.7	4.0	3.8	3.4	3.7	3.5
Freezing	1.9	1.7	1.9	1.8	2.0	2.0	1.8	1.9	1.8	1.9	1.9
Broccoli, All[1]	6.7	6.9	7.0	7.3	7.1	8.3	8.1	7.4	7.4	8.3	8.2
Fresh	4.4	4.3	4.5	5.0	5.0	6.2	5.9	5.4	5.4	5.7	5.8
Freezing	2.3	2.6	2.5	2.3	2.1	2.1	2.3	2.0	2.1	2.6	2.4
Cabbage, All	10.3	9.5	9.3	10.4	9.8	8.8	10.3	10.1	9.5	8.6	9.0
Fresh	9.1	8.1	8.3	9.0	8.4	7.6	8.9	8.8	8.3	7.5	7.9
Canning (kraut)	1.2	1.4	1.0	1.4	1.4	1.2	1.4	1.3	1.2	1.1	1.1
Carrots, All[2]	16.9	15.4	16.9	18.2	13.7	13.1	13.0	12.7	11.5	11.9	11.5
Fresh	12.7	11.2	12.4	14.1	9.5	9.3	9.2	9.4	8.4	8.8	8.4
Canning	1.4	1.6	1.7	1.5	1.4	1.4	1.1	1.9	1.2	1.6	1.5
Freezing	2.8	2.6	2.8	2.6	2.8	2.4	2.7	1.5	1.9	1.5	1.7
Cauliflower, All[1]	2.6	2.2	2.2	2.2	2.2	2.3	2.3	2.0	1.7	2.0	2.2
Fresh	2.0	1.6	1.7	1.8	1.5	1.8	1.7	1.5	1.4	1.7	1.7
Freezing	0.6	0.6	0.5	0.4	0.8	0.5	0.6	0.5	0.3	0.4	0.5
Celery	7.2	6.9	7.0	6.5	6.5	6.5	6.3	6.4	6.3	6.1	6.2
Sweet Corn, All[3]	27.4	28.5	29.1	27.5	28.4	28.3	27.1	27.1	26.1	26.9	27.8
Fresh	8.2	7.8	8.3	8.3	9.3	9.1	9.0	9.2	9.0	9.7	9.7
Canning	10.1	10.4	10.4	9.1	9.2	9.1	9.0	8.7	7.8	8.3	8.6
Freezing	9.1	10.3	10.4	10.1	9.8	10.1	9.0	9.3	9.3	9.0	9.5
Cucumbers, All	10.2	10.6	10.0	11.6	10.5	10.9	11.2	10.0	11.9	9.7	11.2
Fresh	5.4	5.6	5.9	6.4	6.5	6.7	6.4	6.3	6.5	6.1	6.3
Pickling	4.8	5.0	4.1	5.2	4.0	4.2	4.9	3.7	5.4	3.6	4.9
Melons	25.4	26.1	28.9	28.2	27.3	29.0	27.2	28.1	27.3	26.8	27.2
Watermelon	15.0	15.2	16.6	15.5	14.3	15.2	13.8	15.0	14.0	13.8	14.0
Cantaloupe	8.4	9.0	10.3	10.5	10.6	11.4	11.1	11.2	11.1	10.8	11.0
Honeydew	2.0	1.9	2.0	2.2	2.3	2.5	2.3	2.0	2.2	2.2	2.2
Lettuce, All	30.7	28.1	27.4	30.5	28.9	32.5	31.8	31.0	32.1	30.9	31.3
Head lettuce	25.0	22.2	21.6	23.9	22.3	24.9	23.5	23.0	22.5	21.4	21.3
Romaine & Leaf	5.7	5.9	5.8	6.6	6.6	7.6	8.4	8.0	9.6	9.5	10.0
Onions, All	17.8	19.1	19.1	19.7	19.5	20.8	20.4	19.5	20.4	20.3	20.5
Fresh	16.9	17.8	18.3	18.8	18.4	18.5	18.9	18.5	19.3	18.9	19.1
Dehydrating	0.9	1.3	0.8	0.9	1.1	2.3	1.6	1.0	1.1	1.4	1.4
Green Peas, All[4]	3.5	3.7	3.4	3.5	3.3	3.4	3.7	3.3	2.8	3.2	3.3
Canning	1.4	1.6	1.5	1.5	1.4	1.4	1.5	1.4	1.1	1.3	1.3
Freezing	2.1	2.1	1.9	2.0	1.9	2.0	2.1	2.0	1.7	1.9	1.9
Peppers, All	10.7	9.9	11.7	10.9	11.1	11.4	12.1	12.0	12.5	12.4	12.9
Bell Peppers, All	6.4	6.2	7.1	6.4	6.4	6.7	7.0	6.9	6.8	7.0	7.2
Chile Peppers, All	4.3	3.7	4.6	4.5	4.7	4.7	5.1	5.1	5.7	5.4	5.7
Tomatoes, All	92.5	91.4	90.5	89.4	91.7	89.2	88.2	83.7	88.4	87.7	88.9
Fresh	16.2	16.8	17.4	16.8	17.7	18.0	18.0	18.2	19.2	18.1	19.1
Canning	76.3	74.6	73.1	72.6	74.0	71.2	70.1	65.5	69.2	69.6	69.8
Other, Fresh[5]	8.9	8.4	8.8	9.2	10.0	10.5	17.7	16.6	17.1	17.8	18.3
Other, Canning[6]	2.6	2.4	2.2	2.3	2.1	2.5	2.6	2.7	2.4	2.5	2.5
Other, Freezing[7]	2.9	2.8	3.1	3.0	2.9	3.2	3.2	3.1	4.2	4.0	4.1
Subtotal, All[8]	284.4	279.7	284.7	288.1	283.4	289.4	294.3	284.9	290.1	287.9	293.8
Fresh	155.6	151.1	158.1	163.0	157.8	165.1	171.0	169.3	170.1	168.1	171.3
Canning	106.1	104.5	102.6	101.9	102.2	99.6	100.0	94.3	97.5	97.2	99.1
Freezing	21.8	22.8	23.2	22.3	22.3	22.5	21.8	20.3	21.4	21.2	22.0
Potatoes, All	136.7	136.9	145.0	141.4	138.1	136.5	138.8	138.2	132.3	138.8	136.0
Fresh	49.6	49.2	49.9	48.5	47.0	48.0	47.3	46.4	44.6	47.0	45.6
Processing	87.1	87.7	95.1	92.9	91.1	88.5	91.5	91.8	87.7	91.8	90.4
Sweet Potatoes	4.5	4.2	4.3	4.3	3.8	3.7	4.2	4.4	3.8	4.7	4.3
Mushrooms	4.0	3.8	3.9	4.0	3.9	4.1	4.1	3.9	4.1	4.1	4.2
Dry Peas & Lentils[9]	0.6	0.7	0.5	0.5	1.5	1.4	0.9	0.6	0.8	0.6	0.6
Dry Edible Beans	7.9	7.6	7.5	7.4	7.3	7.8	7.6	7.0	6.7	6.6	6.7
Total, All Items	438.1	432.9	445.9	445.7	438.0	442.9	449.8	439.0	437.8	442.7	445.6

[1] All production for processing broccoli and cauliflower is for freezing.   [2] Industry allocation suggests that 27 percent of processing carrot production is for canning and 73 percent is for freezing.   [3] On-cob basis.   [4] In-shell basis.   [5] Includes artichokes, brussels sprouts, eggplant, endive/escarole, garlic, radishes, and spinach.   [6] Includes beets, chile peppers (1980-94, all uses), and spinach.   [7] Includes green lima beans, spinach, and miscellaneous freezing vegetables.   [8] Fresh, canning, and freezing data do not add to the total because onions for dehydrating are included in the total.

[9] Preliminary.   [10] Forecast.   Source: Economic Research Service, U.S. Department of Agriculture (ERS-USDA)

VEGETABLES

Average Price Received by Growers for Broccoli in the United States   In Dollars Per Cwt.

Year	Jan.	Feb.	Mar.	Apr.	May	June	July	Aug.	Sept.	Oct.	Nov.	Dec.	Season Average
1997	36.80	27.80	25.90	24.20	23.10	30.30	27.50	23.30	31.20	40.70	27.00	30.20	29.10
1998	34.90	27.10	31.70	40.50	27.10	29.60	23.30	27.60	29.20	32.80	25.80	31.20	30.20
1999	27.70	20.10	23.20	20.20	18.60	23.10	18.70	27.40	29.30	23.00	21.60	39.20	24.10
2000	22.60	20.10	27.40	23.20	44.30	30.00	31.50	25.20	27.70	34.10	56.00	34.10	31.20
2001	22.70	32.30	24.70	26.90	25.50	27.00	23.60	27.10	22.90	24.20	22.20	20.00	26.50
2002	55.30	44.40	33.80	24.00	20.80	28.40	27.00	29.60	40.60	24.00	37.10	35.00	31.40
2003	25.20	40.90	28.10	27.10	29.70	24.60	27.00	29.80	49.10	38.90	48.00	40.00	32.70
2004[1]	33.60	28.50	21.60	23.90	27.20	28.70	24.20	29.70	57.00	43.90	43.70	44.00	33.70

[1] Preliminary.   Source: National Agricultural Statistics Service, U.S. Department of Agriculture (NASS-USDA)

Average Price Received by Growers for Carrots in the United States   In Dollars Per Cwt.

Year	Jan.	Feb.	Mar.	Apr.	May	June	July	Aug.	Sept.	Oct.	Nov.	Dec.	Season Average
1997	15.00	14.70	13.40	12.60	12.60	12.60	12.60	13.10	12.70	12.10	12.50	16.80	12.90
1998	14.00	13.00	13.00	12.60	12.00	11.90	10.60	10.80	10.60	10.90	11.60	11.00	12.20
1999	16.10	19.60	21.50	26.50	25.40	22.80	17.20	13.30	10.10	10.50	11.30	11.50	16.80
2000	9.49	11.60	11.80	12.30	13.80	14.70	15.70	14.50	14.00	14.20	14.30	15.50	13.10
2001	15.90	16.70	17.30	17.30	17.60	20.10	22.00	19.90	15.70	17.50	18.50	19.50	17.10
2002	19.30	19.70	21.10	21.20	21.30	21.60	20.60	20.10	18.10	17.90	18.70	19.50	19.10
2003	19.30	19.10	18.70	19.40	19.90	20.00	19.90	20.50	19.80	19.10	21.60	24.30	19.10
2004[1]	24.50	24.90	24.60	24.20	24.90	22.50	20.20	17.90	16.80	16.70	17.10	18.00	20.30

[1] Preliminary.   Source: National Agricultural Statistics Service, U.S. Department of Agriculture (NASS-USDA)

Average Price Received by Growers for Cauliflower in the United States   In Dollars Per Cwt.

Year	Jan.	Feb.	Mar.	Apr.	May	June	July	Aug.	Sept.	Oct.	Nov.	Dec.	Season Average
1997	30.40	34.70	32.90	27.90	20.70	31.20	38.90	23.40	34.60	47.10	27.60	36.20	32.30
1998	39.10	43.20	49.10	44.70	35.50	26.40	23.20	26.10	32.30	25.90	33.20	37.50	34.50
1999	29.40	31.10	42.80	46.40	23.40	25.50	19.60	25.40	21.70	22.30	35.10	55.50	29.70
2000	22.90	30.20	32.00	34.80	46.00	31.20	37.50	25.20	25.40	21.60	65.30	28.00	32.10
2001	25.70	37.00	23.50	46.50	26.30	37.40	25.60	25.50	24.80	21.70	20.10	20.00	29.20
2002	65.50	30.80	44.10	25.10	26.40	32.70	27.80	24.00	24.70	22.50	37.60	50.00	32.20
2003	24.60	30.70	30.80	20.70	39.50	46.30	27.60	25.30	40.30	25.80	57.00	75.50	35.10
2004[1]	27.30	42.20	24.20	23.60	28.80	46.20	27.50	26.00	31.00	37.30	43.10	51.80	33.00

[1] Preliminary.   Source: National Agricultural Statistics Service, U.S. Department of Agriculture (NASS-USDA)

Average Price Received by Growers for Celery in the United States   In Dollars Per Cwt.

Year	Jan.	Feb.	Mar.	Apr.	May	June	July	Aug.	Sept.	Oct.	Nov.	Dec.	Season Average
1997	16.20	16.20	12.30	10.50	15.40	9.89	19.30	17.00	14.30	13.40	18.40	19.10	14.70
1998	11.20	11.40	16.40	13.80	15.40	12.40	10.60	10.30	10.50	10.40	11.90	14.00	11.70
1999	9.51	8.47	8.35	10.20	12.80	18.30	14.00	10.30	10.60	9.14	12.80	17.20	12.00
2000	19.20	16.00	12.90	21.20	25.60	29.10	18.30	20.30	15.30	12.90	19.40	21.50	18.50
2001	14.60	15.00	15.80	19.10	24.00	33.70	13.50	9.33	9.43	8.22	9.01	13.00	14.40
2002	10.10	19.50	23.50	18.60	12.30	9.37	10.80	10.90	11.70	9.98	15.30	9.50	12.80
2003	8.29	11.80	12.60	17.00	11.00	9.34	12.80	11.90	13.30	15.90	23.40	14.50	13.40
2004[1]	20.80	24.40	13.90	15.60	15.00	13.80	11.70	9.43	11.40	14.90	18.10	13.40	15.10

[1] Preliminary.   Source: National Agricultural Statistics Service, U.S. Department of Agriculture (NASS-USDA)

Average Price Received by Growers for Sweet Corn in the United States   In Dollars Per Cwt.

Year	Jan.	Feb.	Mar.	Apr.	May	June	July	Aug.	Sept.	Oct.	Nov.	Dec.	Season Average
1997	29.00	25.80	33.90	26.10	21.20	17.10	18.60	18.00	16.60	15.20	18.90	19.90	17.70
1998	18.70	31.60	24.20	20.10	17.10	14.00	16.40	16.40	18.10	25.30	24.80	14.30	17.20
1999	19.60	23.30	21.80	18.90	18.50	15.00	17.30	16.60	17.30	16.50	28.40	40.70	16.90
2000	31.50	25.10	19.30	18.70	14.40	18.00	22.00	20.70	20.10	24.00	16.80	33.00	18.50
2001	32.70	34.00	26.10	18.10	24.60	18.60	19.80	19.20	19.00	23.80	24.80	22.60	19.50
2002	24.80	23.50	26.30	19.40	20.80	18.80	27.90	21.80	22.50	25.80	15.50	18.30	19.20
2003	29.00	24.00	18.90	14.90	16.60	23.20	21.30	20.10	19.70	23.70	30.70	22.60	19.30
2004[1]	30.80	20.70	20.20	19.80	19.90	15.20	20.20	22.10	21.60	26.20	28.00	16.60	21.30

[1] Preliminary.   Source: National Agricultural Statistics Service, U.S. Department of Agriculture (NASS-USDA)

Average Price Received by Growers for Head Lettuce in the United States   In Dollars Per Cwt.

Year	Jan.	Feb.	Mar.	Apr.	May	June	July	Aug.	Sept.	Oct.	Nov.	Dec.	Season Average
1995	13.40	9.32	27.00	48.20	47.00	15.60	12.60	15.20	25.60	13.30	11.50	16.10	23.50
1996	11.30	14.90	16.50	13.20	13.30	15.20	12.70	23.50	13.70	15.40	17.70	8.87	14.70
1997	14.90	9.58	13.50	15.70	10.40	14.90	17.10	22.80	22.30	34.80	22.20	25.10	17.50
1998	19.00	10.90	12.50	27.20	14.30	11.80	15.50	16.40	14.00	21.00	10.80	12.50	16.20
1999	10.30	15.50	16.30	20.20	14.00	11.40	12.70	12.00	13.10	13.10	10.70	16.20	13.30
2000	14.60	9.28	14.10	22.80	23.60	13.50	15.00	19.20	29.40	16.20	19.90	12.00	17.30
2001	13.60	22.80	15.10	21.60	18.80	12.10	16.40	26.90	26.20	11.50	10.90	10.00	17.90
2002	26.20	44.10	86.40	14.10	10.20	10.60	11.30	14.60	14.30	13.50	11.90	30.00	21.10
2003	12.10	11.80	9.64	12.50	21.20	32.20	11.90	21.50	23.90	26.30	31.70	21.30	18.10
2004[1]	15.40	19.80	10.40	14.70	10.50	13.30	21.00	17.10	15.20	24.10	17.00	14.00	16.80

[1] Preliminary.   Source: National Agricultural Statistics Service, U.S. Department of Agriculture (NASS-USDA)

Average Price Received by Growers for Tomatoes in the United States   In Dollars Per Cwt.

Year	Jan.	Feb.	Mar.	Apr.	May	June	July	Aug.	Sept.	Oct.	Nov.	Dec.	Season Average
1995	41.10	29.80	37.10	20.50	14.70	35.70	24.40	19.60	19.50	22.50	33.10	25.00	25.50
1996	18.40	40.00	81.70	50.50	24.40	24.20	26.00	22.10	23.40	28.30	29.70	30.40	28.10
1997	32.10	45.90	57.40	24.90	32.20	30.30	29.20	27.60	25.90	26.50	43.60	40.80	31.70
1998	26.40	44.00	34.00	37.20	36.50	29.00	40.90	25.10	28.40	43.00	42.10	42.20	35.20
1999	33.50	23.40	22.30	23.70	21.00	29.00	23.10	25.00	26.50	21.30	26.00	28.90	25.80
2000	21.40	21.10	33.00	34.80	23.10	21.80	24.60	33.90	29.50	42.60	47.80	37.60	30.70
2001	43.80	29.10	56.40	19.00	37.80	28.50	27.40	27.60	23.50	28.60	28.50	25.00	30.00
2002	40.50	26.60	38.50	34.30	29.60	33.00	28.50	25.80	23.70	27.60	40.10	38.00	31.60
2003	47.20	31.70	53.30	30.00	23.70	45.70	37.60	41.00	35.70	30.10	30.50	29.10	37.40
2004[1]	34.50	36.30	42.20	47.90	34.90	21.90	22.90	37.70	36.70	71.10	124.00	47.10	37.20

[1] Preliminary.   Source: National Agricultural Statistics Service, U.S. Department of Agriculture (NASS-USDA)

Frozen Vegetables: January 1 and July 1 Cold Storage Holdings in the U.S.   In Thousands of Pounds

	2000	2001		2002		2003		2004		2005[1]
Crop	July 1	Jan. 1	July 1	Jan. 1	July 1	Jan. 1	July 1	Jan. 1	July 1	Jan. 1
Asparagus	15,494	11,359	14,705	10,686	10,954	6,988	10,977	7,368	14,064	9,280
Limas, Fordhook	4,670	14,353	6,742	14,304	7,323	13,068	4,646	5,984	1,960	8,450
Limas, Baby	24,550	32,577	17,169	50,358	30,017	45,544	20,570	46,383	21,716	48,955
Green Beans, Reg. Cut	48,483	147,391	49,355	140,311	48,312	167,669	55,559	126,175	51,147	151,229
Green Beans, Fr. Style	16,481	28,568	8,955	20,517	7,398	19,726	7,272	23,166	6,596	22,925
Broccoli, Spears	35,731	33,295	35,926	38,035	56,679	49,326	53,689	30,185	50,314	35,882
Broccoli, Chopped & Cut	99,478	74,665	89,062	76,491	66,486	67,727	81,782	47,135	58,843	57,607
Brussels sprouts	14,913	19,632	12,244	17,595	10,645	20,220	11,053	18,961	11,588	23,519
Carrots, Diced	46,718	110,335	60,047	89,361	47,110	99,188	36,340	98,398	49,485	117,745
Carrots, Other	133,499	185,041	101,103	186,831	91,705	143,368	90,741	154,404	75,288	140,440
Cauliflower	37,597	44,974	26,866	36,443	25,589	35,635	16,083	28,146	12,518	37,123
Corn, Cut	121,653	315,297	97,601	351,820	137,242	402,164	176,505	494,490	227,404	502,025
Corn, Cob	105,327	255,615	74,548	263,457	85,566	262,338	108,477	288,957	109,612	242,271
Mixed vegetables	47,855	46,312	47,647	51,453	45,248	41,396	42,360	43,537	56,156	46,892
Okra	53,942	47,217	42,863	35,939	35,964	46,616	35,847	37,596	33,111	33,875
Onion Rings	12,284	14,485	7,799	6,978	8,619	9,636	7,772	6,915	8,426	6,587
Onions, Other	53,534	40,420	38,277	29,893	32,143	29,844	28,757	31,717	28,862	33,278
Blackeye Peas	3,517	4,438	3,257	4,473	5,896	6,323	5,340	3,292	3,004	2,693
Green Peas	254,497	295,784	240,139	224,715	198,452	171,161	162,836	180,850	206,413	230,326
Peas and Carrots Mixed	7,512	7,770	8,571	8,847	6,746	6,597	7,897	6,581	5,674	5,641
Spinach	99,820	50,765	97,278	63,368	106,198	56,193	104,522	46,492	83,287	34,724
Squash, Dummer/Zucchini	41,097	42,572	31,839	43,198	36,878	44,617	33,549	43,614	31,326	45,724
Southern greens	36,237	38,934	28,131	35,861	26,478	22,986	20,243	18,749	16,330	17,328
Other Vegetables	280,841	340,043	248,289	336,555	24,187	313,421	265,556	329,499	248,416	363,579
Total	1,595,730	2,201,842	1,388,413	2,137,489	1,369,523	2,081,751	1,388,373	2,118,594	1,411,540	2,218,098
Potatoes, French Fries	929,810	959,035	1,083,484	1,010,098	937,933	877,292	900,194	869,521	864,111	838,438
Potatoes, Other Frozen	256,500	230,628	271,650	229,659	285,605	253,920	281,594	250,897	263,341	236,381
Potatoes, Total	1,186,310	1,189,663	1,355,134	1,239,757	1,223,538	1,131,212	1,181,788	1,120,418	1,127,452	1,074,819
Grand total	2,782,040	3,391,505	2,743,547	3,377,246	2,593,061	3,212,963	2,570,161	3,239,012	2,538,992	3,292,917

[1] Preliminary.   Source: National Agricultural Statistics Service, U.S. Department of Agriculture (NASS-USDA)

Wheat

Wheat is a cereal grass, but before cultivation it was a wild grass. It has been grown in temperate regions and cultivated for food since prehistoric times. Wheat is believed to have originated in southwestern Asia. Archeological research indicates that wheat was grown in the Nile Valley about 5,000 BC. Wheat is not native to the US and was first grown here in1602 near the Massachusetts coast. The common types of wheat grown in the US are spring and winter wheat. Wheat planted in the spring for summer or autumn harvest is mostly red wheat. Wheat planted in the fall or winter for spring harvest is mostly white wheat. Winter wheat accounts for nearly three-fourths of total US production. Wheat is used mainly as a human food and supplies about 20% of the food calories for the world's population. The primary use for wheat is flour, but it is also used for brewing and distilling and for making oil, gluten, straw for livestock bedding, livestock feed, hay or silage, newsprint, and other products.

Wheat futures and options are traded on the Mercado a Termino de Buenos Aires (MAT), Sydney Futures Exchange (SFE), London International Financial Futures and Options Exchange (LIFFE), Marche a Terme International de France (MATIF), Budapest Commodity Exchange (BCE), the Chicago Board of Trade (CBOT), the Kansas City Board of Trade (KCBT), the Minneapolis Grain Exchange (MGE), the Mid America Commodity Exchange (MidAm) and the Winnipeg Commodity Exchange (WCE). The Chicago Board of Trade's wheat futures contact calls for the delivery of soft red wheat (No. 1 and 2), hard red winter wheat (No. 1 and 2), dark northern spring wheat (No. 1 and 2), No.1 northern spring at 3 cent/bushel premium, or No. 2 northern spring at par.

Prices – Wheat prices on the CBOT nearest futures chart showed strength in early 2004 and reached a 2-year high of $4.24 per bushel in April, but then moved sharply lower in the second half of 2004. Wheat futures closed 2004 at $3.07-1/2 per bushel, down 18% from the 2003 close of $3.77. Wheat prices showed strength in early 2004 in sympathy with soybean prices and due to strong export demand. However, wheat prices then fell sharply in the latter half of 2004 due to the ideal growing season in the US and the fact that Europe and Australia had plenty of wheat available for export later in the year. The US wheat crop in 2004-05 of 2.158 billion bushels wasn't large and was below the 10-year average of 2.209 billion bushels, but it was higher than the poor crops seen in 2001-02 and 2002-03 and that allowed stocks to rise. Specifically, carryover stocks in 2004-05 rose a bit to 553 million bushels from 546 million in 2003-04 and the 8-year low of 491 million bushels seen in 2002-03. Another bearish factor for wheat was that export demand in the 2004-05 marketing year, as of February 2005, was running 11% behind the previous year's pace.

Supply – World wheat production in the 2004-05 marketing year rose +12.5% yr/yr to 622.194 million metric tons, which was a new record high. The world's largest wheat producers are the European Union with 22.0% of world production in 2004-05, China (14.5%), India (11.6%), the US (9.4%), Russia (7.3%), France (5.6%), Canada (4.2%), and Australia (3.5%). China's wheat production in 2004-05 rose +4.18% yr/yr to 90.000 million metric tons, well below its record of 113.880 million metric tons in 1999-00. India's wheat production rose +10.7% yr/yr to 72.080 million metric tons, which was well below its record of 76.369 million metric tons. The world land area harvested with wheat in 2004-5 rose +3.8% yr/yr to 217.4 million hectares (1 hectare equals 10,000 square meters or 2.471 acres), rebounding upward from 209.5 million hectares in 2003-04, which was the smallest wheat harvest area since 1970-71. World wheat yield in 2004-05 posted a new record high of 2.87 metric tons per hectare, up from 2.64 metric tons per hectare seen in 2003-04.

US wheat production in 2004-05 fell –8.0% yr/yr to 2.158 billion bushels, which was well below the record US wheat crop of 2.785 billion bushels seen in 1981-82. The US winter wheat crop in 2004-05 fell –12.7% yr/yr to 1.499 billion bushels, which was well below the record winter wheat crop of 1.097 billion bushels seen in 1981-82. US production of durum wheat in 2004 fell –7.0% yr/yr to 89.893 million bushels. US production of other spring wheat rose +7.1% yr/yr to 568.918 million bushels. The largest US producing states of winter wheat are Kansas with 21.0% of US production in 2004, Oklahoma with 11.0%, Washington with 7.8%, and Texas with 7.2%. US farmers planted 59.674 million acres of wheat in 2004, which was down –4.0% yr/yr from the previous year and was just mildly above the 3-decade low of 59.597 million acres seen in 2001. US wheat yield in 2004-05 was 43.2 bushels per acre, which was just slightly below the record yield of 44.2 bushels per acre seen in 2003-04. Ending stocks for US wheat for 2004-05 are projected by the USDA at 558 million bushels, up +2.2% yr/yr from 546 million bushels in 2003-04.

Demand – World wheat utilization in 2004-05 was 608.0 million metric tons, which was a new record high. US consumption of wheat in 2004-05 rose +1.2% yr/yr to 1.217 billion bushels, which was 12% below the record of 1.381 billion bushels seen in 1998-99. The consumption breakdown shows that 74.8% of US wheat consumption in 2004-05 went for food, 18.5% for feed and residuals, and 6.7% for seed.

Trade – World trade in wheat in 2004-05 rose +3.0% yr/yr to 108.2 million metric tons, and accounted for 17% of world production. US exports of wheat in 2004-05 fell –13.7% yr/yr to 1.000 billion bushels from 1.159 billion bushels in 2003-04 and were well below the record of 1.771 billion bushels of exports seen in 1981-82. US imports of wheat in 2004-05 were only 65.0 million bushels, which was the lowest level of US wheat imports since 1991-92.

World Production of Wheat   In Thousands of Metric Tons

Year	Argentina	Australia	Canada	China	European Union	India	Iran	Pakistan	Kazak-hstan	Russia	Turkey	United States	World Total
1995-6	8,600	16,504	24,989	102,215	86,161	65,470	11,300	6,490	17,002	30,100	15,500	59,404	537,948
1996-7	15,900	22,925	29,801	110,570	98,506	62,097	11,000	7,700	16,907	34,900	16,000	61,980	582,571
1997-8	15,740	19,224	24,280	123,289	94,181	69,350	10,000	8,950	16,650	44,200	16,000	67,534	609,958
1998-9	13,300	21,465	24,082	109,726	103,085	66,350	12,000	4,700	18,694	27,000	18,000	69,327	589,931
1999-00	16,400	24,757	26,941	113,880	114,741	70,780	8,500	11,200	17,854	31,000	16,500	62,475	585,819
2000-1	16,230	22,108	26,519	99,640	124,197	76,369	8,000	9,100	21,079	34,450	18,000	60,641	581,377
2001-2	15,500	24,299	20,568	93,873	113,553	69,680	9,500	12,700	19,023	46,900	15,500	53,001	580,930
2002-3[1]	12,300	10,132	16,198	90,290	124,483	71,810	12,400	12,600	18,226	50,550	16,800	43,705	566,963
2003-4[2]	13,500	26,231	23,552	86,490	106,615	65,100	12,400	11,500	19,192	34,100	16,800	63,814	552,828
2004-5[3]	16,000	21,500	25,850	90,000	136,725	72,060	13,500	9,950	19,000	45,300	17,700	58,738	622,194

[1] Preliminary.   [2] Estimate.   [3] Forecast.   *Source: Foreign Agricultural Service, U.S. Department of Agriculture (FAS-USDA)*

World Supply and Demand of Wheat   In Millions of Metric Tons/Hectares

Crop Year	Area Harvested	Yield	Pro-duction	World Trade	Utilization Total	Ending Stocks	Stocks as a % of Utilization
1995-6	218.8	2.46	537.9	99.2	544.8	155.3	28.5
1996-7	230.2	2.53	582.6	104.0	573.4	164.5	28.7
1997-8	228.4	2.67	610.0	104.5	577.3	197.1	34.1
1998-9	225.0	2.62	589.9	102.0	579.0	208.1	35.9
1999-00	215.4	2.72	585.8	112.6	585.0	208.9	35.7
2000-1	217.5	2.67	581.4	104.0	583.8	206.5	35.4
2001-2	214.6	2.71	580.9	110.8	585.4	202.1	34.5
2002-3[1]	214.0	2.65	567.0	110.0	601.4	167.6	27.9
2003-4[2]	209.5	2.64	552.8	105.0	589.3	131.0	22.2
2004-5[3]	217.4	2.87	623.8	108.2	608.0	146.8	24.1

[1] Preliminary.   [2] Estimate.   [3] Forecast.   *Source: Foreign Agricultural Service, U.S. Department of Agriculture (FAS-USDA)*

Salient Statistics of Wheat in the United States

Crop Year	Planting Intentions	Winter	Spring	All	Average - All Yield Per Acre in Bushels	Value of Production $1,000	Domestic Exports[2]	Imports[3]	Flour	Cereal
			1,000 Acres				-- In Millions of Bushels --		In Pounds	
1995-6	69,031	40,987	19,973	60,955	35.8	9,787,766	1,241.1	67.9	140.0	4.1
1996-7	75,105	39,574	23,245	62,819	36.3	9,782,238	1,001.5	92.3	147.0	4.0
1997-8	70,412	41,340	21,500	62,840	39.5	8,286,741	1,040.4	94.9	147.0	3.9
1998-9	65,821	40,126	18,876	59,002	43.2	6,780,623	1,045.7	103.0	143.0	3.9
1999-00	62,664	35,436	18,337	53,773	42.7	5,593,989	1,086.5	94.5	144.0	3.8
2000-1	62,549	35,002	18,061	53,063	42.0	5,782,107	1,062.0	89.8	146.0	3.8
2001-2	59,597	31,295	17,338	48,633	40.2	5,440,217	962.3	107.6	141.0	3.8
2002-3	60,318	29,742	16,166	45,824	35.0	5,637,416	850.2	77.4	137.0	3.7
2003-4	62,141	36,753	16,310	53,063	44.2	7,929,039	1,159.4	63.0	----	----
2004-5[1]	59,674	34,462	15,537	49,999	43.2	7,191,798	1,025.0	65.0	----	----

Header note: ------------- Acreage Harvested -------------; ------- Foreign Trade[5] -------; Per Capita[4] ------- Consumption -------

[1] Preliminary.   [2] Includes flour milled from imported wheat.   [3] Total wheat, flour & other products.   [4] Civilian only.   [5] Year beginning June.
Source: Economic Research Service, U.S. Department of Agriculture (ERS-USDA)

Supply and Distribution of Wheat in the United States   In Millions of Bushels

Crop Year Beginning June 1	On Farms	Mills, Elevators[3]	Totl Stocks	Production	Imports[4]	Total Supply	Food	Seed	Feed & Res-idual[5]	Total	Exports[4]	Total Disappear-ance
1995-6	163.4	343.2	506.6	2,182.7	67.9	2,757.2	882.9	103.5	153.7	1,140.1	1,241.1	2,381.2
1996-7	74.6	301.4	376.0	2,277.4	92.3	2,745.7	890.7	102.3	307.6	1,300.6	1,001.5	2,302.1
1997-8	154.6	289.0	443.6	2,481.5	94.9	3,020.0	914.1	92.5	250.5	1,257.1	1,040.4	2,297.5
1998-9	224.2	498.3	722.5	2,547.3	103.0	3,372.8	909.7	80.4	390.7	1,381.1	1,045.7	2,426.9
1999-00	277.7	668.2	945.9	2,299.0	94.5	3,336.0	921.0	91.7	279.3	1,299.7	1,086.5	2,386.2
2000-1	226.8	723.0	949.7	2,232.5	89.8	3,267.7	949.6	79.5	300.4	1,329.5	1,062.0	2,391.6
2001-2	197.3	678.9	876.2	1,957.0	107.6	2,931.2	926.4	83.4	182.0	1,191.8	962.3	2,154.1
2002-3	216.8	560.3	777.1	1,605.9	77.4	2,460.4	918.6	84.4	115.7	1,118.7	850.2	1,968.9
2003-4[1]	132.1	359.3	491.4	2,344.8	63.0	2,899.2	906.6	79.7	207.1	1,193.3	1,159.4	2,352.8
2004-5[2]	131.9	414.6	546.4	2,158.2	65.0	2,769.7	910.0	77.0	200.0	1,187.0	1,025.0	2,212.0

Header note: ------------- Supply -------------; ------------- Domestic Disappearance -------------; Stocks, June 1

[1] Preliminary.   [2] Estimate.   [3] Also warehouses and all off-farm storage not otherwise designated, including flour mills.   [4] Imports & exports are for wheat, including flour & other products in terms of wheat.   [5] Mostly feed use.   *Source: Economic Research Service, U.S. Department of Agriculture*

WHEAT

Stocks, Production and Exports of Wheat in the United States, by Class   In Millions of Bushels

Year Beginning June 1	Hard Spring Stocks June 1	Hard Spring Pro-duction	Hard Spring Exports[3]	Durum[2] Stocks June 1	Durum[2] Pro-duction	Durum[2] Exports[3]	Hard Winter Stocks June 1	Hard Winter Pro-duction	Hard Winter Exports[3]	Soft Red Winter Stocks June 1	Soft Red Winter Pro-duction	Soft Red Winter Exports[3]	White Stocks June 1	White Pro-duction	White Exports[3]
1995-6	193	475	230	26	102	39	194	825	384	37	456	250	57	325	238
1996-7	106	631	300	25	116	38	154	759	286	35	420	140	55	352	237
1997-8	166	491	240	31	88	57	143	1,098	358	45	472	180	59	332	205
1998-9	220	486	247	26	138	40	307	1,180	453	80	443	105	90	301	198
1999-00	233	448	230	55	99	44	435	1,051	486	136	454	170	87	247	160
2000-1	218	502	230	50	110	50	458	846	403	133	471	176	91	303	203
2001-2	210	476	216	45	84	50	411	767	349	135	400	199	75	232	147
2002-3	230	351	259	33	80	32	363	620	309	78	321	105	73	233	148
2003-4	145	500	272	28	97	44	188	1,071	512	55	380	140	75	297	192
2004-5[1]	157	525	295	26	90	28	227	856	377	64	380	130	72	306	195

[1] Preliminary.   [2] Includes Red Durum.   [3] Includes four made from U.S. wheat & shipments to territories.   *Source: Economic Research Service, U.S. Department of Agriculture (ERS-USDA)*

Seeded Acreage, Yield and Production of all Wheat in the United States

Year	Seeded Acreage -- 1,000 Acres Winter	Seeded Acreage Other Spring	Seeded Acreage Durum	Seeded Acreage All	Yield Per Harvested Acre (Bushels) Winter	Yield Other Spring	Yield Durum	Yield All	Production (1,000,000 Bushels) Winter	Production Other Spring	Production Durum	Production All
1995	48,686	17,010	3,436	69,132	37.7	32.2	30.5	35.8	1,544.7	535.7	102.3	2,182.6
1996	51,445	20,030	3,630	75,105	37.1	35.1	32.6	36.3	1,469.6	691.7	116.1	2,277.4
1997	47,985	19,117	3,310	70,412	44.6	29.9	27.6	39.5	1,845.5	548.2	87.8	2,481.5
1998	46,449	15,567	3,805	65,821	46.9	34.9	37.0	43.2	1,880.7	528.5	138.1	2,547.3
1999	43,331	15,348	4,035	62,714	47.8	34.1	27.8	42.7	1,696.6	503.1	99.3	2,299.0
2000	43,393	15,299	3,937	62,629	44.7	38.4	30.7	42.0	1,562.7	556.6	109.8	2,232.5
2001	41,078	15,609	2,910	59,597	43.5	35.2	30.0	40.2	1,361.5	512.0	83.6	1,957.0
2002	41,766	15,639	2,913	60,318	38.2	29.1	29.5	35.0	1,137.0	388.9	80.0	1,605.9
2003	45,384	13,842	2,915	62,141	46.7	39.5	33.7	44.2	1,716.7	531.4	96.6	2,344.8
2004[1]	43,350	13,763	2,561	59,674	43.5	43.2	38.0	43.2	1,499.4	568.9	89.9	2,158.2

[1] Preliminary.   *Source: Economic Research Service, U.S. Department of Agriculture (ERS-USDA)*

Production of Winter Wheat in the United States, by State   In Thousands of Bushels

Year	Colorado	Idaho	Illinois	Kansas	Missouri	Montana	Neb-raska	Ohio	Okla-homa	Oregon	Texas	Wash-ington	Total
1995	102,600	58,520	68,110	286,000	47,970	54,800	86,100	73,810	109,200	57,750	75,600	133,300	1,544,653
1996	70,400	68,800	41,800	255,200	48,750	61,380	73,500	51,870	93,100	58,680	75,400	164,500	1,469,618
1997	86,400	68,800	66,490	501,400	58,320	55,100	70,300	68,670	169,600	53,790	118,900	141,900	1,845,528
1998	99,450	63,140	57,600	494,900	57,500	48,750	82,800	74,240	198,900	52,930	136,500	136,500	1,880,733
1999	103,200	53,960	60,600	432,400	44,160	36,860	81,600	72,100	150,500	29,610	122,400	96,860	1,696,580
2000	68,150	65,700	52,440	347,800	49,400	44,550	59,400	79,920	142,800	45,260	66,000	131,400	1,562,733
2001	66,000	51,830	43,920	328,000	41,040	19,140	59,200	60,300	122,100	28,000	108,800	106,750	1,361,479
2002	36,300	48,510	30,870	270,600	33,440	21,840	50,160	50,220	103,600	29,820	78,300	104,400	1,137,001
2003	77,000	57,600	52,650	480,000	53,070	67,340	83,720	68,000	179,400	47,940	96,600	117,000	1,716,721
2004[1]	45,900	63,000	53,100	314,500	48,360	66,830	61,050	55,180	164,500	47,580	108,500	117,250	1,499,434

[1] Preliminary.   *Source: Crop Reporting Board, U.S. Department of Agriculture (CRB-USDA)*

Official Winter Wheat Crop Production Reports in the United States   In Thousands of Bushels

Crop Year	May 1	June 1	July 1	August 1	September 1	Current December	Final
1995-6	1,638,211	1,608,396	1,529,950	1,552,230	1,552,230	-----	1,544,653
1996-7	1,363,851	1,369,861	1,484,836	1,494,716	-----	-----	1,477,058
1997-8	1,561,470	1,603,580	1,780,554	1,855,474	-----	-----	1,845,528
1998-9	1,706,784	1,743,294	1,898,719	1,914,359	-----	-----	1,880,733
1999-00	1,614,799	1,611,559	1,673,222	1,688,582	-----	-----	1,696,580
2000-1	1,648,805	1,621,966	1,588,376	1,594,321	-----	-----	1,561,723
2001-2	1,341,381	1,321,126	1,366,192	1,385,048	-----	-----	1,361,479
2002-3	1,300,726	1,237,671	1,178,320	1,158,710	-----	-----	1,137,001
2003-4	1,563,314	1,626,376	1,715,912	1,712,150	-----	-----	1,716,721
2004-5[1]	1,550,395	1,530,742	1,469,735	1,489,408	-----	-----	1,499,434

[1] Preliminary.   *Source: Crop Reporting Board, U.S. Department of Agriculture (CRB-USDA)*

Production of All Spring Wheat in the United States, by State   In Thousands of Bushels

			Durum Wheat						Other Spring Wheat					
Year	Arizona	California	Mon-tana	North Dakota	South Dakota	Total Durum	Idaho	Minne-sota	Mon-tana	North Dakota	Oregon	South Dakota	Wash-ington	Total Other
1995	8,514	6,800	7,950	77,760	896	102,280	44,800	70,400	133,000	221,400	5,928	33,600	20,470	535,658
1996	14,760	13,800	7,000	79,380	720	116,090	50,400	105,000	106,600	313,500	6,405	83,250	18,170	691,680
1997	8,010	13,680	7,540	57,860	513	87,783	45,030	75,200	118,900	210,000	6,600	63,000	23,220	548,155
1998	15,120	15,750	12,040	94,400	624	138,119	39,270	78,720	108,000	211,200	4,560	59,200	20,925	528,469
1999	7,275	8,925	9,450	72,000	1,512	99,322	50,560	78,000	108,000	168,000	5,049	59,850	27,280	503,108
2000	8,075	9,700	13,160	78,300	468	109,805	42,750	95,550	77,500	233,600	8,280	60,040	33,480	556,632
2001	7,917	8,505	11,880	54,600	576	83,556	33,320	79,200	65,550	234,600	4,650	64,350	25,830	512,008
2002	8,928	9,000	12,995	48,750	147	79,960	29,900	61,200	75,900	165,200	4,680	24,000	25,370	388,917
2003	11,500	11,500	14,490	58,410	621	96,637	27,060	104,400	60,500	252,800	5,600	56,280	22,345	531,402
2004[1]	9,603	9,000	17,600	53,760	450	89,893	38,710	89,650	89,900	246,000	8,400	71,910	26,250	568,918

[1] Preliminary.   Source: Crop Reporting Board, U.S. Department of Agriculture (CRB-USDA)

Grindings of Wheat by Mills in the United States   In Millions of Bushels (60 Pounds Each)

Year	July	Aug.	Sept.	Oct.	Nov.	Dec.	Jan.	Feb.	Mar.	Apr.	May	June	Total
1995-6	69.8	77.8	74.2	78.4	74.8	70.0	70.1	72.4	72.1	69.4	72.6	67.7	869.1
1996-7	73.6	77.4	75.1	82.7	73.7	71.3	69.6	66.9	70.3	73.2	72.5	72.2	878.6
1997-8	76.4	75.8	78.4	82.7	75.3	74.8	-----	215.5	-----	-----	216.6	-----	895.5
1998-9	-----	224.7	-----	-----	238.6	-----	-----	213.5	-----	-----	228.0	-----	904.9
1999-00	-----	234.0	-----	-----	242.2	-----	-----	225.6	-----	-----	226.8	-----	928.7
2000-1	-----	244.7	-----	-----	247.7	-----	-----	223.8	-----	-----	221.3	-----	937.5
2001-2	-----	230.2	-----	-----	238.7	-----	-----	217.0	-----	-----	217.6	-----	903.6
2002-3	-----	230.3	-----	-----	224.4	-----	-----	215.8	-----	-----	217.4	-----	888.0
2003-4	-----	231.8	-----	-----	224.2	-----	-----	210.9	-----	-----	212.3	-----	879.1
2004-5[1]	-----	223.1	-----	-----	218.9	-----	-----						884.0

[1] Preliminary.   Source: Bureau of the Census, U.S. Department of Commerce

Wheat Stocks in the United States   In Millions of Bushels

		On Farms				Off Farms				Total Stocks		
Year	Mar. 1	June 1	Sept. 1	Dec. 1	Mar. 1	June 1	Sept. 1	Dec. 1	Mar. 1	June 1	Sept. 1	Dec. 1
1995	335.3	163.4	743.6	477.0	633.8	343.2	1,137.5	861.3	969.1	506.6	1,881.1	1,338.3
1996	220.6	74.6	824.5	584.2	602.9	301.4	899.7	634.7	823.5	376.0	1,724.2	1,218.8
1997	320.8	154.6	794.4	604.0	501.1	289.0	1,282.0	1,015.2	821.8	443.6	2,076.3	1,619.2
1998	399.9	224.2	885.7	680.2	766.6	498.3	1,499.6	1,215.5	1,166.6	722.5	2,385.3	1,895.7
1999	471.2	277.7	888.1	647.4	979.2	668.2	1,557.0	1,236.3	1,450.4	945.9	2,445.0	1,883.7
2000	424.7	226.8	808.4	623.4	991.8	723.0	1,544.3	1,182.7	1,416.5	949.7	2,352.7	1,806.1
2001	384.8	197.3	696.9	517.9	953.6	678.9	1,459.0	1,105.6	1,338.4	876.2	2,155.8	1,623.5
2002	338.5	216.8	580.2	384.8	871.3	560.3	1,170.8	935.1	1,209.8	777.1	1,751.0	1,319.9
2003	236.3	132.1	687.3	491.9	670.3	359.3	1,351.7	1,028.4	906.6	491.4	2,039.0	1,520.3
2004[1]	257.9	131.9	790.6	531.0	762.7	414.6	1,147.8	899.7	1,020.6	546.4	1,938.4	1,430.7

[1] Preliminary.   Source: National Agricultural Statistics Service, U.S. Department of Agriculture (NASS-USDA)

Wheat Supply and Distribution in Canada, Australia and Argentina   In Millions of Metric Tons

	Canada (Year Beginning Aug. 1)					Australia (Year Beginning Oct. 1)					Argentina (Year Beginning Dec. 1)				
		Supply		Disappearance			Supply		Disappearance			Supply		Disappearance	
Crop Year	Stocks Aug. 1	New Crop	Total Supply	Domestic	Exports[3]	Stocks Oct. 1	New Crop	Total Supply	Domestic	Exports[3]	Stocks Dec. 1	New Crop	Total Supply	Domestic	Exports[3]
1995-6	5.7	25.0	30.7	7.8	16.3	2.4	16.5	18.9	3.7	13.3	.2	8.6	8.8	4.2	4.5
1996-7	6.7	29.8	36.5	8.2	19.5	2.0	22.9	24.9	3.3	19.2	.2	15.9	16.1	4.9	10.2
1997-8	9.0	24.3	33.3	7.3	20.1	2.4	19.2	21.6	4.0	15.3	1.0	15.7	16.7	4.8	11.2
1998-9	6.0	24.1	30.1	8.1	14.7	2.3	21.5	23.8	4.5	16.5	.8	13.3	14.1	4.9	8.6
1999-00	7.4	26.9	34.4	8.1	19.2	2.8	24.8	27.6	5.2	17.8	.7	16.4	17.1	4.9	11.6
2000-1	7.3	26.5	33.8	7.0	17.3	4.6	22.1	26.7	5.3	15.9	.6	16.2	16.8	5.0	11.3
2001-2	9.7	20.6	30.2	7.6	16.3	5.5	24.3	29.8	5.4	16.4	.6	15.5	16.1	4.9	10.1
2002-3	6.7	16.2	22.9	8.2	9.4	8.0	10.1	18.2	6.2	9.1	1.1	12.3	13.4	5.2	6.8
2003-4[1]	5.7	23.6	29.3	7.6	15.8	3.1	26.2	29.4	6.0	18.0	1.5	14.0	15.5	5.2	9.4
2004-5[2]	6.1	25.9	31.9	9.2	15.0	5.5	21.5	27.0	5.6	17.0	.9	16.0	16.9	5.5	10.5

[1] Preliminary.   [2] Forecast.   [3] Including flour.   Source: Foreign Agricultural Service, U.S. Department of Agriculture (FAS-USDA)

WHEAT

Quarterly Supply and Disappearance of Wheat in the United States — In Millions of Bushels

Crop Year Beginning June 1	Supply				Disappearance						Ending Stocks		
	Beginning Stocks	Production	Imports[3]	Total Supply	Domestic Use				Exports[3]	Total Disappearance	Gov't Owned[4]	Privately Owned[5]	Total Stocks
					Food	Seed	Feed & Residual[6]	Total					
1994-5	568.5	2,321.0	92.0	2,981.4	852.5	89.2	344.9	1,286.6	1,188.3	2,474.9	142.1	364.5	506.6
June-Aug.	568.5	2,321.0	30.7	2,920.2	213.2	1.6	376.3	591.1	259.6	850.7	146.4	1,923.1	2,069.5
Sept.-Nov.	2,069.5	-----	21.4	2,090.9	229.3	61.1	-28.8	261.6	338.2	599.8	142.8	1,348.3	1,491.1
Dec.-Feb.	1,491.1	-----	17.7	1,508.8	201.5	2.2	25.6	229.3	310.4	539.7	142.3	826.8	969.1
Mar.-May	969.1	-----	22.2	991.2	208.5	24.3	-28.2	204.6	280.1	484.7	142.1	364.5	506.6
1995-6	506.6	2,182.6	67.9	2,757.1	882.9	104.1	153.0	1,139.9	1,241.1	2,381.1	118.2	257.8	376.0
June-Aug.	506.6	2,182.6	22.7	2,711.9	215.3	8.0	305.0	528.3	302.5	830.8	141.5	1,739.6	1,881.1
Sept.-Nov.	1,881.1	-----	16.3	1,897.4	232.2	64.9	-98.7	198.3	360.8	559.1	141.2	1,197.1	1,338.3
Dec.-Feb.	1,338.3	-----	11.8	1,350.0	215.8	3.0	13.3	232.1	294.5	526.6	137.5	686.0	823.5
Mar.-May	823.5	-----	17.2	840.7	219.6	28.2	-66.5	181.3	283.4	464.6	118.2	257.8	376.0
1996-7	376.0	2,277.4	92.3	2,745.7	890.7	102.3	307.6	1,300.6	1,001.5	2,302.1	93.0	350.6	443.6
June-Aug.	376.0	2,277.4	14.9	2,668.3	223.7	8.7	377.5	610.0	334.1	944.1	109.5	1,614.7	1,724.2
Sept.-Nov.	1,724.2	-----	20.7	1,744.9	233.8	59.9	-76.0	217.8	308.3	526.1	96.1	1,122.7	1,218.8
Dec.-Feb.	1,218.8	-----	27.1	1,245.9	212.7	1.8	30.3	244.7	179.3	424.1	95.3	726.5	821.8
Mar.-May	821.8	-----	29.7	851.6	220.5	31.8	-24.2	228.1	179.8	407.9	93.0	350.6	443.6
1997-8	443.6	2,481.5	94.9	3,020.0	914.1	92.5	250.5	1,257.1	1,040.4	2,297.5	94.2	628.3	722.5
June-Aug.	443.6	2,481.5	22.7	2,947.8	227.9	3.1	352.2	583.2	288.2	871.4	93.2	1,983.1	2,076.3
Sept.-Nov.	2,076.3	-----	22.8	2,099.1	238.7	58.6	-113.4	183.9	296.0	479.9	93.1	1,526.1	1,619.2
Dec.-Feb.	1,619.2	-----	23.8	1,643.0	219.2	2.1	.3	221.6	254.9	476.4	93.0	1,073.6	1,166.6
Mar.-May	1,166.6	-----	25.7	1,192.2	228.3	28.7	11.4	268.4	201.3	469.8	94.2	628.3	722.5
1998-9	722.5	2,547.3	103.0	3,372.8	909.7	80.5	542.1	1,532.4	1,042.2	2,574.6	127.9	818.0	945.9
June-Aug.	722.5	2,547.3	24.4	3,294.2	225.7	1.0	424.9	651.6	257.3	908.9	99.8	2,285.5	2,385.3
Sept.-Nov.	2,385.3	-----	23.9	2,409.2	240.7	54.9	73.8	369.5	291.8	661.2	126.6	1,769.1	1,895.7
Dec.-Feb.	1,895.7	-----	27.7	1,923.4	213.2	1.4	11.6	226.2	246.8	473.0	124.2	1,326.2	1,450.4
Mar.-May	1,450.4	-----	27.0	1,477.4	230.1	23.2	31.8	285.1	246.3	531.5	127.9	818.0	945.9
1999-00	945.9	2,299.0	94.5	3,339.4	924.7	91.6	283.8	1,300.1	1,089.5	2,389.6	103.9	845.8	949.7
June-Aug.	945.9	2,299.0	30.6	3,275.5	230.5	6.4	270.0	506.9	323.6	830.5	132.2	2,312.8	2,445.0
Sept.-Nov.	2,445.0	-----	19.5	2,464.5	241.1	54.6	-8.0	287.7	291.3	579.0	115.0	1,770.6	1,885.6
Dec.-Feb.	1,885.6	-----	19.4	1,905.1	220.9	2.3	30.7	253.9	235.9	489.8	108.7	1,306.6	1,416.5
Mar.-May	1,415.3	-----	25.0	1,440.3	232.2	28.4	-8.8	251.8	238.8	490.6	103.9	845.8	949.7
2000-1	949.7	2,228.2	89.8	3,267.7	949.6	79.5	300.4	1,329.5	1,062.0	2,391.6	97.0	779.2	876.2
June-Aug.	949.7	2,228.2	20.4	3,198.3	238.8	1.1	317.9	557.8	287.8	845.6	108.9	2,243.8	2,352.7
Sept.-Nov.	2,352.7	-----	25.1	2,377.8	253.0	49.8	-24.5	278.4	293.3	571.6	102.9	1,703.2	1,806.1
Dec.-Feb.	1,806.1	-----	21.4	1,827.5	228.2	3.5	11.4	243.1	246.1	489.1	104.4	1,234.0	1,338.4
Mar.-May	1,338.4	-----	22.9	1,361.3	229.7	25.2	-4.5	250.3	234.8	485.1	97.0	779.2	876.2
2001-2	876.2	1,947.5	107.6	2,931.2	926.4	83.4	182.0	1,191.8	962.3	2,154.1	99.0	678.1	777.1
June-Aug.	876.2	1,947.5	25.7	2,849.3	233.8	3.5	237.9	475.2	218.3	693.5	97.7	2,058.1	2,155.8
Sept.-Nov.	2,155.8	-----	29.0	2,184.9	245.1	51.6	-23.1	273.6	287.8	561.4	96.9	1,526.6	1,623.5
Dec.-Feb.	1,623.5	-----	27.6	1,651.0	221.1	2.0	-6.6	216.5	224.7	441.2	96.9	1,112.9	1,209.8
Mar.-May	1,209.8	-----	25.2	1,235.0	226.4	26.3	-26.2	226.4	231.5	457.9	99.0	678.1	777.1
2002-3	777.0	1,606.0	85.0	2,468.0	923.0	85.0	119.0	1,127.0	851.0	1,978.0	66.0	425.4	491.4
June-Aug.	777.0	1,606.0	27.0	2,410.0	233.0	3.0	185.0	421.0	240.0	661.0	91.4	1,657.6	1,749.0
Sept.-Nov.	1,751.0	-----	23.0	1,772.0	238.0	55.0	-75.0	218.0	235.0	453.0	80.9	1,239.0	1,319.9
Dec.-Feb.	1,320.0	-----	16.0	1,336.0	219.0	3.0	17.0	239.0	190.0	429.0	74.0	832.6	906.6
Mar.-May	905.0	-----	19.0	926.0	233.0	24.0	-8.0	249.0	186.0	435.0	66.0	425.4	491.4
2003-4[1]	491.0	2,345.0	73.0	2,909.0	912.0	79.0	212.0	1,203.0	1,160.0	2,363.0			546.0
June-Aug.	491.0	2,345.0	19.0	2,855.0	233.0	2.0	317.0	552.0	265.0	817.0	60.0	1,979.0	2,039.0
Sept.-Nov.	2,039.0	-----	23.0	2,062.0	242.0	53.0	-59.0	236.0	305.0	541.0	60.0	1,461.1	1,520.0
Dec.-Feb.	1,520.0	-----	14.0	1,534.0	214.0	2.0	5.0	221.0	293.0	514.0			1,021.0
Mar.-May	1,021.0	-----	17.0	1,037.0	223.0	22.0	-51.0	194.0	297.0	491.0			546.0
2004-5[2]	546.0	2,158.0	72.0	2,776.0	930.0	104.0	410.0	1,444.0	1,174.0	2,618.0			
June-Aug.	546.0	2,158.0	17.0	2,722.0	226.0	4.0	267.0	497.0	286.0	783.0			1,938.0
Sept.-Nov.	1,938.0	----	19.0	1,957.0	239.0	48.0	-62.0	225.0	301.0	526.0			1,431.0

[1] Preliminary. [2] Forecast. [3] Imports & exports include flour and other products expressed in wheat equivalent. [4] Uncommitted, Government only.
[5] Includes total loans. [6] Includes alcoholic beverages. *Source: Economic Research Service, U.S. Department of Agriculture (ERS-USDA)*

Wheat Government Loan Program Data in the United States   Loan Rates (Cents Per Bushel)

| | | | ------------- Farm Loan Prices ------------- | | | | | | ------------- Stocks Ending May 31 ------------- | | | | |
Crop Year Beginning June 1	National Average[3]	Target Rate[4]	Corn Belt (Soft Red Winter)	Central & Southern Plains (Hard Winter)	Northern Plains (Spring & Durum)	Pacific Northwest (White)	Placed Under Loan	% of Production	Acquired by CCC Under Program	Total Stocks	Total CCC Stocks	CCC Loans	Outstanding Farmer-Owned Reserve	"Free"
										In Millions of Bushels				
1996-7	258	NA	253	257	258	271	194	8.5	0	444	93	72	0	351
1997-8	258	NA	253	257	258	271	264	10.6	0	722	94	134	0	629
1998-9	258	NA	253	257	258	271	363	14.2	0	946	128	140	0	818
1999-00	258	NA	253	257	258	271	154	6.7	0	950	104	62	0	846
2000-1	258	NA	253	257	258	271	181	8.1	0	876	97	42	0	779
2001-2	258	NA	NA	NA	NA	NA	197	9.9	0	777	99	78	0	678
2002-3[1]	280	386	NA	NA	NA	NA	120	7.4	0	491	66	51	0	425
2003-4[2]	280	386	NA	NA	NA	NA				546	61	45	0	485

[1] Preliminary.   [2] Estimate.   [3] The national average loan rate at the farm as a percentage of the parity-priced wheat at the beginning of the marketing year.   [4] 1996-97 through 2001-02 marketing years, target prices not applicable.   NA = Not avaliable.   *Source: Agricultural Marketing Service, U.S. Department of Agriculture (AMS-USDA)*

Exports of Wheat (Only)[2] from the United States   In Thousands of Bushels

Year	June	July	Aug.	Sept.	Oct.	Nov.	Dec.	Jan.	Feb.	Mar.	Apr.	May	Total
1996-7	73,715	108,437	145,840	125,910	98,302	75,245	50,979	63,431	59,039	55,936	69,821	47,640	974,295
1997-8	65,654	92,465	123,141	119,029	89,331	79,528	80,906	97,090	68,972	63,914	64,623	68,359	1,013,012
1998-9	67,372	86,605	96,664	90,507	109,168	81,913	96,486	73,017	63,794	65,522	86,066	85,057	1,002,171
1999-00	90,594	110,814	107,168	91,438	96,154	89,211	84,460	71,763	64,198	68,836	73,815	87,789	1,036,240
2000-1	88,581	82,739	104,944	113,785	82,716	86,034	94,705	60,743	85,797	71,502	83,157	68,908	1,023,611
2001-2	59,190	64,911	89,582	86,941	94,598	99,800	81,369	72,114	63,446	78,070	84,211	58,449	932,681
2002-3	63,219	78,013	92,345	73,606	78,866	75,678	69,485	62,769	48,618	65,990	55,764	59,438	823,791
2003-4	54,665	88,042	115,869	125,312	101,168	76,222	79,811	109,607	94,480	96,685	102,588	91,917	1,136,366
2004-5[1]	80,599	97,962	103,222	119,965	92,634	83,947							1,156,658

[1] Preliminary.   [2] Grains.   *Source: Economic Research Service, U.S. Department of Agriculture (ERS-USDA)*

United States Wheat and Wheat Flour Imports and Exports   In Thousands of Bushels

| | --------- Imports --------- | | | | | --------- Exports --------- | | | | | | |
Crop Year Beginning June 1	Wheat — Suitable for Milling	Wheat — Unfit for Human Consumption	Grain	Flour & Products[2]	Total	P.L. 480	Foreign Donations Sec. 416	Aid[3]	Total Concessional	CCC Export Credit	Export Exhancement Programs	Total U.S. Wheat Exports
			--- Wheat Equivalent ---				In Thousands of Metric Tons					
1995-6	47,753	----	47,753	20,180	67,933	1,530	0	NA	1,530	5,662	570	33,708
1996-7	71,727	----	71,727	20,605	92,333	1,009	0	NA	1,155	4,844	0	24,526
1997-8	73,245	----	73,245	21,556	94,801	1,453	0	NA	1,727	5,460	0	25,791
1998-9	79,766	----	79,768	23,219	102,987	556	4,682	NA	5,334	3,621	0	28,806
1999-00	72,408	----	72,407	22,104	94,512	674	2,635	NA	3,436	3,691	0	27,838
2000-1	66,313	----	66,313	23,511	89,824	1,294	1,638	NA	3,109	4,026	0	25,275
2001-2	82,615	----	82,615	24,935	107,551	1,093	875	NA	2,035	4,614	0	25,353
2002-3[1]	49,743	----	49,742	27,638	77,380	1,475	213	NA	1,836	3,610	0	24,434

[1] Preliminary.   [2] Includes macaroni, semolina & similar products.   [3] Shipment mostly under the Commodity Import Program, financed with foreign aid funds.   NA = Not available.   *Source: Economic Research Service, U.S. Department of Agriculture (ERS-USDA)*

Comparative Average Cash Wheat Prices   In Dollars Per Bushel

| | | --- Minneapolis --- | | | | | | | | | ------- Export Prices[2] (U.S. $ Per Metric Ton) ------- | | | |
Crop Year Beginning June 1	Received by U.S. Farmers	No. 2 Soft Red Winter, Chicago	No. 1 Hard Red Ordinary Protein, Kansas City	No. 2 Soft Red Winter, St. Louis	No. 1 Dark Northern Spring 14%	No. 1 Hard Amber Durum	No. 1 Soft White, Portland, Oregon	No. 2 Western White Pacific Northwest	No. 2 Soft White, Toledo	Australian Standard Wheat	Canada Vancouver No. 1 CWRS 13 ½%	Argentina F.O.B. B.A.	U.S. Gulf No. 2 Hard Winter	Rotterdam C.I.F. U.S. No. 2 Hard Winter
1997-8	3.38	3.29	3.71	3.43	4.31	5.97	3.81	3.41	3.12	192	181	157	160	209
1998-9	2.65	2.46	3.08	2.40	3.83	4.06	3.02	2.64	2.27	154	163	120	126	181
1999-00	2.48	2.19	2.87	2.39	3.65	4.22	3.02	2.72	1.94	143	152	114	112	NA
2000-1	2.62	2.39	3.30	2.39	3.62	4.59	2.99	2.72	2.98	145	149	118	114	163
2001-2	2.78	2.69	3.25	2.80	3.61	4.99	3.56	3.67	2.67	157	149	121	125	161
2002-3	3.56	3.40	4.22	3.50	4.47	4.25	3.95	4.58	3.34	185	194	158	160	189
2003-4	3.40	3.66	4.03	3.76	4.39	5.31	3.95	4.24	3.59	179	179	162	156	198
2004-5[1]	3.30-3.45	3.01	4.03	3.36	4.66		3.94	4.07	3.11				153	

[1] Preliminary.   [2] Calendar year.   NA = Not available.   *Source: Economic Research Service, U.S. Department of Agriculture (ERS-USDA)*

WHEAT

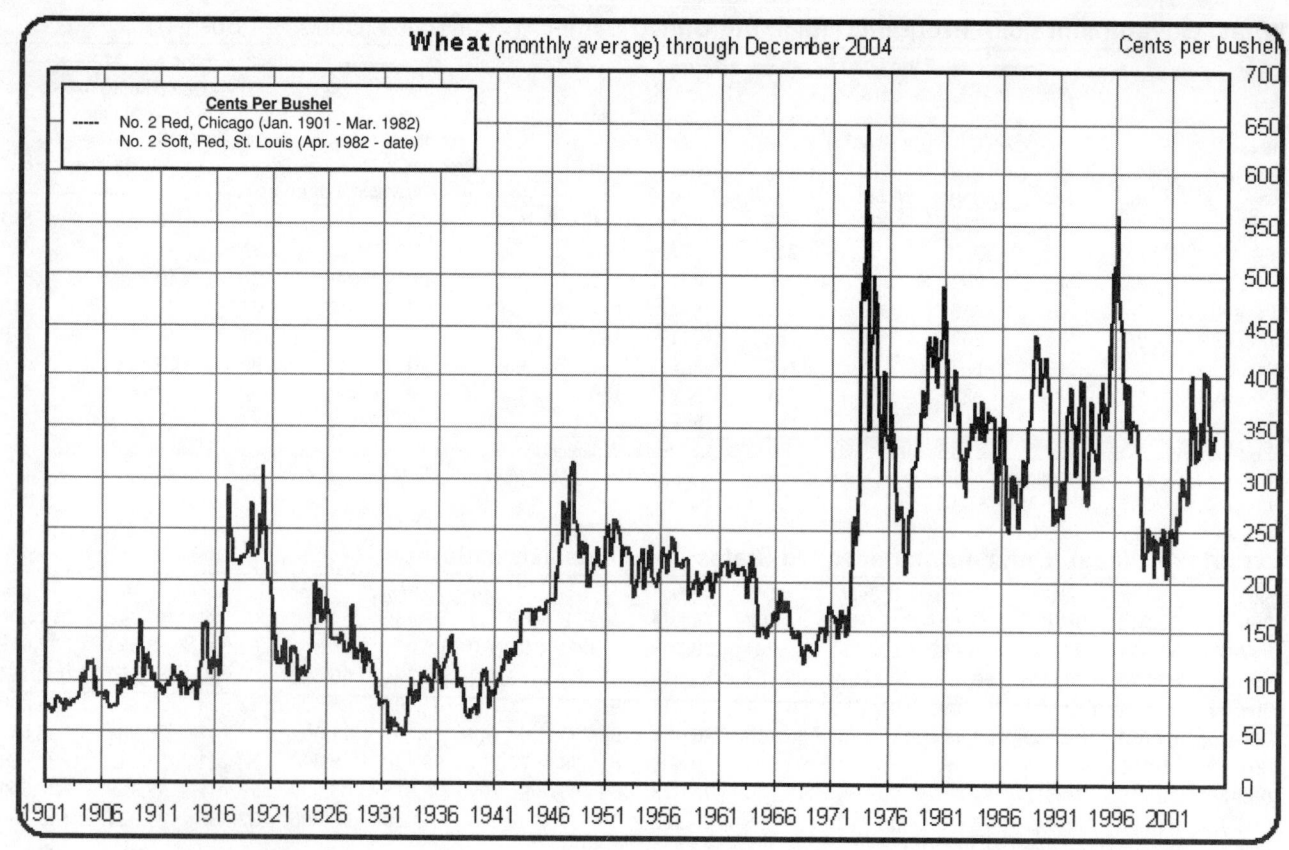

Wheat (monthly average) through December 2004   Cents per bushel

Cents Per Bushel
----- No. 2 Red, Chicago (Jan. 1901 - Mar. 1982)
No. 2 Soft, Red, St. Louis (Apr. 1982 - date)

Average Price of No. 2 Soft Red Winter (30 Days) Wheat in Chicago   In Dollars Per Bushel

Year	June	July	Aug.	Sept.	Oct.	Nov.	Dec.	Jan.	Feb.	Mar.	Apr.	May	Average
1995-6	3.91	4.41	4.28	4.53	4.72	4.85	5.04	4.92	5.10	4.99	5.65	5.57	4.83
1996-7	4.94	4.64	4.49	4.33	3.96	3.57	3.54	3.47	3.29	3.49	3.77	3.57	3.92
1997-8	3.38	3.30	3.52	3.49	3.51	3.44	3.31	3.27	3.26	3.25	2.91	2.87	3.29
1998-9	2.72	2.51	2.39	2.32	2.56	2.58	2.49	2.46	2.28	2.63	2.31	2.24	2.46
1999-00	2.20	1.94	2.09	2.12	1.98	1.96	2.12	2.34	2.38	2.34	2.30	2.45	2.19
2000-1	2.41	2.14	2.08	2.13	2.36	2.42	2.47	2.57	2.49	2.56	2.52	2.51	2.39
2001-2	2.40	2.56	2.57	2.57	2.68	2.75	2.83	2.96	2.74	2.76	2.75	2.73	2.69
2002-3	2.81	3.19	3.42	3.92	3.89	3.85	3.53	3.32	3.44	3.14	3.08	3.25	3.40
2003-4	3.11	3.23	3.63	3.46	3.42	3.87	3.92	3.90	3.84	3.85	3.92	3.73	3.66
2004-5[1]	3.46	3.26	2.92	2.97	2.82	2.79	2.88						3.01

[1] Preliminary.   *Source: Economic Research Service, U.S. Department of Agriculture (ERS-USDA)*

Average Price[1] Received by Farmers for Wheat in the United States   In Dollars Per Bushel

Year	June	July	Aug.	Sept.	Oct.	Nov.	Dec.	Jan.	Feb.	Mar.	Apr.	May	Average
1995-6	3.84	4.10	4.26	4.53	4.72	4.81	4.88	4.83	4.98	5.07	5.32	5.73	4.55
1996-7	5.25	4.73	4.58	4.37	4.18	4.14	4.06	4.03	3.88	3.93	4.11	4.09	4.28
1997-8	3.52	3.23	3.56	3.67	3.55	3.50	3.45	3.33	3.27	3.32	3.15	3.06	3.38
1998-9	2.77	2.56	2.39	2.41	2.79	2.97	2.87	2.80	2.74	2.65	2.62	2.53	2.68
1999-00	2.50	2.22	2.53	2.58	2.57	2.66	2.52	2.51	2.54	2.59	2.57	2.59	2.53
2000-1	2.50	2.32	2.41	2.44	2.68	2.83	2.87	2.85	2.83	2.87	2.86	2.98	2.70
2001-2	2.74	2.70	2.73	2.85	2.87	2.87	2.88	2.87	2.83	2.87	2.83	2.81	2.82
2002-3	2.92	3.21	3.63	4.21	4.38	4.25	4.06	3.89	3.70	3.55	3.37	3.33	3.71
2003-4	3.08	2.95	3.35	3.39	3.44	3.61	3.68	3.68	3.77	3.84	3.89	3.82	3.54
2004-5[2]	3.58	3.37	3.27	3.36	3.44	3.46	3.39	3.42	3.38				3.41

[1] Includes an allowance for unredeemed loans and purchases.   [2] Preliminary.   *Source: Economic Research Service, U.S. Department of Agriculture*

Average Price of No. 1 Hard Red Winter (Ordinary Protein) Wheat in Kansas City   In Dollars Per Bushel

Year	June	July	Aug.	Sept.	Oct.	Nov.	Dec.	Jan.	Feb.	Mar.	Apr.	May	Average
1995-6	4.72	4.98	4.76	5.00	5.28	5.34	5.51	5.40	5.67	5.63	6.60	7.02	5.49
1996-7	6.12	5.34	5.01	4.70	4.76	4.78	4.70	4.61	4.52	4.58	4.78	4.61	4.88
1997-8	4.08	3.57	3.84	3.86	3.88	3.87	3.72	3.61	3.64	3.61	3.39	3.41	3.71
1998-9	3.16	3.02	2.74	2.81	3.30	3.42	3.31	3.27	3.05	3.02	2.94	2.89	3.08
1999-00	2.93	2.68	2.85	2.92	2.80	2.89	2.81	2.90	2.94	2.91	2.84	2.95	2.87
2000-1	3.07	2.97	2.89	3.13	3.41	3.45	3.47	3.54	3.35	3.45	3.41	3.49	3.30
2001-2	3.32	3.20	3.15	3.18	3.28	3.37	3.26	3.29	3.25	3.23	3.24	3.21	3.25
2002-3	3.55	3.92	4.29	5.04	5.10	4.76	4.40	4.06	4.08	3.80	3.79	3.87	4.22
2003-4	3.63	3.34	3.87	3.74	3.79	4.21	4.31	4.32	4.25	4.30	4.35	4.28	4.03
2004-5[1]	4.13	3.97	3.73	4.01	3.95	4.22	4.22						4.03

[1] Preliminary.   Source: Economic Research Service, U.S. Department of Agriculture (ERS-USDA)

Average Price of No. 1 Dark Northern Spring (14% Protein) Wheat in Minneapolis   In Dollars Per Bushel

Year	June	July	Aug.	Sept.	Oct.	Nov.	Dec.	Jan.	Feb.	Mar.	Apr.	May	Average
1995-6	4.89	5.52	5.06	5.27	5.52	5.63	5.80	5.62	5.82	5.81	6.53	7.14	5.72
1996-7	6.73	6.04	5.29	4.63	4.69	4.64	4.51	4.62	4.45	4.62	4.78	4.58	4.97
1997-8	4.44	4.36	4.49	4.36	4.35	4.42	4.27	4.12	4.15	4.26	4.29	4.24	4.31
1998-9	4.01	3.89	3.58	3.53	4.03	4.15	3.97	3.92	3.78	3.79	3.65	3.61	3.83
1999-00	3.73	3.68	3.58	3.55	3.70	3.78	3.64	3.37	3.59	3.65	3.69	3.80	3.65
2000-1	3.78	3.50	3.29	3.17	3.69	3.77	3.52	3.79	3.68	3.63	3.73	3.88	3.62
2001-2	3.81	3.72	3.54	3.52	3.71	3.69	3.59	3.55	3.51	3.51	3.55	3.59	3.61
2002-3	3.64	4.03	4.37	5.24	5.20	4.99	4.47	4.34	4.52	4.36	4.22	4.20	4.47
2003-4	4.12	4.00	4.15	4.03	4.31	4.59	4.43	4.44	4.64	4.63	4.69	4.69	4.39
2004-5[1]	4.56	4.31	4.12	4.68	4.87	5.14	4.93						4.66

[1] Preliminary.   Source: Economic Research Service, U.S. Department of Agriculture (ERS-USDA)

Average Farm Prices of Winter Wheat in the United States   In Dollars Per Bushel

Year	June	July	Aug.	Sept.	Oct.	Nov.	Dec.	Jan.	Feb.	Mar.	Apr.	May	Average
1997-8	3.42	3.16	3.39	3.47	3.42	3.31	3.25	3.16	3.16	3.15	2.94	2.90	3.23
1998-9	2.68	2.47	2.25	2.29	2.66	2.76	2.68	2.70	2.55	2.53	2.48	2.34	2.53
1999-00	2.32	2.12	2.35	2.46	2.47	2.42	2.27	2.32	2.37	2.37	2.32	2.44	2.35
2000-1	2.43	2.23	2.31	2.37	2.63	2.70	2.76	2.77	2.74	2.85	2.77	2.94	2.63
2001-2	2.68	2.67	2.71	2.81	2.82	2.82	2.78	2.81	2.75	2.81	2.75	2.73	2.76
2002-3	2.90	3.19	3.63	4.15	4.32	4.18	3.87	3.66	3.52	3.30	3.19	3.19	3.59
2003-4	2.94	2.89	3.28	3.31	3.37	3.56	3.62	3.66	3.67	3.76	3.79	3.72	3.46
2004-5[1]	3.47	3.32	3.19	3.26	3.34	3.39	3.34	3.27	3.24				3.31

[1] Preliminary.   Source: National Agricultural Statistics Service, U.S. Department of Agriculture (NASS-USDA)

Average Farm Prices of Durum Wheat in the United States   In Dollars Per Bushel

Year	June	July	Aug.	Sept.	Oct.	Nov.	Dec.	Jan.	Feb.	Mar.	Apr.	May	Average
1997-8	4.21	4.61	5.23	5.35	5.09	5.25	5.17	5.02	4.71	4.68	4.45	4.29	4.84
1998-9	3.98	3.39	3.23	3.03	3.04	3.08	3.05	3.20	2.84	2.82	2.80	2.84	3.11
1999-00	2.93	2.89	2.76	2.29	2.30	2.64	2.96	2.90	2.88	2.63	2.89	3.02	2.76
2000-1	2.71	2.90	2.33	2.32	2.42	2.97	3.03	2.94	2.60	2.40	2.52	2.53	2.64
2001-2	3.37	2.74	2.38	3.02	2.91	3.04	3.41	3.44	3.49	3.33	3.33	3.41	3.16
2002-3	3.41	3.44	3.54	4.18	4.43	4.52	4.26	4.23	4.28	4.14	3.93	3.99	4.03
2003-4	3.99	3.85	3.78	3.95	3.89	3.95	3.95	3.96	4.08	4.14	4.22	4.21	4.00
2004-5[1]	4.40	4.11	3.85	3.90	3.89	3.77	3.57	3.62	3.59				3.86

[1] Preliminary.   Source: National Agricultural Statistics Service, U.S. Department of Agriculture (NASS-USDA)

Average Farm Prices of Other Spring Wheat in the United States   In Dollars Per Bushel

Year	June	July	Aug.	Sept.	Oct.	Nov.	Dec.	Jan.	Feb.	Mar.	Apr.	May	Average
1997-8	3.74	3.66	3.75	3.64	3.49	3.55	3.51	3.45	3.34	3.42	3.41	3.31	3.52
1998-9	3.22	3.08	2.69	2.62	3.04	3.23	3.19	3.12	3.09	3.00	2.95	2.92	3.01
1999-00	3.01	2.93	2.86	2.86	2.79	2.94	2.87	2.82	2.82	2.85	2.89	2.92	2.88
2000-1	2.90	2.74	2.59	2.59	2.80	2.97	2.98	2.96	2.99	2.99	3.05	3.13	2.89
2001-2	3.03	2.78	2.84	2.87	2.96	2.91	2.96	2.88	2.86	2.90	2.91	2.91	2.90
2002-3	2.98	3.31	3.66	4.30	4.45	4.26	4.15	4.03	3.82	3.72	3.48	3.55	3.81
2003-4	3.45	3.31	3.42	3.42	3.53	3.68	3.72	3.67	3.84	3.92	3.94	4.01	3.66
2004-5[1]	3.87	3.55	3.38	3.48	3.51	3.56	3.46	3.60	3.55				3.55

[1] Preliminary.   Source: National Agricultural Statistics Service, U.S. Department of Agriculture (NASS-USDA)

WHEAT

Wheat Futures - Chicago Board of Trade
(weekly close) as December 31, 2004

Cents per bushel

Average Open Interest of Wheat Futures in Chicago   In Contracts

Year	Jan.	Feb.	Mar.	Apr.	May	June	July	Aug.	Sept.	Oct.	Nov.	Dec.
1995	66,715	67,768	55,973	55,612	67,875	90,208	101,351	90,800	91,505	103,987	102,475	99,422
1996	102,718	104,807	91,378	98,260	93,378	81,211	69,222	66,128	65,561	65,639	60,810	58,533
1997	63,388	71,304	76,747	85,516	84,721	83,675	92,815	105,320	104,587	108,480	101,089	90,386
1998	96,870	99,103	97,585	114,193	115,199	116,008	121,794	127,240	125,747	131,322	130,186	116,249
1999	119,096	131,961	118,503	117,905	111,541	117,075	120,365	129,748	128,403	135,884	140,798	124,063
2000	127,419	135,316	123,980	128,462	130,938	133,527	139,194	144,953	141,803	150,592	153,287	134,997
2001	145,802	146,927	137,377	138,876	134,051	151,951	142,399	143,574	136,514	126,772	113,456	104,975
2002	118,192	118,484	112,469	112,870	96,050	98,047	118,041	131,303	129,913	114,544	101,354	82,934
2003	92,679	99,882	95,464	99,500	97,750	96,230	92,484	119,817	110,703	109,449	125,335	120,376
2004	130,101	137,459	141,239	155,383	127,086	135,322	154,623	166,422	154,431	156,290	172,064	182,357

Source: Chicago Board of Trade (CBT)

Volume of Trading of Wheat Futures in Chicago   In Contracts

Year	Jan.	Feb.	Mar.	Apr.	May	June	July	Aug.	Sept.	Oct.	Nov.	Dec.	Total
1995	353,603	302,950	316,330	279,099	345,455	598,762	507,876	527,716	436,145	472,794	454,352	359,985	4,955,067
1996	628,340	510,138	455,981	660,722	531,979	512,883	452,690	345,626	305,448	362,047	359,005	261,108	5,385,967
1997	312,680	373,411	368,547	567,099	422,935	469,158	470,992	493,225	401,277	405,978	432,621	340,722	5,058,645
1998	363,511	473,114	452,186	514,557	432,167	601,149	401,508	490,242	475,766	543,680	539,488	394,201	5,681,569
1999	426,524	597,448	710,375	559,211	444,696	674,580	523,516	665,897	536,014	437,689	613,633	380,442	6,570,025
2000	467,050	691,068	522,394	490,694	627,722	759,371	461,068	572,879	388,237	466,328	596,581	364,139	6,407,531
2001	551,756	595,312	536,141	579,992	537,836	720,350	695,339	600,341	385,930	629,479	614,734	354,331	6,801,541
2002	602,956	593,112	501,142	563,072	419,272	689,807	586,449	651,607	682,906	609,435	594,373	378,760	6,872,891
2003	438,021	526,001	411,017	496,770	638,590	661,840	585,073	689,593	536,452	778,863	739,791	465,405	6,967,416
2004	656,879	771,699	783,139	786,167	606,051	786,542	501,733	747,393	520,923	478,674	913,669	402,286	7,955,155

Source: Chicago Board of Trade (CBT)

Commercial Stocks of Domestic Wheat[1] in the United States, on First of Month   In Millions of Bushels

Year	July	Aug.	Sept.	Oct.	Nov.	Dec.	Jan.	Feb.	Mar.	Apr.	May	June
1995-6	92.3	161.7	201.1	234.3	228.3	200.2	178.7	170.8	156.6	137.7	107.6	87.2
1996-7	86.3	112.9	128.0	145.3	117.2	94.9	89.0	80.4	77.0	75.6	68.1	64.6
1997-8	80.1	186.3	235.2	268.1	258.1	231.4	196.8	178.1	170.6	158.0	146.4	145.7
1998-9	209.8	265.0	314.9	325.6	307.3	291.3	272.9	265.7	256.8	251.5	236.7	218.3
1999-00	248.6	294.9	335.8	354.0	334.6	301.5	277.4	273.7	267.8	266.3	247.6	240.3
2000-1	285.5	310.3	335.3	335.5	306.2	286.6	263.7	251.7	243.2	243.7	224.5	221.0
2001-2	271.0	296.6	318.7	321.9	291.9	251.8	224.5	224.6	217.2	195.6	177.3	176.0
2002-3	193.9	207.7	237.2	241.0	237.7	218.8	195.1	179.7	158.3	133.1	107.2	93.8
2003-4	133.3	171.9	212.0	226.3	220.7	198.1	145.0	126.3	113.1	94.0	89.6	85.4
2004-5	118.3	147.6	174.3	173.5	161.6	137.8	129.8	122.5	113.4			

[1] Domestic wheat in storage in public and private elevators in 39 markets and wheat afloat in vessels or barges at lake and seaboard ports, the first Saturday of the month.   Source: Livestock Division, U.S. Department of Agriculture (LD-USDA)

Stocks of Wheat Flour Held by Mills in the United States   In Thousands of Sacks -- 100 Pounds

Year	Jan. 1	April 1	July 1	Oct. 1	Year	Jan. 1	April 1	July 1	Oct. 1
1993	5,487	4,863	6,197	5,882	1999	7,544	5,920	5,697	4,265
1994	5,611	5,904	5,834	6,020	2000	5,099	5,217	5,062	5,244
1995	7,060	6,496	6,312	6,582	2001	5,241	5,506	5,178	5,393
1996	6,869	6,927	6,400	6,350	2002	5,377	5,164	4,632	4,184
1997	6,671	6,040	5,820	6,330	2003	4,265	4,707	4,622	4,554
1998	6,343	6,245	6,210	7,345	2004[1]	4,764	4,029	4,067	4,097

[1] Preliminary.   Source: Bureau of the Census, U.S. Department of Commerce

Average Producer Price Index of Wheat Flour (Spring[2])   June 1983 = 100

Year	Jan.	Feb.	Mar.	Apr.	May	June	July	Aug.	Sept.	Oct.	Nov.	Dec.	Average
1995	110.7	108.5	107.9	109.8	113.5	118.6	127.4	126.7	129.5	132.6	132.3	133.5	120.9
1996	130.4	138.0	136.6	137.6	160.1	146.8	138.0	127.0	121.5	125.7	121.7	121.4	133.7
1997	119.4	119.3	116.6	121.8	120.8	117.4	112.1	113.5	115.1	112.6	111.5	111.1	115.9
1998	106.8	108.1	111.5	110.1	109.9	106.4	105.5	101.8	100.9	106.6	107.8	104.8	106.7
1999	104.8	102.7	105.0	100.5	102.2	102.7	100.7	103.5	101.4	99.8	101.4	96.8	101.8
2000	99.9	99.9	100.2	99.4	100.1	101.7	100.2	100.4	101.2	105.2	103.6	104.4	101.4
2001	104.7	105.1	106.2	105.7	106.9	108.2	107.9	106.8	107.4	110.0	109.5	108.8	107.3
2002	109.6	109.6	110.6	106.5	108.2	108.8	112.6	115.5	120.9	123.0	119.3	116.6	113.4
2003	119.4	121.6	120.2	120.3	122.6	121.6	119.2	122.2	120.4	117.2	121.1	122.4	120.7
2004[1]	123.5	125.1	123.9	124.0	127.6	126.4	125.2	121.0	128.8	126.7	130.9	128.5	126.0

[1] Preliminary.   [2] Standard patent.   Source: Bureau of Labor Statistics, U.S. Department of Commerce (BLS) (0212-0301)

World Wheat Flour Production (Monthly Average)   In Thousands of Metric Tons

Year	Aus-tralia	France	Germany	Hungary	India	Japan	Kazak-hstan	Rep. of Korea	Mexico	Poland	Russia	Turkey	United Kingdom
1995	112.6	473.1	382.3	84.0	400.0	389.3	131.0	139.9	210.7	156.9	274.6	119.7	358.0
1996	123.8	450.0	394.2	75.1	400.0	389.6	132.7	141.2	215.9	164.1	309.7	132.1	371.0
1997	129.7	NA	404.8	77.7	412.5	388.1	127.3	145.9	216.0	175.3	361.9	159.1	369.0
1998	146.8	NA	407.5	70.1	430.6	382.0	128.8	143.5	213.2	172.1	347.8	152.6	377.0
1999	154.8	NA	423.6	69.1	182.2	386.7	105.2	152.8	204.8	125.0	360.0	156.6	NA
2000	NA	NA	405.5	73.9	202.5	386.0	79.5	155.9	206.0	125.4	405.0	162.0	381.0
2001	NA	NA	403.1	84.4	197.2	407.9	78.2	142.8	221.1	126.8	450.9	145.2	372.5
2002	NA	NA	415.3	79.2	211.6	382.0	128.6	151.2	218.1	135.2	436.1	139.6	NA
2003[1]	NA	NA	424.4	69.1	234.1	384.4	138.1	149.3	218.6	143.1	455.0	159.8	NA
2004[2]	NA	NA	412.3	69.4	240.9	381.9	132.7	158.8	212.6	135.5	435.6	171.2	NA

[1] Preliminary.   [2] Estimate. NA = Not available.   Source: United Nations (UN)

WHEAT

Production of Wheat Flour in the United States — In Millions of Sacks (100 Pounds Each)

Year	July	Aug.	Sept.	Oct.	Nov.	Dec.	Jan.	Feb.	Mar.	Apr.	May	June	Total
1996-7	33.9	35.6	34.6	37.5	33.1	32.0	31.3	30.0	31.8	33.1	32.6	32.5	397.9
1997-8	34.0	34.3	35.1	37.2	33.8	33.5	-----	96.0	-----	-----	96.2	-----	400.1
1998-9	-----	100.2	-----	-----	106.5	-----	-----	96.1	-----	-----	103.5	-----	406.3
1999-00	-----	104.2	-----	-----	108.2	-----	-----	101.1	-----	-----	101.6	-----	415.2
2000-1	-----	108.8	-----	-----	109.7	-----	-----	99.4	-----	-----	97.2	-----	415.1
2001-2	-----	102.1	-----	-----	105.8	-----	-----	96.0	-----	-----	96.3	-----	400.2
2002-3	-----	102.1	-----	-----	100.3	-----	-----	95.9	-----	-----	96.8	-----	395.0
2003-4	-----	103.1	-----	-----	100.5	-----	-----	95.7	-----	-----	95.8	-----	395.1
2004-5[1]	-----	100.1	-----	-----	98.2	-----	-----	-----	-----	-----	-----	-----	396.6

[1] Preliminary.   Source: Bureau of the Census, U.S. Department of Commerce

United States Wheat Flour Exports (Grain Equivalent[2]) — In Thousands of Bushels

Year	June	July	Aug.	Sept.	Oct.	Nov.	Dec.	Jan.	Feb.	Mar.	Apr.	May	Total
1996-7	2,006	2,008	1,669	3,133	2,496	2,748	2,240	1,347	1,920	2,521	1,259	2,125	25,472
1997-8	1,803	2,900	1,621	3,101	2,524	1,634	3,118	1,426	2,725	1,309	1,269	963	25,393
1998-9	1,971	1,740	2,027	2,914	3,812	2,354	6,838	2,551	3,341	4,126	3,105	1,948	36,728
1999-00	4,160	3,638	2,586	6,503	4,576	2,332	3,023	2,924	6,108	2,615	3,193	1,286	42,944
2000-1	3,620	3,805	1,623	3,174	4,165	2,332	2,741	2,236	2,365	2,200	3,868	2,163	34,292
2001-2	1,412	661	1,990	1,005	3,226	2,534	2,479	2,207	3,294	2,301	2,802	2,759	26,670
2002-3	1,474	1,547	753	1,373	2,437	2,854	4,645	1,049	884	1,146	1,083	541	19,786
2003-4	824	1,074	3,444	1,087	765	1,295	1,673	1,789	1,342	1,020	732	1,386	16,431
2004-5[1]	742	1,220	885	770	834	1,005							10,912

[1] Preliminary.   [2] Includes meal, groats and durum.   Source: Economic Research Service, U.S. Department of Agriculture (ERS-USDA)

Supply and Distribution of Wheat Flour in the United States

Year	Wheat Ground - 1,000 Bu. -	Millfeed Production - 1,000 Tons -	Flour Production[2]	Flour & Product Imports	Total Supply	Exports Flour	Exports Products	Domestic Disappearance	Total Population July 1 - Millions -	Per Capita Disappearance - Pounds -
					In 1,000 Cwt.					
1996	878,070	7,042	397,776	8,574	406,350	10,651	881	394,818	269.5	146.5
1997	885,843	6,886	404,143	8,684	412,827	11,038	1,167	400,622	272.8	146.9
1998	902,532	7,301	403,880	9,830	413,625	12,574	1,353	394,817	276.0	145.9
1999	917,797	7,040	411,968	9,295	416,354	21,297	1,633	393,377	279.3	142.6
2000	944,868	7,374	421,270	9,666	403,936	16,005	1,693	413,238	282.4	146.3
2001	914,036	7,273	404,521	10,130	414,651	10,507	1,695	402,449	285.6	140.9
2002	889,414	6,893	394,700	11,289	411,747	9,266	1,729	400,752	288.6	138.9
2003	889,188	7,029	396,215							
2004[1]	865,130	6,561	389,865							

[1] Preliminary.   [2] Commercial production of wheat flour, whole wheat, industrial and durum flour and farina reported by Bureau of Census.
Source: Economic Research Service, U.S. Department of Agriculture (ERS-USDA)

Wheat and Flour -- Price Relationships at Milling Centers in the United States — In Dollars

Crop Year (June-May)	At Kansas City — Cost of Wheat to Produce 100 lb. Flour[1]	Wholesale Price of Bakery Flour 100 lb. Flour[2]	By-Products Obtained 100 lb. Flour[3]	Total Products Actual	Total Products Over Cost of Wheat	At Minneapolis — Cost of Wheat to Produce 100 lb. Flour[1]	Wholesale Price of Bakery Flour 100 lb. Flour[2]	By-Products Obtained 100 lb. Flour[3]	Total Products Actual	Total Products Over Cost of Wheat
1995-6	12.97	13.35	1.93	15.28	2.31	13.04	13.03	1.68	14.71	1.67
1996-7	11.22	11.89	1.92	13.81	2.60	11.32	11.68	1.87	13.54	2.22
1997-8	9.03	9.99	1.43	11.41	2.38	9.83	10.62	1.34	11.96	2.12
1998-9	7.91	9.06	1.08	10.15	2.23	8.76	9.80	1.02	10.82	2.06
1999-00	7.74	8.86	.98	9.84	2.10	8.29	9.30	.95	10.24	1.95
2000-1	7.95	9.36	1.06	10.42	2.48	8.24	9.28	.97	10.24	2.01
2001-2	7.64	8.98	1.14	10.11	2.48	8.20	9.11	1.10	10.21	2.01
2002-3	9.66	11.04	1.16	12.20	2.54	9.80	11.03	1.15	12.17	2.38
2003-4	9.17	10.38	1.34	11.72	2.55	9.90	10.50	1.10	11.61	1.71
June-Aug.	8.68	10.20	1.03	11.23	2.55	9.33	10.33	.96	11.29	1.96
Sept.-Nov.	8.85	10.15	1.39	11.54	2.69	10.10	10.15	1.15	11.30	1.20
Dec.-Feb.	9.98	10.78	1.60	12.39	2.41	10.27	11.03	1.20	12.23	1.97

[1] Based on 73% extraction rate, cost of 2.28 bushels: At Kansas City, No. 1 hard winter 13% protein; and at Minneapolis, No. 1 dark northern spring, 14% protein.   [2] quoted as mid-month bakers' standard patent at Kansas City and spring standard patent at Minneapolis, bulk basis.   [3] Assumed 50-50 millfeed distribution between bran and shorts or middlings, bulk basis.   Source: Agricultural Marketing Service, U.S. Department of Agriculture (AMS-USDA)

Wool

Wool is light, warm, absorbs moisture, and is resistant to fire. Wool is also used for insulation in houses, for carpets and furnishing, and for bedding. Sheep are sheared once a year and produce about 4.3 kg of "greasy" wool per year.

Greasy wool is wool that has not been washed or cleaned. Wool fineness is determined by fiber diameter, which is measured in microns (one millionth of a meter). Fine wool is softer, lightweight, and produces fine clothing. Merino sheep produce the finest wool.

Wool futures and options are traded on the Sydney Futures Exchange (SFE), where there are futures and options contracts on greasy wool, and futures on fine wool and broad wool. All three futures contracts call for the delivery of merino combing wool. Wool yarn futures are traded on the Chubu Commodity Exchange (CCE), the Osaka Mercantile Exchange (OME) and the Tokyo Commodity Exchange (TOCOM).

Prices – Average monthly wool prices at US mills in 2004 (through November) fell -2.3% yr/yr to $2.36 per pound from the 9-year high of $2.41 posted in 2003. Wool prices in 2004 were still more than double the 3-decade low of $1.09 posted in 2000. The value of US wool production was only $15.311 million in 2001.

Supply – World production of wool has been falling in the past decade due to the increased use of polyester fab-rics. Wool production in 2002, the latest reporting year for the data series, fell -1.4% yr/yr to a new record low of 1.292 million metric tons. The world's largest producers of degreased wool in 2002 were Australia with 31% of world production, followed by New Zealand (15%), and China (12%).

US wool production of 10,000 metric tons in 2002 accounted for only 0.8% of world production. US production of wool goods fell -17.0% yr/yr in 2003 to a new record low of 23.0 million yards, which is only 12% of the wool produced a decade earlier in 1993. The US sheep herd in 2002 fell -3.5% yr/yr to a record low of 5.500 million sheep, which is roughly half the herd size seen 10 years ago.

Demand – US consumption of wool has dropped sharply, along with production, and fell to a record low of 36.015 million pounds in 2002. The breakdown of US mill consumption in 2002 showed that wool usage for carpets was 6.892 million pounds, which was a record low. Wool usage for apparel production also plunged to a record low of 36.015 million pounds. The plunge in wool demand by US mills reflects the fact that textile manufacturing is increasingly moving to countries with low labor costs such as China.

Trade – US exports of domestic wool in 2002 rose +38.1% to 8.500 million pounds, while imports fell -33.5% to 10.526 million pounds.

World Production of Wool — In Metric Tons--Degreased

Year	Argentina	Australia	China	Kazak-hstan	New Zealand	Pakistan	Romania	Russia	South Africa	United Kingdom	United States	Uruguay	Total
1994	48,000	570,000	130,000	55,000	214,000	31,000	17,000	73,000	40,000	47,000	16,000	50,000	1,693,000
1995	44,000	475,000	141,000	35,000	214,000	32,000	16,000	56,000	35,000	48,000	15,000	46,000	1,512,000
1996	39,000	457,000	152,000	25,000	199,000	32,000	16,000	46,000	37,000	46,000	13,000	43,000	1,459,000
1997	36,000	472,000	130,000	21,000	228,000	34,000	13,000	36,000	34,000	46,000	13,000	46,000	1,440,000
1998	34,000	452,000	141,000	15,000	219,000	23,000	12,000	29,000	32,000	48,000	12,000	42,000	1,388,000
1999	36,000	437,000	144,000	13,000	220,000	23,000	13,000	24,000	34,000	47,000	11,000	34,000	1,369,000
2000	32,000	452,000	146,000	14,000	202,000	23,000	11,000	20,000	32,000	45,000	11,000	32,000	1,356,000
2001[1]	32,000	416,000	149,000	14,000	199,000	24,000	10,000	20,000	32,000	39,000	10,000	32,000	1,310,000
2002[2]	31,000	395,000	152,000	14,000	199,000	24,000	12,000	20,000	32,000	42,000	10,000	27,000	1,292,000

[1] Preliminary. [2] Estimate. Source: Food and Agriculture Organization of the United Nations (FAO-UN)

Production of Wool Goods[2] in the United States — In Millions of Yards

Year	First Quarter	Second Quarter	Third Quarter	Fourth Quarter	Total	Year	First Quarter	Second Quarter	Third Quarter	Fourth Quarter	Total
1995	46.8	45.9	35.2	34.3	162.2	2000	17.9	18.0	13.4	17.4	66.7
1996	44.8	43.6	30.8	32.8	152.0	2001	20.8	12.4	11.0	9.0	53.2
1997	42.7	49.7	42.3	40.5	175.2	2002	7.4	8.6	6.2	5.5	27.7
1998	38.8	37.5	29.6	26.3	132.2	2003	6.5	6.4	5.2	4.9	23.0
1999	25.0	20.9	17.4	14.6	77.9	2004[1]	5.5	5.9	4.2	4.2	19.8

[1] Preliminary. [2] Woolen and worsted woven goods, except woven felts. Source: Bureau of the Census, U.S. Department of Commerce

Consumption of Apparel Wool[2] in the United States — In Millions of Pounds--Clean Basis

Year	First Quarter	Second Quarter	Third Quarter	Fourth Quarter	Total	Year	First Quarter	Second Quarter	Third Quarter	Fourth Quarter	Total
1995	36.3	35.5	29.4	28.1	129.3	2000	17.4	16.1	14.6	13.9	63.0
1996	39.1	36.2	27.4	26.8	129.5	2001	17.0	13.5	11.6	10.9	53.0
1997	33.1	33.8	30.6	32.8	130.4	2002	11.0	10.5	6.5	W	36.0
1998	29.3	29.6	21.9	17.5	98.4	2003	W	W	W	W	W
1999	17.3	16.8	15.8	13.6	63.5	2004[1]	W	W	W	W	W

[1] Preliminary. [2] Woolen and worsted woven goods, except woven felts. Source: Bureau of the Census, U.S. Department of Commerce

WOOL

Salient Statistics of Wool in the United States

Year	Sheep & Lambs Shorn[4] -1,000's-	Weight Per Fleece -In Lbs.-	Shorn Wool Pro- duction 1,000 Lbs.	Price Per Lb.	Value of Pro- duction 1,000 $	Payment Support --Cents	Rate Per Lb.--	Total Wool Pro- duction	Raw Wool (Clean Content) Domestic Pro- duction	Exports Domestic Wool	Dutiable Imports for Consump- tion[3] 48's & Finer	Total New Supply[2]	Duty Free Imports (Not Finer than 46's)	Mill Consumption Apparel	Carpet
										In Thousands of Pounds					
1995	8,138	7.80	63,513	104.0	64,277	212	108.0	63,513	33,535	6,042	63,781	116,313	25,039	129,299	12,667
1996	7,279	7.79	56,669	70.0	39,659	----	----	56,159	29,921	5,715	54,063	99,575	20,971	129,525	12,311
1997	7,032	7.70	53,889	84.0	45,172	----	----	53,578	28,630	4,732	51,484	100,003	24,295	130,386	13,576
1998	6,428	7.70	49,255	60.0	29,415	----	----	49,255	30,321	1,700	45,760	94,814	23,121	98,373	16,331
1999	6,150	7.60	46,549	38.0	17,860	----	20.0	46,549	24,800	3,694	21,251	63,955	20,723	63,535	13,950
2000	6,100	7.60	46,400	33.0	15,377	----	40.0	46,446	24,500	6,629	23,874	62,785	20,003	62,041	15,205
2001	5,700	7.60	43,000	36.0	15,311	----	----	43,016	22,712	6,154	15,843	52,128	19,727	52,969	13,310
2002	5,476	7.50	41,322	53.0	21,876	100	18.0	41,322	21,818	8,461	10,526	38,042	14,159	36,015	6,891
2003[1]	5,057	7.50	28,114	72.0	27,408	100		38,100	20,100	11,100	4,986		15,841	43,869	6,017

[1] Preliminary.   [2] Production minus exports plus imports; stocks not taken into consideration.   [3] Apparel wool includes all dutiable wool; carpet wool includes all duty-free wool.   [4] Includes sheep shorn at commercial feeding yards.   *Source: Economic Research Service, U.S. Department of Agriculture (ERS-USDA)*

Shorn Wool Prices

Year	U.S. Farm Price Shorn Wool Greasy Basis[1] -Cents/Lb.-	Australian Offering Price, Clean[2] Grade 70's Type 61	Grade 64's Type 63	Grade 64/70's Type 62	Grade 60/62's Type 64A	Grade 58's-56's 433-34	Market Indicator[3] -Cents/Kg.-	Graded Territory Shorn Wool, Clean Basis[4] 64's Staple 2 3/4" & up	60's Staple 3" & up	58's Staple 3 1/4" & up	56's Staple 3 1/4" & up	54's Staple 3 1/2" & up
		In Dollars Per Pound						In Dollars Per Pound				
1995	104.0	3.22	2.81	3.01	2.49	2.33	888	2.49	1.93	1.77	1.63	1.53
1996	70.0	2.81	2.34	2.54	1.96	1.84	619	1.93	1.54	1.43	1.31	1.22
1997	84.0	3.56	2.57	2.90	2.06	1.95	615	2.38	1.78	1.64	1.43	1.14
1998	60.0	2.60	1.84	1.92	1.64	1.60	663	1.62	1.31	1.21	1.06	.94
1999	38.0	2.53	1.48	1.66	1.36	1.33	524	1.10	.85	.74	.66	.59
2000	33.0	2.80	1.50	1.69	1.37	1.30	764	1.08	.75	.65	.57	.53
2001	36.0	2.42	1.66	1.69	1.60	1.54	841	1.21	.91	.77	.66	.65
2002	53.0	2.87	2.68	2.70	2.63	2.55	1,051	1.90	1.41	1.40	1.19	1.02
2003	72.0	3.23	3.14	3.16	3.02	2.81	821	2.41	1.73	1.79	1.48	1.24

[1] Annual weighted average.   [2] F.O.B. Australian Wool Corporation South Carolina warehouse in bond.   [3] Index of prices of all wool sold in Australia for the crop year July-June.   [4] Wool principally produced in Texas and the Rocky Mountain States.   *Source: Economic Research Service, U.S. Department of Agriculture (ERS-USDA)*

Average Wool Prices[1] --Australian-- 64's, Type 62, Duty Paid--U.S. Mills   In Cents Per Pound

Year	Jan.	Feb.	Mar.	Apr.	May	June	July	Aug.	Sept.	Oct.	Nov.	Dec.	Average
1995	281	297	302	302	307	308	292	284	266	236	242	237	280
1996	240	237	238	234	242	245	236	234	228	220	225	232	234
1997	234	261	254	261	279	287	NA	270	262	250	245	240	258
1998	218	225	247	205	214	179	NA	144	144	140	156	147	184
1999	158	150	157	156	150	149	152	148	139	139	143	137	148
2000	154	146	144	156	156	154	155	151	149	146	140	148	150
2001	160	168	164	158	164	166	167	172	169	159	166	183	166
2002	218	243	250	251	249	259	255	254	268	312	322	328	267
2003	344	346	326	333	296	326	316	308	306	292	285	290	314
2004	304	294	288	281	261	275	277	263	255	255	270	271	275

[1] Raw, clean basis.   NA = Not available.   *Source: Economic Research Service, U.S. Department of Agriculture (ERS-USDA)*

Average Wool Prices --Domestic[1]-- Graded Territory, 64's, Staple 2 3/4 & Up--U.S. Mills   In Cents Per Pound

Year	Jan.	Feb.	Mar.	Apr.	May	June	July	Aug.	Sept.	Oct.	Nov.	Dec.	Average
1995	245	252	265	288	295	285	261	250	235	185	208	192	247
1996	188	192	197	197	195	192	192	192	192	192	190	190	192
1997	190	190	208	228	248	255	255	255	255	255	260	260	238
1998	236	195	195	188	177	170	170	150	115	115	115	115	162
1999	115	115	115	110	117	122	116	110	105	100	110	95	111
2000	95	95	101	110	125	125	125	120	107	105	105	97	109
2001	95	100	108	129	137	125	127	122	126	130	122	127	121
2002	134	150	170	181	189	200	200	200	198	204	223	233	190
2003	236	260	258	250	223	234	239	243	243	243	232	233	241
2004	233	239	240	240	235	229	233	236	240	236	230	230	235

[1] Raw, shorn, clean basis.   *Source: Economic Research Service, U.S. Department of Agriculture (ERS-USDA)*

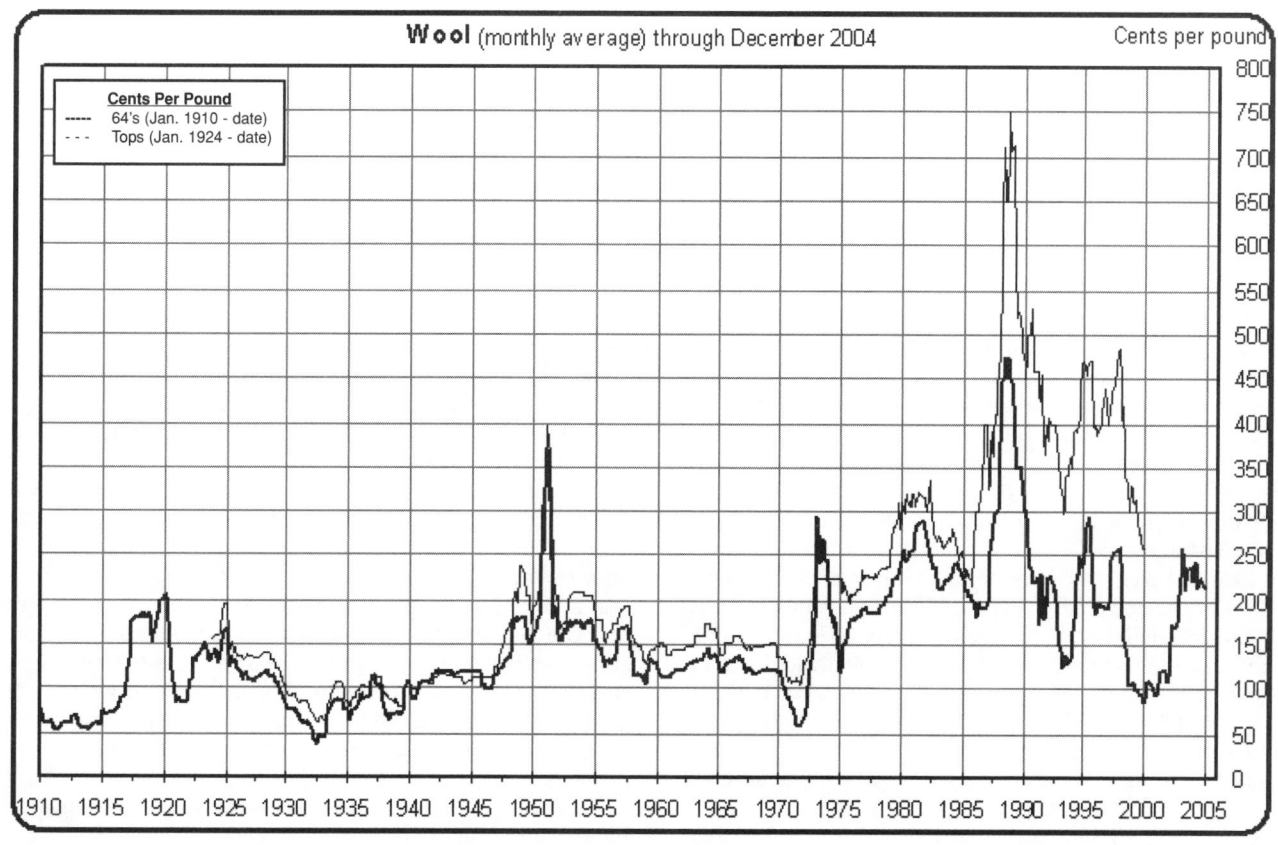

Wool (monthly average) through December 2004 — Cents per pound

Cents Per Pound
- ── 64's (Jan. 1910 - date)
- --- Tops (Jan. 1924 - date)

Wool: Mill Consumption, by Grades in the U.S., Scoured Basis   In Millions of Pounds

	Apparel Class[1]							
	Woolen System			Worsted System			All	Carpet
Year	60's & Finer	Coarser Than 60's	Total	60's & Finer	Coarser Than 60's	Total	Total	Wool[2]
1994	35,960	26,038	61,998	59,599	16,966	76,565	138,563	14,739
1995	30,211	27,089	57,300	54,980	17,019	71,999	129,299	12,667
1996	42,141	27,575	69,716	46,057	13,752	59,809	129,525	12,311
1997	49,038	21,303	70,341	48,153	11,892	60,045	130,386	13,576
1998	31,258	15,079	46,337	42,243	9,793	52,036	98,373	16,331
1999	18,379	10,772	29,151	27,429	6,955	34,384	63,535	13,950
2000	18,503	13,432	31,935	NA	NA	30,106	62,041	15,205
2001	16,062	9,849	25,911	NA	NA	27,058	52,969	13,310
2002[3]	9,627	8,482	18,109	NA	NA	17,906	36,015	6,891
2003[4]	6,681	5,309	11,990	NA	NA	NA	NA	6,017

[1] Domestic & duty-paid foreign.   [2] Duty-free foreign.   [3] Preliminary.   [4] Estimate.   *Source: Economic Research Service, U.S. Department of Agriculture (ERS-USDA)*

United States Imports[1] of Unmanufactured Wool (Clean Yield)   In Millions of Pounds

Year	Jan.	Feb.	Mar.	Apr.	May	June	July	Aug.	Sept.	Oct.	Nov.	Dec.	Total
1995	10.4	7.7	10.8	6.0	11.5	5.2	7.3	7.3	4.9	7.9	7.7	4.1	90.6
1996	9.6	9.1	8.8	5.6	7.0	5.9	5.3	6.6	3.1	4.6	4.6	5.1	75.3
1997	5.1	5.8	5.8	6.6	5.8	4.2	4.9	4.2	4.8	8.5	7.3	8.6	71.5
1998	8.8	5.4	5.4	7.2	5.9	5.5	5.7	4.4	3.3	7.3	4.9	4.3	68.0
1999	6.2	3.6	3.9	7.9	3.5	3.0	3.7	3.1	2.6	3.8	2.8	2.5	46.3
2000	4.9	3.8	3.8	4.6	5.1	2.7	3.2	3.7	4.3	3.2	3.5	2.4	45.0
2001	4.9	4.3	4.3	1.5	2.9	2.8	4.0	1.9	2.0	2.8	1.3	1.3	34.1
2002	1.9	1.8	2.6	2.4	2.3	1.5	1.6	1.2	1.9	2.4	2.1	3.1	24.6
2003	2.5	2.8	2.3	2.2	2.1	1.8	1.2	1.1	0.8	1.6	1.1	1.2	20
2004[2]	1.3	1.5	2.1	1.8	1.4	2.8	1.6	1.9	2.7	2.4	1.9	1.2	

[1] For consumption.   [2] Preliminary.   *Source: Economic Research Service, U.S. Department of Agriculture (ERS-USDA)*

Zinc

Zinc (symbol Zn) is a bluish-white metallic element that is the 24th most abundant element in the earth's crust. Zinc is never found in its pure state but rather in zinc oxide, zinc silicate, zinc carbonate, zinc sulfide, and in minerals such as zincite, hemimorphite, smithsonite, franklinite, and sphalerite. Zinc is utilized as a protective coating for other metals, such as iron and steel, in a process known as galvanizing. Zinc is used as an alloy with copper to make brass and also as an alloy with aluminum and magnesium. There are, however, a number of substitutes for zinc in chemicals, electronics, and pigments. For example, with aluminum, steel and plastics can substitute for galvanized sheets. Aluminum alloys can also replace brass. Zinc is used as the negative electrode in dry cell (flashlight) batteries and also in the zinc-mercuric-oxide battery cell, which is the round, flat battery typically used in watches, cameras, and other electronic devices. Zinc is also used in medicine as an antiseptic ointment.

Zinc futures and options are traded on the London Metals Exchange (LME). The LME zinc futures contract calls for the delivery of 25 metric tons of at least 99.995% purity zinc ingots (slabs and plates). The contract trades in terms of US dollars per metric ton. Zinc first started trading on the LME in 1915.

Prices – Zinc prices in 2004 rose to a monthly average of 52.31 cents per pound, up sharply by 29.6% from 2003. However, the 2004 average was still mildly below the 7-year high of 56.15 cents posted in 2000. The record average monthly high price for zinc is 75.37 cents posted in 1988.

Supply – World smelter production of zinc in 2003 rose +2.4% to 9.880 million metric tons, which was a new record high. The world's largest producer of zinc is China with 23% of world smelter production, followed by Canada with 7.1%, Japan with 6.9%, and Australia with 5.6%. US smelter production accounted for only 3.1% of world production in 2003. Australia's production rose rapidly in the 1999-2002 period and the 2003 level of 557,000 metric tons was just below the record high of 571,500 metric tons seen in 2002. China's production of 2.300 million metric tons in 2003 was more than four times its production level of 550,000 metric tons seen in 1990. US zinc smelter production in 2003 of 303,000 metric tons was less than half of its production of 796,300 metric tons seen in 1970.

US mine production of recoverable zinc fell -3.6% yr/yr to an annualized 711,840 metric tons in 2004 (through October), which was a 7-year low. US production in 2003 of slab zinc on a primary basis rose by +2.7% to 187,000 metric tons, while secondary production rose +2.7% yr/yr to 116,000 metric tons.

Demand – US consumption of slab zinc in 2003 fell by –7.7% yr/yr to 1.080 million metric tons, which was an 11-year low. US consumption of all classes of zinc fell by –5.6% yr/yr in 2003 to 1.34 million metric tons, which was a 10-year low. US consumption of slab zinc by fabricators in 2004 (through October) rose slightly by +0.1% yr/yr to an annualized 423,960 metric tons. That was mildly above the record low of 403,600 metric tons in 2002.

The breakdown of consumption by industries for 2003 showed that 52% of slab zinc consumption was by galvanizers, 22% by the zinc-base industry, 17% for brass products, and the rest for other miscellaneous industries. The consumption breakdown by grades showed that 61% was special high grade, 22% prime western, 12% high grade, and 6% re-melt and other. Within that grade breakdown, prime Western consumption has fallen by nearly half in the past 3 years.

Trade – The US in 2003 relied on imports for 57% of its consumption of zinc, up sharply from the 35% average seen in the 1990s. US imports for consumption of slab zinc fell by –13.3% yr/yr to 758,000 metric tons in 2003, while imports of zinc ore rose by +34.4% yr/yr to a 2-decade high of 164,000 metric tons. The dollar value of US zinc imports in 2003 fell by –5.4% yr/yr to a 10-year low of $840 million.

The breakdown of imports in 2003 shows that most zinc is imported for blocks, pigs and slabs (758,000 metric tons), followed by ores (164,000 metric tons), dust, powder and flakes (27,500 metric tons), dross, ashes and fume (14,100 metric tons), waste and scrap (10,300 metric tons), and sheets, plates and other (1,790 metric tons).

Salient Statistics of Zinc in the United States   In Metric Tons

Year	Slab Zinc Production Primary	Slab Zinc Production Secondary	Mine Production (Recovered)	Imports for Consumption Slab Zinc	Imports for Consumption Ore (Zinc Content)	Exports Slab Zinc	Exports Ore (Zinc Content)	Consumption Slab Zinc	Consumption Consumed as Ore	Consumption All Classes[3]	Net Import Reliance as a % of Consumption	High-Grade, Price -Cents/Lb.-
1994	216,600	139,000	570,000	793,000	27,374	6,310	389,000	1,180,000	2,400	1,400,000	35	49.26
1995	232,000	131,000	603,000	856,000	10,300	3,080	424,000	1,230,000	2,400	1,460,000	35	55.83
1996	226,000	140,000	586,000	827,000	15,100	1,970	425,000	1,210,000	1,400	1,450,000	33	51.11
1997	226,000	141,000	605,000	876,000	49,600	3,630	461,000	1,260,000	----	1,500,000	35	64.56
1998	234,000	134,000	722,000	879,000	46,300	2,330	552,000	1,290,000	----	1,590,000	35	51.43
1999	241,000	131,000	808,000	1,060,000	74,600	1,880	531,000	1,430,000	----	1,700,000	30	53.48
2000	228,000	143,000	805,000	915,000	52,800	2,770	523,000	1,330,000	----	1,630,000	60	55.61
2001	203,000	108,000	799,000	813,000	84,000	1,180	696,000	1,150,000	----	1,420,000	60	43.96
2002¹	182,000	113,000	754,000	874,000	122,000	1,160	822,000	1,170,000	----	1,420,000	60	38.64
	187,000	116,000	738,000	758,000	164,000	1,680	841,000	1,080,000	----	1,340,000	57	40.63

¹ Preliminary.   ² Estimate.   ³ Based on apparent consumption of slab zinc plus zinc content of ores and concentrates and secondary materials used to make zinc dust and chemicals.   *Source: U.S. Geological Survey (USGS)*

World Smelter Production of Zinc[3]   In Thousands of Metric Tons

Year	Australia	Belgium	Canada	China	France	Germany	Italy	Japan	Kazak-hstan	Mexico	Spain	United States	World Total
1994	328.0	306.2	691.0	306.0	359.9	203.6	713.0	172.4	209.2	154.4	294.7	356.0	7,330
1995	325.0	301.1	720.3	300.0	322.5	180.4	711.1	169.2	222.7	162.7	358.0	363.0	7,370
1996	331.0	234.4	715.6	324.3	327.0	269.0	642.3	190.0	221.7	163.1	360.8	366.0	7,610
1997	317.0	243.6	703.8	346.1	251.7	227.7	650.2	189.0	231.4	171.0	364.2	367.0	7,920
1998	322.0	205.0	745.1	321.0	334.0	231.6	652.7	240.7	230.3	175.0	360.0	368.0	8,170
1999	348.5	232.4	776.9	1,700.0	333.1	333.0	152.8	683.6	249.3	218.9	393.0	371.0	8,550
2000	494.5	251.7	779.9	1,980.0	350.0	356.0	170.3	698.8	262.2	235.1	386.3	371.0	9,090
2001	558.5	259.3	661.2	2,040.0	347.0	358.3	177.8	684.1	277.1	303.8	418.0	311.0	9,340
2002[1]	571.5	260.0	793.5	2,100.0	350.0	360.0	176.0	673.9	286.3	302.1	488.0	294.0	9,650
2003[2]	557.0	244.0	700.0	2,300.0	253.0	388.0	123.0	686.1	295.0	310.0	530.0	303.0	9,880

[1] Preliminary.   [2] Estimate.   [3] Secondary metal included.   *Source: U.S. Geological Survey (USGS)*

Consumption (Reported) of Slab Zinc in the United States, by Industries and Grades   In Metric Tons

Year	Total	By Industries					By Grades			
		Galvanizers	Brass Products	Zinc-Base Alloy[3]	Zinc Oxide	Other	Special High Grade	High Grade	Remelt and Other	Prime Western
1994	859,000	395,000	107,000	196,000	68,300	92,400	486,000	112,000	68,400	192,000
1995	1,240,000	390,000	91,500	194,000	70,900	90,800	135,000	98,200	54,400	251,000
1996	788,000	398,000	87,400	142,000	[4]	161,000	385,000	111,000	54,000	238,000
1997	672,000	347,000	76,800	107,000	[4]	141,000	319,000	88,700	57,200	207,000
1998	647,000	320,000	60,300	122,000	[4]	145,000	331,000	72,800	51,700	192,000
1999	614,000	308,000	78,200	105,000	[4]	124,000	317,000	58,400	55,400	184,000
2000	640,000	293,000	82,800	123,000	[4]	NA	332,000	60,600	41,500	206,000
2001	543,000	281,000	74,400	91,200	[4]	NA	294,000	54,000	30,300	165,000
2002[1]	496,000	265,000	86,800	103,000	[4]	NA	294,000	61,400	28,000	113,000
2003[2]	506,000	264,000	87,400	113,000	[4]	NA	310,000	60,000	27,600	109,000

[1] Preliminary.   [2] Estimated.   [3] Die casters.   [4] Included in other.   *Source: U.S. Geological Survey (USGS)*

United States Foreign Trade of Zinc   In Metric Tons

Year	Imports for Consumption							Zinc Ore & Manufactures Exported						
	Ores[1]	Blocks, Pigs, Slabs	Sheets, Plates, Other	Waste & Scrap	Dross, Ashes, Fume	Dust, Powder & Flakes	Total Value $1,000	Blocks, Pigs, Anodes, etc. — Unwrought	Unwrought Alloys	Sheets, Plates & Strips	Angles, Bars, Rods, etc.	Waste & Scrap	Dust (Blue Powder)	Zinc Ore & Concentrates
1994	27,374	793,482	475	51,676	12,152	11,954	878,100	13,220	----	----	----	58,297	6,603	389,488
1995	10,300	856,000	332	42,300	10,900	11,700	1,018,620	----	----	----	----	55,900	8,840	424,000
1996	15,100	827,000	16,900	31,900	14,500	10,300	1,001,800	----	----	----	----	45,500	11,100	425,000
1997	49,600	876,000	19,200	29,600	----	11,700	1,340,390	----	----	----	----	46,100	9,980	461,000
1998	46,300	879,000	16,900	29,200	----	17,600	1,098,690	----	----	----	----	35,000	5,530	552,000
1999	74,600	966,000	22,600	26,600	20,000	21,300	1,133,890	----	----	----	----	28,200	5,050	531,000
2000	52,800	915,000	9,380	36,500	15,500	26,700	1,272,750	----	----	----	----	36,100	4,830	523,000
2001	84,000	813,000	7,240	39,300	12,000	26,700	937,110	----	----	----	----	44,000	4,690	696,000
2002[2]	122,000	874,000	1,640	31,200	15,500	30,900	887,785	----	----	----	----	47,700	5,660	822,000
2003[3]	164,000	758,000	1,790	10,300	14,100	27,500	839,705	----	----	----	----	50,200	6,550	841,000

[1] Zinc content.   [2] Preliminary.   [3] Estimate.   NA = Not available.   *Source: U.S. Geological Survey (USGS)*

Mine Production of Recoverable Zinc in the United States   In Thousands of Metric Tons

Year	Jan.	Feb.	Mar.	Apr.	May	June	July	Aug.	Sept.	Oct.	Nov.	Dec.	Total
1995	49.8	48.1	52.8	45.6	54.5	50.0	50.2	55.0	48.1	52.0	47.8	48.1	601.0
1996	52.4	48.9	49.7	45.5	50.7	49.9	53.7	48.1	46.8	43.4	43.1	42.6	600.0
1997	46.2	45.7	45.8	47.9	49.7	45.3	45.9	49.8	53.0	47.6	44.2	48.4	574.0
1998	50.1	48.3	56.5	56.2	56.7	55.0	59.5	57.2	60.1	55.7	62.0	61.9	722.0
1999	61.4	57.6	63.0	67.0	61.7	62.8	68.2	72.1	60.8	67.8	61.2	65.9	808.0
2000	64.4	56.6	68.5	64.5	70.2	65.3	68.1	71.4	59.6	62.3	63.5	67.2	814.0
2001	68.4	60.5	62.2	65.2	66.9	66.1	66.7	67.6	60.9	67.1	54.0	55.4	799.0
2002	61.3	60.4	67.8	55.2	63.4	63.8	66.0	67.2	54.4	68.3	61.3	65.5	754.6
2003	65.2	60.2	62.7	54.0	65.2	64.0	64.5	59.6	63.3	58.6	61.0	60.5	738.8
2004[1]	60.4	55.3	57.9	58.5	56.1	59.0	60.8	62.0	61.6	61.6	56.8	56.1	706.1

[1] Preliminary.   *Source: U.S. Geological Survey (USGS)*

ZINC

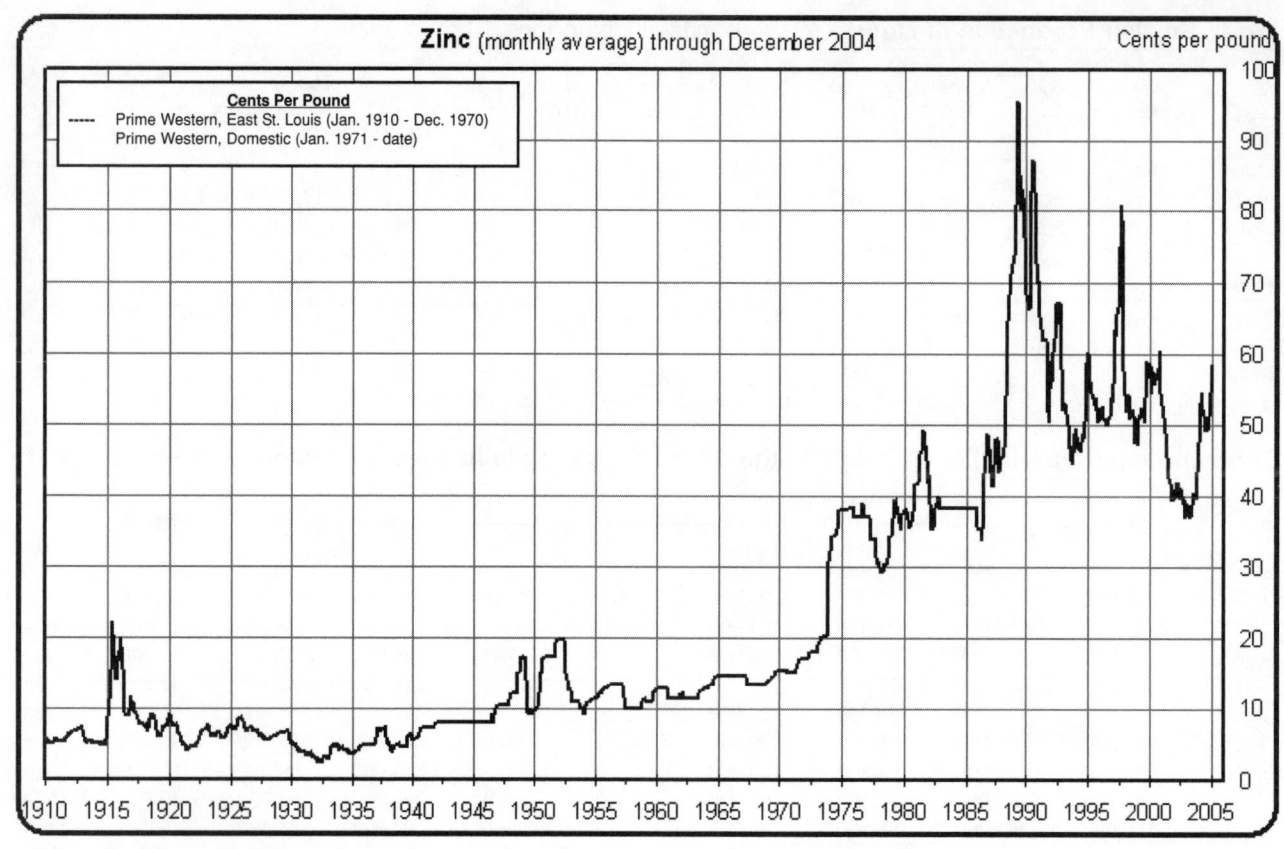

Consumption of Slab Zinc by Fabricators in the United States   In Thousands of Metric Tons

Year	Jan.	Feb.	Mar.	Apr.	May	June	July	Aug.	Sept.	Oct.	Nov.	Dec.	Average
1995	51.3	57.8	56.3	57.9	53.4	58.0	44.0	44.0	58.8	57.0	56.0	54.5	838.0
1996	56.3	55.6	59.3	55.7	56.3	55.9	48.9	48.1	54.4	56.4	54.2	53.1	788.0
1997	47.2	43.1	48.6	50.1	48.1	45.3	45.1	45.5	50.9	49.6	44.3	46.2	588.0
1998	46.3	45.2	47.4	44.8	45.4	49.0	46.0	45.0	45.9	45.9	40.5	43.9	647.0
1999	40.5	45.4	43.8	40.3	42.5	47.1	37.8	40.1	42.0	42.8	41.1	39.7	614.0
2000	41.8	44.6	47.7	45.6	44.4	49.1	42.0	43.3	42.6	47.5	43.8	40.2	640.0
2001	45.4	43.5	44.1	42.7	43.6	38.2	30.6	39.2	37.7	35.7	32.1	27.3	543.0
2002	31.2	31.3	30.4	33.1	34.9	34.4	34.3	35.8	36.1	36.1	32.7	33.3	403.6
2003	33.1	33.1	34.4	35.2	34.7	38.2	34.2	35.5	36.8	36.8	35.3	36.4	423.7
2004[1]	35.1	36.2	36.6	36.7	35.9	37.0	33.7	33.6	33.8	34.6	34.3	33.4	420.9

[1] Preliminary.   *Source: U.S. Geological Survey (USGS)*

Average Price of Zinc, Prime Western Slab (Delivered U.S. Basis)   In Cents Per Pound

Year	Jan.	Feb.	Mar.	Apr.	May	June	July	Aug.	Sept.	Oct.	Nov.	Dec.	Total
1995	60.11	55.44	54.84	56.08	54.61	53.08	53.75	52.00	50.77	50.42	52.52	51.60	53.77
1996	51.38	51.86	52.66	51.03	50.76	49.75	49.86	50.86	51.22	51.76	53.81	53.39	51.53
1997	55.64	59.82	63.28	62.62	65.65	67.78	75.29	80.89	78.96	62.55	57.83	54.45	65.40
1998	55.43	51.86	51.98	54.31	52.77	50.78	52.23	51.64	50.29	47.63	48.74	48.44	51.23
1999	47.29	51.11	51.68	51.07	52.20	50.35	53.73	56.28	59.12	57.07	56.91	58.75	53.84
2000	58.44	54.67	55.60	56.14	57.44	55.67	56.52	58.04	60.53	54.67	53.07	53.00	56.15
2001	51.82	51.29	50.55	48.95	47.54	45.56	43.62	42.53	41.14	39.53	39.99	39.25	45.15
2002	40.98	39.97	42.15	41.66	39.97	39.70	41.01	38.91	39.26	39.08	36.99	38.52	39.64
2003	38.88	38.46	38.48	36.99	37.86	38.57	40.30	39.77	39.84	43.44	44.11	47.60	40.36
2004	49.61	53.31	54.63	51.89	51.88	51.53	49.85	49.31	49.37	53.36	54.61	58.32	52.31

Source: American Metal Market (AMM)

CRB Yearbooks CD

Table of Contents

Chapter 1: Installation

Installing QuickSearch

To run QuickSearch, you will need:
• A computer with a 120 Mhz or faster processor, running any current Windows or Macintosh operating system
• At least 32 MB of total RAM installed on your computer; for best performance, we recommend at least 64 MB
• A CD-ROM drive

To Install:
1) Place the disc in the CD-ROM drive. If installation does not start automatically proceed to step 2.
2) Click Start; Select Run
3) Type D:\Autoplay, where D is the letter representing your CD-ROM drive. Press the enter key and follow the instructions.

Chapter 2: Searching and Browsing

Selecting Text to Search

Searches can be conducted across all the text in a *QuickSearch* document (full-text), restricted to a specific field (fielded search), or restricted to a selected table of contents section.

Everywhere in text - searches the full text of the *QuickSearch* document (except for user-defined notes and bookmarks). Choose **Everywhere in text** in the Search dialog box to specify a full-text search.

Fielded Search - searches a specific field and ignores all text outside of that field. To specify a fielded search:

1) Click **Selected field** under **Select where to search.**
2) Select a field from the list of available fields.

Current Table of Contents section - restricts a re-search only to a Table of Contents (TOC) section.

1) Click the TOC section in the TOC window.
2) Click the Search button on the toolbar OR select Search/Search from the main menu.
3) Click *Current Table of Contents section* under *Select where to search.*

Note: Search results will represent the selected TOC Section and its sublevels.

Types of Searches

Search for Phrase
Type an exact phrase you wish to find, e.g. "Business is the key." Use quotation marks around the search text to distinguish a *phrase search* from a *word search* or choose *Search for phrase* in the **Search/More>>** dialog box. The QuickSearch default setting is a phrase search.

Search for Words
Two types of word searches may be conducted - single words or words in proximity as determined by **Search Operators**. To conduct a word search, choose *Search for word(s)* in the **Search/More>>** dialog box.

1) **Single Word** - Enter any single word, e.g. BUSI-NESS, to find all occurrences in the document.

2) **Words in Proximity** - Enter any series of words that you wish to find near each other (e.g. BUSINESS INCREASE). Before conducting a *proximity search*, define a search range/proximity in the **Search/ More>>** dialog box. The default setting is 4 words. A typical sentence has 10 words, a typical paragraph has 25 words, and a typical page has 500 words.

Refine Last Search

The **Refine last search** feature can be used to modify your most recent search. (See the Advanced Searching section of this chapter.)

Search Operators

Boolean, wildcard and phrase search operators are available by selecting **MORE>>** in the **Search** dialog box. Double-click on any operator to add it to the Search command line *or* type the operator in the **Type the text to find** box.

To see example of each operator:

- Click the **Search** button and then the **More>>** button.
  OR
- Select **Search/Search** from the main menu and **More>>**.
- Click once on the operator you wish to view.

The following operators are available for a word search:

AND (&) - BUSINESS <u>AND</u> INCREASE - Returns all occurrences of BUSINESS and INCREASE in the specified search range that are near each other. "Near" is defined using the Word Proximity setting in the **Search/ More>>** dialog box.

OR (|) - BUSINESS <u>OR</u> INCREASE - Returns all occurrences of the words in the specified search range without regard to proximity.

NOT (~) - BUSINESS <u>NOT</u> INCREASE - Returns all occurrences of the word BUSINESS that are <u>not</u> near the word INCREASE in the specified search range. "Near" is defined using the Word Proximity setting in the **Search/ More>>** dialog box.

Wildcard (*) - Use the asterisk (*) at the end of any part of a word to represent any character or combination of characters. For example, BUSI* may return hits such as *business, businesses, busing,* and *Businowski*. The wildcard operator cannot be used in a phrase search.

Conducting a Search

Basic Searching

1) Click the Search button on the Reader toolbar <u>OR</u> select <u>S</u>earch/Search from the main menu.

2) In the **Search** dialog box, select where to search choosing one of the following:
- Everywhere in text
- Selected field*
- Current Table of Contents

*Note: Click a field or a TOC entry before choosing Selected field or Current Table of Contents section.

3) Type the search text (word, words within proximity or phrase) in the *Type the text to find* box or double click on any entry in the **Word Wheel** to select it as search text.

4) Click **Search** in the dialog box. "Hits" will be highlighted in the text and displayed in context in a separate **Hit List** window. The number of hits also will be displayed on the status bar at the bottom of the screen.

Advanced Searching

Search for Words

1) Begin a search by completing steps 1-3 of a Basic Search.

2) Select **More>>** to expand the Search dialog box and change to a *Search for Word(s)* and/or select other **Search Operators** which alter the nature of the search to be conducted. A *Search for Phrase* is conducted unless you select another type of search.

3) Specify the **Word Proximity** in the **Search/ More>>** dialog box, if you are conducting an AND or NOT search. The default proximity is 4 words.

4) Click **Search** in the dialog box. "Hits" will be highlighted in the text and displayed in context in a separate **Hit List** window. The number of hits also will be displayed on the status bar at the bottom of the screen.

Refine Last Search

To refine the last research:

1) Begin a search by completing steps 1-3 of a Basic Search. Click the **More>>** button on the **Search** dialog box to access all search parameters.

2) Click the **Refine last search** box in the lower left corner of the **Search** dialog box.

3) Select the **Boolean** operator to be applied to the refined search (just to the right of the *Refine last search* check box).

4) Preview the format for the refined search in the *Refined Search box* at the bottom of the **Search** dialog box.

5) Type the **[New text to Find]** word(s) in the *Type the text to find* box at the top of the **Search** dialog box.

6) Click **Search**.

Example:

Your first search in the Constitution was for the word "House." If you want to narrow the search results to include only hits of "House" which are not near "senate," you can return to the **Search** dialog box, select **Refine last search**, select the *NOT* operator, specify the word proximity, type "Senate" in the *Type the text to* find box at the top of the **Search** dialog box and click the **Search** button. The **Hit List** will display only hits of "House" which were not located near "Senate" ("near" depends on the proximity that you specified). The final search command would look as follows:

(House) ~ (Senate)

This search could be further refined by selecting **Refine last search** and repeating the steps above.

Example:

If you want to find only occurrences of "House *NOT* Senate" which are near "Representative," return to the Search dialog box, select **Refine last search**, select the *AND* operator, specify the word proximity, type "Representatives" in the *Type the text to find* box at the top of the **Search** dialog box and click on the **Search** button. The **Hit List** would display only hits of "House" which were near "Representatives" but not located near "Senate" ("near" depends on the proximity that you specified). The final search command would look as follows:

[(House) ~ (Senate)] & (Representatives)

Search Results

Browsing Search Results

Hit List

After conducting a search, each occurrence of the e search text in the document will be displayed in context in a separate **Hit List** window. Double click on any entry in the **Hit List** to move to the corresponding section of text.

Highlighted Hits in the Text

After conducting a search, each occurrence of the search text is highlighted in the text of the document.

1) Click the **First/Previous/Next/Last (Hit)** buttons to move between highlighted hits in the text.
2) The number of the current hit being viewed and the total number of hits are displayed in the Status bar at the bottom of the screen.

Removing the Hit List

1) Click the **Clear** button on the toolbar **OR** select **Search/Clear Search** from the main menu to remove the current **Hit List** window and the highlighting from the hits in the text.
2) Turn off the **Hit List** for future searches by selecting **Edit/Preferences** to open the **Document Preferences** dialog box. Click the **Reader** tab to open **Reader Preferences.** Deselect *Show Hit List?.*

Reader Preferences

Select **Edit/Preferences** from the main menu to open the **Document Preference** dialog box. The box includes three tabs: **Reader, Author,** and **Stopper Word List.**

Reader Preferences include:

CD-ROM Drive Letter

Every CD-ROM player is assigned a drive letter. (It is usually the last drive letter after your other drives.)

Default Word Search Proximity

Set the default proximity (the number of words between selected words) to be applied in multiple word (non-phrase) searches.

Show Hit List?

Click **Show Hit List?** to open a **Hit List** automatically after conducting a Search. The Hit List shows "hits" - items found - when you do a search. Browse hits by clicking the **Next/Previous Hit** buttons on the toolbar or selecting **Search/Search** from the main menu. All hits will be highlighted in the text even if a **Hit List** is not activated.

TOC Window Color

Click the **TOC Window Color** button to open a dialog box containing table of Contest background color options. Select from a present color chart, or create a custom color and select it. Click **OK.**

SAVE YOUR DOCUMENT after you select preferences!

Table of Contents Browsing

Hyperlinks

The Table of Contents (TOC) provides a convenient method for accessing any section of the *QuickSearch* document. Each TOC entry is hyper-linked to the corresponding section of text; just click on an entry and *QuickSearch* automatically will move the corresponding section to the text window.

Multiple Levels

QuickSearch TOC's may include up to 32 levels. If there are sublevels in a TOC section, a "+" will appear in front of the TOC entry. To open the next level, click on the "+".

Automatic Tracing

As you move through a *QuickSearch* document (scroll, Next Hit, Previous Hit, etc.) the Table of Contents will "track" your location in the document automatically. A box outline indicates the current TOC section.

Chapter 3: Viewing Images

A *QuickSearch* document may contain *hyperlinked* or *embedded* images. Different methods are used for finding and viewing each type of image

Finding Images

Finding Hyperlinked Images
You can find hyperlinked images in a *QuickSearch* document by using any of the following options:
- **List** of images
- **Next/Previous Image** buttons or menu selections
- **Search** feature
- **Special formatting**/camera icon

Image List - Open a comprehensive list of hyperlinked images in the document.
1) Click the **Image List** button on the Toolbar *OR* select **Search/Image List** from the main menu.
2) Double click on an image title in the **Image List** to open the image.

Browsing Images - You can browse through images using the **Next/Previous Image** buttons or menu selections.
1) Select Nest/Previous Image buttons OR Search/First (Nest, Previous, Last) Image from the main menu.
2) The **Next and Previous Image** buttons or menu selections move the reader sequentially through images in the document.
3) The **First** and **Last Image** menu selections move only to the first or last image in the document.

Searching for Words in Hyperlinked Image Titles - As each hyper-linked image file is added to a *QuickSearch* document, it is given an *Image Title.* The Image Title appears with an optional camera icon at the point you have chosen in the text window. The Image Title is indexed with other text and may be found using a word or phrase search (see Chapter 1 - *Searching & Browsing*).

Look for Special Formatting/Camera Icon – Hyperlinked images can be found by looking for words that have special formatting (the default is double-underlined text). Double click on the specially formatted text to open the image. A camera icon may precede the specially formatted image title. The image can also be opened by clicking on the camera icon.

Finding Embedded Images

Embedded images appear in the text at the point you have chosen. They may be found by:
- Scrolling through text
- Conducting a search for words/phrases that appear near the image.

Scrolling for an Embedded Image
Use the vertical scroll bar to scan text and locate embedded images.

Searching for an Embedded Image*
Search for text that has been placed near an image and marked as hidden.

*Note: **Titles of embedded images will** NOT **appear on an Image List.** The Image List feature is only for hyperlinked images.

Zooming Hyper-linked Images

Marquee Image Zooming*

Marquee Image Zooming allows you to select a portion of a **hyper-linked image** and enlarge it to the size of the image window. *QuickSearch* allows you to zoom to a single pixel.
*Note: Marquee Image Zooming **is available ONLY for hyper-linked images.**

1) Click a **hyperlinked image title** or camera icon to open the image window.
2) Click on and hold the **left mouse** button and drag a box around the image area you want to enlarge.
3) When the area is defined, release the mouse button. The area selected will fill the **Image Window**.
4) Steps 2 and 3 may be repeated to continuing zooming.
5) To return the image to its original size, click once on the image with the **left mouse** button.

Image Panning

Image Panning allows you to use the horizontal/vertical scroll bars* to move around a **hyperlinked** image that has been enlarged by Marquee zooming.
Click an arrow on the scroll bar *OR* click and drag the horizontal or vertical scroll bar button to move the image across the screen.
*Note: **Scroll bars do not appear on-screen until an image has been zoomed.**

Scale to Gray

Some 1 bit (black & white) hyperlinked images can be sharpened by using the **Scale to Gray** feature. **Scale to Gray** will fill in missing pixels to improve the quality of an image. This feature is particularly useful for viewing scanned document images.

To use Scale to Gray:
1) Open a hyperlinked image
2) Select **View/Scale to Gray** from the main menu
3) **Scale to Gray** will remain active until it is deselected.

Chapter 4: Printing

The **Print** feature will print **text** and **images** in the following forms:
- Highlighted lines or blocks of text
- Selected Tables of Contents section(s)
- Search results ("hit" lists)
- Embedded images
- Hyper-linked images
- Zoomed portions of Hyper-linked images

Print Hints

Highlighted text, images and TOC sections will print in order as they are found in the document.

The printed size of Zoomed and Hyper-linked images may vary between portrait and landscape page orientation settings (found via **File/Print Setup**).

You can print *multiple* TOC sections by:
- Using the **Shift** key to select a series of *adjacent* TOCs.
- Using the **CTRL** key to individually select *specific* TOCs.
- Using the **Shift** and **CTRL** keys alternately to select specific TOC groupings.

Printing specifications can be set from the Windows Print Manager utility.
Make **Print Setup** modifications *before* you **Print.**

Printing Text or Images

To Print portions of a document:
1) Highlight lines and/or block(s) of text.
2) Click the **Print** button on the toolbar.
OR
Select the **File/Print** from the main menu.
OR
Press **CTRL+P.**

To Print a Single TOC section:
1) Click the TOC heading in the **Table of Contents** window.
2) Click the **Print** button on the toolbar.
OR
Select the **File/Print TOC selection(s)** from the main menu.
OR
Click the **right mouse** button and select **Print TOC selection(s).**
OR
Press **CTRL+P.**
*Note: All the sublevels in the TOC section will be printed.

To Print Multiple TOC sections:
1) Click the first TOC section you want to print from the **Table of Contents** window.
2) Press and hold the **CTRL** key while you click the order TOC sections you want to print. They do not have to be adjacent.
3) When you have finished selecting TOCs, click the **Print** button on the toolbar.
OR
Select **File/Print TOC selection(s)** from the main menu.
OR
Click the **right mouse** button and select **Print TOC selection(s).**
OR
Press **CTRL+P.**

To Print adjacent TOC sections:
1) Click the *first* TOC section you want to print from the **Table of Contents** window.
2) Press and hold the **Shift** key, and click the last TOC section in the series (all TOC sections between the first and last will be selected automatically).
3) Click the **Print** button on the toolbar.
OR
Select **File/Print TOC selection** from the main menu.
OR
Click the **right mouse** button and select **Print TOC selection(s).**
OR
Press **CTRL+P.**

*Note: **Multiple TOC Selection functions (highlighting using the** Shift **and/or** CTRL **keys) can be used in combination to select specific TOC groupings.**

To Print Embedded Images:
1) Highlight (double click) the embedded image(s) you want ant to print.
2) Click the **Print** button on the Toolbar.
OR
Select **File/Print** from the main menu.
OR
Press **CTRL+P.**

To Print a Hyperlinked Image:
You can print a **Hyperlinked Image** or a zoomed portion of a Hyperlinked Image.
1) Open the image by double clicking the **Image title** and/or the **camera icon.**
OR
Click the **Image List** button on the toolbar and double click the **Image title** from the list.
2) Click the **Print** button on the Toolbar.
OR
Select **File/Print** from the main menu.
OR
Press **CTRL+P.**

Print Setup

The Print Setup option allows you to select printer type, page orientation, paper size, paper source, and printer properties (paper, graphics, fonts, device options). Make these selections **before** you print.

To change the Print Setup:
1) Select **File/Print Setup** from the main menu.
2) In the **Print Setup** dialog box, click the down arrow in the **Name** pull down menu, select a printer type and enter it in the **Name** window (or click **Network** to access Network printer options).
3) To select new printer properties select **Properties** and make modifications.
4) Select **Landscape** or **Portrait.**
5) Select **OK** to exit.

Page Layout
You can adjust the top, bottom, left, and right margins of a printed page as follows:
1) Select **File/Page Layout** from the main menu.
2) In the **Page Parameters** dialog box, set margins (in inches) and click **OK.**

Chapter 5: User Annotations

The reader may customize a *QuickSearch* document by adding "margin" Bookmarks and Notes.

Annotate functions enable the reader to make customized **Bookmarks** in the text and make private, unsearchable comments about a document with **Notes**. The **Bookmark** feature enables the reader to "save his place," while the **Notes** feature allows the reader to "write in the margins" of the text.

Using Bookmarks

To add a Bookmark to a document:
1) Highlight a portion of text or place the cursor where you would like to add the Bookmark.
2) Click on the **Bookmark** icon on the Reader toolbar *OR* select **Annotate/Bookmark** from the main menu or select **Insert Bookmark** from the **right mouse** button menu. If text has been highlighted, it is shown in the **Edit Bookmark/Name** text box. If not, enter a name for the bookmark in the text box.
3) Click **Add** to place the selected text in the **Current Bookmarks** list.
4) Click **Go to** to scroll text to the point where the bookmark appears.
5) Click **Close** to close the Bookmark dialog box.

To go to a Bookmark:
1) Click on the **Bookmark** button on the toolbar *OR* select **Insert Bookmark** from the **right mouse** button menu to open the list of Current Bookmarks.
2) Highlight the bookmark you want to move to in the text.
3) Click **Go to.** The selected text will move to the top of the text window.

To edit a Bookmark:
1) Click on the **Bookmark** icon on the toolbar *OR* select **Annotate/Bookmark** from the main menu *OR* select **Insert Bookmark** from the **right mouse** button menu to open the dialog box containing current bookmarks.
2) In the **Current Bookmarks** list, click on the bookmark you wish to edit. It will appear in the **Edit Bookmark/Name** window.
3) Make changes and click **Add**.

To remove a Bookmark:
1) Click the **Bookmark** icon on the Reader toolbar or select **Insert Bookmark** from the **right mouse** button menu to open the dialog box containing current bookmarks.
2) In the **Current Bookmarks** list, click on the bookmark you wish to remove. It will appear in the **Edit Bookmark/Name** text box.
3) Click **Remove.**

Using Notes

To add a Note to a document:
1) Place the cursor in the text window where you want the note to appear.
2) Click on the **Notepad** button *OR* select **Annotate/Notes/Insert** from the main menu *OR* select **Insert Note** from the **right mouse** button menu to open the **Notepad** dialog box.
3) Type in the note and click **Save**; a Notepad icon appears in the left margin next to the specified line of text.

To View a Note:
1) Double click the **Notepad** icon in the left margin.
2) The **Notepad** dialog box displays the note.

To Edit a Note:
1) Double click the icon of the note you want to edit.
2) Make changes to text.
3) Click **Save.**

To Remove a Note:
1) Place the cursor on the **Notepad** icon and select **Annotate/Note/Delete** from the main menu *OR* select **Delete Note** from the **right mouse** button menu.
2) A dialog box will ask you to confirm the note deletion.
3) Click **Yes.** The icon will disappear after scrolling in the document.